LITIGATION SERVICES HANDBOOK
The Role of the Financial Expert

FOURTH EDITION

Edited by
Roman L. Weil
Peter B. Frank
Christian W. Hughes
Michael J. Wagner

BICENTENNIAL
1807
WILEY
2007
BICENTENNIAL

For general information on our other products and services, or technical support, please contact our Customer Care Department within the United States at 800-762-2974, outside the United States at 317-572-3993 or fax 317-572-4002.

Wiley also publishes its books in a variety of electronic formats. Some content that appears in print may not be available in electronic books.

For more information about Wiley products, visit our Web site at http://*www.wiley.com*.

Library of Congress Cataloging-in-Publication Data:

Litigation services handbook: the role of the financial expert / edited by Roman L. Weil ... [et al.]. — 4th ed.
     p. cm.
  ISBN–13: 978-0-471-76908-8 (cloth)
  ISBN–10: 0-471-76908-8 (cloth)
  1. Forensic accounting—United States.   2. Evidence, Expert—United States.
I. Weil, Roman L.
  KF8968.15.L57 2007
  347.73'67—dc22   2006036638

Printed in the United States of America

10 9 8 7 6 5 4 3 2 1

CONTENTS

PREFACE

The litigation services practice for financial experts continues to expand in size, complexity, and geographic scope. This *Handbook* offers a comprehensive guide for economists, accountants, and litigators involved generally with damages or analytic issues in commercial litigation. The three previous editions, the first of which appeared 16 years ago, have enjoyed critical success as they served to guide readers and practitioners in the litigation services industry.

This fourth edition of the *Litigation Services Handbook* contains 39 chapters, all written by experts—accountants, economists, and litigators—in their field. In addition to the new chapters, this edition consolidates related chapters that appeared in the third edition and presents substantial updates to or complete rewrites of previous chapters. Together, they explain the financial theory behind the demonstrated practical application and clarify relevant case and statute law. This edition also includes an extensive glossary of financial terms.

Organization and Writing.   This edition comprises seven sections, each addressing a different practice area or set of functional tools.

Part I: *The Litigation Environment* (4 chapters) discusses the civil court system, principles and techniques of alternative dispute resolution, and how CPAs and economists function in the litigation environment; it also includes a new chapter on causation issues.

Part II: *Damages Techniques* (12 chapters) addresses the components of damages calculations with eight new chapters on statistical estimation, econometrics, *ex ante* versus *ex post* calculations, prejudgment interest, problems with averages in calculations, losses of new businesses, business valuation and punitive damages.

Part III: *Litigation Tools* (1 new chapter) explains data management in regulatory and litigation environments.

Part IV: *Civil Litigation* (14 chapters) addresses specific types of commercial cases, categorized into five subsections:

1. *Securities and Accountant Liability* (2 chapters, one of which consolidates securities chapters of past editions)
2. *Intellectual Property* (4 chapters, including two new chapters that discuss intellectual property in the entertainment industry and license compliance, respectively, as well as a chapter that consolidates intellectual property chapters of previous editions)
3. *Antitrust/Business Combinations* (2 chapters, including a new chapter that revisits antitrust issues)
4. *Construction and Real Property Disputes* (2 chapters, including a new analysis of construction claims)
5. *Other Civil Litigation* (4 chapters, including a consolidation of previous bankruptcy chapters and a new discussion of federal contract disputes)

Part V: *Family Law* (5 chapters)

Part VI: *Criminal Cases* (1 chapter with a new discussion of tax fraud)

Part VII: *Investigations* (2 new chapters, one of which considers investigations of financial statements and another that expands the discussion to include international considerations)

Glossary of Financial Terms (a new section that comprises an extensive catalog of terms, concepts, and distinctions among them)

Notes on Writing Style.   Many chapters contain a variety of statements of the form, "The expert will measure cash flows and discount them to present value." Often, the authors originally wrote, and mean, "The expert will usually measure cash flows and then, typically, discount them to present value."

Rather than qualify every positive or absolute statement with "typically" or "usually" or "generally," we have omitted those qualifiers. The reader should understand that unless the statement says something like, "always do X," the writer intended to qualify the statement with "typically" or "generally" or the like, not to assert a prescriptive formula. As a result of this style simplification, we think the reader more easily will comprehend the message.

Relation between Authors and Editors.   We acknowledge the cooperation and patience that our contributing authors have shown. We do not agree with everything they say and sometimes indicate that in notes. We prefer to have experts give their own opinions, even when controversial, rather than less specific guidance—like bland committee reports—on which we can all agree. Note to litigators cross-examining us: just because the author of the chapter said it doesn't mean we agree with it.

Acknowledgments.   We thank Debbie Asakawa for her work in managing, editing, and adding consistency and clarity to the manuscript. We also thank Hillary Ruben for her assistance in tracking down dilatory authors in addition to other tasks that helped bring the book to fruition. We acknowledge the excellent assistance of Katherine McGuire and Nicholas Asakawa and the diligent work of our liaisons at John Wiley & Sons: Judy Howarth and Natasha Wolfe.

Roman L. Weil

Peter B. Frank

Christian W. Hughes

Michael J. Wagner

November 2006

ABOUT THE EDITORS

Roman L. Weil, PhD, CMA, CPA, is V. Duane Rath Professor of Accounting at the Graduate School of Business of the University of Chicago. He received his BA in Economics and Mathematics from Yale University in 1962. He received his MS in Industrial Administration in 1965 and his PhD in Economics in 1966, both from Carnegie-Mellon University. He joined the faculty at the University of Chicago in 1965, where he has held positions in Mathematical Economics, Management and Information Sciences, Accounting, and in the Law School. He cofounded and now codirects the Chicago/Stanford/Wharton Directors' Consortium, which trains corporate board members to do their jobs better; his own specialty in that training focuses on financial literacy of audit committees. He has been a CPA in Illinois since 1973 and a CMA since 1974. He has served on the faculties of the Georgia Institute of Technology, New York University Law School and at Stanford University in its Graduate School of Business, Economics Department, and Law School. At Stanford, he has, since its inception, organized the sessions at Directors' College on Audit Committee duties. He has served on the Board of Academic Advisors of the U.S. Business School in Prague and has taught there. He has served on the accrediting committee of the American Association of Collegiate Schools of Business.

He has served as editor or associate editor of *The Accounting Review, Communications of the Association for Computing Machinery, Management Science, Journal of Accounting and Economics*, and the *Financial Analysts Journal.*

He has coedited four professional reference books for McGraw-Hill, Simon & Schuster, Prentice Hall, and John Wiley & Sons. He has coauthored a dozen textbooks for Holt, Rinehart and Winston, The Dryden Press, Harcourt Brace Jovanovich, and Thomson-SouthWestern. His articles have appeared in *Barron's* and *The Wall Street Journal.* He has published over 80 articles in academic and professional journals. He has served as the principal investigator on various research projects of the National Science Foundation.

He served on the Securities and Exchange Commission Advisory Committee on Replacement Cost Accounting. At the Financial Accounting Standards Board, he has served on two task forces—one on consolidations and the other on interest methods—and on the Financial Accounting Standards Advisory Council. He is a founding member of the Independent Directors' Council of the Investment Company Institute. He is a member of the American Accounting Association, the American Economics Association, the American Institute of Certified Public Accountants (AICPA), the American Law and Economics Association, the Illinois Society of Certified Public Accountants, and the Institute of Management Sciences.

Mr. Weil has consulted to governmental agencies, including the U.S. Treasury Department and the Securities and Exchange Commission. He has testified as expert witness or consultant in a variety of litigation matters involving accounting principles, business valuation, damages estimation, regulatory issues, and taxes.

Peter B. Frank recently retired as executive vice president of Daymon Worldwide Inc., in Stamford Connecticut, which he joined after retiring from PricewaterhouseCoopers LLP, PwC. As a partner in PwC, he served as a member of global leadership and as its Global Risk Management Partner. Prior to the merger with Coopers & Lybrand, Mr. Frank was a Vice Chairman of Price Waterhouse. Mr. Frank spent the bulk of his professional career leading the Price Waterhouse dispute analysis, bankruptcy, and business turnaround practice. He served on that firm's Policy Board (Board of Directors) and its Management Committee. For more than 30 years, Mr. Frank acted as a management consultant and expert witness for litigation, government, and industrial clients.

Mr. Frank is a retired Certified Public Accountant. He chaired the AICPA Subcommittee on Litigation Services (1990–1994) and served on the Management Advisory Services (MAS) Executive Committee (1989–1994) and the Professional Ethics Executive Committee (1995–1996) of the AICPA.

Mr. Frank's consulting expertise has been applied to engagements involving analyses of economic, liability, and damages issues in connection with expert testimony. He was consultant to the Christopher Commission's study of the Los Angeles Police Department and the alleged excessive use of force and also acted as special consultant for the Los Angeles Police Commission study (the Webster Commission), organized to assess the city agencies' response following the riots in Los Angeles.

Mr. Frank received his BS in Economics from the University of Pennsylvania. He obtained his MS in Accounting from the Wharton School of the University of Pennsylvania., graduating at the top of his class in both programs.

Mr. Frank has coauthored, in addition to this text, *Bernacchi on Computer Law: A Guide to the Legal and Management Aspects of Computer Technology* (Little, Brown, 1986; Annual Suppl. 1989–1999) and *AICPA Consulting Services Practice Aid 93-4: Providing Litigation Services* (with Michael J. Wagner), 1993. He is a contributing author to the American Bar Association publication *Punitive Damages and Business Torts: A Practitioner's Handbook* (1998) and *Financial Valuation: Businesses and Business Interests*, edited by James H. Zukin (Maxwell Macmillan, 1990).

Christian W. Hughes, CPA, CMA, CFA, CFE, is a partner in Pricewaterhouse-Coopers LLP in its Boston office. As Northeast Regional Advisory leader, he is responsible for the operations of the firm's consulting practices in New England and upstate New York. He is an elected member of the firm's U.S. Board of Partners and Principals and sits on three of its committees, including the Human Resources Committee, which he chairs. He has previously held responsibility for the firm's Dispute Analysis and Investigations practice on the U.S. East Coast.

Mr. Hughes has been associated with PricewaterhouseCoopers (including one of its predecessors, Coopers & Lybrand) since 1989, becoming a partner in 1992. From that time through the present, he has practiced in the areas of dispute analysis, expert testimony, fraud investigation, merger and acquisitions, bankruptcy, and insurance claims, as well as providing consulting assistance to the firm's audit practice. He has testified in state and federal courts, before arbitration panels, and in public oversight and regulatory matters on approximately 30 occasions and at deposition or by expert report in another 30. He has additionally participated in the investigations of a dozen high-profile, and many less notorious, matters involving reporting fraud, investor deception, employee misconduct, and similar matters.

He has also acted in support of disputants or as neutral arbitrator in a large number of postmerger purchase price adjustment disputes and assisted in the preparation, analysis, and settlement of over two billion dollars worth of property and business interruption insurance claims across a diverse range of industries and event types.

Mr. Hughes earned a BSBA in accounting at Babson College. He is a member of numerous professional organizations.

Michael J. Wagner earned his undergraduate degree in engineering from the University of Santa Clara in 1969, his MBA from the University of California at Los Angeles in 1971, and his JD from Loyola University at Los Angeles in 1975. He is a licensed attorney and CPA in the state of California.

A senior advisor at CRA International in their Palo Alto office, Mr. Wagner is the author of over 25 other publications dealing with the litigation services field. He has participated as an expert or consultant in more than 400 litigations and has testified over 97 times in court and over 220 times in deposition. His primary areas of expertise are in the computation of commercial damages or the valuation of businesses. He has also testified a number of times on the subject of alter ego.

Mr. Wagner's consulting experience ranges over most of the major industries in the United States over the last 30 years. He has particular expertise in high technology and biotechnology. One of his principal focuses has been on determining the economic value of intellectual property including patents, copyrights, trademarks, and trade secrets.

Mr. Wagner has testified 27 times in alternative dispute resolution forums and has acted as an arbitrator in a number of commercial arbitrations based on his extensive business consulting experience and his legal training. He was an arbitrator for the American Arbitration Association. He has served on the Litigation Services Committee, the Litigation Services Conferences Steering Committee, the MAS Practice Standards Committee, and the Business Valuation Standards Task Force for the AICPA. He is also a member of numerous professional organizations.

Mr. Wagner is married to Jolon Wagner and has four adult children. He lives in Los Altos Hills, California.

ABOUT THE CONTRIBUTORS

Mark A. Allen, JD, is vice president of Applied Economics Partners. He analyzes documents, data, and testimony in a wide variety of cases involving the application of economic theory to issues in litigation and regulation. He also assists in the preparation and writing of expert reports and works with experts to prepare for direct and cross-examination testimony in depositions and at trial. Prior to joining Applied Economics Partners, Mr. Allen worked as a trial lawyer in Washington, DC and Virginia and participated in appellate practice before the U.S. Supreme Court, federal courts of appeals, and the Virginia Supreme Court. He holds a JD and BA from the College of William and Mary.

Joe Anastasi, CPA, CMC, leads LECG's Corporate Forensics, Analytics and Restructuring Services (CFARS) practice. He has 30 years of experience in managing and directing the analysis and forensic investigative efforts related to complex commercial disputes. Previously, he was the Global Practice Leader for Deloitte's Forensic & Investigative Services practice; prior to that he spent 23 years with Price Waterhouse, where he led a portion of their Dispute Analysis and Corporate Recovery practice. Mr. Anastasi specializes in financial consulting engagements regarding matters of litigation, insurance claims, business disputes, loan restructuring, bankruptcies, and business planning for large and small entities. Mr. Anastasi has extensive consulting experience in industries as diverse as consumer business, semiconductors, manufacturing and distribution of personal computers and peripherals, high-tech communications, cable television, real estate and lodging, manufacturing, international shipping, waste disposal, and retailing.

Bilge Astarlioglu, MSc, is a manager in PricewaterhouseCoopers LLP's Dispute Analysis and Investigations practice in Washington, DC. Ms. Astarlioglu has a Civil Engineering degree and an MS in Construction Engineering and Management. She has domestic and international experience in both engineering and financial areas and extensive skills in using IT and databases to increase effectiveness and efficiency. Her experience includes review of project controls, contract management and procurement, project audits, construction claims, project termination, analysis of productivity, financial statement and general ledger analysis, and quantification of lost profits. Her numerous assignments have included significant projects related to airport, power plant, transportation systems, manufacturing plant, correctional facility, tunnel, highway, retail chains, and pipeline construction.

Christopher D. Barbee, CPA, is a partner in the Advisory Services practice of PricewaterhouseCoopers LLP, where he specializes in forensic accounting investigations and dispute-related services. Mr. Barbee has conducted numerous investigative and forensic accounting projects both in the United States and internationally on behalf of companies, audit committees, and shareholders related to financial reporting fraud, securities litigation, management or employee embezzlement, and tax fraud, including appearances before the Securities and Exchange Commission and the Department of Justice. Mr. Barbee has also provided dispute consulting services and expert witness testimony related to measurement and presentation of damages and lost profits claims; accountant malpractice; securities fraud matters; business interruption claims; and determination of asset allocation upon partnership and corporate dissolution. Mr. Barbee is a frequent speaker on the topics of forensic accounting investigations, and securities litigation.

Peter A. Bicks, JD, a litigation partner at Orrick, Herrington & Sutcliffe LLP in New York, has extensive litigation and trial experience nationwide in the areas of mass tort, contracts, intellectual property, corporate governance, and bankruptcy. He is the author of *Defending a Company in a Punitive Damages Case: A Comprehensive Approach to Defeating Punitive Damages in Light of Present Day Juror Attitudes* (Aspatore Books, 2005). Among other representations, Mr. Bicks is a member of the Orrick team acting as National Counsel to the Union Carbide Corporation in connection with asbestos-related personal injury lawsuits. Mr. Bicks has successfully tried several cases to verdict, including *Kelly Moore v. Union Carbide Corp.*, in which Mr. Bicks obtained one of the largest defense verdicts in 2004. Mr. Bicks received his BA from Pomona College and his JD from the Georgetown University Law Center.

Deborah K. Bothun, CFA, MBA, is a partner in the Advisory Services practice in the Los Angeles office of PricewaterhouseCoopers LLP. Ms. Bothun leads the U.S. Advisory Entertainment and Media practice as well as her company's Digital Convergence initiative, focusing on assisting clients in adapting to the changing content and distribution marketplace. Ms. Bothun specializes in financial due diligence for entertainment transactions and financings, licensing and contract compliance, and intellectual asset management including economic valuation for insurance claims and legal disputes. She is an author and editor of numerous PricewaterhouseCoopers publications, including several pieces on the topic of digital convergence. Ms. Bothun is quoted regularly by the press on emerging entertainment and media industry issues and is a featured speaker at industry conferences. She holds a BS degree from DePaul University and an MBA from Northwestern University's Kellogg School of Management.

Brandi N. Brethour, CPA, MPA, is currently a tax manager, specializing in divorce taxation, at Gursey, Schneider & Co. LLP in Los Angeles, California. Formerly, Ms. Brethour worked as a litigation consultant in the firm's family law practice. Prior to joining Gursey, Schneider & Co. LLP, Ms. Brethour was a senior auditor at KPMG, LLP. She is a member of the California Society of CPAs and holds a BA in Business Economics from the University of California at Santa Barbara and received her MPA from California State University at Northridge.

David B. Burg, MBA, is a principal in the Dispute Analysis & Investigations practice of PricewaterhouseCoopers LLP. He specializes in Forensic Technology Solutions. He has assisted clients in consulting capacities involving the deployment of information technology solutions and their use. He has assisted corporate clients and law firms in matters involving forensic accounting, computer forensic investigations, export control reviews including those governed by International Traffic in Arms Regulations, the Foreign Corrupt Practices Act, cybercrime incident response investigations, and complex data analysis using relational databases in matters involving purchase price disputes, contract disputes, and damages modeling. He has worked on a number of large, international investigative matters including the WorldCom, Adelphia, Royal Ahold, and Computer Associates investigations. He holds an MBA from the College of William and Mary and School of Business and a BA from the University of Pennsylvania.

Jeffrey M. Colón, LLM, JD, is a professor at the Fordham University School of Law. He teaches courses in federal income taxation, international taxation, taxation of derivatives, corporate finance, and corporations. Mr. Colón received his undergraduate and JD degrees from Yale University and his LLM (taxation) from Georgetown University. He has served as legal advisor since 1997 to Fletcher Asset Management, a New York private equity fund. Prior to joining the faculty at Fordham, he was an associate at Groom & Nordberg and Cole Corette & Abrutyn in Washington, DC, where he represented foreign and U.S. multinational firms.

Martha N. Corbett, CPA, CFE, is a partner in the Los Angeles office of PricewaterhouseCoopers LLP and has over 20 years of public accounting and business advisory experience. Her public accounting experience relates to the financial reporting of publicly held companies, internal control reviews and remediation, due diligence reviews, internal corporate investigations, and other business and litigation advisory services. Ms. Corbett is the Advisory Services Leader for Southern California, the West Region Dispute Analysis & Investigations Leader, and a member of the U.S. Dispute Analysis & Investigations leadership team. She serves on the boards of directors of several nonprofit organizations.

Michael A. Crain, CPA/ABV, ASA, CFA, is a managing director in the Fort Lauderdale, Florida office of The Financial Valuation Group. He works extensively in economic damages measurement and the valuation of businesses and financial assets. Mr. Crain is the current chair of the AICPA Business Valuation Committee. He is a coauthor of *Financial Valuation—Applications and Models* and a contributing author to *The Portable MBA in Finance and Accounting*. Mr. Crain has testified as an expert witness on numerous occasions.

Nicholas I. Crew, PhD, is a vice president at Analysis Group, Inc. Dr. Crew applies his background in finance and mathematics to matters involving valuation and damages calculation, with particular emphasis on the valuation and risk analysis of complex financial securities and derivatives including corporate bonds, currency derivatives, and mortgage-backed securities. He also specializes in analyses related to 10b-5 securities fraud cases and stock price behavior. In nonlitigation matters, Dr. Crew has performed pricing analyses, risk assessment, and real option valuation for clients in the pharmaceutical and electric utility industries. He has published research on regulatory policy and risk management. Dr. Crew holds a PhD in management with specialization in finance from the Anderson School of Management, University of California, Los Angeles and a BA in Mathematics from Rutgers College, Rutgers University.

Ronald B. Cushey, CPA, is a director in the Dispute Analysis & Investigations practice, specializing in Entertainment & Media, in the Los Angeles office of PricewaterhouseCoopers LLP. With over 25 years of financial experience in his role as entertainment and media advisor, Mr. Cushey is responsible for overseeing such client activities as acquisition integration analysis, convergence initiatives, market analysis, licensing management, piracy issues, Sarbanes-Oxley compliance, and asset securitization and financial due diligence. Previously, Mr. Cushey worked at several entertainment industry companies, including Media.net Communications and The Harvey Entertainment Company.

Dyan A. Decker, MBA, CFE, is a principal in the Advisory Services practice of PricewaterhouseCoopers LLP and leads the Forensic Technology Solutions (FTS) group in Southern California. The FTS group performs services in the areas of computer forensics, database analysis and management, and application development. Ms. Decker specializes in performing complex data analyses for a variety of issues under dispute, including breach of contract, government investigations, accounting malpractice, and class actions. Ms. Decker also has extensive experience in managing engagements with complex computer forensics and electronic discovery issues. She has worked in numerous industries, including healthcare, entertainment, telecommunications, and retail. Ms. Decker has an MBA from the University of California at Los Angeles and a BA from the University of California at San Diego.

Daniel V. Dooley, CPA, is a partner in the firm of PricewaterhouseCoopers LLP and is the firm's Global Leader of the Securities Litigation and Investigations consulting practice. Mr. Dooley specializes in securities litigation and related investigations, securities regulatory matters, antibribery and anticorruption compliance and investigations, and forensic accounting. He regularly practices before the U.S. Securities and Exchange Commission and U.S. Department of Justice, as well as before other countries' securities regulators. Mr. Dooley's experience with securities litigation and investigations includes, among other matters, Aetna, Ahold (Royal Ahold NV), American Bank Notes, Credit Agricole, Daimler Chrysler, First Republic Bancorp, Integra, Mattel, Maxwell Communications, Microsoft, Paracelsus, Parmalat S.p.A, Royal Dutch Shell N.V., and Vodafone. Mr. Dooley has served as an expert witness on behalf of the Securities and Exchange Commission, the Department of Justice, various U.S. Federal Courts, the U.S. Federal Deposit Insurance Corporation, the U.S. Resolution Trust Corporation, and numerous private parties. He has served as an arbitrator in matters that involved accounting and financial reporting issues. He is chairman of the Editorial Board and editor-in-chief of the Thompson West Group Securities Litigation Report, chairman of the annual London Corporate Responsibilities Conference, and co-chairman of the Securities and Exchange Commission Accounting & Disclosure Conference. He is also the author of articles, monographs, and papers in the areas of forensic accounting, securities litigation and investigations, and accounting and is editor of the PricewaterhouseCoopers Annual Securities Litigation Study.

Michael K. Dunbar, MSME, MBA, PE, is a vice president of CRA International, a litigation and management consulting firm. He has extensive experience in the calculation of damages for infringement of intellectual property rights, including valuing trade secrets, trademarks, copyrights, and patents. He has also assessed damages for a wide variety of other commercial disputes. Mr. Dunbar has published in the areas of valuation of emerging technology and calculation of damages. He holds BS and MS degrees in Mechanical Engineering and an MBA from the Wharton School at the University of Pennsylvania with a concentration in finance.

Bronwyn Dylla, PhD, is the research director at SVB Capital in Menlo Park, California, where she conducts market research in the venture capital industry. She was formerly a manager in the Dispute Analysis & Investigations practice in the Los Angeles office of PricewaterhouseCoopers LLP. Dr. Dylla provided consulting services for commercial litigation, licensing management, and business analytics. She has taught undergraduate courses at the University of California at Los Angeles. Dr. Dylla received her undergraduate degree from Cornell University and a PhD from the University of California at Los Angeles.

Merle Erickson, CPA, PhD, is a professor of Accounting at the University of Chicago's Graduate School of Business where he teaches accounting and tax courses. He is coauthor of *Taxes and Business Strategy* (3rd edition) and is a coeditor of the *Journal of Accounting Research*. Mr. Erickson consults periodically with government agencies, corporations, and individuals on a variety of accounting and tax-related issues.

Elizabeth A. Evans, MBA, JD, CPA, CMA, CFA, is a vice president of Analysis Group Inc. Ms. Evans assists clients in matters involving antitrust, securities, intellectual property, bankruptcy, and general commercial litigation. She analyzes the effects of accounting choices and GAAP on financial statements and stock prices. Ms. Evans evaluates total costs, variable costs, incremental costs, cost-allocation methods, and revenue-recognition policies. She has also valued various types of assets, liabilities, and firms. Ms. Evans holds an MBA in accounting, finance, and statistics from the Graduate School of Business at the University of Chicago and a JD from the University of Alabama School of Law.

Randi L. Firus is a director in PricewaterhouseCoopers LLP's Dispute Analysis & Investigations practice in St. Louis. In this capacity, she provides consulting services and expert testimony on valuation of economic damages to individuals in toxic tort, aviation, and product liability actions, as well as matters involving claims of discrimination in employment practices, including wrongful termination. Ms. Firus has particular expertise in pension plans, executive stock options, and present valuation of future medical expenses or monitoring. Her testimony experience also includes statistical analysis of liability in connection with employment discrimination claims and quantification of damages in commercial litigation matters involving breach of contract. Ms. Firus regularly performs demographic and labor market studies using government, census, and other data. She holds an MS in Economics from the University of California, Los Angeles.

Donald A. Glenn, CPA/ABV, CFE, CVA, has over 30 years of experience. He is a partner with Glenn & Dawson LLP in Walnut Creek, California. He is frequently a court-appointed expert in California Superior and Federal Bankruptcy Courts. He was the founding chair of the California Society of CPAs Family Law Section and author of the California Society of CPAs Family Law Workshop course. He is a member of the national standards committee of the National Association of Certified Valuation Analysts and has served on the National Board of Directors of the Institute of Management Accountants and the State Board of Directors of the California Society of CPAs. Mr. Glenn is a nationally known lecturer to judges, attorneys, CPAs, and other groups on forensic accounting. He has authored the

AICPA's *Forensic Accounting for Divorce Engagements: A Practical Guide, 2nd ed.*, and numerous articles. He was the first recipient of the California Society of CPAs' Family Law Section's Distinguished Service Award for his contributions to forensic accounting.

Kevin L. Gold, MBA, is a manager at Analysis Group Inc. He specializes in applying statistical and financial principles to complex problems in business litigation. Mr. Gold's consulting experience includes analyzing damages in several securities fraud cases. He holds an MBA from the Anderson School of Management at the University of California at Los Angeles and a BA in Economics and Molecular and Cell Biology from the University of California, Berkeley.

Bonnie J. Goldsmith, CPA, MBA, is a vice president in the Oakland office of CRA International. With over 20 years of experience, she has provided consulting services and expert testimony on various topics including accounting, economic damages, and business valuation. She holds an MBA from the University of California, Berkeley and a BS in Business, with specialties in Accounting and Finance, from the University of California, Berkeley.

Donald L. Gursey, CPA, is a senior partner at Gursey, Schneider & Co. He has authored numerous articles and has lectured on the tax aspects of marital dissolution, business valuation, tracing, commingling, and apportionment. He is former chairman of the Litigation Services Committee of the California Society of CPAs and is the tax editor for the *Family Law News*, a California State Bar publication.

Charles R. Hacker, Jr., CPA, CFE, MBA, is a partner in the Dispute Analysis & Investigation practice in the New York office of PricewaterhouseCoopers LLP. Mr. Hacker's experience includes extensive investigative and forensic accounting analysis related to fraud. As part of these engagements, Mr. Hacker has led numerous investigations and analytical reviews of financial information, evaluation and enhancements to internal controls, and the development and analysis of compliance testing programs, corporate policies, and regulatory guidelines. Mr. Hacker has represented boards of directors, audit committees, and creditors in connection with internal investigations, legal proceedings, and regulatory investigations. Mr. Hacker has assisted and participated in settlement negotiations and made presentations of investigation findings to the Department of Justice, the Federal Bureau of Investigation, the Office of Inspector General, the Securities and Exchange Commission, and the Internal Revenue Service. He has served clients in a number of industries including consumer products, financial services, health care, pharmaceuticals, cable, manufacturing, and food services.

Mark W. Haller, MBA, CPA, CMC, is an advisory partner and leads the Dispute Analysis & Investigations practice of the Chicago office of PricewaterhouseCoopers LLP. He is a founder and leader of the firm's Intellectual Asset Management group, a practice dedicated to better management and value realization from corporate portfolios of intellectual property and related technology assets. He regularly deals with structural and valuation issues around intellectual property transactions and licensing. Mr. Haller also leads the firm's emerging Business Analytics practice, which focuses on rigorous analytical solutions to support business decision making. Additionally, he has significant experience in alternative dispute resolution forums, including as an arbitrator, with particular emphasis on the resolution of merger- and acquisition-related disputes. Mr. Haller holds an MBA from the University of Chicago and a BS in Accounting and Finance from Miami University in Oxford, Ohio.

Greg Hallman, PhD, is a member of the faculty in the Finance department at the McCombs School of Business at the University of Texas at Austin, where he teaches MBA courses in investments and real estate finance. Dr. Hallman has won numerous awards for his teaching in the MBA program at the McCombs School. He previously worked in litigation consulting and was a managing director in the Silicon Valley office of Intecap, Inc. He has worked on a wide variety of engagements in class action securities and securities valuation, commercial damages, business valuation, patent infringement, valuation of intellectual property, and wrongful termination. Dr. Hallman has provided testimony at deposition, arbitration, and trial in both state and federal courts.

Gaurav Jetley, MS, CFA, is a vice president of Analysis Group Inc. in Boston. Mr. Jetley specializes in securities litigation, corporate finance, and valuation of derivative instruments. His securities litigation experience includes working on behalf of large corporations across a variety of industries, including electric utilities, office equipment, biotechnology, and healthcare providers. Mr. Jetley's corporate finance work includes detailed analyses of factors underlying the insolvency of several large property and casualty insurers. He has also worked on several matters involving the valuation of over-the-counter and exchange-traded equity, fixed income, foreign exchange, and mortgage-backed derivative securities. Mr. Jetley holds an MS in Finance from the Carroll School of Management, Boston College. He also holds a CFA designation from the Institute of Chartered Financial Analysts of India.

Glenn K. Jones, JD, is a litigation associate at Orrick, Herrington & Sutcliffe LLP in New York. Mr. Jones received his BA from the University of Vermont and his JD from Georgetown University Law Center. He currently practices in the areas of products liability and commercial litigation. Among other representations, Mr. Jones is a member of the Orrick team acting as national counsel to the Union Carbide Corporation in connection with asbestos-related personal injury lawsuits.

Thomas E. Kabat, MAI, CRE, CCIM, is a principal in the Phoenix office of PricewaterhouseCoopers LLP, specializing in the analysis and quantification of damages to real property affected by contamination, hazard, regulatory constraints, and other influences. Mr. Kabat leads the Real Estate Litigation Support practice of his firm. As a real estate consultant, appraiser, and economist, Mr. Kabat has valued and evaluated properties in all major U.S. markets, with an emphasis on properties influenced by complex environmental, regulatory, and physical conditions. He is a certified general real estate appraiser in several states and the District of Columbia.

Stephen H. Kalos, PhD, is a vice president of CRA International. Dr. Kalos specializes in industrial organization economics and the economics of innovation and intellectual property. He has consulted to corporations, law firms, and government agencies for 30 years. His consulting practice includes three related areas: intellectual property and technology; antitrust; and economic damages. He holds a PhD and an MA in Economics from Yale University and a BA in Economics and Mathematics from Wesleyan University.

Michael S. Knoll, PhD, JD, is the Earle Hepburn Professor at the University of Pennsylvania Law School and Professor of Real Estate at the Wharton School. He teaches courses in corporate finance and taxation in the Law School, the Wharton School, and the Wharton Executive Program. Professor Knoll holds undergraduate and JD degrees from the University of Chicago. He also earned a PhD in economics at the University of Chicago. He has been a visiting professor at Boston University, Georgetown, Penn, and Virginia Law Schools. He clerked for the Honorable Alex Kozinski on the U.S. Court of Appeals, Ninth Circuit, and served as legal advisor to the vice chairman of the U.S. International Trade Commission. Before assuming his current position at Penn, he was a member of the faculty of the University of Southern California Law School. He has published extensively in the fields of corporate finance, international trade, and taxation.

Robert S. Knudsen, CPA, MBA, CFE, is a partner in the Advisory Services practice of PricewaterhouseCoopers LLP. He has over 25 years of experience, including auditing, management consulting, and financial analysis in connection with reorganizations/workouts, business valuation, investigative accounting and commercial litigation. Mr. Knudsen has qualified as an expert and has testified on issues of accounting, valuation, and damages in both state and federal courts. Mr. Knudsen received a BS in Industrial Engineering and Operations Research and an MBA, both from the University of California, Berkeley.

Kevin D. Kreb, CPA, MBA, is a partner in PricewaterhouseCoopers LLP's Investigations practice in Chicago. Mr. Kreb received an MBA from Duke University's Fuqua School of Business and an undergraduate degree in accounting from Iowa State University. Mr. Kreb specializes in conducting forensic accounting investigations. He has conducted investigations relating to asset misappropriation and fraudulent financial reporting issues at both public and private companies. He also specializes in the resolution of disputes arising from merger and acquisition transactions. He has served in the capacity of expert witness and sole arbitrator/neutral accountant on numerous occasions. He regularly consults with clients regarding the resolution of purchase price disputes, earn-out disputes, and breach of representation and warranty claims through negotiation, arbitration, and litigation.

Victoria A. Lazear, MS, is founder and principal of Applied Economics Partners. She has over 25 years of experience in the application of economic theory to issues in litigation and regulation. Ms. Lazear provides expert testimony and directs research for expert testimony in cases involving the estimation of damages and in litigation involving antitrust, telecommunications, high technology, e-commerce and the Internet, pharmaceuticals and chemicals, securities, banking and finance, energy, regulation, and labor issues. Ms. Lazear is coauthor with Robert E. Hall of "Reference Guide on Estimation of Losses in Damages Awards," in the *Reference Manual on Scientific Evidence*. She holds an MS and a BS from the Massachusetts Institute of Technology.

Stephen P. Lechner, MBA, is a principal at PricewaterhouseCoopers where he leads the U.S. Construction Advisory Services practice. He is an engineer and has extensive experience advising clients on cost, schedule and management aspects of construction projects and regulatory matters. He has participated in numerous dispute mediations and settlement negotiations and has submitted expert evidence on delay, productivity and cost accounting issues in various jurisdictions around the world.

Michael W. Maher, PhD, is a professor of Management and Accounting at the Graduate School of Management at University of California, Davis. Mr. Maher has written approximately 50 articles and published 12 books, some in several editions. He has received national awards for research and teaching. His research and teaching has focused on corporate governance and cost management. Mr. Maher holds an MBA from the University of Washington and a BA from Gonzaga University.

R. Jeffrey Malinak, MBA, is a managing principal at Analysis Group Inc. and specializes in financial economics, with particular expertise in damages estimation, applied finance theory, and business and asset valuation. He has provided deposition and arbitration testimony on economic damages issues and directed litigation projects in many industries on issues related to securities (including derivative securities), antitrust, breach of contract, taxation, regulatory economics, and intellectual property claims. Mr. Malinak has frequently addressed class certification and damages issues in securities fraud cases, as well as the myriad economic, financial, and accounting issues common to most damages calculations, such as cost of capital and prejudgment interest issues.

M. Laurentius Marais, PhD, holds graduate degrees in Mathematics, Statistics, and Business administration from Stanford University. His PhD dissertation focused on applications of statistical methods to problems in accounting. He has served on the faculties of the University of Chicago and Stanford University. During his nine years on the regular faculty of the University of Chicago, he was a member of the Institute of Professional Accounting at the Graduate School of Business and taught graduate-level courses in managerial accounting. He is now a vice president and principal consultant at William E. Wecker Associates, Inc., a consulting firm that specializes in applied mathematics and statistical analysis for decision making, corporate R&D, and expert testimony.

David L. Marston, CPA, is a partner in the San Francisco Advisory Services practice of PricewaterhouseCoopers LLP. Mr. Marston has over 25 years of accounting and business experience and for the past several years has focused exclusively on issues related to intellectual property (IP) compliance. He has extensive international experience with multinational companies and focuses on assisting companies with global issues around IP management, primarily in the technology industry. Mr Marston is the leader of the Licensing Management practice area at his firm.

Frederic R. Miller, MBA, CPA, CFE, is a senior partner in the Forensic and Investigations Services practice of PricewaterhouseCoopers LLP. He has over 27 years of public accounting experience. He specializes in forensic accounting investigations and has been the engagement leader on a number of the firm's largest and most complex forensic accounting assignments, including investigations for the Department of Justice and the Securities and Exchange Commission. He coleads the Foreign Corrupt Practices Act practice for his firm and has significant international investigatory experience. He was the engagement partner for his firm's investigation of 27 private and cantonal banks in the Swiss Holocaust Bank Investigation (Volcker Commission). He is also a frequent speaker on international investigation topics. Mr. Miller earned an AB degree from Rutgers College and an MBA from the Cornell University Johnson Graduate School of Management.

Gil A. Miller, CPA, CFE, CIRA, has twenty years experience in public accounting and is the senior managing director of the Advisory Services practice of PricewaterhouseCoopers in Salt Lake City. He has been primarily involved with investigative accounting work, bankruptcy case work, troubled company workouts, breach of contract, contract claims, and fraud examinations. Because of his education and practical experience, he also offers unique expertise in the area of computer applications. Mr. Miller is a member of the Commercial Panel of the American Arbitration Association.

Donald John Miod, CPA, is the founding member and partner of Miod and Company LLP, where he developed and now leads the Forensic Accounting department. In addition to advising a large national and international clientele, he oversees all aspects of the company's accounting services and operations. His background includes the development of leading proprietary asset models, several professional certifications, published articles, and speaking engagements at professional and civic conferences. Mr. Miod is a member of several industry associations and a significant contributor to state industry conferences.

Marnie A. Moore, MBA, is a vice president at Analysis Group, Inc. She specializes in applying statistical and financial analyses to risk management and general commercial litigation. She received a BS in Mathematics from the University of California at Los Angeles and an MBA from the Anderson School of Management at the same university.

John C. Moorman is a principal in PricewaterhouseCoopers' Dispute Analysis & Investigations practice in Chicago. Jack has more than 25 years experience in information technology (IT), the last several of which have concentrated in forensic technology. He leads PricewaterhouseCoopers' Forensic Technology Solutions (FTS) practice for the Midwest, which includes a full range of litigation support analysis services (litigation database, document management, and damages calculation), electronic discovery services, cybercrime prevention and response, and systems failure expert services. Jack has been at the forefront of the FTS investigations tool development in fraud detection and insurances claims allocation. He has testified and been deposed on numerous occasions.

Grant W. Newton, CPA, CIRA, PhD, is a professor of Accounting at Pepperdine University in Malibu, California and the executive director of the Association of Insolvency and Restructuring Advisors. He is the author of *Bankruptcy and Insolvency Accounting: Practice and Procedure* and *Bankruptcy and Insolvency*

Taxation, both published by John Wiley & Sons (updated annually). Dr. Newton was a member of the AICPA's Task Force on Financial Reporting by Entities in Reorganization under the Bankruptcy Code, which resulted in the issuance of Statement of Position 90-7. He is coauthor of *Consulting Services Practice Aid 02-1: Business Valuation in Bankruptcy* and *Providing Bankruptcy & Reorganization Services—Practice Aid*, both published by the AICPA.

Vincent E. O'Brien, MBA, DBA, is a director at LECG LLC in Emeryville, California. He is a leading expert in damages analysis in complex litigation, with over 25 years of experience in applying economic and financial analysis to intellectual property, antitrust, securities, and contract matters. He has developed or critiqued over 400 damages claims and has testified over 170 times in federal and state courts and domestic and international arbitrations. Dr. O'Brien holds masters and doctorate degrees from Harvard Business School, where he taught as a research fellow, and a BS in Electrical Engineering with High Honors from the University of Illinois.

Gregory N. Phelps, MBA, is a director in the Forensic and Litigation Consulting practice of FIT Consulting Inc. located in Los Angeles. He has more than 10 years of experience working on a variety of consulting engagements, including business interruption claims, forensic investigations, and breach of contract disputes. Mr. Phelps has an MBA from the University of Southern California and a BS in Business Administration from the University of California, Berkeley.

Roseanna L. Purzycki, CPA, is a partner in the firm of Gursey, Schneider & Co. LLP in Los Angeles. Previously she was a faculty member of the Graduate School of Business at the University of Michigan. She is a frequent lecturer for organizations providing continuing education for CPAs and attorneys including the American Bar Association and Los Angeles County Bar Association. She specializes in consulting on tax aspects of marital dissolution and Internal Revenue Service procedures and testifies as an expert witness. She earned her MBT from the University of Southern California and MSA from Eastern Michigan University.

Lawrence F. Ranallo, CPA, MBA, is a partner in PricewaterhouseCoopers LLP's Dispute, Advisory & Investigation practice in Dallas. He has more than 29 years of professional experience with the firm as a CPA and is accredited in business valuation and turnaround management. Mr. Ranallo has broad experience in dealing with complex business problems as an auditor, financial consultant, arbitrator, trustee, and expert witness providing expert testimony on economic damages. His audit experience includes responsibility for services at large public multinational corporations, as well as middle market and growing companies. Mr. Ranallo has focused on disputes related to the application of generally accepted accounting principles and the fair presentation of financial reporting disclosures. He is a nationally recognized expert and independent arbitrator in complex purchase price disputes. He has lectured in graduate programs at Carnegie Mellon University and the University of Pittsburgh; he currently is an adjunct lecturer at Southern Methodist University in the "Companies in Crisis" program for the Cox Graduate Business School.

Mohan P. Rao, PhD, is a director with LECG, an international economics and business consulting firm. He specializes in intellectual property, antitrust economics, and economic analysis in complex commercial disputes. His intellectual property expertise includes valuation, business strategy, and the interplay between intellectual property and antitrust issues. He also teaches courses on valuing intellectual property at the Licensing Executives Society. Previously, Dr. Rao was a vice president with Charles River Associates and a professor at the University of California at Los Angeles. He has a BS in Engineering from the University of Michigan, a predoctoral fellowship from Harvard University, and a PhD from the University of Colorado.

Edward M. Robbins, Jr., Esq. is a principal with the law firm of Hochman, Salkin, Retting, Toscher & Perez, PC in Beverly Hills, California, specializing in civil tax controversy and litigation and criminal tax controversy and litigation. Mr.Robbins is a member of the State Bars of California and Hawaii and is a Certified Specialist, Taxation Law, State Bar of California. Mr. Robbins was formerly the chief of the Tax Division of the United States Attorney's Office for the Central District of California. Mr. Robbins was named the IRS Criminal Investigations Outstanding National Criminal Tax Prosecutor in 2004.

Ali Saad, PhD, is the managing partner of Resolution Economics LLC. He has a PhD in Economics from the University of Chicago. Prior to founding Resolution Economics, Dr. Saad was a partner at Deloitte & Touche LLP and at Altschuler, Melvoin and Glasser LLP. Prior to his consulting career, Dr. Saad served as an Assistant Professor of Economics at Baruch College of the City University of New York. Dr. Saad's experience is extensive in the areas of statistical and economic analysis of liability and damages related to employment litigation matters, as well as consulting on a variety of nonlitigation employment issues. He is also experienced in designing, implementing, and analyzing surveys and observation studies related to exempt/nonexempt status, hours worked, uncompensated time, meal and rest breaks, and other wage and hour issues. Dr. Saad has testified a number of times at both deposition and trial.

Sam L. Savage, PhD, is consulting professor in Management Science & Engineering at Stanford University, senior associate of the Judge Business School at Cambridge University, and president of AnalyCorp Inc., a firm that develops executive education programs and software for business analysis. Sam holds a PhD in computer science from Yale University, and has published a wide array of technical and non-technical articles with recent contributions to the *Washington Post*, *Harvard Business Review*, *Journal of Forensic Accounting* and *Journal of Portfolio Management*. His book, *Decision Making with Insight,* has been called "a Must Read" by Harry Markowitz, Nobel Laureate in Economics.

Peter P. Simon, PhD, is a vice president at Analysis Group, Inc. Dr. Simon specializes in applied microeconomics and econometrics, and their application in complex financial litigation. He has conducted damages analyses in a wide range of areas including patent infringement, antitrust, statistical sampling, business valuation, and general damages. His intellectual property analyses have been in the area of patent infringement, covering industries from semiconductor manufacturing equipment to graphical programming software. Previously, Dr. Simon was a lecturer at Princeton University. He holds PhD and MA degrees in

Economics from Princeton University and a BA in Mathematical Economics from Pomona College.

Steven L. Skalak, CPA, MBA, is an Advisory Services partner at Pricewaterhouse-Coopers LLP and the national leader of the Corporate Investigations practice and additionally serves on the leadership teams for Dispute Analysis & Investigations and Advisory Services. His work has focused on defending companies, their officers, and their directors in matters brought by the Securities and Exchange Commission, U.S. Attorneys, or civil litigants alleging violations of the Securities and Exchange Acts, particularly in respect to noncompliance with generally accepted accounting principles. Mr. Skalak has also conducted significant investigations in the financial services industry and has served major domestic and international clients in a variety of other industries such as communications, insurance, publishing, real estate, consumer products, and international trading. He is a past member of the Professional Ethics and Cooperation with Bankers Committees. He received his BA from Dickinson College and his MBA from Columbia University.

James K. Smith, CPA, JD, LLM, PhD, is an associate professor of Accounting at the University of San Diego, where he teaches accounting and tax classes. He received his BA, MBA, and JD from Tulane University, his LLM from the University of San Diego, and his PhD from the University of Arizona. He has published articles in a number of journals, including *Journal of the American Taxation Association*, *Tax Notes*, *Accounting Horizons*, *The Journal of Accountancy*, *Tax Adviser*, *Practical Tax Strategies*, *The CPA Journal*, and *Journal of State Taxation*. Prior to teaching, he worked for four years in the tax department at KPMG Peat Marwick and for five years as a tax attorney.

Laura B. Stamm, CPA, MBA, is a managing principal in the Boston office of Analysis Group, Inc., an economic and financial consulting firm. Ms. Stamm specializes in the application of finance and accounting to problems in complex business litigation. She has testified on several occasions on damages arising out of general commercial disputes and intellectual property matters. She has also analyzed issues relating to the valuation of financial instruments and has provided valuations of privately held companies. Outside of litigation, Ms. Stamm has assisted numerous businesses in a variety of industries with the development of business plans and financial projections, often through the use of complex integrated financial models. She has an MBA from the MIT Sloan School of Management.

James W. Thomas, CPA, is a partner at PricewaterhouseCoopers LLP, where he leads the firm's U.S. Advisory Aerospace & Defense Sector and Washington, DC Government Contracts Practice. With over 20 years of experience in federal procurement rules, he provides advice to commercial companies, nonprofit organizations, and educational institutions on the pricing, costing, and administrative requirements of federal contracts, grants, and other agreements. Mr. Thomas has testified as an expert witness in government contract disputes on the requirements of the Federal Acquisition Regulation, Cost Accounting Standards, and generally accepted accounting principles. He has authored many publications on government contract subjects and is an instructor for Federal Publications Seminars, LLC and ESI International. He has a BS in Accounting from Pennsylvania State University; prior to joining PricewaterhouseCoopers he was with McDonnell Douglas Corporation.

Patricia D. Tilton is a principal in PricewaterhouseCoopers LLP's Advisory Services Group and practices in the Dispute Analysis & Investigations area. She is based in Houston, Texas. Ms. Tilton has over 20 years of experience providing financial consulting services to clients facing disputes or in need of forensic accounting investigations. This experience includes assisting clients with damage assessments and other financial analysis in the context of commercial litigation matters and disputes resolved through arbitration. Ms. Tilton's experience includes quantification of damages, valuations, projecting cash flows, financial and accounting fact finding, reconstruction of financial transactions, asset or transaction tracing, and assessment of internal controls. Ms. Tilton's international experience includes arbitration, litigation, and forensic investigation work in western Europe, Russia, the Ukraine, Mexico, Brazil, and Venezuela. She has a BA in Economics from Bucknell University and an MBA from Rice University.

Vincent Torres, MBA, is a manager in the Advisory Services group and Intellectual Asset Management practice of PricewaterhouseCoopers LLP's Chicago office. Mr. Torres has applied his knowledge of finance, valuation principles, and economic theory to the evaluation of commercial development opportunities and transactions and to the analysis of economic damages pursuant to commercial litigations, specializing in issues involving intellectual assets. He has also assisted clients in developing license compliance programs related to out-licensing initiatives and in identifying, assessing, and mitigating risks related to internal intellectual asset management processes. Mr. Torres holds a BA in economics from Duke University and an MBA from the Fuqua School of Business at Duke University.

Christian D. Tregillis, CPA, MBA, is a managing director in the Los Angeles office of the Financial and Litigation Consulting practice of Kroll Inc., and he is the national leader of its Intellectual Property Services group. In these roles he analyzes financial, accounting, statistical, economic, and market issues, primarily in regard to disputes, valuations, and transactions. He has participated in mediations and has testified in deposition, hearings, and arbitration and at trial in both state and federal courts. Mr. Tregillis has worked on over 400 matters in his 17 years of financial consulting and investigations. Previously, he was a partner in the Financial Advisory Services practice at Deloitte & Touche. He has also served as the CFO of the Center for Law in the Public Interest and is a current board member of this organization.

Keith R. Ugone, PhD, is a principal at Analysis Group, Inc. and has been analyzing economic- and damages-related issues in a litigation context since 1985. Dr. Ugone's areas of expertise include antitrust, breach of contract, intellectual property, securities, and loss of earnings. On the economics side, Dr. Ugone's work has included analyzing the economic environment surrounding a damages claim, analyzing stock price movements, defining relevant markets, assessing market power, and analyzing the level of competition in a market. On the damages side, Dr. Ugone has developed complex damages models, including conducting lost sales analyses, incremental cost analyses, and lost profit and/or lost earnings analyses. He has testified in state and federal courts. Dr. Ugone has a BA from the University of Notre Dame, an MA from the University of Southern California, and a PhD from Arizona State University, all in Economics.

Marc Van Allen, JD, is a partner with the Chicago office of Jenner & Block, where he is a member of the litigation practice group. He joined Jenner & Block immediately upon his graduation from the University of Michigan Law School in 1992. He has a BA in economics from the University of Chicago.

Frank A. Voorvaart, PhD, is a manager in the Dallas office of Analysis Group, Inc. Dr. Voorvaart specializes in the evaluation of economic damages in complex commercial disputes. Prior to joining Analysis Group, Dr. Voorvaart was a director in the Real Estate Litigation practice of PricewaterhouseCoopers where he assessed damages to real property matters. He has over nine years of experience in real estate litigation consulting, economic analysis, and econometrics and has testified on matters pertaining to appropriate valuation and damages estimation methodology. He holds a PhD in economics from Arizona State University.

Leigh Walton, JD, is a member of the Nashville law firm of Bass, Berry & Sims PLC, concentrating her practice in corporate, securities, and health law matters. She received her BA from Randolph-Macon Woman's College and her JD degree from Vanderbilt University. She currently serves on the Corporate Laws Committee and the Committee on Negotiated Acquisitions of the American Bar Association (ABA). Ms. Walton serves as a cochair of the Practicing Law Institute's annual *Nuts and Bolts of Securities Laws.* She lectures annually at the ABA's *Annual Mergers and Acquisitions Institute* and participates in many other seminars and programs on corporate, securities, and healthcare matters. She served as a lecturer at Vanderbilt University Law School from 1980 to 1987. She is a fellow of the Tennessee Bar Foundation. Ms. Walton also serves on the Metropolitan Development and Housing Agency of Metropolitan Davidson County.

William E. Wecker, PhD, is president of William E. Wecker Associates, Inc., a consulting firm specializing in applied mathematics and statistics. He also serves as consulting professor of Law at Stanford University. He has authored numerous professional articles on statistical theory and methods.

Diana L. Weiss, JD, is a partner in the Washington, DC office of Orrick, Herrington & Sutcliffe LLP. She represents companies, professional firms, and individuals in complex financial and securities litigation and regulatory investigations. Previously, Ms. Weiss practiced in New York and Washington, DC with Donovan Leisure. She received her JD from Cornell Law School in 1991.

Michael R. Young, JD, is a litigation partner at New York's Willkie Farr & Gallagher LLP, where he specializes in financial reporting with a particular emphasis on accounting irregularities. His publications include *The Financial Reporting Handbook* (Aspen, 2003) and *Accounting Irregularities and Financial Fraud* (Aspen, 2nd ed., 2002). He is a graduate of the Duke University School of Law and Allegheny College.

John D. Zante, CPA, is a proprietor of Zante & Co., CPA. He holds a BS in Accounting and an MS in Taxation. Since 1973, he has provided consulting and expert witness services in business dissolutions, business interruption, business valuations, contract disputes, damage analyses, lost profits analyses, marital dissolutions, real estate disputes, and tax disputes.

THE LITIGATION ENVIRONMENT

THE ROLE OF THE FINANCIAL EXPERT IN LITIGATION SERVICES

Peter B. Frank
Christian W. Hughes
Michael J. Wagner
Roman L. Weil

CONTENTS

The authors acknowledge Michael G. Ueltzen, who authored "Professional Standards in a Litigation Service Environment," which appeared in the second edition of *Litigation Services Handbook*. This chapter includes some material from that chapter.

1.1   INTRODUCTION

(a) Rationale for the Book.   Anyone who considers undertaking the role of financial expert will find this book valuable. It will help experienced practitioners stay up to date and will guide them in other areas in which they can apply their experience.

This book is a current reference for certified public accountants (CPAs) and other financial experts involved in typical litigation cases and includes technical approaches and case-specific tools in use today. Although not exhaustive on any topic, it addresses the roles that financial experts play in litigation in commonly encountered cases. We incorporate advice from practitioners with extensive experience in litigation services.

(b) Expert Opinions and Admissibility: The Rules of the Road.   Over time, the role of experts has expanded in the American legal system. Originally, courts allowed expert testimony only when the facts became too complex for an average juror to understand, and no expert could express an opinion on the ultimate issue. The Federal Rules of Evidence[1] have liberalized this and other rules applying to experts, thereby increasing their use. Rule 702, Testimony by Experts, states:

> If scientific, technical, or other specialized knowledge will assist the trier of fact to understand the evidence or to determine a fact in issue, a witness qualified as an expert by knowledge, skill, experience, training, or education may testify thereto in the form of an opinion or otherwise, if (1) the testimony is based upon sufficient facts or data, (2) the testimony is the product of reliable principles and methods, and (3) the witness has applied the principles and methods reliably to the facts of the case.

Rules 703 through 705 of the Federal Rules of Evidence also relate to expert testimony. Rule 703 allows experts in reaching their opinion to rely on otherwise inadmissible facts or data if they are "of a type reasonably relied upon by experts in the particular field in forming opinions or inferences upon the subject." Experts can, for example, rely on hearsay evidence, posing the risk that their testimony will expose jurors to evidence from which the Rules of Evidence aim to insulate them. For this reason, Rule 703 requires judges to guard against the expert acting as a "smuggler of hearsay" to the jury:

> Facts or data that are otherwise inadmissible shall not be disclosed to the jury by the proponent of the opinion or inference unless the court determines that their

probative value in assisting the jury to evaluate the expert's opinion substantially outweighs their prejudicial effect.

Rule 704 allows experts to give an opinion on the issue that the trier of fact will ultimately decide. (The only exception relates to an alleged criminal's mental state.) Thus, an expert can give an opinion on such issues as liability or the amount of damages.

The U.S. Supreme Court guided federal trial court judges as to the admissibility of expert testimony in *Daubert v. Merrell Dow Pharmaceuticals*, 113 S. Ct. 2796 (1993). The trial judge has broad discretion to act as a gatekeeper to forbid expert testimony based on mere subjective belief or unsupported speculation. Although the Court decided in the context of scientific expert testimony, the decision applies to any expert testimony including financial, economic, and accounting testimony; the Court provided this clarity in *Kumho Tire Co. v. Carmichael*, 526 U.S. 137 (1999).

Although *Daubert* and its progeny provide no exclusive list or set of tests that the expert's testimony must meet to be admissible—and thus survive the judge's gatekeeping function—one does well to consider the factors that the decision enumerates:

- Is the theory or technique testable? Has it been tested?
- Has it been subjected to peer review or publication?
- Is the potential rate of error known?
- Is it generally accepted within the relevant community of experts?

These *Daubert*-originated factors, bowing to the scientific method, reflect the scientific nature of the expert evidence at issue in that case. We reiterate that these are examples, not tests or a checklist, and one's testimony can flunk a given test yet be judged admissible by the court; similarly, a court will exclude a testimony that meets all the factors if it lacks relevance, doesn't relate to the facts of the case, or otherwise proves unreliable. The Advisory Committee's Note to Amendment (to Rule 702) effective December 1, 2000 includes some bases for doing so, as well as good standards to apply when evaluating one's own prospective testimony:[2]

> Whether testimony is based on research conducted independent of the litigation or was expressly undertaken for the purpose of the testimony;
>
> Whether the expert has unjustifiably extrapolated from an accepted premise to an unfounded conclusion;
>
> Whether the expert has adequately accounted for obvious alternative explanations;
>
> Whether the expert applies the same degree of intellectual rigor within the courtroom as without;
>
> Whether the field of expertise claimed by the expert is known to reach reliable results (for example, astrologers may observe some principles generally accepted within their community but not, per the Committee, within the courtroom).

Diligent, experienced attorneys with adequate time and funding will take the time and care needed to maximize the likelihood of the testimony's admissibility. Many cases lack such resources, and the experts must then apply care and thoughtfulness to avoid exclusion. In the short term, admissibility will avoid the prejudice to the client (and embarrassment to the expert) of a testimony's exclusion. Excluded testimony will also have long-run repercussions: the misfortune will become a topic of discussion in future depositions and *voir dire*[3] proceedings. It will also require a *yes* answer to one of the first questions that most attorneys will ask an expert whom they consider retaining: "Has a court ever excluded your testimony?"

Before one can confront the perils of qualifying to testify in the courtroom, the court must allow the expert to enter. Federal Rules of Civil Procedure Rule 26(a)(2) provides the requirements for federal cases:

(2) Disclosure of Expert Testimony.

(A) In addition to the disclosures required by paragraph (1), a party shall disclose to other parties the identity of any person who may be used at trial to present evidence under Rules 702, 703, or 705 of the Federal Rules of Evidence.

(B) Except as otherwise stipulated or directed by the court, this disclosure shall, with respect to a witness who is retained or specially employed to provide expert testimony in the case or whose duties as an employee of the party regularly involve giving expert testimony, be accompanied by a written report prepared and signed by the witness. The report shall contain a complete statement of all opinions to be expressed and the basis and reasons therefor; the data or other information considered by the witness in forming the opinions; any exhibits to be used as a summary of or support for the opinions; the qualifications of the witness, including a list of all publications authored by the witness within the preceding ten years; the compensation to be paid for the study and testimony; and a listing of any other cases in which the witness has testified as an expert at trial or by deposition within the preceding four years.

(C) These disclosures shall be made at the times and in the sequence directed by the court. ..." [The expert should consult with the retaining attorney regarding the specific provisions that follow.]

Section 1.3(d) of this chapter discusses the nature and content of expert disclosures, including the report substance. Note that the states' requirements for expert disclosure and discovery have important differences and, in a practical sense, have more variation than do the standards for admission of expert testimony.

(c) Role of the Financial Expert in Litigation.   Lawyers use financial experts in litigation for the same reasons that businesses retain financial experts as advisors: lawyers need quality advice when litigating, and financial experts offer this service because they give advice in the real world to real companies with real problems. Juries understand and respect this practical experience. Because accounting is the language of business, accountants can often clarify business transactions and explain the records reflecting them to lawyers, judges, and the jury. Because economists help companies apply the principles of market definition, price theory, economic modeling, and market risk, they can help interpret the effects of a firm's behavior on competitors or other related entities. Financial experts have the quantitative skills required to undertake and perform the analyses necessary to interpret the technical evidence required in complex commercial cases.

The ideal expert (1) has never testified before and has no relationship with the hiring attorney, firm, or client, so that the jury will be disinclined to regard him as a hired gun but (2) has substantial experience in litigation analyses, testimony, and response to cross-examination. This prospective expert does not exist. The lawyer must weigh the risks and rewards each case presents in making the selection.

This book focuses on the financial expert's role as an expert witness, because litigation practitioners most often serve in this comprehensive role. As Section 1.4(b) discusses, however, experts frequently play a behind-the-scenes role as consultant to the legal team or, occasionally, as arbitrator.

(d) Tasks Undertaken by Financial Experts. Attorneys most often retain financial experts to compute or rebut the plaintiff's damages claim for loss resulting from the defendant's legal wrong. They also provide analysis and testimony on liability issues where their expertise suits them to prepare relevant analyses or to discuss compliance with professional standards in malpractice and similar cases. In addition, financial experts sometimes address the business issues in a case: economists and CPAs with suitable experience often consult or testify on issues involving marketing, economics, and industry practices.

Financial experts can organize and synthesize data. Hence, lawyers rely on them to review collections of documents to extract, store, and analyze information relevant to discovery and trial. Chapter 3 discusses the complementary strengths of accountants and economists and the interaction between the two fields of expertise.

1.2 THE CIVIL COURT SYSTEM

(a) General Process. With the exception of criminal activities related to fraud, this book examines civil disputes. Those disputes fall into tort or contract causes of action. A tort is a wrongful act or inaction unrelated to a contract, such as negligence, fraud, or interference with prospective economic relations. Contract causes of action arise from a breach of a contract's essential terms.

Judges and juries resolve disputes. Judges determine the applicable law in all courts; in *bench trials* (i.e., trials heard by judges, without a jury), they also identify the facts when those are in controversy. Parties also have the right to demand a jury to decide disputed facts in trials before most courts of general jurisdiction, but not in trials involving family law, probate and estate, and equitable issues.[4] In addition, the litigants in some special courts—including tax court and the U.S. Court of Federal Claims—have no right to a jury. Appellate courts have no juries because the trials held in them address only legal issues, not factual issues. Even when parties can demand a jury trial, many prefer that the judge resolve all matters in dispute.

Parties have a right to appeal a decision at a trial court to the first level of the appellate process in either state or federal courts. After that, they have a right of appeal to the higher court(s) but with a diminished likelihood of that court exercising its discretion to hear the case: these higher courts of appeal (usually the supreme court of the jurisdiction) accept or decline to hear cases based on their perception of a matter's importance. Normally, they consider cases in which a number of the lower courts of appeal disagree on an issue that has some societal importance. The courts do not, however, usually consider the matter's importance to the individual appealing the lower appellate court's decision.

Courts of appeal can sustain the lower court's decision, reverse it, or partially sustain and partially reverse it. They can remand the case for retrial on whatever issues they consider appropriate and, in certain circumstances, resolve the matter with a trial *de novo,* an unusual proceeding in which the appeals court in effect retries the case itself based on the original trial record.

(b) Financial Experts' Involvement.   Lawyers for the party involved in litigation interview and retain CPAs and economists for their financial expertise and ability to communicate their opinions effectively. The retention usually occurs after the plaintiff files the complaint but before trial. During the pretrial period, the financial expert consults with the lawyers. The expert can assist in discovery by educating the lawyers as to the types of business records to ask for, drafting relevant interrogatory and deposition questions, and suggesting requests for document production.

Once the lawyers receive information, financial experts will analyze it and explain its relevance. Experts then typically reach opinions based on their analyses. If the lawyers deem these opinions helpful to the trial issues, they designate the CPAs or economists as expert witnesses who testify at trial as to their opinions.

CPAs or economists designated as expert witnesses often have to appear and testify at a deposition in which the opposing lawyer will test their expertise and probe for the bases of their opinions.

(c) Federal District Court System.   The federal system's trial court is known as a *district court*. To qualify as a plaintiff in a federal case, either the plaintiff must raise a question of federal law, or diversity of citizenship must exist between plaintiff(s) and defendant(s). This means that at least one of the defendants must reside in a state different from that of the plaintiffs. When a federal court tries a case because of diversity of citizenship, it will apply state law.[5] Federal law applies only when the plaintiffs bring the cause of action under a federal statute. To file a case in federal court, the amount in controversy must exceed a statutory amount ($75,000 as of 2005).

The federal system has 11 numbered and 2 unnumbered circuits, geographically organized as follows:

Federal Circuit: Jurisdiction not geographically based

District of Columbia Circuit: Washington, DC

First Circuit: Maine, New Hampshire, Massachusetts, Rhode Island, and Puerto Rico

Second Circuit: New York, Connecticut, and Vermont

Third Circuit: New Jersey, Pennsylvania, Delaware, and Virgin Islands

Fourth Circuit: Maryland, Virginia, West Virginia, North Carolina, and South Carolina

Fifth Circuit: Texas, Louisiana, and Mississippi

Sixth Circuit: Tennessee, Kentucky, Ohio, and Michigan

Seventh Circuit: Illinois, Indiana, and Wisconsin

Eighth Circuit: Arkansas, Iowa, Minnesota, Missouri, Nebraska, North Dakota, and South Dakota

Ninth Circuit: California, Arizona, Nevada, Oregon, Washington, Idaho, Montana, Alaska, Hawaii, Guam, and Northern Mariana Islands

Tenth Circuit: Colorado, Kansas, New Mexico, Oklahoma, Utah, and Wyoming

Eleventh Circuit: Alabama, Georgia, and Florida

Each state in each circuit has at least one separate district court. More populous states have more than one district court. For example, California and New York each have four judicial districts. Depending on the population and the court's budget, districts will have different numbers of judges, but each case has only one judge.

The plaintiff selects the district in which it files the case, subject to the restriction that one of the parties must reside in the district.

(d) Federal Courts of Appeals. The federal circuit courts hear appeals from district court decisions. The trial court jurisdiction dictates the appellate court jurisdiction. A federal court of appeals will accept appeals only from district courts in its circuit, with specific exceptions (e.g., appeals involving intellectual property cases) which are heard in the U.S. Court of Appeals for the Federal Circuit. A party has a right to appeal a district court decision to the appropriate court of appeals. Normally, a panel of three judges, selected at random, will hear cases on appeal. Through an *en banc* petition, a party can request that the entire panel of judges in a particular circuit hear the appeal, but the circuit can deny such a request.

(e) U.S. Supreme Court. A party must have a decision from the federal court of appeals before it can petition the U.S. Supreme Court for review. Rare exceptions occur for matters of extreme importance and urgency. The Supreme Court found the antitrust case between the United States and Microsoft insufficiently urgent to require an expedited appeal. A party has no absolute right of appeal to the Supreme Court, which accepts cases of broad relevance only. If the issue affects only the immediate parties, the Supreme Court likely will hear the case only if an unsettled question of law needs clarification, for example, when different circuits have decided a matter differently.

(f) Special Federal Courts

(i) Tax Court. Complex tax law often requires judges with training and experience in taxation to resolve disputes expeditiously. An entity with a federal tax dispute can choose to litigate either in district court or in a special tax court, which exists solely to resolve cases between the Internal Revenue Service and taxpayers. The procedural requirements for filing in tax courts differ from those in district courts. Chapter 37 addresses tax fraud cases.

(ii) U.S. Court of Appeals for the Federal Circuit. Federal district courts hear patent, copyright, and trademark issues, which are collectively referred to as intellectual property disputes and discussed in Chapters 20 through 23. Appeals from district court decisions on such cases do not go to the corresponding circuit court of appeals but to the U.S. Court of Appeals for the Federal Circuit in Washington, DC. The Federal Circuit also hears appeals from the Court of Federal Claims, which we discuss next.

(iii) U.S. Court of Federal Claims. This court renders judgment upon any claim against the United States based on the Constitution, any act of Congress, regulation of an executive department, or an express or implied contract with the United States. Although the U.S. Court of Federal Claims hears most claims for damages against the federal government, district courts have concurrent jurisdiction of certain claims against the United States (e.g., certain tax claims) and exclusive jurisdiction of most tort claims. Chapter 31 describes the handling of federal contract disputes in detail.

(iv) Bankruptcy Courts.   Each federal district has a bankruptcy court to hear cases filed under Title 11 of the United States Code covering bankruptcy matters. The bankruptcy court has exclusive jurisdiction over all of the debtor's property once a filing for bankruptcy has occurred. Chapter 28 discusses bankruptcy procedure and practice.

(g) State Courts.   Similar to the federal system, state court systems have trial courts, courts of appeals, and a supreme court to handle final appeals. State court systems usually have several different types of trial courts, and the nomenclature varies across states.

(i) Courts of Limited Jurisdiction.   Some state trial courts limit the amount of damages that the plaintiff can collect or the subject matters upon which they can decide. A small claims court is an example of such a court. Many courts of limited jurisdiction cannot hear felony cases but only civil and criminal misdemeanor cases.

(ii) Courts of Unlimited Jurisdiction.   Each state has general purpose trial courts, similar to the district courts in the federal system. These courts handle cases that involve major issues, whether for large monetary damages or for felony matters in criminal cases. The financial expert involved in state court most often works in these courts.

(h) Choice of Courts.   A plaintiff sometimes can choose the court in which to file a lawsuit. If the suit involves only state law issues but meets federal diversity standards, the plaintiff can file in either state or federal court. If the plaintiff elects to file in federal court, more than one federal court often presents a proper venue (location) for the trial.

A plaintiff considers several factors before deciding in which court to file: the judges' reputations, existing law, and the length of wait to trial. The plaintiff might also consider the number of jurors necessary to reach a verdict (this can differ by court—federal district courts require a unanimous decision by 6 jurors; many states require 12 jurors, but not all states require a unanimous decision) as well as the record and apparent attitude of the related appeals court. Commentators often belittle this decision process regarding which court to file in as forum shopping, an attempt to find the court that will exhibit the most sympathy for the plaintiff's position. Certain states have a reputation of presenting rosier prospects for class plaintiffs (e.g., Alabama), for commercial defendants (e.g., Delaware), or for conferring a home-field advantage in dispensing justice (e.g., Texas). Whether one credits these prejudices or not, most litigants will find it more economical to proceed in their local courts than to bring or defend an action on the other side of the country.

(i) Applicable Rules Governing Litigation

(i) Evidence.   All judicial systems have rules of evidence governing what the parties can present to the trier of fact for deliberation. The judge rules on objections to the admissibility of evidence. Mistakes in evidential rulings, if material, become grounds for appealing the trial court decision.

Financial experts who offer litigation services should become familiar with the rules of evidence of the court systems in which they work. Article VII of the

Federal Rules of Evidence deals with opinions and expert testimony. Article IX addresses authentication and identification of evidence. These rules affect the work of financial experts.

The rules of evidence in state courts vary. Many follow the Federal Rules of Evidence, but some do not. Of particular significance are the hearsay rules. All courts exclude hearsay, which is evidence offered based on something other than the personal experience of the witness. Some exceptions to the hearsay rule exist, such as business records kept in the normal course of operations. Hearsay can, however, form the basis of expert opinions in some circumstances in some courts, and experts should understand the requirements of their venue. The hearsay rules have evolved as common-sense safeguards against unjust trial results, and understanding the logic of the rules can help experts present their testimony more clearly and thoughtfully.

(ii) Procedure.   Courts differ in their methods of operation. *Procedure* is the set of formal steps that guides the judicial process between the filing of the complaint and the culmination of the trial and appeals. It is the machinery by which litigants resolve their disputes.

Criminal and civil courts differ in their procedures. This book emphasizes civil cases, so it discusses civil procedure. As with evidence, formal rules govern procedure. These rules, enacted by statute in each state and by the United States, set out the particular discovery devices that lawyers can use and when they can use them. Section 1.3 of this chapter explains typical discovery tools and their use. In addition to controlling discovery, the rules of civil procedure explain the requirements that pleadings and other motions before the court must meet.

One important rule of civil procedure that affects experts is Federal Rule of Civil Procedure 26, which governs the discovery permitted of experts and consultants. Section 1.3(d) of this chapter discusses this rule.

(iii) Local Rules.   Local court rules supplement the rules of civil procedure in federal and some state courts. The rules of civil procedure do not cover all situations at the detailed level that some judges prefer. Therefore, some judges supplement them with additional procedures that litigants must follow in their courts. Typical local rules deal with page limits on motions, time limits on depositions, mandatory mediation provisions for certain types of action, and similar matters of efficiency in practice. Failure to follow the local judge's special rules can cause delay and the court can refuse to accept legal filings.

(j) Alternative Dispute Resolution (ADR).   Many perceive the United States to have a slow and expensive court system. Several reasons account for this: the ease with which plaintiffs can initiate cases and the limited supply of judicial resources. Moreover, the rights to extensive discovery and the difficulty of scheduling attorneys' time add to the delay. These factors have encouraged disputants to pursue other means of resolution, including arbitration, minitrials, and mediation. (Chapter 4 further discusses ADR.)

(i) Arbitration.   Arbitration involves the submission of a dispute to one or more unofficial persons who will resolve the dispute privately. A contract, the law, or agreement of the parties can set the procedures. Such bodies as the American Arbitration Association, the National Association of Securities Dealers, and private

arbitration providers have established arbitration procedures, some tailored to specific types of dispute (e.g., employment or construction disputes). Arbitration offers the benefit of finality: although most settings offer certain rights of appeal through the formal legal system, judges are slow to revisit the findings of an arbitrator—often a technical expert selected by the parties for that reason—absent fraud or a material undisclosed conflict of interest.

(ii) Minitrials.   The minitrial forum resulted from efforts to involve business people early in the resolution of commercial disputes. In a short trial, usually no longer than a day, both sides present their cases to senior management, such as the chief executive officers of the companies, who has authority to settle the matter. The process does not bind the parties, nor can they use information learned in the proceeding in a subsequent trial on the issues in dispute.

The minitrial has no formal rules of procedure or evidence. Each lawyer presents arguments or a few witnesses. When each side has heard the best arguments of the other, the decision makers discuss the case, with no lawyers present, in an attempt to resolve the dispute.

The minitrial has proved most successful when a commercial settlement seems feasible, the parties share an interest in their ongoing relation, and the parties retain a facilitator or pseudo-judge to conduct the proceeding. They often appoint a retired judge or a person experienced in the industry. The facilitator has no power to decide the matter but can ask questions of the parties, meet individually with them, and lead the discussion between them, giving an informed view of the strengths and weaknesses in each side's case. The Center for Public Resources[6] has a list of individuals qualified to serve in the role of facilitator.

(iii) Mediation.   Marital dissolution cases make the most use of mediation. A mediator works with disputants in an attempt to arrive at a settlement. A mediator helps the parties recognize the strengths and weaknesses of their own and each other's positions; mediators can also suggest compromises and strategies to resolve the dispute.

Similar to a minitrial, this process is nonbinding. A decision requires agreement by all the parties. Success often depends on the parties' desire to resolve the dispute and the skill of the neutral participant.

1.3 THE LEGAL PROCESS

(a) Overview of a Lawsuit.   This section discusses the steps in a typical litigation that proceeds to trial. The expert who understands this structure can work better in the process and communicate better with the lawyers on the team. Litigation comprises five major stages, some of which occur concurrently: pleadings, discovery, trial, the outcome, and appeal.

(b) Legal Pleadings

(i) Complaint.   The complaint is the first pleading in a civil case, in which the plaintiff sets out the actions (or inactions) that prompted the lawsuit. The complaint contains a list of the defendants, the name of the court in which it is filed, the laws and legal theories under which the plaintiff seeks relief, the remedies sought, and whether the plaintiff demands a jury (when that option exists).

Jurisdictions and causes of action differ in the amount of detail the complaint must include. Some courts require the plaintiff to list all known material facts used to support the claims. Other courts require minimal disclosure of facts in the complaints, requiring little more than that the plaintiff notify the defendant of the lawsuit.

(ii) Demurrer.   A defendant who believes that the plaintiff has not met the legal standards of a proper complaint can file a demurrer. This pleading disputes the legal sufficiency of the complaint (or other pleading). It aims to eliminate, at the outset, tangential or nonmeritorious claims. A demurrer states that, even assuming the facts alleged by the plaintiff are true, no cause of action exists that imposes any legal liability on the defendant. The demurrer states that the court need not decide an issue of law and requests the court to dismiss the complaint.

This device often forces the plaintiff to clarify the complaint (or other pleading) because the plaintiff must provide additional information in responsive pleadings. Sometimes the plaintiff must also amend the complaint to make it sufficient. The demurrer also provides time for the defendant to respond to the complaint.

(iii) Answer.   The answer by the defendant responds to the plaintiff's complaint. Normally, defendants admit the allegations in the complaint with which they agree and deny the allegations with which they disagree. Defendants can also plead affirmative defenses based on the facts pled in the complaint, which, if successful, preclude the plaintiff from prevailing.

The answer can also contain a cross-complaint in which the defendant will make claims against the plaintiff (cross-defendant), which the plaintiff will have to answer and defend at trial. Generally, the defendant must file an answer within a short time of receipt of the complaint (20 to 30 days, unless the court grants an extension).

(c) Discovery—Introduction.   Discovery occurs in the time between filing the original pleadings and the trial. In discovery, each party attempts to ascertain the other party's facts and theories. Most litigation never advances to the trial stage but settles during the discovery phase or shortly before trial. Resolving confusing sets of facts and expanding client and counsel's knowledge of the economic landscape decreases the uncertainty of the litigation's outcome, increasing the likelihood of a settlement.

Experts perform most of their work during this period. Before identifying and collecting information, counsel and the financial analyst should educate each other: counsel educates the financial analyst about the legal issues in the litigation; the financial analyst educates counsel on the economic and financial propositions that relate to these legal issues and on the analyses that could develop them. Then the expert, with the assistance of counsel, collects the necessary facts, analyzes them, develops any assumptions, and forms expert opinions.

Lawyers can use various legal tools in discovery to help their experts perform their work. The following sections describe the major discovery tools and their uses.

(d) Discovery—Written Reports.   Federal Rule of Civil Procedure 26(a)(2)(B) requires that experts prepare and sign a written report. (Section 1.1(b) of this chapter contains the full text, including required elements.) Counsel must disclose this report to the other parties before the court will allow the expert to testify at trial. Local rules of the court, or agreement of the parties, or the trial judge will often set the date of this disclosure. Otherwise, counsel must disclose the report at least 90 days before trial. If counsel retains an expert strictly to rebut the testimony of an opposing expert, counsel must disclose the report of this rebuttal expert within 30 days of the disclosure of the other expert's report.

The written report's content should permit full discovery by the opposing side of all the opinions and bases for the opinions. In addition, if the expert has any changes to the report (or subsequent deposition) that correct, complete, or add to the report, counsel must disclose these before trial, or the court can preclude the expert from testifying to these additional opinions or new reasons for the previously disclosed opinions.

District courts can opt out of the requirement for a written report. Financial experts should check with the attorneys who have retained them to ascertain the requirement of the district court in which the plaintiff has filed the case as well as any agreements specific to the case.

Many state court systems model their rules of civil procedure after the Federal Rules of Civil Procedure, requiring written expert reports as well.

(e) Discovery—Interrogatories.   Interrogatories are written questions that one party asks of the adversary, who must answer in writing under oath. The financial expert's special knowledge of business or a particular industry can help counsel construct questions to develop a thorough understanding of the adversary's systems, documentation, files, and structure. For example, the nature and extent of the opposing party's financial reporting and management information systems present possible areas of inquiry. A party can learn the names and titles of officers or principals in the business to enable further discovery of pertinent files or to identify potential sources of deposition testimony.

(f) Discovery—Requests for Production of Documents.   A request for production of documents requires one party to provide documents that the other considers relevant to issues in the case. These requests usually follow interrogatories. If the requests do not name documents with great specificity, the opposing party often will not produce them, even when the request makes clear the information sought.[7] When possible, therefore, the request should state exact titles of reports, which the lawyer has learned from the information obtained through previous interrogatories or depositions.

The party responding to the request often does not copy the documents. Instead, it makes the documents available, typically at its attorney's offices, where the requesting party can review them and decide which ones to copy at its own expense.

The requesting party's attorney often will want the financial expert to review financial and other business records produced to aid in identifying and copying the relevant documents. In addition, the financial expert and the attorney will review the documents copied, so costs will increase as the number of documents discovered increases. Knowledgeable experts can reduce unnecessary copying (and subsequent review costs) by identifying the types of financial and business records that they will need to prove the issues and by helping the attorney efficiently select which of the opponents' documents to review. Section 17.4 of Chapter 17 discusses how to find and obtain data, including e-mail files and traffic.

(g) Discovery—Requests for Admissions. A request for admission seeks the opposing party's verification of information as fact. The request must relate to the litigation. Verifying the information as fact usually proves adverse to the interest of the party making the admission.

Admissions help narrow the factual issues that the parties will litigate at trial. The trial need not address undisputed facts, which decreases the time for trying a case. Judges like admissions. Financial experts can suggest the types of facts within their area of expertise that opposing parties might admit prior to a civil trial. The expert can also assist the attorney in developing arguments about why the party should or should not admit certain business facts prior to trial.

(h) Discovery—Depositions. A deposition is the oral testimony of a witness questioned under oath by an attorney, who can use the written record later at trial under certain circumstances.

(i) Deposition of a Financial Expert. When a CPA, economist, or other financial analyst serves as an expert witness, the opposition's attorney usually deposes the expert to learn his or her background and the bases for the opinions in the case. The attorney uses the deposition to evaluate the expert as a trial witness, find strengths and weaknesses, and develop a comprehensive understanding of the opinions, studies, and analyses. In rare cases, some experienced attorneys omit the deposition, in part because it can educate the expert. A deposition sometimes allows an expert to test theories or approaches and then correct them as needed for the trial. Depositions present a final risk for the adverse party in that the expert can use the deposition as an opportunity to correct deficiencies in previous disclosure that might otherwise lead to exclusions by the judge for failure to comply with Rule 26.

Questions at the deposition usually cover all work that the financial expert performed, including rejected analyses, blind alleys, and information obtained but not used. In addition, the opposing lawyer can use the deposition to narrow the scope of the expert's testimony at the trial, because the lawyer can use information from the deposition to impeach the expert's credibility at the trial. The expert must give consistent testimony in the deposition and at trial or be prepared to explain why they differ.

Federal Rule of Civil Procedure 26(b)(4)(A) covers the taking of depositions of experts in federal cases. Counsel can take a deposition of any person whom the opposing side has identified as an expert who may testify at trial. The deposition cannot occur, however, until after counsel has disclosed the written report required by Federal Rule of Civil Procedure 26(a)(2)(B).

(ii) Assisting in a Deposition. Although only an attorney can ask questions at a deposition, a financial expert (retained as either a witness or a consultant) can assist the attorney during the examination, particularly of people in the financial or accounting areas. Attorneys also ask the financial expert for assistance at a deposition of the opposition's expert. The expert knows the language of business and can often detect a witness's uninformative answer or a sign of weakness that the

attorney might miss. The financial expert can suggest additional questions to the attorney by passing notes or by discussions during breaks in the deposition. In this way, the expert can help identify an inconsistency, suggest a follow-up question, or expose a flaw in the testimony. Although the financial expert has no right to attend another expert's deposition, the attorneys will often agree on an attendance policy for all depositions.

Even when the financial expert does not attend the deposition, the attorney often will request the expert to provide questions for the attorney to ask. These questions have two aims: (1) to clarify the opinions the opposing expert is likely to express at trial and the analytical work that supports it and (2) to point out problems, inconsistencies, and errors in the analysis.

Some lawyers do not want to alert the witness to analytical flaws during the deposition. They prefer to hold this information for use at the trial. Others prefer to use the deposition to point out the weaknesses in their opponent's case, thus encouraging settlement or, at a minimum, forcing the expert to correct the analysis before use at the trial.

(i) Discovery—Subpoenas.   Most often, parties comply with requests for documents and witness appearances. For those situations where a party does not cooperate with such requests, the attorney can use a subpoena to compel such cooperation. The subpoena *ad testificandum* commands a person to appear and testify as a witness. The subpoena *duces tecum* commands a person to produce documents. Practice varies by jurisdiction: serving a subpoena on a party or expert can be an insult in one forum; failing to do so may constitute malpractice in another.

Frequently, only the subpoena will obtain information from third parties not related to the litigation. The court can hold an uncooperative recipient of a subpoena in contempt and impose sanctions as severe as incarceration.

Any party or subpoena recipient, including the financial expert, can object to a subpoena, thus requiring a hearing on the relevance and propriety of materials demanded. A financial expert who objects to a subpoena for documents might thereby delay the trial and generate costly legal fees. Sometimes, however, the expert must object, as when a subpoena requests materials related to other clients. Often the opposing attorneys agree on how much they will try to discover from the experts and thereby avoid unproductive controversy.

The opposing counsel may wish to explore the records of other nonparty clients of the financial experts using the subpoena and deposition process. CPAs must avoid violating Ethics Rule 301 of the American Institute of Certified Public Accountants (AICPA) Rules of Professional Conduct, which requires the CPA to maintain client confidentiality with past as well as current clients. Because CPAs have a duty to comply only with a validly issued subpoena, they may need to test the subpoena's validity before revealing confidential client information.

(j) Trial

(i) Opening Statements.   For a jury trial, the court and attorneys first pick the jury. Each side's attorney then makes an opening statement. (The defendant can choose to delay an opening statement until presenting its case.) The attorneys explain the issues of the case as they view them, the conclusions that the trier of fact should reach on these issues, and the evidence they will present.

The attorney uses this time to educate the trier of fact about the entire case. Although the opening statement does not present evidence, some observers believe that many cases turn on opening statements.

(ii) Plaintiff's Case.   The plaintiff carries the burden of proof at trial and in most civil cases must meet the standard of a preponderance of the evidence, 51 percent in layman's terms. The plaintiff presents its case first. Normally, witnesses present evidence, and the normal process of examination proceeds, as discussed in the following sections.

(iii) Direct Examination.   Direct examination is the first examination of a witness by the attorney who calls the witness. During this question-and-answer session, the plaintiff must introduce the evidence that proves its case.

Formal rules of evidence apply, and the opposing counsel can object to defective questions or to questions intended to elicit inadmissible evidence; the judge can either allow the question or sustain the objection.

Experts serve themselves and their clients well if they understand the typical grounds for objection. Such grounds include questions that call for hearsay evidence or lead the witness, or testimony that misstates prior testimony or assumes facts not in evidence. As with the rules of evidence, understanding the elements of proper questioning can help the expert provide clear and accurate testimony that the court will respect.

(iv) Cross-Examination.   Cross-examination is the first examination of a witness by the attorney for the opposing party. It immediately follows the end of direct examination. The opposing side will try to discredit the witness or to obtain evidence favorable to its case.

In principle, opposing attorneys must limit cross-examination to issues raised in the direct examination of the witness. If attorneys for the opposing side wish to raise other issues, they must call the witness as an adverse witness in their own case and then conduct direct examination. Some judges, however, allow fairly wide cross-examination, particularly of expert witnesses.

Unlike direct examination, cross-examination rules permit leading questions— those that suggest a particular answer. In addition, the opposing attorney can read (if germane) prior deposition or other testimony or writings of the witness into the record in an attempt to impeach the witness. Courts have increased the use of video to replace reading from a deposition transcript.

(v) Redirect Examination.   This examination immediately follows cross-examination of a witness. Rules of procedure limit redirect examination to issues raised on cross-examination. An attorney who forgets to ask about a matter on direct examination cannot raise the matter for the first time during redirect unless it relates to issues raised in the cross-examination. In redirect, counsel tries to rehabilitate the witness if necessary and possible or, if applicable, to demonstrate that the cross-examining attorney has treated the witness unfairly or employed artifice in an attempt to mislead the jury.

(vi) Recross-Examination.   This examination immediately follows redirect examination, and the attorney must limit it to issues raised in the redirect examination. Recross-examination normally has a narrow scope. In theory, iterations of re-redirect

and re-recross can proceed indefinitely. In practice, few judges have the patience to permit such excess, and most lawyers know better than to test that patience.

(vii) Defendant's Case.   The plaintiff will present all of its witnesses and exhibits before the defendant begins its case. When the plaintiff rests, the defendant can request a *directed verdict*, discussed in Section 1.3(k)(iv) of this chapter. Unless the judge grants such a motion, the defendant presents all of its witnesses. The examination proceeds as described previously in *(iii)* through *(vi)* for the plaintiff's case.

If the defendant believes that the plaintiff has not proved its case but no directed verdict has been granted, it can decide against presenting a case and simply rest. The defendant in these circumstances hopes it has made its case through cross-examination and recross-examination of the plaintiff's witnesses. Attorneys usually find this strategy difficult and ineffective because most of the plaintiff's witnesses will prove hostile to the defendant's positions. In the words of an experienced trial attorney: "If your best defense is that the plaintiff hasn't carried his burden, you need another defense."

(viii) Plaintiff's Rebuttal Case.   After the defendant rests its case, the plaintiff has a chance to rebut the defendant's case. This occurs through witnesses and documents as described previously in *(vii)* for the defendant's case. The plaintiff must limit the rebuttal's scope to issues raised in the defendant's case. Some judges and jurisdictions do not allow a rebuttal case. Financial experts often participate in rebuttal when the defendant has sufficiently discredited the plaintiff's damages theory or study so that the plaintiff must present a revised damages study to address the problems raised by the defendant.

(ix) Defendant's Surrebuttal Case.   Some jurisdictions permit the defendant to respond to issues raised by the plaintiff's rebuttal case. Courts refer to this response as *surrebuttal* and restrict it to issues raised in the plaintiff's rebuttal case. Other jurisdictions do not allow surrebuttal or leave it to the judge's discretion.

(x) Closing Arguments.   Once both sides have rested, the plaintiff (in a civil trial) will make its closing arguments first, followed by the defendant. The attorney will summarize the evidence from the trial record and try to persuade the trier of fact why his or her client should prevail.

(xi) Post-Trial Briefs and Findings of Fact.   The judge often will ask the attorneys to file briefs summarizing points that the lawyers think they have proved and the relevant law that the court should apply to the case. This helps the judge write an opinion in a bench trial (i.e., a trial heard only by a judge without a jury).

These briefs contain suggested findings of fact and conclusions of law. Financial experts sometimes assist the lawyer in drafting a portion of the brief, particularly the part summarizing the expert's testimony. The findings of fact must refer only to evidence admitted in the trial. The facts must be part of the record in the trial and cannot result from new or objectionable evidence.

(k) Types of Outcomes

(i) Verdict.   The verdict is the decision rendered by a jury (or a judge in a bench trial). It presents the formal decision or finding made by a jury and reported to the court upon the matters or questions submitted to them at trial. The jury can render

a general or a special verdict. In a general verdict, the jury finds in favor of the plaintiff or defendant on all issues. In special verdicts, the jury decides only the facts of the case and leaves the decisions on the application of the law up to the judge. A special verdict results when a jury must make separate decisions as to different issues in the case. This most often occurs through interrogatories to the jury.

(ii) Judgment.   A judgment is the court's official decision as to the rights and claims of the litigants. If the court (i.e., the judge) accepts the jury's verdict, that verdict becomes the judgment. In almost all cases, the judge makes this judgment with no further comment or opinion. If the court does not accept the jury's verdict, the judge can make a judgment, as explained later in *(v)*. If the judge is the trier of fact, the judge's decision becomes the judgment.

(iii) Opinion.   Judges will state the reasons for their decision and their understanding of the application of the relevant law. These writings, if appealed and sustained, become the precedents that form the basis for court-made law in our judicial system.

In some cases, a party asks the judge to rule on part or all of the case even before the trial begins. The party moving for such a *summary judgment* argues that even if all the facts alleged by the opponent hold true, no triable issue of law exists. In other words, the facts alleged do not violate the laws or legal rights asserted by the opponent. Even though full dismissal of an action on motion for summary judgment occurs rarely (many judges have a bias in favor of allowing parties their day in court), they often prove effective in paring away pieces of an action, reducing the complexity, required time, and, of course, cost of an ensuing trial. Additionally, many attorneys believe they can educate the judge to their perspective in the case, creating a more favorable starting point for them at trial.

(iv) Directed Verdict.   At the close of the plaintiff's case, the defendant requests a directed verdict when the defendant believes the plaintiff has not proved its case either factually or as a matter of law. If the judge grants the directed verdict, the case concludes (although the judgment can be appealed, like any other), and the defendant does not have to present its case.

(v) Judgment as a Matter of Law.   In a jury trial, the jury decides the case and renders a verdict. Before the court (i.e., the judge) accepts the verdict, the losing party can request—or the judge can volunteer—a decision contrary to the verdict rendered by the jury. In effect, the court does not accept the verdict of the jury and renders an opposite decision. This is called a *judgment as a matter of law* (JMOL).

(l) Appeal.   A losing party in a trial who believes that the court has committed an error at the trial can appeal to a superior court to reverse the decision of the lower court. The appeals court does not offer a forum for a new trial of the facts. The appeals court will accept the record of the original trial court and decide whether the lower court committed any legal error in procedure or reasoning. Because the appeals focus on analysis of law rather than facts, financial experts rarely assist in this phase.

1.4   TYPICAL ROLES OF THE FINANCIAL EXPERT

(a) Expert Witness.   An expert witness renders an expert opinion at trial. The financial expert's opinion usually relates to business issues in which the expert has special education, training, or work experience. The trier of fact lacks this knowledge or expertise, so the financial expert's opinion will help it reach a decision.

One party retains the CPA, economist, or other expert and identifies the individual(s) to the opposing party as expert witnesses. Once a party has identified an expert, the opposing side likely can discover all the work the expert performs—or has already performed—related to the litigation. Sometimes the parties agree to limit such extensive discovery. In addition, some issues are poorly settled in certain jurisdictions, notably the question of whether all or only certain communications between expert and retaining counsel are subject to claims of privilege and are hence undiscoverable. The expert should obtain an early understanding with counsel on that attorney's philosophy,[8] including the related topic of whether the best practice of discarding draft expert work-product is appropriate to the circumstances of the case. Many experts believe that they should retain any drafts of reports shown to attorneys. They believe the negative implications (including possible preclusion from testifying) of destroying these drafts far outweigh any cross-examination related to subsequent changes that one makes to the drafts. Regardless of anyone's views, the expert should conduct the engagement from the outset assuming that all work, communications, and documents will be subject to discovery.

(b) Consultant.   The attorney hires the CPA or economist as consultant to advise about the facts, issues, and strategy of the case. The consultant does not testify at trial. Consequently, the opposition often never knows of the financial consultant. The attorney work-product doctrine generally protects the consultant's opinion, discussions, workpapers, and impressions from discovery by the opposition. If a financial analyst progresses from consultant to expert witness, all the analyst's work product, writings, workpapers, and even notes likely will become discoverable. For large cases, attorneys often have one CPA or economist as a consultant and designate another to provide expert testimony. Coordinating their roles without exposing the consultant's work to discovery demands some care and close communication with counsel.

The work of a consultant usually includes analyzing, and advising on how best to discredit, the opposing expert's work. Sometimes the consultant also examines the strengths and weaknesses of the client's case and how best to represent these facts at trial.

Attorneys retain consultants on occasion to evaluate the effects of particularly troublesome facts not shared with the testifying expert. Philosophies vary on the advisability of this practice. If the opposing side knows the troublesome information, it could surprise the unprepared expert at deposition or, worse, at trial. If counsel is curious as to how the expert might respond to a difficult question, performing the experiment in front of the jury can be a costly adventure.

(c) Who Is The Client?   The expert retained to perform a litigation services engagement has two potential clients: the law firm and the party to the lawsuit.

Most attorneys believe that to protect a nontestifying expert consultant's work from discovery, the expert must work for the lawyer. If the disputant hires the expert, the attorney work-product doctrine likely will not apply, nor will the attorney-client privilege, which protects communications only between a client and its attorney. Commercial considerations can enter into the discussion when an attorney has concerns over the client's ability or willingness to pay and prefers to stay out of the contracting loop. Section 1.8 of this chapter addresses such issues.

(d) Trier of Fact.   The court can appoint the financial expert as special master who will decide certain facts in a dispute. In effect, the financial expert will act in this function as the judge and jury. The special master becomes useful when a case has difficult accounting or financial issues that only a CPA or economist can understand. On rare occasions, the judge retains the expert to advise the judge in deciding these issues. Sometimes the parties want to agree on an individual to make these decisions in an effort to get an informed decision, accelerate the process, or save expenses. (Chapter 4 discusses the financial expert's role as a neutral person in alternative dispute resolution.)

1.5   FINANCIAL EXPERT SERVICES IN THE LITIGATION ENVIRONMENT

(a) Discovery Assistance.   Business litigation often depends on documents to prove or disprove an issue at trial. As a result, the parties undertake voluminous document discovery and production. Business records become crucial to a number of issues in most cases. Financial experts can assist in finding, understanding, and explaining the information from these documents.

Lawyers need to know the types of documents that exist in managing a business so they can formulate precise requests for documents. This knowledge also helps the lawyer to assess the responsiveness of particular productions and to understand what other documents might exist (*see* Chapter 17, Data Management).

Depositions of financial and management people often relate to technical business issues. Attorneys need help in understanding the real issues and in formulating effective questions. Because technical people will often answer questions in jargon that has a special meaning in a particular industry or business discipline, attorneys often need assistance in understanding the answers and developing follow-up questions. Financial experts can assist in this area.

Lawyers need information about the opposing expert's work to effectively cross-examine and rebut the opposing expert's opinion. When the expertise involves business, financial experts can assist lawyers in analyzing the expert's work and the strengths and weaknesses of its support.

(b) Proof of Business Facts.   In commercial litigation, factual evidence—except that derived from testimony—comes principally from the business records of the parties or from industry and market sources. Financial experts can help lawyers obtain, understand, authenticate, organize, and explain this information.

Experts can base opinion testimony on either facts or assumptions. They usually base assumptions on facts or presumptions from facts. In either case, the expert must lay a proper foundation as to the source of the information. Financial experts can help to develop these facts by collecting the relevant business or industry data to support their own or other experts' opinions. Federal Rule 702 requires that experts reliably apply their methods to the facts of the case. Accordingly, even when testifying based on hypothetical premises, the expert must have confidence in the reliability of those premises. The expert who accepts the-moon-is-cheese assumptions is fishing with his reputation for bait.

(c) Computation of Damages.   Financial experts often calculate damages in commercial litigation, and this topic dominates much of the remainder of this book. Numerous types of damages occur—such as actual losses of cash, or equivalents, or other property, or expected profits—and practitioners have developed methods to compute them. The type of damages that the expert must compute can be a question of fact or opinion, but the law limits recovery of certain types of damages in certain causes of action.

The financial expert should communicate with the attorney to agree on the type of damages to calculate and an appropriate method of computation. Otherwise, the court can rule a calculation inadmissible as inappropriate to the circumstances.

Actual loss incurred defines one type of damages recovery. Experts compute this form of restitution, which applies in many fraud cases, as the difference between what the plaintiff paid for something and the actual value received, or as the value of something once, but no longer, possessed.

The expected profits from a proposed contract or deal represent another common type of recovery. Practitioners often refer to this as the benefit-of-the-bargain approach of computing damages in contract disputes. Plaintiffs often claim lost profits in business litigation. One measures this as the amount by which the plaintiff's actual earnings fall short of the earnings that would have occurred but for the defendant's illegal actions. Practitioners most often state this formula as the difference between but-for profits (i.e., those that would have been earned but for the defendant's improper act) and actual profits. More generally, most damages analyses require the use of assumptions and projections about what would have happened if certain behavior of the defendant had been different.

Other examples of damages claim types include reasonable royalty analyses in patent infringement, actual cash value computations under business property insurance policies, and monetary cost to restore the plaintiff back to the starting point under equitable rescission theories in some contract cases.

(d) Development of Strategy.   Financial experts who serve as litigation consultants can suggest approaches to the business issues in a case. Even the best trial lawyers usually lack the business experience and insights that such financial experts have learned from their business consulting, experience, training, and education.

Lawyers need independent analysis of the positions they believe they must prove to win the case. The financial expert can help the lawyer identify errors and devise different approaches, perhaps using different facts. Although financial consultants, in contrast to experts who are impartial, may be in an advocacy situation, they should maintain as much objectivity and independence as the circumstances permit. Their clients will find these qualities most useful, and often in short supply, on the trial team.

(e) Document Management. Financial services firms frequently have expertise in management information, information technology (IT), and computer systems. Such experts can help attorneys collect, organize, and summarize the large volume of documents that often arises in a business case. They usually use IT systems to manage the large databases of documents or images created for the case. Chapter 17 discusses techniques involved in such management issues.

Small cases that do not justify the cost of automated document retrieval systems nevertheless need some system. The expert can help organize the documents so that lawyers can locate relevant evidence.

(f) GAAP/GAAS Rules and Compliance. Some CPAs have the qualifications to render opinions on generally accepted accounting principles (GAAP) and generally accepted auditing standards (GAAS). Such issues arise when a party questions the accuracy of financial statements or the care with which they have been audited. Accountants will frequently structure such testimony as an *attestation engagement* (*see* Section 1.6 of this chapter).

GAAP and GAAS issues arise when a plaintiff sues an accounting firm for violating these standards, alleging harm because it relied on the accuracy of the financial statements. Chapter 19 discusses accountants' liability.

GAAP issues also arise when a dispute relates to the purchase or sale of a business and one party questions the accuracy of the prior financial statements or those on which a post-closing working capital adjustment is based. GAAP issues can also arise in any damages computations that rely on financial statements.

1.6 OPINION TESTIMONY

(a) Expert Opinion. Expert opinion is testimony by a person qualified to speak authoritatively because of some combination of special training, skill, study, experience, observation, practice, and familiarity with the subject matter. Expert knowledge is knowledge not possessed by laymen or inexperienced persons. State or federal rules of evidence define the scope and nature of admissible expert opinion testimony.

The courts consider CPAs and some others with appropriate experience and training as experts on accounting matters. Economists and some CPAs (depending on training and experience) have expertise in the application of economic, financial, statistical, and econometric techniques. Either of these types of expert frequently possess industry expertise as well. We encourage experts to objectively weigh their qualifications for any opinion they are asked to give and to do so early in the case lest they find themselves and their clients harmed by a successful *Daubert* challenge (*see* Section 1.1(b) of this chapter).

(b) Audit Opinion. Experts develop their own findings, conclusions, and opinions. In an attest engagement, which requires a CPA's expertise, the CPA expresses a conclusion about the reliability of a written assertion that is the responsibility of another party—the asserter. Only rarely does a litigation services engagement call for an attest opinion. Although an audit opinion is an expert opinion, it differs from an expert witness opinion given at trial.

Sometimes the opposing lawyer tries to confuse the trier of fact by muddling audit opinions with expert opinions. The lawyer might ask whether the CPA performed an audit and can render an audit opinion. When the CPA answers "no," the attorney might suggest incorrectly that the CPA with no audit opinion can have no expert opinion.

1.7   SKILLS COMMONLY REQUIRED OF FINANCIAL EXPERTS

As Section 1.5 of this chapter shows, financial experts provide many services throughout the litigation process. The discussion that follows lists the special skills such experts need to competently perform such work. Of course, crossover can occur where an accountant has training in economic analysis and an economist understands accounting principles. Chapter 3 discusses the interaction between accountants and economists.

(a) Auditing.   Litigation services engagements frequently use the skeptical attitude, investigative skills, and accounting knowledge required by the audit function. Examples include investigation of fraudulent transactions and reconstruction of financial statements.

(b) Financial Analysis.   Development and analysis of financial ratios and relations often aid in understanding the causes of a litigant's business problems. The financial expert can also modify ratio analysis to derive assumptions as to what would have happened but for the alleged unlawful action. Financial experts often perform present value analyses, capital market theory applications, and business valuations.

(c) Economic Analysis.   Economists and accountants perform both macro- and microeconomic analyses in a litigation services engagement. Development of elasticity functions can prove important in claims for antitrust damages or for price erosion claims in a patent infringement matter.

(d) Marketing Analysis.   Much marketing analysis focuses on the collection of quantitative data. Financial experts can help collect and assess the required data. Examples include the number of competitors in a particular market or computation of the market share of each participant based on sales.

(e) Statistics.   Economists and many accountants understand statistical techniques such as sampling and regression analysis. An expert uses sampling when analysis of an entire population is too time consuming or expensive for the case. Regression analysis can help to project sales or suggest cost relations.

(f) Cost Accounting.   The calculation of damages often requires cost accounting skills. For example, cases in which the plaintiff is a multiline product manufacturer or service provider require allocation of common costs to each product line affected by the defendant's actions.

1.8   FEE ARRANGEMENTS AND ENGAGEMENT LETTERS

Practitioners bill most litigation services engagements as they do other consulting engagements, with fees based on hours extended by hourly rates, plus expenses. The expert can also perform work for a fixed fee, although the unpredictable course of litigation can make this a risky proposition for all but the most narrowly focused topics of testimony.

Some lawyers want the attorney work-product doctrine to apply and yet do not want the responsibility of paying the experts' fees. Such lawyers will ask the expert to send bills directly to the party and may ask the expert to sign a retainer agreement expressly disclaiming any recourse against the lawyer for payment of the expert's bills. The lawyer needs to contemplate and understand the risk to the applicable attorney work-product protection arising from this type of arrangement.

The expert could consider both the lawyer and the litigants as clients. Most experts recognize that the litigant ultimately pays their fees and that lawyers engage the expert as an agent for their clients. Some experts insist on holding the lawyer equally or solely responsible for fees, even at the risk of losing the engagement.

(a) Contingent Fees.   The American Bar Association and many state bars make it an ethical violation for a lawyer to proffer testimony from an expert witness who receives contingent compensation. The AICPA does not prohibit a CPA from charging contingent fees in litigation services engagements, except for audit clients of the CPA, although most state boards of accountancy prohibit such fees.

Even if the witness concludes, and counsel concurs, that a contingency arrangement is permissible, one should avoid it in any testifying role. An expert witness working on a contingency basis loses independence and objectivity. Opposing counsel likely will effectively impugn the testimony of an expert whose compensation depends on the outcome. Experts working as consultants rather than witnesses need to decide on the wisdom of accepting contingent arrangements.

(b) Retainers.   Financial experts require a retainer in some litigation services engagements. A retainer will protect the expert's billing only if the expert holds it as security for payment of the final bill. Experience shows that unfavorable outcomes often lead to unpaid bills.

The final outcome of marital dissolution actions usually makes both parties unhappy. Paying spouses feel that they have lost too much, and receiving spouses feel that they have obtained too little. Many financial experts who practice in the marital dissolution field always require a sizable retainer.

An expert should investigate the client's financial ability to pay if the litigation proves unsuccessful. If the client cannot pay in this situation, the financial expert should consider obtaining a retainer against the full anticipated final bill. We recommend this practice regardless of the client's ability to pay. Otherwise, the judge and jury could view the expert as working effectively on a contingent fee basis.

(c) Engagement Letter.   The financial expert should consider whether to use an engagement letter in a litigation engagement, and the authors strongly encourage this practice. Some experts believe that an engagement letter unnecessarily restricts and limits the areas of testimony; however, this argument lacks merit. In fact, the contrary holds true: most attorneys prefer that the engagement letter be inexplicit as to the nature and content of the opinions they hope the expert will develop. At a minimum, experts should reach a clear oral agreement with the attorney regarding the services they will render.

Most engagement letters describe the engagement's scope and limit the use of data or reports that the financial expert prepares to the litigation (e.g., the client cannot use a valuation opinion developed for a litigation to subsequently market the company for sale). The scope should identify the nature of the services and state whether such services include an audit or review (for CPAs). The letter should restrict use of the expert's work product to the case and prohibit distribution to others. Most engagement letters specify hourly rates and fees and call for reimbursement of expenses. Some letters provide for a retainer that will apply against the final billing (discussed in Section 1.8(b)). The letter can also specify that the client will reimburse any costs that the expert's firm incurs for related and necessary legal counsel during or after the case. The engagement letter might also address the possibility that the client could change attorneys, give the expert the option to withdraw, provide for the return of original documents, and state that the expert implies no warranty or prediction of results.

An engagement letter benefits both the expert and the attorney, setting forth an agreement on the engagement's terms and each party's responsibilities. The expert's insurance carrier or professional standards may require one.

1.9 WORKPAPERS

A financial expert in a litigation engagement will generate workpapers or analyses that develop and document opinions. The workpapers and analyses do not follow a prescribed format. As Section 1.1(b) of this chapter explains, the Federal Rules of Civil Procedure require the witness to identify the bases and underlying data supporting the opinion (Rule 26(b)(2)), and the Federal Rules of Evidence require the witness to disclose, if asked, the facts or data underlying the opinion (Rule 705).

Opposing counsel will likely gain access to all materials prepared: notes, any drafts retained, calculations, correspondence, and materials to which an expert witness refers. For an expert serving as a consultant, the attorney probably can assert a work-product privilege, and opposing counsel likely will never discover and analyze such workpapers. Nonetheless, we suggest that experts maintain their files free of superseded drafts, completed to-do lists not otherwise needed, and other such extraneous materials.

Once the lawyer and expert agree on the expert's role, the expert should understand that notes of meetings can include preliminary opinions, draft schedules, and reports. After preparing final versions, the expert will usually find it unnecessary and even inadvisable to retain the preliminary work product so long as the expert can trace the final conclusions and opinions back to source documents.

Lawyers, as a matter of professional principle, will generally not instruct an expert witness to destroy notes, files, and outdated work. More often, they will ask what the expert's normal practice is and suggest that practice be followed.

Most experienced experts keep lean files, retaining only current versions. This procedure reduces the problems caused in comprehensive discovery but can cause the witness extra work to become familiar again with items once learned and since forgotten or to recreate discarded work later deemed useful. Such extra work can generate extra costs for the client, but most lawyers prefer that procedure. The expert who maintains lean files should announce to the lawyer a policy of not keeping notes and extensive files, giving the lawyer an opportunity to provide any differing guidance, rather than waiting for the lawyer to suggest such a policy.

1.10 GUIDELINES FOR A FINANCIAL EXPERT

The AICPA, through its standards and code of professional conduct, has set criteria for its members to help maintain the integrity of the profession and its members. We discuss many of these here as prudent guidelines for *all* financial experts providing litigation services.

(a) Competency. Experts should "undertake only those professional services that the member or the member's firm can reasonably expect to complete with professional competence."[9] Experts embarking on their first litigation engagement can find themselves ill equipped, ill prepared, and lacking foundation for some of their opinions. The attorney retaining the expert frequently cannot evaluate the expert's abilities. An expert uncertain of competence for the engagement should not accept it.

(b) Confidentiality. Experts bring to the courtroom all their prior experience and knowledge of clients and their practices, operations, and trade secrets. The expert should not disclose information obtained during other professional engagements except with the client's consent or pursuant to an appropriate order of the court. Experience in similar cases enables someone to render expert opinions, but the expert must protect confidential information obtained in previous engagements. Often the expert will not need to disclose any confidential information but must recognize the dual responsibility of truthfulness and honesty while preserving past and present clients' confidential information.

  If experts rely on specific information obtained in an unrelated client engagement and use that information as a basis for their opinion, a judge can require them to disclose the information's source. If the expert refuses, the judge can preclude use of the testimony because the opposing counsel could not take discovery on the information providing the basis of the expert's opinion.

(c) Objectivity. Financial experts should avoid taking any position that might impair their objectivity. Although experts can resolve doubt in favor of their client—as long as they can support the position—they must not become blind to objectivity in an effort to please their client. Such a lack of objectivity can become apparent, thus damaging the client's case and the expert's own reputation.

  Any opinions and positions an expert has taken in previous cases can become a matter of inquiry. For example, the expert should not testify in a matter involving an accounting or financial principle from a position inconsistent with one previously taken with similar facts unless the expert can reconcile the apparent inconsistency. Opposing counsel can quickly cast doubt on the expert's objectivity and credibility.

(d) Conflicts of Interest.   Conflicts of interest arise from the expert's ethical obligation to preserve client confidences or from other relations that can affect the expert's ability to present a client's position.

The financial expert must investigate possible conflicts of interest before accepting a litigation engagement and must check whether any adverse party in the litigation, including counsel, is a current or past client of the expert or the expert's firm. This in itself does not create a conflict, but the expert should consider the implications and discuss this with counsel. Although certain professions and professional organizations may impose ethical guidance differing by the expert's discipline, the existence of a legal conflict of interest is rare.[10]

Even when no direct conflict of interest exists, the expert should consider whether to accept an engagement that could prove contrary to the interests of another existing client. For example, civil complaints often identify many persons and entities as defendants. Experts should be wary when asked to work for one defendant when another defendant is a client. A problem can arise if the plaintiff proves joint damages, because then the defendants will lose the unity forged when trying to defeat the plaintiff and will instead dispute the portion that each owes. The defendants often cross-complain against each other in an attempt to escape the ultimate payment of damages. At this point, experts could find themselves opposing a current client.

When a litigation engagement involves a former client as the opposing party, the expert must resolve the question of a conflict on a case-by-case basis. Factors to consider include the length of time since the party was a client, the confidential information the expert possesses that could become an issue in the litigation, and the issues of the case.

The financial expert should consider disclosing all current and former relations with all parties to the litigation to the inquiring lawyer, even though the expert has concluded that no conflict of interest exists. On occasion, duties of confidentiality to a present or former client will not permit that disclosure, and seeking permission to disclose from that client might violate the confidentiality owed to the prospective attorney-client. There is no tidy exit from this box.

(i) Preliminary Interview with Prospective Clients.   When a prospective client approaches an expert regarding a litigation engagement, the client or attorney often gives the expert sufficient information regarding the case to help identify the parties and opposing counsel as well as the key issues in dispute. In describing the matter, the potential client will sometimes communicate confidential information to the expert. Assume that this prospective client does not retain the expert, but the client's opposition subsequently approaches the expert. Should the expert decline the subsequent offer of an engagement to protect the confidential information received previously?

Although the implication of a conflict of interest seems readily apparent, a California appellate court decision, *Shadow Traffic Network, et al. v. the Superior Court of Los Angeles County,*[11] highlights the importance of full disclosure and analysis of any potential conflict of interest in a litigation service environment. In *Shadow Traffic Network*, the plaintiff's law firm interviewed a prospective CPA expert and then decided not to retain the CPA for trial purposes. Subsequently, opposing counsel retained the same CPA to assist in the same litigation even though the CPA expert had informed the new counsel of previous discussions with plaintiff's counsel. When plaintiff's counsel learned that defendant's counsel had retained the rejected CPA firm in the matter, the law firm moved to disqualify the defendant's law firm from further representation of its client because the firm had retained the CPA to whom it had disclosed confidential information. The trial court disqualified the law firm. On review, the appellate court decision upheld the trial court's decision.

The *Shadow Traffic Network* ruling provides aggressive lawyers with an opportunity to foreclose the participation of potential experts by contacting them and disclosing minor bits of confidential information. To avoid the problem, experts will want to limit the information they receive from lawyers before officially being retained and to inform the inquiring lawyers that they have adopted this approach. The authors know of a case in which lawyers for one side contacted many experts and gave each trivial tasks that effectively foreclosed them from working for the other side.

(ii) Simultaneous Consultations.   Particularly with multinational accounting and consulting firms and national law firms, a law firm might engage different experts from the same firm to work simultaneously for and against the law firm's clients in different cases. Consider the following situation: Counsel A has retained Expert A to assist Plaintiff A by valuing an apartment building. Defendant B's attorney in this matter is Counsel B1. Prior to Plaintiff A's case going to trial, Counsel B2 approaches Expert A regarding the valuation of income property for Defendant C. Counsel B2, a partner with Counsel B1, is unaware that Expert A is a consultant or expert opposing B1's case. Does Expert A have a conflict of interest in this situation? In terms of Rule 301 of the Federal Rules of Evidence, the situation does not involve confidential client communications.

This question of conflicts presents more of a problem for counsel than an ethical question for the expert witness. The expert, however, should know the potential for problems in such circumstances and should, given confidentiality constraints, fully disclose such relations to counsel before accepting an engagement or, when this is not possible, alert counsel to the possibility of such an eventuality.

(iii) Regulatory Considerations.   The Sarbanes-Oxley Act of 2002 has transformed the litigation services arena for CPAs whose firms audit companies subject to regulation by the Securities and Exchange Commission (SEC). Such audit clients, once an important source of expert witness and consultant business, can no longer employ partners or staff of their audit firms in this capacity.[12] The AICPA has no similar prohibition for attest clients who are non-SEC-registered issuers, but the profession continues to examine its position in this area through the work of various committees.

(e) Other Guidelines.   In addition to the guidelines discussed elsewhere in this section of the chapter, the AICPA also lists the following standards under Rule 201 of the AICPA Code of Professional Conduct. As stated previously, all financial experts should consider these standards when conducting a litigation engagement.

- **Professional Competence.** Discussed in Section 1.10(a) of this chapter.
- **Due Professional Care.** Exercise due professional care in any performance of professional services.
- **Planning and Supervision.** Adequately plan and supervise the performance of professional services.
- **Sufficient Relevant Data.** Obtain sufficient relevant data to afford a reasonable basis for conclusion or recommendations in relation to any professional services performed.

Rule 202 of the AICPA Code of Professional Conduct adds the following three standards:

- **Client Interest.** Serve the client interest by seeking to accomplish the objectives established by the understanding with the client while maintaining integrity and objectivity.
- **Understanding with the Client.** Establish with the client a written or oral understanding regarding the responsibilities of the parties and the nature, scope, and limitations of services to be performed and modify the understanding if circumstances require significant change during the engagement.
- **Communication with the Client.** Inform the client of (1) conflicts of interest that can occur pursuant to interpretations of Rule 102 of the Code of Professional Conduct, (2) significant reservations concerning the scope or benefits of the engagement, and (3) significant engagement findings or events.

1.11   PROFESSIONAL STANDARDS AND MALPRACTICE CONCERNS

In a California case, *Mattco Forge, Inc. v. Arthur Young and Co.*, an appellate court ruled that experts cannot assert a statutory litigation privilege against their own clients. (A statutory litigation privilege denies the opposing party the right to sue an expert on the other side of the case for anything the expert witness says at deposition or trial. This privilege protects the work of persons assisting in litigation who may otherwise fear that an aggressive adversary will sue them later for their work.) Thus, the opposing litigant cannot sue the CPA, but the court can review the performance of the CPA on behalf of the CPA's client in light of the applicable professional standards. The appellate court stated that

> Applying the privilege in this circumstance does not encourage witnesses to testify truthfully; indeed, by shielding a negligent witness from liability, it has the opposite effect. Applying the privilege where the underlying suit never reached the trial stage would also mean that the party hiring the expert witness would have to bear the penalty for the expert witness's negligence. That result would scarcely encourage the future presentation of truthful testimony by the witness to the trier of fact.[13]

In California, therefore, as a result of the above decision, a CPA who provides expert witness services faces some exposure to the party employing him as an expert, and the applicable professional standards of the accounting profession may determine the appropriate standard of care. Others find similar standards of their professions invoked against them in similar circumstances. In the authors' experience, such cases are rare.

1.12   SPECIAL ISSUES FOR CPAs

CPAs offering litigation services must abide by two sets of rules. First, they must meet the legal standards appropriate to the expert's role, as discussed throughout this chapter, paying particular attention to the requirements of the Sarbanes-Oxley Act with respect to SEC clients. Second, CPAs should adhere to the AICPA's professional standards and their state's Board of Accountancy rules and regulations; they must also ascertain which professional standards apply to the litigation services rendered in the specific case.

As Section 1.6(b) of this chapter discusses, attestation (or auditing) services differ fundamentally from most litigation services engagements. The AICPA has stated that litigation services do not meet the definition of an attestation engagement (and therefore the attestation standards do not apply[14]), except for the rare occasions when a CPA must give an attest opinion during a litigation or when others will receive the written work of the accountant and, under the rules of the proceeding, do not have the opportunity to analyze and challenge the accountant's work. The AICPA recognizes that in a litigation engagement, the opposition and trier of fact will scrutinize the information and conclusions reached by a CPA. CPAs must understand that their opinions will receive the close attention of counsel and, in most instances, an opposing expert or consultant.

CPAs must ensure that anyone using their reports or workpapers understands why the CPA prepared them or has the right to depose or cross-examine with respect to them. A CPA should prevent a third party who does not know of the litigation from relying on the reports; such a person could not challenge or fully understand the underlying assumptions.

The AICPA's Management Consulting Services Division has oversight of litigation services; Statements on Standards for Consulting Services guide the work performed. Section 1.10 of this chapter discusses many of these standards as guidelines for all financial experts, but as specific requirements for CPAs and other professionals employed by accounting firms. As this practice area continues to grow, the AICPA will continue to develop standards and guidelines. We urge all practitioners to remain current on such pronouncements, particularly the current text and any updates or modifications to *AICPA Consulting Services Special Report 03-1*, "Litigation Services and Applicable Professional Standards."

The AICPA has produced a number of publications dealing with litigation services. These include the following:

1. *AICPA Statement on Standards for Consulting Services No. 1*, "Consulting Services: Definitions and Standards"
2. *AICPA Consulting Services Practice Aid 93-4*, "Providing Litigation Services"
3. *AICPA Consulting Services Special Report 03-1*, "Litigation Services and Applicable Professional Standards"
4. *AICPA Business Valuation and Litigation Services Practice Aid 04-1*, "Engagement Letters for Litigation Services"
5. *AICPA Consulting Services Practice Aid 96-3*, "Communicating in Litigation Services: Reports"
6. *AICPA Consulting Services Practice Aid 97-1*, "Fraud Investigations in Litigation and Dispute Resolution Services"

7. *AICPA Consulting Services Practice Aid 98-1*, "Providing Bankruptcy and Reorganization Services"
8. *AICPA Consulting Services Practice Aid 98-2*, "Calculation of Damages from Personal Injury, Wrongful Death, and Employment Discrimination"
9. *AICPA Consulting Services Practice Aid 99-2*, "Valuing Intellectual Property and Calculating Infringement Damages"

The AICPA's Web site contains a comprehensive listing of resources that it publishes or makes available (including this book); the list above simply identifies the most immediately relevant. In addition, the AICPA publishes a quarterly newsletter, *CPA Expert*, that deals with litigation services and business valuation. Experienced practitioners submit articles for publication dealing with all areas of litigation services and business valuation.

1.13   CONCLUSION

This chapter provides an overview of the process and terminology that the financial expert faces when acting as an expert witness or consultant in litigation.

Preparing a complex commercial litigation for trial requires financial experts to accomplish many tasks. They can bring training and expertise to an adversarial proceeding that will challenge and scrutinize their conclusions. The balance of this book discusses the specific types of cases and approaches that the financial expert will face and employ.

NOTES

1. This Rule 702 qualification discussion and the disclosure discussions of Federal Rules of Civil Procedure Rule 26(a)(2) that follow are based on federal court requirements. Most states follow procedures that are similar from a practical point of view, but experts must ensure that they know the standards of the venue that they work in.
2. Available from a variety of Web sites including those of Cornell University and the U.S. Department of Justice. The reader proposing to act as an expert witness is strongly encouraged to read the text of and Note to Rule 702 as well as the short text (11 pages in all) of the *Daubert* and *Kumho* decisions.
3. *Voir dire*, as relevant here, is the procedure by which courts, on their own or a party's motion, hear evidence on whether experts and their opinions are of a standard sufficient to qualify as admissible.
4. *Equitable* actions are those in which the plaintiff seeks an equitable remedy: a nonmonetary order by the court such as issuance of an injunction, the reformation of a contract, the setting aside of corporate liability protection to look through to an owner acting as *alter ego*, or some similar adjustment of the parties' relationship. They are not based on the common law, but on the court's determination of how to achieve fairness in a particular situation. The contrast is to *legal* actions, which seek remedies in the form of monetary damages. Until the early 20th century, many jurisdictions maintained separate courts of law and equity. Today, jurisdictions preserve that distinction rarely, the most prominent example being the Delaware Court of Chancery.
5. On matters of federal law, the rulings of each circuit's Court of Appeals establish precedent within that circuit and, with weaker effect, advisory weight in those other circuits which have not ruled on the issue. When a matter has reached the circuit court due to diversity and, by operation of law or contract, is subject to state rather than federal law, the circuit's ruling carries considerably less predictive value, because the ultimate arbiter of a given state's laws is the highest court of appeals within that state.

6. www.cpradr.org/.

7. This proposition is eroding in many jurisdictions as courts display increasingly limited patience with perceived gamesmanship. Particularly in government-initiated actions, the risks of fines or procedural sanctions for failing fully to respond to discovery requirements tend to outweigh by far the potential tactical or cost-saving advantages of failing to produce arguably responsive documents.

8. For philosophy it is. Skilled, knowledgeable attorneys operating in the same venue and even the same firm will often differ dramatically in their understanding and interpretation of the relevant laws of privilege and protection. Although many describe the concept as "attorney-client privilege," protection under the attorney work-product doctrine is the more relevant concept, since attorney-client privilege is available only to the attorney and client, and the expert is neither.

9. *AICPA Code of Professional Conduct*, Rule 201.

10. One example of a situation in which a legal conflict can occur is when an expert is appointed to a role working for the debtor in a bankruptcy proceeding. The Bankruptcy Code contains a quite restrictive concept of "disinterested person" with which experts must comply lest they see their fees and reputation evaporate.

11. *Shadow Traffic Network v. The Superior Court of Los Angeles County*, 22 Cal. App. 4th 853 (1994).

12. Section 201(a) of the Sarbanes-Oxley Act amends Section 10A of the Securities Exchange Act of 1934 by listing at the latter's (g)(8) as a prohibited activity "legal services and expert services unrelated to the audit."

13. *Mattco Forge, Inc. v. Arthur Young & Co.*, 5 Cal. App. 4th 392 (1994).

14. The AICPA *excludes* consulting—and thus litigation services—from its three general categories of AICPA technical standards: Statements on Auditing Standards (SASs), Statements on Standards for Attestation Engagements (SSAEs), and Statements on Standards for Accounting and Review Services (SSARSs).

CHAPTER 2

CAUSATION ISSUES IN EXPERT TESTIMONY

Lawrence F. Ranallo
Diana L. Weiss

CONTENTS

2.1 INTRODUCTION

Plaintiffs prevail in civil litigation when they prove that the defendant's wrongful conduct has caused them to suffer damages. Testimony of a qualified expert can help the trier of fact—that is, the jury, or the judge in a nonjury trial—decide whether the plaintiffs have proved this causal link.

Causation appears to be a simple concept: Did the defendant's wrongful conduct connect with (i.e., cause) the damages suffered by the plaintiff? In some situations, this connection seems self-evident, such as when a gunshot fired by the defendant hits the plaintiff. Other situations lack such clarity, however. For example, does the study of Latin cause a higher IQ, or is some other factor at work?

The law follows logic in requiring that the plaintiff prove more than correlation to establish causation in the legal sense.[1] Accordingly, courts reject expert testimony concerning causation that only identifies a correlation between two variables.

Courts similarly refuse to find causation when an expert neglects to consider other factors that could have caused, or at least contributed to, the plaintiff's damages, even when the defendant has indisputably engaged in legally actionable misconduct. This refusal makes clear that—to ensure their testimony's credibility

The authors thank Benjamin R. Jacewicz for his considerable assistance in preparing this chapter. They also thank Collen Shackleton for reviewing drafts of the chapter.

and sometimes even admissibility—expert witnesses must understand the applicable causation standards and the relevant facts regarding causation.

The legal standard for establishing causation varies, depending on both the nature of the legal claim (e.g., negligence, common law fraud, or securities fraud) and the law of the relevant jurisdiction. All courts, however, require that the defendant's wrongful conduct *actually cause* the damages allegedly suffered by the plaintiff. A financial expert retained to measure damages consequently must understand and be prepared to explain the following:

- The defendant's wrongful conduct
- How the plaintiff alleges that the defendant's wrongful conduct caused damages to the plaintiff and how the defendant alleges that it did not cause the damages
- The logic that connects the defendant's wrongful conduct and the plaintiff's damages
- Other factors that may have caused and/or exacerbated the plaintiff's damages
- Whether the plaintiff's damages could reasonably be expected to have flowed from the defendant's wrongful conduct

The first half of this chapter focuses on the legal standards for establishing causation in those cases where financial experts most often testify. The second section explains why success often depends on experts accounting for causation in their analyses or assessments.

2.2   FUNDAMENTAL CAUSATION PRINCIPLES

As Exhibit 2-1 illustrates, causation entails two components regardless of the legal claim asserted: (1) actual cause; and (2) legal causes.

This section discusses the standards applied to determine whether each of these components is present in several types of cases in which financial experts often testify or are otherwise involved.

(a) Negligence.   Causation plays a central role in establishing the defendant's liability in negligence cases, including those that involve alleged malpractice by professionals.[2] Plaintiffs bear the burden of proving negligence by a preponderance of evidence,[3] that is, by showing that their allegations are more likely than not to be true.[4]

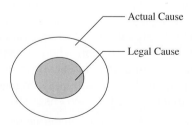

Exhibit 2-1.   Actual versus Legal Cause

> ## Components of Causation
>
> *Actual Cause + Legal Cause = Liability*
>
> *Actual Cause: The defendant's conduct actually causes the plaintiff's damages.*
>
> *Legal Cause: The defendant's conduct gives rise to legal liability for the plaintiff's damages.*

(i) Actual Cause. Although courts lack consensus on a standard for actual cause in negligence cases, "the focus [always] remains on the fundamental and sometimes metaphysical inquiry into the nexus between the defendant's negligent act and the resultant harm to the plaintiff."[5] Regardless of the standard, the plaintiff can use either direct or circumstantial evidence to prove actual cause.[6]

Some courts cast actual cause in negligence cases in terms of a but-for or *sine qua non* (literally, "without which not") test:

> The defendant's conduct is a cause of the event if the event would not have occurred but for that conduct; conversely, the defendant's conduct is not a cause of the event if the event would have occurred without it.[7]

Other courts consider whether the defendant's conduct is a substantial factor in bringing about the plaintiff's damages.[8] Following § 433 of the *Restatement (Second) of Torts*, they have identified several considerations as relevant in deciding whether the defendant's conduct meets this standard, generally referred to as the "substantial factor" test:

- The number of other factors which contribute in producing the harm and the extent of the effect which they have in producing it;
- Whether the actor's conduct has created a force or series of forces which are in continuous and active operation up to the time of the harm, or has created a situation harmless unless acted upon by other forces for which the actor is not responsible; and
- Lapse of time.[9]

These three elements address the concern that—in situations where two independent causes, each by a different defendant, bring about the plaintiff's damages and either cause, by itself, would have resulted in the same damages—courts would absolve both defendants of liability for negligence, to the plaintiff's clear detriment.[10] The test also helps resolve those cases where "a similar, but not identical result would have followed without the defendant's act ... [or] one defendant has made a clearly proved but quite insignificant contribution to the result, [such] as where he throws a lighted match into a forest fire."[11]

Aside from these two situations, the but-for and substantial factor tests should produce the same legal conclusion.[12] This congruence follows from the fact that:

> the substantial factor test subsumes the but-for test. If the conduct which is claimed to have caused the injury had nothing to do with the injuries, it could not be said that the conduct was a factor, let alone a substantial factor, in the production of the injuries.[13]

Standards for Actual Cause in Negligence Cases

- Sine qua non: *but for the defendant's conduct, the plaintiff would not have suffered damages.*
- *Substantial factor: even though it was not the only cause, the defendant's conduct was a substantial factor causing the plaintiff's damages.*

(ii) Legal Cause.   Proof of actual cause is insufficient to establish the defendant's liability for negligence. The plaintiff must show that the defendant's conduct is also the legal cause of his damages.[14] Legal cause "tempers the expansive view of causation [in fact]."[15] As one court has explained:

> The law does not undertake to charge a person with all the *possible* consequences of a wrongful act, but only with its probable and natural result; otherwise, the punishment would often be entirely disproportioned to the wrong, thereby impeding commerce and the ordinary business of life, and rendering the rule [of causation] impracticable.[16] (emphasis in original)

One thus can best understand legal cause as demarcating a certain point beyond which "the law arbitrarily declines to trace a series of events."[17] The determination of this point is not a matter of "logic" but instead of "practical politics," reflecting considerations "of convenience, of public policy, [and] of a rough sense of justice."[18]

- **Foreseeability:** Courts generally define legal cause in negligence cases in terms of foreseeability,[19] which they consider to be an issue of fact.[20] They vary somewhat in how they apply this concept. Some courts consider whether the plaintiff's injury is a "natural and probable consequence" of the defendant's conduct.[21] Others focus on whether a "reasonable person" would have foreseen the conduct causing the plaintiff's injury.[22] Finally, a few courts assess whether the plaintiff's injury is the natural and probable consequence of a negligent act *and* could have been reasonably foreseen in light of all the circumstances.[23] This divergence underscores the importance to the expert witness of understanding the applicable law concerning causation in the jurisdiction in which a case is pending.
- **Intervening Cause:** As Exhibit 2-2 illustrates, legal cause fails to materialize when an independent act of another party intervenes subsequent to the defendant's conduct and produces the plaintiff's damages.[24] In this situa-

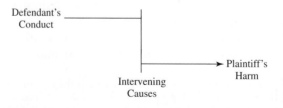

Exhibit 2-2.   Intervening Cause

tion, the independent intervening act supersedes the defendant's conduct as the legal cause, thereby freeing the defendant of liability to the plaintiff.[25] Some courts characterize the occasion of an intervening cause as triggering "a legal metamorphosis [of the defendant's conduct] into a remote cause or 'mere condition.'"[26] To the same effect, other courts provide that "a remote condition or conduct which furnishes only the occasion for someone else's supervening negligence is not a proximate cause of the result of the subsequent negligence."[27] An intervening cause must *not* be foreseeable for it to absolve the defendant of liability for the defendant's prior conduct.[28]

Ventricelli v. Kinney System Rent A Car, Inc., provides an example of how the intervening cause doctrine works. In that case, Joseph Ventricelli rented a car from Kinney System Rent A Car, Inc.[29] The car had a defective trunk lid that did not close satisfactorily.[30] This problem persisted even after Ventricelli returned the car for repair.[31] When the trunk lid later popped open again, Ventricelli parked the car along the street curb, got out and attempted to shut the lid.[32] While Ventricelli was trying to shut the lid, the car of Antonio Maldonado, which was parked behind where Ventricelli was standing, lurched forward and struck Ventricelli, severely injuring him.[33]

The Court of Appeals of New York overturned the jury's verdict that Kinney was primarily at fault for Ventricelli's injuries.[34] This reversal rested on the following reasoning:

> The immediately effective cause of plaintiff's injuries was the negligence of Maldonado, the driver of the second car, in striking plaintiff while he was standing behind his parked automobile. That Kinney's negligence in providing an automobile with a defective trunk lid would result in plaintiff's repeated attempts to close the lid was reasonably foreseeable. Not "foreseeable," however, was the collision between vehicles both parked a brief interval before the accident. Plaintiff was standing in a relatively "safe" place, a parking space, not in an actively traveled lane. He might well have been there independent of any negligence of Kinney, as, for example, if he were loading or unloading the trunk. Under these circumstances, to hold the accident a foreseeable consequence of Kinney's negligence is to stretch the concept of foreseeability beyond applicable limits.[35]

This case illustrates how the unforeseeable intervening conduct of another party can render the defendant's conduct *not* the legal cause of the plaintiff's injuries, thus absolving the defendant of liability to the plaintiff for negligence.

(b) Common Law Fraud. Common law fraud, also known as actual or intentional misrepresentation, arises when, among other things:

- The defendant's material misrepresentation causes the plaintiff to act in reliance of it.
- This reliance causes the plaintiff to suffer damages.[36]

Many courts require the plaintiff to provide clear and convincing evidence to prove common law fraud.[37] Courts recognize clear and convincing evidence as the degree of proof that will produce in the mind of the trier of fact a firm belief or conviction as to the existence of the fact in question.[38] As Exhibit 2-3 illustrates, this requires an evidentiary showing greater than that necessary to prove a fact by

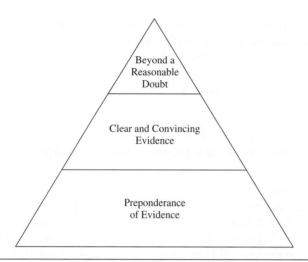

Exhibit 2-3.   Standards of Proof from Least to Most Onerous

a preponderance of the evidence but less than that necessary to prove a fact beyond a reasonable doubt, the standard in criminal cases.[39]

Some courts, by contrast, allow the plaintiff to prove common law fraud by a preponderance of evidence.[40] A few other courts require clear and convincing evidence to establish all the elements of fraud except for damages, which may be proved by a preponderance of the evidence.[41]

(i) Actual Cause.   Reliance equates with actual cause in the context of common law fraud.[42] No consensus prevails on the test for determining actual cause. As with other torts, some courts apply a but-for test, which requires the plaintiffs to show that "but for the alleged misrepresentation …, [they] would not have entered the transaction,"[43] whereas others favor a substantial factor test, which provides that:

> [i]t is not . . . necessary that [a plaintiff's] reliance upon the truth of the fraudulent misrepresentation be the sole or even the predominant or decisive factor in influencing his conduct. . . . It is enough that the representation has played a substantial part, and so has been a substantial factor, in influencing his decision.[44]

Most courts do not permit reliance to be presumed in common law fraud cases,[45] and some have refused to extend the rebuttable presumptions of reliance recognized in federal securities fraud law (discussed in Section 2.2(d) of this chapter) to common law fraud.[46]

(ii) Legal Cause.   Courts generally equate legal causation with foreseeability in the context of common law fraud. They differ in how they characterize foreseeability, however.

Some courts follow the definition of legal cause set forth in Section 548A of the *Restatement (Second) of Torts*, which provides that "[a] fraudulent misrepresentation is a legal cause of a pecuniary loss resulting from action or inaction in reliance upon it if, but only if, the loss might reasonably be expected to result from the reliance."[47] Other courts frame the issue as whether the plaintiff's injury "is the natural and probable consequence of the defrauder's misrepresentation or if the defrauder ought reasonably to have foreseen that the injury was a probable consequence of his fraud."[48] Yet another court focuses on whether "in an appreciable sense . . . the damage flowed from the fraud as the proximate and not the remote cause, and the damage . . . [is] the natural and probable consequence of the fraud."[49]

This divergence in definitions underscores the importance to the expert witness of understanding the applicable law concerning causation in the jurisdiction in which a fraud case is pending.

Causation Elements of Common Law Fraud

Actual Cause = Reliance

Legal Cause = Foreseeability

(c) Breach of Contract.   Causation is also an essential element in breach of contract claims. The plaintiff must prove by a preponderance of the evidence that the defendant's breach of contract caused the damages.[50]

(i) Theories of Contract Damages.   Contract law recognizes three distinct theories of damages to remedy a breach of contract:[51]

- **Expectation Damages** afford plaintiffs the benefit of the bargain by placing them in as a good a position as they would have been in had the contract been performed by the defendant.[52]

- **Reliance Damages** compensate the plaintiff for losses caused by relying on a contractual obligation that the defendant did not perform. They return plaintiffs to the position they would have been in had they not entered into the contract.[53]

- **Restitution Damages** is the amount that returns plaintiffs to their position before they entered into the contract.[54] Unlike expectancy and reliance damages, it focuses on the breaching party, requiring that party, as a matter of equity, to disgorge any benefits received from the plaintiff's performance under the contract.[55]

Theories of Contract Damages

Expectancy: *Provide the plaintiff with benefit of the contract.*

Reliance: *Compensate the plaintiff for losses caused by contract breach.*

Restitution: *Return the plaintiff to pre-contract position.*

(ii) General versus Consequential Damages.   General contract damages seek to compensate the plaintiff for the value of the performance promised.[56] Such damages flow directly from the breach of contract.[57] As one court has explained:

> General damages are those defined as economic injuries that are proximately caused by the breach and are the natural, or "usual" consequences. "Usual" refers to those harms suffered by a plaintiff and that are reasonably foreseeable at the time when the contract is formed.[58]

The plaintiff can seek two distinct categories of damages in a breach of contract case: general or consequential.[59] Each category reflects a particular causal relation between the contract breach and the damages. Depending on the circumstances, either or both categories may be available under the expectancy or reliance theory of damages.[60]

Special or consequential damages compensate the plaintiff for losses other than the value of the promised performance incurred as a result of the defendant's contract breach.[61] They differ from general damages in that "they do not follow as a necessary consequence of the injury complained of, though they may in fact naturally flow from that injury."[62] In other words, one would not ordinarily consider these damages to be a foreseeable result of the contract breach.[63] Examples of consequential damages include lost profits, in those cases where profits are not expressly stipulated for in the contract, as well as interest earned under a loan contract.[64]

When courts ponder causation with respect to consequential damages, they use the same analysis applied in the law of negligence (discussed in Section 2.2(a) above).[65] They first ascertain whether the defendant's breach caused the plaintiff's consequential damages. Most courts rely on the substantial factor test when the actions of multiple parties contribute to the breach of contract.[66] Thus, plaintiffs need not show that they incurred damages solely because of the defendant's breach to prove actual cause.[67]

As in tort actions, the use of the substantial factor test instead of the alternative but-for test to establish actual cause has little legal consequence:

> The only difference between the two tests is that, when there are multiple potential causes, the substantial factor test accounts for the possibility that other causes may have contributed to plaintiff's injury. A plaintiff still must prove that a defendant's breach of contract was sufficiently connected to the plaintiff's damage that it could reasonably be said to have caused the injury, that is, that defendant was the cause in fact of plaintiff's damages.[68]

When considering consequential damages, courts also undertake an analysis analogous to the foreseeability inquiry that decides legal cause in negligence cases.[69] In doing so, they apply the test set forth in the English case of *Hadley v. Baxendale*: whether both parties contemplated the plaintiff's damages when they formed the contract.[70]

Elements of Consequential Contract Damages

Actual Cause: Substantial Factor or Sine Qua Non *Test*

Legal Cause: Foreseeability

(d) Securities Fraud.   The six elements of securities fraud, which plaintiffs must prove by a preponderance of evidence,[71] are as follows:

1. A material misrepresentation or omission
2. Scienter (i.e., the misrepresentation or omission is intended to deceive or defraud investors)
3. A connection between the misrepresentation or omission and the purchase or sale of a security
4. Transaction causation
5. Economic loss
6. Loss causation[72]

Three of these elements (numbers (3), (4), and (6) in the preceding list) address causation. The connection between a material misrepresentation or omission and purchase or sale of a security is self-explanatory. The other two causal elements, transaction causation and loss causation, are discussed next.

(i) Transaction Causation.   Transaction causation, also called *reliance*, requires that the defendant's material misrepresentation or omission cause the plaintiff to engage in the transaction leading to the plaintiff's injury.[73] As such, it is akin to the concept of but-for causation in tort law.[74]

Plaintiffs must show that they either read or heard a material misrepresentation by the defendant and relied on it in buying or selling a security.[75] Put another way, "Reliance . . . generally requires that the plaintiff[s] knew of the particular misrepresentation complained of, have believed it to be true and because of that knowledge and belief, purchased or sold the security in question."[76]

Affirmative proof of reliance is unnecessary in two situations. First, when the defendant has failed to disclose material information to investors, "all that is necessary [to prove reliance] is that the facts withheld be material in the sense that a reasonable investor might have considered them important in the making of [his or her] . . . decision."[77] The defendant can rebut this presumption of reliance by showing, by a preponderance of evidence, that even if it had disclosed the material fact, the plaintiff would not have acted differently.[78]

Reliance is also presumed where the plaintiff has made a trading decision "in reliance on the integrity of the price set in the market, but because of [the defendant's] . . . material misrepresentations that price ha[s] been fraudulently depressed."[79] The defendant can also rebut this fraud-on-the-market presumption of reliance.[80] As the Supreme Court has explained, "[a]ny showing that severs the link between the alleged misrepresentation and either the price received (or paid) by the plaintiff, or his decision to trade at a fair market price, will be sufficient to rebut the presumption of reliance."[81]

The fraud-on-the-market presumption of reliance makes certification of plaintiff investor classes seeking damages for alleged defendant misrepresentations or omissions much easier. Because it permits the class to prove reliance by class members across-the-board, thus obviating the need to prove the reliance of each individual plaintiff, the presumption enables the plaintiff class to satisfy the predominance requirement for class certification under Federal Rules of Civil Procedure 23(a)(2) and 23(b)(3).[82]

The fraud-on-the-market presumption places the central issue of reliance squarely within the realm of expert testimony. In this regard, an expert witness is necessary to establish the critical predicate to establishing entitlement to the presumption that the security in question traded in an efficient market.[83]

Courts have identified the following factors in deciding whether a security is traded in an efficient market:

- Average weekly trading volume expressed as a percentage of total outstanding shares
- Number of securities analysts following and reporting on the stock
- Extent to which market makers and arbitrageurs trade in the shares
- Company's eligibility to file SEC registration Form S-3 (as opposing to Form S-1 or S-2)
- Existence of empirical facts showing a cause and effect relation between unexpected corporate events or financial releases and an immediate response in the share price

- Company's market capitalization
- Bid-ask spread for stock sales
- Float, the shares' trading volume without counting insider-owned shares[84]

Proving Transaction Causation

Reliance on the defendant's material misrepresentation or omission must be shown, except that such reliance is presumed when there has been

- *nondisclosure of material information or*
- *a fraud on the market.*

Both presumptions of reliance are rebuttable.

(ii) Loss Causation.   Loss causation connects the defendant's misrepresentation or omission and the plaintiff's economic loss.[85] It resembles legal causation insofar as it establishes the defendant as legally responsible for the plaintiff's loss.[86] The mere purchase of a security at an inflated price does not by itself prove loss causation.[87]

To establish loss causation, the plaintiff must show that it suffered an actual economic loss as a result of the defendant's misrepresentation or omission.[88] The misrepresentation need not be the sole cause of the economic loss. As one court explained:

> Because market responses, such as stock downturns, are often the result of many different, complex and often unknowable factors, the plaintiff need not show that the defendant's act was the sole and exclusive cause of the injury he has suffered; he need only show that it was a substantial, i.e., significant contributing cause.[89]

Although the defendant's misrepresentation or omission need not be the sole cause of the plaintiff's economic loss to establish loss causation, the plaintiff nevertheless can recover only damages caused by the misrepresentation or omission.[90] Accordingly, in calculating the plaintiff's recoverable damages, the court must isolate and remove other contributing causes.[91] An expert witness often facilitates this task.[92]

Proving Loss Causation

The defendant's material misrepresentation or omission must be a cause of the plaintiff suffering an actual economic loss.

2.3   EXPERT TESTIMONY ON CAUSATION ISSUES

Lawyers sometimes ask liability experts to evaluate whether the defendant has engaged in wrongful conduct without regard to whatever harm has flowed from the conduct. Likewise, they frequently instruct damages experts to assume causation.

These practices, when pursued without proper consideration, can lead to mismatches between the expert evidence and the facts of the case. For example, financial expert testimony quantifying the amount of damages lacks relevance unless one can show that the damages resulted from the defendant's wrongful acts. Similarly, proof that an audit conducted pursuant to generally accepted auditing standards (GAAS) would have detected a misstatement in a company's financial statements is irrelevant unless the misstatement caused the plaintiff's injury.

As these examples illustrate, cases involving financial matters often require expert testimony to resolve whether the defendant's wrongful conduct caused the plaintiff's damages. Such expert testimony is frequently challenged on the following grounds:

- Causation is a fact question that depends on the testimony of fact witnesses rather than experts.
- Causation is a legal issue.

The following discussion addresses these issues. Each case it reviews arises under Federal Rule of Evidence 702, which provides that a court can admit expert testimony relating to scientific, technical, or other specialized knowledge to assist the trier of fact in understanding the evidence or determining a fact in issue so long as it complies with the following requirements:

- The testimony is based on sufficient facts or data;
- The testimony is the product of reliable principles and methods; and
- The witness has applied the principles and methods reliably to the facts of the case.

These requirements ensure that expert testimony "both rests on a reliable foundation and is relevant to the task at hand."[93] They apply to all witnesses offered as experts.[94]

(a) Admissibility of Expert Testimony.   The failure to properly consider causation jeopardizes the admissibility of expert testimony on damages. In evaluating the admissibility of expert testimony under Rule 702, a trial court must consider whether the "expert testimony . . . is sufficiently tied to the facts of the case that it will aid the jury in resolving a factual dispute."[95] Damages experts who fail to take causation into consideration risk a ruling that their testimony lacks this essential tie to the facts of the case.

For example, in *Concord Boat Corp. v. Brunswick Corp.*,[96] the U.S. Court of Appeals for the Eighth Circuit overturned a $133 million antitrust judgment based in part on the conclusion that the trial court should have excluded the damages-related testimony of the plaintiff's financial expert. The court found that the expert's damages model "was not grounded in the economic reality of the ... [relevant] market, for it ignored inconvenient evidence."[97] Among other things, the damages model "failed to account for market events that both sides agreed were not related to any anticompetitive conduct."[98] Based on this and other "deficiencies in the foundation of the opinion," the court held that the expert's conclusions were speculative and unhelpful to the trier of fact.[99]

Concord Boat teaches that an expert cannot ignore whether the defendant's calculated damages flow from the plaintiff's conduct or other events. Indeed, even if the court had not excluded the expert's testimony there, the damages calculation would still have been vulnerable to attack as the expert would presumably have been hard pressed to calculate on the stand the extent to which his damages calculation would have changed in response to changes in the facts.

(b) Expert Testimony versus Fact Testimony.   Expert testimony on causation can prove more reliable than fact testimony in financial cases. A recent breach of contract case in the U.S. Court of Appeals for the Federal Circuit illustrates this situation.

California Federal Bank v. United States[100] is one of a series of so-called *Winstar* cases in which banks that purchased failing thrifts during the savings and loan crisis of the late 1980s and early 1990s sought to recover for damages caused by the passage of the Financial Institutions Reform, Recovery, and Enforcement Act (FIRREA). This act effectively negated beneficial financial statement and regulatory capital provisions of banks' earlier contracts with the federal government to acquire failing thrifts. In *California Federal*, the plaintiff bank, CalFed, alleged that the enactment of FIRREA forced it to sell certain assets, including a large number of adjustable rate mortgages (ARMs), to meet the act's new regulatory capital requirements.[101]

The government was held to have breached its contract with the bank, thus establishing liability. CalFed sought lost profits as damages for this breach, arguing that but for FIRREA's enactment, it would have retained more ARMs, which would have yielded substantial profits. The government countered that FIRREA did not cause the sale of ARMs, which shrunk the size of the bank, and that other factors existed that would have caused the sale irrespective of the changes in regulatory capital requirements effected by the act.

The government sought to debunk the plaintiff's lost profits claim through a financial expert who testified about the economics of the relevant market and presented an analysis of the operations and financial performance of CalFed. Among other things, the expert explained a principle familiar to most financial experts: one would expect the sale of the ARMs to have produced the same amount of profit as retaining them because, in a liquid market, the fair value of the ARMs at the time of their sale would have included the present value of the future cash flow if CalFed had retained them.

The trial court relied on the government's expert in finding that "it was the recession in the California real estate market in the early 1990s that caused Cal Fed to shrink the bank, not the changes to regulatory requirements that resulted from the enactment of FIRREA."[102] On appeal, CalFed argued that "it was improper for the [trial] court to rely on the testimony of the government's experts rather than the testimony of CalFed's fact witnesses, who testified about their own intentions [i.e., that but for FIRREA, they would have retained the ARMs]."[103] The Federal Circuit rejected this argument, explaining that:

> the court, sitting as finder of fact, was entitled to weigh the credibility of CalFed's fact witnesses, taking into account their interest in the outcome of the litigation. At the same time, the court was entitled to consider the government's expert testimony to the extent that it shed light on the economics of finance and banking and thus helped explain why CalFed sold the ARMs following FIRREA's enactment. . . .

> The expert testimony on which the court relied in this case provided an explanation of why a bank such as CalFed might well have chosen to dispose of the ARMs, even in the absence of a breach, and why the sale of the ARMs did not necessarily result in a loss to CalFed. The expert testimony thus satisfied the requirement of Rule 702 of the Federal Rules of Evidence, which permits expert testimony to be admitted "to assist the trier of fact to understand the evidence or to determine a fact in issue."[104]

Accordingly, the court held that "the inability to prove by a preponderance of the evidence that profits would have been made but for the breach" barred the bank from recovering lost profits.[105]

CalFed demonstrates not only how a financial expert can properly present evidence to support or undercut a causation theory but also that such evidence can prove even more useful and credible than fact testimony that appears self-serving to the finder of fact under the circumstances.

(c) Securities Fraud.   Expert testimony on causation is often a critical issue in securities fraud cases. For instance, in *Abrams v. Van Kampen Funds, Inc.*, the plaintiff class alleged that the defendants overstated in various prospectuses the value of loans held by the fund.[106] In this respect, the class "contend[ed] that using available market quotations and properly determining fair market value based on what the loans would currently have sold for would have resulted in lower daily net asset values ("NAV") for the [f]und."[107] To refute the class' calculation of damages caused by the alleged overvaluation of loans held by the fund, the defendants' experts opined that adverse market conditions, in particular an increase in loan default rates and a widening credit spread, accounted for all or a substantial part of a decline in the fund's NAV.[108] The court barred the experts from testifying regarding this opinion, explaining that:

> if plaintiffs prove liability, the burden is on the defendants to show that drops in the NAV were caused by something other than the alleged misstatements in the prospectuses. Here, however, *the experts do not attempt to connect changes [generally] in loan default rates and the credit spread to changes [specifically] in NAV nor do they make any attempt to show how much of an effect there may have been.* Therefore, it has not been shown that this testimony is relevant to the damages issues in this case.[109] (emphasis added)

Similar to *Concord Boat* discussed in Section 2.3(a), this case illustrates that the failure of experts to connect their opinions to facts relating to causation can lead to exclusion of their testimony.

Additionally, expert testimony is important in securities fraud class actions alleging fraud–on–the–market by the defendant. As discussed in Section 2.2(d)(i), in class action involving allegations of fraud on the market, the court presumes the plaintiff's reliance upon the defendant's misrepresentation or omission when the security in question is traded in an efficient market. Assessment of whether the security is traded in an efficient market involves factors (discussed in Section 2.2(d)(i)), best evaluated by experts.

A recent case in U.S. Court of Appeals for the Fifth Circuit illustrates the importance of expert testimony in establishing that a security is traded in an efficient market.[110] Seeking to proceed under the fraud on the market presumption, the plaintiffs submitted an event study by their own expert to establish the existence of an efficient market for the shares at issue.[111]

The trial court, however, found the study "unreliable and purposefully designed to support their market efficiency conclusion."[112] Absent expert evidence, the plaintiffs had to argue that one should presume an efficient market for any stock traded on NYMEX. The Fifth Circuit rejected this argument and affirmed the lower court's denial of class certification.[113]

Finally, expert witnesses should keep in mind the effects of the burden of proof on causation in securities fraud cases. Under Section 11 of the Securities Act, the defendant bears the burden of proving negative causation (i.e., a cause other than the securities violation). Even when the defendant's expert can undermine the plaintiff's case by presenting evidence that other factors *may have* caused the plaintiff's damages, in a Section 11 case, the proof must instead show that *there is a cause in fact* other than the alleged securities law violation.

(d) Expert Sensitivity to Alternative Outcomes.   In cases in which but-for causation becomes an issue, the expert must be prepared to address alternative outcomes. For example, suppose a former client brings a claim against a law firm for improper representation in a bankruptcy proceeding. The plaintiff/debtor contends that, but for the defendant law firm's bad advice, the bankruptcy judge would have confirmed a different plan that provided a superior outcome to either historical equity interests or creditors. The plaintiff's contention hinges on proving that the alternative plan would have

- Been approved for a creditor vote;
- Won approval of the impaired creditors in number and dollar amount;
- Prevailed over any competing topping bids that may have been made at a confirmation hearing; and
- Held by the bankruptcy court to be in the best interests of creditors, feasible, and not likely to be followed by liquidation of the entity.

To carry this burden, the plaintiff would need to show that the required number and amount of creditor interests would have confirmed the alternative plan. Such a showing would necessarily rest on evidence in the bankruptcy regarding (1) the relative value of the alternative plan compared with the confirmed plan, (2) the positions of important interested parties regarding the alternative plan, and (3) whether the alternative plan would serve the highest and best interests of the creditors compared with any other proposed or alternative plans. Given the many financial and bankruptcy issues involved in making this showing, the plaintiff would almost certainly need an expert witness to explain such evidence and its relevance.

This example illustrates why expert testimony is sometimes helpful to, and may be necessary for, the trier of fact to understand whether the defendant's wrongful conduct has caused the damages claimed by the plaintiff. Even if no expert testimony is provided on the issue of causation, the damages expert must nevertheless understand the plaintiff's theory of causation and whether the damages have alternative causes.

NOTES

1. *See*, e.g., *Craig v. Oakwood Hosp.*, 684 N.W.2d 296, 312 (Mich. 2004); *Schafersman v. Agland Coop*, 631 N.W.2d 862, 871 (Neb. 2001).
2. *See*, e.g., *Marlene F. v. Affiliated Psychiatric Med. Clinic, Inc.*, 770 P.2d 278, 281 (Cal. 1989); *Bayly, Martin & Fay, Inc. v. Pete's Satire, Inc.*, 739 P.2d 239, 242-43 (Colo. 1987) (en banc); *Johnson v. Am. Nat'l Red Cross*, 578 S.E.2d 106, 108 (Ga. 2003); *Clampitt v. D.J. Spencer Sales*, 786 So.2d 570, 573 (Fla. 2001) (quoting *Jefferies v. Amery Leas., Inc.*, 698 So.2d 368, 370 (Fla. Dist. Ct. App. 1997)); *Bajwa v. Metropolitan Life Ins. Co.*, 804 N.E.2d 519, 526 (Ill. 2004); *Ulwick v. DeChristopher*, 582 N.E.2d 954, 958 (Mass. 1991); *Case v.*

Consumers Power Co., 615 N.W.2d 17, 20 (Mich. 2000); *Whaley v. CSX Transp.*, 609 S.E.2d 286, 298 (S.C. 2005) (FELA case); *Doe v. Boys Clubs of Greater Dallas, Inc.*, 907 S.W.2d 472, 477 (Tex. 1995).

3. *See*, e.g., *Bayly, Martin & Fay, Inc. v. Pete's Satire, Inc.*, 739 P.2d 239, 242-43 (Colo. 1987) (en banc); *Canonico v. Beechmont Bus Serv., Inc.*, 790 N.Y.S.2d 36, 37 (App. Div. 2005); *Mobil Chem. Co. v. Bell*, 517 S.W.2d 245, 251 (Tex. 1974).

4. *See*, e.g., *Sargent v. Mass. Accident Co.*, 29 N.E.2d 825, 827 (Mass. 1940); *Commonwealth v. $6,425.00 Seized from Esquilin*, 880 A.2d 523, 529 (Pa. 2005); *Cobb v. WVHRC*, 619 S.E.2d 274, 290 n.26 (W. Va. 2005).

The causation standards for negligence extend to the tort of strict products liability, which does not require proof of fault or breach of a duty but does require a showing that the plaintiff was injured as a result of the product's defective condition. *See*, e.g., *Greenman v. Yuba Power Prods.*, 377 P.2d 897, 900 (Cal. 1963); *Hiigel v. Gen. Motors Corp.*, 544 P.2d 983, 987 (Colo. 1975) (following RESTATEMENT (SECOND) OF TORTS § 402A); *Hunt v. Blasius*, 384 N.E.2d 368, 372 (Ill. 1978); *Endresen v. Scheels Hardware & Sports Shop, Inc.*, 560 N.W.2d 225, 229 (N.D. 1997); *Houston Lighting & Power Co. v. Reynolds*, 765 S.W.2d 784, 785 (Tex. 1988) (following RESTATEMENT (SECOND) OF TORTS § 402A). The plaintiff must prove the claim by a preponderance of the evidence and can carry this burden by relying upon either direct or circumstantial evidence. *See*, e.g., *Mays v. Ciba-Geigy Corp.*, 661 P.2d 348, 360 (Kan. 1983); *Waite v. Am. Creosote Works, Inc.*, 204 N.W.2d 410, 291 (Minn. 1973); *Kudlacek v. Fiat S.P.A.*, 509 N.W.2d 603, 610 (Neb. 1994); *Endresen v. Scheels Hardware & Sports Shop, Inc.*, 560 N.W.2d 225, 229 (N.D. 1997).

5. *Yonce v. SmithKline Beecham Clinical Labs., Inc.*, 680 A.2d 569, 576 (Md. Ct. Spec. App. 1996).

6. *See*, e.g., *Henderson v. Cominco Am., Inc.*, 518 P.2d 873, 879 (Idaho 1974); *Kort v. Walter*, 457 N.E.2d 18, 21 (Ill. 1983); *Skinner v. Square D Co.*, 516 N.W.2d 475, 480 (Mich. 1994); *Simmons v. John L. Roper Lumber Co.*, 93 S.E. 736, 738 (N.C. 1917).

7. *See*, e.g., *Dick v. Lewis*, 506 F. Supp. 799, 805 (D.N.D. 1980) (applying North Dakota law) (following PROSSER AND KEETON ON TORTS (1971)); *Gercey v. United States*, 409 F. Supp. 946, 954 (D.R.I. 1976) (Suits in Admiralty Act case) (quoting PROSSER AND KEETON ON TORTS (1984)); *Culver v. Bennett*, 588 A.2d 1094, 1097 (Del. 1991) (same); *Anderson v. St. Francis-St. George Hosp., Inc.*, 671 N.E.2d 225, 227 (Ohio 1996) (same).

8. *See*, e.g., *Lestico v. Kuehner*, 283 N.W. 122, 127 (Minn. 1938); *Toston v. Pardon*, 874 So. 2d 791, 799 (La. 2004); *Hamil v. Bashline*, 392 A.2d 1280, 1284 (Pa. 1978); *Doe v. Boys Clubs of Greater Dallas, Inc.*, 907 S.W.2d 472, 477 (Tex. 1995); *Morden v. Continental AG*, 611 N.W.2d 659, 676 (Wis. 2000).

9. *See*, e.g., *Tennyson v. Brower*, 823 F. Supp. 421, 423-24 (E.D. Ky. 1993) (applying Kentucky law); *Thompson v. Better-Bilt Aluminum Prods.*, 832 P.2d 203, 207 n.6 (Ariz. 1992); *Yonce v. SmithKline Beechan Clinic Labs.*, 680 A.2d 569, 576 (Md. Ct. Spec. App. 1996); *Mack v. Altmans State Lighting Co.*, 470 N.Y.S.2d 664, 667 (N.Y. App. Div. 1984); *Mulder v. Tague*, 186 N.W.2d 884, 887 (S.D. 1971).

For discussion of the situation in which an actor's negligence has merely created a situation harmless unless acted upon by other forces for which the actor is not responsible, *see* infra footnote 27 and accompanying text.

10. *Mitchell v. Gonzales*, 819 P.2d 872, 876 (Cal. 1991); *Culver v. Bennett*, 588 A.2d 1094, 1097 (Del. 1991); *Yonce v. SmithKline Beecham Clinic Labs.*, 680 A.2d 569, 575-76 (Md. Ct. Spec. App. 1996); *Conklin v. Weisman*, 678 A.2d 1060, 1072 (N.J. 1996); *Daugert v. Pappas*, 704 P.2d 600, 605-06 (Wash. 1985) (en banc).

11. *Mitchell v. Gonzales*, 819 P.2d 872, 879 (Cal. 1991) (internal quotations omitted); *Daugert v. Pappas*, 704 P.2d 600, 605-06 (Wash. 1985) (en banc) (same).

12. *Mitchell v. Gonzalez*, 819 P.2d 872, 879 (Cal. 1991); *Fehling v. Levitan*, 382 N.W.2d 901, 904 (Minn. Ct. App. 1986).

13. *Mitchell v. Gonzales*, 819 P.2d 872, 878 (Cal. 1991) (internal quotations omitted).

14. *See*, e.g., *Gercey v. United States*, 409 F. Supp. 946, 954 (D.R.I. 1976) (Suits in Admiralty Act case); *Aetna Cas. & Sur. Co. v. Leo A. Daly Co.*, 870 F. Supp. 925, 936 (S.D. Iowa 1994) (applying Iowa law); *Yonce v. SmithKline Beecham Clinical Labs.*, 680 A.2d 569, 576 (Md. Ct. Spec. App. 1996);)*Craig v. Oakwood Hosp.*, 684 N.W.2d 296, 309 (Mich. 2004); *Skinner v. Square D Co.*, 516 N.W.2d 475, 479 (Mich. 1994).

15. *Paige v. Saint Andrew's Roman Catholic Church Corp.*, 734 A.2d 85, 91 (Conn. 1999).

16. *Smith v. W. Union Tel. Co.*, 83 Ky. 104 (Ct. App. 1885); *see also Doe v. Linder Constr. Co.*, 845 S.W.2d 173, 181 (Tenn. 1992) ("[T]he consequences of an act go forward to eternity, and the causes of an event go back to the dawn of human events, and beyond. Any attempt to impose responsibility upon such a basis would result in infinite liability."); *Blue Chip Stamps v. Manor Drug Stores*, 421 U.S. 723, 729–55 (1975).

17. *Palsgraf v. Long Island R. Co.*, 162 N.E. 99, 103 (N.Y. 1928) (Andrews, J., dissenting).

18. *Id.*, at 103.

19. *See*, e.g., *Ballard v. Uribe*, 715 P.2d 624, 628 n.6 (Cal. 1986); *McCain v. Fla. Power Corp.*, 593 So.2d 500, 503-04 (Fla. 1992); *City of Chicago v. Beretta U.S.A. Corp.*, 821 N.E.2d 1099, 1127 (Ill. 2005); *Wankel v. A&B Contractors, Inc.*, 732 A.2d 333, 349 (Md. Ct. Spec. App. 1999); *Skinner v. Squared D Co.*, 516 N.W.2d 475, 479 (Mich. 1994); *Hurd v. Williamsburg County*, 611 S.E.2d 488, 492 (S.C. 2005).

20. *See*, e.g., *Heatherly v. Alexander*, 421 F.3d 638, 642 (8th Cir. 2005) (applying Nebraska law); *Ballard v. Uribe*, 715 P.2d 624, 628 n.6 (Cal. 1986); *McCain v. Fla. Power Corp.*, 593 So.2d 500, 504 (Fla. 1992); *Derdiarian v. Felix Contracting Corp.*, 414 N.E.2d 666, 670 (N.Y. 1980); *Oliver v. S.C. Dep't of Highways & Pub. Transp.*, 422 S.E.2d 128, 131 (S.C. 1992).

21. *Heatherly v. Alexander*, 421 F.3d 638, 642 (8th Cir. 2005) (applying Nebraska law); *Doe v. Sisters of the Holy Cross*, 895 P.2d 1229, 1234 (Idaho Ct. App. 1995); *Callahan v. Cardinal Glennon Hosp.*, 863 S.W.2d 852, 865 (Mo. 1993) (en banc); *Oliver v. S.C. Dep't of Highways & Pub. Transp.*, 422 S.E.2d 128, 131 (S.C. 1992).

22. *City of Jacksonville v. Ralerson*, 415 So.2d 1303, 1305 (Fla. Dist. Ct. App. 1982) (per curiam); *City of Chicago v. Beretta U.S.A. Corp.*, 821 N.E.2d 1099, 1127 (Ill. 2005); *Kuhns v. Standard Oil*, 478 P.2d 396, 402 (Or. 1970); *Travis v. City of Mesquite*, 830 S.W.2d 94, 98 (Tex. 1992) (identifying "person of ordinary intelligence" as point of comparison).

23. *Lane v. St. Joseph's Regional Med. Ctr.*, 817 N.E.2d 266, 273 (Ind. Ct. App. 2004); *Anderson v. Theisen*, 43 N.W.2d 272, 371 (Minn. 1950); *Mudrich v. Standard Oil Co.*, 90 N.E.2d 859, 863 (Ohio 1950).

24. *See*, e.g., *Riordan v. Corp. of the Presiding Bishop of the Church of Jesus Christ of Latter-Day Saints*, 416 F.3d 825, 832 (8th Cir. 2005) (applying Missouri law); *Lexington Ins. Co. v. Rounds*, 349 F. Supp. 2d 861, 867 (D. Vt. 2004) (applying Vermont law); *Robertson v. Sixpence Inns of Am.*, 789 P.2d 1040, 1047 (Ariz. 1990); *McAuley v. Wills*, 303 S.E. 2d 258, 260-61 (Ga. 1983); *paragon Family Restaurant v. Bartolini*, 799 N.E. 2d 1048, 1054-55 (Ind. 2003); *Mcmillan v. Vliet*, 374 N. W. 2d 679, 681-82 (Mich. 1985); *Delaware v. Valls*, 409 N.W. 2d 621, 624 (Neb. 1987); *Maheshwari v. City of New York*, 810 N.E. 2d 894, 898 (N. Y. 2004); *Adams v. Mills*, 322 S.E. 2d 164, 172-73 (N.C. 1984); *Miller v. Diamond Resources, Inc.*, 703 N.W. 2d 316, 321 (N.D. 2005); *Thompson v. Presbyterian Hosp.*, 652 P.2d 260, 264 (Okla. 1982); *Cramer v. Dep't of Highways*, 870 P.2d 999, 1001 (Wash. Ct. App. 1994).

25. *See*, e.g., *Riordan v. Corp. of the Presiding Bishop of the Church of Jesus Christ of Latter-Day Saints*, 416 F.3d 825, 832 (8th Cir. 2005) (applying Missouri law); *Lexington Ins. Co. v. Rounds*, 349 F. Supp. 2d 861, 867 (D. Vt. 2004) (applying Vermont law); *Robertson v. Sixpence Inns of Am.*, 789 P. 2d 1040, 1047 (Ariz. 1990); *McAuley v. Wills*, 303 S.E. 2d 258, 260-61 (Ga. 1983); *Paragon Family Restaurant v. Bartolini*, 799 N.E.2d 1048, 1054-55 (Ind. 2003); *Mcmillan v. Vliet*, 374 N.W. 2d 679, 681-82 (Mich. 1985); *Delaware v. Valls*, 409 N.W.2d 621, 624 (Neb. 1987); *Maheshwari v. City of New York*, 810 N.E. 2d 894, 898 (N.Y. 2004); *Adams v. Mills*, 322 S.E.2d 164, 172-73 (N.C. 1984); *Miller v. Diamond Resources, Inc.*, 703 N.W.2d 316, 321 (N.D. 2005); *Thompson v. Presbyterian Hosp.*, 652 P.2d 260,264 (Okla. 1982); *Cramer v. Dep't of Highways*, 870 P.2d 999, 1001 (Wash. Ct. App. 1994).

26. *Thompson v. Prebyterian Hosp.*, 652 P.2d 260, 264 (Okla. 1982); *see also Adams v. Mills*, 322 S.E.2d 164, 173 (N.C. 1984); cf. *Paragon Family Restaurant v. Bartolini*, 799 N.E.2d 1048, 1054 (Ind. 2003) (characterizing the supersending or intervening act as being "so remote in time" with respect to the plaintiff's conduct "that is breaks the chain of causation" between the plaintiff's conduct and the defendant's injury).

27. *St. Fort v. Post, Buckley, Schuh & Jernigan*, 902 So.2d 244, 250 (Fla. Dist. Ct. App. 2005); *see also Johnson v. Rice*, 440 S.E.2d 81, 82 (Ga. Ct. App. 1994) (quoting *Logan v. Cincinnati & C.R. Co.*, 129 S.W. 575, 577 (Ky. Ct. App. 1910)).

28. *See*, e.g., *Riordan v. Corp. of the Presiding Bishop of the Churcho f Jesus Christ of Latter-Day Saints*, 416 F.3d 825, 832 (8th Cir. 2005) (applying Missouri law); *Lexington Ins. Co. v. Rounds*, 349 F. Supp. 2d 861, 867 (D. Vt. 2004) (applying Vermont law); *Robertson v. Sixpence Inns of Am.*, 789 P.2d 1040, 1047 (Ariz. 1990); *McAuley v. Wills*, 303 S.E.2d 258, 260 (Ga. 1983); *Paragon Family Restaurant v. Bartolini*, 799 N.E.2d 1048, 1054-55 (Ind. 2003); *McMillan v. Vliet*, 374 N.W.2d 679, 681-82 (Mich. 1985); *Delaware v. Valls*, 409 N.W.2d 621, 624 (Neb. 1987); *Maheshwari v. City of New York*, 810 N.E.2d 894, 898 (N.Y. 2004); *Adams v. Mills*, 322 S.E.2d 164, 172-73 (N.C. 1984); *Miller v. Diamond Resources, Inc.*, 7.3 N.E.2d 316, 321 (N.D. 2005); *Thompson v. Presbyterian Hosp.*, 652 P.2d 260, 264 (Okla. 1982); *Cramer v. Dep't of Highways*, 870 P.2d 999, 1001 (Wash. Ct. App. 1994).

29. *Ventricelli v. Kinney System Rent A Car, Inc.*, 399 N.Y. Supp.2d 237, 237 (App. Div. 1977).

30. *Id.*

31. *Id.*

32. *Id.*

33. *Id.*

34. *See Ventricelli v. Kinney System Rent A Car, Inc.*, 383 N.E. 2d 1149, 1149-50 (N.Y. 1978).

35. *Id.* at 1150.

36. *See*, e.g., *Eternity Global Master Fund Ltd. v. Morgan Guar. Trust Co.*, 375 F.3d 168, 186-87 (2d Cir. 2004) (applying New York law); *Rice v. Strunk*, 670 N.E.2d 1280, 1289 (Ind. 1996); *UPS v. Rickert*, 996 S.W.2d 464, 468 (Ky. 1999); *Kassab v. Michigan Basic Property Ins. Ass'n*, 491 N.W.2d 545, 548 (Mich. 1992); *Specialized Tours, Inc. v. Hagen*, 392 N.W.2d 520, 532 (Minn. 1986); *Spragins v. SunBurst Bank*, 605 So. 2d 777, 780 (Miss. 1992); *Gennari v. Weichert Co. Realtors*, 691 A.2d 350, 367 (N.J. 1997); *Conzelmann v. N.W. Poultry & Dairy Prods. Co.*, 225 P.2d 757, 764-65 (Or. 1974); *Bortz v. Noon*, 729 A.2d 555, 560 (Pa. 1999); *Am. Tobacco Co. v. Grinnell*, 951 S.W.2d 420, 436 (Tex. 1997); *Richmond Metro. Auth. v. McDevitt Street Bovis, Inc.*, 507 S.E.2d 344, 346 (Va. 1998).

37. *See*, e.g., *Racine Fuel Co. v. Rawlins*, 36 N.E.2d 710, 712-13 (Ill. 1941); *UPS v. Rickert*, 996 S.W.2d 464, 468 (Ky. 1999); *Spragins v. SunBurst Bank*, 605 So. 2d 777, 780 (Miss. 1992); *Albright v. Burns*, 503 A.2d 386, 391 (N.J. App. Div. 1986); *Heart River Partners v, Goetzfried*, 703 N.W.2d 330, 339 (N.D. 2005); *Richmond Metro. Auth. v. McDevitt Street Bovis, Inc.*, 507 S.E.2d 344, 346 (Va. 1998).

38. *See*, e.g., *Ullom v. DHS*, 12 S.W.3d, 204, 208 (Ark. 2000); *State v. Michael B. (In re Michael B.)*, 604 N.W.2d 405, 410 (Neb. 2000); *State v. Schiebel*, 564 N.E.2d 54, 60 (Ohio 1990); *State v. Addington*, 588 S.W.2d 569, 570 (Tex. 1979) (per curiam); *Oberbroeckling v. Lyle*, 362 S.E.2d 682, 685 (Va. 1987).

39. *See*, e.g., *State v. Schiebel*, 564 N.E.2d 54, 60 (Ohio 1990); *State v. Addington*, 588 S.W.2d 569, 570 (Tex. 1979) (per curiam); *Oberbroeckling v. Lyle*, 362 S.E.2d 682, 685 (Va. 1987).

40. *Tracinda Corp. v. DaimlerChrysler AG*, 364 F. Supp. 2d 362, 388-89 (D. Del. 2005) (applying Delaware law); *Tew v. Chase Manhattan Bank, N.A.*, 728 F. Supp. 1551, 1564 (S.D. Fla. 1990) (applying Florida law); *Barrett v. Holland & Hart*, 845 P.2d 714, 717 (Mont. 1992).

41. *Kilduff v. Adams, Inc.*, 593 A.2d 478, 487 (Conn. 1991); *Dizick v. Umpqua Community College*, 599 P.2d 444, 448 (Or. 1979).

42. *See*, e.g., *Sandwich Chef of Tex., Inc. v. Reliance Nat'l Indem. Ins. Co.*, 319 F.3d 205, 218 (5th Cir. 2003) (citing RESTATEMENT (SECOND) OF TORTS § 546).

43. *Humana, Inc. v. Castillo*, 728 So. 2d 261, 265 (Fla. Dist. Ct. App. 1999); *see also Shades Ridge Holding Co. v. Coles, Allen & Hall Mortgage Co.*, 390 So. 2d 601, 607 (Ala. 1980).

44. *Engalla v. Permanente Med. Group, Inc.*, 938 P.2d 903, 919 (Cal. 1997) (following RE-STATEMENT (SECOND) OF TORTS § 546); *see also Reisman v. KPMG Peat Marwick LLP*, 787 N.E.2d 1060, 1068-69 (Mass. App. Ct. 2003) (following RESTATEMENT (SECOND) OF TORTS § 546); *Nails v. S &R, Inc.*, 639 A.2d 660, 669-70 (Md. 1994) (following RESTATEMENT (SECOND) OF TORTS § 546 and rejecting the position that the misrepresentation be the sole reason for the plaintiff's actions).

45. *In re Ford Motor Co. Vehicle Paint Litig.*, 182 F.R.D. 214, 221-22 (E.D. La. 1998) (citing cases).

46. *See, e.g., Secs. Inv. Protection Corp. v. BDO Seidman, LLP*, 222 F.3d 63, 72-73 (2d Cir. 2000) (citing cases); *McMahon Books, Inc. v. Willow Grove Assocs.*, 108 F.R.D. 32, 37-38 (E.D. Pa. 1985) (applying Pennsylvania law); *Walco Inv., Inc. v. Thenen*, 168 F.R.D. 315, 335 (S.D. Fla. 1996) (applying Florida law); *In re Soybean Futures Litig.*, 892 F. Supp. 1025, 1031, 1059-60 (N.D. Ill. 1995) (applying Illinois law); *Mirkin v. Wasserman*, 858 P.2d 568, 570-84 (Cal. 1993); *Reisman v. KPMG Peat Marwick LLP*, 787 N.E.2d 1060, 1070-72 (Mass. App. Ct. 2003); *Kaufman v. I-Stat Corp.*, 754 A.2d 1188, 1192-1201 (N.J. 2000).

47. *See, e.g., Sedco Int'l, S.A. v. Cory*, 683 F.2d 1201, 1209-10 (8th Cir. 1982) (applying Iowa law).

48. *See, e.g., Cumberland Oil Corp. v. Thropp*, 791 F.2d 1037, 1044 (2d Cir. 1986) (applying New York law).

49. *Heberer v. Shell Oil Co.*, 744 S.W.2d 441, 443-44 (Mo. 1988) (en banc); *see also Martin v. Heinold Commodities, Inc.*, 643 N.E.2d 734, 746 (Ill. 1994); *Brackett v. Griswold*, 20 N.E. 376, 380 (N.Y. 1889).

    By contrast, a few courts considers foreseeability irrelevant and apply the following test to determine legal cause in common law fraud cases:

    > If, weighing the moral fault of a defendant and applying the rules of causation liberally, the consequences have some reasonably close connection with the defendant's conduct and the harm threatened, and in themselves, using hindsight, are not deemed preposterous or far-fetched, defendant should be held liable. Concepts of policy, fairness and justice are entitled to great weight.

    Shades Ridge Holding Co. v. Cobbs, Allen & Hall Mortgage Co., 390 So. 2d 601, 611-12 (Ala. 1980) (internal quotations omitted) (quoting *Seidel v. Greenberg*, 260 A.2d 863, 875 (N.J. Super. 1969)).

50. *See, e.g., Mannion v. Stallings & Co.*, 561 N.E.2d 1134, 1137-38 (Ill. App. Ct. 1990); *Rinaldi & Sons, Inc. v. Wells Fargo Alarm Serv., Inc.*, 347 N.E.2d 618, 618 (N.Y. 1976); *Pen O Tex Oil & Leasehold Co. v. Fairchild*, 252 S.W. 847, 848 (Tex. Civ. App. 1923).

51. *ATACS Corp. v. Trans World Communications, Inc.*, 155 F.3d 659, 669 (3d Cir. 1998).

52. *See, e.g., S. Cal. Fed. Sav. & Loan Ass'n v. United States*, 422 F.3d 1319, 1334 (Fed. Cir. 2005).

53. *See, e.g., S. Cal. Fed. Sav. & Loan Ass'n v. United States*, 422 F.3d 1319, 1334 (Fed. Cir. 2005); *ATACS Corp. v. Trans World Communications, Inc.*, 155 F.3d 659, 669 (3d. Cir. 1998) (applying Pennsylvania law); *Doering Equip. Co. v. John Deere Co.*, 815 N.E.2d 234, 239 (Mass. App. Ct. 2004); *Reimer v. Badger Wholesale Co.*, 433 N.W.2d 592, 594 (Wis. Ct. App. 1988) (following RESTATEMENT (SECOND) OF TORTS § 344).

54. *See, e.g., Fischer v. Bright Bay Lincoln Mercury, Inc.*, 651 N.Y.2d 625, 626 (App. Div. 1996); *Explorers Motor Home Corp. v. Aldridge*, 541 S.W.2d 851, 853 (Tex. App. – Beaumont 1976).

55. *ATACS Corp. v. Trans World Communications, Inc.*, 155 F.3d 659, 669 (3d. Cir. 1998) (applying Pennsylvania law).

56. *Schonfeld v. Hilliard*, 218 F.3d 164, 175 (2d Cir. 2000) (applying New York law). General damages are also sometimes referred to as market damages because, when the promised performance is the delivery of goods, their measure is the difference between the contract price and the market value of the goods at the time of the breach. *See* id.

57. *Fort Washington Resources, Inc. v. Tannen*, 901 F. Supp. 932, 943 (E.D. Pa. 1995) (applying Pennsylvania law).

58. *Marjan Int'l Corp. v. V.K. Putnam, Inc.*, No. 92 Civ. 8531 (BN), 1993 WL 541204, at *11 (S.D.N.Y. Dec. 28, 1993); *see also Brandon & Tibbs v. George Kevorkian Accountancy Corp.*, 277 Cal. Rptr. 2d 40, 48 (Cal. Ct. App. 1990) ("general damages are ordinarily confined to those which would naturally arise from the breach, or which might have been reasonably contemplated or foreseen by both parties, at the time they made the contract, as the probable result of the breach").

59. *Schonfeld v. Hilliard*, 218 F.3d 164, 175 (2d Cir. 2000).

60. *See Nelson v. Data Terminal Sys., Inc.*, 762 S.W.2d 744, 748 (Tex. App. – San Antonio 1989); 3 Dan B. Dobbs, *Dobbs Law of Remedies* §12.1(1) (1993).

61. *Schonfeld v. Hilliard*, 218 F.3d 164, 176 (2d Cir. 2000) (applying New York law); *Frost Nat'.l Bank v. Heafner*, 12 S.W.3d 104, 111 n.5 (Tex. App. – Hous. [1st Dist.] 1999).

62. *Homes By Calkins, Inc. v. Fisher*, 634 N.E.2d 1039, 1042 (Ohio Ct. App. 1993); *see also Lewis Jorge Constr. Mgmt., Inc. v. Pomona Unified Sch. Dist.*, 102 P.3d 257, 261-62 (Cal. 2004); *Frost Nat'l. Bank v. Heafner*, 12 S.W.3d 104, 111 n.5 (Tex. App. – Hous. [1st Dist.] 1999).

63. *Marjan Int'l Corp. v. V.K. Putnam, Inc.*, No. 92 Civ. 8531 (BN), 1993 WL 541204, at *11 (S.D.N.Y. Dec. 28, 1993).

64. *Brandon & Tibbs v. George Kevorkian Accountancy Corp.*, 277 Cal. Rptr. 2d 40, 48-49 (Cal. Ct. App. 1990).

65. *See*, e.g., *Krauss v. Greenberg*, 137 F.2d 569, 571-72 (3d Cir. 1943) (applying Pennsylvania law); *Point Prods. A.G. v. Sony Music Entm't, Inc.*, 215 F. Supp. 2d 336, 341 (S.D.N.Y. 2002) (applying New York law); *Bird v. St. Paul Fire & Marine Ins. Co.*, 120 N.E. 86, 55 (N.Y. 1918) (Cardozo, J.); *Fowler v. Campbell*, 612 N.E.2d 596, 602 (Ind. Ct. App. 1993) (citing FARNSWORTH ON CONTRACTS § 12.1); *Reiman Assocs. v. R/A Adver. Inc.*, 306 N.W.2d 292, 300-01 & n.11 (Wis. Ct. App. 1981).

66. *See*, e.g., *Vesper Constr. Co. v. Rain for Rent, Inc.*, 602 F.2d 238, 243 (10th Cir. 1979) (applying New Mexico law); *Krauss v. Greenberg*, 137 F.2d 569, 571-72 (3d Cir. 1943) (applying Pennsylvania law); *Point Prods. A.G. v. Sony Music Entm't, Inc.*, 215 F. Supp. 2d 336, 341-44 (S.D.N.Y. 2002) (applying New York law); *Havens Steel Co. v. Randolph Eng'g Co.*, 613 F. Supp. 514, 533 (W.D. Mo. 1985) (applying Missouri law) (following CORBIN ON CONTRACTS § 999); *Bruckman v. Parliament Escrow Corp.*, 235 Cal. Rptr. 813, 820 (Cal. Ct. App. 1987); *Tuttle/White Constrs., Inc. v. Montgomery Elevator Co.*, 385 So. 2d 98, 100 (Fla. Dist. Ct. App. 1980) (following CORBIN ON CONTRACTS § 999); *Thor Elec., Inc. v. Oberle & Assocs., Inc.*, 741 N.E.2d 373, 381 (Ind. Ct. App. 2000); *Reiman Assocs, v. R/A Adver. Inc.*, 306 N.W.2d 292, 300-01 (Wis. Ct. App. 1981) (following CORBIN ON CONTRACTS § 999).

67. *See*, e.g., *Vesper Constr. Co. v. Rain for Rent, Inc.*, 602 F.2d 238, 243 (10th Cir. 1979) (applying New Mexico law); *Nelson v. Lake Canal Co.*, 644 P.2d 55, 59 (Colo. Ct. App. 1981) (following CORBIN ON CONTRACTS § 999).

68. *Point Prods. A.G. v. Sony Music Entm't, Inc.*, 215 F. Supp. 2d 336, 343-44 (S.D.N.Y. 2002) (applying New York law).

69. *Vanderbeek v. Vernon Corp.*, 50 P.3d 866, 870 (Colo. 2002) (en banc); *Reiman Assocs., Inc. v. R/A Adver., Inc.*, 306 N.W.2d 292, 301 n.11 (Wis. Ct. App. 1981).

70. *Hadley v. Baxendale*, 9 Exch. 341, 156 Eng. Rep. 145 (1854). *See also*, e.g., *Krauss v. Greenberg*, 137 F.2d 569, 570-71 (3d Cir. 1943) (applying Pennsylvania law); *Lewis Jorge Constr. Mgmt., Inc. v. Pomona Unified Sch. Dist.*, 102 P.3d 257, 262 (Cal. 2004); *Bay Gen. Indus. v. Johnson*, 418 A.2d 1050, 1057 n.19 (D.C. 1980); *Lawrence v. Will Darrah & Assocs.*, 516 N.W.2d 43, 45 (Mich. 1994); *Pac. Coast Title Ins. Co. v. Hartford Accident & Indem. Co.*, 325 P.2d 906, 907 (Utah 1958); *Reiman Assocs. v. R/A Advertising, Inc.*, 306 N.W.2d 292, 300 (Wis. Ct. App. 1981).

71. *Herman & MacLean v. Huddleston*, 459 U.S. 375, 387-91 (1983).

72. *Dura Pharms. Inc. v. Broudo*, 544 U.S. 336, 341-42 (2005); *Ernst & Ernst v. Hochfelder*, 425 U.S. 185, 199 (1976).

By contrast, plaintiffs alleging claims under Section 11 of the Securities Act, 15 U.S.C. § 77k, based on material misrepresentations in offering materials, need not prove causation. Rather, declines in the value of the securities at issue are presumed to result from the material misrepresentation unless the *defendant* proves otherwise.

73. *Basic Inc. v. Levinson*, 485 U.S. 224, 243 (1988) (four-justice plurality); *Robbins v. Koger Props., Inc.*, 116 F.3d 1441, 1447 (11th Cir. 1997); *Schlick v. Penn-Dixie Cement Corp.*, 507 F.2d 374, 380 (2d Cir. 1974).

74. *Nathenson v. Zonagen Inc.*, 267 F.3d 400, 413 (5th Cir. 2001); *Newton v. Merrill Lynch, Pierce, Fenner & Smith, Inc.*, 259 F.3d 154, 172 (3d Cir. 2001); *AUSA Life Ins. Co. v. Ernst & Young*, 206 F.3d 202, 209 (2d Cir. 2000); *Binder v. Gillespie*, 184 F.3d 1059, 1065 (9th Cir. 1999); *Movitz v. First Nat'l Bank of Chicago*, 148 F.3d 760, 763 (7th Cir. 1998); *Robbins v. Koger Properties, Inc.*, 116 F.3d 1441, 1447 (11th Cir. 1997); *Arthur Young & Co. v. Reves*, 937 F.2d 1310, 1327 (8th Cir. 1991).

75. *Bell v. Ascendant Solutions, Inc.*, 422 F.3d 307, 310 n.2 (5th Cir. 2005); *Shapiro v. Midwest Rubber Reclaiming Co.*, 626 F.2d 63, 69 (8th Cir. 1980); *Zelman v. JDS Uniphase Corp.*, 376 F. Supp. 2d 956, 967 (N.D. Cal. 2005).

76. *Nathenson v. Zonagren Inc.*, 267 F.3d 400, 413 (5th Cir. 2001).

77. *Affiliated Ute Citizens of Utah v. United States*, 406 U.S. 128, 153-54 (1972); *Newton v. Merrill Lynch, Pierce, Fenner & Smith, Inc.*, 259 F.3d 154, 174 (3d Cir. 2001); *Rifkin v. Crow*, 574 F.2d 256, 262 (5th Cir. 1978); *Blackie v. Barrack*, 524 F.2d 891, 905-06 (9th Cir. 1975).

78. *Molecular Tech. Corp. v. Valentine*, 925 F.2d 910, 919 (6th Cir. 1991); *DuPont v. Brady*, 828 F.2d 75, 78 (2d Cir. 1987); *Blackie v. Barrack*, 524 F.2d 891, 906 (9th Cir. 1978).

79. *Basic Inc. v. Levinson*, 485 U.S. 224, 245 (1988) (four-justice plurality).

80. *Id.*, at 245, 250.

81. *Id.*, at 248.

82. *Id.*, at 242.

83. *Bell v. Ascendant Solutions, Inc.*, 422 F.3d 307, 314-16 (5th Cir. 2005).

84. *Unger v. Amedisys, Inc.*, 401 F.3d 316, 323 (5th Cir. 2005) (citing cases from various jurisdictions).

85. *Dura Pharms., Inc. v. Broudo*, 544 U.S. 336, 342 (2005).

86. *Binder v. Gillespie*, 184 F.3d 1059, 1066 (9th Cir. 1999); *Movitz v. First Nat'l Bank of Chicago*, 148 F.3d 760, 763 (7th Cir. 1998).

87. *Dura Pharms., Inc. v. Broudo*, 544 U.S. 336, 341-48 (2005).

88. *Dura Pharms., Inc. v. Broudo*, 544 U.S. 336, 342-46 (2005); *Newton v. Merrill Lynch, Pierce, Fenner & Smith, Inc.*, 259 F.3d 154, 177 (3d Cir. 2001); *Robbins v. Koger Props., Inc.*, 116 F.3d 1441, 1447 (11th Cir. 1997); *Feldman v. Pioneer Petroleum, Inc.*, 813 F.2d 296, 302 (10th Cir. 1987).

89. *Robbins v. Koger Props., Inc.*, 116 F.3d 1441, 1447 (11th Cir. 1997) (following *Wilson v. Comtech Telecomm. Corp.*, 648 F.2d 88, 92 (2d Cir. 1981)).

90. *See* 15 U.S.C. § 78bb(a). The Supreme Court has held that the correct measure of damages is the difference between the fair value of what the plaintiff received and the fair value of that which the plaintiff would have received had there been no fraudulent conduct, except for the situation where the defendant receives more than the plaintiff's actual loss, in which case the damages are the amount of the defendant's profit. *See Affiliated Ute Citizens of Utah v. United States*, 406 U.S. 128, 155 (1972).

91. *Robbins v. Koger Props., Inc.*, 116 F.3d 1441, 1447 n.5 (11th Cir. 1997).

92. *Id.*

93. *Daubert v. Merrell Dow Pharms.*, 509 U.S. 579, 597 (1993).

94. *See Kumho Tire Co. v. Carmichael*, 526 U.S. 137, 147-49 (1999).

95. *United States v. Downing*, 753 F.2d 1224, 1242 (3d Cir. 1985).

96. *Concord Boat Corp. v. Brunswick Corp.*, 207 F. 3d 1039 (8th Cir. 2000).

97. *Id.*, at 1056.

98. *Id.*, at 1056.

99. *Id.*, at 1057.

100. *Cal. Fed. Bank v. United States*, 395 F.3d 1263 (Fed. Cir. 2005).

101. *Id.*, at 1266.

102. *Id.*, at 1268.

103. *Id.*, at 1270.

104. *Id.*, at 1270.

105. *Id.*, at 1268.

106. *Abrams v. Van Kampen Funds, Inc.*, No. 01 C 7538, 2005 WL 88973, at *1 (N.D. Ill. Jan. 13, 2005).

107. *Id.*

108. *Id.* at *9.

109. *Id.*, at *10.

110. *Bell v. Ascendant Solutions, Inc.*, 422 F.3d 307 (5th Cir. 2005).

111. *Id.*, at 314.

112. *Id.*, at 311.

113. *Id.*, at 311-16. *See* Section 2.2(d)(i) of this chapter for a list of the factors in deciding whether a stock is traded in an efficient market.

CHAPTER 3

THE ECONOMICS IN ACCOUNTING FOR LITIGATION

Elizabeth A. Evans

CONTENTS

3.1 INTRODUCTION

Other chapters in this book assist a litigation expert in analyzing a case's issues. This chapter acquaints accountants and lawyers with a group of professionals who offer complementary skills (economists) and their body of knowledge relevant to a wide range of issues in accounting-related litigation (economics).

Economists attempt to understand the structure and performance of the economic entity being examined. Industrial organization economists, for example, know about competitive industries, oligopolies, and the like. Once they analyze industry-specific data, they can forecast likely behavioral patterns. Labor economists understand the market for human capital and factors relevant to the earning power of an individual and occupations. Financial economists will know how the capital markets work. All will use their knowledge to establish a logical framework within which to evaluate the actions of the parties to the lawsuit.

Economists are also familiar with sources of government or other publicly available data. They know where to find the data and what biases the data can have. Finally, many economists know how to use data to devise and test hypotheses using statistical techniques and thereby create empirical proof for theories.

These skills complement those of accountants. Accountants know how financial statements and general business records arise in the normal course of business. They also understand the data supporting financial statements and business records and their limitations. They know how to obtain, organize, and document data. They bring their own analytic abilities to the task. Most important, from auditing, consulting, and tax preparation experience, an accountant will have firm-specific knowledge about the entity that the economist often does not possess.

Every expert witness knows that in litigation at least two sides exist for every case. One side's experts will attempt to discredit the adversary's experts' assertions, assumptions, and reasoning. As a result, experts sometimes obtain the assistance of others whose knowledge does not duplicate but complements their own, in order to buttress their opinions. Economists and accountants have complementary skills. Accountants perform analyses based explicitly or implicitly on certain assumptions; economists can test and prove the correctness (or falseness) of the assumptions. Similarly, economists often have hypotheses to test their theories about how the entity works; accountants provide the correct data for the tests or do the computations involved, or both. Some experts have training in several disciplines and thus combine the expertise of accountants, economists, and statisticians.

Sections 3.2 and 3.3 discuss the strengths of economists and accountants, respectively. Section 3.4 illustrates some of the ways in which economics affects the measurement of lost profits, antitrust, and securities litigation.

3.2   PARTICULAR STRENGTHS OF ECONOMISTS

This section focuses on the areas in which economists have had specific training that other experts cannot easily duplicate. These areas include economic modeling (often using regression techniques), defining markets, and understanding price theory and the implications of market risk.

(a) Economic Modeling.   Economists often understand regression techniques, one use of which is to model what would have happened but for certain events. In fact, an entire branch of economics—econometrics—applies statistical methods to the study of economic data and problems. (Chapter 6 discusses econometrics.) One such method, regression analysis, applies a statistical technique to develop an equation depicting the relation among variables and then uses that equation for prediction.[1] For example, suppose an expert needs to predict the sales that a firm would have made but for the defendant's actions. He could use a regression analysis that models the relation between the firm's sales and other relevant factors (e.g., total industry sales) over a control period preceding the defendant's actions to predict what sales would have been in the absence of those actions. Similarly, if an expert needs to estimate how a share would have performed but for some event, a financial economist can predict this by performing a regression analysis. This regression analysis might relate an investment in the firm's share to an investment of the same size in a portfolio of shares in the same industry or in the market. (*See* Section 3.4(c), "Securities Laws," for a discussion of this point.)

The regression analysis also provides other relevant information such as the statistical significance of the relation among the variables, the degree of explanation afforded by the equation, and the ability to construct confidence intervals around the estimate. Hence, the technique not only provides predictions but also explicitly describes the strength or stability of the predictions.

Assume that an expert has constructed an equation that models the sales of Firm A as a function of total industry sales. Now the expert would like to know whether the sales of Firm A relate to the total industry sales, that is, whether this variable helps explain the movement of the firm's sales. By examining the t-statistic, an economist can ascertain whether the variable has significant explanatory power. The economist can also check the coefficient of determination (often called the R-squared) to measure the amount of the change in the firm's sales explained by the total industry sales.

Although regression analysis produces an unbiased estimate, certain data relations can occur that obscure or overemphasize the estimates. The most common include heteroscedasticity, autocorrelation or serial correlation, multicollinearity, and nonlinear relationships (*see* Pindyck and Rubinfeld, 1998 and Chapters 5 and 6 for more discussion on regression analysis.)

(b) Market Definition.   Even though market definition often relates to antitrust analysis, it can arise in cases such as breach of contract or patent infringement or any case in which the measure of damages equals the plaintiff's lost profits (or the defendant's ill-gotten gains). Analysis of the relevant market can be divided into two areas: the product market and the geographic market. In defining the relevant product market, one must include not only the specific product in the case at hand but also those products that consumers can substitute (demand-side substitution). One must also identify both the firms that currently make the relevant product(s) and the firms that could switch to manufacturing the relevant product(s) (supply-side substitution). Similarly, in defining the geographic market, one must include not only the areas the firms that make the relevant products currently serve but also the areas that firms would ship from if a supracompetitive (or patent monopoly) price were imposed (Posner and Landes, 1981).

Economists can test empirically for a market definition in a way that accounts for relevant factors. First, they can estimate the change that will occur in the quantity sold of a product if the price of that product changes (own-price elasticity). Second, they can estimate the change in the quantity sold of a good when the price of another good changes (cross-price elasticity). These estimates offer useful tools of market definition. For example, if a 10 percent increase in the price of Product A produces a 20 percent decrease in the quantity sold of Product A and a 15 percent increase in the quantity sold of Products B and C, a market defined as Product A alone is too narrow, and one should include Products B and C in the market definition. If, however, a 10 percent decrease in the quantity sold of Product A has no (or only a small) effect on the sales of Products B and C, then one could define the relevant market as Product A alone.

Economists often empirically test the geographic market by correlating the prices of the products in different areas. Correlation analysis measures the strength of the relation between two variables when analysts cannot identify one variable as the cause of the other(s).[2] Economists have found that the prices of products that share the same geographic market will tend to correlate strongly. That is, if the price in Area A and the price in Area B tend to move together, they probably share the same geographic market (Stigler and Sherwin, 1985).

(c) Price Theory. Price theory offers another area of economics important for litigation. By observing prices over long periods, economists have discovered that certain markets behave in certain patterns, most commonly competitive (many sellers of a good and its close substitutes), monopoly (one seller of a good without close substitutes), oligopoly (few sellers of a good and its close substitutes), cartel (a group of firms acting in concert), and monopsony (a firm with monopolistic buying power). For example, economists have observed that, in a competitive market, firms cannot raise the price significantly above the competitive level without decreasing their total revenues and profits, whereas a monopolist who can prevent entry can raise the price profitably. Although most people associate price theory with antitrust and regulation cases, it can apply to any case in which an expert must estimate a firm's behavior in the absence of the injurious conduct. For example, in a breach of contract case, the tools that price theory provides can help identify subsequent sales as replacement sales for the breached amount or additional sales that would have occurred anyway (*see* Section 3.4(a), "Measurement of Lost Profits," for a discussion of this point).

(d) Market Risk. Many empirical studies require consideration of capital market risk.[3] For example, in a present value analysis, an expert discounts cash flows to a specific date, and the discount factor the expert uses should reflect in some cases the market and industry effects of each period. Economists can estimate the appropriate discount rate.

Financial economists often use the Capital Asset Pricing Model (CAPM) to estimate the appropriate discount rate (*see* Chapter 7). CAPM defines the return of a firm as the risk-free rate of return (usually measured by the return on short-term T-bills) plus the difference between the return on the market and the risk-free rate of return (otherwise known as the risk premium) times the firm's beta (the measure of the firm's market risk) (Brealey and Myers, 2000, p. 195). A financial economist using the CAPM could develop a discount factor for the present value analysis that would incorporate not only the effects of cash flows occurring in different time periods but also the return that the market and the specific firm experienced. Hence, an expert could more precisely measure what an expected cash flow occurring in Time Period 6 would equal in Time Period 0.

Financial economists also deal with the effect of leverage (or debt). The presence of debt that a company must pay before the shareholder receives any return makes the shareholders' investment relatively riskier. The discount factor for a firm's assets will therefore differ from the discount factor for the firm's equity by the amount of risk represented by debt (Brealey and Myers, 2000, pp. 231–232). The financial economist understands this distinction, how to change one to the other, and which one will apply to the specific case.

3.3 PARTICULAR STRENGTHS OF ACCOUNTANTS

The accountant has strengths that others would find difficult to duplicate. These include the understanding of generally accepted accounting principles (GAAP), the way in which management uses the underlying data to produce a financial statement (whether for internal or external use), cost estimation, effects of income taxes, and how best to present the results in an understandable fashion.

(a) GAAP. Only one trained in accounting can understand the GAAP used to prepare accounting statements for public use. For example, accountants have a precise meaning for *goodwill*, yet economists often have the more general, lay definition in mind when they use that term. Much empirical data used in lawsuits come from accounting statements. If the economist or other expert does not understand a number's derivation (e.g., goodwill) or what it represents, that expert might base an empirical study on a set of assumptions that does not apply to the case or might use the wrong data altogether. The following discussion highlights some of the areas that nonaccountants understand the least.

One of the most difficult areas involves consolidation of financial entities. After a parent consolidates a subsidiary, economists often need an accountant's expertise to unravel the consolidation to measure unreported items: the amount the parent paid for the subsidiary, the book value of the subsidiary's assets prior to consolidation, the amount of goodwill on the subsidiary's books prior to consolidation, the intercompany transfers, the effect of the subsidiary's being a foreign operation, and so forth. Consolidations become even more complicated when the parent's ownership equals less than 100 percent.

An accountant can explain valuation bases of assets under GAAP. Economists often use balance sheet data over a period of years to perform an empirical study. An accountant can explain when valuations use historical cost and when they use market values. For example, when a case involves a firm's holdings of marketable securities, the accountant will have to ascertain whether the financial statements used a cost or market basis and whether a continuous series of data valued on the same basis exists.

When studying a firm's sales, an accountant will need to explain the effects of revenue recognition at times other than the time of sale. This becomes especially true when the firm has long-term construction contracts, installment or consignment sales, or special-order merchandise.

Inventory presents two difficulties: the valuation of inventory (acquisition cost, current cost, lower-of-cost-or-market, and standard cost) and cost flow assumptions (last in, first out [LIFO], first in, first out [FIFO], and weighted average or the alternative, specific identification). The economist untrained in accounting will not typically know that although LIFO measures the cost of goods sold at current costs, it presents inventory amounts on the balance sheet unrelated to current costs. Even an economist who understands the basics of LIFO may not know how the intricacies of dollar value LIFO, gross margin method, and dollar value retail method LIFO affect accounting data. Regarding capital assets, the accountant understands the differences in the valuation of purchased and self-constructed assets, as well as the valuation of costs subsequent to acquisition (e.g., repairs and maintenance, moving, replacement and improvement, and additions). The concept of *depreciation* causes confusion because the term has different meanings for economists and accountants.

To the economist, depreciation means the decline in an asset's value in a given period that results from reductions in the asset's value caused by (1) physical use and (2) obsolescence, offset by unrealized holding gains (or further reduced by unrealized losses). To the accountant, depreciation means, simply, a process of cost allocation, which assigns cost to periods of use. Over the life of the asset, the accountant will write down the asset's cost to salvage value through some systematic process unrelated to periodic change in value. In contrast, the economist will track the market value of the asset, calling declines in market value *depreciation* and increases *appreciation*.

Economists often do not understand contra accounts. Although assets such as accounts receivable and property, plant, and equipment have contra accounts, each contra account has a different purpose. The *allowance for doubtful accounts* helps estimate the recoverable value of accounts receivable, but the contra account *accumulated depreciation* serves a different purpose. Moreover, an economist may need to know that although tangible assets have separate contra accounts, intangible assets need not have such accounts. However, the nonexistence of a contra account does not mean that firms do not amortize intangible assets in much the same manner as they depreciate tangible assets.

Economists who have mastered the simple process of accounting for marketable securities often do not understand the method used for investments in securities, especially when an equity investment provides significant influence to its owner. One uses market values to value an interest in a firm's equity securities as part of a portfolio in financial statements. In some cases, however, the investor will use the equity method. The balance sheet figure for an investment reported by the equity method does not equal either the cost that the investor paid nor the investment's market value. Instead, it represents a mixture of the original cost to the investor increased by the investor's share of the firm's earnings retained since the time of the investment. Economists, moreover, often do not know that this investor's income statement will report revenue equal to the increase in this investment without the firm's necessarily receiving cash from it.

Accounting for bonds uses accounting conventions that often play an important role in empirical studies. The reporting requirements differ depending on whether the bond is an asset (investment) of the firm or a liability (debt). An economist studying a firm's bond liabilities often does not realize that the amount listed on the firm's balance sheet equals the present value of the bonds' face value and the expected interest payments (evaluated at the effective interest rate on the issue date, unadjusted for subsequent interest rate changes) and not the face value of the bonds. Furthermore, the income statement's interest expense for the bond debtor probably does not equal the cash paid.[4] When studying bond discounts and premiums and their amortization, an economist often needs an accountant's help to calculate the market or face value of what a firm owes or even owns.

Pension plans comprise yet another source of mystery to a nonaccountant; their terminology includes such phrases as *normal cost*, *sweetening*, *actuarial liability*, *vesting*, *defined benefit*, *defined contribution*, *fully funded*, *partially funded*, *contributory*, and *noncontributory*. For an economist, the most important fact concerning pension plans and other postemployment benefits is that a firm's obligations will not always appear—or at least not appear in total—anywhere in the basic set of financial statements.

(b) Understanding Uses of Accounting Data.   An accountant understands how firms record their underlying data for internal purposes and how firms adjust these data to create financial statements for external use. Some accountants, however, do not realize the infirmities of accounting data for economic decision making. In fact, many firms have two different accounting systems—one for financial reporting and one for managerial decision making. The financial accounting system contains the information for preparing reports intended for people outside the firm (e.g., shareholders and banks). The managerial or decision accounting system provides more detailed information for managers or other decision makers within the firm. Managerial or decision accounting data need not comply with GAAP and can include information on such economic concepts as opportunity costs. Accountants also understand that a term used in financial accounting can have a different meaning to economists; such terms include *asset*, *depreciation*, *reserves*, *revenue*, *depreciation*, and *money*. Some words, notably *cost* and *expense*, have different meanings in financial and managerial accounting.

Accountants often use knowledge of the financial data to restate or recreate lost financial records. For example, suppose an issue in litigation relates to only one division or one product line of a firm. An accountant would use internal data to ascertain which income streams and assets belong to the specific entity or product line.

The accountant's understanding of underlying data also becomes critical during analysis of overhead or common cost allocation. When preparing an internal report on a division's profitability, accountants often allocate some corporate overhead costs. The expert witness, however, often needs to know how a division's actual overhead expenditures vary with activity levels. An accountant can ascertain which overhead costs to include in the witness's study. For example, suppose an accountant preparing an internal division profit report attributed one-fifth of the total overhead to the division because the division sales were one-fifth of total sales. The litigation analysis, however, could include only the salary of the division's vice president, because the remaining corporate staff worked on other divisions.

Most accountants understand the issues of transfer pricing and the various methods that firms use to ensure that the overall effect of buying decisions is to earn profits for the firm as a whole (not only for a single division). Some litigation studies will use the market price as the transfer price, however, particularly when the case focuses on a single division. Here accountants can use their expertise to correctly restate transfer prices as market prices.

Some of the litigation studies that economists and accountants perform benefit from cash flow analyses (e.g., the failing-firm analysis in a merger context). Most economists have little experience understanding statements of cash flows, particularly those that use the indirect method for presenting operating cash flow. Accountants can modify historical financial statements to create a cash flow statement for a division or a single product line.

(c) Cost Estimation.   Cost estimation requires an understanding of the underlying data. Often expert witnesses need to identify which costs vary with production or sales and which costs remain fixed. The accountant must always understand the data needed for the expert's study. For example, if the case requires an analysis of incremental costs, the fixed and variable cost definitions often differ from those used in financial reports. Thus, a study of whether the company made more (or lost less) entering into a new market than it would have otherwise requires that the accountant consider the cost of new equipment purchased for this expansion as incremental even though the accountant normally views such costs as fixed. Economists and accountants rarely think about the distinction between marginal costs and incremental costs (Section 3.4(a)(ii) explains the distinction between these terms). Economists more often use the former construct and accountants the latter.

(d) Income Taxes.   In many litigation studies, the expert must consider the effects of income taxes. Although economists know when to consider taxes, they generally have no expertise in calculating the tax effects. The accountant should clarify whether the economist wants to use the average tax rate, the marginal tax rate, the effective tax rate, or even the marginal effective tax rate.[5] For example, a firm's weighted-average cost of capital calculation includes the marginal corporate tax rate, whereas a firm's adjusted present value uses the effective tax rate (Brealey and Myers, 2000, pp. 544, 558).

(e) Presentation of Analysis.   An accountant can help an economic expert present a litigation report or testimony. Often an economist can best present findings to the court as *pro forma* financial statements that an accountant has constructed. Economists make certain assumptions or estimates in their studies and often need to illustrate how these different assumptions or estimates affect the outcome. A sensitivity analysis presented by an accountant that slightly varies the assumptions in several studies helps the parties to identify which assumptions matter most.

3.4   APPLICATIONS OF ECONOMICS IN LITIGATION

The remainder of this chapter discusses three areas of interaction in litigation between accountants and economists: lost profit measurement, antitrust analysis, and securities laws analyses. Because other chapters in this book discuss these topics at length, this chapter focuses primarily on the economic implications of the analysis that a litigation expert will encounter.

(a) Measurement of Lost Profits.   Whether the plaintiff has identified the cause of action as breach of contract, copyright or patent infringement, or violation of antitrust laws, damages usually equal the difference between the profits that the plaintiff would have realized but for the defendant's actions and the plaintiff's actual profits. In other words, the general damages measure equals incremental sales (or revenues) less incremental costs. Although one can measure lost profits in many ways, most measures combine the knowledge of business and financial records with economic assumptions about the relevant industry.

(i) Incremental Sales or Revenues.   In a lost profits study, the analyst must first compute the amount of lost revenues or sales units that the defendant's actions have caused. Analysts use four common approaches to measure this amount:

1. *Before-and-After:* This approach compares the plaintiff's sales level before the defendant's wrongdoing with the plaintiff's sales level after the defendant's wrongdoing; the difference between the two levels represents the lost sales. This approach implicitly assumes that only the defendant's wrongdoing

affected the plaintiff's business volume; otherwise the volume would have been the same. This approach, however, can underestimate lost sales for a plaintiff whose sales were increasing prior to the defendant's actions. Conversely, if the plaintiff's business was declining during the before period, such an assumption can overestimate lost sales. To use such an approach effectively, an expert will often include a market analysis in the lost profits study. For example, an industrial organization economist could characterize the industry as mature and stable during the period under question, indicating that the plaintiff's sales level probably would have remained unchanged but for the defendant's actions.

2. *Statistical Forecast of Sales:* The expert forecasts but-for sales by using a variety of tools such as regression (or other statistical) analysis and then subtracting the actual sales to estimate the lost sales. With this approach, the expert's model (or equation) must adequately predict the sales and use a control period (over which the equation is estimated) that does not contain events that would bias the results; also, the regression equation must not contain biases such as heteroscedasticity, autocorrelation, or other similar factors.[6] The model should also consider all important industry factors that affect the sales of the plaintiff's products. For example, the price of oil can affect the sale of products used in constructing oil rigs. The omission of a significant factor can invalidate the expert's results or make these results seem less credible to a judge and jury. An economist can help ensure that the damages study considers all relevant factors and that the model includes the significant ones.

3. *Yardstick Approach:* The expert gathers an index of firms similar to the plaintiff's firm and compares the plaintiff's performance with the index's performance. This approach assumes that, but for the defendant's actions, the plaintiff would have performed as well as the yardstick. Underlying biases in the data, however, can invalidate this index approach. A plaintiff firm that is smaller or larger relative to the index firms can lead to inaccurate results. For example, if a large plaintiff firm lost market share because of the defendant's wrongful conduct, small firms that acquired those shares could appear to be growing even if the market size remained constant.

4. *Market Share:* Experts consider the plaintiff's market share during the period prior to the defendant's wrongdoing. Here the expert must not only define the relevant market but also ensure that the market remained somewhat stable during the relevant time period. Numerous entrances or exits of competitors could undermine the use of this measure. Also, the analysis should examine the trend of the plaintiff's market share, because if the plaintiff's market share varies greatly over the period before the defendant's actions, this measure can yield unreliable results. As discussed in Section 3.2(b), many economists understand such market definition and structure analyses.

In a less common approach used in some breach of contract cases, the expert begins by assuming that the amounts in the breached contract represent the lost sales. The next step ascertains whether actual sales during the period of breach represented additional sales that would have occurred anyway or were replacement sales for the breached amount.

For example, with a perfectly competitive market for the plaintiff, the expert should assume that the plaintiff sells at the level justified by cost considerations and capacity. Even plaintiffs who could sell more would not unless they were willing to use higher cost capacity or to invest in extra capacity, a consideration we ignore for now. In other words, the seller can get all the customers it wants. Now a customer breaches the contract. In a perfectly competitive market, the expert should assume that the seller could find another customer to take the breaching buyer's amount. The only compensation owed the plaintiff would equal the difference in the two buyers' prices, if any such difference existed (Goetz and Scott, 1979). On the other hand, assume that the market has long-term contracts and few buyers and the seller has extra capacity. Now one of the plaintiff's buyers breaches, and subsequently the plaintiff makes sales to a new buyer (or additional sales to a present buyer). Here one can argue that the new sales do not replace the breached amount and that the court should consider the full amount of the breached contract as lost sales (Goetz and Scott, 1979). Thus, experts who do not first analyze the plaintiff's market and capacity can find their conclusions vulnerable to close scrutiny.

In addition to the direct damages owed to the plaintiff, consequential damages can also occur. Economists find this a natural concept. If damages awards purport to restore the plaintiff to the position it would have been in but for the defendant's actions, the damages claim must encompass every phase of the plaintiff's business affected by the defendant's actions. For example, suppose a buyer breaches a contract for Product A, which is a joint product with Product B, and the breach causes the plaintiff to alter its production of Products A and B. In this case, the breach could also cause damages related to Product B. Consequential damages also arise when a breach affecting the sales of a complicated machine also affect the subsequent sales of replacement parts or maintenance service for the machine. To ascertain whether consequential damages have occurred whenever the plaintiff has an integrated facility requires that the economist conduct the same type of market definition and structure analysis discussed previously not only for any primary product but also for the joint or coproducts.[7]

An expert's most difficult proposition to establish, of course, will be the lost sales or revenues for a newly established or never-established business (*see* Chapter 11). Courts now hold that such businesses can recover damages, provided they have been proved with "reasonable certainty" (Dunn, 1998, vol. 1, p. 345). As a result, the expert needs to ascertain the plaintiff's market structure. If the plaintiff's market contained many small firms or a few large ones, an expert should know where a firm of the plaintiff's expected size would fit along this spectrum. If the plaintiff would have been a small competitor in a market composed chiefly of large competitors, the plaintiff's expert has to prove that the plaintiff still could have competed in such a market. Experts also need to consider ease of entry and the stability of existing firms in the industry. If the plaintiff asserts that its firm would have had an advantage over other competitors because of a patent or other new process but for the defendant's actions, the expert must make some reasonable assumption regarding how long the benefits conferred by the patent or new process would last.[8] Regardless of the method used to estimate the plaintiff's lost sales, the expert should have some economic underpinning for the assumptions.

(ii) Incremental Costs. After estimating the amount of lost sales, the expert must subtract the costs the firm would have incurred to achieve these revenues. Such an analysis will consider many different cost measures:[9]

- *Marginal cost* is the cost of producing one additional unit.
- *Incremental cost* refers to the cost of an unspecified number of additional units or of a new product line.
- *Average cost* equals the total cost divided by the number of units produced.
- *Variable costs* change as the activity (or production) level changes.
- *Direct costs* are the costs of the direct material and direct labor incurred in producing a product.

The expert must decide which cost measure pertains to the particular case. For example, a variable cost estimate will apply only over a certain range of production (called the relevant range). If the estimated lost sales units would increase the production level outside the relevant range, then the use of the variable cost estimate can be incorrect.

The relevant cost measure can vary, of course, depending on whether the business is expanding or contracting. If the business is expanding and the amount of lost sales units would take production past the plaintiff firm's present limits, the expert should consider including the capital costs of investment in new capacity or new equipment as a cost in the lost profit analysis. The expert using incremental costs should include such costs and should also make reasonable assumptions concerning the timing of the investments.

Regardless of the measure used, the expert should consider the time period over which to measure costs. Over a long enough time period almost all costs vary, and over a short enough time period costs remain fixed. Sometimes the case has an obvious time period (e.g., the duration of the defendant's wrongdoing). In other cases, the expert will find that as the appropriate time period shortens, the expert should subtract fewer indirect cost items from the lost sales revenues to estimate lost profits. In any event, experts who ignore this issue can arrive at the wrong answer even though they have correctly made all other assumptions in the analysis.

An expert estimating costs for a firm that would have sold more units but for the defendant's actions should consider the possibility of economies (or diseconomies) of scale. If the model projects a large number of lost units, the plaintiff could achieve large cost savings at that production level. A study using only current costs could underestimate the plaintiff's damages. Similarly, learning curve effects would lead to a higher cost structure in a startup firm than that of a firm that has been in business for some time.

(iii) Other Considerations. If experts use dollar amounts in regression analyses that cover a multiyear time period, the expert can deflate the underlying data to constant dollar values prior to performing the analysis. Failure to perform the analysis in real, instead of nominal, terms sometimes will create or accentuate a trend. Having decided to deflate the underlying data by an index, the expert should choose an appropriate index. Deflating different variables often requires the use of more than one index.

Suppose that a buyer breaches the contract before, or shortly after, the seller has begun performance. Should the seller receive its expected lost profits (referred to as *expectation damages*) or only the costs it incurred in reliance on the buyer's performance (referred to as *reliance damages*)? The answer depends on the situation. A contract formed in a competitive market with symmetrical information between the buyer and seller can call for expectation damages. Otherwise one may find that although expectation damages present a solution to the problem of inefficient breach (i.e., when the costs of the breach exceed the benefits of the breach), reliance damages present a solution to inefficient purchase (i.e., when high-cost customers buy more than the efficient quantity and low-cost customers buy less than the efficient quantity; Friedman, 1989).

When experts complete their lost profit calculations, they should decide whether to calculate the damages on a pretax or after-tax basis. Because the government taxes a lost profits award, some experts prefer to calculate the award on a pretax basis (*see* Chapter 16). This advice, however, can lead to an over- or underestimate of damages by its failure to recognize changes in tax rates. Alternatively, one could calculate the award on an after-tax basis and then gross up the damages amount by the current tax rate (i.e., divide the after-tax damages by one minus the current tax rate). For example, suppose the plaintiff would have made $100 on a pretax basis during Year 1 and had it generated those funds in Year 1, it would have paid $46 in federal income taxes. (This example ignores present value and state tax issues.) Thus, the plaintiff would have had $54 more but for the defendant's wrongdoing. The plaintiff's case goes to trial in Year 7, after the marginal corporate federal income tax rate has dropped to 34 percent. On the one hand, if the court awards the plaintiff the pretax $100 in Year 7, it will pay only $34 in federal taxes and on an after-tax basis will have $66, $12 more than the amount needed to make it whole. On the other hand, had the court awarded the grossed-up amount of the plaintiff's lost profits on an after-tax basis, the plaintiff would have received $82 [= $54/(1 − 0.34)], paid $28 in taxes, and have $54 left. In this example, the plaintiff would have benefited had the damages award been paid on a pretax basis. The results go in the opposite directions if the tax rate increased.

An expert who has used a discounted cash flow analysis to evaluate the plaintiff's lost profits will need an interest rate to bring those cash flows forward to the time of the trial from the base point of the analysis. (This assumes that the jurisdiction or particular cause of action permits prejudgment interest—*see* Chapter 9.) At the very least, this interest rate should reflect the value the plaintiff's funds have lost owing to inflation. This measure, however, will not compensate the plaintiff for the opportunity costs of the use of its funds. This refers to the fact that had the plaintiff not been denied the use of the damages amount, it would have invested it in some enterprise (perhaps in shares, perhaps in the performance of the plaintiff firm) and would have received a return on this amount.

Some experts suggest using the risk-free rate (Fisher and Romaine, 1990) to measure prejudgment interest. Other experts suggest using the plaintiff's cost of capital, that is, a measure of the opportunity cost to the plaintiff (of course, at this point the defendant can argue that it seeks consequential damages). The defendant's borrowing rate offers another measure because it regards the plaintiff's claim as an investment (albeit an involuntary one) in the defendant.[10]

(b) Antitrust. (*See also* Chapter 24 "Antitrust" and Chapter 25 "Mergers and Acquisitions.") Antitrust law relies heavily on economic analysis. In both liability and damages issues, economic analysis plays such an important role that any study failing to consider the economic aspects of the case would become useless in court or administrative hearings. Performing certain calculations has no meaning unless the expert knows what economic concepts those numbers represent and how they fit into the present antitrust framework.[11]

(i) Mergers.   The Department of Justice (DOJ) aims to prevent mergers that create or enhance market power. *Market power* is the ability of a firm (or group of firms) to raise prices above the competitive level for a significant time period. The DOJ has stated that a price increase of five percent for one year in most contexts will constitute a "small but significant and nontransitory" increase in price.[12] The firm (or group of firms) possessing market power can raise prices without losing so many sales that the price increase becomes unprofitable by restricting output (Posner and Landes, 1981).

Merger analysis first defines the relevant product and geographic markets. As Section 3.2(b) discussed, the study must include not only firms directly competing with the parties involved in the merger but also firms producing substitute products and firms that would enter the market or expand their current output should the merged firm impose a supracompetitive price. The DOJ defines the relevant market as all firms that, should they act in concert, would be able to profitably impose a "small but significant and nontransitory" price increase.[13] Note that if the analysis excluded firms that make substitutes for the merged firms' product, a restriction in output resulting in a supracompetitive price would appear on paper to be profitable. In reality, however, because customers would switch to the competitively priced substitutes, the supracompetitive price level would not be profitable. This same reasoning applies to the omission of firms that would enter the market if a supracompetitive price were imposed.

Having defined the relevant product and geographic markets, the expert should now measure the concentration within the markets to ascertain whether the transaction will fall within a safe harbor under the DOJ's guidelines. A common concentration measure (also cited in the DOJ's guidelines) is the Herfindahl–Hirschman Index (HHI). This measure first squares the percentage share of each firm and then compares the sum with preestablished cutoff points.[14] The comparison involves judgment, however, even in a calculation as simple as this. One can measure market shares on the basis of sales (either dollars or units), shipments, production, capacity, or reserves.[15] The correct measure depends on the economic facts of each case. Once one computes the HHI for the correct market, one knows that the DOJ will not likely challenge the transaction if the postmerger HHI is below 1,000, or if the postmerger HHI lies between 1,000 and 1,800 and the merger would produce an increase of less than 100 points, or if the postmerger HHI exceeds 1,800 and the merger would produce an increase of less than 50 points.[16]

Even if the HHI concentration measure does not suggest that the merger would reduce competition, other considerations exist. The DOJ can challenge mergers out of fear of collusion—that is, fear that the number of firms will be so few that they could easily act in concert as one giant firm. Recognized factors exist, however, that facilitate or prevent collusion among a group of firms. Factors that facilitate collusion include scarcity of firms, barriers to entry, homogeneous product, demand inelasticity, level of industry profits, industry social structure, and sealed bidding (availability of price information). Factors that make collusion difficult include irregularity and infrequency of orders, high fixed costs, low transportation costs, frequent technological change, and variations in production costs (Brozen, 1982; Hay and Kelley, 1974). An expert can show that even though one might normally consider the concentration levels within the relevant market to be high, collusion is unlikely; a firm might prefer the gains from cheating on a collusive agreement[17] because of the presence (or absence) of the factors discussed.

The expert should also consider whether reasons exist for this merger other than the purchase of a competitor's exit. The expert should investigate whether the merger will increase output. If the relevant market has high concentration, an expert should consider whether allowing the merger of the third and fourth largest firms would produce an effective competitor to the industry giants positioned as the first and second largest firms. The expert should not neglect, moreover, to perform efficiency studies that will document economies of scale and scope between the merging firms.[18]

Finally, when experts estimate damages in cases alleging that a merger violated the antitrust laws, they must causally link their damages measure to the anticompetitive acts cited in the complaint. In *Brunswick Corp. v. Pueblo Bowl-o-Mat, Inc.*, the plaintiff's damages measure was the profit it would have earned had the defendant not acquired certain bowling centers and these centers had gone into bankruptcy instead. The Supreme Court vacated the lower court's judgment for the plaintiff on the ground that this damages measure bore no relation to the antitrust injury of which the plaintiff complained. The plaintiff would have suffered these injuries had the acquired centers obtained refinancing or been acquired by a nonobjectionable party.[19] Thus, an expert on damages issues should show that the damages relate to those acts that injure competition, not merely to acts that injure a competitor.

(ii) Failing-Firm Defense.   The failing-firm defense relates to merger analysis. However, because it involves such extensive financial analysis, we discuss this defense separately. The economic premise for this defense states that the DOJ should allow an otherwise objectionable merger if the firm to be acquired would otherwise go out of business. In this situation, the law prefers a sale to a dominant firm over removing capacity. To use this defense, the owners of the firm or division to be acquired must have sought and found no other buyers who would continue to run the business. The best financial analysis will nonetheless fail if a less objectionable buyer emerges.

Assuming that the merger meets the shopping requirement, the expert must investigate whether the firm or division to be acquired had such large losses that the present owners will close it rather than continue to incur these losses. First, one must examine the future of the firm or division and estimate whether the future will differ from the recent past. Is competition increasing or decreasing? Is demand increasing or decreasing? Do the firm's competitors have a cost advantage that the failing firm cannot duplicate? If a market analysis demonstrates that the future will not diverge from the past, an expert will find the following rate-of-return experiment useful: using actual cash flows for a five-year period and assuming that everything that has transpired within this period had been known five years ago, would the firm's owners have elected to continue operating the business, or would they have chosen to exit the business?[20]

We use a cash flow rate of return analysis rather than accounting returns because cash flows more accurately reflect whether firms generate sufficient funds to cover variable costs. In the short run, a firm that generates enough cash to cover its variable costs will be able to, and may choose to, remain in operation. The accounting algorithm labels some cash outflows as *operating expenses* and others as *capital expenditures*. It deducts operating expenses from each year's income immediately but depreciates capital expenditures according to a schedule chosen by the accountant. As a result, the accounting return on investment will reflect some cash expenditures made in previous periods and will not reflect some made during the current period. In addition, the reported accounting book value of the assets will not accurately reflect the asset's market value.

One can avoid the problems associated with using the accounting definition of return on investment by using a cash flow internal rate of return (IRR) that incorporates the market or salvage value of the assets. The IRR is the interest rate "that will make the present value of cash proceeds expected from an investment equal to the present value of the cash outlays required by the investment" (Bierman and Smidt, 1980, p. 30). In other words, the IRR is that discount rate that makes the net present value of the project equal to zero (Brealey and Myers, 2000, p. 99).

The expert can compare the firm's IRR with the rate of return the firm could have earned elsewhere with investments of similar risk to ascertain whether the firm would have chosen to exit the business at the beginning date of the analysis had it known the future. If the firm's IRR equals the firm's return on an alternative investment of similar risks, the firm neither profited nor lost from its operations. If the firm's return on alternative investments of similar risks exceeds its IRR, then the firm would have been better off withdrawing.[21] In the extreme case, if an existing business has a cash flow with a negative IRR, the firm not only made less than it could have earned elsewhere, it diminished the value of its original investment as well.[22] In such a case, the firm would improve its position by shutting down the business and selling out, rather than running it and continuing to generate negative cash flow.

To calculate the IRR of a business, the expert should measure each year's cash flow. An expert will adjust a firm's financial statements to a cash basis by, for example, adding noncash items (e.g., depreciation) back to income. The expert will also need to subtract the actual cash spent on capital investments (net of their tax effects). Although the expert will not include any financing effects in the analysis (e.g., interest payments on firm debt), the expert should include a charge for the change in the level of working capital used in operations. The expert should do the analysis on an after-tax basis because tax effects, such as the use of one division's losses to offset the profits earned by another division, can alter the results of the analysis. The expert should also revise the analysis to remove the effects of extraordinary events, such as investment in a major project or the effects of a recession, to disprove the notion that the underlying business is sound but that a large investment in an unsuccessful project or economic conditions that no longer exist caused the firm's difficulties.

The most difficult part of the IRR analysis requires estimating the amounts of the beginning and ending flows. Because the expert needs to ascertain whether the owners would have abandoned the firm had they known the future, the beginning and ending flows should reflect what the firm could expect to have received upon abandonment five years ago, for example, and what the firm could expect to receive upon abandonment at present. In other words, what was the value of the assets at their next best alternative use five years ago outside the industry in which the assets are currently employed, and what is that value today? The expert should ensure that the analysis includes all unrecorded liabilities. For example, large unrecorded environmental cleanup costs can compel the owners to continue operating with minimum losses rather than pay the large lump sum required immediately upon abandonment. Again, one should calculate these beginning and ending flows after taxes, because the owners can deduct losses associated with writing down assets from the firm's other taxable income. Finally, if the potential sales price exceeds the acquired firm's current salvage value, the expert should provide an analysis that explains the acquirer's price (e.g., relating price to cost savings that will accrue to the acquirer because of efficiencies). Otherwise, questions such as why the acquirer is paying more for the whole business than the sum of the values of its individual net assets can undermine the entire analysis.

(iii) Predatory Pricing.   Predatory pricing is pricing a firm's products below cost with the intent of driving one's competitors from the market and thereafter raising the firm's prices to a supracompetitive level.[23] Predatory pricing constitutes an offense under Section 1 (unlawful restraint of trade) and Section 2 (monopolization or attempt to monopolize) of the Sherman Act and Section 2(a) of the Robinson-Patman Act (destroying competition or eliminating a competitor).[24] Although many courts agree with the stated definition, commentators disagree on the appropriate cost measure to use to calculate below-cost pricing in an antitrust analysis.[25]

Professors Areeda and Turner proposed the most widely used cost standard, setting their ideal nonpredatory standard at a price above reasonably anticipated short-run marginal costs.[26] They recognized that analysts seldom have marginal cost data, however, so courts should accept a first approximation price above the reasonably anticipated average variable cost.[27] Nevertheless, courts have held other cost measures relevant to the question of whether the defendant engaged in predatory pricing.[28] The details of the particular case will determine the relevant cost analysis. Although an average variable cost analysis can be appropriate for a firm already in the market, it can be inappropriate for a new entrant who will have to engage in promotional pricing to gain customer loyalty, a capital asset that a long-time competitor already possesses.

Even when the analyst has decided on the relevant cost measure, important aspects of the analysis remain. For example, if the predatory claims relate to a single division (or product) of a multidivision (multiproduct) firm, the expert needs to consider joint costs.[29] The time frame over which the expert analyzes the firm's costs as fixed or variable becomes important: the shorter the period, the fewer the variable costs. The expert should consider whether to analyze costs that vary as production rises and falls within some output range or whether to measure costs that vary as production falls to zero (going-concern versus shutdown analysis). For a firm that has large costs associated with producing one unit that do not increase with the production level (zero-one costs), the level over which one measures costs as variable could determine the outcome of the case.[30]

Important as cost estimation appears to be in predatory pricing analysis, market analysis also has an equally, if not more, significant role. A firm engaging in successful predatory pricing and its anticompetitive effects must recoup its losses, that is, it must obtain and retain market power.[31] If the firm cannot absorb the market shares of its competitors that have failed, demand will remain for the surviving competitors with higher prices, and the firm will have injured itself to no avail.[32] Similarly, if barriers to entry do not exist, the firm that has driven all present competitors from the market by predatory pricing will soon find it has yet another set of competitors and that it cannot maintain supracompetitive prices for the period needed to recoup the losses it has inflicted on itself.[33] If the plaintiff and defendant compete along their full product lines, the analyst should not apply a cost test to a single product line because competitive injury will not occur in the relevant market even if the seller priced that product below cost.[34]

(c) Securities Laws.   Securities cases show the influence of economic analysis. Many developments have centered around fraud-on-the-market cases. In *Basic Inc. v. Levinson*, the U.S. Supreme Court cited academic studies showing that the price of a widely traded share reflects all publicly available information about that share, demonstrating the efficiency of markets.[35]

Accordingly, a plaintiff who can establish that a false, misleading, or omitted statement has affected the share's price can be entitled to recover the difference between the share's actual value and true value (i.e., the value the market would have reached had the truth about the firm been known).[36] The expert in such cases will consider whether the true value of the share differed from the actual value.

Many academic empirical studies have demonstrated that movements in the overall market explain a significant portion of a share's price movement. (Brealey and Myers, 2000, pp. 153–180; Copeland and Weston, 1988, pp. 193–240; Fama, 1976, pp. 41–132). Based on these studies, experts have constructed statistical models (regression equations) that predict share price movements. Using share price data from a period prior to the period of interest, the expert can calculate the relation between the return on a particular firm and the return on a market index (e.g., S&P 500). The expert uses this regression relation (market model) and the actual market return during the period of interest to predict the particular share's return. With a large enough difference between the actual value and the predicted value, analysts consider the firm as having experienced a statistically significant abnormal return. Moreover, some academics have advocated the use of a comparable index, in addition to an event study approach, to ascertain whether the true value of the share differed from the actual value (Cornell and Morgan, 1990).

By combining the efficient market theory and the market model, experts can study the effects of information on a share's price and ascertain whether the effects were material (Fischel, 1982). For example, the expert can compare the actual and predicted return of a firm's share when management discloses corrective information. This comparison will help to estimate whether any abnormal declines in value occurred relative to the share's predicted value at the time an alleged falsehood, misstatement, or omission was corrected. If no abnormal change occurs after management publicly discloses the corrective information, the information is immaterial, and the court should find no liability.

The expert can use this same method to quantify the amount of damages (assuming liability). For example, suppose the plaintiff alleges that the defendant omitted certain information from an annual report and that when the defendant publicly released the information subsequently, the share price dropped. The expert's analysis might attribute any abnormal negative returns occurring when the firm released this information solely to the release of the information and then estimate what the share's price would have been had these abnormal negative returns occurred earlier (i.e., when the plaintiff alleges disclosure should have occurred). Under this type of analysis, the plaintiff who owns shares would be entitled to recover only if the plaintiff bought when the actual price exceeded the predicted price (or true value). A plaintiff who sold the share in question could recover only if the predicted price (true value) exceeded the actual price at the time of sale. In both cases, the amount of damages relates to the difference between the actual value and the true value.

Note, however, that the plaintiff's securities purchase at an inflated price *alone* does not establish the relevant economic loss needed to allege and prove the loss-causation required in securities cases. In *Dura Pharmaceuticals, Inc. v. Broudo*, the U.S. Supreme Court reversed the Ninth Circuit Court of Appeals decision that a purchase of stock at an inflated price owing to a misrepresentation automatically established a causal connection between the misrepresentation and the economic loss. In other words, the U.S. Supreme Court held that an "artificially inflated purchase price" is not itself a relevant economic loss because a misrepresentation possibly might lead to an inflated purchase price without proximately causing any economic loss. Instead, the plaintiff must provide the defendant with some notion of the plaintiff's economic loss and the causal connection between that loss and the misrepresentation. *See* Chapter 18 for more discussion on securities litigation.

NOTES

1. We forego a detailed explanation because other chapters in this book discuss regression analysis in litigation. *See also* Fisher, 1980, for an early, more complete explanation of the construction and use of regressions.
2. If two variables (e.g., the prices of two products) are strongly correlated and one observes a change in one of the variables, one will expect to see a change in the other. If this change in the second variable moves in the same direction as the first, the variables are positively correlated. If the change in the second variable moves in the opposite direction, the variables are negatively correlated. If a change in the first variable results in random fluctuating changes in the second, the two variables are uncorrelated and have no strong relation.
3. Capital market risk results from economy-wide factors that generally benefit or threaten all businesses.
4. Only when bonds are issued at par are the amounts of interest expense and interest paid the same.
5. The average tax rate is the rate found by dividing income tax expense by net income before taxes. The marginal tax rate is the tax rate imposed on the next dollar of taxable income generated. The effective tax rate is the rate that includes the effects of tax shields. The effective marginal tax rate is the marginal tax rate that includes the effects of tax shields.
6. *See also* Chapter 8 in this book.
7. The presence of joint or coproducts in the analysis will also have implications for mitigation. Minimizing the losses for one product and minimizing a division's losses may result in two different sets of actions.
8. Most patents have a legal life of 17 years. Their effective life, however, may be less if the market has frequent technological changes or one can easily design around the patent.
9. These definitions are taken from the Glossary of Financial Terms found in this book.

10. *See* Patell et al. (1982). Note that the defendant's interest rates used to bring the damages to present value should be the effective after-tax rate to reflect the realities of the plaintiff's alternative uses of cash. To do otherwise would have investments in damages claims grow more rapidly than real investments of similar risk. The final amount, of course, should be grossed up by the plaintiff's tax rate, as discussed previously.

11. *See* Rosenfield (1986), for a detailed discussion of the widespread influence of economics in antitrust analysis.

12. U.S. Dept. of Justice, *Merger Guidelines*, 49 Fed. Reg. 28, 823 (1984).

13. *Id.*

14. A firm that had 10 percent of the market would have an HHI number of 100 (= 10 × 10). A market that had 100 firms with a 1 percent share would have an HHI of 100. A market with one firm would have an HHI of 10,000 (= 100 × 100).

15. U.S. Dept. of Justice, supra.

16. *Id.*

17. *See* Stigler (1968) for a more complete discussion of modern collusion theory.

18. With economies of scale (i.e., increasing returns to scale), a firm can increase productivity or lower average costs of production by increasing production. For example, if a firm increases inputs by 10 percent and total output increases by more than 10 percent, the firm is better off with the higher production (assuming that price does not fall). With economies of scope, a firm can achieve lower costs by producing multiple goods together. For example, a firm that produced both clocks and watches might be more efficient than two firms, one of which made clocks and the other of which made watches, because the first firm could share industry-specific knowledge and machinery across both product lines (Samuelson and Nordhaus, 1992, p.735).

19. *Id.*, at 487–488

20. The choice of a five-year period is purely arbitrary. The facts of each individual case will determine the appropriate period to use. If the future appears to differ from the past, the expert will do the same type of analysis, only with projected cash flows. Of course, this experiment may not be as strong as the first because the projected cash flows are less reliable.

21. An expert will find the after-tax return on U.S. government securities to be a useful and conservative benchmark, because people often disagree on what return the firm could expect from alternative investments of similar risks. Certainly a firm that earns less than it could from investing in risk-free government securities would be better off withdrawing from its operations.

22. For example, if the IRR is 210 percent, an initial investment of $100 will be worth only $90 at the end of the year.

23. *See*, e.g., *Cargill, Inc. v. Monfort of Colorado, Inc.*, 479 U.S. 104 (1986); *Matsushita Elec. Ind. Inc. Co. v. Zenith Radio Corp.*, 475 U.S. 574, 584 (1986). For those readers interested in a detailed analysis of the economic aspects of predatory pricing (and for potential expert witnesses in this area), the following are recommended: Bork (1978), 144–160; Easterbrook (1984); Easterbrook (1981), 263; Koller (Summer 1979), 283; McGee 1980, 289.

24. 2 CCH Trade Reg. Rep. 1 6500.

25. In *Brooke Group v. Brown & Williamson Tobacco*, 113 S. Ct. 2578, 125 L. Ed. 2d 168, 186 n. 1 (1993), the Supreme Court declined to resolve the conflict among the lower courts concerning the appropriate cost standard in a predatory pricing case because the parties agreed that the relevant measure of cost was average variable cost.

26. Areeda and Turner (1975), 697 and Areeda and Turner (1978), ¶ 711–722.

27. Areeda and Turner (1978), ¶ 711d.

28. Areeda and Hovenkamp (*1988*), ¶ 711.1c; *MCI Communications Corp. v. American Tel. and Tel. Co.*, 708 F.2d 1081 (7th Cir. 1983).

29. In *Marsann Co. v. Brammal, Inc.*, 788 F.2d 611 (9th Cir. 1986), the Ninth Circuit held that the relevant average variable cost is that of the items sold at the challenged price, rather than that associated with the production of the total output.

30. Remarks about cost estimation made previously in this chapter also apply here.
31. *Brooke Group v. Brown & Williamson Tobacco*, 113 S. Ct. 2578, 125 L. Ed. 2d 168 (1993).
32. *Cargill Inc v. Monfort of Colorado*, Inc. 107 S. Ct. at 494 n. 15; Elzinga and Mills, (1989).
33. *Matsushita Elec. Ind. Co. v. Zenith Radio Corp.*, 106 S. Ct. at 1359 n. 15 (citing Easterbrook, 1984).
34. *Liggett Group, Inc. v. Brown & Williams Tobacco Corp.*, 748 F. Supp. 344 (M.D.N.C. 1990).
35. *Basic Inc. v. Levinson*, 108 S. Ct. at 991 n. 24; *see also Flamm v. Eberstadt*, 814 F.2d 1169, 1179 (7th Cir. 1987).
36. *Id.*

LIST OF CASES

Arthur S. Langenderfer, Inc. v. S. E. Johnson Co., 729 F.2d 1050 (6th Cir. 1984)
Basic Inc. v. Levinson, 485 U.S. 224 (1988)
Bayou Bottling, Inc. v. Dr. Pepper Co., 725 F.2d 300 (5th Cir. 1984)
Brooke Group v. Brown & Williamson Tobacco, 113 S. Ct. 2579, 125 L. Ed. 168 (1993)
Brunswick Corp. v. Pueblo Bowl-o-Mat, Inc., 429 U.S. 477 (1977)
Cargill, Inc. v. Monfort of Colorado, Inc., 479 U.S. 104 (1986)
D&S Redi-Mix v. Sierra Redi-Mix & Contracting Co., 692 F.2d 1245 (9th Cir. 1982)
Dura Pharmacuticals, Inc. v. Broudo, 544 U.S., 336, 125 Sup. Ct. 1627 (2005).
Flamm v. Eberstadt, 814 F.2d 1169 (7th Cir. 1987)
Liggett Group v. Brown & Williamson Tobacco, 748 F. Supp. 344 (M.D.N.C. 1990)
Marsann Co. v. Brammall, Inc., 788 F.2d 611 (9th Cir. 1986)
Matsushita Elec. Ind. Co. v. Zenith Radio Corp., 475 U.S. 574 (1986)
MCI Communication Corp. v. American Tel. and Tel. Co., 708 F.2d 1081 (7th Cir. 1983)

BIBLIOGRAPHY

Areeda, P., and D.F. Turner, "Predatory Pricing and Related Practices under Section 2 of the Sherman Act," *Harvard Law Review* 88 (1975): 697

Areeda, P., and D.F. Turner, *Antitrust Law*, 1978. Boston: Little, Brown

Areeda, P., and H. Hovenkamp, *1988 Supplement to Antitrust Law.* Boston: Little, Brown

Bierman, H. Jr., and S. Smidt, *The Capital Budgeting Decision* 5th ed., 1980. New York: Macmillan

Bork, R.H., *The Antitrust Paradox*, 1978. New York: Free Press

Brealey, R., and S. Myers, *Principles of Corporate Finance*, 6th ed., 2000. New York: McGraw-Hill, Inc.

Brozen, Y., *Concentration, Mergers and Public Policy*, 1982. New York: Macmillan

Copeland, T.E., and J.F. Weston, *Financial Theory and Corporate Policy*, 3rd ed., 1988. New York: Addison-Wesley Publishing Co.

Cornell, B., and R.G. Morgan, "Using Finance Theory to Measure Damages in Fraud on the Market Cases," *UCLA Law Review* 37 (June 1990): 883.

Dunn, R.L., *Recovery of Damages for Lost Profits*, 5th ed., 1998. Coronado, CA: Cromwell-Smith Services

Easterbrook, F.H., "The Limits of Antitrust," *Texas Law Review* 63 (1984); 1.

Easterbrook, F.H., "Predatory Strategies and Counterstrategies," *University of Chicago Law Review* 48 (1981): 263.

Elzinga, K.G., and D.E. Mills, "Testing for Predation: Is Recoupment Feasible?" *Antitrust Bulletin* 34 (Winter 1989): 869.

Fama, E., *Foundations of Finance* (1976). New York: Basic Books

Fischel, D., "Use of Modem Finance Theory in Securities Fraud Cases Involving Actively Traded Securities," *Business Lawyer* 38 (1982): 10.

Fisher F.M., "Multiple Regression in Legal Proceedings," *Columbia Law Review* 80 (1980): 702.

Fisher, F.M., and R.C. Romaine, "Janis Joplin's Yearbook and The Theory of Damages," *Journal of Accounting, Auditing and Finance* (1990): 145–157.

Friedman, D.D., "An Economic Analysis of Alternative Damage Rules for Breach of Contract," *Journal of Law and Economics* 32 (October 1989): 281.

Goetz, C.J., and R.E. Scott, "Measuring Sellers' Damages: The Lost-Profits Puzzle," *Stanford Law Review* 31 (1979): 323.

Hay, G.A., and D. Kelley, "An Empirical Survey of Price Fixing Conspiracies," *Journal of Law and Economics* 17 (1974): 13.

Koller, R.H., II, "When Is Pricing Predatory," *Antitrust Bulletin* 283 (Summer 1979).

McGee, J.S., "Predatory Pricing Revisited," *Journal of Law and Economics* 23 (1980): 289.

Patell, J.M., R.L. Weil, and M.-A. Wolfson, "Accumulating Damages in Litigation: The Roles of Uncertainty and Interest Rates," *Journal of Legal Studies* 11 (1982): 341.

Pindyck, R.S., and D.L. Rubinfeld, *Econometric Models and Economic Forecasts*, 4th ed., 1998. McGraw-Hill Inc.

Posner, R.A., and W.M. Landes, "Market Power in Antitrust Cases," *Harvard Law Review* 94 (1981): 937.

Rosenfield, A.M., "The Use of Economic Analysis in Antitrust and Securities Litigation," *Columbia Law Review* I (1986): 49.

Samuelson, P., and W.D. Nordhaus, *Economics* 14th ed. 1992. New York: McGraw-Hill, Inc.

Stickney, C.P., and R.L. Weil, *Financial Accounting*, 10th ed., 2003. Ohio: South-Western College Publishing (Thompson).

Stigler, G.J., "A Theory of Oligopoly," in *The Organization of Industry* 39 (1968).

Stigler, G.J., and R.A. Sherwin, "The Extent of the Market," *Journal of Law and Economics* 28 (1985): 555.

U.S. Department of Justice, "Merger Guidelines," 49 *Federal Register* 28, 823 (1984).

CHAPTER 4

ALTERNATIVE DISPUTE RESOLUTION

Patricia D. Tilton

CONTENTS

4.1 INTRODUCTION

(a) Definition and Overview. Alternative Dispute Resolution (ADR) refers to processes for resolving a dispute between two or more parties other than through formal litigation in a court system. Several formats can resolve disputes outside of litigation; these range from enforceable determinations by a third party to facilitated negotiations between the parties. The most common forms of ADR are arbitration (an enforceable determination) and mediation (a facilitated settlement). Alternatives to the court system for resolving disputes have existed at least since 1925, when the U.S. Congress passed legislation recognizing the right of parties to agree to resolve disputes using arbitration. Since that date, the use of ADR has increased.

Parties now use ADR for any type of dispute, and it has become the most common method for resolving certain issues, such as construction disputes and disputes under purchase agreements in corporate acquisitions.

The author acknowledges Gerry Lagerberg and Laura Hamilton-Fedotov for their assistance on the chapter.

- Specification of the types of disputes the clause covers
- Limitations on what the parties can claim in a dispute and the available remedies
- Method of resolution (litigation or ADR, and type of ADR)
- Procedures for resolution (timelines, discovery, use of experts, hearings, etc.)
- Method for selecting the neutral(s) and identification of the neutral(s)
- Other possible elements
    - Limitations on what disputes can be brought (e.g., time limitations)
    - Confidentiality of the fact of the dispute and the resolution of the dispute
    - Choice of law (if not otherwise covered in the contract)
    - Form for reporting the decision
    - Binding or appealable nature of the decision

The elements shown here relate to domestic arbitration. For international arbitration matters, the clause should also include a discussion of the language in which the arbitration will be conducted, the governing law for the contract, the seat of the arbitration (which will determine the procedural law for the proceeding), the venue (location of the arbitration), and the composition of the tribunal.

Exhibit 4-1.   Common Elements of a Commercial Dispute Resolution Clause

Most contracts now include a dispute resolution clause specifying one or more forms of ADR. Exhibit 4-1 lists the elements that such clauses include. Parties often use ADR after formal litigation has commenced, many times because of prodding by the judge. Court-ordered, nonbinding mediation has almost become the rule as judges face increasingly overcrowded dockets.

(b) Advantages and Disadvantages of ADR.   ADR offers several potential advantages over litigation. Many people think that ADR achieves results more quickly, less expensively, and less disruptively. As ADR has matured and users of ADR have become more sophisticated, not all ADRs realize these advantages. Certain features of ADR that practitioners often consider advantages may depend on one's position in the dispute. For example, lack of punitive damages in ADR gives an advantage to the defendant at the expense of the plaintiff.

Other features distinguish ADR from litigation. These vary depending on the type of ADR, and include the following:
- Consent of parties
    - Parties initiate ADR only by mutual consent, often granted in an underlying contract. They cannot draw third parties involuntarily into the proceeding.
- Confidentiality
    - Parties to ADR can choose to make the content of the proceedings, the outcome, and even the fact of the dispute confidential.
- Flexibility
    - ADR has more flexibility than litigation and affords the parties more control, such as selecting the decision makers, establishing the procedures, and crafting the solutions.

- Parties can select decision makers with specialized expertise relevant to the dispute.
- The parties can choose the procedures or allow the decision maker to establish procedures.
- A greater range of available remedies exists, although ADR seldom offers interim remedies (e.g., precluding a party from selling in a specific location until a final resolution of the dispute). Solutions can consider ongoing business relations: parties, for example, can structure settlements involving future adjustments to their relationship rather than a one-time payment of damages. This fact, and the generally less adversarial nature of ADR, can help preserve business relations.
- Discovery
  - ADR typically provides for less discovery.
- Precedent
  - Decisions relate only to the dispute at hand and create no precedent.
  - Decision makers can consider precedent in making determinations but are not required to do so.
- Appealing a decision
  - Parties have limited or no ability to challenge an outcome, and decision makers are less accountable than in litigation.
- Enforceability
  - The different types of ADR create differing powers to enforce an award.

ADR creates certain unique advantages in international disputes. When the parties come from different countries, use of international arbitration removes possible local bias and a need to proceed under unfamiliar rules and in a foreign language. When the dispute involves a state or parastatal entity, international arbitration enables a sovereign nation to avoid submission to the laws and courts of another country. Arbitration eliminates the possibility that a foreign investor has to dispute a government body in a national court where that same government appointed the judges. Parties may find it easier to enforce an international arbitration award than an award rendered by a national court as a result of the New York Convention on the Recognition and Enforcement of Foreign Arbitral Awards (adopted in 1959 and ratified by the U.S. Congress in 1970).[1] Signatories to the convention recognize and enforce both agreements to arbitrate and arbitral awards. The award recipient can attach a judgment-loser's property located in a country that is a signatory to the convention.

4.2 FORMS OF ALTERNATIVE DISPUTE RESOLUTION

(a) Arbitration

(i) Description.   Arbitration is probably the most common of alternative dispute resolution mechanisms. Arbitration typically involves the appointment of one or more neutral individuals[2] to adjudicate rights and act as a decision maker. The parties may enter into arbitration voluntarily after a dispute arises, or a contractual arrangement between the parties may require such participation.[3] Without a

contractual requirement, one party cannot compel another to participate in arbitration; one cannot unilaterally institute arbitration.

The arbitrator has the authority to decide the dispute, including issues of fact and law, and to issue an award. Arbitrators base their decisions on the parties' legal rights and obligations (determined by contract and applicable law). Most arbitrations lead to final and binding decisions, and few circumstances allow for a challenge to an award in arbitration.

(ii) Procedures.   Arbitration provides flexibility regarding deadlines and timing, the amount and nature of discovery, the number of arbitrators, the selection of the arbitrators, the nature of hearings before the arbitrator, whether the arbitrator provides an explanation for the final decision, and so on. The arbitrator establishes procedures not specified in the contract or not mutually agreed on, often with input from the parties, but taking into account the governing laws. Domestic arbitrations often use standard procedures such as those recommended by the Center for Public Resources (CPR) or American Arbitration Association (AAA); these provide comprehensive guidelines and increase predictability. International arbitral institutions, such as the International Chamber of Commerce (ICC) and the London Court of International Arbitration (LCIA), have standing rules for cases under their administration. For arbitrations that such organizations do not administer (referred to as *ad hoc*), the parties can develop their own procedures or can adopt procedures published by organizations such as the United Nations Commission on International Trade Law (UNCITRAL). Section 4.4 discusses the rules used in international arbitrations.

(iii) Mechanics.   The mechanics of arbitration include many of the elements of litigation, such as hearings, discovery, and written submissions, but arbitration limits the scope of these elements and increases the involvement of the adjudicator. At the outset, the arbitrator will work with the parties to clarify procedures, set a schedule, and define the issues and facts in dispute. Discovery is typically more limited in arbitration compared with litigation. Discovery involves an exchange of hardcopy documents but normally does not include electronic discovery. Witnesses provide written statements but do not always give depositions. The parties' written submissions—which may be submitted simultaneously in certain cases—state their positions comprehensively.

The final arbitration hearing has many of the same elements as a court trial. One difference lies in testimony: witness statements can substitute for direct testimony, resulting in brief or no direct testimony, and the witnesses appear at the hearing primarily for cross-examination and examination by the arbitrator. Parties often submit post-hearing briefs. Months often pass between the conclusion of the proceedings and the arbitrator's decision. The arbitrator can communicate the decision as only the final numeric result or as a "reasoned" award that reflects not only the final decision, but also the basis for that decision in some detail.

(b) Mediation

(i) Description.   Mediation is another common ADR procedure. Mediation involves the use of a neutral third party to facilitate the parties' negotiations. The mediator renders no decision and has no authority to impose any outcome on the parties, who retain decision-making authority and remain responsible for resolving the

dispute. This voluntary process requires the cooperation of the parties. As with arbitration, however, contractual obligations may require that a party participate in mediation. Additionally judges can order litigating parties to participate in mediation. No requirement exists, however, that mediation continue until the parties resolve the dispute. As a result, mediation does not carry the risks of arbitration or litigation because failure to resolve the dispute has no consequences other than lost time.

(ii) Mechanics.   Mediation involves a less formal process than arbitration and thus requires less time and money.[4] The individuals attending a mediation include one or more representatives of each party (for best results, the representative should have authority to resolve the dispute), counsel for each of the parties, and the mediator. Even though fact witnesses normally do not attend, it is becoming more common for expert witnesses to attend.

The mediator's particular style will govern the process used at mediation. Regardless of style, the mediator needs to maintain control over the proceedings. The typical mediation includes a meeting with all the parties, after which the mediator separates them and has a series of private discussions with each. Occasionally, the mediator will hold additional joint sessions.

During the opening joint session, each party outlines its understanding of the facts giving rise to the dispute, its assessments of its legal rights, and any claims it is making. In some mediations, dialogue between the parties occurs at this opening joint session. During the private caucuses, the mediator evaluates each party's position in more detail. To be effective, the mediator must listen carefully to the arguments of the parties and evaluate unspoken motivations or hidden agendas. The mediator obtains additional information to assess the strengths and weaknesses of each party's positions, identifies areas in which each party may be willing to concede or negotiate, identifies nonstarters (i.e., areas that the parties refuse to concede), and presents the arguments of the opposing parties. The mediator then shifts to evaluative mediation to offer his or her assessment of the relative strengths and weaknesses of the parties' arguments and the likely outcome were the parties to litigate.

Through this process, the mediator attempts to find or create common ground between the parties, identify mutually beneficial solutions, and facilitate a settlement. A persistent and creative mediator can work through impasses and help the parties conclude the matter.

Multiple parties can participate in mediation. The mediation can resolve the dispute between some, but not all, of the parties or can resolve some, but not all, of the issues in dispute. Any of the parties can withdraw from the mediation at any time.

(iii) Resolution of the Dispute.   The mediator can base the proposed solution on business interests in addition to (or as opposed to) legal obligations. The parties can design the solution, which may also address business issues beyond the scope of the dispute. The parties to the dispute must negotiate with each other (directly or through the mediator) to resolve the dispute, rather than convince an arbitrator of their legal rights and their understanding of the facts. The outcome of the mediation is not binding, unless the parties enter into a settlement agreement. Mediation facilitates ongoing business relationships better than litigation and arbitration do because it minimizes the adversarial aspect and requires less time.

Mediation might not resolve the dispute. The parties typically agree that information revealed during the course of mediation remains confidential, and parties cannot use it for any other purpose, including subsequent arbitration[5] or litigation, if the mediation fails to achieve a settlement. Similarly, if the mediation leads to resolution, parties cannot make the outcome public without an agreement to do so.

(c) Other Forms of ADR.   Other ADR mechanisms include private judging, early neutral fact-finding or evaluation, summary jury trials, mini-trials, and moderated settlement conferences. Parties can develop whatever variations suit their situation. These other forms of ADR resemble mediation more than they do arbitration in that each method aims to facilitate a negotiated settlement between the disputing parties, rather than to have an independent party determine the outcome. Nonetheless, a third party participates in each of these, with roles varying from evaluating the parties' positions to simply moderating their discussions.

Often, a dispute resolution clause will include a combination of mechanisms that the parties execute simultaneously or sequentially. Similarly, a judge presiding over a litigation matter could require that the parties employ a combination of mechanisms in an effort to resolve the dispute. For example, in one case, a judge presiding over a litigation ordered the following sequence of alternatives: The parties must first participate in nonbinding arbitration. The arbitration does not aim to resolve the dispute but to provide information to the disputing parties as to how an arbitrator views their liability and damages arguments. The judge then has the parties proceed to nonbinding mediation. The judge expects that the arbitrator's perspective will increase the likelihood of resolving the dispute at mediation. Failing a resolution at that stage, the parties can return to court and proceed with the litigation.

The following gives a brief overview of other forms of ADR:

- **Private judging** involves the use of independent third parties, typically former judges, in the role of judges. These independent third parties preside over private trials and render a nonbinding judgment.

- **Early neutral fact finding or evaluation** involves appointing neutral experts (experts on law, financial matters, industry issues, and so on, as appropriate for the situation) to evaluate and analyze facts and data and report their findings to the parties. The fact finders' assessments often include their views on the likely outcome at trial; these perspectives often improve settlement discussions.

- **Summary jury trials** are abbreviated trials presented to mock juries. The juries render a nonbinding decision, which the judges use to facilitate settlement discussions.

- **Mini-trials** form a panel consisting of representatives with decision-making authority from each of the disputing parties and, in some cases, an independent third party. Counsel for the parties argue their case before the panel. The panel then attempts to negotiate a settlement, moderated by the independent third party.

- **Moderated settlement conferences** are negotiations moderated by independent parties, often judges. Moderators facilitate the discussions and may share their evaluation of the parties' positions and arguments.

4.3 DOMESTIC ADR

(a) Rules Governing the Use of ADR.   A substantial body of law governs the conduct of litigation in U.S. courts. Even though ADR offers more flexibility than litigation does, a similar, though narrower, basis in statute and common law supports ADR. Congress enacted the Federal Arbitration Act in 1925. This act recognized the right of parties to agree to resolve disputes using arbitration—including binding arbitration, which limits the right to appeal an arbitrator's decision—and recognized written arbitration agreements as enforceable in federal courts. It allowed a judge to stay a litigation and refer the case to arbitration. The act granted various authorizations related to private arbitration, including such things as authorizing the courts to appoint arbitrators under certain circumstances and granting certain powers to the arbitrator(s). Additionally, the act recognized arbitration awards, rendering them enforceable in federal court, and established the circumstances under which courts could set aside awards.

In response to increased reliance on ADR to resolve disputes, Congress passed further legislation. In 1990, Congress passed the Civil Justice Reform Act and the Administrative Dispute Resolution Act, which addressed the use of ADR with the federal government. In 1998, Congress passed the Alternative Dispute Resolution Act. This act granted courts the power to use ADR in all civil matters and provided related directives and guidance to the courts. As a supplement to federal arbitration laws, individual states have enacted arbitration laws, most of which add detail to the procedural aspects of the Federal Arbitration Act.

In addition to legislation, various interested bodies have established standard procedures for conducting ADR, as well as established codes of conduct for those serving as neutrals. Entities involved in ADR and the standard-setting processes include the AAA, the American Bar Association (ABA), the CPR, the Society of Professionals in Dispute Resolution (SPIDR), and Judicial Arbitration and Mediation Services (JAMS).

Procedural rules established by these organizations cover subjects such as commencement of the dispute resolution process; appointing the neutral(s) (including the number and qualifications); authority of the neutral; confidentiality of the proceedings; conduct of the proceedings (including submissions, hearings, etc.); and the award.

Three organizations[6] collaborated to establish the Code of Ethics for Arbitrators in Commercial Disputes. They designed the code to ensure fairness and integrity in the arbitration process. The elements of this code include disclosure of any relation that might impair impartiality, prohibition of *ex parte* communications, maintaining confidentiality, and clear and complete communication of the award. Model standards for mediators[7] include recognition that mediation is a process of self-determination by the parties, impartiality, disclosure of any potential conflicts of interest, serving only when qualified, and confidentiality. Arbitrators and mediators should comply with any other standards applicable to the forum or their profession.

(b) The Neutral.   The parties have the right to decide the number (normally either one or three) and identity of neutrals. In disputes that have three neutrals, the parties will choose a chairperson. If the parties do not make a decision within a particular time period or cannot reach agreement related to the neutrals, the organization (such as the AAA) administering the resolution process will select the neutral(s) according to its rules. Many of these organizations have standing panels of qualified neutrals. Any neutral must be independent of the parties to the dispute, must have no vested interest in the outcome, and must demonstrate objectivity. One should consider the specific skills or expertise required of the neutral. Most cases require a background in law, as the legal rights and obligations of the parties often determine a fair decision. In some cases, however, specialized industry or technical knowledge may have importance. For example, a postacquisition purchase price dispute would require that the neutral understand accounting.

When not otherwise specified by the parties (by agreement or through adoption of certain institutional procedures), the neutral has the right to establish the timetable; administrative procedures; extent of discovery; nature, number and timing of submissions; and the nature of the information communicated in rendering the decision. In most cases, neutrals can engage their own independent experts, although this rarely occurs. Apart from engaging their own experts, neutrals do not perform their own research but rather rely on information that the parties present.

(c) The Role of Financial Experts.   Parties will typically engage financial experts to evaluate financial issues in the dispute, similar to the use of experts in litigation matters. These issues most frequently involve damages claimed. Financial experts can also perform financial analysis and related fact finding to help establish the facts supporting liability arguments. In addition to fact finding through a review of the accounting, financial, and related records, many financial professionals have skills in investigations or specific industry expertise, so they can help find information not produced through discovery.

The specific analysis employed by experts will rely on established damages theory or financial analysis practices and will not vary based on the forum for resolving the dispute.[8] Arbitration's limited discovery reduces the financial experts' access to information compared with that of litigation; they often have to rely more heavily on data of comparable companies, industry data, or reasonable assumptions rather than company-specific information. Experts present the information to a neutral, rather than a jury, and should tailor the communications accordingly. Experts have less opportunity to explain the analysis through testimony, so their report should clarify the analysis and results. In any case, the expert should consult with the client's legal counsel on these matters.

As mentioned in Section 4.3(b), neutrals sometimes engage independent experts to perform analyses and advise them on technical matters. Financial experts can fill this role in ADR. The expert should perform the analysis as if working for one of the disputants, although the needs of the neutral will determine the nature of communications.

Financial experts can also serve in the role of a neutral. This would most likely occur when the dispute focuses on financial, rather than legal, issues. In this case, the expert will evaluate the parties' submissions and make a final determination in the dispute.

4.4 INTERNATIONAL ARBITRATION

(a) Differences from Domestic Arbitration. The rules of procedure and evidence in international arbitration cases can vary from that of arbitrations in the United States. Most arbitral institutions give flexibility to the parties and to the arbitral tribunal to tailor procedures for each dispute. Depending on the parties, the arbitrators, and the place of arbitration (referred to as the seat), the rules can contain elements from various legal systems around the world—common law, civil law, and other traditions. Different rules often affect elements such as discovery and the expert's duty. The influence of civil law limits international discovery more than that of U.S. litigation and even that of U.S. domestic arbitration. Some cases exchange only documents on which the owner of the documents intends to rely in building their affirmative case. Outside the United States, arbitrations use depositions rarely or never, relying instead on written evidence rather than oral testimony. Individual states' Data Protection Acts also affect the extent of discovery and the ability to use certain data.[9]

(b) Rules Governing International Arbitration. To prove effective as dispute resolution mechanisms, arbitrations need the force of law: the results must be binding and the awards enforceable. Most countries have national laws that give arbitrations such authority, and many have entered into treaties that support arbitration. Finally, many countries have entered into multistate conventions that address the resolution of disputes and the enforcement of related awards. For example, 140 countries have signed the 1959 New York Convention on the Recognition and Enforcement of Foreign Arbitral Awards, under which the signatory states have agreed to recognize arbitral awards as binding and to enforce them according to the rules of procedures of the territory that enforces the award.

The rules of procedure and evidence vary in each case. The International Bar Association has issued rules of evidence for use in international disputes, which international arbitrations often use.

Various institutions that administer arbitrations, listed in Section 4.4(c), have established procedural rules for the conduct of arbitrations. These rules also provide a framework in which a tribunal can set procedures and timetables for each case.

An arbitration proceeding fully administered by one of the arbitral institutions provides more certainty and less opportunity for disagreement surrounding procedures. These institutions periodically update their procedures to incorporate their experience in administering arbitrations, so the procedures address most issues that will likely arise. An arbitration conducted under institutional rules can have more credibility and, under certain circumstances, will facilitate the enforcement of an award. Arbitrations most often use the procedures propounded by the ICC, the LCIA, and the International Center for Dispute Resolution (ICDR), the international branch of the AAA. Most institutional rules include provisions related to the following items:

- Powers and authority of the institutional administrator
- Commencement of the proceedings
- Appointment of the tribunal, including challenges to an appointed arbitrator

- Presentation of evidence[10]
- Powers of the arbitrator(s)
- Methods for deciding the language of, site of, and applicable law for the arbitration

In *ad hoc* arbitrations that an institution does not administer, the parties have greater flexibility to create their own rules and process. Although this maximizes flexibility and autonomy, it creates a risk of slowing progress if the parties cannot reach agreement as to how the arbitration will proceed. Both the CPR Institute and UNCITRAL have developed procedures for use in *ad hoc* arbitrations. The CPR Institute developed the CPR Rules for International Non-Administered Arbitration. UNCITRAL adopted arbitration rules in 1976.

The UN General Assembly established UNCITRAL in 1966 to reduce obstacles to the flow of trade. UNCITRAL arbitration rules provide a comprehensive set of procedural rules for conducting arbitral proceedings and blend common law and civil law features. *Ad hoc* arbitrations and some administered arbitrations use these rules.

(c) Arbitral Institutions. Numerous arbitral institutions (listed here) administer international arbitrations and have their own procedural rules.

- AAA/ICDR—New York and Dublin
- British Columbia International Commercial Arbitration Centre (BCICAC)—Vancouver
- Cairo Regional Centre for International Commercial Arbitration (CRCICA)—Cairo
- China International Economic and Trade Arbitration Commission (CIETAC)—Beijing
- Deutsche Institution für Schiedsgerichtsbarkeit (German Institution of Arbitration; DIS)—Frankfurt
- Hong Kong International Arbitration Centre (HKIA)—Hong Kong
- Inter-American Commercial Arbitration Commission (ICAC)
- International Chamber of Commerce International Court of Arbitration (ICC)—Paris
- International Centre for the Settlement of Investment Disputes (ICSID)—Washington, DC.
- London Court of International Arbitration (LCIA)—London
- Netherlands Arbitration Institute (NAI)—Rotterdam
- Stockholm Chamber of Commerce (SCC)—Stockholm
- Singapore International Arbitration Centre (SIAC)—Singapore

Of these institutions, disputants most frequently use the ICC, LCIA, ICDR, and SCC. Over half of the cases heard by the ICC have disputed amounts in excess of $1 million. ICC arbitrations offer the most supervised of arbitration proceedings. In addition to its arbitration rules, banks apply the rules of the ICC's Uniform Customs and Practice for Documentary Credits (UCP 500) to finance billions of dollars worth of annual world trade.

(d) Arbitration with a State or Parastatal Entity. Resolving a dispute with a governmental entity presents special challenges. Section 4.1(b) discussed the advantages of resolving such a dispute through arbitration rather than a local court system. These disputes arise either from a direct contractual relation with the state or through guarantees or other commitments provided in an investment treaty.

(i) Investment Treaties. Investment treaties are agreements between two or more state governments that govern the terms of the economic interactions between the states. Investment treaties protect and encourage investment between companies in the signatory countries so as to facilitate cross-border investment. Bilateral investment treaties involve two states, and multilateral investment treaties include three or more states.

These treaties provide an important right and protection for private company investors: the right to sue the host government. Foreign investors can use the dispute resolution terms contained in the investment treaty even if the contractual agreements underlying their transactions do not address a dispute resolution mechanism or contradict the mechanism laid out in the investment treaty. If an investment treaty contains an agreement to arbitrate investment disputes, the treaty itself normally constitutes the host state's consent to an arbitration.

(ii) Rules for Investment Treaty Arbitration. Most investment treaties specify the rules for arbitrations. Most treaties will suggest ICSID arbitration or *ad hoc* arbitration using UNCITRAL rules.

The Washington Convention on the Settlement of Investment Disputes between States and Nationals of Other States established the ICSID in 1965. As the title of the convention implies, it aimed to resolve investment related disputes between a state and a national of another state. ICSID is a part of the World Bank.

Currently, approximately 140 countries have signed the convention. Signatory countries agree to recognize and enforce the obligations imposed by ICSID awards. This applies to any ICSID award, whether or not it involves the particular signatory.

(e) The Tribunal. In most international arbitrations, the parties determine the size and composition of the arbitral tribunal. Most often, they use a three-member panel: each side proposes one arbitrator (who should serve in an unbiased manner even though selected by one of the parties), and the other two members of the panel or the arbitral institution selects a neutral chairman. The chairman is usually a lawyer. The other members are often also attorneys or have a particular technical expertise (e.g., accountant or engineer).

(f) The Role of Financial Experts. Financial experts in an international arbitration perform the same tasks as those of domestic arbitration, with some additional considerations. They will need to understand in each case to whom they owe their duty and to check whether any special rules exist (arising from either the tribunal or the seat of the arbitration) that might govern the conduct of the assignment.

Just as attorneys work with local counsel, experts who lack experience in the local country should consider working with someone in the country where the transactions and dispute occurred. A local contact can provide insight into the local culture and business practices, will understand local tax and accounting rules and regulations (and therefore be better able to interpret and evaluate locally prepared financial information), will know how to locate publicly available information, and will have familiarity with local laws for CPA licenses. A local contact should also know the local data protection laws.

When preparing financial models, other issues come into play in the international arena. For example, one must consider the choice of currency or the timing of currency conversions. Discount rates should reflect political risk.

An expert in international arbitration will usually have to produce a written report of the evidence, explaining the approach, method adopted, evidence seen, and conclusions reached. Sometimes the experts appointed by each side will meet before the hearing and produce a joint report that sets out the areas of agreement and disagreement in their evidence. A recent trend is for witness conferencing. Most often, the expert will not participate in a deposition. If a tribunal appoints the expert, each of the disputing parties will cross-examine the expert at the final hearing.

4.5   CONCLUSION

ADR has become common for resolving disputes; it is increasing in popularity both domestically and internationally. As a result, governments and private arbitral organizations have implemented legislation, procedural rules, codes of conduct for arbitrators and mediators, international investment treaties, international conventions, and foreign legislation in support of this dispute resolution process. Many participants perceive ADR as superior to litigation as a method for resolving disputes. Some of those advantages depend on one's vantage point. Parties can best realize advantages if they understand the ADR process.

In ADR, a financial expert can serve in the role of an expert for one of the parties, or as a neutral expert assisting the arbitrator, or as the neutral. The financial expert can face different procedures for resolving the dispute and a different manner for communicating the results of analysis in ADR. The nature of the analysis and the method of approaching the analysis remain the same as that of a dispute resolved through litigation.

NOTES

1. The Inter-American Convention on International Commercial Arbitration (or the Panama Convention) has provisions similar to those of the New York Convention. It was adopted in 1975, and most Latin American countries are signatories.

2. The use of party arbitrators (serving as advocates for a party rather than as a neutral) is no longer common.

3. In international arbitration matters (discussed in Section 4.4), investment treaties can also require arbitration.

4. Of course, the overall process of resolving the dispute will be quicker only if the mediation is successful.

5. An occasional exception is seen in hybrid proceedings, usually under construction contracts, in which the mediator, if no settlement is reached, becomes the arbitrator in the subsequent arbitration proceeding.

6. The organizations cooperating on this effort include the Arbitration Committee of the Section for Dispute Resolution of the ABA, AAA, and CPR Institute for Dispute Resolution.

7. The organizations establishing standards for mediators include the ABA, AAA, and SPIDR.

8. Certain damages theories that are built on case law may be appropriate for use in arbitration.

9. For example, the Data Protection Act adopted by the European Union in 1998 protects the privacy of personal information that may be contained on an individual's company-issued computer, data storage device, e-mail, and so on. This can complicate the discovery process.

10. Most rules provide for significant flexibility in the presentation of evidence. Much of the decision-making authority related to evidence is granted to the tribunal.

BIBLIOGRAPHY AND SUGGESTED SOURCES

American Arbitration Association. *A Guide to Mediation and Arbitration for Business People.* 2003. www.adr.org

American Arbitration Association. *Commercial Arbitration Rules and Mediation Procedures (including Procedures for Large, Complex Commercial Disputes).* 2003. www.adr.org

American Arbitration Association. *Drafting Dispute Resolution Clauses—A Practical Guide.* 2004. www.adr.org

American Arbitration Association. *Model Standards of Conduct for Mediators.* 2004. www.adr.org

American Arbitration Association. *The Code of Ethics for Arbitrators in Commercial Disputes.* 2004. www.adr.org

Baker, C. Mark, and Ali, Arif H., "Risk Management in International Commercial Transactions: Arbitration and Alternative Dispute Resolution." Presented at the Twenty-Fourth Annual Corporate Counsel Institute seminar, sponsored by the University of Texas School of Law and the Corporate Counsel Section of the State Bar of Texas, 2002.

Bond, Stephen R. "How to Draft an Arbitration Clause (Revisited)." The ICC International Court of Arbitration Bulletin, Vol 1/No 2; December 1990; pp. 14–21.

Bowman, John P., "Dispute Resolution Planning for the Oil and Gas Industry." *Foreign Investment Law Journal* 16 (Fall 2001), International Centre for Settlement of Investment Disputes, pp. 332–407.

Bowman, John P. "Dispute Resolution with Host Governments: What the International Petroleum Negotiator Should Know." 2002.

Center for Public Resources Institute for Dispute Resolution. *CPR Model Dispute Resolution Clauses.* 2004. www.cpradr.org

Center for Public Resources Institute for Dispute Resolution. *Highlights of CPR Procedures and Rules.* 1998. www.cpradr.org/adr

Cummis, Adam S., Mark W. Haller, Kevin D. Kreb, and George G. Strong. "Roles and Techniques of a Financial Expert in Alternative Dispute Resolution." In *Litigation Services Handbook. The Role of the Financial Expert*, 3rd ed. New York, John Wiley & Sons, 2001.

Emmert, Michael P., Mark Mosely, Donald O'Connor, and Mark Richardson. "International Trade Litigation." *In Litigation Services Handbook. The Role of the Financial Expert*, 3rd ed. New York, John Wiley & Sons, 2001.

Federal Arbitration Act, 9 U.S.C. Section 1 *et seq.*

International Bar Association Rules on Evidence in International Commercial Arbitration, 1999. www.ibanet.org

International Centre for the Settlement of Investment Disputes. *ICSID 2004 Annual Report.* www.worldbank.org/icsid

International Chamber of Commerce International Court of Arbitration. *Resolving Business Disputes Worldwide.* www.iccwbo.org

JAMS. *JAMS Guide to Dispute Resolution Clauses for Commercial Contracts.* 2004. www.jamsadr.com

JAMS. *JAMS Comprehensive Arbitration Rules and Procedures.* 2005. www.jamsadr.com

Karl, Joachim. "On the Way to Multilateral Investment Rules—Some Recent Policy Issues." In *UNCTAD, International Investment Instruments: A Compendium*, vol. IV. New York/Geneva, 2000, 107.

National Arbitration Forum. *NAF Code of Conduct for Arbitrators.* www.arbitration-forum.com

National Arbitration Forum. *NAF Drafting Mediation and Arbitration Clauses.* 2005. www.arbitration-forum.com

SPIDR. *Ethical Standards of Professional Responsibility.* www.spidr.org

United Nations Conference on Trade and Development. *International Investment Disputes on the Rise.* New York: UN, 2004. www.unctad.org

United Nations. *United Nations Convention on the Recognition and Enforcement of Foreign Arbitral Awards*, commonly known as the New York Convention. New York: UN, 1958.

DAMAGES TECHNIQUES

CHAPTER 5

STATISTICAL ESTIMATION OF INCREMENTAL COST FROM ACCOUNTING DATA

Michael W. Maher
M. Laurentius Marais
William E. Wecker
Roman L. Weil

CONTENTS

5.1   INTRODUCTION

Litigation assignments often require a computation of damages that the plaintiff suffered. Such damages reflect the incremental revenues less costs the plaintiff would have realized but for the defendant's actions or inactions. This chapter introduces advanced issues arising in the calculation of incremental costs for such damages cases.

The incremental cost is the additional cost of producing and selling additional units. Experts use statistical regression analysis of accounting data to estimate the incremental cost. Properly applied, regression analysis provides an accurate and reliable estimate of incremental cost. Improperly applied, however, regression analysis sometimes produces a biased and misleading estimate of incremental cost. This chapter shows how a regression analysis of accounting data can produce a biased or misleading result.

5.2   ACCOUNTING DATA: USES AND LIMITATIONS

In estimating incremental costs for most firms under most circumstances, the analyst will have data only from a firm's accounting system. One can usually rely on the accuracy of such data because the firm has collected them in the ordinary course of business and someone has verified, if not audited, them. Nonetheless, such accounting data have serious limitations if an analyst mechanically uses them to measure incremental costs. This section describes the accounting data usually available and the difficulties they present.

Analysts usually need to ascertain by how much costs would have increased had production and sales increased by a specified amount. We refer to this as the *but-for* scenario in litigation engagements.

(a) Cost Behavior.   Accountants and economists distinguish over 50 different terms involving the word *cost*. The glossary of this book presents a taxonomy (under the entry for *cost terminology*) for these terms and defines them. This chapter focuses on incremental costs (not marginal costs; *see* glossary for this distinction, often ignored by economists not savvy about accounting data) over either the long run or the short run. The time frame will depend on the specifics of a given assignment.

(i) Long Run and Short Run.   Long-run cost behavior differs from short-run cost behavior. Over sufficient time spans, all costs vary with changes in production: plants can open or close; a firm can hire or fire salaried executives; a business can shut down entirely. Over short time spans, virtually all costs are fixed. Therefore, estimating cost increases that given production and sales increases generate requires a statement of the time span over which the increases would have occurred.

Exhibit 5-1 illustrates this phenomenon. The curve A-B shown in Exhibit 5-1 describes typical long-run cost behavior. If a company has sufficient time, say several years, to adjust manufacturing processes to growth in production from $Q0$ to $Q1$, costs will increase gradually along the curve A-B from $C0$ to $C1$.[1]

The curve C-D describes short-run cost behavior. If production increases from $Q0$ to $Q1$ over a short time span, say one month, costs will increase—from $C0$ to $C2$—more than they would over a long time span.

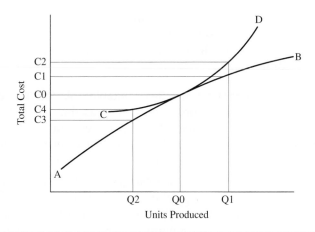

Exhibit 5-1.   Long-Run and Short-Run Cost Behavior

The greater cost increase for the short-run production increase occurs because firms do not add capacity as efficiently in a month as they do over several years. To add capacity quickly, the firm may have to add extra shifts, involving overtime wages, or management may have to bring less efficient manufacturing equipment out of mothballs and put it back to work.

(ii) Expansion and Contraction.   Similarly, when production decreases over a short period, costs decrease less than they do over a long period. If production decreases from Q0 to Q2 over a short time span, say one month, then costs per unit will decrease from C0 to C4 rather than from C0 to C3. The lower unit-cost decrease for short-term contractions results from such factors as machinery put into mothballs or left idle, rather than sold right away. In addition, management may keep workers on the payroll longer than otherwise necessary to maintain favorable labor relations.

(iii) Implications for Using Accounting Data.   In estimating additional costs that additional production and sales generate, the analyst needs to distinguish between two notions of additional costs: *marginal* costs and *incremental* costs. The economist restricts the term *marginal cost* to the cost of producing one more unit or even an infinitesimal fraction of a unit. Thus, the next fraction of a unit has a marginal cost; to double output has an incremental cost. Accountants rarely need to deal with marginal costs in this sense. If a firm produces and sells a new product, financial experts should refer to the related new costs as *incremental*, not *marginal*.

In Exhibit 5-1, note that the initial cost increase from the point Q0 is, to the naked eye, indistinguishable on the short-run cost curve, C-D, from that of the long-run cost curve, A-B. Accounting data collection rarely has the distinction between the long run and the short run in mind. Accounting records often obscure the difference between long-run and short-run cost behavior, because the general ledger accounts reflect costs as incurred and do not distinguish costs incurred during periods of rapid growth from those of gradual growth. Nor do they distinguish costs incurred during periods of expansion from those of contraction. Thus, a mechanical analysis of general ledger accounting data likely fails to recognize the different economic eras that might underlie the costs.

A regression analysis that fails to distinguish long-run cost behavior from short-run cost behavior is unlikely to yield meaningful results, as is a regression analysis that fails to distinguish costs occurring during expansions from costs occurring during contractions.

(b) Unadjusted General Ledger Data May Be Unsuitable. Accounting data collected from the ordinary books and records, referred to as the *general ledger data*, frequently reflect accounting estimates. These estimates, although appropriate for accounting purposes, can sometimes bias a statistical analysis of incremental costs, as we discuss in this section.

(i) Depreciation as an Example of an Incorrect Capacity Cost Measure. Both income tax and financial accounting assign depreciation schedules to new equipment (most often different schedules for the two reporting purposes). The subsequent accounting will record the resulting amounts charged for depreciation and, once recorded, will not change them, even if the accountant later learns that the original estimate of useful life is incorrect.

Suppose the firm expects that the equipment at acquisition will have a useful life of 12 years and no salvage value. Assume the firm uses straight-line depreciation and that at the end of the eighth year of use, market conditions change so that the firm will use the equipment for only 10 years, not 12.

In retrospect, the plant costs over the 10 years during which the equipment is used should reflect one-tenth of the equipment cost each year. The accounting data correctly accumulated in the general ledger under generally accepted accounting principles will, however, reflect one-twelfth of the cost for each of the first eight years and one-sixth of the cost for each of the last two years, Years 9 and 10.[2]

Thus, whenever the depreciable life of plant and equipment has changed during its life, the accounting data recorded for depreciation will not meaningfully represent the year-to-year costs of using capacity. Whether accounting data can measure incremental costs of capacity is an open question not discussed here.

(ii) Salaries as an Example of Too Much Smoothing. Some manufacturing and sales employees receive salaries rather than pay for piecework (in manufacturing) or via commission (in sales). Companies usually quote such salaries on an annual basis but charge them into the general ledger accounts in equal monthly amounts. Sometimes an accurate measure of additional costs associated with increased production (or sales) activity would require changing the salaries to months in proportion to effort during those months, rather than uniformly across months. Generally accepted accounting principles do not require firms to adjust the monthly record of costs at year end so that monthly amounts reflect monthly effects.

Thus, the general ledger data for such salaries, without adjustment, will show more uniformity (less variability) of costs through time than the effort to produce and sell additional units requires. The data in the general ledger accounts are too smooth. Use of accounting data afflicted with this problem will underestimate incremental costs. Further difficulty arises from lags in the result from effort expended, such that the increased output or sales often will not occur in the same month as the increased effort.

(iii) Accounting Adjusting Entries as an Example of Too Little Smoothing. For other general ledger accounts, the data are not smooth enough. At the end of each accounting

period, usually a calendar quarter but sometimes a year, the accountant makes adjusting entries.

Typical adjusting entries affect inventory valuation, bad debt expense, rent expense, insurance expense, and other items for which the firm records charges for several months at a single time, usually when the firm makes an expenditure covering several months.

Consider bad debt expense, which the firm incurs as it makes sales. Typically, once per quarter or once per year the accountant makes an entry to recognize all bad debt expense for that period. Suppose the accountant records the entry on December 31 for the fourth quarter sales. Then December's data will show three months of bad debt expense, whereas October's and November's data will show none. Each month's general ledger accounts do not match the actual cost incurred each month; statistical analysis of such data will often understate incremental costs because the analysis will fail to detect the relation between sales and bad debt expense.

(iv) Adjusting for Lags in Recording Costs.   Suppose a supervisor receives a lump sum, year-end bonus for extra effort. Unless adjustments spread the one-time bonus back to the periods when the supervisor earned it, the general ledger will understate costs for the overtime periods and overstate costs for the period of bonus payment. Failure to adjust for this phenomenon will underestimate incremental costs derived in a statistical regression analysis because the analysis will likely fail to detect the relation.

(v) General Ledger Data Omit Some Additional Costs.   The accounting records do not include all costs of additional production and sales. An example is the added cost of carrying additional working capital to produce and sell additional units. As production and sales expand, a firm will need to carry more inventories and more accounts receivable. These items have a carrying cost that accounting usually does not recognize explicitly.

(c) Additional Information Omitted in General Ledger Accounts

(i) Factors Affecting Incremental Cost Relations.   The accountant will sometimes know of a change that influences cost relations. For example, some cost data accumulate over a period when an important technology change occurs that alters the incremental cost of production.

(ii) Product-Specific Costs.   Sometimes the accountant can associate certain costs (typically direct material and direct labor costs) with particular products, thereby identifying a relation that accounting records do not. The analyst can exclude such costs from the statistical procedures.

5.3 SIMPLE COST BEHAVIOR: VARIABLE COST ASSOCIATED WITH A SINGLE COST DRIVER

Estimating the relation between costs and activities involves two key issues: (1) identifying the cost drivers and (2) estimating the cost behavior (i.e., the nature of the association of cost with the driver). In a common but simplistic approach, analysts use only one cost driver and assume that costs linearly relate to the cost driver.

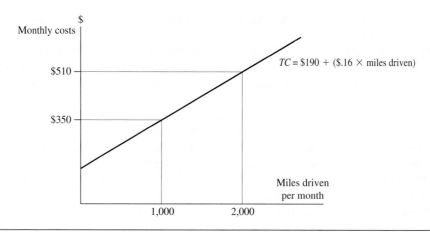

Exhibit 5-2.   Simple Model

The simplest cost behavior pattern separates costs into fixed and variable components. Variable costs change proportionately with changes in total activity levels. In a simple model with one cost driver, costs divide into fixed and variable components; when costs increase linearly with the cost driver, analysts estimate the following cost equation:

$$TC = F + V \times X \tag{1}$$

where

TC = total costs

F = fixed costs that do not vary with the cost driver

V = variable costs per unit for the cost driver (V is the change in the total cost TC caused by a one unit increase in the number of cost driver units X)

X = the number of cost driver units.

Exhibit 5-2 contains a picture of this simple relation in which the cost driver is number of miles driven for an automobile and the costs are hypothetical fixed (e.g., car payment, insurance, etc.) and variable costs (e.g., gasoline and wear on tires) related to the units (miles driven).

This simple cost breakdown into fixed and variable components misses important additional types of cost behavior that we discuss in the next section. Nevertheless, many analysts use this simple model, and it can often satisfy a cost-benefit test better than a more complex, albeit more accurate, cost model.

5.4   MORE COMPLEX COST BEHAVIOR: SEVERAL COST DRIVERS

(a) Cost/Benefit Test.   A more complex model recognizes multiple cost drivers and more complex cost behavior than indicated above. The expert chooses how complex to make the cost estimation model. Generally accepted rules do not exist for how simple or complex to make the model, but good sense dictates that one should apply cost-benefit considerations to the choice of model complexity.

Because analysts probably will not know the costs and benefits of a particular model until they have estimated it (and perhaps not even then), they face the difficult task of applying an approximate cost-benefit analysis before they have a good idea of either costs or the benefits.

(b) More Complex Cost Behavior.   Costs follow a wide variety of patterns in the real world. Unlike the simple model presented in Section 5.3, many costs increase in steps or in curvilinear patterns as activity levels increase.

A diagram of step costs appears in Exhibit 5-3. A step cost, also called a semi-fixed cost, is any cost that increases in steps as cost driver volume increases. Many labor costs are step costs. In Exhibit 5-3, the costs are the costs per hour for quality control inspectors. Assume, for example, that one person can perform quality control inspections for 50 items per hour. The cost driver is the number of units to be inspected. If the company needs less than 50 units inspected per hour, the company hires one quality control person. If the number of units increases to the 51 to 100 units per hour range, then management increases the number of quality control people to two, and so forth, as shown in Exhibit 5-3.

Step costs occur when a firm hires people in time increments, such as hourly, daily, or monthly. Examples include nurses in a hospital, where the number of nurses increases in steps as the number of patients increase (but they won't be called in until the next shift); waiters and waitresses in restaurants (where the midafternoon hours will have fewer servers, but the dinner hour will have more servers); and teachers at a university (where the number of teachers changes with each term, as enrollment changes). In our experience, analysts often ignore these steps, assuming the step costs are either purely fixed or variable.

Analysts also rely on the concept of relevant range to deal with step costs. The relevant range is the range of activity over which one expects a pattern of cost behavior to apply reasonably accurately. Such a pattern might not hold true outside of the relevant range, however. For example, assume that a company does not produce more than 50 units per hour. Then management and analysts could assume that 1 to 50 units per hour comprises the relevant range, as Exhibit 5-3

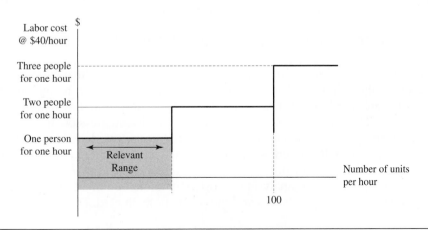

Exhibit 5-3.   Step Costs: Labor Costs for Quality Control

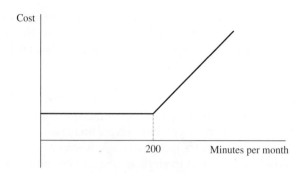

Exhibit 5-4.   Semivariable Costs: Cellular Telephone

shows. As long as management uses one quality control person, then it is reasonable to consider quality control a fixed cost (within the relevant range of 1 to 50 units). If, however, the number of units per hour increases to 75—outside the initial relevant range—then an analyst can no longer assume validly that quality control is a fixed cost.

(c) Semivariable Costs.   Semivariable costs have both a fixed and variable component. Many utilities offer products (e.g., electricity and water) for a fixed cost up to a particular volume, after which they charge per unit. Exhibit 5-4 shows the semivariable cost for a cellular telephone plan that charges a fixed amount per month for up to 200 minutes per month of usage and then charges per minute for each minute used over 200 minutes.

Costs can also exhibit a curved behavior as number of units changes. Suppose a company receives a discount based on the volume of materials it buys, with the discount percentage increasing as the volume purchased increases. Curve A in Exhibit 5-5 represents this pattern, with variable costs decreasing per unit as volume per period increases. Curve B represents variable costs that increase per unit as volume per period increases. For example, energy costs often increase per unit of production as total production per hour increases because managers bring on line machines with inferior energy efficiency.

5.5   STATISTICAL COST ESTIMATION USING REGRESSION ANALYSIS

This section discusses the use of regression analysis to estimate the relation between costs and cost drivers, which we sometimes refer to as *activities*. Regression analysis is a statistical method used to create an equation relating independent (or X) variables to dependent (or Y) variables. Regression analysis uses data from the past to estimate relations between costs (the dependent variable) and activities (the independent variables) that will have validity in the future or in a hypothetical, but-for world.

When using regression analysis for cost estimation, one must first establish a logical relation between activities and the cost to be estimated. These activities are

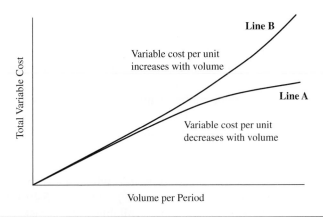

Exhibit 5-5.   Variable Cost Behavior

the X terms or independent variables of a regression equation. Independent variables are the activities that the analyst believes cause, or at least correlate meaningfully with, the dependent variable, costs. The analysis aims to estimate the dependent variable, or the Y term, which represents cost. Dependent variables have a causal relation, or at least correlate with, independent variables. We refer to the Y term as TC because the Y variable always provides some measure of total cost (TC) in our analyses. Depending on the context, TC can refer to the total costs of the organization, total overhead costs of the organization, or some other measure of total cost.

Regression analysis generates an equation (or visually, a line or curve) that best fits a set of data points. In addition, regression techniques provide information that helps a manager or analyst measure how well the estimated regression equation describes the relation between costs and activities.

Popular computer spreadsheet software such as Microsoft Excel®, as well as more powerful statistical packages such as SAS and SPSS have the capacity to perform regression calculations. We leave descriptions of the computational details to statistics books and documentation that come with software packages. Instead, we deal with regression from the standpoint of accountants and experts who must interpret and use regression estimates.

(a) Does a Logical Relation Exist between Costs and Activities?   One must first identify the activities that generate costs. If the relation between costs and activities have followed a particular pattern in the past and one expects that pattern to continue in the future, then one could reasonably use data from the past to estimate cost driver rates. If the past relation no longer has validity, however, then one must adjust the cost driver rates to reflect the changed circumstances.

Over time, the cost-activity relation can change for several reasons. Technological innovation, change in product characteristics, and change in costs can make the past inappropriate for estimating the future. This particularly holds true for many high-tech companies and companies that have products with short life cycles.

Although the use of past data for future cost estimation has limitations, it often works quite well. The use of past data provides a relatively inexpensive analysis for experts because firms have easy access to the data in their records. Section 1.3 of Chapter 1 discusses how to obtain relevant data from the opposing side of a litigation. Past data do show the relations that held in prior periods and often provide at least a meaningful starting point for estimating costs as long as the analysts recognize their limitations.

(b) Relevant Range.   The range of activity within which a cost projection has validity forms the relevant range for that estimate; *see* Section 5.4(b). Extrapolation beyond the relevant range supported by available data is risky, and requires special caution and scrutiny.

(c) Simple Model: A Single Cost Driver.   Section 5.3 discussed the single-driver cost model. This model provides a useful way to obtain a basic understanding of how to apply regression analysis to cost management. Sections 5.5(d) and (e) discuss more complex and realistic models.

With one cost driver and costs divided simply into fixed and variable components, analysts estimate the following cost equation:

$$TC = F + V \times X$$

where

TC = total costs
F = fixed costs that do not vary with the cost driver
V = variable costs per unit for the cost driver (V is the change in the total cost TC caused by a one unit increase in the number of cost driver units X)
X = the number of cost driver units (the independent variable)

In cost estimation, the independent variable is the cost driver. Although regression programs are mechanically capable of accepting almost any data for the Y and X terms without generating error messages, entering numbers that represent no relevant, logical relation will yield cost estimates that lack meaning and can mislead the analyst.

(i) Application of the Simple Model.   Assume we wish to estimate the variable cost per unit (V in the equation in Section 5.5(c)). From the company's records, we collect and input the data shown in Exhibit 5-6 into a regression program. Assume that we have 24 months of data that report the total costs of operating the company and the total units sold for each month. (We do not show every month to save space and tedious reading.)

When reading the output of a regression program for cost estimation purposes, analysts often treat the constant term ($16,086 in the results portion of Exhibit 5-6), or intercept, as an estimate of fixed costs. This interpretation will not always prove reliable because the constant term corresponds to zero activity, which usually lies

Month	Costs	Units
January, Year 1	$63,377	112
February, Year 1	75,703	141
.	.	.
.	.	.
.	.	.
November, Year 2	73,797	139
December, Year 2	54,388	86

Results

The regression equation is Total Costs = $16,086 + $423 × units

Predictor	Coefficient	Standard Errors	t-statistic
Constant	16,086	7,664	2.11
Units	423	81	5.22
$R^2 = .74$			

Exhibit 5-6. Simple Regression Input Data from the Company's Past Records

outside the relevant range of observations. The coefficient V of the X term (in this example, $423 per unit) provides an estimate of the variable cost per unit within the relevant range.

The cost estimation equation based on this regression result is

$$\text{Total Costs} = \text{Constant} + (V \times \text{units of activity})$$

$$\text{Total Costs} = \$16,086 + (\$423 \times \text{units sold})$$

The standard error listed in the results section of the regression program's output measures the uncertainty in the coefficient V. The larger the standard error, the greater our uncertainty in the costs estimated by the coefficient. The t-statistic is the coefficient divided by the standard error associated with the coefficient. For example, for units of activity the t-statistic is 5.22 (= 423 ÷ 81). The t-statistic provides us with information regarding whether the coefficient differs from zero. Analysts generally consider a t-statistic greater than 2.0 sufficiently high to infer that the coefficient reflects a genuine, persistent association of activity X with total costs. The t-statistics in Exhibit 5-6 are large enough to support such an inference.

R-squared (R^2) is the proportion of the variation in the dependent variable (TC in our case) explained by the X or independent variables (the activities in our case). The R^2 statistic varies from 0 to 1.00, with 0 indicating no measured linear relation and 1.00 indicating a perfect measured linear relation between the independent variables and the dependent variable. R^2 indicates the fraction of the amount variation in the dependent variable that the independent variable explains. Exhibit 5-5 shows R^2 to be .74, meaning that the variation in the activity—number of units sold—explains 74 percent of the variation in total costs.

(ii) Using Regression Results for the Simple Model. Suppose the financial expert needs to estimate total costs for a month in which he or she expects the total volume of

units sold to be 100 units. With an estimated variable cost per unit of $423 and a constant within the relevant range of $16,086, the estimated total costs for the month would equal $58,386 [= $16,086 + ($423 × 100 units)].

(d) Using Regression Analysis to Estimate Costs with Multiple Cost Drivers.   Multiple regression extends the analysis to an equation with more than one independent variable. Using multiple regression analyses, financial experts often learn much about cost behavior that simple regression cannot reveal. In general, multiple regression has greater explanatory power than that of simple regression: including more independent variables (cost drivers) will explain more of the variation in the dependent variable (total costs). However, multiple regression typically requires more data than simple regression. As discussed in Section 5.5(d)(i), one can use a diagnostic test (based on R^2) to assess whether adding another independent variable provides a justifiable increase in explanatory power.

When performing multiple regression, one must first identify the activities that logically determine cost. Some organizations use many cost drivers, sometimes more than 100. More cost drivers require more data but often provide better cost information. As a practical matter, however, the additional information from an additional cost driver beyond some level of refinement will not justify the effort required to obtain the data.

To illustrate the mechanics of multiple regression, we will use a manufacturing example with four cost drivers:

- **Units.** These are the number of units sold.
- **Batches.** Batches require setup costs for each batch of product. Further, stopping one batch and starting another often reduces production efficiency and increases quality costs.
- **Products.** Each additional product requires specifications, blueprints, instructions, and other costly items.
- **Customers.** Customer-related costs include the cost of customer files, billing costs, costs of obtaining additional customers, and the costs of dealing with irate customers.

(i) Application of Multiple Regression.   To estimate the relation of total costs with each of multiple cost drivers, the analyst needs total cost and the number of units for each cost driver as shown in Exhibit 5-7.

The results for the multiple regression appear at the bottom of Exhibit 5-7. Note the adjusted R^2 replaces the R^2 generated for the simple regression example. The adjusted R^2 serves the same purpose as the R^2 discussed in Section 5.3(c)(i), but its calculation takes into account the increased number of independent variables in the regression. Adding an independent variable to a multiple regression usually makes the resulting output appear to fit the data better (at least never making it worse), but this always has the cost of reducing the degrees of freedom. Indeed, if analysts use as many independent variables as they have data points, they will always get a regression output that *appears* to fit the data perfectly. To account for this effect appropriately, analysts use the adjusted R^2, not the R^2, to judge the quality of a multiple regression. At 0.78, the adjusted R^2 is high, indicating that the independent variables in the multiple regression succeed in explaining much of the variation in total costs.

Month	Costs	Cost Driver Volume			
		Units	Batches	Products	Customers
January, Year 0	$122,674	11,202	161	15	28
February, Year 0 ...	145,703	14,106	183	11	39
·	·	·	·	·	·
·	·	·	·	·	·
·	·	·	·	·	·
November, Year 3 ..	133,797	13,991	114	13	21
December, Year 3 ..	123,797	11,114	125	12	33

Regression Results

The regression equation is
   Total costs = 40,177 + \$3.98 × Units + \$106 × Batches + \$986 × Products
                  + \$406 × Customers

Predictor	Coefficient	Standard Error	t statistic
Constant	40,177	8,443	4.76
Units	.98	1.16	3.43
Batches	106	45	2.36
Products	986	309	3.19
Customers	406	117	3.47
Adjusted R^2 = 0.78			

Exhibit 5-7. Multiple Regression Input Data from the Company's Records

Assume we wish to estimate total costs for a month in which we estimate producing and selling 10,000 units, with 100 batches, 10 products, and 20 customers. Using the cost equation,

$$\text{Total Costs} = \$40{,}177 + \$3.98 \times \text{Units} + \$106 \times \text{Batches}$$
$$+ \$986 \times \text{Products} + \$406 \times \text{Customers}$$

we insert the number of planned cost driver units, as follows:

$$\text{Total Costs} = \$40{,}177 + (\$3.98 \times 10{,}000 \text{ units}) + (\$106 \times 100 \text{ batches})$$
$$+ (\$986 \times 10 \text{ products}) + (\$406 \times 20 \text{ customers})$$
$$= \$108{,}577$$

(e) Estimating More Complex Cost Relations. The analysis can adapt multiple regression to accommodate a variety of complexities that often arise in cost relations. For example, one can use indicator variables (also known as *dummy variables*), that assume only two values: zero or one. Indicator variables can represent transitions between adjacent activity ranges associated with step costs, for instance. Analysts set the indicator variable to zero or to one, depending on the activity range within which the corresponding observation falls. The analysis can also accommodate curved relations of total costs to activities (such as those shown in Exhibits 5-1 and 5-5). Appropriate statistical analysis of these and other related complexities require expertise and are, in any case, beyond the scope of this introductory chapter. Chapter 6 of this book reviews some of these issues.

5.6   ISSUES ARISING IN REGRESSION ANALYSIS OF ACCOUNTING DATA

To illustrate issues common to regression analyses of accounting data, consider a hypothetical firm that manufactures and sells widgets. Exhibit 5-8 shows a scatter plot of hypothetical cost and production data for a period of several years. Each point shown in Exhibit 5-8 represents the number of units produced (horizontal axis) and the total cost of production (vertical axis) in a single accounting period.

A regression analysis of the data begins by specifying the form of the relation between the two variables. In this example, the two variables have a straight-line relation, wherein the regression calculation will estimate the coefficients for intercept and slope of the straight line. The choice of a straight line is but one of many possibilities, and the analyst must ensure that the functional form chosen correctly represents the pattern that the data exhibit. To illustrate the point that a straight-line regression may not be the correct choice, consider the data shown in Exhibit 5-9. These data evidently do not conform to a uniform straight-line relation. We can approximate a curved relation, such as that in the exhibit, with a series of straight-line segments or with some other nonlinear form, as Chapter 6 discusses.

In addition to assuming a particular functional form, the regression analysis assumes that the costs in each month are influenced by random (unsystematic) factors that differ each month in their effect. These random factors represent noise

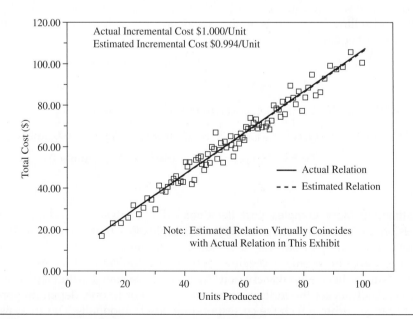

Exhibit 5-8.   Monthly Total Costs versus Units Produced

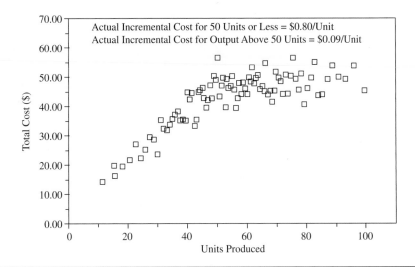

Exhibit 5-9.   Monthly Total Costs versus Units Produced

in the data, which obscures the underlying relations between the variables. When the noise is systematic, however, as with accounting adjustments or short-run departures from the long-run cost function, the regression calculation will not produce reliable results. Scrutiny of the regression residuals will often reveal such deviations in actual cost data from the basic assumptions of regression analysis. The residuals are the discrepancies between the data points and the fitted regression line. (Textbooks on regression methods discuss this topic under the heading of Residual Analysis.)

The solid line in Exhibit 5-8 presents the actual relation between cost and units produced. The dashed line (which virtually coincides with the solid line in this figure) results from an estimated regression calculation. Because the assumption of a straight-line functional form is correct in this example and because the noise is unsystematic, the regression line accurately measures the long-run incremental cost of producing an additional widget.

(a) Inaccuracies Arising from Accounting Allocations.   To illustrate the potentially biasing effect of accounting allocations on regression estimates of incremental costs, we modified the data underlying Exhibit 5-8 by spreading 20 percent of each period's cost across the remaining periods—which resulted in too much smoothing. This introduces systematic noise in the data, which violates regression assumptions. The modified data appear in Exhibit 5-10. A regression analysis of the modified data estimates incremental cost at $0.793, which estimate falls approximately 20 percent below the correct $1.00 per unit cost because of the hypothetical accounting allocations.

(b) Inaccuracies Arising from a Changing Incremental Cost.   In the sample shown in Exhibit 5-8, the incremental cost of production remains constant, and the relation between total cost and units produced, as in Equation (1), is a straight line. Sometimes the incremental cost of production does not remain constant, and a straight-line regression as in Equation (1) is not appropriate. Whether to use a

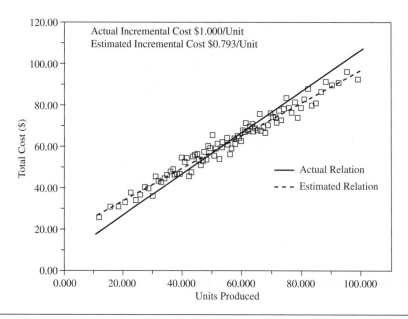

Exhibit 5-10.   Monthly Total Costs Including Accounting Adjustments versus Units Produced

series of straight-line segments or polynomial or exponential or some other closed form of nonlinear function is usually a matter of expert judgment based on analysis of the data. Occasionally, the economic model underlying the cost structure will suggest a particular nonlinear functional form. The following discussion considers three examples of phenomena that change incremental cost: changes in price level, economies of scale and changes in product mix.

(i) Changes in Price Level.   A changing incremental cost can arise as an artifact of inflation when cost data reflect material changes in price levels, with or without corresponding changes in real costs. Restating costs in terms of constant dollars, rather than adding unneeded complications to the chosen regression model, best accounts for an artificial, inflation-induced change in incremental costs.

(ii) Economies of Scale.   Exhibit 5-9 shows hypothetical data on total cost and units produced when the incremental cost of production does not remain constant. The hypothetical data shown in Exhibit 5-9 show lower incremental costs at higher levels of production—a common phenomenon termed *economies of scale*. The change in incremental cost results in a relation between total cost and units produced that does not conform to a uniform straight line. If the analysis overlooks this changing incremental cost and assumes a uniform straight-line regression, the result will show the dashed line in Exhibit 5-11. This straight line underestimates incremental cost at low levels of production and overestimates incremental cost at high levels of production. In this example, an adequate solution fits separate straight lines to the two relevant ranges.

Note that the linear regression estimate of incremental cost shown in Exhibit 5-11 is not grossly in error. The regression estimate of $0.352 lies between the actual val-

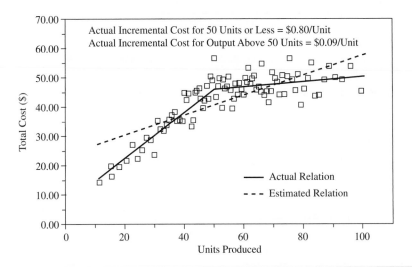

Exhibit 5-11.   Monthly Total Costs versus Units Produced

ues of $0.80 and $0.09, and perhaps may be regarded as a reasonable approximation of the correct values of $0.80 and $0.09 for some purposes, but not in litigation where importance attaches to the expert's standing in the eyes of the fact finder. Unfortunately, this lucky outcome is a happenstance feature of this example—it does not generalize. In general, an apparently small change in incremental cost can have a large and materially misleading effect on the regression estimates if the analysis does not properly account for the change.

(iii) Changing Product Mix.   The relation between total cost and units produced can also change when the analysis treats a group of different products as a single product. Exhibit 5-12 shows two products with different incremental costs that analysis can properly treat as a single product because the firm sells the two products in a constant proportion: here, two units of Product 2 for each unit of Product 1. This is sometimes termed a constant *product mix.* The line that emerges from a regression analysis of total cost versus total units produced (Product 1 and Product 2 combined) appears in Exhibit 5-13. The regression estimates incremental cost

Time Period	Units of Product 1	Units of Product 2	Total Units	Cost
1	10	20	30	$ 20
2	20	40	60	40
3	30	60	90	60
4	40	80	120	80
5	50	100	150	100

Exhibit 5-12.   Two Products Sold in a Constant Proportion
Total cost = $1.0 × (Units Produced Product 1) + $0.50 × (Units Produced Product 2)

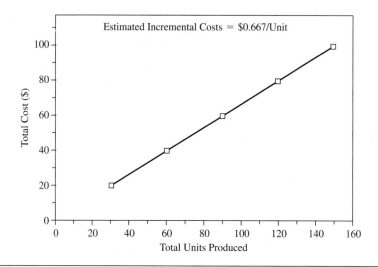

Exhibit 5-13. Regression Analysis of Data Shown in Exhibit 5-12

of \$.67/unit as the correct average incremental cost per unit of one item of Product 1 plus two items of Product 2: $0.67 = \$2.00/3$; $\$2.00 = \$1.00 \times 1 + \$0.50 \times 2$.

Exhibit 5-14 shows two products with different incremental costs that analysis should not treat as a single product because the firm does not sell the two products in a constant proportion; the product mix changes. In this case, the estimated incremental cost (shown graphically in Exhibit 5-15) that results from incorrectly treating the two products as a single product is $0.00/unit. The analysis should split the data into separate series, one for each of the products, when the product proportion does not remain constant.

(c) Inaccuracies Arising from Multicollinearity. A phenomenon termed *multicollinearity* occurs when the numbers of units produced of one product rise and fall in close synchrony with the numbers of units produced of another product. When the production data are collinear, it becomes difficult or impossible for a regression analysis to distinguish the influence on total cost of the two products separately. To illustrate how multicollinearity can make it impossible to separate the influence of two products on total cost, consider the incremental cost of making a suit of clothes

Time Period	Units of Product 1	Units of Product 2	Total Units	Cost
1	10	100	110	$60
2	20	80	100	60
3	30	60	90	60
4	40	40	80	60
5	50	20	70	60

Exhibit 5-14. Two Products Sold in a Varying Proportion
Total cost = $1.0 × (Units Produced Product 1) + $0.5 × (Units Produced Product 2)

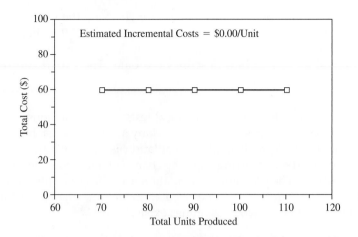

Exhibit 5-15.   Regression Analysis of Data Shown in Exhibit 5-14

comprising one coat and one pair of pants. Suppose, if known, the incremental cost of making the coat is $60 and the pants $40, for a total cost of $100 per suit. Production data will show the cost of making 10 suits to be $1,000 and that of 20 to be $2,000, and a quick calculation will reveal the production cost of a suit to be $100. However, these aggregate data alone will not enable the analyst to separate the $100 cost of the suit into its components—the $60 cost of the coat and the $40 cost of the pants.

The synchrony of production for the two products need not be a perfect lock step to render a regression analysis unable to separate the incremental costs effectively. A commonly cited rule of thumb suggests that a degree of correlation greater than 0.8 to 0.9 (a correlation of 1.0 corresponds to perfect synchrony) likely renders a regression incapable of making the required separation, but a detailed assessment of the potential effects of multicollinearity in a particular case requires statistical expertise.

(d) Inaccuracies Arising from Missing Data and Outliers.   Extreme observations, including missing data, of cost-activity relations can affect cost estimates. Consider, for example, a hurricane's effect on the recorded data for a Florida company in August. Experts have various methods of dealing with outliers, including using indicator variables, trimming, and winsorizing, but these methods go beyond the scope of this chapter. (Chapter 6 discusses some of the relevant diagnostic methods.)

5.7   DETECTING FLAWS IN A REGRESSION ANALYSIS

(a) Informal Methods.   Informal methods to critique regression analyses rely on subjective impressions, usually gained from graphical displays of data. Despite their subjective nature, informal methods are important tools of the applied statistician. Moreover, the informal methods often prove more intuitive and meaningful to laymen than a formal statistical test and therefore can more effectively demonstrate to a layman an error in a regression analysis.

Exhibit 5-9 illustrates an informal method for checking the validity of a regression analysis. The visual impression gained from Exhibit 5-9 is that of deviation from a simple straight line, indicating that a bent line or a curved relation rather than a simple straight line best describes the data. The expert can use formal statistical tests to provide further support.

(b) Formal Statistical Tests.   Formal statistical tests detect violations of the underlying assumptions of a regression analysis. Many such tests exist, but they all use the same basic logic. A mathematical calculation is made of the probability of some feature of the data occurring (e.g., the chance of a fair coin landing heads 10 times in succession). The probability calculation uses the assumptions that the test is to check (e.g., the coin is fair). If the calculation yields a small probability for an observed outcome, one of two possibilities exists.

- The small calculated probability is correct (i.e., the data are simply extraordinary).
- The small calculated probability is incorrect (i.e., one (or more) of the assumptions on which the calculation was based is violated).

When the calculated probability is sufficiently small (a commonly used standard is 0.05 or less), we tend to conclude that the latter of the two possibilities is the more consistent with the observed data.

We illustrate the logic of a formal statistical test with a coin flipping example (because it is simpler than regression). Suppose we flip a coin 10 times, resulting in 10 heads and zero tails. Assuming a fair coin, the probability of such an occurrence is $(0.5)^{10} = 0.00098$, or less than one chance in one thousand. Although such low probability events can occur, it is reasonable to conclude that the coin is not a fair coin.

Some statistical tests are powerful at detecting specific violations of particular assumptions. These specialized tests are appropriate when the analyst suspects a specific violation. Other statistical tests are less effective than the specialized tests at detecting any particular violation but have the ability to detect a broad range of violations.

(c) F-Test to Detect a Changing Incremental Cost.   Exhibit 5-11 illustrates the idea of the F-test (sometimes called the *Chow* test). The analyst divides the data into two portions and calculates a separate straight-line regression on each of the two portions of data. If the data in fact conform to a single straight-line regression (unchanging incremental cost), the two regression estimates of incremental cost will have a small difference. If, however, the data exhibit a changing incremental cost, the two regression estimates of incremental cost will have a large difference. One can calculate the probability of a dissimilarity as large as the observed dissimilarity occurring as a matter of mere chance, under the assumption that the actual relation is that of a single straight line. In the case shown in Exhibit 5-11, the probability calculation shows that the difference in the two estimated incremental costs is too large to be explained by chance fluctuations in the data and reveals instead a changing incremental cost. In the language of the statistician, the test rejects the hypothesis of a single straight line. Chapter 6 also discusses the F-test.

(d) Tests of Reasonableness.   In addition to the formal and informal methods, statisticians test the reasonableness of regression results. If the regression results differ from experience and common sense, one should consider them with skepticism. For example, a regression estimate showing a negative incremental cost or an incremental cost exceeding the product's selling price can indicate a violated assumption rather than a remarkable economic anomaly.

5.8   OTHER METHODS FOR ESTIMATING INCREMENTAL COSTS

In the interests of completeness, this chapter describes two other methods that some experts use to estimate costs in litigation. The authors have never, however, seen a case in which the first of these, account analysis, yields sounder results than does statistical cost analysis of the sort described elsewhere in this chapter.[3] We have seen the second—the engineering method—used by companies when trying to estimate future costs. However, absent a carefully documented foundation, the courts will likely find the use of such methods in litigation too speculative.

(a) Account Analysis Method.   The account analysis method is based on the past costs associated with each cost driver. Account analysis requires more data because the analyst must further separate total costs into categories that correspond to the cost drivers. For the example in Exhibit 5-7, one would analyze the cost accounts over the past 36 months to divide total monthly costs into four categories related to the four cost drivers, plus one category for fixed costs that we assumed were estimated by the constant term:

1. Unit costs
2. Batch costs
3. Product costs
4. Customer costs
5. Fixed costs

Analysts generally use account analysis in simple cases that have few observations and one or a few cost drivers.

(b) Engineering Method.   Statistical methods and account analyses rely on data from the past. By contrast, the engineering method works with the present and future. Analysts make engineering estimates of costs by first measuring the work involved in the activities that go into a product and then assigning a cost to each of those activities. Analysts prepare a detailed step-by-step analysis of each activity required to make a product, together with the costs involved.

The engineering method has two disadvantages. Because the engineering approach analyzes each activity, it can become expensive. Furthermore, analysts often base engineering estimates on optimal conditions.

Analysts can usually obtain engineering estimates of the materials required for each unit of production from drawings and product specification records. People in the company's accounting and purchasing departments have data on the cost of materials that experts can use to price the materials required to make a product. Analysts can perform time-and-motion studies or look at labor time records to ascertain the time required to perform each step. Labor records also provide typical wage rates for various jobs. Coupling those wage rates plus benefits with the time required to perform activities yields the estimated labor cost.

One can estimate other costs similarly. For example, analysts can estimate the size and cost of a building required by production that would have occurred in the but-for world based on area construction costs and space requirements. They can estimate the necessary number of supervisors and support personnel based on a direct labor time estimate.

Some argue that the engineering approach has an advantage over other cost estimation methods because it details each step required to perform an operation. Also, this approach does not require data from prior activities in the organization. Hence, analysts can use it to estimate costs for totally new activities.

Using the engineering method for the four cost drivers in our example plus fixed costs proceeds as follows:

1. **Unit Costs.** To estimate unit costs, estimate the materials required from blueprints and product specification lists and the costs based on information from vendors. To estimate labor costs, figure the time required to perform the tasks required to produce a unit. Multiply the time by a wage cost that includes an allowance for payroll taxes and benefits.

2. **Batch Costs.** Batch costs are mostly labor costs, but they may include some machine parts or even new machines. Preparing a batch includes taking the order, obtaining materials and workforce, providing instructions and training, setting up machines, obtaining parts for machines, moving the batch within the organization, delivering the product, and following up with the customer. Analysts estimate the labor and materials required for each step from order taking to customer follow-up.

3. **Product Costs.** For each product added to the portfolio of products, companies incur costs of specifications, record keeping, training, quality testing methods, prototypes machine dies, computer coding, marketing, and administrative activities.

4. **Customer Costs.** Customer costs are those that increase as the number of customers increase. Clearly, these costs include credit checking, billing, distribution, dealing with customer complaints, and marketing costs incurred to increase the customer base.

5. **Fixed (and Other) Costs.** After estimating the costs related to cost drivers, analysts usually find that some unexplained costs remain. These can include administrative costs and fixed costs of operation that do not vary with any of the cost drivers.

5.9 CONCLUSION

Regression analysis can provide a valid, useful method for estimating incremental cost. However, unadjusted accounting data seldom conform perfectly to the basic assumptions of a regression analysis. Therefore, a regression analysis of unadjusted accounting data will often produce unreliable results. Formal statistical procedures, informal statistical methods, and tests of reasonableness can detect and expose such unreliable results. Proper application of these methods requires an appropriate degree of relevant training and experience.

NOTES

1. We show a curved line so the reader will not think that we understand all cost behavior to be linear.
2. Refer to Clyde P. Stickney and Roman L. Weil, *Financial Accounting: An Introduction to Concepts, Methods, and Uses*, 11th ed. (Mason OH: Thomson Publishing, 2006). Pages 354–355 describe and illustrate the accounting methods for changing estimates of equipment life, and pages 555–557 explain why these methods are a part of generally accepted accounting principles.
3. In the mid-1980s, in *Polaroid v. Eastman Kodak*, the district court judge not only allowed introduction of regression analyses to prove costs but found them "much more accurate, credible, and appropriate" than the account analysis method used by the plaintiff. *Polaroid Corp v. Eastman Kodak Co.*, 16 U.S.P.Q.2D (BNA) at 1527.

CHAPTER 6

ECONOMETRIC ANALYSIS

Mohan P. Rao
Christian D. Tregillis

CONTENTS

The authors thank Laurentius Marais of William E. Wecker Associates, Inc. and Michael D. Ward of the University of Washington for their valuable comments and Lia Han for research support.

Editors' Note: Refer to the matrix appended to this chapter, developed by its authors, Mohan Rao and Christian Tregillis. The matrix summarizes case law grouped into several areas of econometric issues, including statistical significance, choice of variables, multicollinearity, R-squared, serial correlation, and acceptance of statistics. For each case, the matrix includes the type of case, the title of the case, the court that heard the case, and a summary or excerpt of the court's position on the issue.

6.1   INTRODUCTION

Econometrics is the application of statistical methods to understand economic relations. It is an analytical tool that can be used to systematically find answers to questions posed to the economics or financial expert in legal proceedings.

Regression analysis—one of the key techniques in econometrics—provides a statistical framework for understanding the relation between two or more variables. Financial experts often use regression analysis when they must reconstruct a world absent the alleged act, but hold all else constant. For instance, in an intellectual property dispute, the expert must estimate the patent owner's sales absent the infringer's products in the market, while holding constant the economy, the entrance of noninfringing substitutes into the market, and pricing. Similarly, in an employment discrimination case, the expert needs to understand how factors such as education, skill, and experience contribute to wage levels in an occupation or industry to assess what an employee would have earned in the same situation, absent the alleged discrimination.

Courts have recognized the usefulness of regression analysis in a wide range of applications. Other chapters in this book address many of these applications. This chapter examines some of the more subtle elements of regression analysis that frequently emerge in the litigation context, with particular focus on some of the common violations of assumptions related to the least squares regression. It also discusses common diagnostic tests and ways to undertake corrective action when necessary.

The chapter and the appendix (Case Law Summary on Issues in Econometrics) address the substantial case law that now exists on many of these topics within the context of regression analysis. The discussion assumes that the reader understands the basics of regression analysis, including parameter estimation and hypothesis testing. Those who need an introduction or a refresher to regression analysis can look at Chapter 5 or other sources recommended throughout the text and in the Notes at the end of this chapter.[1] This chapter will emphasize how to implement the techniques discussed rather than provide a rigorous theoretical foundation for the various tests and recommended corrections.

6.2   THE ROLE OF ECONOMETRICS IN LITIGATION

Although some courts and areas of law have long embraced econometric analysis, it received a boost following the 1993 ruling by the United States Supreme Court in *Daubert v. Merrell Dow Pharmaceuticals, Inc.*[2] In *Daubert*, the Supreme Court called for the trial judge to ensure that the testimony of an expert has "a reliable foundation" and is "relevant to the task at hand." In addition, the Court outlined five factors for assessing reliability: testability, peer review, a known or potential rate of error, whether there are standards controlling the technique's operation and general acceptance in the relevant scientific community.[3] The *Daubert* factors and standard, which have been adopted in federal courts and in several state courts, are neither exclusive nor dispositive.[4] Rule 702 of the Federal Rule of Evidence, as amended in the year 2000, calls for expert testimony to be "the product of reliable principles and methods that have been reliably applied to the facts of the case."[5]

Econometric analysis has proved well suited to meet the *Daubert* Rule 702 standard. Not only does econometrics provide the expert with a comprehensive toolkit to systematically test substantive arguments, it also offers a framework for systematically calculating the rate of error. Further, when the litigation involves large quantities of data or pathological data (e.g., missing observations or errors in measurement), econometric analysis, and, more broadly, statistical analysis often provides the best way to summarize the available information and to make systematic inferences. As a result, courts have generally found econometric analysis a reliable and well-established method. In some cases, courts have excluded experts' testimony for *failing* to perform such analysis. For example, in *Zenith Electronics Corporation v. WH-TV Broadcasting Corporation*, a breach of contract/defect case in which the plaintiff accused the defendants of delivering substandard satellite boxes and the expert proffered testimony attempting to quantify the lost sales that stemmed from the alleged defect, the district court found that

> the supposed "uniqueness" of a market does not justify substituting a guess for careful analysis. Cities differ in size, average income, levels of education, availability of over-the-air TV signals, and other factors that might affect the demand for multipoint multichannel digital system (MMDS) service. But social science has tools to isolate the effects of multiple variables and determine how they influence one dependent variable—here, sales of MMDS service. Perhaps the leading tool is the multivariate regression, which is used extensively by all social sciences. Regression analysis is common enough in litigation to earn extended treatment in the Federal Judicial Center's Reference Manual on Scientific Evidence (2d ed. 2000). ... [WH-TV's expert] neither employed any of the methods covered in the Reference Manual nor explained why he hadn't.[6]

At the same time, courts have excluded expert testimony on numerous occasions for the misuse of econometric analysis.[7]

6.3 A REGRESSION MODEL

Regression analysis provides a statistical framework for understanding the relation between two or more variables. Regression analysis can explain the change in one variable (the dependent variable) as a function of one or more other variables (independent variables).

Much of the discussion in this chapter will reference the following hypothetical example. Suppose that franchisees of a large national DVD rental business, Mega Video, have a dispute with the franchisor about whether the franchisor could legally open an online rent-by-mail service, MV*flix*, in competition with the franchisees. Through MV*flix*, customers can order and have their DVD rentals shipped directly to home and return them via regular mail. Two key issues require analysis in this litigation:

1. Whether rent-by-mail sales cannibalize retail store sales (i.e., whether the two parties compete with each other); and
2. Calculation of lost sales, if any, to retail store owners (the plaintiffs).

In 2000, Mega Video has several hundred stores throughout the United States and annual revenues of about $500 million. The court needs to know what factors explain the sales of Mega Video in order to estimate how the rent-by-mail service, MV*flix*, has affected retail store sales. Research shows that sales of a firm relate to three major factors: (1) economy-wide factors; (2) industry-specific factors; and (3) firm-specific factors.

Using this information, one can state the model as follows: The dependent variable is Mega Video *retail sales*, measured as the dollar value of sales per month in the retail stores. The model has three independent variables:

1. *Disposable personal income (DPI)*, reported as part of the U.S. National Income and Product Accounts by the Bureau of Economic Analysis, as a proxy to capture the state of the U.S. economy;

2. *Movie industry sales*, as measured by domestic box office receipts; and

3. *Sales of MVflix.*[8]

Other factors may influence Mega Video retail store sales, but these three variables likely capture the most important influences.[9]

Assuming that the influences of these variables on retail sales act linearly and independently, we can write the econometric model as follows:

$$\text{Retail Sales} = b_0 + b_1 \, \text{DPI} + b_2 \, \text{Box Office Sales} + b_3 \, \text{MV}\textit{flix}\, \text{Sales} + e$$

The Mega Video model has been estimated using annual data from 1981 to 2000 in SAS, a widely used statistical program, and the results are listed in Exhibit 6-1.[10] The discussion will refer to these results throughout the chapter.

The goodness of fit, as measured by R-squared (R^2), equals 0.97 (*see* Section 6.11 for a discussion of R^2). The parameter estimates show that b_1 (the coefficient of DPI) is positive and statistically significant and b_2 (the coefficient of Box Office Sales) is positive and statistically significant, indicating that both the economy-wide and industry-specific factors influence Mega Video retail sales. The third parameter of interest, b_3 (the coefficient of MV*flix* Sales), is negative but not statistically significant. Thus, we cannot reject the null hypothesis that no relation exists between MV*flix* sales and Mega Video retail store sales. An analyst can use these results to assess whether a statistically significant cannibalizing effect exists and to quantify the amount of that effect.

After estimating the model parameters and assessing their statistical significance, the next step is to examine whether the sample data follow several assumptions of the least squares regression model. If the data violate any of these assumptions, the analyst will need to undertake corrective action before relying on the estimated parameters and their standard errors. Section 6.4 considers some common violations and recommended corrective actions.

6.4   VIOLATION OF ASSUMPTIONS

(a) Multicollinearity.   The least squares model assumes that no linear relations exist among the independent variables. For example, if DPI and Box Office Sales perfectly correlate in the Mega Video model, the regression model cannot distinguish the separate contributions of these two variables on Mega Video retail store sales. (Section 5.6(c) of Chapter 5 discusses multicollinearity.)

Although only a strictly linear relation between two variables will violate the least squares model's assumption, a high, but less than perfect, correlation

Dependent Variable: Annual Retail Store Sales of Mega Video 1981–2000

Independent Variable		VIF
1. Intercept	**66.29**	0
	(10.76 / 6.16)	
2. Disposable Personal Income (DPI)	**0.000016**	16.98
	(7.60E-6 / 2.10)	
3. MVflix sales	−0.5	5.36
	(0.49 / −1.01)	
4. Box Office Sales	**0.15**	9.95
	(0.03 / 5.00)	
R^2	0.97	
Number of Observations	20	
Durbin-Watson Statistic (First Order Serial Correlation)	**0.94**	
	(0.0006)	

	White Test	Breusch-Pagan
Heteroscedasticity Test	8.42	3.24
	(0.49)	(0.52)
Chow Test	Break Point: 1994	Break Point: 1995
F-Value	2.92	2.78
Pr > F	(0.07)	(0.08)

Coefficients in **bold** are significant at the 5 percent significance level.
First number in parentheses is standard error, second number is *t*-statistic.
Single number in parentheses is significance level corresponding to the test statistic.
The model was estimated in SAS using PROC AUTOREG.

Exhibit 6-1. Results of Regression Analysis for Mega Video

between variables will likely cause problems with the least squares estimates. Even though the least squares estimates remain unbiased, this condition will lead to large standard errors, thereby leading to poor resolution of the effects being measured and, consequently, to weak inferences. Statisticians describe this condition as *multicollinearity*. One popular test for detection of multicollinearity is the variance inflation factor (VIF), available in most statistical programs. Formally, VIF is the inverse of $(1 - R_i^2)$ where R_i^2 is the R^2 from regressing the ith independent variable on all the other independent variables. As a rule of thumb, a VIF of more than 10 indicates that multicollinearity could be a concern.[11]

Multicollinearity is essentially a data problem. It can arise because of an approximately linear relation among the independent variables in the sample under consideration, even if no such actual linear relation exists among any of the regressors. As a result, statisticians often recommend gathering more data in the hope that a larger sample size would provide additional information and, therefore, reduce variances (and standard errors). In most circumstances, however, one cannot follow this advice because analysts typically use all the available data in the initial analysis.

Alternatively, the analyst could delete one of the variables with a high VIF value from the equation or combine two or more variables with high VIF values into a single variable. For instance, one might consider a model of economic growth that includes inflation and unemployment as independent variables. If inflation correlates with unemployment, the analysis could leave one of the variables out of the model or, alternatively, combine these two variables to create what economists call a *misery index* (unemployment rate + inflation rate). Of course, if economic theory guides model choice, we need to evaluate whether dropping or combining variables will lead to misspecification of the underlying model. In other words, dealing with multicollinearity should not create more serious issues with model misspecification (discussed in Section 6.5).

Another potential approach to dealing with multicollinearity is to do nothing. If the eventual use of the model does not need to distinguish between unemployment and inflation, then correcting for multicollinearity may not be as important. For example, if the analyst wants to assess the influence of gender bias on wages, then an explanatory model of wages that includes both unemployment and inflation as separate variables may prove satisfactory even though one cannot, as a result of multicollinearity, find the separate statistical relations between wages and unemployment or between wages and inflation. Even though the model needs to include unemployment rate and inflation as control variables, gender is the key variable of interest. As long as gender does not highly correlate with other independent variables, the "do nothing" approach may be sufficient.

As Exhibit 6-1 illustrates, the VIFs in the Mega Video model are 5.36 for MV*flix* sales, 9.95 for Box Office sales and 16.98 for DPI. Both Box Office sales and DPI are close to or above 10, suggesting that multicollinearity may present an obstacle to drawing inferences from these data. However, the key variable of interest in this model is MV*flix* sales, which has a VIF of only 5.36. Absent a need to characterize the individual statistical relations between Retail Store sales and DPI or Box Office sales, the model may suffice as currently specified.

Courts have tended to understand the challenge in dealing with multicollinearity in regression analyses. In *Estate of Hill v. ConAgra Poultry*, the district court found that

> a multicollinear model makes it difficult to establish that an individual explanatory variable influences the dependent variable. Thus, even if two explanatory variables should be included in the regression, if multicollinearity is serious it may be necessary to drop one of them. This, in turn, may cause problems associated with

omission of variables, but those problems might, in certain circumstances, be acceptable in the face of more serious problems of multicollinearity. Hence, if multicollinearity exists, the probability will be increased that the net impact of group status will be judged statistically insignificant, even in cases in which there are actual differences in the treatment.[12]

In *Denny v. Westfield State College*, the district court wrote that

because multicollinearity increases standard errors, its presence means that results found to be significant in the analysis are likely to be even more significant than they appear. Because the plaintiff's expert's results demonstrated statistical significance for each year studied except one, the Court does not find that the presence of multi-collinearity detracts from the validity of her findings.[13]

(b) Nonconstant Variance.   The least squares model assumes that the disturbances have uniform variance, known as *homoscedasticity*. With homoscedastic disturbances, all values of Y corresponding to various values of X have equal importance. But what if the variance of the disturbance is related to the size of the independent variable? For instance, consumption will likely be a function of the level of income and may deviate more from the base relation at higher levels of income (*see* Exhibit 6-2). In other words, the larger the independent variable, the larger the variance of the associated disturbance. If the disturbances have nonconstant variance, they are said to be *heteroscedastic*.

With heteroscedasticity, least squares estimates of the coefficients remain unbiased but the standard errors are biased, thereby leading to incorrect statistical inferences. One simple test to detect heteroscedasticity is visual inspection. For instance, the larger residuals to the right of the graph in Exhibit 6-3 indicate a positive relation between the error variance and the independent variable. More formal tests to detect heteroscedasticity include the Goldfeld-Quandt test, the Breusch-Pagan test, and the White test.[14]

Many statistical software programs report the White test or the Breusch-Pagan test for detecting heteroscedasticity. The White test examines whether any

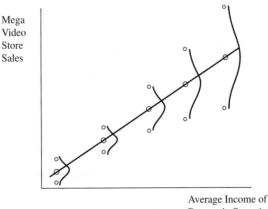

Average Income of
Renters in Store Area

Exhibit 6-2.   Variation in Mega Video Store Sales by Income of Renters in Store Area

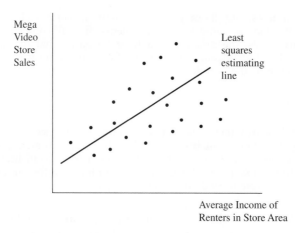

Exhibit 6-3. Evidence of Heteroscedasticity

heteroscedasticity present in the data causes the true variance-covariance matrix of the least squares estimates to differ from that estimated by the formula for the homoscedastic case. Breusch-Pagan tests the hypothesis that the independent variables have no explanatory power on the error terms. Both these tests are asymptotically distributed as Chi-square distributions.

For a simple illustration of heteroscedasticity, consider the example from Greene, which models the average public school spending in the 50 states plus the District of Columbia in the year 1979 as a function of per capita income by state and its square (i.e., per capita income^2).[15] The top half of Exhibit 6-4 displays the least squares regression results. The R^2 test to measure goodness of fit results in a relatively high score of 0.66. All the coefficients are statistically significant at the five percent level of significance, with per capita income having a negative coefficient and per capita income squared having a positive coefficient. Both the White test (21.16) and the Breusch-Pagan test (15.83), however, are statistically significant well below the five percent level of significance, indicating that the null hypothesis that no heteroscedasticity exists can be rejected.

Analysts can use several methods to correct for any detected heteroscedasticity.

- Explore whether the heteroscedasticity results from improper model specification. For instance, the variables in the model may not have linear effects, the data may have subgroup differences, or the model may have excluded some of the important variables. In such cases, fixing the model misspecification problem often resolves the heteroscedasticity problem as well.

- Generate robust standard errors. As discussed previously, heteroscedasticity causes biased standard errors. The least squares estimator assumes that the errors are independent and identically distributed. One calculates robust standard errors by relaxing that assumption. The coefficient estimates remain the same as before, but the test statistics and inferences often change as a result of the corrected standard errors.

- Use a weighted least squares calculation. In the preceding example, a plot of the residuals suggests that the errors exhibit more variance in states with

Least Squares Results

Independent Variable	Dependent Variable: Average Public School Spending in the U.S.
1. Intercept	**832.91** (327.3 / 2.54)
2. State Per Capita Income	**−1,834.2** (829.0 / −2.21)
3. State Per Capita Income Squared	**1,587.04** (519.1 / 3.06)
R^2	0.66
Number of Observations	51
Heteroscedasticity Test	White Test **21.16** (0.0003) · Breusch-Pagan **15.83** (0.0004)

Weighted Least Squares Results
Weight: 1 / (State Per Capita Income Squared)

Independent Variable	Dependent Variable: Average Public School Spending in the U.S.
1. Intercept	**664.58** (333.6 / 1.99)
2. State Per Capita Income	−1,399.28 (872.1 / −1.60)
3. State Per Capita Income Squared	**1,311.35** (563.7 / 2.33)
R^2	0.6
Heteroscedasticity Test	White Test 9.31 (0.0538) · Breusch-Pagan 5.23 (0.0733)

Coefficients in **bold** are significant at the 5 percent significance level.
First number in parentheses is standard error, second number is *t*-statistic.
Single number in parentheses is significance level corresponding to the test statistic.
The model was estimated in SAS using PROC AUTOREG.

Exhibit 6-4. Analysis of Per Capita Public School Spending in 1979

higher levels of per capita income. We can use this information to correct for the heteroscedasticity by specifying $1 \div$ (per capita income)^2 as the weight in a weighted least squares model. In other words, the smaller the error variance, the more heavily one weights the observation. The bottom half of Exhibit 6-4 shows the weighted least squares results. The income coefficient is no longer statistically significant at the 5 percent level. But now both the White test (9.31) and the Breusch-Pagan (5.23) test suggest that the null hypothesis that no heteroscedasticity exists cannot be rejected at the five percent level (although just barely in the case of the White test). Weighted least squares is a superior option when one can implement it, but it requires that the analyst have *a priori* information on the error variances. Perhaps for this reason, calculation of robust standard errors is a more common approach to dealing with heteroscedasticity.

In the Mega Video example in Exhibit 6-1, neither the White test (8.42) nor the Breusch-Pagan test (3.24) indicates that heteroscedasticity presents a problem in that model.

(c) Autocorrelated Errors.   The least squares model assumes that the disturbance terms are not correlated across observations. Time series data frequently violate this assumption. In time series data, random shocks often have effects that persist in subsequent time periods. A natural disaster or an unexpected spike in the price of oil can affect the economy for several months (or even years) after the event. A firm might experience a disruption from one of its suppliers that can affect its sales for several periods after the initial disruption. In each of these cases, the disturbance terms will likely correlate across observations over time. One can also have autocorrelation in cross-sectional analysis if the observations have spatial dependence. For instance, a health epidemic or an economic shock in one state or country will likely affect neighboring states or countries. Misspecification of the model, such as an omitted variable or the wrong functional form, can produce errors that correlate with each other.

As in the case of heteroscedasticity, the time series type of autocorrelation produces unbiased estimates, but with incorrect standard errors, thereby leading to incorrect inferences. The spatial correlation is more complicated and even produces biased estimates with the least squares estimator.[16]

As in the case of heteroscedasticity, a simple test to detect autocorrelation is visual inspection of the residuals. Exhibit 6-5, which plots residuals across time, illustrates one such example. An obvious pattern in the residual plot—such as a series of positive residuals followed by a series of negative residuals or an alternating pattern of positive and negative residuals—often indicates the presence of autocorrelation. A more formal test to detect autocorrelation is the Durbin Watson *d* statistic, which is calculated from the residuals of a least squares regression and is used to test for first-order autocorrelation. The Durbin Watson statistic ranges from 0 to 4, where a *d* value of 0 indicates perfect negative autocorrelation, 2 indicates no autocorrelation, and 4 equals perfect positive autocorrelation.

If the Durbin Watson test indicates autocorrelated errors, one should first explore whether the autocorrelation results from improper model specification such as an omitted variable or an incorrect functional form. As in the case of

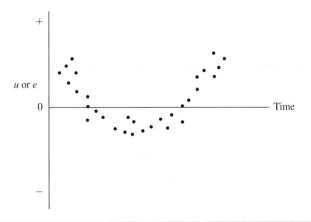

Exhibit 6-5.   Evidence of Autocorrelated Errors

heteroscedasticity, fixing the model misspecification problem often resolves the autocorrelation problem as well.

A more rigorous approach to deal with autocorrelation in time series data is the Durbin two-stage method. Under this method, the regression includes the independent variables, as before, but also lagged dependent and independent variables. The estimated coefficient on the lagged dependent variable provides an estimate of the first-order serial correlation, which one can use to generate the main regression results. Other approaches to deal with autocorrelation include the Cochrane-Orcutt iterative least squares test and the Hildreth-Lu search procedure. A full discussion of these tests and techniques lies beyond the scope of this chapter. *See* Greene's *Econometric Analysis* for a more complete discussion.[17]

As Exhibit 6-1 shows, the Durbin Watson d statistic for first-order serial correlation in the Mega Video model equals 0.94 (with probability of observing a number smaller than this, Pr < DW, of 0.0006), indicating negative first-order serial correlation. Therefore, we recalculate the Mega Video model correcting for this serial correlation. Exhibit 6-6 presents the results, also estimated in SAS. The Durbin Watson d statistic now equals 1.97 (Pr < DW is 0.25). The autoregressive parameter (ρ) is negative and statistically significant at the 10 percent level of significance (coefficient estimate equals -0.56 with a t-value of -1.92). The model has an R^2 of 0.98. When considering the model parameters, DPI no longer has statistical significance, Box Office Sales are positive and statistically significant, and MV*flix* sales are still not statistically significant.

(d) Problematic Models in Litigation. Courts have criticized econometric models afflicted with heteroscedasticity or autocorrelation. For example, in *Rossini v. Ogilvy & Mather*, the district court did not agree with the expert's conclusions and wrote that "plaintiff's expert's regression analysis (which is afflicted with serial correlation) systematically overstates the statistical significance of the regression coefficients and makes the significance of the differences between the salaries of males and females appear larger than should be the case."[18] In *Arcata Forest Products v. United States*, the court wrote that "the Durbin Watson test result of 0.194 showed a high degree of serial correlation, meaning that the model does not

Maximum Likelihood Estimates

Dependent Variable: Annual Retail Store Sales of Mega Video

Independent Variable	1981–2000
1. Intercept	**66.45**
	(15.75 / 4.22)
2. Disposable Personal Income (DPI)	0.00001
	(0.00001 / 0.82)
3. MV*flix* sales	−0.21
	(0.54 / −0.39)
4. Box Office Sales	**0.17**
	(0.05 / 3.42)
AR (1)	−0.56
	(0.29 / −1.92)
R^2	0.98
Number of Observations	20
Durbin-Watson Statistic (First Order Serial Correlation)	1.97
	(0.25)

Coefficients in **bold** are significant at the 5 percent significance level.
First number in parentheses is standard error, second number is *t*-statistic.
Single number in parentheses is significance level corresponding to the test statistic.
The model was estimated in SAS using PROC AUTOREG.

Exhibit 6-6. Analysis of Mega Video Retail Sales Corrected for Serial Correlation

capture the underlying relationship between the two indices."[19] However, in *Denny v. Westfield State College*, in which the plaintiff's expert admitted that heteroscedasticity probably existed to some degree, but that its effect was not significant, the court did not find that the possible presence of heteroscedasticity itself detracted from the validity of the plaintiff's study.[20] In *Estate of Hill v. ConAgra Poultry*, the plaintiff's expert's regression model contained heteroscedastic disturbances, but he did not correct for them.[21] The district court, however, allowed the analysis because the defendants did not point to any evidence that contradicted the plaintiff's assertions. Therefore, experts should consider these potential violations and their effect on substantive inferences as well.

6.5   TYPES OF SPECIFICATION ERRORS

The least squares regression model assumes correct specification of the model. An analyst usually develops the model based on economic or financial theory but can misspecify it in several ways. Consider the consequences of some of these problems on the estimated coefficients and their standard errors.

(a) Omitting a Relevant Variable.   Suppose that the true model is

$$Y_i = \beta_0 + \beta_1 X_{1i} + \beta_2 X_{2i} + u_i$$

and we fit

$$Y_i = \alpha_0 + \alpha_1 X_{1i} + v_i$$

Omitting X_2 leads to several consequences:

- Biased and inconsistent least squares estimators of $\hat{\alpha}_0$ and $\hat{\alpha}_1$ if X_2 correlates with X_1
- Biased $\hat{\alpha}_0$, but unbiased $\hat{\alpha}_1$ if X_1 and X_2 do not correlate
- Incorrectly estimated σ^2
- $V(\hat{\alpha}_1)$ is a biased estimator of $V(\hat{\beta}_1)$
- Potentially misleading confidence intervals and hypothesis testing

Omitting variables that the model should include mistakenly ascribes to the included variables the influences that the missing variable would explain. This often leads to incorrect conclusions about the explanatory power and coefficients of the variables in the model.

As articulated by the Supreme Court in *Bazemore v. Friday*, and consistent with other cases, "[n]ormally, failure to include variables will affect the analysis' probativeness, not its admissibility. Importantly, it is clear that a regression analysis that includes less than 'all measurable variables' may serve to prove [the opponent's] case."[22] In this opinion, the Court recognized that the opposition can argue that the omission hides the true effect of the variable in question. In *Bickerstaff v. Vassar College*, the district court went further by granting the *Daubert* motion to exclude an analysis because it omitted major variables.[23] The deciding factor as to admissibility appears to be the importance and impact of the omitted variable, because courts seem to understand the importance of parsimony and that the equations cannot include every potentially influential variable. However, merely pointing out that the model omitted some key variables may not prove sufficient to demonstrate that the model could be misleading. In *Bazemore v. Friday*, the appellate court wrote that

> lower courts should be cautious about dismissing plaintiff's statistical studies as not probative simply because defendant offers some nondiscriminatory explanation for the disparities shown. In most cases, a defendant cannot rebut statistical evidence by mere conjectures or assertions, without introducing evidence to support the contention that the missing factor can explain disparities as a product of a legitimate, nondiscriminatory selection criterion.[24]

(b) Including an Irrelevant Variable.   Suppose that the true model is

$$Y_i = \beta_0 + \beta_1 X_{1i} + u_i$$

and we fit

$$Y_i = \alpha_0 + \alpha_1 X_{1i} + \alpha_2 X_{2i} + v_i$$

The least squares estimates remain unbiased and consistent; σ^2 is estimated correctly; and the confidence intervals and hypothesis testing remain valid. The irrelevant variable, however, leads to inefficient estimated coefficients: the irrelevant variable can remove some of the relevant variable's predictive power when some correlation does exist between the irrelevant variable and other independent variables. In such a case, the incorrectly specified model will have larger standard errors than those of the coefficients in the correctly specified model. As a result, the analyst will more likely not reject the null hypothesis in the misspecified model, thus leading to incorrect inferences.

Given that the consequences of including an irrelevant variable create a lesser problem than excluding a relevant variable, one may feel tempted to include an irrelevant variable when in doubt. Analysts need to resist this temptation. Ideally, economic and financial theory should drive the choice of a parsimonious model. A model with many variables becomes hard to interpret. Moreover, independent variables that correlate often create other problems.

Analysts can choose from several techniques to test whether a model has omitted a relevant variable. One such technique is known as the regression error specification test, (RESET), which looks for a trace of the omitted variable in the error term of the incorrect model after including one or more variables as a proxy for the omitted variable in the model. One can then use an *F*-test to test the null hypothesis that the additional coefficients equal zero. We can also use RESET to test for nonlinear functional forms.

In *EEOC v. Sears Roebuck*, the court articulated the balance in the decision to include variables with the following:

> If too many factors are added that do not significantly affect the dependent variable, the model can become distorted and then may not accurately estimate how much the independent variables influence the dependent variable. For a regression analysis to be meaningful, it is therefore important to strike a balance by including all factors which significantly affect the dependent variable, and excluding those variables which do not significantly affect the dependent variable.[25]

6.6 CHOICE OF FUNCTIONAL FORM

The least squares regression model assumes that the dependent variable is a linear function of the independent variables. Theory and an understanding of the relations among the variables guide this important assumption. Economic theory often suggests not only the relevant model variables, but also its functional form. However, economic theory can be incorrect or fail to suggest a specific functional form.

In such instances, the expert should first test whether the data fit the linear functional form as opposed to some nonlinear functional form. Several such tests exist, including that developed by Bera and Jarque, which simultaneously tests for functional form and other issues related to the least squares model.[26]

Second, the expert should explore estimating a model with a more flexible (nonlinear) functional form. Sometimes, one can transform a nonlinear functional form and estimate it using the linear regression model. Nonlinear functional forms that one can estimate in this way include log-linear, semi-log, reciprocal or inverse, and polynomial. Exhibit 6-7 illustrates these forms, which are discussed in this section.

- **Log-linear models.** Used widely in economics to estimate the Cobb-Douglas production function, price elasticity models, or the gravity model in international trade, the log-linear model involves taking logarithms of the

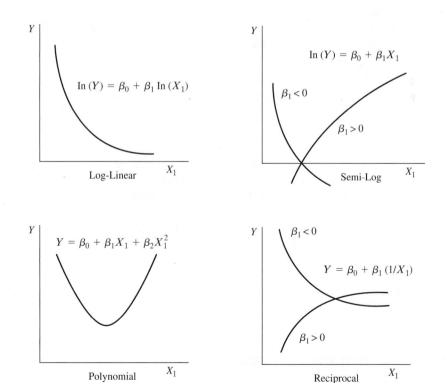

Exhibit 6-7. Graphs of Some Common Nonlinear Functional Forms

dependent and independent variables of the form shown below, where the error term is log normally distributed:

$$\ln Y = \beta_0 + \beta_1 \ln (X_i)$$

One can now interpret the slope coefficient as an elasticity whereby a *percent* change in X_1 leads to some corresponding *percent* change in Y (e.g., a 1 percent increase in price results in a β_1 percent decrease in quantity sold).

- **Semi-log models.** These take the following form:

$$Y = \beta_0 + \beta_1 \ln (X_1)$$

or

$$\ln (Y) = \beta_0 + \beta_1 X_1$$

In the first model, a *percent* change in X_1 leads to some corresponding *unit* change in Y. In the second model, a *unit* change in X_1 leads to some corresponding *percent* change in Y.

- **Reciprocal models.** A reciprocal (also known as inverse or hyperbolic) model typically takes the following form:

$$Y = \beta_0 + \beta_1(1/X_1)$$

This implies that as X_1 gets larger, the marginal effect on Y becomes smaller. This model is often used in macroeconomics to estimate inverse relations such as the Phillips curve, where the dependent variable is the inflation rate and the independent variable is the unemployment rate (modeled as $1/X_1$). One would expect that as the unemployment rate increases, the expected effect on the inflation rate should decrease.

- **Polynomial.** A quadratic (polynomial degree 2) has the following functional form

$$Y = \beta_0 + \beta_1 X_1 + \beta_2 X_1^2$$

Analysts use this model when diminishing returns occur as a variable's numerical value increases. For example, in an employment discrimination case, one could expect that experience has a large effect on earnings in the early years of an employee's career but becomes less important over time. Analysts can capture such an expected relation by specifying a squared term of experience in the regression model. The interpretation on all the other coefficients remains the same as in the linear model. One can no longer interpret the two earnings coefficients (β_1 and β_2) individually, however, because if one of these changes, the other must also change. Therefore, to ascertain the effect of experience on earnings, one must evaluate both coefficients together. The marginal effect, the derivative, of a unit change of experience on earnings is now given by $\beta_1 + 2\beta_2 X_1$.

6.7   SENSITIVITY TESTING OF ESTIMATED RESULTS

Once analysts have estimated the parameters of interest, they must ensure that the inferences they make are not too sensitive (or fragile) to minor variations in model specification or data. Sensitivity testing is a vast topic in statistics and can become complicated quickly, but one can use at least two simple tests to check the sensitivity of the estimated model parameters. The first tests the stability of model parameters for different subsets of data and the second tests for the stability of model parameters for slight variations in functional form.

(a) Chow Test for Different Subperiods. To investigate whether the model parameters shift for different subperiods, analysts can use a Chow test. The Chow test tests the null hypothesis of no difference in parameters by comparing the sum of squared residuals from the two subperiod models to the overall model.[27]

The Chow test for the Mega Video example in Exhibit 6-1 indicates that the null hypothesis that the parameters of our model are stable between the two periods 1980 to 1994 and 1995 to 2000 cannot be rejected at the five percent level. The F-values for breaks for years 1994 and 1995 are 2.92 and 2.78, respectively, which are statistically significant at the 10 percent level. One explanation for the difference in parameters for these two subperiods may lie in the emergence of the Internet as a major medium for entertainment distribution around 1995. The analysis can account for this factor by including an indicator variable (a binary variable that takes on the value of 0 for the 1980 to 1994 period and 1 from 1995 to 2000; also known as a *dummy* variable). Exhibit 6-8 presents model results with the indicator variable. The F-values for the same subperiods as before (1.76 and 1.98, respectively) are no longer significant even at the 10 percent level.

Although perhaps the most popular model for testing for parameter stability (i.e., constancy), the Chow test has its limitations. First, it assumes knowledge of the two subperiods *a priori*, and second, the test is sensitive to the specification of the subperiods, making the first concern even more important. Further, the Chow test assumes constant parameters within the subperiods that change only across the subperiods, thus ruling out gradual evolution of the parameters. More modern techniques for estimating varying coefficient models exist, but such a discussion lies beyond the scope of this chapter.[28]

(b) Tests for Sensitivity of Model Parameters. One can also test for sensitivity by introducing alternative independent variables that follow different, but still plausible, theoretical frameworks. If the parameter on the key variable (or variables) in the model does not change by much, analysts can have greater confidence in their results.[29]

To illustrate, consider the set of regressions in Exhibit 6-9 in which the dependent variable is the share price of a major entertainment conglomerate. In this case, the plaintiff claimed that the defendant's share price increased upon the launch of a domain name that infringed the plaintiff's federally registered trademark. The plaintiff claimed that damages equaled the difference between the actual increase in the share price and what the share price would have been in the but-for world. The plaintiff's expert used changes in the Standard & Poor's (S&P 500) Index as a proxy for how the defendant's shares would have performed in the but-for world. The expert did not perform any statistical analysis.

The defendant's expert used regression analysis to assess whether the change in share price related to the introduction of the domain name. As in the Mega Video example, independent variables that explain movements in the share price could include economy-wide factors, industry wide-factors, and firm-specific

Independent Variable	Dependent Variable: Annual Retail Store Sales of Mega Video
	1981–2000
1. Intercept	**59.08**
	(17.85 / 3.31)
2. Disposable Personal Income (DPI)	0.00002
	(0.000015 / 1.08)
3. MV*flix* sales	−0.31
	(0.63 / −0.49)
4. Box Office Sales	**0.16**
	(0.05 / 3.09)
5. Internet Dummy	−17.19
	(−0.91 / 18.85)
6. AR (1)	−0.54
	(0.33 / −1.63)
R^2	0.98
Number of Observations	20
Chow Test	Break Point: 1994	Break Point: 1995
F-Value	1.76	1.98
Pr > F	(0.21)	(0.17)

Coefficients in **bold** are significant at the 5 percent significance level.
First number in parentheses is standard error, second number is *t*-statistic.
Single number in parentheses is significance level corresponding to the test statistic.
The model was estimated in SAS using PROC AUTOREG.

Exhibit 6-8. Analysis of Mega Video Retail Sales with Internet Dummy Variable

Dependent Variable: Daily Closing Stock Price
January 1, 1998 to December 31, 2000
Length of Event Window

Independent Variable	2 Days	1 Week	1 Month	2 Months	3 Months
	8/16/99 to 8/17/99	8/16/99 to 8/20/99	8/16/99 to 9/16/99	8/16/99 to 10/16/99	8/16/99 to 11/16/99
1. Intercept	**2.555**	**2.578**	**2.548**	**2.496**	**2.247**
	(1.1444/2.23)	(1.1454/2.25)	(1.1437/2.23)	(1.1199/2.23)	(1.0617/2.12)
2. S&P 500 Index	**0.004**	**0.004**	**0.004**	**0.004**	**0.004**
	(0.0011/3.39)	(0.0011/3.36)	(0.0011/3.40)	(0.0011/3.43)	(0.0011/3.54)
3. Dow Jones Entertainment and Leisure Index	**0.012**	**0.012**	**0.012**	**0.012**	**0.013**
	(0.0044/2.66)	(0.0044/2.68)	(0.0044/2.65)	(0.0044/2.70)	(0.0044/2.88)
4. Event Window Dummy Variable	0.057	-0.240	0.001	0.017	0.004
	(0.2669/0.21)	(0.2667/0.90)	(0.2662/0.00)	(0.2650/0.06)	(0.2636/0.01)
5. R^2	0.97	0.97	0.97	0.97	0.97
6. Number of Observations	755	755	755	755	755

Coefficients in **bold** are significant at the 5 percent significance level.
First number in parentheses is standard error, second number is *t*-statistic.

Exhibit 6-9.   Model with Alternative Specifications

factors. The analysis used the S&P 500 Index as a proxy for economy-wide factors and the Dow Jones Entertainment and Leisure Index as a proxy for entertainment industry factors. The defendant's expert also used a dummy variable for time periods, called an *event window*, during which investors use new information affecting a firm to reevaluate the firm's share price. (Chapter 18 discusses event study methods.) Economists often specify an event window of two days, because one cannot be certain whether the release of information into the market occurred before or after the market closed on the day of release.

In the present case, the plaintiff's expert used a three-month time period after the launch of the domain name as the event window. The defendant's expert used the event window dummy variable to evaluate whether a statistically significant up-tick occurred in the price of the defendant's stock. Further, the defendant's expert used the typical two-day event window used by economists, as well as the three-month window used by the plaintiff's expert (along with some intermediate event windows) to evaluate whether a relation existed between the launch of the domain name and the price of the defendant's shares.

As Exhibit 6-9 shows, the fit of all five (alternative) models is quite good (R^2 of 0.97). The coefficients of both the S&P 500 Index and the Dow Jones Entertainment and Leisure Index are positive and statistically significant, as one would expect. But the event window dummy variable proves statistically insignificant across all the models representing different event windows, including the three-month window proposed by the plaintiff's expert. These results show that, independent of which event window one uses, no statistically significant relation exists between the launch of the domain name and the defendant's share price. In other words, the conclusion is robust (i.e., resistant) under various alternative specifications of the event window. One could try additional alternative specifications in which the independent variables vary across the different models.

6.8   ATTRIBUTES OF A GOOD MODEL

A good model should exhibit *parsimony*. Good practice encourages a model with a few key variables to capture the essence of the relation under study and to ensure that analysts relegate all minor and random influences to the error term, to the extent that this strategy does not introduce specification errors. Courts and experts often have difficulty interpreting a model with too many variables. Similarly, a better model often emerges by using more sophisticated functional forms and estimators with a few key variables rather than expanding the list of variables to improve the model's fit. This also relates to assessing the *goodness of fit* of models. With regression, analysts want to explain as much of the variation in the dependent variable as possible with explanatory variables included in the model, and in so doing explain the relations among the variables. R-squared (R^2), explained in Section 6.10, indicates this explanatory power, but maximizing R^2 itself is not the objective, because overfitting often leads to coefficients that fit the data but misstate the actual relation among the variables.

Once analysts have estimated the model's coefficients, they need to check for *theoretical consistency*. Do the estimated coefficients follow the hypothesis? Do the estimated coefficients make substantive sense? In other words, when converted into dollars or some other units, does the relation between a unit change in the independent variable and the corresponding change in the dependent variable make sense?

Finally, a strong model exhibits *predictive power.* This is especially relevant in the litigation context, in which an expert often fits a model to historical data and forecasts future values to represent what would have happened in the but-for world. If the model has weak predictive power, the forecast values will not represent the but-for world. This has importance because the difference between the but-for world forecasts and actual realizations usually drives the measure of damages.

6.9 CHOOSING THE CORRECT SIGNIFICANCE LEVEL

Whether to reject a null hypothesis depends critically on α, the level of significance. This also reflects the probability of committing a Type I error (rejecting a true null hypothesis). A Type II error is that of accepting a false hypothesis. For a given sample size, trying to reduce the possibility of a Type I error by lowering the significance level increases the possibility of a Type II error, and vice versa. In other words, a trade-off exists between these two types of errors. As a result, one must weigh the relative costs of the two types of errors to establish an appropriate trade-off threshold between the possibilities of the two errors.

In a criminal trial, for example, a Type I error is that of convicting an innocent man. Here, the null hypothesis is that the man is not guilty; a Type I error incorrectly rejects the hypothesis and convicts the man. Statistical testing measures the probability of committing this error, according to the chosen level of significance. Conversely, one cannot be certain of the correct conclusion, so the possibility of a Type II error—that of letting a guilty man go free—exists. Diminishing the probability of convicting an innocent man (which could occur by letting almost everybody go) would increase the probability of not convicting a guilty man. Someone's position on the spectrum depends on a preference between letting guilty people go free instead of convicting the innocent or convicting the innocent rather than letting guilty people go without punishment. In general, one can reduce the probability of both types of errors only by increasing sample size.

This tradeoff in statistical testing resembles—but should not be confused with—trade-offs that occur in the judicial system. For instance, civil and criminal litigation have different burdens of proof ("a preponderance of the evidence" compared with "beyond a reasonable doubt"), which could affect the level of significance required in performing hypothesis tests. In the matter of *In re Winship*, Justice Harlan wrote the following:

> The standard of proof influences the relative frequency of these two types of erroneous conclusions. If, for example, the standard of proof for a criminal trial were a preponderance of the evidence rather than proof beyond a reasonable doubt, there would be a smaller risk of factual errors that result in freeing guilty persons, but a far greater risk of factual errors that result in convicting the innocent. Because the standard of proof affects the comparative frequency of these two types of erroneous outcomes, the choice of the standard to be applied in a particular kind of litigation should, in a rational world, reflect an assessment of the comparative social disutility of each.[30]

Justice Harlan went on to say that:

> a preponderance of the evidence standard therefore seems peculiarly inappropriate for, as explained most sensibly, it simply requires the trier of fact "to believe that the existence of a fact is more probable than its nonexistence."[31]

Courts have offered different opinions as to what level of statistical significance establishes that an event is not random (e.g., indicates gender discrimination). Many courts have embraced the 5 percent level as offering prima facie evidence of the relation in question. In *Magistrini v. One Hour Martinizing Dry Cleaning*, the district court wrote that "a study is statistically significant if the *p*-value attributed to that study is less than 0.05."[32] However, in *Vuyanich v. Republic Nat'l. Bank* the district court wrote that "[i]t has become a convention in social science to accept as statistically significant values which have a probability of occurring by chance 5% of the time or less. Speaking purely from a statistical point of view, this does not mean that only results significant at the 5% level should be considered; less significant results may be suggestive."[33]

In testing for statistical significance, the expert must decide whether to perform a one- or two-tailed test. To test the relation between the variables for statistical significance in one direction based on *a priori* expectations (e.g., a decrease in sales volume due to an increase in price), one could use a one-tailed test. A one-tailed test requires a lower threshold *t*-score than a two-tailed test. Courts, however, have generally favored two-tailed tests, which offer a stricter standard, as they call for a higher *t*-score for the same level of significance. For example, in *EEOC v. Federal Reserve Bank of Richmond*, the appellate court wrote that one can report the analysis of data based on two-tailed probability levels without apology, whereas one must almost always "explain away" the use of one-tailed probability levels. Further, "the Court is not persuaded that it is at all proper to use a test such as the 'one-tail' test, which all opinion finds to be skewed in favor of plaintiffs in discrimination cases, especially when the use of all other neutral analyses refutes any inference of discrimination, as in this case."[34]

6.10   STATISTICAL VERSUS PRACTICAL SIGNIFICANCE

Even though statistical significance refers to the probability that a relation exists among the variables in question, practical significance refers to the concept of whether the analysis yields meaningful results, given the data analyzed. For example, in a gender discrimination analysis with a *t*-score of 25.00 on a male gender dummy variable explaining annual salary, the data suggest that, all else being equal, gender likely influences salary. However, a coefficient of 1.20 indicates that firms pay similarly situated men a salary of $1.20 per year more than women. In such a case, statistical significance is high, whereas practical significance is not. Analysts are cautioned against overemphasizing statistical significance, as articulated by the court in *United States v. Test*:

> The mathematical conclusion that the disparity between these two figures is "statistically significant" does not, however, require an a priori finding that these deviations are "legally significant."[35]

6.11 *R*-SQUARED (*R^2*)

R^2 is a summary measure of the goodness of fit of the fitted regression line to a set of data. Formally, R^2 is defined as the ratio of explained sum of squares (variation of estimated Y values about their mean) to total sum of squares (total variation of Y values about their sample mean). R^2 ranges from 0 to 1, where 0 reflects that no variation in the dependent variable is explained by the independent variables and 1 reflects that all of the variation in the dependent variable is explained by the independent variables.

Because of the heuristic simplicity of R^2, it is a widely used measure of the goodness of fit of a least squares model. However, maximizing R^2 itself is not the objective of regression analysis within the context of litigation. R^2 attests to the predictive power of the model within the given sample, but we are interested in more than that. Typically, theoretical consistency of the model (are the estimated coefficients in the hypothesized direction?) and the statistical and substantive significance of the estimated coefficients are more important in shedding insight on the underlying relation of importance in the litigation. Therefore, one should not accept or reject a model based solely on R^2.

Moreover, the addition of variables to a model generally will increase its R^2. But a model with a large number of variables and a higher R^2 does not necessarily provide additional understanding of the relation between the key variables of interest and the dependent variable. (*See* the discussion of adjusted R^2 in Section 5.5(d)(i) of Chapter 5.) Estimated coefficients and their standard errors are more important for this purpose. Further, a model with a large number of variables is harder to interpret. As discussed earlier, parsimony is a desired criterion in model specification, and one should resist the temptation to increase the number of independent variables solely to increase its R^2. One should use theory to drive model specification.

Courts have generally understood the importance of theory and parsimony, as well as the importance of seeing the bigger picture in evaluating an econometric model. In *Reynolds v. Alabama Department of Transportation*, the court wrote that it "need not determine whether a higher R^2 value necessarily means that the result is more accurate to conclude that, on the facts of the case, the defendants' argument is not without merit."[36] Similarly, in *Windy Boy v. County of Big Horn*, the court wrote that "courts should not place too much reliance on R^2 analysis in ruling on the issue of racial polarized voting. Other evidence should be considered."[37] In *Vuyanich v. Republic Nat'l. Bank*, the court wrote that "a high R^2 does not necessarily indicate model quality. For instance, the addition of more explanatory variables to the regression equation can never lower R^2 and is likely to raise it. Thus, one could increase R^2 by simply adding more variables, even though, because of 'over inclusion' and 'multicollinearity,' it may be improper econometrically to do so."[38]

In summary, although one may feel tempted to "overfit" a regression equation to sample data to strengthen statistical diagnostics such as R^2, this practice can pose problems. Before developing an econometric model, one must use sound economic theory to support decisions regarding what data to collect, which variables to include, and what functional form to use in the model.

6.12   CONCLUSION

The use of econometrics as an analytical method requires insight and well-founded decision making to yield maximal value. It can provide a powerful tool for those with the patience and thoroughness, as well as education and training, to examine the data, study the results, and consider the implications. Otherwise, the analysis can provide misleading or statistically invalid results or inaccurate conclusions.

When implemented properly, conclusions based on competent econometric analysis have a compelling logic even for the noneconomist and can often uncover insights that are compelling to clients, judges, and juries.

NOTES

1. There are several excellent introductory textbooks on econometrics. Two such books are: G.S. Maddala, *Introduction to Econometrics*, 2nd ed. (New York: John Wiley & Sons, 1992); Jan Kmenta, *Elements of Econometrics*, 2nd ed. (Ann Arbor: University of Michigan Press, 1997). A good companion book to any econometrics textbook is Peter Kennedy, *A Guide to Econometrics*, 4th ed. (Cambridge, MA: MIT Press, 1998). At a more advanced level, see William H. Greene, *Econometric Analysis*, 5th ed. (Upper Saddle River, NJ: Prentice Hall, 2000); and George G. Judge, W.E. Griffiths, R. Carter Hill, Helmut Lutkepohl, and Tsoung-Chao Lee, *The Theory and Practice of Econometrics*, 2nd ed. (New York: John Wiley & Sons, 1988).

2. *Daubert v. Merrell Dow Pharmaceuticals, Inc.*, 509 U.S. 579, 595 (1993).

3. *See also Frye v. United States*, 293 F. 1013 (D.C. Cir. 1923). In *Kumho Tire v. Patrick Carmichael*, 526 U.S. 137, 147 (1999), the Supreme Court clarified that *Daubert* factors were to be applied to "scientific, technical, and other specialized" experts, which includes economists and financial experts.

4. In state courts, many have adopted a standard similar to that proffered in *Daubert*. In others, the admissibility of expert testimony is governed by the standard set forth in *Frye v. United States*, 293 F.2d 1013 (D.C. Cir. 1923), which requires "general acceptance of the scientific premises on which the testimony is based."

5. Courts both before and after *Daubert* have found other factors relevant in determining whether expert testimony is sufficiently reliable to be considered by the trier of fact. These factors include

   • Whether experts are "proposing to testify about matters growing naturally and directly out of research they have conducted independent of the litigation, or whether they have developed their opinions expressly for purposes of testifying." *Daubert v. Merrell Dow Pharmaceuticals, Inc.*, 43 F.3d 1311, 1317 (9th Cir. 1995).

   • Whether the expert has "unjustifiably extrapolated from an accepted premise to an unfounded conclusion" *See General Elec. Co. v. Joiner*, 522 U.S. 136, 146 (1997) (noting that in some cases a trial court "may conclude that there is simply too great an analytical gap between the data and the opinion proffered").

   • Whether the expert has "adequately accounted for obvious alternative explanations." *See Claar v. Burlington* N.R.R., 29 F.3d 499 (9th Cir. 1994) (testimony excluded where the expert failed to consider other obvious causes for the plaintiff's condition). Compare *Ambrosini v. Labarraque*, 101 F.3d 129 (D.C. Cir. 1996) (the possibility of some uneliminated causes presents a question of weight, so long as the most obvious causes have been considered and reasonably ruled out by expert).

   • Whether the expert "is being as careful as he would be in his regular professional work outside his paid litigation consulting." *Sheehan v. Daily Racing Form, Inc.*, 104 F.3d 940, 942 (7th Cir. 1997). *See Kumho Tire Co. v. Carmichael*, 119 S.Ct. 1167, 1176 (1999) (*Daubert* requires the trial court to assure itself that the expert "employs in the courtroom the same level of intellectual rigor that characterizes the practice of an expert in the relevant field").

- Whether the field of expertise claimed by the experts is "known to reach reliable results for the type of opinion the expert would give." *See Kumho Tire Co. v. Carmichael*, 119 S.Ct. 1167, 1175 (1999) (*Daubert's* general acceptance factor does not "help show that an expert's testimony is reliable where the discipline itself lacks reliability, as, for example, do theories grounded in any so-called generally accepted principles of astrology or necromancy."); *Moore v. Ashland Chemical, Inc.*, 151 F.3d 269 (5th Cir. 1998) (en banc) (clinical doctor was properly precluded from testifying to the toxicological cause of the plaintiff's respiratory problem, where the opinion was not sufficiently grounded in scientific methodology); *Sterling v. Velsicol Chem. Corp.*, 855 F.2d 1188 (6th Cir. 1988) (rejecting testimony based on "clinical ecology" as unfounded and unreliable).

6. *Zenith Electronics Corporation v. WH-TV Broadcasting Corporation* 395 F.3d 416 (2005).

7. *See* the appendix of this chapter, "Case Law Summary on Issues in Econometrics."

8. DPI measures the dollar amount of take-home pay after accounting for taxes. DPI increases as the economy expands and contracts as the economy shrinks. Since DPI forms the basis for personal consumption by consumers, it could influence sales of firms such as Mega Video. However, the direction and magnitude of the relation will likely vary by industry. For instance, some sales tend to positively correlate with the state of the economy. Examples include luxury goods and discretionary goods. Other goods tend to be countercyclical to the state of the economy, thereby doing well when the economy is performing badly and poorly when the economy is strong. Examples could include auto repair shops and pawn shops.

9. Instead of the aggregate model described here, one could use a similar model to estimate retail sales for each store. The latter may be preferable if we are calculating damages for individual stores. A store-by-store model also allows us to consider local competition (from new stores of competitors or cannibalization from new Mega Video franchisees) and local economic factors (which can differ from national economic trends). Furthermore, if the franchisees are involved in class action litigation, the expert can use a store-by-store analysis to evaluate whether the impact of MV*flix* will likely be similar across class members—analysis that could prove useful at the class certification stage of the litigation.

10. In addition to being an industry standard for complex data management and statistical analysis, SAS also has excellent manuals. Especially relevant for the discussion in this chapter are *SAS/STAT* and *SAS/ETS* user guides. *See* www.sas.com for further information.

11. Peter Kennedy, *A Guide to Econometrics*, 4th ed. (Cambridge, MA: MIT Press, 1998), 190.

12. *Estate of Hill v. ConAgra Poultry Co.*, 1997 WL538887 (N.D. Ga. 1997).

13. *Denny v. Westfield State College*, 669 F. Supp. 1146, 1987, U.S. District Court for the District of Massachusetts.

14. T.S. Breusch and A.R. Pagan, "A Simple Test for Heteroscedasticity and Random Coefficient Variation," *Econometrica* 47 (1979): 1287–1294; and H. White, "A Heteroscedasticity-Consistent Covariance Matrix Estimator and a Direct Test for Heteroscedasticity," *Econometrica* 48 (1980): 817–838.

15. William H. Greene, *Econometric Analysis*, 5th ed. (Upper Saddle River, NJ: Prentice Hall, 2000); *see also SAS/ETS User's Guide* for additional discussion of this example. Economists often incorporate the squared version of a variable into the model to capture diminishing returns as a variable's numerical value increases. For instance, one would expect that average school spending increases with increases in per capita state income up to some point but further increases in per capita income do not increase school spending by as much.

16. Luc Anselin, *Spatial Econometrics: Methods and Models* (Dordrecht: Kluwer Academic Publishers, 1988).

17. William H. Greene, *Econometric Analysis*, 5th ed. (Upper Saddle River, NJ: Prentice Hall, 2000); *see also SAS/ETS User's Guide*.

18. *Rossini v. Ogilvy & Mather*, 597 F. Supp. 1120, 1984, U.S. District Court for the Southern District of New York.

19. *Arcata Forest Products v. United States*, 18 Cl. Ct. 93; 1989 U.S. Cl. Ct.

20. *Denny v. Westfield State College*, 669 F. Supp. 1146, 1987, U.S. District Court for the District of Massachusetts.

21. *Estate of Hill v. ConAgra Poultry*, 94-CV-0198-HLM, 1997 U.S. District Court for the Northern District of Georgia.

22. *Bazemore v. Friday*, 478 U.S. 385, 400 (1986); *see also Smith v. Virginia Commonwealth University*, 84 F.3d 672 (4th Cir. 1996).

23. *Bickerstaff v. Vassar College*, 196 F.3d 435, 449–50 (2nd Cir. 1999).

24. *Bazemore v. Friday*, 478 U.S. 385, 400 (1986).

25. *EEOC v. Sears Roebuck*, 628 F. Supp. 1264, 1986, U.S. District Court for Northern District of Illinois.

26. A.K. Bera and C.M. Jarque, "Model Specification Tests: A Simultaneous Approach," *Journal of Econometrics* 20 (1982): 59–82.

27. G.C. Chow, "Tests of Equality Between Sets of Coefficients in Two Linear Regressions," *Econometrica*, 28, 591–605, 1960.

28. *See*, for example, T. Hastie and R. Tibshirani, "Varying-Coefficient Models," *Journal of the Royal Statistical Society*, B 55 (1993): 757–796.

29. *See*, for example, E. E. Leamer, "Let's Take the Con out of Econometrics," *American Economic Review*, 73 (1983): 31–43.

30. *In re Winship*, 397 U.S. 358, 371 (1970).

31. *In re Winship*, 397 U.S. 358, 371 (1970).

32. *Magistrini v. One Hour Martinizing Dry Cleaning*, 180 F. Supp. 2d 584, 2002, U.S. District Court for New Jersey.

33. *Vuyanich v. Republic Nat'l. Bank*, 505 F. Supp. 224, 1980, U.S. District Court for Northern District of Texas.

34. *EEOC v. Federal Reserve Bank of Richmond*, 698 F.2d 633, 1983, U.S. Court of Appeals for the Fourth Circuit.

35. *United States v. Test*, 550 F2d 577, 1976, U.S. Court of Appeals for the Tenth Circuit.

36. *Reynolds v. Alabama Department of Transportation*, 996 F. Supp. 1156, 1998, U.S. District Court for Middle District of Alabama.

37. *Windy Boy v. County of Big Horn*, 647 F. Supp. 1002; 1986 U.S. District Court for Montana.

38. *Vuyanich v. Republic Nat'l. Bank*, 505 F. Supp. 224, 1980, U.S. District Court for Northern District of Texas.

	Case Type	Case Name	Court	Court's Position
Acceptance of Statistics and Regression	Age Discrimination	*Durwood Currier v. United Technology Corp.*	326 F. Supp. 2d 145, 2004, U.S. District Court for the District of Maine	"Statistical analyses are admissible in disparate treatment cases 'unless they are so incomplete as to be inadmissible as irrelevant' (*McMillan v. Mass. Society for the Prevention of Cruelty to Animals*, 140 F.3d 288, 303 (1st Cir. 1998)."
Acceptance of Statistics and Regression	Antitrust	*State of Ohio v. Louis Trauth Dairy, Inc.*	925 F. Supp. 1247, 1996, U.S. District Court for the Southern District of Ohio	"Econometric and regression analyses are generally considered reliable disciplines." The court further noted that defense expert conceded that plaintiff's regression analysis was "testable, generally accepted and reproducible." Moreover, while statistical evidence cannot prove the existence of an agreement, "regression analysis is not unhelpful in determining whether illegal collusion has occurred."
Acceptance of Statistics and Regression	Antitrust	*Norman Law v. NCAA*	94-2053-KHV, 1998, U.S. District Court for the District of Kansas	"The court believes that a jury could find antitrust injury based on [plaintiff's expert's] non-statistical testimony, without considering the data analysis in his final report." "Nowhere does [the defendant's expert witness] testify that accepted economic principles required [the plaintiff's expert] to perform a regression analysis . . . nor does he suggest that the scientific community would condemn [the plaintiff's expert's] . . . failure to perform regression analysis. Furthermore, [the defendant's expert] does not claim that regression analysis is even capable of accounting for variance based on intangible factors such as relationships with head coaches and student athletes, job performances of RECs and reference coaches, and so forth. He does not claim that 'there [is] a standard statistical economic tool for taking a look at such a thing, or that available data permitted such analysis.'"

Appendix: Case Law Summary on Issues in Econometrics

	Case Type	Case Name	Court	Court's Position
Acceptance of Statistics and Regression	Antitrust	*Auley Crouch III v. Crompton Corp.*	02-CVS-4375, 03-CVS-2514, 2004, North Carolina Superior Court, New Hanover County	This case involves a product used in the manufacturing process, and as such a "regression analysis would be required to disaggregate any effect of other changes in the manufacturing process for each manufacturer for each product category. Further regression analyses would be required to disaggregate the impact on price, if any (by product category and by manufacturers), of other influences on the manufacturer's price. As the product moved down the distribution chain into various avenues of distribution, each step would require additional regression studies to disaggregate other impacts on prices until the final price paid by a consumer for different products purchased in different markets is determined."
				At a minimum, "regression analysis addresses supply and demand factors by looking at price trends over time. A prudent economist must account for these differences and would perform a minimum regression analysis if utilizing the 'before and after' model."
				"The price of tires may be affected by external factors such as high gas prices, which could lower demand. Each variation in manufacturer's process, price, size, quality, market, distribution method and changes in applicable externalities requires individual supply and demand analysis and may require multiple regression analyses in order to eliminate the speculative nature of any damage calculation. Given the many variables, the issues surrounding allocation of the alleged price fixing fund in this case would be exceptionally complex and the results of economic analysis speculative."

Appendix: Case Law Summary on Issues in Econometrics (Continued)

	Case Type	Case Name	Court	Court's Position
Acceptance of Statistics and Regression	Antitrust	*Piggly Wiggly Clarksville v. Interstate Brands*	100 Fed. Appx. 296, 2004, U.S. Court of Appeals for the 5th Circuit	The district court "did not believe given the numerous independent factors that go into both the price that should have been paid and the price that was actually paid, that there could be any general formula for calculating damages with precision, amounting to more than speculation, without requiring some degree of inquiry into the individual facts of 52,000 plaintiffs and potentially thousands of transactions. Given the unique nature of the individual transactions, the court concludes that it is not reasonable to assume that a generalized formula can be created."
Acceptance of Statistics and Regression	Appraisal of Shares	*Cede Co. v. Technicolor*	Civil Action No. 7129, 2003 Del. Ch., Court of Chancery of Delaware, New Castle	Several federal cases recognized that "regression analysis is a well-recognized statistical technique that has met with widespread judicial acceptance." However, "a statistical technique is very different from a valuation technique. With one exception, all the cases that … use regression analyses merely to demonstrate a connection between the dependent and independent variables (a statistical technique), not to forecast costs, revenues, or profits (a valuation technique)."
				For "regression analysis to be an appropriate tool for forecasting economic relationships, the analysis must be based on a mature business with stable economic relationships. Further, there should be a significant relationship between the dependent (factor) and independent (response) variables throughout the historical period from which the regression is derived. It should also be reasonable and expected that this relationship will continue throughout the forecast period."
				Scholars of regression analysis have said, "it is not advisable to use an estimated regression relationship for extrapolation. That is, the estimated model should not be used to make inferences on values of the dependent variable beyond the range of observed x-values. Such extrapolation is dangerous, because although the model may fit the data quite well, there is no evidence that the model is appropriate outside the range of the existing data."

Appendix: Case Law Summary on Issues in Econometrics (Continued)

	Case Type	Case Name	Court	Court's Position
Acceptance of Statistics and Regression	Breach of Contract	*Lifewise Master Funding v. Telebank*	374 F. 3d 917, 2004, U.S. Court of Appeals for the 11th Circuit	The district court "rejected LifeWise's damages model, which was based on regression analysis, because they were found to be deficient under Rules 403 and 702."
Acceptance of Statistics and Regression	Breach of Contract	*Zenith Electronics Corp. v. WH-TV Broadcasting Corp.*	395 F. 3d 416; 2005 U.S. App. LEXIS 1022; 66 Fed R. Evid. Serv. (Callaghan) 345, U.S. Court of Appeals for the 7th Circuit	"The supposed 'uniqueness' of a market does not justify substituting a guess for careful analysis. Cities differ in size, average income, levels of education, availability of over-the-air TV signals, and other factors that might affect the demand for multipoint multichannel digital system (MMDS) service. But social science has tools to isolate the effects of multiple variables and determine how they influence one dependent variable—here, sales of MMDS service. Perhaps the leading tool is the multivariate regression, which is used extensively by all social sciences. Regression analysis is common enough in litigation to earn extended treatment in the Federal Judicial Center's Reference Manual on Scientific Evidence (2d ed. 2000). Regression has its own chapter (Reference Guide on Multiple Regression, prepared by Daniel L. Rubinfeld, at Reference Manual 179–228) and plays a leading role in two more: David H. Kaye & David A. Freedman, Reference Guide on Statistics, at Reference Manual 83–178, and Robert E. Hall & Victoria A. Lazear, Reference Guide on Estimation of Economic Losses in Damages Awards, at Reference Manual 277–332. [WH-TV's expert] Shapiro neither employed any of the methods covered in the Reference Manual nor explained why he hadn't."
Acceptance of Statistics and Regression	Civil Antitrust	*Weisfeld v. Sun Chemical*	84 Fed. Appx. 257, 2004, U.S. Court of Appeals for the 3rd Circuit	The "expert planned to use two approaches, multiple regression and yardstick analysis, as common proof that the 'no hire' agreements artificially depressed the compensation levels of class members. The District Court stated that it was 'not convinced' that Weisfeld's expert 'will be able to prove impact on a classwide basis.'" The District Court "found that Weisfeld's expert provided only 'naked conclusions' that common proof would demonstrate injury to class members."

Appendix: Case Law Summary on Issues in Econometrics (Continued)

	Case Type	Case Name	Court	Court's Position
Acceptance of Statistics and Regression	Copyright Infringement	*Estate of Vane v. The Fair, Inc.*	849 F. 2d 186, 189, 1989, U.S. Court of Appeals for the 5th Circuit	The appeals court upheld the district court's finding that the expert's testimony was speculative regarding how much of the profits of the defendant were to be apportioned to the use of infringing copyrighted photos in television commercials. The regression model had apportioned profits to the entire advertisement, but not to its component pieces (e.g., noninfringing photos, the logo and other parts of the commercials). As a result, the use of a regression in apportionment was not found to be inappropriate—it was that the regression had not been designed to determine the value contributed by only the infringing material.
Acceptance of Statistics and Regression	State-law fraud and Breach of Contract	*Lucius Adkins v. Cagle Foods*	411 F. 3d 1320, 2005, U.S. Court of Appeals for the 11th Circuit	The district judge "gave little attention to the statistical regression analysis presented by Plaintiff as the regression analysis cannot establish a causal link."
Acceptance of Statistics and Regression	Gender Discrimination Title VII	*Chang v. University of Rhode Island*	606 F. Supp. 1161, 1985, U.S. District Court for the District of Rhode Island	"Although statistical analyses serve an important role in employment discrimination cases, they are neither irrefutable nor necessarily definitive." The court must "deal with probativeness, not with perfection."
Acceptance of Statistics and Regression	Gender Discrimination Title VII	*EEOC v. Sears Roebuck*	628 F. Supp. 1264, 1986, U.S. District Court for the Northern District of Illinois	"Statistical evidence, like other evidence, must not be accepted uncritically. The usefulness of statistics depends, to a large extent, on the 'existence of proper supportive facts and the absence of variables which would undermine the reasonableness of the inference of discrimination which is drawn.' *White v. City of San Diego*, 605 F.2d 455."
				"Courts must carefully evaluate all the assumptions and data underlying the statistical analyses to determine whether they are sufficiently related to reality to provide any useful information to the court."
				"Statistical significance and practical significance are two completely different concepts. Statistical significance can be determined merely by calculating the standard deviation or some other test statistic. To determine the practical significance of statistical results, a court must look at the theories and assumptions underlying the analysis and apply common sense."

Appendix: Case Law Summary on Issues in Econometrics (Continued)

	Case Type	Case Name	Court	Court's Position
Acceptance of Statistics and Regression	Gender Discrimination Title VII	*Palmer v. Schultz*	815 F. 2d 84 (D.C. Cir 1987)	"A statistical analysis of a disparity in selection rates can reveal the probability that the disparity is merely a random deviation from perfectly equal selection rates. Statistics, however, cannot entirely rule out the possibility that chance caused disparity. Nor can statistics determine, if chance is an unlikely explanation, whether the more probable cause was intentional discrimination or a legitimate nondiscriminatory factor in the selection process."
Acceptance of Statistics and Regression	Gender Discrimination Title VII	*Dolphine Olda v. State of Washington*	111 Wn. App. 79; 44 P. 3d 8; 2002, Court of Appeals of Washington, Division One	"The 'inherently slippery nature' of statistical evidence has caused many courts to be cautious about allowing the necessary inference of a discriminatory motive to arise solely from disparities shown by a statistical model." Thus, the Supreme Court has said that "an individual plaintiff can support a disparate treatment case with statistics, but cannot establish a *prima facie* case of disparate treatment with statistics. If a plaintiff presents only the circumstantial evidence of statistics in lieu of all other proof of discriminatory intent, the case ordinarily becomes a case of disparate impact, not disparate treatment." The district court noted, "statistical evidence necessarily ignores the peculiar, particular facts of individual cases. Statistical evidence is simply the overall effect of individual cases viewed in the aggregate. Because statistical evidence may both illuminate and distort reality, a court relying on such evidence must constantly look from the statistics to the factual realities in order to gauge the probative value of the statistics."
Acceptance of Statistics and Regression	Gender Discrimination Title VII	*Deborah Cullen v. Indiana University Board of Trustees*	338 F. 3d 693, 2003, U.S. Court of Appeals for the 7th Circuit	In Title VII cases, "statistical evidence of discrimination may be very useful, but 'it will likely not be sufficient in itself.'"

Appendix: Case Law Summary on Issues in Econometrics (Continued)

Case Type	Case Name	Court	Court's Position
Acceptance of Statistics and Regression	*Trout v. Secretary of Navy and Commanding Officer*	354 U.S. App. D.C. 384; 317 F. 3d 286; 2003, U.S. Court of Appeals for the District of Columbia	The district court "accepted the regression analysis demonstrating sex discrimination in the Navy's hiring, promotion, evaluation, and assignment of women. The court also accepted the findings that the Trout class's regression analysis should be used to determine the amount of backpay."
Acceptance of Statistics and Regression	*Betty Dukes v. Wal-Mart Stores, Inc.*	222 F.R.D. 137, 2004, U.S. District Court for the Northern District of California	Both parties rely on their regression analysis. They agree that "regression analysis is an appropriate and scientifically valid statistical technique which has gained general acceptance, indeed a general preference, by the courts." The court "recognized that even with the serious flaws infecting plaintiffs' regression analysis, it would have been improper to exclude it from evidence."
Acceptance of Statistics and Regression	*Lava Trading, Inc. v. Hartford Fire Insurance Company*	03 Civ. 7037 (PKC) (MHD), 2005, U.S. District Court for the Southern District of New York	An "expert who seeks to estimate 'but for' sales cannot rely on his 'industry expertise' or its equivalent as a substitute for a methodology that looks to specific data and proceeds to make statistically or scientifically valid inferences from the data. The witness must look to comparable markets, and if they differ from the market for which he is offering predictions, he must utilize professionally accepted methods of making comparisons—even of 'unique' markets—that will take into account the uniqueness of the comparators. Availability of multi-variate regression analysis is one tool for permitting such comparisons."
Acceptance of Statistics and Regression	*Johnson Elec. N. AM v. Mabuchi Motor Am. Corp.*	88 Civ. 733, 2000, U.S. District Court for the Southern District of New York	"Numerous courts have held that regression analysis is a reliable method for determining damages and a 'mainstream tool in economic study.'"
Acceptance of Statistics and Regression	*SPX Corp., Petitioner v. County of Steele*	File No. C1-00-350, 2003, Minnesota Tax Court, County of Steele, 3rd Judicial District, Regular Division	The Tax Court has not accepted the use of a multiple regression analysis, and a "multiple regression analysis is not widely accepted within the appraisal community."

Appendix: Case Law Summary on Issues in Econometrics (Continued)

	Case Type	Case Name	Court	Court's Position
Acceptance of Statistics and Regression	Racial and Gender Discrimination Title VII	*Vuyanich v. Republic National Bank*	505 F. Supp.224, 1980, U.S. District Court for the Northern District of Texas	"A measure of statistical significance ... provides a basis for inferring whether there is, in fact, some disparity in results for the minority and majority groups." "Practical significance, in contrast, refers to the magnitude of the disparity between the results for the two groups." "It has been argued that no model in the social sciences ever meets the requirements for the perfect regression analysis. But this does not mean that because a model is subject to challenge, its results are valueless. Small departures from assumptions necessary for a perfect regression may have small deleterious effects. The value of a regression would obviously be affected by problems in the underlying data or by mismeasurements of the explanatory variables."
Acceptance of Statistics and Regression	Racial Discrimination Title VII	*Hazelwood v. United States*	433 U.S. 299, 1977, 97 Supreme Court	"Statistics, when properly authenticated, constitute an accepted form of circumstantial evidence of discrimination and may sometimes be sufficient to establish, without more, *prima facie* proof of discrimination."
Acceptance of Statistics and Regression	Racial Discrimination Title VII	*Boykin v. Georgia Pacific*	706 F. 2d 1384, 1983, U.S. Court of Appeals for 5th Circuit	"Validity of statistical proof as means of proving a *prima facie* Title VII case has long been" accepted by the courts.
Acceptance of Statistics and Regression	Racial Discrimination Title VII	*EEOC v. Federal Reserve Bank of Richmond*	698 F. 2d, 633, 1983 U.S. Court of Appeals for 4th Circuit	"Statistics, when properly authenticated, constitute an accepted form of circumstantial evidence of discrimination and may sometimes be sufficient to establish, without more, *prima facie* proof of discrimination."
Acceptance of Statistics and Regression	Racial Discrimination Title VII	*McCleskey v. Kemp*	481 U.S. 279, 1987, 107 Supreme Court	The Supreme Court "has accepted statistics in the form of multiple-regression analysis to prove statutory violation under title VII of the Civil Rights Act of 1964."

Appendix: Case Law Summary on Issues in Econometrics (Continued)

Case Type	Case Name	Court	Court's Position
Acceptance of Statistics and Regression	Racial Discrimination Title VII	RE: Proportionality Review Project (II)	165 N.J. 206; 757 A.2d 168; 2000, Supreme Court of New Jersey	"Creating reliable multiple regression models has been the biggest challenge in systemic proportionality review." But "when properly designed, a series of multiple regressions can be a valuable technique for measuring whether race affects the death-penalty system in this state. Moreover, multiple regression techniques have an advantage not shared by bivariate techniques: multiple regressions control for other factors and therefore isolate the effects of race on capital sentencing."
Acceptance of Statistics and Regression	Racial Discrimination Title VII	Concrete Works v. City and County of Denver	321 F. 3d 950, 2003, U.S. Court of Appeals for the 10th Circuit	The Supreme Court stated that the "inference of discriminatory exclusion can arise from statistical disparities. Accordingly, Denver can meet its burden through the introduction of statistical and anecdotal evidence alone."
Acceptance of Statistics and Regression	Securities Fraud	In re Oracle Securities Litigation	829 F. Supp. 1176, 1993, U.S. District Court for the Northern District of California	"Use of an event study or similar analysis is necessary [to] more accurately isolate the influences of information specific to Oracle which defendants allegedly have distorted."
Acceptance of Statistics and Regression	Securities Fraud	Joe Miller v. Asensio & Co.	364 F. 3d 223; 2004, U.S. Court of Appeals for the 4th Circuit	"An event analysis is often required to support an expert's damages calculation and generally involves the computation of a statistical regression analysis or, at minimum, the compilation of a detailed analysis of each particular event that might have influenced the stock price."
Acceptance of Statistics and Regression	Securities Fraud	Oscar Private Equity Investments v. Royce Holland and Anthony Parella	Civil No. 3:03-CV-2761-H, 2005, U.S. District Court for the Northern District of Texas, Dallas Division	The plaintiffs "provided the report of an expert who conducted a regression analysis to determine statistically significant stock movements. Although Defendants argue that the stock was highly volatile, [plaintiff's] regression analysis incorporates an analysis of stock volatility with statistical support. Defendants' general qualitative assertions and minute-by-minute and general stock price trend analyses regarding the volatility of Allegiance stock do little to undermine [plaintiff's] analysis, which identified statistically significant stock price movements, despite the volatility of Allegiance stock ... The Court is satisfied with the confidence levels in the expert report and notes that despite a general decline of Allegiance stock prices during the putative Class Period, Allegiance stock may still have been artificially inflated by the alleged misrepresentations."

Appendix: Case Law Summary on Issues in Econometrics (Continued)

	Case Type	Case Name	Court	Court's Position
Acceptance of Statistics and Regression	Valuation Analysis of Merger	*Tracinda Corp. v. DaimlerChrysler AG*	364 F. Supp. 2d 362 (D. Del. 2005)	"Defendants contend that [plaintiff's expert, Dr. Silber's] methodology of using the allocation of board seats to determine the appropriate premium to be paid violates the basic statistical principle that correlation is not tantamount to causation and ignores other factors that go into the negotiation of a premium in a business combination. Defendants contend that Silber's methodology is demonstrably unreliable, because it failed to accurately predict the premiums paid in sample transactions to which his methodology is applied. Defendants also point out that Silber himself testified that his model could only predict a premium within 20% of the actual premium and that it could only be that accurate two-thirds of the time, meaning that one-third of the time actual results would vary by more than 20% from a predication made based on Silber's model." The court concluded that the plaintiff's expert testimony is admissible because the "methodology and analysis used by Silber is a standard regression analysis that has been used by other academic studies."
Acceptance of Statistics and Regression	Voting Discrimination	*State of Georgia v. Ashcroft*	195 F. Supp. 2d 25, 2002, U.S. District Court for the District of Columbia	"The Supreme Court has relied on regression analysis to assess the severity of racial bloc voting and whether existing voting patterns would prohibit a minority population from electing candidates of choice. This regression analysis is also referred to as 'ecological inference' methodology, and allows political scientists to infer voting behavior from aggregate information."
Dummy Variables	Racial and Gender Discrimination Title VII	*Vuyanich v. Republic National Bank*	505 F. Supp. 224, 1980 U.S. District Court for the Northern District of Texas	"The weighting on the dummy variable would not be as readily interpretable as a weighting on a more usual type of explaining characteristic, but the question of the overall effect of the characteristic represented by the dummy variable could be answered.

Appendix: Case Law Summary on Issues in Econometrics (Continued)

	Case Type	Case Name	Court	Court's Position
Durbin-Watson	Contract Dispute	*Arcata Forest Products v. The U.S.*	18 Cl. Ct. 93, 1989 U.S. Claims Court	Plaintiff's expert conducted a linear regression analysis of the relationship between two price indices. The plaintiff's expert "testified that the Durbin-Watson statistic of 0.194 meant that [his model] would consistently over or under predict the North Coast prices." He then concluded that the "high degree of serial correlation would lead [him] to believe that [his model] does not capture the underlying relationship between these two indices. They do not move together."
Evolving Model	Antitrust	*In re Polypropylene Carpet Antitrust*	93 F. Supp. 2d 1348, 2000, U.S. District Court for the Northern District of Georgia	"The fact that plaintiff's regression model has evolved since the class certification stage raises no serious issue so long as the model satisfies plaintiff's burden under Rule 23." The court stated that "sound econometric practice requires the identification of potential independent variables 'before any empirical testing of the appropriate-ness of potential independent variables'."
Heteroscedasticity	Gender Discrimination Title VII	*Denny v. Westfield State College*	669 F. Supp. 1146, 1987, U.S. District Court for the District of Massachusetts	Plaintiff's expert admitted that heteroscedasticity was probably present to some degree, but suggested that its effect was not significant. The court "does not find that the possible presence of heteroscedasticity itself detracts from the validity of plaintiff's study."
Heteroscedasticity	Weighing Poultry	*Estate of Bud Hill v. ConAgra Poultry*	94-CV-0198-HLM, 1997, U.S. District Court for the Northern District of Georgia	Plaintiff's expert agrees that "his regression model contains heteroscedastic disturbances, and that he did not correct these disturbances before reaching the conclusions in his report." He cites two reasons for this: (1) to "compute t-statis-tics for forumulas that are based on very large sample sizes, a regression analysis may use an estimate of the standard errors for its coefficients in lieu of the classic least squares estimates for these coefficients. This procedure eliminates the need to correct for heteroscedasticity; (2) the "disturbance creating the heteroscedasticity varies systematically." "Defendants point to no evidence that contradicts [the plaintiff's expert's] asser-tions. Plus, the Court "is aware of several studies that have been admitted into evidence or published in journals in spite of the presence of heteroscedasticity in regression formulas."

Appendix: Case Law Summary on Issues in Econometrics (Continued)

	Case Type	Case Name	Court	Court's Position
Logit	Age Discrimination Title VII	Csicseri v. Bowsher	862 F. Supp. 547 D.C., 1994, U.S. District Court for the District of Columbia	The defendant's expert used the logit model, which "increased the predictive power of her tests between 2% and 6% for each factor considered, and it increased the predictive power up to 50% when all factors are taken out of the model. Using this logit model, her successful prediction rate was between 67% or 68% and 75%."
Logit	Gender Discrimination Title VII	Craik v. Minnesota State University Board	731 F. 2d 465, 1984, U.S. Court of Appeals for the 8th Circuit	The court's decision "is not based on any holding that multiple linear regression or logistic regression fitting analysis is superior to the other as matter of law. They are simply two different ways of analyzing facts, and they may or may not be persuasive in any given case."
Logit	Patent Infringement	Polaroid v. Eastman Kodak	17 USPQ2d 1711, 1990, U.S. District Court for the District of Massachusetts	Defendant expert used a "nested logit model, which was found to be rejectable because it ran contrary to findings about the crucial influences on the demand for instant photography."
Multicollinearity	Gender Discrimination Title VII	Craik v. Minnesota State University Board	731 F. 2d 465, 1984, U.S. Court of Appeals for the 8th Circuit	"If two variables are correlated (because they are determined by or measure the same thing), inclusion of either one will be sufficient to capture the entire effect of their joint variation, but inclusion of both will decrease the coefficient that each would have independently, by splitting up the effects of their variation between them ... In a properly designed regression model, therefore, the independent variables must be independent of each other. Choosing the proper independent variables is therefore critical to the success of a regression model."
Multicollinearity	Gender Discrimination Title VII	Chang v. University of Rhode Island	606 F. Supp. 1161, 1985, U.S. District Court for the District of Rhode Island	Plaintiff "used two variables, years since degree and prior experience, which are arguably correlated with each other. That is, the value of years of prior experience will change, at least to some extent, with the years since degree ... While less multicollinearity is better than more, the problem is not severe."

Appendix: Case Law Summary on Issues in Econometrics (Continued)

	Case Type	Case Name	Court	Court's Position
Multicollinearity	Gender Discrimination Title VII	*Denny v. Westfield State College*	669 F. Supp. 1146, 1987, U.S. District Court for the District of Massachusetts	"From the evidence presented, the Court accepts the testimony of Dr. Ash that the presence of multicollinearity would merely tend to overestimate the amount of error associated with the estimate of difference in salary by sex. In other words, p-values will be artificially higher than they would be if there were no multi-collinearity present. Thus, the presence of multicollinearity means that results found to be significant in the analysis are likely to be even more significant than they appear."
				Because plaintiff's expert's results "demonstrated statistical significance of each year studied except one, the Court does not find that the presence of multicollinearity detracts from the validity of her findings."
Outliers	Antitrust	*In re Polypropylene Carpet Antitrust*	93 F. Supp. 2d 1348, 2000, U.S. District Court for the Northern District of Georgia	The court noted that "exclusion of outliers is a common practice in statistical analysis."
Probit	Racial Discrimination Title VII	*Green v. United States Steel Corp.*	570 F. Supp. 254, 1983, U.S. District Court for the District of Pennsylvania	Defense expert "admitted that USS' applications file was incomplete and that the weighting and validity of his entire probit analysis were affected by the incompleteness of his data source."
Probit	Voting Discrimination	*State of Georgia v. Ashcroft*	195 F. Supp. 2d 25, 2002, U.S. District for the District of Columbia	"While it appears true that probit analysis is a standard statistical technique, no court has relied on such an analysis in reviewing a reapportionment plan." "We do not suggest that a probit analysis may never be a valuable tool, but merely that the one offered by the State in this case is entirely inadequate to that task."

Appendix: Case Law Summary on Issues in Econometrics (Continued)

Case Type	Case Name	Court	Court's Position
R^2	Gender Discrimination Title VII	*Valentino v. United States Postal Service*	511 F. Supp. 917, 1981, U.S. District Court for the District of Columbia.	Plaintiff's expert admitted that his regression did not take into account many factors which would logically affect an employee's salary and obtained an R^2 of 0.284. However, "this is not a case in which a low R^2 can be excused on the theory that the plaintiff has 'included all seemingly relevant factors identified through discovery' and thereby passed the burden to the defendant to bring forward additional bona fide qualifications." Defendant's expert contended that a "desirable R^2 for complex phenomenon such as salaries would be 0.9." Defendant's expert measured a model with more variables that yielded an R^2 of 0.882. The court found in favor of defendant.
R^2	Racial Discrimination Title VII	*Vuyanich v. Republic National Bank*	505 F. Supp. 224, 1980, U.S. District Court for the Northern District of Texas	"The higher the R^2 the greater the association between movements in the dependent and independent variables. There are problems, however, associated with the use of R^2. A high R^2 does not necessarily indicate model quality. For instance, the addition of more explanatory variables to the regression equation can never lower R^2 and is likely to raise it. Thus one could increase R^2 by simply adding more variables, even though, because of 'over inclusion' and 'multicollinearity' it may be improper econometrically to do so."
R^2	Racial Discrimination Title VII	*McCleskey v. Kemp*	481 U.S. 279, 1987, 107 Supreme Court	The district court "noted the inability of any of the models to predict the outcome of actual cases." The "R^2 value of Baldus's most complex model; the 230-variable model, was between 0.46 and 0.48. Thus, as the court explained, 'the 230-variable model does not predict the outcome in half of the cases.'"
R^2	Racial Discrimination Title VII	*Reynolds v. Alabama Dept. of Transportation*	996 F. Supp. 1156, 1998, U.S. District Court for the Middle District of Alabama	"The court need not determine whether a higher R^2 value necessarily means that the result is more accurate to conclude that, on the faces of this case, the defendants' argument is without merit. ... Further, because the defendants admit that it is possible that simply reducing the number of people in the cohort group could increase the R^2 value, good statistical practice does not necessarily support their position."

Appendix: Case Law Summary on Issues in Econometrics (Continued)

	Case Type	Case Name	Court	Court's Position
R^2	Racial Polarized Voting	*Windy Boy v. County of Big Horn*	647 F. Supp. 1002, 1986, U.S. District Court for the District of Montana, Billings Division	Plaintiff's expert conducted a "bivariate regression analysis (computing R^2 coefficients) which he used to determine whether there was a correlation between the number of Indian voters in a precinct and the number of votes for Indian candidates." His studies concluded that 93.2%, 91.5%, 96.7%, 90.9%, 87.4% and 98.7% of the variation could be explained by a number of factors. "Clearly there is a strong correlation between the race of the voter and the race of the candidate for which that voter votes. Indians generally vote for Indian candidates and whites for white candidates." "There was no statistical analysis by defendants, computing correlation by *r*-squared values or by any other technique, to prove either that the correlation between race of voter and race of candidate did not exist, or that some other factor (e.g. income or party affiliation) could better explain the pattern of voting." The "court does not believe the findings of the [plaintiff's expert] study alone are sufficient evidence on which to base a finding of racial polarized voting. Courts should not place too much reliance on *r*-squared analysis, such as that done by [the plaintiff's expert], in ruling on the issue of racially polarized voting. Other evidence should also be examined."
Relevant Range and Sample Size	Appraisal of Shares	*Cede Co. v. Technicolor*	Civil Action No. 7129, 2003 Del. Ch., Court of Chancery of Delaware, New Castle	"If it can be shown that the regression analyses are more reasonable and accurate, it may still be appropriate to use them for determining the inputs to the DCF framework."
Relevant Range and Sample Size	Racial Discrimination Title VII	*Ronald Obrey v. Hansford Johnson*	400 F. 3d 691, 2005, U.S. Court of Appeals for the 9th Circuit	"Considerations such as small sample size may, of course, detract from the value of such evidence, and evidence showing that the figures for the general population might not accurately reflect the pool of qualified job applicants would also be relevant."

Appendix: Case Law Summary on Issues in Econometrics (Continued)

	Case Type	Case Name	Court	Court's Position
Serial Correlation & Autocorrelation	Gender Discrimination Title VII	*Rossini v. Ogilvy & Mather*	597 F. Supp. 1120, 1984, U.S. District Court for the Southern District of New York	Plaintiff's expert's regression analysis "systematically overestimates the statistical significance of the regression coefficients and makes the statistical significance of the differences between the salaries of males and females appear larger than should be the case." Court dismissed most individual claims raised by named plaintiffs; and reserved decision on salary claims of the class and one named plaintiff.
Statistical Significance	Age and Gender Discrimination	*Rhonda Thomas v. Deloitte Consulting*	NO. 3-02-CV-0343-M, 2004, U.S. District Court for the Northern District of Texas, Dallas Division	"Most courts have rejected the arbitrary application of a 5% threshold. 'Whether a given [test result] should be regarded as statistically significant must be determined on a case by case basis since the value signifying statistical significance is dependent upon sample size. It is for the judge to say, on the basis of the evidence of a trained statistician, whether a particular significance level, in the context of a particular study in a particular case, is too low to make the study worth the consideration of judge or jury.'" "Daubert instructs that a court should consider the known or potential rate of error when assessing the scientific validity or reliability of expert testimony. The court is unaware of any employment case where the jury was allowed to consider statistical evidence of discrimination that approached the 10% level used" by the plaintiff's expert. "Given the relatively small sample size used by [the plaintiff's expert] the court has little difficulty in concluding that a statistical deviation of 7% to 10% does not adequately rule out that the alleged disparities identified in her report were due to chance." Therefore, the plaintiff's expert "will not be permitted to offer testimony regarding the results of her statistical analysis."

Appendix: Case Law Summary on Issues in Econometrics (Continued)

Case Type	Case Name	Court	Court's Position
Statistical Significance	*EEOC v. Sears Roebuck*	628 F. Supp. 1264, 1986, U.S. District Court for the Northern District of Illinois	This court will "generally consider that differences between actual and expected values that exceed three standard deviations may be statistically significant. However, it is important to emphasize that the standard deviation and other measures of statistical significance merely attempt to eliminate chance as the reason for the results. They do not prove what in fact caused the results." The Supreme Court "has not laid down any hard and fast rules for evaluating statistical or practical significance in every case, and the Court's 'two or three' standard deviation approach should be applied with caution."
Statistical Significance	*Ottaviani v. SUNY*	875 F. 2d 365, 1989, U.S. Court of Appeals for the 2nd Circuit	A finding of two standard deviations in statistical studies on salaries is not, as a matter of law, *prima facie* proof of discrimination." "When the results of a statistical analysis yield levels of statistical significance at or below the 0.05 level, chance explanations for a disparity become suspect, and most statisticians will begin to question the assumptions underlying their predictions." "Courts should use tests of statistical significance only as 'an aid to interpretation' and not as 'a rule of law.'"
Statistical Significance	*Castaneda v. Partida*	430 U.S. 482, 1977, 97 Supreme Court 1272	"As a general rule for large samples, if the difference between the expected value and the observed number is greater than two or three standard deviations, then the hypothesis that the jury drawing was random would be suspect to a social scientist."
Statistical Significance	*Vuyanich v. Republic National Bank*	505 F. Supp. 224, 1980, U.S. District Court for the Northern District of Texas	"It has become a convention in social science to accept as statistically significant values which have a probability of occurring by chance 5% of the time or less.... Speaking purely from a statistical point of view, this does not mean that only significant results may be suggestive." "Considering that arbitrary nature of the adoption of the 5% level of significance, it is not surprising that courts show flexibility in determining what level of significance to be required in a legal context."

Appendix: Case Law Summary on Issues in Econometrics (Continued)

Case Type	Case Name	Court	Court's Position
Statistical Significance Racial Discrimination Title VII	*Lewis v. Bloomsberg Mills*	773 F. 2d 561, 1985, U.S. Court of Appeals for the 4th Circuit	Statistical "hiring rate of black women was in the range of 5-8 standard deviations below the 'expected' level. Unchallenged expert opinion testimony established that such a disparity was statistically significant."
Statistical Significance Racial Discrimination Title VII	*EEOC v. Federal Reserve Bank of Richmond*	698 F. 2d, 633, 1983, U.S. Court of Appeals for the 4th Circuit	"An easily avoided problem is the treatment of the test of statistical significance as a rule of a law rather than as an aid to interpretation." "A test of significance is treated as a rule of law when the court asks whether the observed disparity is statistically significant at the 0.05 level or whether it satisfies the two or three standard deviations rule. If the answer is yes, the *prima facie* case is established or the evidence is credited. If the answer is no, the *prima facie* case fails or the evidence is discredited." "The Supreme Court itself, though disclaiming any intention 'to suggest that precise calculations of statistical significance are necessary in employing statistical proof,' has stated that standard deviations of more than 'two or three' represent a minimum for statistical significance. From all this, we conclude that courts of law should be extremely cautious in drawing any conclusions from standard deviations in the range of one to three (*Equal Employment Opportunity Com'n v. Am. Nat. Bank*, 652 F.2d at 1192)." "Above this range, with standard deviations of more than three, the analysis may perhaps safely be used absolutely to exclude chance as a hypothesis, hence absolutely to confirm the legitimacy of any inference of discrimination."
Statistical Significance Racial Discrimination Title VII	*Reynolds v. Alabama Dept. of Transportation*	996 F. Supp. 1156, 1998, U.S. District Court for the Middle District of Alabama	"The court can be convinced to a 95% degree of certainty that the average black salary is actually higher than the average white salary, and that this difference is not due to chance. At this degree of confidence, the court can be certain that, despite the defendants' class-wide discrimination, the members of that particular cohort group did not suffer economic harm because of the discrimination." The parties have agreed that the "difference must be statistically significant, and a difference of 1.65 standard deviations is sufficiently statistically significant."

Appendix: Case Law Summary on Issues in Econometrics (Continued)

	Case Type	Case Name	Court	Court's Position
Statistical Significance	Racial Discrimination Title VII	Guerrero v. Reno	98 864, 2000, U.S. District Court for the Northern District of Illinois	"The larger the number of standard deviations, the less likely it is that a disparity is attributable to chance." To demonstrate a statistically significant disparity, one must have a disparity of at least two standard deviations.
Two-tailed Test	Age Discrimination Title VII	Csicseri v. Bowsher	862 F. Supp. 547 D.C., 1994, U.S. District Court for the District of Columbia	Plaintiff's expert "used a one-tail test in drawing his conclusions, when a two-tailed test is generally preferred in this circuit."
Two-tailed Test	Gender Discrimination Title VII	Palmer v. Schultz	815 F. 2d 84 (D.C. Cir. 1987)	Generally (in the District of Columbia), "two-tailed tests are more appropriate in Title VII cases.... the hypothesis to be tested in any disparate treatment claim should generally be that the selection process treated men and women equally, not that the selection process treated women at least as well as or better than men."
Two-tailed Test	Racial Discrimination Title VII	EEOC v. Federal Reserve Bank of Richmond	698 F. 2d 633, 1983, U.S. Court of Appeals for the 4th Circuit	"Analysis of data bases on two-tailed probability levels can be reported without apology, while it is almost always necessary to 'explain away' the use of one-tailed probability levels." The court is "not persuaded that it is at all proper to use a test such as the 'one-tail' test, which all opinion finds to be skewed in favor of plaintiffs in discrimination cases, especially when the use of all other neutral analyses refutes any inference of discrimination, as in this case." "Both the District Court and the plaintiff's expert recognized that the 'one-tail' test is a dramatically stricter standard for statistical significance than the 'two-tail' test. ... A commentator has made the same observation about the 'one-tail' test, describing it as 'data mining' which is the statistician's term for manipulating data to prove a desired result."
Variables— Inclusion and Definition	Age Discrimination Title VII	Csicseri v. Bowsher	862 F. Supp. 547 D.C., 1994, U.S. District Court for the District of Columbia	The selection of variables should be accurate and valid. "It is crucial to know which variables are used as they can have profound effect on the final result." "Under regression models, there is a danger that the variables will be chosen in order to influence the outcome or that the inclusion of a particular variable may be inherently invalid."

Appendix: Case Law Summary on Issues in Econometrics (Continued)

Case Type	Case Name	Court	Court's Position
Variables—Inclusion and Definition	Antitrust	*In re Polypropylene Carpet Antitrust Litigation*	93 F. Supp. 2d 1348, 2000, U.S. District Court for the Northern District of Georgia	"Unless the party challenging a regression model proffers evidence that an omitted variable 'is correlated with the dependent variable and is likely to affect the result of the regression analysis,' the Court will not find that omission of the variable implicated the reliability of the model. Merely pointing to economic conditions that may affect the dependent variable is not enough to call into question the reliability of an econometric model."
Variables—Inclusion and Definition	Antitrust	*Piggly Wiggly Clarksville v. Interstate Brands*	100 Fed. Appx. 296, 2004, U.S. Court of Appeals for the 5th Circuit	The plaintiff's expert stated "that multiple regression analysis could be used to calculate damages under a before and after approach." The expert proposes that "regression analysis could measure the effect of illegal price fixing with a before and after method that compares prices during a period when there was no illegal activity and controls for other variables such as input costs and the size of the account." However, "the expert did not offer a formula based on regression analysis, but merely opined that one could be found. The expert does not explain how to model 'negotiating ability' or the geographic market, factors which the district court thought were relevant."
Variables—Inclusion and Definition	Breach of Contract	*University Computing Company v. Management Science America, Inc. and Larry Smart*	810 F. 2d, 1987, U.S. District Court for the Northern District of Texas	Plaintiff's expert failed to "conduct regressions or provide a statistical test to show that other factors (identified as 'considerations' that the rejected) could not have caused the degree of variation in the sample data points. ... [T]his does not comport with established norms of statistical methodology; such reasoning violates statistical logic, which first requires a determination as to whether ordinary events could have created the variation before looking to attribute unusual (or any) causes. Small influences can often result in large perturbations when conjoined; it is precisely these influences that adequate statistical tests are designed to assess."

Appendix: Case Law Summary on Issues in Econometrics (Continued)

Case Type	Case Name	Court	Court's Position
Variables— Inclusion and Definition	Cornelius Cooper v. Southern Company	390 F. 3d 695, 2004, U.S. Court of Appeals for the 11th Circuit	The district court "noted that Plaintiff's statistical reports did not incorporate variables that would allow for the comparison of individuals who were similarly situated with respect to managerial decision makers, job types, locations, departments, and the specific criteria relevant for the jobs in question. Plaintiff's report did not tailor the analysis to the specific positions, job locations, or departmental and organizational structures in question. The district court concluded that these methodological deficiencies rendered it 'impossible to determine what the [salary and promotions] gaps were, whether they were statistically significant, or whether factors other than race were involved.'"
Variables— Inclusion and Definition	Trout v. Hidalgo	517 F. Supp. 769, 1983, U.S. District Court for the District of Columbia	"Plaintiffs cannot legitimately be faulted for gaps in their statistical analysis when the information necessary to close the gaps was possessed only by defendants and was not furnished either to the plaintiffs or to the Court." "It is commonly accepted that it is inappropriate to include as an independent variable a factor within defendant's control unless it has been established that they did not discriminate in exercising that control."
Variables— Inclusion and Definition	Melani v. Board of Higher Education of the City of New York	561 F. Supp. 769, 1983, U.S. District Court for the Southern District of New York	"Title VII regression studies need not account for every factor that conceivably might explain differences in salaries or promotions. The omission of a variable does not negate the probative value of the studies."
Variables— Inclusion and Definition	Craik v. Minnesota State University Board	731 F. 2d 465, 1984, U.S. Court of Appeals for the 8th Circuit	"It is important to note that the choice of variables should be the result of theoretical determination, made before the data are examined, of what factors are likely to be relevant; the proper variables cannot be identified statistically, because statistically correlated relationships may be accidental, lacking practical significance."

Appendix: Case Law Summary on Issues in Econometrics (Continued)

	Case Type	Case Name	Court	Court's Position
Variables—Inclusion and Definition	Gender Discrimination Title VII	*EEOC v. Sears Roebuck*	628 F. Supp. 1264, 1986, U.S. District Court for the Northern District of Illinois	"The assumptions underlying any statistics must be critically examined by the court. In a regression analysis, this requires a careful evaluation of the variables included in the model, the ability to accurately measure these variables, and the importance of variables not included in the model, including variables which cannot be measured on a mathematical scale. In short, the court must evaluate 'the fit' of the model to the reality of the facts and circumstances." The "EEOC's statistical analyses are so flawed that they lack any persuasive value. Its database has serious errors, it omitted important variables from its analyses, and it used a model that fails to consider Sears' method of actually compensating individual employees."
Variables—Inclusion and Definition	Gender Discrimination Title VII	*Sobel v. Yeshiva University*	839 F. 2d 18, 1988, U.S. Court of Appeals for the 2nd Circuit	"The validity of the influence attributed to a particular variable will depend heavily on how accurately the model mimics the actual factors influencing the dependent variable." Regression analysis must actually demonstrate failure to adjust for disparities. The failure to "include a relevant variable (or the inclusion of an irrelevant or multi-collinear variable) will go to the probative value of the analysis, not its admissibility." "A defendant challenging the validity of a multiple regression analysis has to make a showing that the factors it contends ought to have been included would weaken the showing of a salary disparity made by analysis."

Appendix: Case Law Summary on Issues in Econometrics (Continued)

	Case Type	Case Name	Court	Court's Position
Variables—Inclusion and Definition	Property Tax Valuation	*Department of Revenue v. Grant Western Lumber Co.*	(TC 4394) 2001, Oregon Tax Court, Regular Division	The court believes "that it would be error to conclude the slope coefficient establishes that the price for the subject mill would fall within a range of $7.93 to $22.41 per board foot of capacity. That inference would be true only with regard to one variable. Other variables can move the price outside that range in either direction." "Regression of one independent variable is not reflective of a 'few' or 'a handful' of variables that would explain 80 or 90 percent of the mill's price. It does not take an expert to know that some of those variables are age, condition, location, and other similar characteristics. Those important factors were not regressed or incorporated into the study."
Variables—Inclusion and Definition	Racial and Gender Discrimination Title VII	*Vuyanich v. Republic National Bank*	505 F. Supp. 224, 1980, U.S. District Court for the Northern District of Texas	"Central to validity of any multiple regression model and resulting statistical inferences is the use of a proper procedure for determining what explanatory variables should be included and what mathematical form the equation should follow. The model devised must be based on theory, prior to looking at the data and running the model on the data. If one does the reverse, the usual tests of statistical inference do not apply."
Variables—Inclusion and Definition	Racial Discrimination	*Craig and Georgia Bonton v. City of New York*	03 Civ. 2833 (SAS), U.S. District Court for the Southern District of New York	"To determine whether there is causal link between race and the observed disparity in remand rates, it is necessary to conduct a multiple regression analysis to control for explanatory variables such as parents' income level or employment status." The district court and the majority decided "that because the plaintiff's statistical evidence failed to control for all variables that may have impacted the decisions made at the challenged stages, it is insufficient to establish causation." The statistical evidence "does not show that the reason black applicants failed to proceed at the interview selection stage and position selection stage was their race. Factors such as presentation in the interview, answers to interview questions, demeanor, and ability demonstrated in the interview of course entered into the judgment of the members of the panel as to the candidate who received a position that was being filled." However, "statistical evidence does not have to control for every single variable in order to be sufficient."

Appendix: Case Law Summary on Issues in Econometrics (Continued)

	Case Type	Case Name	Court	Court's Position
Variables—Inclusion and Definition	Racial Discrimination Title VII	*Bazemore v. Friday*	478 U.S. 385, 1986, U.S. Supreme Court	"The Court of Appeals erred in stating that petitioner's regression analyses were 'unacceptable as evidence of discrimination' because they did not include 'all measurable variables thought to have an affect on salary level.' The court's view of the evidentiary value of the regression analyses was plainly incorrect. While the omission of variables from a regression analysis may render the analysis less probative than it otherwise might be, it can hardly be said, absent some other infirmity, that an analysis which accounts for the other major factors 'must be considered unacceptable as evidence of discrimination.' Normally, failure to include variables will affect the analysis' probativeness, not its admissibility."
Variables—Inclusion and Definition	Racial Discrimination Title VII	*RE: Proportionality Review Project (II)*	165 N.J. 206; 757 A.2d 168; 2000, Supreme Court of New Jersey	Judge Cohen noted "that the multiple regressions were inherently unreliable because they were not parsimonious, a requisite for a reliable regression." A parsimonious model is a statistical model with a relatively small number of well-crafted parameters. The lack of parsimony creates "a risk of overfitting, possibly resulting in the false attribution of effect to a variable. In other words, considering the relatively small number of cases in the database, particularly death-sentenced cases, the regression models contained an excessive number of variables and, thus, statistical results suggesting racial discrimination may have reflected a methodological flaw rather than reality." However, "the inability to design parsimonious regression models for individual proportionality review does not necessarily prevent the development of parsimonious regression models for systemic proportionality review."
Variables—Inclusion and Definition	Racial Discrimination Title VII	*Campaign for Fiscal Equity v. State of New York*	187 Misc. 2d 1; 719 N.Y.S. 2d 475; 2001, Supreme Court of New York, New York County	The defense expert's analyses are not persuasive because "the studies are flawed by their reliance on analyses of single years of data ... Education is a cumulative enterprise, and student outcomes are dependent not just on the resources that they receive in a single school year, but on the resources that they receive over years of schooling. The [defense expert's] analyses are not probative because they rest on the premise that students' test results in a single year can be compared to the resources available to the student in that single year to gauge the effectiveness of resources."

Appendix: Case Law Summary on Issues in Econometrics (Continued)

	Case Type	Case Name	Court	Court's Position
Variables—Inclusion and Definition	Racial Discrimination Title VII	*Cynthia Carter Reynods v. Sodexho Marriott Services*	349 F. Supp. 2d 1, 2004, U.S. District Court for the District of Columbia	Regression analysis "can account for more factors simultaneously than a pools analysis. Hence, regressions are better suited to consider 'major variables,' which in turn may help to explain the decision-making process. The importance of including the major variables is clear; failure to do so may mask the true cause of a statistical disparity between races." Analyses that "exclude major factors may be 'so incomplete as to be inadmissible as irrelevant' (Coward, 140 F.3d at 274, quoting Bazemore, 478 U.S. at 400 n.10)." The defendant's content ion that plaintiff's "statistical methodology is 'so flawed' (because plaintiff did not consider the major, nondiscriminatory variables (education and experience) that purportedly played a role in the promotion decisions at issue) that it should be deemed inadmissible as a matter of law is rejected; the issue is one of the evidence's weight, not its admissibility."
Variables—Inclusion and Definition	Weighing Poultry	*Estate of Bud Hill v. ConAgra Poultry*	94-CV-0198-HLM, 1997, U.S. District Court for the Northern District of Georgia	"The Second Circuit observed that the ideal manner for a party challenging the omission of a major variable from a regression analysis is to perform its own regression analysis establishing statistical significance of the omitted variable. Given this law, the Court concludes that, in order to show that the plaintiff's expert omitted significant variables from his regression analysis, defendants must proffer evidence showing that each omitted variable is correlated with the dependent variable and is likely to affect the result of the regression analysis."
Weight/Admissibility	Breach of Fiduciary Duty and Contract	*Pepe & Hazard v. Richard D. Jones*	(X02) CV960151601S, Superior Court of Connecticut, Judicial District of Waterbury	"Questions about the methodological validity of proffered scientific testimony will generally go to the *weight* of such evidence, not to its admissibility. Courts should exclude scientific evidence, however, when such concerns render the techniques, and the resulting evidence, incapable of assisting the fact finder in a sufficiently meaningful way." Courts and commentators have treated multiple regression as scientific.

Appendix: Case Law Summary on Issues in Econometrics (Continued)

	Case Type	Case Name	Court	Court's Position
Weight/ Admissibility	Gender Discrimination Title VII	*Palmer v. Schultz*	815 F. 2d 84 (D.C. Cir. 1987)	Defendant must "present credible evidence that the statistical proof is defective and, second, present a plausible explanation of how the asserted flaw is likely to bias the results against the employer."
				Defendant must present sufficient evidence that preference explains the disparity in order to undermine the probative weight of the plaintiff's statistics.
Weight/ Admissibility	Gender Discrimination Title VII	*Sobel v. Yeshiva University*	839 F. 2d 18, 1988, U.S. Court of Appeals for the 2nd Circuit	The district court should have "discounted the weight to be accorded plaintiff's regression analysis because of the failure to include an explanatory variable only upon a showing by the defendant that the missing variable is a determinant of salary and correlates with sex, and thus is likely to cause a demonstrable, rather than an assumed, under adjustment bias."
Weight/ Admissibility	Labor	*Bickerstaff v. Vassar College*	196 F. Supp. 224, 1980, U.S. District Court for the Northern District of Texas	Court affirmed district judge's exclusion of an expert's statistical report based on the court's determination that the report lacked probative value.
				Recognizing that although as a general proposition, defects in methodology go to the weight of the evidence and not its admissibility, the Second court upheld the trial court's determination that the expert evidence should be excluded because it not only "included less than all the relevant variables" (a factor that would go to weight) but also because "it omitted the major variables" (which goes to admissibility).
Weight/ Admissibility	Racial Discrimination Title VII	*Cynthia Carter Reynods v. Sodexho Marriott Services*	349 F. Supp. 2d 30, 2004, U.S. District Court for the District of Columbia	"In a disparate treatment claim, failure to perform a multiple regression analysis is not a basis for Daubert exclusion of evidence, but instead goes to the weight of the evidence."

Appendix: Case Law Summary on Issues in Econometrics

CHAPTER 7

ESTIMATING THE COST OF CAPITAL

Gaurav Jetley
R. Jeffrey Malinak
Laura B. Stamm

CONTENTS

7.1 INTRODUCTION

That funds have time value (often called the *time value of money*) affects proper valuation of both damages and businesses. The value of any asset results from its ability to provide future cash flows. The value of a project, a company, or an investment equals its future cash flows discounted to the present. This chapter focuses on the concept of the rate used for that discounting, that is, the opportunity cost of capital, the underlying factors affecting the rate, and methods of estimating it.

Section 7.2 reviews the concept of opportunity cost of capital and identifies the economic factors affecting it; Section 7.3 presents the theoretical models that courts and practitioners use for estimating the cost of capital; and Section 7.4 applies the most common methods to calculate the cost of capital for selected companies in the retail industry.

7.2   OPPORTUNITY COST OF CAPITAL

Investment in any asset, whether a corporate venture or a marketable security, implies a foregone opportunity to invest in alternative assets. For an investment to be sensible, it must have an expected return at least equal to the expected return from alternative, comparable investments foregone. To be an acceptable investment, it must have a positive present value of the cash flows discounted at the return that comparable investments yield—the opportunity cost of capital.

What constitutes a comparable investment? Developing a new biotechnology product differs from buying a corporate bond issued by a Fortune 500 company. Nonetheless, in terms of cash outlays and inflows, the two investments differ in only two ways: (1) the timing of the cash flows and (2) the potential variability of the cash flows. Because discounting cash flows to the present eliminates timing differences, the investments differ only in potential variability—the risk due to the uncertainty of an investment's expected payoff. This risk alone determines the return required of an investment.

Suppose an investor faces a choice of two investments, A and B. Investment A, a 20-year zero-coupon Treasury bond, will produce a sure payoff (barring collapse of the U.S. government) of $1,000. Investment B will also produce a single payoff in 20 years; investment B has a 50 percent chance of a $2,000 payoff and a 50 percent chance of no payoff. Both investments have the same expected value of $1,000 [$=(50\% \times \$2,000) + (50\% \times \$0)$]. If the two investments had identical prices, a risk-averse investor would prefer investment A because it offers the same expected payoff with less risk. To attract investors, investments with higher risk must offer a higher return, that is, investment B must have a lower price.

This relation between risk and return makes the opportunity cost of capital the appropriate discount rate. Investments with like risks should offer similar returns; therefore, the opportunity cost of an investment should equal the return offered by a comparably risky endeavor. Because the uncertainty in the payoff of an investment affects its potential return, estimating the cost of capital requires understanding and measuring the types of risk inherent in investments. Factors affecting the cost of capital include the following:

- **Inflation.** A dollar repaid in the future will have smaller purchasing power than it has today. An investor requires additional compensation for expected inflation as well as for the risk of inflation exceeding expectations.
- **Real risk-free rate of interest.** This factor compensates an investor for the use of the investor's resources for the duration of the investment. If the payback is certain and investors expect no inflation, the opportunity cost equals the real risk-free rate of interest.
- **Default risk.**[1] Under a debt agreement, the borrower promises the lender payments according to a fixed schedule; however, the borrower may not meet the repayment schedule and may default on the loan.
- **Market risk.** Most investments are sensitive to prevailing economic conditions, and portfolio diversification cannot eliminate this sensitivity.

Each of these factors influences the certainty of promised cash flows and hence the cost of capital. Observing the historical relation between risk and return for selected investments clarifies how each type of risk influences investments.

Type of Investment	Average Annual Return 1926–2003	Standard Deviation 1926–2003
Short-term Treasury Bills	3.8%	3.1%
Long-term Treasury Bonds	5.5	9.4
Long-term Corp. Bonds	6.2	8.6
Large Company Stocks	12.4	20.4
Small Company Stocks	17.5	33.3
Inflation	3.1	4.3

Source: Ibbotson Associates 2004.

Exhibit 7-1. Average Annual Returns, 1926–2003

Exhibit 7-1 shows the average annual return and standard deviation of return for selected groups of investments. The variability of returns indicates differential risk exposure. Risk-free assets have constant real returns, whereas the returns on assets sensitive to market risk vary over time. The standard deviation, a statistical measure of the variation in average returns, quantifies the risk associated with holding a diversified portfolio of a particular investment type. As expected, investors receive higher average returns for investments with greater risk.

(a) Risk-Free Rate of Interest (and Inflation). Debt obligations of the U.S. Treasury, backed by the credit of the U.S. government, have such small probability of default that most analysts say that such obligations have zero risk or are risk free. The prevailing return offered by Treasury securities is the nominal risk-free rate, because it includes an inflation component that compensates for expected future lost purchasing power. To find the real risk-free rate, one must subtract the inflation rate from the Treasury bill rate over the same time period. As shown in Exhibit 7-1, the short-term real risk-free rate has averaged around 0.7 percent (the average short-term nominal risk-free rate of 3.8 percent minus the inflation rate of 3.1 percent).

Exhibit 7-1 also illustrates the pattern of interest rates over different investment horizons (i.e., the term structure) in the 1.7 percent difference between the returns of short- and long-term Treasuries. The term structure fluctuates, but long-term securities have historically offered higher yields than short-term securities. If this difference reflected only expectations regarding future interest rates, one would expect the historical average yields to be equivalent.[2] Higher returns required to compensate for the uncertainty of either future interest rates or future inflation can explain the observed historical term premium.

(b) Default Risk. Default means that the debtor missed a payment of interest or principal, or paid late, or promised a new set of smaller or later (or both) payments (net, a diminished financial obligation) to retire the original debt. Because default seldom results in a total loss of principal, a lender, estimating the required return on an investment, must consider both the probability of default and the expected recovery in the event of default. Agencies such as Standard & Poor's and Moody's assign quality ratings designed to rank the relative probability that a company will default. These agencies base their ratings on the likelihood that a company will not meet its financial obligation, the company's willingness to make timely payment of interest and principal, the provisions of the obligation, and the protection afforded the lender in the event of bankruptcy or reorganization.

According to Fons and Kimball (1991), lower-rated unsecured debt issuers defaulted at average rates considerably greater than higher rated unsecured debt issuers across investment horizons spanning one to twenty years. Quality ratings, however, only imperfectly indicate default risk. The market must interpret the information that the quality ratings convey. When different agencies assign different ratings to the same company (split ratings), the ratings can hinder rather than aid an investor's ability to assess default risk. Studies have shown that, given a split rating, risk-averse investors tend to place more weight on the lower rating, therefore increasing promised yields on debt (Chandy and Hsueh, 1989).

Covenants and security provisions of debt reduce the lender's cost of potential default risk. The default risk of a subordinated or convertible debenture exceeds that of a senior, unsecured, nonconvertible debenture from the same issuer; the default risk of an unsecured debenture exceeds that of a secured bond from the same issuer. The inverse relation between default risk and increased security results from the lender's expected recovery in case of bankruptcy or reorganization. A secured bondholder can obtain postpetition accrued interest and has priority among creditors. A debenture investor has priority over a subordinated debenture investor. Although certain provisions can reduce default risk, some risk remains even with insured debt, owing to transaction costs and the probability of delayed payments in case of default.

As a result of default risk, the promised return in the capital markets exceeds the expected return on debt investments. Historically, the annualized difference between the realized total returns for corporate bonds and Treasuries for the 10-year period ending in 1992 ranged from 0.27 percent for Aaa-rated debt to 1.82 percent for Baa-rated debt.[3] For investment-grade debt with low default risk, the expected return approaches the promised return. For lower grade debt, the difference increases. For example, a bond rated B may have a promised yield of 12.5 percent. Assuming a 20.0 percent likelihood of default (in which case the investor receives no interest but a return of principal, for a realized return of 0 percent) and an 80.0 percent likelihood of no default (for a realized return equal to the promised return of 12.5 percent), the expected return declines to 10 percent.

(c) Market Risk. *Market risk* is the sensitivity of an investment to economy-wide events. The difference between the returns of common shares and Treasuries indicates the compensation that investors have realized for bearing market risk. For the period 1926 through 2003, Exhibit 7-1 reflects an average market-risk premium (the difference between large-company common stock arithmetic average returns and Treasury bill returns) of 8.6 percent. An investor who bore the risks inherent in the aggregate securities market could have expected to earn a similar premium over this period. As with default risk, the degree of market risk varies among equity investments; note the higher premium, 13.7 percent, that a portfolio of small company securities earned.

Since an equity investment entails an ownership position in the future profits and losses that a company's assets will produce, the market risk of equities in part reflects the risk of the underlying assets. Financial leverage further increases the market risk of equity. The market risk of equity investments in two identical businesses will differ if one finances more heavily with debt. In many cost of capital applications, one must evaluate business opportunities, not securities or debt agreements. For investment opportunities financed by a combination of equity and debt, the cost of capital should reflect the market risk of the assets, irrespective of financing, and not the market risk of the equity alone.[4] The next section discusses theoretical models that attempt to explain the relation between the market risk and expected returns.

7.3 THEORETICAL MODELS OF THE COST OF CAPITAL

This section describes the theoretical models that analysts commonly use to estimate the opportunity cost or expected return on an asset or a group of assets.

(a) Capital Asset Pricing Model. The Capital Asset Pricing Model (CAPM) has become the most common model for estimating the cost of capital.[5] Several variants of the model exist, but this chapter focuses on the Sharpe-Lintner-Mossin (SLM) single-factor model and the multifactor variant first developed by Merton (1973). We also refer the reader to Sharpe (1985) and Haugen (1990), who discuss the different models and their underlying assumptions.

(i) CAPM—Market Risk versus Unique Risk. As Section 7.2(b) discussed, investors bear risk related to uncertain cash flows on their investments. Such risk arises because unforeseen events can change the investment's cash flows. Events that could affect an investment in a particular company include the following:

- A competitor develops a better product.
- Oil prices fall, lowering the company's costs of manufacturing.
- Union workers go on strike.
- A personal income tax increase reduces consumer spending, which results in lower sales.

These events fall into two categories: those unique to a particular investment, such as a competitor's developing a better product, and those that affect all companies to some extent, such as the tax increase. All capital asset pricing models incorporate this distinction.

Consider first events that reflect a firm's unique or specific risk—the risk, for example, that its products will fail or that a fire will destroy its factory. The CAPM assumes that investors seek to eliminate unique risk by diversifying their portfolios of investments. Some investments in the portfolio will yield higher than expected returns because of unforeseen events; others will yield lower than expected returns. In a large enough portfolio, one would expect neither favorable nor unfavorable events to dominate.

Other events will affect the economy as a whole, however, and even a well-diversified portfolio does not afford protection from these events, such as tax increases, oil price changes, and wars. The consequences of the event will likely affect the entire portfolio consistently—favorably or unfavorably. This type of risk is called *market risk* or *systematic risk* or *nondiversifiable risk*. We see evidence of market risk in the tendency of share prices to move together. Various types or components of market risk affect different investments in different ways.

Since diversification reduces unique risk to almost zero, investors will not consider such risks in evaluating the expected return from an investment unless diversifying entails costs.[6] Investors cannot escape systematic risk, however, and therefore require a greater return on assets subject to such risk. The CAPM provides a framework for measuring market risk and the premium that investors demand in return for bearing it. In the standard SLM single-factor CAPM, an individual security's sensitivity to changes in the market provides a simple measure of systematic risk. In other models, such as the one developed by Merton (1973), systematic risk has multiple components (risk factors), and each risk factor has a separate effect on the expected return. We present each of these variant models in turn.

(ii) CAPM—Beta.   A security whose price increases (or decreases) by 10 percent when the market—as evidenced by a well-diversified portfolio such as the S&P 500—increases (or decreases) by 5 percent has greater risk than a security whose price increases (or decreases) by only 2 percent when the market increases (or decreases) by 5 percent. This measure of sensitivity is called a security's *beta.* A security whose price tends to rise or fall in the same percentage amount as the market has a beta of 1.00. A security whose price tends to rise or fall by 2 percent for every 1 percent rise or fall in the market has a beta of 2.00 and so on. If a security has a beta of 1.00, the risk premium (the extra return over a riskless investment) investors require should equal that which they would require for holding the market portfolio. If the security has a beta of 1.50, which indicates 50 percent greater risk than the market, its risk premium should exceed the risk premium of the market portfolio by 50 percent.

(iii) CAPM Formulas.   The basic CAPM formula expresses this concept according to the linear equation:

$$R_A = R_f + b(R_m - R_f) \tag{1}$$

where

R_A = the rate of return required by investors for investing in security A
R_f = the risk-free rate of return
b = the beta of security A with respect to the market portfolio
R_m = the market rate of return
$R_m - R_f$ = the market risk premium.

The model is valid only under a set of restrictive assumptions, described in Fama and French (1993). For example, the model requires constant interest rates. The multifactor CAPM, below, developed by Merton (1973), has less restrictive assumptions:

$$R_A = R_f + b(R_m - R_f) + \Sigma\, b_i\,(R_i - R_f), i = 1, 2, 3, \ldots \tag{2}$$

where

R_A = the rate of return required by investors for investing in security A
R_f = the risk-free rate of return
b = the beta of security A
$R_m - R_f$ = the market risk premium
b_i = the sensitivity of security A to risk i
R_i = the return on portfolio securities bearing a specified type of risk i.

This model assumes that more than one factor, including a change in interest rates, can affect the returns on a particular security.

(b) Recent Tests of CAPM. The predictive accuracy of a particular CAPM model, compared with its competitors, suggests which version the expert should use. Testing the CAPM theory presents two difficulties: (1) we can observe actual returns but not expected returns and (2) the market portfolio hypothesized by CAPM consists of all risky assets, not common shares only. To reduce the sampling error associated with calculating betas for individual securities, analysts usually group securities into portfolios. To test expected returns, we estimate betas from a historical period, use the betas to predict subsequent returns, and then compare actual returns in the subsequent period to the predicted returns. Because of data limitations, analysts almost always use a standard common stock index and simply acknowledge the problem of measuring the true market portfolio as a limitation.

In theory, the CAPM beta measure sufficiently explains the cross section of average returns, that is, a regression of returns against beta should produce a slope equal to the expected market risk premium. Early empirical tests of the CAPM, using stock price data from the 1940s to 1960s that Black et al. (1972) conducted, confirmed the expected relation between beta and average returns. Since then, research has identified two primary shortcomings of the model. The model fails to explain fully the higher returns that accrue to investors in small companies. More important, the model cannot explain the lack of a significant relation between a security's historical beta and its subsequent realized return. These findings increased interest in developing multifactor models that correct for these deficiencies.

For example, studies conducted in the 1980s that used data from that period failed to find a relation between beta and average returns. A well-publicized study by Fama and French (1992) found that beta does not explain the cross section of common share returns. These studies led to articles and headlines proclaiming the death of beta. Other well-known academics have refuted such findings. Using different econometric techniques, annual returns instead of monthly returns, or longer time periods, studies continue to find evidence of a strong, positive relation between beta and average returns predicted with CAPM.

Despite the continuing controversy over beta's ability to explain average returns, either by itself or in combination with other variables, theorists and many practitioners continue to believe that only systematic risk affects return. Observed deviations from the CAPM can simply reflect the imperfect nature of the market risk proxy or the measurement of beta. Academics continue to seek additional proxies to supplement or replace the traditional single-factor market risk model or additional factors to enhance the predictive power of the model.

One of the first studies that identified the shortcomings of the CAPM (Banz, 1983), found that size, as measured by market value of equity, also affects average returns. Stated another way, the observed returns of small company stocks have consistently exceeded what beta alone would have predicted. Chan and Chen (1991) studied NYSE stocks and found small firms more likely to be marginal firms, characterized by historically poor performance, inefficient production, high financial leverage, and cash flow problems. Such characteristics make small companies less able to withstand poor economic conditions. Chan and Chen's results suggest that using the CAPM in conjunction with a value-weighted market index (biased toward larger, more stable firms) will not capture the risks associated with all marginal firms.

Other work on multifactor models has found a strong correlation between the returns of smaller companies and the default premium (the spread between high- and low-grade bonds). This premium relates to the changing business cycle. Such evidence adds further support to the notion that a systematic risk component that the traditional CAPM formulation inadequately captures can affect small company returns. Others have suggested that the size anomaly has little to do with risk. They propose that small company securities appear underpriced because investment analysts do not examine all small firms or that small company securities investors require additional return to compensate them for these issues' reduced liquidity.

Other variables such as leverage, dividend yield, price-to-earnings ratio, and book-to-market ratio also show explanatory power. Fama and French (1993) stud-ied these variables in combination and found three variables that best explain the observed returns of common equity securities. Next, we will discuss the results of their work, an extension of the original CAPM model to a three-factor model. This model exemplifies the current ongoing efforts to shape new financial models and tools for estimating the cost of capital.

(c) Three-Factor CAPM Model.   Whereas the traditional CAPM market factor best explains the difference between average returns on equity securities and those of risk-free securities, Fama and French (1993) found that size and the ratio of the book value of equity to the market value of equity best explain the cross section of average returns across common equity securities. Size and the book-to-market ratio capture the effects of other variables such as price-to-earnings ratio and leverage.

Some theorists believe that the book-to-market factor associates with relative earnings performance because companies with high book-to-market ratios persis-tently show low profitability as measured by earnings on assets. Conversely, companies with low book-to-market ratios persistently show high profitability. This information suggests that book-to-market ratios capture a risk factor related to earnings performance.

The work of Fama and French suggests that a three-factor model predicts expected return better than the traditional one-factor CAPM model. The following linear equation expresses this three-factor model:

$$R_A = R_f + b(R_m - R_f) + s(R_s - R_b) + h(R_h - R_l) \tag{3}$$

where

R_A = the return on a security of company A
R_f = the risk-free rate of return
$R_m - R_f$ = the market risk premium
$R_s - R_b$ = the size premium, that is, the difference between the return of small equity securities and the return of large equity securities
$R_h - R_l$ = the book-to-market premium, that is, the difference between the return of equity securities with high book-to-market ratios and the return of equity securities with low book-to-market ratios
b = beta, the sensitivity of equity security A to market risk
s = the sensitivity of equity security A to size risk
h = the sensitivity of equity security A to book-to-market risk.

Fama and French used monthly returns from 1963 through 1991 of all NYSE, AMEX, and NASDAQ securities to measure the variation in returns associated with size and book-to-market ratios. They created six portfolios from the combination of two size groups and three book-to-market groups. The difference in returns between securities with a market capitalization greater than the median capitalization of the NYSE securities and those with a market capitalization below the median capitalization proxied for the size premium. The difference in returns between securities with book-to-market ratios in the top 30 percent of the NYSE and securities with book-to-market ratios in the bottom 30 percent of the NYSE proxied for the book-to-market risk premium.

Using this model specification, the authors found an average market-risk premium of 0.43 percent per month, an average size premium of 0.27 percent per month, and an average book-to-market premium of 0.40 percent per month. As expected, the small securities portfolios were sensitive to the small size factor, and the high book-to-market portfolios were sensitive to the book-to-market factor. Interestingly, the additional two variables in the regression equation cause the betas to move toward 1.0. The market risk sensitivity approached 1.0 for all portfolios, evidence of a strong correlation between market risk and risks associated with size and book-to-market ratios. In addition, these results suggest that the market factor best describes the return premium associated with common shares on average, and the size and book-to-market factors best explain the variation of returns among common shares.

Practitioners often need to compute the cost of capital for small firms and privately held firms. In such cases, firm size can cause significant deviation from the results derived from the single-factor CAPM. Thus, these analysts frequently apply only the size factor, using available estimates necessary for application of a size premium to the CAPM. Section 7.4(b) illustrates how to apply a size premium to the CAPM.

(d) Arbitrage Pricing Theory.   The trend toward multifactor pricing models led to increasing acceptance of the Arbitrage Pricing Theory (APT), first proposed by Ross (1976). Similar to the CAPM, the APT's fundamental tenet asserts that investors diversify away unique risk and that asset returns depend only on the risk from economy-wide influences. Rather than capturing an asset's systematic risk with a single market-related variable as in the CAPM, the APT attempts to model equity returns with multiple factors, such as specific macroeconomic variables and nonequity asset returns, each representing some component of market risk.

Selecting the specific factors to include in the APT equation requires empirical research. Chen et al. (1986) identified four factors as the most important determinants of expected return:

1. Industrial production
2. Inflation
3. The term premium, as reflected in the spread between long- and short-term interest rates
4. The default premium, as reflected in the spread between high- and low-risk bonds

The APT provides the ability to further differentiate investments on the basis of risk. As a result, analysts have so far applied APT to portfolio selection and performance evaluation rather than capital budgeting. The APT requires selecting relevant factors, estimating the risk premium associated with each factor, and estimating the investment's sensitivity to each risk factor. The complexity of these calculations exceeds the complexity required for the CAPM, because experts do not yet agree on the appropriate set of factors, and one cannot easily access the risk premiums associated with the different factors. Consequently, the model has not yet gained a significant following among practitioners.

(e) The Discounted Cash Flow (DCF) Model.   The origins of the CAPM and APT models described in this chapter can be traced back to the development of modern portfolio theory in the 1950s and 1960s (Markowitz, 1952; Sharpe, 1964; Lintner, 1965). The DCF model was in wide use prior to this period. Furthermore, it is consistent with modern portfolio theory and remains useful today, especially in calculating reasonable rates of return for regulated industries. This model reflects the fundamental observation that the value of a share of stock today must equal the present value of all of its future dividends, discounted at the expected rate of return (or cost of capital). The following equation expresses the DCF model:[7]

$$P_0 = \frac{\text{DIV}_1}{r - g} \tag{4}$$

where

$$P_0 = \text{the current stock price}$$
$$\text{DIV}_1 = \text{the expected dividend in the following year}$$
$$r = \text{the rate of return expected by investors, or the cost of capital}$$
$$g = \text{the expected rate of growth in dividends}$$

Solving for r, or the cost of capital, yields the following equation:

$$r = \frac{\text{DIV}_1}{P_0} + g \tag{5}$$

As with the CAPM, regulatory proceedings and other settings use this basic equation to calculate fair rates of return or costs of capital by developing estimates for DIV_1 and g (P_0 is directly observable).

7.4   ESTIMATING THE COST OF CAPITAL

This section applies some of the methods discussed in previous sections. We first focus on the practical application of the single-factor CAPM. Using this model, we estimate the equity costs of capital for a selected group of retail companies. Then we compare the results with the equity cost of capital for the same companies, calculated using a size-adjusted CAPM. The section then discusses adjusting discount rates for leverage and tax effects by using the weighted average cost of capital formulas. The section concludes by providing techniques for dealing with a widely encountered problem—calculating the cost of capital of privately held companies.

(a) Estimating Equity Cost of Capital with Single-Factor CAPM. Calculating the cost of capital with the single-factor CAPM requires three inputs: the risk-free rate, the expected market risk premium, and the beta.

(i) Expected Risk-Free Rate. We use the current market yield on short-term government securities as the expected risk-free rate. Some experts suggest using the yield on a government security with the same duration as that of the investment.[8] Although this yield usually will exceed the short-term return, using it will lower the market premium measured against longer term instruments, offsetting the higher risk-free rate.[9]

(ii) Expected Market Risk Premium. Because practitioners cannot observe the expected market-risk premium in market transactions, they rely on either historical data or survey data to provide insight into investors' expectations.

Practitioners use different methods for analyzing historical return data to estimate the expected risk premium in the United States. To use historical market risk premiums as proxies for expected market risk premiums, we make assumptions about the statistical nature of market returns. For example, we assume that the premium for risk changes slowly over time and that returns are independent. In more technical terms, we assume that a random variable has an expected value equal to the average of its past values.

- **Historical average excess returns in the United States.** One can calculate the historical market risk premium in the United States as the difference between the arithmetic average return on the market portfolio and the arithmetic average return on risk-free securities.[10] According to the CAPM, the market portfolio consists of all risky assets. In practice, we use only common stock portfolios, such as the S&P 500 Index and the NYSE Composite Index. One should use the same market index to calculate the expected market risk premium (i.e., equity risk premium) as that used in the beta estimation.[11]

  Studies express average historical returns for the market in one of two ways:

  1. **Arithmetic mean return:** sums the annual returns and divides by the number of years in the sample.
  2. **Geometric mean:** calculates the average compounded rate of return earned over the period.

With uncertain returns, the arithmetic mean consistently exceeds the geometric mean.[12] With constant returns (i.e., nonstochastic), the arithmetic mean equals the geometric mean. Historical arithmetic mean returns provide the most appropriate basis for estimating the expected equity risk premium for use in the CAPM.[13] In addition to using arithmetic mean data, the historical base period selected for measuring the average market risk premium affects the model. Over short periods, market returns vary more than over the long term, where the market risk premium appears stable. Many experts advocate using the longest period for which data are available. A longer time span better represents the broad range of possible events that could affect the securities market in the future. Also, using a longer term minimizes short-run volatility.

Historical Period	S&P 500 Average Return	Treasury Bill Average Return	Equity Risk Premium
1926–2003	12.4%	3.8%	8.6%
1944–2003	13.4	4.6	8.8
1964–2003	11.9	6.1	5.8
1984–2003	14.3	5.3	9.0
1993–2003	12.8	4.1	8.7

Source: Ibbotson Associates 2004.

Exhibit 7-2.   Historical Equity Risk Premium

Exhibit 7-2 shows the historical risk premiums calculated for various time periods. The data suggest that the choice of time period can affect the cost of equity calculation. When selecting a time period, an analyst should recognize the sensitivity of the premium to the choice of beginning and ending years. For example, a time span beginning at the start of a bull market and ending at the top of a bull market tends to increase the premium. Similarly, the market risk premium is sensitive to short-term swings in the business cycle, as securities tend to perform well in the beginning stages of economic recovery, causing a decline of the expected equity risk premium. In litigation, experts often use the longest period available, to avoid the appearance of cherry-picking the data.

- **Historical average excess returns to U.S. stocks based on fundamentals.** Fama and French (2002) calculate the average expected return from 1872 through 2000 using a DCF model rather than the historical ex-post realized return.[14] For the period 1951 to 2000, they found real equity risk premiums of 2.55 or 4.32 percent (3.83 or 4.78 percent when bias adjusted) using the DCF method, versus 7.43 percent using the average of the realized return.[15] They attribute this difference to unexpected capital gains on U.S. shares during the post-1951 period and conclude that the expected real equity risk premium is lower than that suggested by average actual realized returns.

- **Historical average excess returns for global equities.** Some analysts have suggested that the high returns and associated equity premiums in the U.S. market result from survival bias (e.g., Goetzmann and Jorion, 1999; Brown et al., 1995, as discussed in Goetzmann and Jorion, 1999). In this context, survival bias refers to an upward bias in returns that occur because the U.S. equity markets have not had a major disruption during the measurement period as have markets in other countries. Failure to adjust historical data to account for this possibility could create an upward bias in estimated expected equity risk premiums because little reason exists to expect that the United States will continue its immunity to such disruptions in the future.[16] However, analyses of the historical data suggest that this source of potential bias may not be large.[17]

- **Survey data.** The appropriate equity risk premium to use in the CAPM is, by definition, an expected or forward-looking value and, as shown in Exhibit 7-1, can vary with different time horizons. Thus, one should tie the expected risk premium used for calculating the cost of capital to the expected business conditions over the investment's time horizon. A less certain economic outlook will lead to a higher risk premium. Some practitioners believe that surveys of current investors or expert expectations provide the best data regarding the current equity risk premium. One such approach is to use the DCF (or dividend discount) model to impute the implied expected rate of return on the S&P 500 based on surveys of current analyst forecasts.[18] A second approach is to survey experts regarding their estimates of the current equity risk premium. One such survey of financial economists found that, in 2000, the expected equity risk premiums ranged from 2 percent to 13 percent over a 30-year horizon and averaged 7 percent over 10- and 30-year horizons.[19] In comparison, the expected long-, medium-, and short-horizon expected equity risk premiums based on historical averages from 1926 to 2000 as reported by Ibbotson (2004) were 8.1, 8.5 and 9.4 percent, respectively.

(iii) Beta. The single-factor CAPM formula uses only one investment-specific variable, beta, the sensitivity of an investment to market risk. For a publicly traded company, analysts can calculate beta from the historical movement of the company's share price relative to the market.[20] Moreover, several sources, including Bloomberg, Value Line, Compustat, and Merrill Lynch, publish betas for most publicly traded stocks. Before using such published betas, however, users should understand their calculation procedure, which often includes adjustments to the calculated betas. For example, Bloomberg often reports adjusted betas, which Bloomberg normalizes toward 1.00 by multiplying the calculated or raw beta by 0.67 and adding 0.33, effectively giving a beta of 1.00 a 33 percent weight in all beta calculations. This accounts for reversion tendencies and sampling error.[21]

First, we perform a linear regression[22] with the returns of share A as the dependent variable and the excess market returns as the independent variable. The regression equation resembles the CAPM formula:

$$R_A - R_f = \alpha + \beta (R_m - R_f) + \varepsilon . \tag{6}$$

In this regression model, the slope coefficient, β, provides an estimate of the firm's true beta. The alpha term, α, and the error term, ε, represent portions of the firm's share returns not explained by movements in the market. The number of observed excess returns used for the regression should be large enough to reduce sampling error. Also, one should use a historical time period recent enough to reflect a company's current business risks. Exhibit 7-3 plots the monthly returns of Wal-Mart versus the monthly returns of the S&P 500 during the five-year period 1999 through 2003. The slope of the regression line estimates Wal-Mart's beta, 0.97.

In the absence of information about a company, we expect the beta for its shares to equal 1.00, the market average. Companies less affected by cyclical trends, such as utility companies, have betas less than 1.00. Companies more affected by economy-wide forces have betas higher than 1.00. Financial leverage also affects a share's beta.

Exhibit 7-4 provides beta estimates for a sample of retail companies. The first column shows betas calculated with daily data on share price returns and the S&P 500 index over the period 1999 to 2003. The second column includes betas calculated with daily data for 2003 only. The third column presents betas calculated

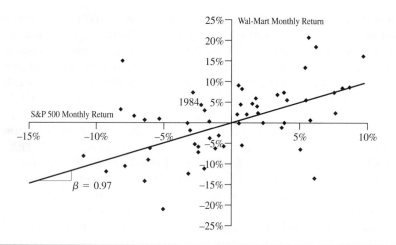

Exhibit 7-3.   Wal-Mart versus S&P 500, 1999–2003

with monthly data for the period 1999 to 2003. Finally, the fourth column contains Bloomberg's adjusted (toward 1.00) betas as of December 31, 2003. Exhibit 7-4 presents Bloomberg adjusted betas calculated on a weekly basis for the two years 2002 and 2003. Note the variation in beta estimates for each firm. In practice, the analyst must understand each firm's relation to the market and how this relation can change over time. The remainder of this chapter will use the betas calculated based on daily returns from 1999 to 2003.

(iv) Historical Data versus Future Expectations.   Studies find that if a business's portfolio of investment projects remains stable over time, its beta also will remain stable. The stability of beta matters because we use the cost of capital calculated with the CAPM in a forward-looking context (for example, discounting future cash flows). To calculate an expected cost of capital, one should use the expected values of each CAPM input. If betas remain stable over time, a company's historical beta should serve as a good proxy for its expected beta.

Estimated betas tend to revert toward 1.00 over time for a number of reasons, including significant sampling error.[23] Over a range of time periods, however, we expect sampling errors to average toward zero. Empirical studies have shown that

	Calculated Beta			
Company	**Daily, 1999–2003**	**Daily, 2003**	**Monthly, 1999–2003**	**Bloomberg Beta**
Wal-Mart	0.97	0.99	0.79	0.94
The Gap	1.13	0.90	1.67	0.94
American Eagle Outfitters ...	1.28	1.27	2.14	1.41
ShopKo Stores Inc.	0.90	1.47	0.44	1.14
Wilsons Leather	0.71	1.24	0.84	0.98

Exhibit 7-4.   Retail Company Betas

securities with betas greater than 1.00 more likely have positive error terms, whereas securities with betas less than 1.00 more likely have negative error terms. Another explanation looks to the tendency of managers to moderate extreme risk positions back toward the average. In this case, the historical beta should exceed the estimate of a future beta. As Section 7.4(a)(ii) discusses, some analysts and services (such as Bloomberg) adjust their estimates of betas toward 1.00 to account for reversion tendencies and sampling error.

(v) Asset Beta. Calculating a beta based on stock price movement results in an equity beta that reflects the riskiness of a firm's equity. Using the equity beta in the CAPM yields the return equity investors expect (i.e., the equity cost of capital). This will not reflect the appropriate rate if we want to evaluate the underlying asset (e.g., a company) rather than the equity stake in that asset. Although the application of CAPM extends beyond equity, measuring an asset's sensitivity to market risk in a way other than through share price movement presents difficulties. The underlying riskiness of a company wholly financed by equity equals the riskiness of that company's equity. For a company financed partially by debt, the riskiness of the equity relative to the riskiness of the assets increases because the lending arrangements entitle debt holders to receive full repayment, regardless of a company's performance.[24] Section 7.4(e) discusses methods for estimating the cost of capital appropriate for a company's assets.

(vi) Calculating the Cost of Equity Capital. Once we have estimated the three inputs of the CAPM formula, we can calculate the cost of equity capital. Exhibit 7-5 shows the cost of equity capital calculated for the sample of retail companies. We performed these calculations using a risk-free rate of 2.1 percent, the recent yield on 30-day Treasury bills, and an expected equity risk premium of 8.6 percent, the average premium for the S&P 500 for the period 1926 through 2003.

(b) Estimating Equity Cost of Capital with a Size-Adjusted CAPM. In the three-factor model presented earlier, the expected return depends on market risk, size premium, and book-to-market premium. As discussed in Section 7.3(c), in practice, practitioners often apply the size premium alone to improve their cost of capital estimates.

Exhibit 7-6 shows the size-adjusted costs of equity capital derived using size adjustments calculated by Ibbotson Associates. Ibbotson Associates classifies firms according to market value as *large-cap, mid-cap, small-cap,* and *micro-cap.* They then calculate the average size premium for each category other than large-cap. For the firms in the exhibit, American Eagle is a mid-cap firm, ShopKo is a

Company	Beta	Cost of Equity
Wal-Mart	0.97	10.5%
The Gap	1.13	11.9
American Eagle Outfitters	1.28	13.2
ShopKo Stores Inc.	0.90	9.9
Wilsons Leather	0.71	8.2

Exhibit 7-5.   Retail Companies—Cost of Equity

Company	Market Value ($ millions)	Cost of Equity Based on CAPM	Size Premium	Size-Adjusted Cost of Equity
Wal-Mart	$221,780	10.5%	—	10.5%
The Gap	19,209	11.9	—	11.9
American Eagle Outfitters	3,745	13.2	0.9%	14.1
ShopKo Stores Inc.	534	9.9	1.7	11.6
Wilsons Leather	122	8.2	4.0	12.2

Source: Ibbotson Associates, 2004.

Exhibit 7-6.   Retail Companies—Cost of Equity Using CAPM Adjusted for Size

small-cap firm, and Wilsons Leather is a micro-cap firm. Exhibit 7-6 adds the appropriate size adjustments as calculated by Ibbotson Associates for the period 1926 through 2003 to each firm's single-factor CAPM cost of equity capital.

(c) WACC: Adjusting for Debt and Taxes.   The appropriate cost of capital for evaluating an investment (e.g., a company) is the required rate of return on the assets that make up the company. Only if the company finances its operations entirely with equity does this required return on assets equal the equity cost of capital. A weighted average cost of capital reflects the returns required by the providers of different types of financing. The rate of return required on the assets themselves does not change. The return required by alternative sources of financing varies, however, according to the risk associated with each form of financing. The weighted average cost of capital (WACC) formula will properly incorporate financing into the cost of capital calculation only if the mix of equity and debt reflects the company's expected financing during the future investment time horizon. The following formula reflects the basic WACC:

$$WACC = R_E + E/V + R_D \times D/V \tag{7}$$

where

R_E = equity cost of capital
R_D = debt cost of capital
E/V = ratio of equity financing to total financing
D/V = ratio of debt financing to total financing.

This formula seems to imply that a firm can lower its cost of capital by increasing its leverage. This incorrect implication fails to consider that leverage increases the cost of equity, which offsets the effect of the lower rate on debt. Increased leverage also increases the cost of debt.

Firms can deduct from taxable income the interest they pay on debt, but they cannot deduct dividends from taxable income. The tax benefit associated with debt reduces the cost of borrowing. The cost of capital used to discount after-tax cash flows should reflect this tax benefit when firms use debt in their capital structure. The WACC formula adjusted for tax effects follows, where *t* equals the firm's marginal tax rate.[25]

$$WACC = R_E \times E/V + R_D(1 - t) \times D/V \tag{8}$$

Company	Cost of Equity	Cost of Debt	After-Tax Cost of Debt	Percent Equity	Percent Debt	WACC
Wal-Mart	10.5%	4.3%	2.8%	87.2%	12.8%	9.5%
The Gap	11.9	5.2	3.4	90.4	9.6	11.0
American Eagle Outfitters	14.1	n/a	n/a	100.0	0.0	14.1
ShopKo Stores Inc. . .	11.6	6.2	4.0	52.5	47.5	8.0
Wilsons Leather	12.2	7.2	4.8	82.9	17.1	11.0

Note: Cost of debt is based on Bloomberg fair market curves for Wal-Mart, The Gap, and ShopKo (using USD Composite five-year yields for different credit ratings: AA for Walmart, BB+ for Gap [based on an average of the BBB and BB yield], and BB- for ShopKo [based on an average of the BB and B yields]). For Wilsons Leather, which is not rated, the cost of debt is taken from Bloomberg's WACC page.

Exhibit 7-7.   Calculation of Weighted Average Cost of Capital (WACC)

We can expand this formula to include additional components of a company's financing, such as preferred stock. Exhibit 7-7 shows the weighted average cost of capital for the sample of retail companies. We use the size-adjusted CAPM model to calculate the cost of equity capital. The cost of debt equals the average expected yield on the company's publicly traded debt. These calculations assume a marginal tax rate of 35 percent for all of the firms. If firms employ other methods to raise capital (e.g., preferred shares), then the WACC calculation should include the appropriate weight and cost of capital. The firms in the exhibit use only debt and common equity instruments.

(d) Calculating Cost of Capital for Privately Held Companies.   The previous sections focused on calculating the cost of capital for publicly traded companies. This section discusses techniques for estimating the cost of capital for privately held companies.

The opportunity cost of capital specific to any single project of a company can differ from the average for the company. Usually, we cannot observe the systematic risk and cost of capital associated with a project. Likewise, we find it difficult to estimate the cost of capital of a privately held company because of the lack of data for historical share price movements necessary to observe systematic risk.

A common approach to such problems uses publicly traded companies engaged in similar activities as a benchmark for measuring risk. Of course, no two businesses are perfectly comparable, but the average cost of capital for a group of carefully chosen companies should provide a good estimate. In identifying comparable companies, one must analyze characteristics that relate to market risk. These characteristics include:

- Industry
- Earnings cycle
- Operating leverage (ratio of fixed costs to variable costs)
- Financial leverage

- Size
- Profitability
- Geographic markets
- Customer and vendor mix

(e) Using Asset Betas.   Because financial leverage affects the cost of equity capital, the average equity beta of a group of comparable companies can differ from the subject company's beta, especially if leverage differs across companies. To adjust for leverage effects, we calculate an asset beta as a first step in computing the equity beta for the specific company. An asset beta reflects the risk associated with a firm's assets, whatever its leverage. This asset beta, also called an *unlevered beta*, equals the equity beta when a firm finances entirely with equity. The equation for an asset beta, B_A, is similar to the WACC formula:

$$B_A = B_E \times E/V + B_D \times D/V \qquad (9)$$

where

B_E = equity beta
B_D = debt beta
E/V = ratio of equity financing to total financing
D/V = ratio of debt financing to total financing.

Analysts often assume that the debt beta equals zero, which implies that the company's borrowing rate should equal the risk-free rate. Borrowing rates, in fact, seldom equal the risk-free rate, because of default risk. Debt betas, however, tend to be small. For a company with little debt and a strong debt rating, assuming a debt beta of zero will not bias the asset beta estimate. For a firm with considerable leverage or a low debt rating, one can measure the debt beta by using the single-factor CAPM formula.[26]

Asset betas do not vary with leverage. Thus, one can compute an average asset beta for a group of comparable companies, and then relever to the specific company's capital structure to estimate the equity beta of the company.

7.5   CONCLUSION

This chapter addresses the risk factors that influence the cost of capital and various methods employed in its calculation. We discuss also the sensitivity of the methods to data and equation inputs, such as the risk premium. Regardless of the model employed, each component of the cost of capital calculation reflects uncertainty and subjectivity. Furthermore, data availability and an analyst's preference or judgment can affect the choice and application of a particular model. Because the final answer depends on so many factors, any litigation will include a debate regarding the correct cost of capital.

NOTES

1. Economists consider default risk a bond-market factor. *See* Fama and French (1993).
2. Yields from short-term securities would equal yields from long-term securities, because periods when investors expect higher future interest rates would counter periods when investors expect lower future interest rates.

3. Data from Lehman Brothers and Miller, Anderson & Sherrerd, as reported in Thomas L. Bennet, Stephen F. Esser, and Christian G. Roth, *Corporate Credit Risk and Reward* (West Conshohocken, PA: Miller, Andersen & Sherrerd, 1993) and re-reported in Frank J. Fabozzi, *Bond Markets, Analysis and Strategies,* (Englewood Cliffs, NJ: Prentice Hall, 1996).

4. Financing does affect the final cost of capital estimate if one considers taxes. *See* Section 7.4(c).

5. The authors of one study found that 74 percent of firms always or almost always used the CAPM to estimate the cost of capital. *See* Brealey and Meyers (2003).

6. Small, investor-operated businesses often fit the category of investments with a high cost of diversification. Individuals cannot diversify their human capital without cost because of moral hazard risks (e.g., shirking). Where diversification is costly, the opportunity cost rises.

7. This formula relies on the mathematics behind annuities and perpetuities and is sometimes referred to as the "Gordon Growth Model." According to Brealey and Myers (2003), the formulas were first developed in 1938 by J. B. Williams (Williams, 1938) and "rediscovered" by Gordon and Shapiro (1956). *See* Brealey and Myers (2003) for a complete discussion and derivation.

8. Duration is a statistical measure of interest rate risk. Duration encompasses more than the relation between yield and maturity, to include the sensitivity of bond price changes to interest rates. Duration is formally defined as the percent change in a bond's price with respect to a 1 percent change in interest rates.

9. For example, if we use the yield on an intermediate-term Treasury bond as the risk-free rate, then we should calculate the market premium as the difference between the average return on the market portfolio and the average return on intermediate-term Treasury bonds.

10. The University of Chicago's Center for Research in Security Prices (CRSP) has data on monthly prices and dividends for all NYSE stocks, dating back to 1926. Ibbotson Associates publishes an annual compendium of annual return data, beginning in 1926, for all major risk classes of securities. As discussed in Mehra and Prescott (2003), Shiller (1990) and Homer (1963) provide data on returns for large company (NYSE) stocks and Treasury certificates, respectively, back to 1871. Schwert (1990) and Siegel (1998) provide data as far back as 1802. Data for the period before 1871 have been described as less reliable than the data after that year (Mehra and Prescott, 2003).

11. For example, if one calculates beta from a regression of stock returns against the NYSE Composite Index, then one should use the risk premium associated with holding this same portfolio rather than the S&P 500. The market risk premium equals the equity risk premium when one uses common stocks as the proxy for the market.

12. If an investment yields a 100 percent return during the first year and a −50 percent during the second year, then the arithmetic mean return is 25 percent, in contrast to the geometric mean of 0 percent.

13. *See* Brealey and Myers (2003), Ibbotson (2005), and Ross, Westerfield, and Jaffe (1990).

14. Section 7.3(e) explains DCF modeling.

15. Fama and French use six-month commercial paper as a proxy for the risk-free rate. They note that using Treasury bills would add approximately 100 basis points to their estimates of the risk premium. This would produce equity premium estimates of 3.55 or 5.32 percent (4.83 or 5.78% on a "bias-adjusted" basis).

16. In this post-9/11 world, it is perhaps easier to imagine such a disruption.

17. Goetzmann and Jorion (1999) found that a globally diversified equity portfolio had capital appreciation returns of 4.0 percent from 1921 through 1996, versus 4.3 percent for the United States. Dimson et al. (2002) found that the average equity premium in the United States above Treasury bills from 1900 to 2000 (about 7.7%) was approximately equal to the simple average of 15 countries (7.4%). They also found that a

gobally diversified portfolio would have had a 6.2 percent premium. Based on these data, the authors conclude that concerns about the use of U.S. returns may have been overstated.

18. The DCF model can be applied to the entire S&P 500 to determine an implied rate of return for holding the market portfolio. This rate of return less the current risk-free rate is the current expected market risk premium.

19. Welch, I., "Views of Financial Economists on the Equity Premium and on Professional Controversies," Journal of Business, 2000, vol. 73, no. 4. pp. 501–537.

20. In statistical terminology, beta = $cov\ (r_A r_m)$, $var\ (r_m)$ where $cov\ (r_A r_m)$ = the covariance of the return of security A and the return of the market, and, $var\ (r_m)$ = the variance of the return on the market.

21. Betas may tend to revert toward 1.00 over time for a number of reasons, including significant sampling error. For example, an event specific to a company that causes its price to rise may by chance occur simultaneously with an event that causes the entire market to rise. In such a case, beta would be overstated. Over a range of time periods, we expect sampling errors to average out to zero. Empirical studies have shown that stocks with betas greater than 1.00 are more likely to have positive error terms, whereas stocks with betas less than 1.00 are more likely to have negative error terms. Another explanation may be the tendency of managers to moderate extreme risk positions back toward the average. In this case, the estimate of a future beta should be lower than the historical beta.

22. Simple linear regression is a statistical tool that determines the best fitting linear relation between two variables, in this instance the excess return on a security and the excess return on the market. Then this linear relation can be used to predict values for one variable based on the value of the other. See Chapters 5 and 6.

23. For example, an event specific to a company that causes its price to rise may by chance occur simultaneously with an event that causes the entire market to rise. In such a case, beta would be overstated.

24. A simple example illustrates why leverage increases the risk of the equity. Suppose a company has assets valued at $1,000 and the assets are expected to increase 10 percent to $1,100 by the end of one year. If the company is financed entirely with equity, then the value of the equity is also $1,000 and will also be expected to increase 10 percent to $1,100 in one year. If, instead, the company is financed with debt of $500, then the value of the equity is $500 (= $1,000 − $500). When the assets increase to $1,100, the debt remains at $500 and the equity increases to $600, a 20 percent return compared with the 10 percent return on the assets.

25. The marginal tax rate should reflect the expected tax position of the company in the future.

26. One can ascertain the debt beta from the single-factor CAPM equation by using the following inputs: the expected yield on debt, the risk-free rate, and the market risk premium.

BIBLIOGRAPHY

Altman, Edward I. "Measuring Corporate Bond Mortality and Performance." *Journal of Finance* XLIV, (September 1989).

Banz, R.W. "The Relationship between Return and Market Value of Common Stocks." *Journal of Financial Economics* (March 1981): 3–18.

Black, Fisher. M.C. Jensen, and M. Scholes. "The Capital Asset Pricing Model; Some Empirical Tests." In *Studies in the Theory of Capital Market* edited by M. C. Jensen. New York: Praeger, 1972.

Brealey, Richard A., and Stewart C. Myers. *Principles of Corporate Finance,* 4th ed. New York: McGraw-Hill, 1991.

Brown, S.J., W. Goetzmann and S. Ross, "Survival," *Journal of Finance* 50 (1995): 853–873.

Chan, K.C., and Nai-fu Chen. "Structural and Return Characteristics of Small and Large Firms." *Journal of Finance,* XLVI (September 1991).

Chandy, P.R., and L. Paul Hsueh. "An Examination of the Yield Spread between Insured and Uninsured Debt." *Journal of Financial Research,* XII (Fall 1989).

Chen, Nai-fu, Richard Roll, and Stephen A. Ross. "Economic Forces and the Stock Market." *Journal of Business,* 59, (1986).

Dimson, Elroy, Paul Marshall, and Mike Staunton. *Triumph of the Optimists, 101 Years of Global Investment Returns.* Princeton, NJ: Princeton University Press, 2002.

Fabozzi, Frank J. *Handbook of Fixed Income Securities,* 3rd ed. Homewood, IL: Business One Irwin, 1991.

Fama, Eugene F., and Kenneth R. French. "Common Risk Factors in the Returns on Stocks and Bonds." *Journal of Financial Economics,* 33 (1993).

———. "The Cross-Section of Expected Stock Returns." *Journal of Financial Economics* 47 (June 1992): 427–465.

———. "The Equity Premium." *Journal of Financial Economics* 57 (April 2002): 637–659.

Fons deromes and Kimball Andrew E. "Corporate Bond Defaults and Default Rates: 1970–1990." *Journal of Fixed Income* (June 1991).

Gordon, M.J and E. Shapiro. "Capital Equipment Analysis: The Required Rate of Profit," *Management Science* 3 (October 1956): 102–110.

Haugen, Robert A. *Modern Investment Theory.* Englewood Cliffs, NJ: Prentice-Hall, 1990.

Homer, S. (1963), *A History of Interest Rates* (Rutgers University Press, New Brunswick, NJ).

Ibbotson Associates. *Stocks, Bonds, Bills and Inflation: 2004 Yearbook.* Chicago: Ibbotson Associates, 2004.

Jorion, P. and W. Goetzmann, "Global Stock Markets in the Twentieth Century," *Journal of Finance* 54 (June 99): 953–980.

Markowitz, H.M. "Portfolio Selection." *Journal of Finance* 7 (March 1952): 77–91.

Lintner, J. "The Valuation of Risk Assets and the Selection of Risky Investments in Stock Portfolios and Capital Budgets." *Review of Economics and Statistics* 47 (February 1965): 13–37.

Mehra, Rajnish and E. Prescott, "The Equity Premium in retrospect," *Handbook of the Economics of Finance* (2003), G.M. Constantinides, M. Harris and R. Stulz, Eds. (Elsevier, B.V.), Chapter 14, pp. 887–936.

Merton, Robert C. "An Intertemporal Asset Pricing Model." *Econometrica* 41 (November 1973): 867–887.

Ross, Stephen A. "The Arbitrage Theory of Capital Asset Pricing." *Journal of Economic Theory* 12 December (1976): 341–360.

Ross, Stephen A., Randolph W. Westerfield, and Jeffrey F. Jaffe. *Corporate Finance,* 2nd ed. Homewood, IL: Irwin, 1990.

Schwert, G.W. (1990), "Indexes of U.S. stock prices from 1802 to 1987," *Journal of Business* 63: 399–426.

Sharpe, William F. *Investments,* 3rd ed. Englewood Cliffs, NJ: Prentice Hall, 1985.

Sharpe, William F. "Capital Asset Prices: A Theory of Market Equilibrium under Conditions of Risk." *Journal of Finance* 19 (September 1964): 425–442.

Shiller, R.J. (1990), *Market Volatility* (MIT Press, Cambridge, MA).

Siegel, J. (1998), *Stocks for the Long Run,* 2nd Edition (Irwin, New York).

Standard & Poor. *Standard & Poor's Stock Guide.* New York: Standard & Poor, September 1993.

———. *Standard & Poor's Bond Guide.* New York: Standard & Poor, September 1993.

———. New York: Standard & Poor, *The Value Line Investment Survey.* December 24, 1993.

Williams, J. B. *The Theory of Investment Value.* Cambridge, MA.: Harvard University Press, 1938.

CHAPTER **8**

EX ANTE VERSUS EX POST DAMAGES CALCULATIONS

Michael J. Wagner
Michael K. Dunbar
Roman L. Weil

CONTENTS

8.1 INTRODUCTION

Economic damage awards in litigation serve a double purpose: they compensate entities that suffered harm from unlawful acts, and they deter future unlawful acts. The optimal compensation award should put an injured entity in the same economic position it would have been but for the act. The optimal deterrent award, putting aside punitive issues, should be equal to the ill-gotten gain derived from the unlawful act adjusted for the probability that someone will detect the act. In many cases these two amounts are the same. Consider an example whereby I steal $100 from you. If I were immediately apprehended and forced to return your money, then your economic loss would be eliminated and my ill-gotten $100 would have been disgorged. Under that circumstance, the compensation amount equals the deterrent amount. I would have no incentive to steal from you, and you would have no incentive to make it easy to be robbed.

In this example of immediate restitution, one can easily find an optimal award that satisfies both the compensation and deterrent purposes. Ideally, plaintiffs would receive instantaneous compensation for the damages they suffered without delay between the date of injury and the award of damages. If a delay occurs between the time of the unlawful act and the date of restitution, however, the victim's harm and the wrongdoer's ill-gotten gain often diverge.

In the real world, a delay always occurs between the date of injury and the date of compensation to the plaintiffs. During the time lag, in addition to the divergence between the damages and ill-gotten gain, information about the value of the unlawful act becomes available, which can change the parties' perception of the damages.

For example, suppose that you buy a lottery ticket for $1. Then suppose I steal it from you before the lottery winner becomes publicly known. Assume that on the date of the injury all lottery tickets had an equal chance of winning and there was no shortage of tickets available for $1. Time passes and it turns out that the ticket I stole from you is the lottery winner and is now worth $32 million. How much should I pay you to make you whole? Do I owe you the expected value of the return from the ticket, about 12 cents, called the *ex ante* value before the event?[1] Or do I owe you the fair market value of the ticket I stole, $1? Or, do I owe you the amount that you would have made had you owned the winning ticket, $32 million, its *ex post* value, or value after the event?

Surely one could argue that if you bought a ticket with an expected value of 12 cents, you were not planning to try to resell it before the winner was announced. If you weren't keeping the ticket through the lottery, you would have been better off not buying it at all. Therefore, after the fact—*ex post*—it is a virtual certainty that you would have won the lottery. One could also argue that the $1 price of the ticket is the risk-adjusted value of that ticket and reflects the value of the low probability of a particular ticket winning.

Given these circumstances, and considering that at the time of the theft you could have bought another ticket with equal probability of winning for $1, few would disagree that on the date of the theft, damages did not exceed $1. However, after the lottery ends and your ticket becomes worth $32 million, few juries would think that me giving you back $1 of my $32 million in winnings presents a just resolution, even with the understanding that I had borne the risk of the ticket's not winning. After all, the case would likely not have gone to trial if the ticket did not win, and therefore, I had borne a small risk of having to pay any restitution at all.

8.2 EXPECTANCY VERSUS OUTCOME DAMAGES

Ex ante is Latin for "from before." A pure *ex ante* analysis would use only information available at the time of the unlawful act to calculate the damages incurred at the time of the act. Practitioners base the analysis, therefore, on the expectancy that they would have if they were to analyze the damage caused by the act contemporaneously with the occurrence of the act. Most business activities resemble lotteries: the firm invests time and money up front in an activity with an uncertain outcome. Thus, the damages expert faces the question of whether to compute damages at the time of the investment (or unlawful act) or after the outcome is known.

Ex post is Latin for "from after." A pure *ex post* analysis uses all the information available up to the date of the analysis. Such an outcome-based analysis considers

	Ex Ante	*Ex Post*
Information	Use information known or knowable on the date of the unlawful act; ignore subsequent events.	Use all available information.
Measurement Date	Date of unlawful act.	Date of analysis.
Discounting	Discount all cash flows back to the date of unlawful act using a rate that reflects the risk of the asset. Calculate prejudgment interest on this amount from the date of the unlawful act to the date of judgment using a rate reflecting either the plaintiff's cost of capital, or the defendant's debt rate.	Bring past cash flows (i.e., damages) to present value using an interest rate reflecting either the plaintiff's cost of capital or the defendant's debt rate. Discount future cash flows (i.e., damages) to the date of judgment.

Exhibit 8-1.   Differences between *Ex Ante* and *Ex Post* Calculations

facts that become known after the unlawful act. For example, an *ex post* analysis would consider a product's success in the marketplace or the increased value of a tangible asset.

One could also perform an analysis that is a hybrid between *ex post* and *ex ante*. For example, analyses often use subsequent information but discount cash flows that occurred after the unlawful act back to the date of the act at a risk-adjusted discount rate.

The differences between *ex post* and *ex ante* analyses lie in which information subsequent to the unlawful act the analyst uses, the date of the damages measurement, and how the analyst discounts future damages. Exhibit 8-1 highlights the differences between the two approaches as practitioners have applied them.

8.3   APPLICATION OF THE *EX ANTE* APPROACH IN LITIGATION

(a) The Mechanics of *Ex Ante* Analyses.   To illustrate the mechanics of *ex ante* analyses, we use the following example. Suppose that on New Year's Day 2000, the defendant stole the victim's 1972 AMC Pacer. At that time, the defendant and others could have bought an identical replacement Pacer for $300. Also, suppose that in early 2005 BMW came out with a remake of the original Pacer and subsequently the fair value of a classic AMC Pacer increased to $10,000.

The car's owner files a lawsuit and trial begins on December 31, 2006. An expert using a pure *ex ante* approach would calculate damages of $300 and then might calculate interest on the $300 from January 1, 2000 to December 31, 2006. Three hundred dollars is the expected value of the car as dictated by the then-current market price. If the plaintiff had a different expectation for the car's future value, he could have mitigated any damages by buying another car for $300 after the theft. In fact, if he had thought the car was worth more than its market value of $300, he should have bought additional cars.

Advocates of *ex ante* analyses point out that using *ex ante* information properly allocates risk.[2] In the example of the Pacer, the car's market price on the date of the theft already incorporates the probability that the model will become a collector car. The market price also incorporates the then-higher probability that the car will ultimately be worth only the salvage value of the metal.

The victim, by having his $300 car stolen, was relieved of the risk that it would ultimately become nearly valueless and deprived of the low probability outcome that it would become a collector car. The market value of the car on the theft date reflects the present value of these two possible outcomes and all future costs and benefits associated with ownership of the car. In this way, using *ex ante* information avoids two significant potential pitfalls of *ex post* analyses: incorrectly accounting for avoided risk and neglecting avoided costs and benefits.

Proponents of the *ex ante* approach would argue that awarding $10,000 would improperly reward the plaintiff for the full current value of the car without taking into account that the plaintiff avoided the costs and risks of ownership. Implicitly, the costs and risks of ownership equal $9,700 (= $10,000 − $300). In other words, an *ex ante* approach properly measures the value of an asset at the time it *was taken*, whereas an *ex post* approach converts a risky investment into a certain outcome.

Even though the *ex ante* approach solves some particularly sticky problems, it presents additional ones. For example, some firms have private information upon which they value particular assets more or less highly than the market does. In that case, do the firms' expectations set the amount of damages? Likewise, the plaintiff may have had a once in a lifetime chance to succeed (i.e., there may have been no additional lottery tickets or Pacers available to replace the stolen one). Additionally, the assets can have unique value to a particular firm. Is this unique value the relevant measure of *ex ante* damages if the firm falls victim to an unlawful act? Proving that an asset has a value that differs from market value can be difficult.

The damages expert can rarely value the act's consequences with accuracy as of the time of the act because of the difficulty of reconstructing the information known when the act occurred. Sometimes contemporaneous forecasts exist, but these can be imprecise information sources. Forecasts produced for different purposes or by different business units in the same organization can vary. Sometimes individuals associated with a project prepare more aggressive forecasts than those prepared by management, whose bonuses rely on performance compared against those forecasts. Banks and venture capitalists prefer conservative forecasts. Firms and industries often have multiple forecasts with widely divergent results. These problems sometimes drive experts to inappropriately rely on forecasts made at the time of the unlawful act that were not reliable for reasons other than the act.

(i) Usable Information.   An *ex ante* analysis relies on information known or knowable at the time of the unlawful act. However, one cannot easily identify all knowable information. Anything in the public dominion is arguably knowable. Private information held by the opposing parties or third parties is also arguably knowable. For example, patent law accepts that the patent holder's private information is knowable. Patent law regards all subsequent information as knowable at the time of the hypothetical negotiation that the courts assume to occur contemporaneously with the act. Section 8.6 of this chapter discusses this concept, also known as the *book of wisdom.*

One way to identify relevant information hypothesizes an analysis that the plaintiff could have performed at the time of injury. The current analysis could include any information that the injured party would have used in performing that contemporaneous analysis. As a practical matter, the expert uses other information from documents dated slightly after the date of the unlawful act on the basis that the information was known or knowable prior to the date that the document memorialized it.

Questions often arise regarding the treatment of subsequent mitigation and investment. If one uses an *ex ante* analysis, one should not consider the outcome of subsequent actual mitigation. Doing so converts the analysis into an *ex post* measure of damages. Similarly, in theft of trade secrets or patent infringement cases, the injured party often makes significant investments after the date of the theft that it might not have made had it been aware of the theft. To ensure consistency, a pure *ex ante* analysis should not consider subsequent information about these actual investments.

(ii) Measurement Date.   The measurement date is the date as of which the expert calculates damages. In the case of an unlawful act that occurs on a single date, say the breach of a contract, the measurement date would be the date of the breach. Some cases have multiple unlawful acts occurring on different dates. For example, one could argue that every time a patent infringer makes, uses, offers to sell, or sells an infringing product, the infringer commits a new unlawful act. In this example, an expert applying an *ex ante* analysis should measure the damages associated with each separate unlawful act on the date that each occurred.[3]

(iii) Probability of Outcome.   If no contemporaneous market price exists, or if for some reason the market price does not reflect the idiosyncratic value to the victim, then the expert can forecast future cash flows with contemporaneous information. Such forecasts lend themselves to assigning relative probabilities to different possible outcomes. Similarly, if contemporaneous analyses do exist, one may find multiple analyses, such as best case, worst case, and expected case analyses. A proper analysis should assign probabilities to the various scenarios and weight the resultant net present values of damages proportionately.

(iv) Ex Ante *Discounting.*   In *ex ante* discounting, an expert applies a risk-adjusted rate of return appropriate for the company or project at issue when discounting the lost cash flows back to the date of damage (or breach). This results in a lump sum equal to the present value of the damages on the date of the injury. The analysis can weight this lump according to the probability of outcome as described in

Section 8.3(a)(iii) of this chapter. The expert subsequently applies prejudgment interest to the damages amount starting from the date of the act and continuing through the restitution date.

As with identifying measurement dates, discounting becomes complicated when the unlawful act is not a one-time event. For example, suppose that two unlawful acts occur on different dates. One could ascertain separate discount rates for each unlawful act and discount the lost cash flows back to the corresponding unlawful act dates. Or, as in the case of the patent infringement discussed in Section 8.3(a)(ii) of this chapter, one should not discount all the cash flows back to the date of first infringement; instead, an expert should discount the separate cash flows (at different discount rates, if necessary) to the date of each lost sale. In summation, if the unlawful act does not occur on a single date, then the expert should calculate damages associated with each unlawful act and discount each back to the appropriate dates at the appropriate discount rate that depends on the date of each unlawful act.[4]

(v) Prejudgment Interest. Some courts allow the computation of prejudgment interest and grant that amount to plaintiffs. One should calculate prejudgment interest from the date of damages to the date of recovery. Because of uncertain recovery dates, the courts often use the date of trial as a proxy for the recovery date. Courts have used a variety of interest rates for prejudgment interest. State law and federal statutes often specify a statutory rate. If no statutory rate exists, it is common and logical to use the defendant's unsecured borrowing rate.[5] This makes sense because the defendant owes the damages to the plaintiff; thus, the analysis can regard the damages as funds that the plaintiff has, albeit involuntarily, lent to the defendant. The appropriate risk-adjusted rate for this loan reflects the defendant's default risk, captured by the defendant's unsecured borrowing rate for loans of similar duration initiated in the same time period. Even though courts sometimes use the plaintiff's opportunity cost as a measure of prejudgment interest rates, this would not be an appropriate rate because this would presume that the plaintiff would have assumed risk that it had not indeed assumed in order to earn its opportunity cost.

(b) The Debate

(i) Advantages. The *ex ante* approach properly accounts for risk. The contemporaneous market price or contemporaneously conducted analyses capture the probability of the entire spectrum of outcomes. Awarding a plaintiff with all the benefits of a successful project without the plaintiff having to assume the project risk would overcompensate the plaintiff. In fact, it would give the plaintiff an incentive to seek harm. Better that I should induce you to deprive me of the right to drill for oil on a site that is likely a dry hole than that I should spend the, say, $1 million to drill for myself. If I can induce you to deprive me of the right to drill, then I can save the $1 million of drilling costs but still collect the value of the oil if, contrary to expectation, it turns out the well would have been a gusher. Additionally, the results of an *ex ante* analysis are independent of when the trial occurs. Therefore, there is no incentive for a plaintiff to attempt to game the court system by timing a potential lawsuit to maximize damage awards. *Ex ante* analyses also provide foreseeability of consequences to potential wrongdoers. Another advantage: it does not penalize the plaintiff for either pursuing or not pursuing mitigation.

(ii) Disadvantages. *Ex ante* approaches often require a complex reconstruction of the world at the time of the unlawful act, likely impaired by a shortage of contemporaneous information. The expert will often need to construct both an actual and a but-for world, neither of which in fact existed. The artificial actual world reflects the cash flow from the next best alternative given the unlawful act. The but-for world is composed of future cash flows that would have followed but for the act.

Another potential disadvantage of the *ex ante* approach lies in its use of contemporaneous markets for valuation at the time of the unlawful act. The notion that the market value at any given time reflects the present value of future cash flows assumes efficient markets and perfect information. However, some markets are not efficient, and perfect information rarely exists. In fact, proponents of the *ex ante* approach agree that private information related to the value at the date of the act provides the best information and therefore the market is not the ultimate arbiter of value.[6] Also, even with complete information, market forecasts can be wrong. Even if one had a broad portfolio of stolen cars, the forecast future value of the cars at the time of the theft will not likely closely match the actual future value if the restitution were many years away.

(c) Case Law and References Supporting *Ex Ante* Analyses. This section cites some cases that reflect court decisions supporting *ex ante* analyses. For each case we provide excerpts from the published opinions, without editorial comment or modification by the authors.

INDU CRAFT, INC. v. BANK OF BARODA, 47 F.3D 490, 495-496 (1995)

Breach of Contract. Indu Craft concedes that it proffered no evidence with respect to fixed costs. Decisional law analyzing the role of fixed costs in damages calculations is sparse since most breaches of contract in a business setting do not result in the termination of a business. Plaintiff relies on our decision in [*Adams v.*] *Linblad Travel*, 730 F. 2d 89, 93 (2nd cir. 1984), for its view that overhead costs need not be deducted from income to calculate damages. That reliance is misplaced. *Linblad* determined that fixed costs should not have been included in the damages calculation where plaintiff was an ongoing business whose fixed costs were not affected by the breach. *Id.*

In the present case, plaintiff's cessation of business may very well have reduced or eliminated fixed overhead costs. Such savings, resulting from the Bank's breach, are properly offset from lost profits. Hence, the failure to deduct fixed costs when utilizing lost profits to calculate damages renders such measurement too imprecise for judicial use. However, proof of lost profits is but one method of proving the amount necessary to restore plaintiff to the economic position he would have been in absent the breach. An alternative methodology, extrapolating the value of a business as an ongoing entity from the company's past earnings, establishes a plaintiff's damages without suffering the same defect. By resorting to past earnings, this methodology already incorporates the necessary deduction of fixed and variable costs, providing an accurate measurement of plaintiff's loss as adjusted for savings resulting from the breach.

In fact, when the breach of contract results in the complete destruction of a business enterprise and the business is susceptible to valuation methods, such an approach provides the best method of calculating damages. *Cf. Sharma v. Skaarup Ship Management Corp.*, 916 F.2d 820, 825 (2d Cir.1990) ("where the breach involves the deprivation of an item with a determinable market value, the market value at the time of the breach is the measure of damages"), *cert. denied*, 499 U.S. 907, 111 S.Ct. 1109, 113 L.Ed.2d 218 (1991). The methodology of determining a business's earnings and applying an earnings multiplier to fix the value of a business that was completely terminated is one we have approved. *See Lamborn v. Dittmer*, 873 F.2d 522, 533-34 (2d Cir.1989).

SHARMA v. SKAARUP SHIP MANAGEMENT CORPORATION, 916 F.2D 820, 825-826 (1990)

Breach of Contract.   It is a fundamental proposition of contract law, including that of New York, [FN3] that the loss caused by a breach is determined as of the time of breach. *See Simon v. Electrospace Corp.*, 28 N.Y.2d 136, 145, 269 N.E.2d 21, 26, 320 N.Y.S.2d 225, 232 (1971). It is also fundamental that, where the breach involves the deprivation of an item with a determinable market value, the market value at the time of the breach is the measure of damages. *See* id at 145-46, 269 N.E.2d at 26, 320 N.Y.S.2d at 233.

Numerous cases illustrate these principles. For example, changes in currency exchange rates subsequent to a breach may not be taken into account in measuring damages. *See Parker v. Hoppe*, 257 N.Y. 333, 178 N.E. 550 (1931). The damage award resulting from a breach of an agreement to purchase securities is the difference between the contract price and the fair market value of the asset at the time of breach, not the difference between the contract price and the value of the shares sometime subsequent to the breach. *See Aroneck v. Atkin*, 90 A.D.2d 966, 967, 456 N.Y.S.2d 558, 559 (App.Div. 4th Dep't 1982) (rejecting claim that value of securities should be based on performance of business in 1979 and 1980 rather than at time of breach in 1978 when value was $0). Where a purchaser breaches a contract to buy real estate, the measure of damages is the difference between the contract price and the fair market value at the time of breach, even though the seller is able to sell the real estate only later and for less than the value on the date of breach. *See Webster v. DiTrapano*, 114 A.D.2d 698, 699, 494 N.Y.S.2d 550, 551 (App.Div. 3d Dep't 1985) (contract price $63,500, value at time of breach $57,500, sold eleven months later for $55,000, damage award should have been $6,000). The same measure applies when a seller of a home breaches and the buyer is forced to assume higher interest rates in purchasing another home as a result of the breach. *See Lotito v. Mazzeo*, 132 A.D.2d 650, 651, 518 N.Y.S.2d 22, 23 (App.Div. 2d Dep't 1987).

Appellants have not led us to any New York authority that even remotely undercuts the numerous contrary precedents. They rely heavily upon *Greasy Spoon, Inc. v. Jefferson Towers, Inc.*, 75 N.Y.2d 792, 551 N.E.2d 585, 552 N.Y.S.2d 92 (1990). However, that case involved a lessor's refusal to execute documents enabling the lessee to obtain municipal licenses and permits to operate a sidewalk cafe adjacent to the lessee's restaurant. The licenses and permits did not have a market value and were not replaceable. Lost profits were therefore the best measure of the loss. Other cases that have awarded lost profits, such as *McLeod, Inc. v. R.B. Hamilton Moving and Storage*, 89 A.D.2d 863, 453 N.Y.S.2d 251 (2d Dep't 1982), are similarly distinguishable. In *McLeod*, a lessee of a crane failed to return it in good condition and thus caused it to be unusable for ten weeks. The court awarded the lessor the profits lost for the period in which it could not be leased. Had the crane been permanently rather than temporarily disabled, damages under New York law would have been the value of the crane on the date of breach. Damages for the temporary loss would be the leasing value for that period, which is the same as lost profits.

M & R CONTRACTORS & BUILDERS v. MICHAEL, 215 MD. 340, 351; 138 A.2D 350, 356 (1958)

Breach of Contract. In the decisions in which plaintiffs were allowed to recover *direct* profits they had lost, we have consistently stated that the measure of damages is the difference between the price specified in the contract and what it would have cost the plaintiff to do, or to complete, the work he had undertaken to perform.

KELLY v. MARX, 428 MASS. 877, 878; 705 N.E. 2D 1114, 1115 (1999)

Breach of Contract. *Discussion.* We affirm the decision of the Superior Court because we reject the "second look" approach, and conclude that a liquidated damages clause in a purchase and sale agreement will be enforced where, at the time the agreement was made, potential damages were difficult to determine and the clause was a reasonable forecast of damages expected to occur in the event of a breach.

BRUSHTON-MOIRA CENTRAL SCHOOL DISTRICT v. FRED H. THOMAS ASSOCIATES, 91 N.Y.2D 256, 261-262; 692 N.E.2D 551, 553-554; 669 N.Y.S.2D 520, 522-523 (1998)

Breach of Contract. The Appellate Division erred, however, in holding that damages are to be measured as of the date of trial. It has long been recognized that the theory underlying damages is to make good or replace the loss caused by the breach of contract (*see*, e.g., *Reid v. Terwilliger*, 116 N.Y. 530, 532, 22 N.E. 1091). Damages are intended to return the parties to the point at which the breach arose and to place the nonbreaching party in as good a position as it would have been had the contract been performed (*see*, e.g., *Goodstein Corp. v. City of New York*, 80 N.Y.2d 366, 373, 590 N.Y.S.2d 425, 604 N.E.2d 1356; Haig, Commercial Litigation in New York State Courts, § 51.3[c], at 31 [4 West's New York Practice Series, 1995]; Restatement [Second] of Contracts § 347, comment a; § 344). Thus, damages for breach of contract are ordinarily ascertained as of the date of the breach (*Rodriguez v. Moore-McCormack Lines*, 32 N.Y.2d 425, 429, 345 N.Y.S.2d 993, 299 N.E.2d 243; *Simon v. Electrospace Corp.*, 28 N.Y.2d 136, 145, 320 N.Y.S.2d 225, 269 N.E.2d 21; *Parker v. Hoppe*, 257 N.Y. 333, 341, 178 N.E. 550).

Upon this amount, interest is awarded pursuant to statutory mandate. CPLR 5001(a) provides that interest shall be recovered upon a sum awarded for a breach of contract. The CPLR further mandates that "[i]nterest shall be computed from the earliest ascertainable date the cause of action existed" (CPLR 5001[b]). The award of interest reflects a recognition of the principle that damages are properly ascertained as of the date of the breach and a recognition that there may be a time lag between the accrual of a plaintiff's cause of action and the resulting damage sustained and actual payment by defendant (*see, Love v. State of New York*, 78 N.Y.2d 540, 544- 545, 577 N.Y.S.2d 359, 583 N.E.2d 1296). If damages were to be computed as of a date other than the accrual of the cause of action the application of CPLR 5001(b) could lead to anomalous results and windfalls for some plaintiffs. In view of the clear statutory direction that interest *must* be computed from the date of accrual, we need not deviate from the general rule that damages should be measured as of that same date. To the extent that the Appellate Division relied on *Kaiser v. Fishman*, 138 A.D.2d 456, 525 N.Y.S.2d 870, supra, which was followed in *Attardo v. Petosa*, 240 A.D.2d 607, 659 N.Y.S.2d 294, those lower court precedents should not be followed and this action should not be treated differently from other breach of contract situations.

Measuring replacement costs as of the date of trial, moreover, might contradict the general principle that the injured party has a duty to mitigate damages (*see, Wilmot v. State of New York*, 32 N.Y.2d 164, 168-169, 344 N.Y.S.2d 350, 297 N.E.2d 90; *Losei Realty Corp. v. City of New York*, 254 N.Y. 41, 47-48, 171 N.E. 899; Haig, Commercial Litigation in New York State Courts, § 39.3[c], at 501 [3 West's New York Practice Series, 1995]; Restatement [Second] of Contracts, § 350). Notably, plaintiff has incurred no expense to repair and has had use of the building during the entire period, nor has it claimed any consequential damages. There would be no incentive to mitigate damages if plaintiff could wait until trial to recover damages measured as of the trial date and, in addition, receive interest from the earlier date of accrual.

8.4 APPLICATION OF THE *EX POST* APPROACH IN LITIGATION

(a) The Mechanics of *Ex Post* Analyses. *Ex post* computations rely on actual outcomes. The expert looks backward from the time of trial and uses actual information. In an *ex post* analysis, experts believe that events that have happened after the date of the unlawful act provide information useful in understanding the economic effect of the act and, thus, affect the cost imposed by the act. Consider our example of the stolen AMC Pacer introduced in Section 8.3(a) of this chapter. The market value on the date of theft was $300 even though the current market value is $10,000. Using *ex post* information, damages would be $10,000 less the avoided costs of ownership between the theft date and today (e.g., costs of maintenance, insurance, and fuel), plus any lost benefits of ownership of the car between the theft date and today (e.g., monetary award in a car show and the cost of replacement transportation services).

The application of *ex post* information raises several questions:

- If subsequent information is available, how should the expert use it?
- If the analysis uses subsequent information, how does this affect the risk profile of the cash flows and, consequently, how does this affect the appropriate discount rate for discounting those cash flows?
- Does the use of subsequent information affect the selection of the present value date used for the calculation of damages?
- How should the analysis treat subsequent mitigation and investment?

(i) Usable Information. In a pure *ex post* analysis, all available information has relevance. Because the analysis aims to value the unlawful act as of the date of

restitution, more recent information about the value becomes particularly important in assessing the current value. If only forecasts are available at the time of computation, the analysis uses recent forecasts, not earlier ones, and also adjusts those forecasts for known differences in assumptions.

Additionally, both the outcomes of mitigation efforts and the actual investments made by the victim provide relevant and important information in *ex post* analyses. For example, if the defendant wrongfully precluded the plaintiff from making a particular investment, an expert should consider what the plaintiff subsequently did or should have done with the funds it could not invest.

(ii) Measurement Date.   Experts measure *ex post* damages as of the date of restitution. Such analyses use the trial date or the analysis date as proxies for the date of restitution. One could also use the expected date of final payment or even the expected date of the resolution of subsequent appeal, depending on the facts of the case and the available information.

(iii) Ex Post *Discounting of Cash Flows.*   The *ex post* approach discounts future lost cash flows at the risk-adjusted rate of return appropriate for the company or project at issue. *Ex post* discounting uses past lost cash flows and brings them forward to the restitution date at a rate sufficient to compensate for the defendant's default risk, but with no other risk considerations. As Section 8.4(a)(ii) of this chapter discussed, the analysis can use various dates as a proxy for the restitution date.

Proponents of the *ex post* approach argue that their method of discounting has merit because it gives the plaintiff the exact recovery that, if invested at the same risk-adjusted rate of return as that of the firm, will reproduce the future stream of lost cash flows. Proponents also argue that the *ex post* approach offers the only means of putting plaintiffs in the same position they would have been in but for the unlawful act. In fact, one could argue that this approach is conservative, because it regards the plaintiff's restitution date as the date of trial when, in fact, restitution often does not occur until much later, particularly if a party appeals the case. In that situation, even though the plaintiff does not receive restitution until years after the initial trial date, the method discounts the amount generated from future cash flows further back than necessary, to the initial trial date.

Critics of the *ex post* approach argue that by discounting only future damages that occur after the restitution date, experts accept pretrial damages as though they were certain and neglect the risk associated with earning those cash flows. The counter arguments have a legal rather than economic basis. In fact, the defendant precluded the plaintiff from taking the risks associated with earning those particular cash flows. If the plaintiff wanted to and could take those risks, the defendant should not benefit from preventing the plaintiff from taking those risks. One could also argue that once the plaintiff proves liability, the benefit of any uncertainty should go to the plaintiff. Section 8.7 of this chapter discusses the case law supporting this concept, known as the wrongdoer's rule. Moreover, critics argue, *ex post* damages reduce the incentive for mitigation—after all, victims could have bought another lottery ticket or another Pacer and restored their economic position as of the time of the unlawful act. If one knows they will collect *ex post* damages, then they have no incentive to mitigate.

(iv) Prejudgment Interest.   Even though *ex post* analyses do not discount past lost cash flows, the cash flows should accrue prejudgment interest from the date the

plaintiff lost them to the date of recovery (or a proxy for such a date). As with *ex ante* analyses, courts have used various interest rates for prejudgment interest. State law or federal statutes often specify a statutory rate. If no statutory rate exists, one can use the defendant's unsecured borrowing rate because the plaintiff is effectively lending the damages amount to the defendant.

(b) The Debate

(i) Advantages.   The *ex post* approach appeals to an individual's sense of justice. If someone steals your lottery ticket that becomes worth $32 million, then even an unskilled lawyer can persuade jurors to award you $32 million in damages, not $1. While proponents of the *ex ante* approach argue that an *ex ante* analysis makes the victim whole as of the *date of the unlawful act*, proponents of the *ex post* approach argue that the *ex post* approach makes the victim whole at *any time*.

The *ex post* approach also provides a social deterrent to violating the legal rights of others. Only cases with significant damages will go to trial. For example, no one will bring a case to trial for a stolen lottery ticket that lost. *Ex ante* damages, therefore, will fail to deter when the plaintiff has little incentive to bring the wrongdoer to justice either because the outcome was small (or negative) or because even when the outcome was large, its expected value was small and the defendants need pay only the expected value. In the real world of potential judicial error and high transaction costs to litigating, this suggests that *ex ante* damages analysis without compensation for both the chance of court error and transactions costs does not properly deter.

Additionally, the *ex post* approach ensures that those who commit unlawful acts do not receive windfalls from doing so. Even though the thief of a losing lottery ticket is not brought to justice, his benefit was small—the small probability of winning and keeping the benefits of winning. This poses a powerful argument for using *ex post* information to calculate unjust enrichment.

(ii) Disadvantages.   The *ex post* approach to measuring damages has disadvantages, one being that damages amounts change over time as new data become available. Because the changing environment influences *ex post* damages, this approach provides incentive for gaming the courts to maximize or minimize damages. For example, a party can intentionally delay proceedings until the stock market improves, or, as in our example, until classic AMC Pacers are valued at $10,000. Second, as Section 8.4(a)(iii) of this chapter discussed, the *ex post* approach unquestionably gives plaintiffs the benefit of the proceeds from a risk that they did not bear. Also, this approach risks overcompensation of the plaintiff. In particular, if the plaintiff can choose between an *ex post* and an *ex ante* remedy, the plaintiff is overcompensated when the *ex post* damages exceed *ex ante* damages. A defendant will argue whichever approach gives the lower damages figure as the correct approach to use.

Frank Fisher puts forth an alternative argument that the *ex post* method can overly deter wrongdoers because the infringer runs the risk of the downside loss. For example, assume that the infringer has a 50 percent chance of a $200 gain and a 50 percent chance of a $100 loss; his expected gain then equals $50 [= (50% × $200) + (50% × −$100)]. The plaintiff will not choose to sue if the infringer incurs a loss but will sue if the infringer makes a gain. The plaintiff's expected recovery equals $100 [= (50\% \times \$200) + (50\% \times 0)]$, and the defendant's expected net loss after disgorgement is $-\$50 [= (50\% \times (\$200 - \$200)) + (50\% \times (-\$100 + \$0))].^{7}$

Thus, the plaintiff may be compensated for risk he did not bear and also the infringer may be hit too hard by both bearing the downside risk and potentially being forced to disgorge the entire upside.

(c) Case Law and References Supporting *Ex Post* Analyses. Courts have often accepted *ex post* analyses. This section cites some cases that reflect *ex post* decisions by the courts. We list each case along with excerpts from the published opinions, without editorial comment or modification.

FISHMAN v. ESTATE OF WIRTZ and *ILLINOIS BASKETBALL, INC. v. ESTATE OF WIRTZ*, 807 F.2D 520, 552 (1986)

Sherman Act and Illinois Law. In this connection, defendants first object to the district court's approach by arguing that damages must be computed as of the date of the injury—in this case, as of July 1972. While this rule may generally govern simple contract damages, it is not necessarily controlling in cases such as the one before us where the injury is continuing or where damages from the injury continue to accrue.... The Bulls did not go out of business but instead continued in business in the hands of CPSC, giving the court, as we have noted, an exceptionally helpful guide to IBI's damages.

Defendants argue that the going-concern value of the Bulls in July 1972 represents a full recovery for IBI because that going-concern value—that is, what a willing buyer given all available information would have paid for the team in 1972—is by definition a future income stream discounted to present value. The district court's valuation, on the other hand, is based on *actual* gain experienced by the Bulls over ten years. (The 1972 going-concern value was affected by a number of *ex ante* predictions, which were proved either true or false and were reflected in the 1982 value). We do not understand defendants' objection to using this adjusted value (which is not speculative, *cf. Farmington Dowel Products*, 421 F.2d 61) because we know of no case that suggests that a value based on expectation of gain is more relevant and reliable than one derived from actual gain. "To correct uncertain prophecies ... is not to charge the offender with elements of value nonexistent at the time of his offense. It is to bring out and expose to light the elements of value that were there from the beginning." *Sinclair Refining Co. v. Jenkins Petroleum Process Co.*, 289 U.S. 689, 698, 53 S.Ct. 736, 739, 77 L.Ed. 1449 (1933) (citations omitted); *see also A.C. Becken Co. v. Gemex Corp.*, 314 F.2d 839, 840 (7th Cir.), *cert. denied*, 375 U.S. 816, 84 S.Ct. 49, 11 L.Ed.2d 51 (1963) ("a *forecast* of tomorrow's weather is always subject to confirmation or modification by tomorrow's *observation*") (emphasis in original); *Twentieth Century-Fox Film Corp. v. Brookside Theatre Corp.*, 194 F.2d 846, 856 (8th Cir.), *cert. denied*, 343 U.S. 942, 72 S.Ct. 1035, 96 L.Ed. 1348 (1952) (passage of time permits better proof of extent of harm).

Authors' note: We know of no requirement that damages must always be computed as of the time of the injury or, if not, reduced by some appropriate discount rate to produce a value as of that date.

TWENTIETH CENTURY-FOX FILM CORP. v. BROOKSIDE THEATRE CORP., 194 F.2D 846, 856 (1952)

Clayton Act. Complaint is made that if the action had been tried at the time it first accrued, it would not then have been possible to make proof of the prospective profits that might reasonably have resulted from a conduct of the business during the period of the leasehold destroyed. That would doubtless have been a misfortune to the plaintiff but it does not change the rule as to the measure of damages nor the admissibility of evidence to prove damages. In Restatement of Torts, Volume 4, Chapter 47, section 910, the rule is stated as follows: Time when the requirement of certainty is satisfied. Although at the time of the commission of the tort or at the time of bringing suit there can be no recovery for a particular resulting harm because its extent was then not definitely ascertainable, if, before the time of trial, the situation is so changed that the extent of harm can be proved with the required degree of certainty, recovery is permitted.... Thus where there has been interference with a business, events antecedent to the trial may indicate that profits which at the time of the tort were apparently speculative would certainly have been made.

PARK v. EL PASO BOARD OF REALTORS, 764 F.2D 1053, 1068 (1985)

Sherman Act. FN23. In addition, since the exact number of residential resales in El Paso can now be determined for much of the damages period, the plaintiff should incorporate these figures into his model rather than rely on projections as he did previously. The plaintiff should also use actual figures rather than projections for the home resale inflation rate, when calculating the commissions he would have received for his lost sales.

A.C. BECKEN CO. v. GEMEX CORPORATION, 314 F.2D 839, 840 (1963)

Civil Antitrust. 1. In our 1959 opinion, supra at 5, we concluded that the court was led into error in finding as a fact and concluding as a matter of law that plaintiff was not damaged as a result of defendant's refusal to sell watch bands to it after August 2, 1956. We said "Damage was proved." We added,

"While the evidence now in the record might be sufficient to justify a direction to the district court to compute there from plaintiff's actual damages sustained and make an assessment accordingly, we feel that the ends of justice would be better served if this cause be remanded for the purpose of considering the evidence already in the record on the subject of plaintiff's damages, as well as any proper evidence to be offered by defendant, and rebuttal evidence of plaintiff, on subject of plaintiff's damages, and fixing the proper amount of said damages." Such proceedings we now direct.

The record before us shows that the district court on remand proceeded along the lines suggested. It heard additional evidence that was devoted to actual occurrences during the time which elapsed while the case was being litigated upon appeal. The court thus put itself in a position where it had the benefit, not only of such projections as might have been reasonably based upon the facts appearing at the first trial, which were at that time projected by plaintiff to prove further damages, but it also had the superior advantage of evidence of conditions which had in fact occurred while the case had been on appeal. We concur in the conclusion of the district court that, under these circumstances, evidence of actual occurrences and experiences between the first and last hearings may be considered in connection with the estimates of future damage introduced at the first hearing. Thus, a forecast of tomorrow's weather is always subject to confirmation or modification by tomorrow's observation. While the evidence at the first hearing was a reliable basis for prognostication and was legally admissible to prove damage, no one can deny that to the extent future events modified its correctness, the entire evidence must be considered together. This the court did in this case and we find no error in that respect.

TRANS-WORLD MANUFACTURING CORP. v. AL NYMAN & SONS, INC., 750 F.2D 1552, 1568 (1984)

Design Patent Infringement.   2. A reasonable royalty is the amount that "a person, desiring to manufacture [, use, or] sell a patented article, as a business proposition, would be willing to pay as a royalty and yet be able to make [, use, or] sell the patented article, in the market, at a reasonable profit." *The Goodyear Tire & Rubber Co. v. Overman Cushion Tire Co.,* 95 F.2d 978, 984, 37 USPQ 479, 484 (6th Cir.1938). *Panduit Corp. v. Stahlin Bros. Fibre Works, Inc.,* 575 F.2d 1152, 197 USPQ 726 (6th Cir.1978). Among the factors to be considered in determining that amount is the infringer's anticipated profit from use of the patented invention, including "[t]he effect of [using] the patented specialty in promoting sales of other products of the licensee." *Georgia-Pacific Corp. v. U.S. Plywood-Champion Papers,* 318 F.Supp. 1116, 1120, 166 USPQ 235, 238 (S.D.N.Y.1970) *mod.* 446 F.2d 295, 170 USPQ 369 (2d Cir.), *cert. denied,* 404 U.S. 870, 92 S.Ct. 105, 30 L.Ed.2d 114, 171 USPQ 322 (1971). 5 Chisum, *Patents* § 20.03[3][b][iv], [v]. *See Deere & Co. v. International Harvester Co.* 710 F.2d 1551, 218 USPQ 481 (Fed.Cir.1983). Evidence of the infringer's actual profits generally is admissible as probative of his anticipated profits. *Locklin v. Switzer Brothers, Inc.,* 235 F.Supp. 904, 906, 143 USPQ 233, 238 (N.D.Cal.1964); 5 Chisum, *Patents* § 20.03[3][b][iv].

By supplying the patented racks for displaying the eyeglasses, Nyman used "the patented [invention] in promoting sales of" the nonpatented eyeglasses. Trans-World may be able to prove that Nyman's infringing use of the displays played an important part in the retail sales of Nyman's eyeglasses. Furthermore, the extent of the profits from such sales could be relevant in determining the amount of a reasonable royalty. If, for example, sales were increased because of the infringing use of the displays, that fact could affect the amount of royalties a potential licensee would be willing to pay.

We therefore disagree with the district court's exclusion of evidence of Nyman's profits from the sale of displayed eyeglasses as not relevant to the determination of a reasonable royalty. In so stating, we express no opinion concerning the weight, if any, to be given such evidence or any conditions that might properly be imposed upon its admission; we indicate only that we do not think the district court should have excluded it.

LAM, INC. v. JOHNS-MANVILLE CORPORATION, 219 USPQ 670, 677 (1983)

Patent Infringement.   Lam's impaired growth was clearly shown in Exhibit PX-6. A high rate of growth is evident from 1974 to 1976. Following years of decreased growth due to J-M's infringement, Lam has since enjoyed an even greater growth rate. Such post-infringement growth rate is certainly admissible evidence to form a basis for inferring that Lam would have grown at the pre-infringement rate had J-M not infringed. Cf. *Sinclair Refining Co. v. Jenkins Petroleum Process Co.*, 289 U.S. 689, 697-99 (1933).

FROMSON v. WESTERN LITHO PLATE AND SUPPLY CO., 853 F.2D 1568, 1575 (1988)

Patent Infringement.   Like all methodologies based on a hypothetical, there will be an element of uncertainty; yet, a court is not at liberty, in conducting the methodology, to abandon entirely the statutory standard of damages "adequate to compensate" for the infringement. The royalty arrived at must be "reasonable" under all the circumstances; i.e., it must be at least a close approximation of what would be "adequate to compensate" for the "use made of the invention by the infringer." 35 U.S.C. § 284.

The methodology encompasses fantasy and flexibility; fantasy because it requires a court to imagine what warring parties would have agreed to as willing negotiators; flexibility because it speaks of negotiations as of the time infringement began, yet permits and often requires a court to look to events and facts that occurred thereafter and that could not have been known to or predicted by the hypothesized negotiators.

MICHIGAN STATE HIGHWAY COMMISSION v. DAVIS, 38 MICH. APP. 674, 679-680; 197 N.W.2D 71, 73-74 (1972)

Eminent Domain.   Since we are dealing here not with the value of the property taken, but rather with the damage done to the residue as a result of the taking, we find no bar to the introduction of evidence bearing on those damages despite the fact that the evidence concerns facts occurring after the date of the taking. The trial court's ruling excluding such evidence was, therefore, in error.

KILPATRICK v. WILEY, REIN & FIELDING, 37 P.3D 1130, 1145 (2001)

Legal Malpractice.   ¶ 72 Defendants contend the trial court erred in allowing the jury to determine plaintiffs' damages resulting from their loss of ownership in the station, i.e., lost ownership and lost cash distribution, as measured *either* from the date of defendants' alleged breaches of fiduciary duty or from the date almost a decade later when the case was ready for trial. We disagree. Defendants rely heavily on *Sharma v. Skaarup Ship Management Corp.*, 916 F.2d 820 (2d Cir.1990), a federal case interpreting New York contract law. The *Sharma* court stated as follows:

Measuring ... damages by the value of the item at the time of the breach is eminently sensible and actually takes expected lost future profits into account.

The value of assets for which there is a market is the discounted value of the stream of future income that the assets are expected to produce. This stream of income, of course, includes expected future profits and/or capital appreciation.

916 F.2d at 826. While such an approach may be appropriate in some cases, "the general objective of tort law [is] to place an injured person in a position as nearly as possible to the position he would have occupied but for the defendant's tort." *Acculog, Inc. v. Peterson*, 692 P.2d 728, 731 (Utah 1984) (citing *State v. Stanley*, 506 P.2d 1284 (Alaska 1973)). We believe that the trial court is in the best position to determine what award of damages will make a plaintiff whole, and, thus, we are willing to permit the trial court to use its discretion in determining the date from which damages will be measured. *See Anchorage Asphalt Paving Co. v. Lewis*, 629 P.2d 65, 68 (Alaska 1981) ("Because the circumstances of individual cases differ drastically, it is impractical to adopt a definite point in time to value damages. It has been found preferable to leave the question to the trial court's discretion.").

¶ 73 In this case, we conclude the trial court's decision was within its permitted range of discretion. By measuring damages at the time of trial, the jury was presented with estimates of the MWT, Ltd., limited partners' lost profits from 1987 to the expected trial date, 1997, as well as the potential fair market value of Channel 13 in 1997. We believe this evidence allowed the jury to come to a reasonable approximation of the damages the MWT, Ltd., limited partners actually incurred as a result of defendants' alleged breaches of fiduciary duty. Accordingly, the trial court's decision was within its permitted discretion.

8.5 HYBRID APPROACH

Experts frequently blend different aspects of both *ex ante* and *ex post* analyses in a hybrid approach. A common hybrid between a pure *ex ante* and a pure *ex post* analysis uses *ex post* information but an *ex ante* measurement date. Experts discount the lost cash flows back to the date of the unlawful act, using a risk-adjusted discount rate based on the actual volatility of the returns in the *ex post* period.

The hybrid approach reasons that if all parties know what the lost cash flows would have been, no rationale exists for ignoring this information. What actually happened was, after all, one of the plausible outcomes at the time of the breach. This hybrid approach also appeals to some individuals' sense of justice because it uses the real world as a basis for the calculation of damages as opposed to a hypothetical expectation of what was known and knowable at the time of the unlawful act. It eliminates some speculation as to what the cash flows would have been.

Advocates argue that we must discount the actual cash flows to reflect the business risk of earning those cash flows. If the analyses do not discount actual cash flows at a risk-adjusted rate, as occurs in a pure *ex ante* approach, plaintiffs enjoy a superior economic position relative to where they would have been but for the unlawful act because the analyses ignore business risk.

Consider the situation in which a person has a choice between earning cash flows associated with some uncertainty and holding a free call option on his future cash flows. This individual would invariably choose the call option, because with a call he avoids down-side risk. Likewise, pursuing a pure *ex post* result in court is like giving the plaintiff a free call on his future lost cash flows, because to obtain those cash flows, but for the unlawful act, the plaintiff would have had to suffer through some level of uncertainty; he avoided such uncertainty when the act occurred.[8]

Discounting the *ex post* cash flows back to the date of the unlawful act at the appropriate risk-adjusted discount rate moves the pure *ex post* result closer to a position that is at risk parity with what would have happened but for the unlawful act. The appropriate discount rate for the hybrid approach should incorporate information from proxy companies in the market. The risk premium would be the market risk premium multiplied by the beta of the proxy companies for a period that parallels the damages period as closely as feasible. This hybrid analysis should calculate prejudgment interest as in the *ex ante* analyses—from the date of the unlawful act to the date of restitution. Therefore, an expert would first discount future lost cash flows to the date of the unlawful act and then apply prejudgment interest to both future and past lost cash flows from the date of the illegal act. When statute does not specify a prejudgment interest rate, a reasonable rate would be the defendant's borrowing rate.

8.6 THE BOOK OF WISDOM

Some hybrid analyses use the concept of the *book of wisdom*. This concept allows damages experts to apply facts established after the date of damage to their calculations. The Supreme Court first set forth the concept of the book of wisdom in 1933 in the landmark case *Sinclair Ref. Co. v. Jenkins Petroleum Co.*, 289 U.S. 689, 698-99, 53 S. Ct. 736, 77 L. Ed. 1449 (1933). In its decision, the Court stated that

> at times the only evidence available may be that supplied by testimony of experts as to the state of the art, the character of the improvement, and the probable increase of efficiency or savings of expense. . . . This will generally be the case if the trial follows quickly after the issue of the patent. But a different situation is presented if years have gone by before the evidence is offered. Experience is then available to correct uncertain prophecy. Here is a book of wisdom that courts may not neglect. We find no rule of law that sets a clasp upon its pages, and forbids us to look within.

Further, the Court opined that facts established after the date of damage do not necessarily change past facts, but rather, they "bring out and expose to light the elements of value that were there from the beginning."

Use of the book of wisdom often persuades courts because one could perceive it as a call for less speculation. In *Transit RR. Comm'rs.*, 197 N.Y. 81, 108, 90 N.E. 456, 465 (1909), the courts ruled that "[c]ertainty is better than conjecture, and injuries actually inflicted a better guide than opinion of experts as to the market values just before and after." Likewise, in *Fishman, et al. v. Estate of Arthur M. Wirtz, et al.*, 807 F.2d 520 (7th Cir. 1986), the Seventh Circuit allowed a damages calculation that applied the book of wisdom, stating that "we know of no case that suggests that a value based on expectation of gain is more relevant and reliable than one derived from actual gain."

In cases involving a measurement of value, the courts have used the book of wisdom to allow an analysis or grant an award based on a lost outcome (i.e., *ex post*) approach, as opposed to a lost expectancy (i.e., *ex ante*) approach. For example, the Seventh Circuit sided with a book of wisdom approach in *Fishman*. The Fifth Circuit also supported a valuation analysis based on the book of wisdom in *Park v. El Paso Board of Realtors*, 764 F.2d 1053 (1985), where it opined that, even though a hypothetical sale at the date of the unlawful act can present a useful analogy for purposes of valuation, a lost going concern value offers a more appropriate measure of loss when the plaintiff has been driven out of business. The court based its support of a lost going concern calculation because nothing in principle prevents a plaintiff with a destroyed business from recovering future profits.

In addition to cases of valuation, courts often apply the book of wisdom in patent infringement cases when deciding the details of the hypothetical negotiation that would have occurred between two parties. In *Fromson v. Western Litho Plate & Supply Co.*, 853 F.2d 1586, 1575-76 (Fed. Cir. 1988), the Federal Circuit, citing *Sinclair*, indicated that one could look at postinfringement events in calculating reasonable royalty damages. In this case, the plaintiff wanted to use the infringer's actual profits as evidence of the value of the patent. The court found that excluding the evidence was erroneous and explained that

> the methodology [of simulating a hypothetical negotiation] encompasses fantasy and flexibility; fantasy because it requires a court to imagine what warring parties would have agreed to as willing negotiators; flexibility because it speaks of negotiations as of the time infringement began, yet permits and often requires a court to look to events and facts that occurred thereafter and that could not have been known to or predicted by the hypothesized negotiators.

Likewise, in *Jamesbury Corporation v. United States*, 207 USPQ 131 (US ClCt 1980), the opining judge found that because he was "aided by the benefit of hindsight, it [seemed] unnecessary to create such a fictional [analysis]" as a hypothetical negotiation might have used.

Courts have, however, on occasion limited the applicability of the book of wisdom. In *TWM Manufacturing Co. Inc. v. Dura Corp.*, 789 F.2d 895, 899-900 (Fed. Cir. 1986), the defendant argued that the plaintiff erred in its damages calculation because it based damages on a gross profit value that the defendant's management had projected in an internal memorandum prior to the defendant's infringement of the patent. The defendant believed that the plaintiff should have considered actual gross profit values, not projected values. The Federal Circuit rejected the defendant's argument and considered its preinfringement memorandum as probative on the reasonable royalty issue. Thus, the court focused on the time the infringement began. Specifically, the court ruled that the book of wisdom did not apply in this case, and evidence of what happened after that time did not mitigate damages. Additionally, in *Odetics Inc. v. Storage Technology Corp.* (CA FC) 51 USPQ2d 1225 (1999), the U.S. Court of Appeals for the Federal Circuit found that the federal district court had not abused its discretion by disallowing a book of wisdom approach and thus excluding evidence of two licenses granted by a patent infringement plaintiff from consideration in calculating a reasonable royalty rate for award of damages. They reasoned that, because the hypothetical negotiation required in reasonable royalty analysis obliges courts to envision the terms of a licensing agreement reached between patentee and infringer when infringement began, the court could not in this case consider the license agreements in question, which were negotiated four and five years after the date of infringement.

Robert Goldscheider reconciles the contrary positions of the courts by saying that "one may employ the book of wisdom only by looking prospectively from the date of the hypothetical negotiation, not retrospectively." He illustrates this concept with the example of an invention that had no noninfringing alternative at the date of the hypothetical negotiation but had one—a design-around—five years later. In this case, the expert cannot use the book of wisdom to say that this alternative technology was potentially available at the time of the hypothetical negotiation just because it was achieved five years later. However, this example shows that it took five years to design around the infringed patent. The expert should use this information in calculating damages. Additionally, Goldscheider writes that "reference should be made by expert witnesses to the book of wisdom whether or not such actual subsequent events were non-foreseeable aberrations. Anything that can contribute to the realism of the exercise should be given serious consideration."[9]

In summation, substantial case law indicates that experts can, and indeed should, incorporate all information, even information relating to events that occurred after the date of damage or after the date of hypothetical negotiation in the damages analysis. One could argue that, if the goal is to ascertain the amount of damages that would return the plaintiff to the same position it would have been in but for the unlawful act, the expert should use all available information in reconstructing the but-for world so that the resulting award reflects all the events that have contributed to or limited the damages suffered by the plaintiff.

8.7   THE WRONGDOER'S RULE

Because precedent has accepted both *ex post* and *ex ante* analyses, how do the courts decide which approach to use? Both experts and courts often overlook the concept of the wrongdoer's rule.

When the court has found liability, the wrongdoer's rule gives the benefit of the doubt to plaintiffs, leaving defendants with the burden of dispelling any uncertainty. In *Story Parchment Co. v. Paterson Parchment Paper Co. et al.*, 282 U.S. 555, 51 S.Ct. 248 (1931), the Supreme Court ruled that "whatever ... uncertainty there may be in [a] mode of estimating damages, it is an uncertainty caused by the defendant's own wrong act; and justice and sound public policy alike require that he should bear the risk of the uncertainty thus produced." The courts can apply this ruling to find in favor of a plaintiff's damages calculation.

Although its application is certainly not limited to *ex post* and *ex ante* cases, the wrongdoer's rule can provide a guideline for courts dealing with these two alternative analyses when deciding which damages calculation to award. Unless proved otherwise by the wrongdoer, courts will not withhold a reasonable damages estimate from the plaintiff. In *Fishman, et al. v. Estate of Arthur M. Wirtz, et al.*, 807 F. 2d 520 (7th Cir. 1986), the Seventh Circuit granted a damages award based on an *ex post* analysis, opining that defendants' objections of speculation were not sufficient as the "defendants ... should not benefit because their wrongdoing made it difficult to establish the exact amount of injury." Additionally, the court held that an *ex post* analysis was a reasonable estimate of damages as "we know of no case that suggests that a value based on expectation of gain is more relevant and reliable than one derived from actual gain." It also cited *Sinclair Refining Co. v. Jenkins Petroleum Process Co.*, 289 U.S. 689, 53 S.Ct. 736 (1933) in saying that "[t]o correct uncertain prophecies ... is not to charge the offender with elements of value non-existent at the time of his offense. It is to bring out and expose to light the elements of value that were there from the beginning." As applied by the Court of Appeals of Maryland in *M & R Contractors & Builders, Inc. v. Michael et al.,* 215 Md. 340, 138 A.2d 350 (1958), the court can use the wrongdoer's rule in awarding an *ex ante* damages calculation. In this case, the court found nothing wrong in a damages calculation based on a profit expectation that was measured as of the signing of the subsequently broken contract. The court advised the district court, "[W]here a defendant's wrong has caused the difficulty of proving damage, he cannot complain of the resulting uncertainty." Citing from *Corbin on Contracts* (1951), the court further expresses "doubts [as to whether the amount of lost profits] will generally be resolved in favor of the party who has certainly been injured and against the party committing the breach."

Courts have not frequently applied the wrongdoer's rule to cases in which *ex ante* and *ex post* have been points of contention, but courts have tested and upheld its applicability on many occasions. In each of these occasions, the defendants complained that the plaintiffs' measures of damages were speculative, but the courts allowed these calculations because, as stated in *Story Parchment*, the uncertainty involved was "caused by the defendant's own wrong act." Following *Story Parchment*, the Supreme Court again applied the wrongdoer's rule in granting damages based on historical performance to the plaintiff in *Bigelow, et al. v. RKO Radio Pictures, Inc., et al.,* 327 U.S. 251; 66 S. Ct. 574 (1946). The wrongdoer's rule as established by *Story Parchment* allowed for the granting of damages "which are definitely attributable to the wrong and only uncertain in respect of their amount." However, in *Bigelow*, the Supreme Court went one step further than it had in *Story Parchment* by saying that even though a jury cannot "render a verdict based on speculation or guesswork ... the wrongdoer may not object to the plaintiff's reasonable *estimate of the cause of injury* and of its amount, supported by the evidence, because [it is] not based on more accurate data which the wrongdoer's misconduct has rendered unavailable" (emphasis added). Few courts, however, have applied the wrongdoer's rule as recognized in *Bigelow* to establish a causal relation between the harmful act and economic damages.

The Second Circuit has also used the wrongdoer's rule to award plaintiff damages when damage has resulted from the defendant's harmful act. *See Contemporary Mission, Inc. v. Famous Music Corp.,* 557 F.2d 918 (1977) and *Indu Craft, Inc. v. Bank of Baroda,* 47 F.3d 490 (1995). As the Second Circuit stated in its *Contemporary Mission* decision, "[U]nder the long-standing New York rule, when the existence of damage is certain, and the only uncertainty is as to its amount, the plaintiff will not be denied a recovery of substantial damages." State courts have also supported the wrongdoer's rule. The Supreme Court of Michigan has ruled that the risk of uncertainty should be thrown upon the wrongdoer instead of upon the injured party. (*Allison v. Chandler,* 11 Mich. 542, 550-556 (1863)) Similarly, in *Tull v. Gundersons, Inc.,* 709 P.2d 940, 945 (1985), the Supreme Court of Colorado granted damages to the plaintiff "although the amounts were not mathematically certain, [because] had we disallowed recovery ... for injuries that had been proven in fact, we would have rewarded the injured party."

In cases of *ex ante* and *ex post*, the courts can use the wrongdoer's rule in siding with the plaintiff's measure of damages. Because both approaches yield arguably reasonable results, defendants carry the burden of showing why the plaintiff's analysis is not appropriate for a specific case. This is especially applicable when the defendant's own acts have precluded an accurate understanding of the but-for world (e.g., cases of antitrust and breach of contract).

8.8   CONCLUSION

The time lag between the date of the unlawful act and the date of restitution will always foster debate as to the merits of using *ex ante* and *ex post* analyses in calculating damages. No single approach will be appropriate for all situations; the decision to apply any particular approach will depend on case specifics. For any method described in this chapter, one can concoct a situation in which the result of applying that method would not satisfy a common perception of fairness.

NOTES

1. Here we ignore the state's vigorish in selling tickets. Because of the state's take from the proceeds before disbursing to the winners, the expected value of all legal lotteries of which we are aware is negative.
2. The statement of this approach appears in J. M. Patell, R. L. Weil, and M. A. Wolfson, "Accumulating Damages in Litigation: The Role of Uncertainty and Interest Rates," *Journal of Legal Studies* XI (June 1982): 341–364.
3. In the case of continuing breach, such as patent infringement, the limiting case occurs when each period approaches zero length. (Recall the limit theorems and analysis of first-year calculus.) In that case, under suitable assumptions of continuity of damages paths, the *ex ante* analysis and the *ex post* analysis will give the same result. The periods are so short that the before-the-fact analysis of each period becomes identical with the after-the-fact analysis of the preceding period.
4. Obviously, this approach merits a measure of common sense. At some point, this exercise becomes so complex that it becomes unfeasible.
5. The first showing of this result appears to be in Patell et al. (*see* n. 2). *See also* Chapter 9 in this book.
6. Franklin M. Fisher, and Craig R. Romaine, "Janice Joplin's Yearbook and the Theory of Damages," *Journal of Accounting, Auditing & Finance* (Winter 1990): 156–157.
7. Sherry, Edward F., and Teece, David J, Some Economic Aspects of Intellectual Property Damages, Practicing Law Institute; Patents, Copyrights, Trademarks and Literary Property Course Handbook Series, PLI Order No. G0-007N, New York City, October 7–8, 1999, Section XI.
8. As stated earlier in the chapter, we assume that courts do not error. If the courts will assume that there is some chance of error, then they should divide the result by the probability of being found guilty.
9. Robert Goldscheider, "The Employment of Licensing Expertise in the Arena of Intellectual Property Litigation," *IDEA: The Journal of Law and Technology* (1996).

LIST OF CASES

A.C. Becken Co. v. Gemex Corporation, 314 F.2d 839, 840 (1963)

Allison v. Chandler, 11 Mich. 542, 550–556; 1863 WL 1202 (Mich.) (1863)

Bigelow v. RKO Radio Pictures, Inc., 327 U.S. 251; 66 S. Ct. 574 (1946)

Brushton-Moira Central School District v. Fred H. Thomas Associates, 91 N.Y.2d 256, 261–262; 692 N.E.2d 551, 553–554; 669 N.Y.S.2d 520, 522–523 (1998)

Contemporary Mission, Inc. v. Famous Music Corporation, 557 F.2d 918 (1977)

Fishman v. Estate of Wirtz and *Illinois Basketball, Inc. v. Estate of Wirtz,* 807 F.2d 520, 552 (1986)

Fromson v. Western Litho Plate and Supply Co., 853 F.2d 1568, 1575 (1988)

Indu Craft, Inc. v. Bank of Baroda, 47 F.3d 490, 495–496 (1995)

Jamesbury Corporation v. United States, 207 USPQ 131 (1980)

Kelly v. Marx, 428 Mass. 877, 878; 705 N.E. 2d 1114, 1115 (1999)

Kilpatrick v. Wiley, Rein & Fielding, 37 P.3d 1130, 1145 (2001)

LAM, Inc. v. John-Manville Corporation, 219 USPQ 670, 677 (1983)

Michigan State Highway Commission v. Davis, 38 Mich. App. 674, 679–680 (1972)

M&R Contractors & Builders v. Michael, 215 Md. 340, 351; 138 A.2d 350, 356 (1958)

Odetics Inc. v. Storage Technology Corp.,51 USPQ2D 1225 (1999)

Park v. El Paso Board of Realtors, 764 F.2d 1053, 1068 (1985)

Sharma v. Skaarup Ship Management Corporation, 916 F.2d 820, 825–826 (1990)

Sinclair Refining Co. v. Jenkins Petroleum Process Co., 289 U.S. 689; 53 S.Ct. 736 (1933)

Story Parchment Co., v. Paterson Parchment Paper Co., 282 U.S. 555; 51 S.Ct. 248

The Board of Rapid Transit Railroad Commissioners of the City of New York, 197 N.Y. 81, 108, 90 N.E. 456, 465 (1909)

Trans-World Manufacturing Corp. v. Al Nyman & Sons, Inc., 750 F.2d 1552, 1568 (1984)

Twentieth Century-Fox Film Corp v. Brookside Theatre Corp., 194 F.2d 846, 856 (1952)

Tull v. Gunersons, Inc., 709 P.2d 940, 945 (1985)

TWM Manufacturing Co., Inv. V. Dura Corp., 789 F.2d 895, 899–900 (1986)

BIBLIOGRAPHY AND SUGGESTED REFERENCES

Adams, Edward S., and Runkle, David E. "Solving a Profound Flaw in Fraud-on-the-Market Theory: Utilizing a Derivative of Arbitrage Pricing Theory to Measure Rule 10B-5 Damages." *University of Pennsylvania Law Review* (May 1997): 1097–145.

Ben-Shahar, Omri, and Bernstein, Lisa. "The Secrecy Interest in Contract Law." *Yale Law Journal* (June 2000): 1885–925.

Bonsack, Konrad. "Damages Assessment, Janis Joplin's Yearbook, and the Pie-Powder Court." *George Mason University Law Review* 13 (Fall 1990): 1–26.

Fisher, Franklin M., and Romaine, R. Craig. "Janis Joplin's Yearbook and the Theory of Damages." *Journal of Accounting, Auditing and Finance* 5 (Winter 1990): 145–57.

Kabe, Elo R., and Blonder, Brian L. "Discounting Concepts and Damages (New)." In *Litigation Services Handbook, 1999 Supplement to the 2nd Edition*. Hoboken, NJ: John Wiley & Sons, pp. 325–54.

Kolaski, Kenneth M., and Kuga, Mark. "Measuring Commercial Damages Via Lost Profits or Loss of Business Value: Are These Measures Redundant or Distinguishable?" *Journal of Law and Commerce* (Fall 1998): 1–354.

Lanzillotti, R.F., and Esquibel, A.K. "Measuring Damages in Commercial Litigation: Present Value of Lost Opportunities." *Journal of Accounting, Auditing and Finance* 5 (Winter 1990): 125–44.

MacIntosh, Jeffrey G., and Frydenlund, David C. "An Investment Approach to a Theory of Contract Mitigation." *University of Toronto Law Journal* Spring (May 1987): 113–82.

Patell, James M., Roman L. Weil, and Mark A. Wolfson. "Accumulating Damages in Litigation: The Roles of Uncertainty and Interest Rates." *Journal of Legal Studies* XI (June 1982): 341–64.

Phillips, John R. "The Rite Way to Discount Damages." Putnam, Hayes & Bartlett, Inc.

Scott, Robert E. "The Case for Market Damages: Revisiting the Lost Profits Puzzle." *The University of Chicago Law Review* 57 (Fall 1990): 1155–202.

Taurman, John D., and Bodington, Jeffrey C. "Measuring Damage to a Firm's Profitability: *Ex Ante* or "*Ex Post*"?" *Antitrust Bulletin* 37 (Spring 1992): 57–106.

Tye, William B., and Kalos, Stephen H. "Antitrust Damages From Lost Opportunities." *The Antitrust Bulletin* (Fall 1996).

CHAPTER 9

PREJUDGMENT INTEREST

Michael S. Knoll
Jeffrey M. Colón

CONTENTS

9.1 INTRODUCTION

Litigants often turn their attention to prejudgment interest only toward the end of a lawsuit. They are often weary, overextended (in terms of their financial and other obligations), and in a rush to conclude the matter. Many have not yet focused on the issue and regard it as an afterthought. Such a mistake can prove expensive because many jurisdictions grant courts wide discretion in calculating prejudgment interest. Thus, lawyers and experts who understand the concepts involved can provide substantial value to their clients.

The authors acknowledge the seminal work in this area: James M. Patell, Roman L. Weil, and Mark A. Wolfson. "Accumulating Damages in Litigation: The Roles of Uncertainty and Interest Rates," *The Journal of Legal Studies*, 11 (June 1982): 341–364. They also acknowledge Roman L. Weil's chapter titled "Compensating the Plaintiff for Asynchronous Payments," which appeared in the 2004 and 2005 Cumulative Supplement of the *Litigation Services Handbook*. This chapter contains material taken from Weil's chapter.

An expert working on prejudgment interest should first ascertain how the relevant jurisdiction views the issue. In the United States, no single set of rules guides prejudgment interest. Instead, different rules apply depending on the relevant jurisdiction and perhaps the cause of action under which the plaintiff seeks recovery. Many states have prescribed simple rules. For example, some states set a fixed prejudgment interest rate by statute; others tie the rate to an established index. *See* Philips and Freeman (2001) for a survey across the states. In these instances, the courts must decide only the length of the prejudgment period.[1]

Litigants and their experts face a different situation under federal law, which has no mandated prejudgment interest rate or index. Instead, federal courts have long recognized prejudgment interest as an element of complete compensation. Thus, a court should grant prejudgment interest in the amount that will compensate the plaintiff for the defendant's use of its funds from the date of injury until the date of judgment.[2] In other words, prejudgment interest should return the plaintiff to the position it would have been in had the defendant compensated it immediately after injuring it. Courts and commentators have also pointed out that prejudgment interest plays an important role in preventing defendants from unjust enrichment.

Although courts have articulated a broad principle—make the plaintiff whole—they have left open the method of calculating prejudgment interest. Although commentators have proposed a variety of different methods, the federal courts have not consistently adopted any single approach. Moreover, the Supreme Court's most recent pronouncement, *Kansas v. Colorado*, 533 U.S. 1 (2001), makes clear that lawyers and their experts have wide latitude in trying to persuade a court of the amount of prejudgment interest that the defendant should pay.[3]

The monetary stakes are substantial. When the injury occurred long before the judgment, prejudgment interest can exceed the original judgment. For example, in its 1986 complaint against Colorado, Kansas sought $9 million in damages going back to 1950, plus $53 million in prejudgment interest. In 1992, the Seventh Circuit awarded $65 million in damages and $148 million in prejudgment interest in a suit arising out of the grounding of the supertanker *Amoco Cadiz* off the coast of Brittany on March 16, 1978.

Even when the legal resolution occurs quickly, if the judgment is large, the amount of interest will also be large, even more so when interest rates are high. Moreover, because of compounding, even small differences in interest rates can have large effects on the final award. For example, in *Amoco Cadiz,* a 1 percentage point (100 basis points) increase in the interest rate would have increased the final award by $20 million. For these reasons, the methods that courts use to calculate prejudgment interest have important practical significance.

This chapter describes the basic principles that should apply in calculating prejudgment interest and extends that analysis to cover a range of special circumstances that frequently arise. This chapter is neither a compendium of the case law nor a survey of the different positions advanced by commentators. Although we discuss cases and other methods when appropriate, this chapter describes what we believe to be the proper method based on sound financial principles.

9.2   THE PROBLEM

Courts most often assess the final award by first calculating a multiplier (denoted by m), which, when applied to the original judgment (J), produces the final judgment *(FV)*:

$$FV = J \times m \tag{1}$$

Thus, once it has decided liability and calculated the original judgment, the court must set the multiplier.

Courts often compute the multiplier, m, as follows:

$$m = \left(1 + \frac{r_m}{n}\right)^{nT}, \tag{2}$$

where r_m is the prejudgment interest rate, n is the number of compounding periods in a year, and T is the prejudgment period in years. Accordingly, setting the multiplier entails three tasks:

1. Set the prejudgment interest rate (r_m)
2. Calculate the prejudgment period (T)
3. Determine the frequency with which to compound interest (n)[4]

9.3   WHICH INTEREST RATE? THE DEFENDANT'S COST OF UNSECURED BORROWING

Courts award prejudgment interest to place both the plaintiff and the defendant in the same position that they would have been in had the defendant compensated the plaintiff immediately after the injury. In awarding prejudgment interest, courts describe their task as looking for the interest rate that will compensate the plaintiff for delay.

This chapter assumes that both parties are publicly traded corporations with access to the capital markets. We also assume that the corporations' investors hold diversified investment portfolios and therefore tie up little of their wealth in the litigating corporations. Section 9.8 briefly discusses how to adjust the calculations when the plaintiff is a close corporation or an individual.

The search for the appropriate interest rate begins by examining the plaintiff corporation's balance sheet (using market, not book, values). As a result of the defendant's wrongdoing, the plaintiff either lost an asset or incurred an additional liability. Either effect would reduce the plaintiff's net worth.

The judicial system compensates the successful plaintiff with a monetary award, an asset. If the award were immediate (and costless to obtain), an award equal to the harm would offset the entire injury, leaving the plaintiff's net worth unchanged. Because the plaintiff does not receive an immediate judgment, the court awards prejudgment interest so that the present value of the eventual judgment equals the present value of the harm.

The assumption that the parties have ready access to the capital markets now comes into play. The term *judgment asset* means the claim that the plaintiff has against the defendant when the defendant injures the plaintiff, later replaced with an award from the court. The court must set the return on the judgment asset that is appropriate for the risk, so that the value of the judgment asset will equal that of the lost asset or offset the new liability. As with other assets, the value of a judgment asset to a plaintiff does not depend on the plaintiff's characteristics, but rather on the judgment asset's risk and return.

The judgment asset has two risks, only one of which should be compensated through prejudgment interest. The first risk is that the courts will not uphold the plaintiff's claim, or, even if they do, they will not grant the plaintiff a judgment that fully compensates for its injury. Although this problem and its solution—for the court to increase its judgment by dividing the harm by one minus the probability of error—are well known in the law-and-economics literature, successful plaintiffs do not receive compensation set by the courts increased for the possibility that they, the courts, might have erred.[5] Moreover, the risk of judicial error lies conceptually outside of the realm of prejudgment interest; one should address it before the calculation of prejudgment interest. Accordingly, courts should not increase the prejudgment interest rate to reflect the risk of judicial error.

The second risk is that the court will grant the plaintiff a judgment equal to its harm but that the plaintiff will not collect the full judgment because the defendant goes bankrupt. Accordingly, if courts fail to compensate plaintiffs for the risk that defendants default, they will undercompensate plaintiffs and enrich defendants. Therefore, to put plaintiffs and defendants back into their positions before the injury occurred, plaintiffs must receive compensation for the risk that defendants will default. This approach was first elucidated in Patell, Weil, and Wolfson (1982) and was endorsed by the Seventh Circuit in *Gorenstein Enterprises, Inc. v. Quality Care-USA, Inc.*[6] Accordingly, the prejudgment interest rate should reflect the risk that the defendant defaults.

As with other debt, the risk that a plaintiff will not collect its debt (the judgment) does not depend on the plaintiff's assets, liabilities, or capital structure, but rather on the defendant's risk of default. The interest rate that reflects the risk that the defendant does not pay its debts is the defendant's borrowing rate. In bankruptcy, courts treat legal claims like unsecured debt. Therefore, to compensate the plaintiff for delay, the court should award prejudgment interest at the defendant's unsecured borrowing rate. Such an award will allow the judgment asset to grow at the interest rate appropriate for the risk the plaintiff bears: the risk that the defendant will default on the judgment.

Some commentators refer to this approach to prejudgment interest as the *coerced loan theory*. That phrase underscores the notion that the defendant, by not immediately compensating the plaintiff for its harm, has in effect forced the plaintiff to make a loan to the defendant equal to the plaintiff's harm. Accordingly, compensating the plaintiff for the delayed repayment requires that the court award prejudgment interest at the rate that the defendant would pay a voluntary creditor on an otherwise identical loan.

(a) Alternative Rates Do Not Properly Compensate Plaintiffs.   Some courts, litigants, and commentators have not accepted the coerced loan theory. The alternative rates they propose include the return on the plaintiff's equity, the plaintiff's cost of capital, the plaintiff's cost of debt, the return on a market index, and the risk-free interest rate. One can divide these proposals into three groups, depending on whether the court bases prejudgment interest on (1) the plaintiff's return on investment, or (2) the plaintiff's cost of raising funds, or (3) an interest rate that is independent of both plaintiff and defendant.

(i) Return on Plaintiff's Capital.   Keir and Keir (1983) argue that the court should assess prejudgment interest at the average return on the plaintiff's equity. Their proffered rationale: had the plaintiff collected the funds, it would have invested in its own business; therefore, the return that the business has produced provides the best measure of the amount the plaintiff lost through delay.

This argument ignores our assumption that the litigants (especially the plaintiff) are two publicly traded companies with ready access to capital markets. Given that assumption, one cannot claim that the defendant's actions prevented the plaintiff from foregoing any attractive investment opportunities and forced the plaintiff to forego the resulting return. If the plaintiff did not have the capital to pursue a desirable project, it could have raised the funds through the capital market.

(ii) The Plaintiff's Cost of Capital.   Keir and Keir (1983) also argue that the minimum prejudgment interest rate is the plaintiff's cost of capital; for a firm with both debt and equity, this equals its weighted average cost of capital.[7] Awarding prejudgment interest at the plaintiff's cost of capital aims to compensate the plaintiff for the cost of tying up its capital. The proponents reason that awarding prejudgment interest at the plaintiff's cost of capital compensates the plaintiff for the cost it incurred to raise the funds denied it by the defendant's wrongdoing. Arguments against this alternative also apply to the plaintiff's cost of borrowing, which we discuss next.

(iii) The Plaintiff's Cost of Borrowing.   Closely related to the plaintiff's cost-of-capital alternative, some argue that courts should award prejudgment interest at the plaintiff's cost of borrowing. Proponents reason that if the injury did not prevent the plaintiff from undertaking any investment, then it most likely caused the plaintiff to increase its borrowing (because public firms rarely issue new equity, but they often borrow). Accordingly, to return the plaintiff to its uninjured state, the defendant should pay interest to the plaintiff at the plaintiff's cost of borrowing additional funds.

Arguments that look to the plaintiff's cost of raising funds (whether cost of capital or borrowing rate) have an obvious intuitive appeal, but they also have problems. Sometimes the injury does not cause the plaintiff to raise additional funds. The plaintiff nevertheless suffers harm because of the defendant's delay in compensating the plaintiff and the risk that the defendant will go bankrupt before paying the plaintiff.

Suppose the plaintiff must raise additional funds by issuing debt.[8] Then the interest rate that the plaintiff pays for that new capital will reflect the risk borne by those new investors. That risk depends on the assets they can look toward for repayment and their priority. Only in rare instances do the new investors invest solely in the claim. In such cases, the new investors bear the same risks as those borne by the plaintiff; one can then measure the cost to the plaintiff of waiting as the interest rate the plaintiff pays to its new investors to bear that risk.[9]

In contrast, when the new investors do not look solely to the claim for repayment, then the risk they bear and hence the interest rate that the plaintiff pays will not reflect the harm caused to the plaintiff by delay. In these circumstances, the interest rate that the plaintiff pays the new investors will reflect their position in the plaintiff's capital structure. If the interest rate that the plaintiff pays its new investors exceeds the defendant's unsecured borrowing rate, it is because the plaintiff's new investors will assume not only the defendant's default risk, but other additional risks as well, for which they demand compensation in the form of a higher interest rate. The defendant should not have to compensate the plaintiff for risks unrelated to the litigation that the plaintiff transfers to new investors. Alternatively, if the defendant's cost of unsecured borrowing exceeds the interest rate that the plaintiff pays to outside investors, then the new investors do not assume the defendant's entire default risk and the plaintiff retains some of the risk of the defendant's default. The court should not fail to compensate the plaintiff for the risk it bears because of the defendant's wrongdoing because the plaintiff raised additional capital without transferring all of that risk to its new investors.

(iv) The Return on a Market Index.   Plaintiffs sometimes seek to receive prejudgment interest at the rate that they would have earned had they received the money earlier and invested it in a diversified portfolio of stocks. The logic follows that the plaintiff could have distributed the money to its shareholders, who would have reinvested it. The return on the market portfolio offers a reasonable market-based return for a diversified investor. For example, in appraisal cases, the Delaware Court of Chancery awards prejudgment interest based in part on the return that the plaintiff could have earned on a diversified portfolio of stocks.[10]

This argument has several problems. First, in the context of litigation between two publicly traded companies, the defendant's actions do not prevent the plaintiff's shareholders from cashing out their stock and investing in a diversified portfolio. They can sell their stock and invest their proceeds as they please. They can also adjust their other investments if they want to increase or decrease their risk exposure.

Second, the return on a diversified portfolio of stocks reflects the risk of that portfolio. That, however, is not the investment that the plaintiff has made (albeit involuntarily) with the funds held by the defendant. Instead, the plaintiff has, perforce, invested them in the defendant's unsecured debt and should receive a corresponding risk-adjusted return. Giving the plaintiff a different return, based on the risk of a diversified portfolio of stocks, does not compensate the plaintiff for the risk it bore through its forced investment in the defendant.

(v) Risk-Free Rate.   Fischer and Romaine (1990) argue that the court should award prejudgment interest at the U.S. Treasury bill rate—the interest rate that the federal government pays when it borrows. They reason that U.S. courts do not compensate plaintiffs for the risks of litigation and that the possibility of the defendant going bankrupt is a risk of litigation.

Weil (1995) has two cogent responses to that argument. First, Fisher and Romaine's argument—that courts should not compensate plaintiffs for litigation costs—does not imply that courts should award prejudgment interest at the risk-free rate. Taken to its logical conclusion, Fisher and Romaine's argument implies that courts should never award prejudgment interest, not that they should award prejudgment interest at the risk-free rate. Because that result conflicts with statutory law, case law, and the logic behind prejudgment interest, one should reject the

argument. Second, awarding prejudgment interest at a fixed or variable rate independent of the defendant's cost of unsecured debt (such as the risk-free rate) will
encourage defendants to increase their risk. The defendant, through its choice of
investments, has some control of its bankruptcy risk. If the prejudgment interest
rate does not reflect that risk, the defendant, by increasing that risk, will be able to
shift some portion of the costs of risky undertakings to the plaintiff. This is an
unnecessary and undesirable feature of a judicial system.

(b) Recent Criticisms of the Coerced Loan Theory Are Unpersuasive.   Several commentators have criticized the coerced loan theory and the proposal to award
prejudgment interest at the defendant's unsecured borrowing rate. We examine
two of these criticisms.

Escher and Krueger (2003) employ a cost-of-carry pricing model. They argue
that the plaintiff's claim for damages or lost profits (i.e., the judgment asset) is in
essence a forward contract that is traded at the time of the harm. The forward
contract entitles the plaintiff to receive an amount in the future when the court
renders the judgment. The delivery price of such a contract—the amount to be
exchanged in the future—is simply today's price (i.e., the harm incurred by the
plaintiff) plus the cost of carry. In their model, the cost of carry is the plaintiff's
implied financing cost or cost of debt capital. Escher and Krueger's insightful cost-
of-carry approach supports the coerced loan theory rather than undercutting it. In
the absence of default risk, the delivery price of a forward contract is the spot (or
today's) price plus the risk-free rate. As Escher and Krueger note, however, if
default risk exists, the difference between the spot price and delivery price should
reflect that risk. In the litigation context, because only the defendant can default,
only the defendant's default risk matters. Thus, the cost-of-carry model leads back
to awarding prejudgment interest at the defendant's cost of unsecured debt.[11]

Barondes (2004) takes a different tack. He argues that the coerced loan theory
fails to distinguish between the plaintiff's equityholders and creditors. Drawing
on the idea of asset substitution in corporate finance (Jensen and Meckling, 1976),
Barondes notes that the judgment asset, even if it has the same present value as
the asset that the plaintiff lost (or the liability it incurred) will likely have different
risk characteristics. Substituting a riskier asset for an asset with the same present
value will usually transfer value from the plaintiff's debtholders to equityholders,
and conversely. As a result, awarding prejudgment interest at the defendant's cost
of unsecured borrowing will not restore the plaintiff's equityholders and
debtholders to their positions before the injury occurred. If the judgment asset is
riskier than the asset it replaces, equityholders will typically gain at the expense of
debtholders, and conversely. The possibility of such a transfer, however, does not
provide a basis for rejecting the coerced loan theory. Modern finance rejects the
view, implicit in Barondes's argument, that equityholders are the only investors in
the firm. Instead, in the contemporary view, debt and equity are alternative methods of investing in a firm, and the firm's investors are the injured parties.
Accordingly, awarding prejudgment interest at the defendant's unsecured
borrowing rate will allow debtholders and equityholders taken together to receive
full compensation for the risk of the judgment asset without being overcompensated. Using any other interest rate to calculate the final award will either
overcompensate or undercompensate some investors in the plaintiff.

9.4   AWARDING PREJUDGMENT INTEREST AT A FLOATING INTEREST RATE

Interest rates usually vary with the duration of an investment. The observed pattern of interest rates from now to various future times is called the *term structure of interest rates.* Typically, long-term rates exceed short-term rates, producing an upward-sloping term structure.

When, as normally occurs, the term structure is not flat, the court must decide whether to use a series of short-term rates or a single long-term rate. Consider, for example, a plaintiff who suffers an injury on January 1, 1996, and receives payment on January 1, 2006. The court, looking backward from the year 2006, might apply the 10-year rate for debt issued by the defendant in 1996 maturing in 2006, or it might apply a series of 10 one-year rates—one for 1996, one for 1997, and so on, through 2006. Because the term structure is not usually flat and because it shifts over time, these two choices will give different answers. Typically, but not invariably, the single 10-year rate will exceed the rate compounded from 10 one-year rates. Should the court use the 10-year rate or the rate compounded from 10 one-year rates? Finance does not provide an answer because either method, if settled on before the injury occurred,[12] would compensate the plaintiff. Knoll (1996), however, argues that the need of the court system to encourage parties to settle their disputes favors the use of short-term interest rates.

If courts used the long-term interest rates, they would interfere with the parties' incentives to settle. If interest rates rise during litigation, defendants will be in effect borrowing at below-market interest rates, which will give them an incentive to prolong litigation. Falling interest rates reverse the incentives. Thus, although one party's incentive to delay is matched by the other party's incentive to expedite, it is easier for one party acting unilaterally to delay litigation than to expedite it. In contrast, short-term rates give neither party an advantage or disadvantage from delay and thus encourage settlement relative to using long-term rates.

The upward-sloping term structure reflects the increasing interest rate risk from fixing an interest rate at the start of ever longer loans. Because courts set prejudgment interest *ex post,* after the events have occurred and all interest rates are known for all past periods, the investor (the plaintiff) bears no risk that those past interest rates will change. Accordingly, courts should calculate prejudgment interest using a series of short-term rates, short enough not to include a premium for interest rate risk. This implies computing prejudgment interest based on floating, variable, or adjustable rates, not on fixed rates. (Chapter 8 discusses *ex ante* and *ex post* calculations.)

Losey, Mass, and Li (2002) disagree. They argue that short-term interest rates will neither discourage foot dragging nor compensate plaintiffs. Instead, they propose that courts should award prejudgment interest at a variable rate with a term premium. That premium serves two functions: compensation for the risk of default and for tying up capital. To the extent that the premium compensates for the risk of default, Section 9.3 discusses that issue. Here, we discuss only compensation for extending credit for a period of time.

The standard explanation for the persistence of the upward sloping interest term structure is that borrowers have shorter time horizons than lenders. Accordingly, to induce borrowers to invest their capital for a long period, they must receive a premium. One must distinguish between a term premium and a liquidity premium. Holders of long-term federal government securities, however, do not have to tie up their funds because such securities have a liquid market. Holders of 1-year bonds can get their money in one year; holders of ten-year bonds can also get their funds in one year, by selling their bonds. The latter, however, face more risk because the price they receive for their bonds will depend on the 9-year interest rate in one year. The term premium reflects this risk, which one can avoid by granting prejudgment interest at a variable or floating interest rate.[13]

9.5   ESTIMATING THE DEFENDANT'S UNSECURED FLOATING BORROWING RATE

We have discussed the coerced loan theory, which posits that courts should award prejudgment interest at the interest rate that the defendant would pay on an otherwise equivalent voluntary loan. Because a judgment award carries the same risk as that of an amount owed unsecured creditors in bankruptcy, courts should grant prejudgment interest at the interest rate that the defendant would pay for unsecured debt to compensate the plaintiff for the risk of default. To avoid the possibility of having both a large winner and a large loser when interest rates change, the court should grant prejudgment interest at a floating or variable interest rate.

Courts can use several methods to estimate the interest rate that the defendant would pay on an otherwise identical voluntary loan. We discuss three methods that one can easily implement. They all yield approximations. Although none of the methods will yield a precise, theoretically correct answer, they will produce credible results when done with some care.

The coerced loan theory states that the prejudgment interest rate should reflect the risk to the plaintiff that the defendant will default. The first and most obvious proxy is a floating interest rate at which the defendant had or could have borrowed unsecured. For companies that can borrow large sums from banks without security, the prime rate is an obvious proxy.

Second, many large companies have access to and regularly borrow through the commercial paper market. Commercial paper is short-term, unsecured promissory notes. Because the commercial paper market is more restrictive than the market for bank loans at prime, the interest rate on commercial paper is regularly 200 to 300 basis points below the prime rate. As a result, only the most creditworthy borrowers can issue commercial paper. Losey, Mass, and Li (2002) take issue with awarding prejudgment interest at the defendant's commercial paper rate. They argue that the short-term commercial paper rate does not compensate the plaintiff for the risk that the defendant will go bankrupt before the plaintiff receives the full award. This occurs because the risk of bankruptcy increases with the horizon, and most plaintiffs have been forced to make a long-term loan (perhaps many years in duration) to the defendant, whereas the holders of commercial paper typically make loans for a year or less.

Accordingly, to compensate for this risk, a court can grant prejudgment interest at the defendant's long-term (unsecured) variable interest rate. Although this represents the conceptually correct interest rate, few defendants will likely have any long-term variable interest rate debt outstanding, because most corporations borrow at fixed rates. This leads to the third approach of a court estimating the defendant's long-term (unsecured) floating interest rate. This rate is typically determined by reference to a market interest rate, such as the rate on Treasury bills or London Interbank Offered Rates (LIBOR) plus an additional amount to reflect the credit worthiness of the issuer.[14]

The court can use several methods to estimate the defendant's long-term variable interest rate. Bond-rating services, such as Moody's and Standard & Poor's, rate the creditworthiness of corporations' unsecured long-term debt. Financial services firms, such as Bloomberg, publish yield curves for corporate debt with different credit ratings. They also calculate yield premiums for bonds with different credit ratings relative to Treasury securities for a range of maturities. The average premium for firms with the same credit rating as the defendant will reflect the additional interest (over Treasury securities) that such firms pay to issue debt for a given maturity. A court can then apply that average premium for long-term debt of a given credit risk and maturity to short-term Treasury interest rates to estimate the appropriate prejudgment interest rate.

9.6   COMPUTING THE MULTIPLIER

This chapter has discussed how the court should select the prejudgment interest rate. To complete the elements of the award multiplier using Equations (1) and (2) in Section 9.2, the court must also decide on the length of the prejudgment period (T) and the choice of compounding period (n). We now turn to these issues.

(a) The Prejudgment Period.   The prejudgment period ends on the award date.[15] That leaves two open issues: when to begin the prejudgment period and whether to award interest for the entire period or to deny interest for a portion of the prejudgment period. To aid in our discussion, consider the following dates (terminology adapted from Weil, 1995): incident date, harm date, filing date, and award date.

Consider first when the court should begin the prejudgment period. Jurisdictions fall into one of two categories: those that begin to accrue interest from the harm date (usually, but not necessarily, the incident date) and those that wait until the filing date. The recognition that prejudgment interest compensates for the defendant's possession of funds that rightfully belong to the plaintiff favors using the harm date. That will place the plaintiff in the same position as if the defendant had immediately paid the plaintiff, the intent of prejudgment interest.

Courts sometimes deny interest to plaintiffs who have unduly delayed filing under the doctrine of laches, which denies plaintiffs compensation for harm they themselves caused by waiting to file. Penalizing plaintiffs for their own delay might be appropriate if the court awards prejudgment interest at a rate that exceeds the defendant's unsecured debt rate. If, however, the court sets the rate correctly, then not commencing the accrual of interest at the harm date undercompensates the plaintiff and undercharges the defendant. Even if the plaintiff has unduly delayed action, accrual of interest over the entire judgment period will not penalize the defendant. The defendant will break even, having held the funds during the delay period, for which it pays interest at its normal borrowing rate.

(b) Choice of Compounding Period.   For the court's last task in setting the multiplier in Equation (2) of Section 9.2, it must select the compounding period—an issue that the parties and the courts frequently overlook. All interest rates explicitly or implicitly assume a compounding period. Consider a stated annual interest rate of 12 percent. With a compounding period of one year, the effective annual rate equals 12 percent. If, however, the compounding period is the calendar quarter, implying a rate of $3(=12/4)$ percent per quarter, the effective annual rate is $12.55(=1.03^4 - 1)$ percent. If the compounding period is one month, implying a rate of $1(=12/12)$ percent per month, the effective annual rate is $12.68(=1.01^{12} - 1)$ percent.

The choice of compounding period on the award can have substantial effects. The defendant pays dollars, not percentages. For example, the *Amoco Cadiz* court awarded interest at the prime rate compounded yearly. The court did not take into account the practice that prime rate loans typically call for quarterly interest compounding. Knoll (1996) estimates that adjusting the interest rate calculation for the more frequent compounding that the quoted rate presumes would have increased the interest component of the award by about $11 million. A court should use the same compounding period in computing the award as the reference interest rate.

9.7   OTHER ISSUES IN THE CALCULATION OF PREJUDGMENT INTEREST

This section discusses several additional issues in the calculation of prejudgment interest: taxes; multiple defendants; the relation between prejudgment interest and currency conversion; and injuries that produce harms at a later date.

(a) Adjusting the Multiplier for Taxes.   Thus far, this chapter has ignored income taxes. To ensure that the award compensates the plaintiff without being overly generous, the court should adjust its calculation for taxes. This holds true because the tax treatment of prejudgment interest does not mirror the tax treatment of corporate bond interest.

The government taxes the interest earned on bonds as it accrues. In contrast, even accrual method plaintiffs do not pay tax on prejudgment interest until the award date. Compared with receiving compensation immediately at the time of harm and investing the proceeds in taxable bonds, the plaintiff has deferred its tax payments on its interest earnings to the award date. To adjust for the benefit of deferral, the court should compound prejudgment interest at the product of the defendant's cost of unsecured borrowing and one minus the plaintiff's tax rate over the prejudgment period[16] and then gross up that after-tax amount by dividing by one minus the plaintiff's tax rate on the award date. When the court takes into account the tax on prejudgment interest, the multiplier, denoted by m'_{AT}, becomes:

$$m'_{AT} = \frac{\frac{(1 + r_m^{AT})^{nT} - 1}{n}}{1 - \tau_T} + 1, \tag{3}$$

where τ_T is the tax rate in year T and r_m^{AT} is the mean after-tax interest rate, with $r_i^{AT} = r_i(1 - \tau_i)$.

The court might also need to adjust the multiplier to reflect the tax treatment of the original judgment. Equations (2) and (3) implicitly assume that the plaintiff would not have paid any taxes if the defendant had immediately compensated the plaintiffs, and so the plaintiff could have invested the entire payment. If, however, the plaintiff would have had to pay taxes on any payment received from the defendant, then the plaintiff would have been able to invest only the after-tax amount and so would not have earned as much interest. Accordingly, when the original judgment is taxable, the multiplier, now denoted by m'_{AT} is

$$m'_{AT} = \frac{(1 - \tau_0)(1 + \frac{r_m^{AT}}{n})^{nT}}{1 - \tau_T} \tag{4}$$

where τ_T and r_m^{AT} are as defined in Equation (3) and τ_0 is the tax rate at the time of injury. Multipliers calculated using Equation (3) will usually exceed those calculated using Equation (4).

Which multiplier the court should use depends on the plaintiff's tax status and the taxability of the award. (Chapter 16 discusses the tax treatment of damages.) If the plaintiff is exempt from tax, the court should use Equation (2). If the plaintiff is subject to tax on taxable interest income, the court should use either Equation (3) or Equation (4). If the award is also taxable, then Equation (4) gives the correct multiplier. On the other hand, if the award is not taxable, then Equation (3) gives the correct multiplier. In general, the award is taxable if it compensates the plaintiff for lost income, but not if it compensates for an otherwise deductible loss.[17] For example, assume a contract case in which the court awards the plaintiff expectancy damages of $1 million comprising $600,000 as compensation for expenses incurred and $400,000 for anticipated profit. The court should then assess prejudgment interest on $600,000 using Equation (3) (because that portion of the payment is in effect untaxed assuming that the deduction was suspended until payment) and on the remaining $400,000 using Equation (4) (because that portion of the payment is taxed).[18] In at least two cases, *Hughes Aircraft Co. v. United States* and *Cement Division, National Gypsum Co. v. Milwaukee*, the defendants argued that the court should adjust the multiplier for the deferral of taxes. In neither case did the court adjust the multiplier for taxes. In *Cement Division*, however, the district court, to which the defendant had submitted a working paper version of Knoll (1996), stated that the proposed adjustment would result in a more accurate calculation. Nonetheless, it declined to do so, noting that the record did not contain sufficient information about the plaintiff's income or taxes to calculate the adjustment and that no other court had previously done so.

(b) Multiple Defendants. In many cases, the plaintiff can collect its judgment, if at all, only from the defendant. In such cases, awarding prejudgment interest at the defendant's cost of unsecured debt compensates the plaintiff for the risk of default. In other cases, however, the plaintiff can collect from more than one source. When the plaintiff can recover from more than one party, the court should take that possibility into account in setting the prejudgment interest rate. In general, because the opportunity to look toward multiple sources increases the likelihood of recovery, it should reduce the prejudgment interest rate.

For example, when the court finds several defendants jointly and severally liable, a successful plaintiff will fail to collect the full judgment only if all liable defendants default. Because the plaintiff will collect the entire judgment if any defendant is solvent, the plaintiff should be awarded prejudgment interest at the market interest rate for an unsecured loan jointly made to (or guaranteed by) all the liable defendants. The interest rate for such a loan cannot exceed—and will usually be less than—the rate paid by the most creditworthy defendant.

When the defendant carries insurance, the successful plaintiff can then look both to the defendant and to its insurance company for recovery. When the plaintiff is covered by insurance that the defendant had in place on the injury date, the plaintiff will recover if either the defendant or its insurer is solvent. In such circumstances, prejudgment interest should not exceed the lesser of the defendant's or its insurance carrier's unsecured borrowing rate.

This issue also arises when the defendant is part of an affiliated group of companies. (*See* Chapter 29's discussion of alter ego.) Under such circumstances, a dispute can arise as to which, if any, companies within the group will have to pay the judgment if the defendant cannot. For example, a wholly owned subsidiary of Amoco operated the supertanker *Amoco Cadiz*. If the court finds the subsidiary liable but not the parent, the plaintiffs could look to only the subsidiary's assets to satisfy a judgment. Although the plaintiffs would *ex ante* be less likely to collect their judgment, they should receive compensation for this additional risk through a higher prejudgment interest rate based on the subsidiary's unsecured borrowing rate only, unprotected by the parent. Accordingly, the court should base the interest rate on the default risk of the subsidiary, or group of companies, whose assets the defendants can reach to satisfy its judgment.[19]

(c) Currency Conversion.   Regardless of where an injury occurs and the currency of the harm's original denomination, U.S. courts usually grant the final award in U.S. dollars. Thus, when the court does not measure the original harm in U.S. dollars, setting the final judgment requires two steps: converting the award into dollars and calculating prejudgment interest.

The court can calculate the final judgment in two ways. First, it can convert the original award to dollars using the exchange rate on the harm date and then calculate prejudgment interest using the defendant's unsecured borrowing rate for dollar-denominated loans. Alternatively, a court can calculate prejudgment interest using the defendant's unsecured borrowing rate in the currency in which the harm occurred and then convert the award to dollars using the exchange rate on the judgment date.

Because exchange rates and interest rates move over time in ways that markets cannot anticipate, the order in which the court performs those two steps matter. Moreover, the wider the fluctuations, the greater the difference in results.[20] Neither sequence is wrong, but courts should not allow either party to choose the method it prefers at the end of litigation. A party would obviously choose the method that proved more advantageous. Instead, courts should develop a consistent approach.

A simple rule would require courts to follow the current jurisprudence on exchange rate conversions. The prevailing approach looks to the jurisdiction in which the plaintiff's cause of action arose to identify when to convert the award into dollars. Only when the plaintiff's cause of action arises entirely under foreign law will the courts convert the judgment on the judgment date. If, however, the plaintiff has a claim arising under U.S. law, the court will convert the judgment into U.S. dollars as of the harm date. We recommend that courts adopt such clear rules for the order of the foreign exchange conversion and prejudgment interest calculation. In the absence of such clarity, as long as the court decides early in the litigation which approach it will use, the parties will have little opportunity for strategic action.

(d) Payment for Subsequent Harms.   This chapter has discussed harms that occur at a single date or over a short period around the time of the injury. Thus, for example, in *Amoco Cadiz*, the harm was the cost of cleaning up the beaches and waterways damaged by the oil spill. Barondes (2004) has shown that there is a risk of double counting when the harm occurs subsequently. In such circumstances, the appropriate response is usually to discount the subsequent harm back to the date of injury (using an interest rate appropriate for the project) and then to calculate prejudgment interest on that amount until the judgment date. That will produce a different result than just bringing the harm to the judgment date whenever the discount rate on the project differs from the prejudgment interest rate (*see* Weil, 2005).

Consider the following example. An oil spill occurs on January 1, 1996, and the court renders a final judgment on January 1, 2006. A portion of the judgment covers the harm from the lost fish catch in 1999 (assumed to occur on January 1, 1999 to keep the arithmetic simple). Because the court rendered its judgment on January 1, 2006, the calculation must bring the payment to that date. The court can use one of two methods: (1) calculate prejudgment interest from 1999 to 2006, a period of seven years, or (2) discount the value of the lost catch from 1999 back to 1996, a period of three years and then calculate prejudgment interest from 1996 to 2006, a period of 10 years.

Which approach the court should use depends on the nature of the injury. If the lost fish catch in 1999 resulted from the 1996 oil spill and was unlikely to be prevented by subsequent remedial actions, then as of 1996, the plaintiff had to look toward the defendant for a damages award to compensate for the lost catch in 1999. Accordingly, the court should discount the value of the catch back to 1996 and then calculate prejudgment interest until 2006. Alternatively, if the defendant could have remedied the harm by taking reasonable remediation steps as late as 1999, but it still failed to prevent the harm, then the plaintiff's injury can be traced to 1999. Accordingly, the court should award prejudgment interest for seven years, from January 1, 1999 to January 1, 2006.

9.8   CLOSE CORPORATIONS AND INDIVIDUAL PLAINTIFFS

If the plaintiff is an individual or small business, one must modify the analysis and conclusions discussed to this point in the chapter. The defendant's unsecured borrowing rate will not be the appropriate rate in all such cases.[21]

The argument for awarding prejudgment interest at the defendant's unsecured borrowing rate has two key premises:

1. The plaintiff had ready access to the capital markets. This premise ensured that the defendant's actions would not prevent the plaintiff from making any desirable investments and removed the argument that the court should compensate the plaintiff for a missed opportunity.

2. Investors in the plaintiff had little of their wealth tied up in the plaintiff and held diversified investment portfolios. This ensured that the investors would value the claim in the same manner as would the market and implied that they would require compensation for the risk associated with the claim at the amount that the market would pay if the claim were a separately traded asset.

Together, the two premises lead to the conclusion that awarding prejudgment interest at the defendant's cost of unsecured debt would compensate the plaintiff (and its investors) for the delay in receiving judgment.

When the plaintiff is a close corporation or an individual and the claim is large relative to an affected individual's wealth, then both premises are likely to be violated. In such circumstances, the defendant's actions could prevent a plaintiff from making desirable investments (or increase the cost of such investments) and force the affected individuals to change their consumption. Clearly, such individuals would be unlikely to value the claim in the same way as would the market.

The actions of diversified investors set the unsecured borrowing rates of publicly traded companies in the marketplace. The market interest rate and, in particular, the excess of the promised rate over the risk-free rate will reflect the expected default loss and, to the extent that the marginal investor is risk adverse, an additional premium over the risk-free rate.

If an affected individual's portion of the claim is large relative to his or her wealth, the forced loan to the defendant would cause such an affected individual to hold an undiversified portfolio and bear unsystematic risk, which risk is not reflected in the defendant's borrowing rate. Thus, the use of defendant's unsecured borrowing rate would undercompensate such an individual. In theory, to adjust this rate properly, a court would need to assess the affected individuals' aversion to risk. These individuals, of course, would have a great incentive to exaggerate their aversion to risk.[22]

In addition, the delay in receiving the judgment proceeds and interest can prevent an affected individual from exercising his or her optimal consumption during litigation. Although adjusting the prejudgment interest rate to reflect the affected individuals' diminished utility has theoretical merit, how to make such an adjustment is unclear because it depends on subjective information from the affected individual.

9.9   CONCLUSION

This chapter has set forth the appropriate method for assessing prejudgment interest in litigation and has demonstrated how to apply the rate in different situations. We argue that in lawsuits between two parties with ready access to the capital markets, courts should calculate prejudgment interest using the defendant's unsecured, short-term borrowing rate with possible adjustment for the risk that the defendant will default. If done well, such an award will compensate the successful plaintiff for the delay in receiving payment and for the risk that the defendant will go bankrupt before the plaintiff can collect. It will also prevent the defendant's unjust enrichment without further penalizing the defendant. Moreover, by calculating prejudgment interest at a floating rate over the prejudgment period instead of at a fixed, long-term interest rate at the start of the period, the court can eliminate the risk of interest rate changes.

Use of the defendant's unsecured, floating borrowing rate has many benefits. Once litigation has begun, this rate will economize judicial resources because neither party has an incentive to delay litigation unnecessarily. This rate will give both parties the proper economic incentives to engage in appropriate behavior prior to litigation because defendants who are found liable must pay and successful plaintiffs will receive complete economic compensation for damages.

NOTES

1. Even in those states in which prejudgment interest is fixed by statute, attorneys and litigation experts can still add value. For example, if the statutory rate differs from the theoretically correct rate, the parties will have incentives to alter their litigation strategies.
2. Postjudgment interest is granted from the date of judgment until the date of payment. Under federal law, postjudgment interest is awarded at the 52–week Treasury bill rate. 28 U.S.C. 1961(a).
3. The dispute arose out of a violation of the Arkansas River Compact. The compact, negotiated by Kansas and Colorado, and approved by Congress in 1949, provided that future development of the river basin could not materially deplete the quantity of usable water available to downstream users.
4. Equation 2 assumes that prejudgment interest will be compounded. Although interest in commercial settings is always compounded, some courts, following the traditional common law rule for prejudgment interest, award simple interest. Courts should, however, award compound prejudgment interest.
5. If the harm is H and the plaintiff's probability of losing at trial is p, then to compensate for the risk of judicial error, the court should award a judgment, not of H, but of $H/(1 - p)$.
6. James M. Patell, Roman L. Weil, and Mark A. Wolfson, "Accumulating Damages in Litigation: The Roles of Uncertainty and Interest Rates," *The Journal of Legal Studies* 11 (June 1982): 341–364. *Gorenstein Enterprises, Inc. v. Quality Care-USA, Inc.*, 874 F.2d 431 (7th Cir. 1989).
7. Keir and Keir (1983) argue that if a firm's historical return exceeds its weighted average cost of capital, the court should award prejudgment interest at the higher rate; otherwise, the court should award prejudgment interest at the plaintiff's cost of capital.
8. Publicly traded firms rarely issue new equity, and so in the text we assume the plaintiff issues debt to raise additional capital. The logic, however, is the same if the plaintiff issues equity except that the return on equity replaces that on debt.
9. The language in the text assumes that the plaintiff is certain to succeed on the merits and be granted a judgment (before calculation of prejudgment interest) of a known amount. As Section 9.3 discusses, prejudgment interest does not compensate successful plaintiffs for their litigation costs or the possibility that they might have lost the case.
10. In appraisal cases, the Delaware courts award prejudgment interest based on an equal weighting of the defendant's cost of borrowing and the return on a "prudent investor" portfolio consisting of a diversified portfolio of stocks, money market instruments, and a bond portfolio. *Gonsalves v. Straight Arrow Publishers, Inc.*, 2002 Del. Ch. Lexis 105.
11. This conclusion is consistent with the financial economist's view that the payoff to a long party of a forward contract (the party purchasing the asset, who, in the litigation setting is the defendant) is economically identical to a fully levered position in the underlying asset. Because the leverage is the obligation of the long party's (defendant), only the long party's (defendant's) default risk is relevant.
12. Obviously, the court should not allow either party to select one of the methods at the end of litigation. That would give the party with a choice a valuable option that would encourage it to delay. The method should be set beforehand. The rates can be determined at the end of litigation.
13. That is not to say that there is no cost to the plaintiff from tying up the money or more accurately that the market does not pay a premium for tying up capital. However, such a premium, if it exists, is not given by the yield curve premium.

14. If a defendant has outstanding long-term variable interest rate debt, the court can use the rate on the that debt, provided that it adjusts for the value of any put and call provisions held by the holder or issuer.

15. The prejudgment period ends when the court issues its judgment. Frequently, because of appeals, collateral litigation, and the possible delays in collection, the plaintiff is not paid until later. The period from judgment to payment is the postjudgment period.

16. Implicit taxes (in the form of lower expected rates of return) on some investments, such as municipal bonds, are taxes for this purpose.

17. In the latter circumstance, no deduction is generally allowed while the case is in litigation.

18. Equations (3) and (4) both include the plaintiff's tax rate. That rate should be the plaintiff's marginal tax rate on the amount at issue. That rate will often differ from the effective tax rate that is reported in the plaintiff's financial reports (Scholes et al., 2005). The appropriate rate is also affected by the tax planning strategies available to plaintiff (Weil, 1995).

19. Parent-subsidiary liability has the potential to create a strategic issue because a defendant whose subsidiary is sufficiently solvent to pay the judgment has an incentive to concede the parent's responsibility assuming the subsidiary is liable at the end of the process in an attempt to keep the prejudgment interest rate down.

20. The possibility of arbitrage will ensure that the two techniques will yield the same final judgment using long-term interest rates over the entire prejudgment period in both markets and the forward foreign currency-dollar exchange rate as of the date of harm. That equivalence, however, does not hold for shorter-term interest rate and spot exchange rates, which is what courts would use if they adopted our method.

21. If the plaintiff is a publicly traded corporation and the defendant an individual or small business, then a court should still award prejudgment interest using the defendant's unsecured borrowing rate. The plaintiff has made a forced loan to the defendant and must be compensated for the risk that the defendant won't pay any final judgment. Unlike the case of corporate defendants, there is no readily available interest rate a court could look to in order to set the appropriate prejudgment interest rate. Home mortgage and car loan rates are not appropriate benchmarks because such loans are secured. The rate on credit card debt is probably better because it is unsecured. Credit cards rates, however, vary greatly and are relatively high. If this benchmark is used, the defendant would greatly benefit by being able to show that he or she would be eligible for a rate on the low end of the range. As explained previously, to the extent that a judgment was covered by insurance, the insurance company's unsecured borrowing rate would be the appropriate rate.

22. If plaintiffs hold employee stock options, we can infer something about the aversion to risk of nondiversifiation from their voluntary exercise of options and disposal of resulting shares.

LIST OF CASES

Cement Division, National Gypsum Co. v. Milwaukee, 950 F. Supp. 904, aff'd, 144 F.3d 1111 (7th Cir. 1998)

Gonsalves v. Straight Arrow Publishers, Inc., 2002 Del. Ch. Lexis 105 (2002)

Gorenstein Enterprises, Inc. v. Quality Care-USA, Inc., 874 F.2d 431 (7th Cir. 1989)

Hughes Aircraft Co. v. United States, 31 Fed. Cl. 481 (1994), aff'd, 86 F.3d 1566 (Fed. Cir. 1996)

In Re Oil Spill by the Amaco Cadiz off the Coast of France on Mar., 16, 1978, 954 F.2d, 1279 (7th Cir. 1992) (per curiam)

Kansas v. Colorado, 533 U.S. 1 (2001)

BIBLIOGRAPHY

Ault, David E., and Gilbert L. Rutman. "The Calculation of Damages Awards: The Issue of 'Prejudgment Interest'." 12 *Journal of Forensic Economics* pp. 97-104 (1999).

Barondes, Royce de R. "Rejecting the Marie Antoinette Paradigm of Prejudgment Interest." *Brandeis Law Journal* 43, pp. 1-27 (2004).

Dilbeck, Harold. "The Time Value of Money." In *Litigation Services Handbook: The Role of the Accountant as Expert*, 2nd ed., edited by Roman Weil, Michael Wagner and Peter Frank, Hoboken, NJ: John Wiley & Sons, 1995. pp. 38-1 to 38-15.

Erickson, Merle, and James K. Smith. *"Tax Treatment of Damages Awards."* In *Litigation Services Handbook: The Role of the Financial Expert*, 3rd ed., edited by Roman Weil et al. Hoboken, NJ: John Wiley & Sons, 2001 and pp. 14.1 to 14.15 2005 Supplement.

Escher, Susan, and Kurt Krueger, "The Cost of Carry and Prejudgment Interest." *Litigation Economics Review* 12, pp. 12-16 (2003).

Fisher, Franklin M., and R. Craig Romaine. "John Joplin's Yearbook and the Theory of Damages." *Journal of Accounting, Auditing and Finance* 145 pp. 145-157 (New Series 1990).

Hoffman, Cornelius A. "Risk-Free Rates." In *Litigation Services Handbook: The Role of the Accountant as Expert*, 2nd ed., edited by Roman Weil, Roman Weil, Michael Wagner and Peter Frank Hoboken, NJ: John Wiley & Sons, pp. 39.1 to 39.8 1995.

Jensen Michael C., and William H. Meckling. "Theory of the Firm, Managerial Behavior, Agency Costs and Ownership Structure." *Journal of Financial Economics*, pp. 305-360 (1976).

Kabe, Elo R., and Brian L. Blonder. "Discounting Concepts and Damages." In *Litigation Services Handbook: The Role of the Accountant as Expert*, 2nd ed., edited by Roman Weil, Michael Wagner and Peter Frank Hoboken, NJ: John Wiley & Sons, pp. 37A.1-37A.16 1995 and Supplement 1997.

Keir, John C., and Robin C. Keir. "Opportunity Cost: A Measure of Prejudgment Interest." *Business Lawyer*, pp. 129-152 (1983).

Knoll, Michael S.,"A Primer on Prejudgment Interest." *Texas Law* Review pp. 293-374 (1996).

Knoll, Michael S. "Primer on Prejudgment Interest." In *Litigation Services Handbook: The Role of the Financial Expert*, 3rd ed., edited by Roman Weil, Michael Wagner, Peter Frank, Hoboken, NJ: John Wiley & Sons, pp. 8B.1-8B.14 2001 and pp. 40A.1-40A.11 2000, Supplement.

Lanzillotti, Robert F., and Amanda K Esquibel. "Measuring Damages in Commercial Litigation: Present Value of Lost Opportunities." *Journal of Accounting, Auditing and Finance* pp. 125-145 (New Series 1990).

Losey, Robert L., Michael Mass, and Jingsan Li. "Prejudgment Interest: The Long and the Short of It." 15 *Journal of Forensic Economics*, pp. 57-70 (2002).

Patell, James M., Roman L. Weil, and Mark A. Wolfson. "Accumulating Damages in Litigation: The Roles of Uncertainty and Interest Rates." *The Journal of Legal Studies*, 11 (June 1982): 341–364.

Philips, John R., and Neill W. Freeman. "Interest as Damages," In *Litigation Services Handbook: The Role of the Financial Expert*, 3rd ed., edited by Roman Weil, Michael Wagner, Peter Frank. Hoboken, NJ: John Wiley & Sons, 2001.

Scholes, Myron S., Mark A. Wolfson, Merle Erickson, Edward Mayhew and Terry Shevlin. *Taxes and Business Strategy*. 3d ed. 2005. Upper Saddle River, NJ: Prentice Hall.

Weil, Roman L. "Compensation for the Passage of Time." In *Litigation Services Handbook: The Role of the Accountant as Expert*, 3rd ed., edited by Roman Weil, Michael Wagner, Peter Frank, Hoboken, NJ: John Wiley & Sons, 1995.

Weil, Roman L. "Compensation for Asynchronous Payments." In *Litigation Services Handbook: The Role of the Financial Expert*, 3rd ed., edited by Roman L. Weil, Michael Wagner, Peter Frank. Hoboken, NJ: John Wiley & Sons, pp. 8A.1-8A.10 2001 and 2005 Supplement.

CHAPTER 10

THE FLAW OF AVERAGES IN LAW AND ACCOUNTING

Sam L. Savage
Marc Van Allen

CONTENTS

10.1 INTRODUCTION

When adjudicating in the face of uncertainty, courts often replace a range of possible outcomes with a single "average" case. This leads to systematic distortions, which we refer to as the flaw of averages (FOA).[1] Although mathematicians have understood these concepts for at least a century, adapting law to science requires a better understanding of basic principles by courts and lawyers.

   This chapter describes the FOA and presents various cases in which courts have ignored it or only partially integrated it. We illustrate how conventional damages studies are subject to the flaw and conclude with suggestions for a more standardized method of illuminating risk and uncertainty that might reduce misunderstandings leading to litigation.

10.2   FLAW OF AVERAGES: DEFINITION

Under its broadest definition, the FOA describes the systematic errors that occur when analysts base calculations on the average (expected value) of uncertain inputs, rather than the entire distribution of possible inputs. We differentiate between two variants of this misunderstanding.

The weak form of the FOA misjudges risk by ignoring the distribution around the correct average value. For example, consider transporting 10 eggs either one by one in individual baskets, or all at once in a single basket. Suppose that a 10 percent chance exists of dropping any particular basket. Then either basket strategy will leave you with an average of nine eggs. However, someone equating these two strategies based on the average outcome of nine remaining eggs would be guilty of the weak form of the FOA. By analyzing the distribution of eggs, it becomes apparent that if you "put all your eggs in one basket," a 10 percent chance exists of losing the entire lot. With the multibasket approach, however, a 99.98 percent chance exists of having at least five eggs at the end of the day.

The strong form of the FOA uses the average case of an input assumption in a calculation and does not derive the correct average for the output. An example involves a drunk wandering down the middle of a busy highway with an average position on the center line. Someone who predicts the future state of the drunk based on his average position errs with the strong form of the FOA, and will claim that the drunk will remain alive. However, his average state is obviously dead.

(a) The Weak Form.   The central idea behind the Nobel Prize winning economics of Harry Markowitz in the 1950s recognizes the weak form of the FOA. In optimizing investment decisions, Markowitz argued that average return was insufficient. Instead, he used a combination of both the average return and uncertainty of return to illuminate a risk/return tradeoff.[2] As a consequence, if two investments have the same average return, the one with the lesser risk has more value.

As an intuitive example of this risk adjusted value, imagine the choice between receiving a $500 million out of court settlement in cash or a 50/50 chance of a jury award of $1 billion or zero. Although both choices have the same average value, most organizations would prefer the first. Although economics accepts this risk/return tradeoff, Johnson et al. illustrate a violation of this principle in accounting rules.[3] The example in their 1993 article in *Accounting Horizons* involves receivables from a counterparty that has a 10 percent chance of defaulting. In spite of the risk, generally accepted accounting principles (GAAP) require the holder to book the face value of the receivables, with no offsetting valuation allowance, stating that "it is not probable that an asset has been impaired." For further incompatibilities of GAAP with the FOA, *see* Sam Savage and Marc Van Allen's article.[4]

(b) The Strong Form.   The strong form of the FOA involves nonlinear formulas[5] that depend on uncertain inputs. The basic principle states that evaluating such formulas using the average values of the uncertain inputs does not result in the average value of the formula. Mathematicians refer to this result as Jensen's Inequality after Johan Ludwig William Valdemar Jensen, a 19th century self-taught mathematician who worked for the Danish phone company.[6] One can find his inequality in the seminal work on the valuation of stock options published by Fischer Black and Myron Scholes in 1972.[7]

- Linear Calculations: the average of $F(x) = F$(average of x) (no bias)
- Convex[8] Calculations: the average of $F(x) > F$(average of x) Example: Options:
- Concave Calculations: the average of $F(x) < F$(average of x) Example: Restrictions

Exhibit 10-1.   Bias Implied by Jensen's Inequality (Strong Form of the Flaw of Averages)

Jensen's Inequality may be understood in terms of a formula, F, which depends on an uncertain number, x. We use $F(x)$ to denote the output of the formula when the input is x. This mathematical result states that the average value of F is not necessarily the value of F based on the average value of x, as summarized in Exhibit 10-1.

The next section frames the concept in more intuitive terms.

(c) Example: Stock Options.   We illustrate the FOA using one of the simplest types of options, a European call option. This contract provides the holder with the right, but not the obligation, to purchase a share of a certain stock at a certain price (the strike price) at a certain time in the future (the expiration date). The payoff for this option is as follows:

$$\text{Payoff at Expiration of Call Option} = \text{The Greater of } \$(S - K) \text{ and } \$0 \qquad (1)$$

where

$\$S$ = the stock price at expiration
$\$K$ = the strike price

If the stock price at expiration exceeds the strike price, the holder will exercise the option to purchase the share at $\$K$, and then sell it on the market at $\$S$, resulting in net gain of $\$(S - K)$. If the strike price exceeds the stock price at expiration, the holder abandons the option as worthless.

Now imagine a hypothetical stock, which at expiration could be worth either $\$(K + 2)$ or $\$(K - 2)$ with an average of $\$K$. Then the payoff will equal either $\$2$ if the stock increases, or $\$0$ if the stock decreases. Thus we have:

$$\text{Average Payoff} = (\$2 + \$0)/2 = \$1 \qquad (2)$$

To demonstrate the FOA, consider substituting the average price of the stock ($\$K$) directly into Equation 1. The result would be

$$\text{Payoff of the Average Price} = \text{The Greater of } \$(K - K) \text{ and } \$0 = \$0 \qquad (3)$$

Thus, in this context, the *average payoff* exceeds the payoff evaluated at the *average stock price*. The FOA—an error—would be to use the valuation for the average stock price instead of the average payoff.

Although stock market analysts and academicians accept the 1972 work of Black and Scholes, case law has yet to embrace it consistently, as discussed throughout Chapter 11, "Valuing Losses in New Businesses." One can, however, observe the progress of its acceptance in some professional communities. In 1995 (more than two decades after Black and Scholes' initial paper), the Financial Accounting Standards Board (FASB) issued *Statement 123,*[9] which acknowledges the basic principles of option theory: that the fair value of an option "is determined using an option-pricing model that takes into account the stock price at the grant date, the exercise price, the expected life of the option, the volatility of the underlying stock and the expected dividends on it, and the risk-free interest rate over the expected life of the option." The word *volatility* in the statement accounts for the distribution of all possible stock prices. Using volatility in the valuation can save the analysis from the error of the FOA. Ignoring volatility will lead to the errors of the FOA.

For accounting purposes, however, firms continued to claim that the options it awarded as performance incentives had no cost, and therefore the award did not increase expense or reduce the company's book value. In 2004, FASB issued a revision of *Statement 123*[10] that requires firms to use "the fair value method" when costing share-based compensation. FASB did not specify the type of model to use but suggested choices based on the original Black-Scholes formula, or the more flexible binomial lattice model proposed by Cox et al. in 1979,[11] or the most general form of modeling uncertainty, Monte Carlo simulation (discussed in Section 10.6 of this chapter and Chapter 11).

Not all segments of the business and legal communities have agreed on how to account for the value of stock options, but after a third of a century, it looks like Jensen's Inequality has won at least this battle. Section 10.2.d.(ii) presents an analogous accounting issue in which current practice violates the FOA.

(d) Three Important Cases of the Strong Form.   Jensen's Inequality in litigation typically falls into one of three classes:[12] (1) linear calculations, (2) those with real options, and (3) those with real restrictions.

(i) Linear Formulas.   When a formula involves only simple sums of uncertain quantities, it is mathematically valid to substitute F(average of x) for the average of $F(x)$. Suppose, for example, that a court has awarded a plaintiff an amount equal to five percent of future dollar sales on some invention in three distinct markets, A, B, and C. Suppose further that both sides agree that the average sales in the three regions are expected to be Avg.(A), Avg.(B), and Avg.(C), respectively. Then it is valid to estimate total average sales as Avg.(A) + Avg.(B) + Avg.(C). Although this computes the correct average, it does not indicate the degree of uncertainty of the sum.[13] In other words, the weak form of the FOA still applies to the linear case.

(ii) Real Options.   If a formula, which we will assume measures a benefit, takes into account the decision maker's ability to make a future decision after the resolution of an uncertainty, then the average value of the formula exceeds the value of the formula evaluated at the average input—that is, the average of $F(x) > F$(the average of x). The stock option hypothetical of Section 10.2(c) presented this situation; the future decision of whether to buy or abandon the option can await the actual outcome, where the decision maker knows the actual share price on exercise date.

Consider a hypothetical case in which the court rules that a plaintiff should receive liquidating payment for a share of a mineral mine. The court will base damages on the mine's value. Both sides agree that the operation can recover one million tons of the mineral and that the incremental cost of mining the material equals $10 per ton. Both sides also agree that the mineral has an uncertain future price, ranging between $4 and $20 per ton, with an average of $12. The defense argues that the court should base damages on the average price (i.e., F(average of x)), leading to a valuation of $2 million ($= 1,000,000$ tons $\times$ ($12 - $10)/ton). The average value of the property exceeds this. If the mineral price drops below $10, the mine has the option to shut down, limiting costs when the low price precludes extraction. On the other hand, if the price rises, no such limitation exists on the upside.

A numerical example demonstrates this asymmetry. Imagine that the mineral has only two equally likely possible future prices: $6 and $18, with an average of $12. If the $6 price appears, then the mine has value of $0 because the operators have the option to shut down rather than lose $4 per ton. On the other hand, the $18 price results in a mine value of $8 million. The average of $0 and $8 million equals $4 million, twice the valuation arrived at by using the average price of $12.

In reality, a trajectory of uncertain prices would exist through time, interspersed with a sequence of production decisions. However, the basic principle remains: the option to halt production ensures a greater value than the value based on average price. Viewed from this perspective, the mine becomes a call option on the mineral, with a strike price equal to the marginal production cost. Thus, one might expect the fair value method of FASB *Statement 123* to apply to its valuation, but it does not. When the SEC addressed a parallel situation related to petroleum reserves, a recent *Wall Street Journal* article reported that "[t]he SEC [Securities and Exchange Commission] stipulates that their evaluations must be based on a snapshot of oil prices at the companies' year end, usually Dec. 31."[14] Given the high volatility of oil price and the expected indefinite, but long, life of an oil reserve, the SEC regulation results in undervaluations for such properties. Jeff Strnad of the Stanford Law School has shown that the inconsistency of tax laws pertaining to the real options underlying petroleum exploration can have an adverse effect on energy development.[15]

Note that in real options, the greater the uncertainty in price, the greater the option value, because now the profit can go even further up but it still can't fall below zero. Similarly in the Black-Scholes option formula: the value of a call option goes up with increasing uncertainty (volatility) in the stock price. It is ironic that when valuing lost profits for a new business (*see* Chapter 11), courts will argue that there is too much uncertainty for there to be any damages, which flies in the face of the fact that the more uncertainty, the more valuable the business can be under the right circumstances. We finish this example by considering a modification in which the price is $12 with certainty, but the future marginal cost of mining is uncertain with an average of $10. If the cost exceeds $12, the mine will halt production, but if the cost is low, the profits will be considerable. Again, the option ensures that the average value of the mine exceeds the value of the mine given the average cost of $10. Estimating average damages by substituting average values of the underlying uncertainties leads to wrong results.

(iii) Restrictions. Just as the real option to act on future knowledge has a value, a restriction of one's actions imposes a cost. Consider a hypothetical litigation that bases damages on one year's profit derived from a manufacturing plant that produces custom-machined parts on an as-ordered basis. Both sides agree that the plant generates a profit per part of $10, and has the capacity to produce 100,000 parts per year. They also agree that the average demand for parts is 100,000 units but that demand could vary between 50,000 and 150,000. The plaintiff argues that

because average demand is 100,000, the profit formula for damages (or F(average of x)) should equal $1 million (= $10/part $\times$ 100,000 parts). In this case, the average profit will be less than $1 million, (i.e., the average of $F(x) < F$(the average of x). Suppose that demand had an equal likelihood of either 60,000 or 140,000 units, with an average of 100,000. The plant's capacity limits production to either 60,000 or 100,000 for an average of 80,000. Thus, average profit would equal $800,000 (= $10/part $\times$ 80,000 parts), not $1 million.

(iv) Summary of the Strong Form of the Flaw of Averages.   The examples of real options and restrictions show that the error inherent in the FOA can result in either over- or undervaluation. Also, it does not require a complex calculation to identify the direction of bias, as summarized earlier in Exhibit 10-1. With real options, the average value is *greater or equal to* the value associated with the average inputs. With restrictions, the average value is *less than or equal* to the value associated with the average inputs.

10.3   FLAWED JUDICIAL DECISIONS

(a) Historical Trends.   For years, courts have succumbed to the FOA when valuing financial options. As Section 10.2(c) discussed, financial options have *more* worth than the difference between the market price of the underlying stock and the option strike price. In the legal system, however, "the relevant black-letter rule to measure damages ... [for] failure to deliver publicly traded securities subject to an option agreement ... [is] the difference between the public market price of the underlying stock on the date of the breach and the option [strike] price specified in the agreement."[16]

For example, over a decade after the Black-Scholes work, in *Richardson v. Richardson*,[17] the court was attempting to value options "to purchase 3,000 shares of the common stock of the Murphy Oil Corporation." The strike price on the options was $13.71 per share and "[o]n the day the case was heard Murphy Oil Corporation's common stock was being traded at $22.50."[18] Based on these facts, the court reasoned that the option holder "could have exercised the options for $41,130 and received Murphy Oil stock worth $67,500." As a result, the court *wrongly* "found that the value of the options was the difference between the cost of exercising them and the worth of the stock."[19]

(b) A New Direction.   In several recent cases, courts have recognized the FOA when valuing options.[20] The facts in *Custom Chrome* are instructive. Custom Chrome (a supplier of Harley-Davidson motorcycle parts) borrowed $26 million from the bank. To obtain the loan, Custom Chrome agreed to issue warrants (in essence, options) to the bank to purchase approximately 12 percent of the stock of Custom Chrome. The strike price was $500 per share, which reflected the estimated market value of the Custom Chrome shares on the day Custom Chrome granted them to the lender.

Custom Chrome petitioned the tax court for a determination as to its right to deduct $3 million as a financing expense because of the option value of the warrants. However, the tax court found that the warrants had no value at the time of issuance because any future value was highly speculative and the warrants were "at the money" (i.e., at the same price as the stock itself).

After losing the issue before the tax court, Custom Chrome appealed. The Ninth Circuit Court of Appeals agreed with the taxpayer and reversed the ruling of the Tax Court. In reaching this decision, the Ninth Circuit found that "the Tax Court's reasoning and the Commissioner's arguments proffered in favor of a zero valuation are unsupportable."[21]

First, the Ninth Circuit noted: "The Commissioner has cited no authority for the proposition that the lack of a well-defined present market value and the uncertainty in the future value of a financial instrument imply that the instrument has no value for tax purposes."[22] *Second*, and more fundamentally, the Ninth Circuit concluded that an option that is "at the money" does not render the option valueless. The court determined that an option has two values: an intrinsic value and a time value and explained that

> the intrinsic value of an option is the difference between the actual value of a share and the exercise price of the option.... The time value reflects the expectation that, prior to expiration, the price of the stock will increase by an amount that will enable an investor to sell or exercise the option at a profit.[23]

With respect to intrinsic value, the Ninth Circuit observed that "because the strike price of the warrants was the same as the nominal trading price at the time of the buyout, the warrants had no nominal intrinsic value."[24] With respect to time value, the court decided that "the warrants had a substantial time value— that is the bank and everyone else expected the stock price to increase significantly so that eventually it would be profitable to exercise the warrants."[25]

Although the Ninth Circuit takes a step in the right direction, its analysis still falls short of the mark. To have time value, such an option needs only an expectation that the stock price will fluctuate, not increase. Thus, the court used a faulty argument to reach its decision, which would have led to an incorrect result if *the bank and everyone else had expected the stock price to fluctuate around its current price but not increase significantly.*

In *Alliant Energy*, the Seventh Circuit extended the valuation concepts for financial options to real options. In *Alliant Energy*, the plaintiff utility sued the State of Wisconsin for damages resulting from Wisconsin's utility regulations that prohibit a utility from selling a 10 percent block of its stock without regulatory approval. The utility argued that this regulation increased its cost of capital. The Seventh Circuit agreed, ruling that this regulation did increase the cost of capital for the utility because it "deprive[d] the firm of an *option* value—that is, of the power to sell a 10% block." (emphasis added) The Seventh Circuit explained:

> Suppose that there is only a 10% chance that the firm would be able to attract an investor willing to buy a 10% block of stock ... [and] the firm will save $1 million compared with the outlay in hiring the same capital from banks. Then the loss from not having *the option* to make the placement is $100,000, and this loss affords standing.[26] (emphasis added)

The Seventh Circuit reasoned that the option to sell 10 percent of one's stock "has a positive value even if *no one* wants to buy today" (italics in the original) and concluded "[a] firm with the ability to sell such blocks in the future ... is worth more in the market today than a firm hamstrung by laws cutting off its opportunities."[27]

10.4 FLAWED ANALYSIS OF THE VALUE OF LITIGATION

Even in lawsuits in which the court does not adjudicate issues involving the FOA, the parties may nevertheless need to address it. Many people assume that a party would litigate only if it anticipated a positive expected (average) outcome. This assumption ignores the FOA. Bebchuk[28] and Grundfest and Huang[29] have shown that the plaintiff might bring a lawsuit even when the expected outcome is negative. This occurs when the suing party has the option to abandon the litigation, as with the following scenario.

Suppose Party A believes that Party B might sue for average damages known by both sides to be $100,000. Also assume that both sides estimate the average cost of litigation to Party B to be $140,000. Then it would appear that B poses no credible threat to A, and stonewalling would be A's rational strategy. Now suppose that B can divide its litigation costs into two segments of $70,000 each, with the option to abandon the litigation after the first half. Then by spending the first $70,000, B has placed itself in a position in which spending the second $70,000 will result in average incremental return of $100,000. Thus, after the first desperate act, B now poses a credible threat, which should motivate A to settle in the first place.

This line of negotiation is reminiscent of the example described by Roger Fisher and William Ury in *Getting to Yes*.[30] Two drivers are playing chicken by speeding toward each other on a narrow road, with the winner being the one who swerves or breaks last. Suddenly one of the drivers throws his steering wheel out the window in clear view of the other driver, ensuring that his worst outcome is a draw.

10.5 DISCRETE EVENTS

The flaw of averages is common in estimating the outcomes of discrete chance events that either do or do not occur. This occurs, among other places, in accounting for contingent losses as a result of legal action or in valuing losses for a new business (*see* Chapter 11). We will address contingent losses first.

(a) Accounting for Contingencies. In *Statement No. 5, Accounting for Contingencies*,[31] FASB provides guidelines so fuzzy that they do not warrant the distinction of either the weak or strong form of the flaw of averages. It states that "the estimated loss from a contingency be accrued by a charge to income if it is probable that a liability has been incurred and the amount of the loss can be reasonably estimated," without providing a definition of either *probable* or *reasonably*. Even if FASB defined *probable*, the idea of a threshold is ill advised. Suppose we define 51 percent to be probable. Then Firm A, which had a pending legal action with a 50 percent chance of a $100,000 judgment, would have no charge, whereas Firm B, with a 51 percent chance, would have a $100,000 charge. Furthermore, Firm C, with 1,000 independent cases of $100, each with a 50 percent chance of judgment, would have no charge. If, instead of a threshold, courts used the correct average (judgments weighted by the probability of occurrence), they would calculate the results as follows for the three firms:

Firm	Calculation	Average Amount
A	50% × $100,000	$50,000
B	51% × $100,000	$51,000
C	50% × 1,000 × $100	$50,000

However, this still commits the weak form of the FOA. Both Firms A and B have essentially even odds of judgments of either $100,000 or zero, whereas Firm C is certain to pay out close to $50,000 in judgments.

(b) Lost Profits from a Risky Venture.   Now we will consider valuing lost profits in a new privately held business with a highly uncertain future. A pharmaceutical firm has licensed a compound with which it has been able to cure all known forms of cancer in rats. Credible experts agree that there is one chance in ten that the Food and Drug Administration (FDA) will approve the resulting drug; if it does, the result will be $1 billion of income over the next five years. Otherwise, there will be no profits.

Just before the licensee submits the drug to the FDA, the licensor breaches the contract. Various cases cited in Chapter 11 point to different evaluations of lost profits in similar situations. The damages might be evaluated based on the most likely outcome, that the FDA does not approve the drug. This results in zero damages. Or the court might require a threshold probability of success (which would no doubt exceed 10 percent) before awarding damages, and again the result would be zero damages. The approach more consistent with modern finance theory takes the average profit of 10 percent of $1 billion (= $100 million) and then applies a risk discount factor appropriate for an investment with this level of risk. We will refer to this as the *market valuation*, because it would reflect the share price if the firm were publicly traded. We would argue that zero is too low and that market valuation is too high.

(c) The Certainty Equivalent.   Instead, we propose a value that will most often lie between the two, based on the certainty equivalent value of the business. The certainty equivalent value of the business is the value at which the shareholders would have sold out before the contract was breached. Surely the plaintiff in the breach could not ask for more than this. To illustrate the concept of certainty equivalent, suppose you meet a stranger on the way home from work who offers the following gamble based on a coin toss. Heads you get $10 million, tails you get nothing, for an average gain of $5 million. Before flipping the coin, the stranger asks if you would take $50,000 in cold cash to forgo the flip. If your answer is yes, then your certainty equivalent for this gamble is less than or equal to $50,000. If you still want to go ahead with the flip, then your certainty equivalent is more than $50,000. The dollar amount at which you would be indifferent to taking the cash or proceeding with the gamble is defined as the certain equivalent. This depends on the decision maker's risk tolerance. In ascertaining your own certainty equivalent ($C) for the above gamble, you can find it useful to imagine losing the toss and then having to explain to your spouse or significant other that you turned down $C for the equal chance of $10 million or nothing.

(d) Certainty Equivalent Must Be Less than Market Value for Firm Trying to Go Public.
If the new firm has stated its intention to go public, then its shareholders believe that the market valuation (the average risk discounted cash flow stream) would exceed the value of the company while privately held. Therefore, had it been offered a buyout before getting to flip the coin with the FDA, it would have settled on less than the public market valuation.[32]

10.6 MONTE CARLO SIMULATION: A POTENTIAL CURE FOR THE FLAW OF AVERAGES

As we have demonstrated, representing an uncertain quantity with a single average number in a calculation may lead to the FOA. To avoid this problem, one must analyze the calculation relative to the joint probability distribution of the uncertain numbers in question. The most general approach to this problem involves drawing numbers repeatedly from the distribution and running them through the calculation in question to reveal the full range of possible outcomes. The mathematician Stanislaw Ulam developed this approach, referred to as *Monte Carlo simulation*, while working on the Manhattan Project. As its name implies, the approach resembles testing a gambling strategy by repeating it over thousands of rolls of dice. Section 11.5(c)(i) explains the mechanics of a Monte Carlo simulation. Financial analysts and academics use it today to test investment strategies under economic uncertainties.

Orange County, California should have used Monte Carlo in the summer of 1994. Interest rates were low and were expected to remain so or fall even further. The county had created such a successful financial portfolio (assuming this expected future behavior) that they had to turn investors away. Had the portfolio managers explicitly considered the distribution of possible interest rate outcomes instead of a single average scenario, they would have likely foreseen the possibility of the now famous adverse change in rates that forced them into insolvency a few months later. Shortly after the debacle, Philippe Jorian[33] of the University of California, Irvine performed a Monte Carlo simulation based on data available in advance that indicated a five percent chance of a $1 billion loss or worse. Exhibit 10-2 presents a schematic of this process.

10.7 PROBABILITY MANAGEMENT

The FOA implies that managers require distributions of strategic metrics, such as Gross Domestic Product (GDP) growth and oil prices, to effectively manage their firms. These managers require distributions to perform their jobs well. Fortunately, plenty of statisticians and econometricians know how to produce distributions.

Probability Management[34, 35] represents an emerging managerial discipline that will allow those with statistical expertise to "certify" important probability distributions and distribute them to others. William F. Sharpe, who shared the Nobel Prize with Markowitz and Miller in 1990, pioneered this area. In 1997, Sharpe founded Financial Engines,[36] a firm devoted to the Monte Carlo simulation of pension funds. By allowing employees at participating firms to visualize the full range of future trajectories of their pensions over time, including the unfortunate outcomes, this sort of simulation should ultimately reduce the likelihood of litigation. Financial Engines has developed a database of distributions of thousands of mutual funds.

We believe that a standard-setting organization based on a generalization of these ideas could maintain libraries of benchmark distributions for strategic uncertainties such as GDP growth, interest rate, oil price, and so on. These could prove useful for evaluating contended properties, settling litigation, and detecting risky management procedures in advance.

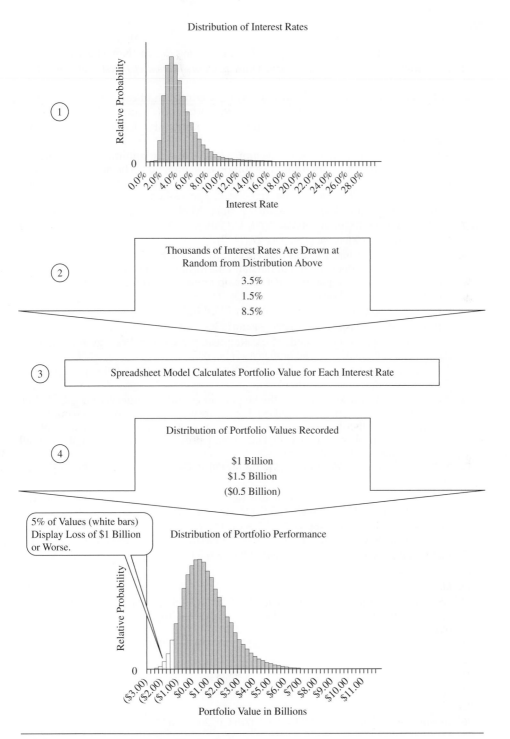

Exhibit 10-2.   Monte Carlo Simulation

NOTES

1. S.L. Savage, "The Flaw of Averages," *Harvard Business Review* (November 2002).
2. H.M. Markowitz, *Portfolio Selection, Efficient Diversification of Investment* (Hoboken, NJ: John Wiley & Sons, 1959).
3. L. Todd Johnson, Barry P. Robbins, Robert J. Swieringa, and Roman L. Weil, "Expected Values in Financial Reporting," *Accounting Horizons* 7 (December 1993): 77–90.
4. S.L. Savage and M. Van Allen, "Accounting for Uncertainty," *Journal of Portfolio Management* (Fall 2002).
5. A formula is said to be nonlinear if its inputs (also known as arguments) enter the formula in a manner other than simple addition or subtraction. The nonlinear formula in the example of the drunk above is known as a step function; if he steps to the left he gets killed, and if he steps to the right he also gets killed.
6. http://www-groups.dcs.st-and.ac.uk/~history/Mathematicians/Jensen.html.
7. Fischer Black, and Myron Scholes, "The Valuation of Option Contracts and a Test of Market Efficiency," *Journal of Finance* 27 (1972): 399-418.
8. A convex function has a graph that curves up (∪), while a concave graph curves down (∩). The reader need not understand the meanings of convex and concave nor the direction of the inequality to get the main point: *F* of average does not equal average of *F* unless *F* is linear.
9. http://www.fasb.org/st/summary/stsum123.shtml.
10. http://www.fasb.org/st/summary/stsum123r.shtml.
11. John Cox, Stephen Ross, and Mark Rubinstein, "Option Pricing: A Simplified Approach," *Journal of Financial Economics* 7(1979): 229.
12. This characterization is modeled on that of Stefan Scholtes of the University of Cambridge Judge Business school.
13. Assume the court asks, "What is the 90-percent confidence interval for sales?" The sum of the averages sheds no light on this. To answer this question, one would need to estimate the distribution of possible sales in each region and the extent of the market's statistical independence. This would provide an estimate of the overall degree of uncertainty in the award.
14. T. Carlisle, "How Lowly Bitumen Is Biting Oil Reserve Tallies," *Wall Street Journal*, February 14, 2005.
15. Jeff Strnad, "Taxes and Nonrenewable Resources: The Impact on Exploration and Development," *SMU Law Review* 55 (2002): 1683–1752.
16. *Mathias v. Jacobs*, 238 F. Supp.2d 556, 575 (S.D.N.Y. 2002) (citing *Hermanowski v. Acton Corp.* 729 f.2d 921, 922 (2d Cir. 1984); *Simon v. Electrospace Corp.* 28 N.Y.2d 136 (1971)).
17. *Richardson v. Richardson*, 280 Ark. 498, 502 (1983).
18. *Id.*
19. *Id.*
20. *See*, e.g., *Custom Chrome v. Commissioner*, 217 F.3d 1117 (9th Cir. 2000) (valuing "financial" options); *Alliant Energy Corp. v. Bie*, 277 F.3d 916 (7th Cir. 2002) (valuing "real" options).
21. *Custom Chrome v. Commissioner*, 217 F.3d 1117 (9th Cir. 2000).
22. *Id.*
23. *Id.*
24. *Id.*
25. *Id.*
26. *Alliant Energy Corp. v. Bie*, 277 F.3d 916 (7th Cir. 2002), at 921.
27. *Id.*
28. Lucian Arye Bebchuk, "Suites with Negative Expected Value," Discussion Paper No. 226 12/1997, in *The New Palgrave Dictionary of Economics and the Law*, (Cambridge, MA: Harvard Law School, 1998, 551–554.

29. J. Grundfest, and P. Huang, "The Unexpected Value of Litigation: A Real Options Perspective," *Stanford Law School Review*, Volume 58, No. 5 March 2006, pp.1267-1336.

30. Roger Fisher and William Ury, *Getting to Yes: Negotiating Agreement without Giving In* (New York: Penguin Books, 1983).

31. Joel G. Siegel, and Marc. Levine, *GAAP 2002 Handbook of Policies and Procedures*, (Englewood Cliffs, NJ: Prentice Hall, 2002).

32. If the firm's shares were publicly traded and the firm had time to announce the impending gamble it was about to undertake, modern finance suggests that market price of the shares would rise to reflect the expected value, whereas the holders of the shares would sell off enough to reduce their investment in the uncertain gamble to acceptable levels.

33. Philippe Jorion, *Big Bets Gone Bad: Derivatives and Bankruptcy in Orange County* (San Diego, CA: Academic Press, 1995).

34. Sam Savage, Stefan Scholtes and Daniel Zweidler, "Probability Management," *OR/MS Today*, February 2006, Volume33, No.1, pp. 20-28.

35. Sam Savage, Stefan Scholtes and Daniel Zweidler, "Probability Management, Part 2," *OR/MS Today*, April 2006, Volume33, No.2, pp. 60-66.

36. www.financialengines.com.

CHAPTER 11

VALUING LOSSES IN NEW BUSINESSES

Mark A. Allen
Victoria A. Lazear

CONTENTS

11.1 INTRODUCTION

We begin by considering a hypothetical example. Suppose that a company has developed a new drug, but then something occurs that prevents the company from bringing the drug to market. The adverse occurrence can be a breach of contract, some type of business tort (i.e., tortuous interference with contractual relations or fraud), or an issue relating to intellectual property infringement.

We then suppose a number of variations to our hypothetical concerning the nature of the business. At one end of the spectrum, imagine an established drug company that has developed a new drug within its area of expertise. Next, imagine an established drug company that decides to produce a drug outside its area of expertise, such as when a manufacturer of drugs for humans finds a use for one of its products in treating animals.

In a situation further removed from the first variation, imagine a startup company that produces an existing drug or an improvement to an existing drug. Finally, imagine a startup company with no expertise in drug development that seeks to design and manufacture a completely new medicine.

This chapter discusses how a damages expert should calculate lost profits in these scenarios. Section 11.2 begins with a discussion of the legal framework for establishing lost profits for a new business, the so-called *new business rule*. As we show in this section, the interpretation of the rule varies across jurisdictions, so the damages expert must have a firm understanding of the law—the legal rules within which the expert must operate—before the expert establishes an approach to calculating damages. Section 11.4 presents an analytical framework for calculating lost profits, using the drug company hypothetical and its variations as examples. We conclude that some courts may disallow lost-profit damages where accepted damages and economic theory fully support an award of such damages.

11.2   THE LEGAL FRAMEWORK FOR ESTABLISHING LOST PROFITS FOR A NEW BUSINESS

The law has progressed from a *per se* rule against recovery of lost profits by new businesses to a rule allowing such profits as long as they are not speculative and the damages expert can establish proof with reasonable certainty. We begin with a general overview of the evolution of the current new business rule—first discussing the former *per se* rule and then explaining why jurisdictions have adopted the current rule-of-evidence formulation for new businesses. Next we consider examples of cases that have allowed lost profits under the new rule as well as those that have not allowed such profits. We show that courts differ in their interpretation of the rule. Finally, we consider the effect of *Daubert* in connection with a crucial element of the plaintiff's proof in new-business cases: establishing the probability of success of the new venture through taking into account the risk of the business.

(a) The Evolution of the Current New Business Rule

(i) The Former New Business Rule.   An often-quoted statement of the former business rule (also referred to as the *per se* rule) comes from *Evergreen Amusement Corporation v. Milstead.*[1] In *Evergreen,* a Maryland appellate court affirmed a trial court's denial of testimony relating to lost profits caused by a contractor's delay in clearing and grading a site for a drive-in theater. The court stated:

> Under the great weight of authority, the general rule clearly is that loss of profit is a definite element of damages in an action for breach of contract or in an action for harming an established business which has been operating for a sufficient length of time to afford a basis of estimation with some degree of certainty as to the probable loss of profits, but that, on the other hand, loss of profits from a business which has not gone into operation may not be recovered because they are merely speculative and incapable of being ascertained with the requisite degree of certainty.[2]

An alternate formulation of the former new business rule states that no business can recover anticipated profits because of their uncertainty, but an exception exists if an established business can prove such damages with reasonable certainty.[3] Courts have occasionally awarded lost profits to new businesses even under this former new business rule, but such cases have involved businesses with an established record of earnings. Examples include franchises or businesses that are new in name only, such as an established business that has changed ownership or has begun operating in a new location.[4]

(ii) The Current New Business Rule.   Today, most jurisdictions have rejected the former *per se* bar against recovery of lost profits by a new business in favor of a rule allowing such damages upon proof of reasonable certainty.[5] As one commentator has stated:

> A *per se* "new business" rule is now widely regarded as having failed in an attempt to control the award of damages. Instead of discarding the "new business rule" caption, courts will often state that the rule is no longer a *per se* rule forbidding the award of lost profits damages to new business, "but rather an evidentiary rule that creates a higher 'level of proof needed to achieve reasonable certainty as to the amount of damages.'"[6]

Courts have used several reasons to justify their departure from the former *per se* rule. Such justifications include the following:

- Denying recovery for lack of a sufficient record of earnings is grossly unfair where the defendant's actions have prevented the plaintiff from establishing such a record.[7]
- The *per se* rule would encourage those contracting with new businesses to breach their contracts.[8]
- Economic forecasting has become more sophisticated.[9]
- "Courts have become sufficiently sophisticated in analyzing lost-earnings claims, and have accumulated sufficient precedent on the standard of undue speculativeness in damages awards, to make the balance of costs and benefits tip against the rule."[10]
- Denying damages proved with reasonable certainty merely because the business venture was newly established is "patently unfair."[11]
- The former new business rule is simply "too draconian" to apply in all cases.[12]

Courts can find additional support for the current new-business rule in the *Restatement (Second) Contracts* and the *Uniform Commercial Code*. Section 352 of the *Restatement (Second) Contracts* states the general rule that the plaintiff must establish damages with reasonable certainty. Comment b to Section 352 explains the general rule in relation to new businesses:

> However, if the business is a new one or if it is a speculative one that is subject to great fluctuations in volume, costs or prices, proof will be more difficult. Nevertheless, damages may be established with reasonable certainty with the aid of expert testimony, economic and financial data, market surveys and analyses, business records of similar enterprises, and the like.[13]

Similarly, Comment 2 to *Uniform Commercial Code* Section 2-708 (Seller's Damages for Non-acceptance or Repudiation) states:

> This section permits the recovery of lost profits in all appropriate cases, which would include all standard priced goods. . . . It is not necessary to a recovery of "profit" to show a history of earnings, especially if a new venture is involved.[14]

The Ohio Supreme Court relied on both sections 352 and 2-708 in recognizing that a new business may recover lost profits, so long as the plaintiff provides a sufficient amount of proof.[15]

Some jurisdictions have adopted the current new business rule by statute. Prior to 2002, for example, Virginia courts still adhered to the *per se* formulation of the rule. The Virginia legislature reversed this case law with the following statute:

> Damages for lost profits of a new or unestablished business may be recoverable upon proper proof. A party shall not be deemed to have failed to prove lost profits because the new or unestablished business has no history of profits.[16]

Most jurisdictions have now adopted the current new business rule, which allows lost future damages where proof is reasonably certain.[17] But when has the plaintiff proved lost profits with reasonable certainty, and, conversely, what constitutes undue speculation for lost profits? The next section seeks to answer these questions.

(b) Decisions Interpreting the Current New Business Rule. The current new business rule allows a new or unestablished business to recover lost profits if it can prove such losses with reasonable certainty. The inquiry is factual, and the evidence necessary to achieve reasonable certainty depends on the circumstances of each case. Courts differ, however, as to the evidence they will deem sufficient for a new business to establish lost profits. Whereas some courts appear amenable to lost profit claims for new businesses, others require more exacting proof.

This section explores several decisions interpreting the current new business rule. We begin by examining decisions that have allowed the recovery of lost profits and then consider those that have denied recovery. Finally, we consider the effect that *Daubert v. Merrell Dow Pharmaceuticals*[18] has had on new business cases, particularly with respect to one element of the plaintiff's proof: the risk of failure of the new venture.

(i) Cases Approving the Recovery of Lost Profits. In *Energy Capital Corp. v. United States*,[19] the court approved a lost damages award where the trial court drew reasonable inferences from the evidence to arrive at an estimate of damages. The government had contracted with Energy Capital, an established lender, to provide loans to make Housing and Urban Development housing more energy efficient, but it breached the agreement before Energy Capital could finalize any loans under this new venture. At trial, the government conceded the breach but argued that Energy Capital had failed to prove lost profits. The trial court awarded $10 million in damages.

The Court of Appeals for the Federal Circuit began its analysis by reciting the general rule for recovery of lost profits—that the plaintiff must prove both the existence and quantum of lost profits, but "if a reasonable probability of damage can be clearly established, uncertainty as to the amount will not preclude recovery."[20] The court then applied this general rule to the special case of the new or unestablished business: "While the nature of a new venture may make it difficult to recover lost profits by establishing all of the elements of the general rule, such damages are not barred as a matter of law."[21]

The court rejected the government's argument that the trial court had engaged in unsupported speculation in arriving at its calculation of the plaintiff's lost profits. Crucial in this decision was the court's recognition that Energy Capital's lost profit damages flowed not from other independent and collateral undertakings but directly from the breached agreement.[22] The court concluded:

> What we have before us is a case in which the trial court drew reasonable inferences based upon the evidence, not a case in which the trial court engaged in unsupported speculation. [citation omitted] ("Certainty [of damages] is sufficient if the evidence adduced enables the court to make a fair and reasonable approximation of the damages. In circumstances such as these we may act upon probable and inferential as well as direct and positive proof." (citations omitted)).[23]

Thus, *Energy Capital* recognized that although the nature of a new business can make it more difficult to prove lost profits, the court can draw reasonable inferences from the evidence to make a fair approximation of damages.

In another case, *Cardinal Consulting Co. v. Circo Resorts, Inc.*,[24] the Minnesota Supreme Court faced a claim of lost profits by a new business. In this case, a Las Vegas hotel breached an agreement to provide accommodations to tour operators who had not previously operated tours in the city. After recognizing the current formulation of the new business rule, the court addressed what types of proof a plaintiff could put forth to support a claim for lost profits—or, in the court's words: "substitutes for past profitability that will remove a plaintiff's anticipated profits from the realm of speculation."[25]

The court listed the following general areas of proof: past performance as an employee plus subsequent success; subsequent success alone; other examples of that type of business; and the plaintiff's skill and expertise together with proven existence of a market for the product.[26] The court then evaluated the plaintiff's evidence of lost profits:

> We agree with Circo that the evidence relating to lost profits that was presented by Cardinal lacks precision. Nevertheless, we can not [sic] say that it was unreasonable for the jury to award lost profits to Cardinal, given the unusual circumstances of this particular enterprise and the devastating effect of Circo's breach.
>
> Although Cardinal was able to demonstrate no past or future profitability, one of several substitutes was available in the evidence presented at trial.[27]

The *Cardinal* court noted that the jury could reasonably have based its decision to award lost profits on evidence of the plaintiff's skill and expertise plus the proven existence of the market, or on evidence of the profitability of similar businesses in the same geographic area at the same time.[28] Further, the court seems to have been impressed with the egregious nature of the defendant's actions—the "devastating effect" of the breach.

In *DSC v. Next Level Communications*,[29] at issue was lost profits relating to the development of a new communications technology. Unlike *Cardinal*, however, the product in *DSC* was completely new. The plaintiff had yet to sell its product and had not established a market. In rejecting a challenge that lost profits were speculative, the court recognized the history of the telecommunications industry, the intensive market research for the product, the revolutionary nature of the product itself, and the plaintiff's past business success.[30] The court concluded:

> While "damages may not be determined by mere speculation or guess, it will be enough if the evidence show[s] the extent of the damages as a matter of just and reasonable inference, although the result be only approximate." [citations omitted.]

- Plaintiff's past performance as an employee
- Profitability of plaintiff and third parties in similar businesses in the same geographic area at the same time
- Proven existence of the market
- Intensive market research for the product
- Plaintiff's prior experience in the same business
- Plaintiff's subsequent business success
- The average experience of participants in the same line of business as the injured party
- Pre-litigation projections, especially when prepared by the defendant[a]
- Expert opinion "supported by tangible evidence with a 'substantial and sufficient factual basis' rather than by mere 'speculation and hypothetical situations'"[b]

[a] *Beverly Hills Concepts v. Schatz & Schatz*, 247 Conn. 48, 717 A.2d 724, 735-37 (1998).
[b] *Kaech v. Lewis County PUD*, 106 Wash.App. 260, 23 P.3d 529, 538-39 (2001).

Exhibit 11-1.   Evidence Considered by Courts Regarding New Business Damages

> It is true these predictions are not guaranteed. No one can definitively say what the future holds for SDV technology, or DSC and Next Level in particular. However, uncertainty surrounding precisely how the industry will evolve does not reduce all analysis about future developments to mere speculation. Sears [plaintiff's damages expert] based his predictions on data obtained from respected sources in the telecommunications market. The jury chose to believe his estimation of damages. There was sufficient evidence presented to support the jury's verdict.[31]

As these cases illustrate, courts confronting the issue of lost profits in a new business have considered the types of evidence listed in Exhibit 11-1.

Thus, the nature of a new business makes proving lost profits with reasonable certainty more difficult. In egregious cases, courts can award lost profits by drawing on reasonable inferences from the evidence and will substitute other facts for past profitability in the new-business scenario to justify their decision.

(ii) Cases That Did Not Allow Lost Profits.   In contrast to the cases discussed in the preceding section, other courts have required more proof for a new business to establish lost future profits. Judge Richard Posner's opinion in *Mindgames, Inc. v. Western Pub. Co.* provides the best statement of this approach.[32] In *Mindgames*, the plaintiff had created a new board game but could not establish a track record through other similar successes on which to establish lost profits. After recognizing the current formulation of the new business rule, Judge Posner stated:

> But that leaves us with the question of undue speculation in estimating damages. Abrogation of the "new business" rule does not produce a free-for-all. What makes MindGames' claim of lost royalties indeed dubious is not any "new business" rule but the fact that the success of a board game, like that of a book or movie, is so uncertain. Here newness enters into judicial consideration of the damages claim not as a rule but as a factor in applying the standard. Just as a start-up company should not be permitted to obtain pie-in-the-sky damages upon allegations that it was snuffed out

before it could begin to operate … , capitalizing fantasized earnings into a huge present value sought as damages, so a novice writer should not be permitted to obtain damages from his publisher on the premise that but for the latter's laxity he would have had a bestseller, when only a fraction of new books achieve that success. Damages must be proved, and not just dreamed, though "some degree of speculation is permissible in computing damages, because reasonable doubts as to remedy ought to be resolved against the wrongdoer."[33]

Judge Posner explained his decision not to allow lost profits even though he found the current new-business rule would apply:

> [The plaintiff] was not in the position of the bestselling author who can prove from his past success that his new book, which the defendant failed to promote, would have been likely—not certain of course—to have enjoyed a success comparable to that of the average of his previous books if only it had been promoted as promised. That would be like a case of a new business launched by an entrepreneur with a proven track record.[34]

Although Judge Posner conceded that some speculation might be appropriate in calculating lost profits, he nonetheless found the new venture before him too uncertain for such an award. His example of the bestselling author who writes a new book suggests that he would allow recovery of lost profits only where the new business was similar to other previously successful ventures by that same plaintiff. To be fair, Judge Posner never said that his bestselling-author illustration was the only circumstance under which he would allow a new business to recover lost profits. But his example resembles the exception to the *per se* rule, noted in Section 11.2(a)(i), involving franchises and other already established businesses. *Mindgames* therefore substitutes the current rule-of-evidence version of the new-business rule for the former *per se* formulation, but the practical result, factoring in the exception, appears similar.

Similarly, in *Schonfeld v. Hilliard*,[35] the court held that, although a new business may recover lost profits, evidence of such profits requires higher scrutiny by the court.

> When lost profits are sought from a business with no, or limited, profit records, alternative evidence must be presented to establish whether any damages even exist, let alone the amount of damages. Such evidence calls for more tenuous inferences to reach a conclusion as to damages, and, therefore, such evidence merits greater scrutiny.[36]

In *Schonfeld*, the shareholder of a closely held cable television corporation brought a derivative suit alleging that the other shareholders breached an oral agreement to fund an interim agreement and that this breach in turn led to the corporation's loss of an exclusive cable television license. The corporation, International News Network (INN), was to create a new cable television channel in the United States devoted to distributing news and information programming of the British Broadcasting Corporation (BBC). To establish lost profits, the plaintiff relied on INN's business plan, revenue projections by Cox Cable Communications in connection with its own BBC news channel, the testimony of the BBC and the defendants that the new cable channel would generate profit, and the expert testimony of two damages experts. One expert derived lost profits from projections contained in the INN business plan and projected profits between $112 and $269 million. The other expert opined that the new venture would have success based on comparisons with other cable channels such as CNN.

In affirming the opinion of the lower court, the Second Circuit Court of Appeals decided, however, that Schonfeld had presented an insufficient lost-profits analysis. First, the court found that Schonfeld's analysis relied on hypothetical speculation—beginning with the sale of untested programming to a hypothetical subscriber base, sold to advertisers at a hypothetical price, and supported by hypothetical carriers and investors.[37] Next, the court rejected Schonfeld's comparison between INN and other operating channels because he had not shown a "high degree of correlation" between INN and the other firms.[38] Finally, the court rejected Schonfeld's argument regarding the "wrongdoer rule." The wrongdoer rule provides that where the defendant's actions have prevented the plaintiff from establishing a sufficient record of earnings, "the burden of uncertainty as to the amount of damage is upon the wrongdoer, and the test for admissibility of the evidence concerning prospective damages is whether the evidence has any tendency to show their probable amount."[39] As discussed in Section 11.2(a)(ii), courts have adopted the current new business rule in part because denying recovery for lack of a sufficient record of earnings is unfair where the defendant's actions have prevented the plaintiff from establishing such a record. Some courts appear more likely to approve lost profits where the defendant has exhibited egregious conduct. But the *Schonfeld* court held that the rule shifts the burden to the defendant only when damages exist without question and the only uncertainty relates to the amount of damages. As the court stated, "The rule does not apply here for the simple reason that the *existence* of lost profit damages cannot be established with the requisite certainty."[40]

As suggested by the *Schonfeld* opinion, courts that use this more stringent approach will more likely find no proof of future damages at all—that the plaintiff has failed to establish the existence of future damages, let alone any particular amount. For example, in *Kids' Universe v. In2Labs*,[41] the court considered a claim of lost profits by an Internet Web site. The plaintiffs sought to establish that their Web site to sell toys online was state-of-the-art; that they would attract a large number of orders for their products through agreements with other prominent Web sites; that they had operated a retail toy store for some time and therefore had the expertise and means to deliver on these orders; that this success would attract venture capital investment; and that the timing of the venture in relation to the development of Internet commerce indicated the Web site would have become a financially successful leader in the e-commerce sale of toys.[42] The court, however, held that the plaintiffs had failed to establish that they would have made any profit:

> As substantial as the plaintiffs' evidence sounds on the surface, we conclude it does not suffice to raise a triable issue as to lost *profits*. The evidence would not allow a reasonable trier of fact to find with reasonable certainty lost net *profits* from the un-launched Web site by a preponderance of the evidence. This is because the evidence, while *suggesting* the Web site would have been viable, is not of the type necessary to demonstrate that a triable controversy exists as *to a reasonable certainty* that the unestablished business would have made a *profit*.[43] (italics in original)

The court found that although the plaintiffs had five years' experience as a toy retailer and had operated a Web site for several years, their *Web site* had never produced a profit. Further, the court noted that the online toy market was a new and unestablished market. The court concluded that the plaintiffs' analysis was "rife with speculation."[44] Similarly, the court in *Tipton v. Mill Creek Gravel, Inc.* characterized the heightened scrutiny given to claims of lost profits by new businesses as a requirement of a greater burden of proof.[45] *Tipton* involved a shareholder derivative action alleging breach of an agreement that prohibited a corporation from mining gravel on the defendant's land. As in *Kids' Universe*, the *Tipton* court found that the plaintiff never proved the possibility of profit with reasonable certainty. The court questioned the plaintiff's projection of an increased demand for gravel in the area. The court held: "Projecting $14 million in lost profits upon a future demand that does not yet exist is exactly the kind of conjectural assumption that is disfavored."[46]

(iii) Reconciling the Cases: Interpreting the Reasonable Certainty Standard.   The previous two sections presented examples of cases in which new or unestablished businesses recovered lost profits and those in which they did not. Can we reconcile these cases, and, if so, how?

One possible answer would lie in distinguishing the two sets of cases based on their facts. But would Judge Posner, or the Second Circuit in *Schonfeld,* or the court in *Kids' Universe* have found lost profits if they faced the facts of *Cardinal* or *DSC?* We think not, which illustrates how courts differ when interpreting the new-business rule.

To understand the difference between the two sets of cases, first consider how the new-business rule fits into the general law of damages. In contract law, for example, plaintiffs must first prove the *fact* of damages. Once they have proved that some loss has occurred, the law allows them to prove the *amount* of damages with less certainty. The U.S. Supreme Court referred to these concepts when it stated: "Certainty in the fact of damages is essential. Certainty as to the amount goes no further than to require a basis for a reasoned conclusion."[47] Proving the fact of damages thus relates to causation—that the defendant's conduct in fact caused the plaintiff damage, whatever the amount. Once plaintiffs have established causation, they need only prove damages to a reasonable certainty.

The current new-business rule then establishes an evidentiary rule that creates a higher level of proof needed to achieve reasonable certainty as to the amount of damages. But mitigating against the new-business rule (potentially) is the wrongdoer rule, which holds that where the plaintiff has proved the existence of damages (or causation)—but where the defendant's actions have left the plaintiff unable to calculate damages with reasonable certainty—then "the burden of uncertainty as to the amount of damages is upon the wrongdoer, and the test for admissibility of the evidence concerning prospective damages is whether the evidence has any tendency to show their probable amount."[48]

All courts agree that a new business faces a tougher challenge relative to an established business in proving lost profits. But the courts seem to disagree whether this tougher challenge is a natural result of the fact that a new business will necessarily have less probative evidence at its disposal with which to prove damages, or whether the standard itself is actually higher for a new business seeking lost profits. The courts in the first set of cases follow the rules for lost-profits damages literally and give due consideration to the wrongdoer rule. The courts in the second set of cases arguably place much less weight on the wrongdoer rule and require more of the plaintiff in terms of establishing that the business would earn a profit in the first instance.

The new-business rule and the wrongdoer rule therefore appear to exist in an uneasy balance. Courts can emphasize the wrongdoer rule to find damages in cases in which the defendant demonstrates egregious conduct. But courts, as with *Schonfeld*, can also circumvent the wrongdoer rule by finding that the plaintiff has failed to establish the fact or existence of damages. Courts base decisions such as *Schonfeld*, therefore, not on an application of the new-business rule, but on a narrow interpretation of the basic law of damages—that the plaintiff has not proved the fact of damages.

This varied interpretation of the new-business rule, and the general law of damages, has a further consequence. Courts employing a narrow interpretation would deny recovery of lost profits in cases in which damages are proper under accepted principles of damages analysis. A plaintiff who can show by a preponderance of the evidence that it had a 45 percent chance of earning $1 million has proved by a reasonable certainty an expectation of $450,000. Yet these courts would probably deny such a recovery because the plaintiff could not show it had a better than 50 percent chance at earning the total. In such cases, the plaintiff is undercompensated. Conversely, consider a plaintiff who can show it had a 75 percent chance of earning $1 million. The plaintiff has proved an expectation of $750,000, yet many courts would award $1 million. In such cases, the plaintiff would be overcompensated. The courts therefore may be confusing the quantum of proof necessary to prove the expectancy with the nature of the expectancy itself. Section 11.4 pursues this issue.

(iv) Effect of Daubert: Failing to Consider Risk.   The cases in Section 11.2(b)(ii) discussed damages analyses based on unsupported or speculative assumptions that failed to prove that the plaintiff's new business would have generated a profit but for the defendant's conduct. Implicitly, these courts found that the nature of the business at issue appeared so risky, or that the plaintiff's proof did not establish a sufficient probability of success, such that the very existence of lost profits became too speculative.

As Chapter 1 of this book discusses, courts have extended the requirements of *Daubert v. Merrell Dow Pharmaceuticals*[49] to economic damages assessments. Thus, for example, experts must consider whether damages resulted from a cause other than that claimed by the plaintiff. The court in *Schonfeld v. Hilliard*, discussed in Sections 11.2(b)(ii) and (iii), suggested that a damages expert who failed to calculate and consider the percentage risk of failure of a new business venture would not survive a challenge under *Daubert*.[50]

In responding to the defendants' argument that the plaintiff's lost-profits analysis was too speculative, Schonfeld argued that his damages expert had taken into account the risk associated with the new venture by providing for a 25 percent variance on the projected cash flows of the business. The Second Circuit disagreed:

> However, Curtis [plaintiff's damages expert] failed to establish that this variance would adequately account for any inaccuracies in the revenue and expense assumptions discussed above as well as any changes in consumer demand for British-style news reporting.

Indeed, Curtis failed to account for the effects of *any* general market risks on the Channel's probability of success. These risks include: (1) the entry of competitors; (2) technological developments; (3) regulatory changes; or (4) general market movements. As the district court correctly noted, "[f]ailure to control for adverse market conditions allows the false inference that plaintiff's venture was an assured success." [citation omitted] Therefore, the court properly held that Schonfeld failed to establish a foundation for the existence of lost profits.[51]

Therefore, the *Schonfeld* court dismissed the plaintiff's claim of lost profits principally because he failed to account adequately for risks relating to the new venture. Further, the lower court suggested that *Daubert* standards would probably exclude the expert's opinion, but it decided the issue on other grounds.

Courts have also considered specific estimates regarding the percentage risk of failure, or the probability of success, of a new business in pre-*Daubert* cases. For example, in *Rancho Pescado, Inc. v. Northwest Mutual Life Insurance Co.*[52] the court found persuasive evidence that the business at issue, catfish farming, had a failure rate of 95 percent.[53] On the other end of the spectrum, an early case espousing the current new-business rule found convincing evidence that the new business involved in the case, a McDonald's franchise, had an amazing record of success—not one McDonald's franchise had ever failed.[54] Specific evidence showing the probability of success or failure of a new business has great value. In this era of *Daubert* challenges, the lack of any analysis of exogenous factors may give a court reason to exclude the expert's entire testimony.

One commentator has argued that if statistical evidence of the failure of a new business does not void the plaintiff's lost profits projections, then the plaintiff could incorporate such evidence into a risk premium and add it to the discount rate applied to the estimate of damages.[55] In *Energy Capital*, discussed in Section 11.2(b)(*i*), the court confronted such an issue, framing it as follows:

> Energy Capital argues that once the Court of Federal Claims determined that its profits were reasonably certain, no further consideration of risk was appropriate, because risk already had been considered in determining whether there had been profits. We disagree. A venture that is anticipated to produce $1 million in profits and that has a 95% chance of success is obviously more valuable than a venture that is anticipated to produce $1 million in profits with only a 90% chance of success—and yet, both ventures would most likely have been determined to have a reasonable certainty of producing profits. Therefore, the fact that the trial court has determined that profits were reasonably certain does not mean that risk should play no role in valuing the stream of anticipated profits. In other words, by finding that Energy Capital's lost profits were reasonably certain, the trial court determined that the probability that the AHELP venture would be successful was high enough that a determination of profits would not be unduly speculative. The determination of the amount of those profits, however, could still be affected by the level of riskiness inherent in the venture.[56]

The *Energy Capital* court remanded the case directing the trial court to calculate the present value of the damages award using a risk-adjusted discount rate.

Section 11.4 of this chapter criticizes the *Energy Capital* court's reasoning. But these cases show that a new venture can pose an inherent risk great enough to negate any claim of lost profits. The *Daubert* requirements further underscore that the plaintiff's damages expert must perform a risk analysis as part of the damages analysis. Defense counsel can use the lack of such an analysis to defeat a lost damages claim, either on its merits or as an attack on the plaintiff's damages expert in a *Daubert* challenge. Further, even if a new business plaintiff succeeds in establishing the existence and amount of lost profits, some courts will require the plaintiff to discount this measure by a risk-premium adjusted rate.

11.3 OVERVIEW OF VALUING ECONOMIC LOSSES FOR A NEW BUSINESS

We began this chapter by posing a hypothetical case for a drug company developing a new drug. Variations to the hypothetical relate to the status of the company, its expertise, and the nature of the product—from an established drug company developing a new drug within its area of expertise, to an unestablished company developing a new drug for a new market, and scenarios in between. Section 11.2 of this chapter presented an overview of the current new-business rule and showed that courts differ in their interpretation of this rule. Thus, the damages expert must understand the applicable law before developing a theory of measuring economic losses.

This section presents an analytical framework for establishing lost profits in the new-business scenario, that is, given the law in a particular jurisdiction, how should the damages expert approach the issue? Using examples relating to the hypothetical drug manufacturer, we begin by defining the issues the damages expert faces. Then we examine techniques for applying the analytical framework to calculate damages. In particular, we consider sources of data, categorization and modeling of risk, and methods for estimating economic losses.

As in most damages calculations, damages are the difference in economic value to the plaintiff of the outcome absent the defendant's misconduct and the actual outcome. In most new-business cases, the new business is the plaintiff, and defendant's misconduct usually destroys any value. Thus, damages are simply the but-for value of the new business absent the misconduct.

11.4 THE ANALYTICAL ISSUES FOR MEASURING ECONOMIC LOSSES

As Section 11.2 explained, the plaintiff must first prove the fact of damages—that the defendant's conduct in fact caused the plaintiff damages. After the plaintiff has proved that some loss has occurred, the law allows the amount of damages to be proved with less certainty, or *reasonable certainty*. Thus, an expert should regard damages as requiring two steps: establishing the fact of loss, with the loss directly linked to the bad acts of the defendant, and calculating the extent of the damages.

These concepts apply to calculating damages for both existing businesses and new businesses. To understand how the differences between the two affect how the damages are calculated, begin by considering the example of a manufacturer of an existing drug that faces competition from a company that infringes the patent on the drug. The plaintiff's damages expert will likely forecast the continued profitability of the drug based on its historic profitability and the combined sales of the patent holder and the patent infringer and then adjust the profitability to exclude competition from the infringer. Although the defendant's expert may alter the analysis to account for other factors such as increased competition from other drugs, both experts will usually rely on the same data obtained from parties in the suit to estimate but-for profitability.

In contrast, the plaintiff's expert estimating damages for a *new* business will likely encounter three additional problems.

1. The expert often faces a paucity of data and therefore will need to use additional resources, such as surveys or other market research, to obtain data that can be used to establish the basis for his analysis.

2. The expert faces a higher level of proof in establishing damages for a new business.

3. There can be more than one likely but-for scenario. For example, a firm seeking to design and manufacture a new drug may face a problem of Food and Drug Administration (FDA) approval. Lost profits differ depending on the FDA's approval or rejection of the drug.

Using the hypothetical drug company as an example, let us now consider how an expert should define the analytical issues.

(a) Establishing Economic Loss.   First, the expert must demonstrate that the plaintiff has, in fact, suffered economic losses. When one is estimating losses for an existing business, it is usually self-evident that the plaintiff has been harmed if the plaintiff wins on liability or if the liability case is strong, and the damages expert can focus on the extent of damages.[57] In new business cases, establishing the fact of damages often needs to be explicit. Unless the misconduct is, for example, theft of an asset that later was shown to produce economic value, the expert will need to demonstrate how the misconduct denied the plaintiff the full value of the asset, where the asset may be an invention, a business concept, or a budding venture. The expert can analyze the different risks the business faces and ascertain whether and how the various outcomes would have generated economic value for the plaintiff but for the misconduct.

This analysis is easiest when the expert can rely on some form of existing evidence. The expert can consider the plaintiff's track record, for example. Proof of success can also be that other, similar ventures have succeeded. The track record of other franchisers in the same business often proves sufficient to establish the plaintiff's success as a franchiser.

When no track record exists, the expert can still establish the likelihood of success. For example, an expert can analyze quantitatively the risks the firm faces and show that the product has a reasonable certainty of success. To do this, the expert can establish the potential market for the product, the willingness of consumers to purchase the product at a profitable price, and the firm's ability to manufacture the product at a cost corresponding to the profitable price.

Sometimes, however, the likelihood of success depends on discrete factors. For example, suppose our hypothetical drug company has two primary risk factors: (1) obtaining financing to reach FDA approval and (2) obtaining FDA approval. Then the likelihood of success equals the product of the probability of obtaining financing and the probability of obtaining FDA approval. If several outcomes exist that would have generated economic losses, then the probability of economic losses would be the sum of the probabilities for these outcomes, as long as the outcomes are independent.

(b) Establishing the Amount of Damages

(i) Multiple Outcomes.   Once the expert has established the fact of damages, the amount can be calculated. Traditionally, damages are calculated based on the expected outcome. However, this approach has two problems. First, the plaintiff may have suffered damages but be unable to show that there is a reasonable certainty of a particular outcome with economic losses—there may be no single outcome that meets the standard of a reasonable certainty, but a damages calculation based on multiple scenarios might show that the plaintiff has suffered losses. For example, consider the hypothetical drug case and assume that the new drug has the following potential outcomes:

- A 40 percent probability of failure
- A 20 percent probability that the drug will be used only for humans
- A 20 percent probability that the drug will be used for animals
- A 20 percent probability that the drug will be used for both

The calculation of damages as the weighted sum of the expected economic losses for the different outcomes will likely demonstrate that the plaintiff incurred damages even though the ultimate use of the drug appears speculative. Courts, however, appear unwilling to award damages in this situation. Thus, courts often seem to confuse the concepts of reasonable certainty of damages with reasonable certainty of success of the venture.

The second problem is how to calculate damages when there are potentially multiple outcomes. One resolution is to compute damages for the most likely outcome. Implicit in this decision to treat the most likely scenario as the only scenario is the assumption that damages for the other, unexpected, outcomes will offset each or that the probability of the other scenarios is minuscule.

This resolution, however, overcompensates some plaintiffs and undercompensates others. Consider our hypothetical drug case, and assume that the plaintiff has a 90 percent chance of receiving FDA approval with losses of $1 million, but a 10 percent chance of not receiving FDA approval with losses of $0. Damages in most jurisdictions will be the economic losses assuming FDA approval or $1 million: the courts will treat 90 percent as near enough to certainty as to ignore the small probability of failure. If, however, the plaintiff has a 90 percent chance that it would have achieved FDA approval and thus sustain losses of $1 million, and a 10 percent chance of not receiving FDA approval and sustain no profits, then damages should be estimated as the economic losses assuming FDA approval times 90 percent plus zero economic losses times 10 percent, or $0.9 million. Thus, most jurisdictions would overcompensate the plaintiff by $0.1 million.

Now suppose the drug has a 40 percent likelihood of FDA approval with economic losses of $1 million and a 60 percent likelihood of not receiving FDA approval with no economic losses. In most jurisdictions, the plaintiff will most likely recover no damages even though the plaintiff's economic loss is the expected value of $0.4 million (40 percent of $1 million plus 60 percent of $0). In this situation, most jurisdictions would undercompensate the plaintiff.

Thus, some courts may erroneously award zero damages if the plaintiff has failed to demonstrate that the likelihood of success exceeds some arbitrary, bright line. Courts also err, however, by awarding excessive damages if the plaintiff can establish with reasonable certainty that the business would have been profitable, because courts often award damages as the most likely, rather than the expected, value of economic losses.

(ii) Calculating Damages with Multiple Outcomes.   So what should an expert do? As we have discussed, the expert can calculate damages as the expected value of all outcomes.

In many cases, damages or economic losses are calculated as the discounted sum of lost earnings or lost economic value. Lost earnings for new businesses usually take the form of lost profits. However, these lost profits must be calculated as lost economic profits, which can differ from lost accounting profits. Economic profits include the cost of capital and should generally include the value of future costs such as the value of stock options.

A mathematically equivalent approach is to estimate damages as the loss of an asset, where the asset is an option to obtain a profit stream. Thus, a new business represents an opportunity to obtain a future stream of profits that may be positive, zero, or even negative, but, according to option theory, has positive value today based on the probabilities of the different outcomes. The lost asset thus has value equal to the capitalization of the expected lost profits. This method is discussed more fully in Section 11.5(c)(ii).

At present, many courts are at odds with current finance practice, which recognizes that an option has positive value even though exercising it immediately would not be profitable. Current court thinking is akin to valuing a call option for a stock as the current price of the stock less the strike price if the option is in the money or as zero if the option is out of the money.[58] Stock options trade actively on national exchanges, where they are observed to have positive value even when out of the money. Thus, we can conclude that the plaintiff whose option to have a successful venture is destroyed may have suffered damages even if the venture had a low probability of success. One way to value such an option is to use an option valuation model such as the Black-Scholes model.

The appropriateness of this approach is borne out by the proliferation of venture capitalists. Venture capitalists provide financing to new businesses in exchange for a share of future profits. Moreover, they invest at all stages of business development, even providing financing when a business is no more than a concept. As Section 11.5(c)(ii) discusses, sometimes an expert can rely on a venture capital valuation to value a new business.

This option framework explicitly incorporates the likelihood of the venture not succeeding into the estimate of damages. Plaintiffs are neither over- nor undercompensated. Whether the expert calculates damages using the expected value of outcomes framework or the option theory framework, the expert must consider the factors that affect the likelihood of the firm's success absent the defendant's misconduct.

11.5   APPLYING THE ANALYTICAL FRAMEWORK

We now discuss how the expert should apply the analytical framework discussed in Section 11.4. In particular, we consider how to do the following:

- Obtain data to perform the analyses
- Identify and categorize the risk factors to show reasonable certainty
- Estimate damages

(a) Data Sources.   As discussed in Section 11.4, experts often face the challenge of lack of data. In particular, quantifying the probabilities of different outcomes can prove challenging, especially when the outcomes are discrete. For example, suppose existing data show that a drug, in general, has a 50 percent probability of surviving the first round of FDA approval. However, this success rate can vary depending on other factors—such as whether the drug is injected, applied topically, or ingested orally—that may affect the probabilities. Similarly, the probability of obtaining funding may depend on several factors, such as the amount of financing required, the time required for the product to become economically self-sustaining, or the track record of the entrepreneurs. Although the expert will likely have access to third-party data on factors such as overall success rates for comparable ventures, the expert often needs to rely on the plaintiff and other experts to refine the probability that the venture will succeed.

If the probability reflects consumer preferences, experts often use market research techniques such as surveys. For example, a survey could measure the probability that a consumer will purchase a product through mail order. The expert can also use market research techniques to evaluate the desirability of a new feature for a product and the premium that consumers will pay for the new feature. Often, the business will have already performed such analyses; in other cases, the expert will need to obtain this information. Using existing studies can prove problematic because many have only qualitative information that the expert cannot readily adapt for quantitative analyses. Conducting studies specifically for the damages analysis is often cost effective and may be the only way to obtain the needed information, but the damages expert will often need to work with an expert in market research to ensure the survey's usefulness for calculating damages.

Other potential sources of information include studies of success rates for venture capitalists. Such studies typically show the success rates for new businesses at different stages of investment and the actual return that venture capitalists have realized.

(b) Risk.   This chapter has described each outcome as a discrete or separate scenario. Alternatively, we can think about different outcomes more generally by focusing on the factors, usually referred to as *risk factors*, which define an outcome. This more general way of thinking about different outcomes guides how an expert should model damages. We will first examine how to categorize risks relating to a new venture and then discuss techniques for modeling the two types of risk, idiosyncratic and systematic.

(i) Categorizing Risks.   Risks can be categorized as idiosyncratic (i.e., a risk specific to the venture) or systematic (i.e., a risk that affects the venture in the same way as

it affects many other businesses). For example, FDA approval for a new drug represents an idiosyncratic risk, whereas inflation represents a systematic risk.

Examples of idiosyncratic risk include the following:

- **Risks that the venture will succeed or not succeed.** This risk can depend on a single favorable or negative decision, such as FDA approval for a drug, or a series of such decisions that affect the firm's ability to become the standard for the market.

- **The ability to obtain financing.** The firm's ability to obtain financing will likely depend on external factors, such as the availability and cost of financing, but can also depend on qualitative factors, such as the entrepreneur's track record or the type of product. For example, in the late 1990s, venture capitalists eagerly financed any venture with an Internet-based product. By 2005, venture capitalists preferred more tangible products.

- **Risk that a competitor will develop a similar product.** Competitive products often affect profits or make the venture untenable.

- **Risks that affect the pricing of the product or the price of competitive products, such as the cost of inputs.** Although usually thought of as a systematic factor, these risks could be idiosyncratic if the venture uses a mix of resources that differs markedly from others in the same market. For example, if the new venture automates a manufacturing process that is labor intensive throughout the rest of the industry, an increase in the cost of labor will increase the price of competitive products but have little effect on the price of the product for the new venture.

Systematic risks are external factors that affect many businesses and include inflation, movements in the stock market, and unemployment. Often, however, systematic risk can be more appropriately modeled using the Capital Asset Pricing Model (CAPM), as discussed in the next section and in Chapter 7.

(ii) Modeling Idiosyncratic Risk. The first two types of idiosyncratic risk discussed in Section 11.5(b)(i), market success and the ability to obtain financing, are almost always discrete because the product will either survive or fail—no middle ground exists. Although we have portrayed these risks as having only two outcomes, similar factors can have a finite number of discrete outcomes. For example, at the time of the injury, the probability that the venture will obtain additional financing may be 0 percent, 50 percent, or 100 percent financing.

Analyses usually model these types of risk as different scenarios, each with a specific probability of occurring. The expert computes the lost profits for each scenario as though it were a certainty, multiplies these lost profits by the probability of the event occurring, and then sums these weighted probabilities to arrive at expected lost profits.[59]

Experts can similarly model the third type of risk discussed in Section 11.5(b)(i), the introduction of a competing product. Often, there are just two scenarios: either a competing product exists or it does not exist. Other cases can have multiple scenarios that reflect factors affecting the competing product's success. In either case, the outcomes may be nested, that is, the expert will need to model the case of a product's success in a market with a competing product as one outcome, and the case of a product's success in a market with no competing product as another.

The probability of the first equals the probability of success multiplied by the probability that a competing product will be introduced, and the probability of the second is the probability of success multiplied by the probability that a competing product will not be introduced.

All these situations assume that the probabilities are independent of each other. For example, consider the following situation for Company A when the expert has the following information:

- 40 percent probability that Company A will not produce a commercially viable product
- 60 percent probability that Company A will produce a commercially viable product
- 20 percent probability that Competitor B will enter the market

In this case, the expert could set up three scenarios with the following probabilities:

- Company A has no commercially viable product, with a probability of 40 percent
- Company A has a commercially viable product without Company B in the market, with a probability of 48 percent $(= (100\% - 20\%) \times 60\%)$
- Company A has a commercially viable product with Company B in the market, with a probability of 12 percent $(= 20\% \times 60\%)$

However, these calculations are correct only if the probability of Company B competing is independent of the probability of Company A succeeding. For example, consider the case in which the expert has available the following additional information: if Company A does not succeed, then the probability of Company B not competing is 100 percent.[60] Now, the probability of Company B entering the market depends on the outcome of Company A, and the probabilities should be

- 40 percent probability that Company A will not produce a commercially viable product
- 60 percent probability that Company A will produce a commercially viable product
- 100 percent probability that Competitor B will not enter the market if Company A does not produce a commercially viable product
- 33.3 percent probability that Company B will enter the market if Company A has a commercially viable product $(=100\% \times 20\% \div 60\%)$[61]

The expert then sets up the same three scenarios but with different probabilities:

- Company A has no commercially viable product, with a probability of 40 percent
- Company A has a commercially viable product without Company B in the market, with a probability of 40 percent $(= (60\% - 33.3\% \times 60\%))$
- Company A has a commercially viable product with Company B in the market, with a probability of 20 percent $(= 33.3\% \times 60\%)$

The fourth type of risk discussed in Section 11.5(b)(i)—risks of factors such as those that affect pricing—are risks that can have an infinite number of outcomes. Consider, for example, a case in which lost profits are a function of the cost of alcohol. Experts usually calculate the expectation of lost profits as the mean of lost profits across all scenarios. However, in this case, the mean of lost profits is equal to the calculation of lost profits where the price of alcohol equals the mean (or expectation) of the price of alcohol.

Even then, unless damages are particularly sensitive to this variable or this variable is potentially subject to an extreme shock, the expert can most likely compute lost profits using the expectation. If not, then an expert can sometimes obtain a closed solution from the distribution of the function of the variable. For example, if lost profits are a function of the logarithm of the cost of alcohol, then if the cost of alcohol is normally distributed, its logarithm is a lognormal distribution, and the expert can compute lost profits as the expected value of the cost of alcohol plus one-half the variance. In other cases, the expert can use more complex mathematical techniques such as a Taylor series expansion of the function and the moments around the mean of the variable.[62]

In other cases, the expert can rely on the economics of the situation to simplify the mathematics. Damages are usually the sum of lost profits, where these lost profits are the difference between profits in the but-for world and profits in the actual world. Further, businesses generally choose to operate so as to maximize profits given the external variables. Thus, small changes in any of the variables will not greatly affect profits. (Technically, a function is maximized at the point where the first derivative of the profit function with respect to any variable is zero). Thus, as one would intuitively expect, experts can usually model the effect of continuous risks by ignoring the variation and using only the expected value of the variable. In our example, this means we could model lost profits using the expected value of the price of alcohol and ignore anticipated price fluctuations unless an extreme change in the price occurred.

(iii) Modeling Systematic Risk. Systematic risk factors reflect general economic variables such as inflation, stock market fluctuations, growth in GDP, or wage growth. These risks can be modeled using the same techniques as those for idiosyncratic risks. Alternatively, these risks can be modeled as for an existing business that relies on market information.

After adjusting for idiosyncratic risks, we have a stream of future lost profits that have been discounted for the probability of failure of the venture, the probability of competing products, the difficulties in obtaining financing, and so forth. However, this stream of lost profits has not been discounted for the risks associated with inflation, the growth in GDP, and other, more global factors; we want to know the tradeoff between this stream of future lost profits and cash today.

Analyses for existing business damages usually discount cash flows for systematic factors using the CAPM, discussed in Chapter 7. The sensitivity of the return of the business to such systematic factors is captured by the standardized covariance of the change in the value of the business with the stock market, called the stock market beta.[63] The CAPM computes the expected excess return for the business as the product of the beta for the business times the risk premium, usually calculated as the excess return for all stocks historically.[64] Using information about the debt structure of the business, the asset beta can be computed from the stock market beta. The CAPM uses this asset beta to measure the cost of capital if the venture is financed entirely with equity; if the company is also financed with debt, the analysis must use the asset beta adjusted for the firm's debt structure.

The expected return for the business, which is the sum of the risk-free rate and the expected excess return, is the discount rate used to discount a business's cash flow.

Because we have adjusted for idiosyncratic factors, the remaining risks to lost profits for a new business are the same as those for a similar, existing business. Thus, experts can adjust lost profits for this systematic risk using the CAPM. They then use the expected excess return of the business calculated from the CAPM as the discount rate for discounting cash flows to present value.

(iv) Discount Rate.   We discount future lost profits to the prior year by dividing the lost profits by one plus the discount rate, described also as computing the present values of the expected cash flows. Usually, the discount rate is that computed from a model such as the CAPM, which incorporates systematic risk factors. If, however, the estimates of cash flow at each point in time have incorporated all risks faced by the new venture, including systematic risk factors such as inflation, then lost profits equal the sum of the future lost profits but for the alleged bad acts discounted for the real-time value of money.[65] Because both the lost profits and the discount rate can vary across years, the discounting should be done year by year.

At the risk of being pedantic, we point out that one cannot model expected lost profits using a discount rate calculated as the sum of the risk of a business failing, for example, and the discount rate from the CAPM model without adjustment. For example, consider a business that has a 25 percent probability of failure, a discount rate of 10 percent, and lost profits of $100 million in the next year if it succeeds. Then, its expected lost profits are $68.2 million (or $100 million $\times$ 75% $\div$ 1.1). This is equivalent to a discount rate of 46.7 percent, not a discount rate that is the sum of 10 percent and 25 percent. Further, when experts choose a more complex model than the CAPM, then they must ensure that they are not duplicating any idiosyncratic factors that they have already considered.

The discount rate for the business can vary across outcomes if the outcomes reflect different kinds of ventures. For example, one outcome may be approval for human use and another may be approval only for animal use. The discount rate for firms that produce drugs for human use can differ from firms that produce drugs for animal use. Thus, the expert must be careful to use the discount rate for each calculation of lost profits that reflects the outcome and the year.

(c) Calculating Damages.   This chapter has identified the risk factors that a new venture often faces and has discussed ways to quantify them. Next we turn to calculating damages.

Calculating expected damages is often straightforward. For example, if a drug has a 75 percent probability of FDA approval and expected profits would have been $100 million with FDA approval but negative $40 million without it, then damages equal $65 million (= 75 percent $\times$ $100 million − 25 percent $\times$ $40 million). In the absence of offsetting actual profits, damages equal the stream of expected lost profits discounted to present value.

When calculating damages, experts should remember the following guidelines:

- Each outcome must be independent of the other outcomes, and the sum of the probabilities for all outcomes must equal 100 percent.
- Lost profits for each outcome must properly reflect all important idiosyncratic risks for that outcome.

- Lost profits must be discounted using the appropriate discount rate for that outcome.

(i) Monte Carlo Simulation.   Sometimes the alternatives and interactions become so complex that the expert needs an alternative approach. One such approach is Monte Carlo simulation, one of the most flexible methods for calculating an expectation when there are multiple potential outcomes or when the outcomes depend to varying degrees on different inputs. (Chapter 10 also discusses Monte Carlo simulation.)

For example, suppose a specific drug has two outcomes: in one outcome, the drug is used only for humans; in another outcome, the drug is used only for horses. If the drug is used only for humans, then the amount of money spent on advertising may be greater than if the drug is used only for horses, because the firm can reach the relevant decision makers for horses with less advertising. Any change in the price of advertising will affect both outcomes, but the impact will differ.

Monte Carlo simulation begins by assigning probability distributions to the factors affecting the outcome. Once the simulation picks a value for each input parameter, the model determines the outcome. The process is repeated to simulate hundreds of different outcomes by selecting different values for the factors based on the probability distribution for each. The average of these outcomes is expected damages.

To illustrate how the model works, suppose a breach of contract has prevented a company from pursuing approval of a drug. To calculate lost profits, we need to estimate the probability of the drug's success under different scenarios. We use the following information:

- Probability of getting FDA approval: 40 percent.
- Probability of success, given FDA approval:

  - 80 percent if advertising cost $<$ \$100 per page.
  - 0 percent if advertising cost $>$ \$100 per page.

- Estimated revenue of \$2 million if the business succeeds.
- Advertising is the only cost to the company.
- Lost profits:

  - \$0 if the drug fails in the but-for world.
  - \$2 million minus (the cost per page of advertising $\times$ 1,000 pages) if the drug succeeds in the but-for world.

Three factors affect the outcome:

- The probability of FDA approval.
- The probability of failure with FDA approval.
- The cost of advertising.

Lost profits associated with the outcome are \$0 if:

- The FDA does not approve the drug.
- The price of advertising exceeds \$100.
- The business fails even though the price of advertising is less than \$100 and the FDA approves the drug.

Lost profits equal $2 million minus the cost of advertising ($= 1,000 \times$ cost per page of advertising) if:

- The FDA approves the drug.
- The cost per page of advertising is less than $100.
- The business succeeds.

The probability distribution for FDA approval can be modeled as a random variable following a Bernoulli distribution.[66] Likewise, the probability of success given that the cost of advertising is less than $100 can also be modeled as a Bernoulli distribution. The cost of advertising would most likely follow a continuous distribution. Thus, it could potentially be modeled as a lognormal distribution with a mean of $75 and a standard deviation of $10.[67]

Thus, one can think of an outcome as a draw from each of three urns. The first urn, representing FDA approval, contains 40 white balls and 60 black balls, where a draw of a white ball represents FDA approval and a draw of a black ball represents FDA rejection. The second urn, representing the cost per page of advertising, contains an infinite number of balls, each with a number between 0 and some practically defined upper bound. The relative proportion of any number is determined by the density function for the lognormal distribution with a mean of $75 and a standard deviation of $10. The third urn contains 80 blue balls, representing success, and 20 red balls, representing failure.

The outcome is defined by the color of the balls from the first and third urns and the value on the ball from the second urn. For example, if one draw produces a white ball from the first urn, a ball with a value of $80 from the second urn, and a blue ball from the third urn, then lost profits equal $1.2 million ($= $2 million $- $80 \times 1,000$). The simulation repeats this process hundreds or thousands of times, and the average of lost profits across all outcomes is the expected damages.[68]

This technique provides an estimate of damages that reflects the risks associated with a venture and thus represents the value of the option to obtain the profit stream for the business. Thus, Monte Carlo simulation proves useful when the alternatives or inputs have a complex discrete distribution or when the relation between the inputs is complicated.

(ii) The Asset-Valuation Alternative to Lost-Profits Damages. Courts sometimes accept the asset-valuation method as an alternative to a calculation of lost profits.[69] Because the value of the asset is the present value of future profits, damages equal the difference between the value of the asset before and after the misconduct and are mathematically equivalent to damages using the methods we have discussed. The main difference then is semantics.

In general, one can describe damages calculations as the difference between two profit streams, one before and one after the defendant's actions. Sometimes, however, the expert can rely on market valuations of the firm. For a publicly traded business, the valuation is implicit in the stock price. For a new venture, the valuation is implicit in financing decisions. Most new ventures are financed by venture capitalists who are willing to invest a certain amount in exchange for ownership in the venture. If the deal is simple, the valuation at that time equals the amount of financing divided by the ownership transferred. If a venture capitalist is willing to invest $1 million for an 80 percent share of the business, then the firm's value at that time is $1.25 million (= $1 million/.80). Sometimes the deal is complicated because ownerships have different liquidation preferences. Other times, the investor may receive the option to purchase additional shares in the future at favorable prices. When such additional benefits complicate the exchange, the expert must consider the value of these benefits in valuing the assets.

The asset-valuation calculation can be particularly simple when a valuation of the venture occurred immediately prior to the defendant's misconduct. For example, the valuation may have been the outcome of the venture seeking financing. The valuation can also be implicit, such as when the plaintiff and defendant enter into a contract. Competing valuations sometimes exist. If the value of the business equals zero after the defendant's misconduct, then the damages equal the first valuation. If the valuation after the defendant's misconduct exceeds zero, then one can calculate damages as the difference between the two valuations.

The expert can sometimes use the mathematics of pricing options as another way to value the economic profits of a business as an asset. As Section 11.4(b)(ii) discussed, one can think of a new business as an option to produce and sell a product or, equivalently, as an option to receive a series of economic profits. Option theory values an asset using information regarding the returns of another security or group of securities that contractually relates in some fashion to the asset.[70] Thus, the mathematics of options can provide a concise way of summarizing a series of economic profits.

(iii) Reconciling Different Estimates.   In general, all valuation methods should generate similar results because the mathematics are the same. A significant difference between two calculations usually means that one calculation has treated a risk factor in a way different from the other calculation. The expert must understand the reason for any significant difference and revise the estimates as appropriate. Sometimes different estimates reflect varying treatment of risk factors that the expert can present for the jury to consider based on alternative interpretations of the law. If so, the expert should explain how the different interpretations affect the outcome.

11.6   CONCLUSION

Valuing losses for a new business is complex, in part because of the inconsistent treatment of the issue by the courts. The current legal climate reflects the difficulties in calculating the profitability of a new business absent the defendant's actions. This chapter has presented an overview of current legal thinking relating to the new-business rule so that experts can understand the issues they must consider in estimating losses for a new business. This chapter also presents different ways that economists think about risk that an expert can use to estimate the loss in value of a new business.

NOTES

1. 206 Md. 610, 112 A.2d 901 (1955).
2. *Id.,* at 618.
3. *Central Coal & Coke Co. v. Hartman*, 111 F. 96, 98 (1901).
4. *See* Robert L. Dunn, *Recovery of Damages for Lost Profits,* 5th ed. (Westport: Lawpress, 1998) § 4.2, 344.

5. A complete statement of the status of the new-business rule in all jurisdictions is beyond the scope of this chapter. For information regarding the law in a particular jurisdiction, *see* Dunn §§ 4.3–4.13, 345-380, note 4.

6. *Corbin on Contracts*, vol. 11, interim ed. (2004 Fall Cumulative Supplement), § 1020A, 91-98 (citations omitted). *See also* Dunn § 4.3, 346 ("What was once a rule of law has been converted into a rule of evidence."), note 4.

7. *Chung v. Kaonohi Center Co.*, 62 Haw. 594, 618 P.2d 283, 291 (1980). Courts sometimes refer to this statement as the "wrongdoer rule," discussed in Chapter 8. *See* the discussion of *Schonfeld v. Hilliard*, 62 F.Supp.2d 1062 (S.D.N.Y. 1999), *affirmed in part, reversed in part*, 218 F.3d 164 (2d. Cir. 2000), in the next section of the chapter.

8. *Vickers v. Wichita State University, Wichita*, 213 Kan. 614, 518 P.2d 512, 517 (1974).

9. *Houston Exploration Inc. v. T.K. Meredith*, 102 Nev. 510, 728 P.2d 437, 438 (1986).

10. *Mindgames v. Western Publishing Co.*, 218 F.3d 652, 658 (7th Cir. 2000).

11. *Rancho Pescado, Inc. v. Northwestern Mutual Life Insurance Co.*, 140 Ariz. 174, 680 P.2d 1235, 1245 (1984).

12. *UST Corp. v. General Road Trucking Corp.*, 783 A.2d 931, 942 (R.I. 2001).

13. *Restatement (Second) Contracts*, § 352, comment b.

14. *Uniform Commercial Code*, § 2-708, comment 2.

15. *AGF, Inc. v. Great Lakes Heat Treating Co.*, 51 Ohio St.3d 177, 555 N.E.2d 634, 638-39 (1990).

16. Va. Code Ann. § 8.01-221.1.

17. A notable exception is Illinois, which, as of this writing, still follows the *per se* rule, with limited exceptions. *See*, e.g., *M.S. Distributing Co. v. Web Records, Inc.*, 2003 U.S. Dist. LEXIS 8078 (N.D. Ill. 2003), *Kinesoft Development Corp. v. Softbank Holdings, Inc.*, 139 F.Supp.2d 869 (N.D. Ill. 2001).

18. 509 U.S. 579 (1993).

19. *Energy Capital Corp. v. United States*, 302 F.3d 1314 (Fed. Cir. 2002).

20. *Id.*, at 1326 (citations omitted).

21. *Id.*, at 1326-27.

22. *Id.*, at 1328-29.

23. *Id.*, at 1329.

24. 297 N.W.2d 260 (Minn. 1980).

25. *Id.*, at 267.

26. *Id.*, at 267.

27. *Id.*, at 268.

28. *Id.*, at 268.

29. 107 F.3d 322 (5th Cir. 1997).

30. *Id.*, at 329.

31. *Id.*, at 339.

32. 218 F. 3d 652 (7th Cir. 2000).

33. *Id.*, at 658 (citations omitted).

34. *Id.*, at 658.

35. 62 F.Supp.2d 1062 (S.D.N.Y. 1999), *affirmed in part, reversed in part*, 218 F.3d 164 (2d Cir. 2000). We discuss *Schonfeld* more completely in the next section of the chapter.

36. *Id.*, at 1073.

37. 218 F.3d at 173.

38. *Id.*, at 174.

39. *See*, e.g., *Contemporary Mission, Inc. v. Famous Music Corp.*, 557 F.2d 918, 926 (2d Cir. 1977).

40. 218 F.3d at 175.

41. 95 Cal.App.4th 870, 116 Cal.Rptr.2d 158 (2002).

42. *Id.*, at 886-87.

43. *Id.*, at 887 (citations omitted).

44. *Id.*, at 887.

45. 373 F.3d 913, 918 (8th Cir. 2004).

46. *Id.*, at 919.

47. *Palmer v. Connecticut Ry. & Lighting Co.*, 311 U.S. 544, 561 (1941).

48. *Contemporary Mission, Inc. v. Famous Music Corp.*, 557 F.2d 918, 926 (2d Cir. 1977) (citations omitted).

49. 509 U.S. 579 (1993).

50. *Schonfeld v. Hilliard*, 62 F.Supp.2d 1062, n.6 (S.D.N.Y. 1999).

51. 218 F.3d at 174. The court did reverse the trial court and allow Schonfeld to recover damages based on an alternate theory of damages—the market value of the lost supply agreements. 218 F.3d at 175. We discuss this issue in the next section of the chapter.

52. 140 Ariz. 174, 680 P.2d 1235 (1984).

53. 680 P.2d at 1246.

54. *Smith Development Corp. v. Bilow Enterprises, Inc.*, 112 R.I. 203, 308 A.2d 477, 483 (R.I. 1973).

55. Patrick A. Gaughan, *Measuring Commercial Damages* (New York: John Wiley & Sons, 2000), 159.

56. *Energy Capital*, 302 F.2d at 1333.

57. This is not to ignore the possibility that a plaintiff can win on liability but not have suffered any economic harm.

58. A call (put) option for stock is the right to purchase (or sell) a fixed number of shares of stock at a fixed price (called the strike price) at any time before or on a given date. A call (put) option is "in the money" if the current price of the stock is greater than (less than) the exercise price. It is "out of the money" if the reverse is true.

59. A full discussion of how to estimate the probability of each scenario lies beyond the scope of this chapter. However, the expert will need to buttress this estimate with as much objective evidence as possible in anticipation of cross-examination.

60. Such a situation could arise when both companies are pursuing the same class of drugs to treat the same condition. Then, if the class of drugs is found to have little benefit, neither company will succeed.

61. This is the probability of Company B entering the market conditional on Company A succeeding. Almost every statistics book discusses this concept. One such book is Alexander M. Mood, Franklin A. Graybill, and Duane C. Boes, *Introduction to the Theory of Statistics* (New York: McGraw-Hill, 1974).

62. Usually such mathematics need only be dredged out under cross-examination to justify the simplifications employed. Further, if a jury needs additional information, the expert can usually provide an intuitive explanation.

63. This is the customary approach. There are other models such as the *k*-factor model or various empirical models that may be used.

64. Discussion of the risk premium can be found in books on corporate finance. However, there has been substantial disagreement about how to calculate its value. The beta for a specific stock is available from databases and analysts. The beta can also be computed from the historical share price.

65. The real-time value of money is usually computed as the expected return on a treasury security less expected inflation.

66. A variable follows a Bernoulli distribution if it can have only one of two values. An example is a variable that is one if a firm succeeds and zero if the firm fails. If the probability of success were 0.25 and the probability of failure were 0.75, then the variable would follow a Bernoulli distribution with parameter 0.25.

67. A range for the lognormal distribution is from zero to infinity; thus, this distribution is often used for variables such as prices that cannot have negative values.

68. In this case, the expected damages could also be computed using information about the Bernoulli distribution and the lognormal distribution, but the process would require calculating the properties of the truncated lognormal distribution. Both calculations, though, will generate the same estimate for expected damages.

69. *See, e.g., Schonfeld v. Hilliard*, 218 F.3d 164 , 176 (2d Cir. 2000).

70. John C. Cox and Mark Rubinstein, *Options Markets* (Englewood Cliffs, NJ: Prentice-Hall, 1985) vii. This text also provides a useful discussion on extending the principles of using options to value other securities.

CHAPTER 12

BUSINESS INTERRUPTION INSURANCE CLAIMS

Joe Anastasi

CONTENTS

12.1 INTRODUCTION

Business interruption insurance policies provide a business with insurance coverage for an unexpected interruption of its earnings stream as a result of a covered peril. Such an interruption can result from natural or man-made disasters. If the interruption relates to the wrongful actions of a third party, the insurance company will cover the alleged loss and then pursue a *subrogation* action, stepping into the insured/plaintiff's shoes in claims against the third party. This type of insurance can also cover ordinary payroll costs as well as costs for expediting mitigation of the loss and other extra expenses that the insured incurs during the recovery of its operations.

This industry niche has its own rules and definitions but always focuses on the amount of recoverable costs or profits. In contrast to tort and most other contract consequential damages claims for lost profits, business interruption insurance claims are calculated by methods specified rather rigidly in the applicable insurance policies. Even though this will sometimes result in recoveries that fail to satisfy the economist, accountant, and claimant, it allows for a predictability of underwriting risk that simplifies premium setting and facilitates policy and claim administration.

Business interruption insurance, available for over 100 years, originally was called *use and occupancy* insurance. Businesses in Great Britain and Canada call it *profits* insurance.

12.2   AFTER THE LOSS EVENT: INVOLVEMENT OF EXPERTS

The insurer typically retains its own set of experts to evaluate whether a physical loss event has a nexus with an associated business interruption loss. To this end, the insurer often retains the services of loss adjusters, engineers, and special coverage counsel to evaluate the facts. These experts attempt to ascertain whether the loss event fits within the contractual coverage provided by the underlying policy. To address the complex issues that such loss events typically pose, insurers often retain an accounting firm to evaluate the calculations that comprise the alleged loss. These accounting firms specialize in serving insurers and therefore depend on the insurers for repeat business.

To an unsuspecting insured, the insurer's array of experts presents a daunting adversary. The insured's failure to retain appropriate experts therefore can be a costly mistake. The insurer's adjuster has no incentive to calculate a large business interruption claim. The adjuster's natural bias favors the insurer when scrutinizing business interruption issues. To balance the claims development and settlement process, the insured should retain competent financial and technical experts. The insured should consider whether to include a professional fee or claims preparation endorsement as part of its property insurance policy. Such an endorsement (part of the original policy the insured purchases—think of it as an additional provision or coverage in the policy) obligates the insurer to reimburse the insured for reasonable professional fees incurred by third-party financial experts, construction engineers, and other consultants in quantifying and preparing the insured's claim.

12.3   ADJUSTMENT PROCESS

After a loss event, the adjuster first needs to help the insurer estimate the extent of the loss, sometimes called *establishing a reserve*. Adjusters can be employees of the insurance company or independent adjusters contracting to it. In either case, their job is as the name implies: to adjust the claim for loss to an amount due under the insurance policy's terms and conditions. One should not confuse them with *public adjusters*, contractors who work for insureds, often on a contingent fee basis, in settling claims. These latter are more typically associated with property damage than business interruption claims.

Insurance companies often evaluate adjusters on their ability to accurately estimate and manage the loss. The insured often encounters difficulty in settling an insurance claim when the adjuster's initial assessment significantly underestimated the amount of the loss. The insured will be better situated when the adjuster's initial estimate is accurate (or even conservatively excessive) because the adjuster can more easily persuade the insurer to reduce a loss estimate rather than increase it. The insured and its retained financial experts can help manage this process by meeting with the adjuster soon after the loss to help develop a preliminary loss estimate. Business interruption claims rarely present simple, straightforward issues. The insurer's claims-reporting bureaucracy often compounds the complexity of the claim development process. Adjusters seldom have the authority to settle significant claims without further authorization. They often have to submit details of the claim to the insurer's regional claims manager, who in turn will need to forward information to the headquarters' claims examiner. This process often repeats for each significant development in settling the claim.

This centralization of the claims settlement process affects the eventual claim resolution and often leads to conservative initial estimates. Adjusters who want to prevent higher levels of the insurance corporate claims group from overruling their judgment will take a conservative position on most issues—at the expense of the insured.

Many states have enacted unfair claim settlement practices statutes that stress the need for timely and responsive communications from the insurer. This creates tension between the parties. Although these laws mandate that the process proceed in a timely fashion, insurance companies often prefer to delay payments. Sometimes litigation will resolve the conflict that arises between an insured who has suffered a loss and the insurer who has not expeditiously settled the claim, with the parties litigating over the insured's allegation of unreasonable delay and lack of good faith and fair dealing on the part of the insurer.

12.4   TENSION BETWEEN CLAIMS ADJUSTER AND POLICY UNDERWRITER

The claims adjuster and corporate claims departments develop and attempt to settle the claim. These departments act independently of the sales or underwriting departments that originated the policy. This separation often causes disruption in smooth claims resolution. For example, sometimes an insurance company's sales and underwriting department originates a new product, such as when e-commerce coverage was first initiated, representing a coverage situation that took some years of experience for adjusters to adapt to.[1] This situation can lead to later confusion in the interpretation of policy coverages when insureds first submit claims for these policies.

Developing a business interruption claim often requires a detailed review of the insured's original intentions. One can consult the broker who placed the coverage as to the intent communicated by the insured when purchasing the coverage. Experts can also consult the insured's corporate risk manager, the insured's insurance broker, the London-based placing broker (if placed through Lloyd's), and the insurance company's underwriting department. When the situation has high financial stakes, the parties often have different recollections of the facts surrounding the placement of the policy.

12.5   PERILS, NUMBER OF EVENTS, AND DENIAL OF ACCESS

(a) Insured Peril.   Business interruption claims center on whether the interruption resulted directly from physical damage caused by an insured peril, as Section 12.9 of this chapter discusses. Business interruption policies cover defined business interruption losses only if physical damage to or destruction of the insured's property resulted from a covered peril. Many court cases conclude that for the business to receive compensation for its interruption loss, the insured must have suffered physical damage from an insured peril.[2] The courts have found that an insured property that becomes untenable as a result of an insured peril satisfies the condition of direct physical loss.[3]

(b) Single or Multiple Events.   Whether a loss is deemed to have a single event as its proximate cause (as opposed to a series of multiple events) can have a significant impact on the calculation of the loss. Multiple events can invoke multiple deductibles, reducing the recoverable loss.

The loss events related to the 9/11 attacks on the World Trade Center towers illustrate this issue. In this case, litigation ensued between the developer/owner of the World Trade Center and its property insurers; the litigation centered on whether the two attacks on the World Trade Center structures comprised multiple events. The recovery of almost $4 billion in losses hung on the answer to this question. In this case, two attacks occurred in separate space and time, each targeting a separate buiding. The attacks destroyed two buildings. One insurance policy was in place, providing approximately $3.55 billion in coverage *per occurrence.* Assume that the total losses will exceed $10 billion. If the losses are deemed to comprise two occurrences, coverage for losses sustained will amount to $7.1 billion; if the losses are deemed to comprise one occurrence, the coverage is half that amount. Each loss event, however, possesses its own set of facts and attendant policy contract language.[4] Making things even more interesting, the insurer had not issued the final policies at the time of the loss, although no one disputes that the risk had been bound (i.e., accepted). Not uncommonly, a policyholder will not have received a policy on a bound risk when a loss event transpires.

(c) Denial of Access.   Business interruption claims can also be compensated under a policy providing coverage for losses resulting from *civil authority denial of access* to the insured's business. For example, a significant hurricane can cause local civil authorities to deny access to the insured's place of business because of the threat posed by the hurricane and its aftermath.

Similarly, the insured sometimes negotiates a specific *denial of access* coverage provision in its business interruption policy. Such a provision will provide for recovery of business interruption losses resulting from denial of access to the property and need not result from a proclamation by the local civil authorities. An example of this would be when earthquake damage at an urban shopping mall has negatively affected retail stores, but the greatest long-term financial impact stems from a complete collapse of the attendent parking structure—hence an argument for denial of access.

12.6 DUE DILIGENCE AND PERIOD OF INTERRUPTION

The typical business interruption insurance endorsement—the Insurance Services Office (ISO) Standard Form—provides business interruption coverage for such length of time as would be required with the exercise of "due diligence and dispatch to rebuild, repair or replace such part of the property herein described as has been damaged or destroyed."[5]

This clause refers to the *period of indemnity,* or *business interruption period.* The insured's business is entitled to recover its actual loss sustained during this defined period of time. The definition of the period of indemnity becomes a fundamental component of quantifying the business interruption loss. The period of indemnity deserves the financial expert's foremost attention, as this factor most directly affects the measurement and magnitude of the loss. The business interruption period is the period necessary for the business, with the exercise of due diligence and dispatch, to restore its damaged structures and fixtures to the state that existed prior to the loss.

The business interruption loss is the actual loss sustained over the period of indemnity, and equals the reduction in gross earnings less any noncontinuing expenses. (Sections 12.9 and 12.11 of this chapter define these terms.) The insured is entitled to a loss recovery such that the business can resume operations and achieve, as the 1982 standard ISO Form states, "the same quality of service that existed immediately preceding the loss."

The extra time required for the business to order and receive (or produce) merchandise to restore the before-loss inventory levels also becomes part of the business interruption period.[6] If the business elects to construct an improved or enlarged structure to replace a loss, one would consider only the time the business would have taken to rebuild a structure similar—of like kind and quality—to the one destroyed.

Adverse circumstances outside the insured's control can lead to a longer business interruption period. For example, consider the hypothetical wherein an insured's landlord causes a delay, which can justify extending the business interruption period.[7] The courts have allowed for construction delays and found that such events expand the period of business interruption.[8]

In some cases, to mitigate its expected loss, the insured's business can resume operations in a temporary facility. Any earnings that result from the resumption of operations in such a temporary facility will reduce the business interruption loss. Both the insured and the insurer benefit from such mitigation because both parties prefer that the insured resume operations as soon as practicable. The resumption of operations in a temporary location does not necessarily terminate the business interruption period, however, which will continue until its "hypothetical conclusion."[9]

12.7 SEASONALITY AND LOSS PERIOD

Many businesses experience seasonal variations in sales and profits, which can affect the calculation of the business interruption loss. This notion of seasonality can also lead to a conclusion that an extension of the business interruption period is warranted.[10] Consider, for example, the hypothetical wherein a toy manufactur-er suffers a fire loss, halting operations for August, September, and early October. Even though this business suffered interruption of business for two-and-one-half months, the real economic measure of its business interruption loss will depend on whether it can meet its sales commitments to place its products (toys) into the distribution channel (the retail toy stores) in time for the holiday selling season. In this case, the economic measure lies outside the strict definition of the period of interruption. To ignore the reality of the seasonal aspect of the insured's business would otherwise distort the economic reality of this insured's business cycle.

In some cases, the courts have increased the business interruption period beyond the time required to physically restore the insured's premises to allow time for the insured to reach its preloss level of business. In one case, the repairs to a restaurant that experienced significant wind damage required three months. The restaurant, however, required an additional seven months to regain the business level it had experienced prior to the loss. In this case, the insurance carrier argued to limit the period of business interruption to the three-month period required to restore the building to the point that the restaurant could reopen. The court ruled that the restaurant was entitled to recover lost earnings to the point at which it reached the previous level of operation.[11] However, an expert should consider the specific contract language of each policy in preparing or evaluating a business interruption insurance claim, and the law of the state with jurisdiction can affect the outcome.

12.8   EXTENDED PERIODS OF INDEMNITY

Some insurance policies provide for an extension of business interruption cover-age for a specified length of time after the loss event. This extended period of indemnity lengthens the business interruption period beyond the time necessary to have damaged structures and fixtures restored to the condition existing prior to the loss event (or beyond other limitations that the policy places on the length of the business interruption period).

This type of endorsement recognizes that after a loss and restoration of structures and fixtures, businesses often need additional time to recover the sales levels they enjoyed prior to the loss. The insured should consider including an extended period of indemnity endorsement as part of its insurance policy because rarely do actual business interruption losses terminate immediately after the repair of physical damages.

12.9   ACTUAL LOSS SUSTAINED

The ISO Standard Form defines the measure of business interruption recovery as follows:

> In the event of such damage or destruction, this Company [Insurer] shall be liable for the ACTUAL LOSS SUSTAINED by the Insured resulting directly from such interrup-tion of business, but not exceeding the reduction in Gross Earnings less charges and expenses which do not necessarily continue during the interruption of business, for only such length of time as would be required with the exercise of due diligence and

dispatch to rebuild, repair or replace such part of the property herein described as has been damaged or destroyed, commencing with the date of such damage or destruction and not limited by the date of expiration of this policy. Due consideration shall be given to the continuation of normal charges and expenses, including payroll expense, to the extent necessary to resume operations of the Insured with the same quality of service which existed immediately preceding the loss (capitals in the original).12

The ISO Form defines gross earnings as the sum of the total net sales and other earnings derived from the operation of the business, less the cost of (1) merchandise sold, (2) materials and supplies consumed directly in supplying the services sold by the insured, and (3) services purchased from outsiders for resale that do not continue under the contract.

Insurance policies stipulating gross earnings calculations provide for the deduction of no other costs in calculating gross earnings. This doesn't matter for loss calculations, which will deduct the remaining variable or saved costs as noncontinuing costs. It does matter, however, in calculating the amount of coverage to buy and hence premium to be paid, because the policies provide for coverage based on gross earnings. The insured is entitled to recover a business interruption loss to the extent there would have been earnings but for the occurrence of the loss event. This condition determines whether the policy covers a business interruption loss.

The definition of gross earnings in the ISO Form provides that, "in determining gross earnings, due consideration shall be given to the experience of the business before the date of damage or destruction and the probable experience thereafter, had no loss occurred." Therefore, the analyst should factor the probable experience of the business but for the loss event into the loss computations. Thus, even a business operating at a loss could have a recoverable business interruption claim as long as the business was earning enough to cover a portion of its operating costs. The business interruption event could have prevented the firm from earning enough to cover all or part of its continuing or fixed (in the short term) cost of operations.

Moreover, a business not operating at all can suffer a recoverable business interruption loss. For instance, a retail store planning a grand opening that is delayed for three weeks because of a fire immediately before the planned event will have suffered a recoverable business interruption loss; one could measure the loss by referring to the business plan for this store or by other historical operating experience of this retailer. Similarly, a software developer who suffers an interruption of operations because of an earthquake, which delayed the introduction of a new software product that was in late-stage beta testing, would also qualify for a business interruption recovery. The relevant measurement criteria include the company's business plan, the operating performance of comparable products that the same software developer had introduced, and the subsequent performance of the affected product. The experienced financial expert can provide the insured with significant benefits in quantifying such losses (*see* Chapter 11, "Valuing Losses in New Businesses").

The court upheld such an interpretation in *General Insurance Co. of America v. Pathfinder Petroleum Co.*[13] In this case, a petroleum refinery experienced a fire that disrupted operations for 90 days. The business had planned to build a polymerization plant that would have provided incremental earnings. The fire loss at the petroleum plant delayed construction of this polymerization plant. The court found that the polymerization plant could have been built and would have earned a profit during the business interruption period. The insurance carrier asserted that the company did not suffer business interruption for the planned polymerization plant during the business interruption period because the plant did not exist at the time of the loss. The court ruled that the planned installation and operation of the polymerization plant provided an essential element of the company's business plan and that the loss of use of the site during the business interruption period prevented the business from earning its planned profits from the polymerization plant.

12.10   MITIGATION OF LOSS

The insured has an obligation to mitigate its loss to the greatest extent practicable. This includes resuming operations at temporary or other locations and using available merchandise or other resources to mitigate the loss. The insurer must reimburse the insured for expenses incurred to mitigate the loss. Moreover, the insured's obligation to resume operations does not require the business to undertake unsound business practices merely to effect a savings to the insurer.[14]

12.11   NONCONTINUING EXPENSES

Noncontinuing expenses are those that do not occur in the absence of sales; they might include sales commissions, sales taxes, bad debt expense, credit card fees, freight-out, and sales discounts. The business interruption insurance contract defines the concept of noncontinuing expenses. In the context of accounting theory or other litigation-related damages models, one can consider these as variable or semivariable costs. The business interruption model, however, treats lost profits as measured over the short run. In some cases, sizable business interruption claims result from a business interruption of only a few days. Costs otherwise believed to be variable need not vary in the context of a brief business interruption.

Consider a retailer who has experienced a two-week business interruption. Valid business reasons often exist for not terminating the sales staff for this interruption period. For example, if a retailer lays off the sales staff for this short period, the sales staff may seek employment elsewhere, forcing the retailer to incur retraining and hiring costs and to reopen with less experienced sales staff. Some retailers will also have concerns regarding customer loyalty to the existing sales staff. The financial expert and insured should discuss these issues to help the client plan its business interruption strategy.

The Standard ISO Form states that "due consideration shall be given to the continuation of normal charges and expenses, including payroll expense, to the extent necessary to resume operations of the Insured with the same quality of service which existed immediately preceding the loss."[15] Payroll expenses include wages, employee benefits, and commissions that often stop because of the business interruption. Most enterprises prefer to avoid laying off their experienced employees in the event of a business interruption, and most business interruption policies allow for this. In effect, this ISO clause provides that all payroll expenses remain a continuing, or covered, expense.

As is apparent, even with a prolonged business interruption, retailers often want to keep most of their employees on the payroll to maintain the integrity of the company and to ensure a smooth resumption of operations. Stephen Cozen, a noted authority on insuring real property losses, states that "for this reason the gross earnings [ISO] form for mercantile and nonmanufacturing insureds assumes that ordinary payroll will be a continuing (and therefore covered) expense."[16]

12.12 ORDINARY PAYROLL ENDORSEMENTS

Payroll is thus a continuing (and therefore covered) expense regardless of the length of the business interruption period. Sometimes, however, a business prefers to purchase insurance to cover less than the entire cost of ordinary payroll in the event of an extended business interruption period. For example, some manufacturing plants plan to lay off all hourly, or unskilled, employees in the event of a prolonged business interruption. For a reduced premium, these companies purchase coverage of the continuing costs of only predefined key personnel. The companies can obtain this limited, and therefore less expensive, coverage through an ordinary payroll exclusion endorsement or an ordinary payroll limited coverage endorsement.[17]

The ordinary payroll *exclusion* endorsement eliminates business interruption coverage for all the ordinary payroll expenses during the business interruption period except for officers, executives, department managers, contract employees, and other key personnel. The ordinary payroll *limited coverage* endorsement covers all ordinary payroll expenses but only for a predefined elected time period (e.g., 90 days, 120 days, 150 days, or 180 days).

12.13 EXPEDITING AND EXTRA EXPENSES

Most businesses need to remain in operation after the loss event. The survival of the business will require a continued presence in the marketplace, which in turn often requires the insured to incur nontraditional expenses (which often exceed that of normal operations) during the recovery period. Therefore, many insurance policies that provide for business interruption coverage also contain *extra expense*, or *expediting expense* endorsements, or both. These endorsements cover costs that the insured incurs during the actual or attempted mitigation of its business interruption loss. Although expediting expenses reduce the total amount of the insured's business interruption loss, extra expenses ultimately increase the total loss but are expended in an effort to provide an overall reduction in loss exposures.

An *expediting expense* endorsement covers costs that exceed normal operating expenses incurred by the insured to make up production or recover from the loss to the extent the costs reduce the business interruption loss. The prohibitive cost involved in the air freighting of a replacement generator weighing a ton or more is one example of an expediting expense. A more traditional shipping method might be by sea or land carrier; in this example, however, the significant cost of the air freighting would be more than offset by the amount of revenue generated by getting back into business within days rather than weeks. To qualify as an expediting expense, the out-of-pocket outlay must relate to the covered loss, must have been incurred to reduce the loss, and traditionally cannot exceed the amount by which it reduces the related loss. Therefore, analysts also refer to expediting expenses as "expenses to reduce the loss."

Three general categories exist for expediting expenses. First, as in the proceeding example, they can accelerate the resumption of operations, ultimately reducing the length of the loss period. For example, the insured can often reduce the business interruption claim by accelerating the rebuild of its damaged manufacturing facility by spending overtime labor premiums, air rather than surface freight for critical parts, and so on. The second category includes expenses that enable the insured to continue its operations, such as the rental of temporary facilities, purchasing finished product from third-party vendors, and customer retention costs. The third category of expediting expenses includes those incurred to build inventory depleted during the business interruption period. These outlays can include the cost of overtime and temporary employees.

An *extra expense* endorsement covers the costs incurred during restoration that exceed the cost the insured would normally have incurred to conduct the business during the same period had no loss event occurred. In contrast to expenses incurred to reduce a loss, the extra expenses increase the insured's total loss claimed. In this case, the insurer reimburses any reasonable and necessary extra expenses that relate to the covered loss and that have been incurred to temporarily continue the business operation. Typical policy language describes them as costs to operate a business in a fashion "as nearly normal as practicable." By definition, as an extra expense, such costs exceed the normal costs that the insured would have incurred had no interruption occurred. Examples of extra expenses include costs to maintain market share, secure damaged property, and retain key employees.

12.14   INVENTORY (CONTENTS) CLAIMS

A typical property or contents insurance policy provides for recovery, at cost, for the inventory lost as a result of an insured peril. An accountant can easily calculate the value of lost inventory for such coverage.

Some policies, however, provide for a different form of recovery for inventory losses. Insured parties often negotiate coverage that provides recovery for inventory damaged by an insured peril, with the recovery amount based on the inventory's net selling value after considering all applicable sales discounts and allowances.

Such recovery for the lost inventory at net selling values compensates the insured for the expected profit on the ultimate sale of the inventory. This inventory replacement coverage simplifies the loss calculation because analysts find it more difficult to quantify a business interruption loss than a contents loss claim. Compensating the insured for lost inventories at net selling price often obviates any need to estimate a business interruption claim, especially with a perceived business interruption period of short duration.

When the insured, however, has suffered a business interruption loss together with a contents loss (which the insurer will compensate at net selling values), the financial expert must avoid double counting an element of profit in the claim. Under some insurance policy requirements, the financial expert will need to reduce the business interruption claim to compensate for the profit on inventory in the contents loss claim measured at net selling value. In effect, the expert reduces the business interruption calculation by the amount of profit inherent in the inventory claim.

The following example illustrates this point. Consider a retailer that has experienced a fire loss that destroyed all of the inventory in the store, which had a cost of $4 million. In this example, the retailer has a contents loss claim of $6 million based on the inventory's net selling value. The retailer's policy provides for contents loss insurance recovery based on the inventory's net selling value, not just the $4 million cost of the inventory. As this example demonstrates, the insurance policy provides a recovery to the insured of $2 million for the gross profit the insured would have earned on the ultimate planned sale of the inventory, but for the fire loss.

Let us further assume that at the time of the loss, the retailer had three months of inventory and the store could not resume operations for fifteen months. Assume also that after considering noncontinuing expenses, the business interruption loss equals $10 million. The calculation of the business interruption period must reflect the three months of inventory that the insurance company has (in effect) purchased from the insured at retail prices. Consider the relation between the contents loss calculation and the business interruption loss calculation: because of the amount of inventory on hand at the time of the loss, the business interruption period would effectively commence three months after the fire loss event. In this example, the business interruption period would equal twelve months, not the fifteen months originally calculated. This modification reduces the business interruption claim to $8 million (= $10 million business interruption loss less the $2 million of compensation for gross profit on the inventory as part of the contents loss claim).

12.15 PERIODIC UPDATES TO THE ADJUSTER

Many insureds present their business interruption claim after the interruption has ceased and normal operations have resumed. This procedure provides the parties the benefit of hindsight in reviewing the events and conditions that affected the amount of the loss. Most appropriately, however, the insured should meet with the adjuster as soon as possible after the loss and periodically thereafter. This initial meeting provides an opportunity to raise at an early stage any issues that can affect the calculation of the business interruption, extra expense, and contents loss. The adjuster will use this information in communicating with the insurer's claims department (which has responsibility for booking a claims reserve). Thereafter, the insured should meet with the adjuster to provide periodic updates regarding the status of the loss because this process minimizes any surprises. Without these updates, amicably resolving a significant claim will prove much more difficult.

12.16 REQUESTS FOR PARTIAL PAYMENT

An insured can seek a partial advance payment from the insurer shortly after the loss. When contending with a business interruption matter comprising a long indemnity period, the insured should request and receive several such advances as the claim progresses. The insured, via its financial expert, should provide adequate documentation to the insurer and its experts to provide reasonable justification for any requested advance. An insurer's unjustified refusal to provide such advance payments could become grounds for asserting a bad faith claim if the refusal makes it impossible for the insured to continue operations.[18]

12.17   MEASURING THE LOSS

The business interruption loss is the earnings stream that would have been achieved but for the loss event, less actual earnings.

To measure the business interruption loss, the courts look to the actual policy language for definition of actual loss sustained. In *Associated Photographers v. Aetna Cas. & Sur. Co.*, the court found the insurance policy language—which limited the recovery of the loss to the "reduction in gross earnings less charges and expenses which do not necessarily continue during the interruption of the business"—to define loss as the difference between the net profit the plaintiff would have earned during the period of interruption and the net profit the plaintiff earned during the period of interruption.[19]

The adjuster and the insurer's financial expert often have a natural bias to assess the claim based on the company's historical financial performance. Sometimes, however, this historical perspective does not adequately reflect what would have happened had the loss event not occurred. For example, nonrecurring adverse market conditions could have existed in the past that will not exist in the future. The plans of the business will likely affect future results. For this reason, the parties should evaluate the insured's prospective business plan in measuring the business interruption loss. The financial expert should, however, compare the claimant's past experience in forecasting actual outcomes with its business plan because some companies make consistently optimistic or pessimistic forecasts.

Financial experts most often review the historical operating performance of the business for one or two years preceding the date of the loss. This gives the financial expert a basis for projecting postloss results.

12.18   PREPARING A PERSUASIVE CLAIM

(a) Visual Documentation of Damage.   Visual evidence of the physical impact of the peril can refresh an adjuster's memory when the insured must present a business interruption claim some time after the business has resumed normal operations. Photographs of the damage and destruction become especially useful. This record also helps to demonstrate how the physical damage led to the interruption of the business. In one case, flooding by a hurricane affected a business 300 miles inland. Approximately one year later, as the insured presented the business interruption claim, the adjuster questioned how such significant flooding could have occurrred in an otherwise dry inland arroyo and whether the impact really had been severe enough to have caused the magnitude of business interruption losses that the claim specified. To address this, the claimant's forensic accountant used news footage to demonstrate the devastation. A video editor pared the hours of raw film stock into a five-minute highlight film. The insured presented this video at a meeting with representatives of the insurance carrier who ultimately paid the claim.

(b) Written Documentation.   Other situations suggest the need to compile memoranda to document the timing and extent of damage. This documentation can describe the condition of the business in terms of its business plan at the time of the loss event and should document any remedial actions that management took to mitigate the loss. For example, the forensic accountant advising a software developer affected by an earthquake decided that the status of the company's quality assurance testing of a new product would be a key factor in defining the business interruption period. As a prophylactic measure, the applicable software engineers, product testing managers, and quality assurance personnel prepared affidavits at the outset of the engagement. This spared the insured numerous intrusive interviews of its key employees and preserved the compelling record that served as the basis for the claim. The forensic accountant presented the affidavits along with all the other claim documentation, which the claims adjuster appreciated.

In other cases, management needs to develop detailed daily or weekly logs to demonstrate the company's efforts to resume business. Similarly, a contemporaneous log detailing the resumption of operations for each department helps to document a business interruption period (which can vary across departments).

The financial expert needs to prepare and present a well-documented claim. The documentation should support each separate claim element. For example, the insurer can request copies of all invoices supporting the claim for extra expenses. The insurer can also request copies of any financial statements, general ledgers, sales or business plans, and annual budgets that the insured's financial expert relied on.

The insured and its experts have the right to develop the initial claim. Conversely, the insurer is not entitled to demand complete access before the insured and its experts have had an opportunity to complete their analysis of the issues and develop the business interruption claim. The insurer and its representatives have legitimite information needs, however. After the insured's experts have analyzed and presented the business interruption claim, the insurer's experts can begin their detailed review and can then ask for additional documentation or clarification on the method. This approach will narrow the scope of inquiries from the insurer and its expert and will minimize any potential disruption of the insured's business operations. Throughout the claims development process, the insured's representatives should hold periodic briefings with the adjuster to maintain an orderly flow of information to the insurer.

The insured and its experts should present the claim and all the supporting documentation at a meeting with the adjuster and the insurer's financial expert. In a face-to-face meeting, the adjuster can assess the claim's completeness and the diligence exercised in its development. At such a presentation, both parties can also develop a timeline to resolve the claim.

12.19 NEGOTIATING A FAVORABLE SETTLEMENT

Although the parties amicably settle many business interruption claims, the insured and its financial expert should recognize that insurance companies and their representatives have experience working in an adversarial environment. Not all insurers use the same approach to resolve claim disputes. Consequently, the insured and its financial expert should prepare to communicate their position clearly and firmly on the business interruption claim.

The insured should insist that a representative from the insurance company with sufficient authority to settle the claim attend settlement meetings. This representative might not be the adjuster.

The insured should request that the insurance company and its representatives state their position on any aspects of the claim that they do not accept. After the insurer's expert has conducted the preliminary inquiries, the insured again should immediately request a response to further define any contentious issues. The insured should document the response of the insurance carrier and its representatives in case of future arbitration or litigation.

The insured will want to retain legal counsel if significant contentious issues exist or if the claims settlement process does not approach resolution. Legal counsel possessing a background in insurance coverage and business interruption claims often has the qualifications for this task; the insurance carrier will likewise consult such specialized counsel. The insured should also understand that, in many instances, insurance policies require the process of arbitration or appraisal rather than traditional litigation.

NOTES

1. Marvin Milton, "Public Adjusters: Fair Players or Fair Game," *Best's Review—Property*, Casualty Insurance Edition (1991).

2. *McDowell-Wellman Engg Co. v. Hartford Accident and Indem. Co.* 711 F.2d 521 (3rd Cir. 1983); *Cleland Simpson Co. v. Fireman's Insurance Co. of Newark*, 392 Pa. 67, 140 A.2d 41 (1958); *Swedish Crucible Steel Co. v. Travelers Indem. Co.*, 387 F. Supp. 231 (E.D. Mich. 1974).

3. *Datatab, Inc. v. St. Paul Fire & Marine Insurance Co.*, 347 F. Supp. 36 (S.D.N.Y. 1972); *Western Fire Ins. Co. v. First Presbyterian Church*, 165 Colo. 34, 437 P.2d 52 (1968).

4. *SR Int'l Bus. Ins. Co. Ltd. V. World Trade Center Properties LLC*, (S.D.N.Y.1:01cv09291).

5. ISO Commercial Risk Services, Jersey City, NJ Insurance Services Offices, Inc. 1982, Sec. 1, Par. 2.

6. *Northwestern States Portland Cement Co. v. Hartford Fire Ins. Co.*, 360 F.2d 531 (8th Cir. 1966); *Compagnie des Bauxites de Guinee v. Insurance Co. of North Am.*, 721 F.2d 109, 116 (3rd Cir. 1983).

7. Steven A. Cozen, *Insuring Real Property* (New York: Matthew Bender-Times Mirror Books, 1994), 3–24.

8. Ibid.

9. Ibid., 3–29.

10. Ibid., 3–35.

11. *Lexington Insurance Co. v. Island Recreation Development Corp.*, 706 S.W.2d 756 (Tex. App. 1986).

12. ISO Commercial Risk Services, Jersey City, NJ Insurance Services Offices, Inc. 1982, Sec. 1, Par. 2. Insurance Services Office, Inc. (ISO) is a leading supplier of statistical, actuarial, and underwriting information for and about the property/casualty insurance industry. All ISO products and services are advisory; insurers can use them, modify them, or not use them as they see fit. The products and services are available to any U.S. property/casualty insurer and its agents. ISO develops standardized policy language for most lines of property/casualty insurance.

13. *General Insurance Co. of America v. Pathfinder Petroleum Co.*, 145 F.2d 368 (9th Cir. 1944).

14. *Gordon Chemical Co. v. Aetna Casualty & Surety Co.*, 632, 266 N.E.2d 653 (1971).

15. ISO Commercial Risk Services., Inc., Jersey City, NJ Insurance Services Offices, Inc. 1982.

16. Cozen, *Insuring Real Property*, 3–14.

17. ISO Form CF 15 17 (Ed.05/77); ISO Form CF 15 18 (Ed.5/77), ISO Commercial Risk Services.

18. Robert M. Morrison, Alan G. Miller, Stephan J. Paris, "Business Interruption Insurance: Its Theory and Practice," (New York: Natl. Underwriter Co.), 1996 p. 239.

19. *Associated Photographers v. Aetna Cas. & Sur. Co.*, 677 F.2d 1251 (8th Cir. 1988).

LIST OF CASES

Associated Photographers v. Aetna Cas. & Sur. Co., 677 F.2d 1251 (8th Cir. 1983).

Cleland Simpson Co. v. Fireman's Insurance Co. of Newark, 392 Pa. 67, 140 A.2d 41 (1958)

Compagnie des Bauxites de Guinée v. Insurance Co. of North Am., 721 F.2d 109, 116 (3rd Cir. 1983)

Datatab, Inc. v. St. Paul Fire & Marine Insurance Co., 347 F. Supp. 36 (S.D.N.Y. 1972)

General Insurance Co. of America v. Pathfinder Petroleum Co., 145 F.2d 368 (9th Cir. 1944)

Gordon Chemical Co. v. Aetna Casualty & Surety Co., 358 Mass. 632, 266 N.E.2d 653 (1971)

Lexington Insurance Co. v. Island Recreation Development Corp., 706 S.W.2d 756 (Tex. App. 1986)

McDowell-Wellman Engg Co. v. Hartford Accident and Indem. Co., 711 F.2d 521 (3rd Cir. 1983)

Northwestern States Portland Cement Co. v. Hartford Fire Ins. Co., 360 F.2d 531 (8th Cir. 1966)

SR Int'l Bus. Ins Co; Ltd. v. World Trade Ctr. Props. LLC, 222 F. Supp.2d 385, 393-95, 398-99 (S.D.N.Y. 2002); *Swedish Crucible Steel Co. v. Travelers Indem. Co.*, 387 F. Supp. 231 (E.D. Mich. 1974)

Western Fire Ins. Co. v. First Presbyterian Church, 165 Colo. 34, 437 P.2d 52 (1968)

BUSINESS VALUATION

Michael A. Crain

CONTENTS

The author thanks Mike Mard of The Financial Valuation Group's office in Tampa, Florida for his
input into this chapter.

13.1   BUSINESS VALUATION IN LITIGATION MATTERS

(a) The Need for Valuation Experts.   In litigation, parties often retain experts to ascertain the value of assets, which one can group into two categories: real assets (e.g., real estate and tangible personal property) or financial assets (e.g., a business, securities, and intellectual property). This chapter will focus on the valuation of certain types of financial assets: businesses and ownership interests in businesses.

Every asset has a value, but some assets or circumstances make valuation more difficult. Experts use similar approaches to value many types of assets. For example, real estate appraisers use three general approaches that resemble those applied in business valuation. The similarities end, however, with the application and inputs needed to value a specific asset.

An analyst measures an asset's value as of a certain date as a function of the future benefits that one expects from owning the asset. Investors will pay a price to acquire an asset based on what they expect the investment will return in the future and their cost of capital. Because the future lacks certainty, investments have risk. Facts often change or information may become available after the valuation date; these often affect earnings, expectations, and the asset's value. For example, the loss of a major customer or a new litigation claim could result in a significant decrease in the earnings and value of a company. Conversely, the business could obtain a major customer, thereby increasing its earnings and value. The variability of future earnings—up or down—is the source of risk to an investor and of holding an investment. In spite of this risk, individuals and institutions make investment decisions every day based on their expectations of the future and their risk tolerance.

(b) Litigation Matters that Require Business Valuation.   Various litigation matters require valuations. Examples include the following:

- A business damages claim measured as a loss of the company's value
- A dissenting shareholder action, requiring the valuation of a party's shares
- A family law matter requiring valuation of the parties' business interests to determine the marital estate
- A failed business purchase transaction that goes to litigation and requires a business appraisal

(c) Common Valuation Issues in Litigation Matters.   Damages claims often require multiple valuations of the same business. For example, the expert values a business before the impairment (but-for value) and values it again after the impairment. The difference between the before and after values reflects the loss of value.

Sometimes a defendant's wrongful action destroys the business. In this case, the expert values the business as of a date just prior to the destruction. The business operations will have no value after its destruction, negating the need for a second valuation. In this case, damages equal the but-for value. Sometimes a company has some assets that survive the destruction; these items provide offsets when the damages are computed.

When the parties disagree over relevant dates for a valuation (such as the date of a contract breach), the expert often provides multiple valuations of a business as of different dates. The client may ask the expert to prepare several but-for values on all possible dates.

Experts also need to decide which information they should consider because litigation sometimes occurs months or years after the event that precipitated the valuation. When the objective is solely to assess the value of a business as of a certain date, the analyst should consider only information that is known or knowable as of the valuation date. In this situation, the expert would ignore new information that arose between the valuation date and the date of trial. One refers to this perspective as *ex ante*. However, in certain litigation situations, the ultimate objective may be more than the value of a business. For example, the situation for some damages claims that intend to make the plaintiff whole can justify using new information that arose after the valuation date (hindsight). One refers to this perspective as *ex post*.

When an expert uses material information that arose after the valuation date (*ex post*), the analysis does not result in the actual value as of that date. However, the value as of a certain date may not be the appropriate damages measure to make the plaintiff whole in some situations. Accordingly, the expert can use hindsight in some damages measurements. For example, assume the plaintiff, a manufacturer, claims a breach of contract that destroyed the business. The breach occurred on July 1, 200X, and the plaintiff wants to use the value of the business on that date as the measure of damages. Suppose a hurricane occurred on September 1, 200X that destroyed the company's sole production facility. In this case, the July 1, 200X value may not be the proper measure of damages suffered by the plaintiff at the time of the trial date because, had the breach not occurred, the business would have suffered losses due to the hurricane.

The expert should consult with the attorney or client to discuss whether the use of information subsequent to the valuation date is appropriate in a particular situation. Such information can take the form of an adjustment to the actual value on the date or the assumption of hypothetical conditions as of the valuation date. Identifying which information to use to ensure fairness proves difficult in many cases. This ultimately becomes a question for the court to decide and most often results in different valuations from the experts (*see* Chapter 8, "*Ex Ante* versus *Ex Post* in Damages Calculations").

(d) Value of Entire Business or Fractional Ownership Interest.   Some valuations consider an entire corporation and others focus on a business unit, division, product line, or single location of a larger firm. In some cases, the expert will need to value all the company's equity or a fractional ownership interest in a firm (i.e., shares of a company's common stock, preferred stock, or some other ownership interest, depending on the type of legal entity).

(e) Quantitative and Qualitative Analysis.   Valuation requires both quantitative and qualitative analysis. Even though a valuation model has quantitative elements, it uses inputs that involve qualitative analysis and judgment. The qualitative analysis provides an important part of the overall conclusion. Qualitative factors often relate to the assessment of risks associated with operating and investing in the business. Several valuation texts describe common types of quantitative and qualitative analyses used in business valuation.[1]

13.2   UNDERSTANDING THE CONCEPT OF VALUE

(a) Standards of Value.   There are different types of value, referred to as *standards of value*. The following lists the most common standards:

- Fair market value
- Investment value
- Intrinsic value
- Fair value—for shareholder rights disputes
- Fair value—for financial reporting under generally accepted accounting principles

The fair market value, investment value, and intrinsic value of an asset are estimates of how investors (either collectively or individually) would value an asset. Valuation is forward-looking and focuses on expected future economic returns and the cost of capital as of a specific date. In this context, valuation theory has its roots in finance rather than the field of accounting.

The term *fair value* has several uses with different meanings. In shareholder rights disputes, fair value is a legal term. State statutes and case law describe the term and, in some cases, prescribe how one should calculate fair value.

Fair value for financial reporting under generally accepted accounting principles (GAAP) is an accounting term. GAAP literature such as that of the Financial Accounting Standards Board provides the relevant guidance. Certain assets (and liabilities) appearing on financial statements and in their related disclosures will be stated at their fair values rather than their historic costs. The fair value of an asset is sometimes the same as its fair market value, but GAAP prescribes a number of exceptions.

Section 13.2(b) explains the definition of each of these terms. Because case or statutory law often specifies the appropriate standard, the expert should obtain the standard of value from the attorney or client.

Jurisdictions often have a definition for a valuation term that differs from the general meaning. For example, some family law courts require a determination of the fair market value of a spouse's business, but they define the term differently from the meaning used in the business community.[2] In these instances, the definition can resemble that of investment value (i.e., the value of the business to the working spouse when no sale is contemplated).

(b) Definitions.   This section defines terms used in this practice area. Appendix A comprises the *International Glossary of Business Valuation Terms*, the source of some of these definitions.

- **Fair market value**

  The price, expressed in terms of cash equivalents, at which property would change hands between a hypothetical willing and able buyer and a hypothetical willing and able seller, acting at arms length in an open and unrestricted market, when neither is under compulsion to buy or sell and when both have reasonable knowledge of the relevant facts.[3]

  Some government agencies have adopted a similar definition in their regulations. For example, the Internal Revenue Service (IRS) has adopted a similar definition in its tax regulations. The IRS requires the use of fair market value when the value of an asset is assessed for federal tax purposes. The definition identifies several aspects that the analyst should consider when assessing fair market value. Key features include a hypothetical willing buyer and seller (i.e., market participants) rather than a specific buyer and seller, a hypothetical sale on the valuation date with cash (or equivalent) terms, and parties having knowledge of all the relevant facts.

In general, an analyst estimates the fair market value of an asset using direct or indirect market observations. A valuation uses direct market observations when the analyst finds identical or similar assets. Analysts will often use indirect market observations as benchmarks when they cannot identify direct comparables.

- **Investment value**

The value to a particular investor based on individual investment requirements and expectations.[4]

A key distinction between investment value and fair market value is the consideration of a *specific* buyer or seller rather than a hypothetical buyer or seller. The specific buyer or seller may not be representative of the market. Corporate acquisitions often have strategic buyers (as opposed to financial buyers) and frequently sell at a premium price. In general, investment value exceeds fair market value because a strategic buyer will often pay a premium due to the unique synergies or cost reductions it obtains from the acquired business.

- **Intrinsic value**

The value that an investor considers, on the basis of an evaluation or available facts, to be the "true" or "real" value that will become the market value when other investors reach the same conclusion. When the term applies to options, it is the difference between the exercise price or strike price of an option and the market value of the underlying security.[5]

A key aspect of this term is that sometimes observable market prices are mispriced and, accordingly, do not represent the true value of an investment. For example, investment analysts frequently use the concept of intrinsic value when they make buy or sell recommendations of marketable securities. When analysts make buy recommendations, they often believe the intrinsic value of the stock exceeds its current market price. Experts usually do not use this standard of value in litigation matters.

- **Fair value for shareholder rights disputes**

The value of the shares immediately before the effectuation of the corporate action to which the dissenter objects, excluding any appreciation or depreciation in anticipation of the corporate action unless exclusion would be inequitable.[6]

This type of litigation usually relates to a claim by a minority dissenting shareholder or oppressed shareholder against a corporation or majority shareholder.[7] Such litigation often requires a valuation of the minority stockholder's shares. Most states have laws that refer to or define the term *fair value* in these actions, adopting the above definition of fair value taken from the Revised Model Business Corporation Act. Some states, however, have not defined *fair value*, even though their statutes use the term. The expert should consult with the attorney or client on the relevant legal definition and interpretations of fair value.

- **Fair value for financial reporting under GAAP**

The amount at which an asset (or liability) could be bought (or incurred) or sold (or settled) in a current transaction between willing parties, that is, other than a forced or liquidation sale.[8]

This relates to certain assets (and liabilities) reflected in financial statements and related disclosures prepared in accordance with GAAP. The analyst performs the fair value measurement of the assets as required by GAAP literature. Current GAAP requirements in the United States rely heavily on market inputs when assessing fair value. However, GAAP literature contains a number of exceptions to fair market value. Accordingly, fair value for financial reporting need not equal the asset's fair market value. Litigation related to financial statements and related issues can use the definition of fair value described in GAAP.

Sometimes an asset will have the same value under two different standards of value. For example, the intrinsic value and fair market value of an asset can be identical.

(c) Premise of Value.   In addition to the standard of value, the analyst identifies the *premise of value*, defined as "an assumption regarding the most likely set of transactional circumstances that may be applicable to the subject valuation; e.g., going concern, liquidation."[9]

The valuation will assume the premise to be either a *going concern* or *liquidation* status for the business and will consider the liquidation as *orderly* or *forced*.[10] The value of the business or business interest can differ depending on the premise of value. For example, the value of a highly profitable business as a going concern exceeds the company's liquidation value. The expert should consult with the attorney or client to identify the proper premise of value.

13.3   VALUATION DATE

(a) Defining the Valuation Date.   Because values of assets vary over time, one must identify the appropriate valuation date according to the law or facts of a case. For example, in a dissenting shareholder action, state law often requires the valuation date to be immediately before the corporate action. A litigation that involves destruction of property will probably use the day before the destruction as the valuation date. Marital dissolutions commonly value the assets as of the petition's filing date. The expert should consult with the attorney or client to identify the appropriate valuation date.

(b) Subsequent Events.   Most business valuations for litigation have retrospective timing. The valuation date precedes the time when the expert develops the opinion, often by months or years.

Values of businesses and business interests vary over time just as they do for shares in public companies, real estate, and commodities. The observation of the time element plays an important role in valuation. Section 13.1(c) discusses the use of information after the valuation date in litigation situations, known as *ex post* analysis.

Some courts have found that a sale of an asset (in an arm's length transaction) after the valuation date indicates its value on the valuation date when no significant changes have occurred. The analyst should investigate any subsequent sales transaction to ascertain the motivations for the sale and its relevance.

13.4 VALUATION MODELS

The two broad types of going-concern valuation models are *relative value models* and *absolute value models*. No one model is superior to the other for every situation. In many cases, analysts use both models and compare the results. A third technique, the *option pricing model*, values options and assets that still require substantial development to achieve their economic potential.

(a) Relative Value Models.   These models calculate the value of an asset relative to the value of similar assets. Some of these models, for example, apply an average price-to-earnings multiple from a group of comparable companies to the earnings of the subject business to arrive at a value. Relative value models require comparable benchmarks that have correct market prices on average[11] (i.e., the benchmarks—individually and collectively—are not mispriced on average).

Section 13.7 discusses the common applications of relative value models in business valuation. Section 13.7(b) presents the general criteria for selecting benchmarks in valuing businesses and business interests. In theory, relative value models that identify and use a representative sample of valid benchmarks result in good measures of the fair market value of an asset. However, one often has difficulty in finding a valid and representative sample of similar assets when valuing private businesses.

(b) Absolute Value Models.   These models establish a value by examining an asset's intrinsic nature. They measure the value of an asset based on its expected future returns without making comparisons with similar assets. Analysts frequently use absolute value models in addition to relative value models in business valuation and compare the results. Absolute value models include present value models and dividend discount models.

Present value models, such as discounted cash flow (DCF) models, calculate the value of an asset based on a series of expected future benefits derived from the asset discounted to the present. DCF models can value either the entire firm or the company's equity. These models often forecast the cash flows the company can pay at the firm level to its debtholders and shareholders or to the equity owners after paying the debtholders. Dividend discount models, such as the Gordon growth model,[*] focus on dividends paid at the shareholder level to value the firm's shares. Analysts also adapt dividend discount models to value the firm. Sections 13.6(e) and 13.6(f) discuss common applications of absolute value models in business valuation.

---

[*]*Editors' Note*: Although financial experts often refer to this model as the *Gordon growth model*—and Myron Gordon did write about it in the 1950s—John Burr Williams described this model in the 1930s.

(c) Option Pricing Models.   These models are a complex form of present value models. Option pricing models either explicitly or implicitly develop multiple scenarios of possible future prices of the asset that underly the option and calculate the resulting worth of the option at each time period. One discounts the resulting potential option values and probabilities to a present value.

Analysts use these models when valuing certain types of *financial assets*, such as put options, call options, and employee stock options. Analysts also use option pricing models when valuing a company's *real assets* such as reserves of natural resources (e.g., oil and gas) and technology assets (e.g., patents) with high future development costs. This technique applies to real assets that have yet to reach full potential and still require significant development costs.

Analysts generally cannot use relative value models to value these types of assets because comparable assets usually do not exist or, if similar assets exist, sufficient data to develop pricing multiples is not available.

When analysts use absolute value models to value real assets, as discussed in Section 13.4(b), some believe the asset's true value is underestimated. These individuals claim that the business options available to management[12] create added value. For example, a firm that owns a real asset such as an undeveloped oil reserve or a pharmaceutical patent in early clinical testing has several business options: it could develop the asset to its full economic potential, sell or license the rights to the asset at any time prior to its full development (e.g., patent licensing), or do nothing now and simply hold the asset in its current condition (e.g., hold and do not develop the oil reserves until oil prices rise). Proponents of option pricing models to value real assets claim that the business options available to a firm create added value that DCF models do not capture.

Common option pricing models include Black-Scholes-Merton models and lattice models (e.g., binomial and trinomial models). Academic researchers have developed other option pricing models. For financial reporting, the Statement of Financial Accounting Standard 123(R) of the Financial Accounting Standards Board (FASB) specifically identifies Black-Scholes-Merton and lattice models as acceptable when valuing and expensing employee stock options under GAAP.[13] The Black-Scholes-Merton (BSM) model is a closed-end derivative (calculus) model requiring only six inputs to calculate the value of an option: current value of the underlying asset, variance (or volatility) of the asset's price, exercise price of the option, life of the option until expiration, risk-free interest rate, and expected dividends on the asset. However, the BSM model makes some simplifying assumptions. Lattice models do not make the simplifying assumptions in the BSM model but require the quantification of numerous factors. For example, lattice models require the forecasting of possible pricing outcomes of the underlying asset at various times under multiple scenarios. A full discussion of option pricing models lies beyond the scope of this chapter; we refer the reader to Damodaran (2002).

13.5   OVERVIEW OF VALUATION APPROACHES

Appraisal literature identifies three approaches to valuation: the income approach, market approach, and asset-based approach. Exhibit 13-1 shows the relation between the models described in Section 13.4 and the three valuation approaches.

Valuation Models	Usage of Model in Traditional Valuation Approaches
Relative value models	Market approach Asset-based approach
Absolute value models	Income approach Asset-based approach
Option pricing models	Income approach

Exhibit 13-1. Relation between Valuation Models and Approaches

Each approach consists of several valuation methods. Exhibit 13-2 presents common valuation methods for each approach. In general, an analyst should consider all three approaches in a valuation but will use only the ones that apply to the specific asset.

13.6 INCOME APPROACH

The income approach is "a general way of determining a value indication of a business, business ownership interest, security, or intangible asset using one or more methods that convert anticipated economic benefits into a present single amount."[14] This approach includes the DCF method, the capitalization of earnings method, and the adjusted present value (APV) method.

Appraisal literature uses the term *income approach*. However, the literature does not use *income* in the same manner as accountants do. The valuation literature broadly uses *income* to mean some form of economic benefits derived from owning an asset. Notwithstanding differences in definitions of income, this approach uses several types of economic benefit streams such as the firm's net income as defined in accounting literature, cash flow, or income on a debt-free basis.

Traditional Valuation Approaches	Common Business Valuation Methods
Income approach	Discounted cash flow method Capitalization of earnings method
Market approach	Guideline public company method Merger and acquisition method Transactions of the subject company's stock
Asset-based approach	Adjusted book value method Excess earnings method (also known as capitalized excess earnings method)[a]

[a]Some valuation texts classify the capitalized excess earnings method as a hybrid of the asset-based approach and income approach.

Exhibit 13-2. Valuation Methods

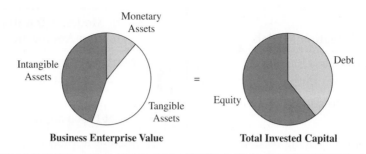

Exhibit 13-3.   Components of a Firm's Business Enterprise Value and Invested Capital

However, analysts frequently use cash flow as the measure of economic benefits from owning a business because published cost of capital data usually develop rates of returns based on cash flows. Cost of capital data on net income is not commonly available.

In theory, the resulting value of an asset should be identical whether one is using the firm's cash flow or income if the analyst properly matches the discount rate to the economic benefit stream. However, timing differences in cash-flow items would cause the values to differ when using a DCF or APV model.

(a) Defining the Subject of the Business Valuation.   Valuations assess the value of either the entire firm or the company's equity. Exhibit 13-3 illustrates these two aspects. The left pie chart represents the value of a firm (also known as the *business enterprise value*). The value of a firm consists of the combined values of its monetary assets, tangible assets, and intangible assets. This value represents all the claims against the company's cash or earnings by debtholders and shareholders (right pie chart). One refers to the combination of a firm's debt capital[15] and equity capital as the firm's total *invested capital*; it represents the capital that debtholders and shareholders have invested in a company. The value of a firm's equity consists of the combined values of the monetary assets, tangible assets, and intangible assets (left pie chart) less the value of the debt (right pie chart).

Defining the subject of the valuation is an important step even though it appears simple. The subject of a valuation could be either the company's equity or the entire firm, depending on the facts of the specific litigation case. The expert usually defines the subject after obtaining information on the case and consulting with the attorney or client. For example, if the plaintiff's business was destroyed but the company must continue to repay its long-term debt, then the subject of the valuation would usually be the firm (the left pie chart in Exhibit 13-3); the analysis would not deduct debt. In this case, the plaintiff would receive the business enterprise value from the defendant and it would then pay off the debt, leaving the plaintiff with the value of its equity.

(b) Valuing a Company's Equity.   Analysts choose from two general methods when they want to value a company's equity using the income approach: the invested-capital method and the direct-equity method. The invested-capital method is a two-step process to value the firm's equity. It begins with the company's cash flows available to pay both the debtholders and equityholders to establish the business enterprise value. The analyst then subtracts the value of the debt. The direct-equity method is a one-step process to value the firm's equity. It begins with the cash flows after payments to the company's debtholders. This method does not assess the business enterprise value.

Exhibit 13-4 summarizes these two methods. A key consideration in choosing which method to use is the capital structure (i.e., proportions of debt and equity) of the firm compared with that of its industry. When the capital structure of the firm differs significantly from that of its industry and a controlling interest is being valued—using fair market value—the invested capital method will more accurately measure the value of the firm's equity.

The capital structure is an important value consideration because the cost of equity capital usually exceeds the cost of debt. The proportion of debt and equity capital affects the company's total cost of capital, which in turn affects its value. As Section 13.2(b) discussed, fair market value considers hypothetical buyers and sellers who represent the market. The hypothetical buyer of a business can have a different capital structure than that of the current business owner(s). For example, a specific business owner can be risk adverse and use no debt to capitalize the firm. Market evidence will likely show that other firms in the industry use a combination of debt (lower cost of capital) and equity (higher cost of capital) to capitalize the business. The firm that uses only equity capital has a higher cost of capital and, therefore, a lower value than a company that uses a combination of debt and equity. The invested capital method will reflect the most likely capital structure that a hypothetical buyer would apply to the firm to value the equity, whereas the direct equity method considers only the firm's current capital structure. The direct equity method often underestimates the fair market value of the firm's equity if the current owner uses little or no debt to capitalize the company.

Invested Capital	Direct Equity
1. Estimate net cash flow to the firm available to all holders of company's invested capital (debt and equity). (*See* Exhibit 13-7.)	1. Estimate net cash flow to equity holders. (*See* Exhibit 13-6.)
2. Apply to the discount rate or capitalization rate on a weighted average cost of capital basis. (*See* formulas in Sections 13.6(e) and (f) for the value of the firm.)	2. Apply to the discount rate or capitalization rate on a cost of equity basis. (*See* formulas in Sections 13.6(e) and (f) for the value of equity.)
3. Results in value of the firm. (*See* Section 13.6(c).)	3. Results in value of company's equity.
4. Subtract value of debt to arrive at the value of the company's equity.	

Exhibit 13-4.   Comparison of Invested-Capital and Direct-Equity Methods

Analysts can apply these methods to both the DCF method (Section 13.6(e)) and the capitalization of earnings method (Section 13.6(f)).

(c) Valuing the Firm. As discussed in Section 13.6(a), the value of the company represents the combined values of its monetary assets, tangible assets, and intangible assets. This amount represents the value of the firm's total invested capital—its equity capital and debt capital. The first column of Exhibit 13-4 summarizes the general method to value the firm when using the income approach (stopping at the third step).

(d) The Cost of Capital. The cost of capital is an important component in the income approach to convert cash flows (or other economic benefit stream) into a value. In finance terms, the cost of capital is the expected rate of return the market requires to attract funds to a specific investment at a specific time. The cost of debt is the company's cost of borrowing new funds as of the valuation date. The cost of equity is the firm's cost to attract equity capital as of the valuation date. A firm's total cost of capital is a blend of its cost of debt and cost of equity, and one frequently measures it as the firm's weighted average cost of capital. Chapter 7 examines cost of capital.

A business with higher risks will have to pay higher costs to attract capital and vice versa. For example, a bank requires a higher interest rate for a high-risk loan. Investors in a high-risk security require higher returns in the form of a lower share price when buying the shares. The cost of capital (or rate of return) becomes the discount rate used in a valuation model using the income approach. The appropriate discount rate for the valuation model represents the market rate-of-return requirements for investments with risk characteristics similar to that of the subject asset. Practitioners also refer to this as the *risk-adjusted discount rate.*

A company's effective cost of capital combines its cost of equity and its after-tax cost of debt.[16] If the valuation uses the direct-equity method, it should use the company's cost of equity as the discount rate, as Exhibit 13-4 shows. If the valuation uses the invested-capital method, it should use the company's weighted average cost of capital as the discount rate.

Analysts cannot make direct observations of a private company's cost of equity because an active market of its equity does not exist. They must estimate its cost of capital with indirect observations. Practitioners often use the capital asset pricing model or the build-up method to estimate a company's cost of equity. A company's cost of equity relates to the conditions of capital markets at the valuation date and the risks associated with an equity investment in the firm. The formulas in Exhibit 13-5 represent common models used to estimate a company's cost of equity.

(i) Capital Asset Pricing Model (CAPM). The first model in Exhibit 13-5 represents the classic CAPM discussed in finance literature and Chapter 7. Financial analysts use the classic model to calculate the cost of equity (required returns) and equity pricing of public companies and larger private companies. The CAPM assumes that investors can diversify their portfolios and that they can diversify away firm-specific risks. Therefore, the classic CAPM does not include any risk premium for nondiversifiable, firm-specific risks. Thus, the CAPM considers

---

Capital Asset Pricing Model (CAPM)

$$E(R_e) = R_f + \beta(RP_m)$$

Modified CAPM

$$E(R_e) = R_f + \beta(RP_m) + RP_s + RP_u$$

Build-up Method

$$E(R_e) = R_f + RP_m + RP_s + RP_u$$

where

e = equity asset being valued
$E(R_e)$ = expected or market-required rate of return on asset e
R_f = risk-free rate
β = beta of asset e
RP_m = equity risk premium required by the market
RP_s = risk premium for small size
RP_u = risk premium for the unsystematic risk associated with the company

---

Exhibit 13-5.   Estimating a Company's Cost of Equity

only systematic (market) risk. Ibbotson Associates, a subsidiary of Morningstar, and other sources provide data for the historic equity risk premiums and size premiums for public companies.

(ii) Modified Capital Asset Pricing Model (MCAPM).   Business valuation practitioners use the MCAPM to estimate the cost of equity of many private companies. Buyers of most private companies do not have diversified portfolios because they invest a substantial portion of their net worth in the private company. Without a larger portfolio, the investor cannot diversify away the firm-specific risks of a particular investment. Accordingly, the MCAPM includes a risk premium for nondiversifiable risks specific to the firm. The MCAPM considers systematic (market) and unsystematic (firm-specific) risks, which includes risks due to smaller size.

(iii) Build-Up Method.   Business valuation practitioners also use the build-up method to estimate the cost of equity of private companies. One challenge in using the CAPM or MCAPM for a private company lies in identifying the stock's beta because the company has no actively traded shares. An analyst cannot directly measure the beta of a private company's shares as one can for shares of public companies. Many practitioners estimate the beta for a private company's shares by relying on the betas of publicly traded companies in the same industry or a subset of the industry group as a proxy.

Accordingly, the beta in CAPM and MCPAM is effectively an adjustment for industry risk when one is valuing a private company's equity. However, analysts make adjustments for industry risk differently in the build-up method. The build-up method avoids beta altogether. The build-up method captures industry risk as part of the unsystematic risk premium. Therefore, the unsystematic risk premium

(RP_u) will not be identical in MCAPM and the build-up method when applied to the same company because each model treats industry risk differently. However, the MCAPM and the build-up method should yield the same cost of equity estimate for a private company in theory.

(iv) Weighted Average Cost of Capital (WACC).   Practitioners calculate a firm's total cost of capital by using the WACC calculation, which blends the company's cost of equity and its after-tax cost of debt in some proportion. Chapter 7 discusses the WACC method. As Exhibit 13-4 shows, practitioners use the company's WACC in the income approach when determining the value of a firm.

(v) Capitalization Rates.   The choice between using a discount rate or a capitalization rate depends on the valuation method. The discounted cash flow method discussed in Section 13.6(e) requires the use of a discount rate. This method forecasts a *series* of returns (e.g., cash flows) and discounts each of them to the present by using a discount rate. The capitalization of earnings method discussed in Section 13.6(f) uses the return for a *single* year—rather than multiple years—and divides it by a capitalization rate. This calculation capitalizes the annual return into perpetuity to arrive at a present value.

As discussed earlier in Section 13.6(d), a discount rate represents a rate of return (e.g., WACC, cost of equity) required for an investment with its risk characteristics at a particular time. The capitalization rate is a number derived from a discount rate. One calculates the capitalization rate using the following formula:

$$\text{Capitalization Rate} = \text{Discount Rate} - \text{Long-Term, Sustainable Growth Rate} \quad (1)$$

(e) Discounted Cash Flow Method.   A common valuation method under the income approach is the DCF method. This method assumes that the value of an asset today equals its expected future cash flows discounted to the present,[17] represented as follows:

$$\text{Value of Equity} = \sum_{t=1}^{n} \frac{CFE_t}{(1 + R_e)^t} \quad (2)$$

$$\text{Value of Firm} = \sum_{t=1}^{n} \frac{CFF_t}{(1 + WACC)^t} \quad (3)$$

where

n = life of the asset
CFE = net cash flow to equity (expected)
CFF = net cash flow to the firm (expected)
R_e = cost of equity
$WACC$ = weighted average cost of capital

One uses the DCF method instead of the capitalization of earnings method (discussed in Section 13.6(f)) when the firm's expected earnings growth rate has not stabilized. For example, a firm with high earnings growth rates that will later stabilize to a lower sustainable rate will use the DCF method in applying the income approach.

One forecasts the firm's earnings for a discrete number of years—we will assume five years—and then calculates the company's terminal value at the end of the forecast period. Analysts select the number of years for forecasts based on when they expect the company's earnings growth rate to stabilize. They commonly use a five-year forecast. In these cases, analysts implicitly expect the firm to reach a stable earnings growth rate in the sixth year. However, forecasts of development stage or other high-growth companies can require forecasts that are longer than five years. After the analyst forecasts the firm's earnings, the model discounts each future amount to the present. In this instance, one can express the calculations as follows:[18]

$$\text{Value of Equity} = \frac{CFE_1}{(1 + R_e)^1} + ... \frac{CFE_5}{(1 + R_e)^5} + \frac{\dfrac{CFE_5 \times (1 + g)}{(R_e - g)}}{(1 + R_e)^5} \quad (4)$$

$$\text{Value of Firm} = \frac{CFF_1}{(1 + WACC)^1} + ... \frac{CFF_5}{(1 + WACC)^5} + \frac{\dfrac{CFF_5 \times (1 + g)}{(WACC - g)}}{(1 + WACC)^5} \quad (5)$$

where

$$g = \text{sustainable growth rate of future cash flows}$$

The mathematical representations above use the cash flow either to the firm or to the equity owners after making payments to the debtholders. Section 13.6(g) describes the components of these cash flows.

(f) Capitalization of Earnings Method. This method derives from a type of dividend discount model used to value shares of public companies commonly known as the Gordon growth model. Analysts use this method instead of the DCF method when the company has reached a stabilized earnings growth rate. A stable growth rate does not mean consistent earnings growth every year. The stable rate of growth in this model reflects the average growth rate sustainable over the long term. This method has another requirement: the growth rate (g) must be less than the cost of equity (R_e) or weighted average cost of capital ($WACC$).

Assuming a stable growth rate over the entire investment horizon, this model represents a simplified mathematical version of the DCF model with the following expressions:

$$\text{Value of Equity} = \frac{CFE_1}{(R_e - g)} \quad (6)$$

$$\text{Value of Firm} = \frac{CFF_1}{(WACC - g)} \quad (7)$$

The cash flows in the above expressions come from the year following the valuation date because the value today depends on expected future returns.

(g) Net Cash Flows. As Exhibit 13-4 shows, the difference between the direct equity and invested-capital methods begins with the cash flows. Exhibits 13-6 and 13-7 define net cash flow to equity (CFE) and net cash flow to the firm (CFF).

	After-tax net income
+	Depreciation and amortization and other non-cash expenses
−	Capital expenditures
−	Increases (or + decreases) in working capital requirements
+	Increases (or − decreases) in long-term debt
=	Net cash flow to equity holders (CFE)

Exhibit 13-6.   Net Cash Flow to Equity

The CFE remains after the firm has made debt service payments of principal and interest to the providers of long-term debt to the company.

The net cash flow to the firm represents the amount available to all capital providers—both equity and debt. It is before debt service payments. Practitioners also refer to this measure as the net cash flow to invested capital.

Exhibit 13-8 compares the cash flow calculations using the two methods. The example demonstrates several points. First, cash flow to equity ($650,000) differs from the company's net income ($1,000,000). In this case, the amounts differ significantly for several reasons. Expected capital expenditures exceed depreciation and amortization expense. In addition, the firm is reinvesting part of its profits back into the business as working capital as the business grows. An analyst incorrectly using net income instead of CFE in a valuation calculation would overstate the valuation conclusion. Second, cash flow at the firm level will exceed cash flow to equityholders, assuming the company has debt. Accordingly, the value of the firm (i.e., business enterprise value) will exceed the value of the company's equity.

The preceding calculations begin with net income, which is the firm's income after income tax expense. A private firm's tax status can present challenges in calculating the cash flow for valuation purposes. Certain types of private firms in the United States do not pay income taxes directly to the government.[19] These entities include S-corporations, partnerships, and limited liability companies electing partnership tax status. For example, a profitable corporation electing S-corporation tax status does not pay any income taxes, and its income statement does not reflect an income tax expense. (Its shareholders pay taxes on the corporation's profit.) An otherwise identical firm with a C-corporation tax status pays

	After-tax net income
+	Depreciation and amortization and other non-cash expenses
−	Capital expenditures
−	Increases (or + decreases) in working capital requirements
+	Interest expense × (1 minus tax rate)
=	Net cash flow to the firm (CFF)

Exhibit 13-7.   Net Cash Flow to the Firm

Assumptions

Net income	$ 1,000,000
Depreciation and amortization expense	400,000
Capital expenditures	600,000
Increase in working capital requirements	250,000
Net increase in long-term debt	100,000
Interest expense	500,000
Tax rate	40%

Cash Flow to Equity (CFE)

	Net income	$ 1,000,000
+	Depreciation and amortization and other non-cash expenses	400,000
−	Capital expenditures	(600,000)
−	Increases in working capital requirements	(250,000)
+	Increases in long-term debt	100,000
=	Net cash flow to equity holders (CFE)	$ 650,000

Cash Flow to the Firm

	Net income	$ 1,000,000
+	Depreciation and amortization and other non-cash expenses	400,000
−	Capital expenditures	(600,000)
−	Increases (or + decreases) in working capital requirements	(250,000)
+	Interest expense $\times$ (1 minus tax rate) [500,000 $\times$ (1−40%)]	300,000
=	Net cash flow to the firm (CFF)	$ 850,000

Exhibit 13-8.   Comparison of Calculations under Cash Flow to Equity versus Cash Flow to the Firm

income taxes directly to the government, and its income statement reflects the income tax expense. Therefore, the net income amounts appearing on the financial statements of these two firms differ because of the tax status even though they have identical operations. The IRS and the U.S. Tax Court have taken the position in certain circumstances that for tax matters an equity interest in a pass-through entity is more valuable because it has lower income taxes. However, one should ask whether the owners of a firm can increase its value simply by filing an S-corporation tax election. No conclusive market evidence exists to prove that ownership interests in pass-through entities sell at higher prices than other types of entities. A full discussion of this topic is beyond the scope of this chapter and we refer the reader to Hitchner (2006, pp. 569–631).

(h) Forecasting Growth.   As Section 13.6 discussed, the income approach establishes a value by discounting the expected future benefits (cash flows) to the present. The cash flow forecast must estimate the company's future growth rates either explicitly or implicitly.

Analysts frequently use three methods to estimate a firm's future growth rate:[20]

1. Project continuation of the company's historic growth rate. This approach proves useful for stable businesses; practitioners find it difficult to apply to firms with high historic growth.

2. Rely on growth estimates of revenues or earnings from industry analysts. Practitioners can use this approach if the industry growth represents that of the subject company.

3. Estimate growth based on the company's fundamentals. Practitioners base this approach on the rate at which the business reinvests its profits back into the company and how it invests those funds. One application of this method estimates growth of a company's net income based on the following basic formula:

$$G = \text{Retention Ratio} \times \text{Return on Equity} \qquad (8)$$

$$G = \text{Growth Rate in Net Income}$$

where

> retention ratio = the percentage of net income retained in the business and not distributed to shareholders as dividends
> return on equity = net income divided by the firm's book value of equity

This basic formula contains some assumptions such as the firm does not raise any new equity and its only source of growth is through retained earnings. It also assumes that the return on equity and retention ratios remain constant.

This formula demonstrates that a firm reinvesting more of its profits back into the business—assuming it earns an appropriate return on those reinvestments—can expect higher earnings growth in the future than a firm reinvesting at a lower level. A firm with higher earnings growth will have a higher value because its shareholders expect greater cash flows in the future.

The analysis can either directly estimate the growth of the cash flows (e.g., 5 percent constant growth on last year's cash flow) or indirectly estimate the cash flows. The indirect analysis would first forecast some element of the company's income statement, such as revenues, and then estimate the relevant expenses and other adjustments to arrive at the projected cash flows.

One can base future growth estimates on the company's historic growth, which assumes that the future will resemble the past. Quantitative techniques that one can apply to past growth include averages (arithmetic, geometric, and weighted) and time series analysis. One can apply averages or use a time series analysis for a financial element (e.g., cash flow, earnings per share, or revenues) or for the historic growth rate itself (e.g., the average growth rate over the past 10 years for a mature company).

Time series analysis is a form of regression analysis. Practitioners use it to explain the past or to predict the future, such as forecasting revenues, when the past is representative of the future. The following provides a simple example using time series analysis.

Assume the following historic revenues for the past 10 years for a company:

Year	Revenues ($ millions)
1	100
2	105
3	98
4	104
5	110
6	120
7	110
8	125
9	131
10	127

A time series analysis on the data results in the selected statistics and trendline plot for the historic 10-year period plus 5 years into the future, shown in Exhibit 13-9. The regression analysis produces the following equation, expressed in millions, for the trendline:

$$\text{Revenues} = 93.40 + 3.56 \times \text{Year}$$

The results of the regression analysis might serve as the basis for the forecasted revenues in a DCF model. For example, the firm's expected revenues for the first year of the forecast (year 11) is $132.6 million ($= 93.40 + 3.56 \times 11$).

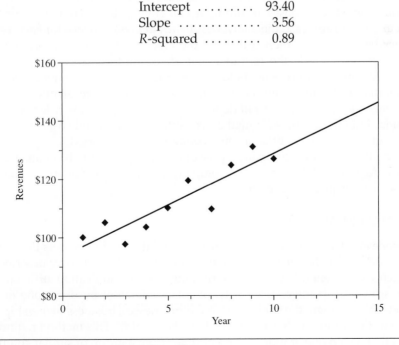

Intercept 93.40
Slope 3.56
R-squared 0.89

Exhibit 13-9.   Statistics and Trendline Plot

(i) Adjusted Present Value Method.   The discounted cash flow (DCF) method to measure the business enterprise value uses the firm's weighted average cost of capital (WACC) as the discount rate (discussed in Section 13.6(e)). Accordingly, the DCF method to calculate the value of the firm assumes that the company will have a constant relative capital structure of debt and equity because the WACC formula assumes a constant capital relation (*see* Section 7.4(c) of Chapter 7).

The adjusted present value (APV) method provides an alternative to the DCF method that does not assume a constant relation between equity and debt. Analysts use an APV model when they expect a significant change in the company's capital structure. A DCF model proves most useful in a business valuation when working with constant debt proportions (e.g., debt will be 40 percent of total capital). The APV method proves most useful when working with specific dollar amounts of debt and allows flexibility for changes over the forecast period. (Appendix B to this chapter discusses APV.)

The basic APV model breaks down the value of a business into two components:

> Value of the company without debt
>
> \+   Present value of the tax benefits from borrowing
>
> \=   Value of the company with debt

The first step values the company as if it had no debt. One can use the DCF or capitalization of earnings method. The analyst estimates the future unlevered net cash flows to the firm (i.e., cash flows assuming the company has no debt) and uses the unlevered cost of equity[21] as the discount rate.

Next, one must estimate the expected tax benefits for a given level of debt and discount them to the present. Firms can deduct interest expense associated with debt for income tax purposes, resulting in a tax savings to the company. For example, in a five-year forecast, the analyst estimates interest expense for each year for a given debt level and then computes the associated annual tax savings. The analysis should include the terminal-year effect for the associated tax savings before discounting all tax benefits to the present. Academics do not agree on the model's discount rate for the tax savings. Finance literature mentions two discount rates: the company's cost of debt and a rate at, or near, the risk-free rate.

A modified form of the APV method considers the risks and costs of bankruptcy for a given level of debt as a third component. In theory, the analysis could maximize the value of a company by assuming 100 percent debt financing using the basic APV model. However, the company's bankruptcy risk and capital costs increase as it assumes more debt.

13.7   MARKET APPROACH

(a) Overview.   The market approach uses the relative value models described in Section 13.4(a). The *International Glossary of Business Valuation Terms* describes this approach as "a general way of determining a value indication of a business, business ownership interest, security, or intangible asset by using one or more methods that compare the subject to similar businesses, business ownership interests, securities, or intangible assets that have been sold." This method requires the analyst to develop one or more price multiples from a group of similar companies and apply the multiple(s) to the subject business to obtain a value.

(b) Methods under the Market Approach. The market approach to valuing a business or business interest has two primary methods:

1. Guideline public company method
2. Merger and acquisition method.

In addition to these two methods, if any relevant sales transactions of the subject company's shares have occurred, the sales price can indicate their value.

An important consideration when applying the two methods lies in identifying similar, or guideline, companies. The American Society of Appraisers describes guideline companies as companies

> that provide a reasonable basis for comparison to the investment characteristics of the company being valued. Ideal guideline companies are in the same industry as the subject company; however, if there is insufficient transaction evidence available in that industry, it may be necessary to select other companies having an underlying similarity to the subject company in terms of relevant investment characteristics such as markets, products, growth, cyclical variability, and other salient factors.[22]

(i) Guideline Public Company Method. The guideline public company method develops price multiples from the shares of guideline companies that actively trade in a free and open market. The sales transactions of the shares represent minority interests of the public companies. Over 10,000 companies in the United States list their securities in publicly traded markets, and one can retrieve company information and their historical market prices from filings with the U.S. Securities and Exchange Commission (SEC) and financial databases. Many private companies exceed or match the size of small public companies, so one can use some public guideline companies in valuations of larger private companies. The analyst develops an appropriate price multiple(s) from the guideline companies and applies it to the subject company to obtain a value indication for the subject company. This method regards the subject interest as a liquid asset because the benchmark is liquid. The analysis should consider an adjustment to the indicated value to reflect any differences in liquidity characteristics between the shares of the public guideline companies and the subject interest.

(ii) Merger and Acquisition Method. This method develops price multiples from sales transactions of significant interests (100 percent or less) in guideline companies, either privately owned or publicly registered. Most of the sales transactions represent controlling interests in the companies. One can obtain data on these types of transactions from proprietary databases[23] and a search of SEC filings. These transactions are less frequent, and the information about them is less systematic than that used in the guideline public company method. Some of the sales transactions reflect strategic acquisitions that involve a premium sales price. In addition, the transactions can include undisclosed factors such as employment contracts and noncompete agreements. Nevertheless, the transactions reflect events in the marketplace even if they do not include all the underlying information. This method values a marketable interest that has less liquidity than that of public company stock transactions on an exchange.

(c) Price Multiples. Price multiples of guideline companies can rely on many financial elements that appear on the income statement (e.g., revenues; earnings before interest, taxes, depreciation, and amortization [EBITDA]; and net income) or the balance sheet (e.g., book value and tangible assets). One can also apply multiples against other factors unique to a certain industry (e.g., price per subscriber).

Prices paid for guideline companies reflect the firms' expected growth. Companies with high expected earnings growth sell at higher prices and multiples, all else being equal. Thus, the anticipated growth of the guideline companies should compare with the growth expectations for the subject company.

One should understand the price multiples obtained from proprietary databases. The multiples sometimes lack consistency across databases because their calculations can vary. In addition, some databases report sales transactions when the seller retains the cash or working capital. These differences often require adjustments in the valuation analysis.

Valuations using some multiples give the value of the firm, whereas the use of other multiples gives the value of the firm's equity. For example, a price-to-EBITDA multiple applied to the subject company's EBITDA gives the value of the firm (i.e., equity and debt capital). A price-to-earnings multiple applied to the company's net income gives the value of the firm's equity.

13.8   ASSET-BASED APPROACH

(a) Overview.   This approach focuses on the individual values of the company's assets and then subtracts its liabilities to value the firm's equity. The asset approach first identifies the company's assets and liabilities and then assesses the value of each item. Analysts use this approach when the firm's assets determine its value rather than its cash flow or income-related value. For example, many real estate holding companies do not generate large amounts of earnings but have substantial value because of their asset holdings. In addition, one can use this approach when a company suffers from poor earnings with no expectation for improvement.

(b) Identification and Valuation of Individual Assets and Liabilities.   This approach first identifies all assets and liabilities of the firm. Most such analyses begin with the company's balance sheet. However, financial statements prepared in accordance with GAAP sometimes do not identify all assets and liabilities of the business. In general, GAAP does not allow a company to record internally developed intangible assets—such as goodwill, assembled workforce, trade name, and customer relationships—onto the balance sheet. Companies usually expense the costs to develop these types of assets rather than capitalize them. However, GAAP requires that companies record intangible assets (such as trade names, leases, mailing lists, and copyrights) on the balance sheet when the company purchases them. A lease with below-market rents represents another asset of the business that does not appear on the balance sheet prepared under GAAP. Unrecorded items on the balance sheet include fixed assets that the company expensed rather than capitalized at acquisition and liabilities such as litigation claims. After identifying the assets and liabilities, the analyst will assess a value to each of them.

One can easily ascertain the value of some types of assets such as cash and marketable securities. Fixed assets such as land, building, and machinery and equipment often require the use of specialty appraisers. Valuing individual identifiable intangible assets can prove difficult. Several texts explain the valuation of individual intangible assets.[24]

Analysts can base the value of the individual assets on the relative value models and absolute value models discussed in Sections 13.4(a) and (b). For example, one can base the values of land and building on relative values from comparable properties. One can value a lease with below-market rents with a present value model, a form of absolute value models. Present value models can value some intangible assets such as patents and trade names.

One can also value individual assets using a cost approach. Analysts use the cost approach when appraising improvements to real property or machinery and equipment. The *International Glossary of Business Valuation Terms* defines the cost approach as "a general way of determining a value indication of an individual asset by quantifying the amount of money required to replace the future service capability of that asset." Practitioners often value inventory using the cost approach. (GAAP requires that financial statements reflect inventories at the lower of cost or market. In most cases, the balance sheet reflects the cost of the inventories, which analysts frequently use as the value.) The cost approach can value some intangible assets, such as the assembled workforce: the costs to hire and train the workforce can provide the basis for its value.

(c) Effect of Control on Value. The asset-based approach assumes that an investor with management control has the ability to reach the underlying values of the individual assets and liquidate the liabilities. Therefore, the value derived from the asset-based approach assumes the ability to control the company and sell the assets. This approach also assumes that a market exists to sell the firm's assets.

13.9 VALUATION ADJUSTMENTS

(a) The Reasons for Adjustments. The value that results from the methods discussed in this chapter often requires further adjustment to reach the final value of the subject asset. This usually occurs because the data or benchmarks used in models often lack an identical similarity to the subject asset.

In analyzing the subject company's historic financial statements, analysts will also need to consider whether to make adjustments to estimate the company's future earnings. Owners of private companies often prepare their financial statements to minimize taxable income. Some owners overstate expenses or understate revenues. In such situations, the analyst makes adjustments to ascertain the economic benefits that a hypothetical investor can expect to receive. If the business had nonrecurring income or expenses in the past, the financial analysis should adjust the projections based on such numbers by removing them.[25]

(b) Valuation Adjustments for Control and Marketability. The analysis will often need to make adjustments when fractional ownership interests become the subject of the valuation. Two common adjustments relate to (1) an ownership interest's ability to exert control on the company and (2) the ability to sell the subject business or business interest and receive the sales proceeds. A noncontrolling, nonmarketable ownership interest has less desirability than a controlling, marketable interest, all else being equal. The value of a more desirable asset exceeds the value of a less desirable asset based on the economic principle of supply and demand.

The first adjustment relates to control. A 100 percent equity interest in a private business wields more control than does a 10 percent interest. An owner of a 10 percent interest in most instances cannot exert control over the business operations or dividend distributions, nor can this owner sell the assets of the company to reach their underlying value. The 10 percent owner of a business lacks the ability to exert control, whereas the 100 percent owner has the ability to exert absolute control.

The second common adjustment relates to marketability. One will find it more difficult to sell a 10 percent equity interest in a private company than a 100 percent interest. A 100 percent owner could sell the entire business through an investment banker or business broker or could take the company public; a 10 percent owner has no such options.

Each valuation method and the underlying data that it uses has implicit assumptions about control and marketability. Analysts often need to make adjustments because the valuation benchmarks differ from those of the subject firm or its ownership interest. For example, the value derived from using the guideline public company method assumes liquid shares in public companies where a sales decision results in the receipt of cash proceeds only three days later. The sale of a private company or fractional interest often requires months or longer before the owner receives the proceeds.

Empirical studies show that buyers and sellers adjust the value for marketability and control factors. Studies demonstrating marketability adjustments fall into two categories: restricted stock studies and initial public offering (IPO) studies. Researchers have conducted fewer control premium studies (applicable to adjustments for lack of control). Analysts use the discounts shown in the studies as valuation benchmarks. The practitioner identifies the control and marketability characteristics of the firm or ownership interest being valued and compares them with the assets in the studies. Any differences result in an adjustment to the benchmark.

When the standard of value is fair market value, the analyst considers valuation adjustments for marketability and control. When litigation matters require a different standard of value, these valuation adjustments are not always appropriate. For example, dissenting and oppressed shareholder actions in many states specify the standard of value as fair value (Section 13.2(b) discusses *fair value*), and statutes or case law frequently define the term to ignore the valuation adjustments for lack of control and lack of marketability of a minority shareholder.

(c) Adjustments for Nonoperating Assets.   Most valuations based on an income approach or market approach use the earnings from the business operations. When a company has a nonoperating asset (e.g., raw land held for investment), the analysis can add the value of the nonoperating asset to the value of the operations, depending on the situation and whether analysis values the entire company or a fractional ownership interest. For example, suppose the expert performs a valuation as a measure of damages for business operations that were destroyed. If the injured party still owns the nonoperating asset and can receive value from it, the damages analysis would not include the value of the nonoperating asset. On the other hand, if the expert needs to value a spouse's company for marital dissolution purposes, the analysis would consider the nonoperating asset.

13.10 BUSINESS VALUATION STANDARDS

Several membership organizations and The Appraisal Foundation, an organization of other appraisal groups, have promoted business valuation standards for many years. The American Society of Appraisers,[26] The Appraisal Foundation,[27] the National Association of Certified Valuation Analysts,[28] the Institute of Business Appraisers,[29] and The Canadian Institute of Chartered Business Valuators[30] have all issued business valuation standards. The American Institute of Certified Public Accountants[31] (AICPA) is developing valuation standards.

The business valuation standards of these organizations consist of developmental standards (criteria necessary to arrive at a valuation conclusion) and reporting standards (disclosures for reporting on the conclusion). Some organizations have special provisions in their standards for valuations that relate to litigation.

13.11 SPECIALTY CERTIFICATIONS IN VALUATION

The following organizations offer a specialty certification in business valuation:

- American Institute of CPAs: Accredited in Business Valuation (ABV)
- American Society of Appraisers: Accredited Senior Appraiser (ASA) and Accredited Member (AM)
- Institute of Business Appraisers: Certified Business Appraiser (CBA)
- National Association of Certified Valuation Analysts: Certified Valuation Analyst (CVA) and Accredited Valuation Analyst (AVA)
- Canadian Institute of Chartered Business Valuators: Chartered Business Valuator (CBV)
- CFA Institute: Chartered Financial Analyst (CFA), a designation that covers an expanded body of knowledge of valuing investments and investment management.

These designations require the successful completion of one or more examinations as well as other criteria.

APPENDIX A: INTERNATIONAL GLOSSARY OF BUSINESS VALUATION TERMS

This glossary was developed by the American Institute of Certified Public Accountants, American Society of Appraisers, Canadian Institute of Chartered Business Valuators, National Association of Certified Valuation Analysts, and The Institute of Business Appraisers. This resource is available on a variety of Web sites including www.aicpa.org/bvfls/resources.

Definitions

Adjusted Book Value Method—a method within the asset approach whereby all assets and liabilities (including off-balance sheet, intangible, and contingent) are adjusted to their fair market values. [*Note:* In Canada, on a going concern basis.]

Adjusted Net Asset Method—*see Adjusted Book Value Method.*

Appraisal—*see Valuation.*

Appraisal Approach—*see Valuation Approach.*

Appraisal Date—*see Valuation Date.*

Appraisal Method—*see Valuation Method.*

Appraisal Procedure—*see Valuation Procedure.*

Arbitrage Pricing Theory—a multivariate model for estimating the cost of equity capital, which incorporates several systematic risk factors.

Asset (Asset-Based) Approach—a general way of determining a value indication of a business, business ownership interest, or security using one or more methods based on the value of the assets net of liabilities.

Beta—a measure of systematic risk of a stock; the tendency of a stock's price to correlate with changes in a specific index.

Blockage Discount—an amount or percentage deducted from the current market price of a publicly traded stock to reflect the decrease in the per share value of a block of stock that is of a size that could not be sold in a reasonable period of time given normal trading volume.

Book value—*see Net Book Value.*

Business—*see Business Enterprise.*

Business Enterprise—a commercial, industrial, service, or investment entity (or a combination thereof) pursuing an economic activity.

Business Risk—the degree of uncertainty of realizing expected future returns of the business resulting from factors other than financial leverage. *See Financial Risk.*

Business Valuation—the act or process of determining the value of a business enterprise or ownership interest therein.

Capital Asset Pricing Model (CAPM)—a model in which the cost of capital for any stock or portfolio of stocks equals a risk-free rate plus a risk premium that is proportionate to the systematic risk of the stock or portfolio.

Capitalization—a conversion of a single period of economic benefits into value.

Capitalization Factor—any multiple or divisor used to convert anticipated economic benefits of a single period into value.

Capitalization of Earnings Method—a method within the income approach whereby economic benefits for a representative single period are converted to value through division by a capitalization rate.

Capitalization Rate—any divisor (usually expressed as a percentage) used to convert anticipated economic benefits of a single period into value.

Capital Structure—the composition of the invested capital of a business enterprise; the mix of debt and equity financing.

Cash Flow—cash that is generated over a period of time by an asset, group of assets, or business enterprise. It may be used in a general sense to encompass various levels of specifically defined cash flows. When the term is used, it should be supplemented by a qualifier (for example, "discretionary " or "operating ") and a specific definition in the given valuation context.

Common Size Statements—financial statements in which each line is expressed as a percentage of the total. On the balance sheet, each line item is shown as a percentage of total assets, and on the income statement, each item is expressed as a percentage of sales.

Control—the power to direct the management and policies of a business enterprise.

Control Premium—an amount or a percentage by which the *pro rata* value of a controlling interest exceeds the *pro rata* value of a non-controlling interest in a business enterprise, to reflect the power of control.

Cost Approach—a general way of determining a value indication of an individual asset by quantifying the amount of money required to replace the future service capability of that asset.

Cost of Capital—the expected rate of return that the market requires in order to attract funds to a particular investment.

Debt-Free—we discourage the use of this term. *See Invested Capital.*

Discount for Lack of Control—an amount or percentage deducted from the *pro rata* share of value of 100% of an equity interest in a business to reflect the absence of some or all of the powers of control.

Discount for Lack of Marketability—an amount or percentage deducted from the value of an ownership interest to reflect the relative absence of marketability.

Discount for Lack of Voting Rights—an amount or percentage deducted from the per share value of a minority interest voting share to reflect the absence of voting rights.

Discount Rate—a rate of return used to convert a future monetary sum into present value.

Discounted Cash Flow Method—a method within the income approach whereby the present value of future expected net cash flows is calculated using a discount rate.

Discounted Future Earnings Method—a method within the income approach whereby the present value of future expected economic benefits is calculated using a discount rate.

Economic Benefits—inflows such as revenues, net income, net cash flows, etc.

Economic Life—the period of time over which property may generate economic benefits.

Effective Date—*see Valuation Date.*

Enterprise—*see Business Enterprise.*

Equity—the owner's interest in property after deduction of all liabilities.

Equity Net Cash Flows—those cash flows available to pay out to equity holders (in the form of dividends) after funding operations of the business enterprise, making necessary capital investments, and increasing or decreasing debt financing.

Equity Risk Premium—a rate of return added to a risk-free rate to reflect the additional risk of equity instruments over risk free instruments (a component of the cost of equity capital or equity discount rate).

Excess Earnings—that amount of anticipated economic benefits that exceeds an appropriate rate of return on the value of a selected asset base (often net tangible assets) used to generate those anticipated economic benefits.

Excess Earnings Method—a specific way of determining a value indication of a business, business ownership interest, or security determined as the sum of (a) the value of the assets derived by capitalizing excess earnings and (b) the value of the selected asset base. Also frequently used to value intangible assets. *See Excess Earnings.*

Fair Market Value—the price, expressed in terms of cash equivalents, at which property would change hands between a hypothetical willing and able buyer and a hypothetical willing and able seller, acting at arms length in an open and unrestricted market, when neither is under compulsion to buy or sell and when both have reasonable knowledge of the relevant facts. [*Note:* In Canada, the term "price" should be replaced with the term "highest price."]

Fairness Opinion—an opinion as to whether or not the consideration in a transaction is fair from a financial point of view.

Financial Risk—the degree of uncertainty of realizing expected future returns of the business resulting from financial leverage. *See Business Risk.*

Forced Liquidation Value—liquidation value, at which the asset or assets are sold as quickly as possible, such as at an auction.

Free Cash Flow—we discourage the use of this term. *See Net Cash Flow.*

Going Concern—an ongoing operating business enterprise.

Going Concern Value—the value of a business enterprise that is expected to continue to operate into the future. The intangible elements of going concern value result from factors such as having a trained work force, an operational plant, and the necessary licenses, systems, and procedures in place.

Goodwill—that intangible asset arising as a result of name, reputation, customer loyalty, location, products, and similar factors not separately identified.

Goodwill Value—the value attributable to goodwill.

Guideline Public Company Method—a method within the market approach whereby market multiples are derived from market prices of stocks of companies that are engaged in the same or similar lines of business, and that are actively traded on a free and open market.

Income (Income-Based) Approach—a general way of determining a value indication of a business, business ownership interest, security, or intangible asset using one or more methods that convert anticipated economic benefits into a present single amount.

Intangible Assets—non-physical assets such as franchises, trademarks, patents, copyrights, goodwill, equities, mineral rights, securities and contracts (as distinguished from physical assets) that grant rights and privileges, and have value for the owner.

Internal Rate of Return—a discount rate at which the present value of the future cash flows of the investment equals the cost of the investment.

Intrinsic Value—the value that an investor considers, on the basis of an evaluation or available facts, to be the "true " or "real " value that will become the market value when other investors reach the same conclusion. When the term applies to options, it is the difference between the exercise price or strike price of an option and the market value of the underlying security.

Invested Capital—the sum of equity and debt in a business enterprise. Debt is typically (a) all interest bearing debt or (b) long-term interest-bearing debt. When the term is used, it should be supplemented by a specific definition in the given valuation context.

Invested Capital Net Cash Flows—those cash flows available to pay out to equity holders (in the form of dividends) and debt investors (in the form of principal and interest) after funding operations of the business enterprise and making necessary capital investments.

Investment Risk—the degree of uncertainty as to the realization of expected returns.

Investment Value—the value to a particular investor based on individual investment requirements and expectations. [*Note:* in Canada, the term used is "Value to the Owner."]

Key Person Discount—an amount or percentage deducted from the value of an ownership interest to reflect the reduction in value resulting from the actual or potential loss of a key person in a business enterprise.

Levered Beta—the beta reflecting a capital structure that includes debt.

Limited Appraisal—the act or process of determining the value of a business, business ownership interest, security, or intangible asset with limitations in analyses, procedures, or scope.

Liquidity—the ability to quickly convert property to cash or pay a liability.

Liquidation Value—the net amount that would be realized if the business is terminated and the assets are sold piecemeal. Liquidation can be either "orderly" or "forced."

Majority Control—the degree of control provided by a majority position.

Majority Interest—an ownership interest greater than 50% of the voting interest in a business enterprise.

Market (Market-Based) Approach—a general way of determining a value indication of a business, business ownership interest, security, or intangible asset by using one or more methods that compare the subject to similar businesses, business ownership interests, securities, or intangible assets that have been sold.

Market Capitalization of Equity—the share price of a publicly traded stock multiplied by the number of shares outstanding.

Market Capitalization of Invested Capital—the market capitalization of equity plus the market value of the debt component of invested capital.

Market Multiple—the market value of a company's stock or invested capital divided by a company measure (such as economic benefits, number of customers).

Marketability—the ability to quickly convert property to cash at minimal cost.

Marketability Discount—*see Discount for Lack of Marketability.*

Merger and Acquisition Method—a method within the market approach whereby pricing multiples are derived from transactions of significant interests in companies engaged in the same or similar lines of business.

Midyear Discounting—a convention used in the Discounted Future Earnings Method that reflects economic benefits being generated at midyear, approximating the effect of economic benefits being generated evenly throughout the year.

Minority Discount—a discount for lack of control applicable to a minority interest.

Minority Interest—an ownership interest less than 50% of the voting interest in a business enterprise.

Multiple—the inverse of the capitalization rate.

Net Book Value—with respect to a business enterprise, the difference between total assets (net of accumulated depreciation, depletion, and amortization) and total liabilities as they appear on the balance sheet (synonymous with Shareholder's Equity). With respect to a specific asset, the capitalized cost less accumulated amortization or depreciation as it appears on the books of account of the business enterprise.

Net Cash Flow—when the term is used, it should be supplemented by a qualifier. *See Equity Net Cash Flows* and *Invested Capital Net Cash Flows.*

Net Present Value—the value, as of a specified date, of future cash inflows less all cash outflows (including the cost of investment) calculated using an appropriate discount rate.

Net Tangible Asset Value—the value of the business enterprise's tangible assets (excluding excess assets and non-operating assets) minus the value of its liabilities.

Non-Operating Assets—assets not necessary to ongoing operations of the business enterprise. [*Note:* in Canada, the term used is "Redundant Assets."]

Normalized Earnings—economic benefits adjusted for nonrecurring, non-economic, or other unusual items to eliminate anomalies and/or facilitate comparisons.

Normalized Financial Statements—financial statements adjusted for non-operating assets and liabilities and/or for nonrecurring, non-economic, or other unusual items to eliminate anomalies and/or facilitate comparisons.

Orderly Liquidation Value—liquidation value at which the asset or assets are sold over a reasonable period of time to maximize proceeds received.

Premise of Value—an assumption regarding the most likely set of transactional circumstances that may be applicable to the subject valuation; e.g., going concern, liquidation.

Present Value—the value, as of a specified date, of future economic benefits and/or proceeds from sale, calculated using an appropriate discount rate.

Portfolio Discount—an amount or percentage deducted from the value of a business enterprise to reflect the fact that it owns dissimilar operations or assets that do not fit well together.

Price/Earnings Multiple—the price of a share of stock divided by its earnings per share.

Rate of Return—an amount of income (loss) and/or change in value realized or anticipated on an investment, expressed as a percentage of that investment.

Redundant Assets—*see Non-Operating Assets.*

Report Date—the date conclusions are transmitted to the client.

Replacement Cost New—the current cost of a similar new property having the nearest equivalent utility to the property being valued.

Reproduction Cost New—the current cost of an identical new property.

Required Rate of Return—the minimum rate of return acceptable by investors before they will commit money to an investment at a given level of risk.

Residual Value—the value as of the end of the discrete projection period in a discounted future earnings model.

Return on Equity—the amount, expressed as a percentage, earned on a company's common equity for a given period.

Return on Investment—*see Return on Invested Capital and Return on Equity.*

Return on Invested Capital—the amount, expressed as a percentage, earned on a company's total capital for a given period.

Risk-Free Rate—the rate of return available in the market on an investment free of default risk.

Risk Premium—a rate of return added to a risk-free rate to reflect risk.

Rule of Thumb—a mathematical formula developed from the relationship between price and certain variables based on experience, observation, hearsay, or a combination of these; usually industry specific.

Special Interest Purchasers—acquirers who believe they can enjoy post-acquisition economies of scale, synergies, or strategic advantages by combining the acquired business interest with their own.

Standard of Value—the identification of the type of value being utilized in a specific engagement; e.g., fair market value, fair value, investment value.

Sustaining Capital Reinvestment—the periodic capital outlay required to maintain operations at existing levels, net of the tax shield available from such outlays.

Systematic Risk—the risk that is common to all risky securities and cannot be eliminated through diversification. The measure of systematic risk in stocks is the beta coefficient.

Tangible Assets—physical assets (such as cash, accounts receivable, inventory, property, plant and equipment, etc.).

Terminal Value—*see Residual Value.*

Transaction Method—*see Merger and Acquisition Method.*

Unlevered Beta—the beta reflecting a capital structure without debt.

Unsystematic Risk—the portion of total risk specific to an individual security that can be avoided through diversification.

Valuation—the act or process of determining the value of a business, business ownership interest, security, or intangible asset.

Valuation Approach—a general way of determining a value indication of a business, business ownership interest, security, or intangible asset using one or more valuation methods.

Valuation Date—the specific point in time as of which the valuator's opinion of value applies (also referred to as "Effective Date " or "Appraisal Date ").

Valuation Method—within approaches, a specific way to determine value.

Valuation Procedure—the act, manner, and technique of performing the steps of an appraisal method.

Valuation Ratio—a fraction in which a value or price serves as the numerator and financial, operating, or physical data serve as the denominator.

Value to the Owner—*[Note:* in Canada, *see Investment Value.]*

Voting Control—*de jure* control of a business enterprise.

Weighted Average Cost of Capital (WACC)—the cost of capital (discount rate) determined by the weighted average, at market value, of the cost of all financing sources in the business enterprise's capital structure.

APPENDIX B: ADJUSTED PRESENT VALUE (APV) METHOD

Bonnie J. Goldsmith
Greg Hallman

This appendix discusses the adjusted present value (APV) approach and describes its benefits. Financial experts will find APV appropriate for valuing future cash flows whether in the damages context, such as lost future profits, or in business valuations. It presents an alternative to the more traditional use of weighted-average cost of capital (WACC) to calculate the present value of a series of cash flows.[32]

The WACC method requires an assumption with respect to the capital structure that may not apply to the cash flows at issue. Specifically, one should not use WACC if the firm's capital structure changes over the valuation period. For example, in a leveraged buyout, the acquired company initially has significant debt scheduled for repayment over time. Using the initial capital structure in the calculation of WACC would lead to an incorrect valuation for the business. Even though many practitioners agree that the analysis should not use the initial capital structure in this situation, the issue becomes one of the appropriate capital structure assumption. One can use APV for calculating damages when the company pays down debt during the damages period. WACC does not allow for this type of varying capital structure. APV offers an advantage over the traditional use of the discounted cash flow (DCF) approach in that it allows for a varying capital structure. It also allows for a varying income tax rate when one is calculating the after-tax cost of debt and valuing the benefits of the tax shield.

BACKGROUND

Stewart Myers helped introduce APV with a leading paper in 1974.[33] Since then, several academic papers have addressed the topic. Corporate finance college and business school textbooks and curriculums include the APV method.[34] Investment banks use it as one of the approaches in the valuation of companies. A 1997 article in the *Harvard Business Review* predicted that "[d]iscounted cash flows will remain the foundations of most formal valuation analyses. But WACC will be displaced as the DCF methodology of choice by adjusted present value or something very much like it."[35] Despite this prediction, most litigation services practitioners do not use APV.

APV METHODOLOGY

APV does not replace DCF but rather offers a refinement in the application of DCF. It separates the investment decisions from the financing decisions when one is calculating the present value of cash flows. It begins with a base case net present value (NPV) analysis that assumes the firm or project has no debt capital (all equity); this represents the investment decisions. The model then adds the effects of financing with debt (i.e., the financing decisions). In its simplified version, the APV model has three steps,[36] which we show in the following equation and examine in the subsequent discussion.

APV = Base-Case Unlevered NPV + PV of Tax Shields − Cost of Financial Distress

Base Case (All-Equity). The base-case NPV analysis assumes the firm is an all-equity firm. Such a calculation discounts the future free cash flows using an unlevered cost of equity capital[37] and then subtracts the initial investment from the present value of the expected future cash flows to calculate NPV.

Valuation of Tax Shields. The analysis next calculates the present value of the tax shields that come with debt financing. One calculates the tax shield by calculating the expected future interest payments and multiplying them by the expected marginal tax rate(s); this amount represents the tax savings that accrue to the firm or project as a result of the debt financing. One can use a varying tax rate over time here if future tax rates will change. The analysis then discounts these expected tax shields using a discount rate that reflects the risk of the tax shields.

Early discussions of the APV method advocated using the cost of debt as the discount rate in calculating the value of the tax shields, based on the logic that the cost of debt by definition reflects the risk of debt (i.e., the risk of making the interest payments) and therefore the risk of the tax shields. More recent literature on the APV has advocated using the unlevered cost of equity as the discount rate in valuing the tax shields under certain scenarios. APV proponents suggest that analysts use the unlevered cost of equity when the amount of debt that a firm has depends on the value of the firm's assets or, equivalently, the firm's success (e.g., a firm that intends to use a particular amount of debt if it prospers but could not secure, or perhaps would not require, that amount of debt if it struggles). When a firm's level or amount of debt depends on its overall value, the cost of unlevered equity captures the risk. *See* Fernandez (2004, 2005) and Ruback (2002) for how to value the tax shields.

Expected Costs of Financial Distress. In the third step of the APV method, the analyst calculates and incorporates the expected costs of financial distress that come from the use of debt financing. Debt financing carries risk, and this third term reflecting the additional risk of bankruptcy that accompanies debt financing incorporates the additional risk of debt that can decrease the firm's overall value. In general, one calculates the expected costs of financial distress by multiplying the probability that the firm ends up in financial distress by the cost of ending up in financial distress (i.e., expected costs of financial distress = probability of bankruptcy [estimated from debt rating] × the severity of bankruptcy [estimated from historical Moody's or S&P data].[38] However, under certain conditions, the failure to explicitly consider financial distress doesn't affect the overall valuation.[39] Use of WACC may not by itself consider the full impact of expected costs of financial distress.

Value using APV. Lastly, one calculates the total value by adding the present value of the tax shields to the base-case all-equity NPV and subtracting the expected costs of financial distress.

BENEFITS OF USING APV OVER WACC

The primary reason for using APV instead of WACC is that APV allows for a varying capital structure during the period under analysis. Analysts cannot calculate an appropriate WACC with a capital structure that changes over time; however, APV valuation allows one to reflect the impact of changing debt levels over time. APV also accommodates a varying tax rate. An assumption regarding the tax rate can vary by period, although it will not likely vary as often as the capital structure. APV also isolates the effects of the financing decisions. The value of the tax shields and the expected costs of financial distress represent separate components of the total value of the project or firm.

WHY LITIGATION PRACTITIONERS DO NOT USE APV MORE FREQUENTLY

Why don't more expert witnesses use APV when valuing businesses or lost future profits? The answer is simple. Today's practitioners used DCF with WACC when they began working. Even though Myers introduced APV in the mid-1970s, corporate finance textbooks did not include it until much later. Today's practitioners have continued to use WACC in spite of its known weaknesses. APV has largely remained within the academic community. Moreover, practitioners find WACC easier to explain, an important consideration in litigation work when selecting methods. Finally, every expert faces challenge on each assumption made, and APV requires differing assumptions from those of traditional DCF or standard WACC.

An example of the use of APV—with enough detail to be useful—is beyond the scope of this appendix. However, one can find several useful examples of the APV method in both practitioner books and academic texts, including the following:

- *Investment Valuation: Tools and Techniques for Determining the Value of Any Asset*[40] contains a short discussion and example of the APV. The discussion provides a clear step-by-step explanation of the mechanics of using APV as well as a guide to implementing the steps. The example includes a useful discussion on the use of and estimating the costs of financial distress associated with debt financing.

- *Corporate Finance*[41] contains discussion and examples for applying the APV in the context of both project valuation and business valuation. Chapter 17 of *Corporate Finance* includes a discussion of the equivalence of the APV and WACC methods as well as some guidelines for choosing between APV and

WACC, depending on the characteristics of the valuation problem at hand. This text also includes an appendix showing the application of the APV method to a leveraged buyout, specifically the RJR Nabisco buyout.

• *Financial Markets and Corporate Strategy*[42] contains the most complete discussion of APV, including a thorough discussion of its theoretical basis. The APV chapter includes topics closely related to and often intertwined with the APV such as debt capacity, the appropriate discount rate for valuing risky debt tax-shields, and the use of APV in a real options approach to valuation.

NOTES

1. For example, James R. Hitchner, ed., *Financial Valuation: Applications and Models*, 2nd ed., (Hoboken, NJ: John Wiley & Sons, 2006) and Shannon P. Pratt, Robert P. Schweihs, and Robert F. Reilly, *Valuing A Business*, 4th ed. (New York: McGraw-Hill, 2000).
2. *See* the conventional definition of fair market value in Section 13.2(b) of the chapter.
3. *International Glossary of Business Valuation Terms*, American Institute of Certified Public Accountants, American Society of Appraisers, Canadian Institute of Chartered Business Valuators, National Association of Certified Valuation Analysts, and The Institute of Business Appraisers. The *International Glossary of Business Valuation Terms* is also available on a variety of Web sites, including www.aicpa.org/bvfls/resources.
4. *International Glossary of Business Valuation Terms.*
5. *International Glossary of Business Valuation Terms.*
6. *See* Hitchner, *Financial Valuation*, 2nd ed., 782; Model Business Corporation Act, 3rd ed., revised through 2002, §13.01(4).
7. A majority of states have laws that address the rights of dissenting and oppressed shareholders. States usually have statutes separated between these two types of shareholders. A dissenting shareholder is a minority shareholder who claims that a proposed corporate action such as a merger adversely affects him or her. The usual remedy is that the corporation purchases the dissenting shareholder's stock. A minority shareholder who claims that a majority of shareholder(s) acted improperly (e.g., mismanagement, fraud) can file an oppressed shareholder action in many states. The remedy can include the purchase of the shareholder's stock.
8. Financial Accounting Standards Board, *Statements of Financial Accounting Standards 142*, June 2001, 117. This is only one of several definitions of *fair value* that one can find in GAAP literature.
9. *International Glossary of Business Valuation Terms.*
10. Appendix A defines these terms.
11. It is generally recognized that publicly traded stocks can become mispriced. See the discussion of intrinsic value in Section 13.2(b). Mispricing occurs when a stock's market price is significantly different from its intrinsic value. For example, if a stock's price temporarily declined because of an unexpected news announcement and then reverted to its original price, one can conclude the price was temporarily mispriced because the company's fundaments did not change. In the late 1990s, many technology stocks were mispriced for a long period largely because of the irrational behavior of investors.
12. Analysts use the term *real options* to describe these features.
13. Financial Accounting Standards Board, *Statement of Financial Accounting Standards 123*, December 2004, 41.
14. *International Glossary of Business Valuation Terms.*
15. A firm's debt capital consists of the debt used to capitalize the firm's operations over the long term. Valuation literature refers to this as long-term debt. This amount

includes the current maturities on the debt. The debt used to capitalize the firm usually excludes trade payables, accrued liabilities, and temporary borrowings.

16. The firm can deduct interest expense for income tax purposes so its effective cost of debt is net of the associated tax benefit (i.e., borrowing costs less avoided taxes equals after-tax cost of debt). The firm cannot deduct dividends it pays to shareholders for tax purposes, and, therefore, the cost of equity has no associated tax benefit.

17. The mathematical expressions for discounting amounts to present value in this chapter make a simplifying assumption that the discount period for a year's earnings should be for an entire year. In reality, most firms earn their cash flows and profits throughout the year. Accordingly, many practitioners use a midyear discounting convention. This convention modifies the mathematical expressions for discounting in this chapter by reducing each time period by one-half year. For example, if the analyst expects next year's cash flows to be $1,000,000, the cash flows would be discounted for one-half year when using the midyear convention rather than a full year.

18. The analyst can use nominal amounts or real amounts in the model. Nominal amounts include inflation whereas real amounts remove the effects of inflation. Formulas (2) through (7) in this chapter use nominal amounts.

19. These firms are "pass-through" entities. The firm's owners—rather than the company—report the taxable income to the government and pay the income taxes.

20. Damodaran, Anwath, *Investment Valuation*, 2nd ed. (New York: John Wiley & Sons, 2002), 268.

21. The unlevered cost of equity assumes the company operates without any debt. Generally, a company without any debt has lower bankruptcy risk and, therefore, a cost of equity that is lower than if it had debt. If the analyst uses CAPM or MCAPM to determine the firm's cost of equity, the analyst "unlevers" the beta, which results in a lower beta. A lower beta results in a lower cost of equity. The reader is referred to the formula to unlever beta in Hitchner, *Financial Valuation*, 2nd ed., 188.

22. American Society of Appraisers, *Statement on Business Valuation Standards 1*, www.bvappraisers.org.

23. The most common databases in the United States are Bizcomps, Done Deals, Institute of Business Appraisers, Mergerstat, and Pratt's Stats, www.bizcomps.com, www.donedeals.com, www.go-iba.org, www.mergerstat.com, www.bvresources.com.

24. *See*, for example, Hitchner, *Financial Valuation*, 2nd ed., Chapter 21; Robert F. Reilly and Robert P. Schweihs, *Valuing Intangible Assets* (Hoboken, NJ: John Wiley & Sons, 1999).

25. The analyst may ask the business owner to identify any underreported income, overstatement of expenses, and nonrecurring items. In some situations, the analyst may not have full access to the owner or management. The client may separately retain the practitioner to investigate the firm's accounting records and identify such items.

26. American Society of Appraisers, www.appraisers.org.

27. The Appraisal Foundation, www.appraisalfoundation.org. This organization publishes the Uniform Standards of Professional Appraisal Practice. Standards 9 and 10 pertain to business valuation.

28. National Association of Certified Valuation Analysts, www.nacva.com.

29. Institute of Business Appraisers, www.go-iba.org.

30. Canadian Institute of Chartered Business Valuators, www.cicbv.ca.

31. American Institute of Certified Public Accountants, www.aicpa.org.

32. A detailed discussion of WACC can be found in Chapter 7, "Estimating the Cost of Capital." It will not be repeated here.

33. Stewart C. Myers, "Interactions of Corporate Financing and Investment Decisions—Implications for Capital Budgeting," *The Journal of Finance* XXIX (March 1974).

34. Two widely used textbooks in MBA finance courses that include a discussion of the APV are: Richard A. Brealey and Stewart C. Myers, *Principles of Corporate*

Finance, 7th ed. (New York: McGraw-Hill, 2003); and Stephen A. Ross, Randolph W. Westerfield, and Jeffrey Jaffe, *Corporate Finance,* 7th ed. (New York: McGraw Hill/Irwin, 2004).

35. Timothy A. Luehrman, "What's It Worth? A General Manager's Guide to Valuation," *Harvard Business Review* (May-June 1997), 135.

36. One can add an additional step to isolate other financing effects, such as cost of issuing debt. However, this discussion will ignore these financial effects.

37. Business valuation and corporate finance literature have detailed discussions on how to determine free cash flows and calculate NPV. The free cash flows used in the APV are equal to the free cash flows used in the more traditional WACC methodology.

38. For a discussion of the estimation of financial distress costs, *see* Damodaran, *Investment Valuation,* in the Bibliography.

39. There will not be a material impact on the valuation if financial distress is not explicitly considered if one of the following conditions exist: (1) bankruptcy is a remote possibility, either because of the firm's size and standing or because of a government guarantee; (2) easy access to capital markets allows firms with good investments to raise debt or equity capital to sustain themselves through bad times, reducing the likelihood these firms will be forced into a distress sale; and (3) projected cash flows that incorporate the likelihood of distress and a discount rate adjusted for the higher risk associated with distress. A final exception exists when the firm will likely receive, in the event of a distress sale, proceeds equal to the present value of expected future cash flows as a going concern. *See* Aswath Damodaran, "Dealing with Distress in Valuation," Stern School of Business, January 2002, for further discussion.

40. Damodaran, *Investment Valuation* Chapter 6, 23–30.

41. Stephen A. Ross, Randolph W. Westerfield and Jeffrey Jaffe, *Corporate Finance,* 7th ed. (New York: McGraw-Hill/Irwin, 2004).

42. Mark Grinblatt and Sheridan Titman, *Financial Markets and Corporate Strategy,* 2nd ed. (New York: McGraw-Hill/Irwin, 2002).

BIBLIOGRAPHY AND SUGGESTED REFERENCES

Damodaran, Anwath. *Investment Valuation.* 2nd ed. New York: John Wiley & Sons, 2002.

Hitchner, James R., ed. *Financial Valuation: Applications and Models,* 2nd ed. Hoboken, NJ: John Wiley & Sons, 2006.

Pratt, Shannon P. *Business Valuation Discounts and Premiums.* New York: John Wiley & Sons, 2001.

Pratt, Shannon P. *Cost of Capital: Estimation and Applications.* 2nd ed. Hoboken, NJ: John Wiley & Sons, 2002.

Pratt, Shannon P. *The Market Approach to Valuing Businesses.* Hoboken, NJ: John Wiley & Sons, 2001.

Pratt, Shannon P., Robert P. Schweihs, and Robert F. Reilly. *Valuing a Business.* 4th ed. New York: McGraw-Hill, 2000.

Reilly, Robert F. and Robert P. Schweihs. *The Handbook of Advanced Business Valuation.* New York: McGraw-Hill, 2000.

Reilly, Robert F. and Robert P. Schweihs. *Valuing Intangible Assets.* New York: McGraw-Hill, 1998.

Smith, Gordon V. and Russell L. Parr. *Valuation of Intellectual Property and Intangible Assets.* 3rd ed. New York: John Wiley & Sons, 2000.

Stowe, John D., Thomas R. Robinson, Jerald E. Pinto, and Dennis W. McLeavey. *Analysis of Equity Investments: Valuation.* Charlottesville, VA: CFA Institute, 2002.

Trugman, Gary R. *Understanding Business Valuation.* New York: American Institute of Certified Public Accountants, 2002.

ADDITIONAL RECOMMENDED READING

Fernandez, Pablo. "The Value of Tax Shields is NOT Equal to the Present Value of Tax Shields." *Journal of Financial Economics*, 73 (July 2004) 145–165.

Fernandez, Pablo. "The Value of Tax Shields is NOT Equal to the Present Value of Tax Shields—a Correction." (February, 2005). *See* http://www.iese.edu/research/pdfs/DI-0581-E.pdf

Fernandez, Pablo. "Reply to Comment On the Value of Tax Shields Is Not Equal to the Present Value of Tax Shields." *Quarterly Review of Economics and Finance*, 45, (February 2005) 188–192.

Ruback, Richard S. "Capital Cash Flows: A Simple Approach to Valuing Risky Cash Flows." *Financial Management* 31 (Summer 2002): 85–103.

CHAPTER 14

LOST EARNINGS OF PERSONS

Randi L. Firus
Keith R. Ugone

CONTENTS

14.1 INTRODUCTION

In personal injury, wrongful termination, wrongful death, medical malpractice, and similar tort cases, the law allows the plaintiff compensation for economic loss when the court finds the defendant liable. The economic loss can include many types of loss the plaintiff suffers (e.g., medical bills), but the plaintiff/decedent's lost earnings usually become the primary component of claimed economic damages. Lost earnings represent the monetary loss, in present-value dollars, stemming from the individual's inability to provide certain services or the ability to provide them only for reduced compensation.

This chapter focuses on the calculation of damages for lost earnings, but an expert may quantify other components of the economic loss. In personal injury or medical malpractice cases, claimed damages often include some or all of past and future medical expenses, rehabilitation services or equipment, special education costs (e.g., in birth injury cases), and loss of household services. Other categories of damages in wrongful death cases include funeral and burial costs and loss of household services. Quantifying damages for these categories usually requires a straightforward summation of past and projected future out-of-pocket expenditures.[1] The plaintiff might also make a claim for lost or reduced pension-related benefits.

Wrongful death cases differ from other types of cases in that the plaintiffs usually are the decedent's survivors. Hence, the plaintiffs' economic loss differs from the decedent's lost earnings; it consists of the portion of the decedent's compensation that would have benefited the plaintiffs. The United States recognizes two different legal causes of action, the *wrongful death action* and the *survival action*, depending on the jurisdiction. These causes of action affect the legal theory of damages in wrongful death cases. The decedent's survivors bring a wrongful death action (the more common), claiming damages or their economic loss as a result of the death. A survival action, brought on behalf of the decedent's estate, changes the damages approach from measuring the loss to the survivors to measuring the loss to the estate.[2]

Finally, plaintiffs increasingly seek *hedonic damages* in personal injury and wrongful death cases. Hedonic damages attempt to compensate for the plaintiff's loss of enjoyment of life, whether the plaintiff is the physically injured party or a survivor of the deceased. Hedonic damages can include such items as the loss of the ability to participate in sports or hobbies and the loss of consortium with a spouse. Whether a plaintiff can receive this category of damages varies by jurisdiction. Jurisdictions that allow hedonic damages may constrain the amount allowed. Experts who quantify damages for lost earnings frequently debate the appropriate methods for quantifying hedonic damages and whether a financial expert should even attempt such quantification.[3]

14.2   BASIC DAMAGES MODEL

Exhibit 14-1 illustrates the basic model generally used in calculating loss of earnings damages. The individual's *but-for* (or *undamaged*) earnings are the earnings the individual would have earned in the absence of the incident (injury/termination/death). *Actual* (or *damaged*) earnings are the individual's projected earnings, given the incident.[4] One calculates the lost earnings or damages as the present value of the difference between these two projections. The damages calculation includes both lost past earnings (i.e., *past losses or damages*) and the lost future earnings (i.e., *future losses or damages*).

(a) Projecting But-For Earnings.   To project the plaintiff's or decedent's earnings stream as if the harmful incident had not occurred, one must understand and compute the individual's base earnings at the time of the incident. The but-for earnings should include all categories of earnings that the incident interrupted or impaired, including salary; incentive compensation such as commissions or bonuses; fringe benefits during the period of employment; deferred benefits such as pensions or stock options; and any relevant perquisites such as company cars. But-for earnings do not include passive income, such as income from stocks or dividends, unless the incident affects that income in some way.[5]

In most cases, the individual's earnings history prior to the incident offers a good source for understanding base-year earnings and predicting future earnings.

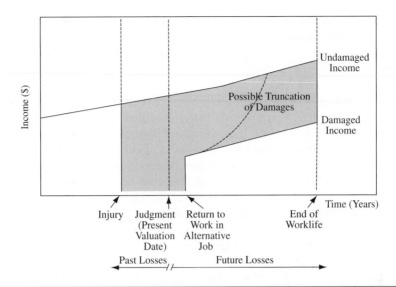

Exhibit 14-1.   Lost Earnings Methodology in Personal Injury Case. *Note:* **Other issues include lost pension benefits and tax effects (where applicable). Case law in some jurisdictions may not allow for the addition of interest to past losses.**

The expert should obtain as full an earnings history as the facts and circumstances of the particular litigation warrant.

If the plaintiff's or decedent's earnings follow a consistent pattern and testimony indicates that the individual intended to stay employed in the same profession or with the same employer, the expert can consider projecting but-for earnings based on the past trend in the individual's earnings.[6] An individual's historical earnings growth, however, can reflect general wage inflation in the economy, merit increases, *and promotions* to higher levels of responsibility. Therefore, an expert needs to understand the individual's place in his or her employer's hierarchy to assess the likelihood of future promotions at the same pace. Without this understanding, one cannot appropriately use the individual's past earnings trend to project future but-for earnings.[7]

If the individual's own earnings history does not adequately predict future growth, the financial expert can consider projecting a life-cycle pattern of earnings based on accepted age, experience, and earnings profiles.[8] Evidence of an impending promotion foregone on account of the incident can impact either the assumed but-for base earnings level, or subsequent growth rates, or both.

Some individuals have an erratic earnings history; the financial expert will have to ascertain the reasons for the pattern and use a different method to project but-for earnings. In some occupations, periods of economic slowdown or economic recovery will distort patterns. For example, bonuses or sales commissions often fluctuate with general or company-specific market conditions. Similarly, in cases involving hourly workers, compensation can go up or down from year to year since many hourly employees do not have a guaranteed minimum number of hours (e.g., unionized construction workers). The earnings pattern will then depend on the number of regular and overtime hours worked.[9] In these instances, the expert can solve this problem by obtaining the earnings of peer workers at the company or in the industry for the past period and use the peer workers' earnings pattern as a proxy for the plaintiff's or the decedent's postincident but-for earnings.[10]

An individual's work history can also exhibit variability owing to periods of not working for reasons other than the job market or economic conditions. The financial expert must ascertain whether the absences reflect personal life-style choices or preexisting health conditions. If the observed pattern will likely recur, the expert should adjust the earnings projection to reflect the individual's work habits or situation. On the other hand, withdrawal for childbirth or child-rearing reasons, or temporary leaves of absence following an accident unrelated to the claim, might not influence the individual's projected future workforce participation.

Contractual arrangements or observed postincident pay increases at the plaintiff's or decedent's former employer often dictate the growth rate of the individual's earnings pattern, at least in the short term. One example of this occurs when a unionized worker suffers an earnings stream interruption.

Experts often find the projection of income streams for the self-employed more difficult than for employees who work for others. Self-employed people often have the ability to move income between salary and business net income. They can also benefit from company expenses such as vehicles, travel and entertainment, insurance, or even placing family members on the payroll. When the company gains or loses value or the individual takes draws or loans, defining a self-employed person's earnings becomes even more complicated. Careful analysis also distinguishes between the self-employed person's earnings on equity (which continues after injury or death) and the earnings from labor services. In this situation, the expert could estimate the cost to pay a manager to do the work the owner was doing and use that as the basis of calculating lost earnings.

In summary, to project but-for earnings, one must

- Understand the plaintiff's or decedent's work history and earnings
- Recognize whether events have altered the individual's future earnings stream relative to the past earnings stream
- Have a good rationale for the approach taken to quantify the claimed future earnings stream

(b) Actual or Mitigating Earnings.   To project the plaintiff's actual or damaged income stream in a personal injury or wrongful termination claim, the financial expert must understand the plaintiff's circumstances following the incident. In most jurisdictions, plaintiffs claiming damages in these types of actions have a duty to mitigate, which requires them to take reasonable steps to minimize the damages they incur by finding alternative employment. In some situations, actual earnings will not appropriately measure mitigating earnings. Examples include a plaintiff who chooses not to return to work despite medical opinions that he or she is capable of working, or a terminated employee who does not make a reasonable effort to obtain comparable or substantially similar employment.

If the plaintiff can return to work, even in alternative employment, the financial expert should project postincident actual or mitigating earnings in the damages analysis. In personal injury or medical malpractice cases, the financial expert usually requires an outside assessment of the plaintiff's ability to return to productive employment. Medical, rehabilitation, and employment experts might assist in this evaluation. A medical expert could assess the likely time before the plaintiff can return to work. A vocational or rehabilitation expert often provides the financial expert with types of occupations the plaintiff could still pursue, given the injury. An employment expert can estimate likely periods of unemployment while the plaintiff conducts a job search. The financial expert can consult government statistics and other data to evaluate the labor market.

The financial expert's role can include researching average earnings associated with the plaintiff's postincident occupational prospects to assess future actual (or damaged) earnings.[11] Absent information on specific occupations that the plaintiff could still pursue, the financial expert can incorporate in the analysis average earnings data by age, gender, years of schooling, and race from the annual March Supplement to the *Current Population Survey (CPS)* by the U.S. Census Department. Alternatively, one can identify sedentary occupations with appropriate worker characteristics and vocational preparation using the *Dictionary of Occupational Titles* published by the U.S. Department of Labor. The financial expert can then incorporate in the analysis earnings data based on these sedentary occupations.

The financial expert should consider the opportunities for advancement in postincident employment. For example, earnings from the new employer may begin lower than with the previous employer but have greater advancement potential, especially if the plaintiff can acquire additional training or education. In particular, similar to the projection of but-for earnings, the financial expert might consider a life-cycle pattern of earnings to project growth on the postincident job, adjusted for fewer years of experience if the plaintiff's preincident work skills do not transfer to the new employment situation.[12]

Sometimes people move from employee status to self-employed status, taking a risk for the chance of higher return. Cases with such facts require care. Earnings from the higher risk business may not measure mitigation appropriately. Defendants will not share in the upside of a business venture and should not underwrite the downside through a lost earnings claim. Under these circumstances, an expert could consider measuring mitigation by the earnings a person might reasonably expect in a similar position as an employee.

Mitigation involves difficult issues. Ultimately, jurors and judges make the final determination as to whether the injured party has properly mitigated claimed damages.

(c) Period of Loss. The *time period of the loss* is the length of the damages period. The expert decides on the method of projecting but-for and actual earnings and the time period of the loss. Government statistics and other studies provide data on worklife expectancies; however, the expert should consider relevant facts in the particular case.[13]

The damages period will not necessarily extend over the plaintiff's or decedent's full statistical worklife expectancy. When establishing the damages period, the expert should consider items such as the individual's preincident health conditions, family circumstances, actual work history, financial incentives such as deferred compensation or early retirement incentives, general market conditions in the individual's industry, and any contracts that directly affect the individual's worklife. In addition, as Exhibit 14-1 shows, the expert must evaluate whether the damages period for an injured or terminated plaintiff will end prior to a projected worklife or retirement date because of a full recovery of the earnings stream. For example, if a plaintiff previously employed as a manual laborer returns to college as a result of being injured, one might reasonably expect that at a future date prior to retirement, the plaintiff's actual earnings will surpass the but-for earnings. In these circumstances, the injury provides the plaintiff with opportunities that would not have arisen but for the injury. In terms of economic loss, past damages still exist, but the plaintiff's retraining will mitigate future economic losses, and damages will end or begin to diminish when the two earnings streams cross.

Wrongful termination cases require special consideration in deciding the length of the damages period. The probability that a person will work at a *specific* job is less than the probability of the person working at *any* job. Since worklife expectancy tables consider all employment, one would expect a terminated employee's expectation of staying with a particular employer to be less than the full worklife expectancy.[14] Examining normal employee turnover can help answer the question of how long a person would have stayed with a particular employer but for the alleged wrongful termination. Additionally, wrongful termination cases often have a high likelihood of full earnings recovery prior to expected retirement because the plaintiff can seek and obtain work in the same occupation.

In wrongful death cases, the expert should also consider additional factors to properly assess the time period of the surviving plaintiffs' damages recovery. For example, in the case of the death of a single parent whose only child was 15 years old, the court may limit the loss period on a component of damages to three years, absent evidence that the child would have continued to receive some benefit from the parent's earnings after reaching age 18.

Hence, an analysis of the damages period in loss of earnings cases must assess whether (1) the individual's worklife expectancy yields the appropriate period of damages, or (2) the particular facts and circumstances of the matter warrant a damages period of a different length.

(d) Discounting Lost Earnings to Present Value.   The expert can prepare damages models for lost earnings in either nominal (i.e., observed or actual) terms or real (i.e., inflation-adjusted) terms.[15] A model prepared in inflation-adjusted terms does not require the expert to project inflation separately. Its disadvantages include the difficulty of explaining to a jury the concept of an inflation-adjusted model and the complexity of calculating taxes on inflation-adjusted numbers (when the case requires an after-tax approach). In such a situation, an expert who uses the plaintiff's or decedent's historical earnings growth rates to project future growth must adjust for the inflation that occurred during the historical period, particularly during periods of high or changing inflation.

Whether financial experts use nominal or real models, they must select appropriate growth and discount rates to apply to but-for and postincident earnings. Certain jurisdictions restrict the expert's choices on this topic. Some states have adopted the *total offset* method, requiring experts to assume that the inflation rate and discount rate exactly offset each other.[16] Absent this restriction, the expert must apply a discount rate to but-for and actual earnings that reasonably assesses the risk associated with the individual's future but-for and actual earnings patterns. In addition, the model should maintain expected historical relations in the economy among inflation, overall wage growth, and interest rates. [17]

In projecting earnings, the expert should not treat the individual's future uncertain income stream as a certain one. Some occupations or professions have more inherent risk or higher turnover rates than others. In addition, components of income representing incentive compensation or stock options have more inherent risk than base salary. The computations can incorporate an adjustment for the appropriate risk level apart from the discount rate used to convert future amounts to present value.

Certain jurisdictions dictate that plaintiffs need not accept any risk when investing the lump-sum damages award. For this reason, courts commonly use interest rates on government bonds or annuity rates for triple A-rated insurance companies as discount rates. Some experts also use municipal bond rates to account for the effect of taxes the plaintiff would otherwise pay on the interest received.[18] (Section 14.4(a) discusses the effect of taxes on the damages award.)

In either case, the maturity of the financial instrument used to discount projected lost earnings should match the damages period, in order to best approximate the interest the plaintiff will earn on the lump-sum award. Because one can expect the plaintiff to withdraw the award steadily over the damages period to replace lost earnings, the expert can incorporate more than one discount rate. For example, the expert can use data from instruments with different maturities to derive the term structure of interest rates and then use the implied rate for each period, computed separately. Alternatively, experts who decide to use one discount rate to simplify the analysis may consider a blended discount rate based on yields on securities with maturities up to the end of the damages period, or a discount rate based on yields on securities that mature midperiod.

(e) Personal Consumption Expenditures. In wrongful death cases, the financial expert should deduct the decedent's personal consumption expenditures from lost compensation. Theory suggests that the surviving plaintiffs should receive only the benefits they would have received from the decedent's earnings; this would not include amounts for the decedent's incremental personal consumption.[19]

Data on personal consumption expenditures usually come in the form of consumption percentages of the combined gross income of all family members. Family size and income bracket typically dictate the percentage. Exhibit 14-2 illustrates the basic model used in wrongful death cases. The figure shows personal consumption exhibiting step-function characteristics, because as children reach the age of 18 and leave the home, the personal consumption of either parent generally increases as a percentage of family income. (The consumption function is not derived by dividing all household expenditures among family members. Items such as the family home and a portion of associated utilities, for example, need not change because of one fewer member living at home.)

Common practice uses standard percentages to estimate the decedent's incremental consumption, except in the case of high-income individuals or when data are available. Unfortunately, no standard, accepted source exists for these percentages.

In 1961, Cheit published a pioneering study on personal consumption expenditures in *Injury and Recovery in the Course of Employment*.[20] Based on the results of a

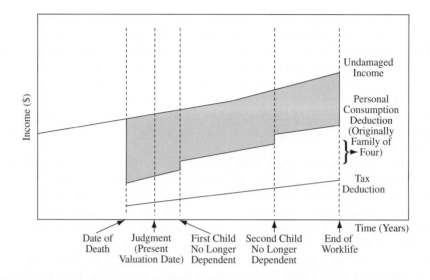

Exhibit 14-2.   Lost Earnings Methodology in Wrongful Death Case. *Note:* **Other issues include lost pension benefits. Case law in some jurisdictions may not allow for the addition of interest to past losses.**

survey he performed, Cheit calculated percentages for the personal consumption of the family breadwinner, based on family size. Financial experts still frequently use Cheit's percentages, although they are dated and do not provide percentages for nonnuclear families, such as single-parent families. In addition, Cheit did not adjust consumption percentages for the income level of the family, a primary determinant of consumption.

More recently, Patton and Nelson published consumption percentages based on research using the *Consumption Expenditures Surveys* published by the U.S. Department of Labor. Their article (Patton and Nelson, 1991) contains tables with consumption percentages based on gender, total family income, and family size. They used a straightforward method that, in cases involving unique facts, a financial expert can use to recalculate a case-specific percentage. This method has also been applied to more recent data (Ruble, Patton, and Nelson, 2000).

In cases involving high-income decedents or meriting the cost of a more detailed analysis, the financial expert can establish a case-specific consumption percentage based on the deceased's actual spending patterns. Provided sufficient information exists on the household's spending habits, the expert can review all family expenditures over an appropriate period and classify them as either personal or joint family expenses. In this way, the expert can arrive at the decedent's personal consumption, adjusted accordingly over time as children become adults and leave the family unit.

In some circumstances, wrongful termination cases also have a personal consumption component. The computation of lost net earnings should include deductions for expenditures formerly incurred as a necessary part of work that are no longer required (e.g., transportation to and from work, licensing fees, costs of required continuing education, trade journals, uniforms, and added meal costs). Job-related out-of-pocket costs could similarly reduce net earnings from a replacement job.

14.3 INFORMATION NEEDED FOR ANALYSIS

Before preparing an analysis of lost earnings, the financial expert will need to obtain case-specific information and relevant statistical data from various reference sources.

(a) Data Specific to the Case. Data specific to the case include personal data, employment/earnings data, and health data.

(i) Personal Data. Making case-specific use of governmental statistical data requires personal information about the plaintiff or the decedent, such as age, gender, race, and educational level. One needs to know the date of birth to estimate the statistical dates of retirement and death from worklife and life expectancy tables. In wrongful death cases, the dates of birth and health conditions of all immediate family members and the decedent's marital status influence the estimation of the portion of the household income spent by the decedent on personal consumption. The date of actual injury or death establishes the beginning of the loss period.

(ii) Employment/Earnings Data. The financial expert should obtain a complete employment history of the plaintiff or decedent as far back in time as the facts and circumstances of the case warrant. Many employers keep personnel files containing records of all raises and promotions, as well as termination letters specifying severance pay and benefit options under COBRA. Employee handbooks often contain statements of benefits and examples of how to compute pensions. (These calculations may be employee specific.) Handbooks for companies with cafeteria benefit plans will show what options employees have and the portion the employer paid. Employers sometimes have records showing the vested portion of the employee's pension plan, as well as information on any stock option plans or 401k plans. The financial expert should request that counsel subpoena employment records directly from the employers rather than rely on the plaintiff to produce relevant records.

Personal income tax returns contain potentially useful data, but most jurisdictions protect these documents from discovery in civil litigation. The plaintiff or survivors can elect to produce tax returns, however, to support a claim for lost earnings based on income that employment records may not document, such as income from self-employment. When the financial experts cannot obtain tax returns, W-2s, 1099s, and year-end pay stubs prove useful.

Whatever the source, the expert should obtain available data regarding the plaintiff's or decedent's salary, job titles and promotions, and benefits. When evaluating benefits and retirement plans, the expert will need to identify the differences in the benefit and retirement plans in the undamaged and damaged projections. In cases involving unionized employees, the financial expert needs to clearly understand the benefits the union provided versus those the employer provided.

In wrongful death and survivor actions, the expert should collect employment and earnings information for other household members and plaintiffs in order to establish household income and evaluate dependency.

(iii) Health Data. Although the financial expert does not assess the plaintiff's physical condition, the financial expert should have a reasonable foundation for an opinion on the plaintiff's ability to return to the same job in the future or to obtain alternative employment. In personal injury cases, the attorney usually retains a medical expert. If the plaintiff requires long-term care on account of the injury, the attorney will often retain a rehabilitation or vocational expert. The financial expert should review any reports these other experts prepare and base any assumptions regarding physical ability to work on their testimony. The financial expert should also consider a medical expert's opinion regarding any physical impairment of the plaintiff prior to the harmful incident. If preexisting physical impairments would have adversely impacted the individual's earnings, the financial expert would adjust any damages calculation accordingly.

(b) Data from Reference Sources. To calculate lost earnings, the financial expert must often estimate or project certain inputs. Government statistics can help in estimating the following inputs when the financial expert cannot obtain case-specific data.

(i) Worklife Expectancy. The financial expert must estimate the plaintiff's or decedent's remaining worklife had the incident not occurred. Unless the individual's preincident family or health circumstances were extraordinary, one source of average worklife is the article by Ciecka, Donley and Golman (1999-2000) "A Markov Process Model of Work-Life Expectancies Based on Labor Market Activity in 1997–98." This article contains worklife expectancies by age, gender, race, and education. The calculations use the increment-decrement model first published by the Bureau of Labor Statistics (1986) in *Worklife Estimates: Effects of Race and Education.* These publications provide total time measured in years of remaining labor force participation, not years until final separation from the workforce.[21] Depending on the facts of the particular case, the expert should consider adjusting the worklife expectancy to reflect intermittent periods of unemployment. The financial expert should also consult any retained medical and vocational experts in injury cases to ascertain whether the plaintiff's health condition will adversely affect worklife or life expectancy.

(ii) Life Expectancy. Analyzing lost pension and other retirement benefits such as Social Security requires an estimate of the plaintiff's or decedent's life expectancy. The National Center for Health Statistics (2004) lists life expectancies by age, gender, and race. In cases that evaluate lost household services, a publication entitled *Healthy Life Expectancy* provides an alternative measure of life expectancy that combines mortality and morbidity (health status) data.[22]

(iii) Average Earnings. The expert will generally project but-for earnings based on the plaintiff's or decedent's specific work history and occupation or profession. In cases without case-specific data, the expert may have to rely on data regarding the average earnings of similarly situated individuals. The annual March Supplement to the *Current Population Survey (CPS)* by the U.S. Census Department provides

national average earnings data by age, gender, and education level. The Bureau of Labor Statistics publication *Occupational Employment Statistics (OES) Survey* lists annual earnings data by occupation for selected metropolitan areas. For certain occupations or in certain industries, private surveys provide more specific average salary information. Data from these various sources also help in projecting actual or mitigating earnings that the plaintiff might be able to earn in alternative employment.

14.4 OTHER CONSIDERATIONS

(a) Taxes.   In 1980, the U.S. Supreme Court ruled in *Norfolk & Western Railway Co. v. Liepelt*[23] that courts should calculate compensation for lost earnings net of income taxes. The decision resulted from the insight that the plaintiff receives tax-free damages stemming from injuries in these types of actions, whereas the lost earnings that provide the basis of the award would have been taxed as regular income to the plaintiff. Therefore, excluding taxes from the analysis would produce a windfall to the injured plaintiff.

In contrast, the recipient must pay federal income taxes on the entirety of an award for lost earnings in employment-related lawsuits including wrongful termination. For this reason, lost earnings calculations in these matters ignore income taxes.

Despite the Supreme Court's decision, a number of jurisdictions have decided against considering taxes because of an offsetting reverse tax effect. Although injured plaintiffs escape taxation on their lost earnings when the analysis excludes taxes, plaintiffs usually receive personal injury damages awards as a lump sum representing the present value of the lost earnings. The court generally expects the plaintiff to invest this lump sum in some risk-free financial instrument that earns interest. The plaintiff, however, often pays income taxes on the interest earned on the risk-free financial instrument.[24] Projecting lost income before tax increases the present value of the damages award, whereas ignoring the taxes that the plaintiff must pay on interest earnings decreases the plaintiff's postinvestment cash flow (thereby jeopardizing the intended income stream to the plaintiff).

Because the two effects of considering taxes have opposing consequences, some argue that courts can ignore taxes altogether. However, the two effects need not offset each other. The reduction in damages awards caused by using after-tax earnings varies with the plaintiff's income levels both before and after the injury and the assumed real growth rate in the projected earnings. The increase in the damages award required to cover the taxes on the interest earnings varies with the time period of projected loss and the nominal discount rate used.

In deciding whether to consider income taxes in damages calculations for lost earnings owing to injury or death, the financial expert should understand the applicable law. If the law allows consideration of income taxes, one should first calculate both the but-for earnings and the projected actual earnings on an after-tax basis, taking into account the applicable tax brackets (assuming the award itself is not taxable). To avoid having to project plaintiff-specific allowable deductions, a reasonable approach uses average tax rates by income level, published by the Internal Revenue Service.[25] Second, the expert must adjust for the taxes the plaintiff will pay on the interest earnings projected from the damages award. One approach is to use municipal bond rates as a discount rate, since the federal government does not tax interest on municipal bonds. If the individual has relatively low net income, analysts should not use this approach, since investors in the highest tax brackets drive the demand for, and price of, municipal bonds, making them inefficient for those in lower tax brackets. Another approach models the investment account for the lump-sum damages award and adjusts the damages award upward by an amount required to pay the taxes on the interest income.

In any event, the loss-of-earnings expert needs guidance as to the legality of an after-tax analysis in a particular jurisdiction. If the jurisdiction allows, the analysis should consider taxes in personal injury and wrongful death actions.

(b) Pension Benefits. In some cases, lost compensation—especially pension benefits—extends beyond the worklife expectancy or retirement date. Employer-sponsored pension plans usually fall into one of two categories, *defined contribution* or *defined benefit.*

Defined contribution plans generally do not require the expert to project the plan benefits to be received after retirement. The expert needs only to ascertain the employer's contribution rate as a percent of pay and then add the computed but-for contributions to lost earnings in the years the employer would have contributed to the pension plan.[26] Employer contributions to this type of plan differ from additional salary only in that the employee excludes pension contributions from taxable income in the year received.

Defined benefit plans require the financial expert to project the actual monthly pension annuity payable beginning at retirement. The typical formula for the annual defined pension benefit includes parameters for years of service, salary levels, and the retirement date. The expert then calculates the present value of the stream of annual pension benefit payable from retirement through life expectancy either with or without cost of living adjustments, as set forth in the particular pension plan guidelines.[27]

(c) Other Fringe Benefits. Lost compensation includes lost fringe benefits. The financial expert should obtain details of the actual benefits the individual was receiving prior to the incident and the benefits a plaintiff will receive subsequent to the incident and then make a projection of lost fringe benefits. The expert may need to consider the replacement cost of lost benefits as well.

Calculating lost fringe benefits as a percentage of the plaintiff's or decedent's undamaged and damaged income is a common error. Although this approach has merit for benefits linked to salary such as employer savings and retirement plan contributions, in the case of health benefits, for example, the individual's health coverage may be a function of whether the plaintiff has employment, not whether the plaintiff's income is higher or lower. Hence, although an individual may hold a lower paying position post injury or post termination, this does not necessarily imply a loss of health insurance benefits.

When no data are available or the individual was not working at the time, a government publication entitled *Employee Benefits Study* provides standard fringe benefit rates by industry or occupation group.[28]

(d) Social Security Retirement or Disability Benefits. Many cases must consider Social Security benefits, either as lost but-for income or as mitigating income. In some jurisdictions, when the injury permanently impairs but does not eliminate a plaintiff's earnings capacity, the plaintiff can claim lost Social Security retirement benefits. The financial expert would base this claim on the reduced benefits derived from lower earnings, and thus lower Federal Insurance Contributions Act (FICA) taxes, prior to retirement.[29] This claim would be moot if the plaintiff's actual earning capacity still exceeded the income threshold to which the FICA tax applies. There might also be no net loss if the individual's savings in FICA tax payroll deductions on account of lower postincident earnings until retirement exceed the difference in lifetime benefits after retirement.

A permanently disabled plaintiff sometimes receives Social Security disability benefits. In some specific jurisdictions and types of cases, the financial expert deducts actual benefits when estimating damages. The financial expert should consult with the counsel who has retained the expert for legal guidance in this area.

The government has straightforward formulas for computing Social Security benefits, basing retirement, disability, and survivor benefits on the individual's annual earnings subject to FICA tax over a specific number of years prior to the date when the beneficiary begins to receive benefits. For a normal retirement, the calculation includes the individual's highest 35 years of income indexed by an adjustment factor.[30] For a permanently disabled individual, the calculation shortens the time period on a sliding scale based on age at the time of the injury. Inserting the average of the indexed earnings subject to FICA tax over the applicable period into the benefit formula for the year of disability or retirement or death yields the individual's primary insurance amount (PIA). The individual's family status and age (for retirees) then determine the Social Security benefit payable. William Mercer & Co. and CCH Incorporated both publish annual guides to Social Security[31] that explain the calculations in detail and give helpful examples. The Social Security Administration Web site (www.socialsecurity.gov) also provides excellent information.

(e) Cases Involving Children. Cases involving children as the harmed party present other difficulties, primarily that of projecting a but-for earnings stream, since the child has no established profession or earnings history and usually no significant education. To deal with these issues, an expert can use national average earnings by age, gender, and education level published in the annual March Supplement to the *Current Population Survey (CPS)* by the U.S. Census Department. The data require an assumption regarding the child's educational attainment. Experts can estimate probabilities of the child reaching specific educational levels based on the parents' education level.

Cases involving an injury or death of a child must consider the beneficiary of the child's but-for earnings stream. Although neither the law nor economic analysis suggest that a parent would have received any benefits from the child's future employment, the parents can introduce evidence that they would have. If permitted by law, potential damages in this instance should be evaluated net of the estimated costs of child raising.[32]

Cases involving babies can entail issues of either wrongful death or wrongful birth. In wrongful death cases, the plaintiffs generally seek damages based on the child's projected future earnings; however, in wrongful birth cases the plaintiff parents generally seek damages for the costs associated with raising a child. The law in many jurisdictions has not yet evolved on this point and inconsistently views children at times as a net financial asset and at other times as a net financial liability.

(f) Personal Services.   Damages often include a claim for lost household services formerly performed by the decedent or injured plaintiff. For household services that can be characterized as basic chores, one can value the lost services by estimating the cost for an outside person to perform the service. For example, in the case of a decedent, one can hire a gardener to perform the yard care the deceased would otherwise have performed.

Injured people typically provide reduced services for themselves and others than they once did. In some cases, however, because of the interruption in the employment, injured plaintiffs may increase their production of these services. If an injured plaintiff performs services that were otherwise paid for (day care, for example), then this becomes an element of mitigation. Similarly, the injured employee could relieve a spouse, who then earns an income not previously earned. This also would present an element of mitigation.

Experts cannot easily establish the value of certain types of household services, especially parental nurturing. Some studies, however, have attempted these valuations and should be consulted if personal sevices are to be an element of the damages claim.[33]

14.5   CONCLUSION

Calculating lost earnings in personal injury, wrongful termination, and wrongful death cases requires an assessment of an individual's undamaged compensation stream, damaged compensation stream, and the time period of the loss. The financial analyst then computes the present value of the difference in these two compensation streams. From these easily stated principles springs an array of complicating issues and puzzles, which have been detailed in this chapter.

NOTES

1. When quantifying damages for future medical or rehabilitation expenses, the financial expert usually relies on the medical or rehabilitation expert's opinion on the types and current cost of the required treatments. An analysis of the medical components of the Consumer Price Index can then guide the analyst in projecting future treatment costs to be discounted to present value.

2. This chapter will not discuss the differences in damages quantification in these types of actions. However, the financial expert must be aware of such differences when calculating damages. In general, the financial expert also should consult with the legal counsel retaining the expert for legal guidance when quantifying damages.

3. This chapter does not discuss the concept or the calculation of hedonic damages. For discussions on quantifying hedonic damages, *see Economic/Hedonic Damages* by Michael Brookshire (listed in the Bibliography).

4. The start of *damaged* earnings upon return to work in an alternative job may follow a period of unemployment. The return to work can occur before or after the trial date.

5. Experts should consider passive income when computing the appropriate tax rates for an after-tax analysis. *See* discussion of taxes in Section 14.4(a).

6. One can do this using either least squares regression analysis or a simple average of the historical real (i.e., inflation-adjusted) increases in the plaintiff's earnings. Care must be exercised to ensure that some future event will not render a simple projection of past growth rates inappropriate.

7. For example, a diminished likelihood of future promotions relative to past promotions warrants adjusting downward projected growth rates compared with past observations.

8. Real life-cycle wage increases (in excess of inflation and overall productivity growth) can be derived from data on average full-time year-round earnings by age bracket reported from the Current Population Survey (CPS), Annual Demographic Survey, March Supplement. The detailed personal income tables by education level are contained in Table PINC-04, available on the Joint BLS/U.S. Census Bureau Web site (https://www.census.gov). To project the individual's earnings in nominal terms, the real life-cycle or experience-based increases are then combined with cost of living adjustments and overall productivity growth.

9. For example, in the construction industry, a worker's earnings can fall substantially during a recessionary period and then increase rapidly as the recession ends.

10. In such an analysis, it is necessary to compare the individual's past work history with that of the peer group and adjust the peer group's postinjury performance used to project the individual's future earnings to account for this relation.

11. One source of market-equivalent average wages by geographic location is the yearly National, State, and Metropolitan Area Wage Estimates, *Occupational Employment Statistics (OES) Survey*, U.S. Department of Labor, Bureau of Labor Statistics. Several states also have employment development or labor departments that monitor and report data for regional job markets.

12. Life-cycle increases should be applied to actual or starting wages only. If median or mean earnings in the postincident occupation are used to estimate the basis of the individual's expected postincident earnings, the average already accounts for life-cycle increases.

13. Expected worklife, as defined by the Bureau of Labor statistics, is the remaining time, measured in years, that an individual is expected to be a labor force participant (either working or actively seeking work) before ultimate retirement. For simplification, some financial experts assume that these years run consecutively beginning from the date of incident, but in actuality, the remaining "years" of worklife are expected to be spread over a longer time interval to ultimate retirement that includes some periods not in the labor force.

14. For a plaintiff or decedent previously employed by one employer for most of his or her career, the distinction between total remaining worklife and remaining worklife at the one employer is likely less significant.

15. *Nominal dollars* include the effects of inflation and deflation. *Real dollars* are inflation-adjusted dollars that remove the effect of inflation from the figures.

16. For a convenient listing of the legal guidelines of various states, *see* Chapter 12 of *Economic/Hedonic Damages* by Michael Brookshire. In addition, the expert should consult with the retaining counsel concerning legal restrictions on the calculation of damages in the relevant jurisdiction. Recent issues of the *Journal of Forensic Economics* have contained special sections assessing economic damages in personal injury and wrongful death litigation in various states.

17. The relationship between these variables is demonstrated and discussed in the "Economic Assumptions and Methods" section of the yearly, *Annual Report of the Board of Trustees of the Federal Old-Age and Survivors Insurance and Disability Insurance Trust Funds*, Social Security Administration Web site (https://www.ssa.gov/OACT/TR/) (Actuarial Publications).

18. The financial expert should ask for legal guidance concerning which rules affect the selection of a discount rate in the relevant jurisdiction.

19. Some jurisdictions that provide for survival causes of action, rather than wrongful death actions, do not allow deductions for personal consumption expenditures. In addition, some jurisdictions allow deductions only for personal needs without necessarily being clear as to whether this restricts the deduction to necessities only.

20. Earl Cheit, "Measuring Economic Loss Due to Death and Disability," in *Injury and Recovery in the Course of Employment* (New York: John Wiley & Sons, 1961), 76–82.

21. If the financial expert assumes that the years of remaining worklife run consecutively beginning from the date of incident, this effectively "front-loads" the losses to earlier years and overstates the calculated damages because future amounts are stated in present value. For this reason, some financial experts project losses through the individual's ultimate retirement date instead of expected worklife but adjust each year's amount by the ratio of remaining worklife to time until retirement or another measure of labor force participation.

22. *Healthy Life Expectancy: 1999 Tables* (Shawnee Mission, KS: Expectancy Data, 2001).

23. *Norfolk & Western Railway Co. v. Liepelt*, 444 U.S. 490 (1980).

24. U.S. Treasury securities are taxed at the federal level but not at the state and local level. The issuing jurisdictions do not tax state and municipal bonds.

25. Data on "Individual Tax Statistics" by state are available on the Internal Revenue Service Web site, U.S. Department of the Treasury (http://www.irs.gov/taxstats/index.html). The 2002 tables, for example, are titled "Tax Year 2002, United States Selected Income and Tax Items for Individual Income Tax Returns: Forms 1040, 1040A & 1040EZ, by State and Size of Adjusted Gross Income, Filing/Processing Period: January 1, 2003 to December 31, 2003."

26. In a defined contribution plan, the beneficiary bears the risk of market fluctuation, and in many companies, employees themselves control the investment of their assets. For this reason, it is unnecessary to project interest on the annual employer contributions as an element of loss because the plaintiff is able to replace the interest income through investment of these amounts in funds or other investment vehicles with similar risk.

27. This method of projection is termed the *expected life approach*. An alternative method, the *probabilistic approach*, instead multiplies the annual pension benefit by the probability of the individual surviving from the present date until each future age, through the theoretical maximum-life age and then sums the products. The expected life approach is more frequently used by financial experts because it is easier to use and easier to explain. In all realistic situations, when the projected discount rate does not change much from year to year and the probability of remaining alive at the end of each year declines through time, the expected life approach will give a higher amount for a life-contingent payment stream than will the actuarially sound probabilistic approach.

28. The most recent version of this annual study by the U.S. Chamber of Commerce is the *2005 Employee Benefits Study* (Washington, DC: U.S. Government Printing Office, 2005).

29. Social Security payroll taxes are collected by the government under authority of the Federal Insurance Contributions Act (FICA). Under current law, social security taxes paid by the employee and employer each represent 6.20% of earnings up to the taxable maximum ($94,200 per year in 2006). The Medicare portion of FICA is 1.45% of all earnings without limit.

30. The retirement benefit formula includes 35 years, regardless of whether the individual had 35 years of earnings.

31. *See Social Security and Medicare: A Professional's Reference* (Louisville, KY: William M. Mercer, Inc.); and *Social Security Explained* and *Social Security Benefits Including Medicare* (listed in the Bibliography).

32. *See Expenditures on Children by Families*, U.S. Department of Agriculture (listed in the Bibliography).

33. *See The Value of a Day: 1999 Dollar Valuation*, Expectancy Data (listed in the Bibliography).

LIST OF CASES

Norfolk & Western Railway Co. v. Liepelt, 444 U.S. 490 (1980)

BIBLIOGRAPHY

Boudreaux, Kenneth J. "A Further Adjustment Needed to Estimate Lost Earnings Capacity." *Monthly Labor Review* (October 1983): 30–31.

Brookshire, Michael L. *Economic/Hedonic Damages: The Practice Book for Plaintiff and Defense Attorneys.* Cincinnati: Anderson Publishing Company, 1990.

Cheit, Earl. "Measuring Economic Loss Due to Death and Disability." In *Injury and Recovery in the Course of Employment.* New York: John Wiley & Sons, 1961, 76–82.

Ciecka, James, Thomas Donley, and Jerry Goldman. "A Markov Process Model of Work-Life Expectancies Based on Labor Market Activity in 1997–98." *Journal of Legal Economics* 9 (Winter 1999–2000): 33–68.

Davidson, Sidney, Clyde P. Stickney, and Roman L. Weil. *Financial Accounting: An Introduction to Concepts, Methods and Uses,* 2nd ed. Hinsdale, IL: Dryden Press, 1979.

Eck, James R., and Jeffrey L. Ungeren. *Structuring Settlements.* New York: McGraw-Hill, 1987.

Expectancy Data. *Healthy Life Expectancy: 1999 Tables.* Shawnee Mission, KS: Expectancy Data, 2001.

Expectancy Data. *The Dollar Value of a Day: 1999 Dollar Valuation.* Shawnee Mission, KS: Expectancy Data, 2001.

Patton, Robert T., and David M. Nelson. "Estimating Personal Consumption Costs in Wrongful Death Cases." *Journal of Forensic Economics* 4(1991): 233–240.

National Center for Health Statistics. *United States Life Tables, 2002.* National Vital Statistics Reports vol 53, number 6. Hyattsville, MD: National Center for Health Statistics, 2004 (annual).

Ruble, Michael R., Robert T. Patton, and David M. Nelson. "Patton-Nelson Personal Consumption Tables, 1997–98 Update." *Journal of Forensic Economics* 13(2000): 303–307.

Sacks, Avram. *Social Security Explained, 2004 Edition.* Riverwoods, IL: Human Resources Products.

Sacks, Avram and Katherine Lerner. *Social Security Benefits Including Medicare, 2004 Edition.* Riverwoods, IL: Human Resources Products.

William M. Mercer, Inc. *Social Security and Medicare: A Professional's Reference.* Louisville, KY: William M. Mercer, Inc., 2004.

U.S. Chamber of Commerce. *Employee Benefits Study.* Washington, DC: U.S. Government Printing Office (annual).

U.S. Department of Agriculture, Center for Nutrition Policy and Promotion. *Expenditures on Children by Families.* Miscellaneous Publication No. 1528-2003, April 2004.

U.S. Department of Labor, Bureau of Labor Statistics. *Occupational Employment Statistics (OES) Survey.* Washington, DC: U.S. Government Printing Office.

U.S. Department of Labor, Bureau of Labor Statistics. *Worklife Estimates: Effects of Race and Education.* February 1986, Bulletin 2254. Washington, DC: U.S. Government Printing Office.

U.S. Department of Labor, Employment and Training Administration. *Dictionary of Occupational Titles,* 4th ed., vols. 1–2. Revised 1991. Washington, DC: U.S. Government Printing Office.

U.S. Department of Labor, Employment and Training Administration. *Selected Characteristics of Occupations Defined in the Revised Dictionary of Occupational Titles.* 1993. Washington, DC: U.S. Government Printing Office.

U.S. Department of the Treasury. *Individual Tax Statistics.* Internal Revenue Service Web site (https://www.irs.gov/taxstats/indtaxstats/index.html).

U.S. Social Security Administration. Annual Report of the Board of Trustees of the Federal Old-Age and Survivors Insurance and Disability Insurance Trust Funds. Washington, DC: U.S. Government Printing Office.

CHAPTER 15

PUNITIVE DAMAGES

Peter A. Bicks
Martha N. Corbett
Glenn K. Jones
Gregory N. Phelps

CONTENTS

15.1 INTRODUCTION

Punitive damages aim to punish and deter wrongful conduct, but these damages should not exceed the level necessary to punish and deter. No standard formula exists to quantify punitive damages and ascertain the appropriate level of punishment. When juries award damages that exceed the amount of actual damages sustained, they intend for punitive damages[1] to punish reprehensible conduct and deter future wrongdoers. Ironically, both the strength and weakness of this type of award lies in its unpredictability. On the one hand, if potential wrongdoers could predict the punitive damages amounts, they could include the cost of potential

The authors revised this chapter from its predecessor in the previous edition, Chapter 12, *Litigation Services Handbook,* 3rd ed. The authors of the earlier chapter were Peter B. Frank, Christopher Kelkar, and Erika Sulkowski, whose efforts are acknowledged and appreciated. The authors would also like to acknowledge Joseph J. Welch, Esq. for his contributions to the present chapter.

awards into the cost of doing business, which could result in a failure to deter harmful conduct.* On the other hand, the lack of clear standards has lead to some wildly unpredictable results with punitive damages awards more than 100 times the actual damages sustained. Recent court cases have clarified the economic issues related to quantifying damages. A financial expert witness can direct the trier of fact's attention to these more objective and quantifiable measurements rather than subjective and emotional considerations.

15.2 BACKGROUND

Punitive damages serve a purpose different from compensatory damages, which aim to compensate plaintiffs for their actual harm. Triers of fact, therefore, tend to measure compensatory damages more objectively. The subjectivity that arises in punitive damages relates to an appropriate level in economic terms that would serve the purpose of punishment and retribution. Constitutional limits exist for punitive damage awards, in particular the due process clause of the Fourteenth Amendment, which prohibits the imposition of grossly excessive or arbitrary punishments. The Supreme Court has become increasingly concerned about arbitrary punitive damages awards and has set down more precise ground rules that courts in the United States have followed in varying degrees.

(a) Basic Issues Arising in a Punitive Damages Action.   A jury's decision of whether to award punitive damages comprises a two-pronged analysis. First, a jury must decide whether the defendant's conduct justifies an award of punitive damages. The jury will base this decision on the state law standard. For example, in California, a jury can award punitive damages only if it finds that, based on "clear and convincing" evidence, the defendant engaged in the alleged wrongful conduct with "malice, oppression or fraud." If the jury makes this threshold decision, it must then decide on the proper amount of punitive damages. (California does not have a limit on punitive damages; some states do, however.)

The U.S. Constitution does not limit the amount of punitive damages that a jury can award. Two Supreme Court decisions, *BMW of North America v. Gore* and *State Farm Mutual Automobile Insurance Company v. Campbell* (discussed in Section 15.2(b)), shape the jurisprudence concerning the constitutionally acceptable level of punitive damages. Through these two opinions, the Court has established three guideposts that juries should consider in determining a punitive damages award:[2]

1. The degree of the conduct's reprehensibility.
2. The disparity between the harm or potential harm suffered and the punitive damages award.
3. The difference between the punitive damages award and the civil penalties authorized or imposed in comparable cases.

Courts will consider any challenged award of punitive damages in light of these factors. Even though every state must follow the Supreme Court's rulings,

---

*Editors' Note: Most economists believe that there is an optimal level (from the point of view of conserving society's scarce resources) of law breaking that is not zero; clearly enunciated punitive damages policies will help allocate those scarce resources in the way society prefers.

different states interpret the Court's decisions in different ways. Section 15.2(b) discusses examples of these interpretations.

(b) Supreme Court Decisions

(i) Pacific Mutual Life Insurance Co. v. Haslip (1991). In its opinion in *Pacific Mutual Life Insurance Co. v. Haslip,*[3] the Supreme Court for the first time addressed a Fourteenth Amendment due process challenge to an award of punitive damages. The case involved a claim brought by an insured against a life insurance agent for fraud. The plaintiff alleged that the life insurance agent continued to charge the plaintiff for an insurance policy that had long since expired. The Court decided that a punitive damages award that was four times the compensatory award did not violate due process, although it "may be close to the line."[4] The Court noted that, although this amount significantly exceeded a comparable statutory civil fine for the alleged misconduct, a criminal context could have required imprisonment.[5] Although the Court noted its concern about punitive damages awards that "run wild," the Court also felt that well-tailored jury instructions and the state's posttrial procedures for appellate review of punitive damages awards address due process concerns.[6] The Court's opinion in *Pacific Mutual* raised numerous issues that subsequent Supreme Court decisions would pursue, such as the ratio between compensatory damages and punitive damages, comparable civil and criminal penalties for the misconduct at issue, and the degree of reprehensibility of the defendant's conduct.

(ii) TXO Production Corp. v. Alliance Resources Corp. (1993). Two terms later, in *TXO Production Corp. v. Alliance Resources Corp.,*[7] the Supreme Court again faced a Fourteenth Amendment challenge to a punitive damages award. In that case, a joint venturer in an oil and gas development project brought a declaratory judgment action against lessor and lessees of the development rights to resolve a purported title problem. Lessor and lessee counterclaimed, alleging slander of title. The jury awarded the lessor and lessee $19,000 in compensatory damages and $10 million in punitive damages, a ratio of 1 to 526. The Supreme Court ruled that, in light of TXO's extremely reprehensible conduct and the large loss to Alliance, the punitive damages award was not "grossly excessive" notwithstanding the disparity between punitive damages and compensatory damages.[8]

(iii) BMW of North America, Inc. v. Gore (1996). The Supreme Court's decision in *BMW of North America, Inc. v. Gore*[9] first articulated the three guideposts listed in Section 15.2(a). The plaintiff, Dr. Gore, brought an action against BMW, BMW's American distributor, and the car dealership where he bought his BMW. The distributor had failed to disclose that the car had been damaged and then repainted prior to delivery. Dr. Gore alleged that his car had lost 10 percent (approximately $4,000) of its value. He based his claim for punitive damages on the fact that BMW had sold nationwide approximately 1,000 refinished cars as new without disclosing that it had repainted the cars. Dr. Gore requested $4 million in punitive damages (= 1,000 cars × $4,000 damages per car). According to Dr .Gore, this amount would represent an appropriate penalty for knowingly selling 1,000 cars worth less than the sales price. The Alabama lower court awarded Dr. Gore $4,000 in compensatory damages and $4 million in punitive damages. On appeal, the Alabama Supreme Court affirmed the lower court but reduced the punitive

damages award to $2 million. BMW appealed this decision, and the Supreme Court held that the award of $2 million was "grossly excessive."

In deciding that the $2 million punitive damages award was excessive, the Supreme Court considered the three guideposts listed in Section 15.2(a).

1. The first and most important guidepost relates to the degree of reprehensibility of the nondisclosure.[10] The Court noted that the damages should reflect the severity of the offense.[11] Among other things, the fact that economic interest drove BMW's harmful conduct—not an indifference to or reckless disregard for the health or safety of others—rendered it not sufficiently reprehensible to warrant a significant sanction in addition to compensatory damages.[12]

2. The second guidepost considered the relation between the amount of punitive damages and the $4,000 compensatory award.[13] The Court noted that "[t]he principle that exemplary damages must bear a 'reasonable relationship' to compensatory damages has a long pedigree."[14] Even though the Court rejected the establishment of a categorical approach for what it considered an appropriate ratio, it clearly considered the 1 to 500 ratio in *BMW v. Gore* excessive and noted a prior decision that described a 1 to 4 ratio as not "cross[ing] the line into the area of constitutional impropriety."[15] The Court did point out that low awards of compensatory damages can properly support a higher ratio than high compensatory awards.[16]

3. The third and final factor compared the punitive damages award with the civil and criminal penalties that the defendant could receive for comparable misconduct.[17] The Court noted that the maximum civil penalty authorized by the Alabama Legislature for a violation of its Deceptive Trade Practices Act is $2,000. Other states provide sanctions ranging as high as $10,000.[18] The Court concluded that the $2 million punitive damages award exceeded the relatively low sanctions imposed by the state for the alleged wrongful conduct.[19]

Another significant holding comes from *BMW v. Gore*: when awarding punitive damages, the jury can consider only the conduct that occurred within the state where the defendant committed the injury. Dr. Gore had argued that inducing BMW to change its nationwide practices would require a large punitive damages award.[20] The Court, however, disagreed: "Alabama does not have the power to punish BMW for conduct that was lawful where it occurred and that had no impact on Alabama or its residents. Nor may Alabama impose sanctions on BMW in order to deter conduct that is lawful in other jurisdictions."[21] Thus, the calcuation of punitive damages could not reflect the fact that BMW sold repainted cars in other states. This holding recognized that principles of state sovereignty and comity (the principle by which the courts of one jurisdiction accede to the laws or decisions of another) forbid a state to enact policies for the entire nation or to impose its own policy choices on neighboring states.[22]

(iv) State Farm Mutual Automobile Insurance Company v. Campbell (2003).   Seven years after its decision in *BMW v. Gore*, the Supreme Court used its decision in *State Farm Mutual Automobile Insurance Company v. Campbell*[23] to revisist the three guideposts in an opinion that many consider the Court's most extensive explanation of the due process constraints on awards of punitive damages under the U.S. Constitution. In *State Farm*, the Supreme Court gave more precise constitutional guidance to lower courts reviewing punitive damages awards.

In *State Farm,* the plaintiff, Campbell, was involved in a multiple-car accident that killed one driver and permanently disabled another. Campbell faced a wrongful death and tort action for the death and injuries of the other drivers. Campbell asserted his innocence for the accident. His insurer, State Farm, decided to contest liability and declined to settle the case with the two injured plaintiffs for the policy limit of $50,000. Instead, State Farm decided to try the case against the injured parties and assured Campbell that State Farm would assume his defense. The jury found Campbell liable and awarded the plaintiffs $185,849. State Farm paid the policy limit of $50,000 but refused to cover the remaining $135,849 and refused to pay for an appeal. Campbell appealed the jury verdict with his own counsel. During the appeal's pendency, Campbell and the two injured parties agreed that the injured parties would not seek the remaining $135,849 from Campbell if Campbell agreed to pursue a bad faith action against State Farm and if Campbell agreed to give the two injured parties 90 percent of any recovery he received in that action. The court denied the appeal, at which time State Farm paid $135,849.

Campbell nevertheless pursued his action against State Farm, claiming bad faith, failure to settle within the policy limits, fraud, and intentional infliction of emotional distress. During the punitive damages phase of the bad faith trial, Campbell argued that State Farm's decision to take his automobile accident case to trial was part of a national scheme to meet corporate fiscal goals by capping companywide payouts on claims. The trial court permitted the plaintiff to introduce evidence of State Farm's nationwide business practices over twenty years. The jury awarded the plaintiff $2.6 million in compensatory damages and $145 million in punitive damages. The trial court judge reduced these awards to $1 million and $25 million, respectively. On appeal, the Utah Supreme Court, after applying the factors established in *BMW v. Gore,* reinstated the $145 million punitive damages award. The U.S. Supreme Court ruled that the $145 million punitive damages award was excessive and violated due process.

In its opinion, the Supreme Court first addressed the reprehensibility guidepost established in *Gore* and found that the Utah Supreme Court failed to focus on the reprehensibility of State Farm's treatment of the Campbells but instead punished the perceived deficiencies of State Farm's national operation.[24] The Court explained that "a defendant's dissimilar acts, independent from the acts upon which liability was premised, may not serve as a basis for punitive damages. A defendant should be punished for the conduct that harmed the plaintiff, not for being an unsavory individual or business."[25] The Court's analysis thus served to restrict lower courts' ability to use the reprehensibility guidepost to expand the scope of a case so as to expose a defendant to punitive damages for any malfeasance.

The Court also reaffirmed its holding in *Gore* that a court cannot use a punitive damages award to punish a defendant for lawful out-of-state conduct unrelated to the specific alleged bad conduct at issue.[26] The Court, however, acknowledged that "[l]awful out-of-state conduct may be probative when it demonstrates the deliberateness and culpability of the defendant's action in the State where it is tortious, but that conduct must have a nexus to the specific harm suffered by the plaintiff."[27] The Court expanded on this principle, writing that a state does not have a legitimate concern in imposing punitive damages to punish a defendant for *unlawful* acts committed outside the state's jurisdiction.[28] *State Farm* thus makes clear that, when assessing punitive damages, a court cannot consider a defendant's out-of-state conduct—whether lawful or unlawful—that bears no nexus to the alleged wrongful in-state conduct.

Finally, the Court outlined five specific factors to consider when performing the reprehensibility analysis, all of which came from the holding in *Gore*:

1. The action caused physical harm as opposed to economic.
2. The tortious conduct evidenced an indifference to or a reckless disregard of the health or safety of others.
3. The target of the conduct had financial vulnerability.
4. The conduct involved repeated actions rather than an isolated incident.
5. The harm resulted from intentional malice, trickery or deceit, or mere accident.[29]

The Court noted that the existence of any one of these factors in the plaintiff's favor might not prove adequate to justify a punitive damages award and the absence of all of them renders an award suspect.[30]

In *State Farm*, the Court also addressed the second *Gore* guidepost: the ratio between the harm or potential harm to the plaintiff and the punitive damages award. The Court first reiterated its reluctance to articulate a hard-and-fast limit on this ratio, but it used far more specificity than the *Gore* decision had employed in fashioning a standard.[31] The Court stated that "few awards exceeding a single-digit ratio between punitive and compensatory damages, to a significant degree, will satisfy due process."[32] The Court also reaffirmed its holding in Gore that where "a particularly egregious act has resulted in only a small amount of economic damages" a higher ratio can meet the due process requirement.[33] It also noted the converse as true: with high compensatory damages, a lower ratio, such as 1 to 1, can reach the outer limits of the due process guarantee.[34] Applying these considerations to the facts of *State Farm*, the Court found the 145 to 1 ratio excessive and noted that the compensatory award of $1 million was itself high and that compensatory awards themselves contain a punitive element.[35]

In its discussion of the second guidepost, the Court also addressed the issue of the defendant's wealth as a justification for a large punitive damages award. The Court, citing a statement from *Gore*, held that "[t]he wealth of a defendant cannot justify an otherwise unconstitutional award."[36] Although this statement does not foreclose a court's ability to consider wealth, it does raise questions about the appropriateness of wealth in calculating punitive damages.

The *State Farm* decision gave little insight into the third and final guidepost (the disparity between the punitive damages award and the statutory penalties authorized or imposed for comparable acts by defendant), perhaps because applying this guidepost to the facts of the *State Farm* decision produced a very clear result. The Court noted that the relevant sanction under the Utah law was a $10,000 fine for an act of fraud, an amount "dwarfed" by the $145 million punitive award. Nevertheless, the Court did consider certain additional principles. The Court noted that juries should look to criminal penalties that could be imposed if the case were tried in criminal court; this bears on the seriousness with which a state views the wrongful conduct.[37] However, the Court also noted the limited relevance of criminal sanctions to punitive damages because criminal prosecution has additional due process protections such as a higher burden of proof.

The Court also cautioned that punitive damages do not present a substitute for the criminal process.

In conclusion, the Court in *State Farm* held that, based on the *Gore* guideposts and the high compensatory award, an award of punitive damages equal to or near the compensatory award was justified and characterized the award of $145 million as "an irrational and arbitrary deprivation of the property of the defendant."[38] Many observers consider *State Farm's* articulation of the single-digit ratio standard as the most significant development in the law of punitive damages.

(c) Post-*State Farm* Punitive Damages Decisions.   State and U.S. District Courts have generally abided by the guidelines that the U.S. Supreme Court laid out in *State Farm* and *BMW v. Gore* to protect due process, and we see no evidence of any systematic or statewide efforts to circumscribe these due process guidelines. However, individual judges have issued opinions that have interpreted these cases to loosen the due process limits on punitive damages in ways that neither *State Farm* nor *Gore* authorized. State courts that have wanted to award large punitive damages have tried to recharacterize what qualifies as compensatory damages for the purpose of the single-digit ratio cap. The larger the portion of total damages characterized as compensatory, the larger the punitive damages can be without exceeding a 9 to 1 ratio—thereby avoiding a red flag regarding the award's constitutionality.

(i) Williams v. Philip Morris (2003).   For example, in *Williams v. Philip Morris*,[39] the plaintiff was the estate of a man who died of smoking-related lung cancer. The estate sued Philip Morris for its fraudulent attempt to create a scientific controversy about the health hazards of smoking cigarettes. Prior to the *State Farm* decision, the Oregon state courts had assessed compensatory damages of approximately $500,000 and punitive damages of approximately $79.5 million, a ratio of approximately 160 to 1. The Supreme Court vacated and remanded this award for reconsideration in light of *State Farm*. On remand, the Oregon appellate court supported the reinstitution of its previous award of $79.5 million in punitive damages based in part on its assumption (supported by the evidence) that the defendant had injured at least 100 other Oregonians in the same way as it had injured the plaintiff; the court then noted that if it considered these hundred plaintiffs' compensatory damages, the ratio, reduced by 100-fold, would lie within the single-digit multiplier and even within the more typical 4 to 1 standard outer bound of constitutionality.[40]

(ii) In re Exxon Valdez (2004).   In a litigation consolidating thousands of oil spill claims following the notorious Exxon Valdez disaster,[41] the district court had concluded that the actual harm done to plaintiffs was $513 million in compensatory damages, and the jury awarded plaintiffs $5 billion in punitive damages. Following the *State Farm* decision, the Ninth Circuit vacated the punitive damages verdict and remanded the litigation to the District Court of Alaska for further consideration in light of *State Farm*. The district court, following intensive review of the unique facts surrounding the Exxon Valdez, found the $5 billion dollars in punitive damages justified by the facts and not so excessive as to deprive Exxon of due process. However, because the circuit court had instructed the district court to reduce the amount of the punitive damages award, and in light of the single-digit

multipliers promoted in State Farm, the district court reduced the punitive damages award to $4.5 billion dollars, for slightly less than a 9 to 1 ratio of punitive to compensatory damages.[42]

(iii) Romo v. Ford Motor Company (2003).   The plaintiffs were the survivors in a family, three of whom had died when their car, a 1978 Ford Bronco, rolled over in a car accident.[43] In a trial prior to the *State Farm* decision, the jury awarded the plaintiffs nearly $5 million in compensatory damages and $290 million in punitive damages, based on a broad view regarding what of the defendant's conduct merited punishment.[44] On appeal, the U.S. Supreme Court vacated the $290 million punitive award and remanded the case for further consideration in light of its then new decision in *State Farm*. On remand, the California appellate court interpreted *State Farm* as permitting it to consider only the defendant's conduct that had resulted in outrage and humiliation to the plaintiffs.[45] In determining the appropriate amount of punishment based on this conduct, *Romo* further interpreted *State Farm* to promote use of the historically common low single-digit damages multipliers. The court found that the defendant's conduct had been extremely reprehensible, because its "reckless disregard of consumers' safety and lives ... caused a high degree of physical harm" to victims who "were financially vulnerable relative to defendant's financial resources."[46] As a result, the court on remand awarded punitive damages of $23.7 million, consisting of two parts: $13.7 million, which equalled three times the amount of compensatory damages, and $10 million ($5 million for each deceased parent, based on the public policy of deterring malicious conduct resulting in death).[47]

(iv) Johnson v. Ford Motor Company (2005).   A subsequent decision by the California Supreme Court, in the unrelated case of *Johnson v. Ford Motor Company*,[48] took a broader view as to which of a defendant's actions a court could consider when assessing punitive damages. *Johnson* indicated that the court could consider a defendant's entire wrongful course of conduct rather than considering in isolation those actions that harmed the plaintiff.

(v) Mathias v. Accor Economy Lodging (2003).[49]   Bedbugs bit the plaintiffs while the plaintiffs stayed at the defendant's hotel. Prior to the plaintiff's stay at the hotel, the defendant had admitted to a "major problem with bed bugs" to its exterminator but declined to pay the cost of spraying the rooms and instead directed its employees to lie about the bugs to minimize guests' alarm. The Seventh Circuit, in an opinion written by Judge Richard Posner, affirmed the jury's award of $5,000 in compensatory and $186,000 in punitive damages.[50] The court recognized that the 37.2 to 1 ratio of punitive to compensatory damages appeared high in the wake of *State Farm*.[51] However, the court justified this ratio by noting that punitive ratios can increase with a low chance of litigation or a potentially lucrative harmful act and that the case fit both categories: "If a tortfeasor is 'caught' only half the time he commits torts, then when he is caught he should be punished twice as heavily in order to make up for the times he gets away."[52] The plaintiffs incurred small economic damages; their damages were harms to dignity and thus hard to quantify. Thus, if the award reflected only compensatory damages or a small multiple thereof, potential plaintiffs would have only a slight incentive to sue, thereby allowing the defendant to pay off any suits without giving it sufficient incentive to

fix its behavior. The court in *Mathias* also noted that situations require higher punitive damages when the defendant aggressively defends minor litigation to "invest ... in developing a reputation intended to deter plaintiffs."[53] Even though the precise number of $186,000 in punitive damages appears arbitrary, the Seventh Circuit did not find it excessive and noted that a certain amount of arbitrariness was inevitable, because "[t]he judicial function is to police a range, not a point."[54]

(d) Differences among State Laws. In addition to the guidelines established in *State Farm* and *Gore*, states have their own body of statutory and case law concerning punitive damages. This section summarizes the variations among states on several issues concerning punitive damages. This summary does not present a 50-state survey of the law on punitive damages but rather discusses some highlights. No substitute exists for a close examination of the specific law of the state when the reader has an engagement related to a punitive damages matter.

(i) Bans on Punitive Damages. A handful of states do not have any punitive damages or allow punitive damages only in narrow, specified circumstances. These states include New Hampshire and Louisiana (by statute) as well as Massachusetts, Nebraska, and Washington (by common law).

(ii) Burden of Proof. Over twenty states require plaintiffs to meet a higher burden of proof to win punitive damages than to win a finding of regular liability. Most of these set this burden at clear and convincing evidence. To receive punitive damages under Colorado law, a plaintiff must prove that such damages are due beyond a reasonable doubt. Over half of all states require plaintiffs to show that the defendant's *mens rea* (i.e., culpable mental state) was especially intentful or criminal to receive punitive damages. Even though these states do not apply one consistent, uniform mental standard, the two most common elevated standards require either "willful and wanton" action by the defendant to injure the plaintiff, or some action by the defendant that showed its "deliberate disregard" of injury likely to affect the plaintiff. Some states, such as Montana, apply higher standards, which require the plaintiff to show "actual malice or actual fraud" to receive punitive damages. Other states have lower scienter requirements than willful and wanton conduct or deliberate disregard; several states allow punitive damages upon a showing of reckless disregard, and at least one state (Florida) allows punitive damages with a showing of gross negligence.

(iii) Limits on Punitive Damages. At least twenty states have statutory caps on punitive damages. Such caps often limit punitive damages to the greater of either a fixed sum in the low-to-middle six figures or a low multiple of the compensatory damages. (For example, Idaho law limits punitive damages in a given trial to the greater of either $250,000 or three times the amount of the plaintiff's compensatory damages). The exact values of both the multiple and the alternative fixed-sum cap vary by state. Several states that have caps on punitive damages remove those caps in certain statutorily prescribed circumstances (for example, Nevada's statutory caps on punitive damages do not apply to claims of product liability). Other states either raise their caps on punitive damages (or do not apply them at all) when plaintiffs show that a defendant fits certain heightened intent requirements. In Texas, if plaintiffs show that the defendant's conscious indifference toward the

rights of others caused their damages, plaintiffs receive punitive damages not exceeding Texas's standard cap—the greater of $200,000 or two times the plaintiff's economic damages plus the plaintiff's noneconomic damages (e.g., pain and suffering or loss of consortium) up to $750,000; however, if plaintiffs can prove that the defendant's tortious actions were a knowing or intentional felony, no limit exists on the amount of punitive damages. A few states tie their statutory caps on punitive damages to the defendant's wealth (e.g., Kansas's default cap on punitive damages is the lesser of $5 million or the defendant's adjusted gross income). Virginia has the strictest cap on punitive damages: a flat maximum of $350,000.

(iv) Bifurcation.   At least 15 states either require or permit the court to separate a trial into multiple parts when punitive damages become an issue. Some states separate the punitive damages portion of the trial in its entirety; other states assess general liability and liability for punitive damages at the same time but separate out a portion of the trial concerning the precise amount of punitive damages. Segregating some or all of the punitive portion of the trial ensures that the jury deciding only punitive damages will hear evidence that could prove prejudicial (such as the defendant's financial status or prior similar actions by the defendant) when presented to the jury deciding the defendant's liability for compensatory damages.

(v) Pleading Limitations.   A few states do not allow plaintiffs to seek punitive damages without some preliminary showing of evidence supporting punitive damages, or perhaps even a showing that a claim for punitive damages will likely succeed. In Illinois, for example, a plaintiff who seeks punitive damages cannot ask for them in the original complaint but must instead make a subsequent motion for a hearing at which the plaintiff must show a reasonable chance of success at trial.

(vi) Split Awards.   Traditionally, punitive damages assessed against a defendant have gone to the plaintiffs who sued for them. Now, however, approximately ten states direct only a portion of these damages to the plaintiff, most frequently giving the remainder to the state itself or to one of its agencies. For example, in Missouri, after attorneys' fees and expenses are deducted, half of the punitive damages goes to the plaintiff, and the other half goes to Missouri's Tort Victims Compensation Fund, designed to assist plaintiffs whose defendants might be judgment proof (i.e., lacking funds to pay an award, or protected by a corporate veil, or otherwise beyond the court's jurisdiction).[55] In theory, award splitting lowers overall punitive damages by reducing the plaintiffs' incentive to aggressively litigate for those damages. It also raises serious potential conflict-of-interest questions.[56] A state with budget woes can reduce or even solve this problem over the short term by assessing large punitive damages against out-of-state corporate defendants with deep pockets. In at least one instance (California), the statute that authorized award splitting acknowledged that its main purpose was not a better justice system but a better bottom line for the state government.[57] To the extent that punitive damages are predictable in a state that splits punitive awards, the statute authorizing split awards may give the parties a strong incentive to settle the case for an amount between what the plaintiff would receive from a split award and the whole punitive damages award that the defendant would pay.

(vii) Other Variations. The categories of statutory limits on punitive damages that we have described represent only the most common and widely applicable limits. Many individual states have wrinkles in these limitations, or other niche limitations that apply in a specific case.

15.3 THE EXPERT'S ROLE

Although financial experts generally do not opine on the issue of a defendant's liability for punitive damages, an accountant or economist or other expert can provide objective information valuable to a trier of fact in determining the amount of punitive damages to award once the plaintiff establishes liability. Whether testifying for the plaintiff or the defendant, the financial expert can define the defendant's financial status, describe its gains from the alleged unlawful conduct, educate the jury in the world of a financial statement analysis, and describe how corporate entities work. The economist can explain the theory of deterrence and the optimal size of punitive awards in future deterrence.

Historically, juries or other triers of fact have received little guidance about how to set an appropriate punitive award. The plaintiff usually will brandish corporate financial statements and focus on data (e.g., gross sales or total assets) that imply a wealthy defendant with substantial cash available. The defendant argues about the conduct, the company's debts, its small net worth, or its limited cash position. Neither approach provides guideposts that are useful to the trier of fact.

A financial expert should present information that will help a trier of fact show the defendant's financial position, the effects of possible punitive awards, and other information deemed relevant to the choice of an appropriate award to help a jury. The *State Farm* decision further clarified that the amount of punitive damages levied should bear some reasonable relation to the harm caused as estimated by the compensatory damages. Thus, the expert should address the reasonableness of the award in light of the alleged harm as well.

(a) Identification of the Party to be Punished: Corporate Identity. Before deliberations can begin on a reasonable award, the testimony should identify the party that merits punishment or deterrence. If the defendant is a corporation, does the entire corporation—or only a division or other segment of the firm—have responsibility for the conduct? This issue becomes critical when an expert evaluates the effect of a punitive award on the corporation. One must also differentiate the products and services produced by a corporation that do not relate to the lawsuit in question. The calculation of compensatory damages does not depend on the defendant's economic status, but such status has primary importance when setting punitive damages. The fact finder cannot evaluate an award's reasonableness without knowing the financial circumstances of the entity.

Corporations are amalgams of businesses, products, services, and functions, often operating through largely autonomous divisions. Each division may have its own financial statements, management organization, and business culture. Understanding the organizational structure, geography, customer base, and how the business units make decisions will help the fact finder focus on the conduct at issue. Disaggregating corporations into their components will help a jury understand that these complex organizations comprise people performing a variety of tasks at all organizational levels.

For example, suppose the ABC Lighting Company has a small division that manufactures and sells neon lamps. After years of successful operations, it becomes apparent that these particular lamps turn people's hair blue. The other operations of ABC deal only in fixtures and incandescent lamps, which have no adverse health effects. The neon division has its own general manager and management team, and their compensation depends partially on the neon division's operations and results. One might argue that the measure of punitive damages necessary to punish and deter ABC should relate only to the neon division's operations. A punitive award that proves sizable in relation to this division will affect the careers and financial rewards of the responsible people even though the award is not material in relation to ABC as a whole. The effect on other managers both within ABC and at other organizations could prove substantial when they see what has happened to the neon division. The financial expert can explain the realities of large organizations from a financial and organizational point of view.

One could expect the plaintiff's expert to make the opposite argument: a punitive damages award must have a significant effect on the firm as a whole to punish or deter effectively. Unless the award is large in relation to the entire firm, central management will have no incentive to closely monitor the division's future activities. Additionally, the misbegotten profits benefited the entire company, even if they registered directly on the income statement of only one division.[*]

In some situations, by the time the punitive issue comes before a judge or jury, people associated with the wrongful conduct might no longer work with the neon division, or even with ABC Lighting. This fact alone may not prove sufficient to absolve ABC of any exposure to punitive damages, but the jury should know it. On the one hand, a punitive award today may harm other people at ABC even though they had nothing to do with the conduct and may be part of its clean-up and solution. On the other hand, since public policy intends that punitive damages deter future harm, a complete amnesty will likely fail to achieve a societal goal. But the jury should know whom it is punishing and the likely effect of the punishment. One could also educate the jury as to who the company's stakeholders are. Union pension plans, mutual funds, small shareholders, and others will likely own large, publicly held U.S. corporations; a jury should understand whom the punitive damages will punish.

(b) Relevant Financial Information.   The plaintiff and defendant will argue over which financial information has relevance, given the circumstances. In some states, the plaintiff can discover and admit into evidence a defendant's net worth for the limited purpose of assessing punitive damages. The relevance of net worth comes into question frequently when determining an award. Financial statements measure net worth as the total assets minus total liabilities—in other words, the shareholders' equity and accumulation of profits over time of a company as presented in its financial statements. Depending on the industry, accounting principles may require that a financial statement reflect most assets and equity accounts at their original book value rather than their current fair market value.

---

[*]*Editors' Note:* We find that lay people often commit errors by focusing on percentages rather than on dollar amounts. We think this is another example. Middle-level and top managers likely will notice a fine in proportion to its dollar amount, not its percentage of overall corporate wealth.

Fair market values of assets, liabilities, and equity can vary significantly from those recorded in the fiancial statements. Some practitioners argue that fair evaluation of a defendant's net worth is its current market capitalization—in other words, the total outstanding shares multiplied by the market share price. Others argue that the market value of net worth does not offer a relevant measure because it does not represent resources currently available to the company.

The net worth review should also evaluate the defendant's capital structure, which can be complex. Capital restructurings, such as debt for equity swaps, enter into the calculation of the defendant's net worth. The judge or jury should perhaps consider such restructurings.

The reference to net worth in valuing punitive damages awards appears to have two purposes. First, one could argue that net worth data measure a defendant's ability to absorb and survive an adverse award. However, such data do not help in analyzing the defendant's ability to raise cash. Second, net worth can help in calculating an amount that the defendant will find significant. Thus, large corporate defendants face risk simply because of their size. For example, one could argue that a company with $1 billion in net worth would not suffer any consequences of a $1,000 judgment. Such a relatively small judgment would not prove punitive enough to satisfy the goal of discouraging similar actions in the future. Conversely, one could argue that a punishment equaling significantly less than some percentage of net worth or corporate-wide profits would prove consequential in relation to the resources of the identified perpetrator, whether it be a product-line division, a management unit, or an individual.

Ascertaining the defendant's ability to absorb the cost of the payment and whether a defendant will suffer any punitive effect of the award requires more than examining the defendant's adjusted net worth. One should also look at the form that the assets take. Can the firm easily convert the assets to cash? Does their conversion to cash cause additional hardships that compound the award's punitive effect? For example, assume that the assets of a company with a net worth of $1 billion consist of factories, warehouses, and other fixed assets. The company might have limited cash resources such that the punitive award would force liquidation of fixed assets important to the company's ongoing operations, causing labor force displacement and increased hardship.

In addition to evaluating the venture profits and the relevant entity's net worth, the ability of an entity or individual to generate cash flows has relevance in the punitive damages analysis. An entity's ability to pay relates to the amount of time required for the entity to generate cash. The longer it takes for the defendant to earn the punitive damages assessed, the greater the deterrent effect.

When evaluating an entity's ability to generate cash, one should focus on the future ability, not the past. Many industries face rapid changes resulting from competition or demand for their products or services. As a result of past success, some companies have generated a large net worth, but because of these changes, they now earn little. Startup companies incur large development expenses or require significant capital infusions to get started and have a large negative net worth, but currently or in the future they have the ability to earn substantial profits. If the decision maker ignores cash flow and focuses on the entity's net worth, the punitive damages award can overdeter some companies and underdeter others.

Various measures of earnings ability—including operating profit, profit before tax, net income, cash flow from operations, cash flow before tax, and net cash flow—can shed light on an entity's ability to pay and to absorb costs. Other financial information that juries should consider includes the defendant's borrowing capability, working capital, and the amount of dividends or payments to owners over the recent past.

When reviewing net worth, the expert should avoid using information that would prejudice a theoretically impartial decision maker who should evaluate punitive awards as punitive awards, not supplements to a plaintiff's compensatory damages. Reviewing net worth can cause the focus to move from deciding punitive awards based on the egregious action to recommending punitive awards simply because a harmed plaintiff exists and a defendant has the funds to pay. In other words, rather than looking at the action's maliciousness and the need for deterrence, the decision maker looks at a harmed victim and the defendant's deep pockets.

(c) Product or Venture Profitability.   Most analysts use profitability to measure the success of a company's products or ventures. Profitability relies on some level of customer satisfaction and thus should assume a level of product safety. One could consider removal or disgorgement of the profitability or benefit gained from wrongful conduct as an element of punishment. The profits gained (or in some cases profits expected to be received, as identified by projections, forecasts, or business plans) by the defendant from the malicious action will, in part, affect punitive damages. Thus, one can consider the profits eliminated by compensatory damages as containing an element of punishment.

Examination of the profit the defendant made, or expected to make, can frame the amount of damages that would have caused a reasonably prudent defendant not to have taken the egregious action in the first place. For example, assume that ABC Lighting Company's neon lamp, which caused blue hair, netted them a profit of $1 million. The fact finder's decision forced ABC to incur costs for removing the product from the market and workplace and for compensatory damages resulting from personal injury claims to make whole those people who will live the rest of their lives with blue hair. If the amount the company spent to resolve the compensatory and economic damages claims does not exceed the profit earned selling the product, one might argue that ABC incurs little or no implicit punitive damages. When the compensatory and out-of-pocket amounts exceed the profit earned, one could argue that the total damages the defendant paid already include an element of punishment. With hindsight, any reasonably prudent defendant would not make the same investment again. If the amount the company spent to resolve the costs and compensatory and economic damages do not exceed the profit earned selling the product, one might argue that the fact finder must award punitive damages at least in the amount needed to eliminate the profit in excess of the compensatory damages.

A financial expert can provide the jury with an independent assessment of the financial results of the wrongful act. The expert can base this analysis on both historical product-line economic detail, product-specific business plans, financial projections based on market factors, and other indications of likely profitability.

When evaluating product or venture profitability, the plaintiff often focuses on the gross or net sales. Plaintiffs sometimes argue that because ABC Lighting Company has annual sales of $1.5 billion, it will require a punitive award of hundreds of millions of dollars to get the company's attention. Accountants and business people reject such analyses as absurd. Recent court decisions seem to reject this as well by focusing on a reasonable multiple of punitive damages to compensatory damages—the maximum ratio of 9 to 1, set forth in *State Farm* and discussed in Section 15.2(b)(iv). However, the defendant who assumes that the jury shares the financial expert's understanding of this absurdity treads on thin ice. The accountant appearing in the defendant's case must teach the jury through a minicourse in accounting for nonaccountants. Using simple examples, analogies, and demonstrative charts and exhibits, the financial expert can illustrate that revenue does not equate to cash or profits. More elaborate explanations might deal with cash flow and projected financial results, depending on the facts at hand.

(d) Degree of Harm Caused to the Plaintiff.   As outlined in *BMW v. Gore*, the extent of the actual harm sustained by the plaintiff and the potential harm the plaintiff was exposed to as a result of the defendant's conduct have relevance for the punitive damages calculation, especially when one is considering the ratio of the punitive damages award to the compensatory damages. The decision maker must consider the claim and its deterrent effect.

An expert testifying about the plaintiff's profits lost because of the defendant's wrongdoing calculates the harm that the plaintiff sustained in a business tort or other commercial case. To identify an appropriate ratio of punitive damages to compensatory damages, the trier of fact could also consider the potential harm threatened by the defendant's conduct. The expert, therefore, sometimes will also testify to the amount of profits that the plaintiff *could have lost* if the defendant had carried its wrongdoing to completion.[58]

(e) Awards for Large Classes and Multiple Awards for the Same Act.   In mass tort actions and other cases in which the defendant faces multiple lawsuits from a single incident, the act in question may have affected more than one plaintiff. We think, but not all commentators agree, that the fact finder should evaluate the expected effect from other, related cases. In these cases, the fact finder might consider the entire compensatory, economic, and punitive amounts paid to the class when evaluating the punitive amount for any individual.

Assume that ABC Lighting's blue hair reaction does not always manifest immediately. Perhaps our defendant has resolved 100 claims for an average of $10,000 each. ABC Lighting Company may still expect to pay an additional 200 claims in the future as more potential claimants' hair turns blue. An expert might present to the jury the estimated future cost of satisfying these claims and the extent to which these claims eliminate profitability.

In many cases in which the plaintiff seeks punitive damages, the defendant may already have incurred costs associated with correcting the alleged wrongful conduct, and the jury should include these costs in evaluating the overall deterrent effect. Some examples of a corporation's efforts to correct any wrongful conduct include recalls, owner notification programs, and technical service bulletins. The costs associated with these efforts include, but are not limited to, program administrative costs, parts costs, and labor costs. The testifying expert must explain the proper method of accounting for these costs to the jury and will find financial statement disclosures useful in this regard.

The plaintiff's expert can argue that the defendant will understate any such accounting estimates to avoid alarming investors looking at the company's financial performance and will point out that accounting guidelines require that when the estimated loss is a range, the firm should book the lower end of that range. The plaintiff's expert will suggest that these estimates represent the minimum punitive damages that the jury should consider, effectively establishing a floor for the calculation.

(f) Comparable Statutory Penalties.   The decision in *BMW v. Gore* allows the expert to use other comparable statutory penalties (civil or criminal) as a guidepost for assessing punitive damages. One should use this assessment as a benchmark relative to the existing facts and circumstances. In most cases, a punitive damages award will vastly exceed comparable civil or criminal penalties. Defense experts, with the assistance of counsel, should become familiar with civil or criminal penalties so as to contrast them with the plaintiff's proposed punitive damages award.

(g) Insurance.   The plaintiff's expert will want to present the amounts of the costs and compensatory damages covered by insurance as relevant to establishing an appropriate amount of punitive damages, particularly if the defendant expects to present an argument relating to the burden that the defendant already suffered. Defendants typically do not present insurance information, and their financial expert needs to discuss such a disclosure with the client. Juries will find a picture of extensive cost burdens misleading, however, if insurance policies cover the bulk of the burden. For example, if ABC has insurance to cover all the costs and compensatory damages resulting from the claims, then the profit made on the product still equals $1 million.

We have discussed areas and issues in accountants' testimony relating to financial information that they present to a jury evaluating punitive damages. Because the law has defined few specific guidelines, accountants can bring a broad spectrum of training, expertise, and creativity to the engagement.

(h) Tax Treatment of Punitive Damages.   As Chapter 16 (Tax Treatment of Damages Awards) discusses, defendants can deduct punitive damages associated with the defendant's breach of contract, fraud, mismanagement, or other improper actions, assuming the damages have an origin in the taxpayer's trade or business.

NOTES

1. Also referred to as *exemplary* or *vindictive* damages.
2. *BMW of North America, Inc. v. Gore*, 517 U.S. 559 (1996), at 574-575.
3. *Pacific Mutual Life Insurance Co. v. Haslip*, 499 U.S. 1 (1991).
4. *Id.*, at 23.
5. *Id.*
6. *Id.*, at 18 and 19-21.
7. *TXO Production Corp. v. Alliance Resources Corp.*, 509 U.S. 443 (1993).
8. *Id.*, at 462.
9. *BMW of North America, Inc. v. Gore*, 517 U.S. 559 (1996).
10. *Id.*, at 575.

11. *Id.*

12. *Id.*, at 576.

13. *Id.*, at 580.

14. *Id.*

15. *Id.*, at 581.

16. *Id.*, at 582.

17. *Id.*, at 583.

18. *Id.*, at 584.

19. *Id.*

20. *Id.*, at 572.

21. *Id.*, at 573-574.

22. *Id.*, at 572.

23. *State Farm Mutual Automobile Insurance Company v. Campbell*, 538 U.S. 408 (2003).

24. *Id.*, at 422-423.

25. *Id.*

26. *Id.*, at 421.

27. *Id.*, at 422.

28. *Id.*, at 421.

29. *Id.*, at 419.

30. *Id.*

31. *Id.*, at 424.

32. *Id.*, at 425.

33. *Id.*

34. *Id.*

35. *Id.*, at 426.

36. *Id.*, at 427.

37. *Id.*, at 428.

38. *Id.*, at 429.

39. *Williams v. Philip Morris*, 193 Ore. App. 527 (Ore. App. 2003).

40. *Id.*, at 562.

41. *In re Exxon Valdez*, 296 F. Supp. 2d 1071(D. Alaska 2004).

42. *Id.*, at 1110.

43. *Romo v. Ford Motor Company*, 113 Cal. App. 4th 738 (Cal. App. 5th Dist. 2003).

44. By "broad view," the Court in *Romo* meant a view in which the courts undertake to deter a practice systematically by depriving the wrongdoer of profit from its general course of conduct. In *Romo*, for example, this might involve stripping the defendant of at least some of its profits from the entire line of vehicles that shared a defect with the car used by the plaintiffs. This broad view is in contrast to a narrower goal of punishing the defendant based primarily on what the defendant had done to the present plaintiff and not based on the defendant's general incorrigibility or wealth. *Id.*, at 748-749.

45. *Id.*, at 749-750.

46. *Id.*, at 755.

47. *Id.*, at 763.

48. *Johnson v. Ford Motor Company*, 35 Cal. 4th 1191 (2005).

49. *Mathias v. Accor Economy Lodging* 347 F.3d 672 (7th Cir. 2003).

50. *Id.*, at 678.

51. *Id.*, at 675-676.

52. *Id.*, at 677.

53. *Id.*

54. *Id.*, at 678.

55. *See* Mo. Ann. Stat. 537.673.3.

56. *See*, e.g., Victor E. Schwartz, Mark A. Behrens, and Cary Silverman, "I'll Take That: Legal and Public Policy Problems Raised by Statutes That Require Punitive Damages Awards To Be Shared with the State:" 68 Missouri. L. Rev. 525 (2003).

57. *See* Cal Civ. Code §3294.5.

58. *See BMV v. Gore.*

LIST OF CASES

Adams v. Murakami, 54 Cal. 3d 105, 110 (1991)

Barton v. Alexander Hamilton Life Ins. Co. of America, 110 Cal. App. 4th 1640, 1644 (2003)

Beliz v. W.H. McLeod & Sons Packing Co. 765 F.2d 1317, 1332 (5th Cir. 1985)

BMW of N. America, Inc. v. Gore, 517 U.S. 559, 575-76 (1996)

Boerner v. Brown & Williamson Tobacco Co., 394 F.3d 594 (8th Cir. 2004)

Brewer v. Second Baptist Church, 32 Cal. 2d 791, 800 (1948)

Brown v. Farkas 511 N.E. 2d 1143, 1148 (Ill. App. Ct. 1986)

Browning-Ferris Indus. Inc. v. Kelco Disposal Inc., 492 U.S. 257, 282 (1989)

Buzzard v. Farmers Ins. Co. 824 P.2d 1105, 1116 (Okla. 1991)

Chandler v. Denton 741 P.2d 855, 868 (Okla. 1987)

Chavez v. Keat, 34 Cal. App. 4th 1406, 1415 (Cal. Ct. App. 1995)

College Hospital, Inc. v. Superior Court, 882 P.2d 894, 908, 8 Cal. 4th 704, 712 (Cal. 1994)

Cooper Indus., Inc. v. Leatherman Tool Group, Inc., 121 S. Ct. 1678, 1685 (2001)

Dynamed, Inc. v. Fair Employment & Housing Comm., 43 Cal.3d 1379, 1387 (1987)

Dzinglski v. Weirton Steel Corp. 191 W.Va. 278, 281, 445 S.E.2d 219, 222, 226 (1994)

In re Exxon Valdez, 270 F.3d 1215, 1244 (9th Cir. 2001)

In re Exxon Valdez, 296 F. Supp. 2d 1071 (D. Alaska 2004)

Ferguson v. Lieff, Cabraser, Heimann & Bernstein, 30 Cal. 4th 1037, 1051 (Cal. 2003)

Honda Motor Co. v. Oberg, 512 U.S. 415, 432 (1994)

Johnson v. Ford Motor Company, 35 Cal. 4th 1191 (2005)

Lakin v. Watkins Associated Industries, 6 Cal. 4th 644, 664 (1993)

Lane v. Hughes Aircraft Co., 993 P.2d 388, 400-01 (Cal. 2000)

Maiorino v. Schering-Plough Corp. 302 N.J. Super. 323, 356-358, 695 A.2d 353, 370 (1997)

Mathias v. Accor Economy Lodging, 347 F.3d 672 (7th Cir. 2003)

Memphis Community School Dist. v. Stachura, 477 U.S. 299, 307 (1986)

Mirkin v. Williamson, 5 Cal. 4th 1082, 1106 (1993)

Neal v. Farmers Ins. Exch., 12 Cal. 3d 910, 928 (1978)

New York Cent. R. Co. v. Johnson, 279 U.S. 310, 319 (1929)

Nortica v. State Comp. Ins. Fund, 70 Cal. App. 4th 911, 953 (Cal. App. 2d Dist. 1999)

Pacific Mut. Life Ins. Co. v. Haslip, 449 U.S. 1, 21 (1991)

Protectus Alpha Navigation Co. v. North Pac. Grain Growers, Inc., 767 F.2d 1379, 1385 (9th Cir. 1985)

Romo v. Ford Motor Co., 6 Cal. Rptr. 3d 793, 805 (Cal. App. 2003)

Romo v. Ford Motor Company, 113 Cal. App. 4th 738 (Cal. App. 5th Dist. 2003)

Rosado v. Santiago 562 F.2d 114, 121 (1st Cir. 1977)

Rowlett v. Anheuser-Busch, Inc., 832 F.2d 194, 206 (1st Cir. 1987)

Smith v. Wade, 461 U.S. 30, 52 (1983)

State Farm Mut. Automobile Ins. Co. v. Campbell, 538 U.S. 408, 419 (2003)

CHAPTER 16

TAX TREATMENT OF DAMAGES AWARDS

Merle Erickson
James K. Smith

CONTENTS

16.1   INTRODUCTION

Attorneys need to contemplate the tax implications of damage awards for both the plaintiff and defendant from the beginning of the dispute process. For the plaintiff, a properly worded complaint or settlement agreement can lead to the exclusion of the damages from gross income or their taxation as a capital gain (rather than as ordinary income). For the defendant, a properly structured settlement can allow the deduction of damages and related legal expenses in full in the year paid. The best-case scenario for failure to recognize the tax consequences of damages awards is lost opportunities, and the worst-case scenario is a possible malpractice claim against the erring attorney.[1]

   The tax consequences of damages are the same whether they are received in a judgment or through a settlement.[2] Internal Revenue Code (IRC) § 61 mandates that all income, including damages, is taxable to the recipient.[3] Plaintiffs, can, however, exclude damages from gross income in a limited number of situations. The most significant exclusion results from IRC § 104(a)(2), which allows exclusion of damages (other than punitive damages) from gross income if received for personal physical injuries or physical sickness. Less significant exclusions apply to damages received for medical care caused by emotional distress, punitive damages received under a state wrongful death statute where punitive damages are the only remedy, and damages received for amounts that another IRC section would have excluded (e.g., gifts or inheritances). If the damages replace a cost or expense that the plaintiff did not deduct, then gross income will not include the award.[4] Damages not excluded by these exceptions are generally taxable as ordinary income or as capital gains, depending on the plaintiff's underlying legal claim.

Defendants paying damages in judgment or settlement can often deduct the damages and associated legal expenses as trade or business expenses under IRC § 162 or as production of income expenses under IRC § 212. Defendants , however, cannot deduct damages if the dispute originates from personal matters, even if the tort adversely affects the defendant's business. In addition, taxpayers cannot deduct fines and penalties paid to a government and must capitalize, and then amortize, damages considered to be capital expenditures.

Attorneys play a pivotal role in helping clients obtain desired tax results for damages received or paid in legal disputes. For example, characterizing disputes with multiple potential theories as personal physical injuries often increases the plaintiff's after-tax damages award. In other cases involving personal physical injuries, the plaintiff's attorney sometimes encourages a settlement to avoid taxable punitive damages or set up periodic payments (i.e., a structured settlement) to maximize the benefit received from the exclusion. In nonphysical personal injury cases, attorneys often avoid characterizing damages as back wages to avoid employment taxes or specify that a portion of the damages received represent payments for medical care related to emotional distress to allow for an exclusion. Attorneys in business injury cases often portray the damages received as compensation for harm to capital assets to justify their tax treatment as capital gains or as a return of capital. Finally, defense attorneys often prefer to settle disputes involving potential fines or penalties to increase the likelihood of a deduction for damages paid. Effective client service requires attention to the tax consequences from the start of the dispute and a clear statement as to the purpose (i.e., the origin of the claim) served by the payment in the settlement agreement.

16.2 ORIGIN OF THE CLAIM TEST

The origin of the claim test determines the tax consequences of damages received and damages paid for judgments and settlements. For damages received, the test establishes whether the damages are excludable and, if taxable, whether they are taxable as ordinary income or as capital gains. For damages paid, the test determines whether the defendant can deduct the damages and related legal expenses. The test has its origins in the U.S. Supreme Court case of *Hort v. Commissioner*, in which the taxpayer received a $140,000 settlement payment for the cancellation of a lease.[5] Because the origin of the claim was a lease agreement, the court treated the cancellation fee received by the lessor as the rent payments it replaced and found it to be ordinary income.

The origin of the claim test places taxpayers in the same tax position they would have been in if they had not suffered the injury. To accomplish this, the damages received attract taxes in the same manner as the item they replace. Thus, damages received for lost profits become ordinary income, damages received for harm to capital assets become a return of capital, and damages received for excludable items (e.g., gifts, inheritances, property settlements in a divorce, or nondeductible costs) or physical personal injuries do not become gross income. Tax rules exclude damages received for personal physical injuries or physical sickness from gross income on the theory that the origin of the claim is the taxpayer's physical well-being, a nontaxable commodity.[6]

The courts have often used the origin of the claim test to decide whether damages received by a plaintiff replace lost profits and therefore become ordinary income. For example, the court found that amounts received by a taxpayer for losses he anticipated to his oyster beds due to laying of an oil pipeline were ordinary income.[7] The courts have used the test to establish whether damages received by a taxpayer compensated for harm to capital assets and therefore become taxable to the extent they exceeded the taxpayer's basis in the capital asset. For example, the court held that damages received for the fraudulent taking of the taxpayer's securities became a capital gain to the extent it exceeded her basis in the securities.[8]

The origin of the claim test also determines the defendant's tax consequences. Assuming that the origin of the claim is the taxpayer's business or profit-making activity, the taxpayer can deduct damages and related legal expenses as business expenses or as production of income expenses.[9] The facts of many cases make it difficult to decide whether the origin of the claim is the taxpayer's business or personal affairs. For example, in *United States v. Gilmore,* the origin of the claim test decided whether a taxpayer could deduct legal expenses for a divorce as trade or business expenses.[10] The court held that even if the legal expenses allowed the taxpayer to retain his controlling interests in three corporations, the origin of the claim was a personal situation and as a result the taxpayer could not deduct the legal fees. The origin of the claim rule also determines whether the payor receives a current deduction for deductible damages or must capitalize them.

Attorneys can affect the tax results to the parties involved in a controversy by documenting the origin of the claim in the complaint and the settlement agreement. Settlement agreements that specify the origin of the claim to be a physical personal injury or harm to capital assets make it easier for taxpayers receiving the damages to justify excluding the damages from gross income or treating them as a capital gain. The IRS looks to the complaint, the settlement agreement, and the court's ruling as the primary sources for evidence on the origin of the claim.

16.3   TYPES OF DISPUTES

(a) Physical Personal Injuries.   IRC § 104(a)(2) excludes any damages (other than punitive damages) received on account of personal physical injuries or physical sickness. Once a taxpayer has established the origin of the claim to be a physical injury or physical sickness, then the taxpayer can exclude from gross income *all* damages (other than punitive) that flow therefrom.[11] As a result, the § 104(a)(2) exclusion extends to damages received for items such as lost wages, medical expenses, pain, suffering, and emotional distress, as long as they originate from a personal physical injury or physical sickness.

> *Example 1:*   Assume that a taxpayer suffers injury in an automobile accident and as a result incurs costs of (1) $5,000 of medical expenses, (2) $15,000 in lost wages, and (3) pain, suffering, and emotional distress not precisely measured. If the taxpayer settles a resulting lawsuit for $30,000 (and if the taxpayer has not previously deducted his or her medical expenses), the taxpayer can exclude the entire $30,000, according to § 104(a)(2). The taxpayer received payment for medical expenses, lost wages, and pain, suffering, and emotional distress all on account of personal physical injuries.[12]

IRC § 104(a)(2) did not always require personal injuries or sickness to be physical. Prior to its amendment by the Small Business Job Protection Act of 1996 (SBJPA), IRC § 104(a)(2) excluded damages received "on account of personal injuries or sickness."[13] During the 1980s and early 1990s, many courts broadly interpreted the phrase *personal injuries* within this code section to exclude damages received for injury to reputation,[14] injury to constitutional rights,[15] and discrimination based on age, sex, or race.[16] The current version of IRC § 104(a)(2) applies to damages received pursuant to judgment or settlement after August 20, 1996 and narrows the exclusion to damages (other than punitive damages) received on account of personal *physical* injuries or *physical* sickness.

The current version of IRC § 104(a)(2) does not allow an attorney the same flexibility in extending its exclusion to nonphysical injuries as the older version of the code section allowed. In a limited number of disputes involving multiple potential legal theories, an attorney can, however, allow the plaintiff to employ the IRC § 104(a)(2) exclusion through the wording of the settlement agreement.

> *Example 2:*   A trainer at a zoo suffers physical injuries from a lion attack after failing to follow standard procedures for handling the animal. The zoo decides to terminate the trainer's employment contract for her breach of the rules. The trainer hires an attorney and threatens legal action. The zoo, eager to avoid unfavorable publicity, offers to settle the dispute for $250,000. If the plaintiff's attorney drafts the settlement agreement to specify that the zoo is paying damages for the personal physical injuries suffered by the trainer, the settlement likely will escape taxation under § 104(a)(2). If the IRS, however, were to decide that the damages compensate for wrongful termination of an employment contract or gender discrimination, the $250,000 would be taxable ordinary income. The drafting of the settlement agreement therefore can materially affect a claimant's after-tax wealth.

IRC § 104(a)(2) does not require the physical personal injuries to occur to the person receiving the damages for them to be excludable. Damages received for wrongful death and loss of consortium due to the physical injury or physical sickness of a spouse are excludable, despite the lack of physical injury or physical sickness to the damages award recipient.[17]

The damages received under § 104(a)(2) are excludable whether received in a lump sum or as periodic payments.[18] As a result, the expert can structure damages settlements to provide for payments over a number of years, with all the payments excludable from the recipient's gross income. This tax treatment allows attorneys great flexibility in designing structured settlements to provide tax advantages to both the plaintiff and the defendant.

(i) Medical Expenses.   The IRC § 104(a) exclusion for damages received for physical injuries or sickness does not apply to reimbursements of medical expenses that the taxpayer has deducted on prior year tax returns.[19] This rule prevents taxpayers from receiving a double tax benefit from the deduction and exclusion.

> *Example 3:*   Assume that the taxpayer in Example 1 receives $5,000 in damages for medical expenses incurred but has deducted the $5,000 in medical expenses on a prior year tax return. In deducting the $5,000 in medical expenses on the prior year return, she took a deduction of $1,250 after applying the 7.5 percent adjusted gross income (AGI) limitation. As a result, her exclusion for the damages received for the medical expenses is limited to $3,750.

(ii) Punitive Damages.   The recipient must include in taxable income punitive damages received for personal physical injuries or physical sickness. This rule came about as a result of the 1996 U.S. Supreme Court case of *O'Gilvie v. United States* and the SBJPA of 1996 amendments to § 104(a)(2).[20] The only exception is found in IRC § 104(c), which allows the recipient to exclude punitive damages if the court awarded them under a state wrongful death statute and the only remedy available under the statute is punitive damages.

The difference in the tax treatment of compensatory and punitive damages in physical injury cases makes settlement of such disputes more attractive for plaintiffs. If the case goes to judgment, the plaintiff must include any punitive damages awarded in taxable income. On the other hand, if the plaintiff settles the dispute and drafts the settlement agreement to reflect only compensatory damages, the damages can escape taxation. Defendants will often cooperate with the wording of such settlement agreements to avoid the stigma of paying punitive damages.

(b) Nonphysical Personal Injuries.   Damages received for nonphysical personal injuries, such as for claims originating in employment discrimination (e.g., age, race, or sex discrimination), injury to reputation, or invasion of privacy, are taxable to the recipient under IRC § 61. Two exceptions apply to this rule, but they provide limited relief. First, § 104(a) allows taxpayers to exclude damages received for medical care (as defined by IRC § 213(d)) attributable to emotional distress. Second, taxpayers can exclude receipts of damages for nonphysical personal injuries if they originate in a claim that is excludable from gross income (e.g., gifts, inheritances or life insurance).

> *Example 4:*   John loses his job and sues his employer under the Age Discrimination in Employment Act (ADEA). He settles with the employer and receives $20,000 for back pay, $15,000 for emotional distress, and $8,000 for medical expenses to treat the emotional distress through psychiatric care. The $35,000 received for back pay and emotional distress are both ordinary taxable income, but he can exclude the $8,000 for medical expenses from gross income under IRC § 104(a).

Taxpayers look for theories to exclude damages received as a result of non-physical personal injuries. One approach seeks coverage under § 104(a)(2) by claiming a physical injury or physical sickness brought on by the emotional distress of the nonphysical injury. For example, suppose the sex discrimination at her workplace has so distressed the plaintiff that she has a bleeding ulcer. Likewise, the age discrimination at his workplace has so distressed the plaintiff that it leads to his heart attack. This approach will not likely work, because the language in the amended § 104 Conference Committee Report indicates that nonexcludable emotional distress claims include those with physical symptoms (e.g., insomnia, headaches, stomach disorders).[21] Courts have, so far, shown reluctance in allowing an exclusion under § 104(a)(2) when the physical injury claimed by the plaintiff appears to be tax motivated and not the true origin of the claim.[22]

In another approach to seeking exclusion for nonphysical personal injuries under § 104(a)(2), plaintiffs try to convert them to a physical injury by claiming some type of physical contact. For example, in sexual harassment cases plaintiffs sometimes claim nonconsensual physical contact in an attempt to use the exclusion under § 104(a)(2). The success of this approach depends on the extent of the physical contact. The IRS has adopted a hard-line stance on this in letter rulings, requiring "observable bodily harm such as bruises, cuts, swelling, and bleeding."[23]

(i) Payroll Taxes.   Damages received for back wages in employment disputes are subject to payroll taxes and income tax withholding.[24] The payroll taxes due on back wages include FICA (Federal Insurance Contributions Act or Social Security taxes) and FUTA (Federal Unemployment Tax Act taxes). Characterizing damages received in an employment dispute as being for something other than wages (e.g., emotional distress) can increase the plaintiff's after-tax damages award. This strategy also applies in disputes involving back pay for self-employment income, which is subject to the self-employment tax.[25]

(ii) Punitive Damages.   Punitive damages received on account of nonphysical personal injuries are taxable to the recipient.[26]

(iii) Damages Received In Lieu of Nontaxable Sources.   Damages are not taxable if they originate in claims that are not taxable. For example, damages received in lieu of gifts, inheritances, or property settlements from a marriage are not taxable to the recipient.[27] The receipt of gifts, inheritances, life insurance proceeds on a key employee, and property settlements from a marriage are not taxable income, so damages received to compensate plaintiffs for these items should not be taxed either.

(iv) Reimbursement of Expenses (Costs).   Damages received to reimburse plaintiffs for past expenses or costs are not taxable, unless the taxpayer deducted the expense on a previous tax return.[28] For example, taxpayers can exclude damages received from an accountant that represent additional income tax paid as a result of the tax adviser's error.[29] The logic behind this ruling is that the damages place the plaintiff in the same position he or she would have been in if the error had not occurred and, therefore, there is no economic gain to be taxed.

Two exceptions apply to this rule. First, if the plaintiff received a tax benefit from a deduction of the expense on a previous tax return, then the reimbursement is taxable income.[30] Second, the direct payment of a plaintiff's tax or indemnity payments for bad tax advice to a plaintiff have been held to be taxable income.[31]

This second exception is designed to prevent investment schemes planned to reduce or eliminate tax liabilities.

(c) Business Injuries.   The tax treatment of damages received for business injuries depends on the origin of the claim. If the origin of the claim is lost profits, the damages are ordinary income.

> **Example 5:**   In *H. Liebes & Co. v. Commissioner,* the taxpayer received $106,517 in damages from the government, which wrongfully seized the taxpayer's boats and prevented the taxpayer from catching seals. The court determined the origin of the claim to be lost profits, so the damages were ordinary income.[32]

In contrast, if the origin of the claim is harm to capital assets or injury to goodwill, the damages are taxable only to the extent they exceed the basis of the capital asset.[33] If the damages exceed the capital asset's basis, the excess is a capital gain.

> **Example 6:**   In *Wheeler v. Commissioner,* the taxpayer demolished a building on his land after a third party promised to obtain capital to finance a new building. The third party failed to obtain the necessary financing and ended up paying the taxpayer $30,000 in damages for the demolished building. The court found damages to be taxable as a capital gain to the extent they exceeded the taxpayer's basis in the destroyed building.[34]

Finally, if the plaintiff receives the damages award in lieu of items that are not taxable, then the damages are not taxable. For example, damages due to a corporation for a loss of promised tax deductions resulting from the U.S. government's change in the tax law were not grossed up for taxes because the court ruled that the damages would not be taxable.[35] The logic behind this ruling follows *Clark v. Commissioner.*

(i) Harm to Capital Assets.   To classify damages received as payments for harm to capital assets, the taxpayer has the burden of proof that the origin of the claim is harm to capital assets.[36] In addition, taxpayers need to establish their basis in the capital asset if they want to treat the damages received as a nontaxable return of capital.[37] For example, when a corporation could not establish the basis of its asset, the court held that the damages received for the destruction of the asset were taxable.[38]

(ii) Tax Planning.   Plaintiffs have a greater chance of obtaining capital gains treatment for damages received if their attorneys clearly state the origin of the claim to be harm to capital assets in the complaint and the settlement agreement. The taxpayer also needs to document the basis of the capital asset. When a taxpayer receives a lump sum, the settlement should allocate payments between capital and lost profits. A defendant can reduce the pretax cost of any settlement by agreeing to language giving the plaintiff tax-favored treatment in the agreement.

(iii) Antitrust.   Business injury damages received from antitrust judgments or settlements have unique tax consequences for two reasons. First, plaintiffs will likely receive punitive damages from the trebling of antitrust judgments. Thus, plaintiffs have tax incentives to inflate the compensatory damages sought in the complaint

and then settle the dispute without allocating any of the damages in the settlement agreement to punitive damages. Assuming that the origin of the claim is harm to the plaintiff's capital assets (e.g., goodwill), this allows the plaintiff to report the entire damages received as a capital gain or a return of capital.

16.4   SUBSTANTIATING TAX TREATMENT

Most plaintiffs pursue legal disputes under several theories or claims. For example, a plaintiff can initiate a lawsuit seeking damages for lost wages, emotional distress, damage to property, physical personal injuries, and punitive damages. How the court or arbitration characterizes the damages awards can have a big impact on the participant's after-tax results. Attorneys improve a client's tax position for the damages by properly substantiating the allocation of the damages award. Properly wording the complaint and the settlement agreement or asking the court to allocate the damages awards to particular claims, or both, are the best ways to substantiate the tax treatment of damages received or paid in a legal dispute.

Disputes resolved through a judgment by a court need not allocate the damages to the plaintiff's particular claims. Attorneys can influence whether and how the damages award is split in the judgment by requesting the court to allocate the award to particular claims. Plaintiffs occupy a better position if they have a court's written finding to substantiate their tax treatment of the damages award. The IRS, however, has ruled that a written finding by a judge regarding the characterization of damages received is a "relevant factor, but not a conclusive factor" in deciding the tax treatment of the damages.[39]

Attorneys have a greater opportunity to characterize damages in disputes that they settle. They can best substantiate the tax treatment of damages received in a settlement with documents filed in court (e.g., complaint, motions, pleadings) and the settlement agreement. The IRS regards the complaint as the most persuasive evidence for characterizing the damages received through a settlement.[40] To use the complaint as substantiation, attorneys need to consider the tax consequences of the damages award early in the dispute. Substantiating the tax treatment of damages in a complaint becomes difficult when the plaintiff pursues multiple approaches or claims in the dispute. The settlement agreement, on the other hand, gives the attorneys greater control in substantiating an advantageous allocation of the damages award. For example, an attorney settling a personal physical injury case will want to allocate as little as possible of the award to punitive damages. Courts have held the allocations in a settlement agreement to be binding for tax purposes in several cases.[41] The attorney, however, must document that the parties negotiated the allocations in the settlement agreement at arm's length. The courts often do not recognize settlement agreements that allow the plaintiff complete discretion in allocating the damages award.[42]

16.5   STRUCTURED SETTLEMENTS

Structured settlements refer to damages awards paid in a series of payments, sometimes over a number of years, as opposed to a lump sum payment. Although any type of dispute can result in a structured settlement, parties use it primarily for settlements of personal physical injuries or physical sickness because of the wording of IRC § 104(a)(2). This rule allows taxpayers to exclude damages received for personal physical injuries or physical sickness whether received "as lump sums or as periodic payments." Thus, taxpayers can exclude the entire amount of periodic payments received for personal physical injuries, which will exceed the lump sum alternative. In contrast, structured settlements for nonphysical injuries lack such advantages. The primary tax advantages that result from structured settlements for nonphysical injuries comprise tax deferral and the shifting of income between periods.

The primary disadvantage to plaintiffs of periodic payments is the risk that the defendant will not make the payments as promised. The restrictions the IRS places on parties regarding the security arrangements allowed for structured settlements magnifies the risks. The plaintiff cannot be in constructive receipt (that is, have a substantial economic interest in the entire series of payments) or have an economic benefit in the structured settlement. A structured settlement that prohibits the plaintiff from accelerating the payments or receiving their discounted present value avoids constructive receipt.[43] The plaintiff avoids having an economic benefit in the structured settlement by owning nothing more than an unfunded, unsecured promise to pay in the future.[44]

For the defendant, a structured settlement can be attractive if the lump sum payment required for settling the dispute exceeds the present value of the periodic payments. Comparing the cost of the lump sum payment with the cost of periodic payments is usually easy because defendants can assign the obligation of making the periodic payments to a third party by paying the third party a single amount. The disadvantage to the defendant of structuring a settlement lies in the uncertainty of the timing of the deduction for the damages payment. If the defendant makes a qualified assignment of the obligation to make the periodic payments to a third party, the defendant can immediately deduct the cost of the assignment. IRC § 130 permits qualified assignments only in workmen's compensation claims or disputes involving personal physical injury or sickness.[45]

16.6 TAX TREATMENT OF PAYMENTS BY PAYOR

The IRC does not have a code section that allows for the deductibility of damages paid in a legal dispute. The defendant, however, can generally deduct damages paid as a trade or business expense under IRC § 162 or as a production of income expense under § 212.

(a) Business Expenses under § 162. The origin of the claim test establishes whether a defendant can deduct damages paid in a legal dispute as trade or business expenses under IRC § 162. Assuming that the origin of the claim is the defendant's business, courts have held that defendants can deduct damages paid under judgment[46] and damages paid in settlement[47] as trade or business expenses.

> *Example 7:* In *Musgrave v. Commissioner*, an accounting firm could deduct the $193,500 in damages it paid to settle a lawsuit brought by a client after the accounting firm's employees embezzled money from the client.[48] The court held the damages to be ordinary and necessary business expenses that arose from the accounting firm's business. As a result, the damages were deductible under IRC § 162.

If the origin of the claim, however, is not the taxpayer's business, but instead is a personal matter, the defendant cannot deduct the damages.

> *Example 8:*   In *McCaa v. Commissioner,* the taxpayer tried to deduct $10,000 in damages paid to his son's mistress in an attempt to avert a scandal that might have resulted in the cancellation of the taxpayer's Chevrolet automobile franchise.[49] The mistress had suffered injuries in a scuffle with the taxpayer. The court held that the defendant could not deduct the damages because the origin of the claim was personal. The fact that the business might have suffered harm if the defendant did not pay the damages did not matter.

The origin of the claim between business and personal is sometimes difficult to identify, particularly in cases involving automobiles. The courts generally require that damages paid in connection with an automobile accident relate directly and closely to the taxpayer's business rather than function as incidental to the business.[50] For example, the origin of the claim for an automobile accident in the commute home from the office was personal, even though the taxpayer was taking work home from the office.[51]

For the defendant to deduct damages under IRC § 162, it must meet the requirements of that code section. As a result, the expenses must be ordinary, necessary, and reasonable. Assuming taxpayers meet the requirements of IRC § 162, they can deduct all damages, including punitive damages. Taxpayers cannot deduct fines and penalties and must capitalize, then amortize, damages considered to be capital expenditures.

(b) Production of Income Expenses under § 212.   The origin of the claim test decides whether taxpayers can deduct damages paid in connection with their income-producing activity under IRC § 212. One can deduct damages paid as a result of a dispute that has an origin in the taxpayer's income-producing activity, assuming the expenses meet the ordinary-and-necessary requirements of IRC § 212. For example, the court held that damages paid to settle an action brought by the Securities and Exchange Commission to impose trusts on the taxpayer's corporate shares were deductible as an ordinary and necessary expense paid for the collection or production of income under IRC § 212.[52]

(c) Fines and Penalties.   IRC § 162(f) disallows the deduction of "any fine or similar penalty paid to a government for the violation of any law." Taxpayers faced with the potential of large fines have considerable incentives to convert the fines into deductible damages. The press reported that Exxon avoided a fine by settling its liability over the Exxon Valdez oil spill with the U.S. government for $1.1 billion in damages, which it subsequently deducted on its tax return. As a result, the after-tax cost to Exxon was only $524 million. This approach will not always work, as evidenced by *Allied-Signal v. Commissioner,* in which the court held that amounts paid to a private nonprofit clean-up fund were nondeductible fines even though the taxpayer did not pay them to a government.[53] One could attribute the result in *Allied-Signal, Inc. v. Commissioner* to the district court judge's guarantee that he would reduce the associated criminal fine of $13.24 million in return for a contribution of $8 million to the cleanup fund.[54]

The limitations on the deductibility of trade or business expenses under IRC § 162 determine whether trade or business expenses are deductible.[55] As a result, taxpayers can deduct punitive damages and damages paid for their fraud, mismanagement, or other improper actions under IRC §162, assuming that the damages have an origin in the taxpayer's trade or business.[56]

(d) Expensing or Capitalizing.   The origin of the claim test establishes whether the taxpayer can currently deduct or must capitalize damages paid in a legal dispute. The taxpayer must capitalize damages when the origin of the claim is the acquisition of a capital asset. The taxpayer can amortize the capitalized damages if the related capital asset has a readily ascertainable useful life.

> *Example 9:*   In *Mathiasen v. Commissioner,* the court denied the petitioner a deduction for damages paid to a third party that put the taxpayer in touch with persons who aided in the financing of oil tankers. The taxpayer claimed it made the payments to the third party to protect his business reputation, but the court held that the payments were for services that helped the taxpayer acquire title to property (i.e., oil tankers). Therefore, the court considered the payments capital expenditures and not deductible as ordinary and necessary expenses of a trade or business.[57]

16.7   DEDUCTION OF LEGAL FEES

(a) Legal Fees Unrelated to Contingency.   The IRC does not have a code section that expressly allows for the deductibility of legal fees paid in a lawsuit. Taxpayers can, however, sometimes deduct damages paid as a trade or business expense under IRC § 162 or as a production of income expense under § 212. Whether legal fees are deductible, capitalized, or not deductible depends on the origin of the claim test. When the origin of the claim is the taxpayer's business or profit-making activity, the taxpayer can deduct legal fees under IRC § 162 or § 212. Likewise, the taxpayer must capitalize legal fees when the origin of the claim is the acquisition of a capital asset or the defense of title to property.[58] If the origin of the claim is a personal matter, the taxpayer cannot deduct the related legal fees. However, taxpayers can deduct legal fees paid for tax advice in a personal dispute such as divorce.

(b) Contingent Fees.   The tax treatment of the contingent fee portion of a damages award to an individual plaintiff has been subject to great debate. Plaintiffs have tried to report only the net amount received (gross amount of damages award minus the contingent fees paid to the attorney), but the IRS has required taxpayers to report the entire damages award as income with a miscellaneous itemized deduction for the contingent legal fees paid. This approach limits the benefit from the miscellaneous itemized deduction through the alternative minimum tax (AMT) and the phase-outs that apply to miscellaneous itemized deductions and itemized deductions. In extreme situations, plaintiffs can end up with little or no money after paying taxes on the gross amount of the damages award.

> *Example 10:*   Plaintiff receives a damages settlement of $100,000 for which her attorney was paid $60,000 under a contingent fee agreement (including

reimbursement for expenses). If the plaintiff is subject to AMT, she will report the $100,000 as income but will be denied a benefit from the $60,000 miscellaneous itemized deduction. Assuming the plaintiff is in the 40 percent tax bracket (combined federal and state), she is left with $0 of the damages award after taxes.

Congress addressed this situation by adding IRC § 62(a)(19) under the Jobs Creation Act of 2003, which allows taxpayers to deduct the contingent fee portion of a damages award for AGI. Unfortunately, this new code section only applies to damages received for specified claims against the United States and claims of unlawful discrimination.[59] Other situations are covered by the 2005 Supreme Court case of *Commissioner v. Banks*, which requires plaintiffs to use the IRS approach of reporting the entire damages award as income with the contingent fee portion taken as a miscellaneous itemized deduction.[60]

In disputes with multiple causes of action, attorneys can increase their client's after-tax damages by allocating a greater portion of the damages award to qualifying claims of unlawful discrimination in a clearly written settlement agreement.

16.8   CONCLUSION

Financial experts and attorneys need to understand the tax rules regarding damages received and damages paid in order to serve their clients properly. Tax rules play an important part in the decision on whether to settle or litigate and the wording of the complaint and the settlement agreement. Litigators who fail to grasp the importance of the tax implications of damages paid or received place their clients in a poor position for tax purposes. They reduce a client's after-tax amount of damages received or prevent the client from an immediate deduction for damages paid. Litigating attorneys should consult with a tax professional early in each case to arrive at the correct tax strategy for the dispute.

NOTES

1. Cases involving malpractice claims against attorneys for failure to consider the tax consequences of damages include *Graham v. Harlin, Parker & Rudloff,* 664 S.W.2d 945 (Ky. Ct. App. 1983) and *Philips v. Giles,* 620 S.W.2d 750 (Tex. Civ. App. Dalls 1981).
2. *Logino v. Commissioner,* 32 T.C. 904 (1959).
3. However, in *United States v. Gotcher* 401 F.2d 118, the court noted, "The concept of economic gain to the taxpayer is the key to section 61. This concept contains two distinct requirements: There must be an economic gain, and this gain must primarily benefit the taxpayer personally." *See also* Rev. Rul. 81-277, and PLR 8604065.
4. *See Clark v. Commissioner,* 40 BTA 333 (1939), Rev. Rul. 57-47, 1957-1 CB 23, Rev. Rul. 81-277, Field Service Advice 685 (1993), and PLR 9041072.
5. *Hort v. Commissioner,* 313 U.S. 28 (1941).
6. IRC §104(a)(2).
7. *Collins v. Commissioner,* 18 CCH TCM 756 (1959).
8. *Megargel v. Commissioner,* 3 T.C. 238 (1944).
9. Trade or business expenses are deductible under IRC § 162, and production of income expenses are deductible under IRC § 212.
10. *United States v. Gilmore,* 372 U.S. 39 (1963).

11. The Court in *Commissioner v. Schleier,* 515 U.S. 323 (1995) held the phrase "on account of personal injuries" to include damages received for lost wages, medical expenses, pain, suffering, and emotional distress as long as they originate in a personal injury. Also, the language in the Conference Committee Report to § 104 makes it clear that the §104(a)(2) exclusion applies to all damages received, including damages for emotional distress, as long as they are attributable to a physical injury or physical sickness.

12. This example, with slight adjustments, is taken directly from *Commissioner v. Schleier,* 515 U.S. 323 (1995).

13. Pre-SBJPA of 1996 §104(a)(2).

14. Rev. Rul. 85-98, 1985-2 C.B. 51 held that damages for libel or slander to a taxpayer's personal reputation were excludable from gross income.

15. *Bent v. Commissioner,* 835 F.2d 67 (CA-3, 1987) held that damages received for a violation of the taxpayer's right to free speech was excludable from gross income under § 104(a)(2).

16. Although later overruled by *Schleier v. Commissioner,* 515 U.S. 323 (1995), the Third Circuit held in *Rickel v. Com.,* 900 F.2d 655 (CA-3, 1990) that damages awarded for age discrimination were excludable. Although later overruled by *United States v. Burke,* 504 U.S. 229 (1992), the Sixth Circuit held in *Burke v. United States* 929 F.2d 1119 (CA-6, 1991) that back pay awarded in settlement of Title VII of the Civil Rights Act of 1964 (i.e., sex discrimination) was excludable. Likewise, prior to *Burke v. United States* 504 U.S. 229 (1992) the Tax Court held in *Stocks v. Com.* 98 T.C. 1 (1992) that damages for racial discrimination were excludable.

17. *See* support for this approach in the discussion in the House Report No. 736, 104th Cong. 2d Sess., 1589 (1996). Also, the IRS ruled in PLR 200121031 that damages received for loss of consortium and wrongful death were excludible under IRC §104(a)(2).

18. *See* language in parentheses of § 104(a)(2): "whether as lump sums or as periodic payments."

19. § 104(a): "Except in the case of amounts attributable to (and not in excess of) deductions allowed under section 213 (relating to medical, etc., expenses) for any prior taxable year, gross income does not include."

20. *O'Gilvie v. United States,* 519 U.S. 79 (1996).

21. House Report No. 736, 104th Cong. 2d Sess., 1589 (1996).

22. *See Emerson v. Commissioner,* TC Memo 2003-82, and *Prasil v. Commissioner,* TC Memo 2003-100.

23. PLR 200041022.

24. Income tax withholding required under Rev. Rul. 78-336, 1978-2 C.B. 225. FICA required under *Social Security Board v. Nierotko,* 327 U.S. 358 (1946).

25. *Erickson v. Commissioner,* 64 CCH TCM 963 (1992); *aff'd in unpub. op.* 1 F.3d 1231 (1993).

26. The only time punitive damages are excludable is under IRC § 104(c), which allows punitive damages to be excluded if they are awarded under a state wrongful death statute and the only remedy available under the statute is punitive damages.

27. *Lyeth v. Hoey,* 305 U.S. 188 (1938), *Vincent v. Commissioner,* TC Memo 1992-21, *Green v. Commissioner,* TC Memo 1987-503.

28. Field Service Advice 685 (1993) states, "The tax benefit rule requires the inclusion of recovery of amounts previously deducted. It also requires the exclusion of recovery of amounts that have not been so deducted."

29. *Clark v. Commissioner,* 40 BTA 333 (1939), Rev. Rul. 57-47, 1957-1 CB 23, Rev. Rul. 81-277, and various PLRs including PLR 8604065. The court in *Clark* summed up these concepts when it stated "Moreover, so long as petitioner neither could nor did take a deduction in a prior year to this loss in such a way as to offset income for the prior year, the amount received by him in the taxable year, by way of recompense, is not then includable in his gross income."

30. IRC § 111(a).

31. Reg. § 1.61-14(a) and PLR 9833007.
32. *Liebes & Co. v. Commissioner,* 90 F.2d 932 (CA-9, 1937).
33. *Raytheon Production Corp. v. Commissioner,* 144 F.2d 110 (CA1, 1944). The court in *Raytheon* explained the logic of its analysis of the tax treatment of the damage payment when it noted: "The test is not whether the action was one in tort or contract but rather the question to be asked is *'In lieu of what were the damages awarded?'"*
34. *Wheeler v. Commissioner,* 58 T.C. 459 (1972).
35. *Centex Corporation, et al. v. United States,* 55 Fed. Cl. 381 (2003).
36. *Raytheon v. Commissioner,* 144 F.2d 110(CA-1, 1994), *cert. den.* 323 U.S. 779 (1944).
37. *Raytheon v. Commissioner,* 144 F.2d 110(CA-1, 1994), *cert. den.* 323 U.S. 779 (1944).
38. *Telefilm, Inc. v. Commissioner,* 21 T.C. 688 (1954).
39. Private Letter Ruling 8437084 (June 13, 1984).
40. Rev. Rul. 85-98, 1985-2 C.B. 51 (1985).
41. *Mckay v. Commissioner,* 102 T.C. 465 (1994) and *Bagley v. Commissioner,* 105 T.C. 396 (1995), *aff'd,* 121 F.3d 393 (CA-8, 1996).
42. *Robinson v. Commissioner,* 102 T.C. 116 (1994), *aff'd* 70 F.3d 34 (CA-5, 1995), *cert. denied* 117 S.Ct. 83 (1996).
43. Rev. Rul. 79-220, 1979-2 C.B. 74 (1979).
44. Rev. Rul. 79-313, 1979-2 C.B. 75 (1979).
45. IRC §130(c).
46. *Hales-Mullaly Inc.,* 46 BTA 25 (1942), *aff'd* 131 F.2d 509 (CA-10, 1942).
47. *International Shoe Co.,* 38 BTA 81 (1938), *acq.*
48. *Musgrave v. Commissioner,* 73 CCH TCM 1721 (1997).
49. *McCaa v. Commissioner,* 26 CCH TCM 711 (1967).
50. *Freedman v. Commissioner,* 35 T.C. 1179 (1961), *aff'd* 301 F.2d 359 (CA-5, 1962).
51. *Hall v. Commissioner,* 41 CCH TCM 282 (1980).
52. *Guttmann v. United States,* 181 F. Supp. 290 (W.D. Pa. 1960).
53. *Allied Signal, Inc. v. Commissioner,* 54 F.3d 767 (CA-3, 1995).
54. *Allied Signal, Inc. v. Commissioner,* 54 F.3d 767 (CA-3, 1995).
55. *Commissioner v. Tellier,* 383 U.S. 687 (1966).
56. *See* Rev. Rul. 80-211, 1980-2 C.B. 57 (1980), *Helvering v. Hampton,* 79 F.2d 358 (CA-9, 1935), and *I. Talley Industries Inc.,* 68 CCH TCM 1412 (1994), *rev'd & rem'd on other issue* 79 AFTR 2d 97-3096 (CA-9, 1997).
57. *Mathiasen v. Commissioner,* 20 CCH TCM 1681 (1961), *aff'd* 310 F.2d 738 (CA-3, 1962).
58. Reg. § 1.263(a)-2(c).
59. *See* IRC § 62(a)(19) for what qualifies as a claim against the U.S. and IRC § 62(e) for a complete list of what qualifies as "unlawful discrimination."
60. *Commissioner v. Banks,* 543 U.S. 426 (2005), 95 AFTR 2d 2005-659.

BIBLIOGRAPHY

Hanson, R.L., and J.K. Smith, "Taxability of Damages," *The CPA Journal,* May 1998.

Khokhar, J.A. "Tax Aspects of Settlements and Judgments," *BNA Tax Management Portfolios,* No. 522-2nd.

Raby, W.L. "Why Should Anyone Pay Taxes on Litigation Settlements?" *Tax Notes Today,* April 5, 1994.

Wood, R.W. "Navigating the Tax Maze of Workplace Winnings," *Tax Notes Today,* Mar. 24, 1997.

Wood, R.W. "Taxation of Damage Awards and Settlement Payments," Tax Institute, 1998.

CHAPTER **17**

DATA MANAGEMENT

David B. Burg
Dyan A. Decker
John C. Moorman

CONTENTS

17.1 INTRODUCTION

Financial experts working in a litigation environment need to understand data management for several reasons:

- The best evidence in litigation often resides in its original form within electronic data sets.

- The expert involved in a fraud investigation, or Securities and Exchange Commission (SEC) investigation, or other regulatory action will find that opposing counsel and experts have a superior capability in data management

The authors acknowledge Brian Wycliff for his assistance with the chapter.

that may give them an advantage in credibility and impact of evidence in support of their theories.

- Counsel will expect the financial expert to assist in the complex issues of electronic discovery.

In the normal course of business, companies manipulate, analyze, and discard data—often unbeknownst to the employee who created it. Effective management of data—collecting it, transforming it into useful information, providing it on a timely basis to decision makers, and disposing of irrelevant data—has become an important consideration for most enterprises. This comes into focus when a dispute or investigation erupts. The effectiveness of data management—by the company, its counsel, or external service providers—can make the difference between success and failure. This chapter discusses issues relating to the management of data before, during, and after a legal proceeding.

Consider some of the ways that data originate:

- The business day dawns, and each swipe of a parking pass and building access card creates a record in a security database.
- A manager e-mails his colleagues instructions on how to conduct business; a server—possibly several—stores the e-mail in the manager's and recipients' mailboxes.
- The same manager forwards a funny e-mail to a select few friends. Again, servers store the e-mail in multiple locations throughout the organization.
- A sales representative inputs activity from each sales call; the Customer Relationship Management (CRM) system generates a record of the information.
- A clerk inputs a batch of invoices, and the accounts payable module in the company's Enterprise Resource Planning (ERP) package creates a series of records.
- A member of the Information Technology (IT) department comes to the office late at night, copies proprietary program code to a Universal Serial Bus (USB)[1] storage device, puts it in her pocket, and goes home. Management did not detect this act, but the computer's registry recorded it.
- An assistant schedules a lunch meeting on his manager's calendar. Three devices record this meeting: the Exchange e-mail server; the manager's personal data assistant (PDA), such as a BlackBerry or Windows CE device; and the manager's home computer when she launches Web access from her home.
- A manager charges lunch on the corporate credit card. Several systems record this transaction: the merchant's systems, the issuing bank's systems, the acquiring bank's systems, and the payment processor's systems.

These simple actions occur daily, creating data trails that might prove central should a dispute arise. An e-mail that a manager sent for seemingly innocuous purposes could become evidence of his frame of mind in an employment dispute. An invoice input by the accounts payable clerk to a vendor who does business at the clerk's apartment building address might become circumstantial evidence of fraud. The computer registry file showing that someone copied proprietary information to a portable device might point to intellectual property theft. Access logs, phone records, and other information routinely captured in the normal course of business often have significant value when disputes arise.

Most businesses now have ERP software packages that collect and interpret data from accounting, human resources, sales, production, and other business functions. Both business and personal communication use e-mail and instant messaging systems so broadly that the line between the two has blurred. Identifying what lies within the scope of subpoenas and production requests has become a complex, imprecise, and costly process. Customer relations, research and development, and similar databases can contain other information important to certain litigation matters. And because companies regularly back up these systems, multiple copies of similar information—some relevant, some not; some up-to-date, some superseded—exist throughout the organization.

Discovery orders and subpoenas address many general types of systems, and the list changes as new technologies arise. A list of generic systems that contain potentially responsive sets of electronic data includes the following:

- Personal computers
- Peripheral devices such as BlackBerrys and PDAs
- Other ancillary media such as compact disks, DVDs, and USB or "thumb drives"
- Servers used for file-sharing purposes
- Servers used for e-mail, BlackBerrys, and other wireless hardware
- Systems used to host ERP systems such as SAP, PeopleSoft, Oracle Financials, and JD Edwards
- Systems used to store research and development data
- Application systems including Web-based systems
- Systems used for various compliance purposes
- Litigation repositories
- Backup systems, including routine and disaster recovery

Consequently, knowledge of clients' collections of electronic data can be significant (in connection with current proceedings) in managing future risks by retaining only legally or operationally required information.

Because courts established most of the rules for document production when firms created and stored most business records in hard copy, many of the rules have become obsolete. The current case law on electronic discovery provides conflicting opinions about how parties should produce information and what information they should retain. Fortunately, as of this writing, the U.S. Supreme Court has approved several amendments to the Federal Rules of Civil Procedure (FRCP), many of which concern electronically stored information. The prosed changes will take effect December 1, 2006 unless Congress chooses to reject, change, or delay the adoption of the amendments. These changes, many of which are discussed in later sections, will provide some clarity in the areas of electronic document discovery and retention but will still leave room for well-crafted discovery motions. Thus, the several think tanks of lawyers, judges, consultants, technologists, and others knowledgeable in this field have more work to do before we have clear and consistent standards. Until then, the volume and complexity of data created and retained in modern businesses will continue to present new challenges.

Technologies that harness the power of data enable us to conduct business faster, more efficiently, and differently from the past. More useful technology brings additional opportunity for misuse. Robert S. Mueller, III, the director of the Federal Bureau of Investigation, noted that

> we live in the age of globalization, and our world grows smaller every day. Airplanes, e-mail, fax machines, and mobile phones made it possible for us to coordinate this summit and travel here to Budapest. Modern technology has made international boundaries less and less relevant. Unfortunately, modern technology has also made it easier for crimes as diverse as drug trafficking, corporate fraud, organized crime, and terrorism to jump from Krakow to Kabul with the stroke of a computer key or the push of a cell phone button.[2]

This chapter does not present a comprehensive discussion of data management issues, but rather comprises a series of observations and key considerations for financial experts working with large, complex data sets. First, the chapter addresses the dynamics behind the changing landscape of electronically stored information—how systems create and store it, and how participants use it in a litigious or investigative context (*see* Sections 17.2 and 17.3). The bulk of the chapter focuses on specific considerations for the two types of electronic information: (1) electronic communications (e.g., e-mail and instant messaging; *see* Section 17.4); and (2) structured data (e.g., accounting system entries and system access logs; *see* Section 17.5). The chapter concludes with a brief discussion about items to consider when completing a case.

17.2   THE CHANGING LANDSCAPE

The area of data management in litigation has changed primarily in the volume of information now handled, the external regulatory requirements imposed on organizations, the prevalence of internal investigations, which create information that can become discoverable, and the global nature of modern business enterprises.

(a) Proliferation of Electronically Stored Information.   Every year brings more ways to store more data less expensively and to do so at costs that approach inconsequential. What costs little is little valued, and the value of scrubbing repositories of redundant or outdated data no longer merits the cost in terms of labor. With litigation, moreover, other costs arise, and even the nonspecific threat of potential litigation can impose bewildering choices.

ERP systems, such as SAP and Oracle/PeopleSoft, enable organizations to share information in real time across the enterprise. These systems and their related data warehouses often store many years' worth of detailed transactional information—information that can relate to litigation matters and can be discoverable. E-mail repositories and ERP systems create a trail of facts that may prove powerful when reviewed in a litigation or investigative climate, in which one has the luxury of time and hindsight to assess and critique decisions.

(i) Electronic Communications.   Many e-mail users neglect caution and discretion when they create messages. The candor engendered by e-mail's illusion of privacy can create a trail to establish intent and awareness. Consequently, lawyers often find that electronic communications provide compelling evidence of the intent of the parties, a key element of white-collar crime investigations. Deputy U.S.

Attorney General James Comey noted that "E-mail is a window into the mind."[3] Expert witnesses and investigators find e-mail valuable because, unlike shredda-ble paper, e-mail can sometimes prove difficult to destroy, and because the author's guard may be down, thereby revealing intent.

Another widely used form of communication is instant messaging. In the past few years, instant messaging has moved from the campus to the corporation. It enables the user to know which colleagues are presently on line and to transport information in many forms. People often use instant messaging to send text to multiple participants, but instant messaging can also transport files, video, and even voice communication.

A 2004 Opinion Research Corp. survey found that 27 percent of companies used instant messenger to communicate at work, an increase from 16 percent in 2003.[4] A 2003 study of risks associated with instant messaging found that over 60 percent of respondents (IT security professionals and business managers) allowed unrestricted instant messaging use in the corporate environment. The study also found that companies do not necessarily track who uses the applica-tion, what they use it for, or what content they pass outside the corporate infor-mation technology security layers.[5]

(ii) Structured Data.   Other types of electronic information that often relate to a liti-gation or investigative matter include application systems that store business records in complex databases and other computer systems that store data in a structured manner to serve non-record-keeping functions. Examples of each type include the following:

Application Systems with Complex Database Schemas

- ERP systems
- Supply chain management systems
- Time and attendance systems
- CRM systems
- Credit card transactional systems

Other Systems with Structured Data

- Voicemail systems
- Firewall logs
- E-mail server logs
- Telephone switching and private branch exchange (PBX) records
- Audit/log functions of various ERP applications
- Surplus equipment with hard drives that still contain important information
- Journal entries automatically created for users of Microsoft Outlook when-ever someone accesses a Microsoft Office application file (if enabled)

Each of these data sources has its own issues and complexities. For instance, the structured data of application systems can be challenging to retrieve because of various source applications and database formats that can change over time. Computer systems with other structured data do not have as their primary function the storage of business records, so retrieval of data from these sources can be difficult. For example, some voicemail systems interface with e-mail applications, and others store messages in a file format that one can seek when a dispute arises. Many other voicemail systems, particularly those of large corporations, run proprietary applications housed in operating systems such as Unix and can require specialized subject matter experts to effectively retrieve and examine the data.

(b) Regulatory and Litigation-Related Requirements for Retention of Information. Regulatory requirements and industry practices for electronic records retention vary by jurisdiction and industry and are evolving rapidly. A discussion of this topic lies beyond the scope of this chapter, but experts serve their client well by understanding the rules and practices that relate to their area of specialty. This allows for a comprehensive search for discoverable material as well as an ability to assist in identifying risks of trying a case. In an environment in which judges can sanction litigants who have destroyed evidence, businesses run considerable risk when disregarding these retention requirements.

Two common mistakes are overretention and underretention of information. Many companies have established a policy for how long to retain information of various types. These policies are captured in a retention schedule. Sometimes IT personnel inadvertently destroy information on backup tapes well in advance of the time specified in the retention schedule; conversely, they often retain backup tapes for longer than the retention period noted in the schedule, without any business or legal reason to do so. Moreover, if the company enters litigation, these tapes become discoverable and increase the discovery risk to the company.

The use of electronic information in litigation has matured since 1970 when the FRCP amended the definition of documents to include "data compilations from which information can be obtained." Over time, additional clarification has emerged, including the introduction in 1993 of Rule 26(a)(1)(B), which required that parties' initial disclosures to each other encompass not only relevant documents and "tangible things," but also relevant "data compilations." Proposed modifications to Rule 26(a) clarify further that initial disclosures apply to electronically stored information (ESI).

(i) Subpoenas and ESI. Subpoenas often include specific language concerning data compilations that parse the content to include specific systems and the information they contain. For example, a recent investigation of investment banks by New York Attorney General Eliot Spitzer promulgated a request for "all" e-mails once investigators discovered an e-mail that suggested one bank had downgraded an Internet company because the company refused to do underwriting business with it.[6] As Section 17.2(b)(iii) discusses, a request for "all e-mail" has many layers of complexity.

In response to such blanket requests, U.S. District Court Judge Lee H. Rosenthal (S.D. Texas), Chairman of the Federal Rules Advisory Committee on Civil Rules, suggested that "the traditional request to produce 'any and all documents' related to a particular subject is completely outdated." At least some judges, therefore, require that advocates rewrite such requests to create detailed and specific queries, tailored to the facts of each case.[7] This important evolution in the discovery process is reinforced by the proposed changes to the FRCP. For instance, proposed change to Rule 26(b)(2) limits discovery in that "[a] party need not provide discovery of electronically stored information that the party identifies as not readily accessible."[8]

The proposed change includes a provision that the responding party make a showing that the data are "not reasonably accessible" and if that showing is made requires a showing of "good cause" by the requesting party for the court to order discovery.[9] Proposed amendments to Rule 26(f) will likely require greater precision in requests for information.[10] These changes require the parties to develop a discovery plan that includes discussing "any issues relating to disclosure or discovery of electronically stored information, including the form in which it should be produced."[11] The Advisory Committee's notes to the proposed changes makes it clear that these "Meet and Confer" sessions should be held at the outset of the litigation to resolve issues better and avoid problems later in the case.[12]

Responding to discovery requests for electronically stored information can prove cumbersome because of the complexity of and frequently poor controls over such information. An aggregation of common law, state law, and federal law governs the rules of discovery. These regulations have proved inconsistent and uncoordinated, leading some companies to retain excess information subsequent to a subpoena or to rely on their counsel's ability to persuade a judge that the document request is too broad, costly, and burdensome.

(ii) Spoliation and Sanctions. Spoliation is defined as the willful destruction of evidence or the failure to preserve potential evidence for another's use in pending or future litigation.[13] The court can impose several types of sanctions on parties involved, including

- Adverse inference instruction
- Attorneys' fees/costs
- Criminal penalties
- Default or summary judgments
- Other monetary sanctions
- Witness preclusion

The decision in *Zubulake v. UBS Warburg LLC* clarified the duties of parties who anticipate litigation. In this wrongful termination matter, UBS backup systems provided the only source for much of the electronic evidence that was pivotal in the case. The courts' decisions in seven separate opinions[14] commented on several aspects of discovery:

- Once a party anticipates litigation, it must suspend its routine document retention and destruction policy and put in place a "litigation hold" to ensure preservation of potentially relevant documents.
- If a company can identify where key player data resides on backup tapes, the company should preserve this data if one cannot otherwise access the information on the tapes.
- The duty to preserve may be interpreted more broadly: one may have a duty to preserve information stored on active and backup systems where responsive information can reside, regardless of where key players are.

This interpretation does not imply that one necessarily has to produce such information as a matter of course, but one may be required to demonstrate efforts to undertake such preservation efforts.

- A court can order sanctions if it finds intentional or reckless failure to preserve and produce relevant data.

- The parties can negotiate cost sharing for collection and analysis of data when a party seeks inaccessible data (i.e., off-line media, such as backup tapes).

In another example of the potential severity of sanctions, a circuit court levied enormous penalties against a large financial services firm for its failure to promptly and accurately produce e-mails in response to a subpoena. This failure, along with other alleged discovery abuses and the submission of a false affidavit, prompted the judge to levy an adverse inference ruling that shifted the burden of proof for critical elements of the case.

The United States Supreme Court's 2005 decision to overturn the Arthur Andersen[15] obstruction of justice conviction related to the Enron bankruptcy does not mitigate the obligation to preserve information nor signal that organizations can actively purge information. However, in the dicta of the opinion, the Court allowed routine compliance with document retention policies and procedures under ordinary circumstances. The Supreme Court noted, in its unanimous opinion, that

> 'Document retention policies,' which are created in part to keep certain information from getting into the hands of others, including the Government, are common in business.... It is, of course, not wrongful for a manager to instruct his employees to comply with a valid document retention policy under ordinary circumstances.[16]

This decision led to the inclusion of a safe harbor provision in FRCP Rule 37(f): "Absent exceptional circumstances, a court may not impose sanctions under these rules on a party for failing to provide electronically stored information lost as a result of the routine, good faith operation of an electronic information system."

(iii) Various Discovery Standards.   Electronic communications are one of the first paths a litigant will likely pursue in discovery. Given e-mail's potential as a key source of critical business information and perhaps the best place to find a smoking gun, litigants will usually target e-mail. However, when an organization reasonably anticipates litigation (before a party files a complaint), the American Bar Association's (ABA) Civil Discovery Standards suggest that the organization should preserve potentially relevant documents. The legal community has debated the concept of reasonable anticipation because of its ambiguity and because many companies receive scores of demand letters from customers, suppliers, and the like that do not result in litigation. One could construe each demand letter as triggering the duty to preserve potentially relevant documents, and an organization adopting a conservative approach will incur heavy costs for more nonevents than for matters that actually ripen to litigation.

Common law imposes certain duties associated with data preservation, which also apply to electronic communications. We list two examples below:[17]

1. Courts typically hold litigants to a reasonableness standard when delineating their duty to preserve evidence.
2. Service of a complaint often puts parties on notice of a duty to preserve potentially relevant evidence if they are sufficiently aware of the relevant issues.

The ABA's Civil Discovery Standards cited a sample request letter prepared by an electronic discovery consultant requesting preservation of the following types of electronic documents:

• All e-mail and information regarding e-mail (including message contents, header information, and logs of e-mail usage)
• All databases (including all records and fields and structural information in such databases)
• All word processing files and file fragments
• All electronic data and file fragments
• All electronic data and file fragments created by application programs that process financial, accounting, and billing information
• All electronic data and file fragments created or used by electronic spreadsheet programs[18]

As Section 17.2(b)(i) discussed, some organizations cannot preserve all the aforementioned items, given the diversity of information systems and the amount of redundant information that they contain. Counsel often petitions the court to allow the resumption of rotating backup media that a litigant suspends because of the duty to preserve potentially relevant documents.

(c) Impact of Internal Investigations.   Enforcement agencies not only collect vast quantities of electronically stored information for their own review and analysis, they also request and obtain copies of information collected as part of company-conducted internal investigations. Discovery requests related to litigation follow this strategy.

Government regulators often request the report or workpapers—including data analyses and keyword searches—prepared during an independent, internal investigation conducted at the direction of a company's audit committee or board of directors. When a company turns over the findings of an internal investigation to the government, it should anticipate that other parties will access this information as well. These other parties include criminal prosecutors, regulators, and civil litigators bringing securities or class action litigation against the company.

(d) Global Challenges and Complexities.   Global organizations must grapple with additional complexity when addressing document retention and litigation production requirements. Countries differ on data privacy requirements, presenting challenges in complying with discovery requests when data reside in a different jurisdiction from the court. In addition, global firms must manage the regulatory requirements associated with cross-border data flows.

Consider an employee's right to privacy, for example: in the United States, courts generally presume that data created or stored by an employee on the employer's systems belong to the company if it publishes its privacy policies and makes employees aware of them. The employee's awareness of the company's privacy policy removes their expectation of privacy and puts them on notice that the company could use the data when, for example, responding to a discovery request. The law in this area is evolving. For instance, eight states have extended the right to privacy to public employees, but private employees do not have a right to privacy in e-mail communications, with the notable exception of California residents.[19] A recent study indicates as many as one-third of U.S. and U.K. companies monitor e-mails.[20] Privacy rights are more expansive overseas. Consider the E.U. Data Directive 95/46/EC1,[21] which calls for a more robust right to privacy and addresses transfers of personal data across borders.[22] Likewise, privacy laws in South America, Asia, and Africa resemble those in the European Union. Some foreign jurisdictions have contrasting views as to how employers can monitor employee e-mail, and employers face limits on disclosure to third parties, such as those involved in litigation.

These varying privacy laws and regulations affect the discovery process of any litigation or investigation involving non-U.S. companies or foreign operations of U.S.-based companies. To gather information from many foreign entities, one must obtain consent of the employees who created the information in the course of their employment. Even after receiving consent, one often cannot transmit personally identifiable information to the United States.

The E.U. data directive contains provisions that allow for the transfer of personally identifiable information given circumstances that meet the following conditions:[23]

- The data are necessary for the purpose of, or in connection with, any legal proceedings (including prospective legal proceedings).
- The data are necessary for the purpose of obtaining legal advice.
- The data are otherwise necessary for the purposes of establishing, exercising, or defending legal rights.

Given the complexity and diversity of privacy requirements, one should consult local counsel before beginning data collection for each engagement.

Also, when collecting data outside the United States, one will encounter information stored in a foreign language. In planning, the analyst should consider

- The volume of non-English information
- The language(s) used
- The language-processing capabilities of any software analytical packages being used
- The need for a human translator

17.3   MEET AND CONFER CONSIDERATIONS

Counsel will often meet with opposing counsel to negotiate the document preservation obligations, the scope of the analysis, and the process by which the parties will exchange documents. In both the litigation and investigations arenas, given the dynamic nature of electronically stored information, these early discussions should mitigate the potential for miscommunication between parties on these often contentious issues of discovery, and they can greatly reduce unnecessary expenditure. As Section 17.1 mentioned, the proposed changes to FRCP Rule 26(f) will require these discussions early in the discovery process. The topics to discuss include the following:

- **Scope of the preservation obligation.** Disclose what has been done to preserve documents and why; discuss the ability and timetable to cease retaining everything and resume rotation of backup tapes.
- **Scope of analysis.** Approach for reviewing documents and leveraging technology; prioritization of what to review first; protocols for revisiting these issues as the case evolves and the litigants refine the issues.
- **Associated costs and timing.** The costs and related timing associated with the production of electronically stored information will vary widely depending on the decisions reached regarding the scope of preservation and analysis.
- **The form of production.**

The last item, form of production, is an important consideration. For example, under current law, parties can produce relevant e-mail messages in hard copy form, as an image file (e.g., TIFF or PDF), or in its native e-mail message form. A party can also produce transactional data in various formats, including a hard copy printout, a copy of the data converted into an agreed-on format (e.g., a fixed width or delimited text file), or a copy of the data in its original format.

However, the proposed changes to the FRCP, specifically changes to Rules 33, 34, and 45, set out a procedure for determining the form that production of electronically stored information will take. Under the proposed changes, the requesting party can specify the form that production is to take, and the responding party can object. If the parties cannot agree as to form, the default provision specified in Rule 34(b)(ii) will be controlling: "if a request for electronically stored information does not specify the form of production, a responding party must produce the information in a form in which it is ordinarily maintained, or in an electronically searchable form."[24]

17.4 ELECTRONIC COMMUNICATIONS: USE OF E-MAIL IN LITIGATION TODAY

(a) Paper versus Electronic Discovery. In litigation matters and corporate investigations, participants have considered managing data in the discovery process as either a necessary evil or a tremendous opportunity. As of the mid-1980s, most key data existed only in paper form, so document management necessarily involved digging through warehouses of documents to find and control a set of relevant documents.

Times have changed. E-mail has become "the 20th century's gift to law enforcement,"[25] providing powerful evidence of the knowledge, awareness, and intent of witnesses.

Discovery of e-mail differs from paper discovery in several respects. E-mail messages multiply rapidly because they are stored in multiple e-mail servers, multiple in-boxes, personal e-mail archives, server backup tapes, PDA devices, and the like. E-mail messages contain metadata (i.e., data about data), which provide information such as when and by whom a document was created, when someone last accessed it, and other information that investigators find relevant. E-mail messages can also become long conversation threads as recipients reply to or forward the message on an iterative basis.

(b) E-mail Processing Considerations.   Many providers of electronic discovery services continue to process information and price their services based on the paper discovery model. This method converts all information processed, regardless of whether it responds to the pertinent issues, to image file format (e.g., the common .tiff or .pdf file formats). The entities discuss and price the volume in units of pages, rather than documents or messages. Applying traditional discovery methods to electronic discovery has proved to be an expensive and inefficient process because electronic discovery generates more duplicative documents.

Other providers take advantage of software capabilities to gain efficiencies in processing the vast amounts of electronic information. The capabilities differ, depending on the software package used, but they include:

- Classic tools of date range and keyword searches
- Removal of duplicate copies of messages
- Concept searching (i.e., searching for documents containing a given concept)
- Data visualization (i.e., preparing a graphical representation of the documents based on concepts, word groupings, or network analysis)

These providers go through the costly exercise of converting information to image formats only for documents that have passed through these processes and that the respondent will produce.

Some providers have changed their pricing model accordingly, away from a flat cost per page. One new pricing model charges a rate per gigabyte of data processed and a rate per page produced to TIFF format.

When comparing costs, one should also consider the amount of time required to manually review documents for responsiveness. Using technology to minimize the number of duplicate copies of e-mail messages and to run complex searches and visualization algorithms reduces the amount of information that one must review.

Even though the shift to electronic discovery provides opportunities to process a given amount of information more efficiently, it also poses new challenges. The amount of raw information is exploding. Thus, parties sometimes seek to shift or share processing costs, especially when one party holds almost all the information relevant to the case, such as in a class action litigation. The parties also struggle with how to authenticate the validity of a production set and ensure its admissibility into evidence.

(c) Collection of Information from E-mail and Instant Messengers.   Collecting information from electronic communications requires extensive effort because of its high volume and dispersion across various systems. As Section 17.1 discussed, electronic information resides in a multitude of formats, and in a myriad of systems and IT platforms.

The use of noncorporate or nonauthorized systems such as Web-based mail imposes complexities that make collecting electronic communications costly, be they e-mail or instant messenger. Review the need to collect such communications and to include such effort in the early case strategy to accommodate fiscal constraints.

One can choose from several levels of effort to recover electronic communications. Recovering logically active content requires the simplest level of effort. (Section 17.4(e) explains logical copy). A complexity of dealing with logical files lies in the variety of e-mail and instant messenger applications (and file types) and how these applications store the communications. E-mail or instant messenger data stored in an uncommon or proprietary format often requires the creation of a matching environment with the same hardware and software configuration as the original to analyze the information.

Analysts can probe deeper, to the physical layer (as Section 17.4(e) will discuss), recovering communications from unallocated, swap, and slack space of the media—if the information captured is an exact bit-for-bit copy. Depending on the type and configuration of the end-user's e-mail or instant messaging system, the physical layer can recover vast quantities of information. However, recovery of such communications can be time consuming and costly because the recoverable content sometimes includes only a portion of the original file.[26] In this case, analysts use forensics tools beyond the original application to work with the content of such files.

Managing duplication presents another complexity, particularly when one is dealing with numerous sets of backup media. This problem occurs with any type of analysis.

Analysts must also consider password-protected and encrypted communications. Several tools are commercially available to crack passwords or decipher encrypted communications; however, these tools process data slowly, and some are expensive. These issues arise only when one is working with adverse parties' data, but it can also arise in cases such as review of ex-employees' files in a poorly administered client IT environment.

(d) Understand Underlying Systems.   One should identify who uses what systems and the location of the relevant data. Many companies maintain asset tracking systems to control accountability over fixed assets, including IT assets. Even an incomplete asset tracking system often provides an effective starting point; the analyst should supplement any review of asset tracking information with interviews of knowledgeable people from the company's IT staff. During this process, one must locate as many relevant computers and data storage locations as possible, including systems that physically reside at employees' homes and systems that the company has recently moved to surplus or transferred to other employees. This effort should include backup media.

Several elements make it difficult to analyze backup systems:

- Firms use several different media types to save backup data—including tapes, hard drives, storage area networks, and disaster recovery systems.

- Firms can choose from many software backup packages and can change strategies, effectively "orphaning" older backup data.
- Restoring backup information can be difficult, either because the backup was incomplete or the backup media has failed from overuse or improper storage (i.e., exposed to excessive heat, humidity, or other conditions).
- If an organization has outsourced part of its business operations, the outsourcing provider may have comingled data from several clients onto one set of backups. This creates complexities because the other clients will likely have no involvement in the litigation.

Assessment of the foregoing elements will likely require interviews with the relevant responsible parties. These responsible parties will typically fall within the IT group and include IT staff with varying functional and technical responsibility. A conversation with the chief information officer often does not suffice, and apparent disconnects between policy and practice make the assessment all the more important as well as challenging.

(e) Preserve and Collect Data.   After identifying systems that contain relevant or potentially responsive information, one must preserve the information. People with formal training and experience in this capacity should perform this task because the accuracy of the data collected and the qualifications of the person who collected it have often come into question during contentious dispute matters. (*See* the discussion of *Daubert* challenges in Chapter 1.)

These qualified analysts can copy data stored on personal computers, PDAs, BlackBerrys, servers, CDs, DVDs, and other electronic media in two ways: (1) capturing a physical bit-for-bit copy of the media, or (2) capturing a logical copy of the media. Each method has costs and benefits:

- **Physical copy:** A physical bit-for-bit copy of a hard drive inside a personal computer or a server replicates the entire media. A physical copy will include active files (those the end-user can see via the operating system), deleted but recoverable files, and information stored in unallocated and slack space.

  A file that a user has marked as deleted will sit intact in unallocated space until another file overwrites all or a portion of the file. File slack[27] is a portion of an active file that contains information from a previously active file; although not related to the active file itself, it may contain meaningful information randomly selected from computer memory.

  A physical copy of a hard drive also captures vast amounts of additional useful information, such as metadata, and useful fragments of files that one can use to reconstruct Internet surfing histories as well as instant messenger communications.

  - **Advantage:** A physical copy has the greatest chance of recovering useful information from unallocated as well as file slack space.

  - **Disadvantage:** Information beyond what a litigant means to produce may in fact be produced, and the reliability of the information may be called into question.

- **Logical copy:** A logical copy of media captures only the content visible to the device's operating system. A logical copy of a hard drive will not include files marked for deletion even if the file still resides in the unallocated space.

  - **Advantage:** A logical copy does not preserve slack or unallocated space, which limits or clarifies which information is being produced to another party.

  - **Disadvantage:** A government entity or litigator who knows the value of physical bit-for-bit media can challenge the completeness of compliance with the associated discovery requests.

Either copying method, performed properly, will include metadata related to each file. One can change metadata without being aware that one has done so. For example, opening a Microsoft Excel file without saving the file alters the last accessed date related to the file. One can preserve the metadata in its preexamination state by using forensic examination software, such as Guidance Software's EnCase software or NTI's SafeBack software. Metadata are complex and sometimes unreliable and should be treated as such.

Qualified experts should perform the task of capturing a logical or physical copy of media, because this process can inadvertently alter data, particularly on volatile systems such as personal computers. For this reason, one must use proper procedures, such as a write-blocking device that prevents alterations of data on the hard drive.

(f) Evidence Integrity.   Establishing evidence integrity can be a layered process that includes interviewing relevant individuals, validating IT asset tracking systems, and conducting analyses of the electronic information itself to identify factual inconsistencies. Factual inconsistencies may be uncovered using techniques such as verification of data integrity. One method of verifying data integrity includes using Message Digest 5 algorithm (MD5) or US Secure Hash Algorithm 1 (SHA1)[28] hash analysis, a process of calculating a digital fingerprint of a data set. The likelihood that any two nonidentical files have the same MD5 hash value[29] is extremely low.

(i) Authentication Issues.   Evidence authentication is complex, but experts should document identifying aspects of the system, such as serial number and model, and capture independent data that often ties the use of the system to a particular employee. These independent corroborating systems can include asset tracking systems, help desk support applications, purchase order documents, and human resources records.

One should also tie the components to the device itself. For example, one should collect the serial number of the hard drive and then cross-reference the component serial numbers to information that one can find on the manufacturer's Web site. Dell Computers, for example, allows anyone to enter a system serial number and see the serial numbers and specifications of the components. This will reveal whether someone has changed component parts such as the original hard drive. A PC with new hardware components should raise a red flag: someone may have attempted to mask content that the original media would store.

(ii) Maintaining an Audit Trail.   Whether assisting the client to respond to production or preservation requirements, or gathering information at an adversary's site, one must maintain a clear audit trail and record of work performed. One should document interviews with the IT staff while working to understand the IT systems. Analysts should also document each information request in writing, noting who requested what information and when they requested it. Such documentation has obvious benefits, but in the frenzied early stages of a litigation project, many people shortcut careful, thorough note taking. Such documentation will often prove critical, particularly if the litigation uses fact witness testimony.

A best practice in the area of documentation includes the use of standardized forms, checklists, and procedures for each step of the project, including the following:

- Data request form
- Evidence receipt form
- Evidence handling procedures and checklist
- Chain of custody form
- Imaging procedures and checklist
- Specific procedures and checklists for various operating systems (e.g., Windows and Linux)
- Analytical procedures
- Overall computer forensic lab maintenance procedures[30]

The degree of formality can vary according to the size, stakes, and nature (e.g., civil versus criminal) of the project, but a party that decides to invest in such a project will face a negligible incremental cost of doing it correctly and possible severe penalties for doing it incorrectly.

One will encounter situations that vary from standard procedures. One should document the variations from the departures and the associated rationale. These best practices will serve to (1) ensure compliance with all steps; (2) increase the efficiency of the quality control process on the procedures performed; and (3) document all steps performed to support any subsequent testimony and any written or oral report of findings. Also, many projects have extended or multiple lives, such as an internal investigation followed by an SEC inquiry and finally civil litigation. When one takes up a long-dormant project, or when project personnel change, a set of organized and detailed workpapers is a godsend.

(g) Analyze Data.   Information storage differs from pages in a banker's box (which holds approximately 2,000 pages of 8 x 11 paper). To help put electronic volumes into perspective, Exhibit 17-1 lists the approximate equivalent number of printed pages that various amounts of electronic information will yield if printed.

Take the example of "an employee that operates a laptop that can store 20 gigabytes of data which must be sifted and analyzed. A gigabyte of data can produce anywhere from 25,000 to 75,000 pages or images, enough paper to fill the bed of a full-sized pickup truck."[31] Cases commonly involve terabytes of information—the equivalent of 2,500,000 to 7,500,000 printed pages. (A terabyte equals 1,000 gigabytes.)

Electronic Measurement	Tangible Equivalent	Example Media
1 byte (8 bits)[a]	One character	
10 bytes	One word	
2 kilobytes[b]	Typewritten page	An Excel file with 72 addresses, no formatting ~ 23 KB (KB = kilobyte)
1 megabyte[c]	Small novel	Compact disks hold ~ 700 MB (MB = Megabyte)
1 gigabyte[d]	The bed of a pickup truck filled with paper	Most hard drives are > 40 GB, some are 300 GB (and getting bigger by the day) (GB = gigabyte)
1 terabyte[e]	50,000 trees made into paper and printed	A file server used for file sharing purposes could easily be multiple TBs (TB = terabyte)

[a]The most basic information unit used in computing and information theory. A single bit is a one or a zero, a true or a false, a "flag" which is "on" or "off," or in general, the quantity of information required to distinguish two mutually exclusive states from each other. *Source:* http://www.answers.com.
[b]Kilobyte = 1,024 bytes.
[c]Megabyte = 1,048,576 bytes.
[d]Gigabyte = 1,073,741,824 bytes.
[e]Terabyte = 1,099,511,627,776 bytes.

Source: Adapted from James S. Huggins at www.jamesshuggins.com/h/tek1/how_big.htm

Exhibit 17-1.   Electronic Measurement

So what's a legal team to do? Common practice converts electronically stored information into its paper form equivalent, usually in TIFF or PDF format. In addition, the processes feed the content of the electronically stored information into databases that allow the team to narrow their focus based on keywords or phrases searching.

Functionally, these databases containing images and searchable content do not significantly differ from those that were built decades ago on mainframe and minicomputers by scanning and coding paper document populations. As with those older databases, reliance on keyword searching continues to have its limitations, including the following:

- Misspelled words or paraphrased expressions in target documents leave them unidentified in a keyword search.

- Search parameters need to strike the right balance between precision and recall. Highly precise searches (i.e., exact word searches) will likely retrieve a manageable number of highly relevant documents but can miss many relevant documents. Fuzzy searches with less precision retrieve high volumes of documents including many false hits.

In recent years, legal technology providers have attempted to use other tools to augment keyword searching and to help the legal team understand large data populations more rapidly. These include the following:

- **Concept searching.** Concept searching is the retrieval of documents based on common subject matter, rather than the existence of specific words. Thus, a concept search tool might recognize that a search for the word "fraud" should also retrieve synonyms such as "cheat" or "deception." It automatically identifies the most significant patterns in any text and uses these compound terms to rank results based on an understanding of meaning rather than simply finding the required words. This is meant to be more adaptive and flexible than exact phrase or proximity searching. Also, the analyst can express queries in natural language, with no need for complex query syntax associated with traditional Boolean techniques.

  Many legal professionals use concept searching in an attempt to make the document review process quicker, more accurate, and more efficient than either paper review or keyword searching. Concept search tools attempt to learn the meanings of words from the documents it reads and not just the presence of keywords so reviewers can focus on the most relevant documents first, instead of wasting time reviewing documents in random order.

- **Data visualization.** Charts, graphs, and other images used to simplify the presentation of vast quantities of information have long been standard tools of the expert witness. However, applying similar visualization tools to understand large bodies of textual information is a relatively new approach. Data visualization tools (discussed later in this section) allows the user to explore data through a graphic interface instead of (or in addition to) traditional word or phrase searches.

- **Social network analysis.** Grouping information based on communication among groups of individuals can be an effective means of selecting subsets that may be germane to key issues. Core groups of individuals are often cognizant of key issues, and focused searches—including communications among these groups—can isolate such content.

- **Timeline analysis.** Timeline analysis can reveal trends in patterns of activity. Such analysis can lead to indications of missing information as well as clearly demonstrate spikes in activity perhaps occurring in proximity to important events.

- **Visualization tools.** An increasing number of applications imbed various visualization capabilities to enable a reviewer to discern relations among sets of information. These tools rely on a variety of taxonomic and other linguistic aggregation or clustering techniques. Such techniques, in theory, accelerate review efforts by logically grouping or organizing information based on the textual content. In certain situations, analysts use such technology to identify content that responds to specific discovery requests. In other cases, the technology facilitates review of information for relevance. However, these tools are evolving, and many complexities are associated with their use; for instance, some visualization tools dynamically "learn" while in use, making it difficult to replicate review efforts.

17.5 STRUCTURED DATA: USE OF TRANSACTIONAL DATA IN LITIGATION TODAY

(a) Understand Underlying Systems.   After identifying which systems to analyze (customer relation management, general ledger, etc.) the analyst should obtain from each system administrator an explanation of how it functions and how the data elements in the system relate to each other. One can also learn of other related and important systems while working with the system administrator. For example, one may learn that interrelations or interfaces exist among subsidiary systems or even subsidiary entities.[32] One could also learn that various data consolidation steps occur in subsidiary systems before the data pass to the system under review. Analysts could also find that the ledger system does not consolidate and report the financial information but that such activity occurs in a separate system (e.g., On-line Analytical Processing [OLAP] solutions) used for management purposes.

Identification of OLAP systems will help the analyst reconcile the underlying data to historically published financial data because the analyst needs to understand how the OLAP application aggregates the components of the financial statements. Moreover, many OLAP applications allow the end-user to make unidirectional adjustments that the user does not post to the underlying general ledger, known as *top side* entries.

(b) Request Data.   When collecting transactional data from client systems,[33] the analyst should articulate the request in detail. The request should include written instructions for specific tables, fields, time periods, and control totals used for reconciliation purposes. The request should also specify the preferred method to extract the data from source systems and preferred media types for the data delivery. Firms sometimes encrypt sensitive data when complying with a request, providing the key only to the data analyst.

When extracting data from proprietary or outdated systems, the analyst should interview system operators to learn about system design, functionality, and available documentation. Sometimes little documentation or knowledge will exist. One can usually extract at least some of the data, but the complexities associated with obtaining and reconciling it will prove more laborious and time consuming.

When encountering nontypical operating systems or applications, one can contract with a third-party firm or consultant with experience in such systems or applications. Alternatively, one might find third-party applications that can export the information to more conventional applications or file formats.

(c) Collect Data.   After identifying and understanding the transaction systems containing the target data, one must decide on the scope and means of data collection. Many companies have multiple ledgers because of mergers, acquisitions, and international operations. Sometimes companies phase in new accounting or ERP applications so that not all divisions will have their accounting or other applications on the same platform. These situations make it difficult to view the data in a consolidated or consistent manner across the enterprise.

To consolidate data from diverse systems, analysts should apply the data management principles discussed in Section 17.5(d) and collect any available system-descriptive information (e.g., data dictionaries, recollections of IT personnel, etc.) from the client. This information will help the analyst identify the types of data stored in various tables in fields, so that the consolidator can map common elements from diffuse systems together. For example, in accounts payable data, it is critical to understand which fields contain which amounts—for instance, invoice amount, payment amount, and adjustment amount—for each line item of each invoice when one is mapping that information to summary journal entries of accounts payable activity. This data mapping becomes even more complicated when the system stores the same data variables in different formats (e.g., metric units in one system, English in another) or currencies.

Analysts can physically collect the transactional system data (such as general ledger data) in various ways. The simplest method uses the end application itself (e.g., the company's normal general ledger package) to produce various reports in electronic or paper form. This method captures only a summary of the data, however. A more comprehensive approach is to copy all data tables. In addition to understanding the relation among key tables, this approach gives the expert flexibility to run nonstandard analyses.

(d) Validate Completeness of Data Set.   Once the analysts have understood the systems and requested the data, they need to perform the following tasks upon receipt of the information:

- Log all incoming data sets to create an inventory of information received and to track what remains outstanding. The inventory follows the format of the data request and should include at least the following information for each receipt:[34] date received, sender, recipient, shipment method with tracking information included, Bates number (if provided), media (e.g., CD-ROM, DLT tape), description of the file, and file name(s). An inventory of the data will prove critical to maintaining an audit trail and to managing the large volume of data often received in complex litigation matters. The inventory is also a helpful project management tool to track its progress of receiving data.

- Select the analytical software with the appropriate power and functionality for the data sets. Common tools include Excel for smaller data sets; Oracle, SQL Server and Access for relational database uses; SAS and SPSS for statistical needs.

- Load the data into the selected data analysis tool. One should copy the data set to create a working data set, thereby ensuring the integrity of the original data. One should add the location of the copy to the data inventory.

- Confirm that the data received conform to the expected data model. This step consists of comparing the data received with any previously gained information about the data, including record layouts, data dictionaries, answers to interrogatories, deposition testimony, and interviews with IT personnel. The team documents deviations from the expected data model into an issue log that a team member will track for resolution.

(i) Processing Special Data Formats.   For unknown file type formats, an Internet search frequently identifies the original application and methods to read the data. For example, one can transform report files (noted with a *.prn prefix) into a table format using third-party software products such as Monarch, or custom-generated PERL, or Visual Basic scripts. One can extract data within certain PDF files using custom software applications available for purchase.

In addition to unknown file type formats, the opposing side could produce data sets in non-ASCII character sets. Hexadecimal is a common character set when one is working with EBCDIC data retrieved from older mainframe systems. Available tools to convert hexadecimal to ASCII include the MKS Toolkit and the statistical package SAS. Many vendors specialize in the conversion of data from legacy systems. International character sets have become more common and one can load these into most database tools, if this is noted upon loading.

Analysts also encounter unexpected values within a data set. These include nontextual objects, such as embedded objects or images; unusual date formats, such as YYYYMMDD; and European numeric formats (e.g., 2.000.000,00 representing two million). When working with currencies in international data sets, one must note the currency used.

(ii) Reconciling Data.   Once analysts have loaded the data into the data analysis tool(s), they identify any problems with the data and reconcile the data to summary reports. The summary reports take the form of financial statements or other internal reports. Analysts often identify multiple problems with the data and perform reconciliations iteratively.

The analyst prepares a report listing summary statistics for each column in the data table. The report provides the following for different types of columns, as the following table shows.

Column Type	Statistics
Numeric	Minimum value Maximum value Average Standard deviation Total across all rows The number of zero values The number of null values
Categorical	Category values with frequencies
Text	The number of null values
Date	Minimum value Maximum value Count by period (e.g., month, year) The number of zero values The number of null values

Some analyses will require additional information, depending on the data set. For example, if the summary report identifies a minimum sales date of January 1, 1990, in a data set of sales for years 2000 through 2004, the team will further analyze the data to identify whether the 1990 sales date is a one-time occurrence or whether multiple records exist with pre-2000 sales dates. Another example relates to the consistency of data across time periods. The team can query the number of records and total sales volume for each month during 2000 through 2004. This query will identify abnormalities or gaps in sales activity. Analyses that were once time consuming and expensive continue to become quicker and cheaper as software and hardware tools become more powerful. Nonetheless, the best analysts use experienced judgment in deciding the nature and extent of testing.

In addition to inconsistencies identified within a given data table, the team prepares a report analyzing known relations between tables. Using our sales data example, assume the analyst also has a product lookup table that describes the products for sale. The report analyzes how many products in the lookup table do not appear in the sales data and how many sales transactions list products for which no value exists in the lookup table. The report also identifies any duplicate key values, such as two identical product codes in the lookup table.

Once analysts have investigated issues within individual data sets and between data sets with known relations, they create a log of the inconsistencies and give it to the client (or opposing attorney, for adversary's data) for follow-up. As analysts resolve problems with the data, they should make note of the resolution in the data issue log. Problems often occur with the data received from a client or opposing side.

After investigating and resolving the issues within the data, one must reconcile the data to financial reports or other summary reports. For example, one should be able to trace the contents of an accounts receivable subledger system up to the comparable line item(s) in a public company's report on Form 10-K. Depending on the circumstances of the data and related problems, the analyst will either reconcile the data to summaries with no variance or within a level of tolerable error. In any event, the team must confirm that the data used for analysis have the same information as other summary reports.

Without confirming the data's completeness and accuracy, the parties cannot rely on any analysis of the data. Analysts should continue to verify the data's integrity and comprehensiveness at various stages of data analysis.

(e) Analyze Data

(i) Organizing Data for Efficient Processing.   Before the data analysis begins, the team selects the conceptual and physical design of the database. An important aspect of the database design is the choice of software package in which the data are housed. Typical packages used are spreadsheet applications such as Microsoft Excel, database applications such as Microsoft Access and Oracle, and statistical applications such as SAS and SPSS. The selection depends on five factors:

1. **The types of anticipated analyses:** The team should describe what the interim work product and final analyses will look like in order to ascertain the complexity of the calculations underlying the analyses. For instance, statistical

applications often contain built-in functionality for complex regression modeling that is not feasible without custom programming in a spreadsheet or database application.

2. **The expected volume and complexity of the data:** In general, the larger the volume of the information to be analyzed, the more efficient a database or statistical application will be over a spreadsheet application. The same holds true for the complexity of the data.

3. **The number of concurrent data users:** The team should examine whether many different people will need to access and analyze the information simultaneously. Most spreadsheet applications will allow "write" or "edit" access by only one individual at a time, thus slowing the team's ability to update the data or to perform calculations.

4. **The dynamism of the data** (i.e., whether the data will change during the course of the litigation): Static data based on historical activity (such as journal entries posted into a general ledger) are factual in nature, and dynamism will not affect them. However, data included in a spreadsheet that is electronically linked to a database will change if the data in the underlying database change. Also, if the team anticipates updates of new activity as time passes, the data set is considered dynamic.

5. **The timing and cost associated with implementing the database design:** Review of information contained in a spreadsheet may be the least costly approach at first glance. However, if the spreadsheet itself contains vast data or is linked to underlying databases or other spreadsheets, the complexity of reviewing data using such an application will likely impact cost. Sometimes, a team can manage large sets of data only by using database applications that have their own cost implications. Another aspect that affects timing and cost is the original application that stored the data. If the team has access to the original application, it must consider whether that application is sufficient to prepare the required analyses, compared with moving the data to another application.

Assessment of the appropriate application to conduct the analysis is a large consideration that should take place early on in the lifecycle of the matter to minimize cost and optimize value.

Exhibit 17-2 provides a comparison of each category of data management applications.

After the team selects the data management application, it must decide how much refinement to put into the original data on the front end to expedite the analysis stage. This depends on the specific situation and objective and on the factors noted in the preceding list. The types of changes the analyst will consider fall into three categories:

1. **Normalization.** decomposing data,[35] into the smallest logical units to decrease the amount of data storage necessary and increase the efficiency of analysis process. Although this may seem unnecessary in an age of cheaper resources, it is a valuable technique for large data sets. Exhibit 17-3 shows a simple example of normalization. Note that in this example, normalization

	Excel Spreadsheet	Database Application	Statistical Application
When Used	• Data contains fewer than 65,536 rows and fewer than 256 columns • Analyses do not require complex calculations • Analyses do not require complex matching between different data sets • Only one user at a time has edit rights to the data	• Data exceeds Excel's capacity. • Data consists of multiple, related tables • Analyses require complex, nonstatistical calculations[a] • Multiple users access the data concurrently	• Data exceeds Excel's capacity • Data consists of multiple, related tables • Analyses require complex statistical calculations, such as complex regression modeling
Example(s) of Analyses	• Calculation of average sales amount by product type • Examination and preparation of pro-forma financial statements • Graphing and simple statistical analyses, such as statistical significance tests	• Lost profits calculation using detailed sales order data and payment history data covering 10 years • In class action, calculation of number of potential class members and claim amounts, using a large set of customer billing history data • Complex matching algorithms, such as with name and address	• Statistical tests for alleged gender or age biases using historical personnel data • Statistical sampling

Exhibit 17-2. Comparison of Data Management Applications

	Excel Spreadsheet	Database Application	Statistical Application
Dynamism of Data	• Subject to inadvertent effects of dynamism if values are linked to other changing data sources • If data values are changing, the accuracy of calculations based on those values should be reverified after each change	• Analyses can be readily updated with changing and expanding data	• Analyses can be readily updated with changing and expanding data
Timing and Cost Considerations	• Typically the lowest cost and quickest solution with smaller, less complex data sets	• Varying cost dependent on volume of information and source application • Typically more time required to analyze information than with spreadsheet	• Varying cost dependent on volume of information and source application • Typically more time required to analyze information than with spreadsheet

[a] For example, consider an analysis that requires identification of commonalities among millions of records that meet various criteria and the subsequent transformation of those records in a specified manner.

Exhibit 17-2. (Continued)

Original sales order information received:

Sales Order #	Product Code	Product Name	Quantity	Cost per Unit	Total Cost
1001	A-123	Widget A	5	$500	$2,500
1002	A-123	Widget A	10	500	5,000
1003	B-456	Widget B	8	750	6,000
1004	C-789	Widget C	7	400	2,800
1005	B-456	Widget B	12	750	9,000

Normalized data sets—sales order listing and product code listing:

Sales Order #	Product Code	Quantity	Total Cost
1001	A-123	5	$2,500
1002	A-123	10	5,000
1003	B-456	8	6,000
1004	C-789	7	2,800
1005	B-456	12	9,000

Product Code	Product Name	Cost per Unit
A-123	Widget A	$500
B-456	Widget B	750
C-789	Widget C	400

Exhibit 17-3.   Normalization of Data

reduces the number of data cells from 30 to 29, about 3 percent. The efficiency increases exponentially as the volume of data increases. The efficiencies are exponential because they are proportional to the reduction in the number of records.

2. **Standardization.** creating consistency among similar data to ease the analysis of large amounts of data, for example, conforming one file's European dating convention to another's American format, or ensuring that a database of petroleum products lists volume in gallons or barrels, but not both.

3. **Supplementation.** adding additional columns of data to ease analysis. Examples of supplementation include:

   • Parsing the columns containing multiple pieces of information (e.g., one field containing city, state, and zip code; or one field containing both a department code and an account number).

   • Grouping the data rows into distinct sets (e.g., employees with salaries in distinct ranges; customers with account types of active, delinquent, or terminated).

- Calculation of various values within a data row (e.g., adding freight, tax, and product costs to get total invoice price).

One should document all refinements to the data so an outside party can recreate the changes. Analysts should not modify the original data, but instead place the modified values into additional data columns or tables, as necessary, using a consistent naming convention for the column and table names. Also, the team should maintain the programming scripts used to populate the new columns in an organization scheme that mirrors the column and table naming convention. The programming script should also contain information about when it was run and the purpose of the script. Section 17.4(f)(ii) discussed the importance of documenting all changes to the data as critical to maintaining a proper audit trail for any analyses introduced into evidence.

(ii) Preparing a Summary of Data.   The analyst then prepares a summary of the data so that the team will know what information is available for analysis. This summary includes a brief description of the information and statistics relevant to the particular data set. These statistics include the time frame represented, total transaction amount, number of e-mail messages by the custodian, and the like. The analyst can also print out a listing of sample records from the data set as further illustration of the available information.

(iii) Common Pitfalls to Avoid.   Faulty analysis often occurs when one rushes to obtain answers from the data before understanding them and ensuring their completeness and accuracy. Analysts often need to produce answers soon after they receive data, but faulty answers can jeopardize the case strategy. Another common problem results from careless project management. A team that fails to track the data processing at every step and cannot recreate its steps breaks the audit trail, and any resulting analyses can become worthless. The team can avoid both these pitfalls with proper planning and communication between all parties.

(iv) Preparing the Analyses.   Analysis of electronic data occurs throughout the litigation process: answering interrogatories, drafting class certification motions, preparing attorneys and witnesses for deposition, and quantifying damages. Because case strategy evolves as more evidence comes to light, the team must stay in communication with counsel and the client to advance and inform the case strategy. The evolution of the strategy will affect the types and substance of the data analysis performed—sensitivity, time series, regression, and the whole range in the analyst's tool kit, as described in the other chapters of this book. When working with data sets, however, one must test for reasonableness and completeness, as this will identify many of the most common problems arising in data management.

After preparing each analysis, the team confirms its accuracy through reasonableness and completeness tests. Reasonableness tests compare the expected results of the analysis with the actual results. One can derive expected results of the analysis from specific case knowledge, review of the company's financial statements, or general industry knowledge. For example, consider an analysis that calculates Cost of Goods Sold (COGS) as a percentage of Gross Revenue. One can analyze COGS/Gross Revenue ratios for the same company over time as well as compare such ratios with industry comparables. As illustrated in Exhibit 17-4, an

Firm	COGS/Gross Revenue	
	Company A	Comparable
Q1	80.0%	79.0%
Q2	83.0	78.0
Q3	81.0	81.0
Q4	65.0	80.5
Average COGS/Gross Revenue	78.44%	
Standard Deviation COGS/Gross Revenue	5.63	
Upper 1 STD	84.07	
Lower 1 STD	72.81	

Exhibit 17-4.   Analysis of Quarterly Data

analysis of the quarterly COGS/Gross Revenue for Company A and Comparable shows that Company A's Q4 ratio fails the reasonableness test since the ratio exceeds one standard deviation from the mean for the data represented. Even though it flunks the reasonableness test as designed, a one-in-four failure rate presents an expected result, by definition, of a standard deviation. Accordingly, the expert must specify the calibration of what the analysis will consider an outlier with due consideration given to the size of the data set and the time available to analyze the results.

When a data point exceeds the reasonableness threshold, the team performs manual recalculations of any functions or calculations to verify their accuracy. Slight but important errors in calculations that can lead to big differences in the final calculation might present themselves only when one is recalculating potential anomalies.

Completeness tests check the accuracy of the analysis by comparing record counts and transaction amounts with known control totals for the data sets. For example, consider a complicated analysis that involves matching customer invoices and the transactions involving those invoices, such as payments or adjustments. If the join between the two data sets fails to consider whether any duplicate entries of customer invoices exist, the system will count information two, three, or four times, depending on the number of duplicate entries. Likewise, if the join does not consider whether any invoices do not have associated transactions, the analysis might remove the information for those invoices.

17.6   INFORMATION ARCHIVAL

As the team drafts, revises, and produces analyses for individuals, it needs to log and track analyses to maintain control over the most current version and to track who has which version. As in all litigation matters, and with information generally, the fewer copies existing in the first instance, and the more rigorous the (recommended) process for calling back superseded drafts,[36] the less the risk of later confusion or of others relying on information that is no longer up to date. The team should maintain archival copies (and the supporting workpapers) of all analyses distributed to other parties.

At the project's conclusion, the team follows preset procedures to archive the original information received through the litigation, as well as the work product and analyses that the team created. If confidentiality agreements or protective orders are in effect, one should use this time to revisit and complete compliance requirements.

NOTES

1. Universal Serial Bus storage devices are the now ubiquitous penknife-sized memories that have replaced floppy disks in sneaker nets. These are very small and cheap storage devices commonly used by office and home computer users. They are, in essence, small, portable hard drives.
2. Remarks prepared for delivery by Robert S. Mueller, III, director, Federal Bureau of Investigation, http://www.fbi.gov/pressrel/speeches/muller051205a.htm.
3. http://aol.businessweek.com/magazine/content/04_08/b3871100.htm.
4. Jennifer Saranow, "Use of IM at Work Grows, New Survey by AOL Shows," *The Wall Street Journal Online*, August 25, 2004, D4.
5. "Securing Instant Messaging," Pricewaterhouse Coopers UK.
6. Scott Fletcher, Vinson & Elkins LLP, "Emerging Issues in Electronic Discovery," *Litigation News* (Winter 2003). http://www.vinson-elkins.com/lawyer/lawyer_detail.asp?H4AttyID=321183105.
7. "Rules Committee Chair Suggests How Trial Practice Will Change If Rule Amendments Are Enacted," *Digital Discovery & e-Evidence* (June 2005). http://ddee.pf.com
8. Committee on Rules of Practice and Procedure of the Judicial Conference of the United States, *Report of the Civil Rules Advisory Committee*, revised August 3, 2004, 6. www.uscourts.gov/rules/
9. Ibid. The court can specify terms and conditions for discovery so ordered. www.uscourts.gov/rules/
10. The committee will complete its reassessment in December of 2006 or later. "Federal Judicial Panel Approves New Rules on Discovery of E-data," *Digital Discovery & E-evidence* 5 (July 2005). Published by Pike & Fischer, a subsidiary of The Bureau of National Affairs, Inc.
11. Committee on Rules of Practice and Procedure of the Judicial Conference of the United States, *Report of the Civil Rules Advisory Committee*, revised August 3, 2004, 9.
12. Ibid., 17.
13. *Trigon Ins. Co. v. U.S.*, 204 F.R.D. 277 (E.D. Va. 2001).
14. *See Zubulake v. UBS Warburg LLC et al.* 217 FRD 309 S.D.N.Y. 2003; *Zubulake v. USB Warburg LLC et al.* 230 FRD 290 S.D.N.Y. 2003; *Zubulake v. UBS Warburg LLC et al.* 216 FRD 280 S.D.N.Y. 2003; *Zubulake v. UBS Warburg LLC et al.* 220 FRD 212 S.D.N.Y. 2003; *Zubulake v. UBS Warburg LLC et al.* 229 FRD 422 S.D.N.Y. 2004; *Zubulake v. UBS Warburg LLC et al.* 231 FRD 159 S.D.N.Y. 2005; *Zubulake v. UBS Warburg LLC et al.* 382 F. Supp. 2d, S.D.N.Y. 2005.
15. This facts and circumstances-based case turned on whether Andersen had reached the point at which it should recognize that a litigation hold should commence, suspending its normal retention policies with respect to certain Enron-related documents.
16. *Arthur Andersen LLP, Petitioner v. United States*. Argued April 27, 2005; Decided May 31, 2005, docket number 04-368.
17. Fletcher, "Emerging Issues in Electronic Discovery."
18. Ibid.
19. Sarah DiLuzio, Comment, Workplace Email: It's Not as Private as You Might Think, 25 Del. J. Corp. L. 741, 741 (2000). (*see* Diluzio, supra this note 2, at 745. *See also* Porten v. University of San Francisco, 134 Cal. Rept. 839, 842 (Cal. Ct. App. 1976)

(recognizing a state constitutional violation even when there is no state action). Copyright (c) Sidley Austin Brown & Wood , London 2003.

20. "Outbound E-mail and Content Security in Today's Enterprise," 2006, Proofpoint, Inc. Cupertino, CA, http://itresearch.forbes.com

21. "Directive 95/46 EC of the European Parliament and of the Council of 24 October 1995 on the protection of individuals with regard to the processing of personal data and the free movement of such data" *EU Regulation of Transborder Data Flows* (Sidley Austin Brown & Wood LLP, April 9, 2003).

22. Although each EU member country is governed by the Data Directive, many member countries have additional data privacy regulations that supersede the EU Data Directive.

23. Sidley Austin Brown & Wood LLP, *EU Regulation of Transborder Data Flows* (Sidley Austin Brown & Wood LLP, April 9, 2003).

24. Committee on Rules of Practice and Procedure of the Judicial Conference of the United States, *Report of the Civil Rules Advisory Committee*, revised August 3, 2004, 27.

25. Deputy U.S. Attorney General James Comey, quoted at http://aol.businessweek.com/magazine/content/04_08/b3871100.htm.

26. In most systems, "deleting" a file doesn't erase its content but simply redefines the space it occupies as available for future overwriting. Thus, most storage media will contain fragments of partially overwritten but partially preserved files.

27. For more information on this issue *see* http://www.forensics-intl.com. (c) 2003-2004 Guidance Software, Inc. 215 North Marengo Avenue, Pasadena, CA 91101.

28. *See* the following Web site for more information: http://www.itl.nist.gov/fipspubs/fip180-1.htm.

29. *Guidance Software EnCase Forensic Edition User Manual Version 4 Revision 1.*

30. Chris Davis, Aaron Philipp, and David Cowen; *Hacking Exposed: Computer Forensics* (New York: McGraw-Hill, 2005).

31. www.jamesshuggins.com/h/tek1/how_big.htm.

32. An example might be an automated vendor reordering system talking to the inventory ledger system.

33. Throughout, these concepts applicable to "client" systems also apply to work done on an adversary or investigative target's systems. It is of critical importance that legal counsel be involved in working out the protocols to be followed where such access and cooperation is afforded, because system integrity, degree of access, and the likely inability to continuously re-access systems, premises and personnel are all potential issues and constraints that need to be addressed definitively.

34. Whether one is tracking receipts from adversary or client, clear records of custody and control enhance reliability and evidentiary value.

35. This is a technique of database structuring and optimization, not to be confused with normalization of the data points themselves, such as seasonal adjustments, price-adjusting history for subsequent stock splits, and so on.

36. Consistent with our advice throughout, the analyst must ensure that counsel understands and agrees with any protocols that result in the deletion or destruction of data.

PART **IV**

CIVIL LITIGATION

CHAPTER 18

FEDERAL SECURITIES ACTS AND AREAS OF EXPERT ANALYSIS

Nicholas I. Crew
Kevin L. Gold
Marnie A. Moore

CONTENTS

18.1 INTRODUCTION

This chapter discusses areas of expert analysis arising from cases involving alleged violations of the Federal Securities Acts. We first provide a brief summary of portions of the acts that an economic expert will find relevant. Next, we review legal measures of damages proscribed by these acts and case law. Finally, we discuss three areas in which economic experts often provide analysis: the event study, the but-for price or true-value line, and aggregate damages estimation.

The authors revised and consolidated this chapter from predecessor chapters in the previous editions. The authors of the earlier chapters were M. Laurentius Marais, Katherine Schipper, David I. Tabak, Fredrick C. Dunbar, Nicholas I. Crew, Patrick G. Goshtigian, Marnie A. Moore, Atulya Sarin, Harinda de Silva, Nancy Lo, and Tara Nells.

18.2   FEDERAL SECURITIES ACTS

The Securities Acts of 1933,[1] the Securities Exchange Act of 1934,[2] and the Private Securities Litigation Reform Act of 1995[3] constitute the federal regulatory instruments of interstate securities transactions. These laws attempt to ensure that the investing public has sufficient information to enable it to rely on the integrity of the securities market while also protecting securities issuers against abusive litigation.

(a) Securities Act of 1933.   The 1933 act regulates the registration requirements and initial distribution of a security.

(i) Section 11: Civil Liabilities on Account of False Registration Statement.   Section 11 provides cause of action to a security's purchaser if the issuer's registration statement falsifies or omits a material fact.[4] A material fact is any information a rational investor would use to make a well-informed investment decision. Plaintiffs can charge the issuer, its directors, or any party that prepared or certified the registration statement (or any report or valuation related to the statement), such as accountants, appraisers, or underwriters. Defendants can avoid liability by proving that, at the time of acquisition, the plaintiff knew of the untruth or omission.[5] However, plaintiffs do not need to prove a defendant's scienter (i.e., guilty knowledge or intent) to establish a Section 11 claim.

(ii) Section 12: Civil Liabilities Arising in Connection with Prospectuses and Communications. Section 12(1) allows the purchaser in an offering to file a cause of action against any person who offers or sells a security in violation of Section 5, which prohibits the sale or delivery of unregistered securities.[6] Section 12(2) prohibits the selling of securities through distribution of a prospectus or oral communication that omits or falsifies material facts via interstate commerce or the mail.[7] As with Section 11, defendants can avoid liability by proving that the purchaser knew of the untruth or omission. The seller can avoid liability by proving that it did not know, or could not have known, of the omission or untruth.

(b) Securities Exchange Act of 1934.   The 1934 act addresses security transactions in the aftermarkets (i.e., securities traded after the initial public offering [IPO]). It requires periodic filings with the Securities and Exchange Commission (SEC) and deems as unlawful activities such as fraudulent transactions, insider trading, market manipulation, omitted material information, and misstatements in filed documents.

(i) Section 9: Prohibition Against Manipulation of Security Prices.   Section 9 prohibits any person from engaging in any action that gives a false or misleading appearance with respect to the market for the security.[8] This includes market manipulation such as creating a misleading appearance of active trading; misrepresenting the price of a security through a series of transactions; broker-dealers circulating information intended to manipulate a security's price; and abusing the trading of options to induce the security's purchase or sale.[9]

(ii) Section 16: Directors, Officers, and Principal Stockholders.   To prevent the unfair use of information by persons who have access to privileged information, § 16(b)

places restrictions on an issuer's directors, officers, or principal stockholders from realizing a profit from the sale or purchase of the security within six months of the initial transaction. Recovery of such profits under § 16(b) requires that the defendant buy and sell the security within a six-month period. Rule 10b-5 addresses insider sales outside the six-month period.

(iii) Rule 10b-5: Employment of Manipulative and Deceptive Devices.   Rule 10b-5, promulgated under § 10(b) of the Securities Exchange Act of 1934, deems it unlawful to make use of any means or instrumentality of interstate commerce, or of the mails or of any facility of any national securities exchange, to do the following:

- Employ any device, scheme, or artifice to defraud
- Make any untrue statement of a material fact or to omit to state a material fact necessary in order to make the statements made, in the light of the circumstances under which they were made, not misleading
- Engage in any act, practice, or course of business which operates or would operate as a fraud or deceit upon any person, in connection with the purchase or sale of any security[10]

(c) Private Securities Litigation Reform Act of 1995.   The 1995 Reform Act creates and redefines provisions of the 1933 act and 1934 act. The new and amended provisions aim to reduce abusive litigation on issuers and provide a limitation on damages, while improving the quality of information provided to investors. Specifically, § 101 adds three provisions to the acts related to the certification filed with the complaint, the appointment of the lead plaintiff, and the disclosure of settlement terms to the class. Added sections require heightened pleading standards. Section 102 adds a safe harbor provision for forward-looking statements made by companies. Section 105 amends the acts to require that the loss resulted from the fraud. Section 201 addresses proportionate liability, and Section 301 to the 1934 act establishes new requirements for auditor fraud detection and disclosure.

(i) Section 101: Private Securities Litigation Reform.   Section 101 aims to reduce abusive litigation by imposing new requirements on the plaintiff class that, in effect, authenticate the plaintiff's intentions. These requirements require that the lead plaintiff file a certification with the complaint. They aim to deter the "professional plaintiff."[11] In addition, § 27(a)(3) of the 1933 act and § 21D(a)(3) of the 1934 act require that the court appoint a lead plaintiff to represent the best interests of the plaintiff class. The plaintiff has the responsibility to give early notice to all potential members of the plaintiff class of the action taken against the defendant company. Within 60 days of the required (widely published) notice, any member of the class can request to be appointed as the lead plaintiff by the court.[12] Prior to the Reform Act, the plaintiff in the first complaint filed became the lead plaintiff. The new provision gives the plaintiffs with a higher financial stake in the security, such as institutional investors, more control over the litigation. Section 27(a)(7) of the 1933 act and Section 21D(a)(7) of the 1934 act require that the communication to plaintiffs report the settlement amount of damages both on an aggregate and on a per-share basis. Also, if counsel seeks an award of attorneys' fees or costs, counsel must disclose the amount on a per-share basis and include a brief explanation of the charges.[13]

Amendments to the 1934 act target abusive litigation by requiring heightened pleading standards. These amendments include the following:

- **Misleading Statements and Omissions.** Section 21D(b)(1) of the 1934 act requires that, for actions taken against issuers for making misleading statements (or omitting material facts), the complaint must clearly state why the statement is misleading (or why the omitted information is material).[14]
- **Required State of Mind.** As stated in Section 21D(b)(2), for each misstatement or omission of material fact made by the defendant, the complaint must "state with particularity facts giving rise to a strong inference that the defendant acted with the required state of mind" for the plaintiffs to collect any awarded damages. Plaintiffs must justify each allegation addressed in the complaint with the defendant's intentions and the facts explaining the reason for the false statement or omission and the defendant's intentions.[15]

(ii) Section 10: Safe Harbor for Forward-Looking Statements. The Securities Reform Act of 1995 creates a new provision of the 1933 and 1934 acts that restricts plaintiffs' causes of action regarding management's plans for the future. Section 27A of the 1933 act and Section 21E of the 1934 act states that a defendant is not liable for untrue statements or omission of material facts if the statement or omission was made in a forward-looking statement. Issuers or any party directed by the issuer making the statement must clearly identify it as a forward-looking statement; "meaningful cautionary" language outlining factors that could cause the forward-looking statement to change materially should accompany the statement.[16] A forward-looking statement includes management plans for future operations, forecasted economic performance, and projections of revenues and earnings.

(iii) Section 105: Loss Causation. Section 105 amends § 12(b) of the 1933 act and § 21D(b)(4) of the 1934 act to require plaintiffs to show that the defendant's actions caused the loss in the security's value. Specifically, § 105 defines the actionable loss as "the depreciation in value of the subject security resulting from such part of the prospectus or oral communication, with respect to which the liability of that person is asserted, not being true or omitting to state a material fact required to be stated therein."[17] Section 21D(b)(4) states, "In any private action arising under this title, the plaintiff shall have the burden of proving that the act or omission of the defendant alleged to violate this title caused the loss for which the plaintiff seeks to recover damages."[18]

(iv) Section 201: Proportionate Liability. The 1995 Reform Act adds § 21D(g) to the 1934 act. This addition states that plaintiffs cannot coerce peripheral defendants into settlements. Only those who knowingly committed a violation of the securities law are liable. For instance, the defendants are liable if they knew of the false statement or the omission and also knew that investors were reasonably likely to rely on the misrepresentation or omission.[19]

(v) Section 301: Auditor Fraud Detection and Disclosure. Section 301 of the 1995 Reform Act adds Section 10A(a) to the 1934 act. It requires that the audit performed by an independent public accountant shall include

(1) procedures designed to provide reasonable assurance of detecting illegal acts that would have a direct and material effect on the determination of financial statement amounts; (2) procedures designed to identify related party transactions that are

material to the financial statements or otherwise require disclosure therein; and (3) an evaluation of whether there is substantial doubt about the ability of the issuer to continue as a going concern during the ensuing fiscal year.[20]

If the audit reveals fraud, the accountant has a responsibility to report the illegal acts to the appropriate parties.[21]

18.3   ALTERNATIVE DAMAGES MEASURES

Plaintiffs who prevail on the merits of their securities litigation can recover based on rescission,[22] profits, or unspecified damages, by statute or court rulings, depending on the circumstance.

Plaintiffs file most federal securities claims under §§ 11 and 12 of the 1933 act and § 10(b) of the 1934 act. The 1933 act specifies the damages method, but the 1934 act lacks distinct provisions for calculating damages, leaving the appropriate measure of damages to the court's discretion. Some of these measures use the plaintiff's injury as a benchmark to measure damages, whereas others consider the defendant's gain in the transaction. The Reform Act of 1995 includes additional guidelines on estimating damages.

(a) Section 11 of the 1933 Act.   Section 11 provides three alternative measures of damages. The plaintiff can recover the difference between the amount paid for the security (not to exceed the offer price) and the following:

1. The value of the security at the time the plaintiff brought the suit; or
2. The price at which the seller sold the security prior to the suit; or
3. The price at which the seller sold the security after the plaintiff filed the suit, if the resulting damages are less than that calculated under (1) above

Furthermore, § 11 reduces damages by price declines that the defendant can prove relate to factors other than the misrepresentations in the registration statement.

(b) Section 12 of the 1933 Act.   If the court finds the issuer liable under § 12, the plaintiff may recover the consideration paid for such security with interest thereon, less the amount of any income received thereon, upon the tender of such security, or for damages if the plaintiff no longer owns the security.[23] As with § 11, § 12 includes a loss causation provision so that the plaintiff cannot recover the portion of the loss that defendants can prove does not relate to the fraud.

(c) Section 9 of the 1934 Act.   We are not aware of any case law on the measure of damages under § 9 of the 1934 act.[24] In *Piper v. Chris-Craft Industries, Inc.*, however, the Supreme Court's language suggests that if a court finds liability, it should compute damages as the difference between the security's transaction price and the price absent the manipulative act.[25]

(d) Section 16 of the 1934 Act.   Section 16(b) provides that the plaintiff recover the profit the defendant realized in connection with insider trading abuses. It does not define profits, and in the event of multiple sales and purchases at different prices, the issue of profit calculation becomes ambiguous. In *Smolowe v. Delendo Corp.*, the court chose to calculate profits by matching[26] the highest sale price to the lowest purchase price, matching the next highest sale price to the next lowest purchase price, and so on.

(e) Section 10(b) of the 1934 Act and Rule 10b-5.   The courts have not reached consensus on the appropriate measure of damages under § 10(b) and Rule 10b-5. Section 10(b) contains no statutory remedy,[27] and because the parties settle most Rule 10 b-5 cases, few court decisions on the measure of damages exist.[28]

Following a strict interpretation of the term *actual damages* in § 28(a) of the 1934 act, and the lead of the Supreme Court in *Affiliated Ute Citizens of Utah v. United States*, many courts have adopted the out-of-pocket rule as the traditional measure of damages in Rule 10b-5 cases.[29]

The out-of-pocket measure rule defines damages as "the difference between the contract price, or the price paid, and the real or actual value at the date of the sale, together with such outlays as are attributable to the defendant's conduct. Or, in other words, the difference between the amount parted with and the value of the thing received."[30] Typically, courts measure this as the plaintiff's purchase price less the true value at the time of the transaction. The true value is the price of the security in the absence of fraud or misrepresentation (*see* Section 18.4(b) of this chapter). Strictly applied, the out-of-pocket rule does not permit damages that depend on increases or decreases in the security's price during the plaintiff's class period (i.e., from the date of the fraud to its disclosure) because the plaintiff agrees to bear market risk by undertaking the transaction.[31] Some courts have adopted a modified out-of-pocket rule, however, which evaluates damages at the disclosure date of the fraud, or at a reasonable time thereafter.

Although courts most commonly apply some version of the out-of-pocket rule, they have the discretion to apply other measures of damages to suit the remedy to the specific harm.[32] Other measures adopted by the courts—and summarized in the following discussion—include the Chasins measure, cover, rescission, restitution (also called windfall profits, disgorgement, or unjust enrichment), consequential damages, and benefit of the bargain.

(i) Chasins Measure.   The Chasins measure, derived from *Chasins v. Smith, Barney & Co.*,[33] awards to the defrauded buyer the total economic loss resulting from the defendant's fraud. The court used this measure of damages because of the lack of evidence as to the true value of the acquired security.[34] Other circumstances in which a plaintiff can seek damages under the Chasins measure occur when the harm to the plaintiff does not relate directly to the price paid for the security, or when a broker-dealer violates Rule 10b-5.[35]

(ii) Cover.   Under the cover remedy, the defrauded seller receives the difference between the highest value the security achieved within a reasonable time after the disclosure of the fraud and the consideration received upon sale of the security. The leading case applying the cover measure is *Mitchell v. Texas Gulf Sulphur.*[36] The defendant, Texas Gulf Sulphur, made an initial press statement denying rumors of an ore discovery; in a later press statement, however, the company admitted that it had made a valuable finding. The Tenth Circuit held that "the measure of damages used should award the reasonable investor the amount it would have taken him to invest in the TGS market within a reasonable period of time after he became informed of the [correct release] ... The award proposed

would permit one to 'cover' by reinvestment and suffer neither loss nor forced sale."[37] The court viewed cover as an appropriate alternative when the defendant does not receive a windfall profit and the rescissionary measure is improper.[38]

(iii) Rescission. Rescission involves the restoration of the counterparties to their pretransaction positions. True rescission involves the return of the security in exchange for the purchase price (plus interest); however, if the holder has already sold the security, the court can use the financial equivalent of rescission, that is, rescissionary damages. Rescissionary damages equal the value of the security that would have been returned, estimated as either the market value at the time of the suit or the highest intervening market value.[39] The courts generally restrict rescission to cases with privity (i.e., direct dealings) between the plaintiff and the defendant, or when a breach of fiduciary duty or unjust enrichment occurs.[40]

(iv) Restitution. In contrast to monetary damages, restitution, sometimes called *windfall profits* or *disgorgement* or *unjust enrichment,* focuses on the defendant's gain rather than on the plaintiff's loss. Unlike rescission, restitution does not require privity between the counterparties.[41] In *Affiliated Ute Citizens of Utah v. United States,*[42] the Supreme Court approved the restitutional measure, citing *Janigan v. Taylor,* for subsequent resale of the stock.[43] The First Circuit Court of Appeals held in Janigan that "[I]t is more appropriate to give the defrauded party the benefit even of windfalls than to let the fraudulent party keep them."[44] This ruling follows from the interpretation that federal securities laws attempt both to compensate defrauded parties and to deter fraudulent acts.[45]

(v) Consequential Damages. Plaintiffs can pursue consequential damages—costs they incurred as a result of the fraud—in connection with general, rescissionary, or restitutional damages. Examples of consequential damages established in case law include dividends on shares sold by a defrauded investor, dividends on shares that the plaintiff would have purchased absent the fraud, brokerage fees incurred in the fraudulent transaction, and expenses related to repurchasing the security that the defrauded investor had sold.[46] The courts have usually imposed two restrictions on consequential damages:

1. The plaintiff must establish a causal relation between the expense and the fraud.
2. Consequential damages cannot duplicate the recovery from other damages measures.[47]

In general, the latter restriction does not bind when the court adopts the out-of-the-pocket rule or restitution as the measure of damages.[48]

(vi) Benefit of the Bargain. The benefit of the bargain measure awards the plaintiff the difference between the gain had the misrepresentations been true and what the plaintiff actually received. Courts have found that "a claim for benefit of the bargain damages must be based on the bargain that was actually struck, not on a bargain whose terms must be supplied by hypothesis about what the parties would have done if the circumstances surrounding their transaction had been different."[49]

(f) Section 21D(e) of the Reform Act of 1995 (Limitation on Damages). Plaintiffs and defendants have presented numerous variations of damages partly attributed to the stock price fluctuating widely for a period of time following the curative disclosure. Section 21D(e) of the Reform Act of 1995 seeks to reduce the variation of damages by allowing a look-back or bounce-back period. Section 21D(e) stipulates that damages cannot exceed "the difference between the purchase or sale price paid or received, as appropriate, by the plaintiff for the subject security and the mean trading price during the 90-day period beginning on the date on which the information correcting the misstatement or omission that is the basis for the action is disseminated to the market."[50] There is also an exception provision: if the plaintiff sells or repurchases the security before the expiration of the 90-day period, the plaintiff's damages "shall not exceed the difference between the purchase or sale price paid or received … and the mean trading price of the security during the period beginning immediately after dissemination of information correcting the misstatement or omission and ending on the date on which the plaintiff sells or repurchases the security."[51]

18.4   THE EXPERT'S ROLE

This section discusses three areas in which economic experts often provide analysis:

1. **Event study.** A well-recognized technique to examine share price movement associated with the release of information. It can help establish materiality of the information and loss causation.
2. **But-for price line.** The value of the security absent the fraud each day during the class period, which is used in the out-of-pocket measure of damages.
3. **Aggregate damages to the class.** Based on actual trading records or estimates of trading behavior using a trading model.[52]

(a) Event Study Methods.   When a dispute or litigation requires an analysis of security price changes in response to a news disclosure, experts must often distinguish the materiality and magnitude of the disclosure. An event study is a statistical approach that experts often use to analyze these two issues.

(i) Definition of Event Study.   An event study is an empirical analysis of an intervention in a time series. In its most common form, an event study involves a statistical regression analysis of a time series of security returns, with the objective of identifying and measuring firm-specific effects of identified information releases, referred to as *events*.

(ii) Illustrative Example.   Exhibit 18-1 lists the daily closing prices and returns of the shares of hypothetical Firm S and a market index for a 51-day period surrounding a hypothetical announcement date. Date "0" (date zero) is the date of the event in question. As the exhibit shows, on date zero, the securities return of the firm was negative 5.03 percent, and the market return was +1.40 percent. The event study provides a way of assessing how much of the firm's return on date zero results from market effects and whether the residual return (i.e., the remaining portion of the firm return after controlling for market effects) is unusual in a statistical sense.

For the 51 days listed in Exhibit 18-1, Exhibit 18-2 shows a scatter plot of Firm S returns against those of the market index. Each observation shows the firm return (shown on the vertical [y] axis) with the market return on the same day (shown on

	Firm S				Firm S		
Event Date	Closing Price	Stock Return	Market Return	Event Date	Closing Price	Stock Return	Market Return
−25 ..	$34.00	10.66%	−1.41%	1 ..	$32.05	4.68%	1.41%
−24 ..	33.46	−1.58	0.57	2 ..	31.91	−0.46	−0.85
−23 ..	33.48	0.05	1.39	3 ..	31.03	−2.75	−0.30
−22 ..	32.69	−2.36	−0.49	4 ..	31.23	0.65	−2.00
−21 ..	31.70	−3.03	−0.55	5 ..	30.59	−2.07	−0.75
−20 ..	31.95	0.79	−0.78	6 ..	32.11	4.98	−0.06
−19 ..	31.69	−0.80	−0.090	7 ..	32.21	0.32	1.49
−18 ..	32.06	1.15	−0.48	8 ..	33.41	3.72	−0.45
−17 ..	32.78	2.27	−0.50	9 ..	31.95	−4.38	−0.92
−16 ..	32.74	−0.12	0.67	10 ..	32.27	1.01	0.63
−15 ..	31.65	−3.33	−0.35	11 ..	33.39	3.48	−0.44
−14 ..	33.18	4.83	1.23	12 ..	34.42	3.08	1.60
−13 ..	32.14	−3.13	1.17	13 ..	35.01	1.72	−0.66
−12 ..	32.23	0.29	0.07	14 ..	35.77	2.16	−0.81
−11 ..	32.10	−0.41	−1.33	15 ..	36.63	2.41	−0.34
−10 ..	30.94	−3.62	0.57	16 ..	37.05	1.16	−0.79
−9 ..	31.88	3.05	0.96	17 ..	36.64	−1.12	1.62
−8 ..	32.18	0.93	0.79	18 ..	37.79	3.14	1.33
−7 ..	31.64	−1.68	0.19	19 ..	38.21	1.12	−0.31
−6 ..	31.85	0.67	−0.10	20 ..	37.31	−2.35	0.38
−5 ..	32.43	1.82	0.28	21 ..	38.27	2.56	1.16
−4 ..	32.24	−0.58	0.18	22 ..	39.83	4.10	1.18
−3 ..	30.22	−6.29	−0.72	23 ..	38.53	−3.28	0.13
−2 ..	30.61	1.29	1.42	24 ..	38.87	0.89	0.16
−1 ..	32.24	5.35	1.18	25 ..	39.90	2.65	−0.64
0 ..	30.62	−5.03	1.40				

Exhibit 18-1. Daily Closing Stock Price and Returns for Period of 51 Trading Days Surrounding Announcement Events for Firm S

the horizontal [x] axis). The solid sloping line is the estimated regression line from applying ordinary least squares regression (a standard statistical method to estimate a linear relation) to the available data shown in the exhibit (excluding the date zero return). This line shows the estimated relation between the firm's return and the market return, based on the data in the exhibit. As the exhibit shows, a positive relation exists, meaning that, on average, higher market returns typically occur with higher returns of the firm. In the exhibit, the date zero's point is filled in. Because this point falls below the estimated regression line, the firm return on date zero is lower than expected, based on the normal day-to-day relation estimated between the market and firm. Practitioners refer to the difference between this point and the solid line (shown in the exhibit by a dotted line) as the firm's *residual return*. The event study provides a way of measuring whether this residual return differs statistically from zero (i.e., whether it is an unusual movement in a statistical sense).

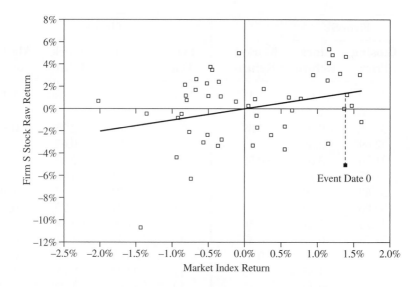

Exhibit 18-2.   Firm S Returns versus Market Index Returns

Appendix A provides a more detailed discussion on the method for conducting an event study.

(iii) Ascertaining Materiality with Event Studies.   In securities cases, counsel often asks the expert to opine on the materiality of information related to the case.[53] For instance, some experts have to ascertain whether false statements or curative disclosures were material in securities cases. Experts frequently use an event study to answer two related questions:

1. Did the disclosure cause a change in the security's value? (*materiality* of the event)

2. If so, what was the size and direction of the net price reaction to the disclosure, after accounting for the effects of other factors? (*magnitude* of the event)

This section discusses how experts use event studies to measure the impact of information in the context of securities. Courts have admitted testimony based on appropriate event studies but have excluded testimony based on an infirm event study.[54]

An event study can provide useful evidence in ascertaining materiality of an event under consideration. All can agree that important events are material, but this raises the question of how to measure importance. Imprecise standards require subjective determinations that vary from case to case. For example, how should a trier of fact ascertain what a reasonable investor would consider material? One could ask a long-time investor to serve as an expert on materiality, and even though this might provide useful insight, it introduces a degree of subjectivity that could vary with each case. Instead, the tools of financial economics provide a scientific and objective way to measure materiality as the probability that a share price movement resulted from chance and not from the news about a particular event. One can quantify materiality with an event study in a manner comparable across cases and events.

In ascertaining materiality, statistical analysis can provide information on the likelihood that the price movement occurred only because of chance. Formally, a materiality test based on an event study provides a statistical answer to the question: How likely is it that the observed share price movement in the event window would have occurred if there were no event that influenced share prices in that window? For example, if an event is material at the 5 percent level, this means that only a 5 percent likelihood exists that the share's normal random price fluctuations could have caused the residual return (or the share price movement after one controls for market, industry, and other effects). Alternatively, if the movement is large enough (as defined using a scientific and statistical definition), we can say that we are 95 percent confident that the size of the residual return exceeds what would be expected based on the share's normal random price fluctuations.

Courts have not specified the level of statistical significance that corresponds to a legal definition of materiality. As with much academic research, they commonly use the 95 percent confidence level but also recognize the 90 percent and 99 percent levels as thresholds for statistical significance. Even though definitive case law does not exist on how statistical confidence levels relate to burden of proof in civil (or criminal) litigation, courts can use event studies to quantify the level of materiality, compare it across cases, and assess it using professional standards from economics literature.

Another issue pertaining to materiality (measured by statistical significance) arises when the cumulative price reaction moves in and out of materiality as time passes. For example, if a share price drops by a large amount on the day of an announcement, the one-day reaction can have statistical significance. However, a rebound on the next day can cause the two-day price reaction to be statistically insignificant, whereas another drop on the third day can cause the three-day price reaction to be statistically significant. In general, experts investigate why the level of materiality changes over the price reaction window. If new information that has no relevance to the case comes into the market, then the analysis should account for this new information in considering the materiality of the event under examination. In addition, experts examine whether the changes in materiality result from the market's reevaluating the importance of the initial event or information, something that experts often deduce from contemporaneous news stories or analyst reports. Some experts test three- or five-day periods surrounding an event to ascertain materiality.

As a general matter, the potential for stock market overreaction might play a role in stock market behavior, although there remains some dispute. This means that if the price initially declines after an event and if, on the second day (or a similar short period), the price returns to a level that makes the event immaterial (with no intervening news event), then an expert might conclude there was short-term overreaction.[55] In addition, in the event of an incomplete disclosure, experts consider subsequent information and price movements to ascertain the full effect of the information.

With some types of material information disclosures, one would not expect to observe statistically significant fluctuations in returns. For example, suppose a company issues an earnings statement that meets market expectations. In such a case, one would not expect to see the company's price change much, even though an earnings announcement that confirms expectations provides important information.

(iv) Magnitude. Experts also use event studies to measure the size of a security price movement as the basis for a damages calculation. For example, as discussed previously in this section, experts often measure the movement in a share price in the wake of a curative disclosure, after controlling for market, industry, and other company-specific influences, to measure the inflation per share. As a result, experts often use event studies to quantify damages in securities fraud cases.[56]

(b) Constructing the But-for Value Line.   For the out-of-pocket measure of damages, experts require an estimate of the but-for price, which is an estimate of the value of the security absent (i.e., but for) the fraud.[57] An expert typically estimates the but-for value on a daily basis. The resulting sequence of prices is often called the *but-for price line* or the *value line*. It represents the value of the security on each day if the market knew the truth that should have been disclosed on that and each previous day. The difference between the but-for price and the actual price is the inflation per share.[58] The inflation per share can vary over time. For example, if a firm perpetuated accounting fraud by increasingly understating its liabilities over a number of years, one might expect the inflation to increase over time as the amount of fraud increased, as Exhibit 18-3 illustrates.

Experts use many approaches to estimate the but-for price line. Many of these approaches involve using the event study method discussed in Section 18.4(a) and Appendix A to measure the share price decline associated with curative disclosures. The share price declines on these curative disclosure dates serve as a basis for measuring the inflation earlier in the class period. The logic of the argument is that when the company disclosed the corrective information on the

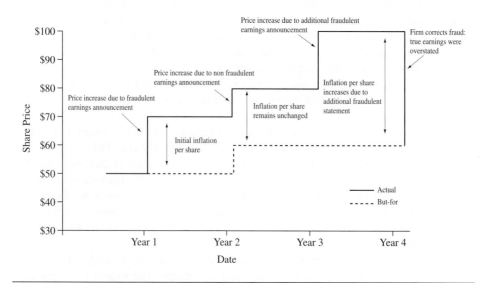

Exhibit 18-3.   Share Price Reactions to Announcements

curative disclosure dates, the share price declined by an amount of X dollars or Y percent, which indicates the decline that would have occurred had the market known the information earlier in the class period. Similarly, experts often measure the share price increases associated with an allegedly false statement to assess how much the share price increased as a result of false information. These price increases can provide guidance as to the extent of the share price inflation until the curative disclosures.

A simple example can help illustrate. Suppose prior to the market opening on Tuesday, a mining firm fraudulently announces it has discovered a valuable mineral deposit worth $100 million. The share price increases $30 per share, or 30 percent, from $100 to $130. The share price does not change until Friday. On Friday, prior to the market opening, the company corrects the fraud by announcing that no valuable deposit exists. The share price declines $30. Exhibit 18-4A illustrates the timeline for this simple example.

The expert's analysis includes a news search, examination of industry and market conditions over the period, and an event study. The expert finds that the relevant industry and market factors did not change on Monday and ascertains that, after controlling for these factors, none of the $30 increase resulted from industry and market factors. After other considerations, which include establishing that no confounding news events occurred on Monday, the expert concludes that the $30 increase results from the announcement. The expert performs a similar analysis for Friday and finds that the $30 decline does not result from other factors and instead results from the curative disclosure. Exhibit 18-4B plots the expert's but-for price line associated with this analysis. As the exhibit shows, the but-for price is $100 per share on each day during the class period. An investor who purchased one share for $130 under the belief that the company had found a

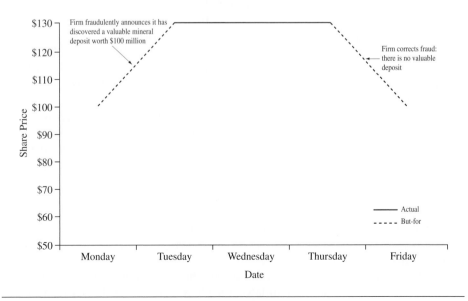

Exhibit 18-4A.   Share Price Reaction to Announcements

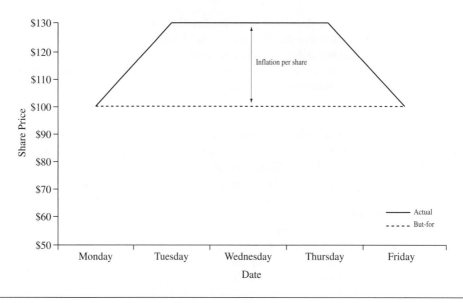

Exhibit 18-4B.   Illustration of Inflation per Share

mineral deposit overpaid by $30. The but-for value (i.e., the value had the truth been known) was, according to the expert's analysis, $100.

Of course, reality is rarely so simple. Many issues complicate the analysis. For example, firms often combine the curative disclosure with other information, making the share price increase or decline an unreliable measure of the fraudulent information at issue. Another complication arises when the disclosed curative information is not relevant for the entire class period. For example, in the case of a company that announces restated financials covering the last three years, one generally cannot attribute the entire decline associated with the full three-year restatement to inflation throughout the entire class period. Class members who purchased early in the class period purchased under less fraud. Early in the class period, the fraud would have a smaller magnitude—in the first fiscal quarter of the class period, only one fiscal quarter of financials would be false, not three years.

A related issue that applies especially to long class periods, surfaces when market conditions change over time so that one cannot conclude that the decline that occurred with the curative disclosure is a reasonable estimate of the inflation earlier in the class period under different market conditions. For example, suppose an announcement of accounting fraud at a firm trading at $1.00 resulted in a price decline of 60 percent, dropping the price to $0.40. Applying the percentage decrease of 60 percent on this date to calculate the but-for price two years earlier may not be reasonable if the share price was trading at $100 two years earlier. Similarly, applying the observed $0.60 decline as the inflation two years earlier when the share traded at $100 may not be reasonable.

Another complication exists in identifying when the inflation entered the share price. Statements that allegedly inflated the share price often do not result in an observed price increase when they were made. For example, one might not expect large increases in share prices for a firm that inflated its stock price by falsely reporting high earnings, if it consistently met market expectations.

To help resolve these issues, experts often incorporate additional analyses beyond the event study. For example, experts have used valuation models, such as discounted cash flow models or multiples models that employ fundamental information, to help estimate the effect of accounting information on the value of the securities. The approaches that experts use to address these issues vary by case.

(c) Estimating Damages.   Under the out-of-pocket measure, the but-for line and a plaintiff's actual trades (or an estimate thereof) provide the basis for estimating a plaintiff's damages. The out-of-pocket measure defines the damages per share for an individual transaction as the difference between the inflation of the share price at purchase and the inflation at sale.[59] In other words, the plaintiff incurs damages to the extent that he or she paid too much (i.e., purchased with inflation); however, the damages diminish to the extent that the plaintiff benefited from selling at too high a price (i.e., sold with inflation). For example, a plaintiff who bought 100 shares with inflation of $5 on the purchase date and sold those shares after a partially curative disclosure reduced the inflation to $1 would incur total damages of $400 (= 100 shares × [$5 − $1]).[60] This calculation is straightforward in principle if the expert knows actual trades; in reality, however, one may not have information on actual trades, and the question of whether an analysis could or should calculate aggregate damages for all class members arises.

In class action lawsuits, there has not been consensus on whether expert testimony on aggregate damages for all class members should be considered. Some courts have indicated that expert testimony on aggregate damages helps to provide context to a jury because a jury should decide aggregate damages.[61] However, some courts have ruled that aggregate damages estimates based on trading models are neither reliable nor necessary. The trier-of-fact need only establish inflation per share at various points in time, and then class members can obtain their award through a proof-of-claim process.[62]

Experts providing testimony on aggregate damages typically obtain class member trading records or more often estimate class member trading behavior and damages using a trading model. The use of actual trading records eliminates the need to model or estimate the trading behavior of those plaintiffs with trading records. However, prior to the proof-of-claim process, actual trading data can be difficult to obtain and will likely be incomplete for all class members.

In the absence of trading data or to supplement it, experts often use trading models to estimate the trading behavior of shareholders during the class period using observable data (such as daily volume and shares outstanding).[63] The idea of a trading cohort helps clarify this type of model. A trading cohort is a group of shareholders that purchases shares at the same time. Most securities cases assume that the same time means the same day. The analysis combines into a single cohort all nonclass members who purchased shares prior to the class period, regardless of the day they purchased shares. The simplest form of the trading model (often referred to as the *proportional trading model*) assumes that on any given day, all shareholders sell the same proportion of their holdings.[64]

Some experts have refined the proportional trading model by developing trading models with richer and more realistic assumptions. Instead of assuming all shareholders are similar, these models allow for different shareholder trading behavior.[65] Two common alternative trading models are the *accelerated trading model* and the *multitrader model*.

The accelerated trading model assumes that on a given day cohorts that have recently purchased are more likely to sell (i.e., they sell a large proportion of their holdings) than cohorts that purchased earlier. In other words, the accelerated trading model attempts to model the concept that shareholders who have held their shares a long time will be less likely to trade than those who have recently purchased their shares.

The multitrader model assumes that the propensity to trade differs among traders. For example, a two-trader model assumes two types of traders—those who trade frequently (*active traders*) and those who do not trade as frequently (*investors*). As a result, active traders trade and retrade more often. A particular cohort consists of both active traders and investors, but active traders are less likely to retain shares than investors.

Estimates of aggregate damages with accelerated and multitrader models are often 20 to 30 percent lower than those calculated by the proportional trading model. Each case is unique, however, and sometimes damages from the alternative models exceed those of the proportional trading model.

Little, if any, scientific support exists in the form of peer-reviewed articles to show that trading models provide an accurate estimate of class member damages. In *Kaufman et al. v. Motorola Inc. et al.*,[66] Judge Gettleman rejected the proportional trading model because it failed to meet any of the four *Daubert* standards.[67] Judge Gettleman found that professional economists did not accept the proportional model, which seemed to have been developed solely for securities litigation. The court also viewed a trading model as unnecessary: "an adequate remedy may be fashioned by having the jury determine a per share damage loss and requiring the filing of claims by each shareholder who claims that he, she or it has been damaged."[68] Despite their additional complexity and more realistic assumptions, the accelerated and multitrading models appear to suffer from the same problems identified by Judge Gettleman.

APPENDIX A: STATISTICAL APPROACH TO THE EVENT STUDY

CREATING A MODEL

Theoretical and Statistical Conditions. At least two theoretical conditions should exist if one plans to use an event study approach in a damages analysis or materiality analysis. First, the security of interest must be traded in an informationally efficient market, that is, one in which prices respond quickly and appropriately to valuation-relevant news.[69] Second, the analysts' statistical model of the return-generating process must be valid throughout the sample period.

An event study proves most useful under the following three conditions:

1. Return data are available that cover the event at issue, and the expert has adequate data to allow estimation of the coefficients on the market and other indices of interest as well as the firm-specific variability of returns (i.e., the standard deviation of returns after abstracting from market and industry effects).

2. The shares trade often enough so that each return covers a short period, such as a day or week.[70]

3. The parties can identify the event in question with one or more announcements that have relatively certain timing, and the event announcement(s) do not contain a great deal of valuation-relevant information unrelated to the issue in question. Such unrelated information is called *confounding events.*

As a practical matter, an expert will have more difficulty identifying interventions in return series for a thinly traded security because fewer returns exist and because (for multiday returns) all the news events during the several days covered by each return can affect that return, introducing confounding information. In addition, the variability inherent in a return series is a function of the time period covered by the return. We would expect two-day returns to have twice the variance of one-day returns and so on.

Model Specification. An event study of security returns seeks to partition the variation of returns to a given security into two components: general marketwide effects (expected to affect multiple firms, albeit in potentially different ways) and firm-specific effects. For example, for a single-factor model in which market performance is the only marketwide factor affecting returns, the regression equation would be:

$$r_{st} = \alpha_s + \beta_s r_{mt} + \epsilon_{st} \tag{1}$$

where

r_{st} = return to security s on day t
α_s = market model intercept for security s
β_s = market model beta for security s
r_{mt} = market index return on day t
ϵ_{st} = firm-specific residual return to security s on day t

The variation over time of $(\alpha_s + \beta_s r_{mt})$, the first component of r_{st}, reflects marketwide effects. Analysts refer to this component as the systematic (or predictable, conditional on knowledge of the market or industry effects) portion of the return. The second component, ϵ_{st}, is the firm-specific effect.

Experts often augment the basic single-factor model expressed in equation (1) by including one or more industry indices. For example, an expert might include a market index such as the S&P 500 and an industry index composed of firms in the same Standard Industrial Classification (SIC) code, which presumably react to the same industry-specific common factors. The resulting augmented market model would be

$$r_{st} = \alpha_s + \beta_{ms} r_{mt} + \beta_{is} r_{it} + \epsilon_{st} \tag{2}$$

This model has two slope coefficients: one for the relation between the subject share's return and the market index, and one for its relation with the industry index r_{it}. Both coefficients measure the sensitivity of share returns to index returns. Studies include these additional factors (e.g., industry indexes) to increase the proportion of the variance of total returns (the left-hand variable), thereby reducing the variance of the firm-specific residual returns.

Model Estimation. Experts usually estimate the relation between the individual share returns and the indices using a statistical estimation method such as ordinary least squares (OLS) on a sample of returns taken from an estimation period.[71] The solid sloping line in Exhibit 18-2 shows the OLS estimate of the regression line, based on all data in the exhibit except the event-day return. Thus the solid sloped line corresponds to the estimated market model equation.

$$r_{st} = a_s + b_s r_{mt} + e_{st} \tag{3}$$

where

a_s and b_s = the OLS estimates of α_s and β_s in Equation (1).

Given a_s, b_s, r_{st}, and r_{mt}, we can compute e_{st}, the estimated counterpart of ϵ_{st}. Whether e_{st}, is a residual or a prediction error depends on whether the estimation sample includes the return for day t. Experts typically compute the estimated event-day residual return e_{s0} as a prediction error. That is, they, as we have done in our example, compute a_s and b_s from an estimation sample without the event-day return and compute e_{s0} as the deviation of r_{s0} from the estimated regression line shown as the solid line in Exhibit 18-2:

$$e_{s0} = r_{s0} - (a_s + b_s r_{m0}) \qquad (4)$$

On the event date, this residual return component corresponds to the dotted vertical line in Exhibit 18-2; it numerically measures the abnormal return or residual associated with the announcement (i.e., the residual difference between the conditional forecast and the actual return). Statistical theory then provides a means to judge the statistical significance of this residual return.

INTERPRETING THE MODEL

Analysts use two measures of the estimated relation between individual security returns and returns to the index (or indices):

1. The magnitude (and statistical significance) of the regression slope (beta) coefficient(s)
2. The explanatory power of the regression expressed in terms of R^2 (i.e., the fraction of the variance of returns explained by the regression).

Beta Coefficient. In the context of the market model, analysts refer to the slope coefficient (β_s in equation 1) as the security's beta or systematic risk. A beta coefficient of 1.0 means that the security returns change, on average, as much as the market index returns in response to the common factors captured in the index. Coefficients greater or less than 1.0 indicate securities whose expected returns vary more or less than average in response to the common factors.

Statistical Significance. The statistical significance of the estimated coefficient measures the reliability of its estimated sign and magnitude, based on the coefficient's standard error. The OLS regression calculations produce a standard error for each estimated coefficient to gauge the size of the discrepancy between the estimated value and the underlying true value.

Statistical theory provides that a confidence interval centered at b_s and extending for two standard errors in each direction will cover the true value β_s approximately 95 percent of the time. Thus, a finding that the two-standard-errors interval does not cover zero indicates at a 95 percent level of confidence that the estimated coefficient b_s has at least the same sign as the true coefficient β_s. In many applications, one can restate this condition as that of requiring that the t ratio, that is, the ratio of the estimated coefficient to its standard error, is greater than two or less than negative two.

Most event studies have greater interest in the statistical significance of the estimated effect of the intervention (i.e., the significance of the residual return on the event day) than that of the slope coefficients.

Standard Deviation of the Return Series. When returns' variability differs substantially across shares, then a return of a given magnitude can be unusual for one firm but frequently observed for another. A common measure of the variability inherent in a given return series is the time series standard deviation of returns, which measures the typical dispersion of returns around their mean over some period.[72]

Statistical theory shows that approximately two-thirds of normally distributed returns should fall within plus-or-minus one standard deviation of the mean return, and about 95 percent of all returns should fall within plus-or-minus two standard deviations of the mean return. Thus, one would observe by chance (i.e., on a day selected at random) a return that exceeded two standard deviations from the mean no more than 5 percent of the time assuming normally distributed returns.

Explanatory Power: R^2. The regression's R^2 (R-squared) measures the explanatory power of the regression. The regression's R^2 (R-squared) measures (in the case of a market model regression) the fraction of the variance in share returns that the market index returns explain. The higher the R^2, the greater the portion of a given security's return explained by the index returns.

Calculating the Statistical Significance of the Event-Day-Specific Return. Standard regression theory provides a means to measure the statistical significance of the estimated residual (i.e., prediction error) on the event date. Analysts often use the augmented market model, expressed in Equation (5), as a computationally convenient approach to calculate the statistical significance of an event-day-specific return:

$$r_{st} = \alpha_s + \beta_s r_{mt} + \gamma_{sA} d_{At} + \epsilon_{st} \tag{5}$$

where d_{At} is an indicator variable for the date of the information event under study; that is, d_{At} equals one on the date of announcement a and zero on all other dates. Analysts often refer to the coefficient γ_{sA} as an event parameter, because it measures the sensitivity of returns of security s to information events of type A.

Let g_{sA} be the OLS estimate of γ_{sA} in a regression that includes both the original estimation sample for Equation (2) and the event-date observation. This event parameter g_{sA} equals the prediction error at the event date as defined previously, and its standard error and t ratio account for the effect of the estimation error in the regression line. If g_{sA} is statistically significant, then the event date return is unusual in a statistical sense.

APPENDIX B: TRADING MODEL DISCUSSION

Trading models typically require two inputs: volume and float. Trading models do not define *volume* as the reported volume (which serves as a starting point), but rather as the number of shares purchased by a particular day's cohort. The *float* is not the shares outstanding (which serves as a starting point) but instead is the shares for which the trading behavior is unknown and that are being modeled.[73] In practice, to implement the trading models discussed throughout the chapter, experts often make the following type of adjustments to reported daily volume and shares outstanding to arrive at the volume and float inputs that go into the trading model.

- **Specialist trading.** Analysts usually reduce reported volume to account for overcounting that results from specialists and market makers in the marketplace.[74] Anderson and Dyl,[75] in a follow-up study to Atkins and Dyl's study on reported trading volumes,[76] estimate a median decrease in reported market transactions of about 50 percent for firms switching from Nasdaq to NYSE, but the volume change varies across firms. They attribute this decrease in volume to the Nasdaq structure in which dealers play a larger role than on the NYSE. Madhavan and Sofianos (1998) report that specialist participation rates (i.e., the ratio of specialist purchases and sales to total reported volume) averaged approximately 25 percent in their sample but varied widely across firms.[77]

- **Intraday trading.** Experts often reduce reported daily volume to account for intraday trades. Because the expert often assumes constant damages per share within a day, traders who buy and sell within the same day do not suffer any damages resulting from fraud. Their gains from inflation at sale just offset their losses due to inflation at purchase.

- **Institutional trading.** Institutions that manage at least $100 million file their holdings each quarter on Form 13 F. These filings can provide information on whether institutions traded or held shares during the class period. Experts often remove from the float the institutional shares that were not traded.

- **Short sales.** In a short sale transaction, an investor sells shares borrowed from another investor. At a later date, the short sale investor buys the shares and returns them to the original owner. The short interest for a given security represents the aggregate short position of investors. When the short interest increases (i.e., short sellers sell more shares short), short sellers have in effect increased the float because the shares they sell are, in effect, borrowed and resold. Many experts increase the float to reflect the additional shares trading as a result of shorting. Also, when the short position decreases, experts often adjust the daily volume to reflect the fact that short sellers have made some of the purchases on that day. Short sellers, who speculate that a share price will decrease, are not considered part of a class harmed by alleged inflation.

- **Buybacks and offerings.** When a company buys back shares, the float decreases by the amount of the buyback. If the reported daily volume includes the buyback, then the expert usually removes the amount of the buyback from the volume on the day the buyback occurs and reduces the float from that point onward. A securities offering increases the float. If the reported daily volume does not include the shares in the offering, the analyst should increase the reported daily volume to reflect the fact that the cohort on the day of the offering also purchased the shares in the offering. Again, to the extent that some investors buy and sell the shares on the offering day (often called *flipping* shares), the volume arising from buying and selling in the same day should not count as part of the cohort purchase for that day.

- **Insiders.** Insiders are often defendants and not part of the class. Experts usually exclude their shares from the float and the volume. When insiders sell to the public, the float usually increases. The shares they held become available for trading and enter the model. When insiders purchase from the public, the float decreases. Also, on days when insiders purchase shares in the open market, the expert can reduce the volume in calculating the volume purchased by the damaged cohort because volume entering the trading model should include only purchases made by class members.

NOTES

1. Securities Act of 1933, Section 1 et seq., 15 USC Section 77a et seq.
2. Securities Exchange Act of 1934, Section 1 et seq., 15 USC Section 78a et seq.
3. Securities Litigation Reform, Report 104-369, November 28, 1995.
4. 15 USC Section 77k(a).
5. Ibid.; *McFarland v. Memorex Corp.*, 96 F.R.D. 357 (N.D. Cal. 1982).
6. 15 USC Section 77(e).
7. 15 USC Section 77l(2).
8. 15 USC Section 78i(e).
9. 15 USC Section 78i(a), (b), and (c).
10. 17 CFR 240, 10b-5.
11. *Securities Litigation Reform*, Report 104-369 and *Joint Explanatory Statement of the Committee of Conference*, November 28, 1995. p. 4.
12. Ibid. p. 8.
13. Ibid. p. 11.
14. Ibid. p. 11.
15. Ibid. p. 12.
16. Ibid. p. 15.
17. Ibid. p. 22.

18. In the *Dura Pharmaceuticals Inc. v. Broudo* case, the Supreme Court ruled that plaintiffs invoking the fraud-on-the market theory must demonstrate loss causation by pleading and proving a causal connection between the alleged fraud and the investment's subsequent decline in price. The court held that only showing that the security's price was inflated at the time of the purchase is insufficient to meet this requirement.

19. *Securities Litigation Reform*, Report 104-369, and *Joint Explanatory Statement of the Committee of Conference*, November 28, 1995. p. 24 http://frwebgate.access.gpo.gov/cgi-bin/getdoc.cyi?dbname=104 cong reports&docid=f:hr369.104.pdf.

20. Ibid. p. 28.

21. Ibid. p. 28 (July 1996), in the Bibliography.

22. Rescission is the cancellation of a contract and the return of the parties to their positions had the transaction or contract not occurred (e.g., the purchaser of the stock surrendering the stock in exchange for the purchase price of the stock).

23. 15 USC Section 771(2).

24. 15 USC Section 78i(e).

25. 430 U.S. 1, 51 L Ed 2d 124, 97 S Ct 926 (1977). Cited in Kaufman (1992), p. 5, in the Bibliography.

26. *Smolowe v. Delendo Corp.*, 136 F.2d 231, 239 (CA2 1943). Cited in Kaufman (1992), p. 12, in the Bibliography.

27. *See* Thorup (1990), p. 25, in the Bibliography.

28. Indeed, in a press release dated February 17, 2005, Bernstein Litowitz Berger & Grossmann (a plaintiff law firm) claimed that the *Clarent* securities litigation was only "the third securities class action to go to trial in the last ten years."

29. *See* Lee (1987), p. 1267, in the Bibliography.

30. *Estate Counseling Serv., Inc. v. Merrill Lynch, Pierce, Fenner & Smith, Inc.* Cited in Mullaney (1977), p. 281, (1990), in the Bibliography.

31. *See* Thorup (1990), p. 32, in the Bibliography.

32. Ibid.

33. *Chasins v. Smith Barney & Co.*, 438 F. 2nd 1167 (1970). *See* Mullaney (1977), p. 287, in the Bibliography.

34. Ibid. p. 287

35. *See* Lee (1987), p. 287, in the Bibliography. .

36. 446 F.2d 90 (10th Cir.), *cert. denied*, 404 U.S. 1004 (1971). Cited in Lee (1987), p. 1277, in the Bibliography.

37. 446 F.2d at 105.

38. 446 F.2d. Cited in Mullaney (1977), p. 286, in the Bibliography.

39. *Myzel v. Fields*, 386 F.2d at 742. Cited in Thorup (1990), p. 40, in the Bibliography.

40. *Mitchell v. Texas Gulf and Sulphur Co.*, 446 F.2d at 105. Cited in Thorup (1990), p. 40, in the Bibliography.

41. *See* Lee (1987), p. 1278, in the Bibliography.

42. 406 U.S. 128, 155 (1972). Cited in Lee (1987), p. 1284, in the Bibliography.

43. 344 F.2d 781 (1st Cir.), *cert. denied*, 382 U.S. 879 (1965). Cited in Lee (1987), p. 1284, in the Bibliography.

44. 344 F.2d at 786. Cited in Thompson (1985), p. 235, in the Bibliography.

45. *See*, for example, *Nelson v. Serwold* (Nelson): 576 F.2d 1332 (1978), Cited in Thompson (1985), p. 236, in the Bibliography.

46. *See* Lee (1987), p. 1276, in the Bibliography.

47. Ibid. p. 1277

48. *See* Dobbs (1973), in the Bibliography. Cited in Lee (1987), p. 1277, in the Bibliography.

49. *Barrows v. Forest Lab, Inc.*, 742F.2d 54 (2d Cir. 1984).

50. *Securities Litigation Reform*, Report 104-369, November 28, 1995.

51. Ibid. It is not clear how the bounce-back rule should be interpreted in the event of partial disclosures, and the authors are not aware of any case law that provides guidance.

52. As discussed later, some courts have ruled that it is not necessary for an expert to calculate damages for the class. A jury can decide inflation per share (with expert testimony as guidance), and class members would establish their damages individually through a proof of claim process in which they provide their trading records.

53. Material information is generally defined as information that would be important to a reasonable investor in valuing a security and making investment decisions.

54. *In re Executive Telecard, Ltd. Securities Litigation*, 94 Civ. 7846 (CLB) (S.D. N.Y. 1997). *See also In re Seagate Technology II Securities Litigation*, C-89-2498(A)-VRW (N.D. Cal.), in which the court accepted some of the defendants' event studies and dismissed certain claims on that basis but ruled that the defendants' other event studies were inadequate and denied their request for summary judgment with regard to those issues. The court also found the plaintiffs' event studies lacking and therefore denied a cross-motion for summary judgment. Also, *see Goldkrantz v. Griffin*, QBS: 02760800 (S.D. N.Y. 1999), in which the court granted summary judgment based on the plaintiffs' failure to contest the defendants' event study analysis.

55. The Private Securities Litigation Reform Act (PSRLA) 90-day bounce-back rule, in effect, recognizes the possibility of overreaction to a curative disclosure.

56. It is, however, not the only way experts compute damages. As will be discussed later, sometimes experts employ a fundamental analysis or perform a larger sample event study by looking to stock price changes based on a sample of stock responding to similar events. Which approach is undertaken depends on circumstances relating to the allegations in the complaint and the reliability of the various types of estimates given the available data.

57. Fraud generally falls into two categories: actively disclosing false information and failing to disclose material information (including correcting previous disclosures that are known to be false).

58. The majority of securities cases are "buyer" suits brought on behalf of purchasers of securities who claim that share prices were inflated as a result of the fraud. However, there are "seller" suits in which sellers claim the price was depressed as a result of the fraud. For example, the seminal case of the *SEC v. Texas Gulf Sulphur* 401 F.2nd 833 (2nd Cir. 1968) was brought on behalf of sellers who sold their securities at prices below what they would have had the company released information related to its mineral deposits discovery. In the remainder of this chapter, almost all of our discussion will assume a purchasers suit in which the wrongdoings are alleged to have inflated prices.

59. There may be modifications to this. For example, as stated in *Dura v. Brouda*, a plaintiff who buys and sells under the same fraud should not be damaged. Individual experts, however, often appear to disagree on exactly how to reconcile this with their but-for price line calculation and the out-of-pocket measure.

60. Future cases will help determine the impact of the *Dura* decision on the measurement of damages.

61. Cases in which the court accepted testimony on aggregate damages include *In re WorldCom Securities Litigation*, 2005 WL 491397 (S.D. N.Y. 2005) and *In re Oxford Health Plans, Inc. Securities Litigation*, 244 F. Supp. 2d 247 (S.D. N.Y. 2003).

62. Cases in which the court did not allow testimony on aggregate damages include *In re Clarent Corp. Securities Litigation* (N.D. Cal. 2005); *Bell v. Fore Systems, Inc.*, WL 32097540 (W.D. Pa. 2002); and *Kaufman et al. v. Motorola Inc. et al.*, No. 95-1069 (N.D. Ill. 2000).

63. *See* Appendix B to this chapter for a more detailed discussion of the potential adjustments to trading model inputs.

64. Note that the proportion of holdings each cohort sells varies each day depending on the day's volume.

65. The financial literature has shown that there are differences in investor behavior. For example, *see* Barber and Odean (2001), in the Bibliography and Odean (1999), in the Bibliography.

66. *Kaufman et al. v. Motorola Inc. et al.*, No. 95-1069 (N.D. Ill. 2000).

67. Chapter 1 discusses *Daubert* standards.

68. *Kaufman et al. v. Motorola Inc. et al.*, No. 95-1069 (N.D. I11. 2000).

69. The efficient market condition provides the foundation of the fraud-on-the-market theory in which plaintiffs do not need to show reliance on a particular piece of false information because the stock price is presumed to impound the information.

70. The first event studies used monthly returns and a large cross-section of firms to examine the average effect of an event undergone by many firms (such as earnings announcements and dividend announcements). In the context of litigation, most event study analysis uses only one firm because the event is specific to the litigation.

71. The appropriate estimation period is case specific.

72. The time series *standard deviation* of the return series equals the square root of its time series variance. Variance is a statistical measure of the spread or dispersion in a distribution from its mean or average. A larger variance means a greater spread in the distribution. The variance of a large sample of observations is the average of the squared deviations of the sample values from the sample mean.

73. For example, experts exclude shares from the float that are known not to have traded in the class period and exclude shares from the float if they are calculating damages on those shares separately.

74. A *market maker* is a bank or brokerage firm that facilitates the trading of shares by posting bid and ask prices along with maintaining an inventory of shares for a particular stock. A *specialist* is a type of market maker that is specific to the NYSE. In a dealer market (as opposed to an auction market), a market maker is on each side of every transaction (buy and sell), causing the trading volume to be overstated. For example, although the same 10 shares of a stock are sold by one investor and purchased by another investor, the dealer reports 20 shares traded for both the buy and sell transactions, causing the trading volume to be overstated by 10 shares.

75. *See* Anderson and Dyl (2005) in the Bibliography.

76. *See* Atkins and Dyl (1997) in the Bibliography.

77. These are examples of difficulties that make trading model testimony susceptible to *Daubert* challenges.

BIBLIOGRAPHY

Atkins, A.B., and E.A. Dyl. "Market Structure and Reported Trading Volume: NASDAQ Versus the NYSE," *Journal of Financial Research* 20 (Fall 1997): 291–304.

Anderson, A. M., and E.A. Dyl. "Market Structure and Trading Volume." *Journal of Financial Research* 28 (March 2005): 115–31.

Barber, B., and T. Odean. "Boys Will Be Boys: Gender, Overconfidence, and Common Stock Investment." *Quarterly Journal of Economics* 116 (February 2001): 261–92.

Dobbs, D.B. *Handbook on the Law of Remedies.* (St. Paul, MN: West Publishing Co., 1973).

Fama, E., and K. French. "The Cross-Section of Expected Stock Returns." *Journal of Finance* 47 (1992): 427–65.

Fama, E., and K. French. "Common Risk Factors in the Returns on Stocks and Bonds," *Journal of Financial Economics* 33 (1993): 3–56.

Gould, J.F., and A.W. Kleidon. "Market Maker Activity on NASDAQ: Implications for Trading Volume," *Stanford Journal of Law, Business & Finance* 8 (1994): 213–63.

Kaufman, M.J. *Securities Litgations: Damages.* Deerfield, IL: Clark Boardman Callaghan, 1992.

Koslow, J. "Estimating Aggregate Damages in Class-Action Litigation under Rule 10b-5 for Purposes of Settlement." *Fordham Law Review* 59 (1991): 811–42.

Lee, R.B. "The Measure of Damages under Section 10(b) and Rule 10b-5." *Maryland Law Review* 46 (Summer 1987): 1266–92.

Madhavan, A., and Sofianos, G. "An Empirical Analysis of NYSE Specialist Trading." *Journal of Financial Economics* 48 (1998): 189–210.

Mullaney, T.J. "Theories of Measuring Damages in Security Cases and the Effects of Damages on Liability." *Fordham Law Review* 46 (1977): 277–94.

Odean, T. "Do Investors Trade Too Much?" *The American Economic Review* 89 (December 1999): 1279–98.

Thompson, R.D. "The Measure of Recovery under Rule 10b-5: A Restitution Alternative to Tort Damages." *Securities Law Review* 17 (1990): 213–62.

Thorup, R.A. "Theories of Damages: Allowability and Calculation in Securities Fraud Litigation." *Securities Regulation Law Journal* 18 (1990): 23–52.

CHAPTER 19

ACCOUNTANT LIABILITY

Christopher D. Barbee
Michael R. Young

CONTENTS

19.1 INTRODUCTION

Accountant liability has become one of the most challenging areas of the law. It is far from straightforward and involves the interplay of generally accepted accounting principles (GAAP), generally accepted auditing standards (GAAS), the use and misuse of financial information, a complex allocation of responsibility for financial reporting, and a network of overlapping—and not always consistent—laws. Both prosecuting and defending claims in this area present challenges.

Events of the past several years have illuminated the potential for accountant liability in connection with fraudulent financial reporting in which plaintiffs allege

The authors acknowledge Harvey R. Kelly, who co-authored with Michael R. Young the version of this chapter that appeared in the third edition.

that the auditors should have detected the fraud earlier. Even though the existence of fraud often doesn't translate to auditor liability, mega-frauds in companies such as Cendant, Enron, WorldCom, HealthSouth, and Adelphia have turned accounting firms into targets of high-profile lawsuits, with billions of dollars at stake.

This chapter will first outline the types of accounting services that may be the subject of litigation. It will then examine the law and some of the legal issues likely found in any accountant liability litigation. Next, it will discuss underlying trends in accountant liability and, in particular, an important evolution of responsibility for financial reporting that began in the mid-1980s and continues. The chapter will also analyze typical strategies and arguments used by plaintiffs and defendants in accountant liability litigation. Finally, the chapter will address the role of accountants as experts in litigation that involves alleged accountant liability.

19.2 TYPES OF ACCOUNTING SERVICES

Accountants today play many roles in business. Major accounting firms (and many smaller firms) have extended their capabilities beyond traditional auditing, tax consulting, and bookkeeping services. Accountants have embraced such fields as business process improvement, litigation consulting, internal audit outsourcing, business turnaround consulting, and risk management consulting (including information technology security). As the breadth of services provided by accountants has expanded, so too has the nature of litigation claims.

Most claims against accountants, however, stem from the traditional services. Users who conclude that the financial statements were inaccurate or incomplete frequently bring actions against accountants who provided services such as review and auditing services with respect to those financial statements (referred to as *assurance services*). Similarly, subsequent business failures of an accountant's client can result in claims by the company's shareholders, creditors, and bankruptcy trustees that the accountant failed to alert interested parties about the severity of the client's financial woes. Indeed, even when an employee embezzles funds, parties sometimes seek recovery of losses from the accountant servicing the company.

Tax accountants, too, are vulnerable to litigation claims. When unanticipated losses result in some way from tax strategies recommended by a tax accountant, that accountant may have to defend an accountant's liability claim. Matters beyond the tax advisor's control can give rise to such claims. For example, when tax laws changed in the 1980s to eliminate the tax savings associated with tax shelters, many companies and individuals initiated claims against their tax advisors who previously advocated investing in such tax shelters.

Accountants have found themselves defending against litigation claims in connection with services provided beyond the traditional accounting and tax realm of accountants. For example, accounting firms have recently defended claims that they provided faulty business restructuring consulting services,[1] litigation consulting services,[2] and financial system implementation services.[3]

Because of the nature of the respective practices, clients of small firms will more likely sue for alleged flawed tax services, and clients of larger firms will more likely sue for alleged flawed assurance services. The greatest liability, by far, has resulted from the latter. This chapter focuses on the most common engagement giving rise to litigation for the larger firms: auditing historical financial statements. The basic legal and strategic concepts, however, will apply to almost any litigation that names an accountant as a defendant.

19.3 AN OVERVIEW OF THE LAW

Comprehension of the role of an expert in accountant liability litigation requires an understanding of certain legal concepts.

(a) The Crux of a Claim: Information. At the crux of accountant liability is the notion that an accountant produces information. That information frequently takes the form of a three-paragraph audit report. As discussed in Section 19.2, however, it can take other forms as well. The accountant may issue a review report, compile financial statements, undertake agreed-on procedures, and prepare tax returns.

Accordingly, the available legal claims against an accountant are those that seek to remedy harm caused by wrong information. Four types of claims predominate: negligence or negligent misrepresentation, fraud, breach of contract, and violations of securities laws.

(b) Claims for Negligence. Of the four types of claims, some plaintiffs find a claim for negligence or negligent misrepresentation the easiest to prove. Such a claim alleges that the accountant, through an unreasonable failure to conform to the accepted standards of the profession, misstated financial information, which caused another harm. In legal jargon, the elements of a negligent misrepresentation claim require a victim to prove the following:

- A misrepresentation
- Of a material fact
- To one to whom the accountant owed a duty
- Upon which the plaintiff justifiably relied
- Proximately causing harm

The starting point, of course, is that the information has to be false. If everything the accountant said was true, the plaintiff has no claim.

All things being equal, one might think that in seeking to sue an accountant one should make a negligence claim the first choice. Negligence claims do not require plaintiffs to prove that accountants deliberately did anything wrong—only that they were too sloppy. For that matter, courts can find an accountant theoretically liable for negligence for an accidental blunder as long as the accident involved an unreasonable failure to conform to the standards of the profession.

However, courts have erected barriers to the prosecution of a negligence claim against an accountant. The courts—sensitive to the vulnerability of the accounting profession to such claims—limit the category of plaintiffs who can assert negligence claims against an accountant, but even today those limits lack precision. The United States has three separate mutually exclusive rules of law.

The inconsistency results from the proximity that the law requires between the would-be plaintiff and the accountant before the plaintiff can assert a negligence claim. The underlying concept has its roots in a historical doctrine known as *privity.* Under this doctrine, only one in privity with a wrongdoer—which means one with whom the wrongdoer had entered a contract—can legally recover on a negligence claim. Throughout the nineteenth century, and part of the twentieth, the privity doctrine impeded negligence claims against anyone—including accountants—when a contract between the parties did not exist.

Not far into the twentieth century, however, the privity doctrine began to erode as the courts realized that a privity limitation, at least in the context of physical harm, had become impractical in an increasingly industrialized society. A significant breakdown in the privity doctrine occurred in 1916, when New York's Court of Appeals (the state's highest court) allowed the driver of an automobile to sue the manufacturer for a defect—an astonishing result (under the law of the time) because a contract did not exist between the driver and the manufacturer.[4] Over the years, the privity doctrine has continued to erode. This historical evolution explains the inconsistencies that today comprise the law of those who can sue an accountant for negligence. Three rules have emerged. Together, they track the evolution of the law from the historical concept of privity to the modern concept of foreseeability.[5]

(i) Privity Rule.   Courts still refer to the first, and most conservative, rule as the rule of privity. Championed most notably by the state of New York, that rule continues to adhere to the principle that only those in privity with an accountant—meaning a contractual relation or its equivalent—can sue for negligence. In 1931, Benjamin Cardozo, then of New York's Court of Appeals, wrote the intellectual justification for this rule, describing the policy as follows:

> If liability for negligence exists, a thoughtless slip or blunder, the failure to detect a theft or forgery beneath the cover of deceptive entries, may expose accountants to a liability in an indeterminate amount for an indeterminate time to an indeterminate class. The hazards of a business conducted on these terms are so extreme as to enkindle doubt whether a flaw may not exist in the implication of a duty that exposes to these consequences.[6]

In 1985, as the concept of privity eroded in other states, New York's Court of Appeals was presented with an opportunity to overturn Cardozo's opinion. However, in *Credit Alliance Corp. v. Arthur Andersen,*[7] the court concluded that Judge Cardozo's opinion still made sense. As a result, New York state continues to adhere to the privity rule. So do 15 other states.

(ii) Foreseeability Rule.   At the other end of the spectrum, some states have ostensibly moved to adopt the *foreseeability rule,* which permits foreseeable victims of wrongdoing to sue. Under that rule, a victim need not have a contractual relation with an accountant or, for that matter, any contact with the accountant whatsoever. Instead, the rule requires that the victim suffer a harm that the accountant should have reasonably foreseen at the time of the accountant's negligence.

In practice, the foreseeability rule has imposed uncertainty on the accounting profession. In the context of financial information, one can arguably foresee just about anything. One court explained the problem as follows:

> Foreseeability is endless because [it], like light, travels indefinitely in a vacuum. [It] proves too much. Although it may set tolerable limits for most types of physical harm, it provides virtually no limit on liability for nonphysical harm. It is apparent that reliance on foreseeability of injury alone in finding a duty, and thus a right to recover, is not adequate when the damages sought are for an intangible injury.[8]

Today, only Mississippi and Wisconsin follow the foreseeability rule to a meaning-ful extent.[9]

(iii) Restatement Rule.   That leaves the middle-ground rule, known as the *restatement rule* (named after a scholarly compendium of law known as the *Restatement of Law*). Under that rule, those victims who fall within "a limited group of persons for whose benefit and guidance [a professional] intends to supply the information or knows that the recipient intends to supply it" can assert a negligence claim. Thus, the restatement rule is not as broad as the foreseeability rule, which would allow claims by those whose harm was foreseeable, nor is it as narrow as the privity rule, which would require the equivalent of a contractual relation. The champion for the restatement rule is the Supreme Court of California, which adopted it (ironically, while at the same time ousting the foreseeability rule from the state) in *Bily v. Arthur Young & Co.*[10] Today, 21 states apply the restatement rule.

Thus, although every victim would prefer to sue an accountant for negligence, not everyone can. If the victim has not entered a contractual relation or its equiva-lent with the accountant, the victim's ability to sue for negligence will depend on the law of the relevant state. Those unable to assert a claim for negligence must resort to the second choice, a claim for fraud.

(c) Claims for Fraud.   Unlike a negligence claim, all states allow a plaintiff to assert a fraud claim against an accountant in the absence of a contract, even when the plaintiff falls outside a limited class. When the plaintiff has met the other elements of a claim, the only limitation on a plaintiff asserting fraud lies in proving that the accountant could have reasonably foreseen, at the time of the wrongdoing, that the accountant could harm the plaintiff. Even though the law makes a fraud claim easier to assert in one respect, it makes assertion of a fraud claim more difficult in another. Unlike a negligence claim, the plaintiff cannot premise a fraud claim on unreasonable sloppiness or a failure to reasonably adhere to the profession's stan-dards, rather, a fraud claim requires proof that the accountant deliberately lied (or, sometimes, at a minimum that the auditor behaved recklessly).

(d) Claims for Breach of Contract.   A claim for breach of contract does not typically figure prominently in most accountant liability litigation for two reasons. First, the category of victims who can assert contract claims has the most limitations—only those who have entered into a contract with the accountant. Second, a typical con-tract will define performance in a way that will require the accountant to conform to the professional standard of care. Accordingly, when a claim exists for breach of contract, a claim will likely also exist for negligence. When both claims exist, the negligence claim frequently plays the more prominent role.

Nonetheless, sometimes breach of contract claims can play an important role, particularly in the context of consulting agreements that define performance in terms of output rather than conformity to the professional standard of care. To prove a claim for breach of contract, the plaintiff must prove the existence of a con-tract, material breach of its terms, and proximately resulting harm.

(e) The Federal Securities Laws.   The federal securities laws may apply when in-correct numerical data affect the public markets for securities. Although only one body of federal securities laws exists, the federal courts have interpreted the laws differently. As with state law, the geographic location of the particular court therefore plays a role regarding the prerequisites of a claim.

Some basic principles, however, command almost uniform consensus. One such principle relates to the main federal claim likely to be brought against an accountant—pursuant to Section 10(b) of the Securities Exchange Act of 1934—which requires proof of "an intent to deceive, manipulate, or defraud." This means that, in most instances, the federal securities laws do not allow a victim to sue for negligence. As under fraud claims pursuant to state law, therefore, proof of unreasonable sloppiness or a failure to reasonably conform to the standards of the profession will not provide adequate grounds for recovery.

This limitation, though, has one important exception. Plaintiffs suing on the basis of false statements made as part of a public offering of securities normally need not prove fraud. In such a circumstance, the federal securities laws allow a claim based on something akin to an unreasonable failure to conform to the standards of the profession. When the accountant liability litigation arises from a public offering of securities, therefore, the liability risk for the accountant increases.

Whether the plaintiff claims fraud or negligence, one aspect of the federal securities laws poses a particular problem for the accounting profession. Unlike the laws of the states, the federal securities laws do not normally require victims to prove that they justifiably relied on the information that the accountant provided. The rationale stems from the assumption that only a rare investor will actually go to the trouble of obtaining from the Securities and Exchange Commission (SEC) a company's financial statements or other information on which the accountant issued a report. Rather than requiring proof of justifiable reliance on the information, the federal securities laws therefore allow plaintiffs to recover if they can prove in substance that they relied on the integrity of a securities market that efficiently processed public information. In other words, if plaintiffs can prove that a false SEC filing constituted a fraud on the market, and therefore artificially increased the price they paid for a security, even though they never personally saw the accountant's work product.

19.4   THE EVOLVING TREND OF ACCOUNTANT LIABILITY

To understand the implications of the legal concepts, one must understand the direction of accountant liability litigation in addition to the case law and statutes discussed in Section 19.3. In particular, one must understand a trend, occurring over the last 25 years, as to who should bear primary responsibility for financial information and should therefore stand first in line as the culprit when an entity reveals or admits flawed financial information. With the advent of new initiatives by the SEC, the evolution continues.[11]

(a) The Way It Was: Blaming the Outside Auditor.   To begin, go back to the early 1980s, when the principal target of blame for financial misreporting seemed straightforward: the outside auditor, often because the auditor had assets. When audited financial statements turned out to be wrong, a typical investor, outside director, or for that matter senior executive, might simply testify, "I relied on the outside auditor."

To make matters worse, some courts seemed to view the accounting profession almost as a vehicle for risk diversification. Thus, one state supreme court justified an expansion of accountant liability through an observation that "independent auditors have apparently been able to obtain liability insurance to satisfy their financial obligations."[12] Data collected by the then Big Six firms showed that those firms by themselves would ultimately end up facing legal liability of around $30 billion. It came to roughly $3.8 million per partner.[13]

By the mid-1980s, the accounting profession had come to view the liability landscape with a blend of frustration and terror. On the one hand, they faced increasing exposure to liability. On the other hand, they had limited ability to discover fraud at its origin. Key members of the financial community came to realize the need to rethink, and to rationalize, the allocation of responsibility for fraudulent financial reporting between the outside auditor and others. The question was how to do it.

(b) The Treadway Commission.   The situation set the stage for the formation of the National Commission on Fraudulent Financial Reporting, later known as the Treadway Commission after its chairman, former SEC Commissioner James Treadway.

The Treadway Commission began a study of financial fraud in 1985 and, over a two-year period, undertook an exhaustive investigation of its causes. The resulting Report of the National Commission on Fraudulent Financial Reporting concluded that corporate executives who stepped over the line into financial fraud almost always did so in response to unreasonable pressure: "unrealistic pressures, particularly for short-term results" or "financial pressure resulting from bonus plans that depend on short-term economic performance" or pressure from "the desire to obtain a higher price for a stock or debt offering or to meet the expectation of investors."[14] The report stated:

> The Commission's studies revealed that fraudulent financial reporting usually occurs as the result of certain environmental, institutional, or individual forces and opportunities. These forces and opportunities add pressures and incentives that encourage individuals and companies to engage in fraudulent financial reporting and are present to some degree in all companies. If the right, combustible mixture of forces and opportunities is present, fraudulent financial reporting may occur.[15]

Any effort to combat financial misreporting, therefore, had to start with management and the proper tone from senior management—an attitude that demanded candor in financial reporting and that removed pressures for unrealistic financial performance. This attitude had to penetrate the organization so that it became part of the corporate culture. The commission summarized: "The tone set by top management—the corporate environment or culture within which financial reporting occurs—is the most important factor contributing to the integrity of the financial reporting process."[16] Supporting the importance of a proper tone from senior management, a study of enforcement actions filed by the SEC between 1987 and 1999 relative to securities frauds found that the company's chief executive had involvement about 70 percent of the time.[17]

The Treadway Commission's findings and recommendations implied that relying on mechanisms outside the corporate structure—in particular, the annual audit function—to prevent fraud would prove inadequate. Indeed, the Treadway

Commission explicitly relegated the outside auditor to "a crucial, but secondary role" and cautioned that outside auditors could not act as "guarantors of the accuracy or the reliability of financial statements."[18] Instead, the mechanisms to prevent and detect fraud must begin within the corporation. Thus, the Treadway Commission's findings and recommendations shifted primary responsibility for accurate financial reporting onto the shoulders of senior management, outside directors, internal audit, and—most importantly—audit committees. Attempts in litigation to place primary responsibility on the accountant became correspondingly more difficult.

Upon its publication in October 1987, the findings and recommendations of the Treadway Commission garnered support. Members of Congress viewed the report's recommendations as authoritative. Legal writers discussed the Treadway report at length and advocated a level of diligence consistent with its recommendations. The national accounting firms separately apprised the directors and officers of their client companies as to new expectations the report placed on them. Thus, the accounting firms published their own monographs, duly distributed to corporate officials, which highlighted the recommendations of the Treadway Commission and outlined their views as to the responsibilities of corporate officials and audit committees. At the same time, the profession revised the standard form of the auditor's report to state explicitly the guidance that had earlier appeared in the underlying literature articulating GAAS: that the "financial statements are the responsibility of the Company's management," whereas the auditor's responsibility was only to "express an opinion on these financial statements based on our audit." Management letters, typically issued at the conclusion of an audit engagement, explicitly or implicitly began to assume Treadway Commission recommendations as important criteria against which to measure the corporate-governance aspects of internal control systems.

A practical consequence of all of this was to lay an evidence trail demonstrating the primary responsibility of management and the auditor's secondary role. Such evidence could later prove helpful to accountants in defending malpractice litigation.

(c) The Sarbanes-Oxley Act of 2002.   Passed in the immediate aftermath of the Enron and WorldCom debacles, the Sarbanes-Oxley Act was Congress' answer to the perception of widespread corporate fraud and the belief that the courts had failed to hold senior management sufficiently accountable. Among other things, the act does the following:

- Regulates the accounting profession by establishing the Public Company Accounting Oversight Board (PCAOB)
- Proscribes auditors from providing certain services to their public audit clients to enhance the perception of auditor independence
- Reiterates and strengthens "the responsibility of management for establishing and maintaining an adequate internal control structure and procedures for financial reporting"
- Requires an annual report containing management's assessment of the effectiveness of the internal control structure and procedures of the issuer for financial reporting

- Requires the auditor to "attest to, and report on, the assessment made by the management of the issuer"

As this book goes to print, auditors are completing the second wave of controls attestation reports; assessing the effect that these reports will have on accountant liability requires more time and hindsight. However, future claims against accountants may call into question their work surrounding the opinion on the financial statements or on the internal control structure, or both.

19.5 THE PLAINTIFF'S STRATEGIES

Thus far, the chapter has presented a background that will help us explain strategies of the plaintiff and defendant in an accountant liability case. We first discuss plaintiff's liability claims against accountants, which involve several basic elements. First, the plaintiff asserts that the financial statements audited by the accountant were materially incorrect. Then the plaintiff contends that the accountant failed to meet its professional responsibilities as an auditor and watchdog. The plaintiff then alleges that the accountant who followed GAAS would have discovered and prevented the financial misstatements. Finally, the plaintiff asserts that it suffered damages as a result of the financial misreporting.

In some cases the plaintiff must prove reliance on the improper financial statements. As discussed in Section 19.3, significant differences exist between federal and state law governing claims against accountants with respect to a plaintiff's burden to demonstrate reliance.

(a) The Financial Statements Have Errors. Most claims asserted against auditors allege that the financial statements on which the accountant rendered an opinion failed to report fairly the company's financial position and results of operations in accordance with GAAP. Even when plaintiffs appear to emphasize a principal allegation other than accounting misstatements, they often include such a claim. For example, in situations involving undetected employee defalcations, the plaintiff may focus on the defalcation itself. Similarly, in matters involving subsequent business failures, the plaintiff may stress the auditor's failure to properly evaluate an entity's ability to continue as a going concern. Even in such cases, allegations that the financial statements improperly failed to disclose relevant issues play a prominent role in the plaintiff's case.

In some circumstances, the plaintiff finds alleging improper financial statements one of the easier claims to assert. This often occurs when the company's restated financial statements become the primary evidence. When material errors or irregularities affecting previously issued financial statements surface, companies sometimes must issue corrected, or restated, financial statements. Those restated financial statements often disclose the extent of the restatement and usually are accompanied by an auditor's opinion (often rendered by the defendant accountant) that the restated financial statements conform to GAAP. In such instances, a plaintiff may conclude that a simple comparison of the original and the restated financial statements constitutes sufficient proof that the previous financial statements contained errors.

In other cases, the question of the financial statements' validity becomes more complex and contentious. For example, armed with the knowledge that a company failed to collect its reported accounts receivable, the plaintiff may claim that the financial statements that reported those receivables as assets violated GAAP. The defendant's expert witness accountant, on the other hand, may assert that the financial statements reasonably considered facts and circumstances known or knowable at the time of issuance.

When the accountant's defense claims that the financial statements were fairly stated, the plaintiff's case necessarily will involve expert testimony concerning the propriety of the financial statements. One can expect the plaintiff's expert to highlight the specific areas of GAAP that the expert contends the financial statements violated. Such testimony will likely quantify the effects of the alleged misstatements and include the expression of an opinion that the financial statements had errors of material magnitude. Plaintiffs' experts frequently claim that events occurring subsequent to the financial statements substantiate their opinions (e.g., "the ultimate failure to collect receivables proves the receivables were overstated").

Rarely does the plaintiff limit the GAAP violation allegations to one area. Plaintiffs and their experts search the document productions for potential misstatements. Where might such experts look? They often begin with the accountant's own audit working papers, which reveal matters identified and questioned by the auditor. In fact, the working papers often contain adjustments recommended by the auditor that management elected not to process in its financial statements.

Subsequent year accounting records constitute another set of documents inspected by plaintiff experts. By examining transactions recorded in a subsequent period, a plaintiff's expert may identify asset write-offs or other adjustments that the expert opines should have served to reduce income reported in an earlier period.

(b) The Auditor Failed to Perform Its Duties. Having asserted that the financial statement numbers contain errors, the plaintiff now turns its attention to the accountant. Notwithstanding the undeniable provision under GAAS that an audit opinion on a set of financial statements does not constitute a guarantee, the plaintiff often designs a strategy to persuade a jury that an auditor's opinion does provide a seal of approval or guarantee the financial statements' accuracy. "How," the plaintiff asks the jury, "could the auditors have done their job and missed this major financial statement problem?" The plaintiff then sets forth a multitude of alleged violations of GAAS.

Those who do not understand GAAS might mistakenly think that GAAS represents a step-by-step set of procedures that all auditors must perform when conducting every financial statement audit. Instead, recognizing the diversity of companies and such key factors as internal control and accounting systems, GAAS represent prescribed standards rather than procedures. Auditing standards, as distinct from auditing procedures, concern themselves with the auditor's professional qualities and the judgment exercised by the accountant in the performance of the audit and in the auditor's report. GAAS, as originally approved and adopted by the American Institute of Certified Public Accountants (AICPA), but now adopted by the PCAOB, read as follows:

General Standards

1. The audit is to be performed by a person or persons having adequate technical training and proficiency as an auditor.
2. In all matters relating to the assignment, an independence in mental attitude is to be maintained by the auditor or auditors.
3. Due professional care is to be exercised in the performance of the audit and the preparation of the report.[19]

Standards of Field Work

1. The work is to be adequately planned and assistants, if any, are to be properly supervised.
2. A sufficient understanding of internal control is to be obtained to plan the audit and to determine the nature, timing, and extent of tests to be performed.
3. Sufficient competent evidential matter is to be obtained through inspection, observation, inquiries, and confirmations to afford a reasonable basis for an opinion regarding the financial statements under audit.[20]

Standards of Reporting

1. The report shall state whether the financial statements are presented in accordance with generally accepted accounting principles.
2. The report shall identify those circumstances in which such principles have not been consistently observed in the current period in relation to the preceding period.
3. Informative disclosures in the financial statements are to be regarded as reasonably adequate unless otherwise stated in the report.
4. The report shall either contain an expression of opinion regarding the financial statements, taken as a whole, or an assertion to the effect that an opinion cannot be expressed. When an overall opinion cannot be expressed, the reasons therefore should be stated. In all cases where an auditor's name is associated with financial statements, the report should contain a clear-cut indication of the character of the auditor's work, if any, and the degree of responsibility the auditor is taking.[21]

Through the years, the AICPA Statements on Auditing Standards (SAS) have described and interpreted these standards and related issues. As a result of the Sarbanes-Oxley Act, the PCAOB has authority for the auditing standards for public companies but can look to other professional groups for input.

Rarely can the plaintiff show by simply quoting GAAS that the auditing standards demand the performance of a specific audit procedure. Thus, instead of exclusively focusing on an accountant's failure to perform an allegedly necessary procedure, the plaintiff must also highlight alleged violations of prescribed standards.

The plaintiff will likely allege that the accountant violated many of the aforementioned standards. The law will often require the plaintiff to demonstrate that the accountant did so knowingly or recklessly. The plaintiff will often attempt to do so by offering a CPA auditor expert witness as the principal means of proving this contention.

The plaintiff wishes to avoid the perception that the case rests on mere hindsight—Monday morning quarterbacking. After all, once people know of an accounting problem, they can envision and describe audit procedures that could have detected the misstatement. This does not necessarily imply that the auditor had an obligation to execute such procedures. Therefore, in the absence of a GAAS requirement to perform a specific audit procedure, the plaintiff must give the trier of fact a reason to believe the accountant should have performed a particular step at the time of the audit.

(c) The Auditor Should Have Discovered the Problem.   Plaintiffs frequently accuse the auditor of ignoring warning signs or red flags. If the accountant had pursued such red flags, the plaintiff and its expert assert, it would have discovered and corrected the financial reporting problem. If the matter involves an intentional fraudulent financial reporting scheme, the plaintiff alleges that an appropriate auditor response to the warning signs would have uncovered and discontinued the scheme. In such circumstances, the plaintiff will likely cite SAS No. 99 (which superseded SAS 82 in 2002), which addresses an auditor's "responsibility to plan and perform the audit to obtain reasonable assurance about whether the financial statements are free of material misstatement, whether caused by error or fraud."[22] Plaintiffs and their experts often assert the following as supposed red flags: known similar problems in the past, aggressive accounting practices employed by the company, significant internal control deficiencies, existing questions about the quality of management representations, and the company's use of demonstrably wrong accounting judgments.

The plaintiff and its expert will examine the available records to find other evidence to bolster claims of GAAS failure. Citing the relevant auditor's working papers (or lack thereof) and testimony, the plaintiff's expert may opine that the auditor failed to obtain "sufficient competent evidential matter" as required by the third GAAS standard of field work. Similarly, the plaintiff's expert may conclude that the audit working papers reflect inadequate planning or an insufficient understanding of the company's internal control system, and thus evidence a failure to comply with the other standards of fieldwork.

19.6   THE STRATEGIES OF THE DEFENDANT ACCOUNTANT

The accountant's defense typically has four contentions.

1. The numbers at issue at the time of the accountant's report had no errors.
2. The plaintiff did not justifiably rely on them in any event (for claims other than those under the federal securities laws).
3. If the numbers have errors, others deserve the blame.
4. The accountant's report was correct and the accountant conformed to professional standards.

(a) The Numbers Were Correct.   The most straightforward defense—and one that defendants almost always present when it is available—is that the numbers in the financial statements had no errors. As proof, the defendant accountant takes the witness stand and testifies that the numbers had no errors. The accountant gives a convincing explanation supporting the numbers' accuracy and then explains why those contending otherwise are wrong. The accountant's expert then repeats the testimony, giving more credibility to the defendant's claim. The accountant's expert, therefore, needs to muster all available evidence from the record supporting the accuracy of the numbers.

Whereas some numbers in financial statements will appear unimpeachably correct, others seem inherently susceptible to second guessing. Plaintiffs will normally select the latter category as the focus of their case. To illustrate, consider the balance sheet line item "cash." Accountant liability trials almost never focus on the reported amount of cash because reliable evidence typically exists (bank statements, for example) that objectively and convincingly demonstrate the number's accuracy. Such evidence leaves little room for argument.

Such objective and convincing evidence does not, however, typically exist as to reported financial statement amounts that result from an application of an accountant's judgment. Revenue recognition and the resulting accounts receivable provide such an example. Regarding the former, not only does GAAP have many rules regarding revenue recognition, many of the rules require the application of subjective criteria. Weighing in with its own view on revenue recognition, the SEC issued *Staff Accounting Bulletin 101 – Revenue Recognition* in 1999. This generated additional questions and was followed by a FAQ document and then a new version, *Staff Accounting Bulletin 104*, issued in 2003, of over 80 pages. Revenue recognition generally results in accounts receivable. GAAP requires that the company record as revenue only receivables that are "reasonably assured" of collection; clearly this provides no guarantee, yet plaintiffs often use hindsight uncollectibility to question not only the level of receivables reported in the financial statements but also the initial recording of revenue that generated them. Securities litigation claims against public companies (which often also name the auditors) contain allegations related to revenue or accounts receivable more than half the time.[23]

Accordingly, in assessing the level of an allowance for bad debts, an accountant must consider the amount of those receivables that the company will not collect. Assessing the potential for lack of collections requires that one predict the future. If the future does not turn out as predicted—and it almost never does—the plaintiff's expert will assert that, had the accountant better used the available information in predicting future events, the accountant would have recorded the amount of receivables at a different number (usually lower).

The accountant's expert must therefore examine the evidence showing that, based on what the accountant knew at the time, the item appeared correct. For receivables, such evidence might be documentation showing historical collections consistent with the receivables item, documentation showing the credit worthiness of those who owed, and testimony of the defendant accountant describing the analysis at the time of the audit and the basis for the assessment. Evidence need not appear in the trial record. In federal court, an expert can consider information and data from outside the trial record as long as it is "of a type reasonably relied upon by experts in the particular field in forming opinions or inferences upon the subject."[24] That means that an accountant's expert seeking to support the accuracy of reported numbers can sometimes use textbooks, economic analyses, studies by academics, and everyday conversation with other professionals.

An accountant's defense, however, will rarely rest on only the accuracy of the reported numbers. When possible, the accountant will almost always use a second defense: asserting an absence of *justifiable reliance.*

(b) No Justifiable Reliance. A defense premised on an absence of justifiable reliance rivets attention on a legal prerequisite that a plaintiff must prove in almost any trial against an accountant except for trials under the federal securities laws. Plaintiffs must prove not only that the reported numbers contained errors. In addition, plaintiffs must prove that they justifiably relied on the incorrect numbers in such a way that caused them harm. This defense relates to causation: if the numbers contained errors but nobody looked at them, any misrepresentation had no consequence. In such an instance, the law bars a recovery.

To understand this defense, one must figure out what the prerequisite of justifiable reliance means. The courts have shown no consensus. On the one hand, many courts require plaintiffs seeking to prove justifiable reliance to demonstrate that they received the financial statements, read them, understood them, and acted sensibly as a result of the information they contained. At the other end of the spectrum, some courts have suggested that plaintiffs can claim justifiable reliance on financial statements that the plaintiffs never saw. Courts interpreting the justifiable reliance prerequisite so loosely, however, have become a shrinking minority, and increasingly they require proof of physical inspection and reliance on the reported information.

Whatever justifiable reliance means, many plaintiffs will find it surprisingly difficult to prove that they justifiably relied on the financial statements because of limits inherent in GAAP. Investors really want to know about future cash flow and present equity value. Financial statements, however, say little about either of these. Reported net income does not necessarily forecast future cash flow. Only rarely does book value correspond to the present value of equity. So the information's user cannot expect the information to reveal everything about a company's current or future situation, rather, a user must start with the information and then adapt it to his or her particular needs. At issue is whether such an individual did in fact rely on the financial information presented. The defense will also question the merits of the plaintiff's analysis of the information.

A good example of GAAP's practical limitations is its requirement that a company record most asset values at cost. Knowing an asset's cost may provide little information about its current fair market value. Almost anyone analyzing financial information will care less about what the asset cost (unless potential gains taxes are an issue) than about what the company could sell it for today or, perhaps, its replacement cost. However, GAAP—which has understandable concerns with objective verifiability—reflects a conscious decision that, in most cases, today's value should not appear on the balance sheet. GAAP often views the fact that the reported number can lack value for forward-looking decisions as secondary to objective verifiability.

Moreover, historical financial statements report on the past—not the future. Plaintiffs seeking to prove justifiable reliance on financial statements, therefore, cannot simply say that they relied on the information with no analysis of the numbers. Instead, they must say that they considered the information in trying to predict what would happen in the future. Thus, they introduce the question of the sensibility of their predictions of the future. Did they adequately consider industry trends? Did they adequately assess economic conditions? Should they have realized that a new competitor was about to enter the market? The defense will frequently raise all such issues.

Proving justifiable reliance on financial statements becomes still more difficult, moreover, because of the internal processes of institutional users of financial information. To illustrate, consider a commercial bank—often a potential plaintiff. When a borrower defaults and the bank received the borrower's financial statements before making the loan, the bank may file suit against the accountant (in those states that will allow a nonprivity party to do so), seeking to recover from the accountant the entire loan amount.

But what happens when the bank tries to prove justifiable reliance on the financial statements? Sometimes the lending committee, which decided to make the loan, never saw the financial statements. Instead, the committee may have approved the loan based on a written credit analysis to which the financial statements were not even attached. True, the credit analysis may have reported net income or other key numbers lifted from the financial statements. But can the bank claim justifiable reliance on financial statements after looking at only one or two numbers, without considering the financial statements as a whole? Without reading the accompanying notes? Without even looking at the auditor's opinion—the document that the bank contends that it relied on? The jury would have to decide.

The plaintiff, of course, may try to circumvent such inconvenient details. First, the plaintiff might testify that the net profit number provided adequate information. Second, the bank's representatives might testify (if they never saw the financial statements) that, had the financial statements said something different—for example, reported a loss rather than a profit—*then* they would have reviewed the information more thoroughly.

Juries often remain unpersuaded by such testimony. Given the wealth of data in financial statements—even without addressing the principles of GAAP that lie behind them—it can sound implausible for a sophisticated financial analyst to argue the sensibility of a quick look at net profit. Similarly, plaintiffs who testify that they relied on a document that they never saw can face an uphill battle—assuming the trial judge lets the jury hear such testimony.

In the end, the worst enemy of plaintiffs seeking to prove justifiable reliance on financial statements can be their own filing cabinets. Rarely will an individual or firm make an important financial decision based on financial statements. Instead, such a plaintiff's filing cabinet usually holds extensive documentation of completely separate and independent financial analysis, inquiry, and investigation into the underlying financial structure and economics of the transaction at issue. In the context of such a blizzard of paper, after-the-fact testimony that such an individual relied on a single set of historical financial statements often sounds hollow. Indeed, sometimes among all the documentation surrounding the financial transaction, one cannot find the audited financial statements.

(c) Others Are at Fault.   Another defense in the arsenal of defendant accountants is that others should bear the responsibility. Most defendants use this argument, which has roots in the structure of a normal accountant engagement. In an audit engagement, for example, the auditor does not have primary responsibility for the reported numbers. Consider again the report of the Treadway Commission, as reinforced by the Sarbanes-Oxley Act, and its effects. The company's management has primary responsibility for reported numbers; the auditor is responsible for formulating an opinion on the financial statements based on a sample of information that was the subject of audit tests. Even statistically derived samples run the risk of sampling error; the sample may not represent the underlying population of transactions being sampled. The auditor may therefore have performed all prescribed tests flawlessly, yet miss fraud or error in the accounts. If the numbers contain errors, however, evidence almost always exists to indicate that management erred.

Different individuals within a company's management, moreover, will bear responsibility for different functions. At the lowest level, all employees have responsibility for acting honestly and in accordance with company policy regarding the processes used to transmit information to the company's accounting department. Individual members of the accounting department, in turn, must perform functions that collectively result in the system faithfully recording transactions. A chief financial officer and senior staff supervise these processes. The chief executive officer or the chief operating officer has responsibility for supervising the chief financial officer.

Moreover, the board, through its audit committee, has increased responsibility for oversight of the financial reporting function. Under the Sarbanes-Oxley Act, the audit committee is also "directly responsible for the appointment, compensation, and oversight of the work of any registered public accounting firm employed by that issuer … for the purpose of preparing or issuing an audit report."[25] Thus, should financial misreporting surface, blame might fall on the individual audit committee members. Their diligence, the faithfulness with which they performed the duties set forth in their written charter, and their attentiveness to the financial reporting system and its potential vulnerabilities may all surface in an accountant liability trial.

The law, the auditor's letter in the financial statements, and management's letter to shareholders all document management's responsibility for the integrity of the financial statements, which will frequently be well documented.[26] Additional evidence will show, for example, that, during the course of audit testing, the audit team recorded management representations in the audit work papers. Similarly, the audit files will likely contain client documentation—marked "PBC" for prepared by client. Senior client executives will have signed a representation letter before the auditor issued a report.

The accountant can often blame others, beyond management. For example, if the books and records include data that a third-party supplier or creditor has improperly confirmed, the auditor may lay the blame there. Similarly, if other financial professionals (such as appraisers) provided analysis, the auditor may blame them. The involvement of another accounting firm in some aspect of reported financial results may give the accountant an opportunity to shift responsibility.

If the company is pursuing a claim, then an attempt to reallocate responsibility may take the form of a *contributory negligence* defense. The accountant will seek to shift blame to the plaintiff by contending that the plaintiff was contributorily negligent or did not justifiably rely on the financial information or incorrectly analyzed the data. Rarely does a plaintiff—at least outside the context of the federal securities laws—emerge from an accountant liability trial completely unscathed.

(d) The Auditor Spoke the Truth. Accountants have another defense. Even if the numbers contained errors, even if the plaintiff justifiably relied on them, and even if others are not available to blame, accountants can claim that they spoke the truth.

The availability of this defense results from what the audit report actually says. A typical audit report on financial statements does not state that the numbers in the financial statements are correct. Instead, it reads as follows:

> We have audited the accompanying balance sheet of X Company as of December 31, 20XX, and the related statements of income, retained earnings, and cash flows for the year then ended. These financial statements are the responsibility of the Company's management. Our responsibility is to express an opinion on these financial statements based on our audit.

> We conducted our audit in accordance with the standards of the Public Company Accounting Oversight Board (United States). Those standards require that we plan and perform the audit to obtain reasonable assurance about whether the financial statements are free of material misstatement. An audit includes examining, on a test basis, evidence supporting the amounts and disclosures in the financial statements. An audit also includes assessing the accounting principles used and significant estimates made by management, as well as evaluating the overall financial statement presentation. We believe that our audit provides a reasonable basis for our opinion.

> In our opinion, the financial statements referred to above present fairly, in all material respects, the financial position of X Company as of December 31, 20XX, and the results of its operations and its cash flows for the year then ended in conformity with generally accepted accounting principles.[27]

Thus, the actual representations boil down to these: First, the auditor audited the financial statements. Second, the accountant conducted the audit in accordance with GAAS. Third, in the auditor's opinion, the financial statements as a whole present fairly in all material respects the company's financial position in accordance with GAAP. Nowhere does the audit report say that the numbers are correct.

In some situations, therefore, the underlying financial statements can be materially wrong while everything that the auditor said still holds true. The auditor can still contend, therefore, that he or she spoke the truth. Moreover, the provisions of GAAS add viability to this defense because they state that the auditor's judgment lies at the heart of any audit. Proof that an auditor violated GAAS, therefore, requires proof that the auditor used indefensible judgment, based on the information then available. Plaintiffs will often find such proof difficult to obtain.

The first class action against an accountant to go through trial pursuant to the securities "tort reform" of the mid-1990s demonstrated the importance of such a defense. The case, *In re Health Management, Inc. Securities Litigation*,[28] involved financial statements that unquestionably contained misstatements. Among other problems, management had fabricated substantial quantities of inventory, falsified accounts receivable data, and recorded improper sales. Fraud had infected the most critical aspects of the company's financial statements.

Nonetheless, the jury exonerated the auditor. At no point did the jury conclude that the financial statements were correct. Instead, the jury distinguished management's responsibility for the numbers in the financial statements from the auditor's function of auditing the financial statements in accordance with GAAS. Thus, the jury distinguished between the inaccuracy of the numbers and the fact that the audit report spoke the truth.

(e) Plaintiffs' Use of Hindsight.   Plaintiffs typically take advantage of hindsight. For example, when a company records a significant increase in its reserve for bad debts, plaintiffs will claim that the increase proves that the prior accounts were in error. However, accounting for any balance sheet item requires the use of estimates: accounts receivable and inventory reserves; goodwill or other long-lived asset impairment; assessing probability relative to whether contingent liabilities will become actual liabilities. Under GAAP, changes in good faith estimates do not require restatement of the financial statements; in other words, GAAP does not consider such changes as errors. Defendant accountants will seek to demonstrate that, based on the information available at the time, they came to a reasonable conclusion. They will try to illustrate that the plaintiffs, in forming their conclusion that the accounts contained errors, rely on information that became available only after the auditor's opinion date.

19.7   THE ACCOUNTANT AS EXPERT

The accountant expert can provide testimony on a number of issues: accounting, auditing, financial analysis, and damages.

(a) The Accounting Expert.   The accounting expert addresses whether the financial statements complied with GAAP. The accounting expert identifies which time periods contained errors in financial statements, quantifies the amount of the alleged misstatements, and opines as to whether the misstatements were material. To the extent that the accounting expert believes the financial statements at issue are correct (as might be the case for a defendant's accounting expert), the expert must rebut the plaintiff expert's allegations that the numbers contained errors. This might involve explaining the necessity of using estimates (rather than precise amounts) in financial reporting and the fact that GAAP requires such estimates.

The accounting expert sets the stage for the audit expert by identifying which company books and records contained the problems. Explaining how the errors affected the books can support the plaintiff's or defendant's position as to the propriety of the auditor's actions. For example, a plaintiff's accounting expert might testify that the auditor should have detected all or part of the misstatements, perhaps because of large dollar value entries with highly suspicious descriptions on a company accounting record. The plaintiff can strengthen the case against the accountant by establishing that the accountant saw or should have seen this company record during the audit.

Conversely, if the defendant's accounting expert establishes that any misstatements resulted from the company's failure to record a transaction that was otherwise not apparent from the accounting records, such testimony can help defend the reasonableness of the audit procedures.

(b) The Audit Expert.   The audit expert must explain the requirements of GAAS and whether the accountant followed GAAS. The audit expert uses several tools to explain what constitutes generally accepted auditing standards. These include the auditing standards approved by the PCAOB (at this time largely adopted from standards originally promulgated by the AICPA, the profession's self-regulatory body prior to the establishment of the PCAOB). Beyond those standards, some audit experts seek to introduce evidence of the general acceptance of specific audit procedures through the use of such materials as textbooks and professional reference books on auditing, the planned audit procedures outlined in the audit working papers of the accountant, and the experience of the audit expert.

The audit expert will then compare or contrast GAAS with the audit in question. Through reference to relevant working papers and testimony of the auditors themselves, the expert will opine as to whether the auditors used appropriate procedures. The audit expert will address the question of whether the auditor obtained sufficient, competent evidential matter before rendering an audit opinion.

The expert will evaluate the qualifications, technical competence, and adequate supervision of the audit team. The audit expert will also assess the level of care and professional skepticism with which the accountant conducted the audits.

The audit expert's opinions will depend on the expert's individual professional judgment. The jury will hear divergent views from the plaintiff's and defendant's audit experts as to what GAAS require and what the auditor should have reasonably known during the time of the audits.

The audit expert should become familiar with the degree to which the plaintiff must demonstrate that the accountant erred. In cases of fraud claims, the effective plaintiff expert convinces the jury that the auditor knowingly or recklessly fell well short of professional obligations. If that expert can further succeed in proving that a proper GAAS audit would have prevented or caused early detection of the financial reporting problem, the plaintiff's audit expert achieved much of the plaintiff's goal.

An effective defendant's expert seeks to defend as reasonable the accountant's judgments made during the audit's planning and execution. If material misstatements eluded the auditor's attention, a skilled defendant's expert can succinctly convey the limitations of GAAS. The defendant's audit expert also seeks to explain how the auditor followed GAAS and why the auditor's actions were appropriate. Usually, this requires that the audit expert differentiate between facts and information discovered after identification of the problem and the information available to the accountant during the time of the audits in question. An effective expert for the accountant helps ensure that the jury does not hold the auditor to a higher standard than the generally accepted standards of the auditing profession and does not judge unfairly based on information discovered after the audit. Finally, the expert will draw a distinction, where appropriate, between acts of commission and acts of omission. In the former, management recorded an accounting transaction(s) in the books and records—erroneously or intentionally—that it should not have recorded. Auditors may find these acts easier to detect than acts of omission, wherein management has failed to record an accounting transaction(s) that it should have recorded.

(c) The Financial Analysis Expert.   An expert in financial analysis can have a pivotal role in accountant liability litigation. The financial analysis expert does not testify as to the audit's conformity with GAAS or whether the financial statements complied with GAAP. Rather, the financial analysis expert testifies about the process of financial analysis and the role and limitations of historical financial statements in the process. In other words, the expert testifies about the plaintiff's justifiable reliance. As part of that testimony, the analyst explains distinctions such as those between cash and accrual-based income, historical and prospective results, cost versus fair market value, and the extent to which GAAP prefer objectivity to usefulness in choosing the basis for reporting accounting data. An effective expert can teach that only foolish analysts and investors rely solely on the bottom line.

(d) The Damages Expert.   The nature of the plaintiff's damages theory will depend on the plaintiff's relation to the financial statements. For example, a creditor of a company that issued improper financial statements might seek to recover amounts owed to it by the company. Shareholders, on the other hand, might assert damages related to an allegedly excess price paid for their shares. If the company that issued flawed financial statements chooses to assert a claim against its auditor, the company's damages expert will develop yet another basis for calculating recoverable damages.

The plaintiff's damages expert and the accountant's damages expert will likely disagree on several fundamental principles and assumptions. The length of the damages period, the economic consequences of company-specific events unrelated to the financial statement errors, and the method of adjusting damages estimates represent some of the primary areas of differences between typical plaintiff and defendant damages calculations in accountant liability cases. *See* Chapters 5 through 16 for further discussion of relevant damages estimation techniques.

NOTES

1. "Ernst & Young Settles Suit with Merry-Go-Round for $185 million," *Dow Jones Business News*, April 26, 1999.
2. Randall K. Hanson et al., "Litigation Support Liability," *The CPA Journal*, March 1995.
3. "Consultants Becoming Deep-Pocket Targets," *Consultants News*, August 1998.
4. *Macpherson v. Buick Motor Co.*, 217 N.Y. 382, 111 N.E. 1050 (1916).
5. *See* generally Richard I. Miller and Michael R. Young, "Financial Reporting and Risk Management in the 21st Century," *Fordham Law Review* 65 (1997): 2013–16.
6. *Ultramares Corp. v. Touche*, 255 N.Y. 170, 179, 174 N.E. 441, 444 (1931).
7. *Credit Alliance Corp. v. Arthur Andersen & Co.*, 65 N.Y.2d 536, 483 N.E.2d 100, 493 N.Y.S.2d 435 (1985).
8. *Bily v. Arthur Young & Co.*, 834 P.2d 745, 762 (Cal. 1992).
9. *Touche Ross & Co. v. Commercial Union Ins. Co.*, 514 So. 2d 315, 318–23 (Miss. 1987) (considering both the *Ultramares/Credit Alliance* and the Torts Restatement rules and rejecting both, approving instead a "reasonably foreseeable" rule, but also noting that "the auditor remains free to limit the dissemination of his opinion through a separate agreement with the audited entity"); *Citizens State Bank v. Timm, Schmidt & Co.*, 335 N.W.2d 361 (Wis. 1983).
10. *Bily v. Arthur Young & Co.*, 834 P.2d 745 (Cal. 1992).
11. *See* generally Michael R. Young, *Accounting Irregularities and Financial Fraud* San Diego, CA; (Harcourt, 2000), 21–340.
12. *H. Rosenblum, Inc. v. Adler*, 93 N.J. 324, 461 A.2d 138, 151 (1983).

13. *See* Michael R. Young, "The Liability of Corporate Officials to their Outside Auditor for Financial Statement Fraud," *Fordham Law Review* 64 (1996): 2155, 2160. *See also* "Accounting Firms Predict Dim Future if Joint and Several Liability Remains, 25 Sec. Reg. & L. Rep. (BNA) Vol 24 at 872 (June 18, 1993).

14. National Commission on Fraudulent Reporting, *Report of the National Commission on Fraudulent Financial Reporting*, October 1987, 6.

15. Ibid., 23.

16. Ibid., 24.

17. Ken Brown, "Auditor's Methods Make It Hard to Catch Fraud by Executives," *Wall Street Journal*, July 8, 2002, C-3.

18. Ibid., 32.

19. *Codification of Auditing Standards and Procedures, AICPA Professional Standards*, vol. 1 AU sec. 200.

20. Ibid., sec. 300.

21. Ibid., sec. 400 and 500.

22. Ibid., sec. 110.02.

23. *PricewaterhouseCoopers 2004 Securities Litigation Study*, 14.

24. Fed. R. Evid. 703. *See also Daubert v. Merrell Dow Pharmaceuticals, Inc.*, 509 U.S. 579, 595 (1993).

25. Sarbanes-Oxley Act of 2002, Section 301(2).

26. *See* generally Michael R. Young, "The Liability of Corporate Officials to Their Outside Auditor for Financial Statement Fraud," *Fordham Law Review* 65 (1996): 2155.

27. *AICPA Professional Standards*, AU §508.08 (June 1, 1999).

28. *In re Health Management, Inc. Sec. Litig.*, No. CV 96-889 (ADS) (E.D.N.Y. 1997).

CHAPTER 20

ECONOMIC ANALYSIS OF NONPATENT INTELLECTUAL PROPERTY RIGHTS AND DAMAGES MEASURES

Elizabeth A. Evans
Peter P. Simon

CONTENTS

The authors thank M. James Call, Cate Elsten, Terry Lloyd, Martha S. Samuelson, Robert A. Sherwin, and George G. Strong for their contribution in writing the chapters on these topics appearing in the first, second, and third editions. This chapter does not intend to endorse or criticize the views presented by various courts as related to trademark, trade secret, false advertising, and copyright cases, but rather focuses on identifying standards and trends. The authors do not recommend any specific method of calculating damages without first considering the facts of a particular case.

20.1   INTRODUCTION

Property means a tangible or intangible resource to which an owner has legal title.[1] *Property rights* refer to the capacity of people or firms to own, buy, sell, and use property in a market economy.[2] Readers familiar with these terms in the context of physical property or financial capital often do not understand the rights of authors or inventors, how the law protects these rights, and the proper compensation if an abuser infringes these rights. Chapter 22 discusses these issues for patents; this chapter focuses on these issues and other considerations as they relate to nonpatent intellectual property.

Section 20.2 introduces the three forms of nonpatent intellectual property rights (copyrights, trademarks and protection against false advertising, and trade secrets) and discusses each form's economic characteristics. Section 20.3 analyzes damages measurement issues unique to intellectual property. Section 20.4 explains how nonpatent intellectual property differs from patent intellectual property. Then Sections 20.5, 20.6, and 20.7 discuss various issues specific to copyrights, trademarks and false advertising, and trade secrets, respectively.

20.2   MAIN FORMS OF NONPATENT INTELLECTUAL PROPERTY RIGHTS

The three main types of nonpatent intellectual property rights are copyrights, trademarks, and trade secrets. This section discusses what protections the law provides, what an owner must do to obtain protection, and the economic implications for each type. Why examine the economic implications for each type of intellectual property? Economics is "the study of how societies use scarce resources to produce valuable commodities and distribute them among different people."[3] Regarding intellectual property as a scarce resource, economists have studied how the law rewards its creation, the cost to society of this reward system, and whether the system's benefits exceed its costs. Hence, this section will also focus on how the law can structure intellectual property rights so that the creator of intellectual property will receive an appropriate return at a minimal cost to society. See the Appendix for a comparison of different types of intellectual property.

(a) Copyrights.   Copyrights protect "original works of authorship fixed in any tangible medium of expression."[4] Section 102 of the Copyright Act lists eight protected categories: literary works; musical works (including any accompanying words); dramatic works (including any accompanying music); pantomimes and choreographic works; pictorial, graphic, and sculptural works; motion pictures and other audiovisual works; sound recordings; and architectural works.[5] Congress listed these categories to be illustrative, not exhaustive.[6] The particular medium containing the work does not affect its right to copyright protection: "A novel is still a novel and protected by copyright whether it is recorded in the form of a manuscript, typescript, computer diskette, printed plates, laser disks, or bubble memory."[7]

Copyright protection never covers the expressed *idea*, only the *expression* of that idea. Section 102 of the Copyright Act states, "In no case does copyright protection for an original work of authorship extend to any idea, procedure, process, system, method of operation, concept, principle, or discovery, regardless of the form in which it is described, explained, illustrated, or embodied in such work."[8] Nor does copyright protection require novelty of the work: that a play reworks the Romeo and Juliet theme will not keep an author from receiving copyright protection. In fact, two people separately can create similar works, yet each of them can receive a copyright and each author can have copyright protection. A patent provides protection against any use, even if the second inventor developed the same idea independently. In contrast, an independently created copy does not infringe a copyright.

As in the case of patents, rights under copyright endure for a limited time. For works created after December 31, 1977, a copyright will continue for 70 years after the death of the work's only or last surviving author.[9] For anonymous works, pseudonymous works, or works made for hire, a copyright lasts for 95 years after the work's first publication or 120 years from its original[10] creation, whichever comes first. When a copyright expires, the public can exploit the formerly protected property freely.

Congress has imposed fair use limitations on the rights of the copyright owner in order to accommodate socially desirable copying (in certain circumstances) that remains fair to the copyright owner. "Fair use" would include copying for purposes such as criticism, comment, new reporting, teaching, and research. To decide what falls within the fair use exception, the courts look to the following:

- The purpose and nature of the use (courts treat more leniently groups using the materials for purposes other than economic gain)
- The nature of the copyrighted work
- The percentage of the copyrighted work used and its importance to the work as a whole
- The effect of the use on the potential market for the copyrighted work or its value[11]

Courts must tailor fair use analysis to the individual case. For example, in *Harper & Row v. Nation Enterprises*, the Supreme Court held that the publication of 300 to 400 words of copyrighted material from memoirs of former President Ford violated the fair use doctrine.[12] Even though the amount of words quoted were an insubstantial portion of the total transcript, the Supreme Court found the words chosen played a key role in the infringing article and the circumstances under which the infringer published them affected the right of first publication, an important marketable subsidiary right. On the other hand, courts allow use of portions of a copyrighted work in a book review because this can benefit the author by establishing his work in a new market.[13]

Recently, however, Congress passed legislation that eliminated some fair use limitations. The Digital Millennium Copyright Act (DMCA), passed in 1998, forbids the creation, distribution, or use of technologies that make circumvention of digital rights management (DRM) systems possible.[14] DRM technology systems allow copyright holders to protect and control access to their copyrighted works. Put simply, DMCA limits the copying of digital material. Prior case decisions defined fair use to include, for example, videotaping of television programs for later viewing.[15] Some observers propose that this law's protection of digital works eliminates the possibility of any fair use of these works.[16]

The issuance of copyrights involves competing social benefits and costs. If a publisher appropriates an author's novel (or other copyrightable work) without compensation, the author will not have received an appropriate return for his or her investment in creativity.[17] However, if the publisher pays the author compensation, such as a royalty, the publisher then will pass on to the public the compensation it pays an author in the form of a higher book price. In other words, one must consider whether the benefits of copyright (the creator has an incentive to create the work) exceed the costs (one must pay to duplicate the work). Litigation related to file sharing forces the courts to balance these interests. For example, in *MGM v. Grokster*, the Supreme Court ruled that duplicating technology in order to encourage infringement infringed a copyright.[18] These considerations parallel those involved in the economic analysis of patent rights.

Economic analysis of copyrights involves at least four considerations:

1. Copyrights protect the expression of the idea and not the idea itself.
2. Copyrights provide a stronger form of protection than do patents, in that copyright holders receive control over derivative works, whereas patent holders do not.
3. Copyrights provide less protection than that of patents, because copyrights do not protect holders from independent duplication, whereas patents do.
4. The ease of private copying leads to varying effects of replication on producer and consumer welfare.

(i) Expression of an Idea.   Courts and authorities have suggested at least two justifications for protecting the *expression* of an idea, rather than the idea itself: (1) the cost of expressing the idea exceeds the cost of creating the idea, and (2) the public benefits by a larger number of competing works.[19] If one could copyright ideas, the public would have fewer works from which to choose, the work being the expression of the idea.

(ii) Derivative Works.   Copyrights provide a stronger form of protection than do patents, in that the author of a copyrighted novel controls all derivative uses of the work—for example, translation into another language or quotes appearing on T-shirts or in calendars. Suppose an inventor receives a patent for a method of combining elements to create a new chemical, and another inventor receives a patent for using this new chemical in a certain way to create a new product. The chemical's inventor will have to pay a royalty to use the new process.[20] Control

over derivative works provides the maximum incentive to produce.[21] Such control encourages the early release of work: in the absence of this protection, the author would delay publication to prepare related translations and other commercial derivatives.[22] This rewards the author while giving the public as many works as possible, and as soon as possible, from which to choose. The prospect theory of Edmund Kitch suggests that giving authors control over derivative works allows them to manage the efficient use of their ideas and to avoid duplicative efforts, such as several translations into a single foreign language.[23] For example, some argue that royalty payments enable an author to maximize the joint value of hard- and softcover editions of the author's work.[24]

(iii) Independent Duplication. Regarding independent duplication, patents provide more protection than do copyrights. Under the patent system, the winner takes all, whereas the author of a copyrighted work has no protection from an independent recreation of the author's work. This inconsistency has an economic rationale: the cost of checking for duplicates in the copyright system exceeds that for the patent system, and accidental duplication of a copyrighted work does not involve free riding on the original author's expression, because the second author must incur the full cost of creating the expression.[25]

(iv) Ease of Copying. One cannot easily assess social gains and losses from copying. Some justify the doctrine of *fair use* by noting that, although most authors will consent to the use of a portion of their work for a slight fee and most users will pay, high negotiation costs preclude such exchanges. Thus, the fair use doctrine provides a benefit to the user and causes little harm to the author.[26]

(b) Trademarks. A trademark is any word, name, symbol, device, or any combination thereof that a business uses to distinguish its goods or services from those of others.[27] Trademarks identify products so that consumers can choose those they know and like; manufacturers can then benefit from building up a strong base of consumer support.[28]

Trademark law protects any "words, designs, shapes, numbers, sounds, or smells,"[29] as well as names like McDonald's, Xerox, and Coca-Cola. Trademarks even protect symbols, slogans, and phrases—such as the flying window associated with the Microsoft Windows programs, the phrase "You're Fired" registered to Donald Trump, and the shape of the old Coca-Cola bottle.[30]

Trademark protection extends to Internet domain names. An individual or company cannot register or use a domain name identical to or confusingly similar to a trademark owned by another entity. An entity that registers another entity's distinctive or famous trademark as a domain name, however, can keep the domain name if it can show that it did not do so in bad faith.[31] For example, an arbitrator ruled that, because no evidence of bad faith existed, qwestcorp.com, owned by Quest Publishing, did not infringe Qwest, Inc.'s trademark.[32]

Whereas patent and copyright law aims to encourage innovation, trademark law aims to avoid deception and confusion of customers and to protect a firm's investment in reputation and goodwill. As a result, one cannot trademark a product feature determined by the product's purpose. For example, the manufacturer cannot trademark the circular shape of a car's tire because its form follows from its rolling function.[33]

Trademarks must have distinctive characteristics. The more distinctive the word, the more likely the trademark protection. To decide which marks, symbols, and names qualify for protection, the law uses a distinctiveness scale with four categories (listed here in ascending order of distinctiveness):[34]

1. **Generic** encompasses many commonly used words and phrases, as well as formerly distinctive words. For example, although once a protected trademark, the word *aspirin* no longer belongs to any one firm, having become common.

2. **Descriptive** contains names that usually describe the product being represented. The trademark law does not give trademark protection to descriptive names unless the manufacturer can prove a secondary meaning that consumers have come to associate the name with a single source (*Honey-Baked*, for example).[35]

3. **Suggestive** includes names or symbols loosely associated with a product. Trademark law does, however, extend protection to suggestive trademarks without proof of secondary meaning.

4. **Arbitrary** or **fanciful** names bear no obvious relation to the product they represent. Trademark law generally protects such names.[36]

Unlike that of patents and copyrights, ownership of trademarks depends primarily on use. The trademark will last as long as the company holding the mark continues to use it. Should the trademark owner cease using the trademark, it will lapse.[37] The licensee must renew a registered trademark every 10 years, with no limit on the number of renewals.[38] Although one can register a mark with the U.S. Patent and Trademark Office and with other state regulatory bodies, one need not do so except to receive the advantage of "a nationwide right of priority, even in areas where the work has not been used."[39] If an owner registers a trademark and an infringer violates those rights, the owner can recover damages through the Trademark Act. An owner who has not registered the mark can recover damages under state common law.

In trademark infringement cases, courts examine the similarity of marks, the similarity of products or services, the geographic area involved, the manner of concurrent use, the strength of the defendant's allegedly infringing mark, evidence of confusion in the market place, and the defendant's intention.[40] Although the owner of a trademark need not prove confusion—only the likelihood of confusion—the owner will find it easier to prevail in a lawsuit if the owner establishes confusion.[41]

As noted previously, trademarks provide rules of orderly marketing. Trademark protection benefits society by reducing consumer search costs and encouraging firms to invest in quality.[42] For efficient trademark protection, the consumer must find it cheaper to search for the trademarked good than for the desired attributes of a product, and the consumer must find past experience a good predictor of the future. In other words, the firm must have products of a consistent quality.[43] This reflects the implicit thinking that guides trademark law. However, some argue that advertising the trademarked good can result in monopolistic rents or wasteful competition if a firm advertises to convince the public without base that the trademarked good exceeds the quality of the same, less advertised, generic good.[44]

Trademarks have legal protection for a different period of time than either patents or copyrights, because trademark names do not consume scarce resources the way manufactured products do. In other words, trademark names do not involve rent-seeking issues. Many of the problems associated with tracing or identifying products that infringe patents, moreover, do not exist with trademarks because trademarks apply to physical, easily identified goods.[45]

Although trademarks are also covered by various common law provisions and state statutes, the primary source of law for trademark infringement is the Lanham Act. Section 43(a) of the Lanham Act prohibits unfair competition, and trademark infringement represents a type of unfair competition.[46]

Another type of unfair competition under the Lanham Act is false advertising. False advertising encompasses false or misleading claims about a competitor (the plaintiff or a third party) or about the originating entity (the defendant). It includes false statements, literally true statements presented in a fashion that tends to deceive or mislead, and failure to disclose material information. Courts have found that obvious hyperbole does not provide a basis for false advertising claims. False advertising laws apply not only to media (broadcast, print or online) advertising, but also acts or materials such as project labeling, general sales pitches or bad mouthing, letters, or oral representations to clients and public relations materials.

False advertising cases allow the same forms of remedy, including monetary damages, as other Lanham Act claims. In practice, of course, the fact patterns for trademark and false advertising cases can differ in ways that affect the relevance of specific damages approaches. Nevertheless, courts often cite case law arising from trademark infringement matters as precedent in false advertising cases and vice versa. Therefore, even though false advertising does not imply an intellectual property issue, this chapter will include it in discussions of damages for trademarks under the Lanham Act.

(c) Trade Secrets. Whereas statutes established patents, copyrights, and trademarks to protect people who have put their works before the public, the intellectual property rights for trade secrets function to keep knowledge hidden from others. Each state sets its own trade secret laws, although all generally agree as to what constitutes a trade secret. According to the Uniform Trade Secrets Act, trade secrets encompass

> information, including a formula, pattern, compilation, program, device, method, technique, or process that: (1) derives independent economic value, actual or potential, from not being generally known to, and not being readily ascertainable by proper means by, other persons who can obtain economic value from its disclosure or use, and (2) is the subject of efforts that are reasonable under the circumstances to maintain its secrecy.[47]

Hence, to receive protection, the knowledge must be secret, the secret must have some economic value, and the owner must make some effort to keep it secret and protect it from any unauthorized use.[48] Courts have found trade secrets in price and cost data, production processes, customer lists, databases, computer programs, computer program algorithms, secret formulas, marketing plans, and books of formulas known in the trade but combined in a way to provide a unique advantage (similar to a football play book).[49]

If one acquires a trade secret by improper means—such as industrial espionage, breach of confidence, bribery, subversion of employees, or breach of contract—one must compensate the owner of the trade secret. This protection endures for an indefinite time. The Supreme Court has ruled, however, that an owner has no protection for a secret discovered by another who used fair and honest means.[50] Courts recognize reverse engineering from a publicly available source as proper, for example.[51]

In some ways, the law extends more protection to owners of trade secrets than to owners of patents. Had Colonel Sanders patented the recipe for Kentucky Fried Chicken, after 20 years anyone could have used it. By maintaining the recipe as a trade secret, the Colonel and his successors in interest have hidden the recipe from the public indefinitely. However, if someone independently develops a method of replicating a secret recipe or other sensitive information, unlike a patent owner, the original secret holder will receive no compensation.

The intellectual property protection extended to trade secrets differs from the others analyzed thus far. First, instead of granting its creator rights for its disclosure—as with patents, copyrights, and trademarks—trade secret protection grants the creator rights only as long as the intellectual property remains secret. Also, unlike patents or copyrights, the damages award for violating this intellectual property right has nothing to do with rewarding creativity. The courts base remedies for its violation solely on its commercial value.

Landes and Posner argue that trade secret protection supplements the protection offered by patents and tends to keep the benefits of innovation accruing to the owner of the trade secret.[52] They also note, however, that the law of trade secrets penalizes industrial espionage, but not reverse engineering, because reverse engineering will frequently generate knowledge about the product that will allow improvements.[53]

Trade secret law does not derive from federal, but rather from state, law. Nevertheless, some federal laws relate to theft of trade secrets. The Federal Trade Secret Act (18 U.S.C.S. (2005) § 1905 *et seq.* at §1905) and the Federal Trade Commission Act (15 U.S.C.S. (2005) § 41-58 at § 46(f)) prohibit disclosure of trade secrets by federal employees who receive such information in their role as federal employees. Further, we note that the Freedom of Information Act (5 U.S.C.S. (2005) § 552 *et seq.*) does not require public disclosure of documents containing trade secrets if the authorized official believes that the government does not normally release such information to the public and that doing so would cause significant competitive harm to the trade secret's owner.[54] Because the Racketeer Influenced and Corrupt Organizations Act (RICO; 18 U.S.C.S. (2005) § 1961-69 at § 1964(c)) allows recovery to anyone injured by interstate theft, an owner might use a RICO action to recover damages for trade secrets that a prepetrator steals and takes across state lines.

20.3 GENERAL DAMAGES MEASUREMENT ISSUES IN NONPATENT INTELLECTUAL PROPERTY CASES

In almost all commercial cases, damages equal the difference between the profits the property owner would have received but for the defendant's actions and the profits (or losses) the owner received. Given the property rights discussed in previous sections of this chapter, however, the owner of intellectual property can suffer in ways not found in most commercial cases. For example, because a copyright grants its owner a monopoly on the copyrighted work and because the behaviors of prices and costs of a monopoly differ from those in a competitive market, the measurement of damages to a copyright holder (whether measured as lost profits, royalties, or unjust enrichment) will differ from measurement of damages in other commercial cases. This section discusses some of the damages measurement issues involved in making the owner of intellectual property whole.

(a) Injuries to Owners of Intellectual Property.   Assume that someone has infringed the rights of an intellectual property owner by illegally using the intellectual property. How has that person harmed the owner? If the owner would have produced the product exclusively, the owner suffers reduced sales and thus lost profits on the infringing sales. The owner may have also lost sales on non-infringed goods as a result of infringement. Profits on these, too, are recoverable. In addition to the lost profits on sales, the infringement further reduced the owner's profits through less obvious effects on the owner's cost structure. For instance, the reduced sales could have resulted in reduced economies of scale, or the unwarranted competition could have caused an increase in costs, such as advertising aimed at maintaining sales. Moreover, price erosion caused by competition from the infringer could have reduced profitability on the owner's sales. In the absence of infringement, the owner would have had a monopoly (to a greater or lesser extent) on the intellectual property and could have charged monopoly prices. With infringement, the owner faced competition from the infringer. Such competition leads to lower prices.

If the owner would have both used the intellectual property and licensed it to others (i.e., a licensor/competitor owner), the court can consider several types of damages:

- To the extent that a competitor infringed, the owner lost sales. Even if the owner would have otherwise licensed to the infringer, the owner suffers losses because the royalty-free infringement reduced the infringer's costs. These lower costs, in turn, afforded the infringer lower prices and increased the number of sales over the sales level that the infringer would have achieved had the infringer paid for the use of the intellectual property.
- The added competition created price pressures on the owner that, because of the lowered prices in the market, lowered the owner's profits on the sales that the owner retained.
- The infringer deprived the owner of royalty payments.
- To the extent that the infringer competed with legitimate third-party licensees, those licensees in turn may have sold less and, as a result, made lower royalty payments to the owner than otherwise.

Would-be licensor/competitor owners will find irrelevant whether they receive reasonable royalties or lost profits because the reasonable royalty model includes lost profit damages. Why is this so? When calculating damages, one often assumes that in the but-for world the infringer would have used the next best alternative to the intellectual property, not the property itself. However, in the licensor/competitor situation, one assumes that in the but-for world the infringer would have licensed the property. The owner would structure the license so that price and total quantity would be as in the situation with no infringement. Thus, the portion of damages that looks like lost profits (part of the lower sales the owner made at lower prices) results from the infringer's not having paid a running royalty, and a reasonable royalty calculation should include that portion.[55]

In addition to lost profit and reasonable royalty damages measures, the owner in some cases can also claim damages based on unjust enrichment (i.e., the amount by which the infringer has profited by the infringement). This remedy, which Section 20.3(e) of this chapter discusses in more detail, can result in a damages measure that exceeds a lost profit calculation when the infringer can use the intellectual property in question more effectively. For example, suppose an infringer could manufacture a product with lower costs using the intellectual property than the owner could; as a result, an award based on the infringer's profits might exceed an award based on the owner's lost profits. Moreover, the amount of the infringer's profits may place a maximum boundary on the amount of reasonable royalty that the owner may seek. In other words, the amount of unjust enrichment represents a first approximation of the maximum amount available for a royalty payment. If the court required the infringer to pay more than the amount of the infringer's profits as a royalty, the infringer would have negative income and the court would invalidate the assumption underlying the reasonable royalty calculation.

(b) Running Royalty versus Lump-Sum Royalty. When examining but-for royalty income, the expert must often decide what form the arrangement would have taken had one existed. Would the royalty have been a running royalty (e.g., a certain percentage of revenues or a per-unit charge) or a paid-up (lump-sum) license fee?

An expert should not arbitrarily choose between a running royalty and a lump-sum license fee. Instead, a variety of factors will favor one over the other. One factor considers the relative importance of the intellectual property. For example, if the expert finds that a relatively small (e.g., 0.1 percent of sales) running royalty would properly compensate the owner, the parties will more likely choose a lump-sum fee because of the relatively low value of the license and the relatively high cost of monitoring sales.

The expert must also decide whether the infringer/licensee would have had an exclusive license. If so, the owner would more likely receive a lump-sum royalty because of a phenomenon known as *double marginalization*.[56] In essence, if the intellectual property has significant value, an exclusive licensee will have a measure of monopoly power. When paying a running royalty, the licensee will take the cost of the running royalty into account in deciding on pricing and production levels, resulting in the licensee producing too few items, at too high a price, to maximize the joint profits of the owner and the licensee under this scenario. A lump-sum royalty solves this problem and increases the profits split between owner and infringer/licensee.

A corollary situation exists in which the infringer/licensee will compete with the owner or with other licensees who pay running royalties. In a competitive situation, the owner maximizes profits attributable to the intellectual property by setting a running royalty at a level that raises total marginal cost (including the royalty) to the monopoly price. If all competitors paid a lump-sum royalty, they would ignore the sunk cost of their licenses and compete the price toward marginal cost. In such cases, the licensees might not recover their sunk costs, thus reducing the incentives to pay a lump sum. Hence, one might expect to see clauses in such licenses that would assure the licensee that the license terms will always equal at a maximum the most favorable license the owner grants.

One reason that the owner of significant intellectual property does not often license it to competitors relates to the following argument. For the owner to avoid putting the licensee at a competitive disadvantage, the owner would have to charge itself the same license royalty rate. An economically sophisticated owner would understand that this charge was a real opportunity cost in making a sale, because the owner takes such a sale from one of its licensees who would otherwise have paid the owner a running royalty. A would-be licensee, however, may wonder whether a sale-maximizing owner might ignore such opportunity costs in day-to-day competition. If so, the result could be a price war that would squeeze or eliminate the owner's profits. Nevertheless, in computing a reasonable royalty, one must assume that in the but-for world some solution to this problem exists and that the owner could convince the infringer (assumed to be a licensee in the but-for world) that the owner would take this opportunity cost into account in competing.

Experts also consider the effects of risk aversion in deciding between running and lump-sum royalties. Relative to a running royalty situation, a lump-sum royalty shifts risks from the licensor to the licensee. Perhaps because of size or other attributes, the expert might find that one party is more risk averse than the other, thus informing the choice between running royalty and lump-sum royalty.

Existing licenses may influence the choice between a running royalty and a lump-sum royalty. One must not, however, use licenses granted in the face of ongoing widespread infringement as evidence without making an appropriate adjustment to remove the effects of infringement. An infringer who makes a small payment for a paid-up license to a third-party competitor must not conclude that he or she has provided persuasive evidence that the court should award a lump-sum royalty in a world without infringement to the owner.

(c) Reasonable Royalty versus Lost Profits.   Nonpatent intellectual property owners can estimate damages based on a reasonable royalty or lost profits. Neither measure serves as a floor on damages. However, an expert should note that a reasonable royalty calculation that includes the other secondary but foreseeable damages from failure to pay the royalty (e.g., reduced sales and prices for the owner or the other licensees) often will result in an amount that exceeds the result from a lost profits calculation. Moreover, for products produced in competitive industries with constant returns to scale and no significant sunk costs, the two measures, when appropriately calculated, should give the same results. In such conditions, an owner will realize the full incremental benefit of intellectual property regardless of whether the owner produces the product, or others do and pay royalties.

To illustrate, assume that a manufacturer of fish lures discovers a lure color and shape vastly superior for catching striped bass and holds this property as a trade secret. The manufacturer uses the same manufacturing process for the new superior lure that it uses for other lures. Assume that striped bass fishermen will pay twice the normal price of $5. In such a case, the owner can produce all the special lures or charge a royalty of $5 per lure or some combination of the two. The manufacturer will receive the same profits in any event.

Slight variations to this basic example show how damages based on either lost profits or a reasonable royalty can yield different calculated damages amounts. Suppose that the manufacturer must advertise the lure to educate buyers. Further assume that a single firm can advertise a specialty product for smaller total cost than the sum of costs for many such firms. In such a case, the owner will probably choose to produce the lure, and damages based on lost profits will exceed those based on a reasonable royalty because a potential licensee would need to make enough over the cost of manufacture, distribution, and royalty payments to purchase its own advertising.

In another scenario, assume that lure manufacturers distribute through various channels. In this case, the owner can maximize profits by licensing enough manufacturers to cover all the major distribution channels. The total profits from licensing would then exceed those from self-manufacture, because the owner would lose no (or fewer) sales as a result of unserved distribution channels. If the infringer sold through channels different from those of the owner (and other existing licensees), a reasonable royalty damages award would likely exceed damages based on lost profits.

What about the case in which the owner has demonstrated that the owner would under no circumstances license the infringer? Should the court pretend such a license exists and then award reasonable royalty damages when, in fact, reasonable royalty damages exceed the owner's lost profits? To do so would make the owner better off than the owner would have been if infringement had not occurred. Hence, courts often compromise when reasonable royalty damages exceed lost profits and when the evidence shows that the owner would not have licensed the infringer. In such cases, the courts should award an amount equal to lost profits (even if the amount is less than reasonable royalty damages) but no less than what a reasonable royalty payment from the infringer alone would have been (i.e., reasonable royalty damages excluding the effects on the owner's own sales and on its other licensees' sales). This exception prevents the infringer from profiting from infringement.

(d) Calculating Sales in the But-For World.   In both lost profits and reasonable royalty damages calculations, the prices charged in the but-for world usually exceed the actual prices. In damages based on lost profits, the unlawful competition from the infringer will have expanded output and lowered the actual price below the but-for price. Similarly, in the case of damages based on a reasonable royalty, the infringer will have likely passed on to customers some or all of the cost savings the infringer enjoyed as a result of infringement. Thus, an expert must decide what prices and sales would have been in the absence of infringement, keeping in mind that higher prices mean lower sales quantities.

In certain situations, however, lower costs due to infringement do not significantly expand output and decrease price. Assume that environmentally contaminated underground tanks cost $10,000 to remove safely using an older technology. Then a firm invents and treats as a trade secret a process that costs $1,000 less. As long as the owner and the infringer (the trade secret thief) did not come to dominate the market (i.e., some competitors continued to use the old technology and retained their market share), then the prices would still be set under the influence of the cost of the old technology. In this type of case, infringement (theft of the trade secret) will not have resulted in a significantly lower price.

In any event, an expert should not make the unrealistic assumption in a lost profits case that the owner would have made all of its sales and all of the infringer's sales and made all of these sales at higher prices. Instead, higher prices should mean a lower combined number of units sold.

(e) Unjust Enrichment.   This discussion has focused on making the property owner whole through payment of damages caused by the infringer. An infringed owner can also claim the infringer's profits (only to the extent such an amount does not duplicate other damages). Including the infringer's profit in the damages calculation will ensure that infringement does not enrich the infringer.[57] The law for each type of nonpatent intellectual property permits recovery of unjust enrichment (either as an explicit award labeled "unjust enrichment," or through allowing recovery of the infringer's profits). We discuss unjust enrichment related to copyrights, trademarks, and trade secrets in Sections 20.5(b), 20.6(c), and 20.7(c), respectively.

(f) Monopoly, Oligopoly, and Game Theory.   Infringement usually changes the nature of competition and, as a result, the prices and quantities in the marketplace. Where owners should have enjoyed a monopoly-like position, they find themselves competing with one other company, the infringer. Instead of a legal monopoly, the owner now faces a more competitive duopoly (i.e., a market with two competitors). Although in theory duopolies can reach the competitive price level, the monopoly price level, or anywhere in between, the expert can often show how much the competition caused prices to fall. If a period of no infringement occurs, the expert can calculate price and cost relations and estimate the but-for prices (adjusted for changes in cost and demand).

Experts often estimate the price effect—even if they lack precise before and after time periods—by using game theory. Economists use game theory to model how competitors interact and to estimate an equilibrium of prices and quantities. Using game theory allows the expert to map out factors such as each competitor's choices or the likely choices of the other competitor(s). Although prices in duopoly can range from fully competitive to monopolistic, game theory helps us find the most likely prices and quantities that would have existed in the but-for world.

Game theory models go beyond the scope of this chapter, although an example can show the power of this approach. Assume that someone discovers a trade secret that lowers the cost of producing an item from $170 to $100; the defendant steals and begins using the trade secret; the defendant and plaintiff each have 50 percent of the market (as a result of their lower costs) with sales of one million units each; and they sell the product for $125. Using these limited data, an expert can derive models that answer such questions as (1) the price the plaintiff would charge if it alone had the trade secret, (2) the volume the plaintiff would sell at that price, and (3) the damages the plaintiff would suffer from theft.

For example, one game theory model of competitor interaction concludes that each competitor in a duopoly (i.e., a two-supplier market) prices according to its residual demand curve. In turn, each firm's residual demand curve equals the industry demand curve less the current production of its competitor. The demand elasticity (i.e., sensitivity to price) for each competitor equals the industry demand elasticity divided by the competitor's market share.[58] Further, using the Lerner index, one assumes that each competitor maximizes its profits at a price that is a markup over cost equal to the inverse of (the quantity of) that elasticity minus one.[59] To sum up, by using the data in the previous example and this game theory model, an expert can estimate that for each 1 percent increase in price, the competitor will lose 5 percent of sales (the residual demand elasticity).[60]

Next the expert can use this residual demand elasticity, coupled with the competitor's share of the market, to estimate the entire market's demand elasticity.[61] The residual demand elasticity (5) times the market share (50 percent) results in market demand elasticity of 2.5. With this information, an expert can estimate the optimal monopoly price that the plaintiff would have enjoyed without the illegal competition. The inverse of (the quantity of) this elasticity minus one is a 66.7 percent (= $1/[2.5 - 1]$) markup over cost, or a but-for price of $166.67. The elasticity also suggests that at this price the plaintiff would have sold 974,000 units.[62] This analysis estimates lost profits at about $40 million, the difference between estimated profits of $65 million and the actual profits of $25 million.

An expert can modify this model to reflect different costs between the litigants, different economies of scale (or lack thereof), and the existence of constraining alternative technologies. For instance, assume that the old way of making the product costs $140 instead of $170. In that case, the owner of the trade secret would set a price just equal to (or slightly less than) $140 to prevent competition from the older technology. At that price, the owner of the trade secret would sell about 1.5 million units, for a total profit of $60 million.[63] Compared with actual profits of $25 million, the lost-profit damages in this scenario would equal $35 million. Of course, if the owner of the trade secret would have made capital expenditures to increase capacity for this additional production, then these saved capital costs offset damages.

20.4   HOW NONPATENT INTELLECTUAL PROPERTY DAMAGES DIFFER FROM PATENT DAMAGES

Differences exist in the fundamental purpose of laws governing the various forms of intellectual property. Patent and copyright laws aim first to protect the inventor or author, to the eventual benefit of the public. However, patent law protects the inventor from all unauthorized uses, whereas copyrights protect authors only from copying and unjustified use. Trademark and trade secret laws focus not on protecting the inventor, but rather on the immediate protection of the public and on maintenance of business ethics, respectively. These differences in fundamental purposes drive differences in damages measurement for patent and nonpatent intellectual property cases. Factors occurring only in nonpatent intellectual property cases comprise the following:

- An ability to claim a damages award based on both the owner's losses and the infringer's gains

- The owner's burden of proving only revenues in a claim for the infringer's profits
- The infringer's burden to prove that the court should attribute only a portion of the infringer's profits to the infringer's wrongful act
- The lack of a floor in damages calculations
- The greater use of nonmonetary remedies
- The lack of a paradigm decision in the courts that addresses the damages calculation method

This section discusses each of these factors. See the Appendix for a comparison of the different types of intellectual property.

(a) Claiming the Infringer's Profits.   The intellectual property owner's ability to claim an award based on the infringer's gains or profits represents the most significant difference between patent and nonpatent intellectual property damages calculations. Although legislation in 1946 (35 U.S.C. § 289) removed the availability of an infringer's profits as a measure of damages in patent cases (except for design patents), an owner bringing an action related to any of the nonpatent intellectual property rights can claim damages based on either the owner's own lost profits, the infringer's profits, or both (to the extent that double recovery does not result).[64] The availability of an infringer's profits as a damages measure means that an owner might recover damages without proving the owner has suffered economic harm. As a result, certain courts require proof of scienter (willfulness or bad faith) on the infringer's part as a prerequisite to recovery of the infringer's profits. For example, in the case of trademark infringement, courts have awarded an infringer's profits only when the infringement was willful or in bad faith. However, the Ninth Circuit has held willful infringement to be necessary for an award of profits under an unjust enrichment theory, but not when used as an estimate of the plaintiff's damages.[65]

(b) Owner's Burden of Proof.   In calculating a claim for the infringer's profits, laws governing nonpatent intellectual property cases generally provide that the owner bears the burden of proving only revenues. The burden of proving the specific costs one should deduct from revenues to calculate the infringer's profits shifts to the infringer. This shift in burden is reasonable, in many cases. Even with discovery procedures, the owner remains at a disadvantage in ascertaining the infringer's cost structure, and in many types of nonpatent intellectual property cases, the infringer's costs are minimal as a percentage of its revenues (e.g., the printing costs of books). Complicating matters, however, is the fact that no consensus among courts exists as to which costs one should deduct in nonpatent intellectual property cases, unlike patent cases in which parties seek to prove incremental costs because courts generally agree on incremental profits as the appropriate measure of damages. Hence, in nonpatent intellectual property cases, the infringer often tries to deduct as many costs as possible.[66] One sees the success of this method when courts have endorsed the deduction of costs that did not increase incrementally with the level of infringing sales but that nonetheless contributed to the realization of those sales.

(c) Apportionment of Infringer's Profits.   The owner's recovery of the infringer's profits in nonpatent intellectual property cases should not exceed the portion of profits attributable to the infringer's alleged wrongful act. As a result, an infringer can argue that its profits result from the presence and influence of factors other than the alleged wrongful act and seek to apportion its computed profit amount based on those factors. For example, in a trademark case the infringer might argue that profits resulted from the functional and aesthetic qualities of its product, the quality of the sales force, and pricing, in addition to or instead of the alleged infringing mark. In a copyright case, the infringer might argue for apportionment when the infringed work is in a book with other works, is part of an otherwise original musical play, or is a subroutine of a computer program. As with the cost calculation, the burden of proving a reasonable approach to apportionment rests with the infringer. The copyright law requires that the infringer prove "the element of profit attributable to factors other than the copyrighted work."[67]

Apportionment methods can and often do split profits even when the alleged infringing activity forms an integral part of an economic whole. This feature of nonpatent actions differs from the entire-market-value rule in patent cases in which the entire profit of a product containing an infringing element becomes a proper basis for recovery despite the contribution of noninfringing elements, provided the patentee shows that the patented characteristic represents a material reason for the sale of the product.[68]

(d) Lack of Damages Floor.   Damages based on a royalty may apply to all types of intellectual property cases, including both patent and nonpatent actions. The patent statute, however, provides that damages in a patent case must equal or exceed a reasonable royalty. Assuming that the damages calculation for patent violation based on lost profits exceeds a calculation based on royalty, the royalty-based calculation sets an explicit floor for damages.[69] In contrast, whereas all nonpatent intellectual property actions permit royalty-based awards, the laws governing such actions do not provide for a royalty floor for damages. Furthermore—unlike patent cases—in trade secrets and most trademark cases, the court can find liability but no damages when the owner cannot establish that the owner lost profits and can neither (1) establish that the infringer realized profits because of its wrongful acts, nor (2) prove willfulness by the infringer in venues requiring this as a prerequisite to recovery of the infringer's profits.

(e) Use of Nonmonetary Remedies.   Several types of nonmonetary sanctions exist for actions involving intellectual property rights. These include temporary or permanent injunction (an enforceable order to stop producing and selling the item), seizing, impounding (the physical taking of the item) and destroying offending goods, excluding importation, and criminal penalties. In applying these sanctions, courts attempt to maintain a balance between free and unfettered commercial competition and protection of the property owner's rights. The courts use these nonmonetary sanctions more often in nonpatent cases.

For example, in the midst of the *Beanie Babies* craze, Goffa International began producing a line of *Bean Bag Friends* strikingly similar to the *Friendly Pebble Pets* made by Imperial Toy Corp. (Neither Imperial nor Goffa sold *Beanie Babies*; *Beanie Babies* are merely mentioned here for context.) Imperial showed that Goffa had copied its work with "substantially similar" elements. The court granted Imperial's motion for a preliminary injunction, enjoining Goffa from "importing, manufacturing, distributing, advertising or selling" nine of the ten toys in its catalog.[70]

Some would say that this decision reflects a historical preference on the part of the courts for injunction as a resolution to Lanham Act matters. Some attribute this preference to the difficulty in isolating the owner's harm or the infringer's gain caused solely by the wrongful act when a complex array of factors contribute to a product's success in the marketplace and the perception that proving monetary damages requires "something more."[71]

In copyright cases, when the court believes that the copyright owner has a *prima facie* case for infringement and will suffer irreparable harm if infringement continues, the court can issue a preliminary injunction or order the seizing and impounding of infringing goods before a trial. If the owner prevails at trial, the court can impose a permanent injunction and order the destruction of impounded goods. The court can also levy criminal sanctions, including fines and prison terms, in cases of willful copyright infringement for "personal profit or commercial advantage."[72]

If the court finds the infringement to constitute counterfeiting, the court can order impounding and destruction of offending goods and criminal sanction under RICO laws.[73] In false advertising cases, courts have ordered recalls of offending advertising material.[74] Finally, the state laws governing theft of trade secrets in some cases provide for criminal penalties.

(f) The Absence of Paradigm Decisions.   Compared with patent law, few decisions in other types of intellectual property cases have attempted to establish frameworks or paradigms for general approaches to damages. The nonpatent intellectual property law has no equivalent to the widely cited Georgia-Pacific Corp. v. United States Plywood Corp.,[75] in which the court presented 15 factors to consider in calculating a reasonable royalty for a patent. (Chapter 22 discusses these factors.) The relative absence of such paradigm cases allows for more creative approaches in calculating and rebutting damages in nonpatent cases but also introduces uncertainty regarding acceptable approaches. Thus, parties involved in these suits should search for any precedents in the particular venue where a court will decide the current case.

20.5   DAMAGES ISSUES SPECIFIC TO COPYRIGHT INFRINGEMENT

The owner of an infringed work has several damages remedies available, including the following:

1. Actual damages to the copyright owner
2. The infringer's profits or unjust enrichment
3. Both (1) and (2) to the extent that double-counting does not occur
4. Statutory damages
5. Other remedies such as costs, attorney's fees, prejudgment interest, and punitive damages
6. Impoundment and injunction, which the courts often employ when the owner has not suffered monetary damages and the infringer has not realized monetary gains

This section of the chapter examines each of these remedies, with the exception of impoundment and injunction, which we discussed in section 20.4(e). See the Appendix for a comparison of various aspects of copyrights with those of other types of intellectual property.

(a) Damages to the Copyright Owner.   The owner of an infringed copyrighted work "is entitled to recover the actual damages suffered by him or her as a result of the infringement" (17 U.S.C. § 504(b)).[76] Actual damages awarded under the Copyright Act of 1976 should compensate the copyright owner for the fair value of the infringed work. Courts follow two approaches, depending on whether the owner and infringer sell their relevant products in the same market: if they do, then one looks to the owners's sales lost to the infringer; if not, one assesses the market value of the property or a reasonable royalty.[77] One commentator summarized the approach to actual damages by noting that "[c]onceptually, all measures of copyright damages are measures of market value. The willing buyer-willing seller measure, the reasonable royalty measure and, indeed, the lost sales measure simply represent different routes to computing market value."[78] Owners use the following five elements to calculate this loss of market value.

(i) License or Usage Rate Established by Earlier Authorized Use or Unfulfilled Contracts. Owners can establish their damages by using the actual royalty rate or other license rate that the owner established prior to the infringement. Royalty rates apply to creative works (e.g., a song), and technical works (e.g., encryption software) and to works that have both technical and creative elements (e.g., architectural plans).[79] For example, in software cases, the owner may have suffered lost profits or damages that one could calculate as the established license rate multiplied by the number of central processing units (or other license units) on which the infringer has used the work.[80]

(ii) Appropriate Trade Customs or Standard Industry Practices.   Parties use industry experts who have negotiated licenses or royalties for comparable works in the past to establish the royalty rate or license fee that the owner should have received. This approach often offers the best method when the copyright holder has not issued licenses to any party.

However, when the owner has not agreed to licensing in the past, an expert can consider the industry standard as the *minimum* amount for damages measurement. Some artists oppose licensing or commercial use of their work to an extent that industry standards or averages might understate the amount it would have required to induce them to license. For example, in *Cary Grant v. Esquire, Inc.,*[81] the court found that a higher than average license rate was appropriate because actor Cary Grant had not previously allowed commercial licensing of his identity. Even though Cary Grant brought this case as a right of publicity issue, it illustrates the importance of looking to the value in the specific situation and how the trier of fact might consider damages.

(iii) Lost Profits of the Copyright Holder.   Experts use this method when the owner and the infringer compete in the same market. Sections 20.3(a) and (d) discussed the factors that an expert should consider in estimating lost sales in the but-for world. After experts make such an estimate, they must subtract the incremental costs

associated with those lost sales to measure the profits the owner would have achieved and for which the infringer should compensate the owner. In other words, from the lost sales revenue, the expert subtracts variable costs—those costs that change as sales vary between the actual level and the but-for level.[82] Note that the longer the period of infringement, the greater the number and level of variable costs: in the long run, all or most costs vary with output.

(iv) Market Value and Reasonable Royalty to the Copyright Holder.   These approaches are very closely related and can be used when the owner and infringer operate in different markets. With the market value method, the expert seeks to approximate an appropriate royalty rate—no more than what the owner would have accepted and no less than what the infringer would have paid—by establishing the license fee the parties would have agreed to through bargaining.[83] This concept is one employed in the patent context when establishing a reasonable royalty. One could use the same term, reasonable royalty, in the copyright context. One could, except the copyright context often uses "reasonable royalty" to refer to an established royalty, earned from a previous license, employed to estimate what the defendant should have paid.[84] Ignoring semantics, these methods seek to estimate what compensation the owner and infringer would have agreed to through bargaining with the reasonable royalty method looking to prior licenses to inform what the outcome of what the outcome of that bargaining would have been. In practice, one may look to prior licenses, and if none exists (but, even when one or more do), turn to the market value method.[85]

(v) Cost to Create or Duplicate.   Experts will find this approach useful only when the duplicated work has no resale value of its own and is mixed in with other, noninfringing material, such as software used in operations. This method focuses on the infringer's cost savings, that is, the cost the infringer would have had to pay to develop or create the work independently (e.g., in-house programmers). These cost savings may be factored into an assessment of market value.[86] The cost approach violates the fundamental axiom that "cost does not equal value" and that the value of the work provides the appropriate measure. This approach also fails to consider any time savings that the infringer achieved by entering the market earlier than it would have had it developed rather than duplicated the product. Experts should consider this a fallback approach.

(b) Infringer's Profits (or Unjust Enrichment).   The Copyright Act of 1976 permits recovery of "any profits of the infringer that are attributable to the infringement and are not taken into account in computing actual damages" (17 U.S.C. § 504 (b)). Hence, one can measure damages as the seller's (infringer's) revenues less the costs it incurred to realize those sales, as discussed in Section 20.4(a). For example, one can measure the infringer's profit by its incremental gross margin, although—as noted in Section 20.4(b)—no consensus exists regarding the nature of costs subtracted to calculate the infringer's profits. In calculating this incremental gross margin, the expert should consider the following elements.

(i) Revenues.   The burden of proof for an infringer's revenues falls on the copyright owner (17 U.S.C. § 504(b)).

(ii) Burden of Proof for Costs.   Once the owner establishes the infringer's gross revenue, the burden shifts to the infringer "to prove his deductible expenses and the elements of profit attributable to factors other than the copyrighted work."[87] If the infringer fails to prove deductible expenses, the owner can recover gross revenues as profits.[88]

The expert can use two approaches when deciding which costs to deduct. The first approach deducts a portion of all common costs shared by an infringing work and other works of the infringer, reasoning that the infringing work is only one of many items that the infringer produces and carries its share of all the costs. The owner prefers the second, opposing approach that the computation should deduct only incremental costs of producing the infringing work, since eliminating portions of overhead costs unrelated to the infringing work from consideration increases the profit of the infringing work. Advocates of this view argue that the infringing work adds incrementally to the infringer's profits so one should evaluate costs in like fashion when evaluating the infringer's profits. For example, assume there is a common cost that does not appear to have increased with the additional production caused by the infringing work. The first approach would result in the deduction of a share of that cost (perhaps based on a percentage of revenues) in ascertaining the profitability of the infringing product. The second approach would subtract the cost only if it appeared incremental to the production of the infringing work. That is, the expert would lower the profits of the infringing work to account for the cost only if he or she could show that production of the infringing work caused this cost to be higher and then only by the increase in cost that the production caused.

(iii) Costs Deductible in Calculating the Infringer's Profits.   Case law indicates that the damages calculation should include only costs that would have been saved but for the production or sale of the infringing product, but it is "an inherent part of the defendant's burden to produce adequate and acceptable evidence to its costs."[89] These represent the variable costs of producing or using the infringing work, such as the license fee that the infringer would have had to pay the copyright owner,[90] the duplications costs,[91] and contractors hired for producing the work.[92]

The decision in *Jarvis v. A&M Records*[93] included an extensive list of deductible and nondeductible items. The court allowed deductions for sales discounts, distribution fees, manufacturing, packaging, artwork, recording costs, and promotion and marketing of the infringing work. The court did not allow deductions for items sold and returned, artist and mechanical royalties, a parent company service charge unrelated to the infringing work, and other overhead.

(iv) Overhead.   "If the infringer is engaged in business activities other than the production, distribution, performance or display of copyrighted works, it must prove that expenses such as rent, salaries, telephone and travel were incurred *because of* the infringement."[94] One court noted that costs "that would be incurred anyway should not be subtracted, because by definition they cannot be avoided by curtailing the profit-making activity."[95] Because "allocating overhead expenses between infringing and noninfringing activities usually cannot be done with precision,"[96] the courts have required only that a "reasonably acceptable formula be established."[97] Courts have barred willful (or knowing)[98] infringers from deducting any overhead costs.[99]

(v) Apportionment (Allocation) of Overall Profitability to the Infringing Component.   In the 1940 case *Sheldon v. Metro-Goldwyn Pictures Corp.*, the U.S. Supreme Court affirmed a lower court's decision to apportion (allocate a value to the infringed work) and award to the copyright owner a part of the total profits earned by a larger work that included the infringing element within it.[100] The Court upheld the award based on "only that part of the profits found to be attributable to the use of the copyrighted material as distinguished from what the infringer himself has supplied."[101] The Copyright Act of 1976 follows *Sheldon* by allowing the infringer to apportion some of the revenues to "the element of profit attributable to factors *other than* the copyrighted work"[102] but places on the infringer the burden of proving those other factors. The House report notes, however, that "where some of the defendant's profits result from the infringement and other profits are caused by different factors, it will be necessary for the court to make an apportionment."[103]

In "doubtful cases, courts should err on the side of generosity."[104] The Ninth Circuit stated that the "burden of proving apportionment (i.e., the contribution to profits of elements other than the infringed property), is the defendant's."[105] The precision of such a calculation does not limit its feasibility. The court in *Sheldon* confirmed that it did not require mathematical exactness but only a "reasonable approximation."[106] The Fourth Circuit, in *Wesley Walker v. Forbes*, notes that "fiendish difficulties" can arise in the calculations and that the courts cannot apply "hard and fast rules."[107]

When estimating damages by apportionment, the expert should not consider the infringing work's quantitative share of the total but rather its *relative value* to the overall work. One court stated that it must "consider the relative quality or drawing power of the [defendant's] show's various components."[108] For example, in a 1991 case, singer Gilbert O'Sullivan sued rap performer Biz Markie and eight others for sampling (i.e., including without permission) a small portion of O'Sullivan's *Alone Again Naturally* in Markie's song, *Alone Again.* The rap work sampled only three words, and eight bars of the music from O'Sullivan's earlier hit, but the court concluded that what it borrowed, particularly the words "Alone again, naturally," was an important part of the work.[109]

Courts have found apportioning sales value a subjective exercise, usually based on expert testimony. Experts find mathematical estimating techniques such as regression helpful, particularly if the infringer sold the work with and without the infringing element under similar conditions. Chapter 21, "Intellectual Property Damages in the Entertainment Industry," discusses additional court cases and methods of analysis.

When the courts cannot calculate a fair apportionment but many items contributed to the infringer's profits, the Copyright Act of 1976 gives the owner all the profits from the infringing sale. The act does not, however, address the proper approach when the infringer does not sell the work directly but uses it as part of an advertisement or the operations of the company, such as proprietary software. Some case law has addressed this question. In *Estate of Vane v. The Fair, Inc.*, the court recognized that the use of copyrighted photographs in a television commercial for a retail store was *not* the only source of profits to the store after the commercial ran.[110]

(vi) Indirect Profits.   Damages can include the profits earned by an infringer from any of its operations that the infringement enhanced. In *Frank Music v. MGM*, the court awarded damages in part on the infringer's increased hotel and gaming

operations that resulted from including a copyrighted work in one of its stage performances.[111] This theory also applies to cases in which the infringer has used a copyrighted work in an advertisement because even though the infringer does not sell advertisements (typically considered an expense), the infringement contributes to the infringer's overall profitability.[112]

A theory adapted from patent practice provides another method for estimating the value of an infringed work when the infringer does not sell the item itself but uses it in business operations.[113] Under this method, the property's overall value equals some multiple of the appropriate royalty rate. Substantial industry experience exists regarding the relation between royalties paid to a patent holder and the profitability of the intellectual property to the licensor.[114] The literature suggests that, on average, the licensed property receives between 25 and 33 percent of the licensor's expected overall profitability from the activity or work incorporating the licensed property. In other words, a work's expected profitability equals three to four times the amount paid to the owner of the contributing intellectual property.[115] The literature itself presents these rates as approximations, and specific, individual results based on all the factors affecting a royalty negotiation will be higher or lower. This approach, however, can provide a useful starting point in the calculation process. Finally, a copyright owner can recover the value of receiving credit as the author and any related loss of goodwill.

(vii) Value in Use.   To estimate the infringer's profitability, courts also consider value in use—the value from the infringer's internal perspective. One case characterized the funds not spent on licensing as available to expand the business and generate additional profits to the infringer.[116] This approach resembles damages suffered when the infringer uses the product in advertising, because the infringer does not directly resell the product, but the infringed work contributes to the infringer's overall profitability. The expert can approximate the value in use by examining

- Other contracts in force or being negotiated by the infringer for an equivalent product
- Appropriate trade or customs in the industry
- A reasonable royalty or license fee found in the industry

This theory also resembles a patent infringement claim because savings realized through lower operating costs can result from an infringed device as opposed to a creative work. Courts apply this approach when the infringer does not sell infringed software but uses it in its operations. Under this approach, any money saved through reduced expenses becomes available, as a result of the infringement, to expand the business and generate additional profits because the infringer has not incurred royalty costs. Courts also apply this approach in cases involving not-for-profit entities because they usually generate little or no revenue from an infringed work.

(c) Statutory Damages.   Unlike patent cases, 17 U.S.C. § 504(c) makes statutory remedies available for copyright infringement. Hence, even when the owner fails to prove lost profits or royalty-based damages and cannot prove enrichment to the infringer, the owner can still receive an award. The amount the owner can elect to receive as statutory damages ranges from $750 to $30,000 per infringement. Owners elect to have statutory damages awarded either by judges or by a jury at any time prior to final judgment.[117] However, the owner must have registered for a copyright at most three months after the first publication of the work to receive statutory damages for a published work. If the owner does not register an unpublished work, the owner cannot seek statutory damages.[118]

If the owner proves willful infringement, the court can increase an award to a maximum of $150,000. If infringers establish that they did not know of the infringement and had no reason to believe that they were infringing, the court can decrease the award to a minimum of $200. Courts can award zero statutory damages when infringers reasonably believe that they acted within fair use of the copyrighted work in the course of their employment by a nonprofit educational institution or public broadcasting entity, library, or archive.[119]

For an example of statutory damages, consider *Sid & Marty Krofft Television Productions, Inc. v. McDonald's Corporation, et al.*, wherein the trial court could not ascertain which sales had resulted from the infringing advertising and which sales had not. Without knowing the infringing sales, the trial court decided that it could not measure the infringer's profits and instead awarded statutory damages based on the following:

- The number of copyrights involved
- The number of infringements
- Whether the plaintiff notified the defendants of the infringement
- The amount that should be awarded for each of the various types of infringement

Hence, the plaintiff received $1,044,000 based on (1) 114 different infringing commercials times $6,000 per infringement, (2) 66 different infringing promotional items times $5,000 per infringement, and (3) 60 other infringing acts times $500 per infringement. Note that the court rejected the owner's claim that each airing of each of the 114 commercials and each sale of the 66 infringing promotional items represented separate infringements. Instead, the court held that a single infringing commercial or promotional item was one part of a single continuous infringement regardless of how many times the defendant aired or sold it.[120]

(d) Other Remedies. The Copyright Act of 1976 states, "In any civil action under this title, the court in its discretion may allow the recovery of full costs by or against any party other than the United States or an officer thereof. Except as otherwise provided by this title, the court may also award a reasonable attorney's fee to the prevailing party as part of the costs." As with statutory damages, these become recoverable only if a party infringes after the copyright owner has registered the work with the U.S. Copyright Office or, if a party infringes before registration, the copyright owner registers within three months of publication. Courts do not agree on whether to award prejudgment interest in copyright matters but the trend is toward awarding prejudgment interest.[121]

"Although courts have not categorically excluded the possibility of punitive damage awards in copyright cases, they award them only rarely."[122] Practitioners suggest that the rate or level of compensatory damages often reflects the trier of fact's outrage at the infringer's willfulness. For example, in *Waits v. Frito-Lay, Inc.*, singer-songwriter Tom Waits received compensatory and punitive damages.[123] He refused to do commercials or allow his music to be used in them. The court estimated the unauthorized use would reduce his fee by $75,000 should he ever change his mind, yet awarded punitive damages totaling $2 million.

20.6   DAMAGES ISSUES SPECIFIC TO TRADEMARK INFRINGEMENT AND FALSE ADVERTISING

As Section 20.2 discussed, the Lanham Act is the primary source of law for trademarks and false advertising and combines the common law remedy of an owner's damages with the equitable remedy of an infringer's profits. Hence, the court can award the owner both its damages and the infringer's profits, as shown in *Veryfine Products Inc. v. Colon Brothers Inc.*[124] An owner, however, generally will not receive compensation for both damages and the infringer's profits for the same sale.[125] The courts intend that awards, whether of damages or profits, compensate for the infringement, although some also regard as acceptable the award of profits as a means of deterring future infringement.[126] See the Appendix for a comparison of various aspects of trademarks with those of other types of intellectual property.

(a) Standards for Injunctive Relief and Monetary Recovery.   A finding of trademark infringement will not necessarily result in a monetary award. Courts tend to distinguish between the standard of proof required to establish a right to injunctive relief and that required to establish a right to damages, as seen in *Camel Hair and Cashmere Institute of America v. Associated Dry Goods Corp.*[127]

Establishing a likelihood of confusion between trademarks will generally support an injunction to prevent continued infringement.[128] However, courts appear to require a standard of proof for monetary recovery that exceeds the rigor of the likelihood-of-confusion standard required for an injunction. In other words, the owner seeking damages must establish actual harm or, at a minimum, confusion resulting from the infringement for an award of damages. The testimony of confused customers found in survey evidence offers one possible proof of confusion,[129] although in at least one case, the court found a simple assessment of the nature of the products and the markets in which they were sold sufficient to establish confusion.[130]

Moreover, some venues require a showing of bad faith for an award of damages or profits. Courts have defined bad faith to include the following:

- Fraud or palming off of one's good as those of another
- Deliberate intent to cause confusion, mistake or deception among purchasers
- Wanton and intentionally fraudulent action
- Any infringement done knowingly and with callous disregard of the mark holder's or competitor's rights[131]

Even though the federal circuit courts lack consensus on how much confusion or bad faith, or both, that an owner needs to show to obtain an infringer's profits, the following framework, approved by the First Circuit and observed in *Aktiebolaget Electrolux v. Armatron,*[132] encompasses many of the criteria applied by different circuits:

1. An owner seeking damages must prove actual harm caused by the infringement, such as lost sales. In demonstrating harm, the owner can establish an adequate basis by showing that confusion existed.
2. An award of the infringer's profits requires that the products compete directly, such that the infringer's profits would have gone to the owner but for the infringement.

3. Guideline (2) becomes less restrictive if bad faith exists, such that a court may presume actual harm.

4. Where the establishment of bad faith bypasses the usual rule of actual harm, courts base recovery on an unjust enrichment or deterrence theory.

In the final analysis, the court's equitable discretion will determine the right to any monetary recovery.[133]

(b) Calculating Damages (Owner's Lost Profits) Owners have advanced several types of claims under the Lanham Act. In economic terms, most represent some type of lost profits, including profits on projected future lost sales, price erosion, and actual and projected remedial costs (for example, corrective advertising). Owners can claim damages by measuring the diminution or dilution in the value of the mark.[134] Although statutes do not provide for the use of a royalty as a measure of an owner's damages, a number of Lanham Act cases have used it. This section discusses each of these damages methods.

(i) Calculating Lost Sales. An owner claiming profits on lost sales must demonstrate that the infringer's wrongful acts caused the loss. Methods used by owners include the examination of three factors:

1. **Sales trends.** Owners often analyze sales trends in periods before and after the commencement of the wrongful acts. In *U-Haul v. Jartran* (a false advertising case),[135] the owner and infringer were the only two significant competitors in the market, and the infringer's advertising directly targeted the owner. Trend analysis showed a noticeable change in the owner's sales trends and a commensurate increase in the infringer's sales following the wrongful acts. Conversely, in *Otis Clapp & Sons v. Filmore Vitamin*,[136] the court found that the owner's sales grew during the infringement period and declined after the infringement stopped, leading the court to conclude that the owner lost no sales.

2. **Projections.** The owner can compare its actual sales following the infringer's wrongful acts with projections prepared in the normal course of business. In *Merriam-Webster v. Random House*, courts attributed the difference between projected and actual sales (reduced to profits) to the infringer's acts.[137]

3. **Market share.** Experts can also use market share approaches similar to those of some patent cases to estimate the additional sales that the owner would have made but for the infringer's wrongful acts. In *BASF Corp. v. Old World Trading Co., Inc.*,[138] the owner calculated its but-for market share of the infringer's sales as the owner's actual market share divided by the market share of all relevant competitors *except* the infringer.

Courts do not limit lost profits claims to the loss of past sales. In *Taco Cabana v. Two Pesos*,[139] a case involving trade dress infringement, the infringer entered a market in which the owner did not do business. The infringer's market entry, however, preempted the owner's entry into the same market, causing the owner to lose anticipated future profits.

In the much-litigated *Alpo Petfoods, Inc. v. Ralston-Purina Co.*,[140] the owner received the present value of future profits lost because the infringer's false advertising claim delayed a new product rollout. In this case, the court based the award on the owner's calculation of profits from projections for the new product rollout that the owner had prepared in the ordinary course of business.

The calculation of profits on lost sales deducts the incremental costs that the owner would have incurred to produce and sell the lost units. Although one can find occasional exceptions, all types of intellectual property cases, including Lanham Act cases, recognize this standard.

(ii) Eroded Prices.   Owners in Lanham Act cases can claim price erosion if they can establish that they could have charged higher prices but for the infringer's wrongful acts. Proving such a premise often becomes difficult in trademark or false advertising cases, however, because many factors influence prices. If the infringer can demonstrate that the other competitors or market forces, or both, influenced the owner's pricing policies, or that the owner would have had to compete with the infringer on price with or without the alleged wrongful acts, a claim for price erosion will fail. For example, in *BASF v. Old World Trading Co.,*[141] the court denied the owner's price erosion claim because the relevant market encompassed several competitors and pricing had historically represented an important competitive tool.

(iii) Profits Lost Because of Actual or Anticipated Additional Costs (Corrective Advertising). Another type of lost profits recovery has involved the owner's actual or project-ed future cost to restore the value of its trademark or correct the misimpression created by false advertising. Courts have awarded two types of such damages: (1) the owner's actual costs, as seen in *Cuisinarts, Inc. v. Robot-Coupe Int'l Corp.,*[142] and (2) the projected future costs, as observed in *Big O Tire v. Goodyear*[143] and *Adray v. Adry-Mart.*[144] The second looks to advertising expense incurred by the infringer as a measure of the harm to the owner's goodwill or the probable level of expenditures needed to correct the harm in the marketplace.

Several courts have criticized the use of corrective advertising as a basis for a damages award, however. In *The Gillette Co. v. Wilkinson Sword,* the court noted that the statute does not specifically provide for cost of advertising as a measure of damages and stated:

> It is a surrogate for plaintiff's profit only if it is reasonable to suppose that every time a defendant spends x amount on an advertising campaign, a competitor (plaintiff) is likely to lose x amount as a result. It is a surrogate for defendant's profit only if it is reasonable to suppose that every time a defendant spends x amount on an advertising campaign, it will enjoy profits of at least x amount on the resulting sales. The Court has no basis for concluding that either of these suppositions is reasonable, or that either supposition fits the facts of this case. In light of the absence of a factual basis for equating cost of advertising with either plaintiff's damages or defendant's profit, we believe that there is no statutory basis for a cost-of-advertising measure.[145]

The future incidence of awards for corrective advertising will depend on the facts of the particular case and the court's disposition.

(iv) Damage to Goodwill.   Claims for damages resulting from harm to goodwill sel-dom appear in Lanham Act cases. Such cases involve some action on the infringer's part that not only infringes but also tarnishes the owner's business, such as dis-paraging advertising or marketing an inferior product under an infringing mark.

Such claims seek a type of present value of future lost profits. As with straight-forward claims for future lost profits, courts sometimes find claims for damage to goodwill too speculative. In *DC Comics, Inc. v. Filmation Associates*[146] and *Taco Cabana v. Two Pesos*,[147] the court rejected such claims or affirmed a jury's lack of award, even when awarding other damages. Recognizing the difficulty of quantifying such damages with precision, courts have on occasion used their discretion to double (*Pioneer Leimel Fabrics, Inc. v. Paul Rothman Ind., Ltd.*)[148] or triple (*Artmark-Chicago v. E. Mishan*)[149] other compensatory awards rather than awarding a separate amount for damage to goodwill.

(v) Reasonable Royalty.   Although statutes do not provide for the use of a royalty as a measure of an owner's lost profits, a number of Lanham Act cases have used it. The nature of the property and the facts of the case, however, must support the use of a royalty award. For example, in *Gillette v. Wilkinson Sword,* the court found a royalty inappropriate because the wrongful act comprised an advertising campaign that emphasized differences between the parties' products. Courts have awarded royalties in cases in which the owner and infringer did not compete directly but the infringement created a false impression of association with the owner, such as in *Taco Cabana v. Two Pesos.* Further, in *Babbitt Electronic, Inc. v. Dynascan Corp.*,[150] the court awarded both an accounting of the infringer's profits (calculated as gross margin) *and* the owner's damages in the form of a reasonable royalty on infringing sales.

Lanham Act case law has no equivalent to the *Georgia-Pacific* case, in which the court established 15 factors for evaluating a reasonable royalty in a patent case (*see* Chapter 22). Nothing prevents an expert on Lanham Act damages from borrowing concepts from *Georgia-Pacific* or other intellectual property cases as a framework for analysis, in spite of a lack of legal precedent for doing so.

Lanham Act case law suggests that one can base a royalty on established royalty, the going rate in the market, a license agreement, an infringer's offer to license, or other acceptable methods. No one method takes precedence. For example, the court in *Holiday Inns, Inc. v. Airport Holiday Corp.*[151] granted the owner a royalty for the infringer's unauthorized use of the Holiday Inn name at the "going rate in the marketplace" instead of the rate in effect during the license agreement prior to the agreement's termination.

Although this section has discussed the use of royalty as a measure of the owner's lost profits, a royalty can also measure the infringer's unjust enrichment as an avoided cost related to the infringed property. Indeed, a royalty's ability to represent *both* or *either* measure of damages appears to provide its appeal to some courts. In *Sands v. Quaker Oats,* the Seventh Circuit reversed the award of profits and remanded, suggesting that a royalty would "more accurately reflect the extent of Quaker's unjust enrichment *and* the interest of (the plaintiff) that has been infringed" (emphasis added).[152]

(c) Calculating the Infringer's Profits.   In trademark infringement and false advertising cases, the court can award the infringer's profits under three distinguishable theories.

1. **Unjust enrichment.** Most cases award the infringer's profits to make the infringer forgo profit it would not have earned but for its wrongful acts and to restore those profits to the owner. Courts refer to such awards as *unjust enrichment.*

2. **Deterrence.** In some cases, the court awards the infringer's profits to deter future infringement, even when the court found the infringer to have acted in good faith. As demonstrated in *Playboy Enterprises, Inc. v. Baccarat Clothing Co., Inc.* and *Otis Clapp & Son v. Filmore Vitamin Company,* courts sometimes view a recovery's primary purpose under the Lanham Act as making infringement an unprofitable activity.[153]

3. **Proxy for owner's damages.** The courts can award an infringer's profits as a proxy for the owner's damages because the infringer's wrongful act prevented the owner from establishing sufficient sales to provide a basis for calculation. Although based on the infringer's profits, awards of this type approximate damages in competitive relations, assuming that the plaintiff would have made each of the infringer's sales.[154]

The following sections discuss issues that experts encounter in calculating an infringer's profits in Lanham Act cases.

(i) Burden of Proof in Establishing Sales.   The owner bears the burden of establishing and quantifying the infringer's sales of the infringing product. In practice, however, an expert for an infringer will almost always make an independent calculation or review the owner's calculation. In cases in which the infringer fails to maintain or produce data adequate to calculate sales with precision, courts have permitted owners to rely on a wide variety of estimation methods.[155]

(ii) Apportioning Sales and Profits.   In the marketplace, many factors influence consumers' choices of the companies with which they do business. In addition to advertising and the brand identity associated with a trademark, these factors include pricing, quality of the sales force, functional and aesthetic features of the product, and convenience. These factors affect both the owner and the infringer in an intellectual property case, to the extent they compete in the same market. The possibility of apportioning the infringer's profits in a Lanham Act case, however, indicates a significant difference in the conceptual approaches to awards based on the owner's damages and those based on the infringer's profits.

When quantifying sales to include in a calculation of the owner's lost profits, one must ask whether the owner would have made the sale but for the infringer's wrongful acts. The owner need not demonstrate that the infringed mark or false advertising offered the sole reason consumers did business with the infringer. The owner must show only that the owner would have made the infringer's sales but for the wrongful act. The owner's lost profits will then equal the profits on the entire sale that the owner would have captured, even if other factors contributed to that sale.

In contrast, an infringer facing claims for the infringer's profits can argue that the court should apportion those profits to reflect the presence and influence of other factors on the consumers' decision to do business with the infringer. If the infringer can present a rational and reasonable means of calculating the effect of factors other than the alleged wrongful acts, the infringer can argue that an award based on the infringer's profits should represent something less than the whole.[156]

The burden for proving the reasonableness of any apportionment method rests with the infringer;[157] however, case law provides little guidance on apportionment. Courts have on occasion accepted theories based on little more than the subjective testimony of fact witnesses. For example, in *Holiday Inns v. Airport Holiday*,[158] the infringer produced testimony by an employee that only 30 percent of its business came from customers specifically seeking a Holiday Inn. The trial court's award of the infringer's profits relied on this testimony when the court ruled that only 30 percent of the infringer's profits related to the unauthorized use of its infringing signs.

In practice, experts can use several analytical techniques to establish apportionment. The simplest method quantifies the proportion of offending content to nonoffending content. For example, the expert can calculate the proportion of square inches of print or seconds of broadcast time devoted to the portion deemed false or misleading in an infringer's total advertising campaign. In other cases under the Lanham Act, as in copyright cases, the court has rejected this approach when the owner could demonstrate that the *value* of the wrongful message or misappropriated mark was disproportionate to its physical representation.

Experts can also use various types of surveys to quantify an apportionment of sales. In addition, when the facts of the case and available data permit, time series analyses of the infringer's sales and profits before and after the alleged wrongful act can help. Finally, experts can compare sales and profits for the alleged infringing product with noninfringing but otherwise comparable products sold by the infringer. This approach resembles the analytical method used in patent cases.

(iii) Deduction of Costs.   As with apportionment, the infringer bears the burden of proving expenses to deduct. When calculating damages based on the *owner's* lost sales, one should use incremental profits. The law lacks this clarity with respect to calculating the infringer's profits. At least two general approaches—incremental and percentage (i.e., fully allocated)—appear acceptable in certain situations, as well as a number of hybrids.

The infringer subject to an incremental cost approach can deduct only those expenses that vary with the production and sale of the infringing products at the level of production relevant to the case. The infringer using a percentage-basis (also known as *fully allocated* or *full absorption*) approach can deduct most or all of its costs of doing business, whether such costs increase incrementally at the relevant level of sales or not. Experts often allocate expenses between alleged infringing and noninfringing sales, when necessary, by applying a common expense percentage. Such percentages could be based on the ratio of total expense to total sales but could also be based on ratios of units produced or percent of labor hours. The percentage-basis approach to cost deduction will result in a lower calculation of profits than a strictly incremental approach.

For example, assume that total expenses are $25 and that total revenues are $100 for infringing and noninfringing sales. Also, assume that expenses increasing with production of the infringing product are only $5 and that the revenues for the infringing product are $50. The percentage-basis approach results in a $37.50 or 75 percent profit for infringing sales. However, the incremental approach results in a $45 or 90 percent profit for infringing sales.

Certain types of costs appear to receive unique treatment in Lanham Act cases without regard to the overall approach taken to cost deductions. Courts can allow (*Carter Products, Inc. v. Colgate-Palmolive Co.*[159]) or deny (*S.C. Johnson & Son, Inc. v. Drop Dead Co.*[160]) deductions for advertising expenses when the content of such advertising forms the basis for the action. In at least one case, specifically *W.E. Bassett Co. v. Revlon, Inc.*,[161] the court denied deduction for the infringer's cost to relabel infringing goods.

Outside the context of litigation, experts may find that any of these methods provides an appropriate approach to calculating profits for certain purposes and that none of the methods follows generally accepted accounting principles governing the presentation of corporate financial information. We advise experts to consider both the facts of the case and any known prejudices of the relevant circuit court in formulating opinions on the deduction of costs.

(iv) Offset of Loss Against Profit—Products and Periods.   When an infringer has some time periods or individual products with profits and others with losses, most courts will allow the owner to include only profitable periods or products in its total damages claim. For example, in *Wolfe v. National Lead Co.*,[162] the Ninth Circuit rejected the infringer's attempt to offset profits made from infringement during certain years with losses from other years. Most courts have followed this approach. For example, in *Burger King Corp. v. Mason*,[163] involving an infringer's profits on multiple restaurant locations, the Eleventh Circuit permitted an infringer to offset profitable years with loss years when a single restaurant experienced both. The court did *not* allow losses at one restaurant location to offset profits incurred at another location, even though the same infringer owned and operated all locations.

(v) Use of a Reasonable Royalty.   Although not provided for by statute, reasonable royalty offers an allowable alternative to other methods of computing an infringer's profits, just as it poses an alternative to computing an owner's lost profits. Courts find royalty (or fractions of revenues) useful in certain circumstances, as demonstrated by the following examples:

- A fraction of revenue used as a measure of an infringer's economic benefit from its wrongful acts when the infringer did not generate profits[164]
- Royalty awarded as an alternative when the court found disgorgement of the infringer's total profits a windfall to the owner[165]

(d) Statutory Damages and Other Remedies.   Owners can claim statutory damages for trademark infringement by counterfeiting even without proof of monetary harm. The owner can choose statutory damages instead of actual damages at any time before the court renders final judgment. Statutory damages for counterfeiting range from $500 to $100,000 per mark per type of product, or up to $1 million for willful infringement. The statutory damages awarded depend on the opinion of the court only.[166] Finally, the Intellectual Property and Communications Omnibus Reform Act of 1999 (also known as the Anticybersquatting Consumer Protection Act) also permits an owner to elect statutory damages of not less than $1,000 nor more than $100,000 per domain name in lieu of actual damages and profits. The act specifically amends Section 43 of the Lanham Act to prohibit the registration and bad faith intent to profit from Internet domain names that the court deems "confusingly similar" to registered, "distinctive" or "famous" marks.

Prejudgment interest in Lanham Act cases compensates the owner for the lost use of funds wrongfully diverted to or realized by the infringer. Economic logic requires award of prejudgment interest when the court awards the owner's lost profits. The economic basis for awarding prejudgment interest lacks such clarity when the court awards the infringer's profits or when the plaintiff and defendant did not compete (*see* Chapter 9, "Prejudgment Interest").

Courts do not, however, consistently base awards of prejudgment interest under the Lanham Act solely on economic principles. Although findings of bad faith lack economic relevance for this issue and the law does not require such findings for awarding prejudgment interest, in practice courts appear more likely to award interest when it considers the violation "intentional" and "outrageous."[167] The Second Circuit found that, even though the Lanham Act does not recognize prejudgment interest, the court can use its discretion regarding prejudgment interest, which nevertheless "is normally reserved for 'exceptional' cases."[168]

No single approach to calculating prejudgment interest has universal acceptance. Calculations at either the prime rate or the owner's borrowing rate have occurred, pursuant to the court's discretion. District courts have upheld compounding, but courts can deny compounding as they see fit.[169] Courts can also look to state statutory interest rates, particularly when the defendant violates state law in addition to actions under the Lanham Act.

Finally, Section 35 of the Lanham Act provides for awards of attorneys' fees in exceptional cases, and such an award becomes automatic in cases of counterfeiting. The court can award other costs related to the action, including experts' fees and other items.[170]

The Lanham Act allows courts wide latitude to adjust an award of damages, either upward (up to a trebling) or downward, as warranted by the circumstances of the case. Such augmentation of damages under federal law must, however, "constitute compensation and not a penalty."[171] Conversely, courts can reduce the award on the grounds that some uncertainty in the lost profits calculation could result in an undue windfall to the owner.

Owners can seek punitive damages in Lanham Act cases under accompanying state unfair competition claims. Federal intellectual property laws do not otherwise provide for punitive damages.

20.7 DAMAGES ISSUES SPECIFIC TO TRADE SECRETS

Trade secret law derives not from federal statute but from common law, state regulations, and case law. A state-by-state discussion goes beyond the scope of this chapter, rather, we will discuss the general themes of damages under trade secret law. For a discussion of the laws for a particular state, we recommend an *American Law Reports* annotation on trade secret damages.[172] See the Appendix for a comparison of various aspects of trade secrets with those of other types of intellectual property.

(a) Standards for Injunctive Relief and Monetary Recovery.   To establish liability, the owner must prove the following:

- The existence of a legally protectable trade secret
- That the infringer had a confidential relation with the secret's owner or improperly discovered the trade secret (such relation can exist by virtue of employment as between a company and its employees or by contract)
- Use of the trade secret[173]

Remedies available to the owner in a trade secrets case resemble those available in other nonpatent intellectual property actions and include injunction, recovery of damages, and disgorgement of the infringer's gains. Unlike copyright and Lanham Act cases, however, trade secret cases rarely result in permanent injunction because many courts presume that others could and would independently develop the secret information. Courts can accommodate this presumption while protecting the rights of the secret's owner by preventing use of the information for the length of time the usurpers would have needed to develop the information using available information and art.[174]

(b) Calculation of the Owner's Damages.   The standards for assessing and calculating monetary damages for trade secrets resemble those applicable to trademark and copyright actions. The owner must prove both the fact of damages and a causal connection between the infringer's actions and the owner's loss.[175] The types of items for which an owner in a trade secrets case may claim relief include profits on diverted sales, eroded prices, remedial costs, future lost profits, developmental costs, harm to reputation, and royalties.[176]

(c) Calculation of the Infringer's Profits.   In most respects, issues in calculating infringer's profits mirror those in Lanham Act cases. The owner can claim both lost profits and the infringer's gains, to the extent this does not result in double recovery. The infringer carries the burden of proving the extent to which a portion of infringer's sales resulted from factors other than the theft.[177] Losses from one accounting period do not offset gains from another.[178] Analysis of damages by year and by product can yield damages where none would emerge at an aggregate level. Just as an owner's lost profits can include not only profits on lost sales but also profits lost through increased costs, any costs saved by the trade secret's unauthorized use represents gain to the infringer, and the courts can disgorge these amounts.[179]

(d) Reasonable Royalty and Punitive Damages.   The courts have awarded a reasonable royalty to the owner as damages, often for the same reasons that one finds such awards in Lanham Act cases.[180] The Uniform Trade Secrets Act recognizes the reasonable royalty remedy as an appropriate measure in certain cases, by stating that "[in] lieu of damages measured by any other methods, the damages caused by misappropriation may be measured by imposition of liability for reasonable royalty for a misappropriator's unauthorized disclosure or use of a trade secret."[181] For example, in *Structural Dynamics Research Corp. v. Engineering Research Corp.*,[182] the court awarded the plaintiff a reasonable royalty of 15 percent. The court intended for the award to address the issue of profit apportionment because the defendants' commingled use of their own skills with the plaintiff's secret information.

No paradigm cases guide royalty calculations for trade secrets cases. An expert calculating a royalty in a trade secrets case will, however, find guidance from *Georgia Pacific* useful if the case involves a technical trade secret or otherwise resembles subject matter similar to that found in patents.

State laws allow punitive damages[183] but subject such awards to the same guidelines and standards as in other tort actions.

TYPE OF INTELLECTUAL PROPERTY

	Patent	Copyright	Trademark	Trade Secret
Protected Elements	The subject matter of a patent must be novel, not obvious, useful, and not a mere idea or suggestion: any person who "invents or discovers any new and useful process, machine, manufacture, or composition of matter, or any new and useful improvement thereof, may obtain a patent . . . "	"[O]riginal works of authorship fixed in any tangible medium of expression"	Any word, name, symbol, device or combination thereof that a business uses to distinguish its goods and services from those of others	"information . . . that (1) derives independent economic value from not being known to . . . other persons who can obtain economic vlaue from its disclosure or use" and (2) is the subject of reasonable efforts to maintain its secrecy
Relevant Law, Act	Patent Act	Copyright Act of 1976 (including Digital Millennium Copyright Act)	Trademark Act of 1946 "Lanham Act" (federally registered trademark infringement; false designation of origin)	Uniform Trade Secret Act (UTSA) (43 states and D.C.); Restatement of the Law (3d) of Unfair Competition (remaining states)

* This table is intended to be used for basic comparisions only. Of necessity, it is highly simplified, and the general statements do not substitute for advice from legal counsel.
# The authors acknowledge Morton Goldberg's suggestions in the preparation of this table.

Appendix: Comparison of Intellectual Property Remedies*#

TYPE OF INTELLECTUAL PROPERTY

	Patent	Copyright	Trademark	Trade Secret
Length of Protection	20 years (from filing of applications) for utility and plant patents; 14 years (from issuance of patent) for design patents;	For new works, 1978 and later: 70 years after the death of the work's only or last author; for anonymous works and works made for hire: 95 years after the work's first publication or 120 years from its creation, whichever comes first	Lasts as long as the entity holding the mark continues to use it. For registration, statement of continuing use must be filed periodically, and registration must be renewed every 10 years, but there is no limit on the number of renewals	Indefinite, but lasts only until the secret becomes generally available through proper means, loses its economic value, or is no longer guarded
Ownership Depends on Use	No	No	Yes	Must make effort to keep secret
Remedies: Not Damages-Related				
Injunctive Relief	Yes	Yes	Yes	Yes

Appendix: Comparison of Intellectual Property Remedies (Continued)

TYPE OF INTELLECTUAL PROPERTY

	Patent	Copyright	Trademark	Trade Secret
Remedies: Not Damages-Related (Cont.)				
Impoundment	No	Yes; infringing material along with equipment used to produce infringing copies; impounded material may be ordered sold or destroyed by the court	Yes; court may order all infringing material and means of making the same to be delivered up and destroyed	UTSA doesn't mention seizures, but the act has been interpreted to allow seizure of "the fruits of misappropriation," such as customer lists or manufacturing blueprints
Exclusion of Importation	Yes	Yes	Yes	N/A
Remedies: Damages-Related				
Lost Profits	Yes; Patent owner is entitled to damages (lost profits or lost royalty income), but not less than a reasonable royalty	Yes; no floor on non-statutory damages	Yes; in most cases, there is no floor on damages	Yes; no floor on damages. Under the Restatement, damages are the greater of lost profits or the infringer's total profits
Lost Profits-Use of Defendant's Profits	Yes, as an estimate of lost profits	Yes	Yes	Yes

Appendix: Comparison of Intellectual Property Remedies (Continued)

TYPE OF INTELLECTUAL PROPERTY

	Patent	Copyright	Trademark	Trade Secret
Remedies: Damages-Related (Cont.)				
Can recover value of credit as the author or goodwill	N/A	Yes; both—can recover value of receiving credit as the author and any related loss of goodwill	Yes, can recover damages to reputation or goodwill	In certain circumstances, courts will award damages for harm to reputation
Can recover value of sales lost on noninfringed goods	Yes, on convoyed (sold with product employing patent) and derivative (made using the patent) sales	Yes	Yes	Yes
Reasonable Royalty	Yes	Yes (usually refers to the use of royalties from previous licenses) can be used to approximate lost profits if the facts warrant	Yes	Yes

Appendix: Comparison of Intellectual Property Remedies (Continued)

TYPE OF INTELLECTUAL PROPERTY

	Patent	Copyright	Trademark	Trade Secret
Remedies: Damages-Related (Cont.)				
Market Value	Not a concept discussed in the patent context. However, the idea (in the copyright context) is one of what a willing buyer and willing seller would agree to, and this is embodied in the hypothetical negotiation in patent damages	Yes; when neither lost sales, reasonable royalty, nor defendant's profits has empirical basis, damages may be based on what a willing buyer would have paid a willing seller for use of the work	N/A	Value of secret: where value has been destroyed through misappropriation, the owner can be awarded the value of the secret at the time of the misappropriation
Cost to Create or Duplicate	This idea is captured by the cost of a "design around" the patent, which is one of the factors in assessing what the infringer would have been willing to pay	Where market value is to be assessed, can be factored in	No, but plaintiff can claim costs of corrective advertising as damages	In cases in which there is no established value for the secret in the marketplace, the owner's investment in the secret is a valid measure of value

Appendix: Comparison of Intellectual Property Remedies (Continued)

TYPE OF INTELLECTUAL PROPERTY

	Patent	Copyright	Trademark	Trade Secret
Remedies: Damages-Related (Cont.)				
Head Start Damages	No	No	Yes. Fifth Circuit accepted idea of a loss to the plaintiff from infringement in geographic areas that it was logical for the plaintiff to expand into	Yes; limits damages period to time up until defendant could have become aware of secret through legitimate means
Statutory	No	Yes; plaintiff can elect to receive statutory damages as a substitute for actual damages and profits, but only if the copyright was registered promptly (usually before infringement)	Yes, as to counterfeit marks and bad faith registration or use of a domain name	No

Appendix: Comparison of Intellectual Property Remedies   (Continued)

	TYPE OF INTELLECTUAL PROPERTY			
	Patent	Copyright	Trademark	Trade Secret
Remedies: Disgorgement				
Infringer's Profits	No, except for Design Patents	Yes, to the extent amount is not taken into account in computing damages	Yes, to the extent amount is not taken into account in computing damages. Lanham Act allows court, in its discretion, to augment or decrease the award without limit (Lanham Act's Equitable Overlay)	Yes; Under the UTSA, to the extent the amount is not taken into account in computing the owner's loss. Under the Restatement, damages are the greater of lost profits or the infringer's total profits. May also recover illicit benefits such as the defendant's cost saving, even if it exceeds the defendant's profits
Apportionment of Infringer's Profit	Not applicable for utility or plant patents, and notably not for design patents (see *Nike v. Wal-Mart Stores* (1998))	Yes	Yes	Yes

Appendix: Comparison of Intellectual Property Remedies   (Continued)

| | TYPE OF INTELLECTUAL PROPERTY | | | |
	Patent	Copyright	Trademark	Trade Secret
Remedies: Disgorgement (Cont.)				
Apportionment of Profit-burden of proof for cost	Not applicable, except for Design Patents, for which Defendant bears this burden	Defendant bears this burden	Defendant bears this burden	Defendant bears this burden (categories of expense deductible vary by state)
In calculating infringer's profits-use incremental cost or not?	Not applicable, except for Design Patents, for which a determination depends on the facts of the case.	No consensus	No consensus	No consensus
Remedies: Costs and Attorneys' Fees	Attorneys' fees only in "exceptional cases;" costs, yes	Court's discretion, with respect to both cost and attorneys' fees, but no award of attorneys' fees is permitted unless copyright was registered promptly (usually before infringement)	Lanham Act provides for the recovery of "the costs of the action"; in "exceptional cases" the courts can award attorneys' fees to the prevailing party	If misappropriation is "willful and malicious," it depends on state law, but for states that have enacted the UTSA, courts can award attorneys' fees Costs, yes

Appendix: Comparison of Intellectual Property Remedies (Continued)

TYPE OF INTELLECTUAL PROPERTY

	Patent	Copyright	Trademark	Trade Secret
Remedies (Cont.)				
Prejudgment Interest	Yes	Not expressly mentioned in Copyright Act. Courts divided, but trend is toward awarding prejudgment interest	Yes, in both counterfeiting and ordinary trademark infringement, but in "exceptional cases" in the latter	Not expressly under the UTSA. Some states allow prejudgment interest in all civil cases; in the majority of states, though it is unavailable
Augmented/ Punitive Damages	Under federal patent statute, a court may award up to three times the amount of damages if infringement was willful	Generally not available. Not categorically excluded by courts, but are awarded only rarely	Lanham Act permits up to a trebling of damages	May be available; depends on state; for states under the UTSA, available where "willful and malicious" misappropriation exists and are limited to double the amount of any compensatory damages, and are at court's discretion

Sources: Dratler, Jay Jr. Intellectual Property Law: Commercial, Creative and Industrial Property (2006: Law Journal Press, New York).
Goldstein, Paul. Goldstein on Copyright, Third Edition (2005: Aspen Publishers, New York).
Kane, Siegrun D. Trademark Law; A Practitioner's Guide, Fourth Edition (Practicing Law Institute, 2004).
McCarthy, J. Thomas. McCarthy on Trademarks and Unfair Competition (2005: Thompson/West).
Pooley, James, Trade Secrets (2005: Law Journal Press, New York).
Ross, Terence P., Intellectual Property Law - Damages and Remedies (2005: Law Journal Press, New York).
USCS Titles 15, 17, 22, 35.
USPTO Website.
Nike v. Wal-Mart Stores(138 F.3d 1437, Federal Circuit, 1998).

Appendix: Comparison of Intellectual Property Remedies   (Continued)

NOTES

1. *American Heritage Dictionary*, 1993, S.V. "Property."
2. P. Samuelson and W. Nordhaus, *Economics,* 15th ed. (New York: McGraw-Hill, 1995), 29–30.
3. Samuelson and Nordhaus, Economics, 4.
4. J. Dratler, Jr., *Intellectual Property Law: Commercial, Creative, and Industrial Property* (New York: Law Journal Press, 2005), 1–15.
5. U.S.C.S. (2005), Title 17, Chapter 1, Section 102(a).
6. *Id.,* Section 102 discussion.
7. Dratler, *Intellectual Property Law*, 1–15.
8. U.S.C.S. (2005), Title 17, Chapter 1, Section 102(b).
9. *Id.,* Section 302(a) and (b).
10. *Id.,* Section 302(c).
11. *Id.,* Section 107.
12. 471 U.S. 539 (1985).
13. W. Landes and R. Posner, *The Economic Structure of Intellectual Property Law* (Cambridge, MA: The Belknap Press of Harvard University Press, 2003), 117–8.
14. U.S.C.S. (2005), Title 17, Chapter 12, Sections 1201(a)(1)(A) and (a)(2).
15. David V. Lampman, "COMMENT: 'A Prologue to a Farce or a Tragedy?' A Paradox, a Potential Clash: Digital Pirates, The Digital Millennium Copyright Act, The First Amendment & Fair Use," *Gonzaga Law Review* 38 (2002/2003): 381.
16. Derek J. Schaffner, "*Note:* The Digital Millennium Copyright Act: Overextension of Copyright Protection and the Unintended Chilling Effects on Fair Use, Free Speech, and Innovation," *Cornell Journal of Law and Public Policy* 14 (Fall 2004): 148.
17. This chapter uses the word "author" to refer to a creator of any type of copyrightable work: artist, choreographer, composer, and the like.
18. *Metro-Goldwyn-Mayer, Inc., et al. v. Grokster Ltd., et al.,* 125 S. Ct. 2764; 75 U.S.P. Q.2d (BNA) 1001. 2005
19. W. Landes and R. Posner, "An Economic Analysis of Copyright Law," *Journal of Legal Studies* 28 (1989): 325, 348–49.
20. In turn, the inventor of the process cannot use his or her process without paying the inventor of the chemical a royalty for its use.
21. S. Besen and L. Raskind, "An Introduction to the Law and Economics of Intellectual Property," *Journal of Economic Perspectives* 5 (1991): 16.
22. Landes and Posner, *The Economics Structure*, 354–55.
23. E. Kitch, "The Nature and Function of the Patent System, *Journal of Law & Economics* 20 (1977): 265.
24. C. Hall, "Renting Ideas," *Journal of Business* 64 (January 1991): 22.
25. Landes and Posner, 1989, *The Economic Structure*, 344–46.
26. Ibid., 115–16.
27. 15 U.S.C.S. Section 1127 (2005).
28. Landes and Posner, *The Economic Structure*, 168 ff.
29. Siegrun D. Kane, *Trademark Law, A Practitioner's Guide,* 4th ed. New York (Practising Law Institute, 2004). Current through Release No. 2 (October 2004), section 1:1:1.
30. Kane, *Trademark Law*, section 1:1:1, and U.S. Patent and Trademark Office, Trademark Electronic Search System, and tess2 uspto.gov/bin/gate.exe?f=tess&state=rsmbse.1.1.
31. Theodore H. Davis Jr., R. Charles Henn Jr., and Christine M. Cason, "The Anticybersquatting Consumer Protection Act of 1999," *Georgia Bar Journal* 5 (February 2000).
32. R. Grabowski, "Adventures in Cyberspace: Strategies for Securing and Protecting Your Firm's Domain Name," *Legal Tech* 17 (Feb. 2000):7, and National Arbitration

Forum Decision in *Qwest Communications International v. QC Publishing*, Claim Number FA0406000286032, September 23, 2004, www.anb-forum.com/domains/decisions/286032.htm.

33. Landes and Posner, *The Economic Structure*, 197–98.

34. Kane, *Trademark Law*, Section 2:1.

35. Ibid., Section 2:1:2.

36. Ibid., Section 2:1.

37. Ibid., Section 1:1 and 1:1.5[D].

38. 15 U.S.C.S. Section 1059 (2005).

39. This advantage flows from the filing date of the application—assuming registration follows. *See* Dratler, *Intellectual Property Law*, 11–28.

40. W. Holmes, *Intellectual Property and Antitrust Law* (New York; Clark, Boardman, Collaghan, 1994), 3–14.

41. J. Thomas McCarthy, *McCarthy on Trademarks and Unfair Competition*, (Eagan, MN: Thomson West, 2005), Sections 23:12 and 23:13.

42. Landes and Posner, *The Economic Structure*, 168.

43. Ibid., 167–68.

44. Ibid., 173 and 186.

45. Ibid., 186.

46. 15 U.S.C.S. (2005) §1051-1129.

47. Uniform Trade Secrets Act with 1985 Amendments, Section 1(4) .

48. Dratler, *Intellectual Property Law*, 1–35.

49. For a listing of some trade secrets, *see Taco Cabana International, Inc. v. Two Pesos, Inc.* 932 F.2d 1113; 19 U.S.P.Q. 2d (BNA) 1253 (5th Cir. 1991).

50. *Kewanee Oil Co. v. Bicron*, 416 U.S. 470, 476 (1974).

51. Landes and Posner, *The Economic Structure*, 355.

52. Ibid., 359. They also argue that trade secret law fits within the prospect analysis of Kitch, because an inventor is not barred from obtaining a patent because someone else has made, but did not make public, the invention (pp. 360–61).

53. Landes and Posner (*The Economic Structure*, 370) cite The Semiconductor Chip Protection Act of 1984 (17 U.S.C. section 901 *et seq*.) in recognition of this point.

54. The U.S.C.S. refers the reader to 52 FR 23781 for this specific point.

55. In this chapter, *lost profit damages* will refer to the damages suffered by the owner when the owner would not have licensed the infringer and, instead, the infringer would have used the next best alternative.

56. Jean Tirole *The Theory of Industrial Organization* (Cambridge, MA: MIT Press, 1998), 174–75.

57. Goldstein, 2005, section 14.0, McCarthy, 2005, section 30:59, Pooley, 2005, section 7.03[2] (*see* Bibliography).

58. W. Landes and R. Posner, "Market Power in Antitrust Cases," *Harvard Law Review* 94, (March 1981), 939–40.

59. Ibid., 944–45 (setting the supply elasticity to zero).

60. The residual demand elasticity equals $P/(P - MC) = 125/(125 - 100) = 5$, where P equals price and MC equals marginal cost.

61. Ignoring the supply response (elasticity) of competitors, the formula for the residual (firm) demand elasticity, $E(i)$, can be rearranged to solve for the market demand elasticity, $E(m)$ as a function of that firm's market share, $S(i)$: $E(m) = S(i) \times E(i)$. *See* Landes and Posner, *The Economic Structure*, 945 (Equation 2). As mentioned previously, this particular model of competitor interaction takes into account the current supply (output) of the other firm but assumes no change in output by that firm in response to a price change. Thus, the expert can assume the supply response (elasticity) to be zero.

62. Assuming a demand curve of constant elasticity. The market demand formula, $Q = a \times P^{-2.5}$, can be solved for a where $P = 125$, $Q = 2$ million, and -2.5 equals the demand elasticity. In such a case, $a = 3.494 \times 10^{11}$. At P equal to 166.67, Q will equal 974,230 units. Alternative assumptions concerning the shape of the demand curve can also be used with this model.

63. Quantity equals $3.494 \times 10^{11} \times 140^{-2.5}$ or 1,506,555 units.

64. Combined awards are similar to split claims in patent cases, in which the plaintiff may claim lost profits damages on the portion of the defendant's sales the plaintiff claims it would have made but for the infringement *and* royalty damages on the balance of the defendant's sales, but not *both* lost profits and royalties on the same sale.

65. McCarthy, *McCarthy on Trademarks*, section 30:62.

66. For more detail on what costs one may deduct from defendant's revenues related to copyright, trademarks, and trade secrets, see the discussions at Sections 20.5(b), 20.6(c)(iii), and 20.7(c).

67. U.S.C.S. (2005), Title 17, chapter 5, Section 504(b).

68. *See* Sections 20.5(b)(v), 20.6(c)(ii), and 20.7(c) for more detailed discussions of apportionment methods.

69. *See* Section 20.3(c), in which we discuss why royalty-based damage measures may exceed lost-profit-based damage measures.

70. *Imperial Toy Corp. v. Goffa International Corp.*, 988 F. Supp. 617 (E.D.N.Y. 1997).

71. McCarthy, *McCarthy on Trademarks*, section 30:58.

72. 17 U.S.C. §1204(a)(1)(2) provides for fines of not more than $500,000 or prison terms of not more than 5 years for the first offense and fines of not more than $1,000,000 or prison terms of not more than 10 years for subsequent offenses.

73. Counterfeiting is not simply an act that creates the possibility or likelihood of confusion as to the origin of the product. A counterfeiter must trade in the counterfeit product intentionally and knowingly use a counterfeit mark. *See* Dratler, *Intellectual Property Law*, section 11.09.

74. *See Toro Co. v. Textron Inc.*, 499 F. Supp. 241 (Del. 1980).

75. 318 F. Supp. 1116, 1121 (S.D.N.Y. 1970); *aff'd* 446 F.2d 225 (1971).

76. *See also* U.S.C.S. (2005), Title 17, Chapter 1, Section 504(a)(1) ("an infringer of copyright is liable for . . . the copyright owner's actual damages").

77. Goldstein, *Goldstein on Copyright*, 2005, section 14.1.1.

78. Ibid., section 14.1.1. *See also Abend v. MCA, Inc.*, 863 F.2d 1465, 1479; 9 U.S.P.Q. 2d 1337 (9th Cir. 1988) (infringing motion picture's impairment of plaintiff's ability to license new derivative works based on its story "would be reflected in the calculation of the damage to the fair market value of the story"), *aff'd on other grounds sub nom., Stewart v. Abend*, 495 U.S. 207 (1990). The courts have frequently described damages as a measure of "the extent to which the market value of a copyrighted work has been injured or destroyed by an infringement." *See also Manufacturers Technologies, Inc. v. Cams, Inc.*, 728 F. Supp. 75, 80 (D. Conn. 1989) ("Although the statute does not define what constitutes actual damages, it has been interpreted to mean the extent to which the market value of the copyrighted work has been injured or destroyed as a result of and during the time of the infringement"); *Frank Music Corp. v. Metro-Goldwyn-Mayer, Inc.*, 772 F.2d 505, 512 (9th Cir. 1985), quoted at *United States v. King Features Entertainment, Inc.*, 843 F.2d 394, 400 (9th Cir. 1988). *See also Sid & Marty Krofft Television Productions, Inc. v. McDonald's Corp.*, 562 F.2d 1157, 1174 (9th Cir. 1977)—market value is "what a willing buyer would have been reasonably required to pay to a willing seller for plaintiff's work."

79. One may construct a house identical to a house depicted in copyrighted plans, but copying the plans themselves constitutes infringement. *See Robert R. Jones Associates, Inc. v. Nino Homes*, 858 F.2d 274 (6th Cir. 1988).

80. *See Bishop v. Wick*, Copyright L. Rep. ¶ 26, 467 (N.D. Ill 1988), in which plaintiffs recovered the fair market licensing value of their computer program multiplied by

each time defendants illegally copied or utilized the program. In addition, plaintiffs recovered all profits defendants made from sales of infringing programs.

81. 367 F. Supp. 876, 881 (S.D.N.Y. 1973).

82. *See Taylor v. Meirick*, 712 F.2d 1112 (7th Cir. 1983), in which the court rejected the trial court's award based on lost sales because it had not taken into account the additional expenses the copyright owner would have incurred to achieve the lost sales.

83. Goldstein, 2005, sec. 14.1.1.b.

84. Ross, pages 2-15 to 2-16.

85. Goldstein, 2005, page 14-14.

86. These cost savings may be factored into an assessment of market value.

87. 17 U.S.C. § 504(b). *See also Szekely v. Eagle Lion Films*, 242 F.2d 266 (2d Cir. 1957); *Sid & Marty Krofft Television Productions, Inc. v. McDonald's Corp.*, 562 F.2d 1157, 1174-75 (9th Cir. 1977). One Ninth Circuit opinion simply states that the "burden of proving apportionment (i.e., the contribution to profits of elements other than the infringed property), is the defendant's" (*Frank MusicCorp. v. Metro-Goldwyn-Mayer*, 772 F.2d 505; 227 U.S.P.Q. 687 [9th Cir. 1985]), citing *Lottie Joplin Thomas Trust v. Crown Publishers, Inc.*, 592 F.2d 651, 657 [2d Cir. 1978]).

88. *Cream Records, Inc. v. Joseph Schlitz Brewing Co.*, 864 F.2d 668, 669, 9 U.S.P.Q. 2d 1568 (9th Cir. 1989); *Blackman v. Hustler Magazine, Inc.*, "Since the statutory scheme calls for subtracting defendant's proof from that of the plaintiff, and since defendant's proof was found to be zero, the figure proven by plaintiff winds up establishing the profits." 800 F.2d 1160, 1163-1164, 231 U.S.P.Q. 51 (D.C. Cir. 1986) (1909 Act) *cert. denied*, 446 U.S. 952 (1980); *Williams v. Arndt*, 626 F. Supp. 571, 582, 227 U.S.P.Q. 614 (D. Mass. 1985); *Whelan Associates, Inc. v. Jaslow Dental Lab, Inc.*, 609 F. Supp. 1307, 1322, 225 U.S.P.Q. 156 (E.D. Pa. 1985) (the plaintiff was entitled to the defendant's gross profits since defendant's statement of expenses was too vague). In *Frank Music*, the court stated "If the infringing defendant does not meet its burden of proving costs, the gross figure stands as the defendant's profits," citing *Russell v. Price*, "[i]f an infringer does not assume this burden or its attempt to do so is found unacceptable by the court, as was the case here, then 'the gross figure is left to stand as the profit factor,'" 612 F.2d 1123, 1130-31 (9th Cir. 1979), *cert. denied*, 446 U.S. 952, 100 S. Ct. 2919, 64 L. Ed. 2d 809 (1980).

89. Howard B. Abrams, *The Law of Copyright*, Eagan, MN vol. 2. Thomson West, 2004), section 17:7.

90. *See Aiken, Hazen, Hoffman, Miller, P. C. v. Empire Construction Co.*, 542 F. Supp. 252, 264 (D. Neb. 1982). "The most straightforward method to avoid double counting in the damage award is to include the actual damages as an expense to deduct from the infringer's gross profits" (Goldstein, *Goldstein on Copyright*, section 14.1.2). *See also Taylor v. Meirick*, 712 F.2d 1112, 1120, 219 U.S.P.Q. 420 (7th Cir. 1983); *Harper House, Inc. v. Thomas Nelson Publishers, Inc.*, 4 U.S.P.Q. 2d 1987 (C.D. Cal. 1987); *Robert R. Jones Associates. v. Nino Homes*, 858 F.2d 274, 281, 8 U.S.P.Q. 2d 1224 (6th Cir. 1988).

91. *See*, for example, *Abeshouse v. Ultragraphics, Inc.*, 754 F.2d 467, 470 (2d Cir. 1985).

92. *See*, for example, *Cream Records, Inc. v. Joseph Schlitz Brewing Co.*, 754 F.2d 826, 829, 225 U.S.P.Q. 896 (9th Cir. 1985).

93. 827 F. Supp. 282, 295 (D.N.J. 1993).

94. Goldstein, *Goldstein on Copyright*, section 14.1.2; emphasis added.

95. *Taylor v. Meirick*, 712 F.2d 1112, 1121, 219 U.S.P.Q. 420 (7th Cir. 1983). *See also Frank Music Corp. v. Metro-Goldwyn-Mayer, Inc.*, 772 F.2d 505, 516, 227 U.S.P.Q. 687 (9th Cir. 1985) ("[D]efendant bears the burden of explaining, at least in general terms, how claimed overhead actually contributed to the production of the infringing work").

96. Abrams, *The Law of Copyright*, section 17.7.

97. *See Frank Music Corp. v. Metro-Goldwyn-Mayer, Inc.*, 772 F.2d 505, 516 (9th Cir. 1985); *Kamar International, Inc. v. Russ Berrie & Co.*, 752 F.2d 1326, 1333 (9th Cir. 1984). The court in *Frank Music* cited *Sammons v. Colonial Press, Inc.*, 126 F.2d 349, *Kamar International*,

and *Taylor v. Merick* 712 F.2d 1112 (7th Cir. 1983) ("It is too much to ask a plaintiff who has proved infringement also to do the defendant's cost accounting").

98. Plaintiffs may show willfulness by showing that defendant recklessly disregarded plaintiffs' rights. *Basic Books, Inc. v. Kinko's Graphics Corporation,* 758 F. Supp. 1522 (U.S.D.N.Y. 1991). The decision cited *Wow & Flutter Music v. Len's Tom Jones Tavern, Inc.,* 606 F. Supp. 554, 556 (W.D.N.Y. 1985); *Lauratex Textile Corp. v. Allton Knitting Mills,* 519 F. Supp. 730, 733 (S.D.N.Y. 1981). Plaintiffs also sustain their burden by showing defendant knew or "should have known" it infringed their copyrights. *Fallaci v. New Gazette Literary Corp.,* 568 F. Supp. 1172, 1173 (S.D.N.Y. 1983). Willful does not mean "malicious," rather, it means "with knowledge," whether actual or constructive. *Fitzgerald Publishing Co., Inc. v. Baylor Publishing Co., Inc.,* 807 F.2d 1110, 1115 (2d Cir. 1986), *aff'd,* 862 F.2d 304 (1988) ("a defendant's actual or constructive knowledge proves willfulness").

99. *Saxon v. Blann,* 968 F.2d 676, 681 (8th Cir. 1992); *Frank Music Corp. v. Metro-Goldwyn-Mayer Inc.,* 772 F. 2d 505, 515, 227 U.S.P.Q. 687 (9th Cir. 1985). *See also Jarvis v. A&M Records,* 827 F. Supp. 282, 295 (D.N.J. 1993), in which the court emphasized the difference between willful and nonwillful infringers' ability to deduct overhead costs.

100. The *Sheldon* decision is found at 309 U.S. 390, 60 S. Ct. 681, 84 L. Ed. 825 (1940). The lower court, affirmed by the Supreme Court, found that the work's overall success was due in part to the infringing portion as well as other factors of the work and upheld the apportionment of profits. The infringing work was a movie based on a play. The Ninth Circuit noted in *Cream Records,* 754 F.2d at 828, "[i]n cases such as this where an infringer's profits are not entirely due to the infringement, and the evidence suggests some division, which may rationally be used as a springboard, it is the duty of the court to make some apportionment." Quoting *Orgel v. Clark Boardman Co.,* 301 F.2d 119, 121 (2d Cir.), *cert. denied,* 371 U.S. 817, 83 S. Ct. 31, 9 L. Ed. 2d 58 (1962). In another case apportionment occurred when the infringer produced a song that infringed the music but had better lyrics; *see Gaste v. Kaiserman,* 863 F.2d 1061, 1069–1070 (2d Cir. 1988).

101. *Sheldon v. MGM,* 309 U.S. 390 at 396.

102. H.R. Rep. No. 1476, 94th Cong., 2d Sess., at 161 (1976); emphasis added.

103. Ibid.

104. In *Sheldon,* the court affirmed the lower court's decision that "it must make an award 'which by no possibility shall be too small'" (309 U.S. 390 at 408). In the 1989 *Frank Music* decision, the Ninth Circuit likewise concluded that "in performing the apportionment, the benefit of the doubt must always be given to the plaintiff, not the defendant" (*Frank Music v. Metro-Goldwyn-Mayer, Inc.,* 886 F.2d 1545; 12 U.S.P.Q. 2d (BNA) 1412 (9th Cir., 1989)). In *Gaste v. Kaiserman,* 863 F.2d 1061, 1070, 9 U.S.P.Q. 2d, 1300 (2d Cir. 1988), the court noted that when "[c]onfronted with imprecision in the computation of expenses, a court should err on the side of guaranteeing the plaintiff a full recovery, but want of precision is not a ground for denying apportionment altogether." *See also Sygma Photo News, Inc. v. High Society Magazine, Inc.,* 778 F.2d 89, 98, 228 U.S.P.Q. 580 (2d Cir. 1985). See also *Update Art, Inc. v. Modiin Publishing, Ltd.,* 843 F.2d 67, 72 (2d Cir. 1988); imprecision due to defendant's unresponsiveness to discovery orders caused the court to award defendant's entire profits.

105. In *Frank Music* at 518, citing *Lottie Joplin Thomas Trust v. Crown Publishers, Inc.,* 592 F.2d 651, 657 (2d Cir. 1978).

106. 309 U.S. 390 at 404 (1940). *See also Abend v. MCA, Inc.,* 863 F.2d 1465, 1480, 9 U.S.P.Q. 2d 1337 (9th Cir. 1988), *aff'd on other grounds sub nom. See also Stewart v. Abend,* 495 U.S. 207 (1990). This is consistent with the language in *Sheldon* that "the defendant, being responsible for the blending of the lawful with the unlawful, had to abide the consequences, as in the case of one who has wrongfully produced a confusion of goods" (309 U.S. 390 at 401).

107. *Wesley M. Walker, Jr., v. Forbes, Inc.,* 28 F.3d 409, 31 U.S.P.Q. 2d (BNA) 1349 (4th Cir., 1994). In a note it added that "each case must be decided on its own set of facts, and that this case sets no rule to be inflexibly applied across categories of works. ... In each

case, the fact finder must simply do its best, keeping in mind the stricture of the law, to grapple with the particular set of facts and determine what profits can be attributed to the infringement." The note appears at 413.

108. *Frank Music* at 1545 and 1548. *See also Blackman v. Hustler Magazine* at 1160 and 1164; *Sygma Photo News, Inc. v. High Society Magazine, Inc.,* 778 F.2d 89, 96, 228 U.S.P.Q. 580 (2d Cir. 1985); *Orgel v. Clark Boardman Co.,* 301 F.2d 119, 133 U.S.P.Q. 94 (2d Cir.). Modification of "show" added for clarity.

109. *Grand Upright Music, Ltd. v. Warner Brothers Records Inc.,* 780 F. Supp. 182 (S.D.N.Y. 1991). *See* additional cases cited in Nimmer and Nimmer (2005), in which the apportionment ranges from a *pro rata* 4.5 percent (one of many songs on an all "hits" album) to 70 percent.

110. Cited at 849 F.2d 186 (5th Cir. 1988), *cert. denied,* 488 U.S. 1008, 109 S. Ct. 792, 102 L. Ed. 2d 783 (1989). The court recognized that the infringed work was only part of the entire commercial, the cost of the photograph was only one cost of the commercial, and it was wrong to base a projection of profits on a ratio of undifferentiated advertising dollars to sales.

111. *Frank Music Corp. v. Metro-Goldwyn-Mayer, Inc.,* 886 F.2d 1545; 12 U.S.P.Q. 2d (BNA) 1412 (9th Cir., 1989).

112. *See,* for example, *Cream Records, Inc. v. Joseph Schlitz Brewing Co.,* 754 F.2d 826, 828, 225 U.S.P.Q. 896 (9th Cir. 1985). Cream was awarded 1/10 of 1 percent of profits from sales of the advertised beverage.

113. It may also be used when the infringer sells the item.

114. For a general discussion and references, *see* Robert Goldscheider, John Jarosz and Carla Mulhern, "Use of the 25 Percent Rule in Valuing IP," *les Nourelles,* December, 2002: 123-133.

115. The inverse of a 25 percent or 33.3 percent royalty rate.

116. *See Deltak, Inc. v. Advanced Systems, Inc.,* 767 F.2d 357, 261, 226 U.S.P.Q. 919 (7th Cir. 1985) ("Each of the [infringing] copies [defendant] ASI distributed had a value of use to it equal to the acquisition cost saved by infringement instead of purchase, which ASI was then free to put to other uses").

117. *C. Elvin Feltner, Jr. v. Columbia Pictures Television, Inc.,* 523 U.S. 340 (1998).

118. 17 U.S.C. § 412.

119. 17 U.S.C. § 504(c)(2).

120. 221 U.S.P.Q. (BNA) 114, (U.S. District Court for the Central District of California, 1983) Ross, page 1-24.

121. *See Goldstein* (2005), 14:20, especially note 52.

122. *Id.,* section 14.1.2.

123. 978 F.2d 1093, 23 U.S.P.Q. 2d (BNA) 1721 (9th Cir. 1992).

124. 799 F. Supp. 240; 25 U.S.P.Q. 2d 1897, 1912 (D.C. P.R. 1992).

125. *See Playboy Enterprises, Inc. v. P.K. Sorren Export Co.,* 546 F. Supp. 987; 218 U.S.P.Q. (BNA) 795; affirmed at 724 F.2d. 977 (11th Cir. 1984). *and Polo Fashions, Inc. v. Extra Special Products, Inc.,* 208 U.S.P.Q. 421 (S.D.N.Y. 1980). A minority of cases appear to affirm awards of both damages and profits on the same sales. *See,* for example, *Conopco, Inc. v. May Dept. Stores Co.,* 784 F. Supp. 648, 680–81, 24 U.S.P.Q. 2d 1721 (E.D. Mo. 1992).

126. McCarthy (2005), 30–117.

127. 799 F.2d 6; 231 U.S.P.Q. (BNA) 39 (1st Cir., 1986).

128. *See Aktiebolaget Electrolux v. Armatron Int'l, Inc.,* 999 F.2d 1; 27 U.S.P.Q. 2d (BNA) 1460 (1st Cir. 1993).

129. *Taco Cabana International v. Two Pesos, Inc.,* 932 F. 2d 1113; 19 U.S.P.Q. 2d (BNA) 1253 (5th Cir. 1991).

130. In *Roulo v. Russ Berrie & Co.,* 886 F.2d 931, 12 U.S.P.Q. 2d (BNA) 1423 (7th Cir. 1989), the court inferred likelihood of confusion because the trade dress of the product was

deemed distinctive, a considerable similarity was perceived between the plaintiff's and defendant's products, and the products were sold side by side at the same stores using similar display racks.

131. *See Carl Zeiss Stiftung v. VEB Carl Zeiss Jena*, 433 F.2d 686, 717 (2nd Cir. 1980), *Fuller Products Co. v. Fuller Brush Co.*, 299 F.2d 772, 777 (7th Cir. 1962), and *Stuart v. Collins*, 489 F. Supp. 827, 831 (S.D.N.Y. 1980).

132. 999 F.2d 1; 27 U.S.P.Q. 2d (BNA) 1460 (1st Cir. 1993).

133. *See,* for example, *Lindy Pen Co. v. Bic Pen Corp.*, 982 F.2d 1400; 25 U.S.P.Q. 2d (BNA) 1570 (9th Cir. 1993).

134. We generally define *diminution* as damage to the value of the mark resulting from misuse by a competitor, whereas dilution is damage resulting from misuse by a noncompetitor.

135. 601 F. Supp. 1140; 225 U.S.P.Q. (BNA) 306 (D. Ariz. 1984).

136. 754 F.2d 738; 225 U.S.P.Q. (BNA) 387 (7th Cir. 1984).

137. 815 F. Supp. 691, 26 U.S.P.Q. 2d (BNA) 1161 (S.D.N.Y. 1993); reversed on other grounds, 35 F.3d 65, 32 U.S.P.Q. 2d (BNA) 1010 (2nd Cir. 1994).

138. 30 U.S.P.Q. 2d 1337 (N.D. Ill. 1992).

139. 932 F.2d 1113, 19 U.S.P.Q. 1253 (5th Cir. 1991).

140. 997 F.2d 949, 27 U.S.P.Q. 2d (BNA) 1455 (D.C. Cir. 1993).

141. 30 U.S.P.Q. 2d 1337 (N.D. Ill. 1992).

142. 580 F. Supp. 634; 222 U.S.P.Q. (BNA) 318 (S.D. N.Y. 1984).

143. 561 F.2d 1365; 195 U.S.P.Q. (BNA) 417 (10th Cir. 1977).

144. 76 F.3d 984; 37 U.S.P.Q. 2d (BNA) 1872 (9th Cir. 1995).

145. 1992 U.S. Dist. LEXIS 1265 (S.D. N.Y. 1992).

146. 486 F. Supp. 1273; 206 U.S.P.Q. (BNA) 112 (S.D. N.Y. 1980).

147. 932 F.2d 1113; 19 U.S.P.Q. 2d (BNA) 1253 (5th Cir. 1991).

148. 1992 U.S. Dist. LEXIS 4187; 25 U.S.PQ. 2d (BNA) 1096.

149. 1992 U.S. Sist. LEXIS 12572.

150. 38 F.3d 1161; 33 U.S.P.Q. 2d (BNA) 1001 (11th Cir. 1994).

151. 493 F. Supp. 1025; 212 U.S.P.Q. (BNA) 208 (N.D. Tex. 1980).

152. 978 F. 2d 947; 24 U.S.P.Q. 2d (BNA) 1001 (7th Cir. 1992).

153. 692 F.2d 1272; 216 U.S.P.Q. (BNA) 1083 (9th Cir., 1982) and 754 F.2d 738; 225 U.S.P.Q. (BNA) 387 (7th Cir. 1984).

154. McCarthy (2005), section 30:59. McCarthy also points out, citing the Restatement (Third) of Unfair Competition, Section 37, comment b (1995), that "The correspondence is clearly imperfect, however, since in most cases there is no reason to expect that every sale made by the defendant has been diverted from the plaintiff, or that the profit margins of the parties are necessarily the same."

155. *See Dive N' Surf, Inc. v. Anselowitz*, 834 F. Supp. 379; Copy. L. Rep. (CCH) P27, 193 (M.D. Fla. 1993) and *Louis Vuitton S.A. v. Spencer Handbags Corp.*, 765 F.2d 966, 227 U.S.P.Q. (BNA) 377 (2nd Cir. 1985).

156. Such arguments do not always succeed. In *Roulo v. Russ Berrie & Co.*, supra, at 942, arguments for apportionment were largely rejected because, although other market factors were undoubtedly present, the defendant was deemed to have appropriated the "total concept and feel" of the plaintiff's product.

157. McCarthy (2005), section 30:65.

158. 493 F. Supp. 1025; 212 U.S.P.Q. (BNA) 208 (N. D. Tex. 1980).

159. 214 F. Supp. 383; 136 U.S.P.Q. (BNA) 348; 136 U.S.P.Q. (BNA) 577 (Dist. of Maryland, 1963).

160. 1965 U.S. Dist. LEXIS 6840; 144 U.S.P.Q. (BNA) 257 (Southern Dist. CA, Central Div, 1965).

161. 435 F.2d 656; 168 U.S.P.Q. (BNA) 1 (U.S. Court of Appeals, 2nd Cir. 1970).

162. 272 F.2d 867; 123 U.S.P.Q. (BNA) 574 (U.S. Appeals Court, 9th Cir. 1959).

163. 855 F.2d 779; 8 U.S.P.Q. (BNA) 1263 (Appeals Court, 11th Cir. 1988).

164. *Otis Clapp v. Filmore Vitamin*, 754 F.2d 738; 225 U.S.P.Q. (BNA) 387 (7th Cir. 1984).

165. *Sands, Taylor & Wood v. Quaker Oats*, 24 U.S.P.Q. 2d 1001 (7th Cir. 1992).

166. 15 U.S.C.S. (2005) §1117(c).

167. *Gorenstein Enterprises, Inc. v. Quality Care-USA, Inc.*, 874 F.2d 431; 10 U.S.P.Q. 2d (BNA) 1762 (7th Cir. 1989); *Artmark-Chicago, Ltd. v. Mishan & Sons, Inc.*, 1992 U.S. Dist. LEXIS 12572 (N.D. Ill. 1992).

168. McCarthy (2005), Section 30:93.

169. Dratler (2005), Section 12.07[1](e).

170. Dratler (2005), Section 12.06[2](b).

171. 15 U.S.C.S. (2005) § 1117(a).

172. Michael A. Rosenhouse, *Annotation: Proper Measure and Elements of Damages for Misappropriation of Trade Secret*, American Law Reports 11 (1995).

173. *See Taco Cabana International, Inc. v. Two Pesos, Inc.*, 932 F.2d 1113; 19 U.S.P.Q. 2d (BNA) 1253 (5th Cir. 1991) for a typical listing based on Texas law.

174. James Pooley, *Trade Secrets*, (New York: Law Journal Press, 2005), 7-34 to 7-39.

175. *Telex Corp. v. IBM Corp.*, 510 F.2d 894 (10th Cir. 1975), *cert. dismissed*, 423 U.S. 802 (1975).

176. Pooley, *Trade Secrets*, 7-40 to 7-41. *See also Dozor Agency, Inc. v. Rosenberg*, 218 A.2d 583 (Pa. 1966) and *University Computing Co. v. Lykes-Youngstown Corp.*, 504 F.2d 518 (5th Cir. 1974).

177. Pooley, *Trade Secrets*, 7-41 to 7-42.

178. *Adolph Gottscho, Inc. v. American Marketing Corp*, 26 N.J. 229, 139 A.2d 281 (N.J. 1958).

179. Pooley, *Trade Secrets*, 7-42 to 7-43.

180. Ibid., 7-43 to 7-44.

181. Uniform Trade Secrets Act § 3(a) (1985).

182. 401 F. Supp. 1102 (E.D. Mich. 1975).

183. *See Telex Corp. v. I.B.M. Corp.*, 510 F.2d 894 (10th Cir. 1975), *cert. dismissed*, 423 U.S. 802 (1975); *Clark v. Bunker*, 453 F.2d 1006 (9th Cir. 1972); *Aladdin Mfg. Co. v. Mantle Lamp Co. of Am.*, 116 F.2d 708 (7th Cir. 1941).

LIST OF CASES

Abend v. MCA, Inc., 863 F.2d 1465, 1480, 9 U.S.P.Q. 2d 1337 (9th Cir. 1988)

Abeshouse v. Ultragraphics, Inc., 754 F.2d 467 (2d Cir. 1985)

Adolph Gottscho, Inc. v. American Marketing Corp, 26 N.J. 229, 139 A.2d 281 (N.J. 1958)

Adray v. Adry-Mart, 76 F.3d 984; 37 U.S.P.Q. 2d (BNA) 1872 (9th Cir. 1995)

Aiken, Hazen, Hoffman, Miller, P. C. v. Empire Construction Co., 542 F. Supp. 252, 264 (D. Neb. 1982)

Aktiebolaget Electrolux v. Armatron Int'l, Inc., 999 F.2d 1; 27 U.S.P.Q. 2d (BNA) 1460 (1st Cir. 1993)

Aladdin Mfg. Co. v. Mantle Lamp Co. of Am., 116 F.2d 708 (7th Cir. 1941)

Alpo Petfoods, Inc. v. Ralston-Purina Co., 997 F.2d 949, 27 U.S.P.Q. 2d (BNA) 1455 (D.C. Cir. 1993)

Artmark-Chicago, Ltd. V. Mishan & Sons, Inc., 1992 U.S. Dist. LEXIS 12572 (N.D. Ill. 1992)

Babbitt Electronic, Inc. v. Dynascan Corp., 38 F.3d 1161; 33 U.S.P.Q. 2d (BNA) 1001 (11th Cir. 1994)

BASF Corp. v. Old World Trading Co., Inc., 30 U.S.P.Q. 2d 1337 (N.D. Ill. 1992)

Basic Books, Inc. v. Kinko's Graphics Corporation, 758 F. Supp. 1522 (S.D.N.Y. 1991)

Big O Tire v. Goodyear , 561 F. 2d 1365; 195 U.S.P.Q. (BNA) 417 (10th Cir. 1977)

Bishop v. Wick, Copyright L. Rep. ¶ 26, 467 (N.D. Ill. 1988)

Blackman v. Hustler Magazine, Inc., 800 F.2d 1160, 1163-1164, 231 U.S.P.Q. 51 (D.C. Cir. 1986) (1909 Act) *cert. denied*, 446 U.S. 952 (1980)

Burger King Corp. v. Mason, 855 F.2d 779; 8 U.S.P.Q. (BNA) 1263 (Appeals Court, 11th Cir. 1988)

C. Elvin Feltner, Jr. v. Columbia Pictures Television, Inc., 523 U.S. 340 (1998)

Camel Hair and Cashmere Inst. v. Associated Dry Goods Corp., 799 F.2d 6; 231 U.S. P.Q. (BNA) 39 (1st Cir. 1986)

Carl Zeiss Stiftung v. VEB Carl Zeiss Jena, 433 F.2d 686 (2nd Cir. 1980)

Carter Products, Inc. v. Colgate-Palmolive Co., 214 F. Supp. 383; 136 U.S.P.Q. (BNA) 348; 136 U.S.P.Q. (BNA) 577 (Dist. of Maryland, 1963)

Cary Grant v. Esquire, Inc., 367 F. Supp. 876 (S.D.N.Y. 1973)

Clark v. Bunker, 453 F.2d 1006 (9th Cir. 1972)

Conopco, Inc. v. May Dept. Stores Co., 784 F. Supp. 648, 680–81, 24 U.S.P.Q. 2d 1721 (E.D. Mo.1992)

Cream Records, Inc. v. Joseph Schlitz Brewing Co., 864 F. 2d 668; 9 U.S.P.Q. 2d 1568 (9th Cir. 1989)

Cream Records, Inc. v. Joseph Schlitz Brewing Co., 754 F. 2d 826; 225 U.S.P.Q. 896 (9th Cir. 1985)

Cuisinarts, Inc. v. Robot-Coupe Int'l Corp., 580 F. Supp. 634; 222 U.S.P.Q. (BNA) 318 (S.D. N.Y. 1984)

DC Comics, Inc. v. Filmation Associates, 486 F. Supp. 1273; 206 U.S.P.Q. (BNA) 112 (S.D.N.Y. 1980)

Deltak, Inc. v. Advanced Systems, Inc., 767 F.2d 357; 226 U.S.P.Q. 919 (7th Cir. 1985)

Dive N' Surf, Inc. v. Anselowitz, 834 F. Supp. 379; Copy. L. Rep. (CCH) P27,193 (M.D. Fla. 1993)

Dozor Agency, Inc. v. Rosenberg, 218 A.2d 583 (Penn. 1966)

Estate of Vane v. The Fair, Inc., 849 F.2d 186 (5th Cir. 1988), *cert. denied*, 488 U.S. 1008, 109 S. Ct. 792, 102 L. Ed. 2d 783 (1989)

Fallaci v. New Gazette Literary Corp., 568 F. Supp. 1172, 1173 (S.D.N.Y. 1983)

Fitzgerald Publishing Co., Inc. v. Baylor Publishing Co., Inc., 807 F.2d 1110, 1115 (2d Cir. 1986), *aff'd*, 862 F.2d 304 (1988)

Frank Music Corp. v. Metro-Goldwyn-Mayer, Inc., 772 F.2d 505, 227 U.S.P.Q. 687 (9th Cir. 1985)

Frank Music Corp. v. Metro-Goldwyn-Mayer, Inc., 886 F.2d 1545; 12 U.S.P.Q. 2d (BNA) 1412 (9th Cir. 1989)

Fuller Products Co. v. Fuller Brush Co., 299 F.2d 772 (7th Cir. 1962)

Gaste v. Kaiserman, 863 F.2d 1061; 9 U.S.P.Q. 2d 1300 (2d Cir. 1988)

Georgia-Pacific Corp. v. United States Plywood Corp., 318 F. Supp. 1116, 1121 (S.D.N.Y. 1970); *aff'd*, 446 F.2d 225 (1971).

Gorenstein Enterprises, Inc. v. Quality Care-USA, Inc., 874 F.2d 431 10 U.S.P.Q. 2d (BNA) 1762 (7th Cir. 1989)

The Gillette Co. v. Wilkinson Sword, Inc., 1992 U.S. Dist. LEXIS 1265 (S.D.N.Y. 1992)

Grand Upright Music, Ltd. v. Warner Brothers Records Inc., 780 F. Supp. 182 (S.D.N.Y. 1991)

Holiday Inns, Inc. v. Airport Holiday Corp., 493 F. Supp. 1025; 212 U.S.P.Q. (BNA) 208 (N.D. Tex. 1980)

Harper & Row v. Nation Enterprises, 471 U.S. 539 (1985)

Harper House, Inc. v. Thomas Nelson Publishers, Inc., 4 U.S.P.Q. 2d 1987 (C.D. Cal. 1987)

Imperial Toy Corp. v. Goffa International Corp., 988 F. Supp. 617 (E.D.N.Y. 1997)

Jarvis v. A&M Records, 827 F. Supp. 282 (D.N.J. 1993)

Kamar International, Inc. v. Russ Berrie & Co., 752 F.2d 1326 (9th Cir. 1984)

Kewanee Oil Co. v. Bicron, 416 U.S. 470, 476 (1974)

Lauratex Textile Corp. v. Allton Knitting Mills, 519 F. Supp. 730, 733 (S.D.N.Y. 1981)

Lindy Pen Co. v. Bic Pen Corp., 982 F.2d 1400; 25 U.S.P.Q. 2d (BNA) 1570 (9th Cir. 1993)

Louis Vuitton S.A. v. Spencer Handbags Corp., 765 F.2d 966, 227 U.S.P.Q. (BNA) 377 (2nd Cir. 1985)

Lottie Joplin Thomas Trust v. Crown Publishers, Inc., 592 F.2d 651 (2d Cir. 1978)

Manufacturers Technologies, Inc. v. Cams, Inc., 728 F. Supp. 75, 80 (D. Conn. 1989)

Whelan Associates, Inc. v. Jaslow Dental Lab, Inc., 609 F. Supp. 1307, 1322, 225 U.S.P.Q. 156 (E.D. Pa. 1985)

Williams v. Arndt, 626 F. Supp. 571, 582, 227 U.S.P.Q. 614 (D. Mass. 1985)

Wolfe v. National Lead Co., 272 F.2d 867; 123 U.S.P.Q. (BNA) 574 (9th Cir. 1959)

Wow & Flutter Music v. Len's Tom Jones Tavern, Inc., 606 F. Supp. 554, 556 (W.D. N.Y. 1985)

BIBLIOGRAPHY

Abrams, Howard B. *The Law of Copyright.* Vol. 2, section 17:7. Eagen, MN:Thomson West, 2004.

American Heritage Dictionary (1993).

Besen, S., and L. Raskind. "An Introduction to the Law and Economics of Intellectual Property." *Journal of Economic Perspectives* 5(1991): 16.

Davis, Theodore H. Jr., R. Charles Henn Jr., and Christine M. Cason. "The Anticybersquatting Consumer Protection Act of 1999." *Georgia Bar Journal* 5 (February 2000).

Dratler, J. Jr. *Intellectual Property Law: Commercial, Creative, and Industrial Property.* New York: Law Journal Press, 2005, 1–15.

Goldstein, Paul. *Goldstein on Copyright.* New York: Aspen Publishers, 2005.

Goldscheider, Robert, John Jarosz, and Carla Malhern, "Use of the 25 Per Cent Rule in Valuing IP," *les Nouvelles,* December 2002: 123–133.

Grabowski, R. "Adventures in Cyberspace: Strategies for Securing and Protecting Your Firm's Domain Name." 17 (February 2000): 7.

Hall, C. "Renting Ideas." *Journal of Business* 64 (January 1991): 21–48.

Holmes, W. *Intellectual Property and Antitrust Law.* New York: Clark, Boardman, Collaghan, 1994, 3–14.

H.R. Rep. No. 1476, 94th Cong., 2d Sess., at 161 (1976).

Kane, Siegrun D., *Trademark Law; A Practitioner's Guide, Fourth Edition.* New York: Practicing Law Institute, 2004.

Kitch, E. "The Nature and Function of the Patent System." *Journal of Law & Economics* 20 (1977): 265.

Landes, W., and R. Posner. "An Economic Analysis of Copyright Law." *Journal of Legal Studies* 28 (1989): 325.

Landes, W., and R. Posner. *The Economic Structure of Intellectual Property Law.* Cambridge, MA: The Belknap Press of Harvard University Press, 2003.

Landes, W. and R. Posner. "Market Power In Antitrust Cases." *Harvard Law Review* 94 (March 1981): 935–96.

Lampman, David V. "COMMENT: 'A Prologue to a Farce or a Tragedy'? A Paradox, a Potential Clash: Digital Pirates, The Digital Millennium Copyright Act, The First Amendment & Fair Use." *Gonzaga Law Review* 38 (2002/2003) 367–407.

McCarthy, J. Thomas. *McCarthy on Trademarks and Unfair Competition.* Eagan, MN: Thomson West, 2005.

National Arbitration Forum Decision in Qwest Communications International v. QC Publishing, Claim Number FA0406000286032, September 23, 2004, www.arb-forum.com/domains/decision/286032.htm.

Nimmer, Melville B., and David Nimmer. *Nimmer on Copyright.* Newark, NJ: Matthew Bender, 2005.

Pooley, James. *Trade Secrets.* New York: Law Journal Press, 2005.

Rosenhouse, Michael A. *Annotation: Proper Measure and Elements of Damages for Misappropriation of Trade Secret. American Law Reports* 11 2004.

Ross, Terence P., *Intellectual Property Law-Damages and Remedies.* NewYork: Law Journal Press, 2005.

Samuelson, Paul, and William Nordhaus. *Economics*. 15th ed. New York : McGraw-Hill, 1995.

Schaffner, Derek J. "Note: The Digital Millennium Copyright Act: Overextension of Copyright Protection and the Unintended Chilling Effects on Fair Use, Free Speech, and Innovation." *Cornell Journal of Law and Public Policy*. 14 (Fall 2004): 148.

Siegrun, D. Kane. *Trademark Law, A Practitioner's Guide*. 4th ed. New York: Practising Law Institute, 2004. Current through Release No. 2, October 2004, section 1:1:1.

Tirole, Jean. *The Theory of Industrial Organization*. Cambridge, MA: MIT Press, 1998, 174–175.

Uniform Trade Secrets Act with 1985 Amendments.

U.S.C.S. Titles 15, 17, 22, 35.

U.S.P.T.O. Website.

INTELLECTUAL PROPERTY DAMAGES IN THE ENTERTAINMENT INDUSTRY

Deborah K. Bothun
Ronald B. Cushey
Bronwyn Dylla
Robert S. Knudsen

CONTENTS

The authors would like to acknowledge Benjamin King and Ernest Fierro for their research efforts and David Daly, Aron Levko, and Matthew Lieberman for their review and comments on previous drafts. Any errors or omissions are the responsibility of the authors.

Industry nomenclature defined in the appendix of the chapter appears in italics at the first appearance in the chapter.

21.1   INTELLECTUAL PROPERTY IN THE ENTERTAINMENT INDUSTRY

The basic legal standards, principles, and approaches to calculating damages related to intellectual property (IP) apply to the entertainment industry as in other industries. Characteristics unique to the entertainment industry include the number of property owners, the multiple and diverse revenue streams related to the same intellectual property, and profit calculation. New profit opportunities from an existing product arising from changes in technology, as well as the nature, terms, and conditions of licensing agreements, also set entertainment IP apart from other IP. Other chapters of this book discuss the principles and approaches to calculating damages in intellectual property cases (*see* Chapters 20 and 22). This chapter describes unique features of the entertainment industry that affect the calculation of damages and highlights how these features affect the application of typical approaches to damages assessment. The entertainment industry has many segments, and this chapter focuses on three of them: film, television, and music. Even though many other entertainment segments exist, from live theatre to video games, this chapter discusses the segments that have been the subject of most entertainment IP litigation.

Entertainment IP differs from IP in other industries. Although patents and trade secrets exist to protect the technological aspects of movie production—from camera equipment and processes to sound reproductions and special effect visuals—the primary forms of entertainment IP consist of trademarks and copyrights.

Entertainment IP differs from other types of IP with regard to its life cycle and the number of entities involved in its production. An entertainment IP can go through a long and costly development cycle, during which *participants* in the process gain rights to various future revenue-generating opportunities of the finished work. The finished work can then appear through multiple distribution channels that incur additional costs and add new participants who also acquire rights to the property. Contracts often allocate front-end costs to various revenue-generating sources that occur at the end of the initial cycle to calculate net profit. Participants or owners of entertainment intellectual property are often uninformed about revenues and costs and must rely on information from another party. The rapid change in technology has presented new avenues to realize income from existing entertainment properties, often not known or envisioned at the time of development. License agreements often contain not only the transfer of IP rights but also the terms for rights to merchandising, distribution, themed events, and the like, which participants need to consider separately from the IP.

21.2   CALCULATING PROFIT IN THE ENTERTAINMENT INDUSTRY

To calculate lost profits or profits to be disgorged in an IP infringement matter related to entertainment, the expert must understand how entertainment companies calculate profit to stakeholders involved in the creation and distribution of the entertainment property. In fact, some stakeholders do not refer to the value they receive as "profit." This section summarizes various definitions of profit used by entertainment companies. In this industry, the definitions of profit (often specified in contracts) can vary across transactions and often differ from standard definitions of accounting profit.

(a) Film. Defining the term "profit" may present the most complex issue in the film industry. Casual observers have cynically viewed Hollywood-style accounting as a method for big studios to cheat individual talent from royalty payments and other earnings. The entertainment industry has complex accounting procedures. It involves different entities (profit participants) as well as *windows* (i.e., markets) through which one sells the intellectual property or delivers it to the consumer, such as theatres, home video, television, and so on. The different entities can include the talent, their representatives, production staff, production studio, distributors, and exhibitors. Entertainment IP realizes revenues for the lifetime of the property through multiple windows. Recent industry trends have seen rapidly changing windows, such as shorter durations and overlaps in timing. Changing technology creates new windows that lead to more channels of distribution.

One frequently hears of film participants receiving a percentage of the gross or net. Hollywood's use of these terms seldom has the same meaning that an accountant or economist would ascribe to gross profit or net profit. Hollywood "net" and "gross" derive their meaning from contractual arrangements, not from generally accepted accounting principles (GAAP). For example, studios can charge their costs such as overhead and distribution to a film at a contractually specified fee or percentage, as opposed to charged or allocated based on actual cost. This does not mean that entertainment companies do not prepare financial statements using GAAP, but rather that profit participants in films depend on a contractually defined "gross" or "net." Common meanings for gross and net exist within the industry, however. For example, the term *gross proceeds* appears in contracts to describe source receipts from distribution in each window. In general, gross proceeds means the remainder after *exhibitors* (i.e., companies owning cinemas) take their share of the box office receipts. Powerful celebrity talent often negotiate contracts as *gross participants* or adjusted gross participants, but more often film participants receive percentages based on net profit.

The definition of *net profit* became the crux of a well-publicized case between Paramount Studios and the humorist Art Buchwald.[1] Art Buchwald was a well-known writer when in 1990 he and movie producer Alain Bernheim successfully sued Paramount Studios for breach of contract in *Buchwald v. Paramount Pictures Corp.* Buchwald and Bernheim charged that Paramount based the 1988 film *Coming to America* on Buchwald's story idea, "King for a Day." Paramount had optioned Buchwald's treatment of this story idea in 1983 but abandoned the project. In 1986, Warner Brothers optioned Buchwald's treatment. The following year, Paramount began to develop a film that resembled Buchwald's story idea but instead credited it to the actor and comedian Eddie Murphy. Warner Brothers then cancelled its version of the Buchwald project because of Paramount's film. When Paramount released *Coming to America* in 1988, it credited the story to Eddie Murphy. Buchwald received neither payment nor credit.

In the first phase of the trial, the court found that Paramount had breached its contract with Buchwald for withholding net profit payments to Buchwald. In the second phase, the court heard the method of calculating *net profits* earned by the film. Paramount argued that despite the film's $350 million in revenues, the studio had spent so much on development and marketing that it made no net profit as calculated by the formula specified in Buchwald's contract. Paramount provided accounting evidence supporting this claim.[2] Buchwald reasoned that claiming that the film had earned zero net profit was "unconscionable," and the court agreed. In the end, the court awarded Buchwald and Bernheim $150,000 and $750,000, respectively, in damages.[3] Paramount appealed the decision, and the parties settled for an undisclosed amount.

The Buchwald case has significance because it brought to the public's attention the method employed by the film industry to calculate net profit. Some commentators believed that this case would be a watershed affecting the net profit formulas in profit participation contracts because the main issue related to studios' disregard of accounting principals to calculate net profit. By contrast, other commentators saw the settlement as a victory for the studios because the judge made no ruling about the procedure for calculating net profit.[4]

Indeed, other cases since Buchwald have also focused on the calculation of profit in film.[5] These include a suit filed in May 1995 by Winston Groom, the author of *Forrest Gump*, against Paramount when a December 1994 financial statement used to calculate net profit receipts showed that the fourth highest grossing film as of 1995 had a $62 million loss.[6] Groom had contracted with Paramount to receive 3 percent of the film's net profits. At the end of 1994, the film had earned more than $350 million at the box office domestically and internationally, but the studio reported a negative net profit after subtracting its distribution fee of 32 percent and about $60 million to the gross percentage participants, such as Tom Hanks. At the time Groom began to question *Forrest Gump's* financial statements, the studio believed that the film would eventually make a profit and that Groom would receive payment from this project. Thus, this dispute also highlighted the timing of revenues received by an entertainment IP from various windows, which affects when net profit participants receive payment from the IP. The parties in the *Forrest Gump* case settled for an undisclosed amount.[7]

The courts have shied away from rulings that alter the traditional profit models in the entertainment industry or define how it calculates profit. More than 10 years after *Buchwald*, the courts ruled that the studio does not have a fiduciary duty to show the support behind their calculation of net profits. Fiduciary duty is defined as the obligation to act in the best interest of a secondary party, in this instance the profit participant. In *Gary K. Wolf et al. v. Walt Disney*, the novelist who wrote *Who Framed Roger Rabbit?* sued the studio for breach of contract and breach of fiduciary duty.[8] Wolf had assigned Disney the rights to the novel as well as all the Roger Rabbit characters. Disney transformed the property into a very successful movie, *Who Framed Roger Rabbit?*, which included film receipts, merchandising, and theme park rides. In exchange for the rights to the property, Disney agreed to pay Wolf a percentage of net profits from a motion picture and 5 percent of any future gross receipts earned from merchandising or other exploitation of the Roger Rabbit characters. Wolfe contended that each time he attempted to exercise audit rights, Disney failed to provide access to pertinent records. In response to the complaint, Disney filed a demurrer, which the court sustained, to the breach of fiduciary duty claim. The court reasoned that distribution agreements do not create a fiduciary relation between the product's owner (the author) and the distributor (in this case, the movie studio).

How can seemingly successful films incur losses? As this chapter will show, a film that is profitable for a studio will not necessarily provide a share in proceeds to all profit participants. Even though some films have box office returns that are less than production costs, more often the revenues generated throughout the life cycle of a film provide a return to senior participants but fall short of providing net profit to the participants positioned last in line for a share of revenues.

To analyze a feature film profit calculation, we first need to understand the components of revenue and costs and how a cost for one participant can become a gain for another participant. Sections 21.2(a)(ii) through (vii) discuss typical revenue received by a film for each of the current windows and the costs associated with these revenues. The film industry is evolving, and calculating revenues and profits for each window will depend on the time since the release date of the film at issue, referred to as age.

(i) Theatrical Revenues. *Box office revenues* are receipts obtained when the public purchases tickets at theaters. Contractual arrangements first divide box office receipts between exhibitors and distributors. The industry refers to the companies that own the theaters, numbering approximately 35,000 in the United States and Canada, as *exhibitors. Distributors* typically prepare the film stock and provide the films to theaters. Distributors can be a division of a studio or a third-party company. The large studios and smaller *independent* companies produce film product but sometimes also distribute their own product into the markets, often creating a confusing situation in which it is unclear who is actually producing and distributing a feature film.[9]

Distributor-exhibitor agreements define box office receipts and *theatrical rentals*, (i.e., the portion that exhibitors remit to distributors from box office receipts). Exhibitors receive the remainder after remitting theatrical rentals to the distributor. When the press reports that a film earns over $200 million at the box office, the distributor receives only a portion of this amount as theatrical rentals. Compared with distributors that are separate from the studio, when studios take on the distribution role, they typically garner more distribution market share and better pricing as a result of a higher volume of product distributed.

Calculating the *theatrical rental* amount paid to distributors can prove complicated. The industry usually computes each week of theatrical release on a seven-day basis initiated from the first day of theatrical exhibition. The percentage amount of box office receipts paid as theatrical rentals usually declines each week per the contract. As a result, the exhibitor often prefers a quality film that may have legs (i.e., one that remains in the theaters for a longer period of time). The amount that distributors ultimately receive from exhibitors can vary. Depending on the size of the distributor and items such as quality of past and future feature films and film genre, a distributor can typically receive from 40 to 60 percent of the box office proceeds throughout the life of the theatrical release, but the sharing ultimately depends on the seven-day calculations. Because the calculation of theatrical rentals is often based on oral agreements and is subject to subsequent negotiation, disputes can arise on this issue. The outcome of these negotiations, which are based on actual box office performance and length of theatrical run, can differ from the results of the originally negotiated seven-day rates. Distributors also receive theatrical rentals from foreign releases of the film.[10] Exhibit 21-1 illustrates the flow of proceeds from exhibitors to distributors to production companies for the theatrical window.

(ii) Theatrical Costs. The major cost items for the production and distribution of a feature film include distribution fees (cost to producer, but revenue to distributor),

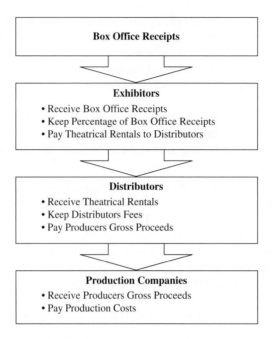

This simplified example is for illustrative purposes only. For instance, many studios have both distribution and production companies.

Source: PricewaterhouseCoopers Analysis.

Exhibit 21-1.   Framework of Entity Arrangements in Film

distribution and marketing expenses (cost to distributor), negative cost (cost to producer to acquire the rights to and then produce the film), and interest (cost to producer).[11] *Distribution fees* are a percentage that the distributor deducts and retains from theatrical rentals. Distribution fees can vary. For *Coming to America*, they amounted to 35 percent of theatrical rentals. Although this percentage was typical for its time, it is usually lower today, depending on factors such as the size of the distributor and the film genre.

Distributors incur costs when preparing the film for distribution. *Prints and Advertising* (P&A) costs relate to the preparation of the film print that goes to the theater for exhibition and advertising costs associated with the box office and home video releases. Whereas distribution fees are a *contracted* cost to net profit participants, albeit a revenue source to the distributor, distribution expenses and marketing are *actual* costs that the distributor incurs and allocates. Depending on the nature of the feature film and the anticipated audience and theaters showing the film, the number of prints can range from 1 to up to 5,000. Although the cost of producing a print has remained relatively steady, average advertising costs for films have steadily increased. As a result, total P&A costs have increased from approximately $6 million per film in 1985 to approximately $34 million per film in 2004 (*see* Exhibit 21-2). In addition, the distributor deducts distribution fees from theatrical rentals to recoup its costs of distributing the film. Third-party gross participation is distributed from theatrical rentals. After making these deductions, the distributor remits the remainder to the production company as the producer's gross proceeds. The production company deducts negative costs and direct and indirect production costs from these proceeds.

Exhibit 21-2 shows the trend in negative costs of producing a feature film. One can divide *negative costs* among direct production costs, indirect production costs, and overhead. Direct production costs related to a film include expenditures on the acquisition of the film rights, talent, and producers. Direct production costs also include sound stage, lab, location, set construction, wardrobe, interest, and other financing costs. The average negative cost of a feature film produced in the United States has increased from approximately $17 million in 1985 to approximately $64 million in 2004. Higher costs for talent and special effects contribute to the increase in production cost during the 1990s.

Indirect production cost items include interest, talent participations, and residuals. The studio charges interest to a film because investing in the film is an alternative to other interest-bearing investments. Interest can accrue on negative cost, overhead, and profit participation payments.[12] Talent and nontalent participations are the costs associated with agreements in which the talent receives a percentage of the contractually defined and agreed-upon revenues or profits rather than or in addition to a flat fee or salary. The industry defines *residuals* as amounts owed to unions and guilds as a result of revenues from domestic and foreign distribution channels other than theatrical exhibition. The parties calculate these amounts per agreements with the union and guild organizations.

Finally, a studio charges overhead to the film. The contract specifies the overhead rate, typically calculated as a percentage of the direct production cost,

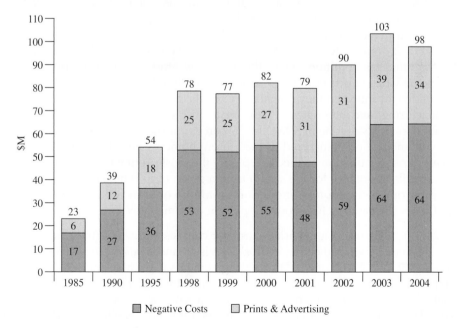

Source: Motion Picture Association Worldwide Market Research. *US Entertainment Industry: 2002 MPA Market Statistics*, pp. 19-20 and *US Entertainment Industry 2004 MPA Market Statistics*, pp. 19-20.

Exhibit 21-2.   Average MPAA Member Company Movie Production Costs

considered to cover all studio overhead. The overhead percentage can vary and is a negotiation point in the contract.

(iii) Home Video Revenues.   Revenues derived from home video generally include receipts from the sale of a product to distributors, wholesalers, or retailers. The industry categorizes distribution to the consumer as either rental or sell-through (i.e., purchase). Distributors usually sell the items as either Digital Video Discs (DVDs) or Video Home System (VHS) cassettes and release them into the market approximately three to six months after the date of initial theatrical release. A current DVD title costs about $5 to manufacture, market, and distribute; it sells for about $15 wholesale.[13] The popularity of home video sales in the past few years has resulted in home video revenues for a film that often exceed box office revenues. The ratio can be as high as two to one, with exceptions exceeding this ratio. Studios also distribute films through services that provide online access to videos through pay-per-view, download-to-own (also known as digital sell-through), and on a subscription basis.

(iv) Home Video Costs.   Home video costs relate to the manufacture and duplication of the home video unit (VHS or DVD) and the packaging and shipping of the units to the wholesaler or retailer. In the past, studios outsourced distribution of home video to other companies and received only about 20 percent of these revenues. Today, however, most studios distribute home video through an in-house department. Studio-distributors will usually include only 20 percent of total home video unit sale revenues for participation calculations. In other words, the studios recognize only 20 percent of revenue from the home video window as revenue to the film's P&L for calculating payment to net profit participants. This 20 percent figure represents a carryover from the inception of the home video market when most distributors outsourced their home video sales efforts and incurred costs to outside manufacturers. The tradition has continued even though many studios-as-distributors manage their home video efforts in-house.[14] Studios claim that the remaining 80 percent of home video revenue that they now receive offsets the costs of hardware, marketing, manufacturing, and other items. Now that most studios retain the home video distribution rights for themselves, the 80 percent portion most likely exceeds the relatively modest costs incurred in the mature home video sales and distribution process.[15] As a result, home video is typically the most profitable revenue stream of all the available sources for the studio from a given film. Whereas studio *ultimates* (i.e., estimated lifetime profit and loss for a film) would include all revenues, net profit for participants includes only 20 percent of home video revenue.

(v) Television.   The television market currently consists of pay-TV (basic and premium) and free TV, which includes *network* television and *syndication.* Studios arrange to release films aired on pay-TV through agreements with cable and satellite television providers typically within 12 months of initial theatrical release. The license fee usually involves a minimum negotiated amount with increases for specified viewer levels. Through arrangements with consumers' cable and satellite providers, films are broadcast on premium pay-TV channels, such as HBO or Showtime (or Canal Plus and BSkyB internationally). In general, pay-TV requires that the studio support the film with (1) a minimum advertising amount and (2) a minimum number of showings on (3) a specified number of theatrical screens for (4) a minimum number of weeks to try to ensure the film's financial potential. The agreement calculates the

purchase price, or license fee, based on the amount of box office gross sales, with a step formula increasing payments for various levels of box office obtained.

Network television in the United States comprises network affiliated stations and independent stations. Studios do not sell packages of films to networks but prefer to sell them individually at a market price that reflects box office receipts. Networks exhibit the films 30 to 36 months after the film's initial theatrical release. The syndication process involves previously exhibited films that various buyers relicense, including independent television stations. Unlike the initial network sale, syndicators purchase films in packages with other films, at the price that the current market will bear. Studios use a subjective allocation of the package price to individual films, based on a rating system of all the films in the package. The ability to exhibit a film through syndication generally begins approximately five years after its initial theatrical release.

Video on Demand (VOD) and subscription VOD (SVOD) offers another window of revenues for films. VOD allows users to select and watch video content over a channel via a network, such as a cable or satellite TV network. Unlike the traditional Pay-Per-View (PPV) system, VOD users can typically pause, fast-forward, and rewind VOD movies. In principle, viewers could watch a selected movie whenever they wanted and how often they wanted. Industry analysts project significant growth of VOD revenues. The leading distributor of VOD and PPV reported a revenue increase of 150 percent in 2004 from 2003, with expectations of a further doubling of revenues in 2005.[16] The accounting and consulting firm of PricewaterhouseCoopers LLP projects that aggregate annual spending on VOD in the United States will grow by about 16 percent annually from 2004 to 2009.[17] Price per film for viewers has held steady through 2005, at around $2.50 for older titles and $4.00 for recent releases; the revenue split between studios and cable companies can vary. Through 2005, studios received about 50 percent of PPV revenues and 60 percent of VOD movie revenues.[18]

(vi) Ancillary Markets.   Films also produce revenue in a variety of ancillary categories that include nontheatrical film rental—such as airlines, military bases, schools, and college campuses—as well as merchandising, music, and other miscellaneous areas. Studios usually base the nontheatrical license fee on a fixed flat fee or a per-viewer negotiated amount. Merchandising, music, and other miscellaneous revenue streams vary depending on the quality and genre of a film, ranging from tens of millions of dollars to zero. License fees vary per film, and the parties negotiate these on a per-film basis. Another relatively new, albeit lucrative, revenue source lies in licensing film rights to video game developers. Owners of film rights typically receive royalties on a per unit basis. Video game publishers typically pay an advance against future royalties, which can be up to 15 percent of projected sales to retailers for most games. Because developing a game requires much time, the parties negotiate these contracts during the film's production and base the fees on expectations of how audiences will receive the film.

(vii) Participant Compensation.   This section has discussed revenue and cost items that affect a film's profitability. However, the studios do not use this profit number as the basis for calculating percentages to allocate profit to participants. The film industry applies accounting treatment to certain key film profit and loss components that result in differences between accrual and cash effects. Exhibit 21-3 provides an example of the timing of some of the main revenue and cost components,

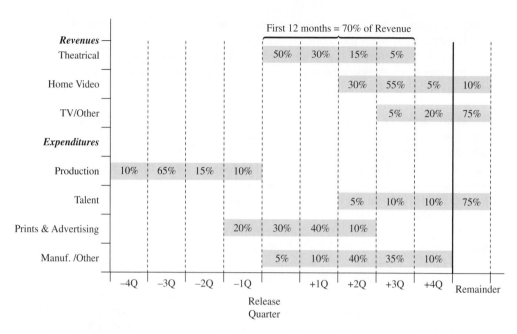

Source: PricewaterhouseCoopers Analysis.

Exhibit 21-3.   Typical Timing of Film Revenue and Costs

highlighting the capital-intensive nature of the film production process during which significant expenditures (production costs) occur well before the receipt of revenues from exhibition.

The discussion of revenue and costs returns us to the question of how a studio can show profit for a film on its income statement but fail to generate profit to all of its participants. The contracted allocations of these proceeds complicate the calculation of receipts to profit participants from the numerous windows. As Section 21.2(a) mentions, powerful celebrity talent at times can negotiate *first-dollar gross participation* even though most other participants receive only net profit participation.[19] Exhibit 21-4 demonstrates the potential differences between payments to net profit participants and those received by gross participants. In this scenario, the film did not earn enough to offset the deductions calculated before the *net participant* receives a percentage of net receipts.

(viii) Film Example.   To see how the concepts discussed above would be used in a typical damages calculation, consider the following example. A film studio and a screenwriter have a dispute. The writer alleges that the studio's most recent blockbuster movie was based on his screenplay, which he accuses the studio of stealing. Indeed, many of the characters and settings in the film resemble those in his screenplay. To date, the film has grossed $200 million in the domestic and international box office, and the studio will release it on home video worldwide in several weeks. The film has not yet aired on television, but the studio has negotiated rights with both a major free-TV network and a major pay-TV network.

The screenwriter is suing the studio under § 106 of the 1976 Copyright Act for damages arising from the alleged theft of his work. Whereas most screenwriters

Domestic Box Office	$ 150.0
Domestic Video Revenues	187.5
International Box Office	150.0
International Video Revenues	90.0

Gross-Based Calculations

Revenues ($m)

Theatrical Rentals

Domestic (53% × $150.0)	$ 79.5
International (43% × $150.0)	64.5

Home Video

Domestic Royalty (20% × $187.5)	37.5
International Royalty (20% × $90.0)	18.0

Domestic TV

Pay TV	21.0
Syndicated	5.0
Network	23.0

International TV

Pay TV	23.0
Syndicated	23.0

Other (licensing, music, etc.)	5.0
Total Revenues	$ 299.5

Gross Talent Participation Amount

Total Revenues	$ 299.50
Gross Participants%	× 10%
Amount Due Gross Participant	$ 30.0

Net-Based Calculations

Costs ($m)

Fees

Domestic Theatrical & TV[a]	$ 38.6
Domestic Video[b]	11.3
International[c]	51.4

Costs

Negative Costs	75.0
Domestic P&A	42.0
International P&A	35.0
Domestic Home Video Costs	N/A
International Home Video Costs	N/A
Residuals	18.0
Talent Participation	30.0
Total Costs	$ 301.3

Net Profit ($299.5 − $301.3)	$ (1.8)

Net Talent Participation Amount

Net Profit	$ (1.8)
Net Participant %	× 10%
Amount Due Net Participant	$ -

a 30% of $79.5 (domestic theatrical) + 30% of $49.0 (Total domestic TV revenue)
b 30% of $37.5 (Domestic video)
c 40% of $128.5 (International theatrical, video and TV)

Exhibit 21-4. Example of Calculations for Film Gross versus Net Participants (all figures in U.S. $Millions)

sell their rights upfront to a studio through a transfer of copyright, the plaintiff claims that he would have been a net profit participant. In the past, the screenwriter had negotiated deals with the studio for previous scripts, for which he received a percentage of net profit. The expert must calculate lost profits to the screenwriter. But for the alleged theft of the screenplay, what would the screenwriter have received from the studio as compensation for the screenplay?

To evaluate the potential lost profits, the expert needs to understand the contractual relations that the studio has executed for this film, including the credited screenwriter. The expert will need to examine the typical arrangements negotiated between the studio and its writers. To do so, the expert would examine current contracts between the studio and screenplay writers as well as the studio and the plaintiff. The expert should have familiarity with the various film exploitation windows and profits captured by the studio. The expert should also review contracts between the studio and distributors and other participants.

A thorough analysis would include a review of financial information relevant to the film, such as the film *ultimate*. The ultimate presents projected revenue and costs for a film across all windows and markets. The ultimate also tracks actual revenue and cost incurred, including participation expense. Exhibit 21-5 illustrates the revenue and cost items the expert would consider to calculate the film's net profit basis (of which the plaintiff claims he would have a share).

The expert should consider the following:

- Theatrical
    - Definition and calculation of theatrical rentals, per the contract between the distributor and the exhibitor.
    - Definition and calculation of distribution fees and expenses recouped by the distributor.
    - Marketing expenditures by the distributor.
    - Net revenue from theatrical rentals received by the studio from the distributor.
    - Production costs to the studio.
    - Box office bonus or break-even payments to talent.
    - Gross profit participants (typically the most select, A-list talent).
- Home video
    - Revenue allocation.
    - Assessment of revenue from sales and rental.
    - Trends in the relation between box office and home video revenue.
    - Costs do not relate to the calculation of net profits because the studio allocates only 20 percent of home video gross revenues to the film.
- Television
    - Licensing rights and fees from free and pay-television networks, per agreements.
- Merchandising
    - Licensing rights and fees from consumer products, publishing, and other deals, per agreements.
- Back-end participants
    - Ascertain whether any back-end participants receive their share prior to the net profit distribution to the screenwriter.

Exhibitors

Revenues
△ Percentage of gross receipts

Costs
△ Cost of exhibits

Film Distributor

Revenues
△ Distribution fees
  • Domestic
  • Foreign

Costs
△ Distribution costs
△ Prints and advertisements

TV Distributor

Revenues
△ Distribution fees
  • Domestic
  • Foreign

Studio

Revenues
△ Percentage of theatrical
△ Percentage of foreign theatrical
△ Pay TV
△ Home video
△ Nontheatrical
△ Free TV
△ Consumer products

Costs
△ Negative costs
△ Direct
△ Indirect costs (talent)
△ Gross participation deferments
△ Net profit participation

Source: PricewaterhouseCoopers Analysis.

Exhibit 21-5. Framework of Revenues and Costs in Film

(b) Television

(i) Free TV.   The landscape of television has changed in recent years. In the past, the three original networks—ABC, NBC, and CBS—provided most television shows; however, cable and new networks (such as Fox, UPN, and The WB) and Spanish language networks (such as Univision) have increased the popularity of their programming. Free TV networks aim to find interesting content to maximize their viewership and sell advertisers access to these viewers.[20] These advertisements provide networks with revenues, which fund the production of programming. Industry observers define *network* television as the Big Three: CBS, NBC, and ABC—and more recently as the Big Four, including Fox. The four networks have similar structures. Each network provides owned and independent affiliate stations with a regular schedule of programming throughout the day for *dayparts*—primetime, daytime, and late-night—as well as news and sports.

Network television can obtain its programming from three sources:

1. Intracompany distribution, such as Viacom (CBS), Disney (ABC), and Fox (Fox)
2. Third-party producers
3. Movie studios, which have separate television production and distribution divisions

Primetime television shows often have negative margins in the first airing of the program until the production companies *recoup* costs through *syndication* and international licensing. According to Fritz Attaway, general counsel for the Motion Picture Association of America (MPAA), the average cost of producing a half-hour situation comedy rose from approximately $994,000 in 2000 to $1.2 million in 2003 per episode.[21]

Networks receive revenues from commercial advertising during the broadcast of the show. Prices for advertising spots vary depending on the number of viewers of a show. For instance, in 2004, Fox sold a 30 second spot on *American Idol* for about $660,000, whereas a 30 second spot on *Smallville* on The WB sold for about $110,000.[22] Networks charge less for local advertising and commercials airing during nonprimetime slots.

The television industry measures the number of viewers through ratings, defined as estimates of the size of a television audience relative to the total television viewership, expressed as a percentage.[23] Shows with better ratings command prices at higher cost per thousand viewers (*CPMs*) (as measured by Nielsen Media Research) because of greater advertiser demand for these spots. Advertisers have an interest in shows with higher ratings because more potential buyers will see their commercials. Furthermore, advertisers often target and pay a premium for programming viewed more by certain demographics, depending on the product they advertise. Recently, the accuracy of Nielsen's measurement system has come under fire, and the company is trying new methods to calculate viewership.

Advertisers negotiate with networks for airtime on primetime television shows. The most watched shows command the highest advertising revenue by the networks. Many advertisers buy large amounts of advertising time in advance of the season to ensure spots on programming with desirable audiences. In *upfront buying*, networks offer advertisers *avails* (i.e., time slots) at discounted prices months before the season begins. Networks begin to sell advertising time on primetime shows in May, just after announcing the schedule for the fall season, and again six months later. The network and the advertiser negotiate the CPM, the list of shows, the dates, and the guaranteed rating. The network sells the remaining spots—most often the least desirable programming for advertisers—closer to program airtime in the *scatter* market.

The industry calculates advertising revenues with the following formula:

$$\text{Advertising Revenues} = (\text{Ratings}) \times (\text{National Clearance}) \times (\text{VPS}) \times (\text{CPM}) \quad (1)$$

where

$$\begin{aligned}
\text{National clearance} &= \text{the percentage of markets that will air the show} \\
\text{VPS} &= \text{viewers per television set in the target demographic} \\
\text{CPM} &= \text{cost per thousand viewers}
\end{aligned}$$

In addition to selling airtime to commercial advertisers, networks buy airtime from their affiliate local stations. Typically, the smaller the market in which an affiliate operates, the greater the percentage of its total revenues that come from network compensation, known as *netcomp*. For the major networks, a typical netcomp formula considers

- Number of commercials per hour
- Ratio of commercials sold nationally compared with locally
- Daypart
- Size and demographic of the audience
- Market size
- Signal strength of the station relative to others
- Length of the program's running time[24]

As with their affiliated network, local stations' main source of revenue comes from selling advertising time. Local stations have airtime in slots that the network leaves open during and between programming and slots available on nonnetwork shows, typically outside of primetime. Commercial time purchased from a local television station is known as the *spot* market. Advertising sales on local television often involve large packages of commercials in many time slots so that advertisers can reach desired demographic groups. Advertisers typically target specific markets and their advertising agency contacts stations in the markets to make an avail request. An avail request will specify the time period, the targeted demographic, the airtime, and the amount of money the advertiser wants to pay.[25] Prices for commercial airtime rely on market conditions, and prices vary accordingly. They also relate to a program's ratings and viewer demographics. Gross sales of commercial time vary by market and across stations within markets.

Affiliates of the major networks have less available time for local advertising sales than do off-network affiliates, such as The WB, since the major networks sell more time directly to advertisers. The available time for local advertising of network affiliates occurs during the news or syndicated programming. *Barter* transactions also reduce a local station's inventory of available commercial time. In a barter deal, a syndicator will provide a program for no fee to the local station but will receive in return advertising slots during the show.

Changes in technology threaten the current advertising system discussed here. Section 21.3(c) explains these changes and some of the ways that networks plan to adapt to these challenges.

(ii) Cable TV.   Cable networks, such as ESPN and CNN, have a revenue model different from that of network television. Large media companies own most cable networks, which the industry categorizes as either basic cable, expanded cable, or pay networks. Basic cable airs commercials during its programming; expanded cable companies and the pay networks (e.g., HBO and Showtime) air shows without commercial advertising and hence charge a premium to their viewers—the cable and satellite subscribers. Established basic cable networks receive a monthly per subscriber license fee from the cable or satellite operators, known as *multiple system operators* (*MSOs*) as well as revenue from commercial advertising. In summary, basic cable networks receive revenue from MSOs and commercial advertising; expanded and pay cable networks receive revenues from premiums charged to cable subscribers through the MSOs.

New networks sometimes pay MSOs to feature their station in their lineup. For instance, Discovery Communications reportedly paid Telecommunications, Inc. (TCI), a cable MSO, $50 million to launch the network Animal Planet.[26] Pay cable networks, such as HBO and Showtime, sell their services to operators at a wholesale price, which the operators then mark up and sell to their subscribers.[27]

(iii) Syndication.   Syndication typically refers to reruns of shows after they have aired in primetime network television. The major networks sell hit broadcast series into off-network syndication typically after the show has completed four seasons in primetime network television. Production companies can also create original shows for off-network syndication. Syndicators are distributors of syndicated programming, and production studios receive a portion of the fees that syndicators receive for advertising spots during the show's off-network run.[28] Exhibit 21-6 illustrates the relations between the key entities in television.

Producers create some television series for airing in their first run on syndication. Examples of first-run syndicated shows include *Xena: Warrior Princess* and *Mutant X.* First-run syndication is booked as episodes air. Hence, first-run syndication is more predictable than off-network syndication and offers a more stable source of revenue to the show. First-run shows are syndicated to television stations and sometimes to cable networks. Because they own most television stations, entertainment conglomerates share in the first-run syndication revenues.[29]

Syndicators typically finance program distribution through a cash and barter system. The cash payment comes from the station or station group to the syndicator. The barter side of the arrangement gives the syndicator the right to sell commercial airtime in the program. In other words, the station barters the value of the airtime by foregoing potential revenue from advertising dollars (which the syndicator now receives), rather than paying all cash for the program.

Through barter arrangements, syndicators acquire commercial airtime to sell to advertisers. To charge high CPMs, a syndicator must guarantee a specific number of viewers of a key demographic to advertisers. Syndicators do not receive additional payment from advertisers if they overdeliver on the ratings of the show, although future fees may be negotiated upward in renewals.

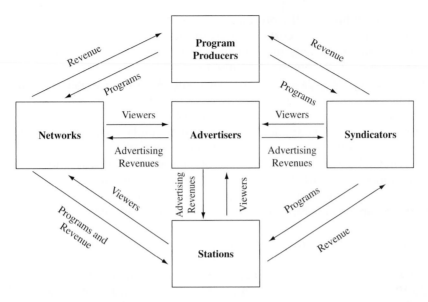

Source: Adapted from Bruce M. Owen, Jack H. Beebe, and Willard G. Manning, Jr., *Television Economics*, Lexington: Heath, 1974.

Exhibit 21-6.   Key Entities in the Television Industry

(iv) Foreign Sales.   The international distribution group of the production studio or the domestic syndication company (if the program was produced independently) distributes network shows to foreign buyers. Studios sell nonsyndicated and syndicated television series to international markets through license fees, which they contract on a per episode basis, one season at a time.

(v) Ancillary Markets.   As in film, television programming also receives revenues from ancillary markets. For instance, some studios release popular television programming on home video and sell related merchandising products. Home video is becoming a lucrative market for television production studios. A recent report stated that television programming makes up about 25 percent of all DVD sales, or about $4 billion annually.[30] Consumer interest in purchasing DVDs of favorite programming also seems to be growing; in the fall of 2005, sales of TV-DVD units were reported to be 26 percent higher than that of a comparable period in 2004.[31]

(vi) Recoupment.   A calculation of profits to a television show would consider the entities involved in bringing the show to market (the producer and the distributor) and the multiple windows in which these entities distribute the television product. Television distribution deals involve multiple investing parties. At the simplest level, the producer negotiates with the distributor to sell and market the property. The producer typically licenses a distributor to sell a property in a specific territory for a particular time, and the distributor in turn receives a percentage of revenues as a fee and reimbursement of certain distribution expenses. The distributor recoups any advance made by the producer, that is, it recovers the initial investment made into the property.

When a party finances the production of a program, the arrangement calls for the recoupment of certain costs incurred by the financing party. For instance, a television network recoups investments in its programs by selling commercial advertising time.[32] Recoupment comes from gross revenues. The calculations increase in complexity as the investment involves more recoupable parties and different levels of investment by the parties.

A successful television program generates revenue for the producer from various revenue streams divided into different amounts to calculate recoupment. For instance, the producer of one property can receive an advance from a distributor covering domestic syndication and another advance from a second distributor covering foreign sales. In this scenario, the distributors would recoup their initial investment only from the markets and territories in which they market the property. Arrangements can also tie revenue streams with the revenues from one market cross-subsidizing the costs in another market.

When calculating profit to different participants, one must ask, "What gets recouped?" Parties to a contract consider costs such as distribution, production, and advances as typical recoupment items and negotiate other items, such as overhead, interest, and indirect costs. With every transfer of recouped costs, revenues shift from the amount shared by net profit participants (*back-end participants*) to recoupment participants (who receive their disbursements from gross revenue to recoup their costs). Back-end participants receive a portion of net profits after recoupments and disbursements to gross revenue participants.

(vii) Television Example.   A copyright dispute arises between an independent film studio and the producers and distributors of a new hit television show. The film studio alleges that the new television program was based on one of their small film releases from 10 years ago. The independent studio owns the copyright of the 10–year old film and argues that this material was used improperly to create the new television program. Under § 106 of the 1976 Copyright Act, the independent studio is suing the television studio and distributor of the new program. In this example, the plaintiff is asking for the disgorgement of profits from the producers (a television studio) and the distributor of the television program as damages. The plaintiff also argues that it was in the process of developing a television show based on the concept of the independent film and now this opportunity has been lost by the film studio because it aired the allegedly infringing television show. The plaintiff will also argue, therefore, that it is entitled to lost profits.

The plaintiff's counsel has asked the expert to calculate profits to the television studio and distributor resulting from this program. To calculate the profit to the infringing television program, the expert will need to understand the contractual arrangements between the parties involved in creating the program. Contracts between the producer and distributor and between the producer and any other parties involved will contain this information. Typically, these agreements state the distribution of proceeds to the profit participants. Agreement terms include the percentage of distribution fee, how to recoup participant costs, the definition of the remaining profit, if any (sometimes referred to as the "pot"), and how to divide this amount among profit participants.

In this case, the television show is in the first season of its first run on a free TV network. The expert finds that the hit television show runs a production deficit during its first season. However, he finds that the distributor has already licensed the show in foreign markets. These foreign sales recoup one-half of remaining production deficit on this half-hour television show.

The expert must assess the likelihood of the show going into syndication. The television show has placed in the top three most watched shows every week for its first season. The expert must assess whether the show will continue to be a hit in future seasons and whether the distributor will sell it to air in syndication and therefore receive revenues in the syndication window. To calculate the amount of revenue in possible syndication, the expert would review typical syndication agreements between studios and syndication companies for similar types of television shows.

The expert should consider cost and revenue items to the studio and the distributors, such as the following:

- Network payments for production
- Selling fee from the network
- Future syndication revenues less distribution fees (if any)
- Foreign licensing sales less distribution fees or other deductions for costs (e.g., dubbing)
- Net revenues from the sale of home video (principles outlined in film section also apply to television shows released on home video)
- Production costs of creating the show, including performers, directors, sets, and props
- Residuals
- Distribution fees received by the distributors in all markets and windows
- Costs to a distributor, such as office overhead and travel
- Revenues from merchandising, if any

(c) Music

(i) Record Companies. A record company produces revenue by selling albums and licensing music in traditional formats such as compact discs (CDs), tapes, vinyl (if any), and, more recently, digital formats. As part of most artist contracts, record companies control the master recordings. Record companies often license the master recording for use by an individual or corporation, for which the record company would receive a *master use license fee.* The record company typically splits this fee equally with the artist.

Music publishing generates revenues for the record company by marketing musical compositions that the record company owns or for which the music publisher administers the rights for the copyright owners. The license fees from exploitation of these copyrighted assets include *mechanical reproduction* fees from the sales of CDs and digital downloads, including albums, singles, and cell phone ringtones and ringbacks that contain musical compositions; *public performance fees* for the performance of compositions on television, radio, and staged venues; and fees for *synchronization* of the copyrighted audio asset to a visual medium such as television, film, or advertisements.

(ii) Songwriters and Artists. Songwriters receive royalties when musicians perform the compositions they own in public performances, when record companies sell

the recorded songs to consumers, and when films, television shows, or commercials synchronize the songwriters' work. Songwriters receive payments from the publisher who administers the music catalog and from various performing rights societies, such as the American Society of Composers, Authors, and Publishers (ASCAP) or Broadcast Music Incorporated (BMI).[33] Artists receive royalties from their record company. This royalty includes a percentage of an album's sales price less stipulated deductions, as well as a percentage share of fees received by the record company for licensing the use of the master recordings for exploitation by others. Artists also derive revenues from public performances (including touring) as well as merchandising, sponsorships, and endorsements. More recently, music has become an integral part of video games, thus generating additional revenues for songwriters, artists, and record companies.

(iii) Recording Artist Agreements.   To record and distribute their music, artists have historically sought a contract with a record company. The artist agrees to provide creative talent, and the record company will provide the capital needed to record, promote, and sell the artist's music. Recording contracts require that the artists render their personal services as recording artists exclusively to the record company for a set period of time and include a recording commitment of, for instance, the number of albums the artist must deliver to the record company. The contract requires that the artist record and deliver acceptable masters to the record company. In turn, the record company will provide a recording advance used to pay the expenses of recording the album, such as fees to the producers, engineers, and other musicians; studio and equipment rental charges; and mixing and editing costs. The record company recoups these recording advances from royalties payable to the artist. Depending on the artist's stature, the recording agreement may provide for an advance of future royalties that the artist will earn. The record company will also recoup these advances from future royalty payments that the record company might owe to the artist.

In addition to recording and production costs, the record company incurs marketing costs for promoting the artist and album. Marketing an album can include in-store merchandising, promotional appearances, and radio and television advertising. The cost of marketing can range from $100,000 to over $500,000 for a major artist. Record labels also promote songs to radio stations, which add only about three or four new cuts per week to their play lists. The intense competition leads to high failure rates in this industry. A rather small proportion of studio releases (about 10 percent) must make a profit large enough to offset the losses of other recordings.[34] From the record company's perspective, every artist signed represents a big risk to the company, although it might receive a huge pay-off.

A recording contract provides that the artist will receive a royalty from the record company upon the sale of recordings of the artist's masters. The royalty is a percentage of a price base, generally defined as the suggested retail list price (SRLP) of recordings sold to the consumer through normal retail channels. In 2003, the SRLP in the United States approximated $7 for singles and $15 to $17 for CDs.[35] Singles have lower royalty rates than those for albums. Royalty rates for mid-line records can be 25 to 66 percent of the normal royalty rate for a top-line album; the royalty rate for a budget record is generally one-half the rate for top-line sales through normal retail channels.[36]

SRLP of a top-line CD	$	16.00
Less packaging deduction:		
SLRP	$	16.00
Packaging deduction rate	×	25%
Packaging deduction		(4.00)
Per CD royalty base	$	12.00
Artist's royalty rate	×	15%
Artist's royalty for each CD sold	$	1.80
Artist's royalty for each CD sold	$	1.80
Assumed sales in units	×	1,000,000
Artist royalty, before cost recoupment	$	1,800,000

SRLP = suggested retailers' list price

Source: PricewaterhouseCoopers Analysis

Exhibit 21-7.   Artist's Royalties (Example)

Exhibit 21-7 provides an example of an artist royalty calculation for a top-line CD sold in the United States with an SRLP of $16. A significant component of the royalty calculation in Exhibit 21-7 is the unit sales. All record companies reduce these sales by a reserve for returns pursuant to the company's standard policy. Most recent recording contracts provide a time period for the release of established reserves. Older contracts, however, are often vague or do not include such a provision. In these cases, the record company has discretion to release such reserves but should have a reasonable policy that addresses this issue.

Exhibit 21-7 calculates an artist's royalty of $1.8 million. In addition to the royalties for the CD sales, the artist would receive a share of master use licenses. The royalty calculation often does not, however, equal the cash payment to the artist. The record company has the contractual right to recoup or recover advance payments made to the artist as well as disbursements made on the artist's behalf. Advance payments made to the artist include recording costs, promotional expenses, video costs, and advances of royalty payments expected to be earned. Other disbursements made on the artist's behalf include advances to producers, producer's royalties, tour support, withholding taxes, and other required or artist-directed payments.

Artists' expenses include professional fees to attorneys, a business manager, an agent, and an accountant as well as costs for travel, touring, promotional appearances, side musicians, studio time, lessons, equipment, and instruments.

(iv) Music Example.   Suppose the 4Cs are a band with a hit song, "Chillin' Homestyle." Their debut album, *Daddy's Little Girls,* topped the charts, and its first single from the album has been the most downloaded track on the digital music services from the date of its release. The track received significant radio play and the band toured internationally, performed at awards shows, and appeared on the talk

show circuit. Another artist served notice to the band and the record label, accusing the band of stealing the music from one of his songs, "Trouble," for their hit song, "Chillin' Homestyle."

The plaintiff's counsel asked the expert to quantify revenues to the record label as well as the 4Cs related to the song. To identify all the revenue streams, the expert reviewed documentation relating to sales and licensing of the song "Chillin' Homestyle." These documents included the following:

- Sales registers for the record label
- Master use license agreements between the record label and third parties
- The band's contract with its record label
- Artist royalty statements from the record label
- Songwriters' royalty statements from the music publisher
- Agreements for appearances and endorsements
- Contracts for concert appearances
- Memberships with and statements from performing rights societies

The plaintiff pursued lost profits under 17 U.S.C. § 504(b) of the 1976 Copyright Act. Based on an analysis of the information produced by the record label, the 4Cs, and other research, the plaintiff's expert compiled a summary of gross revenues including the following:

- Gross album sales by the record label
- Master use license fees
- Royalty advances and earnings from music publishing-related revenues
- Writers' and publisher's share of performance revenues
- Revenues from the 4Cs tour, including gross ticket receipts, merchandising revenues, sponsorship, and concession revenues,
- Appearance fees for award shows, talk shows, and other promotional activities

The plaintiff's expert calculated gross revenues of over $70 million.

As permitted by the applicable sections of the 1976 Copyright Act, the defendant's expert identified costs incurred in generating the revenues for the accused song. The defendant's expert then deducted the following costs from the plaintiff's calculation of net profit:

- Sales discounts and distribution fees
- Recording costs
- Fees to accountants, agents, and lawyers
- Promoter's fees
- Concert production costs
- Other musicians' salaries
- Hall fees
- Marketing costs
- Travel and transportation costs
- Producer's expenses
- Revenues attributable to other 4Cs compositions

The defendant's expert also apportioned the net income of the record label and the 4Cs to other factors that contributed to the album's commercial success. This allocation was based on the relative value of these items—in other words, the track under dispute compared with the other tracks on the album—to the revenues of the album as a whole. The expert further apportioned the allocation of net profits attributable to "Chillin' Homestyle" based on the relative contribution of the material from "Trouble" to the success of "Chillin' Homestyle" as a whole. For this calculation, the music industry expert considered, among other factors, that "Trouble" generated only minimal revenues when it was released.

21.3 TECHNOLOGY AND OTHER TRENDS AFFECTING ENTERTAINMENT IP VALUE

In assessing damages, the financial expert should know the trends in technology that affect distribution, revenue, and costs in the three industry segments discussed in this chapter: movie, television, and music. Technology has created new opportunities for additional revenue and has brought new challenges. When calculating lost profits, particularly future damages, one must understand how to account for the new revenues.

(a) Recorded Music. The music segment leads all others in the entertainment industry in breaking new technological and legal ground. Digital technology and ubiquitous Internet access have affected the promotion and distribution of music. Digital technology not only affects how people listen to music, it also affects how studios distribute, promote, and compensate their artists.

The music business has grown and evolved since 1984, when CDs entered the market and music sales exceeded $4 billion. According to the Recording Industry Association of America (RIAA), this figure rose to $6.25 billion four years later, and, by 1998, sales of combined audio and music video product rose to about $14 billion. Record stores have traditionally been the main retailer of music, but large chain retailers such as WalMart and electronics retailers such as Best Buy have surpassed them. From 1992 to 2001, record store sales fell from 60 percent to about 40 percent of total consumer music sales. The market for licensed digital distribution of music in 2004 accounted for 2 percent of total music sales. The industry expects this percentage to increase to 19 percent of the market, equaling about $3.6 billion, by 2009.[37] With the increasing use of the Internet for consumer purchases, analysts expect that this revenue stream will increase over time. The industry projects that mobile music (i.e., downloading music onto portable devices) and licensed digital distribution will drive spending on music during the next five years, offsetting continued declines in purchases of the physical music product.[38]

Despite strong growth, piracy has inhibited music sales. The RIAA estimates that piracy accounts for the loss of over $4 billion in sales each year.[39] Whereas music piracy has typically involved physical formats, the growth of broadband connections has increased the speed of downloading and distributing digital copies of music illegally without the need for a physical reproduction. The music industry has begun to pay particular attention to digital music formats, such as MPEG audio layer 3—more commonly known as MP3—to control piracy. Many in the industry also see the emergence of digital music formats as a new revenue opportunity.

Even though record companies remain the primary promoters and distributors of today's music, independent musicians now use the Internet to launch, promote, and sell their own music. If these independent musicians develop a solid fan base, they could reduce the percentage of music sales by studio-backed artists. For instance, the independent band Wilco distributed its 2002 album, "Yankee Hotel Foxtrot," on its Web site after the band's record company dropped it.[40] Even studio artists use the new medium to drive campaigns of new releases. For instance, the recording artist Seal first sold his two Extended Plays (EPs)—featuring remixed versions of his songs—on Apple's iTunes download service.[41]

Studio artists and labels have begun to embrace licensed digital distribution. By mid-2005, IP owners had licensed more than a million songs for digital distribution, twice the total at the beginning of 2004. One can routinely find songs available online the same day that radio stations introduce them, and record companies have released some songs to digital services prior to their physical release. In addition, record companies have created separate divisions to serve the digital market. UMG, for example, introduced its Universal Music Enterprises Digital division to make digital-only distribution deals with artists.[42]

More than 36 million Americans have downloaded digital music, legally or illegally, according to the results of a recent survey.[43] The number of downloaders who have used paid services such as Apple's iTunes has risen from 24 percent of all music downloaders in 2004 to 43 percent in 2005. In addition to technology companies providing music over the Internet, major record companies more frequently launch new albums on artists' Web sites. In 2004, the music industry sold about 140 million digital tracks in the United States, compared with about 800 million CDs, cassettes, and other units of music. Industry observers believe, however, that the ratio of legal downloads to illegal downloads is small.

The growth in the usage of legal, paid downloading services demonstrates consumer willingness to pay for digital music as well as the revenue potential for this form of music distribution.[44] The rise in digital distribution has prompted some industry observers to predict the end of physical media. Pricewaterhouse-Coopers estimates that by 2009, album downloads will generate revenues of $820 million annually, and subscriptions will add another $1.2 billion each year.[45] Digital distribution goes beyond computer-based services. In fact, the mobile phone has also become a musical downloading device. In the summer of 2004, Apple and mobile handset manufacturer Motorola concluded an agreement to include a version of the download service iTunes on Motorola's handsets.[46] Such growth of digital distribution on multiple devices will negatively affect music retailers.

How does the digital age affect the revenue model for music? How will record companies attribute royalties from digital downloads? As of mid-2005, record companies have not settled on one method of allocating digital revenues, rather, terms differ by contract. Many standard industry recording agreements do not address the new issues of digital distribution,[47] and contracts predating the new technology do not apply to the new format and mode of distribution. In one case, artists contested the validity of copyright holders extracting profits from works created before digital technology, but the courts established that profits from the digital distribution of copyrighted work is implicit in contracts conceived before the technology existed (*Chambers et al. v. Time Warner, Inc. et al.*).[48]

The issues facing artists and recording companies can range from simple contractual language—does the contract use "record" to mean any forms of reproduction or strictly phonographic recordings?—to royalty calculations. Some recent contracts have used both the terms "record" and "electronic transmission" to distinguish between physical and digital formats. Many current agreements provide for a reduced royalty for electronic distribution of recordings, stated as a percentage of the otherwise applicable royalty rate. Typically, the top-line royalty rate applies only to net sales in the United States through normal retail channels (USNRCs). In this regard, one should consider whether the contract considers sales from online distribution or physical sales via the Internet, also known as "cybersales," as part of normal retail channels (NRCs). If the contract defines NRCs to be record stores or retail stores, does this also include online stores such as Amazon.com?[49]

Similarly, do Internet sales and downloads apply to calculations under royalty escalation provisions? Royalty escalations call for an increase in royalty rates once a work has achieved a specified sales threshold, or level of sales. Some contracts do not count new media sales toward the calculation of the threshold and apply the lower royalty rate to new media sales even when the sum of online and in-store sales reaches the threshold amount. In addition, some contracts calculate advances for a subsequent album on a basis that excludes the earnings of recordings sold over the Internet in a digital or physical format. Distribution through digital downloads also calls into question the standard of reduced royalties for sales outside the United States, because record companies do not incur the higher transaction costs of marketing and manufacturing music abroad. The music industry continues to struggle with these royalty questions and, as of mid-2005, has yet to adopt a standard contract approach to address these issues.[50]

The digital medium also affects the broadcast of music. Webcasting differs from radio broadcast because as consumers listen to music through an Internet webcast, they store a copy of the recording in the computer's cache, or memory. In 1998, Congress passed the Digital Millennium Copyright Act (DMCA), which amended United States Code Title 17, Chapter 5, § 512 to extend copyright while limiting the liability of online service providers (OSPs) from copyright infringement by their users. At the same time, DMCA outlines new restrictions for webcasters of copyrighted musical recordings. Both webcasters and radio broadcasters must obtain a license to broadcast the musical composition.[51] The DMCA also criminalizes production and dissemination of technology to circumvent antipiracy measures and increases penalties for copyright infringement on the Internet.

(b) Film. The number of domestic annual admissions (i.e., ticket purchases in the United States) has increased each year along with a related increase in gross box office dollar amounts. However, this trend changed in 2003, when, for the first time in history, the number of admissions decreased from the prior year (*see* Exhibit 21-8). Escalating ticket prices are offsetting some of the declines in theatre attendance. The increased attraction of varied television content, on-demand television delivery, and other forms of entertainment provide a few of the many appealing alternatives to the increasingly costly cinema attendance.

The development of alternative distribution channels has increased the value and opportunities for the profitability of a feature film with wide audience appeal

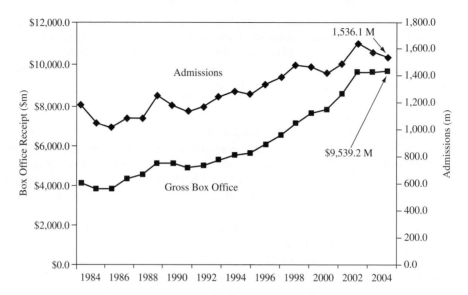

Source: Motion Picture Association Worldwide Market Research, U.S. Entertainment Industry: 2004 MPA Market Statistics, p. 4 and p. 8.

Exhibit 21-8.   U.S. Theatrical Viewership

over time. Historically, theatrical release provided a film's only revenue. The diversification of alternative distribution channels through technological advances has created additional revenue streams. Indeed, some movies begin their life cycles in these distribution channels (such as home video and television) and never have a theatrical release.

The advent of each new distribution channel leads to concerns over the cannibalism of revenues from a prior existing major channel. For example, many believed that television would replace the theatrical revenue stream and, similarly, that home video would reduce theatrical and television revenues. These predictions have gone unfulfilled. To date, every new technological alternative distribution channel has only added additional revenue streams to a feature film. With the expansion of quality home video-viewing hardware and the relatively low cost of home video product, concerns remain that the increasing cost of theater viewing could result in a continual reduction of movie-going audiences and related revenues.

The increased availability and use of digital technology will continue to drive the delivery of product to the consumer, with significant potential changes in associated revenue streams. For instance, the growth of *sell-through* home video came at the expense of the in-store rental market, but industry observers anticipate that the emergence of online DVD rental subscription services distributed through postal or online services will largely offset the decline of in-store rentals over the next several years.[52] Finally, many studios have begun to convert their libraries into a digital format, and some, such as Warner Brothers, will soon have a digital end-to-end system that employs digital techniques to create, distribute, and store filmed entertainment.[53]

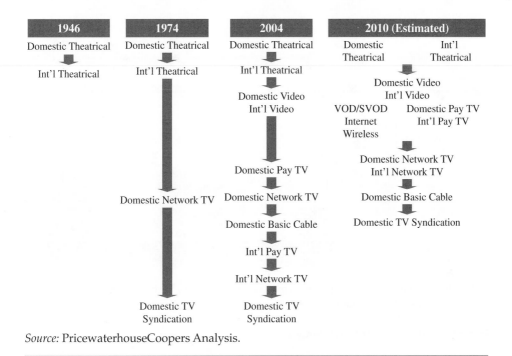

Source: PricewaterhouseCoopers Analysis.

Exhibit 21-9. Diversification of Film Revenue Streams

Finding new channels for film distribution increases the potential for total revenues earned by a film property. Exhibit 21-9 shows the growing number of windows for added revenue streams since the 1940s. In some cases, the more recent windows have become the most lucrative. For instance, revenues from DVD home video sales increased by about 58 percent per annum from 2000 to 2004.[54]

With the development of alternative distribution channels, a change has occurred in the availability of feature films within certain viewing windows. This change has often compressed the timing of windows. For example, at its inception, the home video distribution channel released product to the public one year after the film's initial theatrical release. Due to increased competition and the home video distributors' desire to take advantage of the enormous advertising around the theatrical release, the home video release of the film can now occur as soon as three months after theatrical release. Exhibit 21-10 shows a typical life cycle of a current film and the relative time frames of each window's release availability. The timing of a specific film's windows will most likely differ from that of other films. In general, however, a trend has emerged toward shorter duration windows and new revenue streams from the introduction of new devices to deliver content.

The shift in window timing has also occurred across domestic and foreign release markets. In 2004, the growing use of international day and date releasing, in which a studio releases a film internationally on the same day as its domestic opening, generated a major boost for film revenues. International day and date releasing generates foreign receipts sooner; films benefit from a large opening

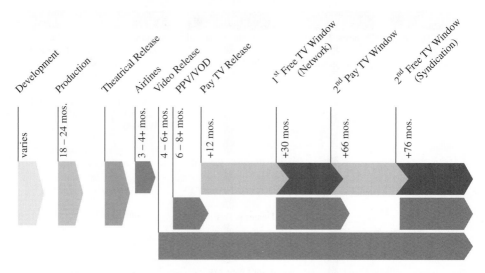

Note: International "windowing" differs by territory; however, the concept remains the same.
Source: PricewaterhouseCoopers Analysis.

Exhibit 21-10.   Current Film Life Cycle

weekend worldwide that also creates less potential for piracy.[55] Receipts from foreign releases contribute an increasing share to a film's revenue. The benefits of international receipts come with a cost, however, with higher print and marketing expenditures to support a worldwide opening compared with a North American opening.[56]

(c) Television.   As Section 21.2(b)(i) of this chapter explained, free television revenues depend on advertising dollars. Growth in the number of households recording television programs with digital video recorders (DVRs) and personal video recorders (PVRs), such as TiVo and Replay, has produced a threat to television advertisers and the traditional advertising model. DVRs give the user the ability to fast-forward through programming advertisements. To combat the reduction in viewership of television commercials, advertisers have begun to use new mechanisms to bring the advertising message to the consumers. Such mechanisms include product placement in television programming, sponsorship of shows, and advertisements shorter or longer than the standard 30-second slot. Industry observers anticipate that about 24 percent of U.S. households will have DVRs by 2009.[57] With so many TiVo users skipping over commercials, advertisers expect a reduction in the effectiveness of television commercials in increasing the sales of their products. As advertisers turn to product placement or technologies such as split screen advertising, the need for metrics around this form of advertising becomes more important.[58] The growth of DVRs also affects the calculation of viewers for ratings purposes. For instance, if DVR users view a delayed playback of programming, do the ratings of a show include viewers who watched it one or two days after the original airing?[59] Nielsen Research launched a service in early 2005 to measure DVR/PVR usage in its local and national people meter samples and will provide national ratings on DVR/PVR usage in 2006.

With competition from cable television, new networks, and other forms of entertainment—such as video games and the Internet—the audience for broadcast network programming has declined among young men between the ages of 18 and 34 years, the most desired demographic. According to Nielsen research, videogame usage was 22 percent higher in this demographic during the fall of 2003 compared with the fall of 2002. Nielsen estimates that young men watched about 8 percent less primetime television programming per day in 2003 than the previous year, part of a 12-year downward trend by this demographic.[60] Many consumer products, such as soft drinks and cars, target young men. As audience numbers have fallen, total share of national advertising spending on network television has also declined since 1980, although network advertising dollars have increased.

Product placement in programming and sponsorships of shows fundamentally alters the typical advertising sales model. In product placement, advertisers pay to conspicuously embed their product in programming. A sponsorship format presents the advertising message at the beginning and end of the show. For instance, Ford Motor Company sponsored the 2005 season debut of the television show *24*. Ford presented the show without commercial interruption. The show included a long-form commercial highlighting Ford's F-150, and the show's content integrated this product.[61] Procter & Gamble (P&G) reduced the purchase of upfront television commercial time, starting with the 2005 fall season. P&G is considering a shift in spending to other forms of television marketing, such as product placement.[62]

Another change in television will come from the companies that deliver pay-TV programming. In the past, cable and satellite operators dominated the market on pay-TV, but telecommunication operators are now expanding into television. The motivation for phone companies entering the TV distribution market stems from competition in the telecommunications market. Cable operators now offer local and long distance telephone services, bundled with standard television and broadband Internet access, and have begun introducing low-cost voice-over Internet Protocol (VoIP) to their broadband subscribers. Aggressive rollouts by telephone companies will create increased price competition.[63] The introduction of a new player—the telecommunications company—will add complexity to the calculation of lost profits to any television property.

21.4   TRENDS IN IP LAW IN ENTERTAINMENT

The calculation of damages in IP cases relies on facts, data, and a clear understanding of the financial aspects of profit and distribution. IP infringement cases in the entertainment industry resemble IP cases in other industries. The law in this area does not regard entertainment litigation differently from other types of IP: and IP cases in entertainment often cite case precedent from other industries. Similarly, entertainment cases have provided rulings for IP law, particularly in the area of copyright. The financial arrangements among the participants who make and distribute the entertainment IP set entertainment cases apart from IP litigation in other industries.

Chapters 20 and 22 discuss the methods used to calculate damages in copyright, trademark, and patent cases. The sections that follow highlight certain entertainment industry-related issues and cases that damages experts should be familiar with. These cases provide insight into how courts have dealt with entertainment industry IP damages issues.

(a) Copyrights.   Damages in copyright cases often consist of the following elements:

- Actual damages suffered by the copyright owner as a result of the infringement (e.g., lost profits and lost opportunities to license or sell)
- Profits made by the infringer from the use of the copyrighted material
- Indirect profits of the infringer (such as promotional benefits derived in other operations through use of the copyright)
- Prejudgment interest
- In lieu of the above, statutory damages (a range of amounts set by statute applied to each act of infringement)

Previous sections of this chapter discussed the complexities of measuring profit in the entertainment industry. The damages expert will also want to consider the industry trends discussed elsewhere in the chapter when projecting future revenue and costs. The damages expert should also understand that when calculating infringer profits, the plaintiff need only show the revenue related to the infringement, and the burden then shifts to the defendant to prove "deductible expenses and the elements of profit attributable to factors other than copyrighted work."[64]

If the plaintiff establishes infringement and demands total profits as compensation, what portion of profit to the infringing property does the court attribute to the copyrighted property? The infringed property often accounts for only a portion of the defendant's product; hence, one must apportion the value as between the infringing and noninfringing elements.

In *Sheldon v. MGM*, the Supreme Court in 1940 affirmed the need to apportion profits between the copyrighted work and other factors.[65] In *Sheldon*, the Court found that the motion picture *Letty Lynton* plagiarized the play *Dishonored Lady*. In arriving at deductible expenses, the Court allowed costs for the actors, scenery, producers, directors, and general overhead. Various defense experts then opined that the portion of profits attributed to the copyrighted play were between 5 and 12 percent, with the most favored estimate at 10 percent. (It does not appear that any empirical analysis supported these opinions.) The appeals court affirmed a decision of 20 percent apportionment as a figure "which will favor the plaintiffs in every reasonable chance of error." Testimony cited by the Court as supporting the apportionment included the following:

- The talent and popularity of the motion picture stars generally constitute the main drawing power of the picture, especially when the title of the picture is not identified with any well-known play or novel.
- The advertising to the public made no reference to the play.
- The picture had been licensed to exhibitors as identified simply with the name of a popular actress.

The Court also stated that principles governing apportionment of profits in patent cases apply to copyright cases, bringing into play concepts such as the entire market value rule (*see* Chapter 20). Not surprisingly, the Ninth Circuit reached similar conclusions regarding the need to apportion profits in the 1988 case *Sheldon Abend v. MCA*.[66] The *Sheldon Abend* ruling cited the need to apportion profits associated with the re-release of the film *Rear Window* between the copyrighted story and the "outstanding performances of its stars—Grace Kelly and James Stewart—and the brilliant directing of Alfred Hitchcock."

Cases related to infringement of musical works often involve apportionment. In *Frank Music Corp. v. MGM*, a segment of the musical revue *Hallelujah Hollywood* performed at the MGM Grand Casino infringed the copyrighted musical *Kismet*.[67] The infringing portion represented 12 percent of the running time of the entire show. In using 12 percent, the court concluded that all the acts in the show were of substantially equal value. The court went on to apportion 75 percent of the *Kismet* portion of the show to the copyright based on the fact that the show copied the music, lyrics, characters, settings, and costume designs. The other 25 percent was credited to defendants related to the creativity of producers, performers, and staging. Thus, the court allocated 9 percent (75 percent of 12 percent) of the total profits of the show to the copyright. This case is also notable for allowing the indirect profits of the casino operations to be claimed as damages. The court attributed 2 percent of the hotel's profits to *Hallelujah Hollywood*, based on consideration of the casino itself, convention facilities, and other entertainment and promotional activities.[68] No empirical basis seems to exist for this amount. (This case lacked an adequate analysis of the revenues and promotional activities at the hotel before and after *Hallelujah Hollywood*). Finally, one should note that the court of appeals directed the award of prejudgment interest and recommended a one-year Treasury bill rate (*see* Chapter 9 for a discussion of prejudgment interest).

In *Louis Gaste and Les Editions Louis Gaste v. Morris Kaiserman aka Morris Albert and Fermata International Melodies, Inc.*, the dispute focused on the medley of the song "Pour Toi," which also became the tune to the infringing "Feelings."[69] To calculate damages, the jury divided profits attributed to the music and to the lyrics of the song. The jury decided to apportion only 12 percent of the song's profits to the lyrics, which the defendant wrote. At trial, a music publisher testified that the normal practice in the industry when the lyrics and music to a song are written by different artists is to split the royalties 50/50. Unfortunately for his client, he could not recall the words to the song on the stand and yet could sing the opening tune. The artist who performed "Feelings" was basically unknown prior to this song, which also appears to have contributed to the relatively high percentage allocated to the tune.

In *Lottie Joplin Thomas Trust v. Crown Publishers, Inc.*, the damages awarded were 50 percent of profits of a complete works album for which about 10 percent of the contents contained copyrighted work.[70] The court decided to award the plaintiff a premium above the straight physical percentage because the use of the copyrighted material made the five album set a complete works set. Other entertainment-related copyright cases dealing with apportionment include *Cream v. Schlitz Brewing*[71] and *Jarvis v. A&M*.[72] These cases indicate that the trier of fact frequently starts with the physical percentage of the work represented by the copyrighted material and then adjusts up or down based on arguments presented regarding its relative value to the overall work compared with other creative contributions. These cases also point out how courts have struggled with these issues and show the need for a solid financial analysis to assist with these allocations of value.

In *Polar Bear Productions v. Timex Corp.*, the Ninth Circuit addressed several topics related to IP damages, notably causation and indirect profits.[73] This dispute involved a portion of a film, *Paddle Quest*, originally produced by Polar Bear and licensed to Timex for use in a commercial advertisement, which Timex later improperly used at trade shows. Polar Bear claimed that because Timex did not pay licensing fees for the use of the film at the trade shows, Polar Bear "lacked the financial wherewithal to sell additional videos." The court found that no causal link existed between Timex's failure to pay a license fee and Polar Bear's lack of business success. On the subject of indirect profits, Polar Bear's expert, an economics professor, testified that $1.5 to $3 million of indirect profits were the result of "brand enhancement" of Timex created by the use of *Paddle Quest*. The expert calculated the brand enhancement damages by taking the average increase in price times the number of watches sold during the period when Timex used the video. The expert then reduced this amount (the complete basis for which is unclear in the record) in part for apportionment to the infringement. Even though the Ninth Circuit did not reject the method, it reversed these damages because the plaintiff did not establish a causal link between the showing of the video at trade shows and consumers purchasing Timex products. The court cited an Eighth Circuit case[74] in which the plaintiff established a causal link to indirect profits. This case involved the use of infringing material in a commercial. The factors cited in connecting use of that material to indirect profits included the following:

- The infringing material was the centerpiece of the commercial.
- The infringer told its dealers the commercial was integral to its launch of the product.
- Sales of the product exceeded projections during the period that the commercial ran.
- The commercial received high ratings and levels of recall on consumer surveys.

(ii) Technology and Infringement.   Widespread Internet usage and the potential for online distribution of digital content give rights-holders a new revenue stream. This new medium brings entertainment product to an array of consumers but has proved vulnerable to violations of copyrights of entertainment properties. Headline lawsuits in music range from the theft of musical ideas to the theft of whole musical properties on a digital medium. As of 2005, the theft of musical property represented the most frequent occurrence of online piracy, but as technology develops and more individuals obtain high-speed Internet access, the frequency of illegal downloads of filmed content will reach the level of musical content. Piracy has become a top issue for media companies, and by the end of 2005, clear case law related to online piracy has yet to emerge; courts simply apply injunctive remedies, unless the plaintiff can establish willful misconduct.

An important online piracy case is *A&M v. Napster,* in which a major record company sued an online peer-to-peer (P2P) service enabling thousands of users to share music and distribute it to each other.[75] The court issued a preliminary injunction preventing Napster from allowing its users to continue to download files yet refrained from imposing compulsory royalties. Compulsory royalties would not only have forced the record company to conclude a licensing arrangement with Napster but would also have allowed Napster to avoid penalties from violating the injunction.

The courts have established a precedent for punitive damages when the plaintiff can establish willful infringement. These cases, however, predate the maturation of the Internet and involve live or recorded performances of the copyrighted music, rather than illegal digital distribution. In an instance in which a club owner did not obtain proper licenses to broadcast copyrighted music, damages awarded equaled approximately three times the amount under past license agreements between the parties (*Chi-Boy Music, et al., v. Charlie Club*).[76] In another case in which an artist was performing the copyrighted music live, the court awarded approximately three times what it would have cost the owner of a bar to purchase a license for her musical performances (*Major Bob Music v. Stubbs*).[77] Many other decisions have awarded payments per occasion of infringement.[78]

Whereas the previous cases involved performances of the infringed properties, calculating damages based on the number of infringements becomes more difficult for cases of online piracy because of the potentially numerous occasions of infringement. However, courts have applied this principle in infringing digital distribution cases in the past. In *UMG v. MP3.com*, the court ruled that the appropriate measure of damages equaled $25,000 per infringed CD that the Internet service My.MP3.com held on its site.[79] The site had copied in an MP3 format a number of CDs and allowed subscribers to listen to this music for free. However, the site restricted users to accessing only music that they proved they already owned.[80] Although the site did not allow users to file share, the court ruled that the unauthorized copying of music that this service performed did not constitute fair use of copyrighted material. Note that the court based damages on the amount of content held by the service, rather than the number of uploads made by the subscribers. The court identified the defendant as willfully infringing the copyrights and set a damages figure (as much as $250 million) that would deter others from engaging in online piracy.

In June 2005, the U.S. Supreme Court ruled unanimously against file sharing companies in *MGM et al. v. Grokster et al.*[81] Among the defendants in the suit were two of the most popular online file-sharing services—Grokster, Ltd. and StreamCast Networks, Inc.—which provide software to allow peer-to-peer online downloading of film and music. The plaintiffs included most of the major studios in music and film.

The defendants argued that they were not liable for the misuse of their software on the basis of the Supreme Court's 1984 decision in *Sony Corporation v. Universal Studios Inc.*[82] In the *Sony* decision, also known as *Betamax*, the studios sued the manufacturers of videocassette recorders for liability in copyright infringement. In *Betamax*, the Court decided that, because consumers primarily used the machines for time shifting—the noninfringing activity of enjoying a protected work in other than its originally broadcast time slot—Sony was not liable for copyright infringement. This decision established the precedent distinguishing between intended use and potential misuse of technology by consumers. By contrast, the plaintiffs in Grokster argued that the sole purpose of the file-sharing software is the distribution of music that has not been licensed for such distribution. Such activity amounts to copyright infringement.

Industry observers anticipated that *Grokster* would establish new precedents in copyright issues resulting from technological innovations, but the ruling does not provide clear guidelines for technology companies. In its decision, the Court stated that "one who distributes a device with the object of promoting its use to infringe copyright, as shown by clear expression or other affirmative steps taken to foster infringement, is liable for the resulting acts of infringement by third parties." However, the Court provided little direction on how to establish whether a company purposefully induced users to trade copyright-protected music or video content illicitly.[83] The ruling sent the case back to the district court. On November 7, 2005, Grokster announced that it would shut down its infringing service in a settlement agreement. As of January 2006, the lawsuits with the other peer-to-peer services had not reached resolution.[84]

(b) Trademarks.   The Lanham Act protects the original user of a trademark or trade name against the infringement of that mark or name. Musicians have used this statute to protect their artist names and trademarks, and film and television producers have used it to protect their films and programming. As with other forms of trademarked property, Lanham Act litigants depend on the so-called Polaroid factors to argue their case. These factors include the following:

- Strength of the mark
- Degree of similarity between the marks
- Proximity of the marks in the market
- Actual confusion by consumers
- Defendant's good faith in using the mark
- Sophistication of likely consumers[85]

Numerous cases have been brought by musical groups against alleged infringers of the groups' name. Such cases include litigation involving Boston, Deep Purple, The Chipmunks, Lynyrd Skynyrd, The Drifters, New Edition and Herman's Hermits, to name just a few. Indeed, artists' names are akin to their trademark or brand. The courts have already established that someone need not register a mark, in this case the artist's name, with the United States Patent and Trademark Office to support a Lanham Act suit.[86] Protection under the Lanham Act extends even to the name of the band after the original group has disbanded but former members of the group continue to perform.[87]

The Lanham Act does not limit the protection of performers' trademarks to their name only; such protection can extend to their persona. For instance, Motown Records sued Hormel, claiming that a television commercial advertisement with a trio closely resembling The Supremes singing about the qualities of beef stew to the tune of "Baby Love" damaged the image of the group and infringed on the song.[88] The court recognized that the Lanham Act could extend to a performer's persona and ordered an injunction against the advertisement.

Some plaintiffs have tried to use trademark law to protect work that had fallen out of copyright. In *Dastar Corporation v. 20th Century Fox*, defendants argued that the Lanham Trademark Act protected their uncopyrighted work from unattributed copying.[89] In this case, to create a documentary series, Dastar had used footage that had previously held a copyright but at the time was in the public domain. The case involved reverse passing-off (i.e., misrepresenting someone else's work as one's own). The Court reasoned that, even though the Lanham Act prohibits reverse passing-off, the rule regarding the misuse of trademarks had no relevance because once a copyrighted work enters into the public domain, anyone in the public can use the work, with or without attribution to the original author. In short, the Supreme Court held that trademark law does not prevent the unaccredited use of an uncopyrighted work.

(c) Patents. Patents have not traditionally been used to a great degree in the entertainment industry to protect IP. However, as media converge and technology plays a bigger role in the delivery of content, the authors expect to see a greater use of patents by entertainment companies.

21.5 CONCLUSION

New technology continues to expand the avenues available for exploiting the value of entertainment-related IP to both owners and potential infringers. The high potential value and complex business arrangements used to finance, produce, and distribute entertainment properties can make for contentious disputes. The developing nature of IP law and its application to the entertainment industry create a degree of uncertainty for disputes in this arena. All these factors point to the need for competent and professional litigation services.

APPENDIX A:
INDUSTRY DATA SOURCES

Adams Media Research
(AdamsMediaReseach.com)
Box office data
Home video data
Special reports

Arbitron (Arbitron.com)
Music ratings data
Special reports

Box Office Guru
(BoxOfficeGuru.com)
Box office data

Box Office Mojo
(BoxOfficeMojo.com)
Industry news
Box office data

The Daily Variety (Variety.com)
Industry news
Box office data

The Hollywood Reporter
(HollywoodReporter.com)
Industry news
Box office data

Internet Movie Database (IMDB.com)
Box office data

Kagan Media Research (Kagan.com)
Box office data
Special reports

Motion Picture Association
(MPAA.org)
Box office data
Attendance data
Special reports

National Association of Theatre
Owners (Natoonline.org)
Special reports
Box office data
Theatrical exhibitor data

Nielsen Media Research
(NielsenMedia.com)
TV ratings data
Special reports

PricewaterhouseCoopers
(pwc.com/entertainmentandmedia)
Entertainment & Media Outlook

The Broadband Future: Interactive Networked and Personalized

IAB Internet Advertising Revenue Report

Big Bets for the U.S. Cable Industry: Key Opportunities for Future Revenue Growth

Competition in the First Mile: Why Fiber to the Premises Is Not the Issue

IP Services Transformation: Beyond the Triple Play

Rentrak Corporation (Rentrak.com)
Box office data
On demand data
Games data
Home video data

Screen Digest (ScreenDigest.com)
International box office data
International home video data
International television data
Special reports

ShowBIZData (ShowbizData.com)
Industry news
Studio market share
Box office data

APPENDIX B:
GLOSSARY OF TERMS USED IN ENTERTAINMENT FINANCE

DEFINITIONS

Avails: Time slots offered to advertisers by networks in upfront buying.

Back-end participation: Profit participation based on net profit, after deductions are made.

Barter: The method in which a syndicator retains a portion of advertising time and sells this time to earn revenue from the programming.

Box office revenues: Sales of tickets purchased by the viewing public at movie theaters.

CPM: Cost per thousand, a term used in conjunction with the price of advertising time on television programming.

Dayparts: Time periods (e.g., prime-time, daytime and late-night) during which programming is aired.

Distributors: Companies, typically film studios, that make films available for release in theaters, home video, television, and so on. Distributors is also a term used for companies that make television programming available for public viewing.

Distribution fee: Funds to distributor on the gross film revenue based on a contracted rate.

Exhibitors: Companies that own movie theatres.

Film rental: Funds paid by an exhibitor to distributor as rental fees for the right to license a film for public exhibition.

First dollar gross participation: Gross receipts minus "off-the-top" deductions, such as trade dues, checking and collection fees, taxes, and residuals.

Gross participant: A profit participant who receives a percentage of gross receipts minus certain pre-agreed deductions. Gross participants include first-dollar gross participants, those who receive a percentage of the gross earnings, and adjusted gross participants, those who receive a percentage of gross receipts minus contracted deductions.

Gross proceeds: Receipts from distribution in each window. In general, gross proceeds are what remains after the exhibitors take their share of the box office receipts. Gross proceeds are also called *gross rentals*.

Gross receipts: Gross receipts include funds paid to theaters by the movie-goers in the form of box office tickets as well as revenues from home video, television airings, soundtracks, books, merchandising, and so on.

Independents: Production and distribution companies other than the major studios and their subsidiaries.

Master use license fee: Licensing by the record company of the master recording for use by an individual or corporation.

Mechanical reproduction fee: Payment based on the mechanical reproduction of a recording, such as CDs, digital downloads, and the like. Also called mechanical royalties.

MSO: Multiple System Operator, a term used to describe cable and satellite operators delivering pay-TV services.

Negative cost: All expenses and costs incurred in the acquisition and production of a motion picture.

Netcomp: Revenues paid by network to affiliate for advertising airtime.

Net participant: A participant involved in the film who shares in the net profits (defined as net proceeds) of the film.

Net profits: The amount remaining from gross receipts after deducting distribution fees, distribution expenses, negative cost, interest, certain gross participations, and so on from film gross revenues.

Network Television: The Big Three: NBC, ABC, and CBS. Fox and UPN are considered new networks.

Participant: See Gross participant and Net participant.

Participation: Contractual terms between a studio and talent that specify contingent compensation due the talent based upon complex calculations that are dependent on product performance.

Prints & Advertising: Prints include costs of preparing prints of the film for distribution; advertising costs are expenditures associated with marketing the box office and home video releases.

Public Performance Fees: Royalties for the performance of compositions on television, radio, and staged venues.

Recoupment: Reimbursing upfront payments with first revenues. Recoupments are paid first from revenues and are deducted when one is calculating allocations to profit participants.

Residuals: Contractual terms between a studio and a trade union that specifies contingent compensation due the union member based on involvement in creation of the product, cash receipts and product exhibition.

Scatter: The way commercial advertising time is sold on television, that is, for spots scattered throughout a number of different television shows.

Sell-through: Process in which a film is released on VHS/DVD with the intended result being a sale to the viewer as opposed to being rented and returned.

Spot: Commercial advertising bought on a specific television show at a specific time.

Synchronization royalties: Royalities based on the synchronization of a recording with elements of a film.

Syndication: Previously exhibited or recorded material that is licensed to a collection of buyers such as independent television and radio stations. Syndication also describes entertainment product that is first aired in syndication, rather than on network stations.

Theatrical rental: Revenues to distributors from the rental, or licensing of the film product, to theatres for public exhibition. The percentage of box office receipts paid to distributors typically approximates 45 to 55 percent.

Ultimate: Term used to describe the total forecasted revenue and cost components during the lifetime of a film. Ultimates can be prepared at any time during a motion picture's life cycle—before, during, or after the film's release.

Upfront buying: Purchases of commercial airtime slots (avails) by advertisers from networks in May when the new fall schedule is announced.

Window: In the film and television industry, the period of time during which contracts permit exclusive exhibition of a product in a specific format of distribution, such as box office, cable, home video, and so forth.

NOTES

1. *Buchwald v. Paramount Pictures*, 13 U.S.P.Q. 1497 (Cal. Super. Ct. 1990).
2. Michael Miller, "Buchwald Award Seen as Victory for Big Studios," *Reuters News*, March 17, 1992.
3. Ibid.
4. Since *Buchwald*, the courts have found that the following elements of damages should be elicited from the plaintiff's witnesses in an action related to a copyright infringement of a screenplay: (1) lost profits from sale of script due to infringement, (2) diminution in market value of script, (3) market value of plaintiff's services, (4) defendant's gross revenues from project associated with infringement, (5) statutory damages under the Copyright Act, (6) costs of the suit under the Copyright Act, (7) attorney fees as costs under the Copyright Act, (8) excess damages from defendant's willful conduct, and (9) expert witness fees (18 *Am. Jur. Proof of Facts*, 3d 721).

5. Other publicized cases include Jane Fonda's suit against Universal for profits of *On Golden Pond* and the suit brought by Robert Wagner and Stefanie Powers against Columbia for allegedly false accounting statements. (Carole Cheatham et al., "Hollywood Profits: Gone with the Wind?" *The CPA Journal*, 66 (1996)).

6. Bernard Weintraub. "'Gump' Still Isn't Raking in Huge Profits? Hmm," *New York Times*, May 25, 1995, B1.

7. It was reported that Groom also cut a "seven-figure" deal for the sequel to *Forrest Gump*, "Gump & Co." ("Writer's Threat to Sue Opens Box of Chocolates," *Sun-Sentinel Wire Service*, June 19, 1995).

8. *Wolf v. Superior Court* (Walt Disney Pictures and Television) 114 Cal. App. 4th 1343 (2004).

9. Studios comprise seven companies: Universal Pictures, Warner Bros. Studios, Paramount Pictures, Sony Pictures, Walt Disney Pictures, Twentieth Century Fox, and Dreamworks SKG.

10. The domestic and international markets generally follow the same release patterns, with the international opening date varying from a date concurrent with the domestic theatrical release to as much as nine months later.

11. It is important to note that even when the distribution is conducted in-house, profit and loss statements for production and distribution are kept separate.

12. Carole Cheatham et al., "Hollywood Profits."

13. John Horn, "DVD Sales Figures Turn Every Film into a Mystery; Studios Closely Guard Details of What Is a Major Source of Profit and a Growing Area of Dispute," *Los Angeles Times*, April 17, 2005.

14. This tradition is based on historical practice, which is currently eroding.

15. *See* discussion in Gabriel Snyder, "H'wood Gets Grossed Out," *Daily Variety*, June 12, 2005.

16. Kathleen Anderson, "InDemand Poised for Big '05," *Hollywood Reporter*, January 19, 2005.

17. PricewaterhouseCoopers (PwC), *Entertainment & Media Outlook 2005*, 165.

18. Matthew Fraser. "Hollywood Has Its Finger on the VOD Pause Button," *Financial Post*, July 3, 2001.

19. Another type of participation is *break-even participation*, a portion of the break-even point when receipts equal the amount paid by the studio. For other participant definitions, *see* Joe Sisto, "Profit Participation in the Motion Picture Industry," *Entertainment and Sports Lawyer* 21 (Summer 2003).

20. This chapter does not discuss public television. For a description of public television, *see* Howard J. Blumenthal and Oliver R. Goodenough, *This Business of Television* (New York: Billboard Books, 1998).

21. From Fritz Attaway's testimony before the U.S. Senate Judiciary Committee, May 12, 2004.

22. Based on a survey of network ad rates by *Advertising Age* magazine, 2004–2005 season. ZapZit.com, September 27, 2004.

23. For instance, if 100,000 households in an area own a television and 15,000 of these households are watching a particular program, the program's rating is a 15.

24. Blumenthal and Goodenough, *This Business of Television*, 19.

25. Ibid., 424.

26. Howard J. Blumenthal and Oliver Goodenough, *This Business of Television*, 70.

27. Ibid., Chapter 5.

28. Ibid., Chapter 3.

29. Morgan Stanley, "Film and Television Studio Economics," October 25, 2004. P. 36.

30. Thomas K. Arnold, "Sony's Sartorial 'Seinfeld' Latest in TV-DVD Marketing," *The Hollywood Reporter*, November 17, 2005.

31. Judith McCourt, "TV-DVD Releases a Lucrative Market for Studios," *Reuters News*, September 2, 2005.

32. Howard J. Blumenthal and Oliver Goodenough, *This Business of Television*, 299–313.

33. The performing rights societies negotiate licenses with and receive fees from users of music (i.e., those who publicly perform compositions.) The users of music include the television stations (e.g., the major networks, public television, cable television); commercial and noncommercial radio broadcasters; background music services; colleges and universities; concert presenters; symphony orchestras; Web sites; and general users of music, such as bars, circuses, hotels, skating rinks, and restaurants.

34. Vogel, *Entertainment Industry Economics*, 163.

35. M. William Krasilovsky and Sidney Shemel, *This Business of Music: The Definitive Guide to the Music Industry*, 9th ed. (New York: Billboard Books, 2003), 17.

36. Ibid.

37. PwC, *Entertainment & Media Outlook 2005*, 213–14.

38. Ibid.

39. This statistic comes from RIAA's Web site, www.riaa.com/issues/piracy/default.asp.

40. John Borland, "Indie Music Riding the Digital Surge; iTunes Is Hot, but the World of Independent Music Service Is Staging a Comeback from the Dot-Bomb Fizzle," *CNETNews.com*, June 21, 2004.

41. Melinda Newman, "Digital Downloads Signify More Than Online Music Sales," *Billboard*, May 1, 2004.

42. PwC, *Entertainment & Media Outlook 2005*, 213–214.

43. Chris Baker, "Artists to Tune in to Court Case; Struggles not Same Old Song after File-Sharing Technology," *The Washington Times*, March 28, 2005.

44. Section 24.4(ii) of this chapter discusses piracy.

45. PwC, *Entertainment & Media Outlook 2005*, 214.

46. Nick Wingfield and Pui-Wing Tam, "Apple Rings up Motorola to Play iTunes Songs on Cellphones," *The Wall Street Journal*, July 27, 2004.

47. The discussion of issues facing the music industry in the digital age comes from Robert Rosenbloom, "Sorting Through the Confusion: Interpreting Standard Recording Agreement Provisions in the Digital Era," *Entertainment Law Reporter* November (1999).

48. *Chambers v. Time Warner Inc.*, 123 F. Supp. 2d 198, 200-201 (S.D.N.Y. 2000).

49. Robert Rosenbloom, "Sorting through the Confusion: Interpreting Standard Recording Agreement Provisions in the Digital Era," *Entertainment Law Reporter*, November 1999.

50. Ibid.

51. Robert Rosenbloom, "Webcasting," http://www.gtlaw.com/pub/articles/1999/rosenbloom99b.htm.

52. PwC, *Entertainment & Media Outlook 2005*, 60.

53. John Healy, "Sony Is Building a Digital Library," *Los Angeles Times*, April 18, 2005.

54. PwC, *Entertainment & Media Outlook 2005*, 60–62.

55. One recent film, *The Sisterhood of the Traveling Pants*, was released on video in China the same day as the U.S. theatrical release in an effort to combat piracy (Jon Healey). "Warner Gets a Jump on Film Pirates in China," *Los Angeles Times*, June 9, 2005).

56. PwC *Entertainment & Media Outlook 2005*, p. 57.

57. Ibid., 121.

58. Daisy Whitney, "Nielsen on Track of Product Placements; Measurement Software Built with NextMedium Quantifies, Gauges Value," *Television Week*, May 31, 2004.

59. Roger Baron, "DVR Threat Real, Growing; With So Many Television Advertisers, Product Placement Can Never Take the Place of Commercial Spots," *Television Week*, October 20, 2003.

60. Christopher Reynolds. "The Lost Demo," *Promo* 17 (February 1, 2004).

61. Ford Motor Company, product press releases http://media.ford.com/products/press_article_display.cfm?article_id=16212 & vehicle_id=8.

62. "Reports: P&G Cutting Advance Buys of Ads." *ABC News*, June 13, 2005, http://abcnews.go.com/Business/print?id=844583.

63. PwC, *Entertainment & Media Outlook 2005*, 158.

64. 17 U.S.C. §504(b).

65. *Sheldon v. Metro-Goldwyn-Mayer Inc.*, 106 F.2d 45.

66. *Sheldon Abend v. MCA, Inc.*, 863 F.2d 1465.

67. *Frank Music Corp. v. Metro-Goldwyn-Mayer Inc.*, 886 F.2d 1545 (9th Cir. 1989).

68. Indirect profit was calculated by deducting direct profits of $6,131,606 from total profit of $395,000,000 and then applying 2 percent of 9 percent (75 percent of 12 percent).

69. *Louis Gaste v. Morris Kaiserman*. 863 F.2d 1061 (2d Cir. 1988).

70. *Lottie Joplin Thomas Trust v. Crown Publishers, Inc.*, 592 F.2d 651, 657 (2d Cir. 1978).

71. *Cream Records, Inc. v. Jos. Schlitz Brewing Co.*, 754 F.2d 826 (9th Cir. 1985).

72. *Jarvis v. A&M Records*, 827 F. Supp. 282 (D.N.J. 1993).

73. *Polar Bear Productions v. Timex Corp.*, 384 F.3d 700 (9th Cir. 2004).

74. *Andreas v.Volkswagen of Am., Inc.*, 336 F.3d 789, 797–98 (8th Cir. 2003).

75. *A&M Records, Inc. v. Napster, Inc.*, 114 F. Supp. 2d 896 (N.D. Cal. 2000).

76. *Chi-Boy Music v. Charlie Club, Inc.*, 779 F. Supp. 527 (7th Cir. 1991).

77. *Major Bob Music v. Stubbs*, 851 F. Supp. 475 (S.D. Ga 1994).

78. *See Swallow Turn Music v. Wilson*, (Swallow turn): 831 F. Supp. 575, 28 U.S.P.Q. 2d 1924, (1993). *Pedrosillo Music v. Radio Musical, Inc.* 815 F. Supp. 511, *Almo Music Corp. v. T&W Communications Corp., Unicity Music v. Omni Communications*, 844 F. Supp. 504 (1994)., *and Chi-Boy Music v. Towne Tavern, Inc.*

79. *UMG Recordings, Inc. v. MP3.com Inc.*, 92 F. Supp. 2d 349, 351 (S.D.N.Y. 2000); and "MP3.com ordered to pay up to 250 million in music copyright case," CNN.com, September 6, 2000.

80. This proof usually involved inserting a CD into the user's computer upon subscribing to the free service, which the service could detect.

81. *MGM Studios, Inc., et al. v. Grokster, Ltd., et al.*, 380 F.3d 1154 (9th Cir. 2004).

82. *Sony Corp. of America v. Universal City Studios, Inc.*, 464 U.S. 417 (1984).

83. Tom Zeller Jr., "Sharing Culture Likely to Pause But Not Wither," *New York Times*, June 28, 2005.

84. Brooks Boliek, "Hollywood Wins as Grokster Agrees to End P2P Service," *The Hollywood Reporter*, November 8, 2005. According to the article, after the settlement was announced, Grokster's Web site stated a warning that the Supreme Court had "unanimously confirmed that using this service to trade copyrighted material is illegal."

85. Elizabeth Williams, J.D., "Trademark Protection under Lanham Act (15 U.S.C.A. §§ 1501 *et seq.*) of Name of Musical Group." *American Law Reports*, 115 A.L.R. Fed., 171 2005.

86. *Bell v. Streetwise Records, Ltd.*, 761 F.2d 67 (1st Cir. 1985).

87. *Noone v. Banner Talent Associates, Inc. (Noone v. Banner)*: 398 F. Supp. 260, S.D.N.Y., 1975., and *Grondin v. Rossington* 690, F. Supp. 200, S.D.N.Y. (1988).

88. *Motown Record Corp. v. George A. Hormel & Co. (Motown)*: 657 F. Supp. 1236, 3 U.S.P.Q. 2d 1124 (1987).

89. *Dastar Corporation v. Twentieth Century Fox Film Corporation*, 123 S. Ct. 2041, 2003.

CHAPTER 22

PATENT INFRINGEMENT DAMAGES

Peter B. Frank
Vincent E. O'Brien
Michael J. Wagner

CONTENTS

22.1   INTRODUCTION

First Co. and Second Co. manufacture competing widgets. First Co. develops a safer and easier-to-use locking mechanism for its widget and applies for a patent but does not, however, add the new lock to its widgets. Patent applications are confidential for the first 18 months from the earliest filing date for which a benefit is sought,[1] so Second Co. does not know of First Co.'s new lock when it introduces one of its own. The new lock becomes popular with customers, and Second Co. increases its share of the market. Two years later, the Patent and Trademark Office (PTO) issues a patent for the lock to First Co., which promptly notifies Second Co. of its infringing product. On advice from counsel, Second Co. disagrees and refuses to change its product. First Co. sues for patent infringement and damages. Second Co. counter sues under the antitrust laws alleging abuse of the patent process.

In another case, Small Co. purchases a patent from the inventor for a new way to wrap meat in plastic. Supermarkets like the new machine, and Small Co. sells a hundred machines in two years. Large Co. has over 60 percent of the market for all equipment used in supermarket meat departments. It has an older machine for wrapping meat and sells a thousand of these a year. Its sales staff visits meat departments in every supermarket every two months. During these visits, the staff learns that Small Co.'s machine offers the best way to wrap meat. In response, Large Co. sets out to develop a new meat-wrapping machine. Engineers and attorneys working for Large Co. review Small Co.'s patents. After spending a half-million dollars, Large Co. introduces its new machine. It becomes successful, and Large Co. sells 1,220 in the first year. Small Co., whose sales have stagnated at 100 per year, sues for patent infringement.

In a third case, Inventor Co. develops a new way to process lead plates for use in automobile batteries, builds a machine based on this process, and sells it to all the major manufacturers of auto batteries except one, Infringer Co. When sales staff for Inventor Co. calls on Infringer Co., Infringer Co. refuses them access to the plant floor. Several years later, a disgruntled employee of Infringer Co. informs Inventor Co. that his employer has installed 80 copies of the machine. Inventor Co. sues for patent infringement and discovers that the machines are exact duplicates.

Each of these patent infringement cases involves the computation of damages, which can involve aspects of economics, industrial engineering, management science, marketing, organizational behavior, finance, accounting, and statistics. A patent case typically requires a working knowledge of some or all of these disciplines to establish evidence of lost profits, the amount of reasonable royalties, or, in certain situations, the infringer's unjust gain.

The question of whether a particular product infringes a given patent involves both technical issues (the product's features) and legal issues (the patent's scope and validity). These issues, which the parties typically dispute, will fall outside the scope of the damages expert's field of professional expertise. Consequently, experts perform damages analyses on the basis of an assumption that the trier of fact will find the patent valid and infringed by (some subset of) the defendant's products. Sometimes the expert needs to calculate several different damages numbers, on the basis of a set of alternative assumptions (e.g., all the defendant's accused sales infringe, or only certain subsets of them do).

This chapter describes the types of damages that a plaintiff can claim in a patent case, examines the analytical tasks used to prove these damages, and discusses the issues that most frequently arise during the litigation.

22.2 PATENTS

Article I, Section 8 of the Constitution of the United States reads "Congress shall have the power to promote the progress of science and useful arts, by securing for limited times to authors and inventors the exclusive right to their respective writings and discoveries." The current operative law relating to patents passed by Congress is Title 35 of the United States Code (U.S.C.). Title 35 provides that the patentee, or his or her licensee, is the sole person allowed to make, use, or sell the invention in the United States. Thus, the ownership of a patent can impart a potential economic benefit that the owner can exploit by either selling a product that incorporates the patented invention, keeping others from selling a product with the patented invention, or licensing the patent to someone else who wants to exploit it. Inventors can obtain patents on products, processes, and software algorithms and designs, but they cannot patent ideas.

Compensation to the patentee for infringement of any patent can take the form of lost profits or reasonable royalty damages. Compensation for infringement of a design patent can also include damages for unjust enrichment. A plaintiff can receive interest on these three types of damages and receive punitive damages if the court finds that the infringement was willful. Punitive damages take the form of a multiple of the other damages proven. The judge assesses this multiple, which can equal as much as triple (the maximum set by statute) the damages amount. (Chapter 14 discusses punitive damages.)

A successful plaintiff can receive damages only for the period beginning after the patent issued or some later date. Identifying this date involves issues of product marking (i.e., marking *patent* on the product) and notification; parties often dispute this date. Practitioners should refer to their clients for the correct date at which to begin the calculations. Sometimes they will need to compute damages using different starting dates.

Even though the patent gives the owner a patent monopoly over the invention's use, it does not automatically give the owner an economic monopoly or even ensure a modicum of economic value. The marketplace will evaluate the technology's economic value. For example, each of the major automobile companies has a large patent portfolio, yet none of them possesses an economic monopoly. In fact, their patents may not even give them an edge against the competition.[2] Courts have often confused a technology monopoly with an economic monopoly.[3] The practitioner should avoid this mistake.

22.3 PATENT DAMAGES

(a) Section 284: Damages.   Title 35 has several sections—most notably 35 U.S.C. § 284—that relate to damages calculations for patent infringement. Section 284 provides that "the court shall award the claimant damages adequate to compensate for the infringement, but in no event less than a reasonable royalty." Thus, if patentees cannot demonstrate economic harm, they can still receive some compensation for the technology's use.

Both § 284 and prior case law emphasize the harm that the patentee suffered, not the gain that the infringer received by infringing. The latter, typically falling under the heading *unjust enrichment*, raises different issues, some of which this chapter discusses later. Also, courts award damages only to the patentee; courts usually do not allow licensees (unless the licensee has an exclusive license), whom the infringement may have also injured, to recover damages.

In summarizing and reaffirming the case law on the question of economic harm, the U.S. Supreme Court in *Aro* stated:

> But the present statutory rule is that only "damages" may be recovered. These have been defined by this Court as "compensation for the pecuniary loss he [the Patentee] has suffered from the infringement, without regard to the question whether the defendant gained or lost by his unlawful acts." *Coupe v. Royer,* 155 U.S. 565, 582. They have been said to constitute "the difference between his pecuniary condition after the infringement, and what his condition would have been if the infringement had not occurred." *Yale Lock Mfg. Co. v. Sargent,* 117 U.S. 536, 552. The question to be asked in determining damages is "how much had the Patent Holder and Licensee suffered by the infringement. And that question [is] primarily: had the Infringer not infringed, what would Patent Holder-Licensee have made?" *Livesay Window Co. v. Livesay Industries, Inc.,* supra, 251 F.2d, 469, 471.[4]

This wording resembles that commonly found in other areas of the law, most notably in the area of antitrust damages where the parties attempt to ascertain what would have happened but for the unlawful act. Such an approach places patentees in the same economic position they would have been in had the infringement not occurred. In this sense, the damages award makes the patentee whole—that is, compensates the patentee—for the infringer's transgression.

Thus, when measuring economic harm in a patent case, one must first discern how the market would have acted absent infringement. This includes assessing the lawful actions available to the infringer, such as the following:

- Would the infringer have entered (or remained in) the market with a competing noninfringing product? What commercially acceptable, noninfringing alternatives (if any) were available to the infringer, or might have become available if the infringer had sought one? What would the cost of developing such a noninfringing alternative have been? How long would it have taken to develop or adopt such an alternative?
- Would the infringer have been able to overcome the advantage of the invention by charging a lower price, or by spending more on marketing, or by relying on a superior distribution system, or by some other competitive move?
- Were any other competitive responses available to the infringer?

Unlike other areas of the law, the courts have not yet widely adopted the *but-for* analysis for such damages. Even though the 1964 *Aro* decision enunciates but-for analysis, courts did not fully adopt the method until the *Grain Processing* decision of 1999.[5] This has two implications. First, practitioners should not slavishly follow earlier cases because they do not always reflect the current legal standard. Second, practitioners must link their analyses to real world situations—data and markets.

Proper damages analysis requires an understanding of the market's structure and the nature of competition absent the infringement.

The second step in calculating patent damages entails assessing the invention's general economic significance. Specifically, how much economic gain can the owner realize from the patent? Will the patent lead to increased sales? Higher prices? Lower costs? More opportunities? If one answers "no" to all these questions, then even the greatest technological achievement will involve little damages.[6] The practitioner needs to investigate the invention and how it affects the competitive picture.

(b) Section 289: Additional Remedy for Infringement of Design Patent.   An owner of a design patent can elect the damages remedies allowed in § 284 as well as the remedies available under § 289. Section 289 provides (along with other out-of-date constraints) that the infringer "shall be liable to the owner to the extent of his total profit."

Only in cases of infringement of a design patent can the patentee obtain an unjust enrichment remedy from the infringer. In all other situations, the courts focus on the economic harm the patentee has suffered as a result of the infringement.

(c) Sections 154 and 173: Term of the Patent.   The patent's term affects damages because it may set the beginning or the end, or both, of the damages period. A patent's term depends on the type of patent. The damages period cannot begin before the date that the Patent and Trademark Office issues a patent. In some situations where the infringer has not received proper notice, the damages period cannot begin until some time after the patent issues. Under some circumstances (discussed in Section 22.5(f) of this chapter), the patentee can claim damages after the patent expires.

Title 35 U.S.C. § 154 sets a term of 20 years from the filing of an application in the United States for a utility patent, one that relates to performing a function (e.g., a machine or part of a machine). If the application for the patent specifically references a previously filed application or applications, then the term is 20 years from the date on which the patentee filed the earliest such application. Title 35 U.S.C. § 173 sets a term of 14 years from the date of grant for design patents.

(d) Section 286: Time Limitation on Damages.   Title 35 U.S.C. § 286 limits recovery of damages to no more than six years prior to the filing of the complaint or counterclaim for infringement in the action. For a case against the U.S. federal government, the six-year statute runs from the date of receipt of a written claim for compensation by the department or agency of the government that has authority to settle such a claim.

(e) Section 287: Limitation on Damages and Other Remedies; Marking and Notice. The patentee cannot hold an infringer responsible for damages unless the infringer has received proper notice, be it statutory notice or actual notice. Patentees who sell a patented article give statutory notice by marking their articles with the word *patent* or the abbreviation *pat*. Even if an infringer is not aware of this marking, § 287 considers the infringer notified by it. The patentee cannot claim damages against the infringer for any acts of infringement that occur before the patentee marked the patented article held for sale in the United States.

A patentee can also notify an infringer by an actual notice sent to the alleged infringer by the patentee. A patentee can also provide this notice by filing an action of infringement. The patentee can hold the infringer responsible for damages only after giving the infringer notice if the patentee did not mark the patented articles held for sale by the patentee.

(f) Section 271(f): Foreign Sales of Components Supplied from the United States. This section expands the royalty base to all the sales of the infringer no matter where in the world the sales occur. It reads as follows:

> This section holds that whoever without authority supplies or causes to be supplied in or from the United States all or a substantial portion of the components of a patented invention, where such components are uncombined in whole or in part, in such manner as to actively induce the combination of such components outside of the United States in a manner that would infringe the patent if such combination occurred within the United States, shall be liable as an infringer.[7]

22.4   CAUSATION

The practitioner must be familiar with the causal link between the infringement and the harm being measured. One cannot assume that the infringement automatically led to the patentee's lower sales and profits. Other market forces, including the introduction of other technologies, can cause the harm. Or the harm could have simply come from the infringer's entry into the market with any product rather than the infringing product. First, the plaintiff must describe a link that could reasonably explain the type and amount of the harm. Then one must examine other factors that could have caused the harm. Finally, one must consider the alternative *lawful* actions that the infringer could have taken. The infringement demonstrates that the infringer intends to have a presence in the market with a competitive product. One must take this into account.

22.5   LOST PROFIT DAMAGES

(a) Evolution of the Law.   Lost profit damages in patent cases have evolved more slowly than in other areas of the law. An unusual case, *Panduit Corp. v. Stahlin Bros. Fibre Works*, dominated thinking about patent damages from 1978 until 1990.[8] Today, it still plays a significant role. In *Panduit*, the court narrowed the definition of noninfringing substitutes for the patented product so as to accept the plaintiff's contention that it would have made all the defendant's sales of the infringing product. In 1990, *State Industries* allowed experts to use a simple market-share approach for estimating lost sales when noninfringing substitutes did not exist.[9] In 1993, *BIC Leisure Products Inc.* involved a more sophisticated examination of the market and competition.[10] Finally, in 1999, the court in *Grain Processing* established the use of a but-for analysis.[11]

Because *Panduit* dominated for so long and because courts have only recently embraced more sophisticated analysis, the practitioner will likely encounter damages claims of widely differing sophistication. Practitioners should understand these cases. They should also adopt a correct conceptual framework; otherwise, the court may reject their testimony (*see* Chapter 1). Finally, patent damages continue to evolve, so the practitioner needs to monitor the appellate decisions.[12]

(b) Panduit. *Panduit* states that a patentee can prove lost profits by meeting four conditions:[13]

1. Demand for the patented product
2. Absence of acceptable noninfringing substitutes
3. Manufacturing and marketing capability to exploit the demand
4. The amount of profit that would have been made

(i) Demand for the Patented Product. The plaintiff generally demonstrates demand for the patented product by showing significant sales of the infringing product. Because patentees usually do not take action against infringers who make few sales, the allegedly infringing product has been successful in the marketplace. Defendants often do not challenge this assertion. When they do, they tend to argue that the product's success did not rely on the patented feature. Because the patented invention's contribution is at the core of the patent's value, the practitioner should pay close attention to these arguments.

(ii) Absence of Acceptable Noninfringing Substitutes. Many courts have used the second condition, absence of acceptable noninfringing substitutes, as a bright line test that the parties often disputed. In those cases, the courts endeavored to decide whether Product A sufficiently resembled Product B that consumers could consider one as a substitute for the other. If the answer was *yes*, then courts disallowed lost profit damages. These cases often undercompensated plaintiffs who held infringed patents.[14] If the answer was *no*, then the plaintiff claimed that it would have made all of the infringer's sales. These cases often overcompensated the plaintiffs.

Many experts, including the authors, find the bright line approach too simplistic. In real markets, product substitution becomes a matter of degree and occurs across a spectrum. Consumers will substitute attendance at a baseball game with viewing the same game on TV, or attending another sporting activity, or going to a movie, or staying home with the family. Sometimes which entity offers the product makes a difference to the consumer. Other times, the product's price affects substitutability.

A product need not duplicate another for users to consider it a suitable substitute. It need only resemble the product enough that consumers would purchase it in place of another product. For the practitioner, this conceptual test becomes key to estimating the sales lost due to an infringement. The behavior of consumers in the marketplace provides the answer—not a particular technical or physical attribute of the product. For example, Internet access over copper telephone lines (commonly called DSL) offers a close substitute for access over coaxial cable (cable TV) even though the technologies differ.

The Court of Appeals in *Panduit* understood the reality of product substitution when it stated, "There are substitutes for virtually every product."[15] Although this overstates the situation, it points out a fatal flaw in the court's penchant for bright line tests: few infringed products would qualify for lost profit damages under *Panduit* if the courts adopted a market-oriented definition of substitution.

Rather than change the lost profits test, the Court of Appeals narrowed the definition of an acceptable substitute to the point at which it would find that most patented products have no substitutes. It did this by focusing on the product's technical attributes and the defendant's behavior during the litigation rather than consumer behavior.

Although courts have looked at consumer behavior in some cases, in others the court has refused to examine consumer behavior.[16] One even went so far as to rule that noninfringing wheelbarrows were not substitutes for infringing wheelbarrows because the latter had a patent.[17] In other words, only an infringing wheelbarrow could be an acceptable substitute. This effectively eliminated the test.

In the real markets for actual products, substitution becomes a matter of degree and varies from one product to another. Some products have none or only a few imperfect substitutes. Most, however, have substitutes that consumers interchange.[18] Thus, *Panduit* offers little guidance to the practitioner interested in measuring actual damages. Almost every lost profits damages claim cites it, however, and practitioners need to familiarize themselves with it.

(iii) Manufacturing and Marketing Capability to Exploit the Demand.   Courts often misapply the third *Panduit* factor, manufacturing and marketing capability, when they focus on whether a patentee had the necessary capacity in place to exploit the opportunity. From a conceptual standpoint, the courts should instead focus on whether the patentee would have been in a position to fulfill the additional sales had the infringement not occurred. Also, the courts often fail to consider other resources, including the managerial foresight and skill, that a successful product requires. In general, the courts have tended to ignore the need for such complementary resources and the prospect that a patentee could have obtained and deployed them. Nonetheless, an analysis of economic harm should consider these elements.

(iv) The Amount of Profit That Would Have Been Made.   Parties often dispute the fourth *Panduit* factor, the amount of lost profits. This involves the standard sorts of issues discussed elsewhere in this book.

If the patentee proves that the market has only two suppliers, then the patentee needs to prove only the third and fourth *Panduit* factors—its manufacturing and marketing capacity and its profit margin.[19]

(c) Market Share Approach.   When the patented product competes with noninfringing substitute products, the practitioner can estimate the patentee's lost sales by several methods. The federal circuit court in *State Industries* approved one of these, the market share approach. This approach looks at the patentee's historical sales in relation to all other competition in the market, except for the infringing sales, to estimate the percent of the infringing sales that the patentee could have sold. This offers an improvement over *Panduit* because it recognizes that the patentee might have made some of the infringer's sales even when substitutes existed. It also recognizes that the patentee might not have made all of the infringer's sales.

This approach, although less simplistic than *Panduit*, also requires simplifying assumptions. A number of factors affect market share, including the introduction of the new technology. If a new technology has a special appeal to consumers, it will presumably lead to an increased market share for the patentee so that using historical shares for the but-for world leads to a lower estimate of the patentee's lost sales than would have in fact occurred.

A more recent case, *BIC Leisure Products, Inc.,* introduced more sophistication into the market share approach. The Court of Appeals for the Federal Circuit Court (CAFC) in *BIC* rejected the plaintiff's application of the historical market share approach because the plaintiff had not properly analyzed the market.

The market in the *BIC* case dealt with sailboards for windsurfing. Windsurfing International made sailboards that fit the specifications of the One-Design competition class, with an average sales price of approximately $600. The plaintiff, BIC Leisure Products, made sailboards called Open Class boards, which did not meet the specifications of the One-Design competition class but were faster, more maneuverable, and more versatile. These sailboards sold for less—around $350 per board. The court found that the people who bought BIC Leisure's sailboards probably would not have bought the more expensive, different sailboards manufactured by Windsurfing. Instead, the court ruled that they would have purchased other low-price sailboards of the same type. If the patentee had used Windsurfing's market share of the Open Class board market rather than the total sailboard market, the court would probably have sustained the award of lost profits. *BIC* needed a proper analysis of the market before the market share approach would accurately calculate lost sales.

BIC and subsequent cases require that the practitioner correctly analyze the market for the product and the competitive forces in that market. The sophistication of *BIC* also suggests that practitioners need not confine themselves to historical market shares. A properly conducted market analysis that concluded the patentee would have increased its market share but for the infringement would be consistent with the ruling in *BIC*.[20]

The market share approach must address other competitors in the market that also arguably infringe the patents at issue. The patentee normally wants to exclude the market share of all potential infringers. Excluding these competitors will increase the but-for patentee's market share and increase the amount of lost profits damages. The most likely candidates for exclusion would be any other competitor that the patentee has sued under the same patents. It can also include those that have received a notice informing them of the infringement. Finally, patentees may want to exclude competitors that the patentees believe infringe their patents. Conversely, the defendant argues that a market share calculation should exclude only competitors that the court has found to infringe. The case law offers no discussion on this issue, except that of *Pall Corp. v. Micron Separations, Inc.*[21] This case holds that if the other suppliers (competitors) "were likely infringers," then the patentee could claim their shares of the market when computing damages based on lost sales. The finding did not define the phrase "likely infringers."[22]

(d) Estimating Lost Sales.   Estimating lost sales in a patent case involves many of the same analyses as in other cases discussed elsewhere in this book. Patent cases, however, almost always involve actual sales of the product, whereas other lost profit claims may not. Both the infringer's and the patentee's sales of the product provide information as to what the sales would have been but for the infringement.

(i) Infringer's Sales. In the past, when the patentee had not licensed its patent to others,[23] both the plaintiff and courts assumed that the patentee would have made all of the infringing sales. For this assumption to hold, all the following conditions must hold: (1) no substitutes existed for the product other than those made by the parties to the suit; (2) the infringer had no noninfringing product to offer (including the current one but without the patented feature); (3) the infringer could not invent around the patent; (4) the companies were identical in every economically significant way; and (5) the infringer priced and promoted the product in a fashion similar to that of the patentee. Often one or more of these conditions will not hold, and the practitioner should make adjustments or even adopt a different approach if necessary.

In any event, the volume of patented items that the infringer sold offers a good starting point for the analysis, because these represent actual transactions. One can then adjust the volume for market realities. Quantifying the historical volume, however, can become complicated. Companies will not likely segregate records by infringing and noninfringing sales. Sometimes analysts have difficulty obtaining even sales by model number.

The practitioner must first identify the infringing products by the product numbers or labels used by the infringer. Sometimes normal discovery produces this information. Technical and industry experts can also prove useful in developing the list of infringing products. Sometimes counsel will simply ask the financial expert to assume that the court will find certain products as infringing. Because the parties often dispute this, one should maintain the separate product identities throughout the calculations.

With a list of infringing products, the analyst can use the infringer's accounting records to ascertain the volume of infringing sales. When the company has no summary sales reports with the information needed to compute the infringing sales, the expert can turn to individual invoices if the company has retained copies. This process takes time and becomes costly, however, and the individual invoices often provide only ambiguous infringing sales information. Counsel may agree that sampling will provide cost-effective information. Analysts can use computerized accounting systems to compile the data. This approach requires the defendant's cooperation because each system requires specialized knowledge. Obtaining such cooperation often proves difficult and rarely will the defendant allow independent verification.

The infringer's production records often provide data for calculating the dollar amount of infringing sales. Sometimes production records include the necessary detail. One must not assume that the company sold all of the infringing production. In the semiconductor industry, for example, companies scrap a significant amount of production that fails to perform as specified. Analysts can estimate the quantity sold, as opposed to manufactured, by evaluating the quantity of infringing goods currently in inventory and by obtaining records of returns, free goods, and other dispositions of production.

One litigation-related analysis used a random sample of customers to examine the products they purchased for the infringing feature. The calculation then multiplied the percentage of these products with the infringing feature by total shipments to estimate the number of infringing units.

Usually the patentee will use an interrogatory to inquire as to the infringer's sales volume. In many cases, the parties agree on the unit volume or at least identify where they disagree. Indeed, accountants retained by one party often work with their counterparts retained by the other party to come to some agreement on the relevant sales or profits, or both. The parties often make such agreements contingent on unresolved disputed issues. For example, the parties often agree that the sales of product X were $Y and the profits on those sales were $Z, without agreeing on whether product X infringed the patent.

When all else fails, the practitioner can rely on the principle that an infringer cannot escape paying damages simply because it has incomplete records. The plaintiff's expert need only rely on the best available evidence. Courts permit reasonable assumptions at times, and the infringer has the burden to prove otherwise.

(ii) The Patentee's Sales.   Examining the patentee's sales can provide information useful for measuring the lost sales. Analysts might examine this information in much the same way as they would examine that of the infringer and then assume that the infringer's customers have the same preference for the patented feature. Also, a change in a patentee's sales trends that coincides with the introduction of the infringing product creates a strong inference of lost sales. The practitioner will find the usual tools of statistics helpful at this point.

If both parties have a small number of units sold, the analyst can examine each customer's purchases. Often, both parties have kept records on each sale that the analyst can review and then use to calculate the infringement's effect on the sale made. One can usually identify the patented feature's effect on the product's functionality. Analysts can then compare the effect with each customer's preference for that function and assess the customer's but-for choice. Often, however, the parties do not want to disturb their customers or reveal any customer-specific information that would have value to a competitor.

(iii) Industry Sales.   If substitute products exist, the practitioner should consider examining sales trends in the entire industry. The methods used could include the simple historical share approach of *Mor-Flo*[24] or more sophisticated models. In some circumstances, the complex models allow the analyst to assess the importance to the consumer of a single patented feature on a product involving multiple features. Thus, the analyst can assess the infringement's effect on the patentee's sales even when many competing products exist, each with a different mix of features.[25]

(iv) Other Considerations.   The analyst also needs to consider brand loyalties. Some of the infringer's customers, for instance, might buy only from the infringer, especially if the industry practice is to consolidate all purchases from one supplier. Or some customers might have been unwilling to purchase from the patentee because of unfavorable past dealings, its reputation, service, or other factors. Sometimes the infringer expands the demand for the product beyond the market that the patentee, alone, could service. This can result from the infringer's superior marketing capability, additional advertising expenditures, different distribution channels, or simply different geographic locations. Perhaps the infringer sold the infringing product at a discount and expanded sales by obtaining a price-sensitive segment

that the patentee did not serve. One must address the standard business considerations in making a sales forecast when estimating lost sales.

(v) Capacity Considerations. After measuring the patentee's potential lost sales, *Panduit* requires the patentee to show it had the capacity to produce and sell the additional units of the patented product. An analysis should also consider whether the patentee had the organizational ability to achieve the increased sales. This would include the ability to recognize the potential for increased sales, the correct strategy for achieving those sales, the skills required to position, market, and distribute the product effectively, and the ability to grow and manage the workforce as needed.

The expert should study the patentee's actual capacity and its use during the infringement period. Many manufacturing companies maintain records of capacity use. Alternatively, a study of the manufacturing process might help identify key or bottleneck resources. The analysis should compare the actual use of these resources with their practical capacity. Production cycles and peaks as well as the use of extra shifts merit consideration. As production facilities and processes become more complex and flexible, measuring the capacity to produce a particular product becomes more difficult. With the increasing use of robotics, computer control, and more complicated machinery, production runs have become shorter, and particular production lines and machines can make several different products. Consequently, one often cannot easily measure the economic effect of dedicating a production line to one particular product. Finally, the decision to manufacture a particular product often affects the costs and the ability to make and sell other products. In such cases, the analyst will need to increase or decrease the estimated damages.

Even without any existing capacity to produce some or all of the infringer's sales, the patentee might show it could have or would have expanded its manufacturing capacity to meet the additional sales. The infringer will argue that this hypothetical expansion of capacity involves speculation. Evidence to rebut the charge of speculation can include a history of plant expansions to meet sales demand, contemporaneous cost analysis of required plant expansion, and sufficient fund-raising ability to pay for the capital expansion. Also, the patentee's strategic and operating plans and budgets often reveal discussions of capacity expansion during the infringement period, or, better yet, capacity adjustments not made because of the presence of the infringer.

If the patentee's history shows a pattern of capacity expansions over time as demand expands, this evidence will support an argument that, but for the infringement, capacity and sales would have expanded. Conversely, a patentee's capacity constraints during periods of high demand can show a reluctance to expand capacity.

The analyst should also consider the infringement's duration. With a longer period, the firm will find it easier to increase capacity. Conversely, with time, the firm often shifts its resources to other products, reducing damages. Likewise, the analyst should consider the magnitude of the lost sales. With larger lost unit sales, the patentee would expand capacity to meet the demand only with difficulty or, in the other direction, with economies of scale (thereby decreasing unit costs).

(vi) Correct Unit Price. To establish lost revenue, the patentee must identify unit prices. Typically, the plaintiff's damages study refers to prices the infringer

charged because they reflect actual transactions by customers. Circumstances sometimes lead to a different but-for price. If the infringer received a higher price because of added value—for example, a better warranty—the patentee should not claim the premium attached to this feature unless the projection also considers the feature's added cost and the likelihood that the patentee would have offered a similar feature. The analysis must compare the patentee's and the infringer's terms of sale (e.g., credit and warranties), that is, the product's total package price. If the infringer's price exceeds the patentee's because of added value, the but-for unit price will differ from the infringer's actual price.

Patentees often argue that but for the infringement, they would have had higher prices because competition from the infringer depressed actual prices for both parties. Under this theory, the patentee has also lost revenues on its actual sales as well as its lost sales, so analysts often treat this element of damages separately. The patentee must establish the amount of price reduction and that the actions of the infringer caused the price reduction.[26] Practitioners refer to these as *price erosion damages,* and they imply that the patentee possessed some form of market power before the infringement. Because defendants in patent cases often file antitrust counterclaims, an implication of market power can have serious consequences for the patentee.[27]

Whenever the patentee asserts that prices in the but-for world would have been different from prices in the actual world, the actual quantities that either party sold may no longer accurately reflect but-for quantities. As prices increase, sales in units normally decrease and vice versa. Consequently, one must analyze the responsiveness of quantity demanded relative to prices charged for the patented product sold.[28] Economists call this the *price elasticity of demand.* The analysis should also study noninfringing alternatives (i.e., substitute goods) and their ability to affect the patentee's price and quantity sold. If analysts can obtain the appropriate data, they can use econometrics to measure the relation of price to quantity (*see* Chapter 3).

(e) Entire Market Value Rule. Patentees often receive damages for lost profits on not only the patented product but also on products that it normally sells along with the patented product. Practitioners often refer to these products as *convoyed* or *collateral sales.* The law awards profits on the convoyed sales because the patentee has the right to the invention's "entire market value."[29]

Over the years, the courts have struggled with mixed results to define convoyed goods. Some courts have opted for a technical analysis of whether the convoyed goods relate to the patented device in such a way that they function together. Others have focused on whether, for marketing reasons, the company sells the goods together. Still other courts have required the patentee to prove that the patented item's sales caused the convoyed good's sales. Recent cases on this topic, *Rite-Hite* and *King Instruments,* appear inconsistent and confusing.[30]

In *Rite-Hite,* the court did not award profits on the convoyed product because it found the unpatented component (dock levelers) did not function together with the patented component (a type of vehicle restraint) or another unpatented component (another type of vehicle restraint) in some manner so as to produce a desired end product or result. The court held that all the components together must be analogous to components of a single assembly or be parts of a complete machine, or they must constitute a functional unit. In this case, the court found that the consumers used the products together, but the company sold the convoyed products with the patented product only for marketing reasons, not because they essentially functioned together.

Conversely, in *King Instruments*, the court allowed lost profits on the spare parts for the unpatented machine that the patentee sold. This case has significance because the court allowed lost profits on products sold by the patentee that did not contain the patented invention. This is because the patent law permits the patentee to exclude others from using the invention; it does not require the patentee to use the invention. Where the patentees believe they will maximize profits by selling other products without competition from others using the invention, the patent laws will allow them to claim lost profits. *King Instruments* expanded this to include lost profits on spare parts as well.

The causation approach has the strongest appeal to those interested in the infringement's economic consequences. How far down the causation chain the courts should go, however, becomes a policy issue. For now, practitioners should consult with their clients before calculating the lost sales of convoyed goods.

The Entire Market Value Rule also relates to reasonable royalty calculations. If the patented feature drives the demand for the product, then courts often consider some or all of the profits from the sale of the product in assessing the appropriate royalty rate. If the patented feature, however, does not drive the demand for the product containing the patented feature, the analyst must apportion the profit before selecting the reasonable royalty rate.[31] (*See* Section 22.6(n) of this chapter, which discusses the thirteenth of the *Georgia Pacific* factors.)

(f) Accelerated Reentry Damages.   A successful patent suit usually results in an injunction against the infringer's further use of the patented technology. Thus, lost profit damages in patent cases usually involve only past lost sales. Some infringements, however, can have lingering effects that lead to future lost profits. Accelerated reentry damages (also called accelerated market entry damages) are a form of lost future profits in a patent infringement case. The theory behind these damages recognizes that the infringer gains a head start by obtaining some market share before the patent monopoly expires. As a result, instead of starting from a base of zero sales at the patent's expiration, the infringer starts from a base of established sales. If the period of infringement lasts through the patent's expiration, the infringer has gained a head start. This will cause the patentee to have lower sales after the patent expires than if the infringer had never infringed during the patent's duration.

Similarly, an infringer can use the period of infringement to develop a noninfringing alternative, thereby protecting or obtaining a market share it would not have had. Some courts have addressed this injury by enjoining the infringer from selling the noninfringing product for a period of time. Others have simply awarded additional damages. In either case, the expert will likely testify as to the temporal issues.

(g) Estimating Costs.   Cost calculations in a patent infringement case resemble those of most other litigation. Therefore, we refer the reader to Chapters 5 through 16 for a full discussion and will list here some issues that an expert should consider.

One needs to include only the incremental costs that arise from the incremental sales. The federal circuit has approved the incremental income approach in *Paper Converting Machine Co. v. Magna-Graphics Corp.*[32] This requires characterizing costs as fixed or variable and identifying the fixed and variable components of semivariable costs. One often uses regression analyses (*see* Chapters 5 and 6), engineering studies (which scrutinize the actual relation between volume and costs), and account analyses (line-by-line categorization of chart of accounts) for this purpose.[33] One must avoid naively analyzing a company's financial statements without first making adjustments. Most companies use absorption accounting, which allocates a portion of fixed manufacturing overhead to the cost of each unit produced, muddling the distinction between fixed and variable costs. Also, the company's time horizon (inherent in the financial reporting system) often lacks relevance to the litigation; differing time horizons affect the characterization of costs as fixed or variable.

Multiproduct companies often have substantial common costs to allocate to individual products, which usually require statistical analysis. The most important consideration in patent cases, however, relates to claims that involve increases in unit sales over long periods. For long-enough time spans, all the costs, even corporate overhead, become variable. Furthermore, the additional sales often require some expenditures not normally shown on an income statement, like capital expenditures.

22.6 REASONABLE ROYALTY

(a) Case Law Guidelines. Patent law awards a patentee no "less than a reasonable royalty for the use of the invention by the infringer."[34] Thus, a patentee who does not use the patent can still collect damages. Furthermore, some courts award a patentee a reasonable royalty if it exceeds the lost profits. Finally, sometimes the court awards royalty damages to a patentee who fails to prove lost profits.

Courts have tended to view the manufacture and sale of each product as a separate act of infringement. Thus, when patentees could not prove they would have made all of the infringer's sales, the courts have awarded the patentee both the profits on the portion of the infringer's sales that the patentee demonstrated it would have made (i.e., its lost sales) and a reasonable royalty on the remainder of the infringing sales. As Section 22.8 of this chapter discusses, this legalistic approach can create a conceptual problem for the practitioner.

(b) Ascertaining a Reasonable Royalty. Actual licenses specify royalties in many ways, including an aggregate dollar amount, or a dollar amount applied to some measure of quantity, or a percentage rate applied to some base (e.g., the selling price or the manufacturing cost), some other negotiated amount, or a combination of these. A reasonable royalty claim can use any of these. The choice usually depends on the situation, including practices in the industry. The analyst will want to examine how the particular industry typically structures licenses.

When the royalty uses either a dollar or percentage rate, the analyst will also need to select the base to which one will apply this rate. In doing so, one should use a rate consistent with the base. For example, if one uses comparable licenses to establish the rate, then the analysis should also use the bases used in those same licenses. The expert cannot use a rate typical for a component and apply it to the entire product.[35]

Regardless of which royalty approach analysts use, they will face the same problem: how does one select a reasonable royalty in the absence of an actual arm's length negotiated agreement between the patentee and the infringer (as a would-be licensee)? Although the insights of game theory can help, solid analytical formulas do not exist. Typically the two parties to the dispute will be far apart on a reasonable royalty. Patent case law provides little enlightenment on the analytics of establishing a rate, but it does suggest a framework for the analysis.

Panduit states that a reasonable royalty equals an amount that a person who wants to manufacture and sell a patented article would willingly pay as a royalty and still realize a reasonable profit on the item. The *Panduit* court also considered the other half of the negotiation, namely, the amount the patentee would have accepted. *Panduit* cited *Egry,* stating that:

> when the patentee's business scheme involves a reasonable expectation of making future profits by the continuing sale to the purchaser of the patented machine, of supplies to be furnished by the patentee, which future business he will lose by licensing a competitor to make the machine, this expectant loss is an element to be considered in retroactively determining a reasonable royalty.[36]

The *Grain Processing* decision in 1999 reinforced this concept.[37] Thus, an expert must analyze the negotiation from both perspectives.

Both of these courts relied on the decision in *Georgia-Pacific* to select the specific royalty rate.[38] The district court in *Georgia-Pacific* summarized 15 factors (discussed in the remainder of this section) used in prior decisions to establish a reasonable royalty. From an economic perspective, some of these factors seem redundant, whereas the court stated others in a fashion that does not reflect all the relevant economic considerations. Moreover, the appropriate weights to place on each factor vary by situation. Finally, the 15 *Georgia-Pacific* factors do not discuss some important economic determinants of a patent's value. Nonetheless, the *Georgia-Pacific* factors provide helpful guidance to the expert. Because courts refer to this case so widely, the practitioner should make explicit use of the 15 *Georgia-Pacific* factors in any reports.[39]

(c) The Hypothetical Negotiation.   The most important *Georgia-Pacific* factor is the last one (number 15), because it summarizes and shapes most of the others. This discusses the hypothetical negotiation that *Georgia-Pacific* defines by stating that a reasonable royalty should equal

> the amount that a licensor (such as the patentee) and a licensee (such as the infringer) would have agreed upon (at the time the infringement began) if both had been reasonably and voluntarily trying to reach an agreement; that is, the amount which a prudent licensee—who desired, as a business proposition, to obtain a license to manufacture and sell a particular article embodying the patented invention—would have been willing to pay as a royalty and yet be able to make a reasonable profit and which amount would have been acceptable by a prudent patentee who was willing to grant a license.[40]

This criterion assumes that a reasonable royalty would be set at the rate that a generic licensor and licensee (who are similar to the parties) would have negotiated at the outset of infringement. Conceptually, this factor, a hypothetical negotiation, blends the other factors in *Georgia-Pacific* and, therefore, provides a sound basis, absent a directly comparable proxy rate, for suggesting the appropriate reasonable royalty rate.

The court in *Panduit,* however, cautions that the law should not carry the fiction of a negotiation too far:

> The setting of a reasonable royalty after infringement cannot be treated as the equivalent of ordinary royalty negotiations among truly "willing" patent owners and licensees. That view would constitute a pretense that the infringement never happened. It would also make an election to infringe a handy means for competitors to impose a "compulsory license" policy upon every patent owner.[41]

The court further pointed out that

> determination of a "reasonable royalty" after infringement, like many devices in the law, rests on a legal fiction. Created in an effort to "compensate" when profits are not provable, the "reasonable royalty" device conjures a "willing" licensor and licensee, who like Ghosts of Christmas Past are seen dimly as "negotiating" a "license." There is, of course, no actual willingness on either side and no license to do anything, the infringer being normally enjoined from further manufacture, use, or sale of the patented product.[42]

In *Panduit*, the court resolves this conundrum by referring to the factors set out in the *Georgia-Pacific* case and suggesting that one also consider the licensee's profits. In contrast, Congress specifically rejected disgorging the licensee's profits when it enacted the current patent law; Supreme Court decisions at that time had also prohibited disgorgement. Unfortunately, the court in *Panduit* did not attempt to reconcile these opposing views. The CAFC has recently ruled that "although an infringer's anticipated profit from use of the patented invention is among the factors to be considered in determining a reasonable royalty, the law does not require that an infringer be permitted to make a profit."[43] The CAFC also found that the infringer could pay a royalty even though the infringer was already selling the infringing product at a loss. The court again stated that "there is no rule that a royalty be no higher than the Infringer's net profit margin."[44]

Likewise, the *Panduit* concern about a compulsory license is inappropriate. As the dissent in *Rite-Hite* pointed out, infringement cases do not grant permanent licenses because they enjoin the infringer from using the technology.[45] *Panduit* acknowledges this.[46] Thus, it appears that the expert should use the conceptual framework of the hypothetical negotiation but not feel bound by it.

(d) The Infringer's Next Best Available Alternative.   *Georgia-Pacific* does not explicitly mention the next most important factor in determining a reasonable royalty: an analysis of the various lawful (noninfringing) alternatives available to the infringer. These would tend to dominate any negotiation and influence the expert's economic analysis of the remaining *Georgia-Pacific* factors. This becomes crucial to establishing what the parties would have agreed to.

Georgia-Pacific does recognize at least one lawful alternative of the infringer: inventing around the patent. Also, *Grain Processing* explicitly states, by the same token, a fair and accurate reconstruction of the "but for" market also must take into account, where relevant, alternative actions the infringer foreseeably would have undertaken had he not infringed. Without the infringing product, a rational would-be infringer is likely to offer an acceptable noninfringing alternative, if available, to compete with the patent owner rather than leave the market altogether. The competitor in the "but for" marketplace is hardly likely to surrender its complete market share when faced with a patent, if it can compete in some other lawful manner. Moreover, only by comparing the patented invention to its next-best available alternative(s)—regardless of whether the alternative(s) were actually produced and sold during the infringement—can the court discern the market value of the patent owner's exclusive right, and therefore his expected profit or reward, had the infringer's activities not prevented him from taking full economic advantage of this right.[47]

This excerpt summarizes the conceptual approach required of an expert calculating either lost profits or reasonable royalties. It states that the goal is to "discern the *market value* of the patentee's exclusive right" (emphasis added) and the infringement's effect on that value. It also indicates that the expert needs to describe a realistic but-for marketplace that includes the defendant's likely lawful behavior. Damages analyses in other areas of the law use such analyses.

As in other areas of the law, one would not expect the court to require a patentee to consider and rule out every possible response by the infringer. Thus, the expert should identify the lawful responses and select the most likely ones to consider. Some obvious behaviors include inventing around the patent, selecting a different and perhaps inferior feature, or eliminating the patented feature altogether. Others include not offering the product at all and employing the resources elsewhere.[48]

An analysis of alternatives addresses legal issues involving the scope of the patent and technical issues regarding the feasibility and cost of noninfringing alternatives, both of which will likely fall outside the scope of the damages expert's professional expertise. Consequently, damages experts often rely on expert testimony by others. Damages experts should make clear the degree to which their opinion rests on such testimony.

(e) The Time of the Negotiation.   *Panduit* and the cases that address the issue of timing generally place the negotiations at the time of the first infringement. This is often unrealistic because no company would develop a product, build the facilities to produce it, and commit itself to launching the product before negotiating a license. Waiting until the last minute would place the infringer in an untenable position. Because case law stipulates a hypothetical situation in which neither party faces coercion, the expert should not consider the pressures that would arise from a last-minute negotiation. Balancing this consideration is public policy that would oppose such benefits to an infringer over an innocent patent owner.

The related issues of timing and coercion present some of the most difficult subjects of the hypothetical negotiation. On the one hand, the *Georgia-Pacific* hypothetical negotiation calls for willing parties. On the other, setting the negotiation at the date of first infringement (or in some cases, a later date of notice) can place the infringer in a must-license position. Some patent owners have excluded investment costs from their calculations of the infringer's profits on the grounds that these are sunk costs at the time of the hypothetical negotiation. Others have argued for unusually high royalty rates on the grounds that the infringer dare not cut off supplies to customers who have purchased or want to purchase infringing products. Because these factors are not present in a conventional royalty negotiation, introducing them reduces the validity and analytical value of hypothetical negotiations. Unfortunately, no case law gives guidance on this important consideration of the hypothetical negotiation.[49]

The timing of the negotiations also becomes important because it can affect the parties' perceptions of their positions, which in turn can affect the royalties they would agree to. When perceptions have changed over time, the parties will likely dispute the timing of the hypothetical negotiation. If the evidence permits, the analysis should consider each party's view of the market, the expected profitability of the patented item, and other benefits at the time of the infringement and at the most likely time that the parties would have negotiated. To the extent that analysts believe that the choice of the relevant date would significantly affect the negotiated royalty rate, they may want to clarify this dependence, as well as the date(s) used in their analyses.

Analysts most often approach the parties' perceptions through a review of past policies and behavior and contemporaneous documents. Ideally, discovery would reveal reliable projections, memoranda, market research, competitive analysis reports, project evaluation techniques, and decision factors such as rates of return and hurdle rates that measure the profitability percentage that a company desires to earn. Also, any documents that suggest either party's view of the invention's value will help the analyst, who can also search relevant trade journals, newspapers, and business periodicals to reconstruct a party's outlook.

(f) Advantages and Disadvantages of Licensing.   When considering the hypothetical license, the patentee and licensee consider benefits and disadvantages for such an arrangement, including those listed in this section.

- **Benefits for the patentee**
  - Licensing can exploit an invention more quickly and can expand the total market for the invention. This usually becomes the case if the licensee has greater resources and skills than the patentee. Such complementary assets include tangible assets such as specialized production facilities and distribution systems as well as intangibles such as market leadership and reputation.
  - If the potential licensee could lawfully enter the market by using a noninfringing alternative, the patentee can expect to lose sales anyway. Licensing, then, presents a way for the patentee to make the best of a bad situation by capturing some profit on the lost sales.
  - Because royalties increase the patentee's own profits and decrease the infringer's profits, licensing can give the patentee a financial advantage over the new entrant.
  - Licensing can reduce risks associated with building the capacity and investing in other activities necessary to exploit the total market, particularly in a cyclical industry.
  - Licensing can also expand the market by creating demand through more than one company's advertising and marketing efforts.
  - The patentee can set a precedent for licensing in case it needs competitors' patented technology in the future.[50]

- Licensing can dissuade others from developing inventions that could make the patented item obsolete.
- Licensing may lead to the patentee's technology becoming an industry standard.[51]

- **Disadvantages for the patentee**

  - The exclusive use of the technology may lead to sales and profits that are higher than normal.
  - Exclusive use of the technology may be key to follow-on inventions or related opportunities.

- **Benefits for the licensee**

  - A license reduces the costs and risks of attempting to invent a similar product without infringing.
  - A license may reduce the time necessary to get to market.

- **Disadvantages for the licensee**

  - The licensee may establish the licensor's technology as an industry standard.
  - The licensee may forego any opportunity to gain technological leadership and may become dependent on the licensor for new technology.
  - Royalties increase the firm's variable costs, making it more vulnerable in a downturn.

(g) Similar Licenses: Patentee and Licensee.   *Georgia-Pacific*'s first two factors state the following:

1. The royalties received by the patentee for the licensing of the patent in suit, proving or tending to prove an established royalty.
2. The rates paid by the licensee for the use of other patents comparable to the patent in suit.[52]

Thus, where arm's length negotiations for the same or similar inventions exist, the rates established in those negotiations should guide the choice of the reasonable royalty for the product at issue.

(i) Complex Licenses.   In practice, disputed patents that go to litigation usually involve complex licenses.[53] For example, the patent owner may have licensed the patent in return for a license on a patent owned by the other party. This is called a *cross-license*. Sometimes, a cross-license also involves a balancing payment or payments from one party to the other. Often, a cross-license involves multiple patents. In those cases, the dispute will likely center around the expert's unraveling of the license or licenses to arrive at an equivalent royalty.

(ii) Comparable Licenses.   When no licenses exist for the patent in suit, experts usually rely on licenses they select as comparable. Then the parties dispute the comparability. Initially, courts were reluctant to consider any licenses for different technologies or licenses negotiated in the context of litigation. Today, the courts differ as to which licenses one should consider as comparable.

As regards the analysis, a comparable license contains similar terms and conditions and involves technology of similar economic value. In trying to assess the economic value, courts often focus on the technology itself. If the technology enabled a similar product feature, courts consider it comparable. The courts have tended to reject royalty rates for technologies that provided for different product features. From an economic perspective, such a focus on technology alone becomes too restrictive because it deprives the expert access to significant relevant information.

Comparability of licenses involves comparisons of economic benefits rather than technology. The market value of the benefits provided by the technology determines actual royalty rates. Courts correctly assume that different technologies providing the same product functionality have equal market values. Courts act in a short sighted manner, however, if they reject licenses for technologies that provide equally desirable but different functionalities. For example, memory chips embody a multitude of patents with no single patent dominating. Even though the circuit designs differ functionally, royalty rates on these patents tend to fall into a narrow range. Thus, even though the technology differs, these licenses provide guidance for the expert.

One should base the test of comparability on the value in the marketplace of the functionality provided by the patent and not on the physical properties of a particular technology. An analysis of licensing rates of other patents embodied in the product or of licensing practices in the industry can help. License rates within an industry tend to cluster.

Courts remain reluctant to allow examination of licenses negotiated in the context of litigation. The authors find this difficult to understand, because parties negotiate all licenses with an eye toward the potential threat of litigation. The only difference lies in how far the litigation proceeded before the parties signed the license. With proper adjustment for the differences, the expert could discern useful information in the actual outcomes of royalty negotiations.[54]

Parties to the suit provide the best available sources for comparable licenses. Ideally, the analyst should review copies of all the licenses of each party. Usually, however, the parties produce only those licenses they deem comparable. The practitioner should suggest a broader production. If the opposing party objects (a likely outcome), the practitioner can support the client's pursuit of the licenses through an affidavit.

(iii) Variability in Licenses. Licenses tend to vary widely in economic terms. Some involve lump sum payments. Others use percentages that the agreement applies to selling prices or certain costs. Still others use combinations of these. The analyst will have to develop a consistent method for expressing the key economic factors, which include the expected cash flows and the appropriate risk-adjusted discount rate.

Analysts should watch out for other licenses that involve payment in kind. Cross-licenses provide a good example of this. Focusing on the cash-only provisions of such licenses, such as the stated royalty payments, ignores the value of these in-kind payments, which (as an economic matter) often dwarf the value of the cash payments.[55]

(iv) High Royalty Rates.   Interestingly, courts have held that royalty rates can exceed those found in practice and may bear little relation to any royalty the parties would have agreed on.[56] The authors find it hard to reconcile this with the concept of a hypothetical negotiation. Some courts have talked about a separate higher royalty for an infringer. Most of these discussions relate to deterrence. Because a separate section of patent damages provides for punitive damages, this practice has little economic justification.

The hypothetical negotiation can, however, provide an economic rationale for a royalty rate that exceeds those observed in practice. Specifically, the hypothetical negotiation assumes that the parties negotiate under the assumption of a valid, enforceable, and infringed patent. In contrast, real-world negotiations often involve uncertainty about validity, enforceability, and infringement, which would tend to depress the negotiated rate. Thus, rates resulting from the hypothetical negotiation can exceed those observed in the real world. The upward adjustment should not come anywhere close to the multiples that some courts use, however. Some license agreements specify a lower royalty rate going forward if later developments prove a patent to be invalid or unenforceable. The analyst can use the difference between this lower rate and the higher rate to estimate a premium for a presumed valid and enforceable patent.

(h) Commercial Considerations.   The third, fourth, fifth, and seventh factors of the court in *Georgia-Pacific* set forth additional commercial considerations in selecting the appropriate royalty rate:

3. The nature and scope of the license, as exclusive or nonexclusive; or as restricted or nonrestricted in terms of territory or with respect to whom the manufactured product may be sold.

4. The licensor's established policy and marketing program to maintain his patent monopoly by not licensing others to use the invention or by granting licenses under special conditions designed to preserve that monopoly.

5. The commercial relationship between the licensor and licensee, such as, whether they are competitors in the same territory in the same line of business; or whether they are inventor and promoter.

7. The duration of the patent and the term of the license.[57]

These four factors raise fact (or descriptive) issues, and the analyst should evaluate them to judge how, if at all, observed royalty rates apply to the infringed product. If similarities exist between an actual license and the hypothetical license, the observed royalty rate can provide a starting point to ascertain the appropriate hypothetical rate. If differences exist between the licensing situations, the expert can make appropriate adjustments.

Courts use *Georgia-Pacific's* third factor to adjust any observed exclusive or restricted royalty rates. The hypothetical always assumes an unrestricted, nonexclusive license because infringement, by its nature, is unilateral.

In the authors' opinion, experts and courts have often misinterpreted the fourth *Georgia-Pacific* factor, patentee practice. They have tended to view an infringement when the patentee has not licensed in the past as a form of coercion that the law should prevent at all costs. This has led them to conclude that a company's historical refusal to license should justify a higher rate than one that hypothetical negotiations would suggest. The courts have also dismissed any consideration that the infringement made everyone better off.[58] In *Santa Fe-Pomeroy Inc. v. P&Z Company, Inc.,*[59] this position led to a reasonable royalty award designed to recover all the patentee's lost profits.[60]

In *Santa Fe-Pomeroy*, the plaintiff did not have a practice of licensing and had intended to profit from its lawful monopoly without licensing. The district court found that with the unusual facts of this case, "particularly where the patentee did not license his patented process, a reasonable royalty equated to expected profit is a satisfactory reasonable approximation."[61] An expert should avoid accepting this as a general proposition because it has no empirical or theoretical basis.

Observed royalty rates do not come close to returning lost profits even when the patentee has reluctantly come to the negotiation table. As Section 22.6(f) of this chapter discusses, a patentee who has not previously granted a license often licenses for something less than expected lost profits. This most likely occurs because the patentee views competition from the would-be licensee as inevitable. If the would-be licensee can enter the market with a noninfringing alternative, even an inferior one, the patentee will often expect to lose some sales anyway. Furthermore, licensing can shift risk from the patentee to the licensee and allow the licensor to avoid the cost of assembling the complementary resources needed for success.

One should interpret the decision of the patentee not to license a particular patent simply as evidence that the patentee views retaining exclusivity as the most profitable exploitation of the patent. Because the patentee adopts this policy prior to any litigation, it provides an unbiased opinion that the expert must consider. The expert, however, needs to distinguish between a specific decision not to license and a blanket policy of not licensing any patents. A company could adopt the second policy even though it does not believe this will maximize profits in every situation. A blanket policy of this sort indicates only that on average the company maximizes profits by not licensing, and the expert cannot conclude anything about a particular patent.[62]

The fifth factor, the relations between the parties, becomes a question of the strategic value of withholding an invention. This merits attention when the company can use the patent to prevent current or future competition. If the patentee cannot use the patent to prevent competition, then it loses any incentive to refuse to license an existing competitor or a new one. In some situations, a patentee can benefit strategically from licensing a competitor if it establishes the owner's technology as a standard or if it discourages the competitor from developing its own possibly superior technology.

The seventh factor, duration of the license, reflects the belief that patents close to their expiration date will command a smaller rate or fee than those with a long remaining life. It enters the analysis because many of the cases involve periods of infringement that are short relative to the current 20 year life of a patent.[63] One would expect that this factor would lead to a lower rate than those observed in practice. The expert, however, should review the context of the historical licenses and the facts of the present case before forming a conclusion. Many experts assume that the duration of the hypothetical license is identical to the term of the patent. The authors disagree with this position, suggesting that if the patent owner is seeking an injunction, the term of the hypothetical license should end at the judgment date.

(i) Effect on Sales of Other Products.   *Georgia-Pacific*'s sixth factor addresses related products:

>   **6.** The effect of selling the patented specialty in promoting sales of other products of the licensee; the existing value of the invention to the licensor as a generator of sales of his non-patented items; and the extent of such derivative or convoyed sales.[64]

The patented product often generates convoyed sales of other nonpatented products, either goods that consumers typically purchase at the same time, or supplies for the patented product, or replacement parts and service contracts. This factor resembles the Entire Market Value Rule discussed in Section 22.5(e) of this chapter. It affects the computation of royalties in two ways: the selection of the royalty rate and the amount of sales to which one applies the royalty rate (i.e., the royalty base). Because the royalty equals the product of the rate and base, theory and practice inextricably link the two.

Suppose that the patent covers a print head for a laser printer. Before choosing a royalty rate, the expert must decide whether to base the royalty on the value of the print head alone, or on the value of the laser printer. If the latter, the appropriate rate will be lower because the base is higher. The expert must maintain consistency between the rate and the base. For example, the expert should not select a rate based on comparable licenses that use the sales of the printer component as a royalty base and then apply that rate to the sales of the entire printer.

Perhaps one could best avoid an error and understand the importance and treatment of convoyed sales by reviewing industry practices. Licenses specify the royalty base and should shed light on the appropriate base(s) for the hypothetical negotiation. Discussions with practitioners in the industry and depositions of the other party's license negotiators also provide useful information. In practice, the license terms often use sales of the entire product as a royalty base rather than the costs of the patented component because they are easier to measure and the rate decreases correspondingly. Equally often and for the same reason, the royalty base is set at all products within a given category (e.g., all memory chips), whether they infringe or not, and the license reduces the royalty rate to reflect the fact that not everything in the royalty base infringes.

Quantifying the effect on the patentee of the lost sales of other products complicates the analysis. First, one must demonstrate that such a relation exists. Then, the analysis must encompass the profits of not only the patented items but also the related items. Lastly, a fair royalty sometimes considers not only the sales and profits of the patented item but also the profitability of related products and services that the licensor expects to follow directly from the item's sales or availability.

If the patented item leads to sales of other products and services, empirical evidence from studies of historical sales performance should prove the connection. The analysis should include both the infringer and the patentee, because each can have different experiences.

One needs to collect the accounting information on sales by product, preferably in unit-volume terms. The analysis requires an understanding of the marketing and sales programs, techniques, and relations. Interviews or depositions should lead the marketing people to identify their perception of product interrelations. Analyses of historical data will confirm or contradict the beliefs of the in-house people.

The simple case would see parallel movement in the sales volumes of the patented article and the related products. One should, however, verify that other independent factors do not cause the volume increases. For example, sales of related products can increase because of changes in demand, general growth in sales, new product introductions, or growth in the economic sector the related products serve. Service sales can grow rapidly, for instance, because consumers own more nonpatented units than previously. Thus, one must ascertain with reasonable certainty that the sales of related products result primarily from the patented item's sales. Tools commonly employed to perform this analysis include graphical analysis of sales performance and regression analysis.

(j) Established Profitability of the Patented Product. *Georgia-Pacific*'s eighth factor relates to profitability:

> **8.** The established profitability of the product made under the patent; its commercial success; and its current popularity.[65]

Profitability, of course, lies at the heart of market value. A license becomes attractive to a licensee if the technology can increase the licensee's profits over what they otherwise would have been. Thus, one must not only measure the infringing product's profitability but also calculate what the profitability might otherwise have been. For example, consider a firm earning 10 percent on the sales of the widgets it manufactures. It also wants to sell turbocharged widgets because it expects to earn 12 percent on sales. In negotiating a license for the turbocharger, the firm would willingly pay only up to the incremental 2 percent on sales and not the full 12 percent.

The analysis should focus on the projected profits of the infringer and the patentee at the time of the hypothetical negotiations. These expectations would have motivated each party. In practice, these expectations usually arrive at a range of rates acceptable to the parties. Because the parties never consummated a license agreement, most likely the evidence will not reveal a consensus. Sometimes the patentee has never participated in any negotiations, and evidence does not exist as to its expectations. In that case, the court might assume that both parties have full knowledge of the patent's extent and value. The expert can then examine the product's actual profitability and assess the likelihood of the parties projecting such success. If the court adopts this approach, the expert should, in forming an opinion, give it less weight than actual evidence of expectations.

Although both *Panduit* and *Georgia-Pacific* consider profitability as a factor, it alone should not control the choice of a royalty rate. Considerable uncertainty or unacceptable speculation can cloud either party's profitability forecast. Also, the forecasters' motivations often bias forecasts in the normal course of business. The expert needs to assess the reliability of any forecast.

Patent cases have addressed the concept of using information available only after the hypothetical negotiation—hindsight—to help arrive at the terms to which the parties would have agreed. Courts refer to this as the *book of wisdom*, discussed in Chapter 8. The U.S. Supreme Court first discussed this concept in its 1933 decision in *Sinclair Ref. Co. v. Jenkins Petroleum Co.*[66] The Court stated:

> At times, the only evidence available may be that supplied by testimony of experts as to the state of the art, the character of the improvement and the probable increase of efficiency or saving of expense [citations omitted]. This will generally be the case if the trial follows quickly after the issue of the patent. But a different situation is presented

if years have gone by before the evidence is offered. Experience is then available to correct uncertain prophecy. Here is a book of wisdom that courts may not neglect. We find no rule of law that sets a clasp upon its pages, and forbids us to look within.[67]

Courts often use the book of wisdom when information that is knowable at the date of the hypothetical negotiation does not exist in contemporaneous records that existed or should have existed at the date of the hypothetical negotiation. Projected financial statements that estimated the profitability of the patented product provide such an example. If the parties cannot find this information, they can substitute actual financial profitability after the date of the hypothetical negotiation for projected ones.

However, two recent decisions of the Court of Appeals for the Federal Circuit appear to limit the use of the book of wisdom. In *William G. Riles v. Shell Exploration and Production Company,* the court stated that "a reasonable royalty determination for purposes of making a damages evaluation must relate to the time infringement occurred, and not be an after-the-fact assessment."[68] In *Integra Lifesciences I, Ltd., et al. v. Merck KGaA, et al.,* the court reached a similar conclusion:

> The first step in a reasonable royalty calculation is to ascertain the date on which the hypothetical negotiation in advance of infringement would have occurred. The correct determination of this date is essential for properly assessing damages. The value of a hypothetical license negotiated in 1994 could be drastically different from one undertaken in 1995 due to the more nascent state of the RGD peptide research in 1994.[69]

Whether a damages expert can rely on the book of wisdom is unclear from the current case law. Experts should discuss this issue with counsel during preparation of their opinion.[70]

One could also use profitability to adjust observed royalty rates. A patent on a product that earns a higher profit, or reaps greater commercial success, should command a higher royalty than the royalty paid for a comparable product that generates less profit.

(k) Utility, Advantages, and Benefit.   The ninth and tenth *Georgia-Pacific* factors have economic similarities but function differently:

9. The utility and advantages of the patented property over the old modes or devices, if any, that had been used for working out similar results.[71]

10. The nature of the patented invention; the character of the commercial embodiment of it as owned and produced by the licensor; and the benefits to those who have used the invention.[72]

Both of these direct the practitioner to consider the invention's advantages. For the damages expert, this would mean those features that ultimately led to an economic advantage. Factor 9 suggests a comparison with the existing and prior methods. For example, the expert might learn that the new invention reduced costs by 5 percent or replaced another technology that was earning a 2 percent royalty. The expert would find this information useful. Factor 10 directs the practitioner to examine how the company and consumers have used the invention. Does it provide distinguishing features to the product or process? Does it lead to attributes that the company can use to promote the product or that customers prefer? Has the company or consumers widely adopted it? Does it provide a significant benefit to those who use it?[73]

Traditional utility analysis is subjective, preferred by royalty experts who were license negotiators. The accounting or economic expert also find it useful because it places the other analyses in context. For example, when Pilkington Glass Works, Ltd., of England developed a new process for making flat glass that more than halved the production cost while increasing quality, it licensed the process at rates that exceeded any industry license in existence.

A utility analysis begins with the section of the patent that describes the utility of the invention. It can also include a review of the party's planning documents and advertising literature. A search of the trade literature and reports of stock analysts often help. Sometimes experts interview the firm's researchers and sales people and depose their counterparts at the opposing firm. Finally, more quantitative research—such as surveys—can shed light on the invention's importance.

Utility and advantage influence the reasonable royalty rate only if they affect the product's market value. An invention can be a major technological breakthrough but have little immediate market value. Some inventions require vast amounts of time, energy, and resources but have little economic value. Thus, although practitioners should understand an invention's technological significance, they must always return to the economic significance of the benefits that the invention provides. The incremental benefit to the user dominates an invention's market value and provides the focus of the other factors discussed elsewhere in this chapter. Even though experts often analyze this factor subjectively, the amount that the user willingly pays for the incremental benefit becomes the issue here. Thus, experts often need to compare prices over time or across products or features.

(l) Value of the Invention to the Infringer. The eleventh *Georgia-Pacific* factor focuses on the invention's value:

> **11.** The extent to which the infringer has made use of the invention; and any evidence probative of the value of that use.[74]

This factor resembles factors 9 and 10, except that it considers value from the infringer's perspective. Because the infringer did use the invention, it offers the expert insight into its value to the infringer. The same questions and analyses discussed earlier also apply here. In addition, the expert can examine other behavior by the infringer. For example, did the infringing entity use the invention for all of its production or just part of it? For all of its products or just some? Did the infringer charge more for products with it than without? Did the infringer's sales increase significantly after it adopted the invention? Did the infringer consider alternatives before selecting the invention? Has the infringer stopped using the invention?[75]

Value arises from the infringer's *incremental* profits on the sale of the product and from the related effects, if any, on the infringer's sales of other products, its business image, or other economic benefits. The analyst should not confuse widespread use of an invention with its utility. This use can simply be incidental to the product's success.

By its nature, this factor requires the use of the book of wisdom hindsight, which uses an *ex post* analysis (discussed in Chapter 8).

(m) Customary Division of Profit. The twelfth *Georgia-Pacific* factor relates to agreements used by comparable businesses:

> **12.** The portion of the profit or selling price that may be customary in the particular business or in a comparable business to allow for the use of the invention or analogous inventions.[76]

This factor focuses on royalties expressed as a percentage of sales and relates to factors 1 and 2. When industry practice expresses royalties in other terms, such as a lump sum, experts can examine documents used to negotiate those licenses to compute the equivalent percentage.

The court here suggests that an expert consider licenses in comparable businesses, licenses for analogous inventions, and industry standards. This contrasts with cases that confined evidence of comparable royalties to technologies providing similar functionality.

The practitioner should search for rates or compilation of rates in published sources. These tend to be scarce. The practices of other competitors with patent portfolios provide additional insight. For example, IBM once had an apparent practice of licensing any one of its patents in a field of use for 1 percent, any two for 2 percent, and any three for 3 percent.[77] At 3 percent, the licensee had a license on all IBM patents in that field of use.[78] One should take care when using IBM as an industry standard, however, because it set these licensing policies and practices when it was being charged with anticompetitive practices as a monopolist and entered into a consent decree that it would charge reasonable rates for its technologies to its competitors.[79]

The customary portion of profit has been the major use of this factor at trial, and parties often dispute it. One or both damages experts often advocate the rule of thumb first advocated by Robert Goldscheider. Supposedly, negotiators generally agree to split profits from an invention, with 25 percent going to the patentee. Experts then make adjustments to that rule, depending on the uniqueness of the situation.

Some practitioners argue that a 25 percent split has no theoretical or empirical basis. Many argue that, based on the sharing of risks in a license agreement, the licensee takes on considerably more risks than the licensor (patentee) and thus, everything else being equal, should receive a larger percentage of the expected profit pool. These risks include manufacturing and marketing risks to successfully bring the product to market. Practitioners debate, however, whether 25 percent represents the proper starting place. The real world factors that evaluate an invention's economic value vary by situation and often justify a profit split far from the 25 percent rule of thumb. Practitioners have no reason to believe that any particular percentage would hold even within an industry.

One study confirms the usage of the 25 percent rule as a starting point in real license negotiations. A survey with 428 useful responses from 2,100 licensing executives shows that 38 percent of these licensing executives begin with the 25 percent as a starting point when licensing-in patents and 27 percent start with this rule of thumb when licensing-out technology.[80] In 1982, the Licensing Executives Society (United States and Canada) published a treatise on licensing entitled "The Basics of Licensing." This treatise recites the rule of thumb for setting royalty rates:

> Many licensing executives use a rule-of-thumb which is that 25% to $33\frac{1}{3}$% of the saving of a new process, or 25% to $33\frac{1}{3}$% of the profits of a new product should go to the licensor. This split recognizes that the licensee typically assumes greater financial risk in commercializing the technology.[81]

A December 2002 article in *les Nouvelles* reported the results of an empirical study that compared royalty rates with two proxies for expected long-run profits (namely, licensee profits and "successful" licensee profits) and found royalty to operating profit ratios of 27 percent and 23 percent, respectively.[82] Both of these studies have been criticized, and at least one of the authors of this chapter does not find them reliable. The strongest argument for the 25 percent rule occurs when the patentee's lost profits equal less than the infringer's incremental profits. In that case, the parties could agree on a range of royalty rates and both gain from the agreement. In other words, licensing would generate a surplus that the parties could share. Then, one might argue that the parties would typically split the surplus 25 percent to 75 percent.[83] Game theorists argue that 50-50 makes more sense under these circumstances.

Courts have also allowed experts to apply the 25 percent rule to the entire profits from the product. Royalty rates depend on the increase in profits from use of the invention. This could include profits from the entire product or just those from the patented component or some combination of these. Again, the expert should calculate the increment to profits that the invention's use has generated. The expert should then apply any customary percentage to these incremental profits only. The authors of this chapter disagree on the validity of the 25 percent rule. They do agree, however, that the courts use it.[84] Thus, the practitioner needs to understand the 25 percent rule of thumb, even if the practitioner does not agree with it.

(n) Profit Attribution. The thirteenth *Georgia-Pacific* factor considers the economic value of the invention relative to the value of the product's other attributes:

> **13.** The portion of the realizable profit that should be credited to the invention as distinguished from non-patented elements, the manufacturing process, business risks, or significant features or improvements added by the infringer.[85]

This factor indicates that the expert must consider the contribution of other resources to the product's profitability. In other words, the expert must base the royalty on the incremental benefit provided by the patent and not the benefit provided by other resources. Presumably, this factor does not confine the other resources to those explicitly stated but would include any resource that improved the product's profitability. That would include the use of a brand name, advertising expenditures, and established customer relations, among others.

Experts often use a but-for analysis that includes a carefully defined *next best alternative* to estimate the value of these resources. Some situations require additional work, however. This includes segregating the resources employed and ascertaining the return required on each so the firm can remain viable.

In practice, courts have also used this factor to account for the other patents embodied in the product. This prevents one patentee from claiming all the profits at the expense of the others.

This factor also encompasses situations in which a company must expend great effort or assume great risk to develop the patented technology into a marketable product. This often occurs with pharmaceuticals and biotechnology products. In other situations, marketing and distribution prove key to a product's success.

(o) Expert Testimony.   The fourteenth *Georgia-Pacific* factor looks to the opinions of experts:

   14. The opinion testimony of qualified experts.[86]

Initially, parties used this factor to introduce the opinions of professionals who negotiated licenses for a living. This led to highly subjective testimony, biased by the experts' negotiating styles and particular experiences. The negotiators seldom based their testimony on quantifiable analysis. Although litigants use such experts less often now, they can provide information on comparable licenses and fill gaps in the more objective evidence. Today, this factor addresses the type of expert testimony that this chapter discusses.

22.7   ROYALTY BASE

Infringement consists of making, using, or selling products in the United States. The royalty base consists of all products with the following characteristics:

- Sold in the United States regardless of where the product is manufactured
- Made in the United States and sold in foreign countries
- Made or sold elsewhere but used in the United States

Defining "made in the United States" can be difficult. The CAFC answered this question recently in *Eolas Technologies Inc., et al. v. Microsoft Corporation.*[87] Eolas claimed royalty damages for both foreign and domestic sales of Microsoft Windows®. Microsoft exports golden master disks to foreign original equipment manufacturers (OEMs) who manufacture the Windows products overseas. Even though the golden master disk itself does not end up as a physical part of the infringing product, the CAFC found that the software code on the golden master disks constitutes components of an infringing product for combination outside of the United States. The CAFC affirmed this logic and reasoning in *AT&T Corp. v. Microsoft Corporation* on July 13, 2005.[88]

In a similar fashion, "sold in the United States" can be difficult to measure. For example, suppose a Korean company infringes on a technology patented in the United States to manufacture a semiconductor chip in Korea. The company then ships the chip to China, where it becomes a component in a computer. The Chinese facility then ships the computers for sale all over the world. Even though the parties agree that some of the infringing chips were inside computers shipped to the United States, they likely will disagree on how to ascertain the exact number.

Experts can find even "produced in the United States" difficult to measure as companies often do not track where products were produced. If they do, they frequently lump United States production with all of North America. The analyst will usually have to rely on sampling and other estimating techniques to identify the infringing base.

22.8 DUAL AWARDS

Several cases have awarded the patentee lost profits on some lost sales and a reasonable royalty on others.[89] This has occurred when the patentee could not prove that all the sales would have been lost but for the infringement. In those cases, the courts have treated each sale as a separate act of infringement.

In allowing dual awards, the courts ignore the fundamental tradeoff that a patentee faces in a real-world licensing negotiation. A patentee who grants a license receives royalties on all the licensee's sales including those the patentee would not have made. Patentees who do not license retain the profits on the sales they make. The owner, in the real world, usually cannot retain the profits on the sales it would have made and receive royalties on the sales it would not have made.

The dissent in *Rite-Hite* noted this and concluded that no economic justification exists for such awards.[90] It reasoned that once the patentee recovered the larger of lost profits or reasonable royalties, they were made whole. This concurs with an earlier and important patent damages case, *Aro,* which prohibited any recovery beyond "damages sufficient to put [the patentee] in the position he would have occupied had there been no infringement."[91] Unless the dual award recognizes the potential for double counting, it encourages litigation rather than licensing.

Assume a patentee has already been made whole through recovery of lost profits. That patentee should be willing to license for the incremental sales of the infringer at a lower rate. The infringer's remaining sales no longer represent competitive sales. These sales come from customers that the patentee would otherwise not reach. Therefore, the royalty rate for this portion of the award should be less than a royalty rate that one would apply to *all* of the infringer's sales that include some sales that would replace the patentee's sales.

Until *Rite-Hite,* defendants had never appealed the awarding of both lost profits and royalties. Each case merely cited earlier cases that had similar awards without comment or granted the award without any citations or discussion.[92] The citation trail eventually leads back to two cases, *TWM Mfg. Co. v. Dura Corp*[93] and *Gyromat Corp. v. Champion Spark Plug Co.*[94] Neither of these resulted in a recovery beyond the actual harm, as occurred in the subsequent cases. In *TWM,* the court awarded reasonable royalties only in those years in which the patentee could not prove lost profits. Furthermore, this was by prior agreement of the parties. *Gyromat* awarded lost profits on one product for which the court found no substitutes and awarded a reasonable royalty on another product for which it found substitutes.

In *Rite-Hite,* the infringer challenged the combined award as excessive.[95] The court responded by citing the earlier cases, which themselves never considered the issue. In *King Instruments,* the federal circuit again affirmed a dual award. Therefore, it appears that the federal circuit accepts dual awards as an appropriate measure of damages. In 2001, the CAFC confirmed its ruling in *King Instruments* in *Crystal Semiconductor Corporation v. Tritech Microelectronics International,*[96] when it stated:

> A patentee receives a reasonable royalty for any of the infringer's sales not included in the lost profits calculation. ... Thus, a patentee may obtain lost profit damages for that portion of the infringer's sales for which the patentee can demonstrate "but for" causation and reasonable royalties for any remaining infringing [sales].

The authors and editors note that dual awards can overcompensate the patentee unless the license fee on the infringer's incremental sales is less than a license fee granted in the absence of lost profits recovery. However, public policy appears to call for compensation to the patent owner on all sales made by the infringer based on current decisions of the federal circuit.

22.9   PROCESS OR METHOD PATENTS

We have framed the previous discussion around apparatus patents, that is, physical devices. One can also patent processes or methods, and practitioners approach damages calculations in those cases similarly. Experts generally calculate damages on process or method patents from the time of first infringement, subject—in some cases—to a six-year statute of limitations. Unlike apparatus patents, no marking requirements affect the allowable damages period.

Infringement of a process patent often does not lead to any lost sales for the patentee. Instead, they lead to reduced costs for the infringer. Because costs comprise the second half of the profit equation, the previous discussions of lost profits and *Georgia-Pacific* factors also apply to process patents.

22.10   DESIGN PATENTS

The Patent and Trademark Office grants design patents on physical features of a product that have no operating function. For example, an inventor may patent the shape of a newly designed chair but not the fact that it has four legs, a seat, and a back. Design patents protect intellectual property that is important to a product's success but is not covered by patent or copyright or trademark law.

The original Coca-Cola bottle provides a well-known example of a design patent. This design, recognized around the world, is a valuable asset of the company. The company still uses it in advertising in the United States, even though it has seldom used the bottle itself for packaging for 40 years.

35 U.S.C. § 284 addresses damages for utility patents. As Section 22.3(b) of this chapter discusses, 35 U.S.C. § 289 allows additional damages remedies for design patents. When a person or entity infringes a design patent, the patentee collects lost profits, a reasonable royalty, or the profits made by the infringer. This represents a holdover from earlier patent statutes that allowed the patentee to elect between recovering its damages and taking away the infringer's unjust enrichment. Trademark law also addresses disgorgement of the infringer's profits and has a similar logic for its use. First, U.S.C. § 289 recognizes that such infringement is particularly harmful because it involves the product's consumers as well as the producers. Second, restoring patentees to their original position or even making them whole will likely prove difficult, if not impossible. Thus, the law designs damages to deter all infringements by making such unlawful acts provide zero or negative net benefit to the infringer.

Calculating the infringer's profit can prove difficult. Experts often struggle with whether to deduct from revenues only the incremental costs associated with the infringing sales, or the fully allocated costs of such sales (including a *pro rata* share of overheads). Furthermore, they often have difficulty obtaining the necessary data. Records might not segregate sales and profits of the infringing products. Invoice data can be too voluminous to review and often do not identify the infringing products. For these and other reasons, the courts give a great deal of leeway to patentees' experts, requiring that they identify only lost sales and gross profit. The burden then shifts to the infringer to show that it incurred additional costs.

Because the law provides for the disgorgement of profits that resulted or flowed from the infringement, the infringer will disgorge its incremental profit, and not some measure of aggregate profits. For example, if an infringer sold 1,000 widgets using the misappropriated design but would have sold 600 without it, the infringer will have to disgorge the profits on the 400 incremental widgets only.

The expert should analyze the infringer's cost structure. The production of the additional 400 widgets could have led to efficiencies that increased the profits on the initial 600 widgets. Because the additional widgets' production caused these efficiencies, the infringer should also disgorge the related profits.

22.11   INTEREST ON DAMAGES

Experts need to state both lost profits and reasonable royalties in current dollars as of the trial date using net present value techniques. Usually, a damages award involves only past damages, so one must compound at some interest rate. Courts usually grant injunctions against further use of the patent so that future damages will not occur.

A study of patent awards granted identified the method used to award prejudgment interest. Almost all of these involved either a risk-free rate of return similar to that of U.S. Treasury bills or a state statutory rate.[97] A minority used some measure of the patentee's cost of capital. Only a few cases have used the infringer's incremental borrowing rate, or surrogates for the infringer's incremental borrowing rate, despite the arguments made in its favor.[98] *Alpex v. Nintendo*[99] presents a well-reasoned opinion on the use of the latter. In that decision, Judge Wood used the infringer's commercial paper rate. She cited Judge Easterbrook's opinion in *Mahurkar*,[100] in which he recommends calculating prejudgment interest at a rate that adequately compensates the patentee for the risk he incurs in giving the infringer a "large, involuntary, unsecured loan to a debtor of uncertain creditworthiness that is doing its utmost to avoid paying."

Some practitioners have argued for use of the patent owner's weighted average cost of capital (WACC). The authors are not aware of any appellate decisions regarding the use of WACC.

When computing prejudgment interest, one can also address whether to calculate it on a pretax or after-tax basis.[101] An economically correct analysis should consider taxes (*see* Chapter 16). Most courts ignore this element of the prejudgment interest calculation because it presents technical difficulties in ascertaining what taxes the patentee would pay.

The timing of royalty payments creates an interesting set of analytical choices. First, the payments usually occur over several time periods. The expert can complicate the analysis by selecting a series of contemporaneous prejudgment interest rates or can simplify it by selecting a single representative rate. In some cases, the difference has been significant, and the parties have disputed the selection.

The second choice involves the assumed receipt of payments. Royalty payments typically are due a fixed number of days (often 30) after the end of predefined periods, such as quarterly, semiannually, or annually. These periods vary by license, so the expert needs to review other licenses of the parties and industry practices.

22.12 INJUNCTIVE RELIEF

Typically, the courts enjoin an infringer from further use of the patent. In May 2006 the Supreme Court in *eBay v. MercExchange*[102] held that:

> the traditional four-factor test applied by courts of equity when considering whether to award permanent injunctive relief to a prevailing plaintiff applies to disputes arising under the Patent Act. That test requires a plaintiff to demonstrate (1) that it has suffered an irreparable injury; (2) that remedies available at law are inadequate to compensate for that injury; (3) that considering the balance of hardships between the plaintiff and defendant, a remedy in equity is warranted; and (4) that the public interest would not be disserved by a permanent injunction. The decision to grant or deny such relief is an act of equitable discretion by the district court, reviewable on appeal for abuse of discretion. These principles apply with equal force to patent Act disputes. A major departure from the long tradition of equity practice should not be lightly implied.

This decision reversed a CAFC decision that articulated a "general rule" unique to patent cases that a permanent injunction will issue once infringement and validity have been adjudged.[103] This decision makes it clear that injunctions are not automatic in patent cases but they are often entered into after a court finds a patent enforceable, valid and infringed. Thus, in most cases the expert will not have to calculate future lost profits.

One exception to this occurs when the patent nears the end of its life. By infringing, the defendant may have achieved a higher market share or level of sales at the time of the patent's expiration than would have otherwise occurred. Thus, the patentee faces a more formidable competitor than it would have absent the infringement. Similarly, the infringement could have maintained the infringer's sales while it developed and introduced a noninfringing alternative. In that case, the infringement denied the plaintiff the opportunity to gain market share at the infringer's expense, and, as a result, the plaintiff has a weaker position than it would have had when the patent expires.

Often, however, a firm enjoined from infringing finds itself in an untenable position. Such firms often cannot recover the investment they have made in the product and the resources needed to make and sell it. If the injunction effectively prevents the infringer from servicing its customers, the firm's reputation can suffer serious harm. Kodak found itself in this position when it was enjoined from making and selling the film for its instant cameras.

In such cases, the patentee often recovers all of the past losses and significant future profits by licensing the infringer. If the infringer cannot profitably employ dedicated resources elsewhere, perhaps the infringer can profitably pay an abnormally high royalty rate on future sales. Sometimes infringers find it beneficial to pay out all of the firm's profits to the patentee in order to maintain its reputation with existing customers.

The courts have not explored the curative effects of an injunction on patent damages, although the threat of injunction has likely influenced settlement negotiations.

22.13 GUIDANCE

Congress and the courts have not developed the law on patent damages as well as that in other areas of the law. Relative to other areas, the courts have only recently decided many of the important damages cases, and even these conflict with each other in various aspects. One important case, *Rite-Hite*, appears internally inconsistent regarding which products a damages calculation should include. Some court precedents ignore basic economics; more changes will likely come.

In such an environment, experts cannot assume that their clients understand patent damages or even current law. We advise experts to stay current on the evolving case law. More importantly, they should base their calculations on sound economic principles—the same principles used in business daily. Experts should ask not "What can the patentee claim?" but "What injury did the patentee suffer?"

NOTES

1. Title 35, § 122 (release date: 2004-11-08).
2. This does not mean that the patents have no value to the automobile companies. It may be impossible to build a competitive car without certain patents. If the key patents are dispersed among several companies, then these companies can enter into cross-licensing agreements so that each can build cars. This is an example of using a patent portfolio defensively and is a common use of patents.
3. In a recent antitrust case, *Independent, Inc. v. Illinois Tool Works*, 2205 WL 147399 (January 1, 2005), the Court of Appeals for the Federal Circuit (CAFC) upheld a long-standing opinion that in tying cases it should be presumed a patent grants the owner market power even though the CAFC noted that many prominent economists and scholars have argued against this presumption.
4. *Aro Manufacturing v. Convertible Top Co.*, 377 U.S. 476, 507 (1964). This is a seminal case on patent damages that every practitioner should read.
5. *Grain Processing Corp. v. American Maize-Products Company*, 185 F.3d 1341; 1999 U.S. App. LEXIS 18223; 51 U.S.P.Q. 2d (BNA) 1556 (Fed. Cir. Aug. 4, 1999).
6. The adjectives *increased, higher, lower,* and *more* are all relative to what would be achieved without the patented technology.
7. Title 35 U.S.C. § 271.
8. *Panduit Corp. v. Stahlin Bros. Fibre Works*, 575 F.2d 1152 (6th Cir. 1978).
9. *State Industries v. Mor-Flo Industries*, 883 F.2d 1573, 1577–80 (Fed. Cir. 1989), *cert. denied*, 493 U.S. 1022 (1990).
10. *BIC Leisure Products Inc. v. Windsurfing International, Inc.*, 1 F.3d 1214 (Fed. Cir. 1993).
11. *Panduit* can be placed within the framework of the subsequent cases by considering it a special case (i.e., low substitution) in which there are few if any substitutes for the patented product.
12. The Court of Appeals for the Federal Circuit in Washington, D.C., is the sole appeals court for patent cases.
13. *Panduit*, 575 F.2d at 1156.
14. *See Kaufman Co. v. Lantech*, 926 F.2d, 1136 (Fed. Cir. 1991).
15. *Id.* at 1162.

16. *See Panduit*, 575 F.2d at 1159; *Enterprise Manufacturing v. Shakespeare Co.*, 141 F.2d 916, 922 (6th Cir. 1966); *TWM Mfg. Co. v. Dura Corp.*, 789 F.2d 895, 898 (Fed. Cir. 1986); *Gyromat Corp. v. Champion Spark Plug Co.*, 735 F.2d 549 (Fed. Cir. 1984).

17. *Radio Steel & Mfg. Co. v. MTD Products Inc.*, 788 F.2d 1554 (Fed. Cir. 1986); 739 F.2d 604, 616 (Fed. Cir. 1984).

18. *See In re Mahurkar Double Lumen Hemodialysis Catheter Patent Litigation*, 831 F. Supp. 1354 (N.D. Ill. 1993) "Competition is not an all-or-nothing process. There are degrees of substitutability."

19. *Micron Chemical, Inc. v. Lextron, Inc.*, 318 F.3d 1119, 1125, 65 U.S.P.Q. 2d 1695 (Fed. Cir. 2203).

20. The CAFC in *BIC* made it clear that it viewed *Panduit* as only one of several ways to prove lost profit damages. It also indicated a willingness to accept market share approaches that used historical shares.

21. *Pall Corporation v. Micron Separations, Inc.*, 66 F.3d 1211, 1223 (Fed. Cir. 1995).

22. The practitioner needs also to consider whether any of these infringers would have been effectively excluded from the market or would have been able to compete with a noninfringing product.

23. When the patentee has licensed the patent to others, some courts have held that determining the patentee's lost sales would be speculative and thus denied lost profits damages. In reality, the analyses would be the same as those used when there are substitutes and other courts have accepted them. The practitioner should be aware that some courts are uncomfortable with the lost sales analyses that are typically undertaken.

24. *State Industries*, 883 F. 2d at 1573.

25. For a general overview of these models, *see* Gregory J. Werden, Luke M. Froeb, and Lucian Wayne Beavers, "Economic Analysis of Lost Profits from Patent Infringement with and without Noninfringing Substitutes," *American Intellectual Property Law Association Quarterly Journal* 27 (Fall 1999): 305–333.

26. *Vulcan Engineering Co., Inc. v. FATA Aluminum, Inc. and FATA Group, S.p.A.*, 278 F.3d 1366 (Fed. Cir. 2202).

27. Of particular concern are claims of price reductions that result in large reductions in present and future revenues. This may be evidence of significant market power prior to infringement. *See* James Gould and James Langenfeld, "Antitrust and Intellectual Property: Landing on Patent Avenue in the Game of Monopoly," *IDEA* 37 (1997) 449–489. Price reductions may also be a response to the defendant's entry into the market rather than its use of the patented technology. A carefully constructed but-for analysis would take this into account. Price erosion damages are sometimes calculated into the future. In those cases, patentees argue that customers will not accept a return to preinfringement price levels.

28. The CAFC states: "Moreover, in a credible economic analysis, the patentee cannot show entitlement to a higher price divorced from the effect of that higher price on demand for the product. In other words, the patentee must also present evidence of the (presumably reduced) amount of product the patentee would have sold at the higher price." *Crystal Semiconductor Corporation v. Tritech Microelectronics International, Inc. et al.*, Docket No. 99-1558 (Fed. Cir. 2201).

29. *Beatrice Foods v. New England Printing & Lithographing Co.*, 889 F.2d 1171 (Fed. Circ. 1990).

30. *Rite-Hite Co. et al. v. Kelley Co.*, 56 F.3d 1538 (U.S. App.) 1995 and *King Instruments Corp. v. Luciano Perego and Tapematic*, 65 F.3d 941 (1995).

31. As of June 2006, Congress was considering amending 35 U.S.C. § 284 with the following language: "(e) DETERMINATION OF ROYALTIES OR DAMAGES FOR COMPONENTS. Whenever the invention is incorporated into, or is made part of, a method or apparatus otherwise known in the art, or is an approved method or apparatus including within it elements otherwise known in the art, then any award of a

reasonable royalty or other damages shall be based only upon such portion of the total value of the method or apparatus as is attributable to the invention alone and shall not include value attributable to the method, apparatus, or elements otherwise known in the art of contributed by the infringer or its licensors."

32. *Paper Converting Machine Co., v. Magna-Graphics Corp.*, 745 F.2d 11, 2(Fed. Cir. 1984).

33. Generally, we would advise caution in using account analysis when the data can support a statistical derivation of incremental costs (*see* discussion in Chapters 5 and 6). In *Polaroid v. Kodak*, 16 US PQ 2d 1481 (Dist. of Mass. 1990), the trial judge was extremely critical of this approach.

34. 35 U.S.C. § 284.

35. For computational convenience, the expert may convert from one rate/base to another as long as the identity ($R_1 \times B_1 = R_2 \times B_2$) is satisfied.

36. *Egry Register Co. v. Standard Register Co.*, 23 F. 2d 438, 443 (6th Cir. 1928).

37. *Grain Processing*, 185 F. 3d 1341.

38. *Georgia-Pacific Corp., v. United States Plywood Corp.*, 318 F. Supp. 1116 S.D.N.Y. (1970); *aff'd*, 446 F.2d 225 (1971).

39. At least one district court opinion has rejected an expert's reasonable royalty opinion on the grounds that it did not explicitly consider the Georgia Pacific Factors. *See Accusan, Inc. v. Xerox Corp.*, 1998 U.S. Dist. LEXIS 14242.

40. *Georgia-Pacific*, 1122; *see also Santa Fe-Pomeroy, Inc. v. P&Z Co.*, 569 F. 2d 1084 (9th Cir. 1978).

41. *Panduit*, 575 F 2d at 1158.

42. *Id.* at 1159.

43. *Monsanto Company v. Kem L. Ralph*, Docket No. 03-1243 (Fed. Cir. 2004).

44. *Golight, Inc. v. Wal-Mart Stores, Inc., et al.*, Docket No. 02-1608 (Fed. Cir. 2004).

45. *Rite-Hite*, 56 F.3d at 1574.

46. *See* the last quoted paragraph above (taken from *Panduit*).

47. *Grain Processing*, 185 F. 3d at 1351, 1352.

48. Most firms have a surplus of investment alternatives. If a patentee insists on a royalty that would leave the licensee with a rate of return below the next best investment alternative, then the licensee is better off not making the product. Note that, for most firms, the foregone return on the next best alternative exceeds the "normal" or "average" return (e.g., the weighted average cost of capital) for the firm. For a thorough discussion of this topic, *see* Mark A. Glick, "The Law and Economics of Patent Infringement Damages," *Utah Bar Journal* (March 1997): 15.

49. A peculiar problem arises in the case of pharmaceuticals. Here, the law allows for the use of a patented invention for research and development. Infringement is only considered to have occurred at the date of first sale of a product using or made with the invention. At that point, hundreds of millions of dollars may have been spent developing a promising invention into a medicine approved by the Food and Drug Administration. Royalty rates for an approved medicine are much higher than royalty rates for unproven technologies. *See Integra LifeSciences I, Ltd., et al. v. Merck KgaA et al.*, 331 F. 3d 860 (Fed. Cir. 2003).

50. Perhaps the most frequent use of patents is to gain access to technology necessary to build a competing product. Without a portfolio of useful patents, a firm can be excluded from a market by any other firm with a patent portfolio. Portfolios enable some firms to cross-license patents with the other firms in the industry. This is common in many industries including semiconductors and photography.

51. Two prime examples of this are the Beta versus the VHS formats for video recording and the DOS versus the Apple operating systems.

52. *Georgia-Pacific*, 1122.

53. This is because situations involving more straightforward licensing of the patent at issue are likely to be resolved without resort to the courts.

54. For further discussion, *see* Jennifer Fearing, Atanu Sahaand, and Roy Weinstein, *Beyond Georgia-Pacific: A New Approach to the Calculation of Reasonable Royalties*, (Los Angeles: Micronomics, *Inc.*), 1997.

55. In some industries, cross-licensing is so common that it is included in all licenses regardless of its value. The analyst should try to determine the significance of any cross-licensing provisions when they are present.

56. F.P. Porcelli and J.M. Skenyon, "Patent Damages—Life in the 'But-For' World," in Franklin Pierce Law Center's Fifth Annual Intellectual Property Litigation Series, *Patent Litigation: Tactics & Tools*, Sept. 15, 1992, 14.

57. *Georgia-Pacific*, 1122.

58. This is known as an efficient breach. It occurs because the infringer is in a better position to exploit the patent than the owner. Thus, the infringer can fully compensate the patentee and still retain a surplus. Society as a whole benefits from the faster and more widespread use of the technology. In part, this social welfare concept is embraced in contract law.

59. *Santa Fe-Pomeroy, Inc. v. P&Z Company, Inc.*, 569 F.2d 1984 (9th Cir. 1978).

60. Note that this methodology effectively introduces an unjust enrichment claim that is otherwise not allowed.

61. *Santa Fe-Pomeroy*, 569 F 2d at 418. If the facts were as the court described, the patentee should have been able to demonstrate lost profits and recover his or her damages. Allowing the patentee instead to use estimated lost profits to ascertain a reasonable royalty would appear then to be a lowering of the standards of proof for lost profits.

62. A one-sided emphasis on deterrence is actually harmful and leads to excessive litigation. If awards are greater than real losses, patentees will tend to refuse to license even on reasonable terms. Instead, they will seek redress in courts. Consider, for example, a company that, upon learning its product may be infringing, seeks a license from the patentee. If the patentee can expect a higher compensation in court, he or she will refuse to negotiate. Like other areas of the law, optimal damages are those that make the patentee whole and no more (assuming that detection and apprehension are certain).

63. Traditionally, U.S. patents have been valid for 17 years from the date of issuance. Recently, the U.S. rights have been made more consistent with those of the rest of the world, i.e., 20 years from the filing date.

64. *Georgia-Pacific*, 1122.

65. *Id.*

66. *Sinclair Ref. Company v. Jenkins Petroleum Company*, 289 U.S. 689, 698–99 (1933).

67. For a contrary view, *see* Franklin M. Fisher and R. Craig Romaine, "Janis Joplin's Yearbook and the Theory of Damages," *Journal of Accounting and Finance* 5 (Winter 1990): 145–157.

68. *William G. Riles v. Shell Exploration and Production Company*, 298 F.3d 1302, 1811 (Fed. Cir. 2002).

69. *Integra Lifesciences*, 331 F. 3d 860 (Fed. Cir. 2003).

70. A discussion of the "book of wisdom" is really a discussion of measuring damages at the time of the unlawful act (*ex ante*) or after the unlawful act (*ex post*). This is a question of policy that can be clarified but not settled by economics. (Economics does tell us that either approach can lead to efficient outcomes but that allowing plaintiffs to choose either one does not.)

71. *Georgia-Pacific*, 1122.

72. *Id.*

73. Although Factor 10 mentions the licensor, use by the infringer or others would provide similar information.

74. *Georgia-Pacific*, 1122.

75. Even though an expert may conclude that an invention has limited value from the infringer's abandonment of it, the reverse is not true. The infringer's continuing use of an invention can simply reflect its opinion that it is not infringing.

76. Georgia-Pacific, 1122.

77. Patents are often licensed for use in a particular field, e.g., the manufacturing of memory chips.

78. IBM's current policy goes to four patents at 4 percent and excludes some "strategic" patents.

79. Currently, IBM has selected some "strategic" patents it does not license under this policy. Also, IBM has signed many licenses at lower rates.

80. Stephen A. Degnan and Corwin Horton, "A Survey of Licensed Royalties," *les Nouvelles*, June 1997, 91–96.

81. *See* William Marshall Lee, "Determining Reasonable Royalty," *les Nouvelles*, September 1992, 124–128, for his conclusion that this rule of thumb is a useful starting place for negotiations.

82. Robert Goldscheider, John Jarosz, and Carla Mulhern, "Use of the 25 Per Cent Rule In Valuing IP," *les Nouvelles*, December 2002, 123–133.

83. This assumes that there is no other overriding factor like the cost of inventing around that would discourage one of the parties from licensing. In a perfect world, parties facing a surplus would agree to a license, and the lawsuit would not be necessary. An expert encountering this situation should carefully check the evidence and his or her analyses and seek an explanation for why the parties didn't agree to a license.

84. The following patent cases (compiled by Lew Koppel of CRA International) have accepted the 25 percent rule: *Busse, et al. v. United States*, 195 U.S.P.Q. 740, 745 (D.C.E. Wis., 1977); *Tights, Inc. v. Kayser-Roth Corporation*, 196 U.S.P.Q. 750 (M.D. N.C. 1977); *Fromson v. Western Litho Plate and Supply Co.*, 5 U.S.P.Q. 2d 1327, 1333 (E.D. Mo. 1987); *Syntex Inc., v. Paragon Optical Inc.*, 7 U.S.P.Q. 2d 1001, 1027 (D.C. Ariz. 1987); *Polaroid Corp. v. Eastman Kodak Co.*, 16 U.S.P.Q. 2d 1481, 1534 (D.C. Mass. 1990); *W.L. Gore & Associates, Inc. v. International Medical Prosthetics Research Associates, Inc.*, 1990 WL 180409 (D. Ariz. 1990); *Mobil Oil Corporation v. Amoco Chemicals Corporation*, 915 F. Supp. 1333, 1357 (D. Del. 1994); *Fonar Corp. v. General Electric*, 41 U.S.P.Q. 2d 1088, 1105 (E.D. N.Y. 1995) and *see also* at 41 U.S.P.Q. 2d 1801 (Fed. Cir. 1997); *The Proctor & Gamble Company v. Paragon Trade Brands, Inc.*, 989 F. Supp. 547, 612 (D. Del. 1997); *Bose Corporation v. JBL, Inc., et al.*, 112 F. Supp.2d 138, 165 (D. Mass. 2000); *Eaton Corporation v. Rockwell International Corporation, et al.*, 2001 U.S. Dist. LEXIS 17054 (D. Del. 2001).

85. *Georgia-Pacific*, 1122.

86. *Id.*

87. *Eolas Technologies Inc. and The Regents of the University of California v. Microsoft Corporation*, 399 F. 3d 1325 (Fed. Cir. 2005).

88. *AT&T Corp. v. Microsoft Corporation.* Docket No. 04-1285 (Fed. Cir. 2005).

89. *See*, for example, *State Industries*, 883 F.2d at 1573 and *Rite-Hite*, 56 F.3d at 1538.

90. *Rite-Hite*, 56 F.3d at 57, 58.

91. *Aro*, 377 U.S. 476 at 512.

92. *See Rite-Hite*, 56 F.3d 1538; 1995 U.S. App.; 774 F. Supp. 1514; 1991 U.S. Dist.; *Amstar Corp. v. Envirotech Corp.*, 823 F.2d 1538 (Fed. Cir. 1987); *Radio Steel & Mfg. Co. v. MTD Products, Inc.*, 788 F.2d 1554 (Fed. Cir. 1986); *Bio-Rad Lab. v. Nicolet Instrument Corp.*, 739 F.2d 604, 616 (Fed. Cir. 1984); and *Schneider (Europe) AG and Schneider (USA) Inc. v. Scimed Life Systems*, 852 F. Supp. 813 (D. Minn. 1994).

93. *TWM Mfg. Co. v. Dura Corp.*, 789 F.2d 895 at 898 (Fed. Cir. 1986).

94. *Gyromat v. Champion Spark Plug Co.*, 735 F.2d at 549 (1984).

95. Given that the infringement began before the patent was issued, that is, when the infringer could not have had knowledge of the patent, and that the award put the infringer into bankruptcy, this had an intuitive appeal.

96. *Crystal Semiconductor Corporation v. Tritech Microelectronics International, Inc. et al.*, 246 F. 3d 1336 (Fed. Cir. 2001).

97. There is no statutory rate for patent damages under the applicable federal law. However, the case law makes it clear that an award of compound prejudgment interest is necessary in order to compensate the patentee fully. The debate is typically over what prejudgment interest rate is appropriate.

98. James M. Patell, Roman L. Weil, and Mark A. Wolfson, "Accumulating Damages in Litigation: The Roles of Uncertainty and Interest Rates," *The Journal of Legal Studies* 11 (June 1982): 341–364.

99. *Alpex Computer Corp. v. Nintendo Company Ltd., et al.,* 34 U.S.P.Q. 2d 1167 (S.D.N.Y. 1994).

100. *In re Mahurkar Double Lumen Hemodialysis Catheter Patent Litigation,* 831 F. Supp. 1354, 1394–95 (N.D. Ill. 1993).

101. In the but-for world, if the patentee had received royalty payments from the infringer, the patentee would have to pay taxes on these royalty payments before reinvesting the proceeds in an interest-bearing security. In *Alpex,* Judge Wood stated that the damages model should calculate prejudgment interest after considering the taxes that Alpex would have paid on the royalties received from Nintendo.

102. *eBay Inc. et al, v. MercExchange LLC* (U.S. Supreme Court No. 05-130 Decided May 15, 2006).

103. *Id.*

CHAPTER 23

LICENSE COMPLIANCE: PERFORMING ROYALTY EXAMINATIONS

Mark W. Haller
David L. Marston
Vincent Torres

CONTENTS

23.1 INTRODUCTION

Intangible assets and intellectual property have become increasingly important to the functioning of the market. These intangible assets take on many forms, including patents, trademarks, trade secrets, copyrights, software, and associated license agreements. Nonetheless, most companies do not regularly make it a business practice or priority to maximize the economic impact of these assets. Intangible assets can and should generate incremental revenue to a company. Moreover, companies should measure and monitor the monetization of such assets, which the company can easily identify. The failure to do so results in foregone revenue in both large and small companies in industries such as software, high technology, biotechnology, pharmaceuticals, entertainment and media, and luxury branding.

This chapter addresses how to maximize the economic benefit from a portfolio of license agreements through the performance of royalty examinations, commonly referred to as royalty audits. A *royalty examination* is an investigation designed to ascertain whether the licensee's payments to the licensor present an accurate and complete representation of the licensee's use of the licensor's intellectual property as dictated by an underlying license agreement between the parties.

The chapter examines the purpose of executing license examinations, offers a work plan overview for executing a royalty examination, provides guidance on settling reporting discrepancies and managing customer reactions, describes certain industry-specific complexities, and offers certain best practices for developing a systematic license compliance program.   Even though this chapter examines intellectual property licenses and contracts, many of the topics discussed also apply to the compliance management and monitoring of other contracts such as franchise, joint venture, research and development, most favored nation or customer, and pricing agreements.

23.2   PURPOSE OF ESTABLISHING A LICENSE COMPLIANCE PROGRAM AND EXECUTING ROYALTY EXAMINATIONS

Recognizing the void in license management activities within their organizations and the potential benefits, companies have begun seeking out consulting firms to help develop license compliance programs. Over time, these licensing management and revenue recovery programs often pay for themselves. A company could have many reasons to implement such a program, as we discuss in this section of the chapter.

(a) Identification of Incremental Revenue from an Existing License Portfolio.   In general, most royalty examinations result in the identification of underreported royalties, thus generating incremental revenue. Licensees might underreport royalties for several intentional or fraudulent reasons, or, in most cases, because of unintentional omissions caused by clerical errors, contract misinterpretations, or lack of controls surrounding the royalty reporting process. For this reason, licensors should have a process for identifying and questioning any suspect royalty reports. They should then implement royalty examinations at selected licensee sites to review books and records. Licensees often find underreporting when they prepare for a royalty exam, and they often report this directly to the licensor before beginning the examination work.

Licensors should select target licensees for examination based on three criteria:

1. Specific facts exist that identify possible underreporting:
   - A current or former employee has provided information
   - Magnitude of royalties reported or the products covered in recent royalty reports are not consistent with historical reports and expectations

- The licensee has a history of untimely or uncooperative reporting and payment of royalties compared with the terms of the license.
2. Systematic risk assessment, including consideration for the following:
   - Length of time since the last royalty examination
   - Products addressed by the licensed technology and transparency with respect to the use of the licensed technology
   - Geography of the licensee
   - Personnel turnover, corporate reorganization, or merger that may have led to the transfer of royalty tracking and reporting responsibilities to new personnel at the licensee
   - Significant growth in sales and product offerings that may fall under the scope of the license
3. Random selection of at least some of the highest revenue-generating licensees to test the reasonableness of the risk assessment process.

(b) Clarification of Potentially Nebulous License Terms and Conditions.   Licensees often misinterpret certain terms of a license agreement. This occurs because the roles of the representatives negotiating the agreement on behalf of the licensee (typically lawyers and engineers) often differ from those of the individuals responsible for reporting compliance and submitting royalties (typically business unit managers and accountants). Unless the agreement or documentation of the licensing negotiations specifies a position, a licensee's business unit manager or accountant can take a position that differs from the licensor's expectations. The summary-level detail submitted in royalty reports that accompany payments do not reveal these assumptions or positions, which become evident only when a licensor examines the details. The parties will have difficulty foreseeing where misinterpretation or disconnect will occur in the royalty reporting process until the licensor performs an examination, putting the agreement language to the test. Moreover, in many cases, a licensor does not have historical standard license agreement language in place or has made numerous acquisitions, including associated licenses and intellectual property rights. As a result, key terms and conditions can vary, even with the same customer.

(c) Motivation for Increased Accuracy of Future Royalty Reporting by Licensees.   In addition to the immediate economic benefits, licensors can also reap substantial intangible benefits from performing regular royalty examinations. Implementing a systematic compliance program and performing royalty examinations, designed to protect the company's intellectual property and licensing rights, sends a clear message to the channel partners that royalty examinations have become a normal part of doing business. Channel partners communicate with one another, and the informal grapevine provides an opportunity for these partners to know which companies do, and do not, police their licensing rights. By implementing such a program, an organization will create a reputation for taking its licensing rights seriously, and the channel will likely respond with more accurate and timely reporting of royalties. Sometimes even the written announcement of a formal compliance policy to the channel results in immediate upward adjustments to previously filed royalty reports.

23.3   EXECUTING A ROYALTY EXAMINATION

Either generally accepted auditing or consulting standards established by the American Institute of Certified Public Accountants can govern the services provided by a practitioner associated with royalty examinations. Depending on the facts and circumstances surrounding the royalty examination, the client and practitioner conducting the examination should pass judgment as to the most appropriate standard to employ. Abiding by the consulting standards allows for greater flexibility in conducting the investigation.

This section outlines a general approach for conducting a royalty examination and highlights several process steps that apply to most such exams. No uniform royalty examination work plan exists for every industry, company, product, technology, or type of agreement. The practitioner should tailor a work plan specific to the relevant agreements and technologies. Even though the work plan provides a guide for the examination, it should allow the practitioner to remain flexible and deviate from the outlined steps as new information becomes available during the investigative process.

(a) Preparation and Prefield Work.   Preparing properly for a royalty examination will lead to a more efficient and effective examination. It will also communicate to licensees that you want to minimize the additional effort and time required of them to complete the examination. The prefield preparation work should include the following:

(i) Understanding the Terms of Existing License Agreements.   A properly crafted license agreement will delineate the relevant royalty rates, the method of calculating the royalty base (units and revenues), any scope restrictions, and the licensor's audit rights. Summarizing the terms contained in the license in advance of the field visit will familiarize the practitioner with potential audit limitations and the existence of any capacity limits with respect to particular products at issue or geographies. It will provide insights into the types of financial documentation necessary to verify the royalty reports.

In many respects, the language of the audit clause will determine the mandate for the royalty examination. The audit clause may outline the time interval for notice required prior to commencing an audit, whether a third-party auditor will perform the examination, the frequency and duration of the audits, the type of information that a third-party auditor can report back to the licensee, and payment responsibilities with respect to the third-party auditor's fees.

(ii) Analyzing Royalty Reports Submitted by the Licensee.   The license agreement will often dictate the amount and type of information supplied on the licensee's royalty report. The practitioner should begin by checking the royalty reports to ensure that they do not contain any arithmetic errors. If a foreign licensee submitted the royalty report, the auditor should check the accuracy of any exchange rates used to adjust the payment due to the licensor. Also, comparing current reports with historical reports can help identify instances of dramatic revenue shortfalls and unexpected adjustments to examine during the site visit.

(iii) Researching the Licensees' Business to Understand Relevant Products and Business Units. This step will give the auditor a general overview of the company and identify

which divisions will likely use the licensed technology. This will educate the practitioner about the products that include the technology and changes to the product landscape since the execution of the license agreement. The sources for this information can include correspondence between the licensee and licensor, press releases as to products and revenues, industry reports or other market intelligence, and, most importantly, information for the licensor's sales and marketing representatives most closely associated with the licensee. The sales representative can reveal information about changes in the relation with the licensee, possible product changes, and details regarding potential areas of revenue leakage.

(iv) Requesting Additional Information from the Licensee.   Upon notifying the licensee of the royalty examination, the practitioner should request specific business documents necessary to validate the royalty reports. This will allow for more complete preparation in advance of the site visit. It also helps in setting expectations as to the examination's rigor and scope. The practitioner should respect the proprietary and confidential nature of the documentation requested of the licensee during the royalty examination. Licensees sometimes require a confidentiality agreement with the practitioner before providing any detailed documentation.

(b) Accuracy and Completeness of Submitted Royalty Reports.   During the site visit, the practitioner needs to evaluate both the accuracy and completeness of the various components of the royalty calculations included in the royalty report. These components typically include the revenue associated with the licensed product, the volume of licensed product, and any agreed-upon adjustments.

(i) Accuracy and Completeness of Revenue Reported.   When verifying the accuracy and completeness of the reported revenue, the practitioner should begin the investigation by reviewing the licensee's workpapers that support the royalty reports. The practitioner should reconcile the royalty reports with the workpapers, relevant sales summaries, general ledgers, and audited financial statements.

A common area of discrepancies uncovered during royalty examinations relates to the prices used in calculating the relevant revenues. License agreements often use terms such as "gross sales price" and "net sales price" to specify the appropriate price. License agreements also include a detailed definition of these terms as they relate to the licensed product. These definitions often differ from the licensee's typical use of these terms in its invoicing process and workpapers, leading to unintentional misreporting of royalties if licensees lack diligence in their royalty report preparation. To verify the price data, one must often use the invoices submitted by the licensee to its customers. In multinational or vertically integrated organizations, transfer pricing practices can also affect the revenue reported. If the license agreement does not specify the proper treatment of transfer prices, the practitioner should consult the licensor for guidance. The practitioner should also review sales to venture partners for price disparities.

When examining reported royalty revenues, one must also verify the categorization or accumulation of particular revenues for different product types or geographies. The license agreement may apply different royalty rates to different product types or accumulated revenue amounts or specify up-lifts to the royalty rate for different geographies. The practitioner should test for the appropriate interpretation and application of these license terms by the licensee.

(ii) Accuracy and Completeness of Volume Reported.   Evaluating the completeness of the volumes reported requires an analysis of the licensee's inventory reports for the licensed products. Understanding the beginning inventory, quantities purchased or manufactured, and ending inventory will allow for a reasonableness check of the reported sales. During this process, one should examine the licensee's distribution of free or promotional product to customers, the internal use by the licensee of licensed product, and any allowances for destroyed or damaged product.

In analyzing the volumes reported, the practitioner should revisit any suspicions of unreported product sales, particularly for recently introduced products. Product schematics and manufacturing reports that detail materials used in production can evidence the use of licensed technology in unlicensed or unreported volumes.

(iii) Accuracy and Appropriateness of Adjustments/Deductions.   As with reported revenues and volumes, agreed-upon adjustments can affect the amount of royalties owed to the licensee. These adjustments can take many forms such as adjustments to revenues, allocations of particular costs, credits for returned products, and allowances for specific tax expenses. A practitioner should investigate the reasonableness of these adjustments with the same level of diligence as the revenue and volume reports by requesting the proper supporting documentation and confirming the allowance of the adjustment in the license agreement.

(c) Closing Meeting with Licensee.   In the closing meeting with the licensee, practitioners should discuss the examination's preliminary findings that they will report to the licensor as well as the supporting documentation. This session allows the licensee to agree to the quantities and revenues of licensed products sold or used or to explain any discrepancies with the findings. If a discrepancy exists because of a contract misinterpretation, the practitioner should notify the licensor. If there is no misinterpretation by the licensee, then the auditor should adjust the preliminary findings. An agreement on units and revenues and an understanding of the supporting documents facilitates the settlement process.

Practitioners can also use this opportunity to discuss any open items that they could not resolve during the field visit. During the meeting, the practitioner should establish the timing and the process for closing any outstanding information request necessary to complete the findings.

23.4   THE SETTLEMENT PROCESS

The parties often give inadequate attention to the settlement processes used to resolve the findings from royalty examinations. The practitioner can help the licensor develop a systematic process for the immediate follow-up and settlement of findings to avoid protracted negotiations with licensees. The licensors' representatives drive the settlement process, however; this limits the practitioner's role to presenting the facts discovered during the royalty examination.

Most parties amicably settle any findings associated with the royalty examination. The parties involved should quickly resolve any differences associated with the royalty examination and focus their energies on maintaining a positive relation. When the parties cannot settle the findings amicably, the dispute can escalate to litigation or arbitration. The practitioner should remain cognizant of this possibility during every royalty examination and should gather sufficient supporting documentation and maintain the workpapers and correspondence necessary to support the findings.

23.5   INDUSTRY-SPECIFIC COMPLEXITIES IN EXECUTING LICENSE EXAMINATIONS

The types of licensed intellectual property, the relative value of intellectual property to the commercial success of the products it affects, and the volume of licensing activity can vary among industries. This particularly holds true when comparing high-technology, entertainment and media, consumer and industrial products, energy, and financial services industries. Even within these industry groupings, sectors exist with unique economic business models, as well as cultural and operational differences that introduce complexities affecting the performance of royalty examinations. The complexities of every industry and sector and their implications for royalties examinations go beyond the scope of this chapter. Instead, this section introduces some of the salient issues that examiners often face in industries with significant licensing activity: software, high-technology, entertainment and media, and pharmaceutical and biotechnology. Even though we discuss many of the complexities in the context of these particular industries, they also arise when one conducts royalty examinations in other industries.

(a) Software.   Software piracy has received significant press in recent years, leading to an increased focus by software companies on compliance testing activities. Performing a license examination related to the deployment of software requires advanced software technical skills, along with the more typical general business and accounting skills required to perform an examination. Depending on the license compliance features built into the specific product, the practitioner may need fluency in various operating system platforms and hardware environments. This will help the practitioner investigate the deployment of the product and to interview the individuals in the licensee's information technology (IT) departments who are most knowledgeable with the deployment of the product. In addition to this fluency, a practitioner should also leverage the know-how related to the licensed product of the licensor's developers and engineers. The developers can often provide insight into more efficient ways of performing the audit as well as weaknesses in the practitioner's work plans.

One can often facilitate software license audits by using asset management and network diagnostic tools. These tools are automated software codes that scan a series of personal computers or an entire network, identifying deployment of specific types of software. The use of these diagnostic tools can result in a more efficient audit and can often provide a more complete understanding of a particular software product's deployment in a given network environment. However, network administrators often hesitate to allow the use of an external scan tool on their networks, unless the licensee already uses the product for other reasons. The practitioner should be prepared to adjust the workplan to evaluate the use of alternative scan tools already used by the licensee or to execute a more manual and tedious audit based on the functionality of the licensed product.

(b) High Technology.   High-technology (hereafter referred to as "high-tech") companies include the manufacturers and suppliers of semiconductors, computing and other electronic devices, telecommunications equipment, and digital media. Most difficulties associated with performing license compliance programs in these high-tech industries occur because of the complicated technologies, complex distribution channels, and global nature of the licenses.

One must understand the specific technology in order to understand its applications and the uses of the technology. The short life cycle of existing products and frequent introduction of new products in these industries can lead to the incorporation of the patented technology in multiple products not contemplated at the negotiation of the license. The prefield work preparation and research of the licensee's product line in advance can spark questions that often uncover unreported uses of the technology.

Complex distribution networks are not unique to high-tech companies, but they prevail in these industries. Investigating the business organization and affiliates provides assurances that the licensee isn't avoiding royalties through complex supply arrangements and that the licensee isn't using artificial pricing and adjustments.

Practitioners working for high-tech companies must often conduct royalty examinations in foreign countries. This can present unique challenges owing to cultural and language differences as well as differences in accounting rules and business practices. Using a practitioner with experience and resources in the licensee's country can help smooth these differences. Prior experiences in the licensee's country sensitizes the practitioner to any cultural difference that can influence interactions with the licensee throughout the process. In addition to navigating the cultural differences, a team member from the licensee's country who fluently speaks the licensee's native language and understands local business practices (including records and tax laws) can prove invaluable in both reviewing and uncovering the necessary business records.

(c) Entertainment and Media. The entertainment and media industry includes content owners and distributors (such as studios), content aggregators that collect, maintain, and distribute content, and telecommunication companies. The content can take on forms such as movies, television programs, music, games, research materials, and other published works. As with software piracy, content piracy in the entertainment and media industry has increased in recent years, thus increasing the focus on monitoring license compliance.

One could attribute many of the increased difficulties in monitoring compliance and protecting intellectual property distribution in the entertainment and media space to advances in the technologies relied on by content owners, distributors, and consumers. Technology convergence trends have increased the number of distribution outlets as well as changed the underlying technology by which entertainment and media companies can deliver content. This situation shows the inadequacy of traditional methods for protecting and monitoring intellectual property. Content consumption is moving away from reliance on stand-alone media and devices such as DVDs and DVD players to networks that can share content across devices and locations. As the practitioner conducting license exams in this industry, it is important to educate yourself as to the increasing number of content distribution outlets, the complex web of distributors and subdistributors, and the infrastructure available to monitor usage.

(d) Pharmaceuticals and Biotechnology. The pharmaceutical and biotechnology industries often use collaboration agreements. In addition (and generally related to technology licensing agreements), companies in these industries often have codevelopment, cocommercialization, comarketing, copromotion, or other joint ventures meant to spread the risk and required capital investment associated with the successful market adoption of the technology involved. In conducting royalty examinations, the practitioner should review the collaboration agreements and identify all the terms that can affect the royalty base. For instance, these agreements outline terms that segregate costs among the parties involved that appear as adjustments to net sales (to which one applies the royalty rate). The adjustments can vary among contracts and among drugs.

23.6 MANAGING CUSTOMER REACTIONS

Companies should not balk at implementing a compliance program because they fear alienating licensees or business partners. The sales and marketing staff will often object to any royalty examination work for this very reason. Companies that do not perform this work, however, send the message that they will not enforce intellectual property rights. Remember that the parties negotiated the audit clause so they could use it as necessary. Royalty examinations need not be adversarial nor burdensome if planned and completed correctly. Practitioners retained to provide these services must show sensitivity to the customer relation. Licensors should follow up with their licensees after the examination to obtain feedback on the royalty examination process.

23.7 SUMMARY OF BEST PRACTICES FOR DEVELOPING A LICENSE COMPLIANCE PROGRAM

Aside from executing royalty examinations, corporations should consider the implementation of a systematic compliance program that outlines an approach for identifying which licensees to examine, the detailed process for conducting the examinations, and a method for monitoring the results of the program. This section will discuss some of the best practices to consider when establishing a compliance program.

Prior to establishing a systematic compliance program, most companies approach license compliance and royalty examinations on an *ad hoc* or exception basis. These companies lack a strategy and an ongoing program for such programs, substituting reactive improvisation for such planning. Rumor, or speculation, or incomplete facts prompt these reactions when the company does not approach license compliance in a systematic manner. A well-planned license compliance program allows management to control inconsistencies and uncertainties better. When considering how to establish such a program, companies should address the following areas.

(a) Ownership. Someone within the organization must own* and control the license management/compliance program. Generally this person will fall under the finance/accounting, legal/contracts, or revenue assurance departments. Establishing an owner within the company allows for a single point of accountability and a decision maker with respect to managing the execution of exams, monitoring the results of the program, and responding to customer questions and concerns.

(b) Support. A best practice compliance program must have support from every member of senior management. This includes the chief executive officer (CEO), chief financial officer (CFO), in-house counsel, vice-president of sales, and vice-president of operations, because any of these positions can affect a successful program. Even though a middle manager has daily responsibilities, the program would not enjoy success without the support of key individuals in upper management. Also, internal dissension among top management will prove disastrous for the program. Staff members who will take on additional commitments associated with establishing and maintaining the license compliance program and those who may interface directly with licensees need to receive a unified strategy and consistent message from management. If the internal staff members receive a consistent message regarding the program, external licensees will more likely receive a consistent message and respect the audit demands. If management seems divided on a compliance program, internal staff members and licensees will fight to avoid the audit or scale down the efforts.

(c) Inventory. Companies need a vehicle to allow for tracking the key data associated with a portfolio of intellectual property agreements. This allows the company to manage the program with real-time information and knowledge. The underlying data would include items such as the relevant royalty rate; the basis of the calculation for payment of royalties, technology, or products addressed; the territories; the termination date; the "owner" of the royalty reporting; and the auditing rights. Such a tool need not be cumbersome, or complex, or expensive. However, companies must find it cost effective, easy to use, and a comfortable interface with existing systems. Typically, companies use generic relational database software packages that they can customize for specific uses to track such information.

(d) Risk Assessment. The organization must do a risk assessment of potential revenue leakage. The 80/20 rule[1] applies in that most revenue leakage will come from a subset of the licensees. In addition to the factors addressed in Section 23.2(a) for selecting licensees to examine, management should also consider possible differences in distribution channels, differences in geographies, and differences in intellectual property rights licensed.

(e) Contract Language. The company must ensure that its license agreements contain best practice contract language. This includes the audits rights clause, the 5 percent rule,[2] definitions of key accounting terms,[3] interest and penalties,[4] and

---

*Editors' Note: This concept of ownership pervades modern writing about organization structure. We believe it refers to establishing a profit center or incentives based on the unit's performance.

approved distribution channels and geographies. Also, the company should convert all license agreements into a single standard format so that managing the license review process becomes more straightforward, and fewer uncertainties arise with respect to contract misinterpretation by the licensees.

(f) Exercise of Audits Rights Clause.   As discussed in Section 23.6, enforcing audit rights clauses sends a message to licensees that the company takes intellectual property rights seriously. The company should use the appropriate level of due diligence to select the licensors to audit; once the company has made this selection, it cannot allow sales teams to arbitrarily or unilaterally cancel the audit. The company must have procedures to overcome both internal objections and customer objections. The company should send a breach letter if licensees do not cooperate as per the terms of the agreement and needs timely support of the audit teams' efforts while in the field.

(g) Communication.   Because customers represent an ongoing asset of the licensor, licensors should ensure constant communication and transparency during the royalty examination process. A letter to all customers introducing and outlining the license compliance program (or reminding them) helps address the inevitable customer concern of unfair treatment. Immediate feedback on the results of an audit helps preserve customer relations.

(h) Closure.   An audit with no closure would preclude the company from realizing the rewards from the expended efforts. The company should address and settle all findings within 60 days if possible, because collection will become more difficult over time. Management should designate an owner for the settlement process.

(i) Follow-Up.   Best practice programs call for the sales representative or account manager to follow up with the customer for feedback. Even if the customer did not like the process, the company should record the feedback regarding the fairness and reasonableness of the examination process. Also, the company should gather feedback on the third-party audit firm's performance to ensure that they serve as good ambassadors for the company in a manner consistent with its corporate culture and image.

(j) Profit Center.   Best practice programs should benchmark their collections/settlements against that of other licensors. Incremental revenue should exceed costs; if it does not, the company should examine the audit process. The concept of cost efficiency (i.e., considering the program a profit center) plays an important role in its success. Regardless of how the company internally allocates identified and collected incremental royalties, the program should demonstrate that it is at least revenue/cost neutral. The compliance program should bring incremental revenues and have a positive cash flow.

23.8 CONCLUSION

An incongruity exists between revenues generated from licensing agreements and the levels of resources companies expend to enforce these agreements. Companies should never assume full compliance by licensees, who know which licensors enforce their agreements. This knowledge influences the accuracy of royalty reporting. If companies derive revenues from licensing, their ongoing business practices should include a compliance program. Failure to do so ensures lost revenue.

NOTES

1. Also known as Pareto's Principle or Pareto's Law, the 80/20 rule suggests that 20 percent of something is always responsible for 80 percent of the results.
2. Most license agreements contain a fee clause that mandates the licensee to cover the costs of the examination if a certain percentage (typically 5 percent) of underreporting is identified. These "5 percent" clauses provide motivation for the licensee to report accurately, because failure to comply requires them to cover the cost of the examination.
3. Among others, the use of the terms gross and net sales are common areas for misinterpretation. The definition of these terms should be clearly outlined in the agreement.
4. Late fees or interest can be used as leverage to expedite the settlement process.

CHAPTER 24

ANTITRUST

Stephen H. Kalos

CONTENTS

24.1   INTRODUCTION

(a) Statutory and Case Law.   The U.S. antitrust laws aim to "promote and protect the competitive process"[1] by "prohibit[ing] a variety of practices that restrain trade, such as price-fixing conspiracies, corporate mergers likely to reduce the competitive vigor of particular markets, and predatory acts designed to achieve or maintain monopoly power."[2] The Sherman Act of 1890 (Section 1) prohibits "every contract, combination ... or conspiracy in restraint of trade." The courts have found that the following practices restrained trade in violation of the antitrust laws:

- **Price fixing.** Agreements among competitors that set or influence price.
- **Allocation of customers or territories.** Agreements among competitors that allocate customers or territories among the competitors.
- **Refusals to deal.** Agreements among firms not to buy from or sell to a particular firm or group of firms.
- **Vertical price fixing.** Agreements between a seller and buyers regarding the price at which the buyers will resell.
- **Territorial and customer restrictions.** Agreements between a seller and buyers limiting the territories within which, and the customers to whom, the buyers can resell.
- **Exclusive selling agreements.** Agreements between a seller and buyer giving the buyer the exclusive right to resell within a specified territory.
- **Exclusive dealing arrangements.** Agreements between a seller and buyer in which the buyer agrees to purchase all of its product requirements from the seller.
- **Bundling and tying.** Bundling refers to an arrangement whereby the seller offers multiple products in a single package. Bundling can be mixed (i.e., the seller also offers the individual products separately, although the package is offered at a discount) or pure (i.e., the individual products are not separately available). Pure bundling is also referred to as tying.

The law regards certain of these practices (e.g., price fixing) as so blatantly anticompetitive as to consider them *per se* unlawful. With such practices, the plaintiff must prove only that, as a matter of fact, the defendant has engaged in the practice to prevail on liability. The "rule of reason" governs others of these practices, for example, territorial and customer restrictions. In such cases, the plaintiff must prove that the anticompetitive effects of the practice in question outweigh the procompetitive effects (i.e., business justifications).

Section 2 of the Sherman Act makes it illegal to "monopolize, or attempt to monopolize . . . or conspire . . . to monopolize" any market. To prevail on a Section 2 claim, the plaintiff must prove that the defendant either has monopoly power or that there is a dangerous probability that the defendant will succeed in acquiring monopoly power.[3] The Supreme Court has defined monopoly power as "the power to control price or exclude competition."[4] In addition, the successful plaintiff must prove that the defendant acquired or maintained its market power willfully (consciously). Monopoly power that results from "superior skill, foresight and industry" is not unlawful.[5]

(b) Elements of the Analysis of Monopolization

(i) Product and Geographic Markets   The first step in analyzing whether the defendant possesses monopoly power is to define the product and geographic markets in which the defendant competes. "[M]arket definition, if it is to be an aid to analysis, has to place in the relevant market those products and services and firms whose presence and actions can serve as a constraint on the policies of the alleged

monopolist."[6] The *Merger Guidelines* jointly issued by the Department of Justice (DOJ) and the Federal Trade Commission (FTC), define markets by focusing on demand substitutability, that is, the ability and willingness of consumers to respond to a price increase by switching away to other products.[7] In defining relevant economic markets, the *Merger Guidelines* call for the use of the "smallest market test."[8]

(ii) Barriers to Entry The plaintiff must show that the defendant has a substantial share in the defined market(s); however, even a 100 percent share does not confer monopoly power if entry is easy. Therefore, the plaintiff must also prove that barriers to entry exist sufficient to prevent potential entry from constraining price to its level absent the anticompetitive practices.

(iii) Harm to Competition Finally, a finding of monopolization requires proof that the defendant's allegedly anticompetitive practices harm competition. That is, the anticompetitive effects of the defendants' conduct must outweigh any procompetitive effects or business justifications. In practice, this generally means that the defendant's conduct must serve to raise prices in the market, although reductions in research and development (R&D), product quality, and service qualify as harm to competition, all else being equal.

(iv) Mergers and Acquisitions Section 7 of the Clayton Act prohibits mergers and acquisitions where the likely effect is to "substantially lessen competition," restrain commerce, or "tend to create a monopoly." The *Merger Guidelines* outline the competitive problems that mergers can cause and the framework for the merger analyses that the agencies use in evaluating whether such problems are likely. Merger analysis begins with an analysis of market structure including market definition, market concentration, and entry conditions. Merger analysis also considers the competitive effects of the merger, that is, either coordinated effects (by which the merger facilitates tacit or express collusion) or unilateral effects (by which differentiated products or capacities distinguish the firms and a merger between close competitors allows unilateral price increases).[9]

(v) Price Discrimination Price discrimination refers to situations in which a firm charges a different price to different customers. The Robinson-Patman Act prohibits price discrimination when it substantially harms competition.

> It shall be unlawful for any person engaged in commerce ... either directly or indirectly, to discriminate in price between different purchasers of commodities of like grade and quality ... where the effect of such discrimination may be substantially to lessen competition or tend to create monopoly in any line of commerce, or to injure, destroy, or prevent competition with any person who either grants or knowingly receives the benefit of such discrimination, or with customers of either of them.[10]

Defendants whom the law has found to have engaged in price discrimination harmful to competition have two statutory defenses: cost justification and meeting competition. The statute allows discrimination based only on "differences in the cost of manufacture, sale or delivery resulting from the differing methods or quantities" sold to the different purchasers.[11] The statute also provides a "meeting competition" defense when "the lower price ... was made in good faith to meet an equally low price of a competitor."[12]

(c) Financial Experts in Antitrust Litigation   The remainder of this chapter will focus on two areas of antitrust in which financial experts have been involved: damages analysis and estimating costs in predatory pricing claims.[13] This chapter introduces the financial expert to issues unique to antitrust damages, identifies the primary issues in antitrust damages, and provides an overview of the legal environment constraining and influencing the calculation of antitrust damages. In particular, the chapter will discuss the following issues:

- The causal connection between the defendant's anticompetitive act(s) and the plaintiff's injury must be proven to a reasonable certainty.
- The courts' requirement that antitrust damages calculations be reasonable and avoid speculation.
- Proof of antitrust injury: the plaintiff's actions must reduce competition.
- Prohibition against recovering damages for indirect antitrust injury (e.g., injury to customers of the firms paying fixed prices).
- Separation of damages attributable to the antitrust from damages due to general market effects, legitimate competition from the defendant, and the plaintiff's failure to mitigate.
- Disaggregation of damages calculations for each challenged act, or groupings of acts.
- Variants of the "before and after" or "yardstick" methods in calculating antitrust damages.
- Use of econometrics to estimate antitrust damages while holding constant factors other than the anticompetitive practices.
- Court-imposed penalties: treble damages but no prejudgment interest for the plaintiff.
- Standard cost allocation methods used in predatory pricing analyses.

24.2   PREREQUISITES FOR ANTITRUST DAMAGES: CAUSATION, ANTITRUST INJURY, AND STANDING

(a) Causation.   To recover damages from an antitrust violation, plaintiffs must first prove causation (also referred to as fact of damage or impact). Plaintiffs must prove that a causal relation exists between the claimed antitrust violation and harm to the plaintiff. The courts require that the plaintiff prove causation with "reasonable certainty."[14]

(b) Antitrust Injury.   The courts also require that antitrust damages result from antitrust injury.

> For plaintiffs to recover treble damages on account of [Section] 7 violations, they must prove more than injury causally linked to an illegal presence in the market. Plaintiffs must prove antitrust injury, which is to say injury of the type the antitrust laws were intended to prevent and that flows from that which makes the defendants' acts unlawful. The injury should reflect the anticompetitive effect either of the violation or of anticompetitive acts made possible by the violation.[15]

Conduct by the defendant that preserves or enhances competition, or has a neutral effect on competition, does not qualify as antitrust injury even if this conduct injures the plaintiff: "The antitrust injury requirement ensures that a plaintiff can recover only if the loss stems from a competition-reducing aspect or effect of the defendant's behavior."[16]

In a series of cases, the courts have identified several types of harm to competitors that fail to qualify as antitrust injury. The Supreme Court first articulated the antitrust injury requirement in *Brunswick Corp. v. Pueblo Bowl-O-Mat*.[17] Brunswick manufactured bowling equipment and operated bowling centers. Brunswick acquired several independent bowling centers that had defaulted on payments to Brunswick for bowling equipment. Pueblo, the owner of several competing bowling centers, filed suit claiming that these acquisitions lessened competition in violation of § 7 of the Clayton Act.[18] According to Pueblo's damages theory, the bowling centers in question would have closed—but for their acquisition by Brunswick—thus allowing Pueblo to profit by capitalizing on increased concentration. The Court denied the plaintiffs antitrust damages:

> At base, respondents complain that by acquiring the failing centers petitioner preserved competition, thereby depriving respondents of the benefits of increased concentration. The damages respondents obtained are designed to provide them with the profits they would have realized had competition been reduced. The antitrust laws, however, were enacted for "the protection of competition, not competitors." It is inimical to the purposes of these laws to award damages for the type of injury claimed here.[19]

In *J. Truett Payne Co. v. Chrysler Motors Corp.*,[20] the Supreme Court held that price discrimination in violation of the Robinson-Patman Act does not, in itself, suffice to prove antitrust injury and thus antitrust damages. The plaintiff, a former automobile dealer, brought suit, claiming that Chrysler's sales incentive programs constituted illegal price discrimination under the Robinson-Patman Act. The plaintiff's damages claims included the amount by which its purchase costs would have decreased had it made its actual purchases at the lower prices paid by its competitors. However, the Court found that simply quantifying the amount of the price discrimination did not warrant an award of antitrust damages and that "a plaintiff must make some showing of actual injury attributable to something the antitrust laws were designed to prevent" and that violation of the Robinson-Patman Act "establishes only that injury may result."[21] For example, a dealer favored with lower costs can simply take the lower costs in the form of increased profits without passing along the decreases to customers or otherwise changing the competitive playing field.

If a defendant(s) uses an antitrust violation such as price fixing to raise its prices, rivals of the defendant benefit from the price increase. That is, such price increases cause antitrust injury not to rivals, but to customers. In *Matsushita Elec. Industrial Co. v. Zenith Radio*, the plaintiffs (Zenith et al.) alleged that the defendants, a group of Japanese consumer electronic product (CEP) manufacturers, had illegally conspired in an attempt to drive American firms out of the market "by engaging in a scheme to fix and maintain artificially high prices for television sets sold by petitioners in Japan and, at the same time, to fix and maintain low prices for the sets exported to and sold in the United States."[22] However, the Supreme Court decided that, given the particular allegations of anticompetitive behavior, the plaintiffs had not incurred antitrust injury and thus should not receive damages.

Nor can respondents recover damages for any conspiracy by petitioners to charge higher than competitive prices in the American market. Such conduct would indeed violate the Sherman Act … but it could not injure respondents: as petitioners' competitors, respondents stand to gain from any conspiracy to raise the market price in CEPs.[23]

In *Atlantic Richfield Co. v. USA Petroleum Co.*, the Supreme Court held that harm to competitors from vertical restraints[24] that reduce prices, but not to predatory levels, does not constitute antitrust injury. Atlantic Richfield, a vertically integrated oil company, encouraged its dealers to match the prices of independent gasoline dealers such as the plaintiff, USA, and succeeded in raising its market share as a result. USA sued, alleging a vertical, maximum-price fixing agreement (in violation of § 1 of the Sherman Act) and an attempt to monopolize local retail gasoline markets (in violation of § 2 of the Sherman Act). According to the Court:

> Although a vertical, maximum-price-fixing agreement is unlawful under § 1 of the Sherman Act, it does not cause a competitor antitrust injury unless it results in predatory pricing…. Low prices benefit consumers regardless of how those prices are set, and so long as they are above predatory levels, they do not threaten competition. Hence, they cannot give rise to antitrust injury.[25]

No clear line separates the types of harm that qualify as antitrust injury and those that do not. Consider, for example, price increases by rival firms that do not participate in a cartel. Economics suggests that rival firms who do not participate in a cartel will raise their prices in response to a price increase by cartel members. Thus, an economist could consider price increases by noncartel members in response to a price increase by the cartel as proximately caused by cartel behavior. However, courts have lacked consistency on whether price increases by nonparticipant cartel rivals constitute antitrust injury.[26]

(c) Antitrust Standing.   Even if a plaintiff has suffered harm proximately caused by an antitrust violation and the harm constitutes antitrust injury, the plaintiff cannot recover antitrust damages if the harm proves indirect. For example, indirect purchasers (i.e., parties purchasing from the customers of firms found to have fixed prices) cannot recover damages under federal antitrust law, even if the intermediate firm passes along some, or all, of the overcharge to them. The courts refer to a party's ability to recover antitrust damages as *antitrust standing.*

In *Illinois Brick*, the Supreme Court denied indirect purchasers the right to recover antitrust damages, except in unusual circumstances.[27] The Court had previously barred defendants in price-fixing cases from reducing damages by proving that plaintiffs (i.e., direct customers) had passed along at least some of the illegal overcharge to their customers (i.e., indirect customers).[28] The Court reasoned that dividing the right to sue among firms in the distribution chain, according to the incidence of overcharge, would overly complicate antitrust litigation and raise a risk of duplicate, or insufficient, recovery. However, some states have enacted "*Illinois Brick* repealer" statutes that permit indirect purchasers to sue under state antitrust law.[29] Under some such state laws, the damages expert must address the questions of whether any of the overcharge was passed through to indirect purchasers and, if so, how much.[30]

24.3   STANDARDS OF PROOF FOR ANTITRUST DAMAGES

(a) Amount of Damages.   The burden for proving the amount of damages has a less exacting standard than that of reasonable certainty used for causation. In *Bigelow*, the Supreme Court stated that "the jury may make a just and reasonable estimate of the damage based on relevant data."[31] The defendant had argued that Bigelow's damages calculation carried too much speculation because one could not predict with certainty the success of the plaintiff's business absent the restraints in question. The Court rejected this argument, reasoning that

> in such circumstances "juries are allowed to act on probable and inferential as well as (upon) direct and positive proof." Any other rule would enable the wrongdoer to profit by his wrongdoing at the expense of his victim. It would be an inducement to make wrongdoing so effective and complete in every case as to preclude any recovery, by rendering the measure of damages uncertain. Failure to apply it would mean that the more grievous the wrong done, the less likelihood there would be of a recovery.[32]

(b) Speculation.   Even though a standard of reasonable certainty does not govern the calculation of the amount of injury, the courts have made it clear that antitrust damages calculations should not rely on speculation. For example, the *Bigelow* Court declared that "even where the defendant by his own wrong has prevented a more precise computation, the jury may not render a verdict based on speculation or guesswork."[33] No clear line separates the disallowed speculative and the allowed reasonable estimate: the courts tolerate some uncertainty in a damages calculation, but not outright guesswork. Blair and Page (1995) provide a comprehensive review of judicial decisions involving speculation in the measurement of antitrust damages and provide examples of assumptions and analyses that have failed to pass muster.[34]

Courts have excluded or discounted expert testimony on damages as speculative when assumptions underlying the expert opinion were inconsistent with the facts of the case.[35] For example, in *Concord Boat v. Brunswick*, the appeals court found that the plaintiff's "expert opinion should not have been admitted because it did not incorporate all aspects of the economic reality of the stern drive engine market and because it did not separate lawful from unlawful conduct. Because of these deficiencies in the foundation of the opinion, the expert's resulting conclusions were 'mere speculation.'"[36]

The plaintiff's expert assumed that, but for the defendant's anticompetitive conduct, the defendant would have been one of two suppliers in the relevant market, with each supplier having a market share of 50 percent. The expert applied a Cournot oligopoly model under the 50-50 market split assumption to calculate a but-for price.[37] The expert calculated the overcharge as the difference between the actual price and the calculated but-for price. The court in *Concord Boat* found two critical problems with the expert's analysis.[38] First, the *assumption* of a duopoly wherein each firm had a market share of 50 percent in the but-for world ignored the fact that the defendant had achieved a 75 percent market share before it began the allegedly anticompetitive conduct. Second, the expert failed to account for several market events unrelated to the anticompetitive conduct that served to increase the defendant's market share and, by inference, the actual price.[39]

(c) Other Factors That Can Affect the Plaintiff.   Factors other than anticompetitive conduct can affect the prices paid, or the profits earned, by an antitrust plaintiff. Potential coincident factors include general market forces (e.g., supply and demand factors), legitimate competition by the defendant in the actual world, compensating benefits from the antitrust violation, legal competitive responses by the defendant in the but-for world, and mitigation opportunities or opportunity costs. Antitrust models should account for these factors whenever possible and exclude their effects from the damages calculations. If a model fails to account for such other factors when it can make such accommodations, the trier of fact will give the model little weight or disregard it altogether.

(i) General Market Forces.   General market forces such as demand and supply can change often. Shifting market forces will either reinforce (i.e., act in the same direction as) or counteract the effects of the antitrust violation(s) at issue. For example, if a cartel begins fixing prices while input costs increase, all else equal, a damages calculation should attribute some of the observed increase in price to the change in input costs. Under such circumstances, to claim the entire price increase as damages would overstate the true damages—an assertion that the fact finder likely would find speculative. Suppose, however, that input costs fall as the cartel fixes prices; any observed increase in price understates the effect of the price fix, assuming no other coincident factors exist. If the plaintiff's damages expert does not disentangle the two effects of the second situation, the trier of fact likely will view the damages estimate as conservative rather than speculative.

(ii) Legitimate Acts by the Defendant.   In some cases, the court will not find every action by the antitrust defendant that harms the plaintiff as anticompetitive. Instead, the fact finder will deem some of the antitrust defendant's actions legitimate, albeit tough, competition. For example, suppose an antitrust defendant who engages in exclusionary conduct also cuts prices to a level that does *not* reflect predatory pricing. The plaintiff's damages should not include the effect of the lower prices, even if the plaintiff lost market share as a result of, or had to lower its own prices in response to, the reduction in the defendant's prices.

(iii) Factors Unrelated to the Defendant.   Courts have excluded expert testimony on damages, or accorded it little weight, when such testimony has failed to account for the effects of factors unrelated to the defendants conduct. For example, in *ILC Peripherals Leasing Corp. v. IBM*, the plaintiff's (Memorex's) expert estimated lost sales as the difference between forecast and actual sales. The court found that this damages calculation failed to isolate the effect of the alleged anticompetitive acts from other explanatory factors including

> (1) Memorex's own mismanagement and the failure of other portions of its business to perform up to expectations; (2) adverse comment on Memorex in the financial community; (3) the recession in the early 1970s; (4) competition from other companies; and (5) lawful competition from IBM.[40]

As a result, the court concluded, "a jury verdict rendered on Memorex's damage evidence would have been speculative."[41]

(iii) Competitive Responses in the But-For World.   Damages models should also reflect the defendant's likely actions in the but-for world. For example, suppose the

defendant engages in exclusionary conduct that prevents the plaintiff from entering a market. Assume that market prices would have fallen in response to the plaintiff's entry as the defendant reduces its prices to retain market share in the face of entry. A plaintiff should not measure damages assuming that but-for prices (with entry) equal the actual prices (without entry).

Courts have excluded expert opinions on damages for failure to account for expected competitive responses in the but-for world. For example, in *Murphy Tugboat Co. v. Crowley*,[42] the trial court issued a judgment notwithstanding the verdict in favor of the defendant, affirmed by the Ninth Circuit, because the plaintiff's damages claim failed to account for an expected competitive response:[43]

> The expert witness's testimony as to Murphy's expected share in the large vessel and flat tow market segment depended upon an assumption that Red Stack [the defendant] would not cut its prices in reaction, even to a loss of over one-quarter of its prior share of this portion of the market.... A reasonable jury could not, however, indulge in the assumption that a competitor would follow a course of behavior other than that which it believed would maximize its profits. ... In a hypothetical economic construction, such as the one underlying Murphy's theory on lost past profits, economic rationality must be assumed for all competitors, absent the strongest evidence of chronic irrationality. Otherwise, it will be impossible to keep chronic speculation in check.[44]

(iv) Mitigation. The antitrust plaintiff needs to account for mitigation opportunities. For example, a firm prevented from entering one market can use the avoided entry costs to make alternative investments, assuming it has not already sunk its entry costs.[45] When firms enter new markets, they bear opportunity costs (i.e., the returns lost from forgoing the next best alternative investment).[46] The amount of damages that the plaintiff suffered in this example would consist of the returns lost by not entering the foreclosed market less the returns still available in the next best investment plus sunk costs, if any. When the plaintiff has not yet sunk any entry costs and has equally attractive investment alternatives, economic theory teaches that exclusionary conduct preventing the plaintiff from entering does not cause the plaintiff to suffer damages.[47]

24.4 DISAGGREGATION OF DAMAGES

(a) Case Law Regarding Disaggregation. When the plaintiff alleges multiple anticompetitive acts, the expert should calculate, if feasible, the amount of damages attributable to each alleged occurrence, referred to as *disaggregation of damages*.[48] The practice of disaggregation arises from the requirement of antitrust injury as a necessary prerequisite for the award of antitrust damages. The court in *Litton Systems v. Honeywell* explained the relation as follows:

> Except in circumstances where disaggregation is shown to be impossible or impractical, an antitrust plaintiff challenging a variety of conduct is required to segregate damages attributable to particular business practices or, at a minimum, to distinguish between losses attributable to lawful competition and those attributable to unlawful anticompetitive conduct. Disaggregation is required because the antitrust laws are only intended to compensate plaintiffs for losses fairly caused by a defendant's unlawful anticompetitive behavior.[49]

Royall (1997) cautions that even though "the courts have not required disaggregation of damages in all antitrust cases, it is also clear that the failure to disaggregate can lead to severe consequences, including the dismissal of the plaintiff's claims."[50] The courts have thrown out some cases or sent back others for retrial on damages because of failure to disaggregate. For example, in *Litton Systems v. Honeywell*, the court ordered a retrial on damages because of problems flowing from Litton's failure to disaggregate its damages claim.[51] The court stated:

> Where an antitrust plaintiff challenges multiple business practices of the defendant yet fails to disaggregate its proof of damages, two related problems arise. First, an aggregated damage study renders it impossible for the trier of fact to be satisfied that the harm complained of flows from the defendant's unlawful acts as opposed to wholly independent factors including the defendant's lawful procompetitive conduct. Second, an aggregated damage model leaves the jury without a reasonable basis for determining the amount by which the plaintiff's damage model figure should be reduced in the event that one or more of the challenged business practices are not found to be exclusionary.[52]

In *ILC* (also known as *Memorex*), the court granted a directed verdict to IBM on the ground that Memorex failed to disaggregate its damages claim and thus failed to provide a basis for the jury verdict that "would not be speculation or guesswork."[53] With respect to damages, the court found Memorex's damages claim speculative because it failed to account separately for damages attributable to the plaintiff's wrongful acts from harm attributable to other causes, including challenged acts found to be lawful.

> In addition, even if the jury found IBM guilty of every violation alleged, there was no basis for it to independently evaluate what the separate effect of each violation was. It would have to take Memorex at its word. In either case, a verdict rendered on the damage evidence offered by Memorex would have been speculative.[54]

To disaggregate a damages claim, the analyst needs to perform a separate damages calculation for each challenged act or, at least, for logical groupings of the challenged acts. Analysts find separate damages calculations straightforward when, for example, one challenged act affects one geographic market and a second challenged act affects a different geographic market.

(b) Inability to Disaggregate.   At the other extreme, the analyst cannot always disaggregate antitrust damages: "When the challenged acts have effects that interact, it is not possible to consider damages separately and add up their effects."[55] Moreover, some cases lack sufficient data to enable an accurate disaggregation.

The inability to disaggregate can pose a mitigating circumstance causing the courts to accept an aggregate damages calculation. In *Spray-Rite Service Corp. v. Monsanto Co.*,[56] the appellate court upheld a damages verdict even though the plaintiff's expert presented an aggregate damages calculation and testified that Spray-Rite's damages were caused by three factors (i.e., three Monsanto practices). However, the plaintiff's expert also testified "that it would be 'very difficult' to apportion the amount of damage caused by each of these factors 'because [the effects of these factors] merge together and interact among themselves.'"[57] The court found that a plaintiff need not disaggregate antitrust damages where doing so would prove difficult or impossible. The court stated: "If the plaintiff shows that such proof is impracticable, the burden shifts to the defendant to demonstrate the contrary."[58]

(c) Other Issues. The expert faces several other issues in disaggregating antitrust damages. Antitrust complaints often challenge numerous practices by the defendant. Some of these practices can have overlapping effects on the plaintiff. For example, suppose International Gadget (IG) and American Widget (AW) compete in the U.S. widget market. IG engages in bundling and predatory pricing in an attempt to take customers from AW and drive it from the market. Assume that the bundling alone would cause 50 percent of AW's customers to switch to IG, predatory pricing alone would cause 40 percent of AW's customers to switch, and that both practices together cause 60 percent of AW's customers to switch to IG. One implication is that even if the expert can reliably estimate these effects, it is not enough to disaggregate damages to the level of the individual practice because the separate effects of each practice do not simply add to yield the total effects of the practices taken together.

The expert should, where possible, also estimate damages for groupings of two or more practices taken together. However, the number of possible groupings grows rapidly with the number of challenged acts; with n acts, there are $2^n - 1$ possible outcomes. For example, when there are five challenged practices, the expert needs to perform 31 damages calculations to enable the fact finder to assess damages for all possible liability outcomes. This may be impractical.

24.5 CALCULATING ANTITRUST DAMAGES

(a) Introduction. The two principal measures of antitrust damages are overcharges and lost profits. The overcharge measure applies when the plaintiff is the defendant's customer.[59] It represents the difference between the price paid by the plaintiff and the price the plaintiff would have paid absent the antitrust violation. The courts measure damages as lost profits when the plaintiff is a rival that the defendant excluded, or attempted to exclude, from the market.[60] Lost profits equal the amount by which the antitrust violation(s) reduced the plaintiff's profits.

The courts use a but-for standard to calculate both overcharge and lost profits damages; this standard compares actual prices or profits and the prices or profits that would have occurred but for the anticompetitive acts. In *Bigelow v. RKO Radio Pictures*, the Supreme Court defined antitrust damages as the "comparison of profits, prices and values as affected by conspiracy, with what they would have been in its absence under freely competitive conditions."[61]

The two most common methods of calculating damages available are the before and after method and the yardstick approach.[62]

(b) Before and After Approach. In the before and after method, the analyst uses the plaintiff's circumstances in the time period before the antitrust violation began (or after it ended) as a benchmark for the anticompetitive period.[63] For example, in a price-fixing matter, the expert would compare prices in the damages period with prices before the price fix began, holding constant the effects of other factors influencing price that differ between the periods. In a lost profits calculation, the expert using a before and after method would compare the plaintiff's profits (or factors explaining those profits such as unit sales, prices, and incremental costs) between the period before (or after) the anticompetitive conduct began and the damage period. Again, the expert needs to be careful to separate, to the extent possible, the effects of the anticompetitive conduct on the plaintiff's profits from the effects of other, unrelated factors.

(c) Holding Other Factors Constant.   Section 24.6 of this chapter and Chapters 5 and 6 discuss one approach to holding other factors constant: the use of econometric methods. However, econometrics often requires more data than are available. One can also hold the other relevant factors constant by basing the damages calculation on measures independent of these other relevant factors. For example, experts sometimes base their antitrust damages calculations on differences in market shares between the periods before or after the antitrust violations and the damage period.[64] By using a market share approach, the expert implicitly accounts for aggregate factors such as supply and demand conditions that tend to affect total market sales without changing market shares. Market share also presents an attractive measure as a driver for an antitrust damages calculation because the defendant's exclusionary conduct often targets the plaintiff's market share. When using a market share approach, the expert should, when possible, take account of any factors other than the defendant's anticompetitive conduct that affect the plaintiff's market share. Such factors could include, among other things, a shift in consumer preferences between differentiated products or mismanagement by the plaintiff.

For example, returning to the hypothetical example from the widget industry, suppose IG has a market share of 75 percent and AW has the remaining 25 percent. Following the commencement of IG's anticompetitive practices, AW's market share declines to 10 percent and IG's share rises to 90 percent. Suppose further that there is a recession at the same time as IG commenced its anticompetitive campaign and that industry sales, sensitive to the economy, decline as a result. If the expert measured AW's lost sales as its sales before the bad acts began less its sales during the damages period, the expert would overstate lost sales because the loss of sales results, in part, from the recession. The expert who, instead, calculates AW's lost sales as its lost market share multiplied by industry sales in a given year, holds the effects of the recession constant.[65] After calculating AW's lost sales, the expert subtracts from lost sales the incremental costs that AW avoided by not producing the lost sales to yield AW's damages.

(d) Yardstick Approach.   The yardstick approach bases the plaintiff's experience in the but-for world on "the experience of a comparable firm in an actual free market."[66] The comparable firm can be the plaintiff in a different market. However, the existence of exclusionary conduct often does not present the only difference between the yardstick market and the market in which the violations occurred. "Cases employing [the yardstick approach] have recognized that product, firm, and market comparability are all relevant factors in the selection of a proper yardstick and have also cautioned that the yardstick firm must be unaffected, one way or the other, by the defendant's antitrust violation."[67]

The yardstick method often faces greater challenges of proof than the before and after method. "Central to this so-called 'yard-stick' approach to proving antitrust damages is the requirement the plaintiff identify a sufficiently comparable firm (the 'yardstick') against which it can measure its quantum of damages."[68]

Failure to select a proper yardstick can prove fatal to a damages calculation, as occurred in *Home Placement Service v. Providence Journal Co.*[69] Home Placement Services alleged that the defendant's refusal to run Home Placement's advertisements injured it and that such injury constituted antitrust injury. To prove damages, the plaintiff, a national chain, offered evidence of its experience in a different geographic market. The court concluded that the geographic market at issue and the yardstick market lacked sufficient similarity to measure damages with accuracy. In particular, the court found that Home Placement failed to account for, among other things, "the impact of industry, rental patterns, unemployment, summer rentals, and colleges" as well as the "relative competition in the rental referral industry in each market."[70]

(e) Using Plaintiff's Business Plans.   Experts have used the plaintiff's business plans to estimate the plaintiff's expected profits in the but-for world. Such plans appear more convincing as a basis of a damages calculation when the company or outside investors have made investments based on these plans. This shows that investors believe in the plan's plausibility. Business plans prove particularly useful when the defendant's conduct has prevented entry by the plaintiff. In such instances, the expert has no historical information on the plaintiff's performance on which to rely. As with other approaches, the expert should hold constant the effects of factors other than the anticompetitive effects on the plaintiff's profits relative to those anticipated in the business plan.

24.6 USE OF ECONOMETRICS TO ISOLATE THE EFFECTS OF ANTITRUST VIOLATIONS

The careful application of econometric methods can help isolate the effects of antitrust violations from other coincident effects. Econometrics uses statistical techniques such as multiple regression analysis to estimate the relations between economic variables. For example, the expert can use multiple regression to calculate the effects on price (the dependent variable) of the various factors that influence price such as supply and demand factors (the independent variables). The estimated regression will contain a series of estimated coefficients or estimated effects of the independent variables on the dependent variable. Moreover, these estimated coefficients reflect the effect of an independent variable, holding constant the effects of the other independent variables included in the regression (*see* Chapters 5 and 6). Accordingly, damages experts often use econometric methods to estimate the effects of anticompetitive behavior on price or sales, holding constant the effects of other relevant variables.

Consider the calculation of an overcharge. The analyst begins by using economic theory to specify a model relating price to a series of variables that influence price, including supply and demand conditions.[71] Experts often specify a single equation with price as the dependent variable and a number of explanatory or dependent variables to identify supply and demand conditions.[72] The expert collects data on these variables (usually over time) to allow econometric estimation of the model. Experts often use regression analysis to estimate the specified model over a time period that includes both the precollusion (or postcollusion) period and the damage period, with a dummy variable for the damage period included as an explanatory variable.[73] The estimated coefficient on the dummy variable measures the overcharge.[74] For example, suppose the model measures price in dollars and estimates the coefficient on the collusion dummy to be 10.5. This implies that, on average, price is $10.50 greater in the collusion period than in the precollusion period, holding constant the model's other factors affecting price.

Alternatively, the expert can use dynamic forcasting methods to "predict" prices in the collusion or damage period. That is, the analyst applies coefficients estimated for the explanatory variables during either the pre- or post-collusion period to actual values of the explanatory variables during the collusion period to predict what the price would have been, absent collusion.

One can use a similar approach to calculate lost profits damages. The critical part of a lost profits damages calculation often lies in determining the plaintiff's but-for sales when the anticompetitive acts present only one of several factors affecting the sales data. Experts have modeled plaintiffs' sales or market share and estimated the model using econometric methods to estimate the effect of the anticompetitive acts, holding constant other effects. For example, in *Spray-Rite v. Monsanto*, the plaintiff's expert used regression analysis to calculate damages.[75] The expert regressed Spray-Rite's sales on total corn and soybean herbicide sales in the relevant geographic regions during a six-year period prior to the illegal acts; the model then used the estimated relation to calculate Spray-Rite's but-for sales given actual corn and soybean herbicide sales in the regions during the damages period.[76]

Even though econometrics, when used properly, becomes a useful tool to calculate antitrust damages, one should not regard it as a panacea. Even econometric methods cannot isolate every effect on prices or sales if the study lacks sufficient data. Moreover, improper use of econometrics can lead to excluded or disregarded testimony.

In a price-fixing case involving corrugated containers, for example, the jury awarded no damages in spite of finding the defendants liable for fixing prices.[77] This was the third in a series of cases brought against the manufacturers of corrugated containers concerning allegations of price fixing. The plaintiff's expert specified his econometric model of price based implicitly on a model of perfect competition. In specifying his model, he assumed that supply equals demand (a standard assumption in the model of perfect competition). He used econometric methods to estimate the model using data from the collusion period. He forecast prices for the postcollusion period by applying his estimated model of collusive prices to data on the independent variables during the postcollusion period. He calculated the overcharge based on differences between actual postcollusion prices and the forecast prices (i.e., the prices that his model projected, would have been changed had collusion continued).

This analysis had several critical flaws.[78] Most importantly, given that the model relied on the economic model of perfect competition, the expert should have estimated the model over the postcollusion period, when conditions were closer to being competitive than during the collusion period, and used that estimated model to predict the (competitive) but-for prices during the collusion period. However, the defendant's expert found that such an approach estimated competitive prices that *exceeded* actual prices during the collusion period.

Obviously, this could not be true. From this, he concluded that the plaintiff's expert had presented a fatally flawed and unreliable model. The jury apparently agreed and awarded zero damages.

24.7 OTHER ISSUES THAT ARISE IN ANTITRUST DAMAGES CALCULATIONS

Several economic issues arise more frequently in antitrust damages calculations than in the calculation of other commercial damages. These include the effects of anticompetitive conduct on costs and prices and the implications of continuing effects of anticompetitive conduct.

(a) Increase in Plaintiffs' Costs.   The economics literature suggests that conduct designed to raise rivals' costs can be anticompetitive.[79] For example, returning to our example from the widget industry, assume that there are only two low-cost suppliers of a raw material input required in the manufacture of widgets. IG would raise AW's costs if it entered into contracts with both raw material suppliers containing restrictive covenants in which the suppliers agree to sell to AW only at prices greater than those paid by IG. Economic theory considers raising rivals' costs as anticompetitive when it allows the defendant to raise prices, because it drives a rival out of the market, prevents new entry, or forces the rival to accommodate or acquiesce to the higher prices.

When anticompetitive acts include raising rivals' costs, the plaintiff's actual costs will exceed what they would have been in the but-for world, at the actual level of sales. The damages calculation should reflect the increased costs imposed on the plaintiff. This means that in addition to accounting for lost profits on lost sales, the damages calculation should also account for lost profits on actual sales resulting from higher costs.[80]

(b) Increase in Plaintiffs' Prices.   As Section 24.2(b) of this chapter discusses, antitrust damages follow from antitrust injury. Antitrust injury typically includes higher prices to customers of the antitrust defendant(s).[81] An antitrust plaintiff that competes with the defendant will benefit from the ability to charge higher prices to its customers. As a result, lost profits calculations in antitrust matters should account for the effects of prices that exceed those in the "but-for world." These effects drive two modifications to the damages model. First, the model should net out from lost profits the benefit to the plaintiff from the higher price. Second, the model should account for the effects of the higher price on total industry sales. That is, because demand curves slope downward, higher prices in a market will result in lower unit sales.

For example, assume that IG has a 75 percent share of the U.S. market for widgets and AW has the other 25 percent. Both competitors charge a price of $20 per widget and have fixed costs of $50 and incremental costs of $15 per unit. Total market sales are 120, that is, IG has unit sales of 90 (= 75 percent of 120) and AW has unit sales of 30. In this example, AW has profits of $100 (=$20 × 30 − $15 × 30 − $50).

Suppose IG engages in exclusionary conduct, for example, tying, that causes it to increase its market share to 90 percent and allows it to raise the price to $25. Although AW matches this price increase, its market share falls to 10 percent. Because of the price increase, total market demand for widgets falls by one-third to 80. Therefore, AW's unit sales fall to 8 (=10 pecent × 80). AW's profits after IG's exclusionary conduct fall to \$30 (=\$25 × 8 − \$15 × 8 − \$50). AW's damages are \$70, that is, the difference between the profits AW would have earned absent the exclusionary conduct (\$100) and the profits AW earned in the presence of the exclusionary conduct (\$30). The plaintiff (AW) would be wrong to claim that it could have made sales of 30 units at a price of \$25 in the but-for world. The defendant (IG) would be wrong to claim that AW would have sold only 20 units (25 percent of 80) in the but-for world at the lower price of \$20.

(c) Future Damages.   The effects of anticompetitive conduct on the prices paid by customers of the defendant and the profits of rivals can extend beyond the end of the anticompetitive conduct and even beyond the time of trial. For example, even after a cartel breaks up, cartel members sometimes continue to price at or near existing levels for a time in the absence of explicit agreement. In the case of exclusionary conduct, a harmed rival often requires some time to recover market share, especially in markets characterized by long-term contracts, switching costs, network effects, or bandwagon effects. Thus, the issue arises in many antitrust cases of how long beyond the cessation of the anticompetitive conduct the damages period will persist.

The analyst has several alternative approaches to calculating future damages. The first approach forecasts the relevant variable(s) (e.g., price in an overcharge calculation) in both the actual and but-for world. The expert continues the forecasts until the actual variable equals the but-for variable (and damages end). The model should then discount future damages back to the date of trial using an appropriate discount rate (*see* Chapter 7 for a discussion on estimating the cost of capital and its use as a discount rate). Alternatively, the expert can cut off the forecast at some reasonable point in the future because forecasts become more uncertain the further into the future they run.

Note that discounting future damages mitigates the potential issue of the uncertainty of forecasts because the values of later years carry a greater discount. Some experts have calculated a terminal value of future damages either instead of one of the above two approaches or at the end of the forecast period. A terminal value calculation requires assumptions about the rate at which damages will decline (or grow) in future years as well as the appropriate discount rate. Depending on how the expert calculates the terminal value, damages are inexplicability assumed to extend forever (although with discounting, little value will attach to the distant future) or for a discrete time period.

24.8   AUTOMATIC TREBLING OF DAMAGES AND PREJUDGMENT INTEREST

In 1914, Congress enacted the Clayton Antitrust Act to regulate business practices that harm competition. Section 4 of that act authorizes private parties to bring suit for damages under the antitrust laws. The Clayton Act requires the courts to treble antitrust damages awards. "[A]ny person who shall be injured in his business or property by reason of anything forbidden in the antitrust laws may sue therefor . . . and shall recover threefold the damages by him sustained."[82] One reason given for trebling is that detecting antitrust violations can be difficult. "Trebling makes up for the fact that antitrust violations are hard to detect and prove."[83] Even though the automatic trebling doesn't directly involve the damages expert, the expert should be aware of trebling.

Several commentators have suggested that the fact that damages will be trebled may compel judges to hold antitrust plaintiffs to higher standards of proof.[84] For example, in the dissenting opinion in the *Visa Check/Mastermoney Antitrust Litigation*, Judge Jacobs wrote: "Enforcement of the mitigation duty may be even more critical in antitrust cases than in cases sounding in contract or tort because an antitrust plaintiff seeking treble damages can profit by avoiding mitigation of loss."[85] Donald Baker, former Assistant Attorney General in charge of the Antitrust Division, maintains: "Mandatory trebling can distort judicial decision making on substantive and procedural questions because it necessarily makes judges more reluctant to impose liability in close cases and more willing to erect narrower standing rules."[86]

Trebling of damages has also moved the courts to preclude prejudgment interest to most antitrust plaintiffs. In *TWA v. Hughes*, the Second Circuit reasoned that:

> it is reasonable to interpret Congress's silence on the matter as indicating that trebled damages are sufficient penalty and that interest need not be included. Moreover, trebled damages will more than adequately compensate TWA for its injuries. Thus, there is no inherent policy reason to award moratory interest here and not doing so avoids difficult questions of proof—including highly abstruse inquiries as to proper rates and the time from which interest should run.[87]

The prejudgment interest rule has two exceptions: the federal government can recover prejudgment interest as well as private plaintiffs in cases in which the defendant has sought to delay the case or otherwise acted in bad faith.[88]

24.9 PREDATORY PRICING AND COST ESTIMATION

(a) Definition. The Supreme Court has defined predatory pricing as "pricing below an appropriate measure of cost for the purpose of eliminating competitors in the short run and reducing competition in the long run."[89] Economists define predatory pricing as

> a price reduction that is profitable only because of the added market power the predator gains from eliminating, disciplining or otherwise inhibiting the competitive conduct of a rival or potential rival. Stated more precisely, a predatory price is a price that is profit maximizing only because of its exclusionary or other anticompetitive effects.[90]

These exclusionary or anticompetitive effects include higher prices or reduced innovation, product quality, or service levels.

(b) Legal Requirements for Predatory Pricing. In its 1993 decision in *Brooke*, the Supreme Court defined the current legal framework for identifying predatory pricing.[91] According to *Brooke*, a successful predatory pricing claim must meet two requirements: "First, a plaintiff seeking to establish competitive injury resulting from a rival's low prices must prove that the prices complained of are below an appropriate measure of its rival's costs."[92] Second, predatory pricing requires "demonstration that the [predator] had a reasonable prospect [in a Robinson-Patman claim], or, under [section] 2 of the Sherman Act, a dangerous probability, of recouping its investment in below-cost prices."[93] Recouping its investment requires "that the predator can later raise price sufficient to recoup its investment in below cost pricing."[94] The recoupment requirement means that the plaintiff must prove that the predatory conduct either has been profitable or could reasonably have been expected, at the time of this investment, to become profitable. The *Brooke* Court specified the recoupment analysis as follows:

> For recoupment to occur, the pricing must be capable, as a threshold matter, of producing the intended effects on the firm's rivals. This requires an understanding of the extent and duration of the alleged predation, the relative financial strength of the predator and its intended victim, and their respective incentives and will. The inquiry is whether, given the aggregate losses caused by the below-cost pricing, the intended target would likely succumb. If so, then there is the further question whether the below-cost pricing would likely injure competition in the relevant market.... The determination requires an estimate of the alleged predation's cost and a close analysis of both the scheme alleged and the relevant market's structure and conditions."[95]

(c) Relevant Cost Measures. No single legal standard exists regarding the appropriate cost measure against which to compare price in a predatory pricing analysis. The courts commonly use average total costs (ATC) and average variable costs (AVC). ATC are the total per unit costs of producing the product in question. AVC are the total costs less the fixed costs of producing and selling the product divided by unit production or sales. Bolton, Brodley, and Riordan summarize the relevant legal precedent as follows:

> Under current U.S. law, a price above ATC is conclusively lawful, while at the other extreme, in most jurisdictions a price below AVC is presumptively unlawful (assuming the other preconditions of Brooke are satisfied). A price between AVC and ATC is either presumptively or conclusively lawful, depending on the Circuit. In Circuits where the price is presumptively lawful, the presumption can be rebutted by other evidence of predation, particularly intent and market structure.[96]

Brooke did nothing to change this situation. Although *Brooke* requires a proof of pricing below "an appropriate measure" of costs, *Brooke* does not specify the appropriate measure(s) of cost in this situation.

Leading economists have proposed other cost measures as standards for proof of predatory pricing, which courts may soon accept, if indeed they haven't already done so. For example, Bolton, Brodley, and Riordan propose replacing AVC with average avoidable cost (AAC), where AAC is defined as "the average per unit cost that [the] predator would have avoided during the period of below cost pricing had it *not* produced the predatory increment of sale."[97] The authors point out that AAC is easier to calculate than AVC because there is no need to allocate costs into fixed and variable buckets and because AAC is more theoretically correct than AVC since it better approximates marginal costs.

Bolton, Brodley, and Riordan also propose replacing ATC with long-run average incremental costs (LAIC), defined as "the per unit cost of producing the predatory increment of output whenever such costs were incurred."[98] LAIC includes all costs specific to the product at issue including R&D and marketing even if those costs were sunk prior to the predatory period. Unlike ATC, LAIC does not require allocation of joint and common costs in the case of a multiproduct firm.

(d) Cost Estimation Methods.   Chapter 5 discusses cost estimation methods. Analysts can use both statistical and nonstatistical methods of estimating costs in a predatory pricing analysis. For example, experts have used multiple regression analysis to measure defendants' incremental costs. The expert regresses total costs on unit sales (or revenues) with the estimated coefficient on sales indicating the incremental costs the seller incurred to sell an additional unit (or dollar). Experts have also used nonstatistical methods such as account analysis in estimating costs for predatory pricing analysis (*see* Chapter 5 for an exposition of nonstatistical and statistical cost estimation techniques.) In some cases, estimates of the plaintiff's incremental costs may be found in discovery documents. For example, if the predation was successful, or almost so, plaintiff may have estimated its incremental costs as part of an exit analysis.

24.10   SUMMARY

Because the antitrust laws aim to protect competition rather than competitors, antitrust damages have a different nature than damages in other commercial litigation. To recover damages from an antitrust violation, plaintiffs first must prove the following:

- **Causation.** The alleged antitrust violations caused their damages.
- **Harm to competition.** The harm to the plaintiff resulted from a competition-reducing aspect of the antitrust violation.
- **Standing.** The plaintiff cannot recover for damages for indirect antitrust injury (i.e., the defendant targets a supplier's supplier).

Plaintiffs face a less exacting burden for proving the amount of damages than the reasonable certainty standard applied to causation. However, the courts have made it clear that antitrust damages calculations cannot rely on speculation or guesswork. Many of the challenges facing the antitrust damages expert involve isolating the anticompetitive effects of the challenged violations from other factors that could have coincidentally harmed the plaintiff—including general market forces, legitimate competition from the defendant in both the actual and but-for worlds, and failure to take advantage of available mitigation opportunities.

Because antitrust claims often include multiple challenged acts—some of which the fact finder might find lawful—the damages expert should disaggregate the damages claim when feasible. Disaggregating damages means calculating damages separately for each challenged act or each logical grouping of challenged acts. Courts have ignored or given little weight to damages calculations that fail to isolate anticompetitive effects from other coincident harm suffered by the plaintiff when such an analysis is possible.

The two most common methods for calculating antitrust damages are the before and after and the yardstick methods. Even though the courts have accepted each, neither method, by itself, solves the challenges of isolating the anticompetitive harm from other harm incurred by the plaintiff. Damages experts often use econometric methods to estimate the effects of anticompetitive behavior while holding constant other factors affecting price or sales. When experts lack sufficient data to perform econometric analyses, experts often isolate the anticompetitive effects by identifying variables (such as market share) that the coincident factors do not affect.

Unlike other commercial damages, the courts automatically treble antitrust damages and do not award prejudgment interest to most plaintiffs.

Predatory pricing (i.e., pricing below cost to reduce competition) requires an analysis of defendant's costs. Experts have used standard cost allocation methods, including both statistical and nonstatistical ones in the predatory pricing context.

NOTES

1. http://www.usdoj.gov/atr/overview.html
2. *Id.*
3. A § 2 claim does not require that the defendant literally have a monopoly, that is, a 100 percent market share in a properly defined market.
4. *United States v. E.I. du Pont de Nemours*, 351 U.S. 377, 391 (1956).
5. *United States v. Aluminum Co. of America*, 148 F. 2d 416, 430 (2nd Cir. 1945).
6. Franklin M. Fisher, "Diagnosing Monopoly," *The Quarterly Review of Economics and Business* (19 1979): 13.
7. Department of Justice and Federal Trade Commission, *Horizontal Merger Guidelines*, (Washington, DC), (Revised 1997) § 1.0.
8. "A market is defined as a product or group of products and a geographic area in which it is produced or sold such that a hypothetical profit-maximizing firm, not subject to price regulation, that was the only present and future producer or seller of those products in that area likely would impose at least a 'small but significant and nontransitory' increase in price, assuming the terms of sale of all other products are held constant. A relevant market is a group of products and a geographic area that is no bigger than necessary to satisfy this test" (Id., § 1.0).
9. U.S. Department of Justice and the Federal Trade Commission, *Horizontal Merger Guidelines*, § 2.
10. 15 U.S.C. § 13.
11. *Id.*
12. *Id.*
13. For more in-depth treatment of the liability issues arising in antitrust matters, *see* Abram Hoffman and Mark Palim, "Antitrust," in *Litigation Services Handbook*, 3rd ed. (Hoboken, NJ: John Wiley & Sons, 2000).
14. William H. Page, ed., *Proving Antitrust Damages: Legal and Economic Issues*, (New York: American Bar Association, 1996), 31, citing several cases.
15. *Brunswick Corp. v. Pueblo Bowl-O-Mat*, 429 U.S. 477, 489 (1977).
16. *Atlantic Richfield Co. v. USA Petroleum*, 495 U.S. 328, 344 (1990).
17. *Brunswick*, 429 U.S. 477 (1977).
18. Section 7 of the Clayton Act prohibits mergers and acquisitions where the effect "may be substantially to lessen competition, or to tend to create a monopoly."
19. *Id.* at 488, citing *Brown Shoe Co. v. United States*, 370 U.S. 320 (1962).
20. *J. Truett Payne Co. v. Chrysler Motors Corp.*, 451 U.S. 557 (1981).
21. *Id.* at 562.
22. *Matsushita Elec. Industrial Co. v. Zenith Radio*, 475 U.S. 574, 574 (1986).
23. *Id.* at 582–583.

24. Vertical restraints, also referred to as vertical restrictions, are conditions imposed by a firm at one rung in the distribution chain, for example, manufacturers, on firms at the next level, for example, distributors. Exclusive sales territories and restrictions on the prices that retailers may charge are examples of vertical restraints.

25. *Atlantic Richfield*, 495 U.S. at 339–340, citing *Brunswick*, 429 U.S. 477.

26. Page, *Proving Antitrust Damages*, 17–18.

27. *Illinois Brick Co. v. Illinois*, 431 U.S. 720 (1977).

28. *Hanover Shoe v. United Shoe Mach.*, 392 U.S. 481 (1968).

29. Page, *Proving Antitrust Damages*, 17.

30. *Id.*, 188.

31. *Bigelow v. RKO Radio Pictures*, 327 U.S. 251, 264 (1946).

32. *Id.* at 264–265, quoting *Story Parchment Co. v. Paterson Parchment Paper Co.*, 282 U.S. 561–564 (1931).

33. *Bigelow*, 327 U.S. at 264.

34. Roger D. Blair and William H. Page, "'Speculative' Antitrust Damages," *Washington Law Review* 70 (1995): 423.

35. For examples of courts rejecting damages claims on account of "assumptions contradicted by experience," *see* Page, *Proving Antitrust Damages*, 49–51.

36. *Concord Boat Corp. v. Brunswick Corp.*, U.S. Court of Appeals for the Eighth Circuit, March 24, 2000, 28 (downloaded from http://www.appellate.net/briefs/), quoting *Virgin Atlantic Airways Ltd. v. British Airways PLC*, 69 F. Supp. 2d 571, 580 (S.D.N.Y. 1999).

37. The Cournot model explains price formation in a noncooperative oligopoly, that is, a market with a small number of firms that act independently but with awareness of each other's existence and actions. *See* Dennis W. Carlton and Jeffrey M. Perloff, *Modern Industrial Organization*, 2nd ed. (New York: Harper Collins, 1994) 233–244.

38. *Concord Boat*, U.S. Court of Appeals at 28.

39. This follows from the fact that a Cournot oligopoly model predicts that price will increase with increases in market concentration, all else being equal.

40. *ILC Peripherals Leasing Corp. v. IBM*, 458 F. Supp. 423, 435 (N.D. Cal. 1978).

41. *Id.*

42. *Murphy Tugboat Co. v. Crowley*, 658 F.2d 1256 (9th Cir. 1981), *cert denied*, 455 U.S. 1018 (1982).

43. For more examples, *see* Page, *Proving Antitrust Damages*, 52–54.

44. *Murphy Tugboat*, 658 F.2d at 1262.

45. Sunk costs are costs that cannot be recovered on exiting a market.

46. *See* William B. Tye and Stephen H. Kalos, "Antitrust Damages from Lost Opportunities," *Antitrust Bulletin* 41 (1996): 637–664 and Roger D. Blair and William H. Page, "'Speculative' Antitrust Damages." The idea that mitigation opportunities are related to opportunity costs was also discussed in *Fishman v. Estate of Wirtz*, 807 F.2d 520, 564–568 (7th Cir.1986).

47. Tye and Kalos, "Antiturst Damages from Lost Opportunities," 648.

48. M. Sean Royall, "Disaggregation of Antitrust Damages," *Antitrust Law Journal* 65 (1997): 311–352. This article provides an extensive discussion of disaggregation including review of leading cases.

49. *Litton Systems Inc. v. Honeywell, Inc.*, 1996-2 Trade Cas. (CCH) 71,559, 77964 (C.D. Cal. 1996), citing *City of Vernon v. S. Cal. Edison Co.*, 955 F.2d 1361 (9th Cir. 1992).

50. Royall, "Disaggregation of Antitrust Damages," 323–324.

51. *Litton Systems*, 1996-2 Trade Cas. (CCH) 71,559.

52. *Id.* at 71, 564–71, 565 (citations omitted).

53. *ILC Peripherals*, 458 F. Supp. at 436.

54. *Id.* at 434.

55. Robert E. Hall, and Victoria A. Lazear, "Reference Guide on Estimation of Economic Losses in Damages Awards," in *Reference Manual on Scientific Evidence*, 2nd ed. (Washington, DC: Federal Judicial Center, 2000): 277–332, 306.

56. *Spray-Rite Service Corp. v. Monsanto Co.*, 684 F.2d 1226 (7th Cir. 1982).

57. *Id.* at 1242.

58. *Id.* at 1243–1244.

59. Although firms often pass along at least a portion of cost increases to their customers, as discussed later in Section, 24.2(c) federal law does not allow indirect purchasers to sue and collect damages for antitrust violations by their suppliers' suppliers.

60. Lost going concern value can also serve as a measure of damages in such instances. Because loss in market value is, in theory, directly related to expected lost profits, economists generally consider loss in market value to be a special case of lost profits.

61. *Bigelow*, 327 U.S. 251 at 264.

62. Blair and Page, "'Speculative' Antitrust Damages," 427–428 and 443–455.

63. Damages experts occasionally use the period after the antitrust violation(s) have ceased as a benchmark for the damages period. The after period is seldom used because the effects of the anticompetitive acts can linger beyond the cessation of the acts, causing a during and after computation to understate the anticompetitive effects.

64. For example, a market share approach to calculating damages was used by plaintiff's expert in *LePage's v. 3M*, 324 F.3d 141 (3d Cir. 2003).

65. The case in which prices rise due to the anticompetitive conduct and industry sales fall as a result is discussed below.

66. *Fishman v. Estate of Wirtz*, 807 F. 2d 520, 551 (7th Cir. 1986).

67. *Home Placement Service, Inc. v. Providence Journal Co.*, 819 F. 2d 1199, 1206 (1st Cir. 1987).

68. *Id.*

69. *Id.*

70. *Id.* at 1207.

71. Such models incorporate assumptions about the form of competition absent the alleged conspiracy.

72. For example, in the case of perfect competition, a "reduced form" equation is derived by solving the equilibrium condition of supply equals demand for price as a function of those variables explaining supply and demand. *See* Michael O. Finkelstein and Hans Levenbach, "Regression Estimates of Damages in Price-Fixing Cases," *Law & Contemporary Problems* 46 (1983): 145–169, 163.

73. *See* Joseph E. Harrington, Jr., "Post-Cartel Pricing During Litigation," *The Journal of Industrial Economics* LII (2004): 517–533, which suggests that strategic behavior by cartel members during litigation (i.e., after the damage period) can raise prices, so that but-for prices calculated on the basis of postdamage period prices are too high.

74. Implicit in this method is the assumption that the overcharge is constant over the entire damage period, either in absolute or percentage terms depending on the specification of the dependent variable.

75. *Spray-Rite*, 684 F. 2d at 1241.

76. *See* Frederick R. Warren-Boulton, "Resale Price Maintenance Reexamined: *Monsanto v. Spray-Rite* (1984)," in *The Antitrust Revolution: The Role of Economics*, 2nd ed., eds. John E. Kwoka, Jr. and Lawrence J. White (New York: Oxford University Press, 1994): 408–411.

77. Franklin M. Fisher, "Statisticians, Econometricians and Adversary Proceedings," presented at the Economic and Social Research Council Econometric Study Group Conference in honor of J.D. Sargan, Oxford, England, March 1984, in John Monz, ed.,

Industrial Organization, Economics and the Law: Collected Papers of Franklin M. Fisher, ed. John Monz (Cambridge, MA: The MIT Press, 1991):282–285.

78. *Id.*
79. Thomas G., Krattenmaker, and Steven C. Salop, "Anticompetitive Exclusion: Raising Rivals' Costs to Achieve Power Over Price," *Yale Law Journal* 96 (1986): 209–293.
80. The plaintiff's marginal costs could have also increased as a result of the acts that raised the plaintiff's costs. If so, the damages expert should be careful to utilize the proper but-for marginal costs in calculating the lost profits on lost sales.
81. Antitrust injury can also follow from effects on other competitive variables including service, product quality, and innovation.
82. 15 U.S.C. § 15.
83. Judge Easterbrook's dissent in *Fishman*, 807 F. 2d 520, 584.
84. Although many antitrust cases are tried before a jury and juries are unaware that damages will be trebled, judicial reaction to trebling is important. First, many cases are decided in whole, or in part, by the courts either before or after trial. Second, even when a jury decision remains unchanged by the appeal process, the jury will consider the damages amount in the context of jury instructions written or approved by the trial judge.
85. *In re Visa Check/Mastermoney Antitrust Litigation*, 280 F. 3d 124, 150 (2nd Cir. 2001).
86. Donald Baker, "Revisiting History—What Have We Learned about Private Antitrust Enforcement That We Would Recommend to Others?" *Loyola Consumer Law Review* 16, (2004): 384.
87. For example, *see Trans World Airlines v. Howard R. Hughes, et al.*, 449 F.2d 51, 86–87 (2nd Cir. 1971), citing *Rodgers v. United States*, 332 U.S. 371, 92 L. Ed. 3, 68 S. Ct. 5 (1947) and *Brooklyn Savings Bank v. O'Neil*, 324 U.S. 697, 89, L. Ed. 1296, 65 S. Ct. 895 (1945).
88. Page, *Proving Antitrust Damages*, 43–45.
89. *Cargill v. Monfort of Colorado*, 479 U.S. 104, 117 (1986).
90. Patrick Bolton, Joseph F. Brodley and Michael H. Riordan, "Predatory Pricing: Strategic Theory and Legal Policy," *Georgetown Law Journal* 88 (2000): 2242–2243.
91. *Brooke Group v. Brown & Williamson Tobacco*, 509 U.S. 209 (1993).
92. *Id.* at 222.
93. *Id.* at 224. Predatory pricing claims can be brought either under Section 2 of the Sherman Act (15 U.S.C. § 2) or the Robinson-Patman Act (15 U.S.C. § 13). A Sherman Act claim involves predation intended to create or maintain the monopoly power of a single firm and requires a "dangerous probability" of monopolization. A Robinson-Patman claim can also involve predatory pricing that facilitates collusion among firms and requires a proof of a "reasonable probability" of "substantial injury to competition."
94. Bolton, Brodley and Riordan, "Predatory Pricing," 2255.
95. *Brooke*, 509 U.S. at 210.
96. Bolton, Brodley and Riordan, "Predatory Pricing," 2271.
97. *Id.* The predatory increment of sale refers to the fact that the predator can expect to increase its unit sales because the price reduction will cause an increase in total market sales through movement along the demand curve and, possibly, by taking sales from the prey if the prey does not match the price reductions.
98. *Id.* at 2272.

LIST OF CASES

Bigelow v. RKO Radio Pictures, 327 U.S. 251 (1946).

Brooke Group Ltd. v. Brown & Williamson Tobacco Corp., 509 U.S. 209 (1993).

Brunswick Corp. v. Pueblo Bowl-O-Mat, 429 U.S. 477 (1977).

Cargill v. Monfort of Colorado, 479 U.S. 104 (1986).

City of Vernon v. S. Cal. Edison Co., 955 F.2d 1361 (9th Cir. 1992).

Coastal Fuels of Puerto Rico, Inc. v. Caribbean Petroleum Corporation, 175 F.3d 18 (1st Cir. 1999).

Concord Boat Corp. v. Brunswick Corp., 207 F.3d 1039 (8th Cir. 2000), *cert. denied*, 531 U.S. 979 (2000).

Conwood Co. v. United States Tobacco Co., 290 F.3d 768 (6th Cir. 2002).

J. Truett Payne Co. v. Chrysler Motors Corp., 451 U.S. 557 (1981).

Fishman v. Estate of Wirtz, 807 F.2d 520 (7th Cir. 1986).

Hanover Shoe v. United Shoe Mach., 392 U.S. 481 (1968).

Texaco, Inc. v. Hasbrouck, 490 U.S. 1105 (1990).

Home Placement Service v. Providence Journal Co., 819 F. 2d 1199 (1st Cir. 1987).

ILC Peripherals Leasing Corp. v. IBM, 458 F. Supp. 423 (N.D. Cal. 1978).

Illinois Brick Co. v. Illinois, 431 U.S. 720 (1977).

In re Visa Check/Mastermoney Antitrust Litigation, 280 F.3d 124 (2nd Cir. 2001).

LePage's v. 3M, 324 F.3d 141 (3d Cir. 2003).

Litton Systems, Inc. v. Honeywell, Inc., 1996-2 Trade Cas. (CCH) ¶ 71,559 (C.D. Cal. 1996).

Memorex Corp. v. IBM, 636 F.2d 1188 (9th Cir. 1980), *cert. denied*, 452 U.S. 972 (1981).

Matsushita Elec. Industrial Co. v. Zenith Radio, 475 U.S. 574 (1986).

Murphy Tugboat Co. v. Crowley, 658 F.2d 1256 (9th Cir. 1981), *cert. denied*, 455 U.S. 1018 (1982).

Reiter v. Sonotone Corp., 442 U.S. 330 (1979).

Spray-Rite Service Corp. v. Monsanto Co., 684 F.2d 1226 (7th Cir. 1982).

Texas Industries, Inc. v. Radcliff Materials, Inc., 451 U.S. 630 (1981).

Trans World Airlines v. Howard R. Hughes, et al., 449 F.2d 51 (2nd Cir. 1971).

United States v. Aluminum Co. of America, 148 F.2d 416 (2nd Cir. 1945).

United States v. E.I. du Pont de Nemours, 351 U.S. 377 (1956).

Unitherm Food Systems, Inc. v. Swift-Eckrich, Inc., U.S.C.A.F.C. (docket no. 03-1472, 2004).

Zenith Radio Corp. v. Hazeltine Research, Inc., 401 U.S. 321 (1971).

BIBLIOGRAPHY AND OTHER SUGGESTED READING

Areeda, Phillip, and Donald F. Turner. "Predatory Pricing and Related Practices under Section 2 of the Sherman Act." *Harvard Law Review* 88 (1975): 697–733.

Baker, Donald I. "Revisiting History—What Have We Learned About Private Antitrust Enforcement That We Would Recommend To Others?" *Loyola Consumer Law Review* 16 (2004): 379–408.

Blair, Roger D., and Amanda Kay Esquibel. "Yardstick Damages in Lost Profit Cases: An Econometric Approach." *Denver University Law Review* 72 (1994): 113–36.

Blair, Roger D., and William H. Page. "'Speculative' Antitrust Damages." *Washington Law Review* 70 (1995): 423–48.

Bolton, Patrick, Joseph F. Brodley, and Michael H. Riordan. "Predatory Pricing: Strategic Theory and Legal Policy. *Georgetown Law Journal* 88 (2000): 2239–330.

Carlton, Dennis W., and Jeffrey M. Perloff. *Modern Industrial Organization*. 2nd ed. New York: Harper Collins, 1994.

Department of Justice and Federal Trade Commission. *Horizontal Merger Guidelines*. Issued April 2, 1992; revised April 8, 1997. Washington, DC.

Hoffman, Abram E., and Mark R. A. Palim. "Antitrust." In *Litigation Services Handbook: The Role of the Financial Expert.* 3rd ed., edited by Roman L. Weil, Michael J. Wagner, and Peter B. Frank. Hoboken, NJ: John Wiley & Sons, 2001.

Fisher, Franklin M. "Diagnosing Monopoly." *The Quarterly Review of Economics and Business* 19 1979: 7–33.

Fisher, Franklin M. "Multiple Regression in Legal Proceedings," *Columbia Law Review* 80 (1980): 702–36.

Fisher, Franklin M. "Statisticians, Econometricians, and Adversary Proceedings," presented at the Economic and Social Research Council Econometric Study Group Conference in honor of J.D. Sargan, Oxford, England, March 1984, In John Monz (ed.), *Industrial Organization, Economics and the Law: Collected Papers of Franklin M. Fisher*, edited by John Monz. (Cambridge, MA: The MIT Press, 1991).

Fisher, Franklin M., and R. Craig Romaine. "Janis Joplin's Yearbook and the Theory of Damages." *Journal of Accounting, Auditing, and Finance* 5 (1990): 145–58.

Finkelstein, Michael O., and Hans Levenbach. "Regression Estimates of Damages in Price-Fixing Cases." *Law & Contemporary Problems* 46 (1983): 145–69.

Hall, Robert E., and Victoria A. Lazear. "Reference Guide on Estimation of Economic Losses in Damages Awards." In *Reference Manual on Scientific Evidence.* 2nd ed. Washington DC: Federal Judicial Center, 2000, 277–332.

Harrington, Joseph E., Jr. "Post-Cartel Pricing During Litigation." *The Journal of Industrial Economics* LII (2004): 517–33.

Jacobson, Jonathan M, and Tracy Greer. "Twenty-One Years of Antitrust Injury: Down the Alley with *Brunswick v. Pueblo Bowl-O-Mat.'*" *Antitrust Law Journal* 66 (1998): 273–312.

Kaye, D.H. "Adversarial Economics in *United States Tobacco Co. v. Conwood Co.*" *Jurimetrics* 43 (2003): 343–52.

Klevorick, Alvin K. "The Current State of the Law and Economics of Predatory Pricing." *The American Economic Review* 83 (1993): 162–67.

Krattenmaker, Thomas G., and Steven C. Salop. "Anticompetitive Exclusion: Raising Rivals' Costs to Achieve Power Over Price." *Yale Law Journal* 96 (1986): 209–93.

Lande, Robert H. "Are Antitrust 'Treble' Damages Really Single Damages?" *Ohio State Law Journal* 54 (1993): 115–74.

Page, William H., ed. *Proving Antitrust Damages: Legal and Economic Issues.* New York: American Bar Association, 1996.

Page, William H. "The Limits of State Indirect Purchaser Suits: Class Certification in the Shadow of Illinois Brick." *Antitrust Law Journal* 67 (1999): 1–39.

Royall, M. Sean. "Disaggregation of Antitrust Damages." *Antitrust Law Journal* 65 (1997): 311–52.

Rubinfeld, Daniel. "Econometrics in the Courtroom." *Columbia Law Review* 85 (1985): 1048–97.

Taurman, J.D., and J.C. Boddington. "Measuring Damage to a Firm's Profitability: Ex Ante or Ex Post?" *The Antitrust Bulletin* 37 (1992): 57–106.

Tye, William B., and Stephen H. Kalos. "Antitrust Damages from Lost Opportunities." *Antitrust Bulletin* 41 (1996): 637–64.

Tye, William B., Stephen H. Kalos, and A. Lawrence Kolbe. "How to Value a Lost Opportunity: Defining and Measuring Damages from Market Foreclosure." *Research in Law and Economics* 17 (1995): 83–125.

Warren-Boulton, Frederick R. "Resale Price Maintenance Reexamined: *Monsanto v. Spray-Rite* (1984)." In *The Antitrust Revolution: The Role of Economics*, 2nd ed., edited by John E. Kwoka, Jr. and Lawrence J. White. New York: Oxford University Press, 1994.

White, Lawrence J. "Lysine and Price Fixing: How Long? How Severe?" *Review of Industrial Organization* 18 (2001): 23–31.

CHAPTER 25

COMMON DISPUTES IN MERGER & ACQUISITION TRANSACTIONS

Kevin D. Kreb
Leigh Walton
Mark W. Haller

CONTENTS

The authors acknowledge that much of the material and language in this chapter comes from two previously published chapters in the third edition (2001) of the *Litigation Services Handbook*: Chapter 27, "Mergers, Acquisitions, and Divestitures: The Nature of Disputes and the Role of the Financial Expert," authored by Mark W. Haller, Kevin D. Kreb, Benjamin W. Perks, and Thomas K. Riordan; and Chapter 4, "Roles and Techniques of a Financial Expert in Alternative Dispute Resolution," authored by Adam S. Cummis, Mark W. Haller, Kevin D. Kreb, and George G. Strong.

25.1   INTRODUCTION

Financial experts provide services during due diligence and negotiation of mergers, acquisitions, and divestitures (M&A) deals, but can also assist with disputes that often arise from M&A transactions, whether resolved through negotiation, alternative dispute resolution, or traditional litigation. This chapter provides an overview of the M&A process and of common clauses in M&A contracts relating to accounting and financial reporting matters. These clauses often affect the purchase price and can therefore cause disputes; we will examine some of the common issues and disputes that arise in connection with these clauses. We will then discuss the financial expert's role in the dispute resolution process.

(a) Overview of the Acquisition/Divestiture Process.   The events surrounding an acquisition or divestiture of all or part of a business typically begin with the initial negotiation on price and contract terms. This negotiation, if successful, usually results in a signed letter of intent, in which each party acknowledges in broad terms its intentions to consummate the transaction. Most letters of intent do not constitute a binding obligation of the parties to proceed with the transaction.

Next comes the negotiation and execution of a purchase and sale agreement. During this phase, the buyer usually conducts due diligence on the target company. Before signing the agreement, the parties seek and obtain the necessary internal approvals for the transaction. Significant transactions usually require approval by the boards of directors.

The length of time between signing the final agreement and closing the transaction depends on a number of factors, including whether the transaction is subject to the Hart-Scott-Rodino Antitrust Improvements Act of 1976, whether the Securities and Exchange Commission (SEC) requires any filings, and whether the buyer needs to arrange financing for the acquisition. The length of the preclosing period varies depending on the transaction but is often one to three months. During the preclosing period, the seller usually manages the business being sold. Typically, the terms of the transaction state that the profits (losses) of the business during the preclosing period will accrue to the seller. For these and other reasons, M&A agreements typically adjust the purchase price to account for results of operations and other transactions during the stub period that occurs between signing (or some other predetermined date) and closing.

Generally, within a specified time period subsequent to closing, often 30 to 60 days, the seller provides the buyer with a closing balance sheet prepared as of the date of closing.[1] This closing balance sheet is usually the basis used to calculate the postclosing adjustment,[2] which accounts for activity during the stub period just defined. The buyer has the right to perform a postclosing review and to make objections to the closing balance sheet in accordance with the purchase/sale agreement. This postclosing review generally identifies any areas that will generate disputes.

(b) Competing Interest of Buyers and Sellers.   Buyers and sellers enter into M&A transactions with different and competing interests. Buyers are typically looking to pay no more than a specified price and receive the related value that they perceive in the company or assets they are purchasing. The buyer generally conducts due diligence to evaluate the liabilities it will assume and the assets it will receive (often with an aim of reducing the purchase price). Sellers, however, want to eliminate ongoing exposure after the sale, to avoid unfavorable post-sale purchase price adjustments and to maintain (or even increase) the consideration actually paid. In keeping with these competing interests, buyers generally prefer to avoid uncertain or contingent liabilities, whereas sellers want the sale to absolve them of exposure to such liabilities. An example of this type of exposure is environmental liabilities, actual or contingent, and the related estimated remediation and associated costs.

These interests collide during the contract negotiations, as both parties seek to identify, quantify, and limit their risks, ultimately agreeing on contract provisions to allocate the risks between them. These provisions typically take the form of representations, warranties, covenants, and indemnifications. Section 25.2 discusses the clauses that purchase/sale agreements typically include, focusing on those related to accounting and financial reporting issues that bear on the purchase price.

25.2 CONTRACT PROVISIONS WITH POTENTIAL ACCOUNTING, FINANCIAL REPORTING, AND PURCHASE PRICE SIGNIFICANCE

(a) Representations and Warranties. Many of the representations and warranties common in purchase/sale contracts relate to accounting, financial reporting, and purchase price issues. From a buyer's perspective, representations and warranties serve three purposes in the agreement: (1) assisting the buyer in understanding the business it is purchasing; (2) enabling the buyer to recover damages if the seller makes inaccurate representations; and (3) allowing the buyer to abort the transaction if it finds the seller's representations incorrect before the closing.

Sellers often represent that they have prepared the financial statements in accordance with generally accepted accounting principles (GAAP). In addition, or as an alternative, some sellers represent that they have prepared the financial statements in accordance with historical company policy or some other basis of accounting. Some jurisdictions—notably Great Britain—require that the agreement specify in some detail the accounting practices that have been or will be applied.

Some sellers also warrant that no undisclosed liabilities exist, warranting, for example, "With respect to financial statements as of a specified date, there were no liabilities of a type required to be reflected on a balance sheet prepared in accordance with GAAP that were not so reflected." This provides the buyer with some assurance that it will assume only those liabilities appearing on the closing balance sheet. Some buyers, however, request that this representation also cover contingent liabilities that would not be required to be shown on a balance sheet prepared in accordance with GAAP. Broadening the representation in this way can increase the seller's exposure to claims for breach.

(b) Postclosing Adjustments. A prospective buyer can employ several methods to value the target and decide on a price. These methods include applying a multiple to earnings or cash flows, measuring the fair value of assets, estimating the value based on amounts paid in other comparable transactions, and calculating a value or adjusting the value based on information regarding potential synergies with a buyer's existing businesses. Whichever method the buyer uses, it will typically select a purchase price based, in large measure, on information in the latest available financial statements and trend of earnings.

Because the business continues, transactions will continue from the signing of a letter of intent until the closing. This means that the closing balance sheet and related financial statements will differ from those on which the buyer computed a purchase price. For this reason, most agreements include a postclosing adjustment clause[3] intended to account for changes in the target's financial position between the preclosing balance sheet date and the closing date balance sheet. This clause usually allocates to the sellers the profits and losses of this "stub" period. It also protects the buyer against potential seller abuses, such as selling inventory without replacement. The seller typically prepares a closing balance sheet. The clause states a calculation of value—often a net asset value—on this closing balance sheet and compares it with the comparable value reflected in the financial statements on which the buyer presumably based the purchase price. If the net asset value increases, the buyer will pay more; if the net asset value decreases, the purchase price will decrease by a corresponding amount. Postclosing adjustment clauses usually call for a dollar-for-dollar adjustment to reflect changes in the net asset value between the preclosing and closing balance, although thresholds and deductibles are becoming increasingly common.

(c) Covenants.   Covenants in purchase/sale agreements serve several functions: they can identify specific actions the parties will take to complete the transaction, they can establish how the seller will operate the business during the period prior to closing, and they can contain no-shop provisions that protect the buyer from competing bids. Certain *operating covenants* govern how the seller will operate the business during the period prior to closing. A common operating covenant obligates the seller to operate the entity in the ordinary course of business during the period between signing the agreement and closing and prohibits the seller from taking actions outside the normal course of business without obtaining prior written approval from the buyer. Operating covenants typically prohibit certain seller actions, such as making capital expenditures not previously budgeted, changing any accounting practices and procedures, or making significant changes to valuation allowances that relate to accounts receivable, inventory, or other asset accounts.

These covenants prevent the seller from undertaking actions that can harm the buyer. For example, a seller anticipating a postclosing adjustment may reduce the allowance for inventory obsolescence or the allowance for uncollectible accounts receivable, thus increasing the closing net asset value and ultimate purchase price. In addition to covenants that protect the buyer from such actions, most agreements require that the seller prepare the closing balance sheet in accordance with GAAP on a basis consistent with the historical statements. When the seller takes actions in preparing the closing balance sheet that violate GAAP, or that are inconsistent with prior financial statements, the seller may be violating its covenant. Inventory and accounts receivable allowances require judgment, however, and a buyer may be unable to establish that the computation of the allowance does not follow historical methods, given the latitude that such judgments allow.

(d) Indemnification. Indemnification relates to breaches of representations, warranties or covenants, typically relating to uncalibrated[4] or undisclosed liabilities. Indemnification clauses cover a wide range of liabilities and vary for each transaction. Typically, the seller agrees to indemnify the buyer for any losses, damages, and expenses arising from a contractually specified matter. The most common such clause provides indemnification for a seller's breach of the agreement's representations, warranties, and covenants. If a seller breaches its representation or warranty, the buyer will have recourse to the extent of the damages suffered. Indemnification clauses may cap the indemnifying party's liability and frequently specify a threshold for a dollar amount of losses (essentially a deductible) before any indemnity obligation arises.

Misunderstandings often arise as to the interpretation of imprecise indemnification provisions. One common—and often disputed—situation occurs when the contract suggests concepts related to thresholds or baskets. For example, one may consider "Seller shall have no liability hereunder until the aggregate of all such damages, losses, liabilities, and expenses exceeds $1 million" as ambiguous language, but consider "Seller shall be required to indemnify buyer only to the extent that the aggregate of all such damages, losses, liabilities, and expenses exceeds $1 million" understandable. We suggest that one include as an exhibit to the agreement an example of the application of any language resulting in a calculation.

In addition to the general indemnification for seller's breach of its representations and warranties, indemnities can also cover specific pending or threatened litigation or claims, taxes due for periods during which the seller had ownership, collectibility of accounts receivable, and environmental issues or exposures (sometimes both known and unknown) that exist at the time of the transaction.

(e) Earnout Clauses. The parties often agree to base a portion of the consideration paid on the future economic and financial performance of the entity. Such provisions are called *earnouts*. Sellers often believe the company has great potential not reflected in current earnings, perhaps because of current research and development projects or products not yet brought to market. In this instance, the parties can establish a purchase price that does not fully reflect the (alleged) potential but provides for additional consideration if the target achieves certain benchmarks. Such provisions require periodic measurement and agreement of any additional purchase price owed to the seller.

These clauses typically involve accounting and financial reporting issues. Therefore, accountants commonly assist in drafting such provisions and help measure the subsequent effect on the purchase price. Earnouts present problems from the seller's standpoint, because the buyer will control the business after closing and may take actions that, in the seller's judgment, lack wisdom or even reflect an intent to reduce the earnout payment amount.

(f) Material Adverse Change. Sellers frequently covenant that no material adverse change will occur in the business through the date of closing. The material adverse change (MAC) clause generally protects the buyer from a significant decline in the financial viability of the business.

A material adverse change may occur when, for example, the company's largest customer terminates its relation with the company. This could impair the company's ability to generate the revenues and profits that the buyer expected when it negotiated for the business. Another example might be a competitor's suing for violation of critical patent rights. Not only could an adverse finding result in a large monetary penalty, but the court can prohibit the company from selling a key product altogether.

Buyers who successfully prove a claim under the MAC clause have several remedies: renegotiation or even termination of an executory transaction, monetary damages from the seller, or even unwinding a completed transaction so that the business reverts back to the seller. Buyers often find it difficult to prove that a material adverse change occurred absent specific contractual parameters defining such a change. An accountant experienced in interpreting accounting literature may have a difficult time defining "material" in this context, and a court can interpret materiality differently than either party intended.

(g) Dispute Resolution.   The preceding sections discussed typical provisions included in purchase and sale agreements. Some provisions grant buyers and sellers the power to raise points of contention. Rather than arguing disputes before a court, parties often prefer to craft an alternative dispute resolution (ADR) mechanism for certain claims. In fact, agreements now contain two ADR clauses: one providing for an accountant to hear postclosing adjustment (including earnout) disputes and a second providing for a suitable arbitrator, typically an attorney, to dispose of other breaches of representations and warranties. (Chapter 4 discusses ADR.)

Several reasons motivate parties to avoid the courts. Often parties feel a court or a jury will lack the technical financial or business knowledge needed to understand the issues in dispute. ADR offers a faster and cheaper means to resolve the dispute. Additionally, parties may wish to avoid the publicity sometimes associated with lawsuits.

25.3   COMMON DISPUTES ARISING FROM PROVISIONS

Disputes arising out of acquisitions and divestitures that involve accounting and financial reporting issues result from three situations: (1) the buyer claims a violation of the seller's representation or warranty, (2) the parties disagree on postclosing adjustments, and (3) the parties disagree on the proper calculation of payments due under earnout clauses. This section discusses common concerns in such disputes.

(a) Representations and Warranties.   Buyers often rely on the target's most recent financial statements in calculating the price they are willing to pay for the company. Buyers can use numerous methods to value a business (*see* Chapter 13, "Business Valuation"). Common methods that incorporate the information contained within financial statements include the following:

- A multiple of an income statement metric such as earnings; earnings before interest and taxes (EBIT); or earnings before interest, taxes, depreciation, and amortization (EBITDA);
- A multiple or discount of the revenues listed on the income statement;
- A multiple or discount of the assets listed on the balance sheet.

The buyer can require the seller to warrant that the financial statements comply with GAAP and do not contain misstatements. After closing, the buyer may contend that the financial statements it relied on in pricing the business do, in fact, contain a misstatement.

For example, a buyer may allege that the financial statements failed to accrue certain expenses, improperly recognized revenues, or improperly classified certain items. These alleged discrepancies, if true, can affect the underlying metric relied on by the buyer in pricing the business. Thus, the buyer will posit that it paid too much for the business based on the misstatements. Buyers, however, often find it difficult to prove that they relied on the financial statements in reaching a definitive price. Buyers often use multiples of metrics to provide broad pricing guidelines, but other significant factors—including negotiating leverage, the presence of competing bidders, tax issues, and synergies—influence the final price.

(b) Postclosing Adjustments. Section 25.2(b) discussed how parties typically agree to a mechanism that adjusts the purchase price by one party compensating the other, depending on the change in, for example, the net asset value in the closing balance sheet from the net asset value in the financial statements presented in negotiations. This section discusses the issues that often prove central to the disputes between the parties.

(i) Notice of Objection. Most agreements limit the period—often to 30 to 60 days— during which a buyer can object to a closing balance sheet and hence propose purchase price adjustments. For example, a contract can state, "Buyer may dispute any amounts reflected on the closing balance sheet or the net asset value reflected thereon, provided that buyer shall notify seller in writing of each disputed item and specify the amount thereof in dispute, within 30 days of receipt of the seller's closing balance sheet."

Some agreements set forth the form and scope of response and require the notice of objection to be specific, whereas some have broader terms. Specific notices identify and explain the item in dispute and require the buyer to state the individual dollar amounts of all its objections at that time. Some general clauses require only that the buyer notify the seller that it objects in general without disclosing details until a later date. Whether a client is the buyer or the seller will influence the specificity desired in the notice of objection.

Parties often dispute whether the buyer can submit new items after the initial objection and whether, and to what extent, it can revise items included in the initial notice. Arbitrators frequently rule on this issue.

Sellers have incentives to carefully define the parameters for the notice of objection, to allow a short time period between sale of the company and the required objection cut-off date, to mandate complete and specific disclosure of the disputed items by the deadline, and to allow little flexibility for changing the basic theory or amount of the buyer's proposed adjustment. Buyers prefer the opposite.

(ii) Changes in Accounting.

- **Preferable versus acceptable GAAP.** As Section 25.2(a) discussed, most agreements contain a clause requiring that the closing balance sheet conform to GAAP consistently applied over a relevant period or point in time that predates the sale. Parties involved in transactions often mistakenly believe that GAAP clearly defines one correct number and that little or no disagreement can arise. Arguments then occur over whether the method the seller selects is more appropriate than the method the buyer prefers. Such disputes arise in at least two situations. First, the buyer proposes an adjustment to the closing balance sheet based on a method different from that applied by the seller. The buyer claims that the seller used a method inconsistent with the buyer's understanding of the purchase agreement terms. Second, the seller prepared the financial statements used in negotiating and executing the purchase agreement according to one accounting method and subsequently switched, often subtly, to a method more favorable to the seller before the closing. This would arguably result in a closing balance sheet prepared using a different accounting method than the historical information provided to the buyer, although GAAP recognizes both methods. These differences can significantly affect the final purchase price.

In these scenarios, each party can make a reasonable argument for its case. The consistent use of an acceptable accounting method, however, usually will prevail over a claim to change to a preferable accounting method. If the financial statements' preparer has consistently applied an accounting principle that is in accordance with GAAP, an accountant would not normally take exception. GAAP is clear, however, that it recognizes no generally accepted methods as preferable to other generally accepted methods. An accounting principle is either generally accepted or not—with no gradations of preferability. The expert should disparage any attempt to invoke a method as being more preferable to another. In any case, GAAP provides no guidance on preferable methods for their application, which becomes a situation-specific matter for the application of professional judgment.

- **Non-GAAP accounting and consistency.** Another common issue relates to the balancing of GAAP and consistency. Conflicts often arise as to whether GAAP or consistency takes precedence when applying an accounting method to a particular transaction or a particular account balance. When GAAP and consistency requirements appear to conflict, arbitrators usually choose GAAP as the higher and controlling standard.[5] For example, a seller may historically have used consistent, non-GAAP accounting. In that case, absent other pertinent contractual provisions, the seller should make adjustments to make the financial statements conform with GAAP.

  Some agreements specify consistency with respect to certain items. In this case, consistency will likely prevail over GAAP, certainly so if the agreement provides for or discloses a non-GAAP presentation. Often, the seller's best course of action is not to make a blanket GAAP warranty without full knowledge that such is the case.

  In addition, disputes can arise over the application of the term *consistent*. For example, consider the following language: the company "consistently provides an allowance for bad debts," versus "provides an allowance using a consistent calculation methodology," versus "provides a consistent amount in the allowance."

(iii) Interim versus Year-End Reporting. The purchase/sale agreement often mandates consistency between the preclosing financial statements used in negotiations and the final financial statements at closing. Because most companies apply more rigorous and in-depth closing procedures at year-end, the question often arises regarding which procedures the seller will use in the financial statements referenced in the transaction. The interpretation of such a clause can differ, depending on whether the closing balance sheet or the financial statements used in negotiations were month- or period-end, but not regular reporting year-end. For example, if the financial statements used in negotiations were for an interim month-end, and the agreement called for consistently applied accounting principles, on what basis should the seller prepare the closing balance sheet if the closing date falls at year-end? Conversely, if the financial statements used in negotiations were the last year's audited financial statements and the closing date is an interim date, on what basis should the seller prepare the closing balance sheet? In the latter situation, absent specific provisions in the agreement, the financial statements prepared (for purposes of closing) at an interim date should follow the same principles and practices as at year-end.

(iv) GAAP versus Company Policy. Companies often represent or warrant financial statements as prepared in accordance with historical company policy as an alternative to GAAP. For example, suppose a clause reads, "The closing balance sheet shall be prepared, and net asset value calculated, in accordance with (i) the accounting principles and practices historically used to prepare balance sheets for the business; and (ii) GAAP, except to an extent inconsistent with the historical company accounting policies." In this instance, historical company policy takes precedence over GAAP. This fairly common situation arises when a subsidiary for sale does not issue its own financial statements, or if the seller decides to sell a division or unit from an existing business. In fact, a seller that warrants that the stand-alone financial statements of a previously unaudited subsidiary conform with GAAP takes a risk, and buyers often dispute such financial statements. The seller often does best with an agreement that pays specific attention to the company's historical accounting policies and their application, or by a warranty of consistency with past practices relating to the application of accounting policies.

(v) Materiality. How and whether to apply the accounting concept of *materiality* can present a hurdle in resolving disputes. In purchase price disputes, the buyer usually will claim that it should receive all properly raised purchase price adjustments, ignoring materiality unless the contract specifically provides to the contrary.

Some agreements provide that the seller has entitlement to postclosing adjustments only if they exceed a specified aggregate dollar amount or threshold. The contract can provide that once the adjustments exceed such levels, the buyer receives the entire amount from the first dollar, or that the buyer will receive only the amount by which the adjustments exceed the specified level. In most cases, however, the agreement does not address materiality. In such a situation, the seller can argue that other contract clauses imply a level of materiality that the parties should apply to the postclosing adjustment process. For instance, an indemnity clause can provide for no payment for breaches of representations and warranties until the associated effects aggregate to 2 percent of the stated purchase price. This argument often meets with little success because (1) most warranty clauses stand alone and (2) most arbitrators believe, not unfairly, that if the parties had wanted to include a materiality concept, they would have done so.

Accountants have traditionally evaluated materiality with respect to the financial statements taken as a whole. Some purchase agreements, however, provide that materiality applies on a line-item basis, thereby reducing its dollar level. We advise those who base purchase prices on multiples of earnings-related numbers to specify low materiality thresholds. An inventory overstatement of, say, 1 percent may be immaterial, but it changes cost of goods sold and pretax income by the same dollar amount. The valuation will then magnify that amount by the multiple factor.

(vi) Right to Offset.   Though the right to offset is seldom written into purchase agreements, sellers often claim it as a defense against paying purchase price adjustments proposed by a buyer who has objected to balances in the closing balance sheet. In reviewing closing statements, buyers typically seek and object to only items favoring them—accounts containing, in their view, overstated assets or understated liabilities.

For example, in its postclosing review, a buyer might note that the vacation liability is underaccrued by $300,000 and that the worker's compensation liability is overaccrued by $300,000. The buyer may ignore the overaccrual and claim $300,000 in a purchase price adjustment associated with the vacation liability. This can lead the seller to claim the right to offset an underaccrual by a corresponding overaccrual. The seller will also assert that the financial statements, taken as a whole, accord with GAAP, because the items offset each other.

Because agreements seldom provide for such rights of offset, the trier of fact can find it difficult to decide whether to adjust the purchase price. The seller will often argue that the financial statements as a whole comply with GAAP and that recording a buyer's proposed entry causes the balance sheet to violate GAAP. Buyers can claim that the seller had ample opportunity, when preparing and presenting the closing balance sheet, to adjust the accounts selectively and that purchase price adjustments protect the buyer against the seller's doing so. Because the parties almost always arbitrate these disputes, and arbitration rests on principles of equity (meaning overall fairness rather than technical legal elegance), it might seem that the arbitrator need only ascertain the fair result. Practical problems arise, however, in establishing whether one or both parties bargained for a position that a Solomonic finding will obliterate. The arbitrator should hope to present each party with the bargain it struck, but this may require more evidence than exists in nature, particularly if the parties gave the matter little or no thought in the negotiating stage.

(vii) Subsequent Events/Proper Cut-off Date.   Disputed issues often relate to events that were unanticipated or uncertain of outcome at the balance sheet preparation date; such issues can have financial reporting ramifications. For example, accounting rules may require a company to record a liability relating to a lawsuit in progress at the balance sheet date, even though resolution will require years. Or a buyer could contend, with the benefit of hindsight, that the sellers reported insufficient reserves for bad debts. In such cases, buyers often rely on facts arising after the

seller has prepared the financial statements. Parties often disagree about the date after which the arbitrator should consider subsequent information (*see* Chapter 8, "*Ex Post* versus *Ex Ante* Calculations").

Buyer and seller typically argue for a cut-off date that will allow or exclude specific information, the better to suit their respective positions. Possible dates include the date of the last transaction covered by financial statements, the date they were issued, the date the seller sent them to the buyer, the due date for the buyer's dispute notice, or even the date on which the parties finalize the purchase price. Although auditing standards establish clear rules for when and how one should regard subsequent events for most periodic financial reporting, their application in a purchase price dispute can produce dubious results, contrary to what the parties may have thought they were bargaining for at a much earlier negotiation date. As with so many other areas of M&A disputes, a foresighted drafting can avoid frustration and confusion in the aftermath.

(c) Earnout Clauses. In some transactions, the entity's future performance can determine part of the purchase price. Such provisions, called *earnouts*, make a portion of the purchase price contingent on the acquired company reaching certain milestones during a specified period after closing. The clauses typically use financial benchmarks such as revenues, net income, cash flow, or earnings per share.

Buyers and sellers often use earnouts when they cannot agree on the target's value. Earnouts prove useful in dynamic or volatile industries, or when the buyer has more pessimistic projections for the target than those of the seller. An earnout arrangement aligns the risk of achieving optimistic projections with the seller who sponsors them. This becomes most appropriate when, as often occurs, the seller owns the business and will stay on to manage the business going forward. We next discuss some common issues associated with the use of earnout provisions.

(i) Earnout Benchmarks. Contracts can include financial or non-financial benchmarks, or both. Common thresholds are the target's net revenue; net income; cash flow; earnings before interest and taxes (EBIT); earnings before interest, taxes, depreciation, and amortization (EBITDA); earnings per share; and net equity. Sellers prefer revenue-based benchmarks: a buyer's postclosing operating decisions and accounting practices will likely have less effect on revenue than other items. Buyers will more likely agree to a revenue benchmark if costs of goods sold and overhead have little variability. Generally, however, buyers oppose revenue-based thresholds because they provide no incentive to the earnout recipients to control expenses and can provide an incentive to generate sales of marginal or even no profitability. Buyers generally favor net income thresholds on the ground that they provide the best indication of the target's success.

Parties most often use cash flow measures such as EBIT or EBITDA as benchmarks. These reflect the cost of goods and services, selling expenses, and general and administrative expenses—but not interest, taxes, depreciation, and amortization, which can vary based on the buyer's capital structure or financing structure for the acquisition. Finally, for a transaction that is initially valued using a multiple of cash flow, the use of EBIT or EBITDA for the earnout appears logical to calculate what becomes, in essence, deferred purchase price.

Regardless of the financial threshold chosen, the parties should carefully analyze the potential of the earnout to distort the incentive for producing long-term, sustainable growth. For example, a revenue target could tempt the earnout recipients to book unprofitable business. An earnout based on cash flow or income could motivate the earnout recipient to slash expenses (e.g., marketing and advertising costs) in order to bolster short-term profitability at the expense of long-term growth. Disputes then arise that will rest on subjective evaluations of the intent behind the parties' actions or what one should consider commercially reasonable when one could fairly subject that concept to a wide range, depending on one's appetite for risk.

(ii) Formula for Calculating Payment Amount.   Parties can stipulate a flat amount of consideration to be paid upon meeting a milestone. More typically, the buyer will pay the seller a specified percentage of the amount by which the target's performance surpasses the threshold. For example, the buyer could make an annual payment to the seller equal to a percentage by which the target's EBITDA for the year exceeds the threshold EBITDA agreed to by the parties. The contract can also adjust the payment so that any shortfall in EBITDA for a previous year will reduce the payment otherwise due for the current year. (Failure to so provide invites manipulation.) An often difficult negotiation ensues regarding whether to prorate payments if the buyer partially achieves the benchmark. The parties can settle this negotiation by establishing a minimum hurdle before any payment occurs and providing a sliding scale or proration after achieving that hurdle.

Parties often disagree on whether income measurements should deduct certain expenses in earnout calculations. Expenses often disputed include integration expenses and expenses associated with restructuring activities (inventory writedowns, for example). Even when the formula anticipates addressing these issues, the parties may ultimately dispute which expenses qualify for such treatment.

(iii) Length of the Earnout Period.   Most earnout periods conclude after the expiration of a specified length of time, generally between two and five years. The appropriate length will reflect the time required to measure the projected value of the target or the period during which the buyer desires to motivate the former owners. Some earnouts are payable upon a specific event, such as the sale of the target, or a change in control of the buyer, or termination of the earnout recipient's employment. Because earnouts can affect the flexibility of the target's postclosing operation and few subsequent purchasers of a business will accept assets burdened by an earnout, a purchaser should negotiate a buyout option for the earnout. Valuing such a buyout usually proves difficult, and parties often rely on a multiple of historical payments or an expert valuation of the target.

(iv) Assessing Whether Performance Has Satisfied the Threshold.   The seller should insist that the buyer maintain separate books and records for the target, division, or other source of the earnout throughout the earnout period. The buyer should covenant that the seller can review these financial records, subject to reasonable notice. The buyer and its accountants typically make the initial assessment regarding whether the target's performance has reached the milestones. The seller then will review the calculations and challenge them if necessary.

Parties often agree on detailed stipulations for the accounting principles used to calculate performance. Because GAAP embraces a wide range of acceptable accounting practices, sellers often have concerns about the ability to manipulate the results of an earnout calculation. Parties need to carefully delineate the calculation principles if the threshold does not use a GAAP financial measure, such as EBIT or EBITDA. Parties often draft agreements that call for a measure calculated "in accordance with GAAP" when GAAP in fact provides no such definition or standard for the benchmark in question.

(v) Earnout Provision Problems. An inadequate earnout provision can hinder a purchaser's efforts to reorient or restructure the target, to misappropriate future value to the wrong party, or to motivate the earnout's recipients to focus on short-term goals that will maximize the earnout. Moreover, earnouts have great potential for engendering later disputes. Disputes often arise when the seller suspects that the buyer is using different accounting techniques during the postclosing period to diminish the payout or is artificially depressing revenues or earnings during the earnout period, particularly in its final year. The seller also fears that the buyer simply will not run the business successfully. Buyers face the risk that the payout formula will overcompensate the seller in some unforeseen way, because of other acquisitions or a change in the buyer's postacquisition business plan that has nothing to do with the target. Reflecting the legitimacy of these concerns, contentious disputes can arise over appropriate accounting, particularly when the earnout provisions apply a multiple that magnifies the effect of any specific accounting treatment.

(d) Issues of Control. Issues of control include situations in which the party in control of the operations can potentially manipulate accounting, and financial reporting to its benefit through the postclosing adjustment process. For example, in a management buyout, the buyer runs the company during the period between signing the agreement and the postclosing adjustment. This time period presents an opportunity for management to manipulate the business operations, accounting, and financial reporting to benefit its members through a postclosing adjustment. For example, manufacturing companies often effect a flurry of shipments at quarter-ends, creating the familiar "hockey stick" pattern of sales. If management simply put the brakes on in advance of a December 31 closing date, making shipments and recording sales in early January, the margin from those sales would go to benefit the buyers rather than becoming an increase to the purchase price due.

Alternatively, when a seller operates the company during the stub period between the date of signing the agreement and the closing date, it may take advantage of its control and drain the working capital from the balance sheet, defer maintenance expenditures, and make other operating decisions to the buyer's detriment. Buyers recognize this potential and therefore require several provisions in the form of representations, warranties, or covenants in the contract to prevent the sellers from doing so.

Earnouts also pose control issues. Both the buyer and the seller often fear mismanagement during the earnout period that could affect the payout. The seller typically has concerns that the buyer will not properly manage the target after the closing. If the contract doesn't retain the seller's management team postclosing, the seller likely will require that the buyer operate the target in the ordinary course of business consistent with past practice and will attempt to reserve, through contractual covenants, some authority regarding major decisions made during the earnout period. The seller will likely demand that the buyer operate the target as a distinct business entity or division so that the seller can verify its results. The seller can require that the buyer adequately fund the target during the earnout period so that it can capitalize on opportunities presented to it. Sellers often establish minimum absolute funding levels. The earnout provisions can acknowledge the parties' agreement or intent to exploit specified opportunities. The buyer will likely resist any limitation of its freedom to run the target as circumstances require.

Often, the seller's management will continue to operate the target post closing. In this situation, the buyer faces a risk that the seller's management team will operate the business so as to maximize the payout amount unfairly or with undue risk. Counsel for the buyer should attempt to provide appropriate controls over the target, including a mechanism for reviewing decisions that can affect the payout. The parties may wish to include detailed postclosing operational procedures in the acquisition agreement to avoid uncertainty.

(e) Dispute Resolution Issues.   Most agreements refer unresolved postclosing adjustment disputes to arbitration before an accountant; earnout and breach of representation and warranty disputes fall under generic arbitration clauses or, less frequently, seek resolution through the courts. This section discusses characteristics of the dispute resolution process.

(i) Standard of Review.   As Section 25.2(g) discussed, the parties often prefer to resolve certain disputes outside the courts for various reasons. The arbitrator's decision is commonly binding upon the parties absent manifest error, or negligence, or fraud. As a practical matter, the courts prefer to avoid reviewing an expert accountant's findings for error, and only the most egregious occasions of negligence or outright fraud will likely result in a successful appeal.

(ii) Submissions.   Parties normally argue their positions to the accountant/arbitrator in written submissions. The parties will need to agree, or the arbitrator to impose, the format, timing, and sequence of submissions.

Sometimes parties choose blind submissions, in which they will not see what information the other presents to the arbitrator. In such cases, the parties have no opportunity to file a response before the arbitrator. Most often, the parties share the submissions and responses with one another and the arbitrator. If they select this approach, the parties and the arbitrator will need to decide how to schedule the submissions. Examples of scheduling include simultaneous submissions, in which the parties submit their opening and then response arguments to the arbitrator simultaneously. Other schedules can include a staggered format, with one party filing an opening submission and the other filing its opening submission at some later date, followed by staggered replies.

(iii) Questions and Answers.   In designing the resolution process, the parties can adopt a formal mechanism for the arbitrator to direct questions to the parties, although the arbitrator commonly reserves the right to ask questions as needed throughout the dispute resolution process. The arbitrator commonly requests additional underlying accounting or financial documents, explanations regarding certain disputed issues, or clarification regarding facts that the parties dispute. The parties and the accountant/arbitrator will set a timeframe and method for responding to the interrogatories.

(iv) Hearing.   In addition to filing written submissions, the parties or the arbitrator may consider whether to hold a hearing. Sometimes they agree that they will or will not have a hearing. Other times, all agree that they do not expect a hearing, but that either party or the arbitrator can request a hearing during the dispute resolution process.

In the hearing, the parties and the arbitrator will convene face-to-face (or by telephone), and the parties will present arguments to the arbitrator. Similar to other elements of the proceedings, the parties negotiate the hearing's format, considering several factors:

- Limiting the time for presenting arguments
- Permitting new information or underlying documents
- Including a court reporter in the proceedings
- Allowing witnesses to testify or undergo cross-examination

In addition, the arbitrator can have additional questions or issues and encourage the parties to address these topics in their arguments during the proceedings.

(v) Decision Letter.   Arbitrators generally communicate their findings in the form of a decision letter. This step usually concludes the resolution process. Arbitrators decide the letter's format and the level of explanation, although the parties can negotiate this matter. Decision letters can cover the spectrum from informing the parties only of the dollar value found, to summarizing the reasons behind the arbitrator's decisions, to providing the detailed logic underlying the decisions.

The transaction agreement and the engagement letter between the parties and the arbitrator establish the arbitrator's powers and duties. The arbitrator should pay specific attention to any language stipulating how to communicate the decision. Also, the arbitrator needs to render a decision that addresses all of the issues—and only those issues—that the parties have submitted for resolution.

25.4 ROLE OF ACCOUNTANTS

Accountants and financial advisors can assist parties involved in M&A disputes. Often companies involved in disputes attempt to use their own accounting personnel to prepare the claim or responses. Although these internal people are familiar with the accounts and the business and may even be involved in the transaction, they may be too close to the issues to offer an objective analysis. Outside accountants can develop independent and unbiased advice in approaching disputes and can identify alternative, strategic options. Moreover, outside accountants do not carry emotional attachments to the transaction. The accountant who serves as consultant or expert witness on behalf of one of the parties, or as an independent arbitrator, can enhance and expedite the dispute resolution process. The remainder of this chapter focuses on the types of services that accountants can provide.

(a) Dispute Formulation.   The accountant can assist a party in formulating the dispute by performing the following tasks:

- **Identifying objections to the postclosing balance sheet.** The accountant can assist a buyer in identifying areas in which the closing balance sheet does not conform to the terms of the agreement. Conversely, an accountant can assist the seller in evaluating the merit of the buyer's claim. With respect to earnout provisions, the accountant can assist in evaluating the appropriateness of specific accounting treatments affecting the calculations.

- **Calculating and supporting objections under purchase price adjustment clauses.** The accountant can assist the buyer in calculating the adjustments necessary to make the balance sheet conform with the agreement. The accountant can also identify and develop the support—in the form of calculations, arguments, or documents—that can convince an arbitrator or counterparty of the merits of a given position.

- **Interpreting technical accounting literature to establish whether a proposed adjustment is warranted under GAAP.** The accountant can provide expertise in interpreting the technical accounting literature and practices that comprise GAAP in the context of the proposed adjustments.

- **Reporting objections in accordance with the terms of the agreement.** A buyer must report its objections in the form and timeframe that the agreement requires. Failure to do so could result in rejection of the proposed adjustments. Listing all agreement sections that the seller has violated will strengthen a buyer's claim. The accountant can help review the agreement and decide which sections apply to various alleged misstatements in the closing balance sheet.

- **Reviewing the opposing party's probable objections and support.** While assisting a buyer in preparing an objection, the accountant can identify strengths and weaknesses in each position and anticipate likely responses from the seller. In addition, the accountant can help a buyer evaluate the seller's responses. Similarly, an accountant can evaluate a buyer's proposed adjustments and assist the seller in responding to them by reviewing contract provisions and providing calculations or other support. Handicapping potential outcomes can prove invaluable, by facilitating settlements and avoiding the cost and time consumed in protracted proceedings.

(b) Discovery.   Although discovery is not available in all proceedings, parties can win or lose a disagreement during discovery. Accountants with experience in M&A disputes can assist during the following steps of discovery:

- **Identifying and requesting pertinent information that the other party must produce.**   Accountants can specifically identify and request documents that could provide relevant information. Documents commonly requested in M&A disputes include financial statements; audit workpapers of independent accountants and internal auditors; internal and external consultants' reports; and analyses prepared during the acquisition, such as those related to the computation of purchase price. Such document requests often overlook internal memoranda on the accounting either for specific transactions or for general company accounting and financial reporting policies. Requesting the documents early in the engagement can help a party access information that otherwise would not surface. In addition, the accountant can help draft interrogatories and identify potential fact witnesses and other individuals to depose.

- **Deposing financial and accounting personnel by preparing deposition questions related to specific technical issues.** Although many trial lawyers generally understand accounting and financial reporting matters, they may lack the detailed accounting knowledge and expertise that the deposition process can require.
- **Organizing and reviewing large volumes of financial and business documents.** As with other disputes, postclosing disputes can become a paper chase; even though the major law firms do not lack for bright young associates, only rarely do they have the training to separate the wheat from the accounting chaff.

(c) Conducting Analyses and Calculating Damages.   By analyzing the facts and documents generated during the discovery process, the accountants can assist clients in proving or disproving liability issues and damages calculations. In M&A disputes, most of this work requires technical accounting skills. Analyses of final balance sheets and income statements and their adjustments usually consist of reviewing disputed items, the applicable contract sections, and technical accounting literature. Liability usually depends on whether the seller breached a contract clause and, if so, whether the breach resulted in a departure in the closing balance sheet from GAAP, consistency, or other contract provisions.

The issue of damages usually arises in computing the appropriate adjustments, if any, that the parties should record to make the closing balance sheet conform with the stated principles, usually GAAP. Damages generally result from two different types of calculations. First, the dollar-for-dollar approach adjusts the final purchase price by the exact amount of the accounting adjustment. Many agreements specify that purchase price adjustments will be made on a dollar-for-dollar basis. Second is the multiple-of-earnings approach. If a buyer has based the purchase price on a historical multiple of earnings of the target company, the buyer can claim that to the extent any misstatements bear on the historical income statements, the buyer should be awarded the adjustment amount multiplied by the earnings multiple it used in establishing the purchase price. For example, assume that a seller underaccrued vacation liability by $100,000 in the income statement provided in due diligence and that the buyer based the purchase price on a multiple of five times earnings. The buyer can claim that by recording the vacation liability properly, income for the period reviewed would decline by $100,000, so that the purchase price would decline by $500,000. Such an underaccrued liability likely results from smaller underaccruals in several preceding periods. The amount by which the current period's income would decline had all periods been accrued correctly is probably less than $100,000.

(d) Trial Presentation.   The accountant must reduce the financial reporting and accounting issues to their essential elements and match their presentation to the sophistication of the arbitrator, judge, or jury.

Accountants can also help prospective witnesses understand key financial data and their effects on establishing liability or damages. They can help counsel cross-examine opposing financial experts by preparing questions for counsel to ask, by briefing counsel on the strengths and weaknesses of the opposing expert's analysis, and by attending the trial and providing commentary on the testimony of other key witnesses.

(e) Dispute Negotiation/Arbitration/Settlement.   If parties retain accountants, the professional services provided will resemble those provided in litigation. Some important differences exist, however. First, accountants can help a client select the appropriate forum for resolving disputes. Accountants can inform their clients of the relative merits of the dispute resolution alternatives, such as mediation or arbitration, and can offer insight into the qualifications the arbitrator or mediator should possess. One must consider whether an accountant, or attorney, or judge, or industry business person is qualified to serve in this role. Frequently the accountant will have specific knowledge of the individuals proposed on a list of prospective arbitrators, which the client may consider valuable.

Second, in litigation, the accounting expert seldom participates in or even knows of settlement discussions between the parties. In an ADR environment, however, the accountant can assume a much greater role in advising the client about the strengths and weaknesses of its position. The accountant can also evaluate proposed settlements by weighing the settlement options against the potential outcome during a trial if the client is considering litigation. In this capacity, the independent accountant can offer an objective assessment to an unavoidably biased client.

Accountants also serve as arbitrators in resolving M&A disputes, because they have experience in the accounting and financial reporting issues on which such disputes usually focus. As arbitrators, accountants set the agenda for the arbitration proceeding by identifying the documents to be filed with the arbitrator, establishing the timeframe for their receipt, and holding hearings on the evidence. In the role of arbitrator, the accountant will evaluate the merits of each party's position and ultimately rule on the items in dispute. Rather than presenting evidence and a position, the arbitrator evaluates the positions of the parties, interprets the purchase/sale agreement, and then renders a decision. Serving as arbitrators allows accountants to experience the role of trier of fact and will enhance their ability to represent other clients in consulting or expert witness roles.

(f) Accountant's Role in Avoiding Disputes.   Accountants experienced in the issues commonly encountered in M&A can serve clients during the acquisition process itself. Some M&A disputes center around poorly worded or ambiguous contract clauses. A review of proposed purchase/sale agreements allows an accountant to inform the client of confusing or conflicting clauses and to recommend language that may prevent subsequent disputes. The accountant can assume an even more important role in drafting and monitoring changes to complex clauses, such as the postclosing adjustment clause and earnout or put-back provisions.

25.5   CONCLUSION

Disputes arising from mergers, acquisitions, and divestitures often involve accounting and financial reporting issues. Breaches of financial representations, warranties, covenants, purchase price adjustment clauses, and earnout provisions can involve issues such as the application of GAAP, the consistent application of accounting and financial reporting procedures, and the concept of materiality. Accountants can use their knowledge of accounting principles, accounting systems, and financial reporting requirements, along with general business understanding, to assist clients in dispute resolution as consultants, expert witnesses, and arbitrators. They can assist clients in dispute formulation, discovery, analysis, and expert testimony on the central issues of the disputes. Perhaps most important, they can help clients understand and stipulate accounting-related issues in the contract to either avoid disputes or ensure a strong position if a dispute arises.

NOTES

1. This chapter assumes throughout that the seller prepares the closing balance sheet, although in practice the buyer may assume this responsibility.

2. Nomenclature differs among agreements when referring to adjustments to the stated purchase price. For purpose of discussion, we define *postclosing adjustment* as the *expected* modification of the purchase price to account for *normal* operation of the company between signing the agreement and the closing date. The adjustment cannot be calculated until some reasonable period after the closing date. Hence, the name *postclosing adjustment*. Later in the chapter the term *purchase price adjustment* refers to modifications proposed by the party who objects to the final balance sheet (generally the buyer) and the final purchase price that it implies.

3. *See* note 2.

4. Liabilities disclosed and valued within the balance sheet are more typically disputed within the battlefield of the postclosing adjustment rather than through litigation of the indemnification clause.

5. Usually, but not always. This bias comes in part from most arbitrators being CPAs who feel uncomfortable coming to a determination that appears to endorse a non-GAAP treatment. Arbitrators, though, should weigh the equities of each situation. Was the treatment known to the seller but not the buyer, and if so, should the seller receive the benefit? Did the buyer learn of it during due diligence and take account of it in bargaining? What interplay exists with representation and warranty claims? Parties seldom draft agreements to express a priority of GAAP or consistency but should at least consider doing so; as an alternative, they can state explicitly that neither is to be an automatic priority and the arbitrator should make determination based on principles of equity.

BIBLIOGRAPHY

Adler, James R. "Accounting Principles: How They Can Be Used in Litigation," *Trial* (Aug. 1988): 37–43.

Getzendanner, Susan, and Steven M. Cook. "Acquisition/Divestiture Transactions and Disputes: The Legal Minefields." 1993.

Kling, Lou R., and Eileen Nugent Simon. "Negotiated Acquisitions of Companies, Subsidiaries and Divisions." *Law Journal Seminars-Press* 1992.

Morgenstern, Marc. H. "Philosophy of Acquisitions." *Corporate Counsel's Quarterly* 1991.

CHAPTER 26

CONSTRUCTION CLAIMS

Stephen P. Lechner
Bilge Astarlioglu

CONTENTS

26.1   INTRODUCTION

The successful delivery of a construction project requires the active management of four major factors: scope, cost, time, and quality. These factors are measured by one or more of the following parameters: contract value, contract schedule, and plans and specifications. Issues and events affecting these factors can force project participants to incur a loss or leave the project owner with a product inferior to that specified in the contract. These consequences often lead to a construction claim for losses and damages. Such losses include the cost of extra work, delay-related costs, and incremental labor and equipment costs resulting from lost productivity associated with project disruption.

    The calculation of losses or damages aims to put the plaintiff in as good a position as it would have been but for the defendant's actions. Calculation of damages often involves complex issues and must work within the limitations of incomplete information. Plaintiffs often develop claims after a project's completion, when

Terms Used within the United States	Terms Outside the United States
General Contractor	Main Contractor
General Conditions	Preliminaries
Bid	Tender
Change Order	Variation
Schedule	Programme
Craft Labor	Trade Labour

Exhibit 26-1.   Sample Differences in Common English Contracting Terms

information and project personnel may no longer be available, restricting an expert's ability to perform a robust analysis. One must show reasonableness and practicality, balancing sound technique with a common-sense, flexible approach to damages.

This chapter discusses various damages models for common construction claims. Construction projects differ, so the methods described in this chapter will not apply to every claim; circumstances of an individual project will require refinements to the methods discussed. Additionally, the case references provided are not exhaustive, and one must consider them within the context of the specific projects to which they relate.

The ideas and methods described in this chapter apply to construction claims inside and outside the United States, but the terminology changes across borders of English speaking countries. Exhibit 26-1 provides some examples of different terms related to common construction concepts.

(a) Types of Claims.   Types of claims differ based on the contractual relation and the pricing arrangement between the parties. Construction dispute claimants can include

- A contractor who seeks additional compensation or extensions of time because of allegedly deficient plans and specifications, unforeseeable or changed conditions, owner or architect interference, or late or deficient owner-supplied materials or equipment.

- An owner who seeks compensation or reduction in contract price because of allegedly deficient or defective performance, late achievement of key project milestones, or damage to owner-supplied materials or equipment.

- Both owner and contractor who seek remedy in the same dispute, especially when the project experiences delays. Each party may argue that the other caused the delay and should provide compensation, or an extension of time, or both remedies.

- Owners and subcontractors who complain of the preceding to each other.

Exhibit 26-2 lists some of the common types of contractor and owner claims.

Major contractor disputes typically include multiple claim elements (or "heads of claim") such as delay, disruption, acceleration, and extra work. For example, a contractor may claim that deficient plans had four consequences: (1) delays owing to extended review and processing time of the updated drawings and postponed

Contractor Claims	Owner Claims
Delay	Delay (Liquidated Damages)
Disruption (Loss of Productivity)	Termination
Acceleration	Lost Profit
Changed/Extra Work	Fraud and Misrepresentation
Termination	Defective Work
Lack of Payment	
Lost Profit	

Exhibit 26-2.   Common Construction Claims

field work; (2) disruption owing to activity resequencing leading to a loss of craft labor productivity; (3) increased labor and equipment owing to acceleration to recover delays; and (4) extra work not included in the original work scope at the time of bid. These consequences may share an origin, but the analysis should treat these claims separately, because the methods for calculating damages differ.

(b) Typical Parties Involved.   Exhibit 26-3 depicts a typical contractual relation among the parties in a traditional construction project. Although any party in this diagram can file a claim, the general contractor, the subcontractors, or the owner most commonly initiate the process. The contractual relation can limit the extent of the claims that the plaintiff can bring against the parties.

The traditional contractual relation has many variations. For example, in a multiple-prime or construction manager without risk arrangement, the owner directly contracts with subcontractors, which significantly reduces or eliminates the risk assumed by the general contractor. In a design-build contract, the owner has only one contract with the general contractor, which also acts as, or subcontracts, the architect/engineer.

Additionally, many other third parties can become claimants or respondents in a construction dispute. These include consulting engineers, material and equipment suppliers, property developers, facility tenants, and financiers.

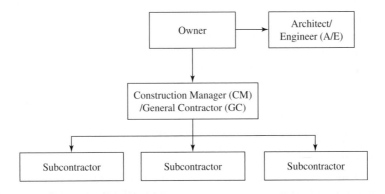

Exhibit 26-3.   Contractual Relation of Parties in Traditional Construction Project

Insurers also play a part in contract projects and disputes when they provide coverage to one or more parties in various forms, such as payment and performance bonds, professional liability, builder's risk, an owner-controlled insurance program (OCIP), and a contractor-controlled insurance program (CCIP). This coverage may render the insurance companies liable for paying damages incurred by an impaired party. In some cases, the insurance companies may directly administer these claims, hiring and directing attorneys and experts, or at least play a key role in dispute resolution proceedings.

(c) Pricing Arrangements. Common pricing arrangements in construction contracts include the following:

- **Fixed-price.** The parties agree on a contract price that they can modify only by approved change orders.
- **Cost-plus.** The contractor invoices the owner its costs plus a predetermined fee, which can be either a fixed amount or a percentage of underlying costs.
- **Guaranteed maximum price (GMP).** The contractor agrees not to charge the owner more than the GMP, which only approved change orders can modify. It operates as a cost-plus contract until the GMP is reached and then becomes in effect a fixed-price contract.
- **Unit price.** Contracts commonly use unit price arrangements in two instances: when the parties do not know the quantity of materials to be installed and when pricing change orders.

Disputes frequently arise from fixed-price contracts when the contractor has to absorb cost overruns unless the contractor proves that the owner or owner's agents[1] have caused the overruns. This commonly occurs in competitively bid fixed-price contracts in which the owner awards the contract to the lowest bidder. In this circumstance, the contractor sometimes underbids the project to secure the job. A contractor underbidding a project would normally not have entitlement to any additional compensation related to the underbid portion unless the owner did not act in good faith (e.g., induced an underbid by providing intentionally misleading information or failing to inform the contractor, and the contractor reasonably relied on the misrepresentations in bidding the contract). *See City of Salinas v. Souza & McCue Construction Co., Inc.* in List of Cases.

In cost-plus contracts, a dispute can arise regarding the types of allowed or reimbursable costs; the parties can also disagree on whether the contractor has misrepresented costs, thereby overbilling the owner. Cost-plus contracts typically have an audit clause, enabling an owner to perform a cost audit. Such clauses require contractors to retain project cost records and supporting documentation and provide them to the owner during the audit. If the audit clause does not detail the type of documents to be retained and provided during the audit, conflicts can arise between the parties regarding access to certain cost records. Owners can also exercise cost audit rights in termination situations to calculate the extent of the costs incurred by the contractor until the termination.

(d) Contract Language. Experts involved in a construction dispute should read the contract(s) prior to preparing or responding to a claim. Sometimes the contract language limits losses recoverable by the parties and outlines how to calculate damages. The court will normally respect the contract's terms unless it finds a

Changes to Work	Termination for Default
Overhead and Profit Markup	Termination for Convenience
Extension of Time	Payment Terms
Liquidated Damages	Contract Audit Rights
Consequential Loss (e.g., Lost Profit)	No Damages for Delay
Conditional Payment	

Exhibit 26-4. Contract Clauses

breach of contract or believes a proposed interpretation would result in unjust enrichment to one of the parties. Disputes also arise when the contract's terms prove conflicting or ambiguous or when they fail to address a point in contention. Exhibit 26-4 lists some important contract clauses.

Contracts in the United States frequently use standard contract templates created by organizations such as the American Institute of Architects (AIA), Associated General Contractors (AGC), and Design Build Institute of America (DBIA). Similar standard contracts exist in many foreign jurisdictions (e.g., The Institution of Civil Engineers [ICE] and the International Federation of Consulting Engineers [FIDIC]). Small owners and contractors who lack the resources or experience to create a comprehensive contract often use these templates. Large owners often maintain a standard contract template that they revise over the years and modify as required to suit specific project needs. The largest owner by far in the construction industry is the U.S. Government. The U.S. Federal Government operates under standards called the Federal Acquisition Regulations (FAR), which governs all federal contracts, unless specifically excluded. Nongovernment owners and contractors can also use the FAR as a guidance. Experts often refer to the FAR on Contract Cost Principles and Procedures (Part 31) and Termination of Contracts (Part 49) as expressions of generally accepted industry practice.

(e) Types of Experts. Contractors and owners often retain separate experts to address the scope, cost, time, and quality aspects of a construction dispute. Cost, schedule, and engineering experts often produce separate reports. Although the reports often overlap, each expert has distinct areas of responsibility. For example, the scheduling expert may assess the number of days of delay caused by an impact event using various delay models. The engineering expert may opine on the quality of the work performed, the adequacy of the drawings, or the effect of the deficient drawings on the work performed. The cost expert develops a damages model to quantify a loss and may rely on the scheduling and engineering experts' opinions to calculate specific elements of damages.

The overlapping nature of construction claims sometimes blurs the experts' boundaries. Some experts have the qualifications to testify in several of these areas. However, experts opining on an area where they lack the necessary qualifications risk a *Daubert* challenge and exclusion of their report. In *William Daubert v. Merrell Dow Pharmaceuticals, Inc.*, the U.S. Supreme Court articulated a new set of criteria for the admissibility of scientific expert testimony, and in *Kumho Tire Co., Ltd., v. Patrick Carmichael*, the Court extended *Daubert*'s general holding to include nonscientific expert testimony.

Contract, Plans, and Specifications	Records of Delays and Disturbance
Change Orders	Progress Reports
Job Cost Ledger	Daily Logs
Bid Documents	Requests for Information (RFIs)
Payment Applications	Meeting Minutes
Engineers Instructions/Submittal Logs	Project Correspondence
Project Schedules (Baseline, Updates)	E-mails
Records of Inspection and Certificate	Project Photos

Exhibit 26-5.   Key Project Documents

(f) Key Project Documentation.   Exhibit 26-5 lists some of the key project documents that experts often need to perform their analyses.

Many projects currently maintain most of these documents in an electronic format. Some owners and contractors use project collaboration systems that store files on a central server or a Web site that all project users can access. A well-managed collaboration system typically reduces document discovery efforts.

When a construction project doesn't store documents electronically, some experts use technologies such as optical character recognition (OCR) to scan and convert hard copies to electronic text, enabling the experts to perform keyword searches. This method works less effectively on data files, such as job cost ledgers or project schedules, than on text files: data files tend to contain information such as scheduling logic or arithmetic operations that scanning technologies have difficulty translating. With electronic data files, such as a job cost ledger, experts can download the information to a database and perform functions such as query, total, filter, group, and link. This process increases the effectiveness of the analysis and often reduces the analysis time.

26.2   COST POOLS

Although not all construction claims are based on cost (some are based on value, or specific contract terms, or both), damages calculations often begin with identifying the costs incurred by the parties. This section explains how contractors typically record project costs, how one can verify these costs, the typical categories of costs (or "cost pools"), and how these cost pools relate to the various heads of claim.

(a) Job Cost Accounting.   Contractors generally use hierarchical job and activity-based costing systems, wherein they record each job in a separate job number with a standard set of division and activity numbers, as shown in Exhibit 26-6. The job-costing hierarchy descends from job → division → activity number. Some contractors have further coding. The terms used at each level depend on the accounting system employed and can differ among companies.

Most contractors have a standard set of division and activity numbers that they use for all projects. Some contractors adopt the standard list of division numbers created by the Construction Specifications Institute (CSI). Most contractors also

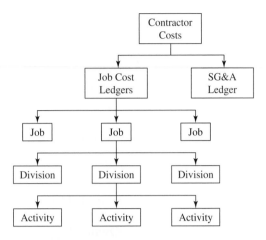

Exhibit 26-6. The Job-Costing Hierarchy

create a separate division number for tracking change order costs separately from the original scope.

(b) Verification of Costs. Experts begin with the job cost ledger to verify the project costs incurred by the contractor. This ledger typically contains all costs allocable to the project except for the home-office overhead costs.[2] Note that the costs recorded in the job cost ledger do not always represent amounts paid by the contractor; the job cost ledger can include unpaid liabilities. In these circumstances, the experts need to identify whether the payment is overdue and the contractor intends to make the payment. Therefore, experts should compare the job cost ledger with the cash and accounts payable ledger. Some contractors produce job cost summary reports that separately report amount incurred, paid, and amount due.

Exhibit 26-7 includes some of the documents, listed by cost type, that experts use to verify the costs recorded in the job cost ledger. Experts can decide to analyze some of these documents on a sampling basis.

(c) Segregation of Cost Pools. Hierarchical job cost accounting systems facilitate the process of segregating cost pools, which experts first separate into two groups: direct and indirect (*see* Exhibit 26-8). The FAR defines direct and indirect costs as follows:

- **Direct costs.** "Any cost that is identified specifically with a particular final cost objective."[3]
- **Indirect costs.** "Any cost not directly identified with a single final cost objective, but identified with two or more final cost objectives or with at least one intermediate cost objective."[4]

These definitions assume that the final cost objective is one of the final accumulation points in a contractor's accumulation system,[5] typically a construction activity.

Exhibit 26-8 illustrates typical project cost pools. Although costs will appear in multiple cost pools along a single vertical strand of disaggregation (i.e., indirect →on-site overhead→time-related), experts need to ensure that costs do not appear

Hourly Labor	**Subcontractor**
Certified Payroll Reports	Subcontract
Union Contracts	Subcontractor Payment Applications
Timesheets	Subcontractor Change Orders
	Canceled Checks
Salary Labor	
Salary/Bonus Information	**Rental Equipment**
Hourly Rate Computations	Rental Agreement
Timesheets	Invoices
	Canceled Checks
Material	
Purchase Order	**Owned Equipment**
Invoices	Equipment Depreciation Ledgers
Canceled Checks	Equipment Internal Rates
	Equipment and Small Tools List
Home-office Overhead	
Audited Financial Statements	
Audited Computation of Overhead Rates	

Exhibit 26-7. Documents Used to Verify Costs Recorded in Job Cost Ledger

in multiple horizontal strands of disaggregation (i.e., appearing in both on-site and home-office overhead), which will lead to double recovery by the contractor. The FAR also favors consistency when categorizing project costs: one cannot assign costs incurred for the same purpose to a final cost objective as both direct and indirect costs.[6]

As Exhibit 26-8 illustrates, contractors can separate indirect costs into two pools: on-site and home-office overhead. They typically record their on-site overhead in their job cost ledger under a separate division called General Requirements (CSI Division 01). Contractors typically record home-office overhead in the Selling, General, and Administrative (SG&A) ledger and do not directly allocate them to the job cost ledger.

One can further segregate on-site overhead to activity-related, time-related, and one-time costs. Sample one-time costs include mobilization, demobilization, and temporary utility set-ups. Time-related costs typically include costs such as temporary utilities, site facilities, site security, and field office personnel. Activity-related indirect costs include costs that cannot be attributed to a single activity but are directly related to the works performed by direct labor forces. Examples of activity-related indirect costs include general support labor, small tools and consumables, and possibly some equipment and supervision costs.

(d) Relation between Cost Pools and Types of Claims.   Experts segregate cost pools to provide a link between costs incurred as a result of the parties' actions. As Exhibit 26-9 shows, each claim type usually relates to a specific cost pool. For

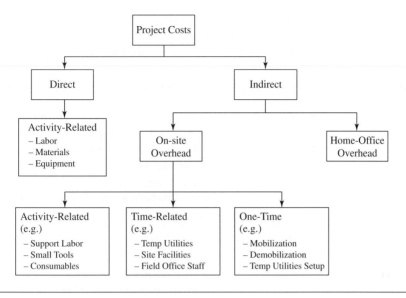

Exhibit 26-8.   Sample Hierarchy of Cost Pools

example, an element of extra work will result in additional activity-related costs. Extended durations at the project site owing to delay will result in additional time-related costs. Segregation of the cost pools allows experts to avoid double-counting cost components in more than one claim type and enables experts to identify cost components that are missing from the individual claim items.

26.3   DAMAGES MODELS

Experts use different damages models for different types of claims, some of which we discuss in this section. When proving and calculating the damages, experts need to remember that not all damages are recoverable. A plaintiff cannot recover damages attributable to the plaintiff's actions; the harm must result from the defendant's actions. Also, to the extent the plaintiff could have mitigated the damages but instead chose not to take any action, the court can deem the plaintiff ineligible from recovering all or a portion of damages even though the defendant caused those damages. *See Edward S. Paine et al. v. John Spottiswoode et al.,* 612 A.2d

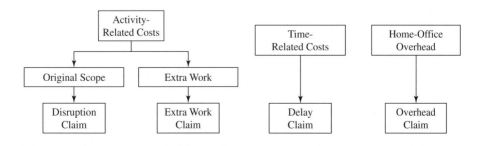

Exhibit 26-9.   Relation between Claim Type and Specific Cost Pool

235 (1992), where the contractor ignored its duty to build in a workmanlike manner and attempted to relieve itself of responsibility for its own negligence by asserting that the contractor need only build in accordance with the plans.

(a) Delay.   Delay (or "prolongation") can be defined as the number of workdays the contractor took to complete the project beyond the contractual completion date.[7] One calculates total delay by subtracting the agreed completion date (plus any extensions granted by the owner) from the actual completion date. In a delay claim, the expert must identify who caused the delay and categorize the delay into one of the four types listed below. Scheduling experts use various delay models to make this determination. A comprehensive discussion of delay analysis is outside the scope of this chapter, but Section 26.4 summarizes some of these models.

1. **Inexcusable delay.** Within control of contractor and outside control of owner (e.g., lack of contractor supervision). Contractor receives neither time extension nor additional compensation.

2. **Excusable delay.** Outside control of both owner and contractor (e.g., unusually severe weather). Contractor receives time extension but not additional compensation unless granted by the contract.

3. **Concurrent delay.** Within control of both owner and contractor (e.g., concurrent inexcusable and compensable delay). Contractor receives time extension but not additional compensation.

4. **Compensable delay.** Within control of owner and outside control of contractor (e.g., extension owing to additional work scope). Contractor receives both time extension and additional compensation.

Both owners and contractors can file delay claims, and the method for calculating delay- related damages (e.g., the number of eligible delay days times a daily rate) remains the same regardless of who files the claim. A contractor's damages reflect compensable costs incurred because the contractor had to maintain a site presence longer than the contractor would have absent the claim issue. The contractor receives a time extension for any excusable, compensable, and concurrent delays and additional compensation for any compensable delays. The owner receives compensation for any inexcusable delays, either as lost profits or contractually-stipulated liquidated damages.[8]

As Exhibit 26-10 illustrates, after the expert identifies the number and type of delay days, the expert multiplies the eligible delay days by a daily rate to calculate the damages incurred by the parties. The expert will use one of two types of daily rates:

1. **Liquidated damages per day.** Applied to contractor-caused inexcusable delays to calculate damages to the *owner*

2. **Time-related costs per day.** Applied to compensable delays to calculate damages to the *contractor*

Even though some contracts prescribe a daily liquidated damages rate to apply in the event of compensable delays to the contractor, others have a "no damages for delay" clause that prevents one or more parties from recovering any delay damages. In some situations, however, courts have made exceptions to no

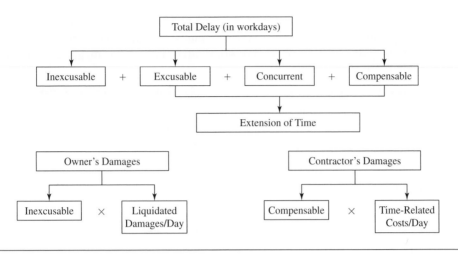

Exhibit 26-10. Delay Claims and Related Damages Calculations

damages for delay clauses. In *Corinno Civetta Construction Corp. v. The City of New York*, the court listed some breach of contract situations in which a contractor can recover delay damages despite the clause. In *Howard Contracting, Inc. v. G.A. Macdonald Construction Co., Inc., & City of Los Angeles*, the court held that a no damages for delay clause contained in the contract did not preclude the recovery of delay damages under Pub. Contract Code, § 7102.

Absent these contract clauses, parties to the dispute rely on cost experts to calculate the daily rate. Delays cause the contractor to be at the site longer than it would have been absent the impacts. Therefore, the daily rate to apply to compensable delays should include only time-related indirect costs. Time-related indirect costs are related to the amount of time the contractor is present at the site. In addition to time-related indirect costs, a delay claim can also include labor and material cost escalation, idle equipment, interest and financing, and weather protection costs owing to the extended stay. Other chapters in this book discuss various methods of calculating lost profit by the owner in the absence of a liquidated damages clause.

(b) Disruption. Disruption on a construction project is any change in project conditions, construction methods, or work sequence relative to the planned work sequencing reasonably contemplated by a contractor at the time of bid or project commencement that affect the contractor's performance. Disruption often results in loss of production or loss of efficiency in contractor labor and equipment and increased costs. Experts generally use activity-related costs—such as labor, equipment, small tools, and trade-specific supervision costs—to calculate losses related to disruption. Various factors, other than the owner's actions, can cause the contractor to spend additional resources that exceed the contract price. For example, the contractor could have underbid the project or contributed to its own inefficiency. The expert must define and isolate the disruption causes and then establish a causal relation between the sources of the disruption and the resulting effects on labor and equipment.

Disruption is typically the most complicated type of claim to quantify and relate to a specific cause. The information available usually determines the choice of method to quantify disruption. We summarize below the major methods of quantifying disruption.

(i) Total Cost (Global) Method.   This method is one of the easiest but also the most disputed method to calculate damages. The contractor needs to demonstrate four conditions to justify using the total cost method:

1. The nature of losses make it impracticable to accurately measure losses using a specific identification method.
2. The bid price was realistic.
3. The actual costs were accurate and reasonable.
4. The contractor was not responsible for increased costs.

Total Cost (Global) Formula:

$$\text{DISRUPTION DAMAGES} = \text{ACTUAL COST} - \text{BID ESTIMATE}$$

The total cost formula typically uses the contractor's bid estimate instead of the contract price because the contract price includes various contractor markups and thus is not comparable to the actual costs incurred by the contractor.

(ii) Modified Total Cost Method.   The modified total cost method overcomes some of the inadequacies of the total cost method. Under this approach, the contractor adjusts the claim to assume some responsibility for bid errors and/or costs incurred. The courts and experts prefer this approach over the total cost method. This method recognizes that most bids are not perfect and that the contractor could have caused or contributed to labor or equipment inefficiency or both.

Modified Total Cost Formula:

$$\text{DISRUPTION DAMAGES} = \text{ACTUAL COST} - \text{BID ESTIMATE} - \text{AMOUNT} \\ \text{UNDERBID} - \text{IMPACTS BY CONTRACTOR}$$

(iii) Productivity Analysis.   Analyzing contractor productivity to assess disruption has become the most commonly accepted method for the courts but also the most complex method for experts to apply. Insufficient data and the consequences of events on contractor performance sometimes make this method impractical. Required information for a meaningful productivity analysis includes details of material quantities installed or other measures of physical progress and labor (or equipment) used for each activity.

The measured-mile approach has become the most commonly used productivity analysis to quantify disruption. In the measured-mile method, experts establish a baseline, defined as the amount the contractor would have spent absent the disruptive event for which the contractor does not have responsibility. The analysis assumes the baseline includes the loss of productivity caused by underbidding and the contractor's own inefficiency, because it represents the contractor's actual performance on the project absent owner impacts.

Measured Mile (Productivity) Formula:

$$\text{DISRUPTION DAMAGES} = \text{ACTUAL COST} - \text{BASELINE}$$

This method establishes a baseline from an area or period of work that the defendant's actions didn't affect. When such an area or period does not exist, the expert will need to adopt alternative methods to establish a normal productivity level based on averages of areas or time periods of minimal impacts or to consider the contractor's performance on other projects that have similar characteristics.

Productivity-based disruption approaches to quantify disruption, when properly used, have been more accepted by the courts than total cost methods. In *Clark Concrete Contractors, Inc. v. GSA*, the court stated that

> The purpose of a measured mile analysis is to permit a comparison of the labor costs of performing work during different periods of time, so as to show the extent to which costs increased from a standard during periods impacted by certain actions. *See U.S. Industries, Inc. v. Blake Construction Co.*, 671 F.2d 539, 547 (D.C. Cir. 1982); *Stroh Corp. v. General Services Administration*, GSBCA 11029, 96-1 BCA 28,165, at 141,132.

The court also stated that

> the ascertainment of damages for labor inefficiency is not susceptible to absolute exactness. *See Electronic & Missile Facilities, Inc. v. United States*, 416 F.2d 1345, 1358 (Ct. Cl. 1969). We will accept a comparison if it is between kinds of work which are reasonably alike, such that the approximations it involves will be meaningful.[9]

One can define productivity as the ratio of input to output (e.g., labor hours required to install a unit of quantity) or vice versa. The method calculates productivity separately for each activity, such as installing cubic yards of concrete, square feet of masonry, or linear feet of cable. To calculate disruption damages using the measured-mile method, the expert performs the following steps for each affected activity. Depending on circumstances, one may need to perform variations of this calculation. The home-office overhead and profit markup is also applied to the damages calculated using the following steps:

- Calculate baseline productivity from the measured mile.
- Calculate actual productivity for the period or area affected.
- Calculate lost productivity by subtracting the baseline from the actual productivity.
- Calculate lost labor hours by multiplying lost productivity by quantities installed in the affected area or during the period affected.
- Calculate labor costs by multiplying lost labor hours by labor rate. Labor rate is derived from the activity-related direct costs, which should include the labor burden.
- Calculate damages by applying the activity-related on-site overhead markup to the labor costs.

These steps reflect a simplified summary of a measured-mile calculation. In actual application, the expert must also consider issues such as the learning curve typically experienced by craft labor on construction projects and potential factors to normalize data to ensure that the actual productivity is comparable to the measured-mile productivity.[10]

Exhibit 26-11 illustrates the calculation of disruption damages for a single activity. This simplified example does not consider issues such as learning curve or other adjustments to normalize work efforts.

		Baseline Productivity (MH/CY)	Total Labor Hours (MH)	Quantity Installed (CY)	Actual Productivity (MH/CY)	Lost Productivity (MH/CY)	Lost Labor Hours (MH)
	Week No.	I	II	III	IV=II/III	V=IV−I	VI=III×V
Period Impacted	16	1.79	362	150	2.41	0.62	93.5
	17	1.79	480	205	2.34	0.55	113.1
	18	1.79	508	230	2.21	0.42	96.3
	19	1.79	466	190	2.45	0.66	125.9
	20	1.79	419	215	1.95	0.16	34.2
				Average	2.26	Total	462.9
Measured Mile	21	1.79	420	240	1.75		
	22	1.79	438	245	1.79		
	23	1.79	395	218	1.81		
	24	1.79	390	215	1.81		
				Average	1.79		

Direct Labor Rate = $32 per hour
Labor Burden = 34%
Burdened Labor Rate = $42.88 per hour

Labor Cost = Burdened Labor Rate × Lost Labor Hours
$\qquad$ = $42.88 × 462.9 = $19,849.15

Activity-Related Field Overhead Markup = 15%

Disruption Damages = Labor Cost × Activity-Related Field Overhead Markup
$\qquad$ = $19,849.15 × 1.15 = $22,826.52

Exhibit 26-11. Sample Calculation of Disruption Damages Using Measured Mile

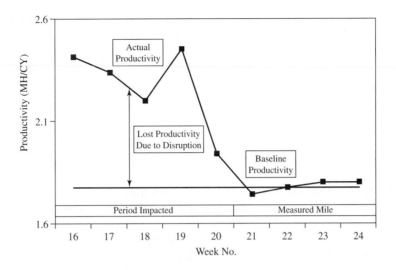

Exhibit 26-11.   (Continued)

(iii) Industry Studies.   Throughout the world, researchers have studied the effect of various conditions on the productivity of craft labor on construction projects. Engineering and construction industry groups, academics, and other construction professionals have studied how certain factors affect productivity and how to quantify the potential productivity losses resulting from these factors. Groups such as the Construction Industry Institute (CII), American Society of Civil Engineers (ASCE), United States Army Corps of Engineers (USACE), and Mechanical Contractors Association of America (MCAA) have performed some of these productivity studies. The industry studies provide useful guidelines and estimates of how certain factors will affect labor productivity and also give a basis for validating the measured-mile calculations used to quantify the disruption resulting from the impact events.

Most of the available productivity studies conclude that certain factors, when present in a construction project, have direct adverse effects on the productivity of craft labor (e.g., pipefitters and carpenters). One of the reports frequently referred to in many industry studies, prepared by the MCAA in the United States, lists sixteen causes of productivity loss and the anticipated percentage loss when the condition is minor, average, or severe.[11] Exhibit 26-12 lists the sixteen productivity loss factors addressed in the study.

Trade Stacking	Beneficial Occupancy
Morale and Attitude	Joint Occupancy
Manpower Reassignment	Site Access
Crew Size Inefficiency	Logistics
Concurrent Operations	Fatigue
Dilution of Supervision	Ripple Effect
Learning Curve	Overtime
Errors and Omissions (and Changes)	Weather

Exhibit 26-12.   Productivity Loss Factors

(iv) Other Methods.   Experts use other methods to quantify disruption or to validate the result of an approach that we have discussed previously. These other methods include

- "Should cost" estimates (e.g., cost estimates based on the actual costs of a similar project)
- Expert opinion
- Time and motion studies

A detailed discussion of these alternative methods to quantify disruption lies beyond the scope of this chapter.

(c) Extra Work.   Owners cause extra work when they alter the contract scope with one of two types of changes: directed and constructive. Owners initiate *directed changes* by asking the contractor to submit a cost proposal for the changes. After concluding price negotiations, the owner usually gives the contractor approval to perform the work. The owner does not formally initiate *constructive changes*, but they nonetheless result from the owner's actions. For example, the owner may instruct the contractor to change its work sequence because of an unforeseen conflict, which may require the contractor to incur additional costs to meet the contractual completion date.

Acceleration is a type of change that can be directed or constructive depending on whether the owner requests and negotiates a price prior to the acceleration. The industry uses the term *scope creep* to describe the cumulative effect of many minor changes that lead to a significant total cost impact. Their size and number make these changes difficult to identify and quantify.

Contractors often encounter conditions during work on the project that require changes and extra work. For example, excavation on a project can reveal a harder rock bed than originally anticipated. Contract terms and conditions typically require the contractor to provide a written notification to the owner, give the owner a chance to evaluate the change, and respond with an action plan. Generally, the contractor should not start performing the changed work until it receives an approval from the owner. Working on an unapproved change puts the contractor at a risk of not receiving compensation for its costs incurred. In some situations, however, the contractor has no choice but to perform the work before obtaining the approval, especially if the owner does not respond to the contractor's notification in a timely manner. In these situations, the contractor has a better chance of recovering its costs if it notifies the owner that it will incur additional costs and reserves its right to submit a claim later.

Most contracts require timely written notification to recover damages associated with extra work. In *Nat Harrison Associates, Inc. v. Gulf States Utilities Co.*, the court listed several situations that can form the basis for written notification waiver:

> (1) when the extra work was necessary and had not been foreseen; (2) when the changes were of such magnitude that they could not be supposed to have been made without the knowledge of the owner; (3) when the owner was aware of the additional work and made no objection to it; and (4) when there was a subsequent verbal agreement authorizing the work. [*See*] *Roff v. Southern Construction Corporation*, La. App., 3d Cir., 163 So. 2d 112, 115-116 (1964).

In many cases, one cannot assess the actual losses associated with the extra work until the contractor completes the project. Most contractors try to capture the costs associated with extra work separately from their original scope. A change clause in the contract typically dictates extra work pricing. Some contracts have predetermined unit rates to use for valuing extra work. In the absence of unit rates, one can use a cost-based approach to price the extra work. Cost-based extra work claims should include only activity-related direct and activity-related indirect costs plus the markup allowed under the contract.

In the United States, the industry uses the term "cardinal change" when the changes become so pervasive or material that the final project becomes fundamentally different from the project the contractor bid on. Proving cardinal change is very difficult. Some experts calculate cardinal change damages under a *quantum meruit* theory, which considers the *value* of work performed under the existing circumstances and does not consider existing contractual pricing provisions, bid values, and overhead and profit assumptions within the bid. The valuation under a *quantum meruit* claim typically considers the liability incurred by the contractor in performing the work, less costs incurred as a result of the contractor's own errors or omissions, plus a reasonable overhead and profit contribution based on the nature of the work performed.

The courts typically do not favor use of *quantum meriut*. In *Amelco Electric v. City of Thousand Oaks*, the court listed two main reasons why allowing contractors to recover under *quantum meruit* would potentially undermine the competitive bidding process:

> (1) Contractors would wait until a project was completed before giving change notices, thus creating uncertainty in the budgeting and financing of construction projects and (2) contractors would bid unrealistically low, with the expectation of numerous changes and therefore, the hope of prevailing on under *quantum meruit.*

The recovery under *quantum meriut* is therefore very limited and even prohibited in some jurisdictions.

(d) Acceleration.   Acceleration is a type of extra work that one could consider directed or constructive, depending on whether the owner requests and negotiates a price prior to the acceleration. It occurs when an owner wants to achieve an earlier completion date, recover excusable delays, or mitigate the effects of its own actions—which would delay the project—to meet the original completion date. The owners typically avoid instructing acceleration overtly, and instead maintain the contractor's obligations to meet the scheduled project completion date. To recover its costs, the contractor needs to prove that, if not mitigated, the owner's actions would result in a delay. The contractor then needs to show the impact of the owner's actions to the project schedule by using one of the delay methods described in Section 26.4 of this chapter. This is a hypothetical analysis, because delay would not occur if the contractor accelerates the efforts and completes the project on schedule.

Even though acceleration is a form of extra work, it does not change the plans and specifications; it changes only the means and methods. During the acceleration, the contractor usually increases manpower and equipment, adds shifts and over-time, and revises its work sequence. Typical acceleration costs include the premium portion of overtime incurred for a labor force required to work extended days or multiple shifts; costs for additional equipment and materials (i.e., formwork) brought in to support the acceleration efforts; and premiums for expedited delivery of materials.

Disruption often accompanies acceleration. For example, a contractor would not likely complete the project in half of its original duration by doubling its man-power. The contractor will lose some of his work force's productivity because of inefficiencies such as overcrowding, as well as dilution of supervision. One can separately calculate losses associated with disruption using the methods described in Section 26.3(b) of this chapter.

(e) Home-Office Overhead.   A contractor generally will not assign or allocate a portion of its home-office overhead to a specific project during the course of con-struction. The fixed nature of home-office overhead means that this amount will typically not increase as a result of a specific project claim. However, when a project is delayed, the contractor can experience extended or unabsorbed home-office overhead.[12]

One can use several methods to calculate unabsorbed home-office overhead. Experts most often include it as a markup to other claims such as delay and disruption. Some experts also calculate a daily rate to apply to periods of com-pensable delay using formulas such as Eichleay (discussed in Section 26.3(e)(ii)).[13] Experts who use both daily rates and markups for various claims in the same project need to avoid double counting the home-office overhead.

(i) Markup.   Experts often calculate home-office markup based on a *pro rata* method, using cost or billings as the distribution base. The FAR also favor distrib-ution of indirect costs such as home-office overhead on a *pro rata* basis using an appropriate allocation base.[14] The calculation first divides allowable home-office overhead by a company's cost base. One then applies the markup to the individ-ual elements of damages related to the project. One can calculate the markup separately for each corresponding year or for the project's entire duration.

(ii) Daily Rate.   Delay claims generally use daily overhead rates. One of the more common methods of establishing a daily overhead rate uses an estimation formu-la referred to as *Eichleay.* The formula originated from a decision by the Armed Services Board of Contract Appeals in 1960: *Eichleay Corp.*, ASBCA No. 5183, 60-2 BCA ¶2688 (1960). The Eichleay formula calculates home-office overhead allocable to the project by dividing the project billings by company billings (or the project costs by total project costs) and multiplying it by allowable home-office overhead. The formula then divides allocable overhead by the actual days of con-tract performance to calculate the daily rate. The last step multiplies the daily rate by number of days of compensable delay to arrive at the unabsorbed home-office overhead. Experts have frequently used the Eichleay formula, and courts have both accepted and rejected it depending on the jurisdiction. Rejections mostly occur on the basis that no direct link exists between the claim and any increased or

unabsorbed home-office overhead. In *Wickham Contracting Co., Inc. v. D.J. Fischer (General Services Administration)*, the court held that the Eichleay formula was the exclusive means available for calculating unabsorbed overhead. However, in *Chilton Insurance Co. v. Pate & Pate Enterprises, Inc.*, the court denied the use of the Eichleay formula.

26.4   DELAY CLAIM CALCULATIONS

Each project comprises a set of activities that the contractor can sequence in a project schedule. The relation between various activities is called scheduling logic. For example, a worker cannot pour a concrete slab before preparing the form. Therefore, the pour and form activities have a finish-to-start logic. Using this logic, schedule development methods can calculate the optimal time period to perform each activity. The most common schedule development method is the Critical Path Method (CPM). Using CPM, one can calculate a range of early and late dates: early start, early finish, late start, and late finish. As long as workers perform the activities between the early and late dates, the project completion date will not change. CPM also identifies critical activities, which have identical early and late dates. Critical activities determine the project duration, because any delay to these activities results in a delay to the project completion. Each project usually has one critical path, which consists of a series of critical activities. Any delay to tasks on the critical path will result, absent mitigation, in a delay to the overall project. The critical path can change during the project, when noncritical activities are delayed beyond their late finish dates and hence become critical.

Most contracts require contractors to submit CPM schedules prior to the start of the work. Most contracts also require contractors to submit periodic (e.g., monthly) updates to the CPM schedules, which reflect the status of the project including the as-built dates (i.e., actual progress through the update) and as-planned dates (i.e., scheduled progress after the update). Experts value reliable CPM schedules when performing a delay analysis. The scheduling experts need to examine the integrity and reasonableness of the CPM schedules, as they may contain flaws or the project may not have been built according to the schedule. The following sections summarize methods to quantify a delay claim; an extensive discussion of these methods is beyond the scope of this chapter.

(a) Impacted As-Planned.   This analysis uses an initial as-planned schedule, sometimes called a baseline schedule. Experts sometimes use this type of analysis when a reasonable baseline schedule exists but no periodic updates. The analysis introduces the effects of the owner's actions to the baseline schedule as activities, and the expert recomputes the project completion date. This analysis requires minimal time but loses merit as a hypothetical calculation. It does not take into account any logical sequence changes, contractor delays, and any as-built information.

(b) Collapsed As-Built.   This method creates an as-built schedule using the available contemporary information such as progressed schedule updates, daily logs, and meeting minutes. The expert removes specific owner-driven (or other) impacts from the schedule and recomputes the project completion date considering an as-built critical path. This method has merit because it relies on actual historical information as to how the project was built, and the adjusted as-built critical path will include the claimant's own delay. This approach is often time consuming, however, and the preparer must address a number of issues, including arguments regarding pacing for noncritical activities.[15]

(c) Windows Analysis.   The windows analysis uses both as-built and as-planned information from the baseline schedule and periodic schedule updates. The time period between the two consecutive schedule updates is called a window. For each window, one compares the as-built dates with the as-planned dates by comparing the two consecutive schedule updates. The expert then identifies the number of days of critical delay, the delay type (inexcusable, excusable, compensable, and concurrent), and the causes for each delay. The final step sums these critical delays by window to calculate the total delay. Courts prefer this method when reliable schedules are available and the expert correctly applies the approach.

(d) Time Impact Analysis.   One can use this method when few owner-driven effects have occurred and one can identify the periods of their impact. This method is most commonly used during the project to assess the effects of change orders. Some owners require the contractors to submit a time impact analysis before granting any time extension for change orders. One can also use this method for delay claims after the project's completion. After-the-fact time impact analysis resembles the windows analysis with one difference: instead of using periodic schedule updates as windows, the expert prepares the adjusted schedule with a status date at the end of the impact period, which the expert then compares with the most recent schedule update prior to the occurrence of impact. The expert repeats this step for each impact.

26.5   CONCLUSION

The conditions surrounding each claim and the types of documents available for each one make every claim unique, and experts must adapt their analyses to these different circumstances. Experts can maintain the integrity of their damages models by following various guidelines from this chapter, summarized in the following list. These guidelines are also helpful in rebutting opposing experts.

- **Maintain objectivity.** When preparing a report for a contractor, the expert needs to account for the amount underbid by the contractor. The expert also needs to identify the damages caused by its client. Ignoring these factors impairs the integrity and reliability of the model and the expert.
- **Avoid double-counting.** Especially when the claim has multiple components, experts need to ensure that they have segregated the cost pools and have not included the same cost components in more than one claim component. For cost-based claims, the expert also needs to make sure that the sum of damages calculated for each claim does not exceed the total damages (i.e., the actual cost overrun).

- **Provide links between cause and effect.** Depending on the availability of the documentation, the expert needs to demonstrate reasonable links between the cause and damages.

NOTES

1. Throughout the remainder of this chapter, we use the term "owner" to represent both the owner and the owner's agents.
2. Home-office overhead is typically recorded in the Selling, General, and Administrative (SG&A) ledger and is not directly allocated to the job cost ledger.
3. FAR Reissue 2005 Effective on May 19, 2006 Part 2.101 Definitions.
4. Ibid.
5. FAR Reissue 2005 Effective on May 19, 2006 Part 31.001 Definitions.
6. FAR Reissue 2005 Effective on May 19, 2006 Part 31.202 Direct Costs.
7. Delay to individual project milestones can also be relevant, depending on individual contract terms and conditions.
8. Construction contracts will often provide a fixed or formulaic amount per day, other period, or event for certain failures of the contractor to perform; this is referred to as liquidated damages. When the amount is derived from a formula, experts will often differ on the result, necessitating a judicial solution.
9. *Clark Concrete Contractors, Inc. v. GSA*, GSBCA 14340, 99-1 BCA at 30,280.
10. A learning, or experience, curve describes the propensity of workers to become more efficient as they perform a task repeatedly, accumulating expertise. A measured mile established before an impact, particularly early in a project, may understate damages; conversely, a measured mile from late in a project applied to an early impact may overstate damages.
11. *Factors Affecting Productivity*, Mechanical Contractors Association of America (MCAA), Bulletin 58, 1976.
12. Unabsorbed overhead results when an owner-caused delay significantly reduces a contractor's cash flow on a project and the contractor's home-office overhead must be absorbed by other projects.
13. The Eichleay formula is one of the more common home-office overhead estimating approaches used in the United States. Outside the United States, other estimating formulas such as Hudson and Emden are sometimes used by contractors and experts. Experts who use both daily rates and markups for various claims in the same project need to avoid double counting the home-office overhead.
14. FAR Reissue 2005 Effective on May 19, 2006. Part 31.203 Indirect Costs.
15. For example, a contractor can "pace" a noncritical activity by reducing resources assigned to the activity, therefore extending the activity duration and creating a critical activity.

LIST OF CASES

Amelco Electric v. City of Thousand Oaks, 27 Cal. 4th 228, 38 P.3d 1120, 115 Cal. Rptr. 2d 900 (2002)

Chilton Insurance Co. v. Pate & Pate Enterprises, Inc., 930 S.W.2d 877 (1996)

City of Salinas v. Souza & McCue Construction Co., Inc., 66 Cal. 2d 217, 424 P.2d 921 (1967)

Clark Concrete Contractors, Inc. v. GSA, GSBCA 14340, 99-1 BCA at 30,280

Corinno Civetta Construction Corp. v. City of New York, 67 N.Y.2d 297, 493 N.E.2d 905, 502 N.Y.S.2d 681 (1986)

Edward S. Paine et al. v. John Spottiswoode et. al., 612 A.2d 235 (1992)

Eichleay Corp., ASBCA No. 5183, 60-2 BCA ¶2688 (1960), *aff'd on recon.*, 61-1 BCA ¶2894

Electronic & Missile Facilities, Inc. v. United States, 189 Ct. Cl. 237; 416 F.2d 1345 (1969)

Howard Contracting, Inc. v. G.A. Macdonald Construction Co., Inc., & City of Los Angeles, 71 Cal. App. 4th 38, 83 Cal. Rptr. 2d 590 (1998)

Kumho Tire Co., Ltd. v. Patrick Carmichael, 526 U.S. 137, 119 S. Ct. 1167 (1999)

Nat Harrison Associates, Inc. v. Gulf States Utilities Co., 491 F.2d 578 (1974)

Roff v. Southern Construction Corporation, La. App., 3d Cir., 163 So. 2d 112 (1964)

Stroh Corp. v. General Services Administration, GSBCA 11029, 96-1 BCA at 28,165

U.S. Industries, Inc. v. Blake Construction Co., Inc., 671 F.2d 539 (D. C. Cir, 1982)

Wickham Contracting Co., Inc. v. D.J. Fischer (General Services Administration), 12 F.3d 1574 (1994)

William Daubert v. Merrell Dow Pharmaceuticals, Inc., 509 U.S. 579, 113 S. Ct. 2786 (1993)

CHAPTER 27

QUANTIFYING DAMAGES IN REAL ESTATE LITIGATION

Thomas E. Kabat
Frank A. Voorvaart

CONTENTS

27.1 INTRODUCTION

This chapter discusses how to quantify damages in real estate litigation, but because each case has different circumstances, the methods presented will not apply to every case. Damages to real estate can arise not only from direct physical impairments but also from indirect factors. Direct impairments include hydrocarbon or heavy metal contamination from a manufacturing facility, noise pollution from a nearby rail yard, or visual impairment from high-voltage transmission towers. Compensation for diminution in property value due to *direct* impairments is a well-recognized concept. Formulating clear arguments for compensation for diminution due to *indirect* effects, however, presents challenges. Such damages, sometimes called *proximity damages*, could originate from the perceived threat of contamination to a property, for example. In such instances, the contaminant doesn't directly affect the subject property, but only an adjacent property. The market might attribute some risk of future contamination to the subject property, which would cause the property to trade at a discount relative to properties not at risk. Whether the landowner can recover compensation for these indirect effects becomes a question for the courts.

Damages to real estate values can arise in situations other than environmental impairment, such as eminent domain litigation or right-of-way acquisition of a portion of a property. In other examples, a developer might sue a city for precluding development of a parcel of land, resulting in an unprofitable investment, or federal laws protecting an endangered species might effectuate a taking of private property.

For discussion purposes, we will refer to the various sources of damages as *environmental conditions*. Additionally, although many professionals—appraisers, real estate economists, accountants, and financial analysts—have some or all of the skills for the analyses discussed in this chapter, we use the term *appraiser* throughout for simplicity.

We first discuss the appropriate analyses given the type of property in dispute. For residential properties, we recommend a combination of statistical measures and individualized analyses; for income-producing properties, practitioners perform property-specific analyses. Given the increasing access to electronic data from assessors, multiple listing services, and data vendors, as well as the proliferation of sophisticated statistical software, we discuss some misconceptions regarding multiple regression analysis (*see* Section 27.3(d)). We conclude by discussing recent federal regulatory developments.

27.2   RESIDENTIAL VERSUS INCOME PROPERTY: GENERAL OBSERVATIONS

(a) Differing Issues.   Important differences exist between owner-occupied residential property and income property. Income property can be owner occupied or it can be investor owned, but appraisers value it in terms of the income it can generate net of operating expenses. Residential apartments and retail, office, industrial, and hotel properties provide examples of property types that one would classify as income property.

Those transacting in income property exercise sophisticated environmental due diligence that deals with the observables—the nature and the extent of any contamination; the regulatory posture with respect to cleanup; the entity responsible for the cleanup and its ability to pay; and any additional risk from contamination that may have migrated to adjacent properties. Both investors and lenders, the two sources of capital (equity and debt), understand the importance of these issues and generally work through them in a systematic way. Their concerns fall into three general areas:

- Cost of remediation and who will pay for it
- Effects of contamination on the utility of the property

- Potential liability to third parties (e.g., adjacent property owners or former employees)

Residential property[1] presents different issues. Most transactions involve no environmental due diligence, even when parties know of significant subsurface contamination. This is because residential property owners are presumably rarely liable for the cleanup of contamination or concerned about third-party liability, rather, prospective buyers and owners focus instead on whether the contamination affects the use of the property. Their perspective, when negative, is not based on an intimate understanding of the details. Instead, it reflects a media-fed perception of the contamination. The litigation itself may influence their understanding.

(b) Different Valuation Methods.   The second major distinction between income and residential property lies in the appropriate valuation approach. Appraisers value residential properties almost exclusively using the sales comparison approach, drawing inferences from actual market transactions. Relevant to our topic, appraisers compare sales of potentially contaminated properties with sales of presumably unaffected properties. Even though appraisers can select from several methods (*see* Sections 27.3 and 27.4), they must base their value of any residential property on market data.

One can analyze income property using any of the three traditional appraisal approaches:

1. **Cost approach.** replacement cost, net of depreciation, plus land value
2. **Sales comparison approach.** value indications from comparable property sales
3. **Income approach.** the capitalized value of anticipated future cash flows from the property

The cost approach has little relevance to assessing the effect of contamination on value. It lacks sufficient sensitivity to either cash flow or risk issues that often accompany environmental contamination.

Similarly, appraisers have difficulty applying the sales comparison approach to contaminated income property. In its basic form, the sales comparison approach analyzes multiple sales with conclusions such as, "Sale No. 1 sold for $34 per square foot but was superior to the subject, and Sale No. 2 sold for $28 per square foot but was clearly inferior to the subject."[2] This approach falls short in recognizing the important differences that exist between the sale properties and the subject property; appraisers cannot easily quantify many of these differences. For example, how does one quantify the implications of petroleum contamination versus heavy metal contamination? How does one value differences in indemnification agreements or the financial strength of indemnitors? How does one weigh the implications of being a source site versus a nonsource site?

Editors' Note: By *income approach,* the authors do not mean accrual accounting revenues less expenses, but rather net cash flows, adopting standard appraisal nomenclature.

The income approach has proved most practicable for analyzing the effects of contamination on the value of income property. Actual transactions can (and must) play an important role in supporting the assumptions used in the income approach, but the appraiser can best analyze the effects of contamination on income property in terms of their effect on anticipated future income and on the risks that lenders and investors attach to these income flows given the facts associated with the contamination.

(c) Summary.   When studying contamination effects, the appraiser can delineate the tasks as follows:

- **Residential property.** What evidence from actual transactions demonstrates that the price of similar but unaffected properties exceeds the sales price of affected properties? Interestingly, the perceptions of buyers, sellers, and brokers determine this increment, often wholly divorced from the technical dimensions of the incident or its cause.
- **Income property.** In this context, appraisers will more likely consider the specific circumstances of the subject property and ask whether the contamination will affect future income flows or the rate at which the market will capitalize this income into value. Appraisers will need to support their conclusions with an examination of the facts of the subject property, discussions with knowledgeable market participants (particularly lenders and investors), and evidence distilled from actual transactions.

Sections 27.3 and 27.4 will examine the methods for evaluating residential property value diminution; Section 27.5 will examine this topic in the income property context.

27.3   STATISTICAL MEASURES OF DAMAGES FOR RESIDENTIAL PROPERTY

Environmental damages to residential property occur when the market reflects a perception that an environmental condition affects the utility of homes. Because homeowners are seldom subject to regulatory action or remediation cost liability, the perceptions of a typical buyer in the relevant market drive the diminution in value.

Appraisers consider single-family residential appraisal a relatively straightforward exercise for most properties in most markets: the appraiser identifies and evaluates comparable sale transactions as a basis for estimating value. Appraisers use the cost approach—developing an indication of the depreciated replacement or reproduction cost of the improvements, and adding the estimated value of the land—as a benchmark to evaluate results of the sales comparison approach.

Quantifying residential property value diminution, especially in a class action or mass tort case, involves a complex analytical process that the appraiser must perform primarily on the basis of empirical real estate market data. The analyst must ascertain the extent to which the market would discount the value of a given property as compensation to a buyer for perceived loss of utility. The analytical process may be complicated by the fact that market participants often lack the sophistication necessary to isolate and quantify the effects of contamination on utility. Sometimes appraisers must perform the analysis with limited or no data for a comparable real estate market. Appraisers may find some survey-based methods appropriate, provided the researcher produced unbiased results. A detailed discussion of survey methods lies outside the realm of this chapter.

An appraiser can use several statistical measures to ascertain whether an environmental condition has affected a class of properties. This chapter does not discuss simple analyses, such as average price per square foot, for two reasons: one can easily understand the methods, and these methods could mislead the appraiser by ignoring relevant factors. Multiple regression analysis, which this chapter discusses, offers a more sophisticated approach.

Multiple regression analysis helps the analyst identify possible relations between various independent or predictor variables and a dependent or response variable. In analyzing the possible effect of environmental conditions on residential property values, one might formulate and test a hypothesis that the condition in question has or has not influenced property values. Then, using actual marketplace transaction data, one develops a mathematical equation that expresses the relation between potentially significant independent variables (such as lot size, number of bedrooms and bathrooms, distance to contamination source, and so forth) and the dependent variable (typically sale price) as a basis for testing the hypothesis. Chapters 5 and 6 discuss regression analysis.

(a) Neighborhood Comparison Approach. Analysts often use the neighborhood comparison and proximity approaches when evaluating whether an environmental condition has affected residential property values. Both methods use multiple regression analysis. After controlling for price differences owing to physical property characteristics (such as lot size, gross living area, age, dwelling type, number of bedrooms, and existence of a basement or porch), one can use multiple regression to test the hypothesis that an environmental condition has a statistically significant effect on the sale prices of properties located within the subject area.

In a neighborhood comparison approach, the regression model tests whether sale prices of homes located within the subject area exhibit a different trend compared with the sale prices of homes within the control area that the model assumes to be unaffected. The proximity approach considers only sales occurring within the subject area but includes a variable that measures the distance from each property sold to the contamination source. The appraiser then analyzes this distance variable to ascertain whether a distance premium (or discount)[3] existed before the environmental condition and whether the premium changed after the environmental condition arose.

Analysts can develop and specify a regression model that measures the location premium associated with a neighborhood and whether the neighborhood premium changes over time. For example, one can test for premiums and year-to-year changes in premiums, or test whether the premium changed after the environmental condition occurred. Consider the following model that one might use to test whether homes located over a plume[4] sold at a discount relative to homes located elsewhere after the plume's discovery.

$$SP = \beta_0 + \beta_1 Z + \beta_2 \text{AFTER} + \beta_3 \text{PLUME} + \beta_4 \text{PL\_AFTER} + \varepsilon$$

where

> SP = sale price
> Z = independent variables such as home size, lot size, age, and number of bedrooms
> AFTER = indicator (dummy) variable indicating whether a sale occurred in the "after" period (i.e., post discovery) or "before" period (i.e., pre-discovery), where 0 = "before" and 1 = "after"
> PLUME = indicator variable indicating whether the property is located in the subject area (i.e., over the plume) or in the control area, where 1 = subject area and 0 = control area;
> PL_AFTER = interactive indicator variable obtained by multiplying PLUME and AFTER indicator variables
> ε = error term associated with the estimated sale price.

One can use the above equation to test whether homes over the plume sold at a premium before the plume's discovery and whether the premium changed over time. Analysts cannot simply test whether a home sold at a discount after discovery of the plume. This would neglect the possibility that houses in the neighborhood over the plume were previously selling at a discount, incorrectly attributing the difference in sale price to the environmental condition.

(b) Proximity Approach. The proximity approach tests for an adverse effect related to proximity of subject area properties to an environmental hazard or contamination source. The regression model includes a variable indicating each property's distance, in feet, from the contamination source. One can estimate such a distance variable through the use of Geographic Information Systems (GIS) and related software. A positive value associated with the distance variable would indicate the existence of a premium for homes located farther away from the contamination source relative to those located near it. An analysis of year-to-year or before-and-after changes in the distance variable coefficient would indicate whether this premium, if any, has changed over time.

This approach uses an equation similar to that shown above:

$$SP = \beta_0 + \beta_1 Z + \beta_2 AFTER + \beta_3 DISTANCE + \beta_4 DIST\_AFTER + \varepsilon$$

where

> SP = sale price
> Z = independent variables such as home size, lot size, age, and number of bedrooms
> AFTER = indicator variable indicating whether a sale occurred in the "after" period (i.e., post discovery) or "before" period (i.e., pre discovery), where 0 = "before" and 1 = "after"
> DISTANCE = continuous variable indicating distance of each subject property to the environmental hazard
> DIST_AFTER = interactive indicator variable obtained by multiplying DISTANCE and AFTER variables
> ε = error term associated with the estimated sale price.

The analyst should not simply examine the coefficient of the distance variable to see whether proximity to an environmental condition has affected values. The distance premium associated with being farther away might have existed before the event occurred. Instead, the analyst must compare the "after" premium with the "before" premium to ensure a statistically significant difference before concluding that the environmental condition has affected property values.

(c) Hybrid Approach. Residential property damages analyses can use a hybrid approach that incorporates elements of both the neighborhood comparison and proximity methods. The analyst can perform sale price trend analysis on the basis of transactions occurring within concentric rings located at successively increasing distances from a source site or identified hazard. One might, for example, wish to evaluate whether home sale price appreciation rates decline at locations nearest to an environmental hazard relative to areas located farther from the source. Assuming that adequate data are available, one could select rings at various intervals of, say, one-quarter mile, one-half mile, three-quarters of a mile, one mile, and so on.

Exhibit 27-1 shows an example of the results of such an analysis. Here, the analyst divided a two-mile-radius study area surrounding an environmental hazard into four subareas, with Study Area A located nearest to the source site (i.e., within one-half mile) and Study Area D located farthest (i.e., from 1.5 to 2.0 miles from the source site). The analysis summarized over 800 sales in the study area and grouped them into five time periods selected on the basis of varying degrees of market awareness of the condition under evaluation.

The regression model used for analyzing the sales transactions included the following variables: house age at the time of sale, square feet of living area, lot size, whether the house had a pool, whether the house had a fireplace, a location variable indicating the study area of the property's location, and a time variable indicating the sale date. These variables produced a stable regression model and

Time Period	Study Area A	Study Area B	Study Area C	Study Area D
1/1/05–4/30/05	$157,748	$158,400	$158,583	$157,121
5/1/05–8/30/05	160,369	159,769	159,649	160,972
9/1/05–12/31/05	158,287	163,183	157,250	159,806
1/1/06–4/30/06	163,834	165,404	163,578	161,135
5/1/06–8/30/06	168,345	168,791	168,727	167,282
Percent Change (1/1/05–8/30/06)	6.72%	6.56%	6.40%	6.47%

[a]Estimated prices are based on a home with average characteristics.

Exhibit 27-1.   Concentric Study Area Price Trends[a]

achieved an adjusted R^2 of 92.9 percent.[5] Each of the housing characteristic variables had the expected sign and was statistically significant.[6]

Exhibit 27-1 shows that home values in Study Area A (the area closest to the source site) appreciated at a rate similar to that of Areas B, C, and D. If the source site had adversely affected property values, one would expect depreciating home values or at least a reduced appreciation rate in Area A relative to Areas B, C, and D. The results shown in the exhibit, however, indicate this result did not occur. Because all four study areas had comparable home price appreciation rates, one would conclude that these data do not support an assertion that the environmental condition has affected property values near the source site.

(d) Prediction versus Hypothesis Testing.   When implementing or reviewing statistical applications based on multiple regression analysis, one must distinguish between hypothesis testing and prediction. In hypothesis testing, the analyst develops a hypothesis concerning the potential effect of the environmental condition and then tests that hypothesis on the basis of the model. For example, one might test the hypothesis that "the environmental conditions associated with site Y have significantly affected sale prices of homes within neighborhood X."[7] The analyst can then use multiple regression analysis as a basis for accepting or rejecting that hypothesis. The reliability of multiple regression is generally well established in this context.

Abuses of the method can and do occur when analysts use the coefficients obtained from the regression model to predict or quantify the loss in value incurred by any particular home within the study population. For example, an analyst might conclude incorrectly that the values of all homes within a subject area have declined by an amount equal to the coefficient of the PLUME variable discussed in Section 27(b)(i).

One can demonstrate the impropriety by analyzing the standard error associated with either the sale price estimate or the estimated coefficient associated with the environmental condition. Suppose a regression model indicates an estimated sale price of $120,000 for a certain home with specified features located within a subject area over a groundwater plume. Such a model could have a standard error of the estimated value of $20,000 or more. A standard error of $20,000 would enable one to conclude with 95 percent confidence that the actual sale price of the home lies between $80,000 and $160,000 (i.e., within a range of plus or minus two standard deviations of the estimate of $120,000). Clearly, a model that indicates a sale price range of plus or minus 33 percent of the estimated value for a given home has little predictive capability. In contrast, market value estimates developed by appraisers using traditional residential valuation methods are typically reliable to within 3 percent to 5 percent of the actual sale price.

The same issue arises with respect to the coefficient of the PLUME or subject area variable. Assume that the coefficient of the PLUME variable in the above example is negative $12,000 and that it has a standard error of $4,800. The t-ratio of the coefficient therefore equals -2.5 (i.e., $-\$12,000/\$4,800 = -2.5$), showing it to be statistically significant at the 95 percent confidence level. Thus, one can accept the hypothesis that the effect of the plume on sale price differs from zero, but it would not support a conclusion that the sale price declines by $12,000 as a result of the plume.

The analyst could, for example, test other hypotheses without rejecting them. These could include "the environmental condition reduces the sale price by $4,000," or "the environmental condition reduces the sale price by $18,000."[8] At the 95 percent confidence interval, the analyst would have to accept both of these hypotheses. This example shows that a correct statement is that the environmental condition has negatively affected home values in the subject area. Analysts can use multiple regression analysis to test hypotheses of whether an effect exists but often cannot use the method to indicate the size of the effect.

(e) Other Quantitative Methods.   Other statistical measures can provide the financial expert with additional insight. These measures include *days-on-market, sale price to list price ratio, turnover ratio*, and *media coverage analysis*.

(i) Days-on-Market.   The average time required to sell a home within the allegedly affected market, submarket area, or neighborhood provides one indicator of whether environmental conditions have affected residential property values. One can obtain such data through local real estate broker listing databases, such as the Multiple Listing Service (MLS).[9]

The analyst wants to evaluate whether any discernable increase has occurred in the number of days required to market and sell a home relative to prior periods or relative to other competing neighborhoods or submarkets. Practitioners typically perform a days-on-market analysis using a representative sample of sale transactions occurring within the affected area. One can make intraneighborhood comparisons to evaluate differences in days-on-market before and after an event, or compare the days-on-market within a neighborhood with that of other similar neighborhoods. Ideally, one should perform a four-way analysis that compares the days-on-market of the *subject* neighborhood *before* and *after* the incident with the days-on-market of the *control* neighborhood also *before* and *after* the event.

Analysts can evaluate days-on-market in one of two ways. They can define it as the number of days between the date listed for sale and the date that the seller accepts a contract for sale, or they can define it as the number of days between the listing date and the date of closing.

The original listing date identified in a database such as MLS need not reflect the date when the seller placed the home on the market. An owner may list the property, delist it, and list it again later, possibly with a different agent or broker. Sometimes owners first try to sell their homes themselves, before listing it with a broker who would enter it into the MLS system. This practice would distort the data but not necessarily the conclusion from the analysis.

(ii) Sale Price to List Price Ratio.   The ratio of sale prices to listing prices for properties located within a potential area of influence provides another possible indicator of contamination effects on residential real estate. The MLS and other sources also provide these data.

Exhibit 27-2 suggests that homes sell at a reduced percentage of their original listing prices relative to the same period of the prior year. The relevant analysis, however, is not whether the ratio changed over time, but whether a disproportionately negative change has occurred with respect to the area nearest to the source site (i.e., Study Area A). The change in Study Area A is more negative than

| | Study Area | | | |
Period	Area A (Median Value)	Area B (Median Value)	Area C (Median Value)	Area D (Median Value)
1 5/1/05–8/31/05	98.78%	98.72%	98.71%	98.08%
2 5/1/06–8/31/06	97.97	98.61	98.11	97.09

Exhibit 27-2.   Sale Price to List Price Ratio

that of Study Area B, which lies farther away. The change in Area A is consistent, however, with that of Area D, which lies outside the potential influence of the hazard in question.

Exhibit 27-2 shows that other nonenvironmental economic influences can affect the willingness of buyers to purchase area homes at or near listing prices. Sellers may have become more aggressive and decide to test the market to see if sufficient demand exists to bear higher rates of appreciation in the near term. Regardless of which factors influence the ratio of sale price to original list price, the data do not indicate a disproportionate burden on properties located nearest to the source of environmental concern.

(iii) Turnover Ratio. Another test or indicator of possible impact is the turnover ratio, which practitioners sometimes refer to as *sales velocity.* This analysis compares the number of homes sold within the allegedly affected area over a specified time period or periods with the total number of properties located within the selected area. In a manner similar to that employed in evaluating days-on-market, one can perform the analysis either on a before and after basis or by comparing a subject neighborhood with a control neighborhood. Assume, for example, that an analyst needs to evaluate the alleged effect of an environmental condition confined to a residential subdivision consisting of 500 homes. Assume further that 45 to 50 of those homes had traded during each of the three years prior to a chemical release that recently occurred within the subdivision. If only 35 homes traded in the year immediately following the release, and the analyst concluded that no other conditions existed in the relevant market that might have caused such a decline, then the environmental condition appears to have affected, at least temporarily, the marketability of homes located within the affected area.

As with days-on-market analyses, a finding of possible impairment indicated by a reduced turnover ratio might not reflect compensable property value damages. These indicators may simply provide insight as to the amount of time necessary to realize the value of the property in question. If a home sale occurs at a price reflecting unimpaired market value, but it takes three or six months longer than it should have (but for the contamination), then the owner/seller of that home may have suffered damages. The damage results from a temporary condition and does not impose a permanent reduction in value. Accordingly, the analyst would base the appropriate damages calculation on an analysis of the time value of the funds that were unavailable to the prospective seller during the extended marketing period.

(iv) Media Coverage Analysis.   In evaluating quantitative measures of possible effects on residential property value, one should consider how much the transaction participants know or knew of the existence and potential severity of the environmental condition. Optimally, the analyst would evaluate transaction data in the context of what was known by, or communicated between, buyers and sellers. The analyst rarely, if ever, can obtain such information, however. This holds true particularly when the defendant in a property damage case has retained the analyst and the plaintiffs are the same local homeowners who would possess this information, so that information received would be subject to bias.

Identifying the appropriate date of impact for comparing before-and-after market conditions presents another hurdle in evaluating residential property value diminution. One can easily identify such a date for catastrophic events, such as oil or chemical spills, which tend to receive extensive and immediate public attention. At the other extreme, some environmental conditions develop over extended periods of time. Public disclosure and recognition of the condition can occur gradually over many years. In these situations, the analysis needs to impute degrees of awareness, based not on what specific buyers and sellers knew as of the date of a particular transaction, but rather on what *reasonably knowledgeable* buyers and sellers in the local market could or should have known about the condition as of a specific date.

Media coverage analysis (as Exhibit 27-3 demonstrates) presents an alternative to direct communication with buyers and sellers and offers an analytical tool that one can use to estimate the date of impact when no identifiable incident or triggering event occurs. This analysis evaluates media exposure of an event or condition over a given period of time. The summation and graphic display show data regarding the number of articles or the number of lines of print, published in relevant local newspapers. Properly applied, media analysis can enable the analyst to draw inferences concerning date of impact and the degree of market recognition of a contamination event or issue.

(f) Summary.   Although one cannot imagine people preferring, for example, a home next to a nuclear power plant that has had a serious accident (other things being equal), the empirical record shows that residential property values around the Three Mile Island Nuclear Station returned to their preaccident levels within two months following the accident.[10] Kinnard and others have documented similar findings with respect to pipelines and electric transmission lines.[11] The literature reports other cases of significant contamination and the resulting effects on property values.[12] Clearly, one cannot evaluate *a priori* the effect of contamination on residential property values, rather, one must evaluate the effect for each case in light of evidence derived from actual market transactions.

27.4   NONSTATISTICAL MEASURES OF DAMAGES FOR RESIDENTIAL PROPERTY

The appraiser can often strengthen residential property value diminution analysis, which draws primarily from statistical and other quantitative methods, by

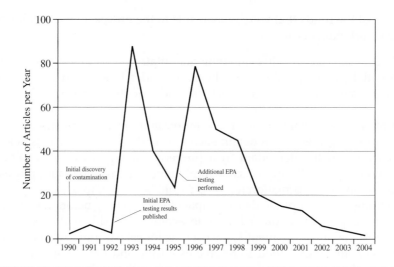

Exhibit 27-3.   Media Analysis Articles by Year

applying qualitative indicators of buyer and seller behavior. This section discusses some of these methods.

(a) Structured Market Participant Interviews.   Interviewing market participants—buyers, sellers, brokers, lenders, and investors—often proves integral to real estate valuation. These interviews can help the analyst frame the questions that need analysis and corroborate or test results obtained through quantitative measures.

The appraiser could use market participant interviews to address issues such as the following:

- Discerning the hierarchy of local market preferences for certain housing characteristics (such as number of bedrooms and lot size)
- Discerning the hierarchy of local market preferences for certain location characteristics (such as proximity to schools and access to public transportation)
- Providing insight regarding the importance or ranking of environmental conditions and influences in the hierarchy of home purchase decision-making criteria

Market participant interviews differ from opinion surveys that analysts use to draw statistically valid conclusions. One must avoid using qualitative interviews as a basis for drawing quantitative conclusions, although analysts can and do use established opinion survey research techniques to develop statistically valid results. Their application lies outside the scope of this chapter.

(b) Retrospective Appraisal Methods.   Although market participant interviews can provide some limited insight into the relative importance of a contamination issue, the appraiser must evaluate and answer questions of whether and to what extent damages have been incurred in the context of market transaction data.

One method of evaluating whether an environmental condition has affected home sale prices compares actual sales prices with what they should have been but for the effect of the condition (i.e., unimpaired value). Retrospective appraisals are one tool to accomplish this. The analyst estimates unimpaired value on the basis of comparable sales transactions occurring outside the potential area of influence. We summarize the method below:

1. **Subject area**[13] **identification.** Evaluate the geographic extent of the potential effect of the environmental condition or event in question. A competent geotechnical specialist or hydrogeologist typically provides the scientific analysis serving as the basis for identification.

2. **Control area identification.** Evaluate nearby residential subdivisions, neighborhoods, or submarket areas for similarity to the subject area in terms of supply and demand characteristics and location attributes other than the environmental condition affecting the subject area.

3. **Identification of subject area sales.** Identify sales of residential properties located within the subject area and occurring after the local market's recognition of the specified event.

4. **Identification and selection of control area sales.** Identify sales of residential properties located within the control area that have features consistent with and comparable to the subject area sale properties to be appraised.

5. **Appraise the subject area sale properties.** Appraise each of the subject area properties, as of their respective dates of sale, on the basis of comparable sales located within the control area. This indicates unimpaired market value as of the date of sale.[14]

6. **Compare the actual sale prices with the values indicated by the appraisals.**

The reliability of the results produced by retrospective appraisal analysis depends largely on the appropriate selection of the control area neighborhood. Although the analyst does not need to select an area with precisely the same supply and demand characteristics as those of the subject area (such combinations rarely exist), one must identify and adjust for any significant differences between the two. The analyst should also specify the basis for quantifying any such adjustments, which, to the extent possible, one should base on both empirical market data as well as local real estate market knowledge and appraisal expertise. When applying the retrospective appraisal process, one must avoid bias in the selection of sale transactions drawn from within the control area.

(c) Interpreting the Results.   As with many forms of residential property value diminution analyses, retrospective appraisals test for differential treatment by market participants—treatment that manifests in a reduction in value, or a discount to market value, in the unimpaired state.

In comparing actual sale prices with the appraised values, a positive deviation indicates that the sale price exceeded the expected value, and a negative deviation indicates that the sale price was below the value indicated by the retrospective appraisal. If an adverse effect associated with environmental contamination does exist, then one would anticipate a predominance of negative deviations for the sales analyzed.

Sale No.	Subject Property Address	Sale Date	Max. Concentration (ppm)	Possible Future Remed. Required	Contamination Disclosed to Buyer	Actual Sale Price	Retrospectively Appraised Value	Nominal Difference	Percent Difference
1	1 Rolling View Drive	05/22/00	110.00	Yes	No	$112,000	$107,000	$5,000	4.46%
2	44–46 West Central Avenue	07/22/00	6.40	No	No	116,000	129,000	(13,000)	(11.21%)
3	15 Cedar Hollow Road	12/01/00	8.40	No	Yes	117,000	108,000	9,000	7.69%
4	277 West Central Avenue	02/22/01	430.00	Yes	Yes	114,000	122,000	(8,000)	(7.02%)
5	8 West Central Avenue	08/10/01	8.50	No	Yes	75,000	79,000	(4,000)	(5.33%)
6	108 North Valley Road	04/04/02	1.50	No	Yes	152,500	145,000	7,500	4.92%
7	277 West Central Avenue	10/04/02	430.00	Yes	Yes	124,900	128,000	(3,100)	(2.48%)
8	34 West Central Avenue	03/13/03	4.00	No	N/AV	127,000	126,000	1,000	0.79%
9	6 Rolling View Drive	10/01/03	9.09	No	Yes	130,000	127,000	3,000	2.31%
10	279 West Central Avenue	02/06/04	180.00	Yes	Yes	125,500	126,000	(500)	(0.40%)

Exhibit 27-4. Subject Property Sales and Retrospective Appraisal Summary, Ten Selected Transactions

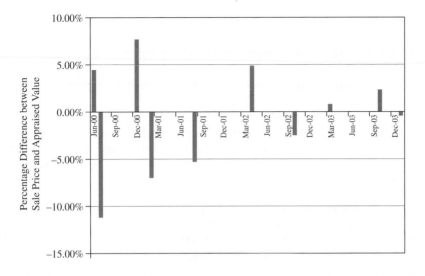

Exhibit 27-5.   Difference between Sale Price and Retrospectively Appraised Value, Ten Selected Transactions

Exhibit 27-4 summarizes the results of retrospective appraisal analysis applied to ten properties affected by heavy metal contamination associated with an adjacent Superfund site. All ten transactions occurred after the EPA initiated an emergency response action, and media coverage of the contamination was widespread for several years after the initial discovery and response action.

Exhibit 27-5 illustrates the difference between the actual or anticipated sale prices of the subjects and the retrospectively appraised values. Both exhibits show the differences chronologically by sale date.

In this example, negative deviations do not predominate. To the contrary, an equal number of sales occurred at a price exceeding appraised value as those that occurred at a price below appraised value. Detailed analysis of the transactions failed to indicate any single characteristic, common to either the positive or negative deviation sales, which would suggest a systematic pricing differential.

27.5   EVALUATING AND QUANTIFYING DAMAGES FOR INCOME PROPERTY

(a) Conceptual Framework.   One can state the critical steps in evaluating damages in simple questions:

- What is the problem?
- What needs to be done about it?
- Whose problem is it?
- Will the problem affect the use of the property?

This approach is consistent with the literature, published largely in *The Appraisal Journal*, of the past several years.[15] Articles by Peter Patchin outline the importance of remediation costs, indemnification, and stigma[16] in valuing contaminated property and show how one can adjust capitalization and yield rates to account for the effects of contamination on a property's mortgageability and marketability.[17] Articles by Bill Mundy[18] distinguish real and perceived risk as determinants of stigma and present a generalized theory of how the value of contaminated property changes over time.

Richard Neustein evaluated the extent that contamination can impair income-generating potential and how such impairment might require a risk premium to attract capital to a contaminated property.[19] Chalmers and Roehr presented a framework on how to quantify these considerations through the income property valuation process.[20]

(b) Direct Capitalization Method. Income property is real property that is developed, purchased, and sold on the basis of the quantity and quality of the income stream that it can generate. It includes property improved for office, industrial, retail, and lodging use and, in some instances, land or unimproved property with near-term development potential.

As with all income-producing assets, the value of income property is a function of the relation between the income produced by the property and a rate of return necessary to compensate an owner for the inherent risks of holding property.[21] Environmental hazards can influence both of these factors, and an impact on either one can influence value.

One can express the value equation for income property in its simplest form as $V = I/R$. That is, value (V) equals actual or anticipated yearly income (I) divided by an appropriate rate of return (R) that reflects the risks inherent in owning the property. This formula is known as *direct capitalization*. Analysts can apply it to all types of income property, but it is most reliable when applied to properties that are improved to their highest and best use[22] and operating at or near stabilized levels (i.e., rental rates, occupancy, and other operational characteristics reflect levels consistent with other competitive properties in the relevant market). Although simple in concept and application, and thus useful for first approximations, this method must be used judiciously, and with full understanding of the potential impact of the key simplifying assumption—a constant or continuously lognormally increasing income stream.

Consider the example in Exhibit 27-6. If one wanted to know the value of an apartment complex capable of generating net operating income (NOI)[23] of approximately $180,000 per year, and one could demonstrate that the overall rate of return[24] for apartment properties within the local area market was approximately nine percent, one might reasonably conclude that the market value of the property will equal approximately $2.0 million (= $180,000/.09 = $2,000,000).

Now assume that an environmental condition arose causing NOI to decline by $10,000 per year to $170,000. This might be caused by ongoing operation and maintenance costs associated with a groundwater treatment system. Holding the capitalization rate constant, one might conclude that value has declined by approximately $110,000 (= $2,000,000 value as if unimpaired, less $1,890,000 value as impaired).

Value Estimate as if Uncontaminated

	Net Operating Income (without Contamination Effects)	$ 180,000
	Overall Capitalization Rate (without Contamination Effects) ..	9.00%
	Unimpaired Value Estimate	$2,000,000

Property Value Diminution Due to NOI Reduction

	Net Operating Income (without Contamination Effects)	180,000
	Less: Annual Cost of Remediation	(10,000)
	Net Operating Income (with Contamination Effects)	170,000
	Overall Capitalization Rate (without Contamination Effects).	9.00%
	Impaired Value Estimate.	1,888,889
	Less: Unimpaired Value Estimate	(2,000,000)
	Property Value Diminution.	$ 111,111
	Rounded:.	$ 110,000

Exhibit 27-6.   Direct Capitalization Analysis, Property Value Diminution due to NOI Reduction

(c) Overall Capitalization Rate.   The rate of return applied in the direct capitalization method is the overall capitalization rate, which represents a weighted average total return to lenders and equity investors active in the financing and acquisition of similar properties. One can quantify incremental risk associated with environmental conditions by adjusting the overall capitalization rate to reflect any alternative loan and investment criteria that apply in light of the specified condition. If the condition evaluated in Exhibit 27-6 were to produce less attractive loan terms for a prospective buyer/borrower, or if an investor were to seek a higher rate of return based on incremental risk, the overall rate of return necessary to attract capital would increase, thereby reducing value further.

Appraisers apply adjustments to the overall capitalization rate via the band-of-investment technique, a weighted average formula expressed by the following:

$$R_o = (M \times R_m) + ((1 - M) \times R_e)$$

where

R_o = overall capitalization rate

M = loan-to-value ratio (proportion of debt financing available, relative to total property value)

$1-M$ = equity ratio (i.e., cash downpayment as percentage of property value)

R_m = mortgage constant (i.e., annual debt service as a percentage of total loan amount)

R_e = equity dividend rate (i.e., annual equity return as a percentage of total equity investment)

Assume that current terms for apartment property loans in a given market include loan amounts of up to 70 percent of acquisition price based on a 25-year term, payable monthly, and an interest rate of 8.5 percent per annum with no discount points. Assume further that investors in apartment properties seek an equity dividend rate, or annual cash-on-cash return, of 7.5 percent. These market-derived indicators would produce an overall capitalization rate of approximately 9.0 percent, calculated as follows:[25]

$$R_o = (M \times R_m) + ((1 - M) \times R_e)$$
$$R_o = (0.70 \times 0.0966) + ((1.00 - 0.70) \times 0.075)$$
$$R_o = (0.0676) + (0.0225)$$
$$R_o = 0.0901 \text{ or } 9.0\% \text{ (rounded)}$$

Now assume that the analyst has interviewed lenders and investors active in the local apartment market in an effort to discern whether a known environmental condition affecting the property being valued would cause them to change their loan terms or investment return requirements. These interviews produce strong evidence that the nature and extent of the environmental condition would not influence investor return requirements, but would cause lenders to adjust the offered interest rate by 50 basis points, from 8.5 percent to 9.0 percent. The corresponding effect on the overall capitalization rate increases it from 9.0 percent to 9.3 percent, producing a corresponding reduction in the value of property:

$$R_o = (M \times R_m) + ((1 - M) \times R_e)$$
$$R_o = (0.70 \times 1.1007) + ((1 - 0.70) \times 0.075)$$
$$R_o = (0.0705) + (0.0225)$$
$$R_o = 0.0930 \text{ or } 9.3\%$$

Exhibit 27-7 presents an example that uses a formula known as direct capitalization. Although owners and prospective buyers occasionally use direct capitalization as an indicator of value, they more commonly use or at least supplement it with other methods, such as discounted cash flow analysis.

(d) Discounted Cash Flow Method. Discounted cash flow (DCF) analysis is a method for evaluating anticipated future cash flows in terms of their present value. Whereas direct capitalization involves cash flows projected in perpetuity at a constant or constantly increasing amount, DCF analysis allows nonconstant cash

---

Net Operating Income (with contamination)	$ 170,000
Overall Capitalization Rate (with contamination)	9.3%
Impaired Value Estimate	$ 1,827,957
Less: Unimpaired Value Estimate	(2,000,000)
Property Value Diminution	$ 172,043
Rounded:	$ 170,000

Exhibit 27-7.   Direct Capitalization Analysis, Property Value Diminution Due to NOI Reduction and Increased Capitalization Rate

flows in future periods. The analysis discounts each of these periodic cash flows according to the number of periods hence when they occur.

DCF analysis is generally accepted in the real estate investment community, and prospective purchasers of multitenant income properties commonly use it as a pricing tool. The method has gained similar acceptance by, and recognition within, the real estate valuation profession. In the context of litigation, however, courts and jurors often view DCF analysis as inherently suspect because of the arguably speculative nature of estimating future cash flows. In some cases, valuation experts have had all or portions of their testimony excluded from evidence because they relied on, or included, DCF analysis in an income property valuation dispute.[26] Courts have demonstrated a general preference for reliance on comparable sale transactions, even when the sales comparison approach may not provide the most reliable indicator of value for the property type in question.

(e) Analysis of Income or Cash Flow Effects. Although DCF requires more complex calculations, it resembles direct capitalization in that they both enable the analyst to estimate value based on the relation of cash flow to a rate of return. If environmental conditions influence either component negatively, the value of the property will decrease. For example, certain portions of an office building or shopping center may be unavailable for occupancy for an extended period of time because of environmental remediation activities. Similarly, a development site may have a deed restriction, necessitated by environmental regulations, thus limiting the size or configuration of permissible improvements. The seller might pass remediation costs on to a willing buyer who may choose to fund the necessary expenditures through operating cash flows. The buyer may incur incremental property management costs in connection with implementation of the remedial strategy. Any of these factors can affect the amount of net cash flow that an income-producing property will generate—and when cash flow decreases, value decreases.

Factors to evaluate for potential effect on cash flow include the following:

- **Occupancy and rents.** Has the environmental condition influenced building occupancy or the rent that tenants will pay?

- **Operating expenses.** Does the existence or remediation of the environmental condition impose incremental operating costs on ownership? Such expenses might include tenant relocation costs, incremental utility charges, repairs and maintenance, insurance expenses, and management fees.

- **Capital expenditures.** Will the buyer need to fund capital expenditures associated with the remediation? Are postremediation structural or cosmetic repairs necessary?

(f) Analysis of Risk Effects. In DCF analysis, one discounts cash flows by a rate of return sufficient to attract both debt and equity capital. Analysts express that rate as an overall property yield, which resembles the overall capitalization rate but reflects other factors such as any anticipated appreciation in the value of the property over the analysis period, rental income and operating expense growth rates, the extent to which debt will be paid down during the anticipated holding period, and any significant depreciation that can influence the property's resale value at the end of the holding period.

		Value Estimate as if Uncontaminated				Value Estimate as if Contaminated		
Year	Cash Flow	Market Yield Rate	Present Value Factor	Present Value	Cash Flow	Adjusted Yield Rate	Present Value Factor	Present Value
1	$ 652,844	12.0%	0.89286	$ 582,896	$ 652,844	13.0%	0.88496	$ 577,738
2	678,958	12.0	0.79719	541,261	678,958	13.0	0.78315	531,724
3	706,116	12.0	0.71178	502,599	706,116	13.0	0.69305	489,374
4	734,361	12.0	0.63552	466,700	734,361	13.0	0.61332	450,397
5	763,735	12.0	0.56743	433,364	763,735	13.0	0.54276	414,525
6	794,285	12.0	0.50663	402,409	794,285	13.0	0.48032	381,510
7	826,056	12.0	0.45235	373,666	826,056	13.0	0.42506	351,124
8	859,098	12.0	0.40388	346,975	859,098	13.0	0.37616	323,158
9	893,462	12.0	0.36061	322,191	893,462	13.0	0.33288	297,420
10	10,796,333	12.0	0.32197	3,476,130	10,796,333	13.0	0.29459	3,180,474

Unimpaired Value Estimate (a)	$7,448,192	
Impaired Value Estimate (b)		$6,997,443
Property Value Diminution (a)−(b)		$ 450,749
Rounded:		$ 450,000

Exhibit 27-8. Discounted Cash Flow Analysis, Property Value Diminution due to Yield Rate Adjustment

Mortgage-equity analysis consists of several possible methods to estimate the appropriate yield rate to apply in discounting future cash flows. A detailed discussion of the appropriate methods for derivation and reconciliation of yield and discount rates appears in various published works.[27]

Exhibit 27-8 shows how one can apply DCF to the analysis of an income property that an environmental condition has allegedly affected. A prior owner will fund the costs of remediating the condition. Assume, however, that the overall required property yield has increased from 12 percent to 13 percent because of investor concerns regarding the risk of future environmental liability.

(g) Summary.   We summarize this section by describing the authors' experience in studying contaminated income properties. We start with the postclosure case: a property in regulatory compliance that requires no further action. Properties in regulatory compliance trade at no apparent discount provided that the parties have handled the closure competently; the contract or statute has identified the responsible party, who will continue in accountability for the historical problem; and no economically relevant restriction exists on the use of the property as a result of its current condition. In particular, the authors find no empirical support for the position that an environmental history necessarily implies a loss of value. This does not suggest that postclosure risk cannot occur. It certainly can, especially if the circumstances do not meet any of these assumptions. Such a conclusion would then require examination of site-specific facts.

At any time before closure, the critical question becomes whether, beyond direct costs, the contamination has affected the cost of capital available to the property in the market. In other words, does the contamination affect the cost or terms under which debt is available or the cost or terms of equity?

The availability of debt—that is, whether the property is mortgageable—becomes the threshold question here. If it has lost its mortgageability, the property's value will depend exclusively on the cost of equity. Further, the equity will be available only at a considerable premium to market rates for unimpaired property. The overall result is a substantial diminution in the value of the property. If the contamination has small and well-defined risks, however, the mortgageability can remain unchanged, and the equity investors may require a sufficiently small risk premium that the property value will show little or no effect from the contamination.

27.6 RECENT FEDERAL REGULATORY DEVELOPMENTS

In 2004, the U.S. Environmental Protection Agency (EPA) published two noteworthy announcements that might affect the real estate expert in quantifying damages of environmentally impaired properties. One concerns the rule on *All Appropriate Inquiry* (AAI); the other revises EPA's prior position on the effect of listing a property on the National Priorities List (NPL) of the Superfund program.

The Small Business Liability Relief and Revitalization Act (the Brownfields Amendments) of January 11, 2002 tasked the EPA with establishing standards for property owners to follow to qualify for Comprehensive Environmental Recovery, Cleanup and Liability Act (CERCLA) liability protection when acquiring potentially contaminated real estate. The AAI rule, which took effect in November 2006, summarizes these standards.[28] As part of the rule, a prospective purchaser must consider "the relationship of the purchase price to the fair market value of the property, if the property were not contaminated." The rule does not require that an appraisal be performed in order to establish fair market value.[29] The language of the rule does, however, suggest that EPA favors the sales comparison approach as a basis for comparing the purchase price with the fair market value of a property. Although the sales comparison approach is clearly an appraisal technique, the authors question its applicability in the contaminated property context. Adequate and reliable comparable sales data seldom exist for an environmentally impaired property, especially for commercial or industrial property. For this reason, the EPA's preference for one approach over another has little practical value. Experts must base the selection of a valuation method on property- and market-specific circumstances. Whether prospective purchasers can select and employ valuation methods in a manner sufficient to meet the requirements of AAI—outside the context of an appraisal—remains to be seen.

The second announcement concerns the EPA's stance on the impact of an NPL listing on the value of area property.[30] The EPA recently summarized the literature in this field and concluded that "evidence suggests that placing sites on the National Priorities List (NPL) of the Superfund program either has no effect on the prices of nearby homes, or may actually raise them." This differs from a prior EPA guidance document stating that a Superfund listing negatively affects property values.[31] We attribute this change in the EPA's position to the inclusion of more current research in its literature review.

NOTES

1. *Residential property* as used here denotes owner-occupied residences, typically single-family detached properties.

2. Sue Ann Adams and Trevor E. Phillips, "How to Use Comparable Sales to Value Contaminated Property," *Environmental Compliance & Litigation Strategy*, Part 1 of 2 (September 1997).

3. Hereafter, "premium (or discount)" is referred to as "premium" to avoid unnecessary repetition.

4. A plume is a space in air, water, or soil that contains pollutants released from a point source.

5. The R^2 of a regression equation indicates how much of the variation of the dependent variable (i.e., sale price) the independent variables explain. Most useful in linear regression, it is more difficult to interpret in multivariate regressions, particularly those with large numbers of variables. *See* Chapters 5 and 6.

6. The t-statistic quantifies the reliability of the calculation (i.e., determines whether the estimate is statistically significant). The most common threshold in the scientific community is the 95 percent confidence level, which requires a t-statistic (the ratio of the estimated coefficient to its standard error) of 1.96 or higher.

7. The mathematical formulation associated with such a hypothesis tests whether the coefficient associated with the environmental condition equals zero.

8. These hypotheses are just two examples selected from a wide range of possible hypotheses that could be tested in this instance. Hypothesis testing does not provide information about which hypothesis is more accurate or precise in quantifying the effect of the environmental condition on home values.

9. MLS, or Multiple Listing Service, is a subscription-based data entry and tracking system used by many local Realtor® boards across the United States to identify, describe, and list the availability and asking prices of residential and smaller commercial or industrial properties. It is typically available only to members of the local Board(s) of Realtors.®

10. The accident at the Three Mile Island nuclear power plant near Middletown, Pennsylvania, on March 28, 1979, has been characterized as the most serious incident at a nuclear power plant in the United States. The sequence of events led to a partial meltdown of the reactor core and cumulated in the off-site release of a small amount of radioactivity. The event, however, did not cause any deaths or injuries to plant workers or members of the nearby community. Comprehensive investigations and assessments by several well-respected organizations have concluded that in spite of serious damage to the reactor, most of the radiation was contained and that the actual release had negligible effects on the physical health of individuals or the environment. For more information on the TMI accident, *see*: http://www.nrc.gov/reading-rm/doc-collections/fact-sheets/3mile-isle.html. For a discussion of the impact on property values, *see* Jon P. Nelson, "Three Mile Island and Residential Property Values: Empirical Analysis and Policy Implications," *Land Economics* (August 1981): 363–372.

11. William N. Kinnard, Jr., Sue Ann Dickey, and Mary Beth Geckler, "Natural Gas Pipeline Impact on Residential Property Values: An Empirical Study of Two Market Areas," *Right of Way* (June/July 1997): 26–29 and William N. Kinnard, Jr., "Tower Lines and Residential Property Values," *The Appraisal Journal* (April 1967): 269–284.

12. Robert W. Hall, "The Causes of Loss in Value: A Case Study of a Contaminated Property," *Real Estate Issues* (April 1994): 23–27.

13. The subject area can be defined as a proposed class area, such as all properties located over a groundwater plume, or any other geographic area alleged to be affected by the environmental condition.

14. When performing retrospective appraisals outside the analyst's local market, it is necessary to engage the services of a competent local residential real estate appraiser who is knowledgeable in the local market dynamics of both the subject and control areas.

15. Richard J. Roddewig, ed., *Valuing Contaminated Properties: An Appraisal Institute Anthology* (The Appraisal Institute, 2002).

16. Peter J. Patchin, "Contaminated Properties: Stigma Revisited," *The Appraisal Journal* (April 1992): 167–172.

17. Peter J. Patchin, "Valuation of Contaminated Property," *The Appraisal Journal* (January 1988): 7–16.

18. Bill Mundy, "Stigma and Value," *The Appraisal Journal* (January 1992): 7–13 and Bill Mundy, "The Impact of Hazardous Materials on Property Value," *The Appraisal Journal* (April 1992): 155–162.

19. Richard A. Neustein, "Estimating Value Diminution by the Income Approach," *The Appraisal Journal* (April 1992): 283–287.

20. James A. Chalmers and Scott A. Roehr, "Issues in the Valuation of Contaminated Property," *The Appraisal Journal* (January 1993): 28–41.

21. The overall rate of return also takes into account that which is necessary to compensate lenders for the risks taken in loan underwriting.

22. *Highest and best use* is defined as "the reasonably probable and legal use of vacant land or improved property, which is physically possible, appropriately supported, financially feasible, and that results in the highest value." *Dictionary of Real Estate Appraisal*, 3rd ed. (Appraisal Institute, 1993), 171.

23. Net operating income is defined as periodic gross rental income, adjusted for vacancy and collection losses, less operating expenses, such as utilities, property management, property taxes, and the like.

24. The overall rate of return, also known as the overall capitalization rate, is effectively a weighted average cost of capital. It typically comprises returns to both debt and equity used in acquiring the property type in question.

25. The mortgage constant (R_m) is calculated as the periodic payment (annualized) required to amortize a loan with the stated term and interest rate.

26. *See*, for example, Memorandum of Decision, *Northeast Economic Alliance, Inc. v. ATC Partnership, et al.*, Superior Court of Connecticut (Case No. CV 940049248S), Sept. 14, 1999.

27. *See*, for example, James A. Chalmers and Thomas O. Jackson, "Risk Factors in the Appraisal of Contaminated Property," *The Appraisal Journal* (January 1996): 44–58.

28. http://www.epa.gov/brownfields/regneg.htm.

29. The rule does, however, acknowledge that an appraisal "may serve as an excellent source of information on the fair market value of the property."

30. http://www.epa.gov/superfund/programs/recycle/property.htm.

31. The prior EPA opinion was listed on the EPA Web site under http://www.epa.gov/superfund/programs/recycle/stigma.htm as of February 2000. However, the link is no longer active.

THE TROUBLED BUSINESS AND BANKRUPTCY

Grant W. Newton
Gil A. Miller

CONTENTS

The authors acknowledge Francis G. Conrad and Dominic DiNapoli, who authored "Bankruptcy Litigation," a chapter that appeared in the third edition of this Handbook. This fourth edition chapter includes material from that chapter.

28.1 INTRODUCTION

(a) A Challenging Area. Troubled business and bankruptcy engagements challenge the financial advisor who helps a failing business. Such engagements require knowledge of and experience in business management, auditing, and taxation. When reorganizing a business in a bankruptcy proceeding, financial advisors often perform the following tasks:

- Assist the debtor in analyzing operational problems, designing a turnaround strategy, and implementing the strategy.
- Provide organization and management evaluation
- Perform consulting activities (management advisory services) that provide information to help the debtor make decisions, including the development of a business plan.
- Assist the debtor in identifying the type of action to take to resolve its financial problems.
- Provide the debtor's counsel with the information needed to prepare the schedules, statement of affairs, and other forms necessary to file a petition.
- Prepare special financial statements, including a balance sheet as of the date the creditor voluntarily, or the debtors, file the petition.
- Provide the usual accounting services for the client, including data management and control services.
- Assist in preparing operating statements to file with the court.
- Perform special investigative services, including an analysis of selected transactions to ascertain whether preferences or fraudulent transfers exist. Section 28.3(y) of this chapter discusses these concepts.
- Reconcile and evaluate creditors' proofs of claims.

- Estimate the value of the business.
- Provide tax advice on several issues including the effect that debt discharge and the terms of the plan will have on the debtor's tax liability.
- Help the client create a plan that meets the approval of creditors and allows the debtor to operate the business successfully.
- Prepare the disclosure statement that the debtor must issue prior to or at the time that it solicits acceptance of the plan.
- Render other services, including assistance in finding sources of credit.

Each case can present problems that differ from those in a general accounting and tax practice. A fundamental premise of historical cost accounting undergirding generally accepted accounting principles (GAAP) is that of the going concern. A company approaching bankruptcy is no longer a going concern, so GAAP does not apply. This chapter explains how accountants and financial advisors can provide special services to a troubled business inside or outside the bankruptcy forum.

(b) Bankruptcy as a Specialty. Bankruptcy-related work has become a specialized profession. Bankruptcy has its own court system, laws, language, and fraternity. One must understand how to apply the Bankruptcy Code and speak the language of the bankruptcy laws before becoming a bankruptcy specialist. The term *specialist* does not reflect a designated title as a licensed specialist but rather refers to the individual who emphasizes and has experience in this practice area.

Those who desire to specialize in this practice area should consider becoming members of the Association of Insolvency and Restructuring Advisors (AIRA) and take advantage of its educational resources and certification program (CIRA).

(c) Bankruptcy Clients. Bankruptcies use financial advisors in a variety of roles. In out-of-court or bankruptcy cases, several different parties also retain financial advisors. In general, the same sources of retention in a bankruptcy case also exist in out-of-court cases except that no examiner role exists. In a nonbankruptcy case, financial advisors often render services for a court-appointed receiver (the analog to a bankruptcy trustee), or can themselves be appointed as the receiver. The following explains the financial advisor's role under the different roles of employment:

- **Debtor, debtor-in-possession, or trustee.** Debtors can retain a financial advisor that served them prior to the development of financial problems or filing the bankruptcy petition, or they can use a different financial advisor during a bankruptcy proceeding. A debtor cannot retain a prior financial advisor for work during bankruptcy unless the advisor forgives any outstanding fees. The debtor's estate pays fees for services rendered during bankruptcy. In both out-of-court and bankruptcy engagements, the financial advisor can help the debtor turn the business around, analyze the company's operations, develop a turnaround strategy, and assist in strategy implementation.
- **Unsecured creditors' committee.** In chapter 11 cases and in many out-of-court settlements, the court will appoint an unsecured creditors' committee that often needs a financial advisor's services. The debtor's estate pays the compensation for the financial advisor.

- **Other creditors' committee.** In large cases, the court appoints additional creditors committees, such as a separate committee for bond holders, various types of secured creditors, and so on. If the court authorizes the appointment of a committee, the debtor pays the cost of the professionals retained, including financial advisors.
- **Equity holders' committee.** In large cases, the court often appoints a committee of equity holders, and the debtor pays the cost of professionals.
- **Individual unsecured or secured creditor.** An individual creditor, secured or unsecured, can retain a financial advisor to evaluate the debtor's financial condition and to provide advice. The individual creditor pays the cost for these services. Under some conditions, however, the debtor pays these costs. In business turnarounds, out-of-court settlements, and bankruptcies, the secured lender retains an accountant or financial advisor.
- **Individual shareholder.** Individual equity holders retain a financial advisor to perform services similar to those listed above for individual creditors. The shareholder pays for these services.
- **Examiner.** The court can order the retention of a financial advisor for the examiner. The debtor's estate pays the fees for an examiner or for the examiner's financial advisor.
- **Trustee.** Financial advisors serve as trustees or as advisors to the trustees in chapter 7 and chapter 11 cases.

(d) A General Overview.   This chapter introduces this practice area and does not substitute for complete authoritative research of legal and taxation issues. More details appear in texts on the accounting and tax considerations in reorganization and bankruptcy proceedings. The bibliography includes a brief list of reference materials that provide additional information on the liquidation or reorganization of troubled businesses.

The Bankruptcy Code and Rules and Guidelines of the Office of the U.S. Trustee provide the essential tools. As with most laws, Congress often amends the Bankruptcy Code, thus requiring continuing education. Four major amendments have modified the Bankruptcy Code since it became law in 1979. The latest modification—Bankruptcy Abuse Prevention and Consumer Protection Act of 2005—became effective for all petitions filed after October 16, 2005. This chapter addresses issues related to chapter 7 (liquidation) and chapter 11 (reorganization) cases under the Bankruptcy Code (Title 11 of the U.S. Code) and includes the modifications made by the 2005 legislation.

28.2   THE BEST PLACE TO START

(a) When.   One can assist a troubled business best by preventing its failure. Accordingly, the optimal time to help occurs before the business petitions for bankruptcy. The bankruptcy system weighs the interest of the debtor, its creditors, and other parties in interest. This can require costly proceedings to establish the facts and appropriate action.

(b) Where.   Banks and other financial institutions often refer troubled companies to advisors prior to the filing of the petition. With such referrals, financial advisors work for either the debtor or the financial institution. Financial advisors should clarify with lenders that neither the bank nor the advisor has assumed management control of the bank customer.

Corporate or bankruptcy attorneys provide referrals in the insolvency/bankruptcy arena. The local bar association can provide the names of those specializing in this area. A business person facing financial difficulties often seeks an attorney's advice before consulting a financial advisor, probably because a lawsuit, or an Internal Revenue Service (IRS) notice, or concern for personal liability have revealed the financial problems.

(c) How.   Financial advisors who concentrate in troubled businesses function much like physicians. Accordingly, before financial advisors can cure an ill, they must first identify it. These steps will help start the process:

- Obtain samples of operating management financial reports.
- Obtain *detailed* financial reports for at least the last five years.
- Complete an internal control questionnaire.
- Obtain and compare industry operating ratios and statistics.
- Obtain information that will help them understand the structure (both legal and operational) of the business and its operations, including the following:
  - Management/organization charts
  - Operating locations
  - A brief description of all its business operations (e.g., the product, competition, major suppliers, customers, and distribution).
- Identify the major assets; ascertain their liquidation and market values; identify which assets the debtor has pledged as collateral for debts.
- Identify the business segments that provided most of the past profits and cash flow.
- Tour the facilities. Be observant and ask questions. Obtain a clear understanding of the business and its operations.
- Interview the management team members individually to ascertain their views of the problems and possible solutions.
- Obtain an aging of the receivables and payables.
- Obtain the terms of all leases, loans, and contracts payable.
- Ascertain the status of deposits for taxes with the IRS and state taxing authorities.

Some management groups cannot identify impending financial problems. The balance sheet, profit and loss statements, and income tax returns alone do not provide adequate information to manage most businesses. Information about operations—including quality of products or services, comparisons with industry, management capability and other aspects of the debtors business—will help in assessing the viability of the business. Detailed financial information, such as the use of aging reports of receivables, will identify potential cash flow problems.

(d) Recognizing the Characteristics.   Business failures have common characteristics. Consider the following typical profile: A person competent in an area of expertise, but with little capital or management experience, starts a business. The business prospers, but as it grows, it fails to grow in management depth. The owner/manager, confident because of earlier success, thinks that the company will continue to grow without additional specialized management help in areas such as marketing, production, accounting, and finance. The owner does not recognize that customers pay for goods and services more slowly than suppliers and vendors demand payment for their inputs. The more a business grows, the more cash it needs to cover the shortfall between payable and receivable dates. The business obtains a bank loan that becomes inadequate. The company enters high-risk transactions to appear successful. Management neglects accounting records and procedures. Excessive salaries and questionable perks (generally personal expenses) continue. The owner/manager has an eternal optimist's outlook. The company acquires new facilities and equipment. Management records questionable transactions and carries doubtful receivables with inadequate allowances for uncollectibles. Payroll taxes go unpaid, and the business must default on the bank loan. The business files a bankruptcy petition. The debtor blames the bank or suppliers because they would not increase the loan amount and extend its repayment terms.

28.3   BANKRUPTCY: AN OVERVIEW FROM BEGINNING TO END

(a) Alternatives Available to Troubled Businesses.   The business might first choose to locate new financing or to merge with another company. If neither of these appears possible, it can seek an arrangement with creditors, either informally (out of court) or through judicial proceedings.

(b) Out-of-Court Settlements.   The informal settlement presents an out-of-court agreement comprising some combination of a time extension (stretch-out), a *pro rata* cash payment for full settlement of claims (composition), and an issue of stock for debt.

The parties can require months, or even years, to develop an agreement that will provide the type of relief that the business needs. For example, International Harvester worked with its creditors for several years before finalizing its out-of-court plan. Such negotiations occur between the debtor's counsel, who should have experience in bankruptcy and workout situations, and the counsel who represents major creditors or committees of creditors. Success in any attempt to work out an agreement with creditors requires the cooperation of some of the largest creditors and those with the most influence over other creditors as soon as financial problems develop.

There are several reasons why debtors should meet with creditors as soon as the creditors realize that they need relief. First, the business still has a considerable asset base. Also, key employees tend to leave when they see unhealthy conditions developing; early corrective action can encourage them to stay. In addition, prompt action can make it possible for the company to maintain some goodwill developed during successful operating periods. Many troubled businesses take no action, and the creditors force the company to call an informal meeting or file a bankruptcy court petition.

(i) Informal Creditors' Committee.   To facilitate the company's work with creditors, the company selects an informal committee of creditors with input from the largest

creditors. Many out-of-court situations do not use an informal committee. No formal procedure exists for forming a committee. Ideally, the committee should comprise four or five of the largest creditors and one or two representatives from the smaller creditors. No legal rules exist for a committee's formation. Although smaller creditors often serve on committees, many committees include only large creditors, either because the small creditors lack interest or because the large creditors dominate. Conflicts of interest arise when creditors compete in the market.

The debtor's financial advisor and attorney should help the debtor prepare a suggested settlement plan to present and discuss with the creditors. No formal guidelines exist for the settlement plan. It can require a combination of a 100 percent payment over an extended time period, cash payments on a *pro rata* basis for full settlement of creditors' claims, and satisfaction of debt obligations with shares. A forecast of operations, based on realistic assumptions developed by the debtor with a financial advisor's assistance, can help creditors ascertain whether the debtor can perform under the plan's terms and operate successfully in the future.

Creditors will accept a plan only if they receive at least as much as they would receive in liquidation. The liquidation amount per dollar of claim equals the sum of a forced-sale value of assets, realizable accounts receivable, cash, and prepaid items *minus* priority claims, secured claims, and administration expenses, all *divided by* the total amount of unsecured claims.

The plan should dispose of all costs of administration, secured claims, and priority claims (i.e., wages and taxes that would be senior to unsecured creditors' interests in a bankruptcy setting) to protect the unsecured creditors. If the debtor's plan includes a cash down payment in full or partial settlement, the payment should at least equal the probable dividend the creditors would receive in chapter 7 bankruptcy liquidation.

A company (or its representatives) will often move from one creditor (or its representative) to another, rather than negotiate directly with a committee of the creditors, especially when an active creditor community does not exist. The business will negotiate first with the secured lender or the largest unsecured creditor or creditors to identify the type of settlement that the parties will accept and then meet individually with the other creditors that have claims similar in legal status, such as unsecured trade creditors and landlords. The company continues this process until the debtor obtains an agreement.

(ii) Advantages and Disadvantages. Today's environment encourages informal settlement for several reasons:

- The out-of-court settlement presents less disruption to a business that continues operation.
- The debtor can benefit from the advice of a committee, especially if some members have considerable business experience (preferably not in the same line of business).
- The informal settlement avoids invoking the Bankruptcy Code provisions and, as a result, can adopt more businesslike solutions.
- A settlement minimizes frustrations and delays by resolving problems informally without court hearings.
- The parties can usually reach an agreement much faster informally than in court proceedings.

- An out-of-court settlement usually costs less to administer than that of a formal reorganization.

Informal (sometimes called *composition*) settlements have the following weaknesses:

- A successful settlement plan requires substantially all creditors' approval, and some creditors will not accept a settlement calling for payment of less than 100 percent.
- A creditor can attack the debtor's assets while a settlement is pending. (If a creditor takes legal action, the debtor could file a bankruptcy petition.)
- The informal composition settlement does not provide a method to resolve individual disputes between the debtor and specific creditors.
- The parties can find executory contracts, especially leases, difficult to settle.
- Certain tax law provisions make filing a bankruptcy petition advantageous.
- The debtor must first pay priority debts owed to the United States under Rev. Stat. § 3466.

(c) Assignment for Benefit of Creditors.   Some states allow a debtor in serious financial difficulties to obtain an assignment for the benefit of creditors. In this procedure, the debtor voluntarily transfers title to its assets to an assignee, who then liquidates them and distributes the proceeds among the creditors. Assignment for the benefit of creditors, an extreme remedy, terminates the business. This informal liquidation device (court supervised in many states) requires that all creditors consent or at least agree to refrain from taking separate action, because appointing a custodian over the debtor's assets gives creditors the right to file an involuntary bankruptcy court petition.

(d) Bankruptcy Code Protection.   Bankruptcy court proceedings usually result when the debtor's financial condition precludes it from acquiring additional funds. When the debtor agrees to, or is forced into, bankruptcy court proceedings, the assets' liquidation value often equals only a fraction of the debtor's liabilities. If the debtor liquidates the business, the creditors receive only part of their claims. The court discharges the debtor from its debts and gives the debtor a fresh start. The parties have lost the business and all the assets, however. Liquidation proceedings result in large losses to the debtor, to the creditor, and also the business community. Chapter 7 of the Bankruptcy Code governs liquidation proceedings. The Code has another option that grants relief to the debtor for sufficient time to negotiate agreements with creditors. Chapters 11, 12, and 13 of the Code govern this procedure, referred to as *reorganization cases.*

(e) The Bankruptcy Code and the Bankruptcy Court.   The bankruptcy law appears in Title 11 of the U.S. Code, which has nine chapters:

Chapter 1	General provisions
Chapter 3	Case administration
Chapter 5	Creditors, the debtor, and the estate
Chapter 7	Liquidation
Chapter 9	Adjustment of debts of a municipality

Chapter 11   Reorganization

Chapter 12   Adjustment of debts of a family farmer with regular income

Chapter 13   Adjustment of debts of an individual with regular income

Chapter 15   Ancillary and other cross-border cases.

Chapters 1, 3, and 5 apply to all proceedings under the Code except chapter 9, to which only specified sections of chapters 1, 3, and 5 apply. The term *Title 11 case* refers to any case under the Bankruptcy Code's chapters 7, 9, 11, 12, 13, and 15.

(i) Bankruptcy Courts.   The Bankruptcy Reform Act of 1978 established a bankruptcy court ("the court") in each judicial district with jurisdiction to decide almost any bankruptcy-related matter. This jurisdiction included not only the traditional case matters (e.g., objections to discharge or claim) but also affirmative actions against third parties (e.g., the recovery of preferential transfers or fraudulent transfer actions). The original act also granted the court jurisdiction to hear matters related to antitrust claims, personal injury claims, wrongful death claims, and any other matter related to the bankruptcy case. A Supreme Court decision, temporary rules, and 1984 amendments, however, restricted this authority to settle all case-related claims.

The Bankruptcy Amendments and Federal Judgeship Act of 1984 provide that a bankruptcy judge can hear and decide all cases and all core proceedings arising in a case that the district court refers to the bankruptcy court. The 1984 act defines *core proceedings* to include the following:

- Matters concerning administration of the estate
- Allowance or disallowance of claims and determination of exemption claims; counterclaims by the estate against persons filing claims
- Orders related to obtaining credit
- Orders related to turnover of the estate's property
- Proceedings to identify or avoid or recover preferences
- Motions to terminate or modify the automatic stay
- Proceedings to identify or avoid or recover fraudulent conveyances; assessing the ability to discharge debts
- Objections to discharge
- Identification of validity, extent, or priority of liens
- Confirmation of plans
- Orders approving the use or lease of property, including the use of cash collateral
- Orders approving the sale of the estate's property
- Other proceedings that affect an estate's liquidation, or the adjustment, of the debtor-creditor or the equity-security holder relation; exceptions are personal injury tort or wrongful death claims heard in the district court where the bankruptcy case is pending or where the claim arose, as determined by the district court where the bankruptcy case is pending

(ii) Office of the United States Trustee.   The Office of the U.S. Trustee is part of the U.S. Department of Justice. It consists of 21 judicial regions, each having one or more

federal districts and headed by a U.S. trustee for that region except the federal districts in the states of Alabama and North Carolina. An administrator within the bankruptcy court handles the functions of a trustee in these two states.

The U.S. trustee has the following duties:

- To monitor applications for compensation and reimbursement for trustees, financial advisors, attorneys, and other professionals filed under § 330 of Title 11 and, whenever the U.S. trustee deems it appropriate, to file comments with the court with respect to any such applications
- To appoint the creditors' committee
- To monitor plans and disclosure statements filed in cases under chapter 11 and file comments regarding such documents
- To monitor plans filed under chapters 12 and 13 and make appropriate comments
- To ensure that the debtor files all required reports, schedules, and fees properly and in a timely fashion
- To monitor creditors' committees under chapter 11
- To notify the U.S. attorney of matters that relate to the occurrence of any action that can constitute a crime under the laws of the United States and, at the request of the U.S. attorney, assist the U.S. attorney in carrying out prosecutions based on such action
- To monitor the progress of cases under Title 11 and take action to prevent undue delay
- To monitor requests for employment of professionals (including financial advisors and attorneys) and, when appropriate, file comments with respect to approval of such requests
- To perform other duties prescribed by the attorney general
- To establish, maintain, and supervise a panel of private trustees who have the eligibility and availability to serve as trustee in chapter 7 cases
- To appoint a trustee or examiner in chapter 11 cases when the bankruptcy court authorizes such appointment
- To move for the appointment of a trustee if reasonable grounds exist to suspect that the current members of the governing body of the debtor, the debtor's chief executive or chief financial officer, or members of the governing body who selected the debtor's chief executive or chief financial officer, participated in fraud, dishonesty, or criminal conduct in the management of the debtor or the debtor's public financial reporting

Litigating parties should serve the U.S. trustee with all case pleadings and other documents filed with the bankruptcy court.

(iii) Chapter Selection.   The Bankruptcy Code consists of five chapters, excluding cross-border filings, under which a party can file a petition. An individual can file under any of chapters 7, 11, 12, and 13. A partnership or corporation can file under any of chapters 7, 11, and 12. A municipality files under chapter 9. The following sections discuss the general provisions of chapters 7, 11, 12, and 13. One can use chapter 15 for cross-border filings.

(iv) Chapter 7: Liquidation. Chapter 7 addresses the liquidation of a debtor. It provides for a trustee's appointment, liquidation of the business, the estate's distribution to the creditors, and discharge of the debtor from liability. All persons and entities can file a petition under chapter 7, except railroads, domestic insurance companies, banks (including savings and loan associations, building and loan associations, and credit unions), and foreign insurance companies and banks engaged in the insurance and banking business in the United States. Although farmers and nonprofit corporations can file voluntary petitions, their creditors cannot bring them involuntarily into the bankruptcy court.

The person filing voluntarily need not be insolvent as defined by the Bankruptcy Code (fair value of assets exceed liabilities) or in the equity sense (book value of assets exceed liabilities); the petitioner must simply have debts. As soon as the court grants an order for relief (the court order that officially commences a bankruptcy case), the U.S. trustee will appoint a disinterested person from a panel of private trustees to serve as the interim trustee. The U.S. trustee can also appoint as interim trustee a person serving as trustee in an involuntary case prior to the order for relief. In accordance with the Bankruptcy Abuse Prevention and Consumer Protection Act of 2005, the bankruptcy court will dismiss a chapter 7 filing by an individual that the trustee identifies as an abuse unless the individual converted the petition to chapter 11 or 13.

A creditors' meeting called under § 341(a) can elect a trustee if at least 20 percent of the dollar amount of the qualifying claims request an election. For voting eligibility, creditors must hold an allowable, undisputed, fixed, liquidated, unsecured claim, cannot have an interest materially adverse to other creditors' interest, and cannot be insiders (i.e., relatives of individual debtors and directors, officers, and persons-in-control of corporate debtors). To elect a trustee, holders of at least 20 percent of the qualifying claims must vote, and the candidate must be elected by a majority (evaluated by the dollar amount of the claims) of those voting. If creditors do not elect a trustee, the interim trustee will serve as trustee. Typically, creditors do not elect a trustee, and the interim trustee continues.

In addition to voting for a trustee, the creditors can also elect a committee of creditors. Each eligible committee member must hold an allowable unsecured claim. The committee will consult with the trustee regarding the estate's administration, make recommendations to the trustee regarding the performance of his or her duties, and submit to the court any questions affecting the estate's administration. Unlike chapter 11 cases, in which the U.S. trustee appoints creditors' committees, a creditors' committee will not serve in a chapter 7 liquidation unless the creditors elect one, a rare occurrence in chapter 7.

Section 723(a) provides that if a partnership's property cannot fully satisfy the claims of the partnership and if a general partner has personal liability, a claim exists against the general partner for the entire deficiency. According to § 723(b), the trustee must seek recovery first from the general partners who are not debtors in a bankruptcy case. The court can order the general partners to provide assurance of payment of the partnership deficiency or can order general partners not to dispose of their property.

The trustee can, with court approval, operate the business for a short time if this will increase the amount available to creditors. After the trustee has liquidated the estate and satisfied the secured claims to the extent allowed, the trustee shall distribute the remaining amount to the claim holders in a specified order. Unless § 510 subordinates a claim, § 726(a) distributes the balance in the following order:

1. Priority claims as set forth in § 507
2. General unsecured claims with a proof of claim filed on time or with such proof filed late because of lack of notice or knowledge of the case
3. General unsecured claims filed late
4. Allowed secured or unsecured claims, not compensation for actual pecuniary losses, for fines, penalties, forfeitures, or damages suffered by the claim holder
5. Interest on the preceding claims at the legal rate from the date of filing the petition
6. Any balance to the debtor

Bankruptcy Code § 726(b) provides for claims within a particular classification that will receive payment on a *pro rata* basis when the funds do not fully satisfy all the claims of a particular classification. This policy has one exception: if the debtor does not have the funds to pay all administrative expenses and part of the administrative expenses related to a chapter 11, 12, or 13 case prior to conversion to chapter 7, then the trustee will first pay those administrative expenses incurred in chapter 7 after conversion. Thus, professionals cannot receive all their fees in a chapter 11 case if funds prove insufficient for all administrative expenses in a subsequent chapter 7. After the trustee has liquidated assets and distributed the proceeds in proper order, the trustee will make a final report and file a final account of the estate's administration with the court. The court will then discharge the trustee from further responsibility.

(v) SIPC Liquidation.   Shareholder liquidation often requires accounting services. The Securities Investor Protection Act of 1970, as amended, and § 741 through § 752 of chapter 7 of the Bankruptcy Code govern a stockbroker or stock dealer liquidation. The Securities Investor Protection Corporation (SIPC) has responsibility for liquidating a troubled stockbroker. The membership of SIPC—a nonprofit corporation—consists of all persons registered as brokers or dealers under § 15(b) of the Securities Exchange Act of 1934. Through an annual assessment from its members, SIPC establishes a fund to cover the costs to customers of a stockbroker's liquidation.

(vi) Chapter 11: Reorganization.   Chapter 11 provides the debtor with court protection, allows the debtor (or trustee) to continue operating the business while developing a plan, and reduces the economic losses associated with liquidation. Chapter 11 allows the debtor to use different procedures depending on the nature of the debtor's problems and the creditors' needs. Agreements under this chapter can affect unsecured creditors, secured creditors, and shareholders. Parties can file either a voluntary or an involuntary petition under chapter 11. Once a creditor has filed the involuntary petition, the court can, at the request of a party in interest, appoint a trustee. The appointment is not mandatory, and the debtor can continue to operate the business as though no bankruptcy petition exists, except that the debtor can avoid certain transactions under the Bankruptcy Code. If the

creditors prove the petition's allegations, the court enters an order for relief, and the case proceeds in a manner identical to a voluntary case. The Bankruptcy Code provides that the U.S. trustee will appoint a creditors' committee in a chapter 11 case. Chapter 11 proceedings include assessing whether the trustee can reorganize the business (or part of it). If the court decides reorganization will not work, then it can order direct sale or liquidation of the business, in which case the debtor can propose a plan to liquidate the business without converting the proceedings to chapter 7.

In chapter 11, the debtor will continue operating the business unless a party in interest requests that the court appoint a trustee for specific grounds, although this is unusual. More typically, the debtor continues operating the business as debtor-in-possession.

When the debtor-in-possession operates the business, it has 120 days after the order for relief to file a plan of reorganization and 180 days after the order for relief to obtain acceptance before other parties can file a plan. Courts sometimes refer to this as the *plan exclusivity period,* and the court can, and often does, extend these deadlines. However, the court can extend the plan exclusivity period for no more than 18 months and the time period to obtain acceptance for no more than 20 months. After the creditors and the equity holders have approved the plan, the court will hold a hearing to confirm the plan and discharge the debts for which the plan does not provide.

A party cannot solicit a plan's acceptance or rejection from the affected creditors and shareholders unless they receive a written court-approved disclosure statement. Section 1125(b) of the Bankruptcy Code requires that the debtor provide this disclosure statement before or concurrent with the solicitation. After notice and hearing, the court must decide whether the disclosure statement contains adequate information.

(vii) Prepackaged and Prenegotiated Chapter 11 Plans. Before filing a chapter 11 plan, some debtors develop a plan, often called a *prepackaged plan,* and obtain approval of the plan by all impaired claims and interests. The court can accept this vote, provided that the debtor complied with all applicable laws (not only bankruptcy laws) governing the adequacy of disclosure when soliciting the acceptance (or rejection). If no nonbankruptcy laws apply, then the solicitation must have occurred after or at the time that the holder received adequate information, as § 1125 of the Bankruptcy Code requires.

Because the costs of a traditional chapter 11 bankruptcy exceed the professional fees and other costs of a prepackaged plan (including the cost of disrupting the business), a prepackaged or prenegotiated bankruptcy can offer the better alternative.

Rather than filing a prepackaged chapter 11 plan, many companies elect to file a prenegotiated chapter 11 petition. This differs from a prepackaged plan in that the company solicits the plan's acceptance after, not with, the filing of the petition. Thus, companies need not file statements with the Securities and Exchange Commission (SEC) because the solicitation occurs after filing the petition. The number of chapter 11 petitions that have been filed in which the major creditors and the debtor have agreed to the terms of a plan before the petition is filed has increased in recent years. In addition to working with the creditors to develop a plan, the debtor—often through financial advisors and workout specialists—addresses any operating problems. When filing the petition, the debtor can also file a disclosure statement and a chapter 11 plan and request a hearing date for the approval of the disclosure statement. The time that the debtor will remain in bankruptcy will depend on several factors, including whether a majority of creditors support the debtor's plan, the progress of the operational turnaround, and whether new issues arise in the case. However, companies that do not need to address operating issues in chapter 11 can complete the solicitation, voting, and confirmation process in a few months.

A debtor often prefers a chapter 11 plan to a nonbankruptcy workout for several reasons:

- The federal government taxes income from debt discharge in an out-of-court workout to the extent that the debtor is or becomes solvent. Although a bankruptcy case can reduce some tax attributes, the government does not tax the gain from debt discharged in a bankruptcy case.

- The debtor can preserve a larger percent of the net operating loss if it files a chapter 11 petition. For example, the provisions of § 382(l)(5) and § 382 (l)(6) of the Internal Revenue Code (IRC) dealing with net operating losses apply only to bankruptcy cases.

- Chapter 11 requires a smaller percentage of creditor approval: only two-thirds of the dollar amount of debt represented by those creditors voting and a majority in number in each class. For any out-of-court workout to succeed, however, the percentage accepting the plan must exceed these thresholds. For example, some bond indenture agreements provide that parties cannot make amendments unless all holders of debt approve the modifications. Because the debtor will not likely obtain 100 percent approval, the debtor will have to file a bankruptcy plan to reduce interest or modify the principal of the bonds.

(f) Commencement of Case.   A voluntary case begins when a debtor files a bankruptcy petition seeking an order for relief and places itself and its property under court supervision.

Creditors with aggregate unsecured claims of at least $12,300 can file an involuntary petition, which they can initiate only under chapter 7 or chapter 11. This amount will increase on April 1, 2007 and each three years thereafter to reflect the change in the Consumer Price Index for all Urban Consumers for the three-year period ending the previous December 31. If 12 or more creditors hold unsecured claims, at least 3 creditors must sign the petition; with fewer than 12, a single creditor suffices. The creditors can force the debtor into bankruptcy if either (1) the debtor fails to pay its debts as they become due; or (2) within 120 days prior to the petition, the court appointed a custodian, or a custodian took possession of all the debtor's property.

Creditors can force only nonfarmer individuals, partnerships, and for-profit corporations into bankruptcy. Creditors cannot file involuntary petitions against governmental units, estates, and trusts.

If the creditors can prove the allegations set forth in the involuntary petition (or the debtor fails to contest them promptly), the court will enter an order for relief, and the case will proceed. Otherwise, the court will dismiss the case.

To discourage creditors from filing unwarranted petitions, § 303(i) provides that the court can require the petitioners to cover the debtor's costs and reasonable attorney's fees and to compensate for any damages resulting from a trustee's taking possession of the debtor's property and, if filed in bad faith, for any damages—including punitive—resulting from the filing.

(g) The Automatic Stay.   A petition filed under the Bankruptcy Code results in an automatic stay of the creditors' actions and prohibits any party—with minor exceptions that include certain unsecured creditors and creditors with a security or adverse interest in the debtor's property—from interfering with the debtor or its property, regardless of the property's location, until the court has modified or removed the stay. The debtor or the trustee can use or sell or lease property (other than cash collateral) in the ordinary course of business without notice or hearing if the court has authorized the business to operate in a proceeding under any of chapters 7, 11, 12, and 13 and the court has not restricted the debtor's or trustee's powers in the order authorizing operation of the business.

Bankruptcy Code § 362(a) lists eight acts and conducts subject to the automatic stay:

1. The commencement or continuation of a judicial, or administrative, or other action or proceeding against the debtor, including the issuance or employment of process, that could have been commenced before the petition date or would be commenced to recover a claim that arose prior to the commencement of the case in the bankruptcy court

2. The enforcement against the debtor or against property of the estate of a judgment obtained before the commencement of the case

3. Any act to obtain possession of property of the estate to exercise control over the property of the estate

4. Any act to create, perfect, or enforce any lien against property of the estate

5. Any act to create, perfect, or enforce against property of the debtor any lien to the extent that such lien secures a claim that arose before the commencement of the case

6. Any act to collect, assess, or recover a claim against the debtor that arose before the commencement of the case

7. The setoff of any debt owing to the debtor that arose before the commencement of the case against any claim

8. The commencement or continuation of a proceeding before the United States Tax Court concerning a corporate debtor's tax liability that the bankruptcy court can determine (*see* § 505) and concerning an individual for a tax period ending before the petition was filed

The stay of an act against the estate's property continues, unless modified, until the estate no longer owns the property. The stay of any other act continues until the court closes or dismisses the case, or grants or denies a discharge to the debtor. The automatic stay does not apply against initiating or continuing a criminal action against the debtor; enforcing governmental police or regulatory powers; or actions by a tax authority to perform a tax audit, make demand for tax returns, and issue a notice and demand for payment for assessment and certain other actions.

Under § 362(d), the court can grant relief, after notice and hearing, by terminating, or annulling, or modifying, or conditioning the stay. The court can grant relief for cause, including the lack of adequate protection of the interest of a secured creditor seeking relief. The court can grant relief for an act against property under chapter 11 if the debtor has no equity in the property and an effective reorganization does not require the property.

For example, suppose that a creditor holds a first mortgage debt of $100,000 on real property owned by the debtor having a value, estimated by the creditor, of $75,000. The creditor will seek relief from the stay by claiming that the debtor has no equity in the property, or that the property lacks importance to the debtor's reorganization, or the infeasibility of reorganization, and that the court should allow foreclosure. The debtor can argue the opposite and claim that the value exceeds the mortgage debt.

(h) Cash Collateral.   Bankruptcy Code § 363(c)(2) requires the debtor-in-possession to receive the consent of the interested creditors or authorization from the court prior to using cash collateral.[1] Section 363(a) defines cash collateral as

> [c]ash, negotiable instruments, documents of title, securities, deposit accounts, or other cash equivalents whenever acquired in which the estate and an entity other than the estate have an interest and includes the proceeds, products, offspring, rents, or profits of property subject to a security interest as provided in § 552(b), whether existing before or after the commencement of a case under the Bankruptcy Code.

Thus, the cash received from the sale of inventory that the company pledged as security for a line of credit is cash collateral. Unless the court has granted an order under § 363(c), the debtor-in-possession must segregate cash collateral from the estate's other assets.

In practice, a debtor can often receive the consent of a creditor that has a security interest in accounts receivable by granting an interest in future accounts receivable. As the debtor collects receivables and makes payments to the creditor, new credit follows, thereby creating a revolving account. Often, the first order for debtor's use of cash collateral covers only a 7- to 14-day period. Subsequent orders can be for a longer period and in some cases continue as long as the company remains in chapter 11, unless the secured lender or a party in interest requests the court to cancel the order.

During the first few days of the case, creditors often restrict the use of cash collateral to the payment of immediate and necessary expenses, including payroll and payroll expenses. The secured creditor releasing the cash collateral usually requests it be used only to support its immediate operations.

(i) Debtor in Possession Financing.   Bankruptcy Code § 364 allows the debtor-in-possession to obtain necessary credit post petition with court approval. The court can give the creditor a super-priority, or secured, or junior-secured status if it cannot otherwise obtain credit on an unsecured basis. The debtor can obtain funds from the existing lenders or new lenders that specialize in making loans to chapter 11 debtors. If good relations exist when the case begins, a debtor will find it simpler to continue with the existing lender(s). The lender will often seek concessions, such as waiving prepetition claims against the bank, stipulating to the validity of its security interests, and cross-collateralizing prepetition debt with postpetition collateral.

(j) Adequate Protection (§ 361). When a creditor's security interest rests in an endangered, dissipating, or depreciating asset, the creditor can move the court for adequate protection and associated limited relief from the automatic stay.[2] Such a motion seeks to ensure maintenance of the *status quo* throughout the duration of the stay.[3] The court has broad discretion in the method it chooses to remedy adequate protection problems.

Even though a creditor can enter an adequate protection motion seeking to continue a foreclosure action or stop the debtor from granting an additional lien on the creditor's collateral, the court can provide an alternative remedy. The court can require the debtor-in-possession to make cash payments to a creditor in instances of decreasing collateral value or a security cushion that erodes as interest accrues. The court can also choose to grant relief from the stay to allow the creditor to seize assets in which the creditor holds a security interest. The court must balance the danger to the interests of the creditor against the necessity of the property to the debtor in the reorganization.

Three Bankruptcy Code sections discuss adequate protection:

1. Section 362 addresses the automatic stay: Unless the creditor's security interest has adequate protection, the court can remove the stay.[4]
2. Section 363 addresses the use, sale, or lease of property (including cash collateral) of the debtor: The court cannot approve the release of cash collateral until the court confirms that creditors have adequate protection.
3. Section 364 addresses new credit: When the debtor-in-possession cannot obtain postpetition financing on an unsecured or junior-secured basis, a creditor can obtain a new lien that primes prepetition liens, but the court must first decide whether credit is otherwise unavailable and that the holder of the previous lien has adequate protection.

Bankruptcy Code § 361 lists three ways to provide adequate protection:

1. Requiring the trustee or debtor-in-possession to make cash payments
2. Providing an additional or replacement lien
3. Granting such other relief, other than entitling such entity to an administrative expense, that will result in the realization by such entity of the indubitable equivalent of the entity's interest

The Bankruptcy Code does not define "indubitable equivalent" which often involves the substitution of one collateral by another of less value in the case of debtor-in-possession financing. The debtor must have the opportunity to realize the indubitable equivalent of the entity's interest in the property and not the value of the property. Thus, if the creditor has adequate protection, the debtor can then substitute less favorable collateral for the existing collateral.

The bankruptcy court can look at the equity cushion or analyze special risk factors when assessing whether the debtor has adequate protection in these cases. An equity cushion is the value in the property, above the amount owed to the secured creditor, that will shield that interest from loss owing to any decrease in the value of the property during the time the automatic stay is in effect.

Shortly after the Bankruptcy Code's enactment, many courts began to evaluate what amount constitutes an adequate equity cushion. The court in *In re McKilips*, 81 B.R. 545 (Bankr. N.D. Ill. 1987) analyzed prior cases and concluded that an equity cushion of less than 11 percent did not provide adequate protection; a range between 12 and 20 percent has divided the courts. Courts have assessed equity cushions that exceed 20 percent as sufficient.

Rather than focusing on the equity cushion to assess adequate protection, some courts have focused on actual or likely diminution in the value of the collateral during the time between the petition date and the confirmation of the plan.[5]

(k) Filing Schedules and the Statement of Affairs.   Bankruptcy Code § 521 requires schedules—a prescribed form for listing the debtor's assets and liabilities. The schedules list assets at market value and briefly describe each asset and its location. Although the schedules indicate that the amounts should record market values, companies—especially larger ones—commonly use historical cost values, properly indicating that the values reflect historical costs. The debtor reports each individual liability in defined classifications:

1. Creditors holding security
2. Creditors having priority (as defined by statute)
3. Creditors having unsecured claims without priority

For secured claims without priority, the schedules report the related collateral and its market value.

The schedules also note whether the debtor disputes the claim's status. The creditor can file an undisputed claim for the amount shown on the debtor's schedules. The schedule can also list claims as contingent, unmatured, and unliquidated. The Statement of Financial Affairs presents answers to a prescribed series of questions concerning the debtor, its business, its financial records, and other historical information.

The debtor files these reports with the bankruptcy court when filing the petition or shortly thereafter. They become the basis for inquiry by creditors, a trustee, and other parties in interest. The debtor's financial advisor often helps prepare these reports.

(l) Employment of Professionals.   In bankruptcy court proceedings, all professionals must, upon applying to the court, obtain an order that authorizes their engagement under § 327. The professional should obtain this order prior to commencing services. If the professional must start work before obtaining such an order, the professional must obtain it shortly thereafter with a *nunc pro tunc* (retroactive) status.

The court must authorize any engagement that will request payment from the bankruptcy estate; otherwise, it can reject any compensation requests even though the professional performed the services.

Engagements that require authorization include services such as financial advisor or expert witness for any of the debtor, trustee, and official creditors' committee; such engagements exclude services such as trustee or examiner where the court's order of appointment suffices. If a creditor or other parties in interest who engage a professional agree to pay for the services, the fee application process does not apply. The application for employment of professionals must disclose all former and current relations between the financial advisor and the debtor or any other parties, including other professionals involved.

Under § 330, professionals can collect fees for services only after the professional submits detailed applications and the court holds a noticed hearing. The fee applications contain more detail than required in other areas of professional practice. The fee application should describe specifically the service performed, the date it was performed, the time (sometimes in tenths of an hour), and charges involved. Each individual working on the engagement must provide descriptive and detailed time records. The court, the U.S. trustee's office, and all parties in interest can challenge the fee application. All compensation must appear reasonable for actual and necessary services rendered; the courts can regard inadequate time records as a basis for reducing or denying compensation.

(m) Debtor-in-Possession.   *Debtor-in-possession* refers to the management of a chapter 11 debtor that continues to control and operate the business. Under § 1107, management has a fiduciary responsibility that it must exercise with utmost care, placing the creditors' interest above the best interest of the shareholders. Many actions of a debtor-in-possession, as with those of a trustee, require the court's prior approval. Such actions include setting wages for key management personnel, hiring professionals, obtaining additional capital by way of loans or issuing new equity certificates, pledging assets, and selling assets (other than goods normally held for sale). Management should consult counsel before taking action in these matters. The Bankruptcy Abuse Protection and Consumer Protection Act of 2005[6] limits the extent to which the debtor-in-possession can use key employee retention plans.

(n) Creditors and Equity Security Holder Committees.   In chapter 11, the U.S. trustee appoints a committee of unsecured creditors soon after the court enters an order for relief. The court-appointed trustee can also appoint other creditor and equity security holder committees, although this usually occurs only in larger cases. The Bankruptcy Code provides that committees consist of the seven largest parties in each class who agree to serve. In larger cases, however, the number appointed to the committee exceeds seven. The 2005 amendments to the Bankruptcy Code also provided for an expansion of the committee to include selected creditors holding smaller claims. Under § 1103, the committees monitor the debtor's activities and serve as the primary negotiating bodies regarding the reorganization plan. The committee members must act in a fiduciary capacity to benefit all members in their class and not for their individual interest. The official committees can apply to the court for authority to engage professionals to assist them. This offers another opportunity for a financial advisor knowledgeable in bankruptcy proceedings to provide service.

Small cases often do not have committees because the U.S. trustee cannot find creditors willing to serve. An active committee can assist the debtor when a good working relation exists. This relation becomes important when the debtor seeks the acceptance of a proposed reorganization plan. Without support, the debtor can have difficulty obtaining a plan's acceptance. Open, truthful, and complete communications between the debtor and the committees help ensure success.

The creditor and equity security holders committee also must actively protect their own interests. All committees must see that adequate controls exist to ensure that the debtor's assets do not dissipate.

(o) Trustee and Examiner.   Under § 1104, the bankruptcy court can, after notice and hearing, authorize the appointment of a trustee for cause, which includes "fraud, dishonesty, incompetence, or gross mismanagement of the affairs of the debtor by current management, either before or after the commencement of the case, or similar cause if such appointment is in the interest of creditors, any equity security holders, and other interests of the estate." After the court has authorized appointment of the trustee, the U.S. trustee makes the appointment. If the court does not appoint a trustee, § 1104(c) states that the court can, upon request of a party in interest and after notice and hearing,

> order the appointment of an examiner to conduct such an investigation of the debtor as is appropriate, including an investigation of any allegations of fraud, dishonesty, incompetence, misconduct, mismanagement, or irregularity in the management of the affairs of the debtor of or by current or former management of the debtor.

The court can authorize the appointment of an examiner upon request if the court finds that such an appointment is in the best interests of any creditors, or equity security holders, or other interests of the debtor's bankruptcy estate, or if the unsecured liabilities exceed $5 million.

A court appointed trustee becomes the company's chief executive and, like a debtor-in-possession, must file operating reports and seek the court's approval for the sale of assets not in the ordinary course of business. According to § 1106, such trustees also have all the duties of a debtor-in-possession and investigate "the acts, assets, liabilities, and financial condition of the debtor, the operation of the debtors' business and the desirability of the continuance of such business, and any other matter relevant to the case or to the formulation of a plan [of reorganization]." Court appointed trustees also prepare a report of their investigation of the debtor's affairs and its current and past management.

An examiner often performs only an investigation and reports the findings. The court can, however, limit or expand these duties and has recently tended more toward expansion. The court can select a trustee or examiner from (1) a panel of people who devote most or all of their time to acting as trustees (listed by the U.S. trustee) or (2) other parties who possess particular expertise in business and financial management. Attorneys, accountants, and financial advisors often fill this role. After the court authorizes the appointment of a trustee in chapter 11, the creditors at a meeting of creditors under § 341 can elect a trustee in chapter 11.

Bankruptcy Code § 326 sets a trustee's compensation based on a percentage of monies disbursed, ranging from 25 percent on the first $5,000 to reasonable compensation not to exceed 3 percent of disbursements in excess of $1,000,000. The court can award less than the percentage formula because a trustee's compensation depends on the case facts and the trustee's ability. An examiner usually receives an hourly rate as established by the court.

(p) Accounting for the Debtor during Chapter 11.   In 1990, the American Institute of Certified Public Accountants (AICPA) issued Statement of Position (SOP)

No. 90-7, *Financial Reporting by Entities in Reorganization under the Bankruptcy Code,* the first major pronouncement issued on financial reporting by companies in bankruptcy. The SOP reduced the significant diversity in accounting for bankruptcies and increased the relevance of financial information provided to debtors, creditors, shareholders, and other interested parties who make decisions regarding the debtor's reorganization and plan. The SOP applies to financial reporting by companies that have filed chapter 11 petitions and expect to reorganize as going concerns and also to companies that emerge from chapter 11 under confirmed plans. It does not apply to companies that are restructuring their debt outside chapter 11 or to those that adopt chapter 11 plans of liquidation. It addresses how to report the activities of the chapter 11 company during the reorganization proceeding and how to report the emergence of the company from chapter 11.

Financial statements issued by the trustee or debtor-in-possession (the "debtor") in chapter 11 should reflect the debtor's financial evolution during the proceeding. Thus, financial statements issued after the filing date should distinguish between transactions and events directly associated with the reorganization and those related to the ongoing operations. Several significant areas of the financial statements reflect this principle.

(i) Balance Sheet.   Paragraphs 23 through 26 of SOP 90-7 provide specific guidance for preparing the balance sheet during the reorganization.

Liabilities subject to compromise (i.e., reduction) should appear separately from those that are not, and from postpetition liabilities. Liabilities subject to compromise include unsecured claims, undersecured claims, and fully secured claims that face impairment under a plan. Paragraph 23 of the SOP indicates that if some uncertainty exists as to whether a secured claim is undersecured or will be impaired under the plan, the balance sheet should include the entire amount with prepetition claims subject to compromise.

The balance sheet will initially report most prebankruptcy claims as liabilities subject to compromise. The collateral can remain unappraised while the trustee or examiner prepares the balance sheet. As the case progresses, actual cash flows from a property can exceed the amount estimated. Some security interests will not have been fully perfected (i.e., they do not meet all the legal notice and recording requirements for a fully enforceable security interest). Because of these and other factors, trustees often find that claims that appeared fully secured at the onset of a case become compromised during the proceedings. Paragraph 26 also indicates that circumstances arising during the reorganization can require a change in the classification of liabilities between those subject to compromise and those not subject to compromise.

The notes to the financial statements should disclose the principal categories of the claims subject to compromise (such as priority claims, trade debt, debentures, and institutional claims). The reporting requirement focuses on providing information about the nature of the claims rather than whether the claims are current or noncurrent.

Liabilities that cannot become subject to compromise consist of postpetition liabilities and liabilities not expected to be impaired under the plan. Debtors report them in the normal manner and thus should segregate them into current and noncurrent categories if debtors present a classified balance sheet.

Debtors should report liabilities that the plan will affect at the amount that they expect the court will allow, even though the debtors expect to settle the liabilities for a lesser amount. In other words, after debtors estimate the allowed amount of existing claims, debtors should adjust the carrying value of the debt to reflect that amount. Paragraph 25 provides that the debtor should view debt discounts or premiums as well as debt issue costs as valuations of the related debt. When the allowed claim differs from the debt's net carrying amount, one should adjust the discount or premium and deferred issue costs to the extent necessary to report the debt at the allowed amount of the claim. If these adjustments prove inadequate, then the debtor must adjust the debt's carrying value and report the gain or loss resulting from the entries to record these adjustments as a reorganization item, as SOP 90-7 explains.

The debtor should report prepetition claims that become known after the debtor files the petition, such as a claim arising from the rejection of a lease, on the basis of the expected amount of the allowed claim and not at an estimate of the settlement amount. Paragraph 48 of the SOP suggests that the debtor should report these claims at the amount that the court allows because it reflects the amount of the liability until it is settled and is consistent with the treatment of other prepetition liabilities.

FASB Statement No. 5, *Accounting for Contingencies,* applies to the process of measuring the expected amount of an allowed claim. Notes to the financial statements should disclose claims that are not subject to reasonable estimation based on the provisions of FASB Statement No. 5. After the debtor satisfies the accrual provisions of FASB Statement No. 5, the debtor should record claims.

(ii) Statement of Operations.   Financial reporting in chapter 11 cases focuses on presenting the results of operations of the reporting entity and clearly separating activities related to the normal operations of the business from those related to the reorganization. Thus, the debtor should separately report revenues, expenses (including professional fees), realized gains and losses, and provisions for losses resulting from the chapter 11 reorganization and restructuring of the business. According to Paragraph 27 of SOP No. 90-7, the debtor should report items related to the reorganization—except for the reporting of discontinued operations that the debtor must report separately—in a separate category within the income (loss) from operations section of the statement of operations. Appendix A in the SOP 90-7 contains an example of the form to use for operating statements issued during a chapter 11 case. The section of the operating statement that relates to the reporting of reorganization items is shown in Exhibit 28-1.

Note that the user can calculate the income generated from continuing operations without reflecting the effects of the reorganization in these totals. Although management will need to use judgment to decide which part of income relates to ongoing operations, a reasonable estimate of the segregation will benefit the reader more than including all items in the same category, as prior practice suggested.

A summary of the provisions relating to the operating statements follows:

- The statements report gains or losses as a result of restructuring or disposal of assets directly related to the reorganization as a reorganization item (unless the disposal meets the requirement for discontinued operations). The gains (or losses) include the gain (or loss) on disposal of the assets, related

Earnings before reorganization items and income tax benefits ..	$ 47

Reorganization Items:

Loss on disposal of facility	$ (60)
Professional fees	(50)
Provision for rejected executor contracts	(10)
Interest earned on accumulated cash resulting from Chapter 11 proceeding	1
	(119)
Loss before income tax benefit and discontinued operations . . .	$ (72)

Exhibit 28-1.   Example of Reorganization Items for an Operating Statement

employee costs, and other charges related to the disposal of assets or restructuring of operations. Note that reporting a reduction in business activity does not result in reclassification of revenues or expenses identified with the assets sold or abandoned, unless the statement classifies the transaction as a disposal of a business segment under the Financial Accounting Standards Board (FASB) Statement No. 144, *Accounting for the Impairment or Disposal of Long-Lived Assets.*

- The statements expense professional fees as incurred and reports them as a reorganization item.
- The statements classify interest income earned in chapter 11 that would not have been earned as a reorganization item, but for the proceeding.
- The statements report interest expense only to the extent that the debtor will pay it during the proceeding or that the court will allow it as a priority or secured or unsecured claim. The notes to the operating statement should reflect the extent to which the reported interest expense differs from the contractual rate; the SEC prefers, however, that the face of the operating statement show this information parenthetically.
- The statements show income from debt discharge as a reorganization item unless the debtor reports it as an extraordinary item in conformity with the Accounting Principles Board (APB) Opinion 30, *Reporting the Results of Operations,* as amended by FASB Statement No. 144. Paragraph 41 of the SOP indicates that debtors not qualified for fresh-start reporting should also follow this procedure.

(iii) Statement of Cash Flows.   Paragraph 31 of SOP 90-7 indicates that the statement of cash flows should separately disclose reorganization items within the operating, investing, and financing categories. The SOP prefers the direct method for reporting reorganization items related to operating cash flows and provides an example in Appendix A of SOP 90-7.

According to the SOP, if the statement uses the indirect method, it should disclose the details of the operating cash receipts and payments resulting from the reorganization in a supplementary schedule or in the notes to the financial statement. The note or supplementary schedule should include the information

Net loss

Adjustments to determine net cash provided		
by operations items before reorganization items		$ (118)
Depreciation	$ 20	
Loss on disposal of facility	60	
Provision for rejection of executory contracts	10	
Loss on discontinued operations	56	
Increase in postpetition liabilities and other liabilities . .	250	
Increase in accounts receivable	(180)	
Reorganization items	49	
Total adjustments		265
Net cash provided by operating activities before reorganization items		$ 147
Net cash before reorganization items		$ 147
Reorganization items:		
Interest received on cash accumulated because		
of the chapter 11 proceeding	$ 1	
Professional fees paid for services rendered		
in connection with the chapter 11 proceeding	(50)	
Net cash provided by reorganization items		(49)
Net cash provided by operating activities		$ 98

Exhibit 28-2.   Statement of Cash Flows

from the reorganization section of the statement of cash flows that appears in Appendix A of SOP 90-7. The debtor can reflect this information in the cash flow statement, as Exhibit 28-2 shows. The cash flow statement should also separately disclose any reorganization items included in financing and investing activities.

(q) Filing Operating Reports.   The court receives monthly operating reports that reflect the financial activities of the bankruptcy estate. The reports detail cash receipts, cash disbursements, and cash position data as well as other financial information in a format prescribed by the U.S. trustee. The operating reports provide the key information linkage between the debtor, the court, and the court-appointed committees (i.e., the official unsecured creditors committee).

(r) Liquidation versus Reorganization.   Should the debtor liquidate or try to reorganize? If the debtor did not analyze and answer that question before filing a petition for relief, it certainly demands top priority immediately after filing a petition.

As Section 28.3(k) of this chapter discusses, the Schedule of Assets and Liabilities initially filed with the court most often reports the debtor's assets at their market value, especially for smaller companies. The optimistic debtor overstates these alleged market values, hoping to reorganize.

Owners should weigh valuing the business as a going concern against selling the business or some of its assets. They often find part of the business marketable as a going concern, whereas the liquidation value of other portions exceeds or equals their value in use.

(s) Going Concern Valuation.   In developing the terms of a plan, one must estimate going concern values as well as liquidation values. Chapter 13 of this handbook describes the methods and the standards that one should use in calculating the value of a business. Financial experts use the same methods to calculate the value of a business reorganizing under chapter 11. One must make certain adjustments, however, which include the following:

- In using the income approach, the beta used for calculating the cost of capital under the Capital Asset Pricing Model (CAPM) must be determined from comparable company data because the company's historical and current (if any) beta is meaningless.
- In applying discounted cash flow analysis, one will need to adjust the cost of equity capital to reflect any additional risk associated with a business in or emerging from bankruptcy; under the market approach, earnings before interest and taxes (EBIT), earnings before interest, taxes, depreciation, and amortization (EBITDA) and similar multiples will require similar adjustment.
- Because of the difficulties in calculating "g" (growth factor in the Gordon growth model), some appraisers prefer to use a multiple, such as EBITDA, to calculate the terminal value rather than using the perpetuity method.*
- When using the market approach, one will need to adjust the debtor's historical earnings to remove the effects of the bankruptcy; alternatively, the debtor can use the earnings projections for the next year or so to allow time for the EDITDA, EBIT, and so on to return to normal.

(t) Other Valuation Needs.   In addition to calculating the value for the purpose of the plan, the proceeding requires valuation analysis for other reasons:

- **Adequate protection (§ 361).** As Section 23.4(j) of this chapter discusses, when a creditor's security interest lies in property that the debtor's actions endangers, depreciates, or dissipates, the creditor can move the court for adequate protection. The court needs valuations to calculate the value of the security interest and the extent to which the creditor needs adequate protection because of the potential decline in the collateral's value.
- **Claims determination.** Valuation is a central issue for several types of claims. For example, under § 506 of the Bankruptcy Code, the bankruptcy court will hold a hearing to identify the secured and unsecured portions of undersecured claims based on the value of the collateral.
- **Recovery action.** The trustee or debtor-in-possession can take action to recover assets based on preferences, fraudulent transfers, and requests for

---

Editors' Note: Common usage refers to the model as the *Gordon Growth Model;* although Myron Gordon did write about these methods in the 1950s, John Burr Williams had already described and used them in the 1930s.

reclamation. Because such actions are viable only if the debtor was insolvent at the time of the initial transfer, the court will need a valuation to perform the required solvency analysis.

- **Reasonably equivalent value.** To bring action under the constructive fraud guidelines,* one must show that the transfer reflects less than reasonably equivalent value. Thus, one needs a valuation of the item transferred, whether it is a single asset or an entire segment of a business.

- **Value of liabilities.** In ascertaining the insolvency of the debtor for purposes of § 547 and § 548, one does not always measure debt at its face value. If the creditor issued the debt at a discount, one values the debt at the initially issued price plus the amortization of the discount based on the effective interest method. For publicly traded debt, the Third Circuit[7] held that one should measure the debt at its face value and not its market value. Note the circularity involved here. The more likely the business is to default on its debt, the lower the market price of the debt. When valuing the claim for contingent debt, one must consider the probability that the court will consider the debt a claim.

(u) Abandonment of Bankruptcy Estate Property.   Bankruptcy Code § 554 provides for the abandonment of property of the bankruptcy estate property under specific conditions. This provision raises controversial issues best illustrated by an example.

Suppose the bankruptcy estate of an individual has real property with the following characteristics:

- A net tax basis of $100,000
- A current net realizable value after selling expenses of $500,000
- Secured debts against such property aggregating $475,000
- Nonessential to the reorganization of the debtor

This situation frequently occurs when the debtor acquired a property that increased in value; then the debtor liquidated that appreciation value by placing additional debt against it and used the additional loan proceeds for other purposes.

At first glance, the property's net realizable value of $500,000 exceeds the secured debt of $475,000 and thus has a pretax equity of $25,000. With a relatively low net tax basis of $100,000, the income tax liability resulting from the sale of this property can prove significant (assume $110,000 for purposes of illustration). This income tax liability is an administrative expense of the bankruptcy estate, thus taking priority over the general unsecured creditors and reducing their potential claims recovery by $85,000

Under these circumstances, the bankruptcy trustee should consider abandoning this property for abandonment back to the debtor, thereby removing this problem of negative net equity (after taxes) from the bankruptcy estate. Sometimes the

---

Editors' Note: Constructive fraud: when the circumstances show that someone's actions give him or her an unfair advantage over another by unfair means (i.e., lying or not telling a buyer about defects in a product), the court can decide from the methods used and the result that it should treat the situation as if fraud occurred even if all the technical elements of fraud have not been proved.

trustee can arrange other transactions to offset this taxable gain with a deductible loss. The combinations of transactions and their overall tax effects merit consideration, as discussed in Section 28.4 of this chapter.

(v) Proofs of Claims or Interests.   A creditor files a proof of claim. An equity security holder of a corporation or a partner in a partnership files a proof of interest.

The courts allow a properly filed claim, under § 502, unless a party in interest objects. If the debtor's schedules filed in a chapter 11 case list the creditor's claim or equity security holders' interest as undisputed and the creditor agrees to the amount and classification (i.e., secured versus unsecured), this presents *prima facie* evidence of the claim's or interest's validity. In such situations, the creditor or equity security holder need not file a proof of claim or interest. In a chapter 7 case, creditors must file a proof of claim. The courts can disallow claims only for specific reasons set forth in the Bankruptcy Code. A creditor filing a collateralized claim can have two classes of claim: a secured claim to the extent of the related equity (based on value) in the collateral, and an unsecured claim for the balance.

Claims administration provides another significant, but often overlooked, opportunity for the financial advisor to service a bankruptcy estate by combining computer and auditing skills with bankruptcy knowledge. Depending on the number of claims and interests involved, the parties often find such services essential. Such services include the following:

- Investigating claims and interests
- Comparing proofs of claims and interests filed with the debtor's books and records and the schedules
- Eliminating duplicate proofs of claims and interests
- Classifying secured versus unsecured claims, different equity security interests, reorganization plan classes, and other descriptive categories
- Calculating the voting results to accept or reject a reorganization plan
- Establishing amounts allowed, allowable, or disallowed
- Ascertaining amounts to be paid for securities (i.e., stock of a corporation) issued according to a reorganization plan
- Maintaining the claim and interests register and the master mailing list

Duplicate proofs of claim and interest and multiple classifications of a single proof of claim commonly occur. Before undertaking such tasks, the accountant or financial advisor should discuss materiality and the extent of investigation with the debtor, trustee, and the case attorney.

(w) Conversion or Dismissal of Bankruptcy Petition.   When a case converts from one chapter to another, § 348(a) provides that the conversion constitutes an order for relief under the new chapter; the petition's filing date, the commencement of the case, and the original relief order do not change. Conversion from one chapter to another terminates the services of any trustee or examiner serving at the time of conversion.

(i) Conversion from Chapter 7.   Bankruptcy Code § 706 allows the debtor to convert a case under chapter 7 to chapters 11, 12, or 13, provided the case was not previously converted to chapter 7. The court can also convert a case to chapter 11 after notice and a hearing, when a party in interest requests such action. Section 707 allows the

court to dismiss a chapter 7 case, after notice and a hearing for cause. Cause includes the debtor's unreasonable delay that is prejudicial to creditors, nonpayment of fees or charges, and failure to punctually file the necessary information and schedules as § 521 requires, but only if the U.S. trustee makes such a motion. The court on its own accord or at the U.S. trustee's request can also dismiss a chapter 7 petition consisting primarily of consumer debts if the granting of relief would abuse chapter 7 provisions. The debtor, rather than have the case dismissed because the filing can be an abuse under § 704, can convert the case to chapter 11 or 13.

(ii) Conversion from Chapter 11.   Bankruptcy Code § 1112 provides that the debtor can convert a case under chapter 11 to chapter 7 unless a trustee has been appointed, or the case commenced involuntarily, or the case converted to chapter 11 from another chapter and not at the debtor's request. A party in interest or the U.S. trustee can request the court to convert a chapter 11 case to chapter 7 or to dismiss the case (whichever lies in the estate's or the creditor's best interest) for cause, which includes the following:

- Continuing losses and absence of reasonable likelihood of rehabilitation
- Inability to implement a plan
- The debtor's unreasonable delay that is prejudicial to creditors
- Failure to propose a plan within the court-imposed deadline
- Denial of every proposed plan and denial of a request for more time to file or modify the plan
- Revocation of a confirmation order
- Inability to consummate a confirmed plan
- The debtor's material default of a confirmed plan
- The plan's termination owing to an occurrence specified in the plan
- Nonpayment of fees and charges

The court, on its own or at the U.S. trustee's request, can convert a chapter 11 case to chapter 7 or dismiss the case (according to the estate's or creditors' best interest) if the debtor fails to file the information and schedules that § 521 requires.

(x) Classification and Priorities Claims and Interests

(i) Classification.   Bankruptcy Code § 1122 classifies claims and interests by their nature, and all claims and interests placed into a particular class (i.e., a common group) must share similar characteristics. The claim's or interest's legal description usually governs its classification. For example, preferred shareholders and common shareholders have different rights and require separate classification. The court will separately classify creditors holding claims collateralized by different property.

(ii) Priorities.   Claims and interests usually receive a priority that does not alter their legal, equitable, and contractual rights. The priority status usually has the following order:

1. Collateralized claims to the extent that they are secured but only against the property pledged
2. Priority claims as defined (listed next)
3. Unsecured claims, including undersecured claims
4. Equity interests

Bankruptcy Code § 507 creates a special priority category of allowed expenses and claims in the following order of priority:

1. Allowed claims for domestic support obligations (debts to a spouse for alimony, maintenance, or child support)
2. Administrative expenses and costs of preserving the bankruptcy estate, including compensation for services rendered to the estate after the bankruptcy proceeding begins
3. Unsecured claims arising after creditors have filed an involuntary case but before the court enters an order for relief
4. Wages earned by individuals within 180 days before the filing date, not to exceed $10,000 per individual
5. Unsecured claims for contributions to an employee benefit plan related to services rendered within 180 days before the filing date, not to exceed $10,000 multiplied by the number of employees so covered, less:
    i. The aggregate amount paid under (4) and
    ii. The aggregate amount paid by the bankruptcy estate on behalf of the employees to any other benefit plan
6. Certain unsecured claims of farmers and fisherman, not to exceed $4,925 per individual
7. Unsecured claims of individuals arising from the deposit of money for the purchase, lease, or rent of property, or the purchase of services that were not delivered or provided; for personal, family, or household use; and not to exceed $2,225 per individual
8. The unsecured claims of governmental units, but only for the following:
    i. A tax measured by income or gross receipts for a taxable year ending on or before the petition's filing date and for which a return (if required) was last due (including extensions) within three years prior to filing the bankruptcy petition
    ii. A property tax assessed before the petition's filing date and last due, without penalty, within one year prior to filing the bankruptcy petition
    iii. A tax collected or withheld in whatever capacity
    iv. An employment tax on wages, and the like, earned from the debtor before the petition's filing date (whether or not paid) for which a return was last due (including extensions) within three years prior to filing the bankruptcy petition
    v. An excise tax relating to a transaction occurring before the petition's filing date for which a return was last due (including extensions) within three years before filing the bankruptcy petition
    vi. Custom duties on merchandise imported within one year before filing the bankruptcy petition

   vii. A penalty related to the priority claims specified above and as compensation for actual pecuniary loss

9. Claims against the debtor for any commitment made to a federal depository institution regulatory agency for the maintenance of capital of an insured depository institution

The dollar amounts just described will increase on April 1, 2007, to reflect the change in the Consumer Price Index for all Urban Consumers for the three-year period ending December 31, 2006, with similar revisions to occur every third year thereafter.

(y) Preferences and Fraudulent Transfers.   Matters relating to preferences and fraudulent transfers provide another major focus of assistance by financial advisors with bankruptcy knowledge. Detecting and confirming such transactions requires the financial advisor to identify when the debtor became insolvent and to perform a liquidation analysis. A trustee can avoid preferences and fraudulent transfers by bringing an action before the court.

Bankruptcy Code § 547 allows the trustee to avoid the transfer of the debtor's property as a preference under five conditions:

1. The transfer benefited a creditor.
2. The transfer was for or on account of an antecedent debt owed by the debtor before making such transfer.
3. The debtor made the transfer when the debtor was insolvent.
4. The debtor made the transfer on or within 90 days preceding the filing date (or one year if that creditor was an insider at the time of the transaction).
5. The creditor received more from the transfer than it would have received if the case were in a chapter 7 liquidation, if the transfer had not occurred, and under other Bankruptcy Code provisions (i.e., under the reorganization plan).

Exceptions to a preferential transfer include the following:

- Contemporaneous exchange for new value
- A transfer made in the debtor's ordinary course of business or a transfer made according to ordinary business terms
- The creation of a security interest in property acquired for new value provided the security interest is perfected (i.e., meets Uniform Commercial Code [UCC] recording or notice requirements) within 30 days.
- A transfer to the extent that subsequent new value is given.

Bankruptcy Code § 548 allows the trustee to avoid the transfer of the debtor's interest in property or any obligation incurred by the debtor, made or incurred within two years (one year for cases filed prior to April 20, 2006) before filing the bankruptcy petition (1) if the debtor made the transfer to hinder, delay, or defraud, or (2) if the debtor received less than reasonable equivalent value and

- Was or became insolvent from such transaction
- Left the debtor with unreasonably small capital
- Intended or believed that the debtor would incur debts that the debtor could not repay as they matured

- Made such transfer to or for the benefit of an insider, or incurred such obligation to or for the benefit of an insider under an employment contract and not
in the ordinary course of business.

In addition to the recovery of property for fraudulent transfers under § 548,
trustees can attack fraudulent conveyances under § 544(b) of the Bankruptcy
Code. This section allows recovery of fraudulent transfers under state fraudulent
transfers laws, based on the Uniform Fraudulent Conveyance Act, the Uniform
Fraudulent Transfer Act, and other statutory or common law. Under state law,
trustees can recover fraudulent transfers between one and six years (some states
allow seven years for actual fraud) prior to the filing of the petition, with the most
common period being four years. Thus, for a transfer made more than two years
(one year for petitions filed prior to April 20, 2006) prior to bankruptcy, any
recovery action due to a potential fraudulent transfer, while administered by the
bankruptcy court, must comply with state law.

Any action to recover a fraudulent transfer or a preference must occur within
two years after the order for relief or, if the court appoints a trustee during the
second year following the order for relief, within one year after the trustee's
appointment.

(z) Discharge of Debts.[8]   he extent to which the court discharges a debt depends
on (1) whether the debtor is an individual or corporation, (2) the chapter under
which the debtor filed the petition, and (3) the debt's nature and priority.

(i) Individual Debtors.   Bankruptcy Code § 523 exempts several debts from an individual debtor's discharge. This section lists the debts that have exemption from
discharge under chapters 7, 11, 12, and 13. The court cannot discharge a tax with
priority under § 507(a)(2) or (7) or related to a tax return that the debtor did not
file or filed late (and within two years of the petition date) or that the debtor willfully evaded.

Section 523(c) provides that the creditor who is owed a debt that might be
exempted from discharge as a result of false statements for fraud or embezzlement
or larceny or for willful or malicious injuries as specified in the section must initiate proceedings to obtain the exception to discharge. Otherwise, the courts will
discharge those debts unless it denies the debtor's entire discharge.

(ii) Chapter 7 Cases.   Bankruptcy Code § 727 contains 11 conditions in a chapter 7
case that will result in denial of a discharge, including the fact that the debtor is
not an individual. Thus, only an individual debtor can obtain a discharge in a
chapter 7 case; a partnership or a corporation cannot. Also, a corporation or partnership liquidating under a plan adopted in a chapter 11 case would not obtain a
discharge. Because a corporation effectively goes out of business as a result of the
liquidation, granting a discharge might appear unimportant. A corporation, however, can continue to exist, and shareholders often keep these shells alive to
reactivate later for tax reasons or to avoid the costs of creating another corporation. A debtor will be reluctant to use these shells under the current bankruptcy
law because the creditors for prebankruptcy debts can attach any assets owned by
the corporation.

(iii) Chapter 11 Cases.   Bankruptcy Code § 1141(d) provides that, in a chapter 11
case, a plan's confirmation discharges the debtor from any debt that arose before

the plan's confirmation except to the extent that the plan provides for such debt. This discharge occurs whether the creditor filed proof of claim or § 502 allows such a claim, or the claim's holder has accepted the plan. Individuals cannot discharge a debt of the type listed in § 523 and discussed in Section 28.3(z)(i) of this chapter. Bankruptcy Code § 1141(d) does not allow a discharge, however, for a tax or custom duty for which the corporation made a fraudulent return or willfully attempted to evade or to defeat.

(aa) Plan of Reorganization.   A plan of reorganization represents the blueprint for satisfying creditors and equity security holders under chapter 11 of the Bankruptcy Code. A plan will not satisfy all creditors and equity security holders because the debtor lacks sufficient assets or earning power to do so.

(i) Provisions.   Section 1123 promulgates mandatory provisions for all chapter 11 plans to

- Designate classes of all claims and interests
- Specify the unimpaired classes
- Specify the treatment of all impaired classes
- Provide for identical treatment for each claim or interest in a particular class (unless a particular party agrees to a less favorable treatment)
- Provide adequate means to implement the plan's provisions such as selling certain assets, merging with other entities, modifying contractual terms, curing defaults, or issuing the debtor's securities
- Prohibit issuing nonvoting equity securities and provide for the seniority of different equity security classes if the debtor or its successor is a corporation
- Select management of the reorganized entity while protecting the best interest of creditors and equity security holders and public policy

A plan can also include the following optional provisions:

- Impair or leave unimpaired any class of claims or interests
- Assume, reject, or assign executory contracts or unexpired leases
- Settle, adjust, retain, and enforce any claim or interest belonging to the debtor
- Sell all or most of the debtor's assets and then distribute the proceeds to holders of claims and interests of the debtor
- Include any other provision that is consistent with the Bankruptcy Code provisions

(ii) Impaired Claims and Interests.   Bankruptcy Code § 1124 states that claims and interests are *impaired* if the plan alters the holder's legal, equitable, and contractual rights, and if the debtor does not cure any defaults and does not compensate for damages. A successful reorganization plan will have to impair some claims and interests; this will affect the plan's acceptance or rejection, as Section 28.3(cc) of this chapter discusses.

Product line information carries particular importance. One or more products (or services) can prove unprofitable when one is considering the assets and debt or capital that they require. Selling or discontinuing such product or service lines can leave the debtor a smaller but profitable business.

With this in mind, one can reuse and present the cash flow forecast for different alternatives. This will then indicate the cash available to service a reorganization plan that should incorporate different alternatives, including debt restructure by principal reduction or term revisions (or both), lease or contract rejections, and conversion of debt to equity.

One should then analyze the alternative plans by giving *pro forma* effect to the current balance sheet in conjunction with the appropriate cash flow forecast over the subsequent plan life (the time required to complete all terms of the proposed plan). One must also consider financial projections for the period between the current balance sheet date and the plan's expected effective date.

The parties can then select the proposed plan from the alternatives. Such decisions must include the entire team of debtor and trustee (if any), their attorneys and financial advisors, and the creditor and any equity security holder committees.

Financial experts should remain realistic about the proposed plan's feasibility. The court can require accountants and financial advisors to testify as to the plan's feasibility.

(bb) Disclosure Statement.   A disclosure statement presents the proposed reorganization plan to the creditors and equity security holders. It resembles a prospectus in its nature and intended use. The Bankruptcy Code does not specify in detail the disclosure's required content, leaving this to the court's discretion. Section 1125 does, however, define adequate information as "information of a kind, and in sufficient detail, as far as is reasonably practical in light of the nature and history of the debtor and the condition of the debtor's books and records, that would enable a hypothetical reasonable investor typical of holders of claims or interests of the relevant class to make an informed judgment about the plan."

Required disclosures vary for each case. One should consider the following matters:

- Opinions, disclaimers, and so on, concerning the statement's content
- A brief description of the debtor and its current business
- A description of the proposed management team including individual profiles and current and proposed compensation
- A summary of the proposed reorganization plan including a description of the classes of creditors and equity security holders and the treatment the plan affords each class
- Disclosure of related parties, affiliates, and major equity security holders under the plan's terms and a description of the transactions that will change the current situation
- A liquidation analysis
- Special risk factors
- Income tax issues
- Financial information, including
    - Historical operating results for pre- and postpetition periods

- Current financial position
- Cash flow and income projections for an extended period (often five years)
- *Pro forma* effect of the plan based on reorganization values
- A statement indicating the plan's implementation
- A brief description of pending legal proceedings
- A valuation of the specific assets and the going concern business (reorganization value)
- Marketing plans
- Major postpetition events and transactions including the appointment and reports of a trustee, examiner, and official creditor or equity security holder committees
- Terms of new debt or security instruments issued or to be issued under the plan's terms

Paragraph 37 of SOP 90-7 states that, although the court evaluates the adequacy of information in the disclosure statement, entities that expect to adopt fresh-start reporting should report information about the reorganization value in the disclosure statement. Reporting this value should help creditors and shareholders make an informed judgment about the plan.

According to the SOP, the *pro forma* balance sheet that shows the financial position of the entity as though the court has confirmed the proposed plan can show the reorganization value.

The court must approve the disclosure statement after a noticed hearing before releasing it. The financial advisor can testify on matters concerning the disclosure statement's content and adequacy.

(cc) Acceptance or Rejection of the Plan.   Each claim or interest holder (i.e., investor) receives a court-approved disclosure statement, the proposed plan, and a ballot. This presents the formal solicitation for the plan's approval in accordance with § 1126. The documents should disclose that promises, representations, and terms of treatment not specifically approved by the plan and disclosure statement are improper and unauthorized.

Each claim or interest holder can vote to accept or reject a proposed reorganization plan. The court, however, presumes that an unimpaired class of claims or interests has accepted the plan and does not require their formal solicitation.

A class of creditor claims has accepted a plan if at least two-thirds in dollar amount of claims voted and more than one-half in number of allowed claims holders that voted accept the plan. A class of interests has accepted a plan if at least two-thirds in dollar amount of allowed interests accept the plan.

The court bases the required vote computations on the total number of claims or interests by each class that actually votes (as opposed to the entire dollar amount and number of allowed claims or interests composing a defined class). The bankruptcy court fixes the voting period when it approves the ballot or performs other related procedures. For any bankruptcy case with a large number of creditors or equity security holders, accountants or financial advisors often mail the voting materials and receive, tabulate, and report the results.

During the first 120 days after a bankruptcy proceeding begins, the debtor has the exclusive right to file a reorganization plan; the bankruptcy court often extends the period. The court cannot, however, extend this right beyond 18 months after it issues the order for relief. After the period, including any approved extensions, other parties in interest can file a plan. Accordingly, the claim and interest holders can simultaneously vote to accept or reject competing plans.

(dd) Confirming the Plan.   Following the vote for a proposed reorganization plan, the plan's proponent will seek its confirmation by the court. Bankruptcy Code § 1128 provides that a court hearing must occur after notice to all parties in interest to give them the opportunity to object to the plan's confirmation.

Section 1129 specifies certain requirements before the bankruptcy court confirms a plan:

1. The plan complies with the applicable provisions of the Bankruptcy Code (Title 11, U.S. Code).
2. The plan's proponent complies with the applicable provisions of the Bankruptcy Code.
3. The parties have proposed the plan in good faith and not by any means forbidden by law.
4. Payments made or to be made related to the case or the plan are reasonable and the court has approved, or will later consider approving, them.
5. The plan discloses management or proposed management, insiders, and affiliates.
6. The plan has obtained approval of governmental regulatory bodies concerning rate changes.
7. The best interest test: each impaired class of claims and interests accepts the plan or will receive or retain under the plan (as of the plan's effective date) an amount not less than the amount such holders would receive or retain if the debtor were liquidated under chapter 7.
8. Each class of claims or interests has accepted the plan (or, if unimpaired, is deemed to have accepted the plan).
9. The plan provides for the treatment of priority claims.
10. At least one class of impaired claims—other than a class held by insiders—accepts the plan.
11. The feasibility test: the plan will not likely be followed by the liquidation or need for further reorganization of the debtor or its successor (if not provided for in the plan).
12. The debtor has paid or provided for all fees payable under § 1930 of the Bankruptcy Code.
13. The plan provides for payment of retiree benefits as required by § 1114 of the Bankruptcy Code.

Notwithstanding requirement 8, the court can, under certain circumstances and upon the proponent's request, confirm the plan if the plan does not discriminate unfairly and if the plan appears fair and equitable with respect to an impaired class of claims or interests that rejected the plan. Practitioners refer to this as the *cram-down* provision. Bankruptcy Code § 1129(b) specifies tests for ascertaining a plan's fairness and equity.

(ee) Cram Down.   As requirement 8 in Section 28.3(dd) noted, before the court confirms a plan, a class of claims or interests must either accept the plan or not be impaired. However, Subsection (b) of § 1129 allows the court under certain conditions to confirm a plan even though an impaired class has not accepted the plan. Before the court will confirm a plan that has a class that has not accepted the plan, the court must ascertain that the plan does not discriminate unfairly and appears fair and equitable, with respect to each class of claims or interest impaired under the plan that has not accepted the plan. The Bankruptcy Code sets forth conditions for secured claims, unsecured claims, and shareholder interests that the court must consider in the "fair and equitable" requirement. Because the subsection uses the word "includes," it does not restrict the meaning of fair and equitable to these conditions. Bankruptcy Code § 1129 (b)(2) provides that for a plan to be fair and equitable, it must include the conditions that we describe in this section of the chapter, which are based on the absolute priority doctrine. This doctrine states that a creditor or interest holder with a higher ranking must be satisfied in full before a lower ranking credit or interest holder can receive any consideration.

(i) Secured Creditors' Test.   Bankruptcy Code § 1129(b)(2)(A) indicates that the plan must provide for at least one of the following in order to prove fair and equitable:

1. The holders of such claims must retain the lien securing such claims, whether the property subject to such lien is retained by the debtor or transferred to another entity, to the extent of the allowed amount of such claims (*see* § 1124). In addition, each holder of a claim of such class must receive on account of such claim deferred cash payments totaling at least the allowed amount of such claim, of a value, as of the effective date of the plan, of at least the value of such holder's interest in the estate's interest in such property,

2. For the sale, subject to § 363(k), of any property that is subject to the lien securing such claims, free and clear of such lien, with such lien to attach to the proceeds of such sale, and the treatment of such lien on proceeds under clause (1) or (3) of this subparagraph, or

3. For the realization by such holders of the indubitable equivalent of such claims.

(ii) Unsecured Creditors' Test.   For holders of unsecured claims, § 1129(b)(2)(B) provides that the plan must satisfy one of the two following requirements for each impaired class that does not accept the plan:

The plan provides that each holder of a claim of such class receive or retain on account of such claim property of a value, as of the effective date of the plan, equal to the allowed amount of such claim.

The holder of any claim or interest that is junior to the claims of such class will not receive or retain on account of such junior claim or interest any property according to § 1129(b)(2)(C).

Members of the class must, if they have not accepted the plan, receive or retain property that has a present value equal to the allowed amount of the claim. Alternatively, the plan can contain any provision for a distribution of less than full present value as long as no junior claim or interest will participate in the plan. Implicit in the concept of fairness is that senior classes will not receive more than 100 percent of their claims and any equal class will not receive preferential treatment.

(iii) Shareholders' Interest Test. The test for equity interests resembles the test for unsecured claims. Bankruptcy Code § 1129 (b)(2)(C) provides that the plan must satisfy one of two standards for each impaired class that does not accept the plan:

1. The plan provides that each holder of an interest of such class will receive, or retain on account of such interest, property of a value (as of the effective date of the plan) equal to the greatest of (1) the allowed amount of any fixed liquidation preference such holder has entitlement to, (2) any fixed redemption price that such holder has entitlement to, or (3) the value of such interest.
2. The holder of any interest that is junior to the interests of such class will not receive or retain under the plan on account of such junior interest any property, according to § 1129(b)(2)(C).

One major provision in the first standard requires that the equity interest receive the greater of liquidation preference, fixed redemption price, or the value of its equity. Thus, a corporation could not file a chapter 11 petition solely to take advantage of the low liquidation value of preferred stock.

(iv) New Value. An emerging exception to the absolute priority doctrine is the granting of new value. This new value corollary states that a junior party (often equity holders) can receive an interest in the reorganized entity provided that the interest resulted from the contribution of new value and not because of a current interest in value. Although the Supreme Court's decision in *Bank of America v. 203 North LaSalle Street Partnership*[9] did not address the merits of new value, it held that one of the following two conditions must exist before a court confirms a plan:

1. The debtor must give up its exclusive right to propose a plan and give the creditors an opportunity to also propose a plan.
2. The courts will not confirm any new value plan filed during the debtor's exclusivity period under § 1121(b) of the Bankruptcy Code unless it uses a competitive bidding process for the equity in the reorganized debtor. This process provides a test to determine if the plan proponents of the debtor are paying the highest value for the equity.

(ff) Accounting for the Chapter 11 Plan. SOP 90-7 also explains how the debtor emerging from chapter 11 should account for the reorganization—both when the debtor should adopt fresh-start reporting and when it cannot. Fresh-start reporting requires the debtor to use current values (going concern or reorganization values) in its balance sheet for both assets and liabilities and to eliminate all prior earnings or deficits.

(i) Requirements for Fresh-Start Reporting. The debtor must satisfy two conditions before it can use fresh-start reporting: (1) the total of all postpetition liabilities and allowed claims exceeds the reorganized value of the emerging entity immediately before the plan's confirmation; and (2) holders of existing voting shares immediately before confirmation retain less than 50 percent of the voting share of the emerging entity.

Paragraph 36 of the SOP indicates that the plan must contemplate a substantive and long-term shift of controlling interest. Thus, the new controlling interest must not revert to the shareholders existing immediately before the parties confirm the plan. For example, if a plan that provides for shareholders existing prior to the confirmation to reacquire control of the company at a subsequent date, the debtor cannot adopt fresh-start reporting. Debtors that meet both of the above conditions will report the assets and liabilities at their going concern values.

Reorganization value is the fair value of the entity before considering liabilities; it approximates the amount that a willing buyer would pay for the assets of the entity immediately after the restructuring. Estimation of the reorganization value focuses on the value of the assets; however, most valuations use discounted future cash flows, resulting in an enterprise value. (Enterprise value represents the value of funded debt plus the value of equity, generally reduced by the amount of cash on hand at the valuation date.) Depending on the circumstances, one can use several approaches to estimate enterprise value.[10] The financial advisor, often with the appraiser's help, converts the enterprise value to reorganization value by adding to the enterprise value the current liabilities (excluding any current liabilities that are part of the funded debt) plus the amount of cash, if any, that one deducts to calculate the enterprise value. Although the financial advisor usually does not decide the debtor's reorganization value (unless the engagement related to business valuation), the financial statements should report the value that the debtor, the creditors', and shareholders' committees and other interested parties have negotiated.

The debtor can use reorganization values only when the debtor satisfies both conditions for a fresh start. For example, most nonpublic companies will not use fresh-start reporting because most often the ownership does not change.

(ii) Allocation of Reorganization Value.   When the value of the liabilities exceeds an entity's reorganization value and the old shareholders own less than 50 percent of voting stock of the emerging entity, the entity can implement fresh-start reporting in the following manner:

- The debtor will allocate the reorganization value to its assets based on the market value of the individual assets and according to the provisions of FASB Statement No. 141, *Business Combinations,* which describes allocation of purchase cost under the purchase method. The debtor should report any part of the reorganization value not attributable to specific tangible assets or identifiable intangible assets as goodwill. Under FASB Statement No. 142, *Goodwill and Other Intangible Assets,* the enterprise does not amortize goodwill but reduces it only if it is impaired.

- The debtor should report liabilities that survive the reorganization at present value of amounts that the debtor will pay with future contractual cash flows discounted at appropriate current interest rates. Thus, the report will show all liabilities at their discounted values.

- The debtor must report deferred taxes in conformity with GAAP. Fresh-start reporting should use benefits realized from preconfirmation net operating loss carryforwards first to reduce reorganization value in excess of amounts allocable to identifiable assets and other intangibles. Once the allocations have exhausted the balance of the intangible assets, the report shows the balance as a direct addition to the additional paid-in capital.

(iii) Disclosure Requirements.   Paragraph 39 of the SOP indicates that when the debtor adopts fresh-start reporting, the notes to the initial financial statements should disclose the following:

- Adjustments to the historical amounts of individual assets and liabilities

- The amount of debt forgiven

- The amount of prior retained earnings or deficit eliminated

- Significant matters relating to the computation of reorganization value

The SOP indicates that the notes should also disclose other significant matters, including the following:

- The method or methods used to calculate reorganization value and factors such as discount rates, tax rates, the number of years for which the report projects cash flows, and the method of estimating terminal value

- Sensitive assumptions (those assumptions with sufficient possibility of variation and that would significantly affect measurement of reorganization value)

- Assumptions about anticipated conditions that management expects to deviate from current conditions, unless otherwise apparent

(iv) Reporting by Debtors not Qualifying for Fresh-Start Reporting.   Debtors that do not meet both of the conditions for adopting fresh-start reporting should state any debt issued or liabilities compromised at the present values of amounts owed. SOP 90-7 prohibits quasi-reorganization for companies reorganizing under chapter 11. Even though these provisions apply only to chapter 11 cases, debtors restructuring out of court will find it difficult to justify not recording liabilities at their value. However, no provisions exist to preclude the debtor from following the guidelines under quasi-reorganization in an out-of-court restructuring.

In March of 1994, the AICPA issued Practice Bulletin 11, *Accounting for Preconfirmation Contingencies in Fresh-Start Reporting.* This bulletin states that the debtor should include adjustments made after the adoption of fresh-start reporting and resulting from a preconfirmation contingency in the income in the period in which the financial advisor quantifies the adjustments. Examples of preconfirmation contingencies include uncertainties concerning the following:

- Amounts that the debtor will realize upon disposing of assets designated for sale by the confirmation plan

- Nondischargeable claims

- Disputed, unliquidated, or contingent claims that remain unresolved at confirmation.

The practice bulletin provides that preconfirmation contingencies do not include allocation of reorganization value to the entity's assets and the deductible temporary differences or net operating loss and tax-credit carryforwards that exist at confirmation.

(gg) Postconfirmation Activities.   After the court confirms a reorganization plan, the parties must implement it. The implementation date is the "effective date of the plan."

If a plan provides for payments equaling some percentage of an allowed claim or the issuance of equity securities based on a formula related to an allowed claim or interest, a financial advisor can develop a program to make these calculations. Professionals can assist with the accounting and taxation issues related to a confirmed plan. The court considers a plan consummated when the parties have implemented the plan according to its terms.

28.4   INCOME TAX CONSIDERATIONS

The income tax effect of certain transactions during the administration period and of tax assessments related to prebankruptcy periods can impose undue hardship on the debtor, who already faces a tenuous financial position. Debtors often realize substantial taxable income from taxable recoveries. Net operating loss carryovers and other offsetting tax deductions sometimes do not nullify the income tax effect. Therefore, in addition to ensuring that the debtor has satisfied all statutory tax reporting and filing requirements at the due dates, the accountant or financial advisor must identify those tax aspects that will preserve and enlarge the bankrupt's estate.

This section identifies items that the debtor (and, to a limited extent, creditors and other interested parties) should consider in solving the problems of financially troubled companies. Newton and Liquerman's *Bankruptcy and Insolvency Taxation* (updated annually) contains a more detailed discussion of these tax issues (*see* Bibliography).

(a) Assessing Tax Liability.   Bankruptcy Code § 505 authorizes the bankruptcy court to assess a debtor's tax liability if the parties did not contest or adjudicate the tax issue before the bankruptcy case began. The calculation would include any fine or penalty relating to a tax or any other addition to a tax. The bankruptcy court establishes the tax claims allowed under § 502 of the Bankruptcy Code and the dischargeability of the tax under § 523 of the Bankruptcy Code. Section 505 applies to all types of taxes, including income tax, excise tax, sales tax, and unemployment compensation taxes. The automatic stay prohibits any effort by the IRS or any other taxing authority to collect the tax during the bankruptcy.

Before the bankruptcy court can establish the estate's right to a tax refund, the trustee must file a claim for the refund and either receive a determination from the IRS or allow 120 days to pass before filing the claim. If the IRS has not made a determination within 120 days, the bankruptcy court can then establish the estate's right to a tax refund.

A debtor facing a tax liability can request the taxing unit, including the IRS, to determine the liability under § 505(b) of the Bankruptcy Code. The tax unit then has 60 days to notify the debtor that an examination will occur. If the tax unit decides to examine the return, it has 180 days from the request date to take action. If the taxing unit does not notify the debtor that it plans to examine the debtor or does not complete the examination, it has no recourse.

(b) Responsibility for Filing Income Tax Returns: Corporation. The receiver (under state law), trustee or debtor-in-possession (under a bankruptcy case), or assignee who possesses title to all or substantially all of a corporation's property or business must file the income tax return for the corporation exactly as the corporation would. The bankruptcy trustee, while acting on behalf of a debtor's estate, acts as a fiduciary. The trustee does not represent a separate taxable entity apart from the corporation. As set forth in IRC Section 1.641(b)-2(b), a corporation in bankruptcy is not a taxable entity separate from the person for whom the fiduciary is acting. Hence, the corporation's tax return should include income and expenses of a debtor corporation's trustee. The trustee uses the debtor corporation's identification number. The Bankruptcy Tax Act of 1980 added § 1399 to the IRC, which provides that no separate tax entity should result from a corporation or partnership commencing a case under the Bankruptcy Code.

A trustee should file a corporate income tax return annually, even if the corporation has no income, so long as the corporation exists for tax purposes. A corporation existing during any part of the year must file a return. A corporation does not exist after it ceases business and dissolves, retaining no assets, even though state law can consider it as continuing for certain limited purposes—such as lawsuits—connected with concluding its affairs. If the corporation has valuable claims for which it will bring suit during this period, it has retained assets and therefore continues to exist. A corporation remains in existence if the court has turned it over to receivers or trustees who continue operations.

(c) Responsibility for Filing Income Tax Returns: Partnerships and Individuals. Whereas well-established procedures exist for corporations, much controversy existed in the past regarding individual and partnership returns. To eliminate the uncertainty as to whether bankruptcy proceedings created a separate entity, the Bankruptcy Tax Act (1980) added § 1398 and § 1399 to the IRC.

(i) Partnerships. IRC § 1399 provides that a partnership filing a case under the Bankruptcy Code does not create a new entity. The trustee must file a partnership information return under § 6031 of the IRC for the period(s) that the trustee operated the business. The legislative committee reports indicate that the trustee has responsibility to file the partnership return, although the statute does not specifically require it.

In a Letter Ruling (8509038), the IRS held that a partnership's trustee must file Form 1065 only for the year that the trustee was appointed and later years. No obligation exists to file Form 1065 for earlier partnership years. The trustee must, however, cooperate with the IRS by providing all relevant tax information available for prior years. This practice area needs definitive rules because of the practical problems that it presents.

(ii) Individuals. Bankruptcy proceedings for an individual's affairs create a separate taxable entity, consisting of the debtor's property before bankruptcy. After the debtor has filed, the bankruptcy estate can earn income and incur expenses. A trustee (or debtor-in-possession) administers these transactions for the creditor's benefit. Concurrently, the individual debtor can also earn income, incur expenses, and acquire property that does not become part of the bankruptcy estate. The separate taxable entities for federal income tax purposes occur in

bankruptcy cases under chapters 7 and 11. Chapters 12 and 13, however, do not create a new taxable entity. When the bankruptcy court dismisses a bankruptcy case involving an individual, the law does not deem the estate to have been a separate taxable entity.

When the individual and bankruptcy estates represent separate entities, they must file separate returns. The estate files Form 1041 for the period beginning with the petition filing date or for any subsequent year if gross income exceeds the exemption amount plus the basic standard deduction, as required by IRC § 6012(a)(9). The individual files Form 1040, as usual, and reports all income earned during the year. This includes income earned before bankruptcy proceedings but not the estate's income. IRC § 6012(b)(4) requires that the estate's fiduciary file the return. The trustee, if appointed, would have this responsibility; otherwise, the debtor-in-possession must file the estate's return.

IRC § 1398 gives an individual debtor under either chapter 7 or 11 the right to elect to close his or her taxable year as of the day before the date bankruptcy commences. The taxpayer using this election must divide his or her taxable year into short taxable years. The government collects the first short year's tax liability from the bankruptcy estate. The government considers the tax a liability before bankruptcy and thus payable by the estate. If the estate does not possess enough assets to pay the tax, the remaining liability is not discharged but is collectible from the individual after the case. The individual must make this election by the fifteenth day of the fourth month after filing for bankruptcy, which is the return's due date without an extension.

(d) Special Rules for Individuals.   IRC § 1398 suggests different considerations for individuals because chapters 7 and 11 create a new estate. The considerations include who—the individual or the estate—must report income and expense items, treatment of transfers between the debtor and the estate, and carryover and carryback of administration, liquidation, and reorganization expenses.

(i) Income and Deductions.   IRC § 1398 provides that the estate's gross income for each taxable year should include the debtor's income to which the estate is entitled under Title 11 of the Bankruptcy Code. This does not include any income that the individual earned prior to the date of the bankruptcy case filing. The gross income of the debtor (the individual as opposed to the estate) will include income earned prior to bankruptcy plus any income items that the estate's gross income does not include.

The original bill passed by the House divided deductions and credits between the debtor and the estate. Congress subsequently modified these provisions to read that if IRC § 1398(e)(3) regards a deduction or credit as belonging to the bankruptcy estate, the debtor cannot deduct the item.

(ii) Transfers between Debtor and Estate.   A transfer (other than by sale or exchange) of an asset from the debtor to the estate does not lead to gain or loss recognition or deductions or credits recapture or income acceleration. Thus, a transfer of an installment obligation would not generate income under IRC § 453(d). The same nondisposition provisions apply when the entities transfer assets (other than by sale or exchange) from the estate to the debtor as provided under § 1398(f).

(iii) Attribute Carryover to Estate.   IRC § 1398(g) provides that the estate should assume the following income tax attributes of the debtor under chapters 7 or 11:

- Net operation loss carryovers under IRC § 172
- Capital loss carryovers under IRC § 1212
- Recovery exclusion under IRC § 111 (relating to bad debts, prior taxes, and delinquency amounts)
- Credit carryovers and all other items that, except for the bankruptcy, the debtor would have to consider with respect to any credit
- Charitable contribution carryover under IRC § 170(d)(1)
- The debtor's basis in and holding period for the character of any asset acquired in the debtor's hand (other than by sale or exchange from the debtor)
- The debtor's accounting method
- The debtor's other tax attributes to the extent provided by U.S. Treasury regulations:
  - The debtor's unused passive activity losses and credit carryovers under IRC § 469
  - The debtor's unused losses from at-risk activities under IRC § 465
  - The debtor's exclusion of $250,000 ($500,000 for married couple) of gains on the sale of a residence

(iv) Attribute Carryover to Debtor.   Upon the estate's termination in chapter 7 or 11 cases, the debtor assumes the following:

- Net operating loss carryover
- Capital loss carryover
- Recovery exclusion
- Credit carryover
- Charitable contribution carryover
- The estate's basis in, holding period for, and the character in the estate's hand of any asset acquired (other than by sales or exchange) from the estate
- The debtor's other tax attributes to the extent provided by Treasury regulations:
  - Unused passive activity losses and credit carryovers under IRC § 469
  - Unused losses from at-risk activities under IRC § 465
  - Unused exclusion of $250,000 ($500,000 for married couple) of gains on the sale of a residence

(v) Carryback of Net Operating Losses and Other Credits Incurred Subsequent to Commencement of Case.   IRC § 1938(j)(2)(A) provides that if the estate incurs a net operating loss (NOL)—apart from the loss passing to the estate from the debtor—the estate can carry back its NOL to the debtor's taxable years before the year in which the bankruptcy proceeding commenced, as well as to the estate's previous taxable years. An individual incurring NOLs cannot carry back these losses to the years preceding the chapter 7 or 11 filing. Similarly, § 1398 allows the bankruptcy estate to carry back excess credits, such as an investment tax credit, to the years preced-

ing the case; it also prohibits the individual from carrying back these credits to the prebankruptcy time period.

(vi) Administrative Expenses.   IRC § 1398(h)(1) allows the estate to deduct any administrative expense allowed under Bankruptcy Code § 503 and any fees or charges assessed under Chapter 123 of Title 28 of the U.S. Code (court fee and costs). This section allows these expenses even though one might not consider some of these trade or business expenses. Other IRC provisions, such as § 263 (capital expenditures), § 265 (expenses relating to tax-exempt interest), and § 275 (certain taxes) disallow some administrative expenses.

The taxpayer can carry back three years—and carry forward seven years—any administrative, liquidation, and reorganization expenses not used in the current year. The unused administrative expenses carry back or carry forward to the estate's taxable years only. IRC § 1398(h)(2)(D) allows only the estate to deduct expenses that are deductible solely through § 1398(h)(1).

Often the estate does not pay administrative expenses until the bankruptcy proceedings conclude, unless the IRC considers them trade or business expenses. Expenses considered trade or business are most often paid in the normal course of business in a chapter 11 proceeding and do not require specific court approval. The 2005 act modified §960 of Title 28 to provide that government entities are no longer required to apply for allowance and for payment of taxes incurred in the conduct of business after a petition is filed. The regulations treat such taxes as trade or business expenses, so the estate should pay them in the normal course of business.

The estate cannot deduct these administrative costs until they are paid, and often income does not exist during the last year of operating the estate to charge these expenses against, which means that these expenses have no tax benefit. To alleviate this problem, IRC § 1398 provides for the carryover and carryback provision, as Section 28.4(d)(v) of this chapter discusses. Note that the restriction on carryback or carryover of administrative expenses to the estate applies only to those deductions allowed solely by IRC § 1398(h)(1). Thus, an expense (even though it is an administrative expense in a bankruptcy case) that the IRC would normally classify as an operating cost can carry forward to the debtor, once the estate terminates, as an item in the net operating loss carryover.

28.5   MINIMIZING TAX AND RELATED PAYMENTS

A debtor in financial difficulty can take several steps to reduce the cash outflow for taxes or to obtain tax refunds.

(a) Estimated Tax.   A company with financial problems can, after paying one or more installments of estimated taxes, decide that it should recompute its estimated tax liability. Downward recomputations show that it does not need to make additional payments. If the company paid too much tax, it can obtain a quick refund by filing Form 4466 immediately after the taxable year ends.

(b) Prior Year Taxes.   The IRS allows companies that owe taxes from the previous year to extend the time for payment to the extent that the tax will decrease because of an expected net operating loss in the current year. Companies make this request on Form 1138. To quickly obtain a refund of taxes that were previously paid, the company must file Form 1139. The company must file this form within one year after the end of the year in which the NOL occurred and only after it has filed Form 1120 for the loss year.

(c) Pension Funding Requirements.   An employer can receive a funding waiver if it can show that substantial business hardship exists and that funding the pension would adversely affect the plan's participants in the aggregate. If the employer does not receive the funding waiver, it can defer payments under Revenue Ruling 66-144.

28.6   TREATMENT OF INCOME DURING THE BANKRUPTCY PERIOD

(a) Income Required to Be Reported.   One does not expect to see positive income during bankruptcy proceedings because insufficient profits have contributed to the insolvency. During the estate's administration, however, transactions can generate taxable income. The estate must report any income derived from selling or operating the debtor's assets as it is earned.

A bankruptcy estate can have many income sources: the sale or liquidation of assets, realized rental income, royalties from patents, dividends from securities, and accumulated interest on savings and other deposits of the debtor (or trustee, who can deposit the bankruptcy estate's funds). A solvent debtor not involved in a chapter 11 proceeding will recognize income to the extent of the debts forgiven.

(b) Deductions Allowed.   In calculating taxable net income, the trustee receives certain deductions, which include the following:

- The costs of administration in general.
- The costs of administration directly associated with the estate's income-producing activities, provided that the trustee constructs them as ordinary and necessary business expenses.
- Payments made to priority and general unsecured creditors if the trustee can allocate such distribution to a debt associated with an item that the debtor would have deducted. Debtors using an accrual basis have already deducted the expense even though the trustee makes actual payment.
- Payments for priority tax claims incurred before filing the petition, which the debtor could have deducted if the debtor had paid them prior to bankruptcy.
- Net operating loss carryovers.

The taxpayer must, however, use care when deducting general administration costs. For example, one cannot deduct expenses connected with a reorganization because IRC § 162 regards them as capital expenditures that will benefit the corporation in future years. IRC § 162 allows the trustee to deduct all costs necessary to operate the business, as they would have been without the bankruptcy proceeding. Note that one can deduct professional fees incurred to improve operations and not solely to reorganize the business. IRC § 162 does not allow the trustees to deduct expenses incurred to sell assets; instead, they must use them to offset the sale proceeds.

(c) Discharging Debts.   Debt cancellations represent one major income source in most insolvency and bankruptcy proceedings. IRC § 61 lists discharge of debts as subject to tax, and Regulation 1.61-12(a) provides that the discharge of indebtedness can result in complete or partial income realization. If a shareholder cancels a debt owed to him or her without consideration, however, the company does not realize taxable income. The amount canceled results in an additional contribution to capital by the shareholder.

In selecting the form of financial relief, a debtor should consider the tax factors related to a gain on debt forgiveness. The rules for out-of-court proceedings differ from those under the Bankruptcy Code. Amended IRC § 108 provides that the company can exclude discharge of debt income from gross income under any of the following conditions:

1. The discharge occurs in a Bankruptcy Code case
2. The discharge occurs when the taxpayer is insolvent
3. The discharge was from farm debt
4. The discharge was from qualified real property business indebtedness

The amount excluded because of insolvency provisions, however, cannot exceed the amount of the debtor's insolvency. Thus, in an out-of-court settlement in which the debt outstanding equals $10 million, the fair market value of the assets equals $7 million, and the court has discharged $4 million of indebtedness, $3 million would fall under the second condition in the preceding list (insolvent debt), and $1 million would be taxed as income from debt discharged. IRC § 108(d) indicates that the taxpayer's indebtedness means debts for which the taxpayer is liable or debts on property owned by the taxpayer such as a nonrecourse mortgage on real property. Thus, § 108 affects both recourse and nonrecourse debts.

In bankruptcy or insolvency cases, IRC provisions do not consider the debt amount discharged as income; however, IRC § 108(b) reduces the tax attributes in the following order:

1. **Net operating losses.** Any net operating loss for the taxable year of discharge and any net operating loss carryover to the year of discharge.
2. **Certain credit carryovers.** Any carryover to or from the year of discharge of a credit under IRC § 38.
3. **Minimum tax credit carryovers.** Any carryover under IRC § 53(b) of minimum tax credit (the excess of the sum of the minimum tax imposed for all prior taxable years following 1986 over the amount allowed as a minimum tax credit for those prior taxable years) as of the beginning of the taxable year immediately after the year of the discharge.
4. **Capital loss carryovers.** Any capital loss for the taxable year of the discharge and any capital loss carryover to the year of discharge under IRC § 1212.
5. **Basis reduction.** The debtor's property reduced according to the provisions of IRC § 1017. These provisions do not require basis reduction to the extent that the basis of assets is less than liabilities immediately after discharge (IRC § 1017(b)(2)).

6. **Passive activity loss and credit carryovers.** Any passive activity loss or credit carryover of the taxpayer under IRC § 469(b) from the taxable year of the discharge.

7. **Foreign tax credit carryovers.** Any carryover to or from the taxable year of discharge of the credit allowed under IRC § 33.

IRC provisions reduce the tax credits 33–1/3 cents for each dollar of debt canceled. The taxpayer can take all other reductions dollar for dollar. The taxpayer takes the reductions after establishing the tax for the year of discharge. For net operating and capital losses, the taxpayer makes the reduction first from the losses for the taxable year and then from the loss carryovers in the order of the taxable years for which the losses arose. Taxpayers reduce the tax credits in the order that they consider the carryovers for the taxable year of discharge.

(d) Election to Reduce Basis First.   IRC § 108(b)(5) allows the debtor to elect to apply, first, any portion of the reduction required owing to debt discharge to reduce the basis of depreciable property. The reduction amount cannot, however, exceed the aggregate adjusted basis of depreciable property held by the taxpayers as of the beginning of the first taxable year subsequent to the taxable year of discharge.

(e) Basis Adjustments.   Two conditions exist under which the debtor can elect or be required to reduce the basis in assets:

1. Under IRC § 108(b)(5), the debtor can elect to apply the gain from discharge to depreciable property before reducing net operating losses, capital losses, or other credits.

2. Under IRC § 108(b)(2)(D), the debtor (whether in bankruptcy or insolvent) must reduce the basis in property if net operating and capital loss carryovers and certain tax credits do not absorb these losses.

Treasury regulations under IRC § 1017 prescribe the order to reduce the basis of assets. The debtor first reduces property that it has pledged as security for the debt. The debtor reduces assets not pledged as security for the debt other than inventories and receivables before reducing the basis in inventory and receivables. One makes the reduction on the first day of the taxable year following the year that the discharge occurred.

(f) Limitations on Deduction.   The basis reduction for a bankruptcy case or an insolvent debtor cannot exceed the total basis of the debtor's property over the total liabilities immediately after the discharge. This limitation does not apply to the extent that the debtor elected first to reduce the basis in property under IRC § 108(b)(5).

(g) Individual's Estate.   IRC § 108(c)(7) provides that the estate as the taxpayer, and not the individual, will make the basis adjustments along with other attribute reductions for debt discharge. Thus, the trustee or debtor-in-possession will make the election to reduce depreciable property and not tax attributes. The estate will make the basis adjustment as of the first day of the taxable year following the discharge. For example, suppose the estate files its final return for a period ending September 15, 2006, and IRC provisions require basis adjustment. Should the individual reduce property as of September 16, 2006 (the beginning of a new taxable year of the estate, if it had to file a return) or January 1, 2007 (the first day of the individual's taxable year)? The Senate Report (96-1035, 96th Cong. 2nd Sess. [1980]) indicates that if the estate must reduce basis owing to debt discharge in the final year of the bankruptcy estate, the estate must make the reduction on the basis of assets acquired by the debtor from the estate and at the time acquired. Thus, in our example, the estate should reduce basis as of September 16, 2006 and cannot include reduction of other property held by the debtor on September 16, 2006. IRC § 1017(c)(1) states that the estate cannot reduce the basis of exempt property. The trustee or debtor-in-possession must make attribute reductions other than basis reduction in the taxable year that the discharge occurred.

(h) Partnerships.   IRC § 108(d) applies at the partner level for discharge of debt in a bankruptcy case or a situation out of court involving either an insolvent debtor or solvent debtor (qualified business indebtedness provision). IRC § 1017(b)3(c) regards a partner's interest in any partnership (whether that partnership's debt was discharged) as a depreciable asset only if a corresponding reduction occurs in the partnership's basis in depreciable property with respect to such partner.

(i) Exchanging Securities for Debt.   Debtors that accept both securities and property to satisfy debt must treat property as having satisfied an amount of debt equal to the value of the property and use the securities to satisfy the balance of the debt. To the extent of its solvency, a corporation will have income from debt discharge on the exchange if the debt exceeds the value of the securities.

IRC § 108 provides that if creditors receive securities for debt that they previously wrote off as an ordinary bad debt deduction, the creditors must recognize subsequent gain on the share's sale as ordinary income to the extent of the loss previously taken. A cash basis taxpayer must consider as a bad debt deduction any amount not taken into account by the method of accounting used.

(j) Purchase-Money Debt Reduction.   When the debt arises from a property purchase, the debtor can treat the discharge as a reduction of the purchase price. To be treated this way, the case must not be a chapter 11 case, or the purchaser must be solvent, and the reduction would otherwise have been treated as income from a discharge of debt.

(k) Tax Planning.   The debtor should consider the tax consequences of any decisions to resolve its financial problems. A company that will become solvent after debt discharge can find a chapter 11 petition better than an out-of-court agreement. Debtors at the beginning of a case should not allow net operating loss carryover to be materially reduced by cancellation of debt income, leaving insufficient net operating loss carryover to absorb subsequent gain on the disposal of assets or operating income.

(l) Corporate Reorganization.   A corporation in bankruptcy or insolvency proceedings can continue operations by—among other methods—transferring all or part of its assets to another corporation. One should structure this transfer as one of the tax-free reorganizations that IRC § 368(a)(1) describes. With a tax-free reorganization, the new entity might assume some of the bankrupt corporation's tax attributes, such as unused net operating losses.

(m) Tax-Free G Reorganization.   Under the tax-free reorganization provisions of IRC § 368(a)(1), the G reorganization category includes certain transfers of all or part of the debtor's assets to another corporation pursuant to a court-approved reorganization plan in a bankruptcy case under the new Title 11 of the U.S. Code, or in a receivership, or a foreclosure, or similar proceedings in federal or state court. G reorganization does not require compliance with state merger laws (as in A reorganizations), does not require that a financially distressed corporation receive only stock of the acquiring corporation in exchange for its assets (C reorganization), and does not require that the former shareholders of a financially distressed corporation control the corporation receiving the assets (D reorganization). The G reorganization provision requires that a corporation's transfer of assets in a bankruptcy case and the acquiring corporation's distribution of stock or securities qualify under § 354, or § 355, or § 356 of the IRC.

(n) Availability of Net Operating Losses.   IRC § 172 provides that a corporation can carry NOLs back two years and carry them forward 20 years. This provision allows a corporation, in most cases, to carry forward for up to 20 years NOLs sustained in a particular tax year and not carried back to prior years. The extent, however, to which the entity can preserve the net operating loss in bankruptcy and insolvency proceedings depends on how one restructures the debt.

The Tax Reform Act of 1986 includes the annual § 382 limitation that minimizes the effect of tax considerations on the decision to acquire loss corporations by limiting potential loss carryovers to a hypothetical income stream that would have been realized had the loss corporation sold its assets at their fair market value and the proceeds been reinvested in high-grade securities. Further conditions for loss survival include the coverage of built-in losses, rules governing changes in ownership, and exceptions for bankruptcy debtor corporations.

One considers net operating loss limitations only when the corporation holding the carryovers changes ownership. IRC § 382 recognizes that an ownership change has occurred when more than half the loss corporation's stock value changes ownership within the past three years. The use of any NOL resulting from operations before the ownership change in any period after the change falls under the § 382 limitation.

This limitation now restricts the absorption of any prechange NOL in a postchange taxable year to the fair market value multiplied by the long-term tax-exempt rate. For example, X Corporation has a net operating loss of $4 million and Shareholder A purchases 60 percent of the outstanding stock for $600,000. The long-term tax-exempt rate equals 6 percent. The value of the loss corporation of $1 million (= $600,000/.60) times the long-term tax-exempt rate of 6 percent results in a maximum use per year of the net operating loss of $60,000 (= $1,000,000 × .06). One adds the § 382 limitation not used in a given year because of insufficient taxable income to the limitation for a following year. When using NOLs, one must focus on the loss corporation's fair market value. For a taxable stock purchase, this valuation becomes relatively simple. When a change in control results from a reorganization in which the purchase price includes stock of a privately held corporation, however, this valuation becomes more difficult.

IRC § 382(l)(5) provides that the § 382 limitation does not apply if, prior to the ownership change, the corporation was in bankruptcy and the historical creditors and shareholders of the loss corporation own 50 percent or more of the value of the loss corporation. To consider a creditor as historical, the related debt must have arisen in the ordinary course of business or have been held by the creditor for 18 months prior to the ownership change. Two special rules apply under the bankruptcy exception:

1. The debtor must reduce the NOL by any interest deducted during the three previous taxable years plus the interest paid in the current taxable year prior to the ownership change on the debt converted to stock.

2. Another change in ownership within the next two years will eliminate the balance of the new operating loss that remained after the first ownership change.

The debtor can elect not to have the bankruptcy exception under § 382(l)(5) apply. IRC § 382(l)(6) provides that, if the debtor elects not to have the bankruptcy exception apply or does not qualify for the § 382(l)(5) exception, one should base the § 382 limitation on the value of the corporation's equity after discharging the debt. When the debtor exchanges a large part of the outstanding debt for shares, the value of the equity of the reorganized corporation will exceed the value before reorganization, which can have negative value in many cases. As a result of this increase in value, the debtor can preserve more of the net operating loss under the § 382 limitation than by using the § 382(l)(5) exception.

NOTES

1. The process for seeking authorization is found in Bankruptcy Rule 4001(b).
2. Creditors can bring a motion for adequate protection under Bankruptcy Code § 362 (relief from automatic stay), § 363 (motion to halt the use of cash collateral), or § 364 (regarding the granting of liens on previously encumbered property).
3. Three seminal cases exist in the adequate protection area: *In re American Mariner Industries, Inc.,* 734 F.2d 426 (9th Cir. 1984), *In re Briggs Transportation Co.,* 780 F.2d 1339 (8th Cir. 1985), and *United Savings of America v. Timbers of Inwood Forest Association,* 484 U.S. 365 (1988).
4. The protection is only for further decline in collateral value after commencement of the case. The creditor is not protected from the shortfall existing at the filing date.
5. *See LNC Investment, Inc and Charter National Life Insurance Co. v First Fidelity Bank, et al.,* 1995 U.S. Dist. LEXIS 5065 (S.D.N.Y 1995) (recent decisions in the Second Circuit have rejected the equity cushion approach in favor of a more individualized analysis of the specific risks threatening the collateral); *In re Lane,* 108 Bankr. 6, 9-10 (Bankr. D. Mass. 1989) (creditor not adequately protected when equity cushion is eroding); *In re 1606 New Hampshire Ave. Assocs.,* 85 Bankr. 298, 309 (Bankr. E.D. Pa. 1988) (adequate protection is largely a function of movements in value of collateral). *In re Hagendorfer,* 42 Bankr. 13, 16 (Bankr. S.D. Ala.) (secured creditor entitled to protection even when there is ample equity, if value of lien decreased following bankruptcy, *aff'd, Hagendorfer v. Marlette,* 42 Bankr. 17 (S.D. Ala. 1984): *In re Alyucan,* 12 B.R. 803 (Bankr. D. Utah 1981) (adequate protection warranted if value of creditor's interest in property is declining, regardless of equity cushion); *In re Johnson,* 90 Bankr. 973, 979 (Bankr. D. Minn. 1988) (focus is on shifts in the ratio of the debt to the value of the collateral in a multifactored analysis).

6. *See* § 503(c) of the Bankruptcy Code.
7. *In re Trans World Airlines, Inc.*, 134 F.3d. 188 (3d Cir. 1998).
8. In bankruptcy, *discharge* refers to releasing a debtor from an obligation.
9. *Bank of America v. 203 North LaSalle Street Partnership.* 526 U.S. 434 (1999).
10. For a discussion of reorganization values, *see* Chapter 11 of Grant W. Newton, *Bankruptcy and Insolvency Accounting: Practice and Procedure,* 6th ed. (New York: John Wiley & Sons, 2000).

BIBLIOGRAPHY

AICPA. *Accounting for Preconfirmation Contingencies in Fresh-Start Reporting—Practice Bulletin 11.* New York: AICPA, 1994.

AICPA. Accounting Standards Executive Committee. *Statement of Position (SOP) 90-7, Financial Reporting by Entities in Reorganization Under the Bankruptcy Code,* New York: AICPA, 1990.

AICPA. *Consulting Services Practice Aid 02-1, Business Valuation in Bankruptcy.* New York: AICPA, 2002.

AICPA. *Providing Bankruptcy & Reorganization Services—Practice Aid.* New York: AICPA, 1998.

AICPA. *Consulting Services Special Report 03-1, Litigation Services and Applicable Professional Standards* (CSSR 03-1). New York: AICPA

APB. *Reporting the Results of Operations—opinion 30.*

Collier Bankruptcy Code and Rules. Albany, NY: Matthew Bender & Co. (issued annually).

Collier Bankruptcy Manual. 3rd ed. Albany, NY: Matthew Bender & Co. (updated annually).

Dykeman, F.C. *Forensic Accounting—The Accountant as Expert Witness.* New York: John Wiley & Sons, 1982.

FASB. *Accounting for the Impairment or Disposal of Long-Lived Assets—Statement No. 144.*

FASB. *Business Combinations—Statement No. 141.*

FASB. *Goodwill and Other Intangible Assets—Statement No. 142.*

Newton, G.W. *Bankruptcy and Insolvency Accounting: Practice and Procedures.* 6th ed. New York: John Wiley & Sons, 2000 (updated annually).

Newton, G.W., and R. Liquerman. *Bankruptcy and Insolvency Taxation.* New York: John Wiley & Sons, 2005 (updated annually).

Pratt, S. *Valuing Small Business and Professional Practices.* Dow Jones-Irwin, 1998.

Robert Morris Associates. *Annual Statement Studies.* Robert Morris Associates (issued annually).

Sulmeyer, I., D.M. Lynn, M.R. Rocheole, and S.L. Esseerman, eds. *2004 Collier Handbook for Trustees and Debtors in Possession.* Albany, NY: Matthew Bender & Co., 2004.

Wagner, M.J., and P.B. Frank. *AICPA Professional Standards,* Vol. 2, Section MS 11.06. New York: AICPA, 1986.

CHAPTER 29

ALTER EGO

Michael J. Wagner
Bonnie J. Goldsmith

CONTENTS

29.1 WHAT IS ALTER EGO?

(a) Legal Doctrine.   Alter ego in Latin means *second self.* Plaintiffs use the legal theory of alter ego to obtain a judgment against the owners of a corporation. It allows the court to remove the protection of the corporate veil and hold the controlling forces behind the corporation individually responsible, whether the owners are corporations, partnerships, individuals, or other forms of organization. If inequity results when one entity controls the corporation with which the plaintiff does business, the court holds the controlling entity liable for the actions of the corporation. The court disregards the separate legal status of a corporation and its owners and declares them to be one legal entity.

    Normally, a plaintiff must prove some legal connection with a defendant to have standing to sue and obtain a judgment against that defendant. In commercial litigation, this legal connection usually results from a contract or a fiduciary duty that the defendant owes to the plaintiff. Alter ego theory permits a plaintiff to win a judgment against an entity that the plaintiff would not have the standing to sue under traditional law.

(b) Equitable Remedy. Alter ego offers an equitable remedy. Equity denotes the spirit and the habit of fairness, justness, and right dealing that would regulate the intercourse between individuals. In a more restricted sense, it offers a system of jurisprudence distinct from the common-law courts and empowered to decree equity in the sense defined.[1] Therefore, the court will disregard the formal legal separateness of the corporation to be fair to the plaintiff. If the court were to recognize the legal separateness of the corporation, an unfair result would occur.

The plaintiff faces a challenge in an alter ego case because the relief sought conflicts with established corporate law. Every state has a body of law its legislature established that governs the conduct of companies incorporated in its state. These laws create a separate and distinct legal entity that has the right to enter into contracts and that presents only limited liability to its owners. Alter ego disregards this established body of law and allows third parties to collect judgments from the owners of the corporation on transactions between the third party and the corporation. In fact, piercing the corporate veil, the term used by courts when referring to such matters, is one of the most litigated issues in corporate law.[2]

The alter ego doctrine applies to close corporations, that is, those owned by a few individuals, limited liability corporations (LLCs), and corporate groups (i.e., a corporate parent and a group of corporate subsidiaries). In fact, in closely held corporations, the fewer the shareholders, the more likely it is that the court will invoke the doctrine.[3] As a result, plaintiffs rarely target shareholders in publicly held corporations using the alter ego theory, because of the large number of shareholders. However, public companies often become targets of alter ego analysis when a subsidiary has insufficient assets to satisfy a judgment and the plaintiff sues the parent company (shareholder) under the alter ego theory.

(c) Mixed Questions of Law and Facts. Although the courts created alter ego as an equitable remedy, the court still requires factual evidence to invoke the doctrine. Case law has discussed the relevant factors—known as *indicia of alter ego*—to pierce the corporate veil. The legal standard for establishing when to set aside "the corporate veil is notably imprecise and fact intensive."[4]

Their knowledge of business facts and corporate structure qualifies Certified Public Accountants (CPAs) to examine many of the indicia of alter ego. The CPA should understand the case law regarding alter ego in order to consider the proper factors. The CPA must use judgment because the courts have no consensus as to key factors, the ranking of their relative importance, and how many factors must exist to invoke the doctrine. Each case stands alone on its own facts.

Although no single approach or coherent set of principles exists to govern when to apply alter ego, all the approaches have similarities. One commentator suggests that, as a general rule, the courts have required that the party seeking to pierce the corporate veil satisfy a two-pronged test: (1) such unity of interest and ownership exists that the corporation and the individual shareholders no longer have separate personalities; and (2) viewing the acts as those of the corporation alone will result in inequity.[5] Other cases require proof of fraud as a third test. These cases define fraud to include intent to defraud[6] or bad faith or a showing that injustice may result if shareholders hide behind the veil.[7]

Frederick J. Powell, in his 1931 publication *Parent and Subsidiary Corporations*, identified 11 circumstances that indicate that the subsidiary is merely an instrument of the parent:[8]

1. The parent corporation owns all or most of the subsidiary's capital stock.
2. The parent and subsidiary corporations have common directors or officers.
3. The parent corporation finances the subsidiary.
4. The parent corporation subscribes to all of the capital stock of the subsidiary or otherwise causes its incorporation.
5. The subsidiary has grossly inadequate capital.
6. The parent corporation pays the subsidiary's salaries and other expenses or losses.
7. The subsidiary has substantially no business except with the parent corporation, or no assets except the ones the parent corporation conveys to it.
8. The papers of the parent corporation or the statements of the officers describe the subsidiary as a department or division of the parent corporation, or refer to its business or financial responsibility as the parent corporation's own.
9. The parent corporation uses the subsidiary's property as its own.
10. The subsidiary's directors or executives do not act independently in the interest of the subsidiary but take their orders from the parent corporation in the latter's interest.
11. The subsidiary does not observe its own formal legal requirements.

In 1991, Robert B. Thompson reported results of his study of how the courts used alter ego to pierce the corporate veil.[9] He studied all cases—1,583 in total—in Westlaw through 1985 that dealt with piercing the corporate veil. This study found that courts pierced the corporate veil in about 40 percent of reported cases. The distribution of results by state is shown in Exhibit 29-1.

As one would expect, this study showed that the states with the major commercial centers—New York, Texas, California, and Illinois—have the largest numbers of alter ego decisions. California and Illinois pierce the corporate veil more frequently than the average, whereas New York and Texas pierce the corporate veil less frequently than the average.

Thompson found certain factors that were most often associated with the courts' decision to invoke the alter ego doctrine and pierce the corporate veil. These factors include the following:

- The subsidiary is the "instrumentality" of the parent.
- The subsidiary is the alter ego of the parent.
- The subsidiary is the "dummy" of the parent.
- The case involved misrepresentation of corporate separateness.

The study found that when a court refused to pierce the corporate veil, the plaintiff most often had failed to prove misrepresentation, the most important factor in the cases that Thompson studied.

State	Number of Cases	Pierce	No pierce	Percentage Piercing	State	Number of Cases	Pierce	No pierce	Percentage Piercing
AK	10	3	7	30%	MT	8	4	4	50
AL	17	11	6	65	NC	21	9	12	43
AR	23	9	14	39	ND	4	3	1	75
AZ	17	7	10	41	NE	12	7	5	58
CA	89	40	49	45	NH	5	0	5	0
CO	13	7	6	54	NJ	20	9	11	45
CT	11	7	4	64	NM	13	2	11	15
DC	10	6	4	60	NV	12	5	7	42
DE	11	0	11	0	NY	212	74	138	35
FED	302	119	183	39	OH	14	8	6	57
FL	46	19	27	41	OK	15	6	9	40
GA	47	18	29	38	OR	16	9	7	56
HA	4	1	3	25	PA	65	20	45	31
IA	12	7	5	58	PR	3	0	3	0
ID	9	6	3	67	RI	6	2	4	33
IL	78	33	45	42	SC	8	3	5	38
IN	16	11	5	69	SD	8	5	3	62
KS	19	15	4	79	TN	18	7	11	39
KY	15	4	11	27	TX	106	37	69	35
LA	67	24	43	36	UT	7	3	4	43
MA	15	6	9	40	VA	16	4	12	25
MD	15	6	9	40	VT	0	0	0	0
ME	8	2	6	25	WA	27	12	15	44
MI	22	6	16	27	WI	16	8	8	50
MN	13	5	8	38	WV	7	3	4	43
MO	30	12	18	40	WY	8	5	3	62
MS	14	5	9	36	Total	1580	634	946	40%

Exhibit 29-1.   Results of 1991 Study by Robert B. Thompson. Piercing the Corporate Veil

The study summarized the courts' actions but did not explain why the courts reached the affirmative result.

In 1999, Thompson extended his 1985 study to include an additional 2,200 cases from the period 1985 through 1996. This additional work increased his database to approximately 3,800 cases.[10] The results of the updated study fit within the pattern of the original study.[11] In 547 of these cases, the plaintiff sought piercing within corporate groups. The courts pierced corporate groups 34 percent of the time, somewhat lower than when the plaintiffs sought piercing against individual shareholders.[12]

29.2 TYPICAL SCENARIOS INVOLVING ALTER EGO

(a) Parent or Subsidiary Is Judgment Proof

(i) Undercapitalized Subsidiary.   The plaintiff has a contract with a corporation that is a subsidiary of a parent corporation. The subsidiary corporation breaches a legal right of the plaintiff, who sues to enforce this right. The plaintiff learns that the subsidiary corporation has insufficient assets to satisfy the judgment owing to the parent's action. If the plaintiff can attribute this to the subsidiary's undercapitalization or to the parent's treating the subsidiary's assets as its own, the plaintiff could try to collect its judgment against the parent corporation.

(ii) Controlling Subsidiary.   In a less common scenario in which a subsidiary controls a parent, a creditor of the parent corporation may try to collect its debt from the subsidiary rather than from the parent. This can happen when the subsidiary becomes larger than the parent and controls the decisions of the corporate group. In the examples in this chapter, the parent controls the subsidiary. If the subsidiary controls the parent, the analogous results hold.

(iii) Sibling Subsidiaries.   Under alter ego, one can sue a sibling corporation that controls another sibling corporation within a single corporate family. This can happen when one subsidiary at the same level as a second subsidiary with a common parent actually controls the second subsidiary.

(b) Corporation Is Judgment Proof but Individual Equity Owners Are Not.   Suppose a corporation has breached a contract with the plaintiff but the corporation does not have funds to pay the judgment. If the individual equity holders have either undercapitalized the corporation or used its assets as their own, the plaintiff can try to collect its judgment against the equity owners.

(c) Plaintiff Was Confused about Corporate Identity.   The plaintiff believes it enters into a contract with Corporation A, or at least that Corporation A guaranteed the contract. In reality, the plaintiff entered into a contract with Corporation B, which Corporation A controlled. Corporation B is judgment proof, so the plaintiff seeks to collect its claim against Corporation A.

(d) Corporation Sells Assets, Leaving Insufficient Capital.   The plaintiff has a contract with Corporation A. Corporation A breaches its contract with the plaintiff.

Corporation A sells all or most of its assets to a new Corporation B for less than fair market value. The owners of Corporation B are essentially the same as those of Corporation A. The plaintiff sues Corporation B under the theory that Corporation B is really the same organization as Corporation A. The courts have also referred to this as the *de facto merger* doctrine; the transaction can also be a fraudulent conveyance.

29.3 INDICIA OF ALTER EGO

Most courts will disregard the corporations' separate identities if their owners have also disregarded the corporations' separateness in their dealings. How the owners have treated the corporation is a question of fact. The relation of the owners and the corporation becomes the subject matter of the indicia. Exhibit 29-2 shows the relation between the main indicia for alter ego and the different tests of alter ego. Although the following sections do not describe all indicia, they do apply as listed in the chart.

(a) Financial Dependence.   A key factor examines whether the debtor corporation financially depends on its owner. Perhaps the owner did not properly capitalize the corporation from the outset: instead of infusing a reasonable amount of equity, the owner lent funds to the company. The owner may have initially properly capitalized the corporation but later let it become undercapitalized. This occurs in several situations, including the following:

- The parent buys most of the subsidiary's assets (or takes them in settlement of a current intercompany debt) and then leases them back to the subsidiary for a monthly fee.
- The parent converts its equity in the corporation to debt. The treatment of the related interest and the existence of scheduled principal payments helps in assessing the validity of this type of transaction.
- The parent allows the subsidiary to become undercapitalized because of corporate operating losses.

One can compare the corporation's debt–to–equity ratio with that of other companies in its industry to measure how the corporation's capital structure differs from that of similarly situated companies. If undercapitalization results solely from operating losses, the courts will not invoke alter ego.

An entity's ability (or inability) to exist as a stand-alone corporation without its owner's help also indicates financial independence (or lack thereof). For example, if no informed lender would lend to the entity without the owner's guarantee, then the entity depends financially on the owner. The inability to obtain credit from sources other than the parent indicates alter ego.

Zero balance accounts, or *sweep* accounts, involve relatively common banking arrangements that move any idle cash to the parent company's account at the end of each business day. This centralized cash-control tool permits an owner of multiple entities or subsidiaries to maintain control of all the cash its companies generate. If a subsidiary does not receive interest on the excess cash it generates or does not pay interest when it has a cash deficit, the arrangement indicates that the parent has financial control.

Test of Alter Ego Indicia	Financial Dependence	Confusion About Corporate Identity	Lack of Separateness	Domination and Control
1. Undercapitalization				
a. Intial undercapitalization	X		X	X
b. Subsequent undercapitalization	X		X	X
2. Inability to operate as a stand-alone corporation	X		X	
3. Use of zero balance accounts without interest	X		X	X
4. Related-party transaction to the benefit of owners	X		X	X
5. Related-party transaction to the benefit of corporation	X		X	X
6. Insolvency	X		X	
7. Sameness (name, banks, directors, officers, offices, business activity, attorneys, accountants, accounting systems, stationery, invoices, purchase orders)		X	X	
8. Lack of corporate formalities			X	
9. Preference over other creditors			X	X
10. De facto merger			X	X

Exhibit 29-2. Alter Ego Indicia (Relation of the Owners and the Corporation)

Financial dependence can also exist when the owners give the corporation special treatment that they would not give a third party. This includes excusing required payments of either principal or interest, charging below-market interest rates or no interest, and no documentation of loan terms (referred to as *evergreen loans*).

(b) Confusion about Corporate Identity. Several factors can confuse a plaintiff about a counterparty, including the following:

- **Same name.** Both the parent and subsidiary use the same name to describe themselves.
- **Same stationery.** Identical letterhead or letterhead that includes the names of both the parent and the subsidiary can misrepresent to the plaintiff the nature of the relation between the two entities.
- **Same banks.** When the entities pay vendors from the same bank, particularly if the parent company and bank reside in the same location but the subsidiary corporation resides in another state, the plaintiff often views the parent as the financially responsible party.
- **Same officers.** Dealing with the same people when working with the parent or the subsidiary can confuse the plaintiff, particularly when the officers do not clearly articulate whom they represent, or intentionally (or negligently) misrepresent whom they represent.
- **Same invoices or purchase orders.** Both the parent and subsidiary identify each other on their invoices and purchase orders or use the same trade name or trademark.

Confusion can also exist because of misrepresentations made by the corporate entity. The three most common types of misrepresentations that arise in piercing cases are the following:

1. The corporation's financial status
2. Statements made involving promises of corporate performance
3. Representations and other actions that lead the plaintiff to believe that someone other than the corporation it seeks to pierce stands behind the debt[13]

(c) Lack of Separateness

(i) Lack of Corporate Formality. The courts will treat a corporation as a separate legal entity only if the corporation follows certain rules. These rules—including those listed below—vary depending on the state in which the corporation is incorporated.

- Holding meetings of the board of directors
- Electing the board of directors annually
- Holding an annual meeting of shareholders
- Electing officers annually
- Enacting and following articles of incorporation and bylaws
- Paying annual fees
- Obtaining shareholder or board approval for major corporate events (e.g., major financings or acquisitions)

(ii) Same Directors.   If both entities' board of directors have the same members, control over corporate governance and policy is identical. The boards of directors for both entities need not have the same members. As long as common directors have control, the plaintiff can treat both companies the same.

(iii) Same Officers.   When the same people manage both companies, they can treat both companies as one. Management often attempts to increase efficiency by managing the two entities as if they were one large company.

(iv) Same Offices.   Confusion can result if the parent and subsidiary operate from the same location, particularly if they share the same building and have identical mailing addresses.

(v) Same Business Activity.   If the parent and the subsidiary are in the same line of business, selling the same products or services, business associates will more likely confuse them than if they have unrelated businesses.

(vi) Same Attorneys.   When the companies use the same lawyer to incorporate and to advise, management appears to regard the companies as one. An even stronger signal arises when the two corporations reside in different jurisdictions but use the legal services of the lawyers from the parent's jurisdiction for both corporations. To defend a claim of alter ego, the two corporations must have different financial interests and motives. If the same attorneys represent both companies in an alter ego case, the conclusion of unity of interest follows.

(vii) Same Accountants.   The parent and subsidiary corporation will have their own sets of financial statements. The fact that both companies use the same accountants for audit, review, or compilation services can indicate that the boards of each company treat the companies the same.

(viii) Same Accounting Systems.   When the companies use identical accounting systems—including general ledgers, subsidiary ledgers, chart of accounts, and financial statements—one may consider them as one accounting entity.

(xi) Transactions Not at Arm's Length.   Circumstances inconsistent with the way unrelated parties deal with each other indicate a lack of corporate separateness. These would include transactions that lack exchange of fair consideration, particularly when one corporation or its shareholders consistently exploit another corporation. Transactions not at arm's length include the following:

- Sale of product at terms different from those to unrelated third parties
- Sale of assets at below market value
- Loans that include extending credit without adequate security, without documentation (e.g., a promissory note), with flexible repayment terms, or with nonmarket interest rates

Although courts consider related party transactions and relations as important indicia to an alter ego case, the simple fact that the corporations are related parties does not allow the court to pierce the corporate veil. If the controlling party inequitably uses its authority to maintain its interests over other third-party creditors, then the courts may find it appropriate to invoke the doctrine.

(d) Domination and Control

(i) Preference over Other Creditors.   Alter ego becomes most clear when a shareholder or parent corporation uses its position of influence to favor itself over others. When the facts and circumstances indicate an unfair preference for the parent over other, less powerful creditors, the court often seeks to protect the third-party creditor.

Although the equity courts do not follow bankruptcy rules, the bankruptcy statutes provide guidance as to when a preference occurs. Section 547 of the Bankruptcy Code lists five conditions that a party must prove to assert a preference in a bankruptcy. The court should also consider these five requirements when assessing the treatment of the outstanding debt to the parent corporation relative to the outstanding debt to other third-party creditors. The five conditions are as follows:

1. The debtor transferred property to or for the creditor's benefit.
2. The debtor used this transfer to satisfy an antecedent debt owed by the debtor before it made the transfer.
3. The debtor transferred the property while the debtor was insolvent.
4. The debtor made the transfer within 90 days before the debtor filed the bankruptcy petition or between 90 days and one year before the date that the debtor filed the bankruptcy petition if the creditor was an insider when the transfer occurred.
5. The transfer of property enables the creditor to receive more than the creditor would receive under a chapter 7 liquidation.

The fourth condition does not involve an alter ego situation. The other conditions, although pertinent, need not be present for a court to find alter ego. For example, the corporation need not be insolvent for a preference to occur under alter ego. An insolvent corporation that transfers assets to owners benefits them over creditors. The fifth test is probably the most important in finding alter ego: did the owner receive more than it would have if the transfer did not occur and the corporation was liquidated pursuant to the order of liquidation designed to treat all creditors fairly?

Section 548 of the Bankruptcy Code also provides guidance. This section deals with unwinding fraudulent transfers and obligations (*see also* Section 28.3(y) of Chapter 28). The provision allows the trustee in bankruptcy to avoid transfers if the debtor either voluntarily or involuntarily

1. Transferred assets with an actual intent to hinder, delay, or defraud any other creditor of the debtor, or
2. Received less than a reasonably equivalent value, and
   a. The debtor was insolvent or became insolvent as a result of the transfer, or
   b. The transaction left the debtor with an unreasonably small capital, or
   c. The debtor incurred debts beyond the debtor's ability to pay them as they became due.

Instructive portions of the fraudulent transfers section of the Bankruptcy Code relate to two situations: (1) when an owner deliberately misrepresents to a third-party creditor who the responsible party is and (2) when an owner gives less than adequate consideration for assets transferred from the related company.

(ii) Transactions Not at Arm's Length. Parents or shareholders advancing their own interests at the expense of the corporation give clear evidence of domination and control. These two become relevant only when the parent uses this domination and control unfairly. To learn the relevant facts, one should analyze the intercompany transactions to assess whether the motives and intent of both parties remained consistent or fair, or both, to other less powerful third-party creditors.

(iii) De Facto Merger. An acquiring corporation that buys the assets of a selling corporation usually does not take on the debts and liabilities of the selling corporation. Some exceptions to this general rule arise when the acquiring corporation contractually agrees to assume the liabilities of the selling corporation or the corporations merge.

The general rule has another exception, known as the *de facto merger doctrine*, which defines part of alter ego law. Four elements must exist to find a *de facto* merger:

1. A continuation of the enterprise of the seller corporation creates a continuity of management, personnel, physical location, assets, and general business operations.

2. A continuity of shareholders results from the purchasing corporation paying for the acquired assets with its own shares, which the seller corporation's shareholders will ultimately own so that they become a constituent part of the purchasing corporation.

3. The seller corporation ceases its ordinary business operations, liquidates, and dissolves as soon as it legally and practicably can.

4. The purchasing corporation assumes those liabilities and obligations of the seller that are ordinarily necessary to the uninterrupted continuation of the seller corporation's normal business operations.[14]

If these conditions exist, creditors of the seller corporation often bring ultimately successful claims against the acquiring corporation.

A claimant can collect against a successor corporation when the transfer of assets to the purchaser allows the seller to fraudulently escape liability for debts.[15] Although the alter ego theory does not require proof of a fraudulent purpose, the courts will likely invoke the doctrine if misrepresentation does exist.

The *de facto* merger doctrine has allowed recovery against the successor corporation because it views the successor corporation as a mere continuation of the seller corporation. California court decisions have held that one or both of the following conditions must exist to consider the successor corporation a continuation of another corporation.

1. The successor gave inadequate consideration for the predecessor corporation's assets that had been available for meeting the claims of the predecessor's unsecured creditors.

2. One or more persons served as officers, directors, or shareholders of both corporations.[16]

The above elements become necessary for contractual and most tort causes of action.

When the cause of action results from manufacturing defects, however, a different standard is used to impose liability on a successor to a manufacturer.

The following elements are necessary when the cause of action results from manufacturing defects:

- The successor's acquisition of the business destroyed the plaintiff's remedies against the original manufacturer.

- The successor has the ability to assume the original manufacturer's risk-spreading role.

- Fairness requires the successor to assume the responsibility for the defect in return for enjoying the goodwill attached to the original manufacturer's operation.[17]

The bankruptcy courts use substantive consolidation to aggregate the assets of related entities. Substantive consolidation effectively merges two or more related, yet legally distinct, entities into a single debtor with a common pool of assets and a common pool of liabilities.[18] One of the several rationales that the bankruptcy courts consider when deciding whether to consolidate is whether the control, operational interdependence, or lack of corporate formalities has made the entities alter egos of one another.[19]

29.4   LIMITED LIABILITY COMPANIES (LLCS)

Limited Liability Companies (LLCs) are a hybrid organization, combining characteristics of corporations and partnerships.[20] By 1996, all states had enacted statutes allowing for the formation of LLCs.[21] LLCs soon became the fastest growing form of business.[22] The statutes allow for limited liability to its members, similar to that of corporate statutes.

LLC statutes set forth the basic premise that LLCs are independent entities that shield their members from personal liability. As with corporations, the LLC statutes do not consistently address the piercing issue. Generally, the states' statutory treatment of the piercing issue can be grouped into three categories:

1. Explicit treatment when states have chosen to explicitly adopt and apply the corporate concept of the piercing issue

2. Implicit treatment when state statutes are more subtle than the explicit treatment yet achieve the same piercing result

3. No treatment when state statutes are silent on the piercing issue

In addition, some states have elected to provide for explicit treatment of a particular piercing factor.[23] Therefore, the practitioner should be familiar with the relevant state statutes when working on such a case.

Even though few cases offer guidance for experts working in an LLC situation, a 2004 study of 14 cases in which the court evaluated the merits of the LLC piercing claims indicates that the courts have applied the traditional corporate standards for piercing the veil with little mention that they are applying the standards to a different form of entity.[24] With the exception of the adherence to corporate formalities factors (such as those described in Section 29.3(c)(i) of this chapter), courts have generally remained true to the corporate veil piercing standards.[25] However, treatment of piercing standards for LLCs may change in the future to distinguish between the LLC form and corporate form of business.

29.5 ROLE OF THE BUSINESS EXPERT IN ALTER EGO ANALYSIS

(a) Dealing with Fact Issues. The indicia described in Section 29.3 translate to factual inquiries involving the relations between the corporation and its owners, whether the owners are corporations or individual equity owners. These relations surpass the normal understanding of the court and the jury. Therefore, an expert in business matters must explain normal and abnormal relations of the corporations and their owners in the particular lawsuit.

Corporate managers, corporate lawyers, business professors, and CPAs all qualify to address most of the indicia of alter ego. In addition to deciding which indicia exist in a particular case, the expert should advise the lawyer about documents needed to analyze the relevant indicia. The expert should know which documents probably exist and should describe them well enough for the lawyer to properly request them.

Although each case will use different documents to illustrate the most pertinent indicia of alter ego theory, the following documents often help:

- **The minutes of boards of directors meetings from the corporations involved.** These often discuss intercompany issues.
- **Letters of incorporation.** These can help identify who originally owned the corporation as well as the officers and directors. The current financial statements will update this information.
- **The entities' audited financial statements.** The information contained within these statements includes an overall financial assessment of the company, related party transactions, information for financial ratios, descriptions of accounting treatments for significant transactions, and the basic composition of all types of assets, liabilities, and equity recorded.
- **Internal financial statements.** Original treatments of intercompany transactions often differ from the reported treatment. The expert should direct attention to internal account names and the accounting systems that each company uses. Suppose a company transfers assets according to the audited financial statements but does not record the transfer in the internal financial statements. This indicates that management views the companies as one entity and does not consider transferring the assets necessary for internal reporting purposes.
- **Correspondence between the parent and the subsidiary as well as between the creditor and the company with which it did business.** Similar letterhead, the manner in which the individual who signed the correspondence represents himself or herself to the plaintiff, and the actual content of the correspondence become important factors to consider. Correspondence between the creditor and the company can reveal how the creditor perceived the business relation.
- **The internal accounting documents of both companies.** These can reveal similarities that confuse third parties dealing with only one of the companies.

For example, identical invoices or invoices that include both the address of the parent corporation and the address of the subsidiary corporation often confuse the third party about the counterparty.

- **Credit ratings or any other type of external documents that show how another third party perceived the entities.** The parent and the subsidiary could have represented themselves as one entity for extension of credit.
- **Detailed general ledger entries of both companies.** Analysis of all intercompany transactions reveals the nature of the accounting treatment of various transactions. Note particularly any commingling of funds or special treatment uncommon in an arm's length transaction.
- **Insurance policies.** Review of insurance policies held by the parent and subsidiary will often establish whether the subsidiary carried sufficient insurance for the normal and reasonably expected risks of its business.

After studying the documents provided, an expert will often conclude that the facts and circumstances indicate an alter ego relation. Even an expert who concludes that the facts do not support alter ego can find evidence of fraudulent or criminal activity and should communicate these findings to the client.

Because alter ego theory involves complex issues, a successful litigation depends on an expert's ability to ensure thorough discovery and to clearly present the information to the judge and jury. The indicia of alter ego do not lend themselves to a linear approach. Instead, a matrix of relevant facts and commonalities most likely will exist, complicating the expert's presentation. Demonstrative exhibits can help relay the pertinent information to the trier of fact.

(b) Explaining the Indicia of Alter Ego.   The expert will need to explain which indicia the judge or jury should consider in deciding whether to pierce the corporate veil. Because the courts lack agreement and precedent on the necessary indicia for a particular case, the experts can explain why, given the facts of the case, they consider certain indicia important and others less important.

(c) Offering an Opinion on the Ultimate Issue.   The trial judge will decide if the expert can testify as to whether, in his or her opinion, the court should pierce the corporate veil. If a judge allows the issue of alter ego to go to a jury, then under the rules of evidence that permit an expert to express an opinion on the ultimate issue (e.g., Rule 704 of the Federal Rules of Evidence), the judge should allow an expert to opine on this question.

Seven states (California, Colorado, Delaware, Louisiana, Washington, West Virginia, and Wyoming) hold that because the alter ego remedy is an equitable one, a judge—not a jury—will render the decision.[26] Fourteen states (plus the District of Columbia) have held that the jury should decide whether to pierce the corporate veil: Florida, Georgia, Iowa, Mississippi, North Carolina, North Dakota, Tennessee, Texas, Alabama, Indiana, Kansas, Montana, Utah, and Virginia.[27]

In all other states, the courts have not clarified who decides the alter ego issue. In federal courts, whether the alter ego claims go to the jury often depends on whether the plaintiff based the claim on state or federal law. Federal law does not address this issue. The Second Circuit Court of Appeals has commented, however, that "whether or not those factors ... that will justify ignoring the corporate form and imposing liability on affiliated corporation or shareholders are present in a given case is the sort of determination usually made by a jury because it is so fact specific.[28] A judge who renders the decision can decide whether an expert's opinion will aid in the decision process.

NOTES

1. *Black's Law Dictionary* (St. Paul, MN: West Publishing), 1968.
2. Robert B. Thompson, "Piercing the Veil within Corporate Groups: Corporate Shareholders as Mere Investors," 13 *Connecticut Journal of International Law* 13 (1999): 379–383.
3. Robert B. Thompson, "Piercing the Corporate Veil: An Empirical Study," *Cornell Law Review* 76 (July 1991): 1038.
4. Susan A. Kraemer, "Piercing the Corporate Veil: Backgound and Theory," *Denver University Law Review* 76 (1999): 729, 730, citing *Crane v. Green & Freedman Baking Co.,* 134 F.3d 17, 21 (1st Cir. 1998).
5. Michael J. Garetner, "Note: Reverse Piercing the Corporate Veil: Should Corporation Owners Have It Both Ways?" *William & Mary Law Review* 30 (Spring 1989): 667–678.
6. *Ministry of Defense of the Islamic Republic of Iran v. Gould, Inc.,* 969 F.2d 764 (9th Cir. 1992).
7. David H. Barber, "Piercing the Corporate Veil," *Willamette Law Review* 17 (1981).
8. Cathy J. Krendl and James R. Krendl, "Piercing the Corporate Veil: Focusing the Inquiry," *Denver Law Journal* 55 (1978).
9. Robert B. Thompson, *op. cit.,* p. 1048. "Piercing the Corporate Veil."
10. Robert B. Thompson, "Piercing the Veil within Corporate Groups," 379–385.
11. Ibid.
12. Ibid., 386.
13. Franklin A. Geburtz, "Piercing Piercing: An Attempt to Lift the Veil of Confusion Surrounding the Doctrine of Piercing the Corporate Veil," *Oregon Law Review* 76 (1997): 853–871.
14. *Keller v. Clark Equipment Co.,* 715 F.2d 1280, 1291 (8th Cir. 1983); *Bud Antle, Inc. v. Eastern Foods Inc.,* 758 F.2d 1451, 1457 (11th Cir. 1985).
15. *Ray v. Alad Corp.,* 19 Cal.3d 22, 28 (1977).
16. *Id.* at 29.
17. *Id.* at 31.
18. Mary Elisabeth Kors, "Altered Egos: Deciphering Substantive Consolidation," *University of Pittsburgh Law Review* 381 (Winter 1998).
19. Ibid., 385.
20. Jeffrey K. Vandervoort, "Piercing the Veil of Limited Liability Companies: The Need for a Better Standard," *DePaul Business & Commercial Law Journal* 3 (Fall 2004): 6.
21. Robert B. Thompson, "The Limits of Liability in the New Limited Liability Entities," *Wake Forest Law Review* 32 (1997): Footnote 1.
22. Jeffrey K. Vandervoort, "Piercing the Veil of Limited Liability Companies," 6.
23. Ibid., 7.
24. Ibid., 10.
25. Ibid., 13.
26. By definition, a judge decides matters of equity as opposed to common law decisions, which a jury decides.
27. Mark A. Oltoff, "Beyond the Form—Should the Corporate Veil Be Pierced?" *University of Missouri KC Law Review* (Winter 1995) pp. 331–333.
28. *William Passalacqua Builders, Inc. v. Resnick Developers South, Inc.,* 933 F.2d 131, 137 (2d Cir. 1991).

LIST OF CASES

Bud Antle, Inc. v. Eastern Foods, Inc., 758 F.2d 1451, 1457 (11th Cir. 1985)
Keller v. Clark Equipment Co., 715 F.2d 1280, 1291 (8th Cir. 1983)
Ministry of Defense of the Islamic Republic of Iran v. Gould, Inc., 969 F.2d 764 (9th Cir. 1992)
Ray v. Alad Corp., 19 Cal.3d 22, 28 (1977)
William Passalacqua Builders, Inc. v. Resnick Developers South, Inc., 933 F.2d 131 (2d Cir. 1991)

CHAPTER 30

EMPLOYMENT LITIGATION

Ali Saad

CONTENTS

30.1 INTRODUCTION

Almost all employers face federal nondiscrimination requirements. In addition, about 30 states have enacted overlapping or additional fair employment practices laws dealing with employment discrimination.[1] These laws attempt to ensure that employers base their employment practices on performance and merit rather than non-job-related characteristics. Legally protected characteristics include race, sex, ethnicity, national origin, religion, age, and disability. Individuals or classes who think they have been discriminated against have several options. In some instances, current employees can use established company grievance procedures or enter into arbitration to resolve their dispute.[2] However, more often than not, current employees and prospective employees do not have these options available to them. These claimants turn to civil litigation.

Employment discrimination allegations often charge an employer with maintaining a pattern or practice of discriminating against members of a protected group. These allegations require plaintiffs to initially demonstrate that a pattern or practice of discrimination exists by analyzing the employer's records and data. Statistical and economic methods have become indispensable in such analyses, and triers of fact often rely on these methods to decide liability. In cases alleging patterns affecting large numbers of persons over significant time periods, statistical evidence sometimes comprises the most important evidence presented. Recognizing that anecdotal evidence from a small number of claimants may not be representative of the experiences of the class, the Supreme Court relied heavily on statistical evidence of discrimination when initially formulating the doctrine of disparate impact analysis[3] (*see* Section 30.4).

This reliance on statistical analysis and systematic data means that an employer need not intentionally discriminate to run afoul of the law; numbers, not purity of heart, govern liability in this branch of law. Even business practices that appear neutral can violate the employment discrimination laws if their effect is to disparately impact protected populations without a clear business justification. Indeed, this increased reliance on statistical evidence in employment discrimination cases causes litigants to seek expert testimony. This chapter will not distinguish between state and federal law but will focus instead on the statistical and economic essentials common to both.

30.2 THE ECONOMICS OF DISCRIMINATION.

Gary Becker initiated the economic theory of discrimination in his groundbreaking work first published in 1957 titled *The Economics of Discrimination* (revised, 1971). The theory predicts that firms practicing discrimination will face higher labor costs or limited business prospects. More specifically, the analysis posits that in a competitive market economy, companies that discriminate against a sector of the labor market will pay a premium for doing so. In other words, a company that chooses to hire, promote, and pay a favored group will incur greater costs of labor than companies that employ members of the discriminated group.

Becker's theory of employment discrimination implies that one should not assume that apparent disparities in employment outcomes between groups of workers are the product of discrimination. To the extent that firms have economic incentives not to discriminate, an analyst must look for other explanations of observed disparities before concluding that the data support the inference of discrimination. In other words, one cannot directly observe pattern and practice discrimination—its presence is inferred only as a residual disparity in worker groups, after accounting for other observable differences in worker groups. Thus, to analyze claims of discrimination, analysts must investigate what other factors could explain observed employment patterns with respect to groups of workers. The analysis applies economic theory to the data in that the analyst must identify the factors that explain the observed pattern and whether those factors are relevant to the jobs in question. The law recognizes this point, by permitting companies to offer a "business necessity" defense to rebut the plaintiff's *prima facie* showing of disparities. Section 30.3(b) further highlights this issue.

30.3 LEGAL BACKGROUND

Statistical evidence can support or rebut claims made under various employment discrimination statutes. The major pieces of federal legislation include the following:

- Title VII of the Civil Rights Act of 1964 (amended in 1991)[4]
- Americans with Disabilities Act (ADA)[5]
- Age Discrimination in Employment Act (ADEA)[6]
- Equal Pay Act of 1963 (EPA)[7]
- 42 U.S.C.S. Section 1981
- Executive Order 11246[8]

All these statutes address improper employment outcomes based on employee characteristics unrelated to a job. Statistical evidence helps explain the nature of those outcomes and provides finders of fact with information for reaching conclusions regarding the allegations in such cases.

(a) Title VII of the Civil Rights Act of 1964 (Amended in 1991). The primary federal statute prohibiting employment discrimination is Title VII of the Civil Rights Act of 1964, as amended. Specifically, Title VII prohibits any employer from refusing "to hire or to discharge any individual, or otherwise to discriminate against any individual with respect to his or her compensation, terms, conditions, or privileges of employment on the basis of race, color, religion, sex, or national origin."[9] *Employer* refers to any person or entity with a minimum of 25 employees and engaged in interstate commerce.[10]

(b) *Bona Fide* Occupational Qualification and Business Necessity. Title VII, the ADEA, and many state employment discrimination laws permit the use of protected characteristics as selection criteria, which would otherwise be unlawful, when the action reflects a *bona fide* occupational qualification (BFOQ) reasonably necessary to the normal operation of a business or enterprise.[11] For instance, being Catholic would constitute a *bona fide* requirement for employment as a Catholic priest.

The law also permits a business necessity exception to employment discrimination claims under federal law arising under the disparate impact claim of discrimination.[12] In a disparate impact claim, a policy or action unintentionally but nevertheless disproportionately and unlawfully affects a group. Title VII requires the employer to defend against a disparate impact claim by proving that the challenged employment practice is job related for the position in question and is consistent with business necessity.[13] For example, suppose an employer required that applicants for an engineering position have an engineering degree and that the educational requirement had a disparate impact on African American applicants. The employer would have to demonstrate that business necessity requires those in the engineering position to hold an engineering degree. Thus, the law allows disparate outcomes as long as the employer can prove that the job requires an engineering degree.

(c) Age Discrimination in Employment Act.   Passed in 1967, the ADEA prohibits age discrimination in the terms, conditions, and privileges of employment.[14] The ADEA extends the Title VII protections to age. The act applies to all private employers with 20 or more employees[15] including the federal government,[16] state governments and their political subdivisions, and any interstate agencies,[17] employment agencies,[18] and labor unions.[19]

As with Title VII, the ADEA allows a BFOQ exception. An employer must establish that (1) the essence of a particular business makes the qualification reasonably necessary,[20] and (2) either a factual basis exists to believe that most members of the protected group cannot perform the job safely and efficiently,[21] or the employer cannot individually evaluate the excluded class members.[22] As in Title VII, exceptions exist under the ADEA, such as BFOQ for police officers and state and local government fire fighters.[23]

(d) Americans with Disabilities Act.   The ADA of 1990 prohibits discrimination against persons with disabilities in the same areas as those of Title VII and the ADEA. The ADA not only prohibits discrimination against qualified workers with disabilities but also requires an employer to make reasonable accommodations for an employee's disability in some circumstances. It applies to labor organizations, employment agencies, joint labor-management committees,[24] and employers with 25 or more employees.[25]

(e) Equal Pay Act of 1963.   The EPA prohibits discrimination in compensation on the basis of sex and became the first federal law dealing with equal opportunity in the workplace for women. The EPA is part of the Fair Labor Standards Act (FLSA), and its coverage requirements are the same as those of the FLSA. Compared with Title VII, the EPA's protections are narrow but overlap with those of Title VII.

(f) 42 U.S.C.S. Section 1981.   As amended by the Civil Rights Act of 1991, Section 1981 prohibits racial discrimination against individuals in the making and enforcing of contracts by governmental and nongovernmental entities.[26] Section 1981 also encompasses the making, performance, modification, and termination of contracts, as well as all benefits, privileges, terms, and conditions of the contractual relation.[27]

Some courts have held that data analysis alone cannot establish a *prima facie* case of employment discrimination under Section 1981 and other early civil rights acts.[28] Other courts have found not only that statistical evidence can provide proof of purposeful discrimination[29] but also that proof of gross statistical disparity can itself constitute a *prima facie* case of violation of early civil rights acts.[30]

(g) Executive Order 11246. Various federal statutes and executive orders regulate the employment practices of employers who do business with the federal government as contractors or subcontractors. Executive Order 11246 prohibits job discrimination based on race, color, religion, sex, and national origin, by contractors and subcontractors operating under federal contracts for any service, supply, use, or construction. This also applies to contractors and subcontractors performing under federally assisted construction contracts.

(h) Fair Labor Standards Act. The FLSA is the federal act that governs wages, hours worked, and working conditions. Of all the areas covered by the FLSA, the most litigated are those sections that deal with whether workers are classified appropriately as exempt or nonexempt for the purposes of overtime. Nonexempt workers are usually paid hourly and are entitled to overtime pay. Exempt workers are ineligible for overtime pay. To be appropriately classified as exempt, the job content and pay level must meet the conditions of one of the exemptions, such as the executive exemption, administrative exemption, or outside sales exemption. Individual plaintiffs or classes of workers can charge employers with improperly classifying employees in certain jobs as exempt workers. If the plaintiffs prevail on the misclassification claim, workers can sue for unpaid overtime.

Many states have additional wage and hour regulations, often with provisions that overlap the FLSA. Litigation of wage and hours disputes has increased in recent years, especially in states with complex wage and hour rules. This is especially true in California, where the test for executive exemption involves a quantitative examination of the percentage of work hours spent on exempt duties, rather than the FLSA's primary duties test, which simply requires that the employee be managing the enterprise, or managing a customarily recognized department or subdivision of the enterprise.

30.4 CATEGORIES OF DISCRIMINATION: ADVERSE TREATMENT AND DISPARATE IMPACT

The courts have identified two types of discrimination:

1. *Adverse treatment* refers to intentional discrimination in which an employer singles out members of a protected class for differential treatment.
2. *Disparate impact*, also known as *unintentional discrimination*, refers to the adverse effects of a seemingly neutral employment policy that inadvertently falls more heavily on a protected group.

An example of adverse treatment includes a company that does not promote women because its management believes they are less capable or less committed than men. Other examples include a company that fails to hire adequate numbers of African Americans, because it believes its customers do not like African Americans, or a firm that terminates older workers because it wants a more youthful image.

Disparate impact occurs when a seemingly neutral employment practice unintentionally has a systematic, negative effect on a protected group.[31] Employment application tests provide a good example of disparate impact. Courts use a two-part test to decide whether such a test violates the law. First, does the test screen out a disproportionate number of protected individuals? If so, the test is *prima facie* discriminatory. Second, does the test serve a clear business purpose? Using an employment test that results in the hiring of disproportionately fewer protected workers can be legal if the test strongly predicts employee performance. In general, unless the employer can prove a test's validity (i.e., performance on a particular employment test correlates with job performance), potential employees can challenge it as discriminatory under a disparate impact theory.

30.5   STATISTICAL BACKGROUND

(a) Statistical Analysis and Tests of Significance.   Most employment litigation hinges on whether a protected group of workers fared differently from others because of a particular employment practice. To decide such questions requires statistical analysis.

(b) Hypothesis Tests.   Employment discrimination cases involve one key question: Do the actual employment experiences of a protected group differ from what one would expect in the absence of discrimination? Answering this question requires the use of both statistical methods and informed judgment in thinking about how the employment situation would look in the absence of discrimination.

In hypothesis testing, an analyst compares an actual with a hypothesized result. The analyst then evaluates the difference between the actual and hypothesized results using tests of statistical significance. A significance test permits the analyst to express an opinion concerning the likelihood that chance, or systematic factors, lead to the difference between an actual and a hypothesized outcome.

The mathematical tools of hypothesis testing do not indicate whether the hypothesis tested relates to the issue at hand. In statistical studies connected with employment litigation, one must formulate an appropriate hypothesis, or benchmark, for the employment result expected in the absence of discrimination. Identifying benchmarks for what was expected often requires effort. The following two sections illustrate the critical nature of the concept of *expected* in employment litigation.

(c) Identifying Expectations in the Absence of Discrimination.   The employment practice of involuntary termination presents perhaps the most straightforward setting to demonstrate the essential preliminary concepts. Consider a company that has recently implemented a reduction in workforce (RIF) that eliminated 100 workers, or 10 percent of its workforce of 1,000. Assume 70 of the 100 layoffs were older than 40, and call them *older workers*. Based on this fact, older workers allege that the company discriminated against them. What rate of termination should the employees have expected? Suppose that among the pre-RIF workforce of 1,000, 60 percent, or 600, were over 40 years old. If termination did not relate to age—and all other employee characteristics considered in planning the RIF did not relate to age—then selections should be random with respect to age, implying that one should expect 60 percent of all terminated employees to be over 40 years old. The hypothesis test then compares the benchmark 60 percent with the 70 percent of the older employees that the firm laid off. Because events such as termination contain a random element, only an appropriate statistical test will tell whether the 10 percentage point difference raises an inference of discrimination or results from random chance.

(d) Representation and Availability.   The example in Section 30.4(c) suggests a simple benchmark, based solely on the *representation* of older workers in the incumbent employee population. The simplest study assumes that other factors that could influence the selection for termination do not relate to age. Suppose instead that one of these factors did relate to age. Suppose that the employees were apple pickers, and the company considered the average number of apples picked per hour (i.e., employee performance) when planning the RIF. Suppose that older workers pick fewer apples per hour than do younger workers. In this scenario, using the simple older worker representation of 60 percent understates older workers' representation among those workers that the employer would most likely target for termination.

If the employer has a valid business reason to terminate one employee rather than another, that employee is said to be more *available* for termination. Even if two randomly chosen employees are equally represented in the workforce, they may not be equally available for a particular employment practice. The first RIF scenario in the preceding paragraph implicitly assumes that representation and availability are identical; the second scenario does not.

To accommodate the potential divergence between representation and availability, the analyst must, in our example, construct a test that adjusts for performance, using one of two methods. The analyst can segregate the employee population into performance groupings and then test the relation between representation and termination in each homogeneous performance grouping. Alternatively, the analyst can perform a multivariate analysis, such as regression analysis, using both age and performance as explanatory variables for termination. Regardless of the method chosen, the analyst must compare two similarly situated individuals.

(e) Review of Statistical Methods.   Although this chapter cannot provide a complete discussion of the statistical methods used in employment litigation, the following discussion will briefly outline several commonly used methods.[32]

The concepts of a population (i.e., the pre-RIF workforce) and a sample drawn from that population (i.e., terminees selected from the pre-RIF population) relate to statistical analysis that seeks to draw inferences concerning the relation between a population and a sample, or between different samples drawn from the same population. Any population or sample has a central tendency, or average: average age, average performance, average pay, average rates of termination, and so forth. Statistical methods permit an analyst to assess the significance of the difference between, for example, the observed average termination rates of workers over age 40 (a sample) compared with the average for all workers (the population), the average pay of women (a sample) compared with that of men (another sample), and so on.

Statistical tests generally refer to a distribution of possible outcomes to compare actual and expected results. Exhibit 30-1 gives an example of the most broadly applicable statistical distribution, the normal distribution. Analysts characterize a normal distribution with two parameters: a mean and a standard deviation. The standard deviation measures the relative dispersion of outcomes around the mean.

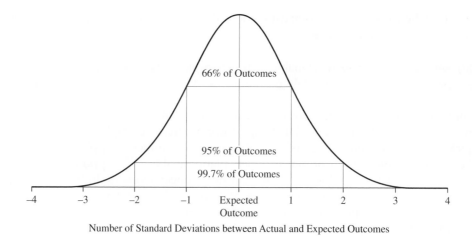

Number of Standard Deviations between Actual and Expected Outcomes

---

Exhibit 30-1.   The Standard Normal Distribution

A normal distribution exhibits a symmetric shape around the mean. In any normal distribution, a fixed proportion of possible outcomes lies within each number of standard deviations from the mean. The approximate proportions of all outcomes lying within one, two, and three standard deviations in a normal distribution are 68 percent, 95 percent, and 99 percent, respectively. The absolute size of the standard deviation depends both on inherent variability in the underlying variable being measured and on the sample size. For a given inherent variability, a larger sample size produces a smaller standard deviation.

If one knows the mean and standard deviation of a particular distribution, one can use the standard deviation to compare the difference between the mean, or actual, value and a hypothesized value. The apple picker example has a mean (observed outcome) for termination of older workers of 70 percent. Suppose the standard deviation equals 10 percent. The hypothesized (i.e., expected) percentage of terminations of 60 percent thus lies one standard deviation below the actual. Based on this, and on the assumption that this pattern would approximately repeat if one made many observations of this company's termination activity, an analyst would conclude that the actual percentage of terminations differs by as much as 10 percentage points from that expected approximately one-third of the time.

Suppose instead that the standard deviation equals 5 percent. Actual and expected terminations now differ by two standard deviations; a difference of two standard deviations or more will occur only 5 percent of the time. To state this result differently, a situation in which the observed and expected numbers of older workers terminated differ by the two standard deviations or more will likely be due to chance only once out of 20 times.

The courts use the 95 percent level of confidence, or the .05 level of significance, as a minimum benchmark of statistical significance in employment cases.[33] Courts judge differences that fail to meet this benchmark as too small or too unreliable to attribute to anything other than chance or measurement error. Conversely, differences that meet or exceed this benchmark level have no more than a 1-in-20

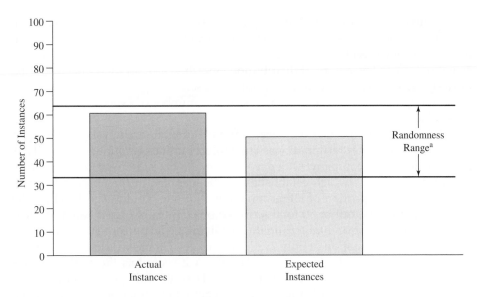

^aEqual to 95% confidence interval around expected number of occurrences.

Exhibit 30-2.   Actual Instances of an Employment Practice Do Not Significantly Differ from Expected if the Actual Number Is within the Randomness Range of the Expected Number

probability of being attributable to chance; thus, courts presume that these differences reflect evidence of possible discrimination.

Exhibit 30-2 compares actual and expected outcomes, using a 95 percent confidence interval randomness range around the expected result. In the example, the number of instances of the employment practice falls within the randomness range of the expected number. One concludes that the actual and expected numbers of instances do not differ in a statistically significant way.

(f) One-Sample Binomial Tests: Z-Scores.   As the example in Section 30.5(e) demonstrates, statistical tests examine whether the effect of an employment practice on a protected class differs significantly from its effect on all employees subject to the practice. The hypothesis is that, absent discrimination, the effect will be equal. A common test to assess this issue is the one-sample binomial test. The test asks, "Does the firm hire, promote, or fire members of the protected class in numbers that differ significantly from what one would expect to find if the firm were selecting from the available population at random?"

One can calculate the expected number by multiplying the percentage availability of protected persons by the total number of persons affected by the practice in question. For example, if African Americans comprised 40 percent of all qualified applicants, and the firm hired 100 people, then one should expect 40 of them to be African American. With a sufficiently large number of observations, the one-sample binomial test will produce the number of standard deviations (also called a *Z-score*[34]) between the observed and the expected numbers of protected class hires. Analysts consider the observed and expected as significantly different from one another if the Z-score has an absolute value exceeding approximately 2, that is, a positive Z-score exceeds 2 or a negative Z-score is less than −2. As explained in Section 30.5(e), two standard deviations correspond approximately to a 5 percent significance level. Z-score tests assume that the underlying population for actual outcomes has a normal distribution, and therefore, in this context, we use the test of Z-scores to approximate the binomial selection process. Such an approximation requires only a certain sample size and number of expected selections to be reliable.

Exhibit 30-3 summarizes a typical standard deviation analysis, focusing on age discrimination in terminations. The table examines termination activity in two divisions of a company. Older workers make up 50 percent of Division I's available workforce, which establishes the benchmark in the absence of other factors for the proportion of all terminations that one would expect to be older employees. Instead, out of 50 total terminations, Division I terminated 35 older workers—70 percent of total terminations. Given the 50 percent availability, one would expect termination of only 25 older workers. Chance could cause this difference between actual and expected layoffs. A Z-score lets the analyst decide whether the actual number of terminations is statistically significant. In this case, the Z-score equals 2.69; this means that actual terminations exceed expected terminations by 2.69 standard deviations, which exceeds the standard deviation benchmark of 2.00. These data indicate that Division I has terminated too many older workers.

Division II has also terminated more older workers than expected: 10 actual compared with 8 expected. In this case, however, the Z-score is only .61—below the threshold of statistical significance. The courts interpret this to mean that chance cannot be ruled out as causing the disparity between actual and expected terminations observed in Division II.

	Data					
	Incumbent Employees			**Employee Layoffs**		
Company Division	**Total**	**Over 40**	**Percent Over 40**	**Total**	**Over 40**	**Percent Over 40**
Division I	500	250	50.00	50	35	70.00
Division II	400	100	25.00	32	10	31.25

	Statistics			
	Calculation of Expected and Z-Score			
Company Division	**Expected Layoffs**	**Surplus/ Shortfall**	**Std Dev**	**Z-Score**
Division I	25.0	10.0	3.54	2.69
Division II	8.0	2.0	2.45	0.61

Exhibit 30-3.   Analysis of Termination

In the one-sample binomial test, one can derive or supply the availability figures from the population external to the firm, making it a useful test for analyzing hiring practices: for example, the outsider can observe the availability of protected persons in a company's external labor market. Promotion analyses also benefit from this feature because the analyst can modify the base availability figures to account for performance, geographic location, and other factors.

(g) Chi-Square Tests. Analysts also commonly use the chi-square test of independence.[35] A chi-square test examines whether two classifications of a population are independent of one another. Rather than produce the number of standard deviations between actual and expected terminations, however, the chi-square test generates a statistic that one can convert directly into a probability. If the probability is less than .05, then data analysts (and courts persuaded by them) reject the hypothesis that age and termination are linked (i.e., a probability less than .05 indicates weak statistical evidence of discrimination).

For example, the test allows one to study the question: "Is being age 40 or older associated with being involuntarily terminated?" A chi-square test compares the age distribution of employees (i.e., under age 40 or age 40 and up) with the distribution of these employees as those who remain employed ("stayers") and those whom the firm terminates ("leavers"). If the distribution of leavers is independent of the distribution of the same employees by age, the proportion over age 40 among all employees should equal the proportion over 40 among both stayers and leavers.

The chi-square test applies to any number of classifications along two dimensions. For example, one can classify employees into age classes of five-year ranges and find the proportion of each class falling into one of, say, the seven reasons a company uses for termination. If the analysis has nine such age classes (such as 20 to 24, 25 to 29, 60 to 65, etc.), then the grouping of membership of each class into seven reasons is a nine-by-seven analysis. The terminology of statistics calls the resulting table of numbers a *nine-by-seven contingency table,* in which each cell represents the number of workers of a given age class terminated for one of the seven reasons. Most often, analysts use the chi-square test to examine situations represented by two-by-two contingency tables. In general, one should not use such large numbers of rows and columns in a contingency table in which most or many cells have zero numbers.

(h) Small-Sample Statistical Tests. On occasion, the sample size will be too small for the tests described in the previous sections. Analysts frequently turn to small-sample tests such as the Fisher's exact test. Consider testing the independence of age and termination. Fisher's exact test computes the number of combinations of older workers who could be terminated in numbers no greater than actually observed. One then divides this figure by the total number of combinations that staying or leaving could be distributed into among all employees without regard for their age group classification. If this probability is less than 5 percent, then current practice rejects the hypothesis that age group and termination status are independent.

Interested readers can investigate other small-sample tests, such as the Mantel-Haenszel chi-square test.

(i) *t*-Tests: Comparing Two Means.   Suppose an investigator in an age-discrimination termination case wants to compare the average ages of stayers and leavers, or of the employee population at different times. Analysts commonly use the *t*-test for these instances.[36] The *t*-test assumes a normal distribution for ages. To compare the average ages of stayers and leavers, we would calculate the *t*-statistic associated with the difference in average age in the two samples. We could then derive a corresponding probability based on this value. The mathematics of the *t*-test and the Z-score are similar: as with a Z-score, if the *t*-statistic exceeds 2 in absolute value, current practice concludes (at the .05 level of statistical significance) that the average ages in the two samples differ significantly from one another.

In general, the greater the number of observations, the more significant a given *t*-test will be. Analysts can use *t*-tests to compare any continuous variables, such as pay, tenure, and time to promotion, between protected and other employees.

(j) Multiple Regression Analysis.   This chapter has stressed the importance of using the correct benchmark when testing for statistical evidence of discrimination. Analysts often have difficulty establishing this benchmark, however, because many variables can simultaneously influence employment patterns. Consider a company being sued for promotion discrimination against women. The company could contend that many other factors influence promotion, such as education, job category, seniority in job category, and performance evaluation. Because these other variables can correlate with sex, the investigator must jointly control for them to discover the relation of sex to promotion.

Statisticians use two methods to control for these kinds of confounding variables. First, the analyst can create multiple strata, perform a series of one-sample binomial tests, and then aggregate the results to reach the overall result. For example, suppose 10 managers are chosen from a pool of 200 employees composed of 100 male analysts and 100 female administrators. Without stratifying the analysts from the administrators, one would expect five male and five female promotions. However, if 80 percent of promotions come from analysts and the other 20 percent from administrators, one would expect eight promotions to be males and two promotions to be females. In this example, the weighted availability of females would be

$$0.80 \times 0.00 \text{ (for analysts)} + 0.20 \times 1.00 \text{ (for administrators)} = 0.20.$$

Multiplying 0.20 by 20 promotions gives a benchmark of two females expected to be promoted.

Suppose, however, that many factors influence the probability of promotion. Such a situation often requires multiple regression analysis. This method controls for differences in multiple individual characteristics. A regression analysis identifies the relation between each of the explanatory variables and the dependent variable (in this case, promotion), while controlling for all other variables. Thus, an analyst using regression techniques can assess the relation between sex and promotion, while adjusting for the influence of other variables, such as experience, seniority, and education. (Chapters 5 and 6 discuss regression analysis.)

30.6 FORMS OF DATA USED IN EMPLOYMENT LITIGATION

The statistical techniques discussed in this chapter depend on the available data. This section surveys the types of information available to the economist or statistical analyst in employment litigation. Most companies maintain two primary kinds of information related to their workforce: human resources, or personnel information, and payroll information. Both can become important sources of data for employment discrimination litigation.

Companies typically store employment-related data in a human resource system (HRS) database. Such a database records employment transactions, such as hiring, termination, promotion, changes in job title, company division, pay type (hourly, salaried), and employment status. The HRS database will also include demographic information, such as race, birthdate, and sex. Most companies retain this information in computerized form. Many companies also maintain a separate payroll system, which records each employee's compensation history. The analyst can combine these data with HRS data using unique identifiers, such as social security number or employee number. Many workforce data systems now combine payroll and personnel information.

The importance of these data to ongoing company operations in principle makes them reliably accurate and complete. Nonetheless, analysts should always look for clerical or data entry errors, as well as incomplete fields. In addition, as companies upgrade their systems, compatibility problems between new and old HRS and payroll formats can develop. The experienced analyst usually can identify these types of problems and through discovery can request the company to provide the information in the most usable format.

In addition to HRS and payroll data, companies also maintain other, less systematic, repositories for employment data. For example, companies often compensate sales personnel through complex incentive schemes. The firm must track this information to evaluate and compensate these employees accurately. As incentive schemes change, the format of these data can change in ways that complicate data analysis.

Many companies also maintain other employment data because the antidiscrimination laws encourage them to do so. For example, the Office of Federal Contract Compliance (OFCCP), which oversees the affirmative action activities of government contractors, requires such companies to maintain records of employment applications in a database called an *applicant flow log*. Many companies do not computerize this information.

For hiring, placement, and recruiting analysis, one can use employment applications, preemployment tests, resumes, and other similar sources. However, because many companies do not computerize this information, the analyst must create the relevant computerized versions of this information, which, depending on the extent of the underlying sources, often requires time and energy. Analysts cannot study all aspects of hiring claims (for example) without such information.

Analysts must often convert the various sources of raw data into statistically useful formats, which involves uniform classification schemes over time. For example, most employment litigation examines a company's employment practices over a particular period of time. Suppose the analyst needs to examine terminations. In such a case, the analyst has to decide how many persons were available for termination at one time, typically either the prior year end or just prior to a reduction in force; this constitutes the pool from which the company selected terminations. To construct such a data set, called an *incumbent file* or *snapshot file*, the analyst would use the dates in the transactions file to see which employees were present on the relevant date. Then the analyst would use the dates and the transaction codes in the transactions file to identify the people terminated in the subsequent period. Only after putting the data into this format can an analyst examine them for statistical evidence of discrimination.

30.7   RECRUITMENT AND HIRING

This section discusses specific types of discrimination allegations. In this context, the word *recruiting* means the process of attracting candidates that the employer considers for hiring. Companies fill positions from both internal and external sources. The internal labor market includes persons available to fill positions through promotion or transfer. The pool available for promotion or transfer consists of a company's current employees. Conversely, the external labor market constitutes the pool available to fill positions via hiring. Not all persons in the external labor market are equally available for all positions. To accurately estimate the availability of protected class workers for recruitment or hire, the analyst needs to evaluate the educational, skill, experience, geographic, and other dimensions of the potential workforce to arrive at what analysts call the *relevant labor market*.

Testing for recruiting discrimination involves a comparison of the company's actual applicant flow to the relevant labor market. If a company's recruiting activities result in fewer protected class applicants than one would expect given the relevant labor market, then one can infer a possibility of discrimination in recruitment.

(a) Defining the Relevant External Labor Market.   As in all statistical analysis in employment litigation, the most critical part of studying a company's recruitment practices is to define the correct benchmark of employment availability. Discovering the relevant labor market allows the analyst to estimate this benchmark availability. The issue is one of representation versus availability. Availability for recruiting or hiring results from the interplay between a company's demand for labor and workers' supply of labor. When a company recruits for a particular job, it requires certain occupational qualifications—which it thinks and expects to prove are *bona fide*, such as education and work experience—before it will consider an applicant. By the same token, workers from different geographic areas and from different educational and work backgrounds will have differing incentives for applying for particular jobs. To compare the expected applicant pool's protected-class composition with the pool of actual applicants, the analyst must recognize that these conditioning factors can by themselves produce nonrandom application patterns among various groups.

From a statistical point of view, the situation resembles that of drawing red, green, and blue balls from an urn containing 100 balls of each color: To have an equal number of balls drawn of each color, balls of each color must have equal probability of being drawn. If the red balls are, for example, more difficult to grasp, then we would expect the number of them drawn to be smaller than the number of green or blue balls. Correspondingly, if persons exist in the external labor market who think their probability of seeking or being selected for work at a company is *a priori* smaller than that of others in the pool, then including them in the external availability without taking this information into account would violate our basic statistical assumptions previously discussed.

The geographic size of the relevant labor market will vary from case to case. Skill levels (qualifications) help determine the relevant labor market area. Economic theory hypothesizes that the geographic size of a labor market positively correlates with skill level. Therefore, when a company hires for low-skill positions, the local labor market and the relevant recruiting area will likely be the same. Both common sense and economic theory provide a rationale for this result. For entry-level laborers or other unskilled and therefore low-paid workers, the cost of relocating would not justify the benefit, so they are unlikely to travel far or relocate. By the same token, companies are less likely to spend time and money conducting a broad search for a candidate to fill a low-level position. At the other end of the spectrum, the relevant recruitment area for high-skilled jobs will extend beyond the local area and—for high-level executive positions—can even encompass the entire nation.

Another factor in defining the relevant labor market, especially for low-skilled positions, is the commuting time to the employer's location. The argument resembles that for relocating: workers evaluate the costs and benefits associated with a job, and those workers whose commuting time exceeds that of others will, all else constant, have less interest in applying for the job. To obtain information on commuting time, the analyst can use various data sources, including the census journey-to-work data. The analyst could also examine the commuting patterns that the addresses of applicants and hires suggest, as well as the availability of public transportation and the proportion of persons with cars.

(b) Estimating Labor Market Protected Class Availability. In practice, data sources from which the analyst constructs external availabilities seldom match the analyst's needs. Instead, the analyst must consult various sources and construct several availability estimates to provide a robust and defensible analysis.

Analysts commonly use the following data sources to estimate protected class availability:

- Public Use Microdata Sample (PUMS), derived from the decennial census
- Equal Employment Opportunity file (special EEO file), again derived from the census
- Annual Current Population Survey (CPS), assembled by the Census Bureau for the Bureau of Labor Statistics (BLS)

The PUMS comprises individual-level data on persons in households and contains demographic and economic variables. Its major advantage of large sample size permits the use of multiple selection criteria, such as race, job type, and geographical location. A disadvantage is that the government collects PUMS data only every 10 years; by the end of the decade after release, availabilities based on it can be outdated. In such instances, analysts can assess the direction of the bias in the dated PUMS availabilities by using the annually updated CPS data. Because the CPS has a relatively small data set, however, analysts should use caution when the availability focus is narrow along a geographic or an occupational dimension.

Finally, the special EEO file, based on the same data as the PUMS, contains only civilian labor force information. It differs from both the PUMS and the CPS in that it does not contain individual data. Instead, the special EEO file presents a summary data set, designed at least in part to permit employers to measure external labor market availabilities conveniently. As such, it contains availabilities for many aggregations by detailed occupation, by educational attainment, and by geographic area. Because it does not contain individual-level data, however, one cannot use it to answer certain specific questions. In addition, it does not provide zip-code-level data, which analysts often need in particularly detailed availability analyses. In addition to these government data sources, private and public sources offer numerous specialized data sets.

(c) Statistical Tests for Recruitment Discrimination.   After analysts have defined the relevant external labor market and computed availabilities, they can evaluate the actual composition of the applicant pool. Here, analysts often use the one-sample binomial test, which compares expected with actual proportions of protected class members in the applicant flow.

Exhibit 30-4 presents an example that considers several definitions of the external labor market for skilled positions in a large metropolitan-area factory. Suppose the plaintiff alleges that a company failed to recruit African Americans adequately. In the city limits, African Americans represent 40 percent of the total population but only 25 percent of the applicant flow. This produces a significant shortfall (a Z-score of -10.58). When the analyst considers labor-force participation, skill level, and commuting time, however, the availability of African Americans falls to 28 percent, which still exceeds applicant-flow representation. The Z-score, even though it is lower than it was prior to considering additional variables, continues to indicate that the number of actual applicants falls significantly below the number expected in the absence of discrimination.

(d) Discrimination Resulting from Employee Referrals.   Recruitment discrimination can occur when a company uses its current employees to recruit new hires. Such a practice often results in an applicant pool with a racial composition more similar to that of the current workforce than to the relevant labor market. If, for example, these employees are white, then recruiting will often deny nonwhites opportunities that would have existed had the company used another recruiting method; therefore, the company could run afoul of disparate impact tests for discrimination. In response, the company can try to show that employee referral offers its only effective means of recruitment, in which case it can make a business necessity defense. In fact, recent research into social networks indicates that extensive job networking occurs because of the surprisingly extensive nature of social contacts.[37]

(e) Hiring Discrimination.   Hiring discrimination resembles recruiting discrimination and as such requires little further discussion. The analyst will use statistics to compare the protected class representation among hires with a benchmark availability for the protected class among applicants. Two primary sources exist for establishing a hiring availability benchmark: actual applicant flow and the relevant external labor market. Analysts often use the latter because of missing or unreliable applicant flow data, or because the analyst believes that the composition of the

Data				
	Availability	Applicant Flow Composition		
Definition of Labor Market	Percent African American	Total Applicants	African American Applicants	Percent African American
City limits				
Total population	40.00%	1,200	300	25.00%
Civilian labor force	38.00	1,200	300	25.00
Skilled labor force	26.00	1,200	300	25.00
Applicants' commuting time[a]				
Total population	36.00%	1,200	300	25.00%
Civilian labor force	33.00	1,200	300	25.00
Skilled labor force	23.00	1,200	300	25.00

Statistical Analysis				
	Calculation of Expected African Americans and Z-Score			
Definition of Labor Market	Expected African Americans	Surplus (+) or Shortfall (−)	Standard Deviation	Z-Score
City limits				
Total population	480.0	−180.0	16.97	−10.58
Civilian labor force	456.0	−156.0	16.81	−9.25
Skilled labor force	312.0	−12.0	15.19	−0.76
Applicants' commuting time[a]				
Total population	432.0	−132.00	16.63	−7.91
Civilian labor force	396.0	−96.00	16.29	−5.86
Skilled labor force	336.0	−36.00	15.55	−2.28

[a]Availability is derived by weighting each time contour commuting ring by the number of applicants coming from that area.

Exhibit 30-4. Analysis of Recruiting Discrimination

applicant flow meaningfully departs from the relevant external labor market. For example, a company's affirmative action initiatives often make the applicant flow excessively rich in the protected class. On the other hand, employers with a reputation for discriminating can chill potential applicants' desire to apply, resulting in an applicant flow deficient in protected classes. Using current employees for recruiting can also produce an applicant flow deficient in protected classes, depending on the composition of the current workforce.

(f) Placement. Initial placement often becomes an important part of hiring cases. Some cases allege that the company not only hired insufficient numbers of protected class members but also placed them in less desirable jobs. To analyze placement disparities, one must analyze hiring by subsets of all positions.

Analysts derive availabilities for placement primarily from the employment and training backgrounds of the applicants, as well as their job interests. One analysis of placement issues creates similarly situated subpools among applicants and conducts, for example, one-sample binomial tests on each subset. The analyst then combines the results of each test into an aggregated one-sample result. In such cases, the analyst must create meaningful previous experience and job interest groupings. Excessive subsetting of the population can result in many cells with small numbers. Alternatively, overaggregation can defeat the purpose of stratifying in the first place—the resulting pools can contain applicants who are not similarly situated.

30.8 PROMOTION PRACTICES

Many, if not most companies fill middle- and upper-level positions by promoting current, lower-level employees. Such companies prefer promotion because of the specific knowledge that current employees acquire with tenure in the company, the employees' demonstrated loyalty to the company and vice versa, and the cost of recruiting higher-level employees from outside the firm.

Because, in general, employees can significantly raise their pay over time primarily through promotion, allegations of promotion discrimination often occur. Recently, however, promotion claims have received heightened publicity, owing to "glass ceiling" claims. Such cases involve instances in which women allege that, although they receive promotions to middle management positions, they do not progress to higher levels. Examples include women who claim that their firms denied them partnership in law, accounting, and consulting firms and denied them access to the vice president and senior vice president levels in corporations. The more typical case, however, continues to be one in which protected class employees in lower-level, nonsupervisory positions claim that the company did not promote them to lower and middle management positions.

(a) Company Hierarchies and Job-Feeder Analysis. By definition, a promotion means a movement from a lower to a higher position. Sometimes an established and explicit company hierarchy requires a specific lower job to feed each higher job. In that case, and in the absence of other promotion-related criteria, the analyst need only identify all incumbents in the feeder job for each promotion job, derive the relevant availability, and perform a one-sample binomial or chi-square test.

Some companies fill higher-level jobs from various lower-level jobs, however, making the task of sorting out their relative importance and combining the results more difficult. Because the relative importance of feeder jobs can vary, and the protected class availability within each feeder can also vary, the analyst must use a weighting method to obtain the overall protected class availability for a particular promotion.

The examples in Exhibits 30-5 to 30-7, which use the one-sample binomial test, illustrate the importance of considering feeder jobs separately. Exhibit 30-5 shows the results of a Z-test that compares actual with expected numbers of promotions of women to management positions. The 7,920 incumbents have a female availability of 37.1 percent. The 1,287 total promotions, when multiplied by

	Data						
All	**Incumbents**				**Promotions**		
Feeders				**Percent**			**Percent**
Aggregated	**Total**	**Women**	**Weight**	**Women**	**Total**	**Women**	**Women**
	7920	... 2940	1.0000	37.1%	1287	348	27.0%

	Statistical Analysis			
All	**Calculation of Expected and Z-Score**			
Feeders	**Expected**	**Surplus/**	**Std**	
Aggregated	**Promotions**	**Shortfall**	**Dev**	**Z-Score**
	477.8	−129.8	17.33	−7.46

Exhibit 30-5. Analysis of Promotion Discrimination, Model I—No Explanatory Controls

37.1 percent, produce 477.8 expected female promotions. The company actually promoted only 348 women, a shortfall of 129.8 promotions. This (negative) difference has a Z-score of 7.46, which is statistically significant. The employer claims that this result is misleading because it fails to consider other factors influencing promotion, such as experience in particular lower-level jobs and employee performance evaluations.

Exhibit 30-6 introduces one of these factors, by disaggregating employees in the incumbent pool into three pools corresponding to feeder jobs. Each of these lower jobs contains an availability, calculated in the usual way. This time, however, the analyst derives *overall* female availability by *weighting* the availability in each feeder job by the number of promotions derived from each of these sources. This reflects the relative importance of various lower jobs to the company as it seeks to fill manager positions.[38] As the aggregated line in the exhibit shows, disaggregating incumbents into feeder groups results in reduced availability of women to 29.7 percent, because of the high concentration of women in Feeder 3, which does not supply a proportionate share of the promotions to manager positions. The aggregated results (Z-score = 22.24) reflect that women continue to be underpromoted (shortfall of 34.6), although to a lesser extent than previously. Note also that Feeder 2 contains a significant shortfall in female promotions.

Finally, Exhibit 30-7 disaggregates by both performance rating and feeder job. This example assumes that women in this company have received lower performance ratings than men. Using performance ratings without some attempt to validate them may be inappropriate, since discrimination could influence such ratings. If the example assumes accurate performance ratings and that the company promotes highly rated employees, the weighted availability of women drops further still, to 27.5 percent. Comparing aggregated observed with expected promotions results in a Z-score of 2.40, which is insignificant at the currently accepted .05 level.

The disaggregation process permits the analyst to uncover differences in promotion rates associated with various strata hidden in the overall results. When a company relies on decentralized decision making, large differences in promotion

	Data						
	Incumbents				**Promotions**		
Job Feeder	**Total**	**Women**	**Weight**	**Percent Women**	**Total**	**Women**	**Percent Women**
Feeder 1	1,320	295	0.2502	22.3%	322	75	23.3%
Feeder 2	2,640	440	0.4514	16.7	581	68	11.7
Feeder 3	3,960	2,205	0.2984	55.7	384	205	53.4
Aggregated & Weighted Results:	7,920	2,940	1.0	29.7%	1,287	384	27.0%

	Statistical Analysis			
	Calculation of Expected and Z-score			
Job Feeder	**Expected Promotions**	**Surplus/ Shortfall**	**Std Dev**	**Z-Score**
Feeder 1	72.0	3.0	7.48	0.34
Feeder 2	96.8	−28.8	8.98	−3.15
Feeder 3	213.8	−8.8	9.73	−0.85
Aggregated & Weighted Results:	382.6	−34.6	15.21	−2.24

Exhibit 30-6. Analysis of Promotion Discrimination, Model II—Divided into Job Feeders

rates can occur. For example, note that the company significantly promotes high-performing, Feeder 2 women in proportions larger than they represent in the population.

Occasionally, the number of variables influencing promotion creates more substrata of the population than the analyst can conveniently handle using a one-sample binomial analysis. The analyst can instead use a multiple regression model, which can include many variables and identify their independent effects on promotion. If the analysis also includes a variable for sex, a statistically significant negative coefficient on that variable indicates that female promotion rates fall short of male promotion rates, even after controlling for other measurable explanatory factors.[39]

As with any multiple regression analysis, one must recognize the difficulty of capturing all variables relevant to promotion, in that some will be unmeasured or unmeasurable. In addition, even if one knows all variables, the analysis often requires a trial-and-error process to find the correct technical specification in a regression equation that properly captures the variables' influence on promotion.*

---

*Editors' Note: This trial and error process may subject the expert to charges of data mining and data dredging. Such preliminary explorations of data, if not clearly related to issues of technical statistical specification, may reduce the probative value of the eventual statistical tests.

Data

Job Feeder	Performance Rating	Incumbents				Promotions		
		Total	Women	Weight	Female Availability	Total	Women	Percent Women
Feeder 1	Low	264	74	0.1677	28.0%	54	10	18.5%
	Medium	528	103	0.2019	19.5	65	14	21.5
	High	528	118	0.6304	22.3	203	51	25.1
Subtotal: Feeder 1		1,320	294	0.2494	22.7%	321	75	23.4%
Feeder 2	Low	792	176	0.1170	22.2%	68	0	0.0%
	Medium	1,584	235	0.4182	14.8	243	27	11.1
	High	264	29	0.4647	11.0	270	41	15.2
Subtotal: Feeder 2		2,640	441	0.4514	13.9%	581	68	11.7%
Feeder 3	Low	528	294	0.0286	55.7%	11	7	63.6%
	Medium	2,508	1,470	0.3880	58.6	149	89	59.7
	High	924	441	0.5833	47.7	224	109	48.7
Subtotal: Feeder 3		3,960	2,205	0.2976	52.2%	383	205	53.5%
Aggregated & Weighted Results:		7,920	2,940	1.0000	27.5%	1,287	348	27.0%

Exhibit 30-7. Analysis of Promotion Discrimination, Model III—Divided into Job Feeders and Performance Ratings Groups

Statistical Analysis

Job Feeder	Performance Rating	Expected Promotions	Surplus/Shortfall	Std Dev	Z-Score
			Calculation of Expected and Z-score		
Feeder 1	Low	15.1	−5.1	3.30	−1.40
Feeder 1	Medium	12.7	1.3	3.19	0.26
Feeder 1	High	45.4	5.6	5.94	0.86
Subtotal: Feeder 1		73.2	1.8	7.51	0.18
Feeder 2	Low	15.1	−15.1	3.43	NA
Feeder 2	Medium	36.1	−9.1	5.54	−1.54
Feeder 2	High	29.7	11.3	5.14	2.11
Subtotal: Feeder 2		80.8	−12.8	8.30	−1.48
Feeder 3	Low	6.1	0.9	1.65	0.23
Feeder 3	Medium	87.3	1.7	6.01	0.19
Feeder 3	High	106.9	2.1	7.48	0.21
Subtotal: Feeder 3		200.4	4.6	9.73	0.42
Aggregated & Weighted Results:		354.4	−6.4	14.83	−0.40

Exhibit 30-7. (Continued)

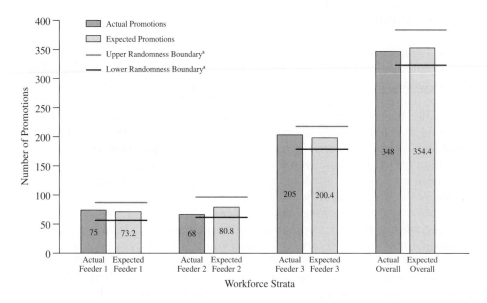

^aRepresents plus or minus 2 standard deviations randomness range around the expected values.

Exhibit 30-8. Graphical Depiction of Statistical Analysis of Promotion

(b) Graphical Depictions of Statistical Findings.   Often the analyst must present the results of complex analyses to lay audiences, such as juries. The expert witness can find simple bar charts effective for this purpose. For example, the expert can display the results in the above table for each of the three feeder sources, and then overall, as in Exhibit 30-8. The chart shows in easily comprehensible form the essential elements of actual and expected promotions and the two-standard deviation randomness range; these can form the basis for the economist or statistician to explain the many elements that entered into the analysis.

(c) Economic Theory and Promotion Analysis.   Promotion cases that consider sex as the protected characteristic can become particularly thorny when a controversial and largely unobservable variable—job or career interest—enters into the analysis. Some economic theory suggests that the desired career paths of male and female workers differ.[40] Under this theory, the economic returns to men from investing in on-the-job training and other qualifications for certain types of career tracks exceed those for women, because women have lower anticipated attachment both to the labor force and to any particular firm. Suggested explanations include the interplay of child rearing with work, the traditional division of labor in the household, and differing innate job interests obtained through socialization. These theories, of course, invite controversy. Nonetheless, the analyst should understand the potential consequences of a largely unobservable promotion interest variable. Strategies for dealing with it include using demographic information and conducting surveys of men and women at the company. (The latter presents its own difficulties and may face a tough road in court.[41])

30.9   TERMINATION

Because employers lay off employees in part to cut costs while scaling back production, companies often attempt to terminate the most expensive workers. These workers tend to be older and more experienced; as a result, many file suit under ADEA or relevant state statutes. Since the early 1990s, which saw an increase in cases related to economic downturn, individual and class action termination cases have continued to be among the most common cases that courts face. At the individual level, so-called *wrongful termination* cases often allege protected status as a motivation for termination. Even though individual termination differs quantitatively from a large-scale layoff, analysts use an identical approach and can use statistical evidence in much the same way.

(a) Large-Scale Layoffs.   One or more plaintiffs often file suit after a large-scale layoff, alleging that the layoff focused on their protected class, or alleging disparate impact. As in all discrimination analyses, the analyst must ascertain the relevant availability for termination. The layoff's business scope most likely will dictate the sections in which the layoffs will occur. The analyst should consult with counsel, and perhaps company documents, on this subject before conducting statistical analysis. Targeted subsections of the workforce could include the employees of any division, department, hierarchical level, plant, geographic area, product line, and job function or skill group. Reductions from multiple but distinct subsections will likely require aggregation to evaluate their overall effects.

Second, the scope of the decision maker's authority can dictate how the analyst delineates the pre-RIF workforce. If the complaint accuses top management of favoring one group over another for discriminatory reasons, then the analyst will need to study the RIF's impact on the entire workforce.

Similarly, the evaluation process used to select for termination can imply relevant groupings of the workforce. In such cases, the analyst should assemble pools of employees who have been compared with each other and who have equal probabilities of selection prior to their evaluation. Because multiple sources exist for the employment practice in question, the analyst should weight the results to obtain correct availabilities.

After setting the incumbent and termination populations, the analyst should identify factors that can influence the probability of termination. Poor performance or low seniority commonly justifies termination. If subjective performance is a factor, the analyst should use comparisons with other objectively quantifiable measures to validate such subjective measures.

(b) Statistical Analysis of an RIF: "Stayer-Leaver" Analysis.   A one-sample binomial or chi-square analysis can usually give a statistical portrait of the RIF. Analysts most frequently use a *stayer-leaver* analysis to study the effects of an RIF. This analysis divides the initial workforce into protected and nonprotected groups. It then further divides each group into stayers and leavers. The analyst then compares the expected number of protected terminees, based on their representation in the workforce, with the actual number and computes either a probability level (for the chi-square) or a number of standard deviations (for the one-sample binomial). In this respect, termination analysis resembles simple promotion analysis, in that all selections come from the workforce pool (i.e., using no externally supplied availabilities and assuming equal selection probabilities). To refine the analysis, one can further disaggregate the groups. For example, if a company uses performance ratings as a basis for an RIF, the analyst can study the effect of such ratings on firing practices. The analyst can also use groupings by company division, decision maker, and geographic location. The analyst can then aggregate availabilities within each strata to reach an overall weighted availability. One can use one-sample binomial methods to perform this disaggregation.

(c) Analysis of Termination over Longer Time Periods. Plaintiffs often allege that a pattern of selecting protected employees for termination has existed for several years. The analyst can apply a stayer-leaver year-by-year approach in such a situation. The most straightforward approach considers terminations from incumbent pools of persons available for termination at the start of each year. This approach, however, does not include persons hired and fired within the year among incumbents or among terminees. In workforce populations with high turnover, this could affect conclusions regarding the relation between age and termination. In general, younger workers have a greater rate of turnover. Therefore, one would expect them to have a greater tendency to be hired and terminated within the same year, compared with older employees.[42]

The investigator should study such variations in turnover rates by age group and adjust for them as necessary. One approach to turnover shortens the analysis period from a year to, say, three months. Another calculates availabilities that include all persons present at any time during the year and considers all terminations during the year. This approach violates the assumption of equal selection probabilities, because people were available for termination for differing amounts of time. Another solution uses multiple regression, which can control for tenure at the company and date of hire.

(d) Age Discrimination in Terminations. Plaintiffs in termination cases most commonly allege age discrimination probably because firms seeking to rid themselves of women or African Americans are less likely to have hired them in the first place. All workers age, however, and therefore every company could have an incentive to reduce the number of higher paid (and typically older) workers or might make business decisions that adversely affect older workers.

The ADEA defines protected workers as those age 40 and above. State laws usually follow this rule as well, although some protect all ages and state that a firm cannot disproportionately terminate any slice of the workforce because of age. As in other employment practices, because termination of older workers can have a legitimate business explanation, the analyst must isolate the influence of age alone on termination.[43]

Firms often attribute the large layoffs of older workers to two underlying productivity-related factors. First, companies terminate workers who have consistently performed relatively poorly but were retained because of the growth in demand for the firm's product or because of high hiring and firing costs. Some companies have lower voluntary turnover of lower-rated workers than that of superior performers, causing them to remain at the company, gradually becoming older workers.

Second, technology disproportionately jeopardizes the jobs of some older workers. For example, until relatively recently, computer-related jobs often did not require a college degree. As the payoff to knowledge-based skills has increased over the past 20 years, new hires have had college degrees in larger proportions than previously. To the extent that on-the-job training does not entirely close the knowledge gap, a relation could exist between training vintage and performance ratings; those with earlier training are most likely older.

Age discrimination cases involve the continuous variable of age: analyses need not treat employees as simply over or under age 40. Although the most probative test of discrimination probably compares observed and expected numbers of older persons selected for termination, analysts often examine differences in the average ages of stayers and leavers. Even if analysts find no adverse impact with respect to the *number* of terminated employees aged 40 or older, the *average age* of terminees could exceed that of the rest of the pool if those terminated are substantially older than 40 than those retained. This implies that an analysis of workers over age 50, for example, might show an adverse impact on such workers.[44]

30.10   COMPENSATION AND PAY

The forms of discrimination discussed in previous sections of this chapter have dealt with dichotomous employment practices—hire or not hire, promote or not promote, terminate or not terminate. Compensation is a continuous variable, in which the issue becomes whether a protected group receives significantly less pay than a nonprotected group, all else constant.

Analyses of pay require that the analyst consider other factors influencing pay, such as education, general and firm experience, department or company division, geographic location, and performance. These factors include worker attributes obtained prior to arrival at the firm (education and prior experience), as well as after arrival (company tenure).

Economists have developed a well-tested and often used economic theory associated with compensation rates and the proper setting of such rates. Adam Smith made the first statement of the modern theory of wages in 1776, in *The Wealth of Nations*. Owing to the competitive nature of business and the labor market, says Smith's theory, employers will closely monitor employee productivity relative to wage levels and will set wages with some care. As a result, because companies spend time evaluating employees with respect to their compensation, a statistical analysis of pay discrimination should try to include those factors the company uses, whether explicit or implicit. Economists have developed and extended the economic theory of pay into the modern human capital model, which provides an econometric framework.[45]

Although most analyses of pay disparities will call for regression analysis, analysts can use *t*-tests if they can simultaneously stratify the data by several criteria simultaneously. For example, suppose one could construct a sample composed of men and women with high school education, 10 years of experience, in the same department, and with the same performance ratings. With such a data set, one could probably use simple *t*-tests to identify differences between men's and women's pay.

Most companies group employees into departments, with salary reflecting hierarchical position. Those workers ineligible to receive overtime under the Fair Labor Standards Act (FLSA), referred to as *exempt,* often have a set of pay grades distinct from those for nonexempt workers. Analysis of pay disparities should take these and other relevant categorizations into account, either by studying separate strata, or by entering appropriate variables in a multiple regression analysis.

In addition to cross-sectional data concerns, the analyst must also consider time series issues. For example, economy-wide business cycles can create group disparities in compensation over time if the composition of protected group hiring varies over the business cycle because compensation increases tend to be lower during economic slowdowns and higher during economic booms. If the firm hired all protected-class workers near the start of a boom, their average pay increases will exceed those for persons hired at the end of the boom. This issue becomes important if the complaint focuses on the size of increases, as opposed to levels.

Labor economists frequently use multiple regression analysis to study pay disparities. Multiple regression allows the analyst to measure the relation between several variables—such as the relation between salary and sex, race, or age— while controlling for the relevant productivity and business-cycle variables. Discrimination often explains any remaining differences in pay between protected and other persons.

The human capital model implies a particular specification for the regression equation, regressing the natural log of compensation on years of education, years of experience, years of experience squared (to capture nonlinearities), and whatever other variables apply. Such variables include measures of performance, pay grade, cohort, department, division, and geographical location. Finally, the analysis includes a variable for the protected class. The example in the next section uses this framework to evaluate whether a company discriminates against women in sales representative jobs.

(a) Sample Analysis of Pay Discrimination. Assume that a female sales representative at Company XYZ files a complaint that XYZ has consistently underpaid her for the past five years because she is female. The company claims that it did not base her pay on sex, but on other factors.

Assume that the company has a total of 100 sales representatives, 55 of whom are female. The company maintains a human resources database containing each employee's name, sex, hiring date, promotion dates, and level of education. Periodically, the company adds other information about each employee to the database. Semiannually, the company tracks actual to budgeted sales, customer response to the representative's handling of the account, and the number of newly acquired accounts. The company has two forms of compensation: base salary and annual bonus. Base salary relates to each employee's experience with the company and annual performance evaluation. The company bases bonuses on the year's sales and the number of new accounts obtained.

Suppose an analysis comparing the gross difference between male and female total compensation indicates that women receive on average $10,000 less per year than men receive. An analyst conducts a regression analysis that sequentially adds explanatory variables to assess the influence of other factors on pay disparities.

Additional Variable Included**	Female Pay ($)	Male Pay ($)	Female Shortfall ($)	Female Coefficient t-statistic
Unadjusted pay differential	50,000	60,000	−10,000	−5.2*
Variables sequentially added:				
Education	51,400	60,000	−8,600	−4.5*
Years as sales representative	53,500	60,000	−6,500	−3.8*
Geographic location	54,000	60,000	−6,000	−3.4*
Performance rating	54,700	60,000	−5,300	−3.1*
Sales last year	56,700	60,000	−3,300	−2.1*
New accounts opened	58,950	60,000	−1,050	−1.2

*Indicates that the difference between male and female pay is significant at the .05 level.

**Analysis is based on regression, where a dependent variable is total pay, and independent variables are sequentially added. *Male pay* is straight average. *Female pay* is straight average for unadjusted. For adjusted female pay, method of calculation is to deduct from the unadjusted differential that amount explained by the independent variables added up to that point (e.g., education explains $1,400 of the initial differential).

Exhibit 30-9.   Analysis of Differences in Male and Female Pay-Scales Representatives

The analyst enters each variable in the regression equation and calculates adjusted female pay and the resultant adjusted pay differential. Exhibit 30-9 summarizes the results of such an analysis.

In this example, larger values for each of the explanatory variables correlate with being male. If the analysis failed to include, for example, tenure as a sales representative, it would attribute the portion of the pay differential owing to this factor to simply being male. For example, the analysis indicates that longer service female employees receive higher pay than do shorter service ones ($53,500 versus $51,400). After the analyst measures and includes other relevant variables in the regression, inspection of the sign and *t*-statistic for the female coefficient identifies whether a statistically significant disparity in pay remains. If the coefficient is negative, and the *t*-statistic exceeds 2.00 in absolute value, the analyst would conclude that a statistically significant shortfall exists in female pay. If the analyst knows, however, that other factors affect pay, but are not available as variables, these factors might explain the remaining differences between male and female sales representatives. In the example here, the remaining difference has a *t*-statistic of −1.2, indicating that the pay differential of $1,050—although still favoring males—is not statistically significant.

30.11   WAGE AND HOURS LITIGATION

Recent years have seen a large increase in a class of litigation commonly referred to as *wage and hour* litigation. Even though this area lies outside the scope of employment discrimination, many practitioners in the analysis of discrimination also provide expert and consulting services in the wage and hour area. Such cases often require statistical analysis of large data sources. For this reason, labor economists and statisticians, as well as survey research experts, often assist counsel.

As Section 30.3(h) noted, the FLSA and similar state statutes provide a set of laws that address whether firms should compensate particular types of employees on an hourly basis and thus make them eligible for overtime wages. These laws specify exemptions from overtime if the job content and salary level meet the requirements for the exemptions. Examples of exemptions include the executive exemption, the professional exemption, the administrative exemption, and the outside sales exemption. Sometimes these exemptions can overlap. For example, often a professional and a managerial exemption can apply simultaneously.

Although there are significant numbers of cases alleging misclassification of exempt status, there are also numerous cases that deal with many other types of wage and hour violations. Examples include time clock violations, off-the-clock work violations, unpaid overtime premiums, failure to pay for reporting time, failure to pay for split shifts, and failure to provide meal and rest breaks.

In wage and hour matters, economists and statisticians focus on three areas. The first area is developing approaches to deal with the immense amount of data involved. Wage and hour cases often have a great deal of available data to manage, including company pay data and company time clock data. When faced with unmanageable amounts of data, analysts often select scientifically designed samples from large populations to study the sample more accurately and project to the population. These situations call for the application of scientific statistical principles.

A situation with no available data also calls for experience and judgmental expertise. For example, assume an employer has classified a particular job as exempt from overtime. Suppose an employee files a claim alleging that the employer should have classified the job as nonexempt and paid employees on an hourly basis with overtime. The first question is whether the job meets the requirements for the exemption. To make that determination, one must design an approach that involves systematically collecting information regarding the job from the employees who worked in that capacity. Generally, one seeks information regarding the nature of their work activities, what tasks they perform, the duration of time they spend performing certain tasks, and the level of discretionary authority they exercise. This information can be matched against the legal exemption requirements to examine the merits of the misclassification claim, the commonality among class members in how they perform their jobs, and the typicality of the representative plaintiffs' experiences.

The classification of employees by companies as exempt from overtime frequently also results in other categories of information for which there are no available data. For example, most exempt workers do not punch a time clock. As a result, the employer does not know how many hours the employees worked per week, or whether they took rest and meal breaks. Thus, to the extent that both the plaintiffs and the employer need to know what these employees did to decide whether they met the specific exemption test at issue, or how many hours class members worked to estimate damages, little or no data exist.

California has seen a great many class action cases against retailers challenging their facility manager exemption classification decisions in the years since 2000, when the state enacted a new law (AB 60). AB 60 requires that, among other things, exempt employees must spend 50 percent or more of their *time* on managerial tasks. It is unlikely that employers collect data on the tasks that different managers perform each day or the amount of time managers spend on those various tasks. Thus, one cannot determine whether managers meet California's quantitative duties test without generating data on managers' activities. Typically, data can be gathered through surveys, observational studies, a review of security videotapes, depositions, sworn statements, and so on. Each method has its virtues and drawbacks, depending on the circumstances.

In wage and hours cases, as in all class actions, class certification is a legal process that precedes the merits phase of litigation. Wage and hours cases present special issues regarding the certification process that the courts have yet to clarify fully. The courts will require input from both technical analysts and the legal profession as they wrestle with the difficult issues in these cases.

30.12   CONCLUSION

Outcomes in employment discrimination litigation cases often hinge on economic and statistical evidence. In a volume titled *Statistical Evidence in Litigation,* Barnes and Conley state, "Perhaps as a result [of the Supreme Court's explicit approval of statistical proof in employment cases] both the quantity and the quality of the opinions discussing statistical evidence far exceed what is found in any other area of the law."[46] Given recent trends indicating that employment cases account for an increasing share of civil cases, and with the increasing sophistication of legal counsel, this pattern will likely continue.

NOTES

1. For a review, *see* Barbara L. Schlei and Paul Grossman, *Employment Discrimination Law,* 2nd ed. (1983) plus subsequent supplements; Michael E. Gold, "An Introduction to the Law of Employment Discrimination," *ILR Bulletin 68* (Ithaca, NY: ILR Press), 1993; and Ronald G. Ehrenberg and Robert S. Smith, *Modern Labor Economics,* 4th ed. (New York: HarperCollins, 1991).
2. Arbitration of employment claims has become increasingly common in recent years. There are industries in which arbitration is, in fact, the rule, rather than the exception. Investment banking, for example, has relied on arbitration and panels of independent arbitrators for years.
3. *Griggs v. Duke Power,* 401 U.S. 424, 3 FEP 175 (1971), was the first case in which the Court systematically applied statistics to a Title VII case. Other notable cases include *Teamsters v. United States,* 431 U.S. 324, 340, 14 1514, 1520-21 (1977); *Havelwood School District v. United States,* 433 U.S. 299, 15 FEP 1 (1977); *Dothard v. Rawlinson,* 423 U.S. 321, 15 FEP 10 (1977); and *New York Transit Authority v. Beazer,* 440 U.S. 568, 19 FEP 149 (1979).
4. 42 U.S.C.S. Section 2000e *et seq.*
5. 42 U.S.C.S. Section 12111 *et seq.*
6. 29 U.S.C.S. Section 621 *et seq.*
7. 29 U.S.C.S. Section 206.
8. 42 U.S.C.S. Section 2000 note.
9. Racial discrimination in other areas (e.g., public accommodation, college admission) was prominently in the news in late 1962 and early 1963 and is dealt with in other parts of the Civil Rights Bill. Although the events in Birmingham in 1963 had to do with public accommodation, and precipitated the drafting of the bill in 1963, public

accommodation cases filed in federal courts have averaged only around 4 percent of employment cases over the past dozen years. For a summary of cases filed in federal district courts, see issues of the "Annual Report of the Director of the Administrative Office of the United States Courts." http://www.uscourts.gov/library/annualreports.htm

10. In 1866 Congress passed Law 42 U.S.C. Section 1981 mandating that all persons be allowed to make and enforce contracts regardless of race. Court rulings and congressional amendments have established that the law protects workers against racial employment discrimination because the employment relation is a type of contract. Section 1981 is broader than Title VII in one respect; the law covers all employers regardless of size.

11. 42 U.S.C.S. Section 2000e-2(e)(1).

12. Employment cases focus on two types of discrimination: disparate treatment (i.e., intentional discrimination) and disparate impact (i.e., a policy or action that unintentionally but nevertheless disproportionately and unlawfully affects a group).

13. 42 U.S.C.S. Section 2000e-k(2)(A)(i).

14. 29 U.S.C.S. Section 623(a)(1). In the initial congressional debates over Title VII, age was suggested as an additional protected characteristic. Since the debates had been so protracted, it was decided not to add age to Title VII, but instead to submit the issue for further study, the result of which was the ADEA in 1967.

15. 29 U.S.C.S. Section 623(a), 623(e).

16. *Id.*, Section 623(a)(1).

17. *Id.*, Section 630(b)(2).

18. *Id.*, Section 623(b), 623(e).

19. *Id.*, Section 623(c)(1)-(2), 623(e).

20. *Id.*, Section 279.

21. *Id.*, Section 280.

22. *Id.*, Section 281.

23. Gold, "An Introduction to the Law," 33–35.

24. 42 U.S.C.S. Section 12111(2).

25. *Id.*, Section 12111(5)(A).

26. *Id.*, Section 1981(c).

27. *Id.*, Section 1981(b).

28. *Hudson v. International Business Machines Corp.*, 620 F.2d 351 (CA 2 1980); *Pouncy v. Prudential Ins. Co.*, 499 F. Supp. 427 (S.D. Tex. 1980), aff'd., 668 F.2d 795 (CA 5).

29. *Gay v. Waiters' & Dairy Lunchmen's Union*, 489 F. Supp. 282 (N.D. Cal. 1980), aff'd 29 BNA FEP Cas. 1027 (CA 9).

30. *Pennsylvania v. International Union of Operating Engineers*, 469 F. Supp. 329 (E.D. Pa 1978).

31. The Supreme Court case that first articulated the theory of disparate impact was *Griggs v. Duke Power*, 401 U.S. 424, 3 FEP 175 (1971).

32. Sources for statistical techniques include the following: David W. Barnes and John M. Conley, *Statistical Evidence in Litigation* (Boston: Little Brown, 1986); Michael O. Finkelstein and Bruce Levin, *Statistics for Lawyers* (New York: Springer-Verlag, 1990); William C. Merill and Karl A. Fox, *Introduction to Economic Statistics* (New York: John Wiley & Sons, 1970); Alan Agresti, *Categorical Data Analysis* (New York: John Wiley & Sons, 1990); Mortis H. Degroot, *Probability and Statistics*, 2nd ed. (Reading, MA: Addison Wesley, 1986).

33. The Supreme Court, in *Hazelwood*, 433 U.S. 299, first established the standard for statistical significance in employment litigation as two or more standard deviations.

34. If a distribution has mean m and standard deviation s, then an actual observation a has a Z-score of $(a - m)/s$.

35. The chi-square test is equivalent to the two-sample binomial test of proportions. *See* Merill and Fox, *Introduction to Economic Statistics*, 299–300.

36. The *t*-test generally requires at least 20 observations to be reliable, although smaller samples can be used, with a corresponding diminution in the power of the test to detect differences.

37. *See* Harry J. Holzer *What Employers Want: Job Prospects for Less-Educated Workers* (New York: Russell Sage Foundation, 1996) and Duncan J. Watts, "Small Worlds: The Dynamics of Networks Between Order and Randomness," in *Princeton Studies in Complexity* (Princeton, NJ: Princeton University Press, 1999).

38. Care should be taken in using feeder pools. The plaintiff can argue that the defendant chose particular feeder pools from which to promote simply because they were male feeders. Therefore, it is important to study the rates of promotion for both men and women from each feeder, as well as aggregated across feeders.

39. Because the dependent variable takes on only two values, promoted or not promoted, the appropriate regression may not be a standard linear form, but instead may be a logistic or probit form. In practice, if the proportion of the sample promoted is somewhere between 25 and 75 percent, the ordinary linear regression will produce consistent and unbiased results. Outside that range, one must use caution and perhaps perform both a linear and a logit or probit regression.

40. The article first treating this issue empirically was Jacob Mincer and S. Polachek, "Family Investments in Human Capital: The Earnings of Women," *Journal of Political Economy*, 82 (Mar./Apr. 1974), S76–S108.

41. A well-known recent case in which the defendant attempted, and failed, to adduce evidence on differential male and female interest in promotion to store management positions by conducting a survey is *Stender, et al. v. Lucky Stores*, C-88-1467 MHP (N.D. Cal., 1989).

42. Research by labor economists demonstrates that younger workers experience higher turnover. *See*, for example, the influential article by Boyan Jovanovic, "Job Matching and the Theory of Turnover," *Journal of Political Economy*, 87 (Oct. 1979), 972–990; *see also* Jacob Mincer and B. Jovanovic, "Labor Mobility and Wages," in *Studies in Labor Markets*, ed. Sherwin Rosen (Chicago: University of Chicago Press, 1981).

43. Gold, "An Introduction to the Law," 41.

44. So-called banding of the workforce into age ranges is accepted in certain circuit courts, if the plaintiff is within a certain band (e.g., age 50 to 60). Clearly, with enough time, and a large enough sample size, an analyst probably can identify some age range with adverse impact. The legal definition of the protected class in a particular circuit, or state, court is therefore important to identify prior to analysis.

45. Gary Becker and Jacob Mincer are credited with first articulating the human capital model. Since that time, there has been an explosion of articles and books, adding theoretical refinements, and conducting numerous empirical tests. Virtually all the tests have found similar results, and hence, the human capital model is regarded as one of the most successful empirical models in economics. *See* Gary S. Becker, *Human Capital*, 2nd ed. (Chicago: University of Chicago Press, 1975); Jacob Mincer, *Schooling, Experience and Earnings* (New York: NBER, 1974).

46. David W. Barnes and John M. Conley, *Statistical Evidence in Litigation* (Boston: Little, Brown, 1986), 587.

LIST OF CASES

Cases Cited in Text

Dothard v. Rawlinson, 433 U.S. 321 (1977)

Griggs v. Duke Power Co., 401 U.S. 424 (1971), often considered the landmark Title VII case establishing this concept

Hazelwood School District v. United States, 433 U.S. 324 (1977)

New York Transit Authority v. Beazer, 440 U.S. 568 (1979)

Stender et al. v. Lucky Stores (C-88-1467 MHP, N.D. Cal., 1989)

Teamsters v. United States, 431 U.S. 324, 14 1514 (1977).

Additional Cases

Albemarle Paper Co. v. Moody, 422 U.S. 405 (1975)

Bazemore v. Friday, 478 U.S. 385 (1986)

Brown v. Board of Educ., 347 U.S. 483 (1954)

Castaneda v. Partida, 430 U.S. 482 (1977)

Connecticut v. Teal, 457 U.S. 440 (1982)

EEOC v. Chicago Miniature Lamp Works, 947 F.2d 292 (7th Cir. 1991)

EEOC v. Federal Reserve Bank, 698 F.2d 633 (4th Cir. 1983)

EEOC v. Sears, Roebuck & Co., 839 F.2d 302 (7th Cir. 1988)

Harris v. Forklift Sys., 114 S. Ct. 367 (1993)

International Brotherhood of Teamsters v. United States, 431 U.S. 324 (1977)

Los Angeles Dept. of Water & Power v. Manhart, 435 U.S. 702 (1978)

Lowe v. Commack Union Free School Dist., 886 F.2d 1364 (2d Cir. N.Y. 1989)

Maresco v. Evans Chemetics, Div. of W. R. Grace & Co., 964 F.2d 106 (2d Cir. N.Y. 1989)

McDonnell Douglas Corp. v. Green, 411 U.S. 792 (1973)

Moore v. Sears, Roebuck & Co., 464 F. Supp. 357 (N.D. Ga. 1979)

Ottaviani v. State University of New York, 875 F.2d 365 (2d Cir. N.Y. 1989)

Price v. Maryland Casualty Co., 561 F.2d 609 (5th Cir. Miss. 1977)

Stastny v. Southern Bell Tel & Tel Co., 458 F. Supp. 314 (W.D.N.C. 1978), *modified*, 628 F.2d 267 (4th Cir. N.C. 1980)

St. Mary's Honor Ctr. v. Hicks, 113 S. Ct. 2742 (1993)

United States v. Warren, 759 F. Supp. 355 (E.D. Mich. 1991)

United States v. Yonkers Bd. of Education, 624 F. Supp. 1276 (S.D.N.Y. 1985), *affd*, 837 F.2d 1181 (2d Cir. N.Y. 1987), *cert. denied*, 486 U.S. 1055 (1988)

Vuyanich v. Republic Nat'l Bank, 505 F. Supp. 224 (N.D. Tex. 1980), *vacated*, 723 F.2d 1195 (5th Cir. Tex. 1984), *cert denied*, 469 U.S. 1073 (1984)

Wards Cove Packing Co., v. Atonio, 490 U.S. 642 (1989)

Watson v. Ft. Worth Bank & Trust, 487 U.S. 977 (1988)

BIBLIOGRAPHY

Agresti, Alan. *Categorical Data Analysis.* New York: John Wiley & Sons, 1990.

Baldus, David, and J. Cole. *Statistical Proof of Discrimination.* Colorado Springs: Shepards McGraw-Hill, 1980.

Barnes, David W., and John M. Conley. *Statistical Evidence in Litigation.* Boston: Little, Brown, 1986.

Becker, Gary S. *The Economics of Discrimination.* 2nd ed. Chicago: University of Chicago Press, 1971.

———. *Human Capital.* 2nd ed. Chicago: University of Chicago Press, 1980.

Ben-Porath, Yoram. "The Production of Human Capital and the Life Cycle of Earnings." *Journal of Political Economy* 75 (1967): 352–365.

Boardman, Anthony E., and Aidan R. Vining. "The Role of Probative Statistics in Employment Discrimination Cases." *Law & Contemporary Problems* 46 (Autumn 1983): 189.

Campbell, Thomas J. "Regression Analysis in Title VII Cases: Minimum Standards, Comparable Worth and Other Issues Where Law and Statistics Meet." *Stanford Law Review* 36 (1984): 1299.

Cathcart, David A., and R. Lawrence Ashe, Jr., eds. *Employment Discrimination Law: Five-Year-Supplement.* Washington, DC: Bureau of National Affairs, 1989.

DeGroot, Morris H. *Probability and Statistics.* 2nd ed. Reading, MA: Addison Wesley, 1986.

Draper, Norman, and Harry Smith. *Applied Regression Analysis.* 2nd ed. New York: John Wiley & Sons, 1981.

Ehrenberg, Ronald G., and Robert S. Smith. *Modern Labor Economics.* 4th ed. New York: HarperCollins, 1991.

Finkelstein, Michael O., and Bruce Levin. *Statistics for Lawyers.* New York: Springer-Verlag, 1990.

Fisher, Franklin M. "Multiple Regression in Legal Proceedings." *Columbia Law Review* 80 (1980): 702.

Gastwirth, Joseph L. "Statistical Methods for Analyzing Claims of Employment Discrimination." *Industrial and Labor Relations Review* 38 (1984): 75.

———. "Statistical Reasoning in the Legal Setting." *American Statistician* 46 (1992): 55.

Gold, Michael Evan. "An Introduction to the Law of Employment Discrimination," *ILR Bulletin 68.* Ithaca, NY: ILR Press, 1993.

Hamennesh, Daniel S., and Albert Rees. *The Economics of Work and Pay.* 3rd ed. New York: Harper & Row, 1984.

Hanushek, Eric A. "When School Finance 'Reform' May Not Be Good Policy." *Harvard Journal on Legislature* 28 (1991): 423.

Kaye, David H., and Mikel Aickin, eds. *Statistical Methods in Discrimination Litigation.* New York: Marcel Dekker, 1986.

Lindemann-Schlei, Barbara, and Paul Grossman. *Employment Discrimination Law.* 2nd ed. Washington, DC: American Bar Association: Section on Labor and Employment Law: BNA Books, 1983 and 1989 Supplement.

Meier, Paul. "What Happened in Hazelwood: Statistics, Employment Discrimination and the 80% Rule, *AM B Found Res J* 139 1984.

Merrill, William C., and Fox, Karl A. *Introduction to Economic Statistics.* New York: John Wiley & Sons, 1970.

Mincer, Jacob. "The Distribution of Labor Incomes: A Survey with Special Reference to the Human Capital Approach." *Journal of Economic Literature* 8 (1970):

———. "On-the-Job Training: Costs, Returns, and Some Implications." *Journal of Political Economy* 70 (Oct. 1962): 50–79.

———. "Investment in Human Capital and the Personal Income Distribution," *Journal of Political Economy* 66 (1958): 281–302.

Mincer, Jacob, and Solomon Polachek. "Family Investments in Human Capital: Earnings of Women." *Journal of Political Economy* 82 (1974): S76–S108.

Paetzold, Ramona L. and Steven L. Willbom. *The Statistics of Discrimination: Using Statistical Evidence in Discrimination Cases.* Colorado Springs: Shepard's/McGraw-Hill, 1994.

Paetzold, Ramona L. "Problems with Statistical Significance in Employment Discrimination Litigation." *New England Law Review* 26 (1991): 395.

Powers, N. Thompson, Paul W. Cane, W. Carl Jordan, and Barry L. Goldstein, eds. *Employment Discrimination Law: 1987–1989 Supplement.* 2nd ed. Washington, DC: Bureau of National Affairs, 1991.

Rosenthal, Robert. "Combining Results of Independent Studies." *Psychological Bulletin* 85 (1978): 185.

Shoben, Elaine W. "Differential Pass-Fail Rates in Employment Testing: Statistical Proof under Title VII." *Harvard Law Review* 91 (1978): 793.

Winkler, Robert L., and William L. Hays. *Statistics: Probability, Inference, and Decision.* 2nd ed. New York: Holt, Rinehart and Winston, 1975.

CHAPTER 31

FEDERAL CONTRACT DISPUTES

James W. Thomas

CONTENTS

31.1 INTRODUCTION

Federal contractors often use consultants and financial experts to resolve administrative or formal contract disputes. There are many occasions to use experts in federal contract matters because disputes can occur well before the award of a contract, any time throughout a contract's performance period, or many years after physical completion. Federal contractors must adhere to complex rules (often confusing and sometimes conflicting) that govern a contract's pricing, costing, and administrative requirements. In a dispute setting, experts who can master the evidence and then apply their key knowledge of the procurement rules can significantly influence entitlement (i.e., liability) as well as quantum (i.e., damages).

This chapter provides an overview of the many types of federal contract disputes and how a consultant or financial expert can assist in the resolution process. The chapter will not explain the many federal procurement rules or analyze related case law interpretations; there are several books on these subjects.[1]

This text will cite laws and regulations to help describe the role of an expert during a federal government procurement dispute.

This chapter focuses on federal, rather than state or local, government procurement contracts. Nonetheless, federal procurement rules and related concepts often apply to state and local contracts. For example, state and local government contracts often incorporate the federal procurement rules or require consistency with the compliance requirements of an organization's federal contracts. Moreover, if the funding for state or local contracts comes from federal procurement appropriations, the federal procurement rules can follow the funding.

This chapter uses the term *contract* in a general context. It refers to the direct relation between the federal government and a contractor (prime contract) but can also apply to subcontracts between the prime contractor and a supplier. Federal procurement rules can flow down from a prime contractor to a subcontractor by statute, regulation, or agreement. Grants and cooperative agreements[2] (used for research and development) must follow compliance requirements separate from contracts (used for supplies and services). However, many of the financial and accounting requirements of grants and cooperative agreements resemble those of contracts.

In federal procurement decisions, courts place considerable weight on the spirit of public policy, contract technicalities, and evidential support of factual assertions raised by one or both parties. Under counsel's interpretation of laws and contracts, the expert will perform financial analyses and measure contract price adjustments, penalties, and damages based on one or more theories of entitlement. As in any other litigation matter, an effective strategy includes exposing the other side's weaknesses. In federal contract disputes, a key weakness in an argument can be an incorrect interpretation of the contract terms governing the accounting and pricing requirements.

In a matter involving a claim against the government, the concept of equity has a special meaning. Although contracting officers must ensure that contractors receive impartial, fair, and equitable treatment,[3] contract price adjustments aim to protect the government. Further, regulations or statutes often limit the remedies that a contractor can receive from the government.[4] Thus, when experts select techniques and methods to value remedies, they should understand not only applicable procurement law and regulations but also how judicial precedent interprets those rules.

There are many unique terms and concepts in the government contracting world, and the extensive use of acronyms can overwhelm new entrants. The regulations themselves or reference material found on the Internet provide glossaries of acronyms.[5] Appendix A provides some of the acronyms that financial experts will encounter and expands all acronyms used in the chapter.

31.2 FEDERAL CONTRACTS AND NATURE OF DISPUTES

Because of the federal government's tremendous volume of procurement transactions, it uses standard procedures and contractual arrangements. The contract types are based on such factors as timing, the contract's dollar value, the complexity of the procured item, the risks assumed by the party performing the contract, the incentives needed to encourage performance, and the need for flexibility during performance. For example, the government uses the Uniform Contract Format (UCF) in sealed bids and negotiated contracts (*see* Appendix B). Although the government's use of a standard approach to contracting can intimidate those unfamiliar with federal procurements, it helps those with deep knowledge of the regulations. In reviewing a standard government contract, the expert can quickly find pertinent financial or administrative provisions and identify additional relevant documents.

One must read contracts in conjunction with the terms and conditions associated with their prescribed use. Experts often refer to the Federal Acquisition Regulation (FAR) Provision and Clause Matrix, a reference table showing each FAR clause and method of incorporation by principal type or purpose of the contract. In negotiated contracts using the UCF, the Order of Precedence clause provides that the government will resolve any inconsistency in the solicitation or contract by giving precedence in the following order:

1. The schedule (excluding specifications)
2. Representations and other instructions
3. Contract clauses
4. Other documents
5. Exhibits and attachments
6. The specifications[6]

Based on this established hierarchy, any financial requirements set forth in the contract's special provisions, which are part of the schedule, take priority over related requirements found in the standard contract clauses.

Under a legal concept called the *Christian* doctrine, the parties should read into the contract any term that a federal government contract should include (as required by law), even though the contract does not include or reference it.[7] The opposite also holds true: when a federal statute or regulation prohibits a term or condition found within the contract, it is deemed to "self-delete" or "read out" of the contract. This is known as the reverse *Christian* doctrine. The *Christian* doctrine affects contract terms related to contract type, payment, changes, and the Cost Accounting Standards (CAS).

FAR guidelines state the following:

> The contract types are grouped into two broad categories: fixed-price contracts (*see* Subpart 16.2) and cost-reimbursement contracts (*see* Subpart 16.3). The specific contract types range from firm-fixed-price, in which the contractor has full responsibility for the performance costs and resulting profit (or loss), to cost-plus-fixed-fee, in which the contractor has minimal responsibility for the performance costs and the negotiated fee (profit) is fixed. In between are the various incentive contracts (*see* Subpart 16.4), in which the contractor's responsibility for the performance costs and the profit or fee incentives offered are tailored to the uncertainties involved in contract performance.[8]

The performance risk placed on contractors makes fixed price contracts conducive to disputes over defective pricing, claims for increased costs from changed work, cost-based billings, and CAS compliance matters. Estimates to complete often play an important role in financial accounting disputes and other matters in which a contractor's responsibility for a loss becomes the focus.

The government bases the value of a cost reimbursement contract on allowable costs. Accordingly, disputes arising under cost type contracts often focus on cost allowability matters and funding limitations. Experts must understand the Allowable Cost and Payment Clause, which sets forth provisions on invoicing (based on FAR 31.2 in effect on the date of the contract), reimbursing costs, final indirect rates, billing rates, quick close-out procedures, and final payment.[9]

31.3   LAWS, REGULATIONS, AND GUIDANCE

As one might expect, the federal government has a highly regulated contracting process. This section discusses some of the relevant statutes, regulations, and guidance, as well as the role and benefit of expert assistance.

(a) Statutes

- **Civil and criminal statutes:** Contractors make numerous representations throughout the contracting process. Inaccurate representations about eligibility and responsibility, compliance with or exemptions from laws or regulations, or the accuracy and completeness of financial data can lead to allegations of civil and criminal infractions under statutes including False Claims Act, False Statements Act, and the Major Fraud Act. Experts can help evaluate the factual basis and data underlying contractor statements and claims.

- **Competition in Contracting Act (CICA):** Provides, among other things, the right to protest a contract award before the Government Accountability Office (GAO) when a contractor (usually an unsuccessful bidder) believes that a government buyer fails to conduct a procurement according to the terms of a solicitation or federal procurement law or regulation.[10] Parties use experts on matters such as cost realism and unbalanced pricing, in which the bidder prices parts of the job below cost and other parts above cost. At the request of a party or the GAO, experts will need to sign a protective order that requires disclosures of relationships to the parties, the extent of any involvement in competitive decision making, and a cooling-off period whereby the experts promise to avoid participating in future related procurements for a specified period.[11]

- **Contract Disputes Act (CDA):** Establishes procedures and requirements for asserting and resolving government or contractor claims subject to the act. It provides for interest payment on contractor claims, a required certification, and a civil penalty for claims that are fraudulent or based on a misrepresentation of fact. Parties use experts and consultants prior to filing a CDA claim in an administrative role to resolve equitable price adjustments, review the certificate for accuracy, and opine on claim elements. Experts also help in assessing the value of the claim.

- **Cost Accounting Standards (CAS):** Maintained by the Cost Accounting Standards Board under Public Law 100-679 (originally under Public Law 91-379) to set forth cost accounting and administrative requirements for covered contracts. Contractors must maintain records, report cost accounting practice changes, and agree to contract price adjustments under certain circumstances.

Mandatory changes, voluntary changes, or compliance violations can lead to price adjustments. Parties can use experts to evaluate CAS compliance issues and calculate a price adjustment if needed. The method for measuring price adjustments depends on the type of contract, type of adjustment, and whether it occurred at the time of pricing or during contract performance.

- **Federal Acquisition Streamlining Act (FASA):** Changed the rules on commercial item contracting.[12] FASA and related legislation combined many clauses into a single clause that resembles a commercial contract. In disputes involving commercial items, experts should understand the special contract provisions and that CAS and the cost allowability rules have limited, if any, applicability.

- **Freedom of Information Act (FOIA):** Requires the government to disclose publicly available information to contractors.[13] Experts can help counsel identify documents available through FOIA, such as contract extracts, agency policies, and audit guidance. Consultants can advise counsel on the types of records maintained and subject to request. As part of a "reverse FOIA" lawsuit, consultants can also help prove how the disclosure of the requested information could harm a contractor in the marketplace.

- **Miller Act:** Requires that contracts for the construction, alteration, or repair of any public building or public work of the United States also have a performance bond that protects the United States and an additional bond that protects persons who furnish material and labor for work related to the contract.[14] Eligible persons can file Miller Act claims for amounts unpaid after 90 days. Parties use experts to help calculate the amount due.

- **Procurement Integrity Act:** Provides restrictions on the disclosure of sensitive procurement information. Experts analyze disclosures and their effect on procurement actions or assist in disputes between contractors.

- **Prompt Payment Act:** Provides for payment of interest to contractors and requires contractors to refund any overpayments back to the government, plus interest. Financial experts will follow the act's provisions to identify the types of payments subject to the act and calculate interest.

- **Public Law 85-804:** Provides authority for agencies connected to national defense contracts to enter into, amend, and modify contracts, whenever the president considers that such action would facilitate the national defense. A contractor seeking a contract adjustment that exceeds the simplified acquisition threshold must submit a certification that the contractor made the request in good faith and that the supporting data are accurate and complete to the best of the contractor's knowledge and belief.[15] Contractors use experts and consultants in connection with their requests for adjustment under the act.

- **Truth in Negotiations Act (TINA):** Requires contractors to furnish current, accurate, and complete cost and pricing data on covered contracts and subcontracts. Violations of TINA lead to price adjustments, an assessment of interest, and perhaps large civil or criminal penalties. Experts and consultants verify cost or pricing data, identify disclosures, analyze financial records relating to reliance defenses, and calculate financial remedies.

(b) Regulations

- **Federal Acquisition Regulations System:** Established for the codification and publication of uniform policies and procedures for acquisition by all executive agencies. The Federal Acquisition Regulations System consists of the FAR (its primary document) and agency acquisition regulations that implement or supplement the FAR. The FAR System does not include internal agency guidance such as designations and delegations of authority, assignments of responsibilities, work-flow procedures, and internal reporting requirements.[16] The FAR contains many financial related requirements, including the Contract Cost Principles and Procedures, Cost Accounting Standards Administration Rules, Contract Financing Rules, and Contract Termination Rules.

- **FAR supplements:** Agencies can issue or authorize the issuance of agency acquisition regulations that implement or supplement the FAR and incorporate agency policies, procedures, contract clauses, solicitation provisions, and forms that govern the contracting process or otherwise control the relation between the agency, including any of its suborganizations, and contractors or prospective contractors. The General Services Administration (GSA) maintains supplemental rules and clauses on Federal Supply Schedule Contracts.

- **FAR deviations:** The head of an agency, or his or her designee, can grant FAR deviations in accordance with agency procedures when necessary to meet specific needs and requirements. However, FAR deviations are not authorized for CAS Board rules and regulations.[17] FAR deviations, for example, have been used to suspend the effective date of a rule and by the Department of Defense (DOD) in relation to the accounting rules for calculating an indirect cost base.[18]

- **Office of Management and Budget (OMB):** Oversees and coordinates executive agency procurement, financial management, information, and regulatory policies. OMB establishes principles and procedures for calculating costs applicable to contracts, subcontracts, grants, and other agreements between the government and noncommercial organizations, such as nonprofits, education institutions, and other governments. The following cost principles apply to noncommercial organizations:

  - **OMB Circular A-21**, Cost Principles for Educational Institutions, provides principles for calculating the costs applicable to research and development, training, and other work performed by educational institutions under contracts with the government.

  - **OMB Circular A-87**, Cost Principles for State and Local Governments, sets forth the principles for calculating the allowable costs of contracts and subcontracts with state, local, and federally recognized Indian tribal governments.

  - **OMB Circular A-122**, Cost Principles for Nonprofit Organizations, sets forth principles for calculating the costs applicable to work performed by nonprofit organizations under contracts (also applies to grants and other agreements) with the government.

- **OMB Circular A-110**, Uniform Administrative Requirements for Grants and Agreements with Institutions of Higher Education, Hospitals, and Other Nonprofit Organizations, sets forth standards for obtaining consistency and uniformity among federal agencies in the administration of grants to and agreements with covered organizations.

- **OMB Circular A-76**, Competitive Sourcing, establishes federal policy regarding the performance of commercial activities and, as supplemented, sets forth the procedures for deciding whether commercial activities should occur under contract with commercial sources or in-house using government facilities and personnel. GAO's bid protest authority under CICA covers protests of agency decisions under OMB A-76. Experts and consultants help counsel with the cost comparisons that government agencies must use to decide whether to contract out a commercial activity or perform it in-house.

- **Other Federal Procurement Rules:** Some agencies follow their own procurement regulations rather than the FAR. For example, the Federal Aviation Administration follows its Acquisition Management System, and the U.S. Postal Service has its own purchasing manual. Although these agencies do not follow the FAR, their procurement regulations resemble those of the FAR, and parties can resolve disputes through the CDA (discussed in Section 31.3(a)).

(c) Guidance

(i) Advance Agreements.   Contractors and contracting officers often reach agreements on the treatment of special or unusual costs to avoid possible subsequent disallowance or dispute.[19] Advance agreements relate to specific costs or to questions about a contractor's disclosures to the government. However, contracting officers do not have authority to use advance agreements to modify specific cost limitations in the FAR.

(ii) Defense Contract Audit Manual (CAM). This manual prescribes auditing policies and procedures and furnishes guidance in auditing techniques for personnel engaged in the performance of the Defense Contract Audit Agency (DCAA) mission. The CAM requires that due professional care should impose a duty on each professional within an audit organization to observe generally accepted government auditing standards (GAGAS).[20] The CAM is neither part of the FAR nor subject to a regulatory process on its own. However, the FAR references it as guidance on what constitutes an adequate final indirect cost rate proposal and supporting data.[21] Additionally, the CAM provides acceptable methods of accounting for certain types of costs (e.g., uncompensated overtime). Although the CAM will prove useful for routine matters, it lacks guidance for gray areas that require contract interpretation or application of accounting principles. A DOD directive established the DCAA to perform all contract auditing for DOD and to provide accounting and financial advisory services—in connection with the negotiation, administration, and settlement of contracts and subcontracts—to all DOD procurement and contract administration activities.[22] DCAA also furnishes contract audit services to other government agencies. Appendix C provides an example of the types of audit reports issued by DCAA.

31.4   THE FINANCIAL EXPERT

(a) Qualifications. Many government contracting disputes do not require a financial consultant or expert. Hundreds of cases each year focus on procurement statutes, implementing regulations, matters of jurisdiction, authority, and procedural requirements without the participation of experts. However, sophisticated contractors will generally retain an expert when legal issues involving a price adjustment, accounting, financial analysis, payment, or cost matter arise.

An expert's qualifications typically include industry experience and background, knowledge of the rules at issue, consulting experience, training, teaching, and areas of study. Disputes over discrete cost rules or standards often require a particular expertise. For example, in a dispute involving the reasonableness of compensation costs, contractors should look to a professional familiar with industry compensation practices. Likewise, pension disputes can require actuaries, construction contracts can require professionals familiar with industry practices, and contracts with nonprofit organizations can require professionals experienced in OMB Circular A-122. Finally, when a contractor faces cost issues that mesh government cost accounting rules with generally accepted accounting principles (GAAP), a certified public accountant can help identify specific guidance and clarify differences between GAAP and FAR or CAS.

When evaluating an expert's qualifications, the courts have focused on whether the expert can help the trier of fact understand the evidence and assess the facts at issue. The law does not permit expert conclusions relating to matters of law.[23] For example, under the Truth in Negotiations Act, one can use a financial expert to verify facts and their relation to future costs. However, the expert cannot opine on the interpretation of what constitutes cost or pricing data, a legal matter for the court to decide.

(b) Role. Experts verify facts, perform financial analyses, assess possible contract price adjustments, calculate add-ons or offsets, and measure penalties and damages, as applicable, under one or more theories of entitlement. The expert must understand the nature of the contract, supplemental regulations, and any special provisions that preempt the general principles. Common special provisions include termination liability, preestablished formulas for computation of equitable adjustments, cost allowability limitations, and price adjustment methods.

Experts must also understand their client's burden of proof. In an appeal from a government claim alleging noncompliance with CAS, the burden of proof lies with the government to demonstrate the specific noncompliance and its cost impact.[24] On the other hand, in matters involving the reasonableness of a specific cost, the contractor has the burden of proof to establish that such cost is reasonable.[25]

Financial experts can perform the following tasks:

- Define the type of cost at issue, applicable or analogous accounting principles, and a contractor's method of accounting. The client can use this determination to identify specific cost allowability limitations and resolve questions about consistency for costs incurred in similar circumstances.

- Identify the indirect or direct relation between a cost and a government contract.

- Verify the reliability and relevance of documents and supporting data used for proposals, billings, or claims.
- Apply GAAP.
- Evaluate the extent to which an allegation of overcharging resulted in an overpayment by the government.
- Apply generally accepted methods of quantifying costs, including the use of statistics, estimating techniques, preestablished formulas, and contract pricing models.
- Use forensic technology to discover evidence.
- Testify on accounting and other financial requirements of contracts.

Common pitfalls that experts need to avoid in a government contract dispute include opining without sufficient information, using unreliable records, failing to correctly apply the contract terms, offering legal advice, or using unconventional financial theories. For example, certain techniques that the government uses for price analysis or price adjustment are designed to meet prescribed guidelines. Therefore, the government's approach to calculating a contractor's monetary relief (i.e., quantum), if reasonable and within the government's discretion, can prevail over an alternative, conceptually superior approach offered by the contractor. An expert must develop a strong link between the basis of entitlement and a fair and reasonable monetary recovery.

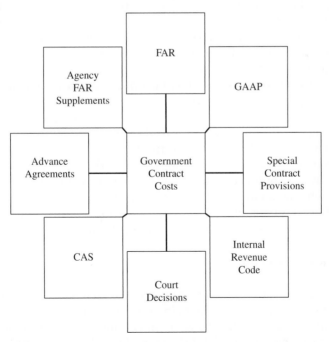

The role of the financial expert includes applying many sources of government contract cost rules

Exhibit 31-1.   Government Contract Cost Rules

31.5 PROTESTS AND PREAWARD DISPUTES

Competing bidders can dispute the process followed by the government leading to the contract award. Interested parties can protest the government's actions for failure to adhere to statutory or regulatory requirements as well as the terms of the government's solicitation. Parties can file protests with the agency awarding the contract, the GAO, or the U.S. Court of Federal Claims either before or after contract award.[26] A financial expert can assist on matters such as contractor representations, financial capability, cost realism, unbalanced pricing, and the cost evaluation.

The government forwards protests over small business representations to the Small Business Administration (SBA) for resolution. If the government awards a contract to a small business, an unsuccessful bidder can challenge the small business size status of another bidder. In an appeal before the SBA, an expert can help independently assess a contractor's small business certification. Small business size standards are either revenue based or employee based. For example, an expert can evaluate whether the annual receipts representation by the contractor is supported by regular financial records, acceptable for federal tax purposes, adjusted for certain allowances, and based on the percentage of completion method of accounting.[27]

Prior to award, the government can conduct a preaward survey of a contractor's ability to perform the contract. Inadequate financial capability, for example, can cause a delay in the award or a decision by the government to use another contractor. An expert can prove useful during this process to calculate or comment on financial ratios, trends, and parent company financial information. The expert can focus on the reasonableness of the contractor's cash flow projections, a key factor in assessing a contractor's ability to perform the contract.

In solicitations for cost reimbursement contracts, the government can adjust a bidder's cost proposal to arrive at the evaluated or probable cost. If the contractor protests the award, an expert can assist in evaluating such probable cost calculations, including performing tests for calculation errors, improper adjustments, and inconsistencies with the solicitation criteria.

The government can reject a bid, or rate it as high risk, if the government finds a distortion in the distribution of costs to line items or unbalanced pricing. An expert can evaluate whether a bid is *mathematically* unbalanced (i.e., below cost for some items and above cost for others) and *materially* unbalanced (a mathematically unbalanced bid that does not result in the lowest ultimate cost to the government).

31.6 CONTRACTOR CLAIMS

(a) Overview. Contractors demanding payment for claims filed under CDA must specify a "sum certain." Experts can help verify a payment demand's clarity and adequate support to ensure that the government understands the amount sought. An error in specifying the amount due can, by itself, lead to a counterclaim from the government under the False Claims Act.

Change orders often occur in government contracting. Many changes are administrative and do not affect the substantive rights of the parties, such as a change in the address of the paying office.[28] Others require a price adjustment.

Although, in a perfect world, one should price change orders before their execution, time limits or other practicalities usually prevent their early negotiation. Disputes and litigation often result from disagreements between the parties over entitlement, the appropriate price adjustment, or both.

The expert should understand the type of change, basis of entitlement, and whether the price adjustment must follow preestablished prices or formulas in the contract. One can use preestablished prices or formulas for options, certain types of construction changes, liquidated damages, delays, and economic price adjustments (inflation factors). In some situations, pre-established prices or formulas must be used even if they do not measure the true financial effects, because the agreement requires their use.

Changes that lack a preestablished pricing mechanism require more detailed analysis. Here, the expert can identify the elements and value of compensation that the contractor can recover. Under standard change order provisions in negotiated contracts, the contractor has entitlement to an equitable price adjustment for increased costs. Courts have measured increased costs as the difference in the reasonable cost of performing the contract before and after the change.[29] Using this approach, experts can develop appropriate price adjustments based on legal theories of entitlement.

When assessing damages, an expert should select the proper approach to calculate a contractor's increased costs based on, in part, the suitability of accounting records and need for using estimates. Contractors should account for changes separately, a practice that the change order accounting clause sometimes requires in contracts.[30] However, when documents do not separately identify the costs of changes, the expert can use estimating techniques or formulas. Quantification methods include the use of statistical analyses, industry standards, estimates by independent technical professionals, formulas deemed acceptable in similar cases (such as the Eichleay formula for delays), contractor estimates, and actual cost records. (For a discussion of the much maligned but generally accepted Eichleay formula for use in construction contracts, *see* Chapter 26.) Contractors do not claim lost profits or loss of income under requests for equitable adjustment because such amounts do not represent increased costs.

The government pays interest on the amount found due and unpaid through the date of payment from the date that (1) the contracting officer receives the claim (certified, if required), or (2) payment otherwise would be due, if that date is later.[31]

(b) Breach of Contract Damages. The expert's approach to calculating breach of contract damages often differs from the approach in a CDA claim, discussed in Section 31.3(a). A breach of contract action against the government is a claim for compensation in addition to or in place of the contract's normal change order or other administrative remedies. Such actions result from the government's misrepresentations, negligent estimates, inappropriate action, use of duress, abuse of discretion, or material out of scope changes. In a breach of contract action against the government, the expert focuses on the value of the harm or loss to the contractor.

The damages elements in a breach of contract case include the same type of costs that the contract allows but disregard contract-specified limits. For example, a breach of contract claim can pursue damages beyond the increased costs of performance of the work or the contract-specified indirect rate limits. It includes the cost or profit elements required to place the contractor in as good a position as it would have been without the breach.

However, even in a breach of contract situation, the government with its unique authority holds the contractor to rigid standards of evidence and rarely allows lost profits or consequential damages. As a prerequisite to recovery, certain courts have held that lost profits must link to the government's actions with both reasonable foreseeability and reasonable certainty.[32] The expert can measure the contractor's loss with values used customarily in the contractor's business, such as the difference between the contract price and the market value of repudiated goods. An alternative approach focuses on the but-for profit (including reasonable overhead) that the seller would have made from full performance by the buyer. This compensation formula, based on lost volume, relies on the expected profit that the injured party would have realized had the government not breached the contract and reflects the benefit of the bargain that the contractor struck at the outset.[33] If the conditions for entitlement exist, the few cases that have allowed lost profits indicate that the expert needs strong evidence and an accurate calculation. For example, in a case in which the government admitted to a breach of contract, the court awarded lost profits, appropriately discounted, for terminated loan processing services to a finance company.[34]

When established contract prices do not provide adequate compensation, the expert can resort to actual costs attributable to the breach. For example, in a cardinal change—one in which the contractor performs duties that are materially different from the original scope of work—the expert can depart from the standard contract pricing mechanism to total actual costs plus a markup.[35] As a rule, the government generally succeeds in denying recovery of consequential damages—such as losses on other contracts and impairment to net worth—as being too remote or speculative.

31.7   CONTRACT PRICING AND CHANGES

(a) Defective Pricing.   The Truth in Negotiations Act (TINA) requires contractors to furnish current, accurate, and complete cost or pricing data as of the price agreement date or, if applicable, another date negotiated by the parties. TINA applies to contracts, subcontracts, and modifications thereto over the threshold, currently $550,000, for which an exception or waiver does not apply.[36] Government auditors perform special postaward, or defective pricing, audits to assess compliance with this rule. In a finding of defective pricing, the government is entitled to a contract price reduction including cost and profit, interest on overpayments, and a penalty equal to the overpayment amount if the contractor knowingly submitted incomplete, inaccurate, or noncurrent data as of the date of final price agreement.[37]

Common defenses that a contractor can raise against an allegation of defective pricing include the following:

- TINA did not apply to the pricing action.
- The contractor submitted current, accurate, and complete data.

- The defective pricing had no, or an insignificant, effect on the contract price.
- Offsets mitigate the defective pricing to an immaterial amount.

Failure to agree on a defective pricing matter can lead to a dispute under CDA. Defective pricing allegations commonly also result in allegations of false claims and false statements.

Financial experts gather facts and evaluate financial information to help counsel assess the validity of the aforementioned defenses against defective pricing. By reviewing documents such as audit workpapers, price negotiation memoranda, and cost submissions, the expert can help assess the extent of cost or price analysis performed by the buyer. Counsel can use this analysis to evaluate a common defense against defective pricing: because of price analysis or adequate price competition, the government ignored the contractor's cost data and instead relied on its own price analysis or what it considered adequate price competition.

Contracts for commercial items and contracts in which law or regulation set the prices are exempt from TINA. However, contract awards that lack an affirmative determination by the contracting officer of an exemption from TINA can lead to allegations of defective pricing. Therefore, when defective pricing is alleged, the applicability of TINA is often a matter for resolution.

To ensure complete cost or pricing data, the contractor must disclose facts that one would reasonably expect to affect price negotiations significantly.[38] The expert can help identify records that have a bearing on the nature and meaningfulness of the contractor's disclosures.[39] For example, one can find evidence of meaningful disclosures in auditor workpapers, forward pricing rate proposals or agreements, other negotiation documents, data submitted in connection with related contracts, CAS Disclosure Statements, make or buy plans, advance agreements, and routine submissions such as invoices. The expert can help identify the contractor's relevant disclosures, whether the government grasped the significance of the disclosures in question, and the effect on the contract price.

Assuming a finding or disclosure of defective pricing occurs, an expert can calculate the appropriate contract price reduction and required repayment amount including interest and penalty, if applicable. The expert will establish the baseline, or starting point, to calculate a defective pricing adjustment. The baseline reflects not only proposal data but also any disclosures up to the price agreement date and any "sweeps data," which the contractor submits after the price agreement with the certificate of current cost or pricing data and before the contract award (the "as of" or cut-off date on the certificate).[40] Sometimes, the expert will need to further refine the price reduction calculation to reflect any adjustment needed for negotiation concession factors.

As part of the defective pricing analysis, the expert also makes observations or evaluates records that relate to potential offsets (i.e., understated cost or pricing data), such as whether the contractor had offset data but did not submit them before the cut-off date. The FAR does not permit offsets if the contractor knew of the understated data or if the government proves that the contract price would not have increased if the contractor had submitted the offset data.[41] Offsets sometimes exceed the defective pricing allegation, that is, understatements may exceed overstatements.

(b) Cost Allowability.   Experts use the FAR cost principles when analyzing cost or when the contract price requires the calculation or negotiation of costs.[42] The FAR group the cost principles and procedures by type of organization, such as commercial, educational institutions, nonprofit, and state, local, and federally recognized Indian tribal governments.[43] This section focuses on contracts for commercial organizations. Many of the theories and rules apply to all organizations even though each set of cost principles has specific allowability factors.

Disputes over cost allowability matters often occur in government contracting—during preaward audits, postaward audits, and routine audits of contractor final indirect cost rate proposals. The financial expert applies the factors required to identify a cost as allowable, including (for commercial organizations) the terms of the contract, cost principle limitations, CAS, GAAP, allocability, and reasonableness.[44] An expert can identify the relevant accounting rules and resolve conflicts between the allowability factors. For example, expenses related to promoting the sale of products sometimes appear as disallowed advertising costs. Upon closer examination, however, they may represent direct selling efforts to a particular customer, an allowed expense.

In resolving disputes over allowability, the expert applies the FAR cost principles in effect on the date of the contract.[45] The rules do not cover every type of cost, so the expert must assess whether a specific cost principle covers the cost element or the cost element resembles or relates to analagous items.[46] When specific rules or contract terms do not cover costs, they follow general rules of reasonableness, allocability, and generally accepted accounting methods. Accordingly, experts will need a specialty in one or more of these areas. A single case can require more than one expert to address these different areas.

One of the more complex areas in accounting for contract costs lies in resolving conflicts between the cost allowability factors. This is an area in which the expert should confirm his or her understanding of the contract with legal counsel. The expert can look to the special provisions of a contract, advance agreements, and individual agency rules for the most specific and strict allowability requirements. Next, one should consider any specific requirements of FAR and CAS. Specific FAR and CAS requirements normally prevail over more general requirements. In matters involving measuring, assigning, or allocating costs, CAS, if applicable and specific to the type of cost at issue, can take precedence over general FAR rules.[47] However, specific FAR rules on allowability can take precedence over specific or general CAS rules.[48] GAAP and industry practices can be used when FAR or CAS provide insufficient guidance because neither FAR nor CAS represent a comprehensive basis of accounting (*see* Exhibit 31-2).

(c) Cost Accounting Standards.   Contracts covered by CAS must follow special rules on the measurement, assignment, and allocation of contract costs. The fundamentals of CAS relate to the amount of cost, the period in which the contractor should record the cost, and the method for charging costs to contracts or other units of accountability. CAS requires contractors to maintain policies, keep certain records, and follow administrative procedures. CAS applies to negotiated contracts and subcontracts that do not qualify for an exemption. Common exemptions include contracts that are sealed bid, valued at $500,000 or under, awarded to small businesses, fixed price for commercial items, set by law or regulation, and

Example	Difference in Treatment
General Rules	The financial accounting rules are focused on the financial health and performance of an entity over time. They deal primarily with the proper classification of transactions and the timing of revenue and expense recognition. The government contracting rules are focused on enforcing public policy and consistency in determining reimbursable costs.
Organizational Structure	An entity's organizational structure is usually at a lower level of reporting for government contracting and can differ from the financial reporting structure or legal structure because the term "business segment" has a special meaning in government contracting.
Asset Capitalization and Depreciation	The government contracting rules require that asset service lives be supported by historical records of disposition and retirement. Asset value adjustments for purchase accounting and impairments under financial reporting rules are generally not recognized for calculating government contract costs.
Miscellaneous Income and Credits	Certain types of income and credits must be treated as an offset to costs for government contracting rather than as income for financial reporting.
Pension and Other Post-Employment Benefits	The amount of expense recognized, period of recognition, and allocation methods can all be different under government contracting compared with financial reporting.
Restructuring Costs	Unlike the financial reporting rules, certain restructuring costs can be deferred for government contracting.

Exhibit 31-2. Differences between Government Contracting and Financial Reporting

firm fixed price awarded on the basis of adequate price competition without submission of cost or pricing data. Once the value of CAS contracts exceeds a cumulative threshold—$50 million for companies and $25 million for educational institutions[49]—contractors must maintain a CAS Disclosure Statement, which is a written description of a contractor's cost accounting practices and procedures.

Disputes over CAS compliance can begin with a disagreement over CAS applicability. An expert can assist counsel in analyzing financial records used in the determination of certain CAS exemptions (i.e., the revenue data for a small business exemption), assessing the factors needed to justify adequate price competition as discussed in the defective pricing section, and reviewing the values of contracts to ascertain whether they surpass the threshold levels.

As with cost allowability issues, experts use their skills in CAS matters to identify the type of cost at issue and whether a specific or general CAS requirement applies. CAS provides general rules on the allocation of direct and indirect costs and very specific rules on certain costs such as home office expenses, general and administrative expenses, pension expenses, and independent research and development costs. Experts use specific rules, if applicable. Otherwise they apply general rules according to established practices, since consistency is a cornerstone of CAS.

In a CAS compliance dispute, courts have held that the burden of proof lies with the government. The expert can provide observations as to whether sufficient evidence exists to support an asserted finding of CAS noncompliance. In a case involving a dispute over whether a contractor was required to maintain separate cost pools for two facilities, the court ruled that the government failed to prove that the contractor violated CAS and to meet its responsibility to determine a cost impact.[50]

CAS disputes often require complex calculations to show the cost increase under various scenarios. Contractors often incur cost increases to correct a noncompliance at the time of price agreement or to correct a noncompliance or change in accounting during contract performance. The CAS rules protect the government against paying increases in costs. For cost-reimbursement contracts, the amount of increased costs equals the amount of costs paid by the government over what it would have paid if the contractor had complied with the applicable standards or had not changed its accounting practices. For fixed-price contracts, the amount of increased costs equals the difference between the agreed contract price and the contract price that would have been agreed to if the contractor had proposed in accordance with the cost accounting practices used during contract performance. If a contractor has multiple contracts covered by CAS and the change or failure affects all of them, a decrease in costs under any of the contracts will offset an increase in costs paid under other contracts.[51] The government's definition of an increased cost on a fixed-price contract seems counterintuitive because it represents a higher profit to the contractor rather than additional payments by the government.

To estimate the cost increases from a CAS practice change or noncompliance during performance, the expert calculates the difference between the estimated cost to complete under the old (or noncompliant) method and the estimated cost to complete under the new (or compliant) method. Depending on the circumstances, offsets can be allowed within contract types or between contract types.

(d) Contract Termination.   The government can terminate a contract for convenience (to serve the government's interest) or default (because of nonperformance or contract noncompliance); in either case, an expert often assists in the final settlement. Because such a termination doesn't resemble a normal business activity, the expert can, as appropriate, apply different rules and accounting techniques compared with those of the contractor's normal practices. In addition, the expert identifies costs that result directly from the termination such as settlement proposal preparation expenses for inclusion in the settlement.

In convenience terminations, financial settlements should not penalize or overcompensate the contractor. The expert applies this theory to avoid altering the contractor's profit or loss position related to contract performance. However, the expected income or loss from a contract can involve complex assumptions that require careful evaluation. The expert must consider the risks assumed by each party. Special cost principles apply to terminations (except commercial contracts) and deal with the treatment for many of the costs that typically become part of the settlement value. Costs related to performance include the following:

- Initial or startup costs
- Costs continuing after termination
- Asset impairment
- Lease costs
- Subcontractors

Experts must apportion incurred costs and commitments among the terminated contract and other activities (or within line items of a partially terminated contract). They can use appropriate accounting adjustments and reclassifications to achieve this objective. The contractor has a duty, however, to use reasonable efforts to mitigate the termination costs by timely actions and use resources on other work if possible.

In evaluating cost adjustments and reclassifications, the expert can review the reasonableness and necessity behind the original business decision to incur the costs in question. If the evidence shows that the contractor incurred the costs because of an identifiable and exclusive need to meet the performance schedule, the costs become eligible for recovery. In a termination for convenience, the government will require an appropriate adjustment to the settlement value if the contractor would have incurred a loss had the contractor completed the entire contract.[52] In such situations, the settlement adjustment results in the contractor absorbing its share, based on a loss ratio, of the cost overrun.[53]

(e) Extraordinary Business Transactions. Unusual major events in business cause large nonrecurring amounts of income or expense in one period. Such extraordinary events and transactions include the sale or closure of a business segment, mass disposition of assets, restructuring or reorganization, asset impairment, contract termination or reformation, loss of a major contract renewal, and involuntary conversions. Under financial accounting rules, the company recognizes the income or expense effects of such transactions in the period in which the event occurs. Under the government's procurement rules, however, extraordinary transactions can create obligations to or from the government under contracts with cost-based prices or terms subject to special price adjustments.

As with other disputes, the expert will look to the specific rules in the contract, FAR or CAS, and accounting practices appropriate to the circumstances. Certain FAR and CAS rules recognize the need for special treatment of extraordinary transactions for each case. A few examples of express provisions for extraordinary or unusual transactions include pension plan terminations, mass disposition of assets, mass severance, continuing costs for idle facilities, and credits and claims after final payment.[54]

Depending on the event and circumstances, the expert can help identify the amount, timing, and allocation of special charges or credits resulting from an extraordinary transaction. Adjustments for pension plan terminations require assistance from actuaries and an analysis to identify the contracts affected along with calculations of the government's historical participation in paying pension costs. A mass disposition of assets, such as the sale of a business park, requires that the contractor apportion gains and losses between depreciable and nondepreciable assets because the government does not share in the gains or losses associated with nondepreciable assets. The government can recover abnormal severance payments based on its "fair share," which often requires an analysis of the contractor's decisions over employment, severance payment practices, and cost mitigation efforts.

Another type of extraordinary transaction relates to unforeseen circumstances, such as the need to reform a fixed price contract into a cost type contract under Public Law 85-804. The expert can identify the risks assumed by each party and an appropriate method of recovery for past and future costs. Another example would require that an expert quantify increased costs associated with unforeseen circumstances on a cost-type contract. The firm might recover these costs despite its failure to follow limitation of funding notice obligations, if the expert can isolate the costs and purge them of reasonably foreseeable costs.[55]

(f) Commercial Contracts.   Disputes and litigation related to contracts for commercial goods and services such as computers, office supplies, and maintenance services typically require less involvement by financial experts because commercial contracts are based on market prices rather than costs. Nonetheless, the government incorporates unique terms and conditions in its contracts for commercial items that lead to disputes over the appropriate prices and other financial requirements. This section discusses two types of commercial contracts: those awarded under the Federal Supply Schedule (FSS) program (awarded under FAR Part 38 and directed by the General Services Administration) and those awarded under FAR Part 12.

(i) FSS Contracts.   Financial experts participate in FSS contract disputes relating to issues such as inaccurate representations made prior to award (defective pricing), failure to provide discounts during contract performance, and failure to remit the proper industrial funding fee. In assessing defective pricing, the expert will look at the completeness and accuracy of disclosures prior to award[56] including disclosures of sales practices, historical sales volumes and prices, discounts and concessions, deviations from written policies or standard commercial sales practices, information provided about suppliers (manufacturers), and sales data by customer category. The penalty for defective pricing under FSS contracts includes the amount of overpayment and simple interest on the amount of such overpayment. The expert can evaluate modifications on remaining items to assess whether they eliminate defective prices.

During performance of any FSS contract, a contractor must offer discounts or other disclosed contract concessions to the government equal to or better than those offered to the most favored customer or category of customers identified in the contractor's FSS contract basis of award document. The FSS contract's price reduction clause contains this contractor obligation. The expert can assist in disputes related to a contractor's triggered obligation under the price reduction clause by analyzing the basis of award documents. Such documents identify the appropriate price lists and price or discount relation offered in the contractor's FSS contract. In evaluating whether prices changed or the contractor provided discounts, the expert will analyze a significant volume of sales data and use forensic technology. Many times, experts can identify errors, offsets, and modifications that negate required price reductions. They can use computer technology to sort and analyze a large volume of sales data based on various price adjustment theories.

Disputes sometimes arise over the payment of the industrial funding fee (charged by the FSS program in order to recoup the program's operating costs) calculated as a percentage of reportable sales.[57] An expert can evaluate the accuracy of the reportable sales baseline by analyzing sales by item, customer, and contract to assess whether the reported sales related to contract items sold to authorized users (including certain state and local governments) and didn't fall under separate FAR or non-FAR contracts. The expert can assess whether the contractor used a consistent accounting method of sales reporting, based on its established commercial accounting practices, such as receipt of order, shipment, invoice, or payment.

(ii) FAR Part 12 Contracts.   Aside from the FSS program, the government acquires commercial items and services using FAR Part 12 contracts, which include a standard clause that replaces many other clauses in a negotiated contract.[58] Compared with a negotiated contract, standard commercial contracts have simple clauses. For example, changes require only a written agreement of the parties, and the contractor need not comply with CAS or the cost principles. Nonetheless, disputes can arise because the parties fail to reach agreement on an appropriate price adjustment when needed.[59]

The expert has a role in commercial contract disputes and can offer opinions on price adjustments using the commercial contract terms. For example, in a convenience termination of a Part 12 contract, the FAR termination cost principles do not apply. Instead, the expert will follow the specific commercial contract language, which states:

> The Contractor shall be paid a percentage of the contract price reflecting the percentage of the work performed prior to the notice of termination, plus reasonable charges the contractor can demonstrate to the satisfaction of the government using its standard record keeping system, have resulted from the termination.[60]

In a CDA claim under a commercial contract dispute, financial experts review the accuracy of the CDA certification and formally attest that "the supporting data are accurate and complete to the best of my knowledge and belief; that the amount requested accurately reflects the contract adjustment for which the contractor believes the government is liable."[61]

31.8 FALSE CLAIMS ACT

The financial remedy under the False Claims Act (FCA) indemnifies the government for its injuries. The financial remedy exceeds the government's contract damages and provides for special and punitive damages as well. For example, the damages elements of the FCA provide that the government has entitlement to three times the amount of its contract damages plus $5,500 to $11,000 per false claim submitted by the contractor. The contractor must also pay for the government's investigation costs. The act does not separately assess interest, although the act includes interest as part of the government's recovery. In an FCA case, the expert can evaluate the government's contract damages and, in cases involving numerous claims (and hence subject to multiple penalties), quantify the number of claims alleged by the government. As part of this effort, the expert can gather and comment on evidence related to the contractor's accounting practices, disclosures, and offsets.

The computation of actual damages depends on the nature of the FCA matter. In cases involving defective items, one can measure damages as the difference between the market value of the goods received and the market value for goods of the specified quality.[62] In cases involving overcharges, one calculates damages using the "would have paid" model based on the difference between what the government paid and what it would have paid absent the overcharges. Under the FCA, a reverse false claim allows the government to recover a civil penalty from any person or entity, who "knowingly makes, uses, or causes to be made or used, a false record or statement to conceal, avoid or decrease an obligation to pay or transmit money or property to the Government."[63]

Calculating how much the government overpaid as a result of the alleged fraud involves more than confirming the existence of an improper pricing or accounting scheme. The expert also needs to evaluate each payment individually, or at least by category, to assess the extent to which the government may have paid more because of the alleged fraud. Specific factors and circumstances can affect the amount of damages; these include the contract type, billing terms, withholdings, rescinded invoices, provisional payments, indirect rate limitations, and other payment considerations.

For example, in a labor mischarging matter, the expert would have to correct not only the labor charges but also indirect cost rates (which contractors often calculate based on labor) and then recalculate contract costs, contract prices, and billings. Depending on the relative size of the contracts, the magnitude of overhead rates, and the mix between fixed-price and cost-reimbursible contracts, the impact can significantly mitigate the damages.

FCA cases can result from defective pricing, disallowed costs, CAS issues, or other noncompliance problems. Other factors that affect the damages calculation include the statute of limitations (which establishes the window of time for claims subject to penalties) and credits for compensatory payments (that the courts will apply either before or after penalties, depending on when the contractor makes repayment).

31.9   *QUI TAM* ACTIONS

FCA cases often originate from allegations made under the FCA's *qui tam* (whistle-blower) provisions. Whistleblowers can work for the contractor, the government, or another entity. Contractor whistleblowers often have job positions related to a function in finance, contract administration, estimating, billing, quality control, or responsibility for signing certifications. FCA requires direct knowledge of the alleged fraud—someone familiar with the act of filing a claim. Whistleblowers have an incentive to bring lawsuits because of the potential for receiving a sizable personal monetary award measured as a percentage of the government's recovery. Although many whistleblowers have received multimillion dollar awards, most of the large cases require many years to resolve.

In response to an allegation of fraud by a whistleblower, an expert can investigate the allegations and assist counsel in evaluating the seriousness of the issues, provide observations on whether an FCA violation exists, and calculate potential damages. The expert should focus on several items:

- Understanding the whistleblower's position, responsibilities, knowledge of the payment process, knowledge of the applicable regulations, and awareness of controls and compliance practices.
- Understanding the specific allegation and potential implications for amounts claimed under government contracts.
- Verifying the accuracy of statements and financial data in support of billings, claims, or proposals.
- Evaluating disclosures to the government such as those through audits, cost submissions, and CAS disclosure statements.

For example, suppose a whistleblower in the contracts department alleges that his employer falsely certified that the contractor's final indirect cost rate proposal excluded disallowed expenses. The whistleblower alleges that, as a result of interest expenses included in the proposal, the contractor submitted false claims that resulted in overpayment. The expert will analyze the indirect cost rate proposal to evaluate whether the indirect rates included disallowed interest expenses and, if so, the effect on invoices and payments from the government. Upon a closer look, the expert may find that the interest costs include some allowable administrative costs of short-term borrowings for working capital. Other portions of the interest expense may be allowable because they were incurred for nonpayment of taxes that resulted from the contracting officer's untimely direction. Lastly, the expert may find that the contractor did not use the final indirect cost rate proposal for billing purposes until a year after submitting it to the government. After making the proper rate adjustments and recalculating invoices, the actual overcharge can become substantially lower than the alleged overcharge—or perhaps disappear.

31.10 FINANCIAL ACCOUNTING DISPUTES

As with all businesses involved in raising capital and conducting corporate transactions, government contractors face disputes over the accuracy of their financial statements and disclosures. A government contractor's financial accounting representations can provide the central element of litigation in acquisitions and divestitures, equity investments, creditor transactions, joint ventures, subcontracts, and teaming arrangements.

An expert in cases involving financial accounting matters should have extensive experience in both GAAP and federal government contracting. Contractors sometimes hire two or more experts for this work. This section discusses typical areas of accounting disputes in government contracts, which include revenue recognition, profit and loss accruals, claims and contingencies, treatment of differences between GAAP and contract accounting rules, receivables, and contract-related liabilities.

Over the years, as contractors have maintained records using practices designed to meet the procurement rules, GAAP have recognized and accepted some of these practices.[64] Differences exist, however, between GAAP and the procurement rules because they have different purposes. Accountants follow GAAP to produce an accurate statement of a company's financial position and operating results. Contractors follow procurement rules to comply with public policies for reimbursing contractors for goods and services bought by the government. As a result of these dual requirements, successful government contractors develop an ability to present financial information under both GAAP and government contract rules. They maintain formal and informal records to track and reconcile the differences between the presentations.

A financial expert experienced in government contracting can help with several areas in these disputes:

- Defining the type of contract and potential price adjustments attributable to actual costs, incentives, audits, and change orders. The contract type and adjustment factors affect the application of accounting literature on topics such as multiple element contracts, revenue recognition, long-term contracts, cost-plus-fixed-fee contracts, precontract costs, service contracts, and industry accounting guidelines.

- Evaluating contract revenue, based on estimated or actual allowable contract costs.

- Assessing contract-related liabilities such as defective pricing, disallowed costs, CAS matters, and other compliance problems.

- Evaluating the realizability of billed and unbilled receivables based on the contractor's compliance with contract terms.

- Analyzing potential gains or losses from extraordinary transactions.

Some of the common differences between GAAP and the government contract accounting rules include accounting for disallowed costs, pensions, restructuring, definition of business segments, home office allocations, treatment of credits and reversions, intangible assets, asset impairments, and cost of money. The expert can assist in explaining these differences and their effect on the timing of revenue and expense recognition.

31.11   THE DISPUTE AND LITIGATION PROCESS

According to the FAR, the government prefers to resolve all disputed contractual issues by mutual agreement at the contracting officer's level.[65] Most often, the parties—not a judicial forum—decide on equitable price adjustments, for example. When the parties cannot reach agreement, a Board of Contract Appeals or the U.S. Court of Federal Claims resolves conflicts over contract awards, performance issues, and other contract matters. Some disputes use alternative dispute resolution procedures (ADR; discussed in Chapter 4) by mutual agreement.[66]

As in other federal cases, experts must meet qualifications under the federal rules of evidence.[67] Agency Board of Contract Appeals (BCAs) procedures include supplemental rules for expert witnesses. The CDA authorizes BCAs to hear the appeals of the contracting officer for final decisions on matters arising under or relating to a contract.[68] The Armed Services Board of Contract Appeals (ASBCA) Rule 20 states:[69]

Hearings: Nature, Examination of Witnesses

(a) Nature of Hearings—Hearings shall be as informal as may be reasonable and appropriate under the circumstances. Appellant and the Government may offer such evidence as they deem appropriate and as would be admissible under the Federal Rules of Evidence or in the sound discretion of the presiding administrative judge or examiner. Stipulations of fact agreed upon by the parties may be regarded and used as evidence at the hearing. The parties may stipulate the testimony that would be given by a witness if the witness were present. The Board may require evidence in addition to that offered by the parties.

(b) Examination of Witnesses—Witnesses before the Board will be examined orally under oath or affirmation, unless the presiding administrative judge or examiner shall otherwise order. If the testimony of a witness is not given under oath, the Board may advise the witness that his statements may be subject to the provisions of Title 18, United States Code, sections 287 and 1001, and any other provision of law imposing penalties for knowingly making false representations in connection with claims against the United States or in any matter within the jurisdiction of any department or agency thereof.

Combined, the BCAs, the Court of Federal Claims, and the GAO process hundreds of government contract controversies (disputes and protests) each year that involve cost issues. Many of these cases relate to matters of entitlement and do not require much financial analysis because the parties do not dispute the financial remedy amount. Other cases require that an expert calculate costs, damages, or penalties under one or more complex theories of entitlement. Such cases require expert financial analysts who have a detailed understanding of the applicable rules and their common interpretation within industry, by government representatives, and through formal proceedings. One must understand not only the litigation process but also the legal matters involved and some of the ambiguities in contract terms that arise when one is dealing with contract accounting issues.

Many court decisions turn on the legal interpretation of terms such as *actual costs, accrued costs, paid costs, increased costs,* and *cost data.* Experts can help evaluate evidence, facts, and prevailing practices relevant to the legal interpretation. However, financial experts must contend with legal interpretations that may conflict with pre-established accounting concepts. As an example, the courts have defined financial terms such as *cost* using a layman's dictionary even though tools of the accounting profession provide a detailed conceptual framework that allows for the specific circumstances in a transaction to influence the meaning.[70]

To present persuasive and usable conclusions, one must communicate an understanding of the circumstances and reason for the dispute—confirming facts, clarifying misconceptions, presenting new evidence as needed, and reaching conclusions based on an appropriate consideration of the evidence and facts. In matters involving cost mischarging, for example, experts perform several tasks:

- Demonstrate an understanding of the contract type and applicable regulations, how costs affect the contract price, billing, and payment provisions, the audit process, industry practices, and the contractor's records.
- Confirm the nature of the costs or transactions at issue, specific contract practices, adherence to regulatory procedures, reliability of records, payments, and contract interpretations.
- Clarify the validity of conclusions that have been reached by contractor personnel, auditors, and government procurement personnel.
- Present new evidence, facts, calculations, and other analyses that conform to contract requirements and generally accepted methods.
- Render conclusions based on the relevant facts and evidence presented as well as on their knowledge, experience, and training.

Experts should keep the presentation simple, but they may find this strategy challenging when the parties disagree over legal definitions of financial terms. Experts must know how to explain these terms and any evidence that supports their clients' position.

APPENDIX A:
SELECTED FINANCIAL ACRONYMS

Acronym	Description
ACO	Administrative Contracting Officer
ACRN	Accounting classification reference number
ACWP	Actual cost of work performed
ACWS	Actual cost of work scheduled
BAFO	Best and final offer
BCA	Boards of Contract Appeals
BCWP	Budgeted cost of work performed
BCWS	Budgeted cost of work scheduled
BEQ	Best estimated quantity
BOE	Basis of estimate
BOM	Bill of material
CAM	Defense Contract Audit Manual
CAS	Cost Accounting Standards
CDA	Contract Disputes Act
CICA	Competition in Contracting Act
CLIN	Contract line item
CRAG	Contractor risk assessment guide
CPSR	Contractor purchasing system review
CSPF	Commercial sales practices format
DCAA	Defense Contract Audit Agency
DOD	Department of Defense
EAC	Estimate at completion
ETC	Estimate to complete
EVMS	Earned value management system
FAR	Federal Acquisition Regulation

FAS	Financial Accounting Standards
FASA	Federal Acquisition Streamlining Act
FCA	False Claims Act
FCCOM	Facilities capital cost of money
FOB	Free on board
FOIA	Freedom of Information Act
FMV	Fair market value
FPRA	Forward pricing rate agreement
FSS	Federal Supply Schedule
FY	Fiscal year
GAAP	Generally accepted accounting principles
GAAS	Generally accepted auditing standards
GAGAS	Generally accepted government auditing standards
GAO	Government Accountability Office
GDMS	General dollar magnitude study
GFE	Government furnished equipment
GSA	General Services Administration
IFF	Industrial funding fee
IG	Inspector General
IGCE	Independent government cost estimate
LCC	Life cycle cost
MAS	Multiple award schedule
MIRR	Material inspection and receiving report (DD250)
MMAS	Material management and accounting system
MRP	Material requirements planning
NPV	Net present value
OMB	Office of Management and Budget
PNM	Price negotiation memorandum
RAM	Regional audit manager
ROM	Rough order of magnitude
SBA	Small Business Administration
TINA	Truth in Negotiations Act
UCF	Uniform Contract Format
W/P	Working Paper

Appendix A: Selected Financial Acronyms

APPENDIX B:
UNIFORM CONTRACT FORMAT

APPENDIX C :
CONTRACT AUDIT REPORTS ISSUED

Type of Audit[1]	Reports Issued	Amounts Examined	Questioned Costs[2]	Funds Put to Better Use
Incurred Costs, Ops Audits, Special Audits	14,747	$ 58,966.8	$855.4	$ 304.2[3]
Forward Pricing Proposals	5,510	64,268.5	—	2,167.0[4]
Cost Accounting Standards	1,312	935.6	93.5	—
Defective Pricing	383	(Note 5)	27.3	—
Totals	**21,952**	**$124,170.9**	**$976.2**	**$2471.2**

($ in millions).
April 1, 2004 through September 30, 2004.

This schedule represents Defense Contract Audit Agency (DCAA) contract audit reports issued during the six months ended September 30, 2004. Both "Questioned Costs" and "Funds Put to Better Use" represent potential cost savings for the government. Because of limited time between availability of management information system data and legislative reporting requirements, the DCAA has minimal opportunity to verify the accuracy of reported data. Accordingly, submitted data are subject to change based on subsequent DCAA authentication.

Source: DCAA Semiannual Report for Transmission to the Congress

---

[1]This schedule represents audits performed by DCAA, which can be summarized into four principal categories:

1. **Incurred Costs:** Audits of direct and indirect costs charges to government contracts to ascertain whether the costs are reasonable, allocable as prescribed by the Federal Acquisition Regulation, Defense Federal Acquisition Regulation, and provisions of the contract. This category includes operations audits—which evaluate a contractor's operations and management practices to identify opportunities for increased efficiency and economy—and Special Audits, which include audits of terminations and claims.
2. **Forward Pricing Proposals:** Audits of estimated future costs of proposed contract prices, proposed contract change orders, costs for redeterminable fixed-price contracts, and costs incurred but not yet covered by definitized contracts.

3. **Cost Accounting Standards:** A review of the contractor's cost impact statement required because of changes to disclosed practices, failure to consistently follow a disclosed or established cost accounting practice, or noncompliance with a CAS regulation.

4. **Defective Pricing:** A review to ascertain whether contracts are based on current, complete, and accurate cost pricing data (the Truth in Negotiations Act).

[2]Questioned costs represent costs that DCAA has questioned because they do not comply with rules, regulations, laws, and/or contractual terms.

[3]Represents recommendations associated with operations audits where DCAA has asserted that a contractor could use funds more effectively if management took action to implement cost reduction recommendations.

[4]Represents potential cost reductions that the government can realize during contract negotiations.

[5]Defective pricing dollars examined are not reported because the original value was included in the audits associated with the original forward pricing proposals.

NOTES

1. *See* Karen L. Manos, *Government Contract Costs & Pricing* (Eagan, MN: Thomson West, 2004); W. Noel, Keyes, *Government Contracts Under the Federal Acquisition Regulation,* 3rd ed. (Eagan, MN: Thomson West, 2004).

2. *See* FAR 35.003

3. FAR 1.602-2(b).

4. Claims against the federal government are subject to specific waivers of sovereign immunity.

5. http://akss.dau.mil/jsp/default.jsp.

6. FAR 52.215-8, Order of Precedence—Uniform Contract Format.

7. *G.L. Christian & Associates v. United States,* Ct. Cl. No. 56-59, July 12, 1963, 32 F.2d 345 (reh'g denied).

8. FAR 16.101.

9. FAR 52.216-7.

10. Competition in Contracting Act, Public Law 98-369.

11. GAO-02-520SP, Guide to GAO Protective Orders, (April 2002).

12. "Commercial item" refers to off-the-shelf goods, or products or services commonly offered in competitive commerce at published prices. A key advantage to commercial item status is that the contractor need not supply—nor the government audit—cost and pricing data, overhead application, and the more administratively intensive provisions of the FAR and Cost Accounting Standards.

13. Freedom of Information Act, Public Law 89-487.

14. Miller Act, Public Law 74-321.

15. FAR 50.303-2(b).

16. FAR 1.101.

17. FAR 1.402.

18. For example, *see* Federal Acquisition Circular 97-24. Also, effective through September 30, 2005, the director of the Department of Defense Procurement authorized a deviation from the requirements of FAR 31.203(c), Indirect Costs, when costs disallowed under FAR 31.205-52, asset valuations resulting from business combinations, are required to be included in the indirect cost base.

19. FAR 31.109.

20. CAM 2-204.

21. FAR 42.705-1.

22. CAM 1-102a.

23. Lockheed Corporation, ASBCA Nos. 36420, 37495, 39195, February 4, 1991, 91-2 BCA ¶23,903.

24. Litton Systems, Inc., ASBCA No. 37131, February 23, 1994, 94-2 BCA ¶26,731.

25. FAR 31.201-3.

26. According to FAR 33.103(e), protests based on alleged improprieties of a solicitation may only be filed prior to bid opening or the closing date for receipt of proposals.

27. FAR 19.101.

28. FAR 43.101.

29. Sante Fe Engineers, Inc., ASBCA No. 48331, February 9, 1995, 95-1 BCA ¶27,505.

30. FAR 52.243-6.

31. FAR 52.233-1(h).

32. *Precision Pine & Timber, Inc. v. United States*, CAFC No. 98-720 C, November 23, 2004.

33. *James S. Lee & Co., Inc. (USA) v. The United States*, Ct. Cl. No. 244-77, January 3, 1986, 9 Cl. Ct. 322.

34. *Energy Capital Corp. v. United States*, CAFC No. 01-5018, August 14, 2002, 302 F.3d 314.

35. Valley Forge Flag Co., Inc., VABCA Nos. 4667, 5103, September 18, 1997, 97-2 BCA ¶29,246.

36. FAR 15.403-4.

37. FAR 52.215-10.

38. The term "cost or pricing data" is defined in FAR 2.101.

39. A proper disclosure of cost or pricing data requires that the contractor adequately explain the elements of its accounting records. *See* Martin Marietta Corp., ASBCA No. 48223, February 25, 1998, 98-1 BCA ¶29,592.

40. CAM 14-120.4. As referenced in CAM 14-111, the Director for Defense Procurement Policy issued policy guidance in June of 1989 to contracting officers for situations in which contractors provide cost or pricing data after price agreement. In these situations, the contracting officer must also include in the price negotiation memorandum a list of all data submitted by the contractor after price agreement and the extent to which these data were relied on in order to establish a fair and reasonable price.

41. FAR 52.215-10.

42. FAR 15.404-1 and FAR 31.000.

43. FAR 31.1.

44. FAR 31.201-2 lists these factors as requirements for allowability.

45. FAR 52.216-7.

46. FAR 31.204.

47. *Boeing North American, Inc. v. James G. Roche, Secretary of the Air Force*, CAFC No. 01-1011, July 29, 2002, 298 F.3d 1274.

48. *Donald B. Rice, Secretary of the Air Force v. Martin Marietta Corp.*, CAFC No. 93-1025, December 29, 1993, 13 F.3d 1563.

49. The CAS Disclosure Statement filing requirements are found at CAS 9903.202.

50. Litton Systems, Inc., ASBCA No. 37131, February 23, 1994, 94-2 BCA ¶26,731.

51. CAS 9903.306.

52. FAR 49.203.

53. The burden of proof is on the contractor to show that its costs are reasonable. *See FAR* 31.201-3(a).

54. *See* CAS 413-50(c)(12), FAR 31.205-16(e), FAR 31.205-6(g)(5), FAR 31.205-17(b)(2), and FAR 52.216-7(h).

55. Dames & Moore, IBCA No. 2553, October 7, 1992, 93-1 BCA ¶25,487.

56. Per GSA 552.215-72(b), the Government will consider information submitted to be current, accurate, and complete if the data are current, accurate, and complete as of 14 days prior to the date they are submitted.
57. GSAR 552.238-74.
58. FAR 52.212-4.
59. Under 52.212-4(d), Part 12 contracts are subject to the Contract Disputes Act of 1978.
60. FAR 52.212-4(l).
61. FAR 52.233-1.
62. *United States v. Bornstein*, U.S. S. Ct. No. 74-712, January 1, 1976, 423 S. Ct. 303.
63. False Claims Act, U.S.C. §3729(a)(7).
64. For example, under the concept of full-absorption costing, contractors may include general and administrative expenses in inventory.
65. FAR 33.103(b) and 33.204.
66. FAR 52.233-1(g).
67. Rule 702.
68. FAR 33.203.
69. Rule of the Armed Services Board of Contract Appeals, July 1, 1997.
70. *See* discussion of the meaning of "cost" in *Donald H. Rumsfeld, Secretary of Defense v. United Technologies Corp., Pratt & Whitney*, CAFC No. 02-1071, January 15, 2003, 315 F.3d 1361.

FAMILY LAW

CHAPTER 32

VALUATION AND DIVISION OF MARITAL PROPERTY

Donald A. Glenn

CONTENTS

32.1 INTRODUCTION

The states have two general approaches to marital property:

1. **Community property.** Arizona, California, Idaho, Louisiana, Nevada, New Mexico, Texas, Washington, and Wisconsin.
2. **Equitable distribution.** All other states, the District of Columbia, and Puerto Rico.

Within states adhering to the same general approach—community property or equitable distribution—substantial differences exist. Differences result from individual state statutes and the courts' interpretation of those statutes.

Current marital property systems have evolved from the English common law notion of presumption of title. English presumption of title affixes ownership to property based solely on title. Women suffered from this because they could not hold title. Upon divorce, a woman would not receive any distribution of property if her husband held title. Equitable distribution methods overcame some of the presumption of title problems, and community property replaced presumption of title within certain limits. Although title can still prove important in determining ownership, many states have recognized the inequity of property ownership based solely on title. Thus, under newer rules, courts award property to nontitled spouses from community property or provide for equitable distributions. Each state has evolved variations of the general rules based on statute or judicially established methods that recognize the contribution of the nontitled spouse to acquire or enhance property during marriage.

Several states have adopted Registered Domestic Partners statutes. Same sex marriage is also an emerging issue. Registered Domestic Partner (RDP) statutes generally apply family law concepts and statutes. However, the Internal Revenue Service has not recognized community or joint income concepts for RDPs filing income tax returns.

(a) Community Property or Equitable Distribution.   Community property rules assume that both spouses jointly own any property acquired during marriage. Personal effort of either spouse during marriage creates community income and property. Each has an equal interest in property acquired during marriage. California Family Code § 760 defines community property as "all property, real or personal, wherever situated, acquired by a married person during marriage while domiciled in this state is community property."

Some exceptions allow separate property, but they limit it to property (1) owned prior to marriage; (2) acquired during marriage by gift, inheritance, or descent; or (3) acquired from separate property or earnings from separate property. Separate property must be traced to establish its character. The party claiming a separate property interest has the burden of proof. Failure to meet the burden of proof results in community property. (*See* Chapter 35, "Marital Dissolution: Tracing and Apportionment of Assets" for an expanded discussion.)

Equitable distribution rules have their source in the old common law presumption of title. Rather than adopt a community property system, equitable distribution allows a court to distribute (divide) property in some equitable or fair manner. In deciding what is equitable, some states list statutory factors that the courts must consider. Other states' courts have developed a judicial list of factors. Still others have no stated guideline for equitable distribution of marital or nonmarital property.

(b) Distributing Separate Assets.   Community property states divide community property equally between spouses. The court *must* award separate property to its separate owner. However, some states have an exception to the equal division of community property: when debts exceed assets, they can allow an equitable division of these negative estates. The court equitably divides the assets and debts considering the superior ability of either spouse to service debts.

In equitable distribution states, the court often has the power to distribute separate assets to either party. In states allowing the award of separate property to either spouse, valuation of individual assets can be less important than the reason for awarding an asset to one party or the other.

(c) What Is Property? *Black's Law Dictionary* defines property as "everything which is subject of ownership, corporeal or incorporeal, tangible or intangible, visible or invisible, real or personal; everything that has an exchangeable value which goes to make up wealth or estate."[1] States have their own definitions of marital property. In some jurisdictions, courts have difficulty locating the dividing line between a mere *expectancy* and the *existence* of property. Retirement plans provide an example of an expectancy that creates property. A spouse who participates in a pension plan not fully vested at the date of divorce has an expectancy of a pension upon retirement. If the employee spouse continues to work and then later fully vest, he or she will receive a pension at normal retirement age. States have recognized the right of the nonemployee spouse to receive a portion of the pension's vesting during marriage.

Some states do not consider a professional license, such as a medical or legal license, as property. However, if a doctor, for example, is also a partner in a medical practice, he or she can have goodwill apart and separate from the value of his or her license. Separating the value of a license (not property) from goodwill (property) of a professional practice can prove difficult (*see* Chapter 34, "Marital Dissolution: Professional Goodwill and Related Intangibles").

(d) What Is Value? The value of marital property depends not only on local statutes and case law, but also on the nature of the subject property. The valuation theory applied to specific marital assets will affect the final results. Each valuation approach requires coordination of asset valuation methods, statutory requirements, and state case law. Early attention to valuation theory focuses the attorney and accountant on issues requiring legal research, analysis or a particular presentation at trial.

(e) Financial Problems. Financial problems often cause a marital dissolution. Otherwise healthy marital estates go into financial distress when separation or divorce creates two households without accompanying increases in income. The parties can likely reach the best solution to this problem through negotiation and compromise, not through litigation. This usually requires a reduction in the standard of living of all of the parties, not only husband and wife, but children as well. Failure to recognize the need to lower consumption to live within the available income will result in accumulation of debt or the dissipation of assets during the pendency of the divorce proceedings. The parties should understand the dollar consequences of certain decisions made immediately after separation so they can appropriately rearrange their financial circumstances and spending.

(f) Spousal Duties. States, to differing degrees, will expect a minimum standard of conduct between spouses. In some cases, the standard of conduct rises to a fiduciary duty. This duty can continue after date of separation and can require full disclosure of all financial information, property, and income. Breach of this duty can have serious consequences. Some states provide for a 100 percent penalty (forfeiture of property) inflicted on spouses who attempt to defraud their spouse's right to property. States will sometimes impose a lesser remedy for a spouse concealing property, requiring the concealing spouse to pay all fees and costs to discover concealed property.

32.2   IMPORTANT DATES

Several dates have importance during the course of a marital dissolution. The significance of these dates depends on local statutes and cases.

(a) Marriage.   The date of marriage is the date on which marital property rights begin. Cohabitation prior to marriage usually does not give rise to marital property rights after marriage. In some states, statutes make remedies available to either spouse for premarital acquisitions.

(b) Separation.   The date of separation is usually the date at which the parties no longer intend to live as man and wife or registered domestic partners (RDP). The date can be the result of one or the other parties physically leaving the marital residence. Separation can occur even though the parties continue to live under the same roof. For example, if, while still living together, one party files a petition for dissolution of marriage, this generally reflects a desire to terminate the marriage or RDP. Identification of the actual date of separation is a legal one.

In some jurisdictions, income earned from personal services after separation is separate property. In other states, personal efforts of either spouse will continue to be community income until the final dissolution of marriage. This can have a substantial effect on high earners or those who create substantial personal income through personal efforts. Postseparation income rules affect professionals, professional athletes, entertainers, and highly compensated business executives.

In states where the date of separation (not dissolution of marriage) terminates community income from personal efforts, the parties often differ about the alleged date of separation. The lower earner usually benefits from a later date of separation.

(c) Valuation.   Valuation of marital property generally occurs at the date nearest trial, subject to exceptions made by local law or judicial precedent. Delaying valuation and division of the property until trial requires spouses to continue sharing the risk of decline in value and the reward of an increase. One party can unilaterally divide some of the marital assets without adequate legal counsel. This occurs often with cash accounts when one spouse takes half of the cash in an account and distributes the other half to the spouse. Division of assets one by one often leaves a large indivisible asset that the parties cannot split. If all other property has been divided, the parties lose the ability to offset the large asset with other several smaller assets. Advisors should warn spouses against dividing property without their attorneys' knowledge and approval.

(d) Property Division.   In community property states, a property division results in an equal division of the community property to each spouse. If property does not divide equally, the spouse receiving the larger share must pay the other to equalize the division.

The property division might not occur all at the same time. Sometimes the parties divide some assets between themselves during the pendency of the proceedings, with a final property division occurring some months or years later. Partial or delayed property divisions have tax implications, which Chapter 36 discusses.

(e) Marital Status Termination.   In some cases, the parties will want to terminate the marital status prior to completing the divorce. Early termination of the marital status can offer significant tax advantages. Furthermore, one of the parties may wish to remarry prior to the completion of the marital property division. The parties should consider the adequacy of medical insurance, as well as employment benefits shared by the nonemployee spouse that may terminate early. Should there be an agreement not to change beneficiaries on retirement plans? The parties should consider new wills and consequences of title held in joint name.

32.3   VALUATION METHODS

Many methods exist for the valuation of marital property. Marital property includes cash, stocks, business interests, limited partnership interests, patents, goodwill, and pensions, among others. Individual states often require different valuation methods for different types of property. This section discusses three common valuation methods.

(a) Fair Market Value.   The *International Glossary of Business Valuation Terms*, adopted by the American Institute of Certified Public Accountants (AICPA), the National Association of Certified Valuation Analysts (NACVA), and other appraisal groups, defines *fair market value* as

> the price, expressed in terms of cash equivalents, at which property would change hands between a hypothetical willing and able buyer and a hypothetical willing and able seller, acting at arms length in an open and unrestricted market, when neither is under compulsion to buy or sell and when both have reasonable knowledge of the relevant facts.[2]

This definition resembles the definitions of fair market value for other types of property. Marital dissolutions, however, can involve significant departure from the fair market value concept. Inherent in many business appraisals are discounts for lack of marketability or risks of transfer to new owners, or both. Many states' statutes or courts do not apply discounts in marital dissolution because the transfer to the managing spouse involves little risk. The transaction requires no marketability discounts because the managing spouse is the purchaser (even if an unwilling one).

(b) Comparable Sales.   An active market for a particular type of property indicates a reliable value by reference to comparable sales of similar merchandise or property or business interest. Comparable sales of complex assets, like business interests, can involve consideration other than cash, such as a note. Consider another complication: the transfer in a divorce often binds the managing spouse to a covenant not to compete or requires that spouse to assist with transition to the new owner. Any of these transition or covenant clauses could relate to value associated with future personal services by the owner after marriage—a separate period. This can raise questions regarding appropriateness or require adjustments to the comparable sale value of a business or other complex property.

(c) Fair Value. *Fair value* refers to a valuation method defined by statute, court cases, or a particular jurisdiction's valuation method. Fair value reflects the unique rules of each state and attributes of a particular property. Most marital dissolution valuations are fair value to reflect the diverse and unique rules of each state.

32.4   MARITAL PROPERTY

Marital property refers to property owned during marriage or property that is subject to division by the court.

(a) Inventory.   The parties prepare an inventory of the marital estate at a date near trial. The inventory should give consideration to transfers, dispositions, and acquisitions of property occurring from the date of separation until the date of trial. The inventory can also include an inquiry to property changes occurring during marriage. The information collected and presented in the inventory can include the following:

- Description
- Current value
- Date valued
- Proposed distribution
- Debts associated with property
- Form of title
- Appraiser's name
- Character: community or separate
- Tax basis and potential gain (if available)

(b) Proposed Division.   All marital property falls into two classifications: community or separate. When dividing a marital estate, the courts have the following options:

- Divide in kind (each owns a portion of the property)
- Sell and divide cash
- Value and award property to one spouse
- Award to either party in an equitable distribution
- Reserve jurisdiction to divide at a later date (generally very limited)

(c) Tax Consequences. Some states do not consider the embedded tax consequences inherent in an asset when assessing its value. In California, *Fonstein* requires the court to consider potential tax liability of a marital asset only in the case of "immediate and specific" tax consequences.

For example, suppose a couple divorces and they have only two assets. Both are rental properties, and each has a value of $1,400,000. Husband's rental has a basis of $1,400,000 (recently purchased) and Wife's rental has a basis of $100,000. Community property rules require an equal division of community property; should the court award the property net of tax consequences and require an equalizing payment from husband to wife? Some community property states will consider this an equal division because each received property worth $1,400,000. The court then would ignore the large imbedded tax gain in Wife's rental property. These states regard the tax consequences as mere speculation unless taxes are *immediate and specific.* If the court ordered Wife's residence sold, however, the income taxes on the sale would become immediate and specific and would reduce the value of Wife's rental. When the court does not consider tax consequences, equity demands that dividing fair market value equally should also require an equal division of the potential tax burdens. This often proves difficult. (*See* Chapter 36 for more discussion of tax implications.)

(d) Liquidity Problems. Some marital estates have substantial value in one unique asset that, by its nature, must be awarded to one spouse. Closely held businesses can represent 80 percent or more of a marital estate's value. For obvious practical considerations, both parties know it will be awarded to the managing spouse. This creates the need for a substantial equalizing payment from the managing spouse. Locating a source of the cash to make equalizing payments can prove difficult. This can lead to further financial problems after the marital dissolution. A dispute over the value of a business isn't always the real problem: the difficulty often lies in finding offsetting assets or liquidity to pay for it after the divorce whatever its value.

(e) Forensic Examinations. Forensic examinations in marital dissolution involve searching for undisclosed assets. Accountants frequently investigate closely held businesses or other personal property or financial assets. Any forensic examination should weigh the professional costs against the potential benefit of discovered assets. Initially, forensic examinations should focus on personal expenses paid by a corporation, loans to family members, transfers of property occurring after the onset of marital discord, or significant evidence of undisclosed income or hidden assets. The examination expands if results warrant.

One can begin such an examination with a yearly analysis of cash flow from personal income tax returns during marriage. The analysis starts with income and converts that to cash flow; it then subtracts expected expenses and net property acquisitions. If remaining cash flow exceeds the living expenses and known property acquisitions, this can indicate undisclosed property acquisitions or undisclosed expenditures for illicit purposes or paramours, which the former spouse can recover under some state rules. This method will not prove effective when the parties' tax returns omit some income.

32.5   INTERPLAY OF PROPERTY ISSUES

The valuation and division of martial property affects other issues in a marital dissolution, as this section discusses.

(a) Income and Support.   A property division that distributes income-producing property to the supported spouse often reduces spousal and child support. Many states use available income as a criterion in establishing the amount of spousal and child support payments. To the extent that an equal division of property results in an award of income-producing property to the supported spouse, the supporting spouse can receive a reduced support obligation.

(b) Liquidity of Property.   The lack of liquidity often requires a large equalizing payment or a transfer of income-producing property to the supported spouse. This leaves the supporting spouse with reduced income. In cases that require an equalizing payment, the supporting spouse will have to pay from earnings a monthly note payment, spousal and child support, and living expenses. The addition of an equalizing payment to the other financial obligations of the supporting spouse can create an untenable financial drain.

32.6   SPECIFIC PROPERTY

(a) Stock Options.   Stock options are a common and significant form of compensation. Stock options received by an employee vest over a period of months or years. Some stock options in the marital estate will have vested before the valuation date, and others will vest afterwards. State rules vary on the treatment of both classes of options. California, for instance, treats the fully vested stock options as of the date of separation as community property but apportions options that vest after date of separation between community and separate property based on the time rule set forth in *Brown* and later incorporated in *Nelson*.

The time rule computes the community portion of an asset by multiplying a fraction by the value or number of shares. The fraction's numerator is the number of months from the date of stock option grant to the date of separation. The denominator is the number of months from stock option grant until full vesting. The *Nelson* decision specified the following formula:

$$\frac{\text{Months from Grant to Separation}}{\text{Months from Grant to Full Vesting}} = \text{Community Options Percentage}$$

$$\text{Community Options Percentage} \times \text{Total Options Grant} = \text{Community Options}$$

Some states allow the time rule to begin at the date of employment rather than the date of grant of the option. The fraction determines how many of the options become community divided (i.e., 50 percent to each party). If the employed spouse loses employment or, for any reason, does not actually vest and receive the options, then neither spouse receives unvested option shares. Stock options, when vested, can represent a source of income available for support. In *Murray*, an Ohio court found that annual appreciation of vested unexercised (but exercisable) stock options represented income available for support. Options that the court divides or awards to both spouses affect support differently. The parties need to consider this issue when dividing property.

(b) Retirement Plans.   The parties can divide retirement plan assets with a qualified domestic relations order (QDRO).

(c) Privately Owned Businesses.   Privately owned businesses represent significant challenges in marital dissolutions. They are difficult to value, illiquid, impossible to divide, and compose a significant part of the marital estate. Both parties understand that the managing spouse will receive the business. Negotiations lack the normal inhibitions that prevent overvaluation of property (for fear of being awarded the property). Absent the restraint of "if you think it's worth that much, you can take it," parties often litigate the value of privately owned businesses. Chapter 34, "Marital Dissolution: Professional Goodwill and Related Intangibles," covers the unique aspects of a professional business. Much of the information applies to nonprofessional businesses. One can find many books dispensing advice on valuing privately owned businesses in marital estates. When valuing a marital business, consider that a court can apply the following fairness criteria:

- Will this business have this value when the managing spouse retires or ceases working in the business?

- Does a readily observable market exist for the sale of this business? Can the owner sell it?

- Considering the salary and profits available to the managing spouse, can that spouse pay the equalizing payment, spousal and child support, and marital debts assigned to him or her?

- How much income is left for the managing spouse's living expenses?

- If the court values the business with an earnings multiple, will this double-count cash flow because the court will use the cash flow from those same earnings to determine support?

In some situations, a reasonable and fair business value creates an untenable financial situation for the managing (purchasing) spouse. One solution reduces the value of the business to accommodate the managing spouse's cash flow. This deprives the nonmanaging spouse of the right to a fair value of the business. These cases prove difficult because they have no fair and equitable answer other than to give the nonreceiving spouse a continuing claim on the cash flow from the business, which itself creates monitoring problems and (perhaps) disincentives to the managing partner. This also forces the parties to continue a link that they want to sever. The court will have difficulty in solving this problem. Litigation that ensues over the value of a business can, in reality, result from an understanding that the business at any reasonable value will produce an untenable financial circumstance. Early identification of this problem can help the parties focus on the ultimate division of property and cash flow, rather than become lost in the expense of valuation litigation.

32.7   CONCLUSION

A leading family law authority, Justice Donald King, once described the role of an experienced accountant expert in marital dissolutions as being similar to that of co-counsel.[3] Accountants who work closely with attorneys can help their clients transition through what will probably be the largest financial event of their lives.

APPENDIX:
FAMILY LAW RESOURCE MATERIALS

California Practice Guide—Family Law

Judge William P. Hogoboom and Justice Donald B. King

Rutter Group, 15760 Ventura Blvd. #630

Encino, CA 91436

(800) 747-3161

Comprehensive Three Volume Loose-Leaf Service—California

Valuation and Distribution of Marital Property

John P. McCahey, J.D., LL.M.

Matthew Bender, 11 Penn Plaza, New York, NY 10001

2101 Webster Street, Oakland, CA 94612; 1275 Broadway, Albany, NY 12201

(800) 833-9844

Comprehensive Three Volume Loose-Leaf Service—National

Deering's California Civil Practice Codes 1994 Edition

Bancroft-Whitney, Law Publishers

3250 Van Ness Avenue,

P.O. Box 7005, San Francisco

CA 94120-7005

(800) 848-4000

Guide to Divorce Engagements

Stanton L. Meltzer, CPA, David A. Rooney, J. Clifford Griffiph, Gary R. Trugman, Jay E. Fishman, Gerald L. Nissenbaum

Practitioners Publishing Company, Fort Worth, Texas

(800) 323-8724

Divorce and Separation

Professor Jerome M. Hesch

Tax Management Inc., a subsidiary of The Bureau of National Affairs, Inc.

1231 25th Street, N.W.

Washington, D.C. 20037

(800) 372-1033

Attorneys Briefcase Legal Research Software

Garrett C. Dailey, Attorney at Law and Honorable James H. Libbey, Commissioner Contra Costa County Superior Court

519 17th Street, Suite 430, Oakland, CA 94612

(510) 836-2743

Legal Research Database for Family Law

NOTES

1. *Black's Law Dictionary* (St. Paul, MN: West Publishing Company, 2004).
2. American Institute of Certified Public Accountants, *International Glossary of Business Valuation Terms* (New York: AICPA 2001). This entire glossary appears as Appendix A in Chapter 13.
3. Justice Donald King, Speech presented to the California Society of CPA's Family Law Conference in San Francisco, 1992.

LIST OF CASES

In re Marriage of Brown 15 Cal. 3d. 838, 126 Cal. Rptr. 633, 544 P.2d 561 (1976)
In re Marriage of Fonstein 17 Cal. 3d 738, 131 Cal. Rptr. 873, 552 P.2d 1169 (1976)
Murray v. Murray (Ohio Ct. App. 1999) CA98-08-097
In re Marriage of Nelson 177 Cal. App. 3d 150, 222 Cal. Rptr. 790 (1986)

CHAPTER 33

CHILD AND SPOUSAL SUPPORT AWARDS

John D. Zante

CONTENTS

33.1 INTRODUCTION

Frequent changes in statutory law and appellate decisions in state and federal courts affect spousal and child support awards. The consultant must become familiar with the changing trends. To comply with law, the court needs financial data of the parties sufficient to assess an appropriate support award.

    This chapter reviews the considerations relevant to child support and spousal support, whereas Chapter 36 addresses the relevant tax implications concerning support issues. Section 33.2 of this chapter provides the statutory and case framework concerning child support; Sections 33.3 and 33.4 discuss the statutory and case law relevant to spousal support. Section 33.5 identifies the typical awards rendered, and Section 33.6 discusses the typical services that a consultant provides in child and spousal support matters. Section 33.7 addresses the preliminary considerations required when one is preparing a report for either a temporary or permanent support award, and the Appendix includes a sample of such a report.

33.2   CHILD SUPPORT

(a) Introduction.   In a dissolution or separation proceeding, the court can order either one or both parents to financially support a minor or dependent child.

(i) Mutual Obligation.   Both parents have mutual responsibility to support and educate their child. Such support must reflect the child's circumstances, considering each parent's earnings or earning capacity.

(ii) Child.   The term *child* applies to *minor child* and can also extend to an adult child who cannot work. Such consideration requires proof of a physical or mental handicap. The term *child* includes adopted, illegitimate, and unborn children.

(b) State Guidelines

(i) Uniform Statewide Guidelines.   By federal mandate, the Family Support Act of 1988 (PL 100-485) required judges for each state to apply state guidelines, considered presumptively correct, for child-support awards. This implies that the court will follow the guidelines absent a compelling reason. Beginning in 1992, the act also required each state to review the guideline amounts for successive intervals every four years. The act bases child-support guidelines on the parents' combined income. The guidelines replaced the subjective criteria previously used among the states and county jurisdictions therein. Deviation from the guideline award can occur because of any of the following: stipulation of the parties, high-earner income, unequal timeshare arrangements, and children with special educational or medical needs.

(ii) Guideline Principals.   The act requested that states observe the following criteria during enactment of their guidelines:

- **Parental responsibility.** Parents should share legal responsibility but divide financial responsibility in proportion to the parents' income.
- **Parental subsistence.** Although support amounts can consider the subsistence needs of parents, in no event should child support be zero.
- **Support standard.** Support should cover the child's basic needs as a first priority. The child (unlike the supported spouse) should share in the improved standard of living of either parent.
- **Support factors.** Each child has a right to share in the parent's income, subject to factors such as the age of the child, income of the parent, income of current spouse, and the presence of other dependents.
- **Paternity.** Each child is entitled to support without regard to marital status of the parents at the time of the child's birth. Hence, guidelines apply equally in cases of paternity, separation, and divorce.
- **Custody.** The guidelines should consider the financial effects provided by the parents in shared custody and extended visitation arrangements.

(iii) Application of Guidelines. Although each of the states has adopted child-support guidelines, each state varies in application of the guidelines, as follows:

- **Calculation of child support.** To calculate child support, the states use different approaches, with the majority of the states applying the *income shares method* and one-quarter of the states applying the *percent of income method*, with the remaining states applying other methods or variants thereof.[1]

- **Income shares.** First, compute the child support amount (using the estimated child costs approved by the state) based on the combined level of income (gross income or net income, depending on the state) of the parents. Second, pro-rate the amount between the parents based on their respective levels of income (gross income or net income). The amount allocated to the noncustodial parent represents the child support obligation.

- **Percent of income.** This method applies a state-approved percentage against gross or net income of the noncustodial parent to arrive at the child support amount. Depending on the state, the percentile rate can differ according to the level of income or number of minor children.

Section 33.2(c) defines the calculation of the terms *gross income* and *net income* (disposable income) as used by various states and as used in this chapter.

- **Other guideline factors.** The states also vary in their treatment of child care costs, health insurance premiums, extraordinary medical expenses, and shared parenting arrangements; a limited number of states consider college support for adult children in setting child support.

- **Primary obligation.** Parents owe a primary obligation in support of their minor children equal to the statutory formula, which in some cases leaves little or no amount available to pay spousal support, except in cases with a high-earner supporting spouse or wealthy families.

- **Computerized programs.** In many states, the courts and counsel use computerized programs to establish guideline spousal or child support, or both.

(c) Income Calculation

(i) Gross Income. The first step in computing a child support award requires a calculation of the parents' gross income. Because rule writers cannot anticipate every possible income source, the states use a definition similar to the Internal Revenue Service (IRS) definition of gross income, which includes all income from any source, except for those items specifically excluded. Hence, even though states include in their definition of gross income a listing of the more common sources of income (i.e., salary, commission, interest, and pensions), the statutory definition will caution that the list is not all inclusive.

Some states also grant the court broad discretion as to inclusion or exclusion of certain items for computing gross income. Items excluded from gross income often include child support from a former marriage or relationship, public assistance payments, spousal support in the current child support proceeding, and the child's cost of health insurance. Resolving the issues of the gross income components for child support has resulted in litigation. California courts held that the following items—not listed in statutes—represented gross income (for full citations for all cases, see the List of Cases at the end of the chapter):

- **Lottery winnings** (*County of Contra Costa v. Lemon*).
- **Gambling winnings** (*Marriage of Scheppers*).
- **Value of selected employee benefits** to the extent benefits reduce the parent's living expenses such as a vehicle or free housing provided by an employer (*Marriage of Schulz*).
- **Veterans disability benefits** not preempted by federal law (*Rose v. Rose*).
- **Bonus or overtime:** Gross income may include historical bonus or overtime (*County of Placer v. Andrade*) The rules may exclude such amounts, if the earner can prove such income will not likely continue. Such proof can take the form of a declaration from the employer, proof of health problems, and the parent/employee's need to spend more time with their children.

Other disputed items include the following:

- **Imputed income:** Relevant cases broaden the scope of what a trial court can use in establishing income for measuring support if the supporting spouse uses assets less than optimally. In California, the court affirmed that imputed income can include what a person could earn from a return on assets, thus imputing a higher rate of income to the husband's rental properties (*In Re Marriage of Dacumos*). Although another court in California acknowledged that an inheritance is not income under the guidelines, the court reasoned that the income from the newly discovered wealth could reduce the supporting spouse's claimed living expenses—thereby increasing the amount available for support (*Kern v. Castle*). One can envision other possible scenarios: (1) if the supporting spouse has low income-producing assets, the court can impute an earning percentage higher than the historical return; (2) if a supporting spouse quits his or her job because of a recent inheritance, the court can impute income from the historical job; and (3) if the supporting spouse lives in a residence free from mortgage, the court can consider as income the fair rental value or portion thereof.
- **Debt repayment:** The court included a husband's voluntary salary withholding to repay a loan to his employer-corporation as part of income, thereby increasing the amount of his gross income for calculation of child support (*Marriage of Kirk*). Had the husband been obligated to repay the debt, the court might have ruled differently. The court reduced income by the amount of debt service the borrower, strapped for cash, incurred to pay for living expenses (i.e., clothing and household items; *County of Lake v. Antoni*). In another matter, however, the court did not reduce income for debt service payments when the obligor-parent faced less severe financial stress than did the obligor-parent in *Antoni* (*County of Stanislaus v. Gibbs*).
- **Stock options:** Employees are increasingly opting for stock options in lieu of a higher salary or bonus, with the expectation of future gains. For child-support purposes, the court can include capital gains in income when they recur but not when they are one-time and not considered income. Thus, the courts held that recurring profits realized on the *exercise of stock options* represented income for child support in California (*Marriage of Cheriton*), in Colorado (*In Re Marriage of Campbell*), and in Connecticut (*Goold v. Goold*), but not in Ohio because it was a one-time event (*Yost v. Unanue*). Later in Ohio, the court decided

to impute *unexercised stock options* as income for child support purposes and explained how to value the unexercised stock options (*Murray v. Murray*).

(ii) Net Income. For the states that use the amount of the parents' net income (also referred to as *disposable income*) as a base for calculating a child support amount, the computations reduce gross income by a limited amount of deductions. Although the guidelines do not always factor in parental discretionary living expenditures (e.g., autos, clothing, food, and residence), permissible deductions generally include state and federal income taxes, employment taxes (i.e., FICA), mandatory union dues and retirement payments, health and disability insurance, job-related expenses, and court-ordered child or spousal support attributable to a preexisting relationship.

(iii) Earning Capacity. In measuring child support based on income (gross income or net income, depending on the state), the court can base such support on the parent's earning capacity rather than actual earnings. The courts apply earnings capacity when they find that the obligor-parent has suppressed income, refused to seek employment, or merely sought a new lifestyle. Such instances often require expert testimony to value the earning capacity of such parent.

33.3 SPOUSAL SUPPORT

(a) Introduction. Spousal support, also referred to as *alimony* or *maintenance*, provides a spouse with funds to accommodate his or her reasonable needs consisting of clothing, food, shelter, and other necessities.

(i) Origin of Support. The alimony concept originated from English common law, which prohibited both divorces and a wife's ownership of property. Thus, alimony represented the husband's continuing obligation to support his wife. This concept has survived in states with community property and common law jurisdictions.

(ii) Current Trend. Each state provides some form of alimony based on factors established by state statute or based on the court's discretion.

(b) Basis for Award

(i) Statutory Factors. Most states have statutes that list factors for the court to consider when setting spousal support levels. Most states consider the standard of living during the marriage and the respective parties' needs and abilities to pay. The states differ, however, on whether to consider marital fault (e.g., adultery) or which spouse has custody of dependent children.

(ii) Broad Court Discretion. As long as the court considers and evaluates the statutory factors, it has broad discretion in the ultimate decision as to amount and duration of spousal support. Failure of the court support order to independently weigh each of the statutory factors could result in reversible error.

(iii) Marital Standard of Living. The evaluation process focuses on finding a support level that will allow the parties to maintain the marital standard of living that existed during marriage. Because of the added costs of maintaining two households, each party usually enjoys a lesser standard of living after separation. The court in

its broad discretion will attempt to balance or assign different weight to each of the relevant statutory factors to obtain the most equitable and just result. Section 33.4 discusses several of these factors.

33.4   RELEVANT FACTORS

(a) Age and Health of Parties.   The factors of age or health, or both, can result in either extending or terminating the support award. A court denied a request to terminate support, citing the supported spouse's limited job skills, earning ability reduced due to advanced age of 61 years, and lack of education, as well as lack of future retirement income (*Marriage of Crobarger*). 178 CA 3d 56, 60, 223 CR 480, 482 (1986). An appeal resulted in reversal of the trial court's denial of support for a marriage of less than eight years, in which the supported spouse had a disease preventing employment and the supporting spouse's income far exceeded the income of the supported spouse (*Marriage of Teegarden*). Alternatively, the appeal upheld a denial of support for a permanently disabled spouse of a 70-month marriage after a support period of 58 months; the court reasoned that enough time had elapsed so that society could take its turn in providing support (*Marriage of Wilson*).

(b) Parties' Assets and Liabilities.   The guidelines require that resources available for support include income from separate property as well as former community property (*Marriage of Epstein, Marriage of Terry,* and *Marriage of de Guigne*). A supported spouse who improperly manages assets that would have provided adequate support can jeopardize an extension or increase in support from the supporting spouse (*Marriage of McElwee,* and *Marriage of Biderman*). Guidelines require that the court must consider income from all property.

(c) Duration of Marriage.   The longer the supported spouse has been out of work during the marriage, the stronger the case for support. Alternatively, the fact of a short-lived marriage can offset the fact of need of the supported spouse, resulting in either a lower amount of support or a shorter period in which to pay support (*Marriage of Bukaty* and *Marriage of Huntington*).

(d) Earning Capacity of Supported Spouse.   A support order must reflect the present capabilities and marketable earning skills of the parties (*Marriage of Prietsch & Calhoun* and *Marriage of Baker*). If the court finds the supported spouse currently unemployable because of a lack of marketable skills or if the supported spouse requires time to develop such skills, it can withhold a reduction in support until the prospects for employment improve. Alternatively, the court can deny support to an employable spouse who fails to seek work (*Marriage of Dennis* and *Marriage of Rosan*). If the supported spouse has not worked for a long time (21 years in the case cited here), the court can consider the supported spouse's earning capacity as permanently impaired (*Marriage of Smith & Ostler*).

(i) Contribution to Spouse's Education.   On occasion, a nonstudent will help a student spouse through school. The court can allow the spouse who later becomes the supported nonstudent spouse to defer work in order to pursue secondary education for a higher earning career position as well (*Marriage of Watt*).

(ii) Employment of Custodial Spouse. Because of the overriding welfare of the children, the court will consider the effect on the children before assessing the need of the custodial spouse to seek employment. In this regard, the court can order indefinite spousal support even for a marriage of short duration, eight years in the case cited here (*Marriage of Aufmuth*).

(e) Needs of the Parties. The court can measure the needs of the parties (not limited to the bare necessities of life) from the standard of living attained during marriage. The standard during marriage serves merely as a reference point because the changed circumstances require that the parties maintain two households after separation. Temporary (*pendente lite*) support awards also provide a reference point, but some guidelines consider them binding on the court's award of a subsequent permanent award. A showing of historical family living expenses incurred during marriage will be less significant if the parties lived unrealistically beyond or below their means (*Marriage of Smith, Marriage of Watt, Marriage of Weinstein,* and *Marriage of Cheriton*). The court can discount the supported spouse's projected expenses to sustain a lifestyle enjoyed during marriage by that spouse's ability to become self-supporting, or by considerations of improved asset management, or by short duration of marriage. Because support terminates upon the death of the supporting spouse, the court can order the supporting spouse to provide a security device if the assets will be insufficient to provide for continuation. The security device can be an insurance policy on the life of the obligor-spouse, or an annuity, or an amount placed into a trust.

(f) Supporting Spouse's Ability to Pay. Although the court relies on the supporting spouse's historical or current record of earnings, it can also consider the supporting spouse's ability to pay (earning capacity) in all cases (*Marriage of Ilas*). The court measures earning capacity from data on historical earnings, including income tax returns. The court will impute income when the spouse suppresses income (*Philbin v. Philbin*). The court can impute income if the supporting spouse quits work to seek higher education (*Marriage of Ilas*). The court should base earning capacity for support purposes on a reasonable work standard and should not hold a spouse accountable to imputed income during marriage that consisted of an inordinate amount of overtime (*Marriage of Simpson*).

Regarding retirement contributions or retirement income, the court has imputed income to the supporting spouse in the following instances, where the supporting spouse can withdraw early without penalty, as an additional income source for measuring support:

(i) Retirement Contributions. The court can consider the amount of voluntary contributions to retirement plans to assess support, whereas it would consider mandatory contributions to government or union plans only if they are available for withdrawal without penalty (e.g., over age $59\frac{1}{2}$ (*Marriage of Olson*)).

(ii) Normal Retirement. Available income need not include retirement income of a participant, age 65, because the supported spouse cannot expect the same level of support after the supporting spouse retires at age 65 (*Marriage of Reynolds*). Alternatively, for retirees reaching age $70\frac{1}{2}$, the court can consider amounts received that exceed the mandated minimum withdrawals (*Marriage of Olson*).

33.5 TYPICAL AWARDS

(a) Voluntary Award. This award represents an agreement between the parties. The paying spouse cannot deduct the award from taxable income, and the receiving spouse need not include it in taxable income. (Chapter 36 discusses voluntary awards and taxes.)

(b) Temporary Award. Initially, the court will order a temporary award during the divorce proceedings designed, if possible, to maintain the economic *status quo.*

(c) Family Support Award. If a written agreement combines both child and spousal support and does not allocate an amount to child support, the combined support award is known as *family support.* The court need not make a separate order for child support. The obligor spouse can deduct family support but cannot deduct child support. The parties prefer this method of payment during the divorce proceedings when the supporting spouse pays income taxes at a higher marginal tax rate than does the supported spouse. The tax savings provides additional funds (*see* Chapter 36).

(d) Permanent Award. At completion of the divorce proceedings, the court will replace the temporary award with a permanent award. If the supported spouse remains unemployed, the court can rely on expert testimony to fix a period in which the supported spouse must obtain suitable employment. The permanent award can include a preliminary step-down provision to take effect at the expiration of the fixed period. The permanent award would also reflect the parties' expected income derived from the property division. The court can include in a permanent award a date by which the court expects the supported spouse to earn income and an amount. Usually, the court holds the spouse to such amount and date unless that spouse has a medical excuse for failure. The courts often use a vocational guidance counselor to establish the supported spouse's potential employability and earnings.

(e) Changes to Award. The court retains jurisdiction in support matters for various reasons, as follows.

(i) Alternative Forms of Payment. When the obligor spouse falls into arrears in making child support payments, the court can issue an order assigning the obligor-spouse's wages to the custodial spouse. New mandated federal forms now exist for assignment of wages. Other alternative payment methods include direct payment of medical costs, special education costs, or payment to a creditor to discharge a minor's debt.

(ii) Modification. Inflation, increased education costs, and the increased expenses incurred as the child grows older can justify modifying and increasing the award. Changes in the parents' income level can also justify an increase or decrease in the award.

(iii) Longevity. In some states that provide for the measurement of all the factors pertaining to spousal support other than the longevity of spousal support,

adverse parties litigate over that provision. The status can include a longevity presumption, such as half the length of the marriage.

(iv) Termination. Generally, child support liability terminates when the child attains the age of majority, which varies from ages 18 to 21. This can vary if the child remains a student. Child support can terminate prior to the child's attaining the age of majority if the child marries, enters the armed services, or receives a judicial declaration of emancipation from the court.

33.6 ROLE OF CONSULTANT

(a) Services Expected. A consultant or expert assists counsel for one or both spouses in estimating child support and spousal support based on the statutory guidelines. Spousal support controversies generally require court testimony more frequently than do disputes involving only child support. To assist counsel, consultants must understand the aforementioned statutory guidelines and their application. They must also understand the relevant case law and the interrelation of child support and spousal support. The services required by the attorney in a support matter will vary, depending on whether the consultant assists in determining a temporary award or a permanent award, explained as follows.

(b) Temporary Award. During this phase of the dissolution proceedings, which generally lasts for one to six months, each of the parties will have incurred the costs of two households with the attendant costs of litigation. Usually the parties have disparate incomes, and frequently one spouse has no earned income. Consequently, the parties often cannot continue the standard of living achieved during marriage. Each of the parties must file declarations showing his or her *disposable income* (gross income reduced by taxes and mandatory deductions, which typically consists of child or spousal support from a prior relationship, health insurance, retirement contributions, and unreimbursed employee expenses) and discretionary *living expenses* incurred during the last 12 months. In rendering services for a temporary award, the attorney often needs advice only by telephone or asks the consultant to provide schedules and be prepared to present the findings in a conference or before a court. During this temporary phase of the dissolution, the court focuses on the parties' declarations of disposable income and living expenes.

(i) Review Services. The attorney often will need only to discuss findings regarding the parties' income sources with the consultant. For this limited purpose, the attorney will forward documents that include declarations summarizing the income and living expenses of the parties and recent tax returns for a period of one or two years. After reviewing the financial data received, the consultant will contact the attorney to confirm or evaluate whether the attorney has reasonably included the correct income sources of the parties in computing a realistic support level. This type of engagement requires a day or less of work for the consultant.

(ii) Formal Schedules. If the parties have substantial assets, including an interest in passive and nonpassive activities (as delineated in the income tax regulations), the consultant will need to review the parties' historical income for a period of three to five years to assess the parties' current income. Because variable income sources

can complicate the income assessment, the attorney will generally ask the consultant to prepare schedules in support of the parties' expected disposable income for presentation in settlement conference or in court. Disregarding the time for settlement conference or trial, the time required to prepare for this type of engagement varies between one day and a week, depending on the extent and nature of the parties' assets.

(c) Permanent Award.   During this phase of the dissolution proceedings, which on average can require as long as 2.5 years, the parties will have changed their lifestyles with attendant changes in income and living expenditures. The parties also will have completed their property division, and the court should consider the earnings on the various properties in deciding the permanent award. During this phase, the attorney will often ask the consultant to update the work previously conducted for the temporary award. In some cases, the consultant supplements the work with additional schedules showing historical living expenditures, which show the parties' standard of living prior to separation. Analysts use two approaches to measure the marital standard of living, both accepted by some courts: the abbreviated *indirect approach* or the more comprehensive *direct approach.*

(i) Indirect Approach.   The indirect approach starts with the parties' historical tax returns for a representative period of two or three years during marriage It then subtracts amounts for net investments and property acquisitions and adds the parties' net increase (or subtracts the net decrease) in debt. The difference represents the parties' discretionary (living) expenditures during marriage. This indirect approach (an annual cash-flow approach) takes less time than compiling a list of all the discretionary (living) expenditures for a similar period. The expert should update such computations to reflect income and expenditures of each spouse for a period subsequent to separation through six months prior to trial to compare the standard of living before and after separation. The total discretionary (living) expenses computed through this method should equal the total of such expenditures shown in the declarations filed by the parties. Disregarding the time for settlement conference or trial, the time required for this type of engagement can vary between two days and a week, depending on the extent and nature of the parties' assets.

(ii) Direct Approach.   In addition to the services explained above, some cases require a comprehensive standard of living analysis. This includes a direct approach, consisting of a cumulative detailed listing of each expenditure for a representative period of two or three years during marriage, with similar information for the period subsequent to separation through six months prior to trial. Cases involving hidden income, prenuptial arrangements, high-income earner, depressed living standards, and instances in which living expenses exceed income sometimes require this direct approach. In these cases, the court focuses on the amount and nature of each living expenditure. Disregarding the time for settlement conference or trial, this type of engagement can require one to two weeks of the consultant's work, depending on the extent and nature of the parties' assets and the parties' compliance during discovery.

33.7 REPORT

(a) Scope of Report. A report showing each party's disposable income and personal living expenses enables the court to evaluate the appropriate level of spousal and child support. A properly prepared report helps the judge assess equitable spousal and child support awards.

The judge is the report's principal user. Both counsels can also use the report to agree on temporary spousal and child support, thereby avoiding a costly formal hearing.

(b) Period of Report.

(i) Temporary Award. The report addresses temporary spousal or child support, or both. When the economic circumstances of either party change, the accountant may need to update the report before the award becomes permanent.

(ii) Permanent Award. This report updates the report prepared for temporary support—assuming that one exists—to reflect the parties' changed economic circumstances, including the property distribution.

(c) Report's Objective. To facilitate the judge's evaluation, the report should include all financial data that a judge needs to render a decision. In California, judges rely on information from each party's Income and Expense Declaration. The report of proposed support, appended to this chapter, addresses several of the elements contained in the Income and Expense Declarations of the parties to facilitate the judge's review.

(i) Income and Expense Declaration. The court may have a standard report for income and expense information. In California (for instance), each spouse prepares a four-page California Judicial Form, which lists sources of monthly income and expenses based on historical and projected information. The parties sign the documents under penalty of perjury, and opposing parties can depose each other about them.

(ii) Disposable Income. The Income and Expense Declaration (or a similar report) must identify the sources of income and mandatory deductions to compute Net Monthly Disposable Income. The mandatory deductions will consist of income and employment taxes and will sometimes include payroll deductions such as health insurance premiums, union dues, and retirement contributions. Other allowed deductions may include court-ordered child and/or spousal support of another former relationship.

(iii) Personal Living Expenses. The declaration also identifies living expenses considered discretionary with respect to type and amount, including food, clothing, shelter, travel, and entertainment.

(d) Elements of Report. Accountants often need from one-half day to a week to compile and analyze the data necessary to prepare a report, subject to difficulty of discovery. Tax planning and spreadsheet software will help identify optional dollar amounts for the variables.

Aside from the supporting schedules, the lead schedule of the report should consist of a single-page summary that compares the parties' disposable income (consisting of income, reduced by permissible deductions and estimated taxes). Disposable income reduced by personal living expenses is intended to show the amount available (needed) for support, as shown in the Appendix to this chapter. Footnotes on the schedule indicate information sources or contain detailed calculations. Judges have found footnotes helpful when an extended time lapse occurs between the hearing and final support evaluation. Accountants should consider the following observations when preparing the report.

(i) Income.   The income number will have more credibility if it reflects the IRS definition of Adjusted Gross Income (AGI) and if it is comparable to the AGI of previous years' tax returns.

(ii) Business Income (Loss).   Experts have difficulty in assessing business income (loss). Ideally, such assessment should immediately follow a business valuation. Without a business valuation, one should use several years of historical income or loss data, heavily weighting recent years' results. If business income substantially declines after separation, discovery should include a review of, and comparison with, industry data to ascertain whether an internal expansion has occurred and a review of unusual expense increases that might include personal legal costs, unreasonable payroll costs, or purchases of unnecessary equipment and extended vacations.

(iii) Passive Income (Loss) Activities.   To assess each party's passive activity losses (PAL), the prior year's tax return will often help estimate the future income/loss stream, although one can find helpful data in two or three preceding years' tax returns. The prior year often best predicts the future year's expected cash flow. When assessing available cash for support from such sources, one should consider the tax effects associated with PAL.

(v) Noncash Expenditures.   This report shows the cash available for support. Accordingly, one makes adjustments to convert taxable income to expected cash flow. Temporary support calculations do not deduct depreciation, but permanent support calculations make the deduction.

(vi) Deductions.   This section of the report comprises deductions permitted by the state jurisdiction in which the divorce occurs. As the appendix shows, the court allowed the supporting spouse to deduct child and spousal support obligations for another marriage. Accordingly, the preparer of the report should know the rules of the specific jurisdiction and should discuss these items with the attorney involved in the matter.

(vii) Personal Expenditures.   In settings involving temporary support, the spouses provide this information in declarations filed with the court. For permanent support hearings, a report with supporting schedules contains this information.

APPENDIX:
SAMPLE REPORT

John and Mary Smith
MONTHLY AMOUNT AVAILABLE [NEEDED] FOR SUPPORT
December 15, 2004

Disposable Income		Temporary Support		
Income:		Petitioner	Respondent	Total
Salary & wages	**A**	$ 300,000	$ 150,000	$ 450,000
Investment income				
Dividends/interest	**B**	6,000	9,000	15,000
Capital loss forward	**C**	0	0	0
Rental income [loss]	**D**	6,000	6,000	12,000
Gross Income		$ 312,000	$ 165,000	$ 477,000
Deductions:				
Child support - other marriage .		$ (15,000)		$ (15,000)
Spousal support - other marriage		(12,000)		(12,000)
Unreimbursed employee expenses		(6,000)	$ (3,000)	(9,000)
Total Deductions		$ (33,000)	$ (3,000)	$ (36,000)
Income Less Deductions ..		$ 279,000	$ 162,000	$ 441,000

Income Less Deductions ..	**E**	$ 279,000	$ 162,000	$ 441,000
Estimated Taxes		(101,210)	(49,978)	(151,188)
Annual Disposable Income		$ 177,790	$ 112,022	$ 289,812
Monthly Disposable Income		$ 14,816	$ 9,335	$ 24,151

Personal Living Expenses

Estimated by Parties	**F**	(14,000)	(12,000)	(26,000)
Excess [Shortfall] of Disposable				
Income		$ 816	$ (2,665)	$ (1,849)

Adjustments to Living Expenses

Rent	**G**		$ 1,500	$ 1,500
Monthly payments	**H**	$ 750		750
Subtotal		$ 750	$ 1,500	$ 2,250
Amount Available Per Month		$ 1,566	$ 1,165	$ 401

A   Based on current wages or wages for prior twelve months

B   Based on prior year return

C   Unused capital loss carryforward of $3,000 each, effecting taxes

D   Cash flow of $6,000 from rental property for each party, consisting of a loss of $12,000, reduced by depreciation of $18,000 for each

E   From previous page

F   Based on Income & Expense Declarations filed by the parties

G   Estimated monthly expenses of $12,000 reduced by $1,500, representing an overstatement of rent expense determined during deposition of party

H   Estimated monthly expenses of $14,000 overstated by $750, representing an automobile payment for an automobile loan which will be paid off the subsequent month

NOTES

1. *Family Law Quarterly 37* (2004).

LIST OF CASES

Marriage of Aufmuth 89 CA3d 466, 459, 152 CR 668, 676 (1979)

Marriage of Baker 3 CA4th 491, 498, 4 CR2d 553, 557 (1992)

Marriage of Biderman 5 CA4th 409, 413, 6 CR2d 791, 793 (1992)

Marriage of Biderman 5 CA4th 409, 413–414, 6 CR2d 791, 793–794 (1992)

Marriage of Bukaty 180 CA3d 143, 150, 225 CR 492, 497 (1986)

In re Marriage of Campbell, 905 P.2d 783 (Colo. Ct. App. 1995)

Marriage of Cheriton, 92 CA4th 269, 286, 111 (2001)

Marriage of Cheriton 92 C4th 269, 308, 111 CR2d 755, 785 (2001)

County of Contra Costa v. Lemon 205 CA3d 683, 688, 252 CR 455, 459 (1988)

County of Lake v. Antoni 18 CA4th 1102, 1106, 22 CR2d 804, 806 (1993)

County of Placer v. Andrade 55 CA4th 1396, 64 CR2d 739, 740 (1997)

County of Stanislaus v. Gibbs 59 CA4th 1417, 1426–1427, 69 CR2d 819, 825 (1997)

Marriage of Crobarger 178 CA3d 56, 60, 223 CR 480, 482 (1986)

In Re Marriage of Dacumos, 76 CA4th 150, 154–155 90 CR2d 159, 161 (1999)

Marriage of Dennis 35 CA3d 279, 283–284, 110 CR 619,621 (1972)

Marriage of Epstein 24 C3d 76, 91, 154 CR 413, 422, fn. 14 (1979)

Goold v. Goold, 11 Conn. App. 268, 527 A.2d 696 (1987)

Marriage of de Guigne 97 CA4th 1353, 1365, 119 CR2d 430, 439–440 (2002)

Marriage of Huntington 10 CA4th 1513, 1520–1521, 14 CR2d 1, 5 (1992)

Marriage of Ilas 12 CA4th 1630, 1638, 16 CR2d 345, 350 (1993)

Marriage of Ilas 12 CA4th 1638–1639, 16 CR2d 350 (1993)

Kern v. Castle, 75 CA4th 1442, 1453, 89 CR2d 737, 740 (1999)

Marriage of Kirk 217 CA3d 597, 606–608, 266 CR 76, 81–82 (1990)

Marriage of McElwee 197 CA3d 902, 909–910, 243 CR 179, 184 (1988)

Murray v. Murray, 128 Ohio App. 662, 668–670, 716 NE2d 288, 293–295 (1999)

Marriage of Olson, supra 14 CA4th 13, 17 CR2d 489

Marriage of Olson supra 14 CA4th 13, 17 CR2d 489 (1993)

Philbin v. Philbin 19 CA3d 115, 119, 121 96 CR 408, 411–412 (1971)

Marriage of Prietsch & Calhoun 190 CA3d 645, 659, 235 CR 587, 592 (1987)

Marriage of Reynolds 63 CA4th 1373, 1377–1378 CR2d 636, 638–639 (1998)

Marriage of Rosan 24 CA3d 885, 896, 101 CR 295, 303 (1972)

Rose v. Rose 481 US 619, 107 S.CT. 2029 (1987)

Marriage of Scheppers, 86 CA4th 646, 651, 103 CR2d 529, 533 (2001)

Marriage of Schulz, 60 CA4th 528–529, 70 CR2d 488, 494–495 (1997)

Marriage of Simpson, 4 C4th 234–236, 14 CR2d 416–417 (1992)

Marriage of Smith, 225 CA CA3d 469, 487, 274 CR 911, 920–921 (1990)

Marriage of Smith & Ostler 223 CA3d 33, 49, 272 CR 560, 569–570 (1990)

Marriage of Teegarden 181 CA3d 401, 409–410, 226 CR 417, 422 (1986)

Marriage of Terry 80 CA4th 921, 930–931, 95 CR2d 760, 766 (2000)

Marriage of Watt 214 CA3d 340, 350, 262 CR 783, 789 (1989)

Marriage of Watt 214 CA3d 340, 351–352, 262 CR 783, 789–790 (1989)

Marriage of Weinstein 4 CA4th 555, 566, 568–569, 5 CR2d 558, 563, 565 (1991)

Marriage of Wilson 201 CA3d 913, 916, 247 CR 522, 524 (1988)

Yost v. Unanue, 109 Ohio App. 3d 294, 671 N.E.2d 1372 (1996)

CHAPTER 34

MARITAL DISSOLUTION: PROFESSIONAL GOODWILL AND RELATED INTANGIBLES

Donald L. Gursey
Donald John Miod

CONTENTS

34.1 INTRODUCTION

Courts change the definition of professional goodwill as they overturn preceding opinions. These decisions come from courts of appeal that have either upheld or overturned a trial court's findings. Because goodwill depends on case law, its definition and treatment present a moving target. We therefore caution readers that this chapter doesn't present the current state of the law in any jurisdiction on any given day. To obtain such information on this subject, financial experts should consult with counsel.

The authors acknowledge Victor A. Levi, who authored the version of this chapter that appeared in previous editions.

This chapter guides the expert in measuring the value, if any, of professional goodwill in a marital dissolution. It deals with the goodwill of sports figures, celebrities, and business executives. Finally, the chapter considers unusual goodwill problems, including the value of professional licenses and education.

34.2   PROFESSIONAL GOODWILL: DEFINITIONS

This chapter uses the term *professional* to mean members of occupations licensed by state or state-authorized agencies. This group includes doctors, dentists, lawyers, accountants, architects, engineers, chiropractors, and acupuncturists.

Frequently licensed, but excluded from the designation as professional, are barbers, court reporters, and the like. Others functionally equivalent to professionals include certified financial planners, real estate appraisers, dental laboratory technicians, and almost any self-employed person or owner-employee of shares in a closely held corporation in which labor, not capital, is the primary income-producing factor.

Practitioners often find goodwill, a future economic benefit, difficult to measure. For our purposes, we define goodwill as:

> the advantage or benefit, which is acquired by an establishment beyond the mere value of the capital, stock, funds, or property employed therein, in consequence of the general public patronage and encouragement, which it receives from the constant or habitual customers, on account of its local position, or common celebrity, or reputation for skill or affluence, or punctuality, or from other accidental circumstances or necessities, or even from ancient partialities or prejudices.[1]

Lord Eldon was more succinct: "The goodwill, which has been the subject of sale, is nothing more than the probability, that the old customers will resort to the old place."[2] The California Business and Professions Code defines goodwill as "the expectation of continued public patronage."[3]

From an accounting standpoint, goodwill is the excess cost of an acquired enterprise over the sum of identifiable net assets.[4] The economics of goodwill relate to the value of characteristics such as good customer relations, loyal employees who voluntarily bring their human capital to work, and the product from the employees' work that exceeds the cost of hiring those employees and giving them the resources to work. These all result in greater than normal earning power.

Professional goodwill has three major elements:

1. **Location.** This element has importance because people usually seek professional services within a small geographical area (*see Spaulding v. Benenatti; In re Marriage of Asbury; In re Marriage of Lukens;* for all full case citations, *see* List of Cases at the end of the chapter).

2. **Reputation** (*Dugan v. Dugan*). Justice Story and Lord Eldon explain the importance of this element in their quotations given previously. In *Wisner v. Wisner*, the husband, a surgeon, argued that he could have no goodwill because he had no repeat patients. Not so, said the court, because the referral base of physicians provides the repetitive business, which supports the finding of goodwill.

3. **Skill and learning in a particular profession** (*Mueller v. Mueller*). When professionals acquire the reputation, skill, and learning in a particular

profession, they often create an intangible but valuable property by winning the confidence of their patrons and securing immunity from successful competition for their business.

All businesses with goodwill have going-concern value, but the reverse is not always true. People incorrectly use the two terms interchangeably. Going-concern value (versus liquidation or exit value) reflects the assumption that the business is an operating entity, which means that its assets are worth more than their net realizable, or disposal, value. Or, as one court stated, going-concern value equals "the amount by which the value of the assets as a whole, assembled together for the conduct of a business, exceeds the aggregate value of the separate items of property" (*In re Marriage of Sharp*). But this is exactly the definition of goodwill in accounting: the excess of the purchase price of a group of assets in excess of their fair value.

Many businesses have an element of goodwill. The question, from a marital dissolution standpoint, is whether it has any identifiable dollar value associated with it.

34.3 PROFESSIONAL GOODWILL IN COURT

The first case dealing with professional goodwill in a domestic relations setting was the 1956 case *Mueller v. Mueller*, which involved a dental laboratory. The court, in reviewing prior cases that found no goodwill, stated:

> Where a person acquires a reputation for skill and learning in a particular profession, as, for instance, in that of a lawyer, a physician, or an editor, he often creates an intangible but valuable property by winning the confidence of his patrons and securing immunity from successful competition for their business, and it would seem to be well settled that this is a species of good-will which may be the subject of transfer.[5]

Mueller was followed by other California cases (*Golden v. Golden* and *Todd v. Todd*), which found goodwill values in medical and law practices. California, as a community property state, treats goodwill as a community asset included in the marital property.

Texas, although a community property jurisdiction, took a different approach regarding small professional practices in *Nail v. Nail*, wherein the court stated:

> [Dr. Nail's] goodwill did not possess value or constitute an asset separate and apart from his person or from his individual ability to practice his profession. It would be extinguished in the event of his death, or retirement, or disablement, as well as in the event of the sale of his practice or the loss of his patients, whatever the cause.[6]

Dr. Nail's goodwill was not community property, said the court. Courts have taken this position in *Austin v. Austin* (Texas), *Depner v. Depner* (Louisiana), *Tortorich v. Tortorich* (Arkansas), and *Walton v. Walton* (Florida). Kansas amended Statute § 23-201(b) to include the goodwill of a professional practice, but only to the extent it is marketable.

Texas took a different posture with larger professional organizations. In *Finn v. Finn*, the husband was a senior partner in a Dallas law firm. The court found that goodwill existed independent of the professional spouse's personal ability and that it had commercial value.

Courts in common law states, which look solely at title to property, do not make these findings of the existence of goodwill. They assigned the practice, without charge, to the practitioner as separate property (*Closson v. Closson*). In an opinion filed in January 2005, the Illinois Supreme Court stated that personal goodwill cannot be divided (*In re Schneider*).

As the use of, and statutory authority for, equitable distribution spread among the common law jurisdictions in the 1960s, the courts in those jurisdictions began to recognize and value professional goodwill. These cases include *In re Marriage of White*, *Stern v. Stern*, *Nehorayoff v. Nehorayoff*, and *Hanson v. Hanson*.

Under community property statutes, a marital interest in property runs only to property acquired during marriage. Under the equitable distribution doctrine, however, the courts can award marital property, legally owned by one party, to the other when the marriage ends. The marital partnership concept, ingrained in community property law, provides the basis for the theory of equitable distribution. Goodwill existing before the marriage is separate property.

34.4   VALUATION METHODOLOGY

The courts that have found goodwill to exist have recognized several methods to measure its value. Depending on the case, the court will allow any reasonable method (*In re Marriage of King*). As a result, the court records discuss several methods.

Most methods assume that prices paid to acquire practices indicate goodwill. These include the following:

- Sale of an entire practice (*In re Marriage of Fortier*)
- Withdrawal rights in a partnership agreement (*In re Marriage of Fonstein*)
- Sale of an interest in a practice (*In re Marriage of Lopez*)

(a) Sale Value.   Some argue that only the sale value—that is, the market price agreed by a willing buyer and seller—properly measures goodwill. Under this theory, one could exclude the value of law practice goodwill, because the California Canons of Ethics prohibit the sale of goodwill; one cannot separate it from the person or persons who generated it (*see Geffen v. Moss*). *See also Williams v. Williams* (Florida), *Berger v. Berger* (Indiana), *In re Marriage of Monoghan* (Washington), and *Ellerbe v. Ellerbe* (South Carolina) regarding the effect of noncompete agreements. Because the owner cannot separate the asset, one might call it human capital, not goodwill.

Opponents of the sale value concept claim that sale values frequently reflect a discount because of the risk of patient/client transfer from one professional to another. Such is not a factor in marital dissolution, however, when owner spouses continue to operate their businesses. Moreover, the valuation need not deduct transactions costs (e.g., brokers fees, legal fees, and commissions) in such cases because the parties already know that the owner spouse will purchase the remaining interest.

Those who reject the sale value concept claim that the value of community goodwill does not always equal the price that a willing buyer would pay for it, but they do not advance a coherent alternative method. They assert that exigencies attendant in marriage dissolutions lead to economic values of goodwill that exceed the market price (*In re Marriage of Foster*). Some professional practices, such as psychoanalytic and psychiatric, entail such close personal relationships between practitioner and patient as to render patient transfer impossible. Under this theory, the practice will have goodwill if it exhibits something called *superior earnings* (also known as *capitalization of earnings*). Measuring the amount of superior earnings and then capitalizing them into a value presents measurement difficulties, as discussed in Section 34.4(c).

Various courts have both accepted and rejected the provisions limiting marketability contained in partnership and professional corporation agreements. They rejected them as nonbinding on the nonprofessional spouse in *In re Marriage of Slater, In re Marriage of Morris*, and *In re Marriage of Fenton*. Courts have accepted them as binding in *Stern v. Stern, Hertz v. Hertz, Stolowitz v. Stolowitz*, and *In re Marriage of Nichols*. Arizona, New Mexico, and Texas lined up with the nonbinding jurisdictions in *Malloy v. Malloy, Cox v. Cox*, and *Keith v. Keith*, whereas Virginia found such an agreement binding in *Kaufman v. Kaufman*. A marketability discount has little to do with marital dissolutions. As stated previously, one does not need to identify the potential buyer: it is the spouse who is part of the partnership or corporation.[7] Convincing a court about the relevance of the market place and the concomitant discount for marketability is difficult.

(b) Formulas/Rules of Thumb. Whatever theory of goodwill value a jurisdiction uses, valuation experts often consider a goodwill measurement based on formulas. Sometimes these formulas result from standards developed by practice brokers and others. They attempt to mimic what happens in the marketplace. For example, general dental practices often change hands for 40 percent of annual gross practice income;[8] accounting practices have sold for prices from 75 percent to 125 percent of the annual gross revenue (*Mitchell v. Mitchell*). Other formulas that courts have accepted include multiples of a month's collections on accounts receivable (*Foster*) and percentages of gross and net income (*Mueller*). Valuation formulas based solely on gross revenue, which ignores profitability, is subject to criticism. Some net profit numbers merit skepticism as being too low, such as those that reflect a large amount of personal expenses in the operating expenses of a business. In such a case, the expert likely cannot ascertain the true profit number; in that event, using a multiple of gross revenue offers a solution. One must understand what the application of a formula results in. Is it only the goodwill or the value of the entire enterprise?

(c) Capitalized Excess Earnings. Applying a single-factor formula, such as one based on gross revenue, to a variety of professional activities has met with numerous questions under cross-examination. A frequently accepted formula for valuing goodwill is the capitalized excess earnings method. This formula contains several subjective inputs that financial experts must justify based on their experience and training.

First, the expert must measure the subject's actual professional earnings. This task requires analyzing the professional's reported income and expenses for some reasonable time period, generally five years.[9] Reject extraordinary results, either high or low, if their inclusion distorts the analysis. Adjust, when necessary, to include only the elements of a professional's income common to all similar practitioners. This removes personal income and expenses from legitimate business costs to obtain a picture of the actual earnings the professional practice generates. These items, commonly referred to as *perquisites*, include additional fees, or profit, or compensation paid to the owner, reducing the business's income.

Experts use their professional judgment to decide whether to use data from one year or multiple years. One could also average the numbers over multiple years to account for business cycles or to smooth out the effect of expenses shifting from one year to the next. The expert should aim to develop an income stream that will repeat itself. Sometimes a single period stream best represents the future; other times, the single period stream is too volatile, as in the case of *In re Marriage of Rosen*, in which the California Court of Appeals applied the method set forth in *In re marriage of Garrity and Bishton*. The *Garrity* decision stated that one should use any period that seems reasonably illustrative of the current rate of earnings as a basis for the calculation.

If the professional belongs to a partnership or a multiowner professional corporation, removing personal expenses can prove complicated. One must review all agreements between the professionals and analyze income and expense accounts to measure the professional's true economic income.

Having measured the professional's economic income, the expert then compares the professional's adjusted income with that of the peer group to estimate a value for goodwill. Some courts (*see Dugan v. Dugan*) have suggested that one should use incomes of employed professionals (i.e., those who work for others under salary and bonus, rather than those who work for themselves) who are similarly educated and experienced, for the comparison. The rationale to this approach is that the employee lacks the goodwill that an owner or partner would have, and a comparison of this group with the subject will establish true excess earnings. Some cases state that the average salaried employee in the same profession does not provide the only valid measure for establishing reasonable compensation under the excess earnings method (*In re marriage of Rosen*).

Establishing reasonable compensation poses a challenge in most cases. Spouses who own businesses will probably claim that high salaries reflect reasonable compensation. However, if one were to ask these spouses what they would pay someone to replace themselves (i.e., operate the business as absentee owners), their answers would likely yield a lesser amount.

Business valuation experts use many terms to describe reasonable compensation. These include *replacement compensation* and *fair value of owner's services*. Regardless of the terminology used, the appraiser wants to convey the cost to replace the owner. This could be the average salaried person or a similarly situated professional.

To properly evaluate the compensation for any particular valuation, one should consider the following areas:

- The employee's role or job description in the company
- The industry in which the business operates
- The location of the business
- The company character and condition
- External compensation comparison
- Company compensation program
- The qualifications necessary to perform the services of the specific job assigned

In the past, available salary data did not allow one to identify the experience level of salaried professionals. Moreover, many salaried professionals are younger, less experienced, or employed by government, with different retirement benefits, working hours, and entrepreneurial incentives than the independent professional whose practice is the subject of the analysis. Factors other than goodwill—such as inborn talent, hard work, and family connections—can cause some individuals to earn more than the averages. The expert should match the job description with the comparison data and understand the source of the underlying data.

Others believe that the proper comparison is with the professional's self-employed peers. James T. Friedman argues that "entrepreneurial drive and acceptance of income uncertainty increase the replacement cost of the professional who is willing to risk self-employment."[10]

Surveys of the earnings of professionals, whether self-employed or employed by professional corporations, can provide appropriate data. Note the date on surveys, which probably occurred at a time other than that of the analysis. Most courts allow updating with relevant price indices.

(d) Capitalization Multiplier.   Last, one must ascertain the proper capitalization multiplier. This multiplier results from a discount rate and the number of years that one can reasonably project excess earnings to continue (given the possibility of retirement, mortality, and ill health), practice risks, clientele and referral source turnover, and other elements. Other factors that affect the capitalization multiplier include past earning power, professional reputation in the community, skill, knowledge, and comparative professional success. One must also consider the nature and duration of the professional's business as a sole practitioner or as a member of a partnership or professional corporation to which the professional has made a proprietary contribution (*Lopez*). *In re Marriage of Rives* required consideration of the professional's (a beekeeper) expressed desire to retire, coupled with his age. There can also be other considerations regarding retirement, such as mandatory retirement for partners in large law and accounting firms.

Few guidelines or empirical bases point to a proper capitalization multiplier. A multiplier of five represents the maximum rate for professional goodwill in most cases. Valuing professional goodwill requires a financial expert's skills, training, and qualitative judgment. One court stated that "for goodwill to be found, … competent, informed and *expert* testimony should be offered to establish that the value of the personal services is less than the net income of the practice" (emphasis added).[11]

Some jurisdictions do not recognize professional goodwill in marital dissolutions. Those jurisdictions prefer to compensate the other spouse, when appropriate, with spousal support. Examples of these cases are *Depner, Matter of Marriage of Fleege, Holbrook v. Holbrook*, and *Powell v. Powell*. When using spousal support, as opposed to valuation in a property division, the spousal support terminates upon the death of the recipient. This could happen on the day after the divorce, and the recipient's estate (beneficiaries) would receive little or no proceeds from the divorce as a result. Certainly, life insurance to secure the support would be wise, but it is not always attainable. A court-ordered spousal support (the same with child support) obligation (even if assigned to a governmental agency) is not dischargeable in bankruptcy.[12]

Wisconsin appears to have changed its position in *In re Peerenboom*, in which the court found that goodwill subject to division, if it exists, has value, and, most importantly, is salable. Oklahoma remains on the other side, preferring the use of support rather than valuing professional goodwill (*Travis v. Travis*).

(e) Going-Concern Value. In some cases, experts must measure a practice's going-concern value. As Section 34.2 explains, going-concern value equals "the amount by which the value of the assets as a whole, assembled together for the conduct of a business, exceeds the aggregate value of the separate items of property" (*Sharp*), which is accounting goodwill. Several courts have suggested that such a value would, at a minimum, equal startup costs. To calculate such costs involves pricing a list of costs typically incurred in starting a professional practice. This list can be simple but should include the following:

1. Value of investigating, negotiating for, and leasing the office space the professional uses, so long as the existing lease has some reasonable term before expiration
2. Value of installing telephones and other specialized equipment, together with the cost of moving furniture, equipment, library, and the like to the occupied space
3. Replacement cost of specialized equipment
4. Value of stationery, other paper goods, and supplies normally on hand at any time
5. Value of hiring and training support staff
6. Value of current client/patient files

The preceding does not include the economic value of a below-market lease, but the valuation should treat it as a separate item. The net value of tangible practice assets represents another marital asset sometimes considered separately from goodwill in the marital estate. If so, eliminate the replacement cost of specialized equipment (item 3) from the list.

34.5 BEYOND GOODWILL

A discussion of professional goodwill should include members of large professional organizations, athletes, celebrities, and business leaders, as well as the interest of a spouse in a professional degree and license.

To find professional goodwill, current case law requires self-employment or a proprietary interest in a professional corporation. Others outside this narrow category may also have goodwill.

Some business community members and sports figures command compensation levels far greater than those of their peers and are not charged with a measure of goodwill upon marital dissolution. Why does this double standard seem to exist? It appears to flow, not from any concept of superior earnings, but rather from the individual's ability to control his or her destiny. If a board of directors or a sports-related injury can terminate an individual's compensation, no court has, to date, found goodwill to exist. The individual's lack of control appears to be the reason. In the California case of *Dubrow v. McTiernan*, the majority concluded that the trial court erred in finding there was $1.5 million of goodwill in husbands practice or career as a motion picture director. The majority opined that a professional individual such as McTiernan may not possess goodwill without having a "business," apparently providing the marital goodwill concept with a set of new elements.

Even though the courts in most of these cases did not find goodwill, we present them here because these issues arise in parallel to the professional's goodwill issues in family law, and the concepts for measuring them parallel the issues for measuring goodwill.

(a) Large-Practice Goodwill.   Consider the professional goodwill of members of large professional organizations, such as an international accounting firm. Some experts make a threshold inquiry as to whether the professional occupies a position in the organization that lends itself to a finding of goodwill.

The argument regarding a lack of control over income might apply to members of large legal, accounting, architectural, and similar firms that operate more like corporations than like small professional organizations. Although each member of the firm has some proprietary interest in the entity's net assets, these interests are often miniscule percentages—frequently less than 1 percent and sometimes much less. This ownership interest resembles that of any shareholder of a company with stock listed on a national exchange: the right to vote but insufficient shares to affect the outcome.

Some courts have recognized the absence of professional goodwill in this situation. In *In re Marriage of Slivka*, the appellate court found substantial evidence to support the trial court's holding that the husband's partnership interest carried no goodwill value. The husband was a partner in the Southern California Permanente Group that provided medical services, under contract, to the Kaiser Foundation Health Plan, Inc. The trial court found that, even though he was a partner, his situation most resembled that of an employee who has no ownership interest and who receives pay for services rendered (*see also In re Marriage of Aufmuth*). Further, in *Iredale & Cates*, the courts valued a small interest in a large law firm at the capital account value—the partner's share of contributed capital and retained earnings—but excluding accounts receivable, work in progress and goodwill of the firm based on the fact that the partner-spouse never acquired an interest in those assets. However, the court found that there was a value to the person's personal goodwill.

(b) Athletes, Celebrities, and Business Executives.   Some courts have discussed the goodwill accruing to professional athletes, entertainment celebrities, and titans of the business world. A 1989 appellate case, *Piscopo v. Piscopo*, affirmed a finding that marital property included celebrity goodwill (*see also Golub v. Golub*).

Elkus v. Elkus dealt with celebrity status constituting marital property. Frederica von Stade Elkus had a successful opera career, to which her husband contributed by being her voice coach and caring for their young children while Frederica became a celebrated artist with the Metropolitan Opera. The appreciation—her ability to command high fees for work—became marital property subject to division. The appellate decision of *Elkus v. Elkus* pursued the concept that celebrity developed during marriage is a marital asset subject to division. During the marriage, Frederica von Stade's annual earnings increased from $2,250 to $621,878.

The appellate court sent the case back to the trial court for a finding as to the value of the marital asset.

In a case reported in the *The Wall Street Journal*, a New York Supreme Court (trial court) judge ordered former New York Jets star, Mark Gastineau, to pay to his ex-wife one-third of the 1988 salary he forfeited to spend more time with his then fiancée, actress Brigit Nielsen.[13] The court found that Gastineau had wasted a substantial marital asset.

Because of their reputations, possibly earned during marriage, substantial income can flow from the sale of celebrities' likenesses and endorsements. Is this income stream an asset divisible upon marital dissolution? What about royalties from an autobiography written post separation but marketable as a result of a reputation built during the marriage? What about security brokers who receive large bonuses when moving from one firm to another—is this a measure of employee goodwill? A valuation expert facing this issue should become familiar with the discussion in "Community Property Interests in the Right of Publicity: Fame and/or Fortune," an article published by the *UCLA Law Review*.[14] A similar question arises with respect to golden parachutes awarded after separation but resulting from efforts expended during the marriage. These and similar situations inevitably will come before appellate courts. The vexing valuation problems may explain why no reported case exists. One would think that, given the great risk associated with many of these occupations, courts would approve only conservative capitalization multipliers.

(c) Professional Education and Licenses.   Some cases have required valuation of professional education and licenses. This area, like so many in the domestic relations arena, changes often. The reader will find an excellent discourse on this subject in "When a Lawyer Divorces" by Skoloff and Orenstein.[15] Another good source is the annual survey published in the *Family Law Quarterly* entitled "Family Law in the Fifty States," which analyzes current thinking in the various courts.[16]

Frequently, a working spouse supports the family while the other spouse pursues an educational program or professional training, and the marriage dissolves prior to any meaningful economic benefit to the family. Here, the courts, charged with arriving at an equitable result, find themselves in a difficult situation. Little or no marital property exists to divide: understandably, the courts until the 1950s rejected the valuation of such intangible and esoteric assets as an education. The courts have considered lump-sum alimony or spousal support reasonable recompense (*Prosser v. Prosser* and *Daniels v. Daniels*). The leading case is *In re Marriage of Graham*, in which the court found that

> An educational degree, such as an M.B.A., is simply not encompassed even by the broad views of the concept of "property." It does not have an exchange value or any objective transferable value on an open market. It is personal to the holder. It terminates on the death of the holder and is not inheritable. It cannot be assigned, sold, transferred, conveyed or pledged. An advanced degree is a cumulative product of many years of previous education combined with diligence and hard work. It may not be acquired by the mere expenditure of money. In our view, it has none of the attributes of property in the usual sense of that term.[17]

This major case has been followed by *Archer v. Archer, Helm v. Helm, Hodge v. Hodge, In re Marriage of Horstmann, Mahoney v. Mahoney, Stevens v. Stevens, DeWitt v. DeWitt, Simmons v. Simmons,* and *In re Marriage of Lee.*

California has codified the issue in the form of a reimbursement. Family Code Section 2641 has delinated the amounts, the time periods related to such a reimbursement, and the conditions upon which reimbursement would be made. Those cases, in other state jurisdictions, with no such enjoyment have compelled the courts to find some value to the contribution one spouse made to the professional education of the other: *Greer v. Greer, Moss v. Moss, In re Marriage of Horstmann, In re Marriage of Rubenstein, Van Bussum v. Van Bussum,* and *Drapek v. Drapek.*

Finally, in 1979, the courts started to recognize professional education as marital property: *Inman v. Inman, Hubbard v. Hubbard, Wisner v. Wisner,* and *In re Marriage of Lundberg.*

Because of that court's high standing in the area of equitable distribution, the New Jersey 1978 decision in *Mahoney v. Mahoney*—which held that a professional education was not property to be divided but instead required a reimbursement of costs incurred in obtaining the degree to the working spouse—became an important stepping stone. The court, quoting *DeWitt,* reasoned that despite the professional education, the recipient might not choose to practice the profession, may fail at it, or may not practice it successfully. In other words, the degree holder may never exploit the value of the education and training. (Compare with goodwill that its owner may never realize for a variety of reasons such as lack of salability, disability, or death.) Because of the risks involved and to avoid the costs of continued jurisdiction in these cases, the court decided against finding a property right subject to distribution. For a contrary holding, *see Cronin v. Cronin.*

Mahoney gave rise to a California case, *In re Marriage of Sullivan,* which concluded, as did *Mahoney* and *Todd,* that a license or degree was not an asset. Mrs. Sullivan worked and had a child while her husband attended medical school and completed his internship and residency. They separated just prior to his commencing practice. Sullivan was appealed to the California Supreme Court, which asked the legislature for guidance. The result was California Civil Code § 4800.3 (now Family Code § 2641), which provided for, under proper circumstances, reimbursement to the community for the following:

- Community contributions to education or training
- Interest at the legal rate
- Any loan taken out during marriage, the proceeds of which were used for education or training

The Supreme Court remanded the case to the trial court for determinations in accordance with the newly enacted code section.

In *Woodworth v. Woodworth,* the appellate court in Michigan stated, however, that a law degree is an asset, as is a medical license in New York (*O'Brien v. O'Brien*) and North Carolina (*Geer v. Geer*).

(d) Not-to-Compete Covenants.   A new line of cases has developed involving the marital interest in a covenant not to compete arising from the sale of a business.

These cases include, *In re Marriage of Monoghan, Ellerbe v. Ellerbe*, and *Berger v. Berger*. For commentary on this subject, *see* the article "New Valuation Tool for Professional Licenses."[18]

34.6   THE DOUBLE DIP

Valuation experts worry about double counting, wherein the courts use the total value of the professional practice in both dividing the marital assets and using the total income therefrom as a measure of the supporting spouse's ability to pay spousal support.

In Illinois, the appellate court reversed the trial court's finding of $117,000 medical practice goodwill because it resulted in a double count of future income, for asset as well as for support purposes (*see Head v. Head*).

Income components from a typical professional practice include the following:

A. Normal earnings (average earnings of similarly educated and experienced practitioners)
B. Excess earnings (a basis for goodwill)
C. Investment earnings (earnings on employment of invested capital)

In assessing the supporting spouse's ability to pay support, courts look to the total earnings, A, B, and C. Supporting spouses argue that they pay the benefits of components B and C in the division of the marital property when the court considers goodwill and invested capital as components of marital property. They claim that under these conditions, counting all the income in computing spousal support payments double-counts the benefits of the goodwill and the invested capital.

34.7   CONCLUSION

Professional goodwill, its existence and value, will generate controversy as long as divorces occur. Courts will struggle to be equitable when valuing marital property and setting support levels. The financial expert can instruct the courts as to the current thinking regarding the existence and value of professional goodwill, both in equitable distribution and in community property jurisdictions.

APPENDIX:
SOURCES OF INFORMATION
REGARDING PROFESSIONAL
PRACTICES AND GOODWILL

Law Practices

Altman & Weil Annual Survey

P.O. Box 472

Ardmore, PA 19003

The American Lawyer

American Lawyer Media, Inc.

600 Third Avenue

New York, NY 10016

National Law Journal

111 Eighth Avenue

New York, NY 10011

Local Bar Associations

Occasionally state or local bar associations will conduct surveys of their members. These can be most useful because the major surveys are broad based in terms of geographical area.

Accounting Practices

State Societies: A number of the major state societies conduct annual surveys. These are frequently broken down into smaller geographical areas. State society addresses can be obtained from the AICPA.

Medical Practices

American Medical Association Annual Survey

Order Department OP22817

P.O. Box 10946

Chicago, IL 60610-0946

Medical Economics

Box 55

Oradell, NJ 07649

This biweekly publication not only conducts an annual survey and publishes the results in a September issue, it also reports during the year on other financial factors of practices, occasionally dealing with specialties. This publication reports on specialties more extensively than does the AMA.
Local Medical Societies: Local societies may also have useful survey material.

Dental Practices

American Dental Association Annual Surveys

211 E. Chicago Ave.

Chicago, IL 60611

The ADA has several publications that can be helpful in valuing dental practices.

Local Dental Societies

Check for publications or surveys conducted by local groups.

Architectural Practices

Local AAA Chapters: State or local chapters occasionally perform salary surveys of their members.

Engineering Practices

Associated General Contractors of America Annual Survey

1957 "E" Street, N.W.

Washington, DC 20006

GENERAL MATERIAL

Davis, Muller. "Valuation of Professional Practices in Dissolution Cases." *Illinois Bar Journal 74* (Sept. 1985). Springfield, IL: Illinois Bar Association.

Dlugatch, H.E., and H. Olds. "Goodwill Determination in Professional Practice Evaluation—Pursuant to a Marriage Dissolution." *Glendale Law Review 4* (1982). Glendale, CA: Glendale University College of Law.

Gerhardt, C.D. "Putting a Value on a Medical Practice." *Family Advocate* 17 (Summer 1984). Section of Family Law. Chicago: American Bar Association.

Goodwill, American Jurisprudence. Vol. 5. *Proof of Facts Annotated.* San Francisco: Bancroft-Whitney Company 1960.

Habeeb, W.R. "Accountability for Goodwill of Professional Practice in Action Arising from Divorce or Separation." *American Law Reports*, 52 (1973): 1344. Rochester, NY: The Lawyers Cooperative Publishing Company.

Hempstead, J.E. "Putting a Value on a Law Practice," *Family Advocate* 17 (Summer 1984). Section of Family Law. Chicago: American Bar Association.

Miod, Donald. "The Double Dip in Valuing Goodwill in Divorce." *CPA Litigation Service Counselor.* New York: Harcourt Brace, 1998.

Pratt, S. *Valuing Small Business and Professional Practices.* Homewood, IL: Dow Jones-Irwin, 1986, 483.

NOTES

1. J. Story, *Commentaries on the Law of Partnership*, 6th ed. (1868), § 99, 170.
2. *Cruttwell v. Lye*, 34 Eng. Rep. 129 (Ch. 1810).
3. California Business and Professions Code, § 4400.
4. Accounting Principals Board Opinion 17, ¶ 24.
5. *Mueller v. Mueller*, 144 Cal. App. 2d 245, 301 P.2d 90 (1956).
6. *Nail v. Nail*, 486 S.W.2d 761 (S. Ct. Tex. 1972).
7. Developing a profile of potential buyers, however, can be part of a method to assess the value for dissolution purposes
8. Santa Clara County Dental Society, *A Guide for Your Practice.* (Santa Clara County Dental Society, 1986).
9. *See,* for example, Revenue Ruling 68–609, 1968–2 Cum. Bull. 327 as one authoritative source.
10. James. T. Friedman, "Professional Practice Goodwill: An Abused Value Concept," *Journal of the American Academy of Matrimonial Law* 2 (1986): 26.
11. *Levy v. Levy*, 164 N.J. Super. 542, 397 A2d 374 (1978)
12. 11 U.S.C. § 523(a)(5).
13. *The Wall Street Journal*, July 2, 1991.
14. "Community Property Interests in the Right of Publicity: Fame and/or Fortune," *UCLA Law Review* 25 (1978).
15. Gary N. Skoloff and Thedore P. Orenstein, *When a Lawyer Divorces* (New York: American Bar Association, 1986).
16. "Family Law in the Fifty States," *Family Law Quarterly.*
17. *In re Marriage of Graham*, 194 Colo. 429, 574 P.2d 75 (1978).
18. "New Valuation Tool for Professional Licenses," *New York Law Journal*, July 9, 1999.

LIST OF CASES

Archer v. Archer, 303 Md. 347, 493, A.2d 1074 (1985)

In re Marriage of Asbury, 144 Cal. App. 3d 918, 193 Cal. Rptr. 562 (1983)

In re Marriage of Aufmuth, 89 Cal. App. 3d 446, 152 Cal. Rptr. 668 (1979)

Austin v. Austin, 619 S.W.2d 290 (Tex. App. 1981)

Berger v. Berger, 648 N.E.2d 378 (Ind. Ct. App. 1995)

Closson v. Closson, 30 Wyo. 1, 215 P. 485 (1923)

Cox v. Cox, 108 N.M. 598, 775 P.2d 1315 (Ct. App. 1989)

Cronin v. Cronin, 131 Misc. 2d 879, 502 N.Y.S.2d 368 (1986)

Cruttwell v. Lye, 34 Eng. Rep. 129 (Ch. 1810)

Daniels v. Daniels, 185 N.E.2d 773 (Ohio App. 1961)

Depner v. Depner, 478 So. 2d 532 (La. App. 1985)

DeWitt v. DeWitt, 98 Wisc. 2d 44, 296 N.W.2d 761 (1980)

Dubrow v. McTiernan, 133 Cal App 4th 1090; 35 Cal Rptr. 3d 287

Drapek v. Drapek, 399 Mass. 240, 503 N.E.2d 946 (1987)

Dugan v. Dugan, 92 N.J. 423, 457 A.2d 1 (1983)

Elkus v. Elkus, 572 N.Y.S.2d 901 (App Div. 1991)

Ellerbe v. Ellerbe, 323 S.C. App. 283, 473 S.E.2d 881 (1996)

In re Marriage of Fenton, 134 Cal. App. 3d 451, 184 Cal. Rptr. 597 (1982)

Finn v. Finn, 658 S.W.2d 735 (Tex. App. 1983)

Matter of Marriage of Fleege, 91 Wash. 2d 324, 588 P.2d 1136 (1979)

In re Marriage of Fonstein, 17 Cal. 3d 738, 552 P.2d 1169, 131 Cal. Rptr. 873 (1976)

In re Marriage of Fortier, 34 Cal. App. 3d 384, 109 Cal. Rptr. 915 (1973)

In re Marriage of Foster, 42 Cal. App. 3d 577, 117 Cal. Rptr. 49 (1974)

In re Marriage of Garrity and Bishton (1986) 181 Cal. App. 3d 675, 226 Cal. Rptr. 485

Geer v. Geer, 84 N.C. App. 471, 353 S.E.2d 427 (1987)

Geffen v. Moss, 53 Cal. App. 3d 215, 125 Cal. Rptr. 687 (1975)

Golden v. Golden, 270 Cal. App. 2d 401, 75 Cal. Rptr. 735 (1969)

Golub v. Golub, 139 Misc. 2d 440, 527 N.Y.S.2d 946 (1988)

In re Marriage of Graham, 194 Colo. 429, 574 P.2d 75 (1978)

Greer v. Greer, 32 Colo. App. 196, 510 P.2d 905 (1973)

Hanson v. Hanson, 12 Fam. L. Rep. (BNA) 1596 (Mo. Ct. App. W. Dist. 1986)

Head v. Head, 168 Ill. App. 3d 697, 523 N.E.2d 17 (1988)

Helm v. Helm, 289 S.C. 169, 345 S.E.2d 720 (1986)

Hertz v. Hertz, 99 N.M. 320, 657 P.2d 1169 (1983)

Hodge v. Hodge, 337 Pa. Super. 151, 486 A.2d 951 (1984)

Holbrook v. Holbrook, 103 Wis. 2d 327, 309 N.W.2d 343 (1981)

In re Marriage of Horstmann, 263 N.W.2d 885 (Iowa 1978)

Hubbard v. Hubbard, 603 P.2d 747 (Okla. 1979)

Inman v. Inman, 578 S.W.2d 266 (Ky. App. 1979)

Iredale & Cates, 121 Cal.App.4th 321, 16 Cal. Rptr. 3d 505 (2004).

Kaufman v. Kaufman, 7 Va. App. 488, 375 S.E.2d 374 (1988)

Keith v. Keith, 763 S.W.2d 950 Tex. Ct. App. (1989)

In re Marriage of King, 150 Cal. App. 3d 304, 197 Cal. Rptr. 716 (1983)

In re Marriage of Lee, 938 P.2d 650 (Mont. 1997)

Levy v. Levy, 164 N.J. Super. 542, 397 A.2d 374 (1978)

In re Marriage of Lopez, 38 Cal. App. 3d 93, 113 Cal. Rptr. 58 (1974)

In re Marriage of Lukens, 16 Wash. App. 481, 558 P.2d 279 (1976)

In re Marriage of Lundberg, 107 Wis. 2d 1, 318 N.W.2d 918 (1982)

Mahoney v. Mahoney, 91 N.J. 488, 453 A.2d 527 (1982)

Malloy v. Malloy, 761 P.2d 138 (Ariz. 1988)

Mitchell v. Mitchell, 152 Ariz. 317, 732 P.2d 208 (1987)

In re Marriage of Monoghan, 78 Wash. App. 918, 899 P.2d 841 (1995)

In re Marriage of Morris, 588 S.W.2d 39 (Mo. 1979)

Moss v. Moss, 80 Mich. App. 693, 264 N.W.2d 97 (1978)

Mueller v. Mueller, 144 Cal. App. 2d 245, 301 P.2d 90 (1956)

Nail v. Nail, 486 S.W.2d 761 (S. Ct. Tex. 1972)

Nehorayoff v. Nehorayoff, 108 Misc. 2d 311, 437 N.Y.S.2d 584 (1981)

In re Marriage of Nichols, 27 Cal. App. 4th 661, 33 Cal. Rptr. 2d 13 (1994)

CHAPTER 35

MARITAL DISSOLUTION: TRACING AND APPORTIONMENT OF ASSETS

Donald L. Gursey
Donald A. Glenn

CONTENTS

35.1 INTRODUCTION

In marital dissolution (death or divorce), property falls into one of four types:

1. Community (or marital)
2. Separate
3. Both community and separate
4. Quasi-community property

Forensic accountants practicing (with legal counsel) in community property states must often characterize property acquired by a couple during marriage. Property acquired prior to marriage and property acquired by gift or personal efforts during marriage compound this task. Furthermore, each state defines its own method of characterization in its statutes and case law. Consultants must research every characterization-related engagement; the case law addressing the issues discussed in this chapter changes often.

The parties need not classify property until a spouse dies or the couple seeks a divorce. At that time, the ability to create community property ceases. Problems that can arise from classifying property while both parties are alive and still married include creditor rights and the individual's liabilities, tax implications, management and control of property, personal injury proceeds, life insurance, property improvements, and postseparation increases in value.

The following definitions help clarify the nomenclature.

(a) Community Property. Community property, both real and personal, is that which a couple acquires through purchase or personal efforts while married and while domiciled in a community property or marital property state. This broad definition of community property descends from a philosophy explained in Ballinger's "A Treatise on the Property Rights of Husband and Wife under the Community or Financial System":[1]

> The principal which lies at the foundation of the whole system is, that whatever is acquired by the joint efforts of the husband and wife, shall be their common property; the theory of the law being, that the marriage, in respect to the property acquired during its existence, is a community of which each spouse is a member, equally contributing by his or her industry to its prosperity, and possessing an equal right to succeed to the property after its dissolution, in case one survived the other.

(b) Separate Property. This is property acquired through purchase, inheritance, or gift that is not community property, with the exception of quasi-community property (discussed in Section 35.1(c)) or some other form of concurrent ownership between the couple. In some states, separate property from personal efforts begins on the date of separation.

(c) Quasi-Community Property. As defined by California and other states, this is property acquired by a current California resident while a nonresident of that state. The property must qualify as community property in all other aspects. This includes any property exchanged for property previously classified as quasi-community property. For property to classify as quasi-community in a divorce proceeding, the spouses must reside in a state that recognizes quasi-community property, and the moving party must file for divorce in that state's court.

The interpretation of the term *acquired* as it relates to quasi-community property frequently results in litigation and leads to tracing of assets. Property purchased during marriage acquires a character identical to that of the funds that purchased it. Identifying the source of the original funds frequently requires tracing.

(d) Domicile. The domicile issue raises additional questions regarding jurisdiction and ultimately the possible recharacterization of property that a married couple held. Domicile is a legal issue that addresses the individual's residency in terms of both physical presence and the intent to continue living in that particular state. The couple's domicile at the time of purchase dictates which state's laws characterize the property; however, the couple's domicile at the time of a spouse's death or a divorce *could* reclassify the property. Individual state laws define domicile as it affects property that a married couple holds, even when the couple has moved from one community property state to another.

35.2 COMMINGLING, TITLE, TRACING, AND APPORTIONMENT: AN OVERVIEW

Case-driven judicial principles use tracing, commingling, and apportionment to identify the separate or community portion of assets. Courts invoke these principles when they find that simply applying legal presumptions leads to inequitable results.

This overview assumes that one spouse has not given the property in question to the other spouse as either a gift or pursuant to a contractual agreement. Having confirmed this qualification, the forensic accountant must ascertain the character of each property held by the two individuals, regardless of the form of the title and the accompanying presumptions. Ascertaining the source of funds used to purchase the property is called *tracing*.

One spouse usually acquires separate property by exchanging other separate property so that the acquired property retains the original property's character. Likewise, exchanging solely community property for other property would characterize the newly acquired property as community property. When the tracing identifies the source to separate property, the emphasis rests on the original source of the funds rather than the acquisition's timing—the *where* rather than the *when*. Some states, however, do not always allow tracing to the original source to classify community property. Circumstances often obscure part or all of the original source of funds. In such a case, the forensic accountant emphasizes the acquisition's timing—the *when* rather than the *where*.

If the tracing does not identify a separate property source and the purchase occurred during marriage, the court presumes a community property classification. Some states, however, either through statute or case law, allow reimbursement—to the extent of the investment—to the spouse who invested separate property in an asset that is classified as community property.

Separate property mixed with alleged community property creates *commingled property*. Identifying the separate and community portions of this property challenges any forensic accountant. The methods for treating an alleged separate property interest labeled as community property are varied, complicated, and receive different emphases from each state.

States generally hold that the form of title at the time of establishing ownership determines the property's characterization. Many states, however, have case law that considers substance rather than the form of ownership in dividing property. In these states, the burden of proof rests on the party claiming an ownership form that differs from that listed on existing property records. In addition, the states do not uniformly regard the static nature of the property's original characterization. For instance, if property purchased before marriage is encumbered at the time of marriage and community funds reduce the encumbrance during marriage, the property's ownership includes an interest vested in the community, regardless of the title's original form. Improvements made to the separate property from community property funds or community effort can also cloud the classification.

The theory of *apportionment* also offers potential problems in identifying the property's character. This theory recognizes not only separate and community funds or property used for initial purchase but also possible fluctuation in the proportionate separate and community ownership. The apportionment theory adjusts the ownership proportions to reflect separate and community funds used to reduce the original encumbrance; it also changes the proportions to reflect improvements or additions to the original property from either source.

35.3   COMMINGLING: PRESUMPTIONS

Commingling combines community property with separate property during marriage. Basic commingling rules help with the initial characterization of the commingled assets. One generally presumes that when separate and community property have become so extensively commingled that one cannot trace the separate property interest, the alleged separate property interest ceases to exist, thus characterizing the entire commingled property as community property (*Estate of Cudworth; see* List of Cases at the end of the chapter). The basic commingling rule does not apply when the community property component comprises a small part of the total property. In such cases, the courts will deem the entire asset as separate property.

(a) Form of Title.   Although an asset's character becomes set at acquisition, the form of ownership (title) does not prove that an asset is separate or community or quasi-community. Louisiana, Texas, and New Mexico allow the form of ownership at the acquisition date to become static unless law or gift or transmutation changes the title. This holds true regardless of improvements made to the original property and payments made on the original separate property from funds that are not the title holder's separate property. In many jurisdictions, the commingling rules defer to title when the couple has, together, taken title as community property, or if they agreed (in writing or orally) that the asset was community property. Some states require a written agreement.

(b) Proportionate Ownership.   If one can establish (trace) the separate and community property interest, the community property presumption relating to the commingled property usually does not apply, and the established nature of each interest remains intact. This creates an ownership proportionate to the percentage of interest that each different asset used to acquire the asset in question bears to the total asset. Most of the states subscribe to this co-ownership form, but the accountant should check individual state laws. Some states do not allow apportioning of certain types of commingled properties. The accountant must allocate the asset's appreciation and depreciation during ownership to the community property and separate property components.

(c) Gain and Income.   Applying the proportionate ownership interest theory requires knowledge of jurisdictional differences regarding an asset's natural appreciation, its income, its purchase from the income of another proportionately owned asset, and an increase in the asset's value through the community's effort. Most community property states do not agree on changes in a married couple's proportionate ownership of an asset. Also, federal and state tax laws' treatment of income does not agree with community property principles, although state laws usually dictate the community property or separate nature of income for federal tax purposes.

Theoretically, community property states have their own rules regarding community effort and separate property income. In practice, interpreting and applying these rules takes effort. The states provide guidance through case law. Texas, Idaho, and Louisiana create community income from some categories of income generated by separate assets during marriage, whereas other income categories remain as separate property (*Arnold v. Leonard*). The remaining community property states allow income from separate property to retain its separate property character. This *American rule* stems from the 1860 California case, *George v. Ransome*. The 1979 Arizona case, *Cockrill v. Cockrill*, has more recently discussed this theory. The law has given little attention to separate property assets—such as oil, gas, and timber—generating income that some states classify as community but whose principal value decreases during marriage.

Some uniformity exists among the community property states in the assumption that spouses' earnings while married are community property. Consequently, in many jurisdictions, the separate property's increased value attributable to community efforts generates a community interest in the separately owned property. The accounting separates this interest generated by community efforts from any appreciation in the separate property attributed to other causes, such as overall market appreciation or accretion. The community property interest equals the portion of the separate property appreciation attributable to the value of the community efforts relative to the separate property's total value. Section 35.6 discusses specific methods used to apportion the community property interest attributed to community effort in separate property.

35.4 TRACING

Tracing finds its source in case law rather than statutes. Accountants use tracing to define an asset's original character or to separate or partition assets that become combined (commingled) during the marriage. Some community property states do not always permit tracing to identify community property interest in separate property. Tracing, however, is the principal procedure to rebut the presumption that property acquired or held in joint estate during marriage is automatically community property. Accountants frequently use tracing to ascertain the taxability of income items and to distinguish an asset's nature vis-à-vis creditors' claims.

An asset's unmixed character is traceable to the character of the asset used to acquire it. If the tracing process establishes that community assets were used to improve or increase separate property assets, a right of reimbursement often exists, such as that found in California (Civil Code §§ 4800.1 and 4800.2) and Louisiana statutes.

(a) Direct Tracing.   *Direct tracing* establishes the source of an asset by recreating the steps through which the asset progresses to its current ownership form. This includes analyzing sales, additional acquisitions, gifts, and the like. One uses tracing to prove that assets can retain their character as separate assets when they are commingled with, or enhanced by, community property assets. Sufficient separate funds in the commingled account to purchase an asset do not always imply that property acquired is separate. In the California case *Hicks v. Hicks*, the court stated:

> Separate funds do not lose their character as such when commingled with community funds in a bank account so long as the amount thereof can be ascertained. Whether separate funds so deposited continue to be on deposit when a withdrawal is made from such a bank account for the purpose of purchasing specific property, and whether the intention of the drawer is to withdraw such funds therefrom, are questions of fact for determination by the trial court.

To substantiate this claim can require disposition of the separate funds and the other spouse's acknowledgment of a particular form of ownership.

The following lists some simple examples of postmarital acquired property that retain their character as separate property and rebut the community property presumption:

- A parcel of real property acquired in exchange for premarital separate real estate property
- An asset purchased with the funds realized from sale of a premarital asset (separate property)
- An asset received by gift or inheritance by one spouse during the marriage and subsequently sold or exchanged for another asset
- Income from separate property (in those states in which it retains its separate nature) used to purchase an asset during the marriage

These examples illustrate the direct tracing of assets acquired during marriage in which one often overcomes the presumption that characterizes an asset acquired during marriage in a community property state solely as community property. The examples do not include, however, complicating factors such as who holds title, transmutations, gifts between spouses during marriage, or community property created from personal efforts during marriage.

(b) Indirect Tracing.   Indirect tracing, also known as the *family expense method*, tries to offer as proof of a property's character the depletion of another class of property that the spouse held. For example, suppose a former spouse proved that the parties had spent all the community property funds on the family's living expenses. By deduction, the remaining property must consist of a different property class than the dissipated community property and must, therefore, be separate property of one or both spouses. To reiterate, if the court considers earnings as community property and assumes that family living expenses came first from these community earnings that have completely dissipated, then expenditures for assets must have come from separate property. The following discussion occurs in the California case of *See v. See:*

> The presumption (of community property) applies when a husband purchases property during the marriage with funds from an undisclosed or disputed source, such as an account or fund in which he has commingled his separate funds with community funds. (*Estate of Neilson* at 742). He may trace the source of the property to his separate funds and overcome the presumption with evidence that community expenses exceeded community income at the time of acquisition. If he proves that at that time

all community income was exhausted by family expenses, he establishes that the property was purchased with separate funds. (*Estate of Neilson*, supra, at p. 742; *Thomasset v. Thomasset* at 127). Only when, through no fault of the husband, it is not possible to ascertain the balance of income and expenditures at the time property was acquired, can recapitulation of the total community expenses and income throughout the marriage be used to establish the character of the property.

In *See*, at p. 785, the court made a statement regarding a theory of reimbursement for community expenses paid from separate property:

> A husband who elects to use his separate property instead of community property to meet community expenses cannot claim reimbursement. In the absence of an agreement to the contrary, the use of his separate property by a husband for community purposes is a gift to the community.

Beam v. Bank of America further limits the scope set forth in *See* to those circumstances in which the accounting can compare total family living expenses with total community income. The court in *Beam* stated that when excess community income was available but commingled with separate income, assets purchased with those commingled funds usually are community assets.

(c) Commingled Bank Accounts. In addition to indirectly tracing funds through the community expense method, practitioners use other methods:

- A chronological schedule of the deposits and withdrawals from the fund. This system applies the first-in, first-out cost flow assumption to the funds analyzed.
- The spouse who does not control the funds traces specific deposits to the commingled account. This could set forth a separate property interest in the funds themselves.
- The spouse without control of the funds establishes a claim against them by tracing funds directly through the account to the purchased assets. This often proves a separate ownership interest in the asset.

(d) Credit Purchases. One should examine borrower collateral, lender intention, and the source of payments to establish separate or community property interests in an asset purchased using credit during marriage. As with other tracing methods, the community property jurisdictions exhibit little consistency in treating such acquisitions. Neither the signatures on the loan documents nor the manner in which the parties hold title always conclusively establish separate versus community ownership.

One complication occurs when separate property provides the down payment for an asset. The collateral used to secure the credit is separate property, but the loan payments come from community property funds. Some community property states do not recognize the payments made toward reducing the debt as establishing a community property interest but look solely to the assets' characterization when the original purchase occurred. Some of the more enlightened community property states, however, have used apportionment in these situations.

Another question arises when the parties refinance separate property with a joint loan and invest the borrowed proceeds in other property. California resolved this question in *Walrath v. Walrath* wherein the court decided that refinanced proceeds from separate property from a joint loan retained their separate character when used to acquire other property.

35.5   TRANSMUTATIONS

Transmutations are voluntary gift-related or contractual changes in the form of property ownership between spouses. Such changes can apply to current assets or to future assets such as earnings. A transmutation of earnings for community property purposes does not change the federal tax treatment of those earnings (*Lucas v. Earl*). Transmutations can change separate property of one spouse to separate property of the other spouse, separate property to community property, and community property to separate property of either or both spouses. In spite of the clarity of this principle, the individual community property jurisdictions have inconsistently interpreted and imposed restraints on transmutations. The practitioner needs to know the laws of each community property state as they apply to the transmutations doctrine.

35.6   APPORTIONMENT

The *inception-of-title doctrine* states that the property's title at acquisition does not change to reflect additional contributions or improvements made after the purchase. This underlying doctrine often forces the courts to consider the extensive commingling of separate and community funds used to purchase an asset or make payments on credit. Frequently, courts have had to take a position regarding improvements made to separate property assets through community efforts (service).

One must distinguish between apportionment and the right to reimbursement. When property is acquired from both community and separate property, the acquired property's ownership is proportionate. This *rule of apportionment* creates a dual ownership that fluctuates during marriage. Conversely, the *rule of reimbursement* dictates that when improvements are made from one categorized property (e.g., community property) to property categorized in another manner (e.g., separate property), the party or parties making the improvements have entitlement to reimbursement of their funds so used.

(a) Definition.   Apportionment establishes ownership by applying the percentage that the separate and community investments bear to the total investment. For example, if tracing established that the husband had $20,000 of separate property, the wife had $10,000 of separate property, and the community had excess receipts over expenses of $20,000, and all these funds were invested in an asset, the property would be owned as follows:

Husband's separate property	$20,000	40%
Wife's separate property	10,000	20
Community property	20,000	40
Total investment	$50,000	100%

Any additions to the investment after the initial purchase would alter the ownership percentages accordingly.

Litigation related to marital dissolution often occurs when one spouse had separate property investments or a separate property business before marriage and the business or property value increased during marriage through the efforts of either or both spouses. Under these circumstances, some courts try to establish a method of carving out a portion of the value increase for which the community should receive compensation for the services rendered. The major issue is in measuring the value or worth of the community services versus the inherent increase in the investments or business value. The courts in community property states have addressed this problem, with findings varying not only among the states but also within each state. California has had numerous cases that deal with apportionment.

Two landmark California cases continue to set precedent both within and outside the state: *Pereira v. Pereira* and *Van Camp v. Van Camp*. In *Pereira*, the court decided "to allocate a fair return on the (husband's separate property) investment (as separate income) and to allocate any excess to the community property as arising from the husband's efforts" (But, *see Estate of Neilson* at p. 740 for "natural enhancement," which may remain separate). This emphasized community labor's primary importance for the separate property's growth during marriage. Conversely, in *Van Camp*, the court concentrated on the original capital and its natural growth as the major factor in the growth of the separate business. Thus, assuming the community property received fair compensation for the working spouse's efforts, all appreciation would be separate.

As stated in *Tassi v. Tassi*, the court wanted "to determine the reasonable value of the husband's services ... allocate that amount as community property, and treat the balance as separate property attributable to the normal earnings of the [separate estate]." Although the courts rely heavily on the *Pereira* and *Van Camp* formulas, even in California they need not use either formula. The courts of New Mexico, Nevada, and Arizona regularly and uniformly apply the formulas specified in these cases. The following discussion applies the *Pereira* and *Van Camp* rules to a hypothetical scenario.

(b) Scenario: *Pereira* and *Van Camp*.   Suppose the husband had a separate property corporation prior to marriage, with a value on the wedding date of $50,000. The marriage lasted seven years, and at the separation date the business was worth $100,000. The husband had worked full-time in this business during the marriage and received an annual salary of $60,000. In the divorce proceedings, the wife includes in her alleged community property a portion of the business value increase during the marriage, claiming that the husband's labors in his business during the marriage were community property.

(i) The Pereira *Rule.*   The theory behind the *Pereira* rule rests on a principle of reimbursements and not on the estimated fair value of the husband's services to the separate property business.[2] Accordingly, the courts would apply a fair rate of return to the value of the husband's separate property business at the time of marriage without ascertaining whether the husband's salary during marriage had adequately compensated the community. Assuming a 6 percent simple interest rate of return on the corporation, the court would allocate as the husband's separate property $21,000 (= 7 × .06 × $50,000) of the $50,000 value increase during

marriage. The remaining appreciation of $29,000 would be attributable to the community efforts of the husband in the business during the marriage. The wife would receive one-half of this $29,000 community property interest, or $14,500.

(ii) The Van Camp *Rule.*   Under the *Van Camp* rule, the court would place a reasonable or adequate compensation test on the husband's services to the corporation during marriage. If the husband received adequate compensation during marriage or did not contribute highly specialized skills to the business, the rule allocates all of the corporation's growth to the separate property investment in the business. The community would have no interest in the increase in value during marriage.

(c) Alternatives under the *Van Camp* Rule

(i) Alternative 1.   Assume that the court finds that the husband should have received an average annual compensation of $65,000. Because he received an average annual salary of $60,000, an underpayment of $5,000 per year for seven years, or $35,000, occurred. A court applying the *Van Camp* rule—and believing that the husband could control his salary level—could allocate the $35,000 salary underpayment to community property. The wife's share would be one-half of the $35,000, or $17,500. The husband would claim as separate property $15,000 (= $50,000 − $35,000) of the corporation's appreciation during marriage. This approach would allocate $14,000 less in separate property appreciation to the husband than he would have received under the *Pereira* rule.

(ii) Alternative 2.   Assume that the court finds that the husband should have received an average annual salary of only $40,000. Theoretically, the community received overcompensation for the seven years of marriage of $140,000. Because the community received more than adequate compensation for services during marriage, the growth in the business resulted from the husband's separate property investment. No precedent exists, however, for the separate property holder to claim reimbursement from the community for this excess compensation.

Neither Texas nor Washington has adopted these apportionment principles, derived from the landmark California cases. Texas has chosen a system that individually categorizes income and gain items. These categories have evolved from case law. Once a court has categorized the items, the Texas courts make an all-or-nothing determination as to rights of ownership. This approach ignores apportionment, although *Jensen v. Jensen* sets forth the following theory of reimbursement:

> The reimbursement theory more nearly affords justice to both the community and separate estates. This theory requires adoption of the rule that the community will be reimbursed for the value of time and effort expended by either or both spouses to enhance the separate estate of either, other than that reasonably necessary to manage and preserve the separate estate in the form of salary, bonus, dividends and other fringe benefits, these items being community property when received.

Washington also does not apply the rules of apportionment unless the spouses have previously agreed to do so. If the separate property business is incorporated, Washington has ruled that the corporation's earnings remain separate property, except for the salary paid to the working spouse or spouses (*Pollock v. Pollock*).

(d) Apportionment: Separate Debt Paid with Community Funds.   Frequently, a spouse brings to the marriage separate property with an accompanying

encumbrance. Payments made on this debt during the marriage can come from the title holder's separate funds or from community funds. California case law has developed formulas that approach this situation in a commonsense manner.

In *In re Marriage of Moore*, the wife purchased a residence shortly before marriage. The mortgage was paid both from her separate funds and from community funds during the marriage. To establish the community interest in the wife's separate property residence, the California Supreme Court applied the following formula:

$$\frac{\text{Mortgage } Principal \text{ Payments Made from Community Property}}{} \div \text{Total Purchase Price} = \frac{\text{Community Percentage}}{}$$

The community interest in appreciation is the appreciation in the asset's value multiplied by the percentage of community interest as measured by this formula. This community interest in the asset's appreciation, when added to the community principal payments made (the numerator), results in the total community property value in the separate property assets. This computation ignores interest payments, taxes, and any maintenance payments that the community made.

The 1982 case *In Re Marriage of Marsden* clarified the formula developed in *Moore*, in which the wife acquired the separate property so soon before the marriage that its precedential value was unclear. In *Marsden*, the court applied the formula's community interest percentage only to the appreciation during marriage and awarded all appreciation before the marriage to the purchaser spouse's separate property interest.

35.7 REIMBURSEMENT

Three situations cause one spouse to seek reimbursement from the other:

1. The use of separate property to improve community property
2. The use of community property to improve separate property
3. The use of one spouse's separate property to improve the other spouse's separate property

Because most community property states lean toward community property status of assets, most cases treat the use of separate property to improve community property as a gift to the community. In 1983, amid much uncertainty and controversy, California adopted Civil Code § 4800.2. This statute provides for reimbursement for any separate property expenditures made to acquire or improve a community property during marriage. The statute does not provide for interest or appreciation on this separate property. The cases have further defined several aspects of this statute. The controversy has centered around the timing of the rule's application. One must research the current status of the section before applying the general rule. In the future, other community property states may reconsider reimbursement as a result of this California legislation.

Improving the separate property of one spouse with the separate property of the other falls outside the general community property rules. A transmutation of this nature has a strong presumption of being a gift in most community property states. One spouse's use of community funds to improve his or her separate property falls under the reimbursement and apportionment theories.

35.8 CONCLUSION

State law identifies the principles to apply when an issue exists as to the property's character. In most states that have apportionment, commingling, and tracing issues, counsel must prove the property's character based on the principles that support the clients' contentions, whereas the duty to maintain meticulous books and records rests with the litigant claiming separate property.

The accountant has to apply the principles underlying state law and use the books and records of the litigants to help counsel establish or rebut a claim of apportionment, commingling, or any form of transmutation. Whatever the result, no single method applies to every case.

NOTES

1. R. A. Ballinger, *Ballinger on Community Property* (San Francisco: BancroftWhitney, 1985).
2. The *Pereira* case provided for a simple interest rate of return pursuant to stipulation by the parties. Presently, the application of either a simple or a compound rate is up to the court's discretion. Either method may be used to obtain justice.

LIST OF CASES

Arnold v. Leonard, 114 Tex. 535, 273 S.W. 799 (1925)
Beam v. Bank of America, 6 Cal. 3d 12, 490 P.2d 257, 98 Cal. Rptr. 137 (1971)
Cockrill v. Cockrill, 124 Ariz. 50, 601 P.2d 1334 (1979)
Estate of Cudworth, 133 Cal. 462, 65 P. 1041 (1901)
George v. Ransom, 15 Cal. 322 (1860)
Hicks v. Hicks, 211 Cal. App. 2d 144, 27 Cal. Rptr. 307 (1962)
Jensen v. Jensen, 655 S.W.2d 107 (Tex. 1984)
Lucas v. Earl, 281 U.S. Ill (1930)
In re Marriage of Marsden, 133 Cal. App. 3d 426, 181 Cal. Rptr. 910 (1982)
In re Marriage of Moore, 28 Cal. 3d 366, 615 P.2d 208, 168 Cal. Rptr. 662 (1980)
Estate of Neilson, 57 Cal. 2d 733, 371 P.2d 745, 22 Cal. Rptr. 1 (1962)
Pereira v. Pereira, 156 Cal. 1, 103 P. 488 (1909)
Pollock v. Pollock, 7 Wash. App. 394, 499 P.2d 231 (1972)
See v. See, 64 Cal. 2d 778, 415 P.2d 776, 51 Cal. Rptr. 888 (1966)
Tassi v. Tassi, 160 Cal. App. 2d 680, 325 P.2d 872 (1958)
Thomasset v. Thomasset, 122 Cal. App. 2d 116, 264 P.2d 626 (1953)
Van Camp v. Van Camp, 53 Cal. App. 17, 199 P. 885 (1921)
In re Marriage of Walrath, 17 Cal. 4th 907, 72 Cal. Rptr. 2d 856, 952 P.2d 1124 (1988)

CHAPTER 36

MARITAL DISSOLUTION: TAX CONSIDERATIONS

Donald L. Gursey
Roseanna L. Purzycki
Brandi N. Brethour

CONTENTS

36.1   INTRODUCTION

Taxpayers must classify transfers between spouses and former spouses into one of four categories:

1. Alimony
2. Child support
3. Property settlement
4. Gift

Internal Revenue Code (IRC or the Code) § 1041 governs the tax treatment of property settlements, and IRC §§ 71 and 215 govern the tax treatment of alimony. Alimony payments can be either taxable or nontaxable. Child support is defined in IRC § 71(c) and is nontaxable. The different tax treatments make it essential to identify and properly classify transfers between spouses. The taxpayer should classify a transfer by first applying the criteria for alimony and child support payments. If a payment does not qualify as alimony or child support, it is either a property settlement or a gift.

36.2   ALIMONY

(a) Overview.   IRC § 71 requires an individual to include in gross income all payments received as alimony or separate maintenance. Accordingly, IRC § 215 allows the payor to deduct the payments that the recipient has included in gross income.[1] The support payments must meet six general requirements to qualify as alimony.

(i) Payments Must Be Obligatory.   A divorce or separation instrument must require the payments. The statute defines three classes of such instruments: (1) a decree of divorce or separate maintenance or a written instrument incident to such a decree, (2) a written separation agreement, or (3) a decree requiring a spouse to pay for the other spouse's support or maintenance.[2] Voluntary payments never qualify as alimony. Furthermore, the existence of a qualified written instrument does not guarantee deductibility. The instrument must specify the amount and timing of the payments. Courts can classify premature alimony payments as voluntary.[3]

(ii) Payments Must Terminate at the Death of the Recipient Spouse.   Prior law required a divorce or separation instrument to expressly state "there is no liability for any period after the death of the recipient spouse to continue to make any payments

which would otherwise qualify as alimony or separate maintenance."[4] However, the Tax Reform Act of 1986 (TRA) modified this provision so that the instrument need not expressly state the end of liability if the state law provides for termination of spousal support at the recipient's death. Payments initiated at or continuing after the recipient's death would also violate the termination requirement.

If a provision for post-death payments exists, the individuals must recharacterize a similar payment amount in the current alimony as nontaxable to the recipient and nondeductible to the payor.[5] For example, assume an instrument requires the husband to pay his former wife alimony of $40,000 per year. The same instrument also provides that, upon the wife's death, the husband must pay $15,000 per year into a trust for the future benefit of their children. Under these circumstances, the husband must treat $15,000 of the $40,000 annual alimony payments as nondeductible payments because the requirement to make the $15,000 payment does not terminate at the wife's death.

(iii) Payments Must Be Made in Cash to or on Behalf of the Recipient Spouse. The payor must make alimony payments in cash to deduct them. Transfers of property do not qualify as alimony under IRC §§ 71 and 215. Payments made pursuant to a divorce decree or written agreement do not have to be made directly to the recipient or specifically for the recipient's support but must be "on behalf of the recipient." Thus, tuition, rent, mortgage, tax liabilities, and attorney fees paid by the payor for the recipient's benefit may qualify as deductible alimony.[6] Section 36.8(d) of this chapter discusses treatment of payments for the marital residence as alimony.

(iv) Payments Must Not Be Designated Nondeductible. The parties can designate all or a portion of the spousal support payments as not deductible by the payor and not includible by the recipient in computing taxable income. Thus, the parties can negotiate their respective tax burdens. This can prove useful in the right economic circumstances. For example, consider a situation in which the support recipient is in a high tax bracket and the payor has a large net operating loss carryforward and will receive no tax benefit from the alimony deduction. To net a given amount of cash flow, the recipient requires a higher alimony payment if it is taxable. By designating some or all of the alimony payments as nontaxable, the parties improve their overall cash flow situation by the tax savings. Such a designation would remain in place until the parties agree to change it.

(v) Parties Must Reside in Separate Households. Support payments will not qualify as alimony if the husband and wife occupy the same household after they have legally separated. Only a decree of divorce or separate maintenance will legally separate the parties. Physical separation of the spouses in the same dwelling unit that they formerly shared does not constitute two separate households. The spouses will not violate this requirement if one of the parties is preparing to depart and does so no later than 30 days after the payor has made the alimony payment.[7]

The separate residence requirement applies to permanent support orders only. Payments required by *pendente lite* orders (i.e., temporary support arrangements) are alimony, if they otherwise qualify, even when the parties occupy the same household.[8]

(vi) Payments Must Not Be for Child Support. Payments intended to support the payor's child(ren) do not qualify as alimony.[9] Payments for the benefit of children

either are fixed or are treated as fixed by the tax law because of their nature. Section 36.3 of this chapter discusses child support.

(b) Alimony-Related Deductions.   An alimony recipient can make an above-the-line tax-deductible IRA contribution. This helps taxpayers over age 50 whom the IRC allows to make an additional catch-up contribution. Additionally, legal fees incurred for the production of alimony can provide a tax benefit to the alimony recipient. Taxpayers can deduct legal fees paid for the production of taxable income on Form 1040 Schedule A as Miscellaneous Itemized Deductions (subject to the limitation of 2 percent of adjusted gross income [AGI]) under IRC § 212.[10] However, the taxpayer does not always receive a benefit from these deductions because the Alternative Minimum Tax (AMT) calculations do not allow such deductions.

(c) Alimony Recapture.   The parties must perform a calculation to ensure that payments between former spouses go toward support and not property division. If the alimony payments decrease too rapidly over a three calendar year period, the statute provides for recapture, and the payments become taxable.

(i) Three-Year Recapture Rule.   The individuals apply the three-year recapture rule in the third post-separation year. The rule does not require a calculation for the second post-separation year or for any year after the third post-separation year. Although the Code defines the first post-separation year as the calendar year in which the payor makes the initial alimony or separate maintenance payment, the Treasury Regulations clarify that payments under a temporary support order do not start the running of post-separation years.[11] The payor does not need to make payments over the entire year. Thus, the actual payment period can be as short as 14 months if the payor makes the first payment in December of the first calendar year and the last payment in January of the third calendar year. The recipient can deduct from gross income the amount that the payor must recapture in gross income.

The payor must recapture in income in the third post-separation year the sum of two amounts computed in two steps:

> Step 1: The payor must recapture the amount by which payments made in the second post-separation year exceed payments made in the third post-separation year plus $15,000.[12]

> Step 2: The payor must average the sum of payments made in the second and third post-separation years, reduced by the recapture calculated in Step 1. The payor must recapture the amount by which the first year payments exceed the total of the computed average plus $15,000.[13] The cases in Exhibit 36-1 illustrate the recomputation analysis required in the third post-separation year.

(ii) Examples.   The cases in Exhibit 36-1 illustrate the peril of front-loading alimony payments. In each case, the alimony payments over three years total $90,000. When payments increase each year (Case 3), no recapture will occur under the recomputation rule. However, when payments decrease between Year 2 and Year 3 by more than the safe harbor amount of $15,000, the payor will recapture some income in the third year.

The third year's alimony payment is key to avoiding or minimizing recapture. A quick method exists to analyze whether the payor must recapture income in the

	Alimony Payments			
	Case 1	Case 2	Case 3	Case 4
Year 1	$ 45,000	$ 45,000	$ 20,000	$ 40,000
Year 2	45,000	40,000	30,000	32,500
Year 3	-	5,000	40,000	17,500
Total Payments	$ 90,000	$ 90,000	$ 90,000	$ 90,000

STEP 1:

Year 2 Payment	$ 45,000	$ 40,000	$ 30,000	$ 32,500
− Less: Year 3 Payment				
Plus $ 15,000	15,000	20,000	55,000	32,500
Amount Recaptured				
from Year 2 **(A)**	$ 30,000	$ 20,000	$ -	$ -

STEP 2:

Year 2 Payment	$ 45,000	$ 40,000	$ 30,000	$ 32,500
+ Add: Year 3 Payment	-	5,000	40,000	17,500
− Less: Amount Recaptured				
From Year 2	(30,000)	(20,000)	-	-
Subtotal	15,000	25,000	70,000	50,000
Divide by 2	2	2	2	2
Average	$ 7,500	$ 12,500	$ 35,000	$ 25,000
Year 1 Payment	$ 45,000	$ 45,000	$ 20,000	$ 40,000
− Less: Average plus $ 15,000	22,500	27,500	50,000	40,000
Amount Recaptured				
From Year 1 **(B)**	$ 22,500	$ 17,500	$ -	$ -
Total Recapture **(A)+(B)**	$ 52,500	$ 37,500	$ -	$ -

Exhibit 36.1. Application of the Three Year Recapture Rules

third year. The payor avoids recapture if Year 2 payments exceed or equal Year 1 payments less $7,500 *and* Year 3 payments exceed or equal Year 2 payments less $15,000. The formula is as follows:

There is no recapture if the payments in

$$Y2 \geq Y1 - \$7,500$$

and

$$Y3 \geq Y2 - \$15,000$$

One can use this guideline to analyze instruments already executed or structure alimony payments in future agreements.

(iii) Exceptions to the Recomputation Rule.   The three-year recomputation rule specifically does not apply to temporary support. The payor desiring to make large payments up front should consider temporary support payments. Temporary support qualifies as deductible alimony if it meets all the general requirements of IRC § 71.

Additionally, alimony recapture will not apply when payments cease because of either of the spouse's deaths or the recipient's remarriage before the end of the third post-separation year. The final exception to the three-year recomputation rule occurs when the instrument calls for "fluctuating payments not within the payor spouse's control." An alimony arrangement made pursuant to a continuing liability to pay for at least three years (a full 36 months) a fixed portion or portions of income from the earnings of a business, property, or services qualifies. The portions of income payable to the recipient can vary as the payor's income varies, as long as the instrument specifies fixed percentages.[14] For example, the payor could be required to pay 30 percent of income up to $50,000 and 20 percent of income between $50,001 and $100,000 and 0 percent of income over $100,001.

(iv) Tax Planning.   A professional can plan to avoid alimony recapture by structuring alimony obligations in the divorce decree. Recapture could inadvertently apply, however, when the timing of the actual payments shifts such that the payor makes delinquent payments with currently obligated payments or prepays alimony. The professional should warn the client that bunched payments can trigger recapture and caution the client to make all payments according to schedule.

Even if payors must recapture some previously deducted alimony in the third post-separation year, he or she may still recognize a tax benefit. The payor can deduct the full amounts in Year 1 and Year 2, even though recapture may occur in Year 3. Thus, the payor derives benefit from the tax deferral. With declining tax rates, this tax deferral becomes advantageous; however, with increasing tax rates, the payor can lose this advantage.

(v) Alimony Trust.   Divorcing parties can consider an alimony trust to fund support obligations in certain situations. The trust minimizes nonpayment risk and protects against a decreasing fluctuation in the payor's income. Parties should consider this alternative for spousal and child support when the payor engages in risky business ventures or has bankruptcy risk.

To qualify as an alimony trust, the trust must satisfy the general requirements of IRC § 71. Subchapter J of the Code governs a § 682 trust, which follows the normal trust rules and, after December 31, 1984, is the only form of allowable alimony trust. The payor spouse will sometimes favor this alternative because it allows a transfer of the trust income with the retention of control over the trust corpus. Also, the recapture rules do not apply to alimony trusts.

The payor spouse (grantor) does not receive an alimony deduction for income reported by the recipient spouse (beneficiary) from the trust. The recipient pays taxes on the trust income received in lieu of alimony. The grantor does not pay taxes on any trust income unless the divorce instrument or trust agreement fixes an amount or portion of payments as child support. Thus, the grantor spouse, by shifting the income to the trust, will achieve the same results as by reporting income offset by an alimony deduction. The parties can tailor trust income changes around potential child-related contingencies. This may avoid taxation of the trust income used for child support to the payor.

36.3 CHILD SUPPORT

(a) Overview.   The payor cannot deduct from and the recipient is not required to include in taxable income any amounts for child support provided for in a divorce agreement or decree.[15] IRC § 71 specifies two child support categories contained in the divorce instrument:

1. Payments clearly identified as support for the payor's child(ren)
2. Payments scheduled to decrease contingent upon a child-related event

IRC § 71 disqualifies payments designated as alimony from alimony treatment when they clearly relate to a child's support.[16] When the sum of required alimony and child support exceeds a payment, one should allocate the payment first to child support and then to alimony.[17] Prior to 1985, the treatment of amounts not expressly identified as child support followed *Commissioner v. Lester.*[18] In *Lester*, the support order did not fix amounts as child support, but the parties agreed to reduce the support payments to the wife by one-sixth whenever any of the three children married, became emancipated, or died. The Supreme Court found this indirect child support designation insufficient for tax purposes and considered all of the payments alimony. The 1984 Deficit Reduction Tax Reform Act (DRTRA) expanded the definition of child support payments to include payments that decrease when a child-related contingency occurs.

(b) Child-Related Contingencies.   IRC § 71 and the Treasury Regulations define child-related contingencies as the child's attaining a specific age, marrying, dying, leaving school,[19] attaining a specified income level, leaving the household, and gaining employment.[20] IRC § 71 will consider the payment reduction related to the contingency as child support from the agreement's inception. For example, assume alimony payments of $2,000 per month drop to $1,500 per month when the payor's child reaches age 18. Of *each* $2,000 payment, $500 will not qualify as alimony includible in the recipient's gross income and deductible by the payor.

(c) Presumed Child-Related Contingencies.   A contingency can be child related and can cause reclassification of the payment to child support, even though the instrument does not appear to include such a contingency. In two circumstances, the Treasury Regulations presume that payments will be reduced at a time clearly associated with the occurrence of a child-related contingency and cause classification as child support.

(i) Six-Month Presumption.   The six-month presumption applies when alimony payments cease or decrease within six months of the child attaining 18, 21, or the local age of majority.

(ii) Multiple Reduction Presumption.   The multiple reduction presumption exists when the parties have more than one child and two or more payment reductions occur within a year *before or after* the different children attain any common age, between 18 and 24 inclusive.

The Treasury Regulations will consider the amount of each payment reduction as child support and not alimony from the agreement's inception.

(iii) Child-Related Contingency Test.   An example from the Treasury Regulations will help clarify the multiple reduction presumption. Assume that divorcing parents have two children: Child A, born on July 15, 1980, and Child B, born on September 23, 1982. A divorce decree dated July 1, 1995, orders payments of $2,000 monthly until January 1, 2001, at which time the payments will decrease to $1,500 per month until January 1, 2005, when they will decrease to $1,000 per month.[21]

The six-month presumption does not apply to this fact pattern, but the multiple reduction presumption does. First, there are two children and two scheduled reductions occurring when the children are between the ages of 18 and 24. The first reduction occurs when Child A is 20 years, $5\frac{1}{2}$ months. Adding 12 months to this age totals 21 years, $5\frac{1}{2}$ months. The second reduction occurs when Child B is 22 years, $3\frac{1}{2}$ months. Subtracting 12 months from this age computes to 21 years, $3\frac{1}{2}$ months. Thus the payment reductions occur close to a common age for both children after adding or subtracting 12 months. The Internal Revenue Service (IRS) will presume that the reductions relate to child support and will classify $1,000 of each $2,000 payment as child support.[22]

The parties can rebut both of these presumptions by showing a reason other than a child-related contingency for reducing alimony payments. For example, alimony can decrease when the recipient sells the personal residence or is required to contribute a greater portion of his or her own support, or when the payor retires. Proof that a reason other than a child-related contingency motivated the alimony reduction should successfully rebut the presumptions.

(d) Family Support.   Some states allow designation of unallocated payments as "family support" instead of alimony and child support. Family support payments are taxable to the recipient if they meet all the requirements of IRC § 71(b), including the requirement that the payments terminate at the death of the recipient spouse. One can use the *Lester* or family support strategy as long as payment reductions do not violate the child-related contingency rules. Family support can be appropriate when the support of young children is at issue in the divorce proceeding and the scheduled alimony payments would cease or decrease before the children reach the age of majority.

36.4   DEPENDENTS

(a) Overview.   For tax years beginning before January 1, 2005, the parent with custody of a child for the greater portion of the tax year was presumed to be entitled to the dependency exemption. For tax years beginning after December 31, 2004, this presumption is superseded by the requirement that the custodial parent (and noncustodial parent in the case of separated or divorced parties) satisfy the qualifying child test requirements to claim the dependency exemption.

(b) Qualifying Child.   To qualify as a child for purposes of the dependency exemption and other dependent-related deductions, an individual:

1. Must be either a child, brother, sister, stepbrother, stepsister of the taxpayer, or descendant of any such relative
2. Must have had the same principal place of abode as the taxpayer for more than one-half of the taxpayer's year

3. Must be under 19 (or 24 if a student) as of the end of the taxpayer's calendar year

4. Must not have provided over one-half of his/her own support[23]

The American Jobs Creation Act of 2004 (AJCA) created the uniform definition of *child*; it defines a child as the taxpayer's son, daughter, stepson, stepdaughter, eligible foster child or legally adopted child.[24]

(c) Multiple Support Agreements.   A multiple support arrangement exists when no one person provides over half the dependent's support. A group including individuals that could have claimed the child as a dependent—except for failing to meet the 50 percent support test—must provide over half of the support. The group can agree that any one of the group who has contributed greater than 10 percent of the support can claim the exemption. The parties in the group who do not claim the exemption must complete Form 2120, *Multiple Support Declaration*, agreeing not to claim the exemption for that year. The individual claiming the exemption must attach the forms to his or her return.[25]

(d) Custodial Parent Releases Claim.   The custodial parent can release the claim to the noncustodial parent. IRC § 152 provides that a child of parents who are divorced or separated under a court decree or written agreement, or who live apart for the last six months of the year, and who together provide over one-half of the child's support and custody can be treated as a qualifying child by the noncustodial parent. The noncustodial parent claiming the dependency exemption must attach to his or her tax return each year Form 8332 *Release of Claim to Exemption for Child of Divorced or Separated Parents* signed by the custodial parent.

(e) Other Dependency Provisions.   The determination of a dependent as a qualifying child is relevant for other deductions and credits. The following list comprises the significant items:

(i) Medical Deductions.   The parent who pays the expense can deduct a child's medical expenses regardless of which parent claims the exemption. The child must receive over half of his or her total support from the parent for this rule to apply.[26]

(ii) Child Tax Credit.   The child tax credit follows the dependency exemption so a waiver of the dependency exemption also waives the child tax credit.

(iii) Dependent Care Credit.   The custodial parent can claim the child-care credit for expenses incurred so that the parent can work. The child must be under 13 or unable to care for himself or herself, must be in the custody of one or both parents for more than half of the year, and must receive more than half of his or her support from the parents. The parent eligible to take the credit is the custodial parent who can claim the dependency exemption or the custodial parent who does not claim the exemption because of the exception to release the claim. The child will not be a qualifying individual for the noncustodial parent even though the noncustodial parent can claim the exemption.[27]

(f) Exemption Phaseout.   The IRS annually adjusts the personal and dependent exemption amount of $3,300 for 2006 by an inflation index. Parties negotiating a divorce should also consider the phase-out when deciding who will claim the dependent exemption, to avoid giving it to a party who will not receive the full benefit.

(g) "Kiddie" Tax.   Prior to the TRA, a tax planning technique within the family unit shifted income from a parent in a high tax bracket to a child in a lower tax bracket. The TRA negated this device by requiring that a minor's unearned income exceeding $700 (in 2006) be taxed at the parents' highest rate. For years before 2006, this provision applies to children under age 14 as of December 31. The Tax Increase Prevention and Reconciliation Act of 2005 increased the age limit to children under the age of 18 at December 31, effective for years beginning after December 31, 2005. In certain circumstances, the custodial parent can elect to include the child's income on his or her income tax return.

The child has to compute his or her regular tax and share of allocable parental tax and pay the greater of the two computations. The allocable parental tax is that which the parent would have paid on the dependent child's unearned income if the parent had received the income.

This becomes complicated with divorced or separated parents. When the parents file a joint return, the child uses the total taxable income on the joint return. When the parents are married and file separately, the child must use the income of the parent with the highest income on the separate return. If the child cannot obtain the required information from the parents, the child can request that the IRS allow a disclosure or inspection of the parent's return.[28] When the parents are legally divorced or separated, the child uses the custodial parent's taxable income as § 152(e) describes, irrespective of which parent claims the dependency exemption.[29]

36.5   FILING STATUS

(a) Overview.   A married taxpayer can file a joint return, a separate return, or—if the taxpayer meets certain requirements—he or she qualifies for treatment as unmarried and can file as Head of Household. The IRS identifies marital status as of the end of the taxpayer's year. Thus, if the taxpayer's year end is December 31 and the taxpayer is divorced under a final decree on December 31, the IRS will consider the taxpayer single for the entire year. State law governs whether an individual is considered married, divorced, or legally separated under a decree of separate maintenance. The IRS recognizes marital status for filing a joint return even if the taxpayers have not lived together for the entire year.

(b) Married Filing Joint.   The IRS holds spouses filing a joint return jointly and severally liable for tax payment obligations plus penalties, additions to tax, and interest,[30] even when a divorce instrument requires one of the spouses to be fully responsible for taxes owed on joint returns. Divorcing taxpayers who elect to file a joint return often execute an Indemnification Agreement whereby they agree to release each other from additional taxes, penalties, and interest resulting from the actions or failures to act of the other party. However, because the IRS is not a party to the agreement, it can hold either party fully responsible for the entire tax obligation. The IRS will try to obtain the tax owed from the taxpayer from whom it can more easily collect. A spouse can obtain relief from joint liability under the innocent spouse rules of IRC § 6015. Section 36.6 discusses innocent spouse. Filing a joint return results in an overall tax savings when one spouse has minimal or zero taxable income.

(c) Married Filing Separate. The tax brackets sometimes discourage married taxpayers from filing separate returns because they cannot fully use the lower brackets. However, separate returns could result in less overall tax in some situations. One such scenario occurs when both spouses have low to moderate income and one spouse has a casualty loss or a large amount of medical deductions for which deductibility is limited based on adjusted gross income. Treasury Regulations place restrictions on married taxpayers filing separate returns, including those listed in the following:

(i) Capital Loss Deduction. The maximum capital loss deductible by a taxpayer on a married filing separate return is $1,500.

(ii) Itemized Deductions. If one spouse itemizes deductions, the other must itemize, because the standard deduction is not available to that spouse. Most often, neither spouse can take the credit for child and dependent care.[31]

(iii) Passive Activity Loss for Active Rental Real Estate. For taxpayers with adjusted gross income under the phase-out level, an exception permits a deduction of up to $25,000 of losses that would otherwise be suspended passive activity losses. These losses must come from real estate rental activities in which the taxpayer actively participates.[32] If married taxpayers file separately and they live together for *any portion* of the taxable year, this exception does not apply, and they cannot claim losses on either return. If the taxpayers file separately and live apart the *entire* year, each taxpayer can deduct up to $12,500 of such losses.

(iv) Education Credits Disallowed. Hope Scholarship and Lifetime Learning Credits are not available to married taxpayers who file separate returns.

(d) Head of Household. Taxpayers qualifying for Head of Household status pay tax at rates lower than those filing as Single or Married Filing Separately. To qualify for this filing status, the taxpayer must provide the primary residence of a dependent child and be unmarried, or considered unmarried, on the last day of the tax year. The IRS will consider a married taxpayer as unmarried and eligible for Head of Household filing status if he or she

1. Files a separate return
2. Has lived apart from his or her spouse for the last six months of the year
3. Has maintained the primary residence for a dependent child for more than half of the year, and
4. Has provided more than one-half of the cost of maintaining such a residence during the taxable year[33]

Some of the restrictions on taxpayers filing as Married Filing Separately are avoided such as the reduction to zero of the standard deduction if one spouse itemizes.

(e) Deciding How to File. The decision to file jointly or separately need not rest solely on considerations of current tax savings. For example, assume parties dispute the character of marital property during a divorce proceeding and must file a tax return; however, before the court adjudicates the property's character, the spouses agree to file jointly. For the parties' joint return, the taxable income and tax are both zero because a business loss of $100,000 offsets other taxable income of $100,000. Assume that the court later decides that the husband's separate property generated the $100,000 of income and the wife's separate business generated the $100,000 loss. If the spouses had filed separate returns, the husband would have had taxable income of $100,000 before deductions and exemptions, and the wife would have had a net operating loss of $100,000. On the joint return, the wife's business loss offset the husband's income of equal amount, resulting in no taxable income and tax. For that year, the parties' overall tax decreased, but the wife lost the $100,000 net operating loss that she could have used against her future taxable income. In retrospect, the wife may not have elected to file jointly so that she could preserve the net operating loss for her future use.

One spouse often files a separate return for reasons unrelated to taxes. Some taxpayers refuse to file a joint return to avoid becoming liable for the other spouse's tax liability. This often occurs with a pending divorce or when one spouse doesn't want to share information about personal finances with the other spouse.

(f) Allocation of Income for Separate Returns.   When married taxpayers file separate returns, state law governing the recognition of community property determines the allocation of income and expenses between the parties.

(i) Allocation of Income in a Community Property State.   In community property states, spouses must divide community property income and deductions evenly on their separate returns and add these amounts to their own income and deductions from separate property. IRC § 66, often called the Abandoned Spouse Rule, protects a spouse who has not filed a joint return from imputation of community property income earned by the other spouse in certain cases.

(ii) Allocation of Income in a Noncommunity Property State.   On separate returns in non-community property states, a spouse must include his or her own income and deductions on his or her own return. In a Tax Court case, *Mahon v. Commissioner*,[34] the taxpayers filed separate returns and split the husband's wages and retirement income evenly on each return. The court held that the husband had to pay taxes on 100 percent of his wages and retirement income because he, by himself, performed the services and earned the income.

(g) Changing the Election to File Jointly or Separately.   Married taxpayers who file separately can change to a joint return any time within three years from the due date of the separate return(s), not including extensions. Taxpayers filing a joint return have only until the return's due date, not including extensions, to change their status to filing separately for that year.

36.6   INNOCENT SPOUSE

(a) Overview.   The IRS Reform and Restructuring Act of 1998 (1998 act) repealed the innocent spouse provisions of highly litigated IRC § 6013(e). The 1998 act clarified the innocent spouse rules by enacting the provisions of IRC § 6015, which protect taxpayers whose spouse violated the tax laws without their knowledge. IRC § 6015 provides three avenues for relief:

1. General relief with liberalized rules to the innocent spouse
2. Separate liability election

3. Equitable relief when the innocent spouse cannot use either of the first two options (Revenue Procedure 2003-61, effective November 1, 2003, clarified the qualifications for equitable relief.)

The spouse seeking innocent spouse relief is called the *requesting spouse.* This section discusses the requirements to seek each type of innocent spouse relief under IRC § 6015.

(b) General Innocent Spouse Relief.   IRC § 6015(b) establishes requirements for innocent spouse relief as follows:

1. The spouses filed a joint return for the year relief is sought.
2. The return understated tax attributable to an erroneous item of the nonrequesting spouse.
3. The requesting spouse establishes that in signing the joint return he or she did not know, and had no reason to know, of the understatement.
4. When considering the facts and circumstances of the situation, it is inequitable to hold the requesting spouse liable for the tax deficiency attributable to the understatement.
5. The requesting spouse makes the election under this section on Form 8857, *Request for Innocent Spouse Relief (and Separation of Liability and Equitable Relief)* within two years of the start of IRS collection activities with respect to the requesting taxpayer.

This provision allows a partially innocent status to the spouse claiming relief. Thus, the requesting spouse may know of the understated taxes but may still obtain relief to the extent that he or she did not know or have reason to know of the full understatement. The requesting spouse cannot receive any benefit from the understatement. Receipt of ordinary support, however, is not considered a benefit for purposes of denying relief. Factors to consider when establishing whether the requesting spouse knew or had reason to know of the understatement include the following:

- The requesting spouse was involved in the family business affairs.
- The parties enjoyed a lavish lifestyle not warranted by the income reported on the tax return.
- Duress or abuse was present in the marital relationship.

These provisions do not protect the intentionally ignorant spouse because every spouse has a duty to make inquiries of the other spouse regarding the contents of the return.

(c) Separate Liability Election.   The requesting spouse can use this election to limit his or her liability when filing a joint return under the following conditions of IRC § 6015(c):

1. Only taxpayers who are no longer married, who are legally separated, or who have not lived together within the last 12 months can use this election.
2. The requesting spouse must make the election no later than two years after the date on which the IRS has begun collection activities in connection with the requesting taxpayer.

3. The requesting spouse has the burden of proving the portion of the deficiency that is allocable to the other spouse.

4. No asset transfers can occur between the requesting spouse and the other spouse. The IRS presumes a transfer to be for tax avoidance purposes if the parties transfer the asset(s) less than one year before the earlier of the payment due date or the date of the notice of proposed deficiency. This presumption shall not apply, however, to any transfer that is governed by IRC § 1041.

5. The requesting spouse cannot have "actual knowledge" of any item giving rise to the deficiency. If the requesting spouse had actual knowledge, then such individual must show that the return was signed under duress.

To deny relief, the IRS must prove actual knowledge of the requesting spouse, as opposed to "reason to know." Therefore, the divorced or separated taxpayer who meets the other conditions will prefer this election. Guidance relating to this relief states that such "actual knowledge must be established by the evidence and shall not be inferred based upon indications that the electing spouse had reason to know."[35]

(d) Equitable Relief.   IRC § 6015(f) provides for equitable relief if the requesting spouse does not satisfy innocent spouse provisions or the separation of liability provisions. If the IRS determines that the requesting spouse does not satisfy the condition's relief under two options outlined above after submitting Form 8857 or Form 8379, *Injured Spouse Claim and Allocation*, then the IRS must automatically consider equitable relief. The IRS considers, by weighing all the facts and circumstances, whether holding the requesting spouse liable for any unpaid tax would be inequitable. The threshold for eligibility for a claim of equitable relief has the following criteria:[36]

1. The spouses must have filed a joint return for the year relief is sought.
2. The requesting spouse cannot obtain relief under the innocent spouse or separate liability rules.
3. The spouse requests relief within two years of the IRS's first collection activity after July 22, 1998 with respect to the requesting taxpayer.
4. No transfer of assets occurred as part of a fraudulent scheme.
5. The requesting spouse did not receive a transfer of disqualified assets.
6. The requesting spouse did not file the return with fraudulent intent.
7. The income tax liability at issue must be attributable to the nonrequesting spouse.

Revenue Procedure 2003-61 added the last requirement but provided safe harbor exceptions that enable the requesting taxpayer to seek equitable relief. A taxpayer can qualify for equitable relief even if (1) the application of community property laws or nominal ownership (unknown to the requesting spouse) created tax liability, or (2) the taxpayer was subject to abuse (but not duress) and did not question the tax returns for fear of retaliation, or (3) the nonrequesting spouse misappropriated funds without the knowledge of the requesting taxpayer.[37]

Factors weighed by the IRS in evaluating equitable relief for the taxpayer include whether the requesting spouse had knowledge or reason to know of the unpaid liability or deficiency; and whether the unpaid liability is attributable to the requesting spouse; and whether the requesting spouse significantly benefited (beyond normal support) from items giving rise to the deficiency. Finally, the IRS also considers the requesting spouse's subsequent good faith efforts to comply with tax laws. The requesting spouse can apply for equitable relief concurrently with either general innocent spouse relief or separate liability relief. For more information on Innocent Spouse relief, *see* IRS Publication 971, *Request for Innocent Spouse Relief (and Separation of Liability and Equity Relief)*.

36.7 PROPERTY SETTLEMENTS

(a) Nonrecognition of Gain on Spousal Transfers. IRC § 1041 governs most transfers of property between spouses and former spouses incident to divorce. Section 1041 addresses "all property" and includes all tangible, intangible, personal, and real property.[38] The Treasury Regulations state that nonrecognition treatment applies "regardless of whether the transfer is of property separately owned by the transferor or is a division [equal or unequal] of community property."[39] A property transfer under IRC § 1041 does not trigger IRC §§ 1245 and 1250 recapture.

IRC § 1041 benefits taxpayers because most assets transferred in a property settlement have appreciated, and divorcing taxpayers can postpone payment of tax on the appreciation until sale to a third party. Professionals should take care to identify significantly appreciated assets and consider the potential tax consequences when negotiating a settlement.

(b) Carryover Basis and Holding Period. Because IRC § 1041 does not recognize gains or losses on property transfers pursuant to a divorce settlement, it follows that the transferee has a carryover basis equal to the transferor's adjusted basis in the property received. This occurs even where the transferred property has liabilities exceeding its basis.[40] The transferor's holding period also carries over to the transferee.[41]

This carryover basis rule applies even when a *bona fide* sale between spouses or former spouses has occurred: the new property owner cannot declare an increase in basis by the amount of the consideration given.[42] IRC § 1041 conveys the taxation on the asset's appreciation from the transferor to the recipient. Future tax consequences should be considered when one is evaluating the equity of a proposed property division.

(c) Related to the Cessation of the Marriage (Six-Year Rule). IRC § 1041 applies to all transfers between spouses and between former spouses if the transfer is "incident to the divorce." IRC § 1041 defines a transfer incident to the divorce as a transfer occurring "within one year after the date on which the marriage ceases, or ... related to the cessation of the marriage."[43] Thus, § 1041 applies to all property transfers between spouses occurring within one year of the divorce regardless of the reason for the transfer.

If the transfer occurs later than one year from the divorce date, then the transfer must relate to "the cessation of marriage" to qualify for § 1041 treatment. The Treasury Regulations regard any transfer that occurs within six years of the divorce date and is made pursuant to a divorce decree as related to the divorce.[44] Hence, any transfer that occurs one to six years after divorce must be pursuant to a divorce or separation instrument, including modifications thereto, to obtain § 1041 treatment.

The Treasury Regulations presume that a transfer occurring more than six years after the divorce date does not relate to the divorce and does not qualify for non-recognition treatment. The parties can rebut this presumption by showing that the transfer did not occur during the prescribed six-year period because of factors that hampered an earlier transfer of the property (i.e., children's welfare and legal or business impediments).

(d) Transfers to Third Parties on Behalf of a Spouse.   If one spouse transfers proper-ty to a third party on behalf of the other spouse, the IRC treats the transaction as two transfers. Assuming that all the requirements of IRC §1041 are met, the first presumed transfer (between spouses) would qualify for nonrecognition, and the second transfer (from the nontransferor spouse to the third party) would be sub-ject to normal rules. The transfer to the third party must occur either (1) pursuant to a divorce or separation agreement, or (2) at the written request of the nontrans-feror, or (3) after the transferor spouse receives a written consent or ratification of the transfer denoting that the parties intend the transfer to qualify under § 1041. The transferor spouse must receive the ratification before filing his or her tax return for the year of the transfer.[45]

(e) Stock Redemptions.   Professionals should understand the regulations issued in January of 2003 regarding the taxation of share redemptions in connection with a divorce. Treasury Regulation § 1.1041-2 attempts to clarify the treatment of trans-actions involving transfers of marital property between divorcing parties and a third-party corporation. Corporate redemptions of stock pursuant to a divorce will result in a taxable event to one of the parties.[46] The parties can negotiate the tax consequences. The regulation applies to redemptions that occur after January 12, 2003, with limited applicability for redemptions that occurred prior to this time pursuant to agreements modified after August 2, 2001. Divorcing parties can structure the property settlement to avoid creating a taxable corporate stock re-demption event.

(f) Passive Activity Interests.   Transfers of passive activity interests with associated suspended losses qualify for IRC § 1041 treatment; however, suspended losses received from a former spouse do not carry forward. IRC § 469 adds these sus-pended losses to the transferor's basis to form the transferee's new basis.[47] If the transferred property is a depreciable asset—an apartment building, for example—the increase in basis allows the transferee to take additional depreciation deduc-tions. One should calculate depreciation in accordance with rules for property acquired by gift. Property acquired by gift after 1986 must follow the Modified Accelerated Cost Recovery System (MACRS) depreciation and recovery rules. If the parties transfer a partnership interest, then the transferee cannot depreciate suspended losses added to the basis.

The AJCA established an exception regarding the transferability of suspended losses and deductions on S-corporation shares due to insufficient basis. The sus-pended losses and deductions accompany S-corporation shares transferred from one spouse to another pursuant to a divorce.[48] The taxpayers treat the losses as though they incurred them in the subsequent year. After transferring the shares and related losses, the owner becomes subject to the existing rules, specifically the at-risk requirements of IRC §465 and the passive activity loss limitations of IRC § 469, regarding the realization of the losses.

(g) *Davis* Rules Apply for Disqualified Transfers.   Prior to DRTRA, the Supreme Court decided in *United States v. Davis*[49] that a transfer of appreciated property pursuant to a divorce decree or separation agreement resulted in a taxable gain to the transferor. The taxable gain amount equaled the fair market value of the transferor's property or interest in the property less the cost basis. The transferee then received a step-up in the property's basis, based on the property's fair market value included in the transferor's gross income. The *Davis* rule trapped the unwary and surprised divorcing parties who found that equally dividing property in a marital dissolution triggered gain recognition.

Under the belief that spouses receive tax treatment as a single economic unit and that the taxing of transfers within the unit is inappropriate, Congress created IRC § 1041, which supersedes *Davis* except in limited circumstances. The *Davis* rules still govern transfers to nonresident alien spouses and transfers of property to a trust when the liabilities exceed the transferor's adjusted basis.[50] With many states recognizing domestic partnerships, the *Davis* rules might emerge as the prominent authority on property division between domestic partners.

(h) Equalizing Note Interest.   When the property division proves unequal, one party often issues an equalizing note to facilitate the division. If the note does not bear interest, the parties need not impute interest even though the note is between related parties.[51] If the note bears interest, the recipient must report the interest income on his or her tax return. The payor cannot automatically deduct the interest because the note, which stems from a divorce, is personal and taxpayers cannot deduct personal interest. However, if payors can identify certain underlying assets that he or she used the note to acquire, he or she can trace the debt to that source and deduct interest accordingly.[52]

36.8 MARITAL RESIDENCE

(a) Overview.   The tax consequences of the ownership, maintenance, and disposition of the marital residence present one of the most important aspects of a marital dissolution. Divorcing parties often decide on an ostensibly equitable property settlement only to find that their arrangement has unintended tax ramifications. The parties need to consider the special rules applicable to a residence and understand the tax consequences of their decisions. Additionally, the professional should obtain all documentation that supports basis in the residence, including the acquisition cost and improvements, at the time of the divorce proceeding. Regulations require that the parties provide all records supporting basis in assets.[53]

(b) Sale of a Principal Residence.   Under IRC § 121, a taxpayer can exclude up to $250,000 of gain on the sale of his or her primary residence. To qualify for the $250,000 exclusion on the sale of a real property, the taxpayer must have owned and used it as his or her principal residence for an aggregate two out of the five years prior to the date of the sale and exchange.[54] For married taxpayers, the exclusion is $500,000 when filing jointly, if (1) either spouse meets the ownership test, and (2) both spouses meet the use test, and (3) neither spouse used the exclusion within the last two years.

If a taxpayer fails to meet the ownership and use provisions, the taxpayer can prorate the gain exclusion when the sale or exchange occurred because of extenuating circumstances such as a change in the place of employment, health, or unforeseen circumstances, including divorce. In addition, the taxpayer cannot have used the exclusion within the last two years.[55] The personal residence gain exclusion is not available for property acquired in a like-kind § 1031 exchange in the previous five years.[56]

(c) Transfer of Ownership Pursuant to Divorce.   When a spouse transfers title to a residence to the other spouse, the transferring spouse's holding period carries over to the transferee spouse. When one spouse moves out of the residence because of the separation or divorce, IRC §121 treats the nonresident spouse as using the property as a principal residence during any period of ownership when one spouse receives exclusive use of such residence under a divorce or separation instrument.[57]

(d) Payments for the Residence.   During a marital dissolution proceeding, one party, often the party who has custody of the children, is granted use of the family residence and the other party vacates the residence. When the parties file separate returns, the property ownership form dictates the appropriate tax treatment in terms of alimony and itemized deductions of mortgage and property tax payments.

(i) Joint Ownership with Right of Survivorship.   If the parties are jointly liable for the mortgage and other obligations on the property (by virtue of joint ownership with the right of survivorship) and the nonresident spouse makes the payments, the payments discharge debts for which both parties are liable. The resident spouse receives a benefit from the discharge of debt. In this instance, the nonresident spouse can report one-half of the mortgage interest and principal reduction as alimony if the payments otherwise qualify under IRC § 71. The nonresident spouse will also deduct one-half of the mortgage interest and all of the property tax deductions as itemized deductions on Schedule A. The nonresident spouse reports all the tax payments because they were made with his or her separate funds and he or she is jointly and severally liable on the entire tax obligation.

(ii) Joint Ownership without Right of Survivorship.   If the parties are separately responsible for obligations on the property by virtue of joint ownership without the right of survivorship and the nonresident spouse makes all of the payments, the payments have two purposes: (1) maintaining the resident spouse and children (and discharging the resident spouse's debt) and (2) discharging debts for which he or she is personally liable. To the extent that the payments otherwise qualify under IRC § 71, the nonresident spouse should deduct one-half of the payments as alimony. The resident spouse must report the same amount as income. The nonresident spouse can deduct the remaining one-half of the mortgage interest and property tax deduction payments as itemized deductions on Schedule A. The resident spouse can deduct one-half of the mortgage interest and property tax deduction payments as itemized deductions on Schedule A.

Given the multitude of property ownership and maintenance arrangements, the parties should review the complicated law that governs this situation before deciding on the property's ownership and arranging for support through mortgage payments.

36.9 RETIREMENT ACCOUNTS

(a) Overview.   A marital division often involves the spouses' interests in individual retirement accounts, various pension and profit-sharing plans, and other employment-related plans. The former spouse could have a significant future interest in these assets based on the employee spouse's services performed during the marriage. The division of these assets affects the retirement planning of divorcing parties.

(b) Individual Retirement Accounts.   Individual Retirement Accounts (IRAs) have different forms, each with different tax consequences. If eligible to make a contribution to a regular IRA, the taxpayer obtains a current deduction for the contribution and defers tax on income earned on the IRA investment until the IRA makes a distribution. The taxpayer cannot currently deduct a contribution to a nondeductible IRA, but income earned on the invested funds remains tax deferred until distributions are made. For a Roth IRA, the eligible taxpayer cannot take a current deduction and does not pay income tax on a distribution from the Roth IRA account. A divorcing spouse will prefer to receive a Roth IRA over a regular IRA because normal distributions from a Roth IRA will be tax free.

When a divorce decree or a written instrument incident to such divorce transfers an IRA owned by one spouse to a former spouse, the transfer is not taxable pursuant to IRC §1041. Thereafter, the IRS will regard the account as maintained for the recipient spouse's benefit.[58] Thus, the recipient spouse can receive distributions from the account without regard to the former spouse. The parties must make transfers pursuant to a written divorce instrument to avoid taxability and should not make them in anticipation of the divorce.

For the purpose of computing eligibility for IRA contributions, the taxpayer can count as compensation alimony included in gross income pursuant to IRC § 71.[59] This helps the spouse receiving alimony who does not currently have earned income. It could offer the only tax-deferred retirement savings vehicle available to that spouse.

(c) Employer Retirement Plans.   A retirement plan is any arrangement that accumulates funds for the future benefit of a retired or disabled employee or beneficiaries. Most plans are qualified in that they allow the employer to receive a current tax deduction for allowed contributions. The IRS does not tax the earnings of most plans, and the plan's participants do not pay taxes on contributions made on their behalf until they receive a distribution from the plan. These plans must qualify pursuant to certain tests in the IRC, such as (1) nondiscrimination rules that prohibit plans designed to cover only select highly paid employees or key employees, and (2) requirements that limit qualified owners of plan assets, and (3) restrictions on plan distributions. These plans must comply with the Employee Retirement Income Security Act of 1974 (ERISA), which provides plan asset protection from creditors' claims. A *nonqualified* plan does not obtain these tax benefits. Two basic categories of qualified retirement plans are *defined contribution plans* and *defined benefit plans*. Before deciding how to divide the retirement plan(s), one must assess the value of the plan assets or the present value of future benefits.

(i) Defined Contribution Plan.   A defined contribution plan maintains a separate account for each plan participant. A participant's eventual distribution amount depends on the employer and employee contributions credited to the account, plan earnings, and some other factors such as vesting. The professional can obtain the value of the defined contribution plan because the plan maintains a separate account for each participant and the value of the plan is calculated based on current asset ownership.

(ii) Defined Benefit Plan.   In a defined benefit plan, a participant accrues benefits payable at some defined future time in an amount defined by formula. The employer contributes to the plan based on actuarially determined amounts necessary to fund the projected benefits of all plan participants. An actuary can calculate the value of the defined benefit plan by estimating the present value of the future benefits based on statistical contingency charts for death, disability, employment termination, and other relevant calculations. Alternatively, for a plan with few participants, one could take the same approach used in defined contribution plans and simply analyze the fair market value of the plan assets. This proves most feasible for plans in which a large portion or all of the plan assets fund only the divorcing participant's retirement benefit. Professionals who have personal service corporations, such as physicians, attorneys, accountants, dentists, architects, and people involved in the entertainment industry (i.e., performing artists, producers, directors, and writers) often have such plans.

(iii) Alternatives for Division.   The IRS recognizes four alternatives for dividing retirement plan assets:

1. The employee spouse retains all interest in the retirement plan and gives a comparably valued asset to the nonemployee former spouse.

2. The parties divide the plan assets pursuant to a *qualified domestic relations order* (QDRO) that assigns all or part of the participant's retirement benefits to the nonemployee alternate recipient. The QDRO's alternate recipient can be the participant's spouse, former spouse, child, or other dependent.[60]

3. The court could retain jurisdiction over the retirement plan until the employee spouse becomes eligible to receive retirement benefits. At that time, the parties can compute the portion of the benefits owed to the nonemployee former spouse based on the percentage of funds resulting from the services performed during marriage.

4. Finally, in cases involving personal service corporations or closely held corporations, the parties could decide to terminate the plan and distribute all the assets according to a mutually accepted property division. Each party can then roll over his or her respective distributions into an IRA, thereby avoiding current taxation on the withdrawal.

Several factors influence the decision regarding which division alternative to pursue. First, the professional should analyze the client's immediate and future cash needs. Plans and other assets have different liquidity and different patterns of cash flow. Consider the cash flow needs of the client as well as the tax consequences.

(iv) Qualified Domestic Relations Order.   If the divorcing parties decide to split the retirement plan asset(s), they must obtain a QDRO to ensure valid and enforceable assignment of the employee's benefits in a qualified retirement plan. The court issues a QDRO for each plan to identify the alternate payee and specify the amount and timing of benefits.[61] The benefit payments to the alternate payee generally begin when payments to the participant begin or would begin. All benefit payment options available to the plan participant also become available to the alternate payee, except for joint and survivor annuities with respect to the alternate payee and his or her subsequent spouse.[62] Some retirement plans will distribute benefits to the alternate payee any time after the court issues a QDRO. However, the plan cannot require the alternate payee to accept an immediate distribution if the present value of the benefits exceeds $5,000.[63]

The earliest date on which the alternate payee can receive benefits depends on whether the plan participant has separated from employment service. If the participant has separated from service, the alternate payee can receive benefits only when the participant can receive them. If the plan participant remains employed by the plan's sponsor, the alternate payee can receive benefits once the plan participant has reached the earliest retirement age. The plan participant's earliest retirement age is the earlier of (1) the date on which he or she is entitled to a distribution under the plan, or (2) the *later* of age 50 or when he or she would become eligible for benefits if he or she had separated from service.[64]

(d) Plan Distributions.   The plan participant or alternate payee will receive distributions as an annuity or a lump-sum distribution. The taxation of the benefits follows the asset's ownership. When the parties divide a plan, the alternate payee becomes the plan's owner and therefore must pay taxes.

(i) Annuity.   The recipient reports amounts received from an annuity as ordinary income but can reduce the taxable portion by a *pro rata* allocation of any employee contributions with after-tax dollars to the plan.[65] The alternate payee receives a portion of the payments in the form of employee contributions when payments result from a QDRO.[66]

(ii) Lump-Sum Distributions.   The IRS considers a payment as a lump-sum distribution if the recipient receives the entire balance credited to the individual's account from a qualified pension or profit-sharing plan. The recipient must receive the distribution within one tax year, and it must be payable on account of (1) the employee's death, or (2) the employee attaining age $59\frac{1}{2}$, or (3) the employee's separation from service or disability.[67] The recipient can partially or totally roll over the distribution into an IRA plan, thereby escaping taxation until the IRA pays benefits. The recipient has 60 days after receiving the benefits to roll over the proceeds.

36.10 STOCK OPTIONS

(a) Overview.   Company performance driven share-based compensation has become a major component of remuneration for executives. Although increased public scrutiny might decrease the future use of such compensation, professionals who advise clients on marital assets should understand the basic types of stock options and the different tax implications of exercising them.

(b) Incentive Stock Options.   Incentive stock options (ISOs) or statutory options meet specific requirements of the IRC and allow deferral of gain on the bargain element in the stock or stock option. If the employee meets certain holding period requirements, he or she does not report compensation income at exercise and reports the income from the shares' sale as capital gain, not ordinary income. The bargain element equals the difference between the exercise price and the fair market value (FMV) of the stock on the day the holder exercises options. The recipient must include the bargain element as a preference item in the year of exercise for alternative minimum tax (AMT) purposes, potentially resulting in an AMT liability. When the ownership of ISOs is transferred pursuant to a divorce, the options lose their ISO status and are converted to nonqualified options. Companies usually restrict the transferability of ISOs.

(c) Nonqualified Stock Options.   Nonqualified stock options or nonstatutory options do not qualify for preferential treatment under the IRC; the recipient recognizes them as ordinary income. If the option has a readily ascertainable fair market value, the recipient recognizes income at the grant date. However, most options (not stock shares) do not have a readily ascertainable fair market value; therefore, the recipient recognizes compensation at exercise rather than grant.[68]

Because the nonqualified stock options are a form of compensation, the employee spouse owes employment taxes on the income from the exercise. Nonqualified options divided between parties pursuant to divorce require coordination between the parties and the employer. As the owner of the transferred stock options, the nonemployee former spouse can elect to exercise the options at his or her discretion. Revenue Ruling 2002-22 requires that the nonemployee former spouse recognize as ordinary income the compensation received through exercising his or her options.[69] Therefore, the former spouse, not the employee, reports the ordinary income recognized on the options that he or she received in the divorce when he or she exercises them. Revenue Ruling 2004-60 clarifies that, even though the nonemployee former spouse reports the ordinary income, the compensation retains its character as wages of the employee for purposes of FICA taxes (Old Age, Survivors and Disability Insurance Tax and Medicare Tax).[70] This is consistent with IRC § 1402, which provides that the party operating a trade or business must pay the self-employment tax even if the sole-proprietorship or partnership income is community income.[71] The professional should address the responsibility of each party for his or her taxes in the marital settlement agreement.

36.11 TAX ATTRIBUTES

(a) Overview.   A far less visible set of marital assets exists in the form of tax attributes, such as overpayments, loss carryforwards, and net operating losses.

Tax attributes are valuable assets, and the divorce decree should divide them between the parties. This has particular importance for the party whom the IRS regards as the spouse and not the (primary) taxpayer because the primary taxpayer's account holds the amounts carried forward from prior years.

(b) Tax Payments. The parties must allocate overpayments that occurred on a joint return filed during a prior year to the party who made the payments. The IRS outlined steps to effect the application of overpayments reported on joint return in a community property state against a separate liability of one spouse. The analysis begins with identifying and characterizing the underlying source of the overpayment. The IRS considers overpayments characterized as community property as owned equally by the parties. If possible, the parties should agree on the division of estimated tax payments. If the parties do not reach an agreement, the IRS divides payments according to the ratio of a taxpayer's separate liability to the couple's combined liability. When the parties credit an overpayment to the next year's taxes, they in effect convert it to an estimated tax payment.[72]

(c) Capital Loss Carryforwards. Loss carryforwards do not stand alone but become part of the parties' financial situation; ownership of the attributes follows the underlying assets that generated the capital losses. If community property assets generated the capital losses, the parties should divide the loss carryforwards. Alternatively, if separate property assets generated the capital losses, the property owner retains the loss carryforward.

(d) Net Operating Losses. The parties divide net operating losses (NOLs) by allocating income and deductions reported on a joint return in a manner that reflects the actual allocation that would have occurred had separate returns been filed. The parties report the resulting NOL as the property of each party.[73] If a divorcing taxpayer anticipates an NOL in a subsequent year, the taxpayer should consider an election to forego the carryback period that includes a joint return year or should include a clause in the marital settlement agreement that allocates the expected refund to the taxpayer who owns the NOL.

(e) Passive Activity Losses. When the IRS disallows passive activity losses and credits for a taxable year, the parties must identify the disallowed items by property and carry them forward under IRC § 469(b).[74] During the dissolution process, the marriage's legal status becomes important because it could affect the classification of the activity to the nonparticipating spouse when the other spouse is a material or active participant in the activity.[75] *See* the discussion of the transfer of passive activity interests in Section 36.7 of this chapter.

(f) Charitable Contributions. When the former spouses have unused charitable contributions carried over from a joint return and the taxpayers file separate returns during the carryover period, then the taxpayers must allocate the contributions as if they had filed separate tax returns instead of joint returns.

(g) Investment Interest Expense. IRC § 163 provides that taxpayers can carry over investment interest in excess of investment income to a succeeding tax year.[76] Section 163 does not prescribe an allocation method. To remain consistent with practice for other carryforwards, however, the parties would base the division on the amounts that they would have allocated to each party, had they filed separate tax returns instead of a joint return.

(h) Special Rules for S-Corporation Suspended Losses.   Suspended losses and deductions that are not transferable because they are limited to the shareholder specifically are transferable to the shareholder's spouse or former spouse pursuant to divorce for transfers occurring after December 31, 2004. The loss will be treated as though it is generated in the succeeding taxable year.[77]

36.12   GIFT AND ESTATE TAX ASPECTS

(a) Overview.   An important and often overlooked aspect of the divorce involves decisions on gift and estate tax planning. Both parties must review and update their wills and trusts. After the divorce, the parties can no longer use the marital deduction for gift and estate tax purposes, and the trustor spouse should reconsider testamentary trusts set up for the other spouse and the children.

(b) Gift Tax.   IRC § 2523 authorizes a deduction for gifts between spouses equal to the gift's value, but it does not allow a deduction for a gift of a life estate or other terminable interest received. It does, however, provide for an election for *qualified terminable interest property* (QTIP) given to the spouse. The election allows a full marital deduction against the donor's taxable gifts, provided the donee spouse includes the gift in his or her gross estate. Consequently, the spouses can avoid any gift tax problems with respect to gifts between spouses during marriage.

IRC § 2516 considers any transfers of property pursuant to a divorce made between spouses to settle marital and property rights and to support their children as exchanges for full and adequate consideration. The parties can avoid gift tax problems pursuant to § 2516 when the divorce occurs within one year before or two years after the settlement agreement date. (For transfers made on or before July 18, 1984, the divorce had to occur within two years after the agreement.) The divorce must occur within this time frame, but the actual property transfer can occur at any time as long as it follows the agreement.

These two code sections help divorcing spouses avoid most gift tax problems. Clients with a gift-giving schedule will want to consider gift splitting with their spouse in the divorce year but prior to the final decree date. The QTIP election could save taxes to the transferor spouse when he or she is transferring assets in trust to the recipient spouse for his or her life with the remainder to the children. The transfer to the spouse can qualify under § 2516, but the remainder interest would be a gift of a future interest to the children without the benefit of the annual exclusion. The transferor spouse should consider the QTIP election on a transfer during marriage in this circumstance.

(c) Estate Planning.   Both parties should review basic estate planning decisions at the time of divorce. The client often wants to change beneficiaries on retirement plans and life insurance policies for which the settlement agreement will affect ownership. The current owner of a life insurance policy may wish to transfer policy ownership at the time of the divorce. This would remove the insurance proceeds from his or her estate (assuming survival of three years after the transfer) and provide a means of support to the former spouse or to children after death. The parties should prefer this arrangement to an agreement whereby the payor spouse's estate continues to pay spousal support.

(i) Marital Residence.   One must also consider the marital residence when planning for the estate. Divorcing spouses frequently wish to retain the residence for some time after the divorce becomes final. If the parties own the residence as joint tenants with right of survivorship, the death of one of the former spouses can trigger unintended results. If the decedent had provided most of the consideration for the residence, then the IRS could argue to include the entire residence in the decedent's gross estate without benefit of the marital deduction. To avoid this result, parties often change title to ownership as tenants in common. Alternatively, the divorcing spouses should consider transferring ownership entirely into the name of the spouse who will occupy the residence.

(ii) Gross Estate Deductibility of Obligations Pursuant to the Divorce.   Prior to DRTRA, no counterpart to § 2516 existed in the estate area. Therefore, whether a gross estate could deduct a decedent's post-death obligation under § 2053 depended on the extent to which "full and adequate consideration in money or money's worth" supported the obligations.[78] DRTRA added § 2043(b)(2), which allows an estate tax deduction for transfers pursuant to claims under a written separation instrument if the transfers satisfy marital or property rights and the agreement would have satisfied the requirements of Paragraph 1 of § 2516. This amendment applies to the estate of a decedent who died after July 18, 1984.

NOTES

1. IRC § 215.
2. IRC § 71(b)(2).
3. *Moore v. United States*, 449 F. Supp. 163 (N.D. Tex. 1978).
4. P.L. 99-514, Act § 1843 (b).
5. *Okerson v. Commissioner*, 123 T.C. 14 (2004).
6. Treas. Reg. § 1.71-1T Q-6.
7. Treas. Reg. § 1.71-IT Q-9.
8. *Id.*
9. Treas. Reg. § 1.71-1T Q-15.
10. IRC § 212(1).
11. Treas. Reg. § 1.71-1T(d) Q-22.
12. IRC § 71(f)(4).
13. IRC § 71(f)(3).
14. Joint Committee on Taxation, *Explanation of the Technical Corrections to the Tax Reform Act of 1984 and Other Recent Tax Legislation*, May 13, 1987.
15. IRC § 71(c)(1).
16. *Id.*
17. Treas. Reg. § 1.71-1T(c).
18. *Commissioner v. Lester*, 366 U.S. 299 (1961).
19. IRC § 71(c)(3).
20. Treas. Reg. § 1.71-1T(c) Q-17.
21. Treas. Reg. § 1.71-1T(c) Q-18.

22. *Id.*
23. IRC § 152(c).
24. IRC § 152(f)(1).
25. IRC §§ 152(e)(3) and 152(c).
26. IRC § 213(d)(5).
27. IRC § 21(e)(5).
28. Temp. Reg. § 1.1(i)1T Q-22.
29. Temp. Reg. § 1.1(i)1T Q-12.
30. IRC § 6013(d)(3).
31. IRS Publication 504.
32. IRC § 469(i).
33. IRC § 7703(b).
34. *Mahon v. Commissioner*, 54 T.C.M. (CCH) 439 (1987).
35. HR Conference Report No. 105-599, 105th Cong., 2d Sess. (1998), Note 4.
36. IRS Publication 971.
37. Rev. Proc. 2003-61.
38. Treas. Reg. § 1.1041-1T(a) Q-4.
39. Treas. Reg. § 1.1041-1T(d) Q-10.
40. Treas. Reg. § 1.1041-1T(d) Q-12.
41. IRC § 1223(2).
42. Treas. Reg. § 1.1041-1T(d) Q- 11.
43. IRC § 1041(c).
44. Treas. Reg. § 1.1041-1T(b) Q-7.
45. Treas. Reg. § 1.1041-1T(c) Q-9.
46. Treas. Reg. § 1.1041-2(c).
47. IRC § 469(j)(6).
48. IRC § 1366(d)(2).
49. *United States v. Davis*, 370 U.S. 65 (1962).
50. *Id.*
51. Treas. Reg. § 1.1274-1(b)(3)(iii).
52. IRC § 163.
53. Treas. Reg. § 1.1041-1T(d) Q-14.
54. IRC § 121(c)(1).
55. IRC § 121(b)(3).
56. IRC § 121(d)(10)[(11)].
57. IRC § 121(d)(3)(B).
58. IRC § 408(d)(6).
59. IRC § 219(f)(1).
60. IRC § 414(p)(8).
61. IRC § 414(p)(1) and IRC § 414(p)(2).
62. IRC § 414(p)(4)(A)(iii).
63. IRC § 411 (a)(11)(A).
64. IRC § 414(p)(4)(B).
65. IRC § 72(b).
66. IRC § 72(m)(10).
67. IRC § 402(e)(4)(D)(i).
68. Treas. Reg. § 1.83-7(a).

69. Rev. Rul. 2002-22.

70. Rev. Rul. 2004-60

71. IRC § 1402(a)(5).

72. ILM 200130036.

73. Treas. Reg. § 1.172-7.

74. IRC § 469(h)(5).

75. Treas. Reg. § 1.469-1T.

76. IRC § 163(d)(2).

77. IRC § 1366(d)(2).

78. F. Sander and H. Gutman, "Tax Aspects of Divorce and Separation: A Detailed Analysis," *The Family Law Reporter* (1986): 220.

LIST OF CASES

R.R. Armacost v. Commissioner, 75 T.C.M. (1998-150)

Durovic v. Commissioner, 487 F.2d 36 (7th Cir. 1973)

Houlette v. Commissioner, 48 T.C. 350 (1967)

Commissioner v. Lester, 366 U.S. 299 (1961)

Mahon v. Commissioner, 54 T.C.M. (CCH) 439 (1987)

Mass v. Commissioner, 81 T.C. 433 (1986)

Moore v. United States, 449 F. Supp. 163 (N.D. Tex. 1978)

Okerson v. Commissioner, 123 T.C. 14 (2004)

Phillips v. Commissioner, 86 T.C. 112 (1983)

Purcell v. Commissioner, 86 T.C. 228 (1986)

J.L. Seymour v. Commissioner, 109 T.C. 279 (1997)

Taylor v. Commissioner, 45 T.C. 120 (1965)

United States v. Davis, 370 U.S. 65 (1962)

Young v. Commissioner, 49 T.C.M. (CCH) 1002 (1985)

BIBLIOGRAPHY

Arthur Andersen & Co. *Tax Reform 1986 Analysis and Planning.* New York: Matthew Bender, 1986.

Asimow, Michael. "Alimony and Marital Property Divisions under the 1986 Act," *Taxes The Tax Magazine* (June 1987); 352–57.

Brown, William J. *Tax Strategies for Separation and Divorce.* New York: McGraw-Hill, 1987.

California Continuing Education of the Bar. *Tax Planning for Marital Termination Settlements.* September/October 1987.

Clemens, Bruce A., and Daniel J. Jaffe. *Employee Retirement and Deferred Compensation Plans on Dissolution of Marriage: Valuation, Distribution, and Tax Aspects.* California Continuing Education of the Bar, Sacramento: October/November 1986.

Gursey, Donald L. *Family Law Symposium: Tax Consequences of Marital Separation and Dissolution.* California Continuing Education of the Bar, November 1985.

Gursey, Donald L. and Roseanna L. Purzycki. "Alimony: A Taxing Situation." *Family Law News* (Spring 1987): 100.

Internal Revenue Service. "Tax Information for Divorced or Separated Individuals." Publication 504 (Rev. 2004).

Internal Revenue Service. "Tax Information on Selling Your Home." Publication 523 (Rev. 2004).

Jaffe, Daniel J. and Roseanna L. Purzycki. "CEO Divorce." Presented to U.S.C. Tax Institute, January 25, 2005.

O'Connell, Madorie A. *Divorce Taxation.* Englewood Cliffs, NJ: Prentice-Hall, 1985.

Poefio, Mark. "The Practical Side of Pensions and Qualified Domestic Relations Orders." *The Family Law Reporter,* Monograph No. 1 (January 5, 1988): 14, FLR 3001.

Randall, Gary C. "Practical Applications of the 1984 Domestic Relations Tax Bill—Trick or Treat?" U.S.C. Law Center Tax Institute (1986): 10–1–10–42.

Rice, David Lee, Gwendolyn K. Hight, and Todd Russell Reinstein. "IRS and the Courts Provide Guidance for Taxpayers Seeking Relief as an Innocent Spouse." *Journal of Taxation* (August 2003). http//checkpoint.riag.com accessed February 20, 2005.

Richman, Bruce L. *Guide to Tax and Financial Issues in Divorce.* New York: John Wiley & Sons, 2002.

Sander, Frank E. A., and Harry L. Gutman. *Tax Aspects of Divorce and Separation: A Detailed Analysis.* Updated for the Tax Reform Act of 1984 by Wicker, William C. Updated for the Tax Reform Act of 1986 by Blake, John F., and Lynn K. Pearle. *The Family Law Reporter.* The Bureau of National Affairs, Inc., Washington DC: (1987).

Van Houten, Margaret D. "Divorce Negotiations Carry Substantial Estate Planning Implications." *Estate Planning* (November/December, 1987); 344–49.

Wofford, Cindy Lynn. "Divorce and Separation." In *Tax Management Portfolios.* 515-2nd ed.,Washington, DC: Tax Management Inc., 2001.

PART VI

CRIMINAL CASES

CHAPTER 37
Tax Fraud

TAX FRAUD

Edward M. Robbins, Jr.

CONTENTS

37.1 INTRODUCTION: CIVIL TAX CASE VERSUS CRIMINAL TAX FRAUD CASE

Since the earliest days of the Internal Revenue Code (IRC) almost 90 years ago, the government and taxpayers have waged an ongoing battle over the assessment and collection of taxes. When courts began refereeing this fight, the terms *tax avoidance* and *tax evasion* emerged. Tax avoidance results in routine civil adjustments, if any, to the taxpayer's tax returns. Tax evasion issues can result in civil and/or criminal tax fraud proceedings often ending with a jail sentence or significant civil fraud penalties, or both.

Tax avoidance generally describes legally permissible conduct, whereas tax evasion connotes intentionally fraudulent designs. A classic description of tax avoidance was penned by Judge Learned Hand:

> Anyone may arrange his affairs that his taxes shall be as low as possible. He is not bound to choose the pattern which best pays the Treasury, there is not even a patriotic duty to increase one's taxes. Over and over again courts have said that there is nothing sinister in so arranging [one's] affairs. … Everyone does it, rich and poor alike, and all do right, for nobody owes a public duty to pay more than the law demands.[1]

In more recent years, the Internal Revenue Manual (IRM) itself has observed the "fine distinction" between tax avoidance and evasion. Nonetheless, after highlighting this delicate distinction, the current manual paints a fairly black-and-white picture distinguishing the two concepts:

> One who avoids tax does not conceal or misrepresent. He shapes events to reduce or eliminate tax liability and, upon the happening of the events, makes a complete disclosure. Evasion, on the other hand, involves deceit, subterfuge, camouflage, concealment, some attempt to color or obscure events, or make things seem other than they are.[2]

The IRS concedes that "any attempt to reduce, avoid, minimize or alleviate taxes by legitimate means is permissible."[3] However, it has also established two tracks to determine if what a taxpayer believes is tax avoidance fits the government's definition of tax evasion. These two tracks—civil fraud audit and criminal investigation—do not operate on strictly parallel courses and, indeed, intersect at various junctures. In the current enforcement climate, born of corporate scandals and increased scrutiny of financial transactions, accountants should familiarize themselves with the IRS's civil fraud and criminal treatment of cases and the process by which an audit can transform itself into a criminal investigation.

Needless to say, accounting computations underlie all tax fraud cases, civil or criminal. In a criminal tax fraud case, the IRS usually assigns a team of experienced special agents from the IRS Criminal Investigation division (CI) and cooperating revenue agents for the investigation, pretrial preparation, and court testimony in tax fraud prosecutions. These well-qualified agents in most cases have much experience in tax fraud and perform an outstanding job. The high conviction rate in tax fraud cases brought to court demonstrates the thorough preparation by these government agents.

In response to any IRS effort to develop a tax fraud case against a taxpayer, the taxpayer needs to assemble his or her own defense team.[4] As discussed in Section 37.11(b) of this chapter, that team should include a tax lawyer who specializes in tax fraud and, necessarily, at least one accountant.

37.2   FOUR MOST COMMON TAX CRIMES

The IRC and Title 18 of the U.S.C. contain a variety of criminal penalties applicable in tax cases; however, almost all criminal tax investigations and prosecutions concern four felony statutes.

(a) 26 U.S.C. § 7201: Attempt to Evade or Defeat Tax. IRC § 7201[5] makes it a felony to willfully attempt to evade or defeat the assessment or payment of any tax. The elements of criminal tax evasion are identical to the elements for a civil fraud penalty. The Supreme Court has stated that § 7201 includes two offenses: (1) the willful attempt to evade or defeat the assessment of a tax and (2) the willful attempt to evade or defeat the payment of a tax.[6] Evasion of assessment entails an attempt to prevent the government from calculating a taxpayer's true tax liability. Evasion of payment entails an attempt to evade the payment of that liability.[7] The government takes the position that § 7201 proscribes a single crime—attempted evasion of tax—that one can commit by evading the assessment of tax or by evading the payment of tax. Whether one views them as separate offenses or as different means of committing the same offense, both evasion of assessment of taxes and evasion of payment of taxes require the taxpayer to take some action, that is, to carry out some affirmative act for the purpose of the evasion. A taxpayer can use several methods to attempt to evade taxes or the payment thereof, and § 7201 expressly refers to "attempts in any manner." The most common attempt to evade assessment of a tax is the affirmative act of filing a false tax return that omits income, or claiming deductions to which the taxpayer does not have entitlement, or both. This results in understated taxes on the return, an evasion of the correct assessment of the tax.

Historically, the principal revenue offense is the crime of willfully attempting to evade a tax through evasion of assessment, as opposed to willfully attempting to evade the payment of a tax. Although the crime has simple basic elements, investigators often find the proof difficult.

The three elements of tax evasion are set forth in § 7201: a tax deficiency must exist, the defendant must commit an affirmative act that constitutes an evasion or attempted evasion of the tax, and the defendant must act willfully.[8] The state-of-mind requirement for imposing the civil fraud penalty is identical to what the IRS must prove in a criminal prosecution for tax evasion under § 7201.[9] "Willfulness" is defined for criminal purposes in all tax crimes as a "voluntary, intentional violation of a known legal duty"[10] and in the civil fraud arena as an "intentional wrongdoing on the part of the taxpayer with the specific purpose to evade a tax believed to be owing."[11] As a practical matter, these two definitions are identical. Thus, the government establishes civil tax fraud and criminal tax evasion through the same elements.

(b) 26 U.S.C. § 7206(1): Fraud and False Statement. Section 7206(1) makes it a felony to willfully make and subscribe a false document if the document was signed under penalties of perjury. Simply stated, § 7206(1) makes it a crime for a person to sign his or her name to a tax return, if the person has in mind that the return is false as to a material matter. The person signing the return does not have to be the taxpayer; it might be an officer authorized to sign for a corporation. Section 7206(1) offers one of the more flexible prosecutorial weapons in the government's arsenal against criminal tax offenses. Practitioners refer to § 7206(1) as the tax perjury statute, because it makes the falsehood itself a crime. Historically, because § 7206(1) does not require proof of a tax deficiency, it permits prosecution in cases that do not involve a tax deficiency,[12] a minimal tax deficiency, or a tax deficiency that the IRS would find difficult to prove.

Section 7206(1) sets forth the four elements of subscription:

1. The defendant must make and sign a return, statement, or other document that contained falsehoods as to a material matter.

2. The return, statement, or other document must contain a written declaration that it was made under the penalties of perjury.

3. The defendant must not believe the return, statement, or other document to be true and correct as to every material matter.

4. The defendant must act willfully.[13]

(c) 26 U.S.C. § 7206(2): Assisting in the Preparation of a False Return.   One court has described § 7206(2) as the IRC's "aiding and abetting" provision.[14] The IRS frequently uses § 7206(2) to prosecute individuals, such as fraudulent tax return preparers, who advise or otherwise assist in the preparation or presentation of false documents. Congress did not limit this statute to preparers, however, but applied it to anyone who assists in filing a false return.[15] Even though the false document will frequently be a tax return or information return, any document filed with the IRS can give rise to the offense.

Section 7206(2) sets forth the three elements of aiding and abetting:

1. The defendant must aid or assist in, procure, counsel, or advise the preparation or presentation of a document in connection with a matter arising under the internal revenue laws.

2. The document must be false as to a material matter.

3. The defendant must act willfully.[16]

(d) 18 U.S.C. § 371: Conspiracy to Defraud the United States (*Klein* Conspiracy).   The criminal tax statutes in the IRC do not include a statute for the crime of conspiracy. As a result, the government prosecutes tax-related conspiracies under 18 U.S.C. § 371, the general conspiracy statute. § 371 sets out two types of conspiracies, but we will concern ourselves only with the most common of the two, the *Klein* conspiracy, or a conspiracy to defraud the United States. "To conspire to defraud the United States means primarily to cheat the Government out of property or money, but it also means to interfere with or obstruct one of its lawful governmental functions by deceit, craft, or trickery, or at least by means that are dishonest."[17] Criminal tax prosecutions typically charge this conduct as a *Klein* conspiracy: the government alleges that the defendant conspired to defraud the United States for the purpose of "impeding, impairing, obstructing and defeating the lawful government functions of the Internal Revenue Service of the Department of the Treasury in the ascertainment, computation, assessment, and collection of the revenue: to wit, income taxes."[18] The *Klein* conspiracy argument presents the most formidable weapon in the tax prosecutor's arsenal because of its breadth.

18 U.S.C. § 371 sets forth the three elements of a *Klein* conspiracy:

1. There must exist an agreement by two or more persons to defraud the United States.

2. The defendant must knowingly and voluntarily participate in the conspiracy.

3. One conspirator must commit an overt act in furtherance of the conspiracy.[19]

Note that, unlike the crimes defined in the IRC, the *Klein* conspiracy does not contain an element for willfulness.

37.3 GENERAL OBSERVATIONS ABOUT THESE FOUR TAX CRIMES

Criminal tax fraud cases differ from other criminal cases and from civil tax cases. In a conventional criminal case the existence of the crime is a foregone conclusion: a bank has been robbed or someone has been stabbed. The government only needs to prove who did it. In a criminal tax case, the government faces the difficult task of proving the existence of the tax crime, which always turns on the defendant's subjective intent or knowledge.

Criminal tax cases also differ from civil tax cases. In civil tax cases, the government and the taxpayer argue over money or technicalities. In a criminal tax case, the government publicly accuses the defendant of committing a crime, with the possibility of time in prison.

37.4 PROOF BEYOND A REASONABLE DOUBT IN A TAX PROSECUTION

Prosecutors find criminal tax fraud difficult to prove. Once the government goes through the monumental effort to put a tax case together, however, the case becomes difficult to defend.

A key distinction between civil and criminal fraud lies in the burden of proof. In a criminal case, the prosecution must prove fraud beyond a reasonable doubt.[20] Civil fraud, however, requires only clear and convincing evidence.[21] If the government establishes that any portion of a tax underpayment relates to fraud, however, the entire underpayment is treated as attributable to fraud, triggering fraud penalties on the full amount of the tax liability. The taxpayer, however, may establish by a preponderance of the evidence that all or a portion of the tax liability is not attributable to fraud.[22]

Whether the government first pursues a criminal or civil case can prove crucial. If the criminal case proceeds first, a conviction under § 7201 precludes the defendant from litigating the issue of civil fraud in any subsequent civil tax proceeding in which the government asserts the fraud penalty.[23] The defendant, however, can still litigate the amount of tax deficiency in the civil proceeding.[24] The collateral estoppel doctrine that results in a finding of civil fraud applies because the willfulness requirement of § 7201 includes the specific intent to evade the payment of tax, which is the same intent requirement for a civil fraud penalty.[25] If the government proves willfulness beyond a reasonable doubt in the criminal case, that finding necessarily meets the clear and convincing standard of the civil fraud case. On the other hand, a criminal felony conviction for subscribing to a false return under IRC § 7206 does not collaterally estop a taxpayer from contesting the civil fraud penalty, since the elements for this offense do not mirror those for the civil fraud penalty.[26]

37.5   SHORTHAND FORMULA FOR A CRIMINAL TAX CASE

Criminal tax fraud focuses on two necessary factors:

1. A solid and substantial tax deficiency.
2. The badges of fraud: provable, sneaky behavior usually (but not always) concerning the tax deficiency.

The criminal tax case becomes stronger for the government as the tax deficiency increases and becomes more evident. The government's criminal tax case also strengthens with the more badges of fraud it can uncover.

37.6   METHODS OF PROVING THE TAX DEFICIENCY

The government considers a tax deficiency a necessary element of the four tax crimes discussed in Section 37.2 of this chapter. Only one of these tax crimes, evasion, found at 26 U.S.C. § 7201, has tax deficiency as an element. The other two Title 26 sections, § 7206(1) (signing a false return) and § 7206(2) (assisting in the preparation of a false return), simply require that the false item on the return be material. The jury must decide whether any alleged false statement was material as the indictment uses that word. The law deems a statement on a tax return as material if it is necessary for a correct computation of the tax due or if it has a natural tendency to influence or impede the IRS in ascertaining the correctness of the tax declared or in verifying or auditing the taxpayer's returns. In theory, a material false statement could have no effect on the calculation of the tax liability, as when a taxpayer lies about whether he or she has signature authority over a foreign bank account. The Klein conspiracy does not refer to a tax item at all.

For obvious reasons, the government usually does not prosecute a taxpayer unless it has evidence of a substantial criminal tax deficiency. The unofficial rule of thumb is a $40,000 criminal tax deficiency total for all years being prosecuted. With a $40,000 tax loss, the defendant goes to jail, even if he or she pleads guilty. A criminal tax deficiency is a deficiency that the taxpayer cannot explain away. Contrast with the civil tax deficiency on a statutory notice of deficiency, which the investigation's target can easily explain, in whole or in part.

The fact that 26 U.S.C. § 7201(evasion) has tax loss as an element makes evasion a lot harder to prove than § 7206(1)(signing a false return) or § 7206(2)(assisting in the preparation of a false return). This is true because to prove the criminal tax deficiency, the government has to deal with every line of a tax return (referred to as *proving up*), which totals 65 lines on a Form 1040, for example. When proving a § 7206(1) subscription or § 7206(2) preparation case, however, the government usually deals with only one line on the return, the line with the material false statement, typically a line containing income or deductions.

(a) Direct versus Indirect Methods of Proving the Deficiency.   In general, the government can use all legal methods available to establish and prove unreported income.[27] We list five of them here and discuss them in subsequent sections.

1. **Specific items method** consists of direct evidence of the items of income received by a taxpayer in a given year, such as testimony by third parties as to

monies paid to the taxpayer for goods or services. The specific items method is the only method of proving false expenses.

2. **Bank deposits method**, an indirect method of proof, reconstructs income by analyzing bank deposits by a taxpayer who has an income-producing business and makes regular and periodic deposits to bank accounts.

3. **Net worth method**, another indirect method of proof, reflects increases in the taxpayer's wealth, as contrasted with reported income.

4. **Expenditures method** (a variation of the net worth method) reflects the expenditures made by a taxpayer. The government uses the expenditures method in the case of a taxpayer who does not purchase durable assets, such as stocks and real estate, but spends monies for consumable items, such as vacations, entertainment, food, drink, and the like.

5. **Cash method**, a variation of the expenditures method, compares the taxpayer's cash expenditures with the known cash sources. As of May 2006, this method has appeared in only one case, in the Seventh Circuit.

The specific items method of proof is a direct method of proof used to establish unreported income. This method of proof differs from the indirect methods of proof (bank deposits, net worth, and expenditures) in that it focuses on specific financial transactions and does not attempt to reconstruct the defendant's overall financial situation. The specific items method primarily relies on direct evidence, although the government can introduce circumstantial evidence. By contrast, the indirect methods generally rely on circumstantial evidence to prove an understatement of income. Using the indirect methods of proof, the government shows "either through increases in net worth, increases in bank deposits, or the presence of cash expenditures, that the taxpayer's wealth grew during a tax year beyond what could be attributed to the taxpayer's reported income, thereby raising the inference of unreported income."[28] The government often resorts to indirect methods of proof when the defendant deals in cash and has maintained inadequate records from which to reconstruct income.

(b) Specific Items Method of Proof.   This method has several advantages: prosecutors can easily present it and juries can easily understand it, the method involves less evidence and has relatively simple criminal computations compared with the indirect methods, and the government does not have to follow all of the technical requirements of the indirect methods of proof. The specific items method aims to prove that a defendant earned more money than the tax returns reflect, or that the tax returns report nonexistent or overstated deductions, expenses, or credits. The government can introduce both testimonial and documentary evidence. This evidence includes the defendant's admissions, the defendant's books and records, bank records, the testimony of inside witnesses (e.g., the defendant's employees and ex-spouse), testimony and documentation of witnesses engaged in the transactions that have been reported inaccurately, and the testimony of the defendant's accountant.

Specific items cases have four categories:

1. Unreported income, where the evidence establishes that the total amount of income received exceeds the amount reported

2. Unreported income, where the evidence establishes that the defendant didn't report identified items of income

3. Failure to report a business or other source of income

4. Overstated deductions or expenses, including fictitious deductions and inflated legitimate deductions

Specific items cases generally deal with income rather than deductions or expenses. The government usually attempts to produce evidence that the defendant received income that the defendant either did not report or underreported.[29]

The government goes through four steps to develop a specific items case that involves unreported income: (1) proving that the relevant amounts are taxable income to the defendant; (2) proving that the defendant received the income; (3) proving that the defendant did not report income; and (4) showing willfulness, in other words, the defendant's personal involvement in the failure to report the income and in the disposition of the unreported income. Although the government must show that the defendant received unreported taxable income, it need not show how the defendant spent the money after it became his or her income.[30]

(c) Bank Deposits Method of Proof.   The bank deposits method of proof is one of the primary indirect methods of proof used by the government in computing taxable income. The bank deposits method of proof has certain features in common with the net worth method of proof (discussed in Section 37.6(d) of this chapter). Both methods develop approximations that seek to show by circumstantial means that the taxpayer had income that the taxpayer did not report.[31]

However, unlike the net worth method, which considers year-end bank balances as well as asset acquisitions and liabilities, a bank deposits case focuses on funds deposited during the tax year. Although "the mechanics of arriving at an income figure are different, both methods involve similar underlying assumptions and afford much of the same inferences for and against the accused."[32]

The Eighth Circuit case of *Gleckman v. United States* presents the classic bank deposits case.[33] As noted in *Gleckman*, "the bare fact, standing alone, that a man has deposited a sum of money in a bank would not prove that he owed income tax on the amount; nor would the bare fact that he received and cashed a check for a large amount, in and of itself, suffice to establish that income tax was due on account of it."[34] The court in *Gleckman* went on to describe the foundation for using the bank deposits method of proof as follows:

> On the other hand, if it be shown that a man has a business or calling of a lucrative nature and is constantly, day by day and month by month, receiving moneys and depositing them to his account and checking against them for his own uses, there is most potent testimony that he has income, and, if the amount exceeds exemptions and deductions, that the income is taxable.

The Gleckman decision and its progeny teach that to use the bank deposits method of proof, the government must initially introduce evidence that shows the following:

- The taxpayer was engaged in a business or income-producing activity from which the jury can infer that the unreported income arose.

- The taxpayer made periodic and regular deposits of funds into accounts in the taxpayer's name or over which the taxpayer had dominion and control.
- The government made an adequate and full investigation of those accounts to distinguish between income and nonincome deposits.
- Unidentified deposits have the inherent appearance of income, such as the size of the deposits, or consistent or variable amounts, fluctuations in amounts corresponding to seasonal fluctuations of the business involved, source of checks deposited, dates of deposits, accounts into which deposited, and so on.[35]

(d) Net Worth Method of Proof. The government has long used this indirect method of reconstructing taxable income in criminal tax cases when the government cannot establish income through direct evidence. For example, consider *United States v. Johnson*,[36] a case that involved gambling transactions in which all records had been destroyed. The net worth method produces an approximation[37] and operates on the concept that if a taxpayer has more wealth at the end of a given year than at the beginning of that year, and the increase does not result from nontaxable sources such as gifts, loans, and inheritances, then the increase represents an approximate measure of taxable income for that year. Because this method adds nondeductible expenditures to any net worth increase, practitioners sometimes refer to it as the *net worth and expenditures method.*

When constructing a net worth computation, one must include only items or transactions that reflect tax consequences. For this reason, the analysis must eliminate nontaxable items received during a prosecution year from the computation of additional taxable income.

A net worth computation identifies not only that the defendant had income but how the defendant spent that income. In essence, the computation depicts the taxpayer's financial life, both prior to and during the prosecution period.[38]

Although endorsing the net worth method, the Supreme Court has cautioned that "it is so fraught with danger for the innocent that the courts must closely scrutinize its use." Despite its reservations, the Supreme Court has approved use of the net worth method a number of times.[39]

The First Circuit described the net worth method as follows:

> The Government makes out a prima facie case under the net worth method of proof if it establishes the defendant's opening net worth (computed as assets at cost basis less liabilities) with reasonable certainty and then shows increases in his net worth for each year in question which, added to his nondeductible expenditures and excluding his known nontaxable receipts for the year, exceed his reported taxable income by a substantial amount. The jury may infer that the defendant's excess net worth increases represent unreported taxable income if the Government either shows a likely source, or negates all possible nontaxable sources.
>
> [T]he jury may further infer willfulness from the fact of underreporting coupled with evidence of conduct by the defendant tending to mislead or conceal.[40]

The Fifth Circuit summarized the steps necessary to establish income when applying the net worth method of proof:

> The government established its case through the "net worth" approach, a method of circumstantial proof which basically consists of five steps: (1) calculation of net worth

at the end of a taxable year, (2) subtraction of net worth at the beginning of the same taxable year, (3) addition of non-deductible expenditures for personal, including living, expenditures, (4) subtraction of receipts from income sources that are nontaxable, and (5) comparison of the resultant figure with the amount of taxable income reported by the taxpayer to determine the amount, if any, of underreporting.[41]

(e) Expenditures Method of Proof.   The expenditures method of proof and the net worth method of proof present accounting variations of the same approach, with the expenditures method a variation of the net worth method.[42]

In *United States v. Johnson* (1943), the Supreme Court approved the use of the expenditures method of proof to establish unreported income.[43] Subsequently, the Third Circuit defined the expenditures method of proof as follows:

> It starts with an appraisal of the taxpayer's net worth situation at the beginning of a period. He may have much or he may have nothing. If, during that period, his expenditures have exceeded the amount he has reported as income and his net worth at the end of the period is the same as it was at the beginning (or any difference accounted for), then it may be concluded that his income tax return shows less income than he has in fact received. Of course it is necessary, so far as possible, to negate nontaxable receipts by the taxpayer during the period in question.[44]

The expenditures method of proof tracks a taxpayer's expenditures for consumable goods and services (i.e., items that do not increase one's net worth), as opposed to any acquisition of assets (i.e., items such as stocks, bonds, or real estate, which increase one's net worth). The expenditures method accounts for the taxpayer who spends his income on consumable items that do not increase net worth, such as food, vacations, travel, or gifts to third parties.

The First Circuit summarized one advantage of using the expenditures method of proof, rather than the net worth method:

> The government proceeded on a "cash expenditure" theory. This is a variant of the net worth method of establishing unreported taxable income. Both proceed by indirection to overcome the absence of direct proof. The net worth method involves the ascertaining of a taxpayer's net worth positions at the beginning and end of a tax period, and deriving that part of any increase not attributable to reported income. This method, while effective against taxpayers who channel their income into investment or durable property, is unavailing against the taxpayer who consumes his self-determined tax free dollars during the year and winds up no wealthier than before. The cash expenditure method is devised to reach such a taxpayer by establishing the amount of his purchases of goods and services which are not attributable to the resources at hand at the beginning of the year or to non-taxable receipts during the year.[45]

The requirements for establishing an expenditures case are identical to those required for establishing a net worth case. Thus, in an expenditures case, the government must do the following:

- establish an opening net worth with reasonable certainty and demonstrate that the taxpayer's expenditures did not result from cash on hand, or the conversion of assets on hand at the beginning of the period
- Establish through independent evidence that the expenditures charged to the taxpayer are nondeductible
- Establish a likely source of income from which the expenditures sprang, or negate nontaxable sources of income

- Investigate all relevant, reasonable leads that are reasonably susceptible of being checked[46]

(f) Cash Method of Proof.   The Seventh Circuit has approved a variation of the expenditures method, referred to as the cash method of proof.[47] This method compares the taxpayer's cash expenditures with the known cash sources, including cash on hand, for each tax period. If such expenditures exceed sources, the government presumes the excess to be unreported income. As of February 2006, this method is limited to the single Seventh Circuit case.

37.7   PROVING INTENT: BADGES OF FRAUD

The second key element in a tax crime is the defendant's intent. Ultimately the jury must read the mind of the taxpayer to decide whether the taxpayer intentionally violated a known legal duty. The government tries to show the jury enough *badges of fraud* to circumstantially demonstrate the taxpayer's criminal intent.

(a) Classic *Spies* Badges of Fraud.   Although each element listed in the following excerpt and discussed in Section 37.7(b) of this chapter can be an innocent error or an anomalous legitimate transaction, such elements may also indicate fraud, particularly when they occur with a frequency or pattern, or combine with other elements. In *Spies v. United States*, the Supreme Court stated the classic list of badges of fraud that provide circumstantial evidence of tax fraud:

> By way of illustration, and not by way of limitation, we would think affirmative willful attempt may be inferred from conduct such as
>
> - keeping a double set of books,
> - making false entries or alterations, or false invoices or documents,
> - destruction of books or records,
> - concealment of assets or covering up sources of income,
> - handling of one's affairs to avoid making the records usual in transactions of the kind, and
> - any conduct, the likely effect of which would be to mislead or to conceal.
>
> If the tax-evasion motive plays any part in such conduct, the offense may be made out even though the conduct may also serve other purposes such as concealment of other crime.[48]

(b) More Badges of Fraud.   The IRM now provides a lengthy list of badges of fraud that can trigger scrutiny by the IRS. The Fraud Handbook[49] described six categories of badges:

1. **Income.** This includes unreported sources of income, unexplained increases in net worth over a period of years, unusually high personal expenditures, and unexplained bank deposits that substantially exceed reported income.
2. **Expenses or deductions.** This includes substantial deductions for personal expenditures claimed as business expenses, lack of substantiation for unusually large deductions, or making a claim for dependency exemptions for nonexistent, deceased, or self-supporting persons.
3. **Books and records.** The IRS will scrutinize taxpayers who keep the classic two sets of books—one for their bank that inflates their net income, and one

for the IRS deflating the same income—or engage in similar mischief with invoices, purchase orders, gift receipts, and the like. The IRS will also examine taxpayers whose business books and tax returns do not reconcile.

4. **Allocations of income.** Taxpayers who move income or deductions out of the correct account and into a more taxpayer-friendly line item, or issue checks to third parties who then endorse them back to the taxpayer, will likewise draw the attention of the IRS. The IRS's fraud spotlight will also shine on distributions of profits to fictitious parties or inclusions of income or deductions in the tax return of a related person whose tax rate differs substantially.

5. **Conduct of taxpayer.** The taxpayer's conduct presents one of the more important variables that can transform a civil inquiry into a criminal investigation. These badges of fraud include hindering examinations by failing or refusing to answer important questions, repeatedly canceling appointments, refusing to provide records or consistently omitting key records, and attempting to threaten or corruptly influence witnesses. When taxpayers assert that they completed their returns on the basis of a good faith reliance on an accountant or lawyer, the IRS will analyze whether the taxpayer followed the advice or fully disclosed the relevant facts to the professional in question. The IRS will also consider the tax sophistication, education, training, and experience of the taxpayer.

6. **Methods of concealment.** If any of the badges of fraud concerning concealment emerge, the likelihood of a criminal referral looms large. Red flags include placing assets in others' names, transferring assets in anticipation of a tax assessment or during an investigation, use of secret bank accounts or entities (particularly offshore entities) to disguise the source and destination of a financial transaction, and use of nominees for property or banking transactions.

A taxpayer's tax counsel should thoroughly investigate the situation for the presence of badges of fraud, both before and during the civil audit. That will provide an opportunity to formulate a strategy for dealing with these sensitive issues, hoping that the parties will conclude the audit without a referral to CI or the assertion of civil fraud penalties. The tax lawyer should also consult criminal counsel to help prevent issues from emerging during the civil audit that could contribute to a CI referral.

37.8   GOVERNMENT'S SOURCES FOR CRIMINAL AND CIVIL TAX FRAUD CASES

(a) Fraud Referral Specialists.   A case works its way from a civil audit to a criminal investigation through the IRS's long-standing fraud referral program. When a revenue agent or revenue officer investigates a case and identifies "firm indications of fraud," the agent or officer must transfer or refer the case to the IRS CI division.[50]

The IRS's Small Business/Self-Employed Division has selected fraud referral specialists (FRS), both on the civil audit side and the collection side, to identify civil fraud cases that have civil fraud penalty and criminal referral potential. Those agents designated as FRS have experience and special training in detecting and developing fraud cases. The IRS has approximately 64 fraud referral specialists, who act as consultants to revenue agents as they conduct civil audits. The FRS help the examining agent identify badges of fraud and develop fraud cases through the gathering of documentation and the interviewing of witnesses, including the taxpayer.

Deciding whether a taxpayer/client should submit to an interview request by a civil agent has become an increasingly sensitive question, since an FRS might be consulting on the audit if it has criminal potential. The government can force the taxpayer to submit to an interview,[51] but the taxpayer can assert constitutional protections if asked a question that could incriminate him or her. Claiming a Fifth Amendment privilege, however, could strengthen the agent's suspicions and could become a factor leading to a referral to CI. Thus, having tax counsel handle all interaction with the agent in the hope of persuading the agent to gather information through means other than a taxpayer interview is often the most prudent strategy.

(b) IRS Criminal Referrals.   If a firm indication of fraud exists, the civil revenue agent suspends the civil audit without informing the taxpayer of the reason and prepares a Form 2797 (Referral Report of Potential Criminal Fraud Cases).[52] The FRS assists the agent in preparing this report, which must specify factors that support the fraud referral, including but not limited to the affirmative acts of fraud, the taxpayer's explanation of the affirmative acts, the estimated criminal tax liability, and the method of proof used for income verification.[53]

The fraud referral report then goes to a CI lead development center, and within 10 days of receipt a referral evaluation conference must take place among the referring civil agent, IRS management, and the FRS.[54] Within 30 workdays thereafter, the same parties, possibly accompanied by IRS counsel, meet again at a disposition conference to discuss the CI's decision to accept or decline the criminal referral.[55] A final decision on whether the referral meets criminal criteria should occur no later than 30 workdays after the disposition conference.[56]

This long, unexplained period of silence after much investigative activity by the revenue agent or officer is but one of the warning signs that the civil agent has consulted an FRS and is contemplating a fraud referral. Civil agents almost always remain silent about this step, so experienced practitioners have learned to identify certain activities (listed and discussed in the following) by the agent, even prior to the period of silence, as indicators of a potential referral to CI.

- In cases involving allegations of unreported income, the agent's request, summonsing, and photocopying of all bank account information could raise the specter of a criminal referral, especially if the agent has stumbled on a side account that was not accounted for in calculating the taxpayer's income. By summonsing the information, the agent ensures that the file will include copies of all bank documents and deposit items that could provide evidence of unreported income.

- A civil agent's questions about the taxpayer's lifestyle, expenditures, and other information indicate that the agent is undertaking a financial status audit[57] to ascertain whether the income reported on the return supports the taxpayer's lifestyle.

- Requests for information about assets and liabilities at the beginning and end of a given year suggest that the agent has ascertained that the taxpayer's books and records do not adequately reflect income and that the agent is considering an "indirect method of proof of income," such as the net worth method.[58]

- The civil agent requests supplier invoices, price lists, customer ledger cards, and the like to use as circumstantial evidence to prove unreported gross receipts.

- The civil agent requests the taxpayer either to submit to an interview or to answer in writing questions concerning the taxpayer's knowledge or intent about the facts and circumstances surrounding the alleged unreported income or false deductions.

- The agent refuses to discuss in detail the status of the audit and the possibility of concluding the audit in the near future.

In considering a fraud referral report, the question of willfulness will heavily influence a decision to proceed with a criminal investigation. Willfulness, a necessary element of every criminal tax felony, including tax evasion, is usually proved through evidence of the taxpayer's conduct. The more egregious the conduct, the more likely a successful prosecution. Thus, CI looks for understatements of income or nonfiling over a period of years (usually three or more) as evidence of willfulness.[59]

In contrast, when a taxpayer understates income for a single year and claims it was a result of a miscommunication with a bookkeeper or gives some other plausible explanation for the income understatement, the government would find it more difficult to prove willfulness. A mere understatement of income by itself, even if it occurs in a pattern over several years, generally does not justify a CI investigation. To buttress the argument for willfulness, therefore, the government often looks for other badges of fraud, such as acts of concealment, destruction of records, altered documents, and other conduct from which one could infer willful behavior.

CI also recognizes that the taxpayer's level of education and sophistication could tip the scales. For example, lawyers educated or experienced in tax law and accountants and business owners familiar with the financial details of their business present better prospects for criminal prosecution than persons who do not have tax or financial training or who operate outside the financial realm of the business under investigation.

Tax practitioners need to understand the process by which a civil tax case works its way through the system, who makes the decisions, and the factors they consider. Practitioners need to master the facts of each case and anticipate which, if any, badges of fraud can emerge in order to prepare a cogent response should these issues arise during the civil agent's examination. Of equal importance, forcefully counseling clients not to accumulate even more badges of fraud during the investigation (including activities such as falsifying, destroying, or altering records; continuing questionable practices into the present and future years; or transferring or concealing assets under investigation) can stave off the final badge that could tip the balance toward a criminal referral.

37.9 INVESTIGATION BY CI: ADMINISTRATIVE VERSUS GRAND JURY INVESTIGATIONS

A CI investigation typically begins with the receipt by CI of information concerning potential criminal violations of one or more of the statutes discussed in Section 37.2 of this chapter. This information can come from the general public, another IRS component, a U.S. Attorney's office, another law enforcement agency, or another CI investigation. Although a division chief must approve the opening of a CI investigation of an individual or entity, he or she can delegate this authority to a branch chief for all but money laundering violations.

Once CI has opened an investigation, a special agent will conduct an investigation and prepare a Special Agent Report (SAR) that the agent's superiors will use to decide whether to refer the case to the Department of Justice (DOJ). If the DOJ decides to prosecute and brings charges against the target, the special agent will assist the prosecutor in the trial of the case.

If the special agent considers an administrative investigation as inviable or inappropriate, he or she will then seek to conduct the investigation through a federal grand jury.[60] Special agents request grand jury investigations when such an option appears more efficient (i.e., the administrative process cannot develop the relevant facts within a reasonable period of time), or when an investigation has proceeded as far as the administrative process allows, but the grand jury process would strengthen the prosecution's case.

37.10   GOVERNMENT'S STANDARD OF REVIEW FOR A CRIMINAL TAX CASE

The government's standard underlying review of criminal tax matters for authorization of prosecution requires that the government have evidence supporting a *prima facie* case, that is, minimal evidence supporting a jury's findings on each element of the crime. The government also requires a reasonable probability of conviction.[61]

Note that the standard is a trial standard. The entire case is investigated, reviewed, and processed with a view toward winning a conviction at trial. If the government has a *prima facie* case, then the government survives the taxpayer's motion to dismiss and the case goes to the jury. Then, if a reasonable probability exists that the government prosecutor's closing argument will persuade the jury to convict, the prosecution will be authorized.

The standard is a "reasonable probability" standard, not a "substantial," or "significant," or "more likely than not" probability. In practice, the criminal tax cases authorized for prosecution have a very high probability of conviction; however, there remains the specter (which happens occasionally) that the government will go forward on a very weak criminal tax case. In such circumstances, because of the highly subjective nature of a criminal tax prosecution, even an innocent taxpayer has reason to be nervous.

37.11   ROLE OF THE ACCOUNTANT IN THE DEFENSE OF A CRIMINAL OR CIVIL TAX FRAUD CASE

Little difference exists between defending a civil tax fraud matter and a criminal tax fraud matter because the six-year statute of limitations for criminal prosecution[62] has not ended in most civil tax fraud cases that the government investigates. As a result, the people defending a civil tax fraud matter must prepare for a potential criminal investigation and prosecution.

(a) Role of the Historical Accountant.   Circumstances limit the role of the historical accountant (i.e., the accountant having some past connection to the tax case when the fraud occurred) to that of witness for the government in a criminal tax case. This holds true because communications between the historical accountant and the taxpayer lack the protection of privilege in a criminal tax matter. The tax practitioner privilege provided by IRC § 7525 applies in civil matters only.[63] Thus, in a criminal tax investigation, the government will look to the historical accountant as a major witness in the criminal case. The government will question the historical accountant with a view toward establishing that the taxpayer did not give the accountant correct information or that the taxpayer made damaging admissions to the historical accountant. An accountant who discovers that a client has engaged in allegedly fraudulent tax activity should know that the government can discover every conversation and every piece of paper generated about the subject. For this reason, the historical accountant should refer the client to an attorney who can have a privileged conversation with the client to plan a defense.

(b) Role of the Kovel Accountant.[64]   After the taxpayer hires a defense attorney, that attorney can formally retain an accountant to help the attorney defend the case. Communications among this accountant, the attorney, and the client during the course of rendering legal advice fall under the protection of attorney-client privilege. Named after the case of its origin, practitioners refer to this as a *Kovel privilege* and refer to an accountant retained by an attorney in these circumstances as a *Kovel accountant*. Likewise, the attorney's work product privilege protects he work product of the Kovel accountant.

The attorney and the Kovel accountant need to document their relation carefully. The attorney should send a retaining letter to the Kovel accountant to clarify several items:

- The accountant is working under the direction of the attorney in connection with the attorney's rendering of legal services to the client.

- The communications between the accountant and the client are confidential and occur solely to enable the attorney to give legal advice to the client.

- The accountant's workpapers are part of the attorney's work product and are subject to the attorney's right to demand the return of his or her work product at any time.

The Kovel privilege may not apply to situations in which the accountant (although working for the attorney) provides accounting services or advice that are distinguishable from assisting the attorney in providing the legal services or advice the accountant is engaged to render. For example, if the Kovel accountant also prepares tax returns for filing, the tax preparation files would not be privileged, despite the Kovel arrangement, because tax preparation files are never privileged. This Kovel privilege does not protect disclosures made to the accountant after the attorney has rendered legal advice or completed his or her engagement.

Kovel accountants help develop the financial data for analyzing the method of proof used by the government. With the current emphasis of the IRS on economic reality audits, the examination division submits fraud referrals with an extensive financial history of the taxpayer. CI and revenue agents assigned to special fraud groups develop evidence that results in the ultimate calculation of unreported income.

If the taxpayer has the financial resources, the defense team will conduct a parallel investigation in a tax fraud case. The Kovel accountant will request copies of bank records and other records that the special agent summons. By following the investigation, the defense team can reconstruct the information and evidence that the IRS has.

(c) Role of the Summary Expert Witness at Trial.   The taxpayer almost always uses an accountant as a summary expert witness at the trial of a tax fraud case, whether civil or criminal. Accountants or other experts can testify as to an opinion with respect to questions of fact. Rule 703 of the Federal Rules of Evidence allows an expert to opine using otherwise inadmissible facts or data if these are reasonably relied on by experts in a particular industry or field of practice.[65] The areas of possible testimony include interpretation of tax law related to a specific case and the use of hypothetical facts on which to base an opinion. Other areas of testimony include the standards of care and responsibility of tax preparers in tax planning, tax preparation, and representation during IRS examinations. An expert will prepare exhibits and charts to use when testifying. The expert must objectively analyze the exhibits of the government's summary witness and rebut the calculations contained therein, if possible. To provide effective rebuttal testimony and demonstrate the taxpayer's lack of willfulness, the summary expert witness must understand indirect methods of proof.

The summary expert witnesses must have the ability to explain complex financial and tax concepts to a group of laypersons: the jury. Taxpayers in criminal tax cases commonly use the defense that they relied on the advice of professionals. The government responds by establishing that the client did not provide all the facts to the tax expert or advisor, who has become just another victim of the taxpayer's fraud. Both parties can call an outside expert to opine as to what facts one would reasonably expect the taxpayer to provide and what questions one would reasonably expect a preparer to ask.

Although the Kovel accountant may have the most knowledge about the facts of the case, placing the Kovel accountant on the witness stand has several drawbacks. When the Kovel accountant becomes a witness for the taxpayer, the defense team may lose the attorney-client and work-product privileges regarding the attorney-accountant relation. Vigorous cross–examination may cause workpapers to surface or be disclosed, including any uncovered facts that can damage the taxpayer's defense. Therefore, this writer recommends use of another accountant to testify.

(d) Civil Tax Fraud Cases with no Criminal Potential.   Rarely, taxpayers defend a civil tax fraud case that has no potential of becoming a criminal case. This occurs when the statute of limitations for a criminal tax prosecution has expired. In such situations, the accountants can take advantage of the tax practitioner privilege provided by IRC § 7525 and the historical accountant will not become the government's star witness. This reduces the need for a separate Kovel accountant, and the historical accountant can participate in the defense. With no criminal potential, the taxpayer need not hire a lawyer before it becomes apparent that the civil tax fraud case will go to trial. The factual and legal development of the civil tax fraud case, as indicated in Section 37.3 of this chapter, will resemble that of a tax evasion case brought under § 7201.

(e) Pre-IRS Referral and Voluntary Disclosure.   The accountant can play a critical role in taking advantage of the IRS's voluntary disclosure policy. Practitioners often struggle with whether a taxpayer can avoid a criminal tax investigation by disclosing prior tax crimes to the IRS. Through such a voluntary disclosure, the taxpayer reports previously undisclosed income (or eliminates previously taken false deductions) through an amended return or the filing of a delinquent return. A taxpayer who makes a voluntary disclosure faces the problem of making a *de facto* confession to the IRS of filing incorrect returns. Thus, the taxpayer runs the risk of conviction of a tax crime on the basis of admissions derived from the voluntary disclosure itself. However, a taxpayer's timely, voluntary disclosure of a significant unreported tax liability becomes an important factor to the IRS in considering whether to refer the matter to the DOJ for criminal prosecution.[66] The DOJ will also consider a voluntary disclosure in deciding whether to prosecute a taxpayer.[67] Properly filed, such a disclosure can lead the IRS to excuse the criminal charges of filing a fraudulent return or failing to file a return.

A voluntary disclosure must be truthful, timely, and complete, and the taxpayer must demonstrate a willingness to cooperate (and must in fact cooperate) with the IRS in calculating the correct tax liability.[68] The taxpayer must make good faith arrangements with the IRS to pay in full the tax, interest, and any penalties that the IRS identifies as applicable.[69] Often the IRS will make the taxpayer pay the civil fraud penalty in a voluntary disclosure. Thus, the voluntary disclosure policy does not help the taxpayer regarding a civil fraud penalty. Additionally, the policy only applies to income earned through a legal business, referred to as *legal source income.* Al Capone could not take advantage of the policy.

The recent revisions to the policy clarify the timeliness requirement of the policy, an issue long troubling to practitioners. To be timely, the IRS must receive the disclosure before the IRS has done the following:

- Initiated a civil examination or criminal investigation of the taxpayer, or has notified the taxpayer that it intends to commence such an examination or investigation
- Received information from a third party (e.g., informant, other governmental agency, or the media) alerting the IRS to the specific taxpayer's noncompliance
- Initiated a civil examination or criminal investigation that directly relates to the specific liability of the taxpayer
- Acquired information directly related to the specific liability of the taxpayer from a criminal enforcement action (e.g., search warrant, grand jury subpoena)[70]

Examples of timely voluntary disclosures include the following:

- A letter from an attorney that encloses amended returns from a client that include complete and accurate data (reporting legal source income omitted from the original returns). This letter should also offer to pay the total tax, interest, and any penalties that the IRS deems applicable and meet the timeliness standard set forth above.
- A disclosure made by a taxpayer of omitted income facilitated through a widely promoted tax evasion scheme for which the IRS has begun a civil compliance project. The IRS considers such a disclosure voluntary if the IRS has already obtained information that might lead to an examination of the

taxpayer but has not yet begun to examine or investigate the taxpayer or notified the taxpayer of such an intent. In other words, the civil compliance project involving the scheme does not yet directly relate to the specific liability of the taxpayer.

- A disclosure made by an individual who has not filed tax returns after the individual has received a notice stating that the IRS has no record of receiving a return for a particular year and inquiring into whether the taxpayer filed a return for that year. The individual files complete and accurate returns and makes arrangements with the IRS to pay the entire tax, interest, and any penalties that the IRS deems applicable. The IRS considers this a voluntary disclosure because the IRS has not yet begun to examine or investigate the taxpayer or notified the taxpayer of such an intent.[71]

Under the revised policy, a voluntary disclosure does not occur until the taxpayer or a representative has contacted the IRS. Therefore, the disclosure must occur as quickly as possible. The IRS will rarely recommend criminal prosecution if a timely voluntary disclosure has occurred. Since returns filed pursuant to a timely voluntary disclosure have significant audit potential, they need to correctly reflect the taxpayer's income items. Various federal-state information sharing agreements suggest that one should contemporaneously file or amend any applicable state returns with the federal returns. One should also contemporaneously file returns for related entities. The taxpayer should resolve questions or doubts in the government's favor. A voluntary disclosure that contains inaccurate information compounds rather than helps the problem.

How many returns must one file or amend? Most practitioners suggest six tax years because the applicable statute of limitations for most tax-related crimes is six years.[72] The disclosure should eliminate any IRS concern regarding a particular tax year for which the applicable statute of limitations for criminal prosecutions has not already expired. Additional returns could be in order since the statute of limitations for a criminal prosecution is tolled (i.e., suspended) for the period of time a taxpayer is outside the United States or is a fugitive from justice.[73]

(f) Pre-CI Referral: The Eggshell Audit. An *eggshell audit* refers to the situation in which an income tax return that could have potential criminal exposure has been assigned to either a revenue agent or an office auditor for examination. The examiner assigned to conduct the audit need not know of the potential criminal exposure. However, the civil examination poses the possibility of turning into a criminal investigation if the routine audit uncovers badges of fraud. In these situations, the attorney and the Kovel accountant must exercise care in ensuring that neither the attorney, nor the client, nor the Kovel accountant provide false or misleading information to the examiner. Professionals involved in an eggshell audit must not mislead the IRS investigation; otherwise, they run a risk of prosecution and loss of their license to practice. Often the best case scenario in an eggshell audit is to limit the taxpayer's exposure to civil liability only, without the IRS addressing the potential fraud-sensitive issues.

The historical accountant should not assume that a notice of exam is just an ordinary computer-generated event. A client's tax situation could have caught the attention of the IRS in many ways that could also predispose the examiner to focus closely on possible badges of fraud.

37.12   CONCLUSION: SOME PARTING ADVICE REGARDING CRIMINAL AND CIVIL TAX FRAUD

So how do you bulletproof yourself and your clients from any possible criminal or civil tax fraud liability? Simple: don't give the government any badges of fraud to work with. Even with an enormous tax deficiency, without badges of fraud, the government does not have a criminal tax fraud case or a civil tax fraud case.

NOTES

1. *Helvering v. Gregory*, 69 F. 2d 809, 810 (2d Cir. 1934), *aff'd*, 290 U.S. 465 (1935).
2. Internal Revenue Manual 9781 §412 (Jan. 18, 1980).
3. I.R.M. 9781 § 412 (January 18, 1980).
4. The rules for tax fraud discussed in this chapter apply equally to people or entities.
5. All references to the Internal Revenue Code are to the Internal Revenue Code of 1986, as amended.
6. *Sansone v. United States*, 380 U.S. 343, 354 (1965).
7. *United States v. Hogan*, 861 F.2d 312, 315 (1st Cir. 1988); *United States v. Dack*, 747 F.2d 1172, 1174 (7th Cir. 1984).
8. *Sansone*, 380 U.S. 343.
9. *Kahr v. Commissioner*, 414 F. 2d 621, 627 (2d Cir. 1969).
10. *United States v. Pomponio*, 429 U.S. 10, 12 (1976).
11. *McGee v. Commissioner*, 61 T.C. 249, 256 (1976), *aff'd*, 519 F. 2d 1121 (5th Cir. 1975).
12. For example, an intentional failure to check the box on a Form 1040 Schedule B showing signature authority over a foreign bank account, if false, would violate § 7206(1).
13. *United States v. Bishop*, 412 U.S. 346, 350 (1973).
14. *United States v. Williams*, 644 F.2d 696, 701 (8th Cir. 1981).
15. *United States v. Searan*, 259 F.3d 434, 443-44 (6th Cir. 2001).
16. *United States v. Searan*, 259 F.3d 434, 441, 443-44.
17. *Hammerschmidt v. United States*, 265 U.S. 182, 188 (1924); *United States v. Collins*, 78 F.3d 1021, 1037 (6th Cir. 1996).
18. *United States v. Klein*, 247 F.2d 908, 915 (2d Cir. 1957).
19. *United States v. Falcone*, 311 U.S. 205, 210 (1940).
20. *Holland v. United States*, 348 U.S. 121, 126 (1954).
21. 26 U.S.C. § 7454(a); U.S. Tax Court R. of Prac. & Proc. 142(b); *Edelson v. Commissioner*, 829 F. 2d 828, 832 (9th Cir. 1987), *aff'g* T.C. Memo 1986-223.
22. *Morrow v. Commissioner*, T.C. Memo 1967-242. *See also* 26 U.S.C. § 6663(b).
23. *Tomlinson v. Lefkowitz*, 334 F. 2d 262 (5th Cir. 1964), *cert. denied*, 379 U.S. 962 (1965); *McKinon v. Commissioner*, T.C. Memo 1988-323 (granting summary judgment against taxpayer for fraud penalties on account of conviction for all years).
24. *Delgado v. Commissioner*, T.C. Memo 1988-66.
25. 26 U.S.C. § 6663.
26. *Wright v. Commissioner*, 84 T.C. 636, 643 (1985).
27. *Holland v. United States*, 348 U.S. 121, 132 (1954); *United States v. Baum*, 435 F.2d 1197, 1201 (7th Cir. 1971); *United States v. Doyle*, 234 F.2d 788, 793 (7th Cir. 1956).
28. *United States v. Black*, 843 F. 2d 146, 148 (D.C. Cir. 1988).
29. *United States v. Marabelles*, 724 F.2d 1374, 1377 n.1 (9th Cir. 1984); *United States v. Horton*, 526 F.2d 884, 886 (5th Cir. 1976). *See also United States v. Genser*, 582 F.2d 292, 295-96 n.1 (3d Cir. 1978); *United States v. Allen*, 551 F.2d 208 (8th Cir. 1977); *United States v. Bray*, 546 F.2d 851, 856-57 (10th Cir. 1976).

30. *United States v. Martin*, 525 F.2d 703, 707 (2d Cir. 1975).

31. *Holland*, 348 U.S. at 129 (1954); *United States v. Hall*, 650 F.2d 994, 999 (9th Cir. 1981); *United States v. Bray*, 546 F.2d 851, 856 (10th Cir. 1976) ("the bank deposits method of proof is not an exact science").

32. *United States v. Hall*, 650 F.2d at 999.

33. *Gleckman v. United States*, 80 F.2d 394 (8th Cir. 1935).

34. *Id.* at 399.

35. *United States v. Abodeely*, 801 F.2d 1020, 1023 (8th Cir. 1986); *United States v. Stone*, 770 F.2d 842, 844 (9th Cir. 1985); *United States v. Helina*, 549 F.2d 713, 720 (9th Cir. 1977); *United States v. Morse*, 491 F.2d 149, 152 (1st Cir. 1974); *United States v. Slutsky*, 487 F.2d 832, 841-42 (2d Cir. 1973); *United States v. Venuto*, 182 F.2d 519, 521 (3d Cir. 1950).

36. *United States v. Johnson*, 319 U.S. 503, 517 (1943).

37. *Holland v. United States*, 348 U.S. 121, 129 (1954); *United States v. Giacalone*, 574 F.2d 328, 332 (6th Cir. 1978). *See also United States v. Gomez-Soto*, 723 F.2d 649, 655 (9th Cir. 1983); *United States v. Schafer*, 580 F.2d 774, 777 (5th Cir. 1978).

38. *Holland*, 348 U.S. at 132; *United States v. Mastropieri*, 685 F.2d 776, 778 (2d Cir.1982).

39. *Massei v. United States*, 355 U.S. 595 (1958); *United States v. Calderon*, 348 U.S. 160 (1954); *Smith v. United States*, 348 U.S. 147 (1954); *Friedberg v. United States*, 348 U.S. at 142 (1954); *Holland*, 348 U.S. at 121; *United States v. Johnson*, 319 U.S. 503.

40. *United States v. Sorrentino*, 726 F.2d 876, 879-80 (1st Cir. 1984) (citations omitted).

41. *United States v. Schafer*, 580 F.2d 774, 775 (5th Cir. 1978).

42. *United States v. Breger*, 616 F.2d 634, 635 (2d Cir. 1980); *Taglianetti v. United States*, 398 F.2d 558, 562 (1st Cir. 1968), *aff'd*, 394 U.S. 316 (1969); *United States v. Caserta*, 199 F.2d 905, 906 (3d Cir. 1952).

43. *United States v. Johnson*, 319 U.S. 503, 517 (1943).

44. *United States v. Caserta*, 199 F.2d at 907.

45. *Taglianetti*, 398 F.2d at 562 (footnotes omitted).

46. *Id.* at 562 (cited in *United States v. Sutherland*, 929 F.2d 765, 780 (1st Cir. 1991)).

47. *United States v. Hogan*, 886 F.2d 1497 (7th Cir. 1989).

48. *Spies v. United States*, 317 U.S. 492, 499 (1942).

49. I.R.M. 25.1.2.2 (Jan. 1. 2003) (Indicators of Fraud).

50. Review of the Internal Revenue Service's Criminal Investigation Division (Apr. 1999) (citing I.R.M. 104.2.4.3 and I.R.M. 4.4565.21(1)).

51. 26 U.S.C. §7602.

52. I.R.M. 25.1.3.2(1) (Jan. 1, 2003) (Preparation of Form 2797).

53. I.R.M. 25.1.3.2(2) (Jan. 1, 2003) (Preparation of Form 2797).

54. I.R.M. 25.1.3.3(1) (Jan. 1. 2003) (Referral Evaluation).

55. *Id.*

56. I.R.M. 25.1.3.3(2) (Jan. 1, 2003) (Referral Evaluation).

57. *See* 26 U.S.C. § 7602(e).

58. The net worth and expenditures method is a recognized indirect method of proof that has been used in reconstructing income in criminal tax cases. *See* I.R.M. 9.5.8.6.2 (Mar. 19, 1999) (Net Worth Investigation); *Holland*, 348 U.S. at 121.

59. *Holland*, 348 U.S. at 121.

60. IRM 9.5.2. (Nov. 5, 2004) (Grand Jury Investigations).

61. U.S. Department of Justice, Criminal Tax Manual, Standards of Review, §6-4.211 (1994).

62. 26 U.S.C. § 6532.

63. § 7525 applies the "same common law protections of confidentiality which apply to communication between a taxpayer and an attorney" to any communication between a taxpayer and "any federally authorized tax practitioner to the extent the communication would be considered a privileged communication if it were between a taxpayer and an attorney" in civil matters only.

64. *See United States v. Kovel*, 296 F. 2d 918, 922 (2d Cir 1961).

65. *Kumo Tire Company, Ltd., v. Carmichael*, 119 S. Ct. 1167 (1999), *Daubert v. Merrell Dow Pharmaceuticals*, 509 U.S. 579 (1993).

66. I.R.M. 9.5.3.3.1.2.1 (9/9/04) (Voluntary Disclosure Practice)

67. U.S. Department of Justice, Criminal Tax Manual, Memorandum From: James A. Bruton, Acting Assistant Attorney General, Tax Division, *re* Tax Division Voluntary Disclosure Policy, February 17, 1993.

68. I.R.M. (9.5).3.3.1.2.1 (12/11/02).

69. I.R.M. (9.5).3.3.1.2.1 (12/11/02).

70. I.R.M. (9.5).3.3.1.2.1 (12/11/02).

71. I.R.M. (9.5).3.3.1.2.1 (12/11/02).

72. 26 U.S.C. § 6531.

73. 26 U.S.C. § 6531.

PART VII

INVESTIGATIONS

CHAPTER **38**

FINANCIAL STATEMENT INVESTIGATION

Steven L. Skalak
Charles R. Hacker, Jr.
Daniel V. Dooley

CONTENTS

38.1   INTRODUCTION

Financial statement investigators seek to establish whether an entity has prepared financial statements in a manner that misleads the users. Such investigations prove difficult, not only because of the complex rules governing the form and content of financial statements but also because investigators must also establish (or disprove) the basic elements of a fraud. Thus, financial statement investigations must consider the following:

- A basis of accounting, most often the U.S. generally accepted accounting principles (GAAP) or International Financial Reporting Standards (IFRS).

- Securities and Exchange Commission (SEC) regulations, or (in various non-U.S. territories) Company Act requirements or the equivalent, as to the form and content of the financial statements. In the United States, these include the Securities Act of 1933, the Exchange Act of 1934, the Private Securities Litigation Reform Act of 1995, and various regulations promulgated pursuant to such acts, such as Regulations S-X, and S-K.
- Concepts of materiality contained in GAAP and SEC standards such as Staff Accounting Bulletin No. 99, *Materiality.*
- The basic elements of fraud:

  - **Misrepresentation.** Presenting false information or withholding information of a material nature
  - **Scienter.** Knowledge that the representation is false, or a reckless disregard for its truth
  - **Reliance.** A plaintiff's reasonable and justifiable reliance on a false representation
  - **Damages.** Financial harm resulting from the first three factors

Generally accepted auditing standards (GAAS) provide a useful definition of financial statement fraud as follows:

- **Misstatements arising from fraudulent financial reporting** are intentional misstatements or omissions of amounts or disclosures in financial statements designed to deceive financial statement users where the effect causes the financial statements not to be presented, in all material respects, in conformity with generally accepted accounting principles (GAAP). Fraudulent financial reporting may be accomplished by the following:

  - Manipulation, falsification, or alteration of accounting records or supporting documents from which financial statements are prepared
  - Misrepresentation in or intentional omission from the financial statements of events, transactions, or other significant information
  - Intentional misapplication of accounting principles relating to amounts, classification, manner of presentation, or disclosure
    Fraudulent financial reporting need not be the result of a grand plan or conspiracy. It may be that management representatives rationalize the appropriateness of a material misstatement, for example, as an aggressive rather than indefensible interpretation of complex accounting rules, or as a temporary misstatement of financial statements, including interim statements, expected to be corrected later when operational results improve.

- **Misstatements arising from misappropriation of assets** (sometimes referred to as theft or defalcation) involve the theft of an entity's assets where the effect of the theft causes the financial statements not to be presented, in all material respects, in conformity with GAAP. Misappropriation of assets can be accomplished in various ways, including embezzling receipts, stealing assets, or causing an entity to pay for goods or services that have not been received. Misappropriation of assets may be accompanied by false or misleading records or documents, possibly created by circumventing controls. The scope of this section includes only those misappropriations of assets for which the effect of the misappropriation causes the financial statements not to be fairly presented, in all material respects, in conformity with GAAP.

Financial statement frauds involving intentional misstatements are often motivated by any of the varied uses of financial statements. Such uses include the acquisition of and continued access to capital through either public markets (e.g., the stock exchanges in countries throughout the world) or private sources (e.g., private equity investors, banks, and private placement of bond offerings). These markets function smoothly when entities provide reliable financial statements, but they expose investors to losses of significant magnitude when entities disseminate false financial statements. Accordingly, financial statement investigations can arise from the following:

- Issuance of false financial statements in initial public offerings of securities
- Issuance of false financial statements to maintain the trading price of publicly traded securities in the secondary market (NYSE, NASDAQ, FTSE, DAX, etc.)
- Bankruptcy
- Theft of assets
- Fraudulent borrowing schemes
- Ponzi-type schemes in which the entity must continue to raise new money to pay off initial investors (e.g., Bennett Funding and Princeton Economics International)
- Employee improprieties that produce losses disguised by false financial statements (e.g., Barings Bank, Sumitomo Corp, Daiwa Bank, and First Allied Irish Bank)
- Tax fraud

Financial statement investigations can help resolve other types of litigation or regulatory issues, for example, when the misstatement arises from a misappropriation of assets, or the valuation of an enterprise requires a thorough investigation and adjustment of the financial statements before they form a reliable basis for calculating claims or damages. Financial statement investigation is often the first step in identifying other types of improprieties, such as payments in violation of the Foreign Corrupt Practices Act, transactions with related parties, and uncovering disbursement schemes to steal corporate assets. In these situations, the financial statements often harbor entries that conceal the wrongdoing; thus, the financial statement investigation will help uncover the scheme. This chapter will not focus on such circumstances, however. Instead, we will discuss situations in which the financial statement itself becomes an integral element of the fraud, not merely an ancillary aspect of covering up a theft or corrupt payment.

Financial statements are essential elements of deceit in many types of schemes, which we divide into two broad categories:

1. Schemes that seek to obtain funds by presenting an overly rosy picture of an enterprise's financial condition. For example, an entity could present false financial statements with a loan application.
2. Schemes that seek to disguise a weakness or disappointing trend to maintain access to credit, support share prices, justify management's compensation, and so on. For example, an entity could fabricate revenue entries to hit the year's budgeted earnings target.

Most of the major financial reporting scandals from 2000 to 2005 belong to this second category: long-serving management teams, often the founders of the business, either improperly burnished otherwise substantial accomplishments or improperly maintained the appearance of success when in fact the business was stagnating or collapsing—circumstances that the stock market punishes with declining share prices. The need for financial statement investigations can arise from bankruptcy, changing business dynamics that lead to losses, rogue employees who overcommit to risky investments and run up substantial losses, management that provides false estimates to meet analysts' consensus earnings, or issues that relate to the personal finances or lifestyle of key executives. Regardless of the underlying incentive or pressure that caused the fraud, a financial statement investigation will likely focus on one or more key themes.

38.2   KEY THEMES OF FINANCIAL STATEMENT FRAUD

(a) Revenue Recognition: The Most Common Financial Statement Fraud.   In spite of its variety and complexity, financial statement fraud nevertheless has several recurring themes and elements. Financial statements mislead when they include a falsehood or omit important information. Practitioners refer to these two basic financial statement manipulations as *inclusive* and *exclusive* fraud. The most common type of financial statement fraud—improper revenue recognition—is an example of an inclusive fraud. Management and shareholders believe more is better when it comes to revenue.[1] Accordingly, many schemes include fictitious revenue transactions or premature revenue recognition that increase the amount reported in financial statements. These include the following:

- Accelerating shipments, including sending customer orders before the agreed shipping dates
- Holding the books open for sales made subsequent to the end of the accounting period
- Recognizing revenue for transactions that do not qualify as sales, such as consignments, bill and hold transactions that do not meet all seven criteria listed in Exhibit 38-1, products shipped for trial purposes, or sales with acceptance conditions that the entity hasn't met
- Executing swaps, round trips, or other sham transactions to increase sales volume
- Manipulating the estimate of the percentage of progress toward completion on long-term contracts
- Allocating all the profit to immediately recognizable elements in multiple-element contracts
- Manipulating necessary valuation estimates for returns, allowances, prompt-pay discounts, or markdowns
- Recording fictitious sales

Except for the last item, recording fictitious sales, investigating any of these schemes will bring the investigator to the two basic principles of revenue recognition contained in both U.S. GAAP[2] and SEC Staff Accounting Bulletins: (1) the earnings process is complete, and (2) collection is reasonably assured. We see these concepts echoed in four basic criteria for revenue recognition first set out in the American Institute of Certified Public Accountants (AICPA) Statement of

1. Risk of ownership has passed to the Buyer.
2. The Buyer has made a written commitment to purchase the goods.
3. The Buyer, not the Seller, requested the bill and hold transaction and has a substantial business purpose in making the request.
4. Delivery must be fixed and on a schedule appropriate to the Buyer's purpose.
5. Seller must not retain any obligations under the arrangement.
6. The "held" goods must be physically segregated from the Seller's inventory and cannot be used to fill other orders.
7. The product must be complete and ready for shipment.

Exhibit 38-1.   Bill and Hold Transaction Criteria for Revenue Recognition

Position 97-2, *Software Revenue Recognition* and later reiterated in SEC Staff Accounting Bulletin No. 104, *Revenue Recognition, Corrected Copy:*

1. persuasive evidence that an arrangement with the customer exists;
2. evidence that the delivery of the goods or services has occurred;
3. evidence that the price of the goods and services is fixed or determinable (including estimates of returns and other allowances that may apply); and
4. reasonable assurance of the seller's ability to collect and the buyer's ability to pay.

The SEC has set forth specific criteria, listed in Exhibit 38-1, under which a seller can recognize revenue from bill and hold transactions. The Commission created these criteria when it suspected that some sellers used bill and hold transactions to accelerate the recognition of sales at or near the end of quarterly financial reporting periods.[3]

(b) Timing: A Key Aspect of Revenue Recognition Schemes.   These revenue recognition standards relate to the concept of timing. Except for fictitious revenue transactions, most improperly recognized transactions will qualify for recognition at some future date. One could consider revenue recognition schemes as robbing the future in that they accelerate to the current accounting period transactions that entities should recognize in a later period. Thus, the financial statement investigator focuses on discovering the facts and circumstances relating to a recognized revenue transaction *at a particular point in time.* This question of timing relates to all the four basic criteria of revenue transactions listed in Section 38.3(a). Accordingly, investigators will need the following information:

1. When the seller finalized the arrangement with the customer or when the customer communicated that acceptance testing or trial periods had been completed
2. When the seller delivered goods or completed their installation
3. When the price became fixed and determinable (this is most often straightforward except when the customer has significant rights of return or other rights leading to price adjustments such as retail markdowns)
4. Whether the buyer had the ability to pay at the transaction date

Some schemes manipulate the justification for when to recognize the transaction or conceal key transaction terms that would set a different date for recording the revenue. These schemes include the following:

- Creating side arrangements that alter the basic terms of transaction documents—often with respect to rights of return—that one can file separately or otherwise conceal.

- Accelerating purchases with channel stuffing, wherein the seller offers extraordinary terms (e.g., a longer time to pay, deep discounts, free shipping, and unlimited return rights). This scheme accelerates customer purchases weeks or months in advance of the customer's need for the products.

- Recording bill and hold transactions, wherein the seller records sales before the customer can or wants to store the goods at its own premises, so the seller holds the goods. In the SEC's view, this type of transaction calls into question seven elements of evidence as to whether an exchange has in fact occurred. (Exhibit 38-1 lists these elements.)

- Sending the product to the customer in advance of agreed-upon delivery dates.

- Recognizing revenue on an entire order when the seller has shipped only a portion.

- Altering the percentage of progress toward completion on long-term contracts to accelerate revenue, most often accomplished by underestimating the total costs at completion.

- Assigning a disporportionate amount of the total sales price to items that the seller immediately delivers. For example, by assigning a disproportionate portion of the contract price to a piece of equipment sold with a monthly maintenance contract, an improper amount of revenue is immediately recognized upon delivery or installation of the equipment. However, the maintenance revenues required to be recognized over the future periods covered by the contract are now artificially reduced.

These examples show that timing is a critical aspect of the fact-finding portion of an investigation into revenue recognition as well as other elements of a financial statement.

(c) Earnings Management. In addition to looking for inflated revenues, financial statement investigators must ascertain whether an entity is or has engaged in earnings management. Earnings management is the improper application of managerial judgments necessary to apply accounting principles or, in its worst form, the creation of fictitious entries. Revenue manipulation is a significant element of an earnings management scheme, but earnings management can affect other elements of the financial statements as well. For example, entities can defer expenses, omit liabilities, or overstate assets.

(i) Inclusive Fraud. As Section 38.2 explains, inclusive fraud manipulates data by including false transactions. Some entities combine inclusive and exclusive fraud schemes to manipulate financial results. Exhibit 38-2 illustrates how the inclusion

Assets or Liabilities	Revenues or Expenses
Accounts Receivable [Overstated]	Revenue [Overstated]
Allowance for Sales Returns [Understated]	Revenue [Overstated]
Doubtful Accounts Allowance [Understated]	Bad Debt Expense [Understated]
Inventory [Overstated]	Cost of Goods Sold [Understated]
Inventory Reserves (for Lower-of-Cost-Or-Market Impairment) [Understated]	Cost of Goods Sold [Understated]
Inventory [Overstated]	Direct Expenses [Understated]
Prepaid or Deferred Assets [Overstated]	Direct, Indirect or Selling, General and Administrative (SG&A) Expenses [Understated]
Accounts Payable, or Accrued Liabilities, or Other Obligations [Understated]	Expenses [Understated]

Exhibit 38-2.   Illustration of Inclusive and Exclusive Fraud Schemes

or exclusion of entries from financial statement accounts commonly used in such schemes results in inflated profits.

As Exhibit 38-2 shows, these types of frauds can involve the creation of fictitious assets, or the omission of actual liabilities, or both. As discussed in Section 38.2(b), such frauds also involve the timing of transactions with the following manipulations:

- Revenues and receivables recognized before they are earned and realizable
- Costs of goods sold deferred beyond when the seller should have accrued them by overstating the value of inventories, or by deferring the recognition of purchases, costs (materials, labor, and supplies), or indirect and overhead expenses
- Contingencies—such as doubtful accounts allowances, sales returns allowances, warranty and product liability reserves, litigation reserves—not recognized when they were first probable and estimable, thus resulting in delayed recognition of associated provision expenses
- Accruals of accounts payable and other liabilities not recognized when the seller incurred the obligations, delaying recognition of the related expenses

With creation of fictitious assets, the two most common frauds involve: (1) recording fictitious revenues (overstating associated receivables), and (2) recording fictitious inventory (understating cost of goods sold). However, when an entity creates a fictitious debit in any balance sheet account, it can create an equal fictitious credit to a revenue or expense account in the profit and loss statement (P&L), thereby overstating earnings.

(ii) Exclusive Fraud.   Exclusive frauds involve the exclusion of liabilities or other obligations (e.g., commitments, guarantees, or contingencies) from a company's balance sheet. The effects of such exclusions include

- Associated understatement of an expense, such as the following:

  - Environmental clean-up expenses and related litigation expense provisions associated with failure to record environmental liabilities
  - Litigation expense associated with a failure to properly record litigation reserves and judgment liabilities
  - Losses associated with debts and other long-term obligations resulting from undisclosed guarantees, commitments, or debt-related contingencies
  - Losses associated with impairments of unconsolidated assets (e.g., equity investments, joint ventures, partnerships)
  - Loss accruals related to, for example, doubtful account allowances, loan loss allowances, inventory reserves, warranty and product liability reserves, and self-insurance reserves

- Associated overstatement of liquidity measures (e.g., debt-to-equity or current ratios) and understatement of the true balance of a company's total liabilities
- Associated understatement of interest expense

(iii) Mischaracterized Transactions and Misleading Disclosures.   Some financial statement frauds intentionally mischaracterize the nature of transactions or create misleading disclosures that deal with (1) the accounting policies and procedures used to account for such transactions or events, (2) the effects of accounting changes, (3) the classification of transactions, or (4) the effect of such transactions on the reported results of operations. Examples include the following:

- Failure to properly disclose the effects of material changes in accounting estimates on both current and, possibly, future operations.
- Misclassification of operating expenses and costs (or losses) as nonrecurring when the entity should reflect such expenses as operating in nature.
- Creation of reserves (most often associated with preacquisition liabilities, restructuring charges, and other one-time charges) that intentionally exceed probable and estimable liabilities expected to be incurred and subsequent release of such reserves to offset unrelated expenses (or increase revenues). Entities often report the provisions of such reserves as nonoperating charges, but improperly report their subsequent release as ordinary course results of continuing operations.
- Misstatement of, or failure to include, key accounting policies or their effect on reported results of operations.

38.3   RESERVE SCHEMES

Another type of financial fraud is the intentional creation of "cookie jar" reserves (i.e., general reserves of the kind prohibited under SFAS No. 5, *Accounting for Contingencies*) while a company enjoys earnings that exceed the company's profit plan and the market's expectations. The company holds these reserves for a rainy day when their release can help the company achieve earnings targets.

Entities can use any allowance, loss accrual, or reserve account as a cookie jar; they simply must intentionally provide or maintain reserves that exceed identifiable, probable, and estimable contingent liabilities.

38.4 ASSET MISAPPROPRIATION AND MISSTATEMENT SCHEMES

(a) Inventory Schemes.   The first report by the Committee of Sponsoring Organizations of the Treadway Commission (COSO) found that fraudulent asset valuations accounted for nearly half of the cases of financial statement fraud,[4] and misstatements of inventory accounted for more than half of asset valuation frauds. Inventory schemes fall into two categories: quantity inflation and overvaluation.

(i) Inflation of Inventory Quantity.   Inflating inventory increases the value of assets against which many banks extend loans and also has the accounting consequence of reducing cost of goods sold expense, thereby increasing income. One or both of these reasons is often behind intentional overstatements of inventory. The simplest way to overstate inventory is to add fictitious items. Companies can create fictitious journal entries, shipping and receiving reports, purchase orders, and quantities on cycle counts or physical counts. Some companies go so far as to maintain empty boxes in a warehouse. In one inventory scheme, the company filled extra boxes with bricks that matched the company's product in size and weight so that auditors would not discover the fraud during the physical inventory count observation if they picked up, moved, or weighed individual boxes or pallets.

Many companies have engaged in fictitious inventory schemes, but perhaps the best known inventory fraud was the salad oil swindle of the 1960s.[5] Entrepreneur Anthony DeAngelis rented petroleum tanks in New Jersey and filled them with seawater, with the exception of one smaller tank, nested inside a larger tank, which he filled with salad oil. He persuaded auditors and lenders that the tanks contained more than $100 million in vegetable oil because the opening for the dipstick accessed the smaller, nested tank. DeAngelis used falsified warehouse receipts confirming the existence of the huge inventory of vegetable oil as collateral for $175 million in loans. Using the borrowed funds to speculate on vegetable oil futures in the commodities market, DeAngelis enjoyed success until vegetable oil prices took a dive and he lost everything. The lenders soon discovered the truth: they now owned tanks of seawater.

(ii) Overvaluation of Inventory: Reducing Cost of Goods Sold.   When a company sells inventory, arriving at the amounts transferred to cost of goods sold (COGS) and included in the income statement as a direct reduction of sales is a multipart exercise. Accountants refer to this as the *inventory equation* or the *COGS equation:*

$$\text{Cost of Goods Sold} = \text{Beginning Inventory} + \text{Purchases} - \text{Ending Inventory}$$
$$\text{Gross Margin} = \text{Sales Revenue} - \text{Cost of Goods Sold}$$

Companies can manipulate any element of the equation to report lower COGS expense and thereby greater profits. One can manipulate income with any of the following irregularities:

- To decrease COGS and Increase Income:
  - Decrease: beginning inventory or purchases or direct labor or overhead costs or reserve charges

- Increase: ending inventory
- To increase COGS and decrease income, reverse the above irregularities

An overvaluation of ending inventory understates COGS and in turn overstates net income.

GAAP require that companies report inventory at replacement cost or market value, whichever is lower.[6] Companies inflate inventory value for various reasons, including the use of inventory as collateral for financing. Inflating inventory value achieves the same impact on earnings as does manipulating the physical count. Companies inflate the value of inventory with the following manipulations:

- Creating false journal entries designed to increase the balance in the inventory account
- Manipulating the unit of measurement to inflate value
- Underreporting reserves for obsolete inventory (especially in industries whose products are being updated or have a short shelf life)
- Delaying the write-down of obsolete or slow-moving inventory because a write-down would require a charge against earnings

The SEC reviewed enforcement actions during the period July 31, 1997 through July 30, 2002 and published its report pursuant to Section 704 of the Sarbanes-Oxley Act of 2002 (704 Report). The 704 Report indicated that 25 enforcement actions involved overstatement of inventory values. One such action involved Rite Aid Corporation, wherein the SEC alleged that Rite Aid overstated its net income by managing the value of its inventory. Senior management allegedly failed to record $8.8 million in shrinkage due to loss or theft. The chief financial officer (CFO) also made adjusting journal entries to lower the reported cost of goods sold.[7]

(b) Accounts Receivable. Receivable schemes include creation of fictitious receivables, kiting (also known as *lapping*), redating, and overstating the value of receivables.

(i) Fictitious receivables. Companies engaging in such schemes often create fictitious orders for either existing or fictitious customers. Recording a fictitious sale in a company's books is as simple as posting a credit to the general ledger. The company then creates false supporting documentation to support the nonexistent sales or services that it never rendered. However, the company will never collect the fictitious account receivable that it created in this scheme. Eventually, this uncollected account receivable will age, that is, it will grow older and become 30 days, then 60, then 90—and more—past due. Long-past-due receivables attract attention; therefore, the company must conceal them to avoid detection of the overall scheme.

Companies can conceal the aged receivables by writing them off in a future period, based on their expectation that future revenues and profits will prove sufficient to permit such a write-off. Thus, such schemes present a form of timing irregularity. However, evidence of the original, fictitious transaction often remains in the books and records, and someone might question the reason for the write-off. One can also conceal the fraudulent transaction by charging it to an account called Sales Returns and Allowances, with the explanation that the customer returned the products for some plausible reason.

Consider the case of medical device supplier Boston Japan, which recognized more than $75 million of revenue from fraudulent sales in fiscal years 1997 to 1998.[8] Sales managers leased commercial warehouses, recorded false sales to distributors, and shipped the goods to the leased warehouses. The distributors never paid for the goods, but Boston Japan masked this by issuing credits to them and then recording false sales of the same goods to other distributors without ever moving the goods out of the leased warehouses.

Company employees even recorded sales to distributors that were not involved in the medical device business but had agreed to collude in the fraud. The company recorded some of the false sales to distributors that never resold any of the goods and never paid Boston Japan for any purported sales. The sales managers and the cooperating distributors further colluded to cover up false sales by falsely confirming the legitimacy of the sales to the company's auditors.

(ii) Lapping.   One can use lapping techniques to conceal the theft of proceeds of valid accounts receivable that have been recorded on the company's books. For example, suppose the perpetrator steals the payment intended for Customer A's account. When the company receives a payment from Customer B, the thief credits it to A's account to conceal the original theft. Thereafter, when Customer C pays, the perpetrator credits that payment to B and so on.

Perpetrators use lapping to conceal fictitious receivable balances that they created to enhance revenue and earnings. The perpetrator establishes a bogus receivable; when the company receives a payment from an unrelated customer, the thief credits it to the fictitious receivable in the same manner as described above.

In 1998, Canadian police arrested a bank manager of the Canadian Imperial Bank of Commerce. The police charged him with forging clients' signatures and using lapping to misappropriate more than $500,000 of client funds. According to police, the manager began by forging a client's signature to cash an investment certificate prematurely. The manager later redeemed a second investment and used it to cover the shortage in the first, with a little left over for personal use. Before that second investment came due, the manager would cash a third to pay the second, and so on.

Lapping is plagued by complexity and usually requires the notorious second set of books to track all the diversions and misapplications and keep a record of which receivables the perpetrator needs to cover and by which misapplied collections. Moreover, these frauds tend to grow as more fictitious entries require an increasing number of deceptions to conceal their existence. Unless the fraudster makes a future reckoning by writing off or repaying some receivable balance(s), this type of scheme becomes a perpetual motion device that must grind to a halt at some point.

(iii) Redating Receivables.   Another type of scheme relates to redating the aged receivables to a more current date. This keeps the amount from capture in the bad-debt reserve. However, auditors can still select the receivable for confirmation.

(iv) Inflating the Value of Receivables.   Inflating the value of legitimate receivables has the same effect as creating fictitious ones. GAAP requires companies to report accounts receivable at net realizable value—the gross value less an estimated allowance for uncollectible accounts.[9] GAAP also requires companies to estimate the uncollectible portion of a receivable, preferring that companies use an allowance

method generally implemented in one of two ways: (1) periodically record the estimate of uncollectible receivables as a percentage of sales or of outstanding receivables, or (2) use a calculation based on the aging of outstanding receivables.

Under the allowance method, the company should record bad-debt provisions on the income statement as a debit to bad-debt expense and as a credit to allowance for doubtful accounts on the balance sheet contra-receivable account. When all or a portion of the receivable becomes uncollectible, the company should charge the uncollectible amount against the allowance account. When the company records receivables at their true net realizable value, the recording of a bad-debt provision decreases accounts receivable, current assets, working capital, and, most important, net income.

Companies circumvent these rules by underestimating the uncollectible portion of a receivable. This artificially inflates the value of the receivable and records it at an amount higher than net realizable value. The overvaluing of receivables also serves to understate the allowance account, so that the provision is insufficient to accommodate receivables that in fact become uncollectible.

A related scheme involves failing or delaying to write off receivables that have become uncollectible. Companies find these schemes easy to execute given the subjectivity involved in estimating bad-debt provisions.

(c) Investment Schemes.   Fraudulent investment schemes provide another method for a company to overstate assets by creating fictitious investments or deliberately overvaluing existing ones. Companies can manipulate their financial statements by inflating the value of investments, misclassifying them, or failing to record unrealized declines in market value for those investments.

GAAP requires that investments in debt securities—that is, bonds and other corporate paper—be classified as either trading, held to maturity, or available for sale.[10] Companies can classify investments as held to maturity only if the holder has the positive intent and ability to hold those securities to maturity. They report held-to-maturity securities at amortized cost with no adjustment made for unrealized holdings gains or losses unless the value has declined below cost and is not expected to recover. In the latter instance, the company writes down the security to fair value and records a loss in earnings.[11]

GAAP requires that investments be classified as trading if companies buy and hold them principally for sale in the near term. Companies should classify investments not classified as trading or as held-to-maturity as available-for-sale securities.[12] The manipulation that results from these requirements first misstates the intent to hold the securities to maturity. A history of sales or reclassification of such securities to other categories can reveal that the company does not intend to hold the securities to maturity. One should ask whether the company has added securities that have lost value to the hold-to-maturity category. The second type of manipulation involves a delay in recognizing permanent market declines, often accompanied by a false explanation as to why the securities might recover in value.

Companies must report trading and available-for-sale securities at fair market value and adjust them periodically for unrealized gains and losses to bring them to fair market value. Unrealized gains or losses from trading securities are included in income for the period. Unrealized gains or losses from securities held as available for sale are reported as a component of other comprehensive income.[13]

Schemes that result in the overstatement of asset values and consequently the deferral of losses most commonly involve mispricing the securities in question. Companies can accomplish this by using a higher price, often from a date other than the balance sheet date. They can also alter a large number of prices by a very small amount that cumulatively yields the desired effect. Investigators can often detect this type of price manipulation for exchange-traded instruments because of the availability of market prices. However, in large portfolios, companies can often hide the altered or improper pricing within the high volume of items.

Companies can classify equity securities only as trading or available for sale. Unrealized gains or losses from changes in fair market value are reported in earnings for trading securities and as a component of other comprehensive income for securities available for sale.

(d) Fixed Assets

(i) Fictitious Fixed Assets.   Similar to the concept of recording fictitious sales or receivables, companies can record fictitious assets to improve the balance sheet and thereby inflate earnings. Fictitious fixed assets include assets on the books and records that do not have an apparent relation to the business, fixed assets that the company never ordered or received, and assets that the company retired but nevertheless continues to include in the financial statements.

(ii) Valuation of Fixed Assets.   One can inflate the value of a fixed asset and correspondingly reduce period expenses by extending its depreciable or amortizable life. Management has leeway to choose any depreciation method that allocates the costs to accounting periods over the useful life in a rational and systematic manner. Some schemes include unusually slow depreciation or lengthy amortization periods and frequent changes to the depreciation rate.

(iii) Improper Capitalization.   As every accountant knows, every credit must have a corresponding debit. When companies spend money or incur costs, they recognize the event by posting a credit to cash, accounts payable, or accrued expenses. The offsetting debit will recognize that either an asset has been acquired or an expense has been incurred. Financial statement fraudsters like to record expenses as assets—that is, to "hang the debit up in the balance sheet." The WorldCom case is perhaps the starkest example of how a company can inflate earnings through improper capitalization of expenses. WorldCom's internal audit department discovered that management had categorized billions of dollars as capital expenditures in 2001 that were, in fact, ordinary expenses paid to local telephone companies to complete calls. The scheme allowed WorldCom to turn a $662 million loss into a $2.4 billion profit.

Perpetrators also record extra liabilities at the time of acquiring a company and recognize the corresponding debit as goodwill. This practice spreads the expense over the goodwill amortization period and can create liabilities that the company can reverse to increase income if they find later that they do not need them. The SEC took action against Pinnacle Holdings Inc., which had acquired certain assets from Motorola, after finding that Pinnacle had improperly established more than $24 million of liabilities that did not represent liabilities at the time of the acquisition.[14] The company entered into a settlement with the SEC as a result of the enforcement action.

Software and research and development expenditures also create difficult accounting judgments that can be manipulated to defer or accelerate expense recognitions.

- **Software development costs.** GAAP requires that companies expense costs associated with software development up to the point of technological feasibility. A company establishes technological feasibility upon completion of a detailed program design or, in its absence, completion of a working model. At that point, the company must capitalize all software production costs and subsequently report them at the lower of unamortized cost or net realizable value.[15]

  Whether software has attained technological feasibility is a subjective decision that some companies abuse. By arbitrarily identifying technological feasibility, management can manipulate income by increasing or decreasing the amount capitalized or expensed.

- **Research and Development (R&D) costs.** GAAP requires that companies expense R&D costs because of the uncertainty of the amount and timing of economic benefits, but a company can capitalize materials, equipment, intangibles, or facilities that have alternative future uses.[16] The SEC has expressed concern about acquisitions in which the purchasers classify a large part of the price as in-process R&D, thus allowing the acquirer to expense the costs immediately.[17] This practice also involves the creation of liabilities for future operating expenses.

38.5 SECURITIES LITIGATION

(a) Frequency of Accounting Schemes. Data accumulated by Pricewaterhouse-Coopers LLP in its annual Securities Litigation Study reveal the frequency of these schemes. The study shows that during 2004 and 2005, 61 and 46 percent, respectively, of all securities class actions filed included one or more allegations of accounting irregularities. This percentage has been somewhat constant since 1999—with the exception of 2002, in which 81 percent of the cases included such allegations. In most years, the most common allegation in accounting-related cases was revenue recognition and revenue accounting irregularities. The other major categories comprise the following:

- Accounting estimates: 26 percent of cases filed
- Overstatement of assets (e.g., accounts receivable, inventory, or long-lived assets): 27 percent of cases filed
- Understatement of liabilities and expenses: 23 percent of the cases filed[18]

Exhibit 38-3 shows the frequency of each of the methods identified in the study.

(b) Fraud on the Market Theory. Fraud on the market is a legal theory that alleviates the need for investors in publicly traded securities to prove that they relied on the misstated financial information. When a company commits an exclusive fraud (wherein the company omits relevant material information from a financial statement or a prospectus), showing reliance on the omission would otherwise

Securities Class Action Lawsuits Filed in 2005

Percentage of accounting cases with specific issues, 2005[a]

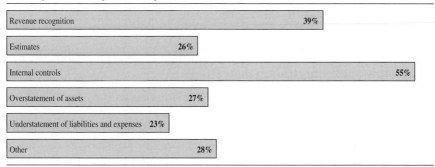

Revenue recognition	39%
Estimates	26%
Internal controls	55%
Overstatement of assets	27%
Understatement of liabilities and expenses	23%
Other	28%

[a]Because the plaintiffs often allege multiple accounting-related violations, the percentages do not total to 100 percent.

Source: Pricewaterhouse Coopers LLP 2005 Securities Litigation Study, p.10.

Exhibit 38-3.   Securities Class Action Lawsuits filed in 2005

prove difficult because at the time of the investment, the investor would not know of the omission. When inclusive fraud occurs (wherein a company includes false entries in a financial statement), the fraud on the market theory also excuses investors from showing that they relied on the false data. The fundamental presumption is that the stock market establishes a fair price considering all available information and that investors purchase shares in reliance on the accuracy or integrity of that price. Thus, if the price is incorrect because of false financial information delivered to the market, investors are relying on a false price for their purchase decision.

The seminal case establishing this principle is *Basic, Inc. v. Levinson*, in which the United States Supreme Court found that there is a rebuttable presumption of reliance on public material misrepresentations to support a fraud claim by an investor in the securities. The Court reasoned that

> the courts below properly applied a presumption of reliance, supported in part by the fraud-on-the-market theory, instead of requiring each plaintiff to show direct reliance on Basic's statements. Such presumption relieves the Rule 10b-5 plaintiff of an unrealistic evidentiary burden, and is consistent with, and supportive of, the Act's policy of requiring full disclosure and fostering reliance on market integrity. The presumption is also supported by common sense and probability: an investor who trades stock at the price set by an impersonal market does so in reliance on the integrity of that price. Because most publicly available information is reflected in market price, an investor's reliance on any public material misrepresentations may be presumed for purposes of a Rule 10b-5 action.[19]

Thus, the Supreme Court recognized that investors need not establish reliance on the actual document alleged to contain false information or omit significant information. This broad doctrine does not eliminate the reliance criteria as a necessary element of fraud. It allows the presumption in cases of widely traded publicly held securities. In situations in which the securities are not public, or no trading market exists, the presumption is generally not sufficient to prove the reliance element of a fraud claim.

Not surprisingly, plaintiffs often allege the omission of significant information when they use the fraud-on-the-market theory to demonstrate reliance. Such a complaint often contains language similar to the following:

Plaintiff will rely, in part, upon the presumption of reliance established by the fraud-on-the-market doctrine in that

1. The defendants made misleading statements and material omissions during the Class Period.
2. Company X securities traded on the New York Stock Exchange, which is an efficient market.
3. Company X stock price effectively reflected new information and announcements concerning the Company that entered the market.
4. Company X is a regulated issuer and, as such, filed periodic public reports with the SEC.
5. The trading volume of the Company's stock was substantial during the Class Period.
6. During the Class Period, Company X was followed by and regularly communicated with securities analysts employed by brokerage and research firms that wrote reports that were distributed to the sales force and certain customers of such firms and that were available on various automated data retrieval services.
7. The misrepresentations and material omissions alleged in this Complaint would tend to induce a reasonable investor to misjudge the value of the Company's stock.
8. Plaintiff and other members of the Class bought the Company's securities between the time the misleading statements and material omissions were made, without knowledge of the omitted and misrepresented facts. (This last point could alternatively be made in the context of selling shareholders).

Despite the lenient view toward proving reliance, plaintiffs must base claims of fraud on substantive allegations that material misstatements occurred. This most often means that the basic financial statements of a company are in error, possibly in one or more of the ways discussed previously in this section.

38.6   PERFORMING A FINANCIAL STATEMENT INVESTIGATION

(a) Investigation Tools and Techniques.   Financial statement investigations can use all the techniques customarily available to investigators of any subject, principally encompassing interviews and documentary review. However, the unique nature of financial accounting information and the legal requirements to maintain adequate books and records[20] make a wealth of information available to the financial statement investigator in the accounting department of most companies. In addition, even though many aspects of the earnings process appear in various operations systems—such as warehouse records of inventory, shipping records, production scheduling records, and payroll records—relevant evidence exists beyond that of the accounting department. Exhibit 38-4 lists records found in many companies.

Financial Reports:
- Audited GAAP financial statements
- Statutory financial statements
- Internal management reports and financial reporting packages
- Debt compliance reports
- Tax returns and supporting records
- Management and internal control letters

Accounting Reports:
- General ledgers and details
- Chart of accounts
- Consolidation records
- Management accounts
- Journal entries and supporting documentation
- Check registers, canceled checks, and bank statements
- Cash registers
- Cash receipt ledgers and bank deposit information
- Wire transfer ledgers and confirmations
- Sales registers
- Accounts receivable ledgers
- Accounts payable registers
- Payroll registers
- Inventory ledgers
- Inventory count sheets
- Purchases register
- Work in process registers

Supporting Records and Documents:
- Press release information, analyst calls, analyst reports, earnings estimates of third parties
- Due diligence reports
- Board and Audit Committee meeting minutes
- Auditor's working papers
- Closing packages prepared for consolidation or auditing purposes
- Closing binders and exhibits from corporate transactions
- Reconciliations of subsidiary ledgers to general ledgers
- Reconciliations of bank records to company ledgers
- Reconciliations of suspense accounts to subsidiary or general ledgers
- Account reconciliations
- Brokerage account statements and confirmations
- Insurance policies, insurance claims, insurance broker reports
- Actuarial computations and reports

Exhibit 38-4.   Financial and Accounting Reports

- Valuation computations, valuations models, valuations assumptions, valuation reports
- Goodwill and other intangible asset valuations and impairment analyses
- Loan and other debt agreements
- Liens or UCC filings
- Sales contracts, terms and conditions of sale, invoices
- Correspondence with customers and vendors by mail, e-mail, or other form
- Sales force communications with customers and sales managers
- Production records
- Shipping records including pick or packing lists, shipping manifests, and common carrier bills of lading
- Warehouse records
- Reserve analyses
- Incentive compensation plans
- Tax accrual computations and supporting records

Policies and Systems:

- Accounting policy and procedures manuals
- Personnel and organization charts
- Computer records relating to access to accounting systems, users' identification, and time of entry

Exhibit 38-4.   (Continued)

Business transactions generally require both a *counterparty*, and, if a payment is involved, a financial intermediary (e.g., a bank or broker-dealer or credit card company). This creates two useful additional sources of information. However, during a private investigation, these sources are not always available to those without subpoena power. A comparison of the customer's understanding of the terms and conditions versus the terms and conditions that the selling company used for revenue recognition will often disclose differences that prove significant to the accounting decisions.

Financial statement investigations have varied elements, but most involve the time at which factual information about transactions or other business events become known, or in some instances, became knowable. Thus, financial statement investigators often prepare timelines to capture the relevant details necessary and to ascertain whether companies have recorded transactions in the proper period. As Section 38.6(b) of this chapter discusses, intent is another key discriminator among ordinary transactions, foolish transactions, and those that involve fraud because the company wants to report a false financial statement result. In this regard, the financial statement investigator seeks to learn whether the transaction(s) had any real economic substance or merely achieved the desired accounting. One should also investigate whether the company based the accounting recognition on all the facts relating to the transaction(s) or whether the company overlooked or withheld information that would alter the accounting.

Investigators base such judgments on the facts discovered through e-mail review, accounting records, transaction records, third-party documents, and interviews with relevant company personnel to establish their recollection and understanding of the origin and completion of the transactions under review. When investigations require subjective judgments regarding risk or probability, the investigator must develop sufficient evidence to credibly establish either that the company made a reasonable judgment based on facts existing at the time and known to those responsible or that the company's explanations lack credibility.

No particular investigative formula or specific set of techniques exists for these investigative tasks. However, the financial statement investigator will frequently examine the following:

- Accounting records prepared in connection with compiling the quarterly financial statements
- Journal entries prepared at or near the end of a financial reporting period, and especially those entries that represent significant managerial judgment
- Reports of internal auditors
- Contracts or terms and conditions of sale for goods or services
- Records relating to customer complaints, returns, short payments, substitutions, or cancellations of orders
- Shipping records and warehouse records relating to the physical custody and movement of goods
- Payments made or received subsequent to the accounting period in question
- E-mails sorted or selected using key word searches from individuals expected to have knowledge of the transactions or practices in question

Even though no one practice applies to every circumstance, many financial statement investigators prefer to review most documents prior to conducting interviews. This aids in assessing the accuracy of interviewees' recollections, provides a basis for challenging inconsistent or self-serving statements, and reduces the possibility that the investigator will accept false or misleading explanations for transactions. Such interviews are often long and detailed; one or more experienced interviewers should conduct them. Interview techniques vary widely and go beyond the scope of this chapter.

(b) Examining Intent. A financial statement investigation must also address intent: the difference between error and fraud in an incorrect financial statement entry depends on whether the entry was erroneous or intentional. Generally accepted auditing standards (GAAS) explain this concept:

> Fraud is a broad legal concept and auditors do not make legal determinations of whether fraud has occurred. Rather, the auditor's interest specifically relates to acts that result in a material misstatement of the financial statements. The primary factor that distinguishes fraud from error is whether the underlying action that results in the misstatement of the financial statements is intentional or unintentional. For purposes of the section, *fraud* is an intentional act that results in a material misstatement in financial statements that are the subject of an audit.[21]

As noted in GAAS, auditors do not make legal determinations of what does or does not constitute an illegal act or a fraud, that is, auditors do not determine *intent.* However, financial statement investigations are directly concerned with determining intent.

Section 10A of the Securities Exchange Act requires that audits include "procedures designed to provide reasonable assurance of detecting illegal acts that would have a direct and material effect on the determination of financial statement amounts."[22] Section 10 A(f) broadly defines illegal acts as: "an act or omission that violates any law, or any rule or regulation having the force of law."[23] This definition is consistent with the definition in GAAS SAS No. 54 *Illegal Acts by Clients:* "The term *illegal acts,* for purposes of this section, refers to violations of laws or governmental regulations. Illegal acts by clients are acts attributable to the entity whose financial statements are under audit or acts by management or employees acting on behalf of the entity. Illegal acts by clients do not include personal misconduct by the entity's personnel unrelated to their business activities."[24] Because these definitions are broad, the matters that require investigation are correspondingly broad-ranging. They often include the following:

- Violations of securities laws and regulations, including the Sarbanes-Oxley Act of 2002
- Violations of antibribery provisions of securities law, such as the Foreign Corrupt Practices Act
- Money laundering, banking crimes, and Patriot Act violations
- Violation of local or foreign laws
- Misappropriation of assets
- Violations of the Employee Retirement Income Security Act of 1974 (ERISA)
- Labor and OSHA rule violations
- Antitrust violations
- Environmental protection law violations

Although some illegal acts committed in the business sector are relatively straightforward factual questions, the most difficult to resolve relate to violations of securities laws and regulations by fraudulent financial reporting.[24] This relates to the nature of fraud as a crime of deceit in which a principal element of the crime is the intent to deceive another person. Therefore, many financial statement investigations must resolve this question of intent. Consider, for example, the issue of revenue recognition of a year-end transaction involving a substantial discount leading to drastically reduced margins. Company A conducts the transaction with its normal terms and discloses that a material amount of sales occurred at year-end to a new customer as part of a strategic initiative to expand its customer base. Company B makes no disclosures and agrees in a side letter that the customer can return the goods without regard to their condition after May 15th of the following year. Both companies desired to record additional sales at the end of the year; however, an investigator will likely infer a different intent regarding the transaction concluded by Company B compared with that of Company A.

The presence or lack of the following factors can have a bearing on whether a transaction was intended to deceive:

- The transaction's economic substance or merit
- The transaction's documentation in the normal course of business
- Hidden terms of a transaction or irregular, unusual, oral, or hidden agreements that relate to a transaction (e.g., side letters)

- The timing of the transaction relative to the end of the financial reporting period or relative to other events such as forecasts
- The incremental impact of the transaction on the financial reporting period in question
- The transaction's function as one part of a reciprocal pair
- The transaction's disclosure in the footnotes to the financial statements and to bankers, bond rating agencies, and the board of directors
- Discussion of the transaction with the internal or external auditors
- Reporting from other parties to the transaction of the same terms and conditions

Even though all these factors will not relate to every financial statement investigation, some of them most likely apply to the majority of cases.

(c) Materiality.   When addressing financial statement fraud, the investigator must consider the issue of materiality that the financial statement preparers (and auditors) used and evaluated. Accounting principles, the SEC, and legal opinions have established criteria for materiality. FASB CON No. 2 defines materiality as

> the magnitude of an omission or misstatement of accounting information that, in light of the surrounding circumstances, makes it probable that the judgment of a reasonable person relying upon the information would have been changed or influenced by the omission or misstatement.[26]

In *TSC Industries, Inc. v. Northway, Inc.*, the Supreme Court shared this view. The Court held that "[t]here must be a substantial likelihood that the disclosure of the omitted fact would have been viewed by the reasonable investor as having significantly altered the 'total mix' of information made available."[27] The SEC defines material items as "information required to those matters about which an average prudent investor ought reasonably to be informed."[28]

Financial management had traditionally used rules of thumb or quantitative benchmarks to assist them in deciding whether an item was material for inclusion in their financial statements. One rule of thumb considered as immaterial any item that fell below a certain percentage, say 5 percent, of income or assets. Auditors would use similar thresholds in their evaluation of financial statements. The SEC in Staff Accounting Bulletin (SAB) No. 99, *Materiality*, sought to clarify its views on materiality and discussed other factors that accountants should consider when assessing the materiality of an accounting transaction, error, omission, and misstatement. SAB 99 indicated that it was not intended to change current law or accounting literature. (In fact, SABs express the staff's view as to the proper interpretation of existing law, regulations, and standards of accounting and auditing but do not change those laws, regulations, or standards). However, most observers view it as a wake-up call to the accounting profession. SAB No. 99 made two key points: (1) exclusive reliance on certain quantitative benchmarks to assess materiality in preparing or auditing financial statements is inappropriate, and (2) misstatements are not immaterial simply because they fall beneath a numerical threshold.

SAB 99 did not reject the use of a numerical threshold, such as five percent, as long as it was an initial step to evaluating materiality. It did emphasize that "financial management and the auditor must consider both 'quantitative' and qualitative' factors in assessing an item's materiality."[29] The SAB noted that certain considerations could cause quantitatively small misstatements to become material and suggested that financial management and auditors assess whether the misstatement does any of the following:

- Arises from an estimate and the degree of imprecision inherent in the estimate
- Masks a change in earnings or trends
- Hides a failure to meet analysts' expectations
- Changes a loss to income or vice versa
- Concerns a segment of the business that has been identified as playing a significant role in the company's operations or profitability
- Affects the company's compliance with regulatory requirements
- Affects compliance with loan covenants or other contractual requirements
- Increases management compensation
- Involves an illegal act

Additionally, the SAB noted that immaterial misstatements that are intentional, in certain circumstances, may be unlawful and therefore material. Thus, in the SEC's view, fraud is always material. This assessment results from the fact that all SEC registrants must, under §§ 13(b)(2)-(7) of the SEC Act, keep books and records in reasonable detail to permit the preparation of financial statements in conformity with GAAP. Accordingly, in the SEC's view an intentional failure to record transactions accurately violates securities law regardless of their materiality.

APPENDIX:
TABLE OF ACCOUNTING PRONOUNCEMENTS APPLICABLE TO REVENUE RECOGNITION

FINANCIAL ACCOUNTING STANDARDS BOARD (FASB) STATEMENTS

FAS 3	*Accounting Changes in Interim Financial Statements*
FAS 5	*Accounting for Contingencies*
FAS 13	*Accounting for Leases*
FAS 16	*Prior Period Adjustments*
FAS 29	*Determining Contingent Rentals*
FAS 45	*Accounting for Franchise Fee Revenue*
FAS 48	*Revenue Recognition When Right of Return Exists*
FAS 49	*Accounting for Product Financing Arrangements*
FAS 50	*Financial Reporting in the Record and Music Industry*
FAS 51	*Financial Reporting by Cable Television Companies*
FAS 60	*Accounting and Reporting by Insurance Enterprises*
FAS 68	*Research and Development Arrangements*
FAS 91	*Accounting for Nonrefundable Fees and Costs Associated with Originating or Acquiring Loans and Initial Direct Costs of Leases*
FAS 107	*Disclosures about Fair Value*
FAS 140	*Accounting for Transfers and Servicing of Financial Assets and Extinguishments of Liabilities*

FASB TECHNICAL BULLETINS

FTB 85-3   *Accounting for Operating Leases with Scheduled Rent Increases*

FTB 90-1   *Accounting for Separately Priced Extended Warranty and Product Maintenance Contracts*

EMERGING ISSUES TASK FORCE (EITF)

EITF 88-18   *Sales of Future Revenues*

EITF 91-6   *Revenue Recognition of Long-Term Power Sales Contracts*

EITF 91-9   *Revenue and Expense Recognition for Freight Services in Process*

EITF 93-11   *Accounting for Barter Transactions Involving Barter Credits*

EITF 95-1   *Revenue Recognition on Sales with a Guaranteed Minimum Resale Value*

EITF 98-9   *Accounting for Contingent Rent*

EITF 99-17   *Accounting for Advertising Barter Transactions*

EITF 99-19   *Reporting Revenue Gross As a Principal versus Net As an Agent*

EITF 00-3   *Application of AICPA Statement of Position 97-2 to Arrangements that Include the Right to Use Software Stored on Another Entity's Hardware*

EITF 00-8   *Accounting by a Grantee for an Equity Instrument to Be Received in Conjunction with Providing Goods or Services*

EITF 00-10   *Accounting for Shipping and Handling Fees and Costs*

EITF 00-21   *Revenue Arrangements with Multiple Deliverables*

EITF 00-24   *Revenue Recognition: Sales Arrangements That Include Specified-Price Trade-In Rights*

EITF 01-9   *Accounting for Consideration Given by a Vendor to a Customer (Including a Reseller of the Vendor's Products)*

EITF 01-14   *Income Statement Characterization of Reimbursements Received for "Out-of-Pocket" Expenses*

EITF 02-16   *Accounting by a Customer (Including a Reseller) for Certain Consideration Received from a Vendor*

EITF 03-5   *Applicability of AICPA Statement of Position 97-2 to Non-Software Deliverables in an Arrangement Containing More-Than-Incidental Software*

EITF 03-10   *Application of Issue No. 02-16 by Resellers to Sales Incentives Offered to Consumers by Manufacturers*

EITF 03-12   *Impact of FASB Interpretation No. 45 on Issue No. 95-1*

EITF Topic D-96   *Accounting for Management Fees Based on a Formula*

FASB CONCEPTS STATEMENTS

CON 2   *Qualitative Characteristics of Accounting Information*

CON 5   *Recognition and Measurement in Financial Statements of Business Enterprises*

CON 6   *Elements of Financial Statements*

ACCOUNTING PRINCIPLES BOARD (APB) OPINIONS

APB 10   *Omnibus Opinion-1966*

APB 20   *Accounting Changes*

APB 21   *Interest on Receivables and Payables*

APB 22   *Disclosure of Accounting Policies*

APB 28   *Interim Financial Reporting*

APB 29   *Accounting for Non-monetary Transactions*

ACCOUNTING STANDARDS EXECUTIVE COMMITTEE (AcSEC) AND AMERICAN INSTITUTE OF CERTIFIED PUBLIC ACCOUNTANTS (AICPA) STATEMENTS OF POSITION

SoP 81-1   *Accounting for Performance of Construction-Type and Certain Production-Type Contracts*

SoP 93-7   *Reporting on Advertising Costs*

SoP 97-2   *Software Revenue Recognition*

SoP 98-5   *Reporting on the Costs of Start-up Activities*

SoP 98-9   *Modification of SoP 97-2, "Software Revenue Recognition," with Respect to Certain Transactions*

SoP 00-1   *Auditing Health Care Third-Party Revenues and Related Receivables*

SoP 00-2   *Accounting by Producers or Distributors of Films*

STAFF ACCOUNTING BULLETINS (SAB)

SAB 104   *Revenue Recognition, Corrected Copy, 17 CFR Part 211 (December 17, 2003)*

NOTES

1. However, some earnings management schemes defer "excess" revenues to future periods, a scheme called "cookie-jarring" and discussed in Section 38.3 of this chapter.

2. *See* Appendix A for a listing of U.S. GAAP pronouncements that contain revenue recognition principles. Particularly note ARB 43, *Revision and Restatement of Accounting Research Bulletins*, Statement of Financial Accounting Standards No. 48, *Revenue Recognition When Right of Return Exists*, Statement of Financial Accounting Concepts No. 5, *Recognition and Measurement in Financial Statements of Business Enterprises*, and SEC Staff Accounting Bulletin No. 104, *Revenue Recognition, Corrected Copy* (17 CFR Part 211 (December 17, 2003)).

3. *See* U.S. Securities and Exchange Commission, *In the Matter of Stewart Parness*, AAE Rel.No. 108 (August 5, 1986).

4. The Committee of Sponsoring Organizations of the Treadway Commission (COSO), *Report of the National Commission on Fraudulent Financial Reporting* (1987), 103.

5. Norman C. Miller, *The Great Salad Oil Swindle* (New York: Howard McCann, 1965).

6. Financial Accounting Standards Board, Accounting Research Bulletin (ARB) No. 43, *Inventory Pricing* (1953), Chap. 4, statement 5.

7. AAER No. 1579 (June 21, 2002).

8. SEA Rel. No. 43183; AAE Rel. No. 1295 (August 21, 2000).

9. Financial Accounting Standards Board, FASB Statement of Financial Accounting Standards No. 5, *Accounting for Contingencies* (March 1975).

10. Financial Accounting Standards Board, FASB Statement of Financial Accounting Standards No. 115, *Accounting for Certain Investments in Debt and Equity Securities* (May 1993), ¶ 6.

11. Id., ¶7.

12. Id., ¶12 (a) and (b).

13. *Other comprehensive income* is generally defined as the change in equity of a business enterprise during a period from all transactions and events except those resulting from investments by owners and distributions to owners.

14. *See In the Matter of Pinnacle Holdings, Inc., Securities Exchange Act of 1934* (SEA) Rel. No. 45135; *Accounting and Auditing Enforcement* (AAE) Rel. No. 1476 (December 6, 2001).

15. *See* Financial Accounting Standards Board, FASB Statement of Financial Accounting Standards No. 86, *Accounting for the Costs of Computer Software to Be Sold, Leased, or Otherwise Marketed* (August 1985).

16. *See* Financial Accounting Standards Board, FASB Statement of Financial Accounting Standards No. 2, *Accounting for Research and Development Costs* (October 1974).

17. Arthur Levitt, "The Numbers Game'" (speech, New York University Center for Law and Business, September 28, 1998), www.sec.gov/news/speech/speecharchive/1998/spch220.txt.

18. Amounts are drawn from 2005 but are good approximations of the experience of the five years then ending.

19. *Basic, Inc. v. Levinson*, 485 U. S. 224 (1988).

20. *See,* for example, the requirement of the Securities Exchange Act relating to a public company's books and records at Section 13(B)2(b)

21. AICPA Statement of Auditing Standards No. 99, *Consideration of Fraud in a Financial Statement Audit*, ¶05, "Types of Fraud in Financial Statements," which appears in Section 38.1 of this chapter.

22. Title III of the Private Securities Litigation Reform Act of 1995 which amends the Securities Exchange Act of 1934 (15 USC 78; -1)

23. Title III of The Private Securities Litigation Reform Act of 1995 which amends The Securities Exchange Act of 1934. *See* Section 10 Af. Definitions.

24. AICPA Statement of Auditing Standards No. 54, *Illegal Acts by Clients*, ¶02.

25. AICPA Statement of Auditing Standards No. 99, *Consideration of Fraud in a Financial Statement Audit*, recognizes two types of fraud that may affect a financial statement: misstatements arising from fraudulent financial reporting and misstatements arising from misappropriation of assets. *See* excerpt of statement in Section 38.1 of this chapter.

26. Financial Accounting Standards Board, Statement of Financial Accounting Concepts No. 2 "Qualitative Characteristics of Accounting Information," Glossary of Terms. May 1980.

27. *TSC Industries, Inc. v. Northway, Inc.*, 426 US 438(1976), Section II c.

28. SEC Financial Statement Requirements Regulation S-X, Rule 1-02 Definition of terms used in Regulation S-X.

29. SEC SAB No. 99, *Materiality*, 3.

CHAPTER 39

INTERNATIONAL INVESTIGATIONS

Frederic R. Miller

CONTENTS

39.1 INTRODUCTION

Investigation work has many similarities, no matter what country an analyst works in. For that reason, most of the guidance in Chapter 38 of this book ("Financial Statement Investigation") applies regardless of a company's location throughout the world. This short chapter addresses some of the additional considerations that can make overseas investigations challenging and, at times, risky or frustrating. The expansion of global trade and development, however, has created a corresponding demand for global forensic services.

The United States and Canadian audience to whom this book is principally oriented informs our perspective and also our nomenclature. Accordingly, this chapter uses *foreign*, *international*, and *global* interchangeably to describe jurisdictions outside those two countries. The chapter uses *local* to describe the experience or resources within those countries, whereas *domestic* refers to the United States and Canada.

Just as the Enron and WorldCom debacles triggered the Sarbanes-Oxley legislation and associated detections in the United States, international practitioners associate names such as Royal Ahold and Parmalat with moves toward a more effective pan-European regulatory structure. Economic growth in Asia and the former Soviet republics continues to flourish using business cultures and legal structures that appear opaque by Western standards or sometimes resemble a toxic brew for enabling fraud. Indeed, Daniel Kaufmann of the World Bank, "a veteran dispenser of third world loans, estimates that illegal transactions cost the world economy some $1 trillion a year."[1] Poorly documented, but believable, speculation suggests that perhaps as much as half such transactions occur directly with government officials. In 2005, the U.S. Department of Justice (DOJ) increased enforcement of the Foreign Corrupt Practice Act (FCPA) cases and listed continued vigilance of this law as a top enforcement priority.[2]

39.2 TYPICAL CASES

International investigations include the following:

- **Financial statement fraud and misstatements.** These cases deal with inappropriate accounting by company insiders in order to misrepresent the global company's financial position. Examples include Parmalat and Royal Ahold NV.[3]

- **Foreign Corrupt Practices Act cases.** FCPA cases investigate alleged bribes or other inappropriate payment by a company representative or agent to a foreign official to gain favorable treatment or advantage. (Examples include *United States v. Syncor* and *United States v. ABB Vetco Gray*.[4]

- **Cross-border asset misappropriation cases.** These cases investigate alleged actions or omissions on the part of members of management in order to divert assets (tangible or intangible) of a company to their own benefit. Examples include contract fraud, receivables lapping, cash theft, and kickbacks.

- **Special purpose case investigations.** These include investigations typically undertaken through the auspices of a blue ribbon international commission to investigate and uncover possible historical wrongdoing. Examples of such investigations include the Swiss Bank Dormant Accounts of Victims of Nazi Persecution Effort (the Volcker Commission) and the International Commission on Holocaust Era Insurance Claims (ICHEIC, or the Eagleburger Commission) and the more recent oil-for-food probe, among others.

Even though these investigations differ widely in size, client, intensity, scope, and nature of work, they share certain characteristics with more mundane domestic investigations.

Thus, domestic and international investigators not only must possess extensive fraud investigatory experience, as well as keen interviewing skills, ample project management skills, and persuasive communication capabilities, but also must have that *sine qua non*, the ability to think like the fraudster. Investigators must put themselves into the mindset of the alleged perpetrator(s) to gauge how and why a fraudster perpetrated the scheme. Without such skills, investigations will require more time and pursue unnecessary dead ends. Successful international investigators, however, must possess additional skills, and this chapter will focus on these supplemental necessities.

39.3 ADDITIONAL CHALLENGES OF INTERNATIONAL INVESTIGATIONS

International engagements require that investigators work in a nonnative country where their typical management and analytical methods often will not apply or will prove less effective. They face several challenges:

- Language barriers
- Limited or nonexistent public information of dubious reliability
- Different laws and legal frameworks
- Different cultural attitudes and values
- Different accounting guidance and standards
- More complex logistics
- Different reporting capabilities and requirements

39.4 PLANNING, PLANNING, PLANNING

To deal with the challenges listed in Section 39.3, one must first develop a strong—but flexible—work plan that contains the key building blocks for the investigation. It should address the following areas:

- The locations and countries involved.
- The language skills needed (resident countries and languages of the interviewees).
- Centralized versus decentralized team organization.
- Logistics: For example, are special work permits or visas required to enter the subject countries and does the location have personal security concerns?
- The nature of the allegations.
- The location of the key records, documents, and electronic media.
- The team members: What skills and analyses does the engagement require? Which countries should the team members come from?[5]
- Local laws and regulations that will affect work in other countries.
- Format of the ultimate report: Oral versus written? Which entities—counsel, audit committee, management—will receive the report? Does the answer differ by country, even within the same investigation?

These elements often affect how the work proceeds. A mistake in planning can result in a flaw from which one can find it difficult to recover.

We now turn to specific examples of considerations one should try to incorporate in a thorough international investigative plan.

(a) Where Are We Going and Why?   A plan must address the number and location of sites involved. Based on the initial briefing with management, outside counsel, and others, one should identify the best locations for efficient information collection. These locations will often change, based on the allegations and subsequent findings.

For example, an investigator would face a simple situation if the alleging party identified some type of irregularity in a specific country's subsidiary, or with a specific employee in a country. But such clear allegations do not always occur. The investigator often faces vague claims of inappropriate marketing behavior in several countries, by persons unknown or unnamed. Fraud investigators often become frustrated when allegations from anonymous tipsters lack specificity or merit. This happens when tipsters use their nonnative tongue and misframe a complaint, or when they complain—out of ignorance or spite—of obnoxious but not improper behavior, or because they lack the perspective to see that an entry in another division or at headquarters will correct an apparent local misrecording of a transaction.

The investigator might have to affirmatively demonstrate (as do some companies in FCPA cases) that the investigation's scope has been broad and thorough enough to satisfy outside regulators (such as the DOJ and the U.S. Securities and Exchange Commission [SEC]). The work plan should support an analysis that attempts to prove a negative—that evidence or illegal activity does not exist in one or more countries. For example, some FCPA investigations have required simultaneous investigations in multiple countries to assess and report to the relevant regulators whether illegal activity found elsewhere is an isolated instance or pervasive problem.

Investigators select the countries to visit based not only on where the subject company conducts business throughout the world but also on the corruption climate in those jurisdictions. For instance, one could compare how the company's locations stack up against the well-regarded Transparency International Corruption Index.[6] Prioritizing site visits based on a recent index, for example, would suggest that Norway and New Zealand might not require early attention but that Nigeria or China might.

Another consideration in deciding where to go is the location of the data—electronic as well as hard copy. Companies with business activities in Country X can have e-mail servers located in Country Y and back office accounting ledgers or supporting documents in Country Z.

Investigators often find that the initial list of selected sites will expand or contract, depending on what they learn during the first several visits.[7] The information they obtain in the field, as a result of interviews, e-mail review, and so on, can send them in directions that differ from the originally identified sites. Therefore, the plan must have the flexibility to accommodate these possibilities.

Thoughtful prioritization of what sites to visit early will prove critical to efficiency, because bad choices can lead to unnecessary visits, travel, and disruption to company personnel and operations. Moreover, memories, records, and guilty consciences can all be perishable commodities; therefore, failing to schedule early visits to key locations can mean missing the opportunity to gather evidence. Finally, as with domestic investigations, international investigators face short time frames, and analysts cannot always recover time lost early in the process with later efficiencies.

(b) Language Issues. Once the team selects the sites for the initial visits, the plan should address the specific language skills required to match those of the interviewees and how best to obtain the necessary information from them. Even though one frequently encounters in global business those who understand and speak excellent English,[8] conducting interviews in the subject's native language will prevent translation issues, capture important nuances better, avoid cultural *faux pas*, and, perhaps most importantly, increase the ease and comfort level of interviewees in already difficult circumstances. Thus, the use of professional translators or local investigators will often lead to a better result, unless one believes that such an arrangement would create problems. For example, some clients prefer to avoid local resources for security reasons. Section 39.6(c) discusses other issues related to conducting interviews.

(c) Legal Issues. One must also remember to actively involve legal counsel as early as practicable for specific reasons that other sections of the chapter discuss. Differences in laws and customs driven by diversity in culture and tradition can surprise many engaged in international business. For instance, on one hand, usury laws in many Islamic countries and certain provisions of libel and slander laws in Great Britain punish behavior that U.S. citizens accept. On the other hand, the United States has laws against some behaviors in tax reporting that international jurisdictions regard in a surprisingly casual manner.

(d) Centralized versus Decentralized. Most teams select from two organization styles:

- **Centralized.** One team will visit most or all of the locations.
- **Decentralized.** Multiple field teams will visit the locations, perform the work, and send updates and results to the core team, which then summarizes the whole.

The number and dispersion of location visits and the deadline for the proposed deliverables will often dictate whether the team should adopt a centralized or decentralized engagement organization. The decentralized organization will prove invaluable if investigators must travel to many countries in a short time. For example, the author once had to conduct and complete an investigation in 18 different countries within eight days. In smaller cases without pressing deadlines, we suggest that one team perform the bulk of the work in all locations to improve consistency, leverage learning curves, and avoid the risk of having all the puzzle pieces but failing to put them together for want of effective communication.

(e) Logistics. Depending on the number and location of the sites the team must visit, logistics can present daunting challenges. In addition to the well-recognized issues of time zone differences and jet-lag fatigue, one must struggle with the following:

- **Timely communication of ongoing results.** For example, clients frequently inquire as to an international investigation's progress and any findings. To accommodate and anticipate such inquiries, the team should develop a central reporting process across all the engagement's relevant time zones in order to digest timely and accurate information and share it with relevant client personnel. Engagements often have daily communication (or multiple communications throughout a day when a team works more than one shift) to capture information while the team members obtain it across the globe.

- **Special visa requirements to enter a location.** One must identify any special visa requirements or other hurdles. For example, when conducting the Swiss holocaust asset investigation, organizers had to obtain special permission that allowed for non-Swiss nationals to conduct work typically performed only by registered Swiss bank auditors. Organizers often need to obtain required work permits for individual team members, depending on the length of stay. Team members who do not have the appropriate work permits risk arrest in some countries.

- **Required immunizations.** Health regulations require inoculations before investigators travel to certain locations. Some of these require more lead time than a trip to the doctor the day before leaving. Speed is often of the utmost essence in conducting these investigations and, of course, you do not want to delay the start of your work unnecessarily.

- **Special security concerns.** In some countries, for instance, foreign nationals need bodyguards and security drivers because of kidnapping risks. If team members will enter such dangerous areas, the planning effort must address this issue. Check with the State Department for areas it suggests that people avoid. The embassy should always know how to contact team members. You may even decide that the information obtained does not merit the risk of obtaining it.

Even though these items can appear obvious, neglecting such tasks can slow or halt the progress of an offshore investigation. The engagement will benefit by addressing such issues in the planning phase.

39.5   OTHER DATA COLLECTION PROBLEMS

(a) Lack of Access to Public Records.   Domestic investigations often exploit publicly available information on a company or individual. For example, in a suspected asset misappropriation case, one can run an asset search on the ownership records of the target individual(s) to ascertain whether they own inexplicably valuable assets given their backgrounds and compensation. Other countries, however, often lack such records or do not allow public access to them. Without these types of tools, forensic investigators need to rely more heavily on other means of extracting this data, such as e-mail searches and interviews.

(b) Caveat E-mail.   Even though some of the best investigative leads and evidence come from e-mail analysis, such work can be difficult and time consuming. E-mail poses special challenges in foreign investigations, particularly when one must capture and analyze e-mail in European Union countries. The rules of the E.U. Privacy and Data Protection Directives regarding the capture and reporting of an individual's e-mail differ dramatically from those of the United States.

When conducting an investigation in multiple countries, one must use different methods to capture and analyze e-mail, depending on its geographic source. Some countries (including some E.U. members) require that the investigator obtain permission from the e-mail's author before capturing it. Additionally, one will generally need the author's permission to remove it from the European Union. To accommodate such laws, some investigations use multiple e-mail analysis centers that have, for instance, separate review teams and centers for E.U. versus U.S. e-mail. Investigators should always obtain legal advice from counsel in the relevant country concerning the appropriate care and handling of such sensitive data.

Investigators must also deal with key word searches of e-mail in multiple languages, some of which use characters (e.g., Japanese and Chinese) or different alphabets (e.g., Cyrillic and Arabic). Some investigators develop software tools to perform this task, and have developed typical key word listings in multiple languages and alphabets.

39.6 DIFFERENCES IN REGULATIONS, PROFESSIONAL PRACTICES, AND CULTURES

(a) Whose GAAP Is It Anyway?   Investigators will also encounter differences between local generally accepted accounting principles (GAAP) for recording the transactions of foreign entities and the GAAP of the United States. Efforts to harmonize international accounting standards have not yet produced consistent financial reporting. Accordingly, the investigation leader must identify any relevant differences between local and U.S. GAAP and educate the teams appropriately.

The financial approaches and techniques favored in the local country often create problems when viewed through the lens of U.S. GAAP or the SEC. One must remember, however, that foreign controllers, not steeped in U.S. GAAP, may think and act differently from a person in a similar role in an SEC registrant company. For instance, reserves use and earnings management concepts often differ in a foreign entity's books and records (assuming it is not a foreign-domiciled filer of U.S. securities).

Some countries have a different ethos or cultural view of financial records. For example, in some countries, one often finds double sets of records: one accurate but another for the local tax authorities. In some countries tax evasion is pandemic and some rogues even consider it a sport.

(b) Other Regulatory Challenges.   Investigators face other regulatory or legal differences. For example, in FCPA cases, U.S. law permits certain small facilitation (sometimes referred to as *grease*) payments. Some Organization for Economic Cooperation and Development (OECD) signatory countries, however, have no such exceptions for facilitation payments, so the investigator must take care when analyzing possible inappropriate payments to identify and differentiate between the relevant rules, because the correct answer in one context can produce a damning admission in another. No substitute exists for legal advice from attorneys (preferably other than the client's general counsel) in the relevant country on these legal and regulatory landmines.

(c) What Happened in That Interview?   Interviews conducted by investigators who prepare beforehand with financial analysis and e-mail review can provide valuable information. But problems can arise when one does not understand the cultural differences that exist when addressing others in person. For example, cultures express and interpret body language differently. Cultural differences can mask or muddy verbal and other clues informed by North American expectations.

A Greek may make an argumentative and defensive-appearing response to a perceived accusation while a Japanese in the same situation may avert his gaze in an attempt to avoid embarrassing you for your silly question. Neither is demonstrating any shade of guilt, but only local culture. If you have experienced these types of situations and found them confusing, imagine what your subject's experience of you might be—you're the foreigner in the context. Conducting interviews via a translator can prove effective, but one must capture the important nuances of the questions and answers. Even if the interviewer has a strong command of the language, no substitute exists for a trustworthy local interpreter who can explain the underlying intention of the responses. Also, one must be careful because different laws and regulations often apply to interviews.

(d) Why Can't We Do That in Our Report?   The international investigation will typically culminate in a written report or an oral presentation. When preparing and presenting such summaries, one should adhere to appropriate standards of quality to ensure the report's accuracy. But one must also verify that the report (as well as interview memos) comports with relevant local laws. For example, some jurisdictions require that the investigator give the targeted individual(s) an opportunity to review the report (as well as interview memos) before the client receives the final version. Others have special caveats or limitations that the report should include to make it consistent with local law and practices. The report could include findings that might lead to allegations of defamation, tortuous interference, or other such charges. For example, the laws of slander and libel differ by country, sometimes in ways that seem wrong-headed to an investigator steeped in the culture of checkout-line tabloids. If allowed by law, we suggest that an independent reviewer (preferably an attorney) vet the report for compliance with local laws and regulations.

39.7   OTHER SUGGESTIONS

Because fraudsters employ innumerable means to perpetrate foreign frauds, we list several methods that have proved valuable in collecting relevant information. These techniques seem to work well in foreign investigations of the nonfinancial statement fraud variety.

- **Interview the local country managers' assistants or secretaries and capture their e-mail.** We find that these individuals often have a wealth of knowledge regarding what has occurred in the subject company in that country. They tend to see or hear about most foreign visitors and local officials visiting the company. They often keep the calendars for the country managers, make their travel arrangements, and handle some or all correspondence. Even though they are often fiercely loyal to their boss, they can provide much data that the country manager lacks or prefers to withhold, even if they let the facts slip out inadvertently.
- **Visually inspect the local books and records.** This is particularly true in the cash disbursement records and petty cash areas. Sometimes the trends and patterns of disbursements or the quantity of and lack of support for petty cash expenditures reveal invaluable information.

- **Review consultant and subcontractor payments.** Who are these entities and what services or goods did they provide? Vague and ambiguously worded contracts with subcontractors that specify ill- or undefined deliverables and fuzzy scopes of work often identify high-value investigative targets.

- **Scan the local employee list.** Relatives, friends, girlfriends, boyfriends, and the like sometimes appear on the employee list but not at the workplace. Comparing purported employee addresses against the addresses of management can also identify areas to investigate.

- **Don't forget to ask.** The response you get might amaze you. While conducting an investigation in a Spanish-speaking country, not too long ago, we simply inquired whether the controller knew about payments made to certain customers, and his response was "Oh, you want to see the *Apoyo* (support) payments. We have files of them right over here." He then proceeded to provide us with several binders documenting all the payments (most of which were inappropriate) made to customers to make sure they bought more product. You never know when you will stumble on an honest person.

39.8 CONCLUSION

International investigations offer some of the most fascinating and intellectually rewarding engagements that one can perform in forensic accounting. Such engagements, however, present different and distinct challenges, not present in their domestic counterparts. This chapter discusses several methods for dealing with these challenges that will help improve the effectiveness of foreign investigations.

NOTES

1. "Shaking Hands, Greasing Palms," The New York Times, May 17, 2005.
2. *See*, for example, "The Sixth Annual Report on Enforcement and Monitoring of the OECD Convention on Combating Bribery of Foreign Public Officials in International Business Transactions as Required by Paragraph (c) (1) of the Senate Resolution of Advice and Consent dated July 31, 1998," available at www.state.gov/documents.
3. The authors have omitted case citations to these and certain other cases because they each spawned numerous, multijurisdictional suits and investigations. What is instructive is not the specific mechanisms or dispositions of the actions, but their global character. Readers seeking more information will find their needs supplied by a simple Web search.
4. *See* U.S. DOJ *FCPA Opinion Procedure Releases 03-01 and 04-02; United States v. Syncor Taiwan, Inc.* (Cr. No. 02-1244) (C.D. Cal. 2002); *Sec v. Syncor International Corp.,* 1:02CV02421 (D.D.C. 2002); *United States v. ABB Vetco Gray, Inc. and ABB Vetco Gray U.K. Ltd.,* (Case No. H-04-279) (S.D. Tex 2004). SEC *v. ABB Ltd.,* Case No. 1: 04CV01141 (D.D.C. 2004).
5. In some places, the "skills" can include gender or religious background. One should consider how to deal with such issues before arriving at the worksite.
6. *See* the Transparency International Web site at www. transparency.org.
7. One might think that corporate management would in nearly all cases be sufficiently knowledgeable to enable the investigator to avoid such false starts, but this is often not the case.
8. Even where English is the true language of the location or *lingua franca* of the company, a New Yorker interviewing in Singapore, or a Glaswegian in London for that matter, can be mystified by the variability of vocabulary and shades of meaning of their mother tongue.

GLOSSARY OF FINANCIAL CONCEPTS*

Roman L. Weil, Editor

The definitions of many words and phrases in the glossary use other glossary terms. In a given definition, we *italicize* terms that themselves (or variants thereof) appear elsewhere under their own listings. The cross-references generally take one of two forms:

1. **absorption costing.** *See full absorption costing.*
2. **ABC.** *Activity-based costing.*

Form (1) refers you to another term for discussion of this bold-faced term. Form (2) tells you that this bold-faced term is synonymous with the *italicized* term, which you can consult for discussion if necessary.

A

AAA. *American Accounting Association.*

Abacus. A scholarly journal containing articles on theoretical aspects of accounting, published by Basil Blackwell for the Accounting Foundation of the University of Sydney.

abatement. A complete or partial cancellation of a levy imposed by a government unit.

ABC. *Activity-based costing.*

abnormal spoilage. Actual spoilage exceeding that expected when operations are normally efficient. Usual practice treats this cost as an *expense* of the period rather than as a *product cost.* Contrast with *normal spoilage.*

aboriginal cost. In public utility accounting, the *acquisition cost* of an *asset* incurred by the first *entity* devoting that asset to public use; the cost basis for most public utility regulation. If regulators used a different cost basis, then public utilities could exchange assets among themselves at ever-increasing prices in order to raise the rate base and, then, prices based on them.

absorbed overhead. *Overhead costs* allocated to individual products at some *overhead rate*; also called *applied overhead.*

*I have developed this glossary over the last 30 years with the help of Sidney Davidson, Michael Maher, Patricia O'Brien, James Schindler, and Clyde Stickney. In addition, Katherine Schipper and Steven Zeff have provided much helpful input. My thanks to all of you. RLW

absorption costing. *See full absorption costing.*

Abstracts of the EITF. See Emerging Issues Task Force.

accelerated cost recovery system (ACRS). A form of accelerated depreciation that Congress enacted in 1981 and amended in 1986, so that now most writers refer to it as *MACRS*, or *Modified Accelerated Cost Recovery System.* The system provides percentages of the asset's cost that a firm depreciates each year for tax purposes. The percentages derive, roughly, from 150-percent *declining-balance depreciation* methods. ACRS ignores salvage value. We do not generally use these amounts for *financial accounting.*

accelerated depreciation. In calculating *depreciation* charges, any method in which the charges become progressively smaller each period. Examples are *double declining-balance depreciation* and *sum-of-the-years'-digits depreciation* methods.

acceptance. A written promise to pay; equivalent to a *promissory note.*

account. A device for representing the amount (*balance*) for any line (or a part of a line) in the *balance sheet* or *income statement.* Because income statement accounts explain the changes in the balance sheet account Retained Earnings, the definition does not require the last three words of the preceding sentence. An account is any device for accumulating additions and subtractions relating to a single *asset*, *liability*, or *owners' equity* item, including *revenues* and *expenses.*

account analysis method. A method of separating *fixed costs* from *variable costs* based on the analyst's judgment of whether the cost is fixed or variable. Based on their names alone, the analyst might classify *direct labor*

(materials) costs as variable and *depreciation* on a factory building as fixed. In our experience, this method results in too many fixed costs and not enough variable costs—that is, analysts have insufficient information to judge management's ability to reduce costs that appear to be fixed.

account form. The form of *balance sheet* in which *assets* appear on the left and *equities* appear on the right. Contrast with *report form. See T-account.*

accountability center. *Responsibility center.*

accountancy. The British word for *accounting.* In the United States, it means the theory and practice of accounting.

accountant's comments. Canada: a written communication issued by a public accountant at the conclusion of a review engagement. It consists of a description of the work performed and a statement that, under the terms of the engagement, the accountant has not performed an audit and consequently expresses no opinion. (Compare *auditor's report; denial of opinion.*)

accountant's opinion. *Auditor's report.*

accountant's report. *Auditor's report.*

accounting. A system conveying information about a specific *entity.* The information is in financial terms and will appear in accounting statements only if the accountant can measure it with reasonable precision. The *AICPA* defines accounting as a service activity whose "function is to provide quantitative information, primarily financial in nature, about economic entities that is intended to be useful in making economic decisions."

accounting adjustments. *Prior-period adjustments*, changes in accounting principles accounted for on a cumulative basis, and corrections of errors. *See accounting changes.* The *FASB* indicates that it will tend to call these items "accounting adjustments," not "accounting changes," when it requires the reporting of *comprehensive income.*

Accounting and Tax Index. A publication that indexes, in detail, the accounting literature of the period. Published by UMI, a subsidiary of Bell & Howell.

accounting changes. As defined by *APB Opinion No. 20*, a change in (1) an *accounting principle* (such as a switch from *FIFO* to *LIFO* or from *sum-of-the-years'-digits depreciation* to *straight-line depreciation*), (2) an accounting estimate (such as estimated useful lives or salvage value of depreciable assets and estimates of *warranty* costs or *uncollectible accounts*), or (3) the reporting *entity.* The firm should disclose changes of type (1). It should include in reported earnings for the period of change the cumulative effect of the change on *retained earnings* at the start of the period during which it made the change. The firm should treat changes of type (2) as affecting only the period of change and, if necessary, future periods. The firm should disclose reasons for changes of type (3) in statements reporting on operations of the period of the change, and it should show the effect of the change on all other periods, for comparative purposes. In some cases (such as a change from *LIFO* to other inventory *flow assumptions* or a change in the method of accounting for long-term construction contracts), *GAAP* treat changes of type (1) like changes of type (3). That is, for these changes the firm should restate all statements shown for prior periods to show the effect of adopting the change for those periods as well. *See all-inclusive (income) concept* and *accounting errors.*

accounting conventions. Methods or procedures used in accounting. Writers tend to use this term when the method or procedure has not yet received official authoritative sanction by a pronouncement of a group such as the *APB, EITF, FASB,* or *SEC.* Contrast with *accounting principles.*

accounting cycle. The sequence of accounting procedures starting with *journal entries* for various transactions and events and ending with the *financial statements* or, perhaps, the *post-closing trial balance.*

accounting deficiency. Canada: a failure to adhere to generally accepted *accounting principles* or to disclose essential information in *financial statements.*

accounting entity. *See entity.*

accounting equation. *Assets = Equities;* Assets = Liabilities + Owners' Equity.

accounting errors. Arithmetic errors and misapplications of *accounting principles* in previously published financial statements. The firm corrects these during the current period with direct *debits* or *credits* to *retained earnings.* In this regard, the firm treats them like *prior-period adjustments,* but technically *APB Opinion No. 9* does not classify them as prior-period adjustments. *See accounting changes,* and contrast with changes in accounting estimates as described there.

accounting event. Any occurrence that is recorded in the accounting records.

Accounting Horizons. A quarterly journal of the *American Accounting Association.*

accounting methods. *Accounting principles;* procedures for carrying out accounting principles.

accounting period. The time period between consecutive *balance sheets;* the time period for which the firm prepares *financial statements* that measure *flows*, such as the *income statement* and the *statement of cash flows*. See interim statements.

accounting policies. *Accounting principles* adopted by a specific *entity*.

accounting principles. The methods or procedures used in accounting for events reported in the *financial statements*. We tend to use this term when the method or procedure has received official authoritative sanction from a pronouncement of a group such as the *APB, EITF, FASB*, or *SEC*. Contrast with *accounting conventions* and *conceptual framework*.

Accounting Principles Board. *See APB.*

accounting procedures. *See accounting principles.* However, this term usually refers to the methods for implementing accounting principles.

accounting rate of return. Income for a period divided by average investment during the period; based on income, rather than discounted cash flows, and hence a poor decision-making aid or tool. *See ratio.*

Accounting Research Bulletin (ARB). The name of the official pronouncements of the former *Committee on Accounting Procedure (CAP)* of the *AICPA*. The committee issued fifty-one bulletins between 1939 and 1959. *ARB No. 43* restated and codified the parts of the first forty-two bulletins not dealing solely with definitions.

Accounting Research Study (ARS). One of a series of studies published by the Director of Accounting Research of the *AICPA* and "designed to provide professional accountants and others interested in the development of accounting with a discussion and documentation of accounting problems." The AICPA published fifteen such studies in the period 1961–73.

Accounting Review. A journal of the *American Accounting Association.*

Accounting Series Release (ASR). See SEC.

accounting standards. *Accounting principles.*

Accounting Standards Executive Committee (AcSEC). The senior technical committee of the *AICPA* authorized to speak for the AICPA in the areas of *financial accounting* and reporting as well as *cost accounting.*

accounting system. The procedures for collecting and summarizing financial data in a firm.

Accounting Terminology Bulletin (ATB). One of four releases of the Committee on Terminology of the *AICPA* issued in the period 1953–57.

Accounting Trends and Techniques. An annual *AICPA* publication that surveys the reporting practices of 600 large corporations. It presents tabulations of specific practices, terminology, and disclosures along with illustrations taken from individual annual reports.

accounts payable. A *liability* representing an amount owed to a *creditor*; usually arising from the purchase of *merchandise* or materials and supplies, not necessarily due or past due; normally, a *current liability.*

accounts receivable. Claims against a *debtor*; usually arising from sales or services rendered, not necessarily due or past due; normally, a *current asset.*

accounts receivable turnover. Net sales on account divided by average accounts receivable. *See ratio.*

accretion. Occurs when a *book value* grows over time, such as a *bond* originally issued at a *discount*; the correct technical term is "accretion," not "amortization." This term also refers to an increase in economic worth through physical change caused by natural growth, usually said of a natural resource such as timber. Contrast with *appreciation*. *See amortization*.

accrual. Recognition of an *expense* (or *revenue*) and the related *liability* (or *asset*) resulting from an *accounting event*, frequently from the passage of time but not signaled by an explicit cash transaction; for example, the recognition of interest expense or revenue (or wages, salaries, or rent) at the end of a period even though the firm makes no explicit cash transaction at that time. Cash flow follows accounting recognition; contrast with *deferral*.

accrual basis of accounting. The method of recognizing *revenues* as a firm sells *goods* (or delivers them) and as it renders *services*, independent of the time when it receives cash. This system recognizes *expenses* in the period when it recognizes the related revenue, independent of the time when it pays cash. *SFAC No. 1* says, "Accrual accounting attempts to record the financial effects on an enterprise of transactions and other events and circumstances that have cash consequences for the enterprise in the periods in which those transactions, events, and circumstances occur rather than only in the periods in which cash is received or paid by the enterprise." Contrast with the *cash basis of accounting*. *See accrual* and *deferral*. We could more correctly call this "accrual/deferral" accounting.

accrue. *See accrued*, and contrast with *incur*.

accrued. Said of a *revenue (expense)* that the firm has earned (recognized) even though the related *receivable (payable)* has a future due date. We prefer not to use this adjective as part of an account title. Thus, we prefer to use Interest

Receivable (Payable) as the account title rather than Accrued Interest Receivable (Payable). *See matching convention* and *accrual*. Contrast with *incur*.

accrued depreciation. An incorrect term for *accumulated depreciation*. Acquiring an asset with cash, capitalizing it, and then amortizing its cost over periods of use is a process of *deferral* and allocation, not of *accrual*.

accrued payable. A *payable* usually resulting from the passage of time. For example, *salaries* and *interest* accrue as time passes. *See accrued*.

accrued receivable. A *receivable* usually resulting from the passage of time. *See accrued*.

accumulated benefit obligation. *See projected benefit obligation* for definition and contrast.

accumulated depreciation. A preferred title for the asset *contra account* that shows the sum of *depreciation* charges on an asset since the time the firm acquired it. Other account titles are *allowance* for *depreciation* (acceptable term) and *reserve* for *depreciation* (unacceptable term).

accumulated other comprehensive income. *Balance sheet* amount in *owners' equity* showing the total of all *other comprehensive income* amounts from all prior periods.

accurate presentation. The qualitative accounting objective suggesting that information reported in financial statements should correspond as precisely as possible with the economic effects underlying transactions and events. *See fair presentation* and *full disclosure*.

acid test ratio. *Quick ratio*.

acquisition cost. Of an *asset*, the net *invoice* price plus all *expenditures* to place and ready the asset for its intended use. The other expenditures might include legal fees, transportation charges, and installation costs.

ACRS. *Accelerated Cost Recovery System.*

AcSEC. *Accounting Standards Executive Committee of the AICPA.*

activity accounting. *Responsibility accounting.*

activity-based costing (ABC). Method of assigning *indirect costs*, including nonmanufacturing *overhead costs*, to products and services. ABC assumes that almost all overhead costs associate with activities within the firm and vary with respect to the *drivers* of those activities. Some practitioners suggest that ABC attempts to find the drivers for all indirect costs; these people note that in the long run, all costs are *variable*, so *fixed* indirect costs do not occur. This method first assigns costs to activities and then to products based on the products' usage of the activities.

activity-based depreciation. *Production method (depreciation).*

activity-based management (ABM). Analysis and management of activities required to make a product or to produce a service. ABM focuses attention to enhance activities that add value to the customer and to reduce activities that do not. Its goal is to satisfy customer needs while making smaller demands on costly resources. Some refer to this as "activity management."

activity basis. *Costs* are *variable* or *fixed* (*incremental* or *unavoidable*) with respect to some activity, such as production of units (or the undertaking of some new project). Usage calls this activity the "activity basis."

activity center. Unit of the organization that performs a set of tasks.

activity variance. *Sales volume variance.*

actual cost (basis). *Acquisition* or *historical cost.* Also contrast with *standard cost.*

actual costing (system). Method of allocating costs to products using actual *direct materials*, actual *direct labor*, and actual *factory overhead*. Contrast with *normal costing* and *standard costing.*

actuarial. An adjective describing computations or analyses that involve both *compound interest* and probabilities, such as the computation of the *present value* of a life-contingent *annuity.* Some writers use the word even for computations involving only one of the two.

actuarial accrued liability. A 1981 report of the Joint Committee on Pension Terminology (of various actuarial societies) agreed to use this term rather than *prior service cost.*

ad valorem. A method of levying a tax or duty on goods by using their estimated value as the tax base.

additional paid-in capital. An alternative acceptable title for the *capital contributed in excess of par (or stated) value account.*

additional processing cost. *Costs* incurred in processing *joint products* after the *split-off point.*

adequate disclosure. An auditing standard that, to achieve *fair presentation* of *financial statements*, requires *disclosure* of *material* items. This *auditing standard* does not, however, require publicizing all information detrimental to a company. For example, the company may face a lawsuit, and disclosure might require a *debit* to a *loss* account and a *credit* to an *estimated liability.* But the court might view the making of this entry as an admission of liability, which could adversely affect the outcome of the suit. The firm should debit expense or loss for the expected loss, as required by *SFAS No. 5*, but need not use such accurate account titles that the court can spot an admission of liability.

adjunct account. An *account* that accumulates additions to another account. For example, Premium on Bonds Payable is adjunct to the liability Bonds Payable; the effective liability is the sum of the two account balances at a given date. Contrast with *contra account*.

adjusted acquisition (historical) cost. Sometimes said of the *book value* of a *plant asset*, that is, *acquisition cost* less *accumulated depreciation*. Also, cost adjusted to a *constant-dollar* amount to reflect *general price-level changes*.

adjusted bank balance of cash. The *balance* shown on the statement from the bank plus or minus amounts, such as for unrecorded deposits or outstanding checks, to reconcile the bank's balance with the correct cash balance. *See adjusted book balance of cash.*

adjusted basis. The *basis* used to compute gain or loss on the disposition of an *asset* for tax purposes. *See also book value.*

adjusted book balance of cash. The *balance* shown in the firm's account for cash in bank plus or minus amounts, such as for *notes* collected by the bank or bank service charges, to reconcile the account balance with the correct cash balance. *See adjusted bank balance of cash.*

adjusted trial balance. *Trial balance* taken after *adjusting entries* but before *closing entries*. Contrast with *pre-* and *post-closing trial balances*. *See unadjusted trial balance* and *post-closing trial balance*. *See also work sheet.*

adjusting entry. An entry made at the end of an *accounting period* to record a *transaction* or other *accounting event* that the firm has not yet recorded or has improperly recorded during the accounting period; an entry to update the accounts. *See work sheet.*

adjustment. An *account* change produced by an *adjusting entry*.

Sometimes accountants use the term to refer to the process of restating *financial statement* amounts to *constant dollars*.

administrative costs (expenses). *Costs (expenses)* incurred for the firm as a whole, in contrast with specific functions such as manufacturing or selling; includes items such as salaries of top executives, general office rent, legal fees, and auditing fees.

admission of partner. Occurs when a new partner joins a *partnership*. Legally, the old partnership dissolves, and a new one comes into being. In practice, however, firms often keep the old accounting records in use, and the accounting entries reflect the manner in which the new partner joined the firm. If the new partner merely purchases the interest of another partner, the accounting changes the name for one capital account. If the new partner contributes *assets* and *liabilities* to the partnership, then the firm must recognize them. *See bonus method.*

ADR. *See asset depreciation range.*

advances from (by) customers. A preferred title for the *liability* account representing *receipts* of *cash* in advance of delivering the *goods* or rendering the *service*. After the firm delivers the goods or services, it will recognize *revenue*. Some refer to this as "deferred revenue" or "deferred income," terms likely to confuse the unwary because the item is not yet *revenue* or *income*.

advances to affiliates. *Loans* by a parent company to a *subsidiary*; frequently combined with "investment in subsidiary" as "investments and advances to subsidiary" and shown as a *noncurrent asset* on the parent's *balance sheet*. The consolidation process eliminates these advances in *consolidated financial statements*.

advances to suppliers. A preferred term for the *asset* account representing *disbursements* of cash in advance of receiving *assets* or *services*.

adverse opinion. An *auditor's report* stating that the financial statements are not fair or are not in accord with *GAAP*.

affiliated company. A company controlling or controlled by another company.

after closing. Post-closing; a *trial balance* at the end of the period.

after cost. *Expenditures* to be made after *revenue* recognition. For example, *expenditures* for *repairs* under warranty are after cost. Proper recognition of after cost involves a debit to expense at the time of the sale and a credit to an *estimated liability*. When the firm discharges the liability, it debits the estimated liability and credits the assets consumed.

AG (Aktiengesellschaft). Germany: the form of a German company whose shares can trade on the stock exchange.

agency cost. The *cost* to the *principal* caused by *agents* pursuing their own interests instead of the principal's interests. Includes both the costs incurred by principals to control agents' actions and the cost to the principals if agents pursue their own interests that are not in the interest of the principals.

agency fund. An account for *assets* received by governmental units in the capacity of trustee or agent.

agency theory. A branch of economics relating the behavior of *principals* (such as owner nonmanagers or bosses) and that of their *agents* (such as nonowner managers or subordinates). The principal assigns responsibility and authority to the agent, but the agent's own risks and preferences differ from those of the principal. The principal cannot observe all activities of the agent. Both the principal and the agent must consider the differing risks and preferences in designing incentive contracts.

agent. One authorized to transact business, including executing contracts, for another.

aging accounts receivable. The process of classifying *accounts receivable* by the time elapsed since the claim came into existence for the purpose of estimating the amount of uncollectible accounts receivable as of a given date. *See sales contra, estimated uncollectibles*, and *allowance for uncollectibles*.

aging schedule. A listing of *accounts receivable*, classified by age, used in *aging accounts receivable*.

AICPA (American Institute of Certified Public Accountants). The national organization that represents *CPAs*. *See AcSEC*. It oversees the writing and grading of the Uniform CPA Examination. Each state sets its own requirements for becoming a CPA in that state. *See certified public accountant*. Web site: *http://www.aicpa.org*. While the AICPA sets many auditing and professional standards for public accountants, the *PCAOB* regulates auditing of public companies and the profession.

all-capital earnings rate. *Rate of return on assets*.

all-current method. *Foreign currency translation* in which all *financial statement* items are translated at the *current exchange rate*.

all-inclusive (income) concept. A concept that does not distinguish between *operating* and *nonoperating* *revenues* and *expenses*. Thus, the only entries to retained earnings are for *net income* and *dividends*. Under this concept, the *income statement* reports all *income*, *gains*, and *losses*; thus, net income includes events usually reported as *prior-period adjustments* and as *corrections of errors*. *GAAP* do not include this concept in its pure form, but *APB Opinions No. 9* and *No. 30* move far in this direction. They do permit retained earnings entries for prior-period adjustments and correction of errors.

allocate. To divide or spread a *cost* from one *account* into several accounts, to several products or activities, or to several periods.

allocation base. The systematic method that assigns *joint costs* to *cost objectives*. For example, a firm could assign the cost of a truck to periods based on miles driven during the period; the allocation base is miles. Or the firm could assign the cost of a factory supervisor to a product based on *direct labor* hours; the allocation base is direct labor hours.

allocation of income taxes. *See deferred income tax.*

allowance. A balance sheet *contra account* generally used for *receivables* and depreciable assets. *See sales* (or *purchase*) *allowance* for another use of this term.

allowance for funds used during construction. In accounting for public utilities, a *revenue* account *credited* for *implicit interest* earnings on *shareholders' equity* balances. One principle of public utility regulation and rate setting requires that customers should pay the full costs of producing the services (e.g., electricity) that they use, nothing more and nothing less. Thus, an electric utility must capitalize into an *asset* account the full costs, but no more, of producing a new electric power-generating plant. One of the costs of building a new plant is the *interest* cost on cash tied up during construction. If *funds* are explicitly borrowed by an

ordinary business, the journal entry for interest of $1,000 is typically:

Interest Expense 1,000
   Interest Payable . . . 1,000
Interest expense for the period.

If the firm is constructing a new plant, then another entry would be made, capitalizing interest into the plant-under-construction account:

Construction Work-
in-Progress 750
   Interest Expense 750
Capitalize relevant portion of interest relating to construction work in progress into the asset account.

The cost of the *plant asset* increases; when the firm uses the plant, it charges *depreciation*. The interest will become an expense through the depreciation process in the later periods of use, not currently as the firm pays for interest. Thus, the firm reports the full cost of the electricity generated during a given period as expense in that period. But suppose, as is common, that the electric utility does not explicitly borrow the funds but uses some of its own funds, including funds raised from equity issues as well as from debt. Even though the firm incurs no explicit interest expense or other explicit expense for capital, the funds have an *opportunity cost*. Put another way, the plant under construction will not have lower economic cost just because the firm used its own cash rather than borrowing. The public utility using its own funds, on which it would have to pay $750 of interest if it had explicitly borrowed the funds, will make the following entry:

Construction Work-in-Progress	750
Allowance for Funds Used during Construction	750

Recognition of interest, an opportunity cost, on own funds used.

The allowance account is a form of *revenue*, to appear on the income statement, and the firm will close it to Retained Earnings, increasing it. On the *statement of cash flows* it is an income or revenue item not producing funds, and so the firm must subtract it from net income in deriving *cash provided by operations. SFAS No. 34* specifically prohibits nonutility companies from capitalizing, into plant under construction, the opportunity cost (interest) on their own funds used.

allowance for uncollectibles (accounts receivable). A *contra account* that shows the estimated *accounts receivable* amount that the firm expects not to collect. When the firm uses such an allowance, the actual write-off of specific accounts receivable (*debit* allowance, *credit* specific customer's account) does not affect *revenue* or *expense* at the time of the write-off. The firm reduces revenue when it debits *bad debt expense* (or, our preference, a revenue contra account) and credits the allowance; the firm can base the amount of the credit to the allowance on a percentage of sales on account for a period of time or compute it from *aging accounts receivable*. This contra account enables the firm to show an estimated receivables amount that it expects to collect without identifying specific uncollectible accounts. *See allowance method.*

allowance method. A method of attempting to match all *expenses* of a transaction with their associated

revenues; usually involves a debit to expense and a credit to an *estimated liability*, such as for estimated warranty expenditures, or a debit to a revenue (*contra*) account and a credit to an asset (*contra*) account, such as in some firms' accounting for uncollectible accounts. *See allowance for uncollectibles* for further explanation. When the firm uses the allowance method for *sales discounts*, the firm records sales at gross invoice prices (not reduced by the amounts of discounts made available). The firm *debits* an estimate of the amount of discounts to be taken to a revenue contra account and *credits* an allowance account, shown contra to *accounts receivable.*

American Accounting Association (AAA). An organization primarily for academic accountants but open to all interested in accounting. It publishes the *Accounting Review* and several other journals.

American Institute of Certified Public Accountants. *See AICPA.*

American Stock Exchange (AMEX) (ASE). A public market where various corporate *securities* are traded.

AMEX. *American Stock Exchange.*

amortization. Strictly speaking, the process of liquidating or extinguishing ("bringing to death") a *debt* with a series of payments to the *creditor* (or to a - *sinking fund*). From that usage has evolved a related use involving the accounting for the payments themselves: "amorti-zation schedule" for a mortgage, which is a table showing the allocation between *interest* and *principal.* The term has come to mean writing off ("liqui-dating") the cost of an asset. In this context it means the general process of *allocating* the *acquisition cost* of an asset either to the periods of benefit as an *expense* or to *inventory* accounts as a *product cost.* This is called *depreciation* for *plant assets, depletion* for *wasting assets* (natural resources), and "amortization" for *intangibles. SFAC No. 6* refers to amortization as "the accounting process of reducing an amount by periodic payments or write-downs." The expressions "unamortized debt discount or premium" and "to amortize debt discount or premium" relate to *accruals*, not to *deferrals.* The expressions "amortization of long-term assets" and "to amortize long-term assets" refer to deferrals, not accruals. Contrast with *accretion.*

amortized cost. A measure required by *SFAS No. 115* for *held-to-maturity securities.* This amount results from applying the method described at *effective interest method.* The firm records the security at its initial cost and computes the *effective interest rate* for the security. Whenever the firm receives cash from the issuer of the security or whenever the firm reaches the end of one of its own *accounting periods* (that is, reaches the time for its own *adjusting entries*), it takes the following steps: It multiplies the amount currently recorded on the books by the effective interest rate (which remains constant over the time the firm holds the security). It debits that amount to the debt security account and credits the amount to Interest Revenue. If the firm receives cash, it debits Cash and credits the debt security account. The firm recomputes the book value of the debt security as the book value before these entries plus the increase for the interest revenue less the decrease for the cash received. The resulting amount is the amortized cost for the end of that period.

analysis of variances. *See variance analysis.*

annual report. A report prepared once a year for shareholders and other interested parties. It includes a *balance sheet*, an *income statement*, a *statement of cash flows*, a reconciliation of changes in *owners' equity* accounts, a *summary of significant accounting principles*, other explanatory *notes*, the *auditor's report*, and comments from management about the year's events. *See 10-K* and *financial statements.*

annuitant. One who receives an *annuity.*

annuity. A series of payments of equal amount, usually made at equally spaced time intervals.

annuity certain. An *annuity* payable for a definite number of periods. Contrast with *contingent annuity.*

annuity due. An *annuity* whose first payment occurs at the start of period 1 (or at the end of period 0). Contrast with *annuity in arrears.*

annuity in advance. An *annuity due.*

annuity in arrears. An *ordinary annuity* whose first payment occurs at the end of the first period.

annuity method of depreciation. *See compound interest depreciation.*

antidilutive. Said of a *potentially dilutive* security that will increase *earnings per share* if its holder *exercises* it or *converts* it into common stock. In computing *primary* and *fully diluted earnings per share*, the firm must assume that holders of antidilutive securities will not exercise their options or convert securities into common shares. The opposite assumption would lead to increased reported earnings per share in a given period.

APB. Accounting Principles Board of the *AICPA.* It set *accounting principles* from 1959 through 1973, issuing 31 *APB Opinions* and 4 *APB Statements.* The *FASB* superseded it.

APB Opinion. The name for the APB pronouncements that compose much of *generally accepted accounting principles*; the APB issued 31 *APB Opinions* from 1962 through 1973.

APB Statement. The *APB* issued four *APB Statements* between 1962 and 1970. The *statements* were approved by at least two-thirds of the board, but they state recommendations, not requirements. For example, *Statement No. 3* (1969) suggested the publication of *constant-dollar* financial statements but did not require them.

APBs. An abbreviation used for *APB Opinions.*

applied cost. A *cost* that a firm has *allocated* to a department, product, or activity; not necessarily based on actual costs incurred.

applied overhead. *Overhead costs* charged to departments, products, or activities. Also called *absorbed overhead.*

appraisal. In valuing an *asset* or *liability*, a process that involves expert opinion rather than evaluation of explicit market transactions.

appraisal costs. *Costs* incurred to detect individual units of products that do not conform to specifications, including end-process sampling and field-testing. Also called "detection costs."

appraisal method of depreciation. The periodic *depreciation* charge that equals the difference between the beginning-of-period and the end-of-period appraised values of the *asset* if that difference is positive. If negative, there is no charge. Not based on *historical cost*, this method is thus not generally accepted.

appreciation. An increase in economic value caused by rising market prices for an *asset*. Contrast with *accretion*.

appropriated retained earnings. *See retained earnings, appropriated.*

appropriation. In governmental accounting, an *expenditure* authorized for a specified amount, purpose, and time.

appropriation account. In governmental accounting, an account set up to record specific authorizations to spend. The governmental unit credits this account with appropriation amounts. At the end of the period, the unit closes to (debits) this account all *expenditures* during the period and all *encumbrances* outstanding at the end of the period.

approximate net realizable value method. A method of assigning joint costs to *joint products* based on revenues minus *additional processing costs* of the end products.

ARB. Accounting Research Bulletin.

arbitrage. Strictly speaking, the simultaneous purchase in one market and sale in another of a *security* or commodity in hope of making a *profit* on price differences in the different markets. Often writers use this term loosely when a trader sells an item that is somewhat different from the item purchased; for example, the sale of shares of common stock and the simultaneous purchase of a *convertible bond* that is convertible into identical common shares. The trader hopes that the market will soon see that the similarities of the items should make them have equal market values. When the market values converge, the trader closes the positions and profits from the original difference in prices, less trading costs.

arbitrary. Having no causation basis. Accounting theorists and practitioners often, properly, say, "Some cost allocations are arbitrary." In that sense, the accountant does not mean that the allocations are capricious or haphazard but does mean that theory suggests no unique solution to the allocation problem at hand. Accountants require that arbitrary allocations be systematic, rational, and consistently followed over time.

arm's length. A transaction negotiated by unrelated parties, both acting in their own self-interests; the basis for a *fair market value* estimation or computation.

arrears. *Cumulative dividends* that the firm has not yet declared. *See annuity in arrears* for another context.

ARS. Accounting Research Study.

articles of incorporation. Document filed with state authorities by persons forming a corporation. When the state returns the document with a certificate of incorporation, the document becomes the corporation's *charter.*

articulate. The relation between any operating statement (for example, *income statement* or *statement of cash flows*) and comparative balance sheets, where the operating statement explains (or reconciles) the change in some major balance sheet category (for example, *retained earnings* or *working capital*).

ASE. American Stock Exchange.

ASR. Accounting Series Release.

assess. To value property for the purpose of property taxation; to levy a charge on the owner of property for improvements thereto, such as for sewers or sidewalks. The taxing authority computes the assessment.

assessed valuation. For real estate or other property, a dollar amount that a government uses as a basis for levying taxes. The amount need not have some relation to *market value.*

asset. *SFAC No. 6* defines assets as "probable future economic benefits obtained or controlled by a particular entity as a result of past transactions....

An asset has three essential characteristics: (a) it embodies a probable future benefit that involves a capacity, singly or in combination with other assets, to contribute directly or indirectly to future net cash inflows, (b) a particular entity can obtain the benefit and control others' access to it, and (c) the transaction or other event giving rise to the entity's right to or control of the benefit has already occurred." A footnote points out that "probable" means that which we can reasonably expect or believe but that is not certain or proved. You may understand condition (c) better if you think of it as requiring that a future benefit cannot be an asset if it arises from an *executory contract*, a mere exchange of promises. Receiving a purchase order from a customer provides a future benefit, but it is an executory contract, so the order cannot be an asset. An asset may be *tangible* or *intangible*, short-term (current) or long-term (noncurrent).

asset depreciation range (ADR). The range of *depreciable lives* allowed by the *Internal Revenue Service* for a specific depreciable *asset.*

asset securitization. *Securitization.*

asset turnover. Net sales divided by average assets. *See ratio.*

assignment of accounts receivable. Transfer of the legal ownership of an account receivable through its sale. Contrast with *pledging* accounts receivable, where the receivables serve as *collateral* for a *loan.*

ATB. Accounting Terminology Bulletin.

at par. A *bond* or *preferred shares* issued (or selling) at *face amount.*

attachment. The laying claim to the *assets* of a borrower (or debtor) by a lender (or creditor) when the borrower has failed to pay debts on time.

attest. An auditor's rendering of an *opinion* that the *financial statements* are fair. Common usage calls this procedure the "attest function" of the CPA. *See fair presentation.*

attestor. Typically independent *CPAs*, who *audit financial statements* prepared by management for the benefit of users. The *FASB* describes accounting's constituency as comprising preparers, attestors, and users.

attribute measured. The particular *cost* reported in the balance sheet. When making physical measurements, such as of a person, one needs to decide the units with which to measure, such as inches or centimeters or pounds or grams. One chooses the attribute height or weight independently of the measuring unit, English or metric. Conventional accounting uses *historical cost* as the attribute measured and *nominal dollars* as the measuring unit. Some theorists argue that accounting would better serve readers if it used *current cost* as the attribute measured. Others argue that accounting would better serve readers if it used *constant dollars* as the measuring unit. Some, including us, think accounting should change both the measuring unit and the attribute measured. One can measure the attribute historical cost in nominal dollars or in constant dollars. One can also measure the attribute current cost in nominal dollars or constant dollars. Choosing between the two attributes and the two measuring units implies four different accounting systems. Each of these four has its uses.

attribute(s) sampling. The use of sampling technique in which the observer assesses each item selected on the basis of whether it has a particular qualitative characteristic in order to ascertain the rate of occurrence of this characteristic in the population.

See also estimation sampling. Compare *variables sampling.* Example of attributes sampling: take a sample population of people, note the fraction that is male (say, 40 percent), and then infer that the entire population contains 40 percent males. Example of variables sampling: take a sample population of people, observe the weight of each sample point, compute the mean of those sampled people's weights (say 160 pounds), and then infer that the mean weight of the entire population equals 160 pounds.

audit. Systematic inspection of accounting records involving analyses, tests, and *confirmations. See internal audit.*

audit committee. A committee of the board of directors of a *corporation*, usually comprising outside directors, who nominate the independent auditors and discuss the auditors' work with them. If the auditors believe the shareholders should know about certain matters, the auditors, in principle, first bring these matters to the attention of the audit committee; in practice, the auditors may notify management before they notify the audit committee.

Audit Guides. See Industry Audit Guides.

audit program. The procedures followed by the *auditor* in carrying out the *audit.*

audit trail. A reference accompanying an entry, or *post*, to an underlying source record or document. Efficiently checking the accuracy of accounting entries requires an audit trail. *See cross-reference.*

Auditing Research Monograph. Publication series of the *AICPA.*

auditing standards. Standards promulgated by the *PCAOB* for auditors to follow in carrying out their *attest* functions. The PCAOB began operations in earnest in 2003, and initially has said that is would use the standards originally promulgated by the *AICPA*, including general standards, standards of field work, and standards of reporting. According to the AICPA, these standards "deal with the measures of the quality of the performance and the objectives to be attained" rather than with specific auditing procedures. As time passes, the PCAOB will substitute its rules for those of the AICPA.

Auditing Standards Board. *AICPA* operating committee that promulgates auditing rules, subject to the higher authority of the PCAOB.

auditor. Without a modifying adjective, usually refers to an external auditor—one who checks the accuracy, fairness, and general acceptability of accounting records and statements and then *attests* to them. *See internal auditor.*

auditor's opinion. *Auditor's report.*

auditor's report. The auditor's statement of the work done and an opinion of the *financial statements*. The auditor usually gives unqualified ("clean") opinions but may qualify them, or the auditor may disclaim an opinion in the report. Often called the "accountant's report." *See adverse opinion.*

AudSEC. The former Auditing Standards Executive Committee of the *AICPA*, now functioning as the *Auditing Standards Board.*

authorized capital stock. The number of *shares* of stock that a corporation can issue; specified by the *articles of incorporation.*

available for sale, securities. *Marketable securities* a firm holds that are classified as neither *trading securities* nor *held-to-maturity (debt) securities.* This classification is important in *SFAS No. 115,* which requires the owner to carry marketable equity securities on the balance sheet at market value, not at cost. Under *SFAS No. 115,* the income statement reports *holding gains and losses* on trading securities but not on securities available for sale. The required accounting *credits* (*debits*) holding gains (losses) on securities available for sale directly to an *owners' equity* account. On sale, the firm reports realized gain or loss as the difference between the selling price and the original cost, for trading securities, and as the difference between the selling price and the book value at the beginning of the period of sale, for securities available for sale and for debt securities held to maturity. By their nature, however, the firm will only rarely sell debt securities "held to maturity."

average. The arithmetic mean of a set of numbers; obtained by summing the items and dividing by the number of items.

average collection period of receivables. *See ratio.*

average-cost flow assumption. An inventory *flow assumption* in which the cost of units equals the *weighted average* cost of the *beginning inventory* and purchases. *See inventory equation.*

average tax rate. The rate found by dividing *income tax* expense by *net income* before taxes. Contrast with *marginal tax rate* and *statutory tax rate.*

avoidable cost. A *cost* that ceases if a firm discontinues an activity; an *incremental* or *variable cost.* *See programmed cost.*

B

backflush costing. A method of *allocating indirect costs* and *overhead*; used by companies that hope to have zero or small *work-in-process inventory* at the end of the period. The method *debits* all *product costs* to *cost of goods sold* (or *finished goods inventory*) during the period. To the extent that work in process actually exists at the end of the period, the method then debits work-in-process and *credits* cost of goods sold (or finished goods inventory). This method is "backflush" in the sense that costing systems ordinarily, but not in this case, allocate first to work-in-process and then forward to cost of goods sold or to finished goods. Here, the process allocates first to cost of goods sold (or finished goods) and then, later if necessary, to work-in-process.

backlog. Orders for which a firm has insufficient *inventory* on hand for current delivery and will fill in a later period.

backlog depreciation. In current cost accounting, a problem arising for the accumulated depreciation on plant assets. Consider an asset costing $10,000 with a 10-year life depreciated with the straight-line method. Assume that a similar asset has a current cost of $10,000 at the end of the first year but $12,000 at the end of the second year. Assume that the firm bases the depreciation charge on the average current cost during the year, $10,000 for the first year and $11,000 for the second. The depreciation charge for the first year is $1,000 and for the second is $1,100 (= .10 × $11,000), so the *accumulated depreciation account* is $2,100 after two years. Note that at the end of the second year, the firm has used 20 percent of the asset's future benefits, so the accounting records based on current costs must show a *net book value* of $9,600 (= .80 × $12,000), which results only if accumulated depreciation equals $2,400, so that book value equals $9,600 (= $12,000 − $2,400). But the sum of the depreciation charges equals only $2,100 (= $1,000 + $1,100). The

journal entry to increase the accumulated depreciation account requires a *credit* to that account of $300. The backlog depreciation question arises: what account do we debit? Some theorists would *debit* an *income* account, and others would *debit* a *balance sheet owners' equity* account without reducing current-period earnings. The answer to the question of what to debit interrelates with how the firm records the *holding gains* on the asset. When the firm debits the asset account for $2,000 to increase the recorded amount from $10,000 to $12,000, it records a holding gain of $2,000 with a credit. Many theorists believe that whatever account the firm credits for the holding gain is the same account that the firm should debit for backlog depreciation. This is sometimes called "catch-up depreciation."

bad debt. An *uncollectible account*; *see bad debt expense* and *sales contra, estimated uncollectibles.*

bad debt expense. The name for an *account debited* in both the *allowance method* for *uncollectible accounts* and the *direct write-off method.* Under the allowance method, some prefer to treat the account as a revenue contra, not as an expense, and give it an account title such as Uncollectible Accounts Adjustment.

bad debt recovery. Collection, perhaps partial, of a specific account receivable previously written off as uncollectible. If a firm uses the *allowance method*, it will usually *credit* the *allowance* account, assuming that it has correctly assessed the amount of bad debts but has merely misjudged the identity of one of the nonpaying customers. If the firm decides that its charges for bad debts have been too large, it will credit the Bad Debt Expense account. If the firm uses the *direct write-off* method, it will credit a *revenue account.*

bailout period. In a *capital budgeting* context, the total time that elapses before accumulated cash inflows from a project, including the potential *salvage value* of assets at various times, equal or exceed the accumulated cash outflows. Contrast with *payback period*, which assumes completion of the project and uses terminal salvage value. Bailout, in contrast with payback, takes into account, at least to some degree, the *present value* of the cash flows after the termination date that the analyst is considering. The potential salvage value at any time includes some estimate of the flows that can occur after that time.

balance. As a noun, the opening balance in an *account* plus the amounts of increases less the amounts of decreases. (In the absence of a modifying adjective, the term means closing balance, in contrast to opening balance. The closing balance for a period becomes the opening balance for the next period.) As a verb, "balance" means to find the value of the arithmetic expression described above.

balance sheet. Statement of financial position that shows Total Assets = Total Liabilities + Owners' Equity. The *balance sheet* usually classifies Total Assets as (1) *current assets*, (2) *investments*, (3) *property, plant, and equipment*, or (4) *intangible assets.* The balance sheet accounts composing Total Liabilities usually appear under the headings Current Liabilities and Long-term Liabilities.

balance sheet account. An account that can appear on a balance sheet; a *permanent account.* Contrast with *temporary account.*

balanced scorecard. A set of performance targets, not all expressed in dollar amounts, for setting an organization's goals for its individual employees or groups or divisions. A community relations employee might, for example, set targets in terms of number of employee hours devoted to local charitable purposes.

balloon. Most *mortgage* and *installment loans* require relatively equal periodic payments. Sometimes the loan requires relatively equal periodic payments with a large final payment. Usage calls the large final payment a "balloon" payment and the loan, a "balloon" loan. Although a coupon bond meets this definition, usage seldom, if ever, applies this term to bond loans.

bank balance. The amount of the balance in a checking account shown on the *bank statement.* Compare with *adjusted bank balance of cash*, and *see bank reconciliation schedule.*

bank prime rate. *See prime rate.*

bank reconciliation schedule. A schedule that explains the difference between the book balance of the cash in a bank account and the bank's statement of that amount; takes into account the amount of items such as checks that have not cleared or deposits that have not been recorded by the bank, as well as errors made by the bank or the firm.

bank statement. A statement sent by the bank to a checking account customer showing deposits, checks cleared, and service charges for a period, usually one month.

bankrupt. Occurs when a company's *liabilities* exceed its *assets* and the firm or one of its creditors has filed a legal petition that the bankruptcy court has accepted under the bankruptcy law. A bankrupt firm is usually, but need not be, *insolvent.*

base stock method. A method of inventory valuation that assumes that a firm must keep on hand at all times a minimum normal, or base stock, of goods for effective continuity of operations. The firm values this base quantity at *acquisition cost* of the inventory on hand in the earliest period when inventory was on hand. Firms may not use this method, either for financial reporting or for tax reporting, but most theorists consider it to be the forerunner of the *LIFO* cost flow assumption.

basic accounting equation. *Accounting equation.*

basic cost-flow equation. *Cost-flow equation.*

basic earnings per share (BEPS). *Net income* to *common shareholders*, divided by the weighted average number of common shares *outstanding* during the period. Required by *SFAS No. 128* and by *IASB. See primary earnings per share (PEPS)* for contrast. Because BEPS does not deal with *common-stock equivalents*, it will almost always give a larger earnings-per-share figure than PEPS.

basis. *Acquisition cost*, or some substitute therefor, of an *asset* or *liability* used in computing gain or loss on disposition or retirement; *attribute measured*. This term appears in both *financial* and *tax reporting*, but the basis of a given item need not be the same for both purposes.

basis point. One one-hundreth (= 1/100). Terminology usually quotes *interest rates* in percentage terms, such as "5.60 percent" or "5.67 percent." The difference between those two interest rates is described as "7 basis points" or seven one-hundreths of 1 percent. Financial writers often extend this usage to other contexts involving decimals. For example, if the mean grade point average in the class is 3.25 and a given student scores 3.30, we might say that the student scored "5 basis points" above the class average.

basket purchase. Purchase of a group of *assets* (and *liabilities*) for a single price; the acquiring firm must assign *costs* to each item so that it can record the individual items with their separate amounts in the *accounts.*

batch-level activities. Work required to ready equipment or people for a production run.

bear. One who believes that security prices will fall. A "bear market" refers to a time when stock prices are generally declining. Contrast with *bull.*

bearer bond. *See registered bond* for contrast and definition.

beginning inventory. Valuation of *inventory* on hand at the beginning of the *accounting period*, equals *ending inventory* from the preceding period.

behavioral congruence. *Goal congruence.*

benchmarking. Process of measuring a firm's performance, products, and services against standards based on best levels of performance achievable or, sometimes, achieved by other firms.

BEPS. *Basic earnings per share.*

betterment. An *improvement*, usually *capitalized*, not *expensed.*

bid. An offer to purchase, or the amount of the offer.

big bath. A *write-off* of a substantial amount of costs previously treated as *assets*; usually occurs when a corporation drops a business line that earlier required a large investment but that proved to be unprofitable. The term is sometimes used to describe a situation in which a corporation takes a large write-off in one period in order to free later periods of gradual write-offs of those amounts. In this sense it frequently occurs when the top management of the firm changes.

Big 4. Final 4. The four largest U.S. *public accounting* partnerships; in alphabetical order: Deloitte & Touche; Ernst & Young; KPMG Peat Marwick; and PricewaterhouseCoopers. *See Big N.*

Big N. The largest U.S. *public accounting* partnerships. When we first prepared this glossary, there were eight such partnerships, referred to as the "Big 8." *See Big 4.* The term "Big N" came into use when various firms of the Big 8 proposed to merge with each other and the ultimate number of large partnerships was in doubt, which it still is, although we don't expect the number to change before 2010.

bill. An *invoice* of charges and *terms of sale* for *goods* and *services*; also, a piece of currency.

bill of materials. A specification of the quantities of *direct materials* that a firm expects to use to produce a given job or quantity of output.

blocked currency. Currency that the holder, by law, cannot withdraw from the issuing country or exchange for the currency of another country.

board. *Board of directors.*

board of directors. The governing body of a corporation; elected by the shareholders.

bond. A certificate to show evidence of debt. The *par value* is the *principal* or face amount of the bond payable at maturity. The *coupon rate* is the amount of the yearly payments divided by the principal amount. Coupon bonds have attached coupons that the holder can redeem at stated dates. Increasingly, firms issue not coupon bonds but registered bonds; the firm or its agent keeps track of the owners of registered bonds. Normally, bonds call for semiannual payments.

bond conversion. The act of exchanging *convertible bonds* for *preferred* or *common shares.*

bond discount. From the standpoint of the issuer of a *bond* at the issue date, the excess of the *par value* of a bond over its initial sales price and, at later dates, the excess of par over the sum of the following two amounts: initial issue price and the portion of discount already *amortized*; from the standpoint of a bondholder, the difference between par value and selling price when the bond sells below par.

bond indenture. The contract between an issuer of *bonds* and the bondholders.

bond premium. Exactly parallel to *bond discount* except that the issue price (or current selling price) exceeds *par value.*

bond ratings. Corporate and *municipal bond* issue ratings, based on the issuer's existing *debt* level, its previous record of payment, the *coupon rate* on the bonds, and the safety of the *assets* or *revenues* that are committed to paying off *principal* and *interest.* Moody's Investors Service and Standard & Poor's Corporation publish bond ratings: Moody's top rating is Aaa; Standard & Poor's is AAA.

bond redemption. Retirement of *bonds.*

bond refunding. To incur *debt*, usually through the issue of new *bonds*, intending to use the proceeds to retire an *outstanding* bond issue.

bond sinking fund. *See sinking fund.*

bond table. A table showing the current price of a *bond* as a function of the *coupon rate*, current (remaining) term *maturity*, and effective *yield to maturity* (or *effective rate*).

bonus. Premium over normal *wage* or *salary*, paid usually for meritorious performance.

bonus method. One of two methods to recognize an excess, say $10,000, when a *partnership* admits a new partner and when the new partner's capital account is to show an amount larger than the amount of *tangible* assets that he or she contributes. First, the old partners can transfer $10,000 from themselves to the new partner. This is the bonus method. Second, the partnership can recognize goodwill in the amount of $10,000, with the credit to the new partner's capital account. This is the *goodwill method.* (Notice that the new partner's percentage of total ownership differs under the two methods.) If the new partner's capital account is to show an amount smaller than the tangible assets that he or she contributed, then the old partners will receive bonus or goodwill, depending on the method.

book. As a verb, to record a transaction; as a noun, usually plural, the *journals* and *ledgers*; as an adjective, *see book value.*

book cost. *Book value.*

book inventory. An *inventory* amount that results not from physical count but from the amount of beginning inventory plus *invoice* amounts of net purchases less invoice amounts of *requisitions* or withdrawals; implies a *perpetual inventory* method.

book of original entry. *Journal.*

book value. The amount shown in the books or in the *accounts* for an *asset, liability,* or *owners' equity* item. The term generally refers to the *net* amount of an *asset* or group of assets shown in the account that records the asset and reductions, such as for *amortization,* in its cost. Of a firm, it refers to the excess of total assets over total liabilities; *net assets.*

book value per share of common stock. Common *shareholders' equity* divided by the number of shares of common stock outstanding. *See ratio.*

bookkeeping. The process of analyzing and recording transactions in the accounting records.

boot. The additional cash paid (or received) along with a used item in a trade-in or exchange transaction for another item. *See trade-in.*

borrower. *See loan.*

bottleneck. An operation in which the work to be performed equals or exceeds the available capacity, thus holding up further operations.

branch. A sales office or other unit of an enterprise physically separated from the home office of the enterprise but not organized as a legally separate *subsidiary.* Writers seldom use this term to refer to manufacturing units.

branch accounting. An accounting procedure that enables the firm to report the financial position and operations of each *branch* separately but later combine them for published statements.

brand. brand name. *See trademark* and *trademark right.*

breakeven analysis. *See breakeven chart.*

breakeven chart. Two kinds of breakeven charts appear here. The charts use the following information for one month. Revenue is $30 per unit.

Cost Classification	Variable Cost, Per Unit	Fixed Cost, Per Month
Manufacturing Costs		
Direct Material	$ 4	
Direct Labor	9	
Overhead	4	$ 3,060
Total Manufacturing Costs	$ 17	$ 3,060
Selling, general, and administrative costs		5
1,740		

Total costs .... $ 22 $ 4,800

The cost-volume-profit graph presents the relation between changes in volume to the amount of *profit*, or *income*. Such a graph shows total *revenue* and total *costs* for each volume level, and the user reads profit or loss at any volume directly from the chart. The profit-volume graph does not show revenues and costs but more readily indicates profit (or loss) at various output levels. Keep in mind two caveats about these graphs:

1. Although the curve depicting *variable cost* and total cost appears as a straight line for its entire length, at low or high levels of output, variable cost will probably differ from $22 per unit. The variable cost figure usually results from studies of operations at some broad central area of production, called the *relevant range*. The chart will not usually provide accurate results for low (or high) levels of activity. For this reason, the total cost and the profit-loss curves sometimes appear as dotted lines at lower (or higher) volume levels.

2. This chart, simplistically, assumes a single-product firm. For a multi-product firm, the horizontal axis would have to be stated in dollars rather than in physical units of output. Breakeven charts for multiproduct firms necessarily assume that the firm sells constant proportions of the several products, so that changes in this mixture, as well as in costs or selling prices, invalidate such a chart.

(a) Cost-Volume-Profit Graph

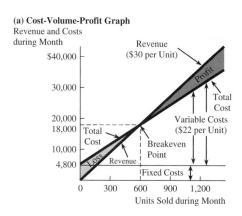

(b) Profit-Volume Graph

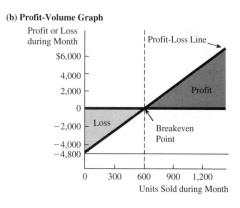

breakeven point. The volume of sales required so that total *revenues* equals total *costs*; may be expressed in units (*Fixed costs ÷ Contribution per unit*) or in sales dollars [Selling price per unit × (Fixed costs ÷ Contribution per unit)].

break-even time. Time required before the firm recovers the amounts it invested in developing a new product.

budget. A financial plan that a firm uses to estimate the results of future operations; frequently used to help control future operations. In governmental operations, budgets often become the law. *See standard costs* for further elaboration and contrast.

budgetary accounts. In governmental accounting, the accounts that reflect estimated operations and financial condition, as affected by estimated *revenues, appropriations*, and *encumbrances.* Contrast with *proprietary accounts*, which record the transactions.

budgetary control. Management of governmental (nongovernmental) unit in accordance with an official (approved) *budget* in order to keep total expenditures within authorized (planned) limits.

budgeted cost. *See standard costs* for definition and contrast.

budgeted statements. *Pro forma statements* prepared before the event or period occurs.

bull. One who believes that security prices will rise. A "bull market" refers to a time when stock prices are generally rising. Contrast with *bear*.

burden. *See overhead costs*.

burn rate. A new business usually begins life with cash-absorbing operating losses but with a limited amount of cash. The "burn rate" measures how long the new business can survive before operating losses must stop or the firm must receive a new infusion of cash. Writers usually express the burn rate in months.

business combination. As defined in *APB Opinion No. 16*, the bringing together into a single accounting *entity* of two or more incorporated or unincorporated businesses. The new entity will account for the *merger* either with the *purchase method* or, outside the U.S., with the *pooling-of-interests method*. *See conglomerate*.

business entity. *Entity; accounting entity.*

but for, but-for. Applied to a computation that attempts to measure a hypothetical outcome if something about the world had differed from the actual outcome. But for the patent infringement, what would have been my profits? But for the fire, what would have been my income? But for the sexual harassment, what would my promotions have been? The goal is to measure the outcome given the but-for assumption so the analyst can compute the difference between that outcome and the actual outcome. The analyst calls the difference the harm (typically, but it could be an advantage) caused by the difference between the actual world and the hypothetical one.

BV (besloten vennootschap). Netherlands: a private limited-liability company.

bylaws. The rules adopted by the shareholders of a corporation that specify the general methods for carrying out the functions of the corporation.

by-product. A *joint product* whose sales value is so small relative to the sales value of the other joint product(s) that it does not receive normal accounting treatment. The costs assigned to by-products reduce the costs of the main product(s). Accounting allocates by-products a share of joint costs such that the expected gain or loss at their sale is zero. Thus, by-products appear in the *accounts* at *net realizable value*.

C

C corporation. In tax terminology, a corporation paying its own income taxes. Contrast with *S corporation*.

CA. *Chartered accountant.*

call. An option to buy *shares* of a publicly traded corporation at a fixed price during a fixed time span. Contrast with *put*.

call premium. *See callable bond.*

call price. *See callable bond.*

callable bond. A *bond* for which the issuer reserves the right to pay a specific amount, the call price, to retire the obligation before its *maturity* date. If the issuer agrees to pay more than the *face amount* of the bond when called, the excess of the payment over the face amount is the "call premium."

called-up share capital. UK: *common stock* at *par value.*

Canadian Institute of Chartered Accountants. The national organization that represents *chartered accountants* in Canada. Web site: *www.cica.ca.*

cancelable lease. *See lease.*

CAP. *Committee on Accounting Procedure.*

capacity. Stated in units of product, the amount that a firm can produce per unit of time; stated in units of input, such as *direct labor* hours, the amount of input that a firm can use in production per unit of time. A firm uses this measure of output or input in allocating *fixed costs* if the amounts producible are normal, rather than maximum, amounts.

capacity cost. A *fixed cost* incurred to provide a firm with the capacity to produce or to sell. Consists of *standby costs* and *enabling costs.* Contrast with *programmed costs.*

capacity variance. *Production volume variance.*

capital. *Owners' equity* in a business; often used, equally correctly, to mean the total assets of a business; sometimes used to mean *long-term assets.* Sometimes used to mean *funds* raised or all assets or long-term financing. This word causes confusion in accounting and finance. Uninformed users mix up the funds (and their uses) with the sources of the funds. Consider the following transactions. A firm raises $100 cash by issuing shares and uses the $100 to acquire *inventory* and *plant assets.* Did the investor "invest capital" of $100 or did the firm "invest capital" of $100, or both? You will hear "invest capital" used for both sides of that transaction. Now focus on the firm who issued the shares and received the cash. Some would say the first transaction, the issue of shares, "raised capital." (If you ask of a person who answers this way, "What is the *capital,* the increase in owners' equity or the increased cash?" you will not get a clear answer, consistent across all such people.) Others would say only the second transaction, spending the cash, raised capital and only then for the plant assets, not the inventory. When a regulator focuses on a bank's capital ratios, it looks to the right-hand side of the balance sheet, not to how the firm has invested its funds. Sometimes bank regulators will take the owners' equity total and subtract from that amount the amount of intangible assets, resulting in a total with no clear conception, which they call "tangible capital." *See cost of capital* for further discussion of the confusion between the cost of raising funds and the return to, or *opportunity cost* of, investing funds. The confusion is so prevalent that we tend to avoid using the word, except to mean *shareholders' equity.*

capital asset. Properly used, a designation, for income tax purposes, that describes property held by a taxpayer except *cash,* inventoriable *assets,* goods held primarily for sale, most depreciable property, *real estate, receivables,* certain *intangibles,* and a few other items. Sometimes writers use this term imprecisely to describe *plant* and *equipment,* which are clearly not capital assets under the income-tax definition. Writers often use the term to refer to an *investment* in *securities.*

capital budget. Plan of proposed outlays for acquiring long-term *assets* and the means of *financing* the acquisition.

capital budgeting. The process of choosing *investment* projects for an enterprise by considering the *present value* of cash flows and deciding how to raise the funds the investment requires.

capital consumption allowance. The term used for *depreciation expense* in national income accounting and the reporting of funds in the economy.

capital contributed in excess of par (or stated) value. A preferred title for the account that shows the amount received by the issuer for *capital stock* in excess of *par (or stated) value.*

capital expenditure (outlay). An *expenditure* to acquire long-term *assets.*

capital gain. The excess of proceeds over *cost*, or other *basis*, from the sale of a *capital asset* as defined by the Internal Revenue Code. If the taxpayer has held the capital asset for a sufficiently long time before sale, then the gain is taxed at a rate lower than that used for other gains and ordinary income.

capital lease. A *lease* treated by the *lessee* as both the borrowing of funds and the acquisition of an *asset* to be *amortized.* The lessee (tenant) recognizes both the *liability* and the asset on its balance sheet. Expenses consist of *interest* on the *debt* and *amortization* of the asset. The *lessor* (landlord) treats the lease as the sale of the asset in return for a series of future cash receipts. Contrast with *operating lease.*

capital loss. A negative capital gain; *see capital gain.*

capital rationing. In a *capital budgeting* context, the imposition of constraints on the amounts of total capital

expenditures in each period.

capital stock. The ownership shares of a corporation. Consists of all classes of *common* and *preferred shares.* In accounting, this term means the *credit* balances showing the sources of funds. In economics, this term usually refers to the *assets* themselves, the *debit* balances, for *inventory*, *property*, *plant*, *equipment* and *intangibles.*

capital structure. The composition of a corporation's equities; the relative proportions of short-term debt, long-term debt, and *owners' equity.*

capital surplus. An inferior term for *capital contributed in excess of par (or stated) value.*

capitalization of a corporation. A term used by investment analysts to indicate *shareholders' equity* plus bonds outstanding.

capitalization of earnings. The process of estimating the *fair value* of a firm by computing the *net present value* of the predicted *net income* (not *cash flows*) of the firm for the future.

capitalization rate. An *interest rate* used to convert a series of payments or receipts or earnings into a single *present value.*

capitalize. To record an *expenditure* that will benefit a future period as an *asset* rather than to treat the expenditure as an *expense* of the period of its occurrence. Whether expenditures for advertising or for research and development should be capitalized is controversial, but *SFAS No. 2* forbids capitalizing *R&D* costs. We believe GAAP should allow firms to capitalize expenditures when they lead to future benefits and thus meet the criterion to be an asset.

carryback, carryforward, carryover. The use of losses or tax credits in one period to reduce income taxes payable in other periods. Two common kinds of carrybacks exist: for net operating losses and for *capital losses*. They apply against taxable income. In general, carrybacks are for three years, with the earliest year first. The taxpayer can carry forward operating losses for fifteen years. Corporate capital loss carryforwards are for five years. Individuals can carry forward capital losses indefinitely.

carrying cost. Costs (such as property taxes and insurance) of holding, or storing, *inventory* from the time of purchase until the time of sale or use.

carrying value (amount). *Book value.*

CASB (Cost Accounting Standards Board). A board authorized by the U.S. Congress to "promulgate cost-accounting standards designed to achieve uniformity and consistency in the cost-accounting principles followed by defense contractors and subcontractors under federal contracts." The *principles* the CASB promulgated since 1970 have considerable weight in practice wherever the *FASB* has not established a standard. Congress allowed the CASB to go out of existence in 1980 but reinstated it in 1990.

cash. Currency and coins, negotiable checks, and balances in bank accounts. For the *statement of cash flows*, "cash" also includes *marketable securities* held as *current assets*.

cash basis of accounting. In contrast to the *accrual basis of accounting*, a system of accounting in which a firm recognizes *revenues* when it receives *cash* and recognizes *expenses* as it makes *disbursements*. The firm makes no attempt to match *revenues* and *expenses* in measuring *income*. *See modified cash basis.*

cash budget. A schedule of expected cash *receipts* and *disbursements*.

cash change equation. For any *period*, the change in *cash* equals the change in *liabilities* plus the change in *owners' equity* minus the change in noncash *assets*.

cash collection basis. The *installment method* for recognizing *revenue*. Do not confuse with the *cash basis of accounting*.

cash conversion cycle. *Cash cycle.*

cash cycle. The period of time during which a firm converts *cash* into *inventories*, inventories into *accounts receivable*, and *receivables* back into cash. Sometimes called *earnings cycle*.

cash disbursements journal. A specialized *journal* used to record *expenditures* by *cash* and by *check*. If a *check register* is also used, a cash disbursements journal records only expenditures of currency and coins.

cash discount. A sales or purchase price reduction allowed for prompt payment.

cash dividend. *See dividend.*

cash equivalent. According to *SFAS No. 95*, "short-term, highly liquid investments that are both readily convertible to known amounts of cash [and] so near their maturity that they present insignificant risk of changes in value because of changes in interest rates.... Examples of items commonly considered to be cash equivalents are Treasury bills, commercial paper, [and] money market funds."

cash equivalent value. A term used to describe the amount for which an *asset* could be sold. Sometimes called *market value* or *fair market price (value)*.

cash flow. Cash *receipts* minus *disbursements* from a given *asset*, or group of assets, for a given period. Financial analysts sometimes use this term to mean *net income + depreciation + depletion + amortization. See also operating cash flow* and *free cash flow*.

cash flow from operations. Receipts from customers and from investments less expenditures for inventory, labor, and services used in the usual activities of the firm, less interest expenditures. *See statement of cash flows* and *operations.* Same as *cash provided by operations.*

cash-flow hedge. A hedge of an exposure to variability in the cash flows of a recognized *asset* or *liability* or of a forecasted transaction, such as expected future foreign sales. The cash flows hedged do not themselves appear on the *balance sheet.* The hedging instrument itself is a *marketable security* and appears on the balance sheet at market value. If the firm uses hedge accounting and the hedging instrument is highly effective, then it will be able to report in *other comprehensive income* the *gains* and *losses*, so these amounts will not appear in periodic net income.

cash flow statement. *Statement of cash flows.*

cash provided by operations. An important subtotal in the *statement of cash flows.* This amount equals the total of revenues producing *cash* less *expenses* requiring cash. Often, the amount appears as *net income* plus expenses not requiring cash (such as depreciation charges) minus revenues not producing cash (such as revenues recognized under the *equity method* of accounting for a long-term investment). The statement of cash flows maintains the same distinctions between *continuing operations, discontinued operations*, and *income* or *loss* from *extraordinary items* as does the *income statement.*

cash receipts journal. A specialized *journal* used to record all *receipts* of *cash.*

cash (surrender) value of life insurance. An amount equal not to the face value of the policy to be paid in the event of death but to the amount that the owner could realize by immediately canceling the policy and returning it to the insurance company for cash. A firm owning a life insurance policy reports it as an asset at an amount equal to this value.

cash yield. *See yield.*

cashier's check. A bank's own *check* drawn on itself and signed by the cashier or other authorized official. It is a direct obligation of the bank. Compare with *certified check.*

catch-up depreciation. *Backlog depreciation.*

cause-and-effect analysis. An identification of potential causes of defects and taking actions to cure the problem found. To use this analysis, first define the effect and then identify the causes of the problem. The potential causes fall into four categories: human factors, methods and design factors, machine-related factors, and materials or components factors. As management identifies the prevailing causes, it develops and implements corrective measures.

CCA. *Current cost accounting; current value accounting.*

central corporate expenses. General *overhead expenses* incurred in running the corporate headquarters and related supporting activities of a corporation. Accounting treats these expenses as *period expenses.* Contrast with *manufacturing overhead. Line of business reporting* must decide how to treat these expenses—whether to allocate them to the individual segments and, if so, how to allocate them.

central processing unit (CPU). The computer system component that carries out the arithmetic, logic, and data transfer.

certificate. The document that is the physical embodiment of a *bond* or a *share of stock*; a term sometimes used for the *auditor's report.*

certificate of deposit. A form of *deposit* in a bank or thrift institution. Federal law constrains the rate of interest that banks can pay to their depositors. Current law allows banks to pay a rate higher than the one allowed on a *time deposit* if the depositor promises to leave funds on deposit for several months or more. When the bank receives such funds, it issues a certificate of deposit. The depositor can withdraw the funds before maturity by paying a penalty.

certified check. The *check* of a depositor drawn on a bank. The bank inserts the words "accepted" or "certified" on the face of the check, with the date and a signature of a bank official. The check then becomes an obligation of the bank. Compare with *cashier's check*.

certified financial statement. A financial statement attested to by an independent *auditor* who is a *CPA*.

certified internal auditor. *See CIA*.

certified management accountant. *CMA*.

certified public accountant (CPA). An accountant who has satisfied the statutory and administrative requirements of his or her jurisdiction to be registered or licensed as a public accountant. In addition to passing the Uniform CPA Examination administered by the *AICPA*, the CPA must meet certain educational, experience, and moral requirements that differ by jurisdiction. The jurisdictions are the 50 states, the District of Columbia, Guam, Puerto Rico, and the Virgin Islands.

CFA. *Chartered Financial Analyst.*

CGA (Certified General Accountant). Canada: an accountant who has satisfied the experience, education, and examination requirements of the Certified General Accountants' Association.

chain discount. A series of *discount* percentages. For example, if a chain discount of 10 and 5 percent is quoted, then the actual, or *invoice*, price is the nominal, or list, price times .90 times .95, or 85.5, percent of invoice price.

change fund. Coins and currency issued to cashiers, delivery drivers, and so on.

changes, accounting. *See accounting changes.*

changes in financial position. *See statement of cash flows.*

channel stuffing. Assume a company's ordinary practices record *revenue* when it ships to customers goods previously ordered. A company engaging in channel-stuffing will ship goods not yet ordered but record them as *sales*, as though a real customer had ordered them. It might even get permission from the customer to ship, saying it will not bill the customer until next period and that the customer will get its usual grace period to pay the bill starting from that later date, next period. Often, sales staff eager to boost their own sales commissions will send a letter to the customer laying out the agreement: the customer will accept the shipment and if asked, confirm that it ordered the goods, but the seller will not send an invoice until later, and the customer need not pay until later or can return the goods. Such a letter is called a "side letter" and even honest managements have a hard time locating these. All a management can do is be diligent and deal severely with employees found issuing side letters.

charge. As a noun, a *debit* to an account; as a verb, to debit.

charge off. To treat as a *loss* or *expense* an amount originally recorded as an *asset*; use of this term implies that the charge is not in accord with original expectations.

chart of accounts. A list of names and numbers, systematically organized, of *accounts.*

charter. Document issued by a state government authorizing the creation of a corporation.

chartered accountant(s) (CA). The title used in British Commonwealth countries, such as Australia, Canada, India, Scotland and New Zealand, for an accountant who has satisfied the requirements of the institute of his or her jurisdiction to be qualified to serve as a *public accountant.* In the UK other than Scotland, members use the initials ACA or FCA: *A* means associate and *F* means fellow; the associate has less experience than does the fellow. A partnership of chartered accountants signs its firm name with the letters *CA.* In Canada, each provincial institute or order has the right to administer the examination and set the standards of performance and ethics for Chartered Accountants in its province. For a number of years, however, the provincial organizations have pooled their rights to qualify new members through the Inter-provincial Education Committee, resulting in nationally set and graded examinations given in English and French. Deviation from the pass/fail grade awarded by the Board of Examiners (a subcommittee of the Inter-provincial Education Committee) is rare.

Chartered Financial Analyst (CFA). A person who has passed three examinations, over at least an 18-month period, covering topics in accounting, economics, financial economics, portfolio management, and security analysis. The Association for Investment Management and Research (AIMR) administers the program though its Institute of Chartered Financial Analysts. Beyond passing examintions,

the person needs to have approved working experience and satisfy standards of professional conduct.

check. The Federal Reserve Board defines a check as "a *draft* or order upon a bank or banking house purporting to be drawn upon a deposit of funds for the payment at all events of a certain sum of money to a certain person therein named or to him or his order or to bearer and payable instantly on demand." It must contain the phrase "pay to the order of." The amount shown on the check must be clearly readable, and the check must have the signature of the drawer. The drawer need not date the check. In the accounts, the drawer usually reduces the *balance* in the *cash account* when it issues the check, not later when the check clears the bank. *See remittance advice.*

check register. A *journal* to record *checks* issued.

CIA (Certified Internal Auditor). One who has satisfied certain requirements of the *Institute of Internal Auditors* including experience, ethics, education, and passing examinations.

CICA. *Canadian Institute of Chartered Accountants.*

CIF (cost, insurance, and freight). In contracts, a term used along with the name of a given port, such as New Orleans, to indicate that the quoted price includes insurance, handling, and freight charges up to delivery by the seller at the given port.

circulating capital. *Working capital.*

clean opinion. *See auditor's report.*

clean surplus concept. The notion that all entries to the *retained earnings* account must record *net income* and *dividends. See comprehensive income.* Contrast with *current operating performance concept.* This concept, with minor exceptions, now controls *GAAP.* (*See APB Opinions No. 9* and *No. 30.*)

clearing account. An account containing amounts to be transferred to another account(s) before the end of the *accounting period.* Examples are the *income summary* account (whose balance transfers to *retained earnings*) and the purchases account (whose balance transfers to *inventory* or to *cost of goods sold*).

close. As a verb, to transfer the *balance* of a *temporary* or *contra* or *adjunct account* to the main account to which it relates; for example, to transfer *revenue* and *expense* accounts directly, or through the *income summary* account, to an *owners' equity* account or to transfer *purchase discounts* to purchases.

closed account. An *account* with equal *debits* and *credits*, usually as a result of a *closing entry.*

closing entries. The *entries* that accomplish the transfer of balances in *temporary accounts* to the related *balance sheet accounts. See work sheet.*

closing inventory. *Ending inventory.*

CMA (Certified Management Accountant) certificate. Awarded by the *Institute of Certified Management Accountants* of the *Institute of Management Accountants* to those who pass a set of examinations and meet certain experience and continuing-education requirements.

CoCoA. *Continuously Contemporary Accounting.*

coding of accounts. The numbering of *accounts*, as for a *chart of accounts*, that is necessary for computerized accounting.

coinsurance. Common condition of insurance policies that protect against hazards such as fire or water damage. These often specify that the owner of the property cannot collect the full amount of insurance for a loss unless the insurance policy covers at least some specified "coinsurance" percentage, usually about 80 percent, of the *replacement cost* of the property. Coinsurance clauses induce the owner to carry full, or nearly full, coverage.

COLA. Cost-of-living adjustment. *See indexation.*

collateral. *Assets* pledged by a *borrower* who will surrender those assets if he or she fails to repay a *loan.*

collectible. Capable of being converted into *cash*—now if due, later otherwise.

collusion. Cooperative effort by employees to commit fraud or another unethical act.

combination. *See business combination.*

comfort letter. A letter in which an auditor conveys negative assurances as to unaudited financial statements in a prospectus or draft financial statements included in a preliminary prospectus.

commercial paper. Short-term notes issued by corporate borrowers.

commission. Employee remuneration, usually expressed as a percentage, based on an activity rate, such as sales.

committed costs. *Capacity costs.*

Committee on Accounting Procedure (CAP). Predecessor of the *APB*. The *AICPA*'s principles-promulgating body from 1939 through 1959. Its 51 pronouncements are *Accounting Research Bulletins.*

common cost. *Cost* resulting from the use of *raw materials*, a facility (for example, plant or machines), or a service (for example, fire insurance) that benefits several products or departments. A firm must allocate this cost to those products or departments. Common costs result when two or more departments produce multiple products together even though the departments could produce them separately; *joint costs* occur when two or more departments must produce multiple products together. Many writers use "common costs" and "joint costs" synonymously. *See joint cost, indirect costs, overhead*; and *sterilized allocation.*

common-dollar accounting. *Constant-dollar accounting.*

common monetary measuring unit. For U.S. corporations, the dollar. *See also stable monetary unit assumption* and *constant-dollar accounting.*

common shares. *Shares* representing the class of owners who have residual claims on the *assets* and *earnings* of a *corporation* after the firm meets all *debt* and *preferred shareholders'* claims.

common-size statement. A *percentage statement* usually based on total *assets* or *net sales* or *revenues.*

common-stock equivalent. A *security* whose primary value arises from its holder's ability to exchange it for *common shares*; includes *stock options, warrants*, and also some *convertible bonds* or *convertible preferred stock* depending on its *effective interest rate* of the time of issue.

company-wide control. *See control system.*

comparative (financial) statements. *Financial statements* showing information for the same company for different times, usually two successive years for balance sheets and three for *income* and *cash flow statements.* Nearly all published financial statements are in this form. Contrast with *historical summary.*

compensating balance. The amount required to be left on deposit for a loan. When a bank lends funds to customers, it often requires that the customers keep on deposit in their checking accounts an amount equal to some percentage—say, 20 percent—of the loan. Such amounts effectively increase the *interest rate.* The borrower must disclose the amounts of such balances in *notes* to the *financial statements.*

completed contract method. Recognizing *revenues* and *expenses* for a job or order only when the firm finishes it, except that when the firm expects a loss on the contract, the firm must recognize all revenues and expenses in the period when the firm first foresees a loss. Accountants generally use this term only for longterm contracts. This method is otherwise equivalent to the *sales basis of revenue recognition.*

completed sales basis. *See sales basis of revenue recognition.*

compliance audit. Objectively obtaining and evaluating evidence regarding assertions, actions, and events to ascertain the degree of correspondence between them and established performance criteria.

compliance procedure. An *audit* procedure used to gain evidence as to whether the prescribed internal controls are operating effectively.

composite cost of capital. *See cost of capital.*

composite depreciation or **composite life method.** *Group depreciation* when the items are of unlike kind. The term also applies when the firm depreciates as a whole a single item (for example, a crane, which consists of separate units with differing service lives, such as the chassis, the motor, the lifting mechanism, and so on), rather than treating each of its components separately.

compound entry. A *journal entry* with more than one *debit* or more than one *credit* or both. *See trade-in transaction* for an example.

compound interest. *Interest* calculated on *principal* plus previously undistributed interest.

compound interest depreciation. A method designed to hold the *rate of return* on an asset constant. First find the *internal rate of return* on the cash inflows and outflows of the asset. The periodic depreciation charge equals the cash flow for the period less the internal rate of return multiplied by the asset's book value at the beginning of the period. When the cash flows from the asset are constant over time, usage sometimes refers to the method as the "annuity method" of depreciation.

compounding period. The time period, usually a year or a portion of a year, for which a firm calculates *interest*. At the end of the period, the borrower may pay interest to the lender or may add the interest (that is, convert it) to the principal for the next interest-earning period.

comprehensive budget. *Master budget.*

comprehensive income. Defined in *SFAC No. 3* as "the change in equity (net assets) of an entity during a period from transactions and other events and circumstances from nonowner sources. It includes all changes in equity during a period except those resulting from investments by owners and distributions to owners." In this definition, "equity" means *owners' equity* or *shareholders' equity. SFAS No. 130* requires firms to report comprehensive income as part of a statement showing *earnings* (primarily from realized transactions), comprehensive income (with additions for all other changes in owners' equity, primarily *holding gains and losses* and *foreign exchange gains and losses*), and comprehensive income plus *accounting adjustments*. The *FASB* encourages the discontinuation of the term "net income." The terms "earnings" and "comprehensive income" denote different concepts, with totals different from that of the old "net income." *SFAS No. 130* requires that the firm report comprehensive income in a format having the same prominence as other *financial statements*. We cannot predict which "income total"— earnings or comprehensive income— users of financial statements will focus on. See the accompanying exhibits for two formats the FASB suggests firms use. General Electric uses a different one, harder to follow.

comptroller. Same meaning and pronunciation as *controller*. Modern users,

---

ONE-STATEMENT APPROACH

Statement of Net Income and Comprehensive Income

Revenues	$100,000
Expenses	(25,000)
Gain on Sale of Securities	2,000
Other Gains and Losses	8,000
Earnings from Continuing Operations before Income Tax .	$ 85,000

Exhibit 1-1.   Reporting Comprehensive Income, Two Allowed Formats

From *Financial Accounting, An Introduction to Concepts, Methods, and Uses 12th edition by Stickney, Weil* © 2003. Reprinted with permission of South-Western, a division of Thomson Learning: *www.thomson-rights.com.* Fax (800) 730-2215.

ONE-STATEMENT APPROACH (*Continued*)

Income Tax Expense		(21,250)
Earnings before Discontinued Operations and Extraordinary Items		$ 63,750
Discontinued Operations, Net of Tax		30,000
Extraordinary Items, Net of Tax		(28,000)
Income before Cumulative Effect of Accounting Change		$ 65,750
Cumulative Effect of Accounting Change, Net of Tax		(2,500)
Net Income (or, as preferred by the FASB, Earnings)		$ 63,250
Other Comprehensive Income, Net of Tax:		
Foreign Currency Translation Adjustments		$ 7,000
Unrealized Gains and Losses on Securities:		
Unrealized Holding Gains Arising during Period	$13,000	
Less: Reclassification Adjustment for Gain Included in Net Income (Earnings)	(1,500)	11,500
Minimum Pension Liability Adjustment		(2,500)
Other Comprehensive Income (Loss)		$ 16,000
Comprehensive Income (Loss)		**$ 79,250**

TWO-STATEMENT APPROACH

Statement of Net Income

Revenues		$100,000
Expenses		(25,000)
Gain on Sale of Securities		2,000
Other Gains and Losses		8,000
Earnings from Continuing Operations before Income Tax .		$ 85,000
Income Tax Expense		(21,250)
Earnings before Discontinued Operations and Extraordinary Items		$ 63,750
Discontinued Operations, Net of Tax		30,000
Extraordinary Items, Net of Tax		(28,000)
Income before Cumulative Effect of Accounting Change		$ 65,750
Cumulative Effect of Accounting Change, Net of Tax		(2,500)
Net Income (or, as preferred by the FASB, Earnings)		$ 63,250

Statement of Comprehensive Income

Net Income (or, as preferred by the FASB, Earnings)		$ 63,250
Other Comprehensive Income, Net of Tax:		
Foreign Currency Translation Adjustments		$ 7,000
Unrealized Gains and Losses on Securities:		
Unrealized Holding Gains Arising during Period	$13,000	
Less: Reclassification Adjustment for Gain Included in Net Income (Earnings)	(1,500)	11,500
Minimum Pension Liability Adjustment		(2,500)
Other Comprehensive Income (Loss)		$ 16,000
Comprehensive Income (Loss)		**$ 79,250**

Exhibit 1-1.   Reporting Comprehensive Income, Two Allowed Formats (*Continued*)

however, tend to use this form for government and not-for-profit entities and *controller* for profit-seeking ones.

conceptual framework. A coherent system of interrelated objectives and fundamentals, promulgated by the *FASB* primarily through its *SFAC* publications, expected to lead to consistent standards for *financial accounting* and reporting.

confidence level. The measure of probability that the actual characteristics of the population lie within the stated precision of the estimate derived from a sampling process. A sample estimate may be expressed in the following terms: "Based on the sample, we are 95 percent sure [confidence level] that the true population value is within the range of X to Y [precision]." *See precision.*

confirmation. A formal memorandum delivered by the customers or suppliers of a company to its independent *auditor* verifying the amounts shown as receivable or payable. The auditor originally sends the confirmation document to the customer. If the auditor asks that the customer return the document whether the *balance* is correct or incorrect, usage calls it a "positive confirmation." If the auditor asks that the customer return the document only if it contains an error, usage calls it a "negative confirmation."

conglomerate. *Holding company.* This term implies that the owned companies operate in dissimilar lines of business.

conservatism. A *reporting objective* that calls for anticipation of all *losses* and *expenses* but defers recognition of *gains* or *profits* until they are *realized* in *arm's-length* transactions. In the absence of certainty, report events to minimize cumulative income. Conservatism does

not mean reporting low income in every *accounting period.* Over long-enough time spans, income is cash-in less cash-out. If a (conservative) reporting method shows low income in early periods, it must show higher income in some later period.

consignee. *See on consignment.*

consignment. *See on consignment.*

consignor. *See on consignment.*

consistency. Treatment of like *transactions* in the same way in consecutive periods so that financial statements will be more comparable than otherwise; the reporting policy implying that a reporting *entity*, once it adopts specified procedures, should follow them from period to period. *See accounting changes* for the treatment of inconsistencies.

consol. A *bond* that never matures; a *perpetuity* in the form of a bond; originally issued by Great Britain after the Napoleonic wars to consolidate debt issues of that period. The term arose as an abbreviation for "consolidated annuities."

consolidated financial statements. Statements that are issued by legally separate companies and that show financial position and income as they would appear if the companies were one economic *entity.*

constant dollar. A hypothetical unit of *general purchasing power*, denoted "C$" by the *FASB.*

constant-dollar accounting. Accounting that measures items in *constant dollars. See historical cost/constant-dollar accounting* and *current cost/nominal-dollar accounting.* Sometimes called "general price level–adjusted accounting" or "general purchasing-power accounting."

constant-dollar date. The time at which the *general purchasing power* of one *constant dollar* equals the *general purchasing power* of one *nominal dollar*; that is, the date when C\$1 = \$1. When the constant-dollar date is midperiod, the nominal amounts of *revenues* and *expenses* spread evenly throughout the period equal their constant-dollar amounts but end-of-period *balance sheet* amounts measured in constant midperiod dollars differ from their nominal-dollar amounts. When the constant-dollar date is at the end of the period, the constant-dollar amounts equal the nominal-dollar amounts on a balance sheet for that date.

constrained share company. Canada: a public company whose *charter* specifies that people who are Canadian citizens or corporations that are incorporated in Canada must own a prescribed percentage of the shares.

constructive liability. *FASB's* term for an item recorded as an accounting *liability*, which the firm has no obligation to pay but intends to pay. An example is the liability with related *expense* that management establishes for future cash payments for severance payments for employees it intends to discharge in a restructuring.

constructive receipt. An item included in taxable income when the taxpayer can control funds whether it has received cash. For example, *interest* added to *principal* in a savings account is constructively received.

Consumer Price Index (CPI). A *price index* computed and issued monthly by the Bureau of Labor Statistics of the U.S. Department of Labor. The index attempts to track the price level of a group of goods and services purchased by the average consumer. The CPI is used in *constant-dollar accounting*.

contingency. A potential *liability.* If a specified event occurs, such as a firm's losing a lawsuit, it would recognize a liability. The notes disclose the contingency, but so long as it remains contingent, it does not appear in the balance sheet. *SFAS No. 5* requires treatment as a contingency until the outcome is "probable" and the amount of payment can be reasonably estimated, perhaps within a range. When the outcome becomes probable (the future event is "likely" to occur) and the firm can reasonably estimate the amount (using the lower end of a range if it can estimate only a range), then the firm recognizes a liability in the accounts, rather than just disclosing it. A *material* contingency can lead to a qualified, "*subject to*" auditor's opinion. Firms do not record *gain* contingencies in the accounts but disclose them in notes.

contingent annuity. An *annuity* whose number of payments depends on the outcome of an event whose timing is uncertain at the time the annuity begins; for example, an annuity payable until death of the *annuitant.* Contrast with *annuity certain.*

contingent issue (securities). Securities issuable to specific individuals at the occurrence of some event, such as the firm's attaining a specified level of earnings.

contingent liability. *Contingency.* Avoid this term because it refers to something not (yet) a *liability* on the *balance sheet.*

continuing appropriation. A governmental *appropriation* automatically renewed without further legislative action until altered or revoked or expended.

continuing operations. *See income from continuing operations.*

continuity of operations. The assumption in accounting that the business *entity* will continue to operate long enough to carry out its current plans. The *going-concern assumption.*

continuous budget. A *budget* that adds a future period as the current period ends. This budget, then, always reports on the same number of periods.

continuous compounding. *Compound interest* in which the *compounding period* is every instant of time. *See e* for the computation of the equivalent annual or periodic rate.

continuous flow processing. Mass production of homogeneous products in a continuous flow. Companies manufacturing with continuous flow processes use *process costing* to account for product costs.

continuous improvement. Modern *total quality management (TQM)* practitioners believe that the process of seeking quality is never complete. This attitude reflects that assumption, seeking always to improve activities.

continuous inventory method. The *perpetual inventory* method.

Continuously Contemporary Accounting (CoCoA). A name coined by the Australian theorist Raymond J. Chambers to indicate a combination of *current value accounting* in which the *measuring unit* is *constant dollars* and the *attribute measured* is *exit value.*

contra account. An *account*, such as *accumulated depreciation*, that accumulates subtractions from another account, such as machinery. Contrast with *adjunct account.*

contributed capital. Name for the *owners' equity* account that represents amounts paid in, usually in *cash*, by owners; the sum of the balances in

capital stock accounts plus *capital contributed in excess of par (or stated) value* accounts. Contrast with *donated capital.*

contributed surplus. An inferior term for *capital contributed in excess of par value.*

contribution approach. *Income statement* preparation method that reports *contribution margin*, by separating *variable costs* from *fixed costs*, to emphasize the importance of cost-behavior patterns for purposes of planning and control.

contribution margin. *Revenue* from *sales* less all variable *expenses*. Contrast with *gross margin.*

contribution margin ratio. *Contribution margin* divided by *net sales*; usually measured from the price and cost of a single unit; sometimes measured in total for companies with multiple products.

contribution per unit. Selling price less *variable costs* per unit.

contributory. Said of a *pension plan* in which employees, as well as employers, make payments to a pension *fund*. Note that the provisions for *vesting* apply only to the employer's payments. Whatever the degree of vesting of the employer's payments, employees typically get back all their payments, with interest, in case of death or other cessation of employment before retirement.

control (controlling) account. A summary *account* with totals equal to those of entries and balances that appear in individual accounts in a *subsidiary ledger*. Accounts Receivable is a control account backed up with an account for each customer. Do not change the balance in a control account unless you make a corresponding change in one of the subsidiary accounts.

control charts. Presentations of warning signals that help management distinguish between random or routine variations in quality and variations that it should investigate. The presentations show the results of statistical process-control measures for a sample, batch or some other unit. These presentations depict variation in a process and its behavior over time. Management specifies an acceptable level of variation and plans to investigate the causes of deviations beyond that level.

control system. A device used by top management to ensure that lower-level management carries out its plans or to safeguard assets. Control designed for a single function within the firm is "operational control"; control designed for autonomous segments that generally have responsibility for both revenues and costs is "divisional control"; control designed for activities of the firm as a whole is "company-wide control." Systems designed for safeguarding *assets* are "internal control" systems.

controllable cost. A *cost* influenced by the way a firm carries out operations. For example, marketing executives control advertising costs. These costs can be *fixed* or *variable. See programmed costs* and managed costs.

controlled company. A company in which an individual or corporation holds a majority of the voting shares. An owner can sometimes exercise effective control even though it owns less than 50 percent of the shares.

controller. A title for the chief accountant of an organization; often spelled *comptroller* when used to identify that person in a government or not-for-profit entity.

conversion. The act of exchanging a convertible security for another security.

conversion audit. An examination of changeover procedures, and new accounting procedures and files, that takes place when a significant change in the accounting system (e.g., a change from a manual to a computerized system or a change of computers) occurs.

conversion cost. *Direct labor* costs plus factory *overhead* costs incurred in manufacturing a product; that is, the cost to convert raw materials to finished products. *Manufacturing cost.*

conversion period. *Compounding period*; also, period during which the holder of a *convertible bond* or *convertible preferred securities* can convert it into *common shares.*

convertible bond. A *bond* whose owner can convert it into a specified number of shares of *capital stock* during the *conversion period.*

convertible preferred securities. *Preferred shares* whose owner may convert them into a specified number of *common shares.*

cookie-jar accounting. A name, most prominently used by a chairman of the *SEC*, to indicate the practice of reporting lower *income* in an early period so that management at its discretion, can report higher income in a later period. Consider, for example, the entry to estimate *warranty costs* for products sold. The *journal entry debits* an *expense account*, reducing income, and *credits* a *liability* account. In some later period, the firm can debit a warranty cost to the liability account, not to an expense account, relieving that later period of the income reduction that an expense would have caused. *See quality of earnings.* Often, users refer to the excess liability amount, the amount in the cookie jar, later available for income enhancement, as a "reserve." *See reserve* for our warnings about using that word in any context.

cooperative. An incorporated organization formed for the benefit of its members (owners), who are either producers or consumers, in order to acquire for them profits or savings that otherwise accrue to middlemen. Members exercise control on the basis of one vote per member.

coproduct. A product sharing production facilities with another product. For example, if an apparel manufacturer produces shirts and jeans on the same line, these are coproducts. Distinguish coproducts from *joint products* and *by-products* that, by their very nature, a firm must produce together, such as the various grades of wood a lumber factory produces.

copyright. Exclusive right granted by the government to an individual author, composer, playwright, or the like for the life of the individual plus 50 years. If a firm receives the copyright, then the right extends 75 years after the original publication. The *economic life* of a copyright can be less than the legal life, such as, for example, the copyright of this book.

core deposit intangible. A bank borrows funds from its customers, called "depositors," who open checking and savings accounts. Those depositors can take out their funds at any time, but usually do not. The amount that depositors leave on deposit for long periods of time are called "core deposits." The bank lends those funds to other customers, called "borrowers," at *interest rates* higher than the amount it pays the depositors for the funds. (For checking accounts, the rate the bank pays depositors is often zero.) The fact that the depositors can remove their funds at any time, but, on average, leave amounts on deposit relatively permanently means

that the bank can lend those funds for relatively long periods of time, usually at higher interest rates, than it can charge for shorter-term loans. (*See yield curve.*) The bank's ability to borrow from some customers at a low rate and lend to other customers at a high rate creates wealth for the bank. Bankers and banking analysts call this wealth the "core deposit intangible." It represents an *asset* not recognized in the financial statements by the bank that created the wealth, although some *SEC* commissioners have expressed the thought that accounting should recognize such items as assets. When one bank buys another in a *purchase*, however, it will pay for this asset and will record it as an asset. Usually, the acquiring bank does not use the specific account title "Core Deposit Intangible," but instead uses the account title *Goodwill*.

corner. The control, of a quantity of shares or a commodity, sufficiently large that the holder can control the market price.

corporation. A legal entity authorized by a state to operate under the rules of the entity's *charter*.

correcting entry. An *adjusting entry* that properly records a previously, improperly recorded *transaction*. Do not confuse with entries that correct *accounting errors*.

correction of errors. *See accounting errors.*

cost. The sacrifice, measured by the *price* paid or to be paid, to acquire *goods* or *services*. See *acquisition cost* and *replacement cost*. Terminology often uses "cost" when referring to the valuation of a good or service acquired. When writers use the word in this sense, a cost is an *asset*. When the benefits of the acquisition (the goods or services acquired) expire, the cost becomes an *expense* or *loss*. Some writers, however, use "cost" and "expense" as synonyms. Contrast with *expense*. The word "cost" appears in more than 50 accounting terms, each with sometimes subtle distinctions in meaning. *See cost terminology* for elaboration. Clarity requires that the user include with the word "cost" an adjective or phrase to be clear about intended meaning.

cost accounting. Classifying, summarizing, recording, reporting, and allocating current or predicted *costs*; a subset of *managerial accounting*.

Cost Accounting Standards Board. *See CASB.*

cost accumulation. Bringing together, usually in a single *account*, all *costs* of a specified activity. Contrast with *cost allocation*.

cost allocation. Assigning *costs* to individual products or time periods. Contrast with *cost accumulation*.

cost-based transfer price. A *transfer price* based on *historical costs*.

cost behavior. The functional relation between changes in activity and changes in *cost*, such as *fixed* versus *variable costs* and *linear* versus *curvilinear cost*.

cost/benefit criterion. Some measure of *costs* compared with some measure of *benefits* for a proposed undertaking. If the costs exceed the benefits, then the analyst judges the undertaking not worthwhile. This criterion will not yield good decisions unless the analyst estimates all costs and benefits flowing from the undertaking.

cost center. A unit of activity for which a firm accumulates *expenditures* and *expenses*.

cost driver. A factor that causes an activity's costs. *See driver* and *activity basis*.

cost driver rate. Rate at which the *cost driver* causes *costs*.

cost-effective. Among alternatives, the one whose benefit, or payoff, per unit of cost is highest; sometimes said of an action whose expected benefits exceed expected costs whether or not other alternatives exist with larger benefit-cost ratios.

cost estimation. The process of measuring the functional relation between changes in activity levels and changes in cost.

cost flow assumption. *See flow assumption.*

cost-flow equation. Beginning balance + transfers in = transfers out + ending balance

$$BB + TI = TO + EB.$$

cost flows. Costs passing through various classifications within an entity. *See flow of costs* for a diagram.

cost hierarchy. Categorizes costs according to whether they are *capacity, product, customer, batch* or *unit costs*.

cost method (for investments). In accounting for an investment in the *capital stock* or *bonds* of another company, method in which the firm shows the investment at *acquisition cost* and treats only *dividends* declared or *interest receivable* as *revenue*; not allowed by *GAAP*.

cost method (for treasury stock). The method of showing *treasury stock* in a *contra account* to all other items of *shareholders' equity* in an amount equal to that paid to reacquire the stock.

cost object(ive). Any activity for which management desires a separate measurement of *costs*. Examples include departments, products, and territories.

cost of capital. *Opportunity cost* of funds invested in a business; the rate of return that rational owners require an asset to earn before they will devote that asset to a particular purpose; sometimes measured as the average annual rate that a company must pay for its *equities.* In *efficient capital markets,* this cost is the *discount rate* that equates the expected *present value* of all future cash flows to common shareholders with the market value of common shares at a given time. Analysts often measure the cost of capital by taking a *weighted average* of the firm's *debt* and various *equity securities.* We sometimes call the measurement so derived the "composite cost of capital," and some analysts confuse this measurement of the cost of capital with the cost of capital itself. For example, if the equities of a firm include substantial amounts for the *deferred income tax liability,* the composite cost of capital will underestimate the true cost of capital—the required rate of return on a firm's assets—because the deferred income tax liability has no explicit cost.

cost of goods manufactured. The sum of all costs allocated to products completed during a period, including materials, labor, and *overhead.*

cost of goods purchased. Net purchase price of goods acquired plus costs of storage and delivery to the place where the owner can productively use the items.

cost of goods sold. Inventoriable *costs* that firms *expense* because they sold the units; equals *beginning inventory* plus *cost of goods purchased* or *manufactured* minus *ending inventory.*

cost of sales. Generally refers to *cost of goods sold,* occasionally to *selling expenses.*

cost or market, whichever is lower. *See lower of cost or market.*

cost percentage. One less *markup percentage; cost* of *goods available for sale* divided by selling prices of goods available for sale (when FIFO is used); *cost* of *purchases* divided by selling prices of purchases (when LIFO is used). *See markup* for further detail on inclusions in the calculation of cost percentage.

cost-plus transfer pricing. *Transfer price* equal to the *cost* of the transferred product plus a *markup.*

cost pool. *Indirect cost pool;* groupings or aggregations of costs, usually for subsequent analysis.

cost principle. The *principle* that requires reporting *assets* at *historical* or *acquisition cost,* less accumulated *amortization.* This principle relies on the assumption that cost equals *fair market value* at the date of acquisition and that subsequent changes are not likely to be significant.

cost-recovery-first method. A method of *revenue* recognition that *credits inventory* as the firm receives cash collections and continues until the firm has collected cash equal to the sum of all costs. Only after the firm has collected cash equal to costs does it recognize *income.* A firm may not use this method in financial reporting unless the total amount of collections is highly uncertain. It is never allowed for income tax reporting. Contrast with the *installment method,* allowed for both book and tax, in which the firm credits *constant* proportions of each cash collection both to cost and to income.

cost sheet. Statement that shows all the elements composing the total cost of an item.

cost structure. For a given set of total costs, the percentages of fixed and variable costs, typically 2 percentages adding to 100 percent.

cost terminology. The word "cost" appears in many accounting terms. Exhibit 1-2 classifies some of these terms according to the distinctions between the terms in accounting usage. Joel Dean was, to our knowledge, the first to attempt such distinctions; we have used some of his ideas here. We discuss some of the terms in more detail under their own listings.

TERMS (SYNONYMS GIVEN IN PARENTHESES)	DISTINCTIONS AND COMMENTS
1. The following pairs of terms distinguish the basis measured in accounting.	
Historical Cost vs. Current Cost (Acquisition Cost)	A distinction used in financial accounting. Current cost can be used more specifically to mean replacement cost, net realizable value, or present value of cash flows. "Current cost" is often used narrowly to mean replacement cost.
Historical Cost vs. Standard Cost (Actual Cost)	The distinction between historical and standard costs arises in product costing for inventory valuation. Some systems record actual costs while others record the standard costs.
2. The following pairs of terms denote various distinctions among historical costs. For each pair of terms, the sum of the two kinds of costs equals total historical cost used in financial reporting.	
Variable Cost vs. Fixed Cost (Constant Cost)	Distinction used in breakeven analysis and in designing cost accounting systems, particularly for product costing. See (4), below, for a further subdivision of fixed costs and (5), below, for the economic distinction between marginal and average cost closely paralleling this one.
Traceable Cost vs. Common Cost (Joint Cost)	Distinction arises in allocating manufacturing costs to product. Common costs are allocated to product, but the allocations are more-or-less arbitrary. The distinction also arises in segment reporting and in separating manufacturing from nonmanufacturing costs.
Direct Cost vs. Indirect Cost	Distinction arises in designing cost accounting systems and in product costing. Direct costs can be traced directly to a cost object (e.g., a product, a responsibility center), whereas indirect costs cannot.

Exhibit 1-2. Cost Terminology: Distinctions Among Terms Containing The Word "Cost"

TERMS (SYNONYMS GIVEN IN PARENTHESES)		DISTINCTIONS AND COMMENTS
Out-of-Pocket Cost (Outlay Cost; Cash Cost)	vs. Book Cost	Virtually all costs recorded in financial statements require a cash outlay at one time or another. The distinction here separates expenditures to occur in the future from those already made and is used in making decisions. Book costs, such as for depreciation, reduce income without requiring a future outlay of cash. The cash has already been spent. See future v. past costs in (5), below.
Incremental Cost (Marginal Cost; Differential Cost)	vs. Unavoidable Cost (Inescapable Cost; Sunk Cost)	Distinction used in making decisions. Incremental costs will be incurred (or saved) if a decision is made to go ahead (or to stop) some activity, but not otherwise. Unavoidable costs will be reported in financial statements whether the decision is made to go ahead or not, because cash has already been spent or committed. Not all unavoidable costs are book costs, as, for example, a salary promised but not yet earned, that will be paid even if a no-go decision is made.
		The economist restricts the term *marginal cost* to the cost of producing one more unit. Thus, the next unit has a marginal cost; the next week's output has an incremental cost. If a firm produces and sells a new product, the related new costs would properly be called incremental, not marginal. If a factory is closed, the costs saved are incremental, not marginal.
Escapable Cost	vs. Inescapable Cost (Unavoidable Cost)	Same distinction as incremental vs. sunk costs, but this pair is used only when the decision maker is considering stopping something—ceasing to produce a product, closing a factory, or the like. See next pair.
Avoidable Cost	vs. Unavoidable Cost	A distinction sometimes used in discussing the merits of variable and absorption costing. Avoidable costs are treated as product cost and unavoidable costs are treated as period expenses under variable costing.
Controllable Cost	vs. Uncontrollable Cost	The distinction here is used in assigning responsibility and in setting bonus or incentive plans. All costs can be affected by someone in the entity; those who design incentive schemes attempt to hold a person responsible for a cost only if that person can influence the amount of the cost.

Exhibit 1-2.   Cost Terminology: Distinctions Among Terms Containing The Word "Cost" (*Continued*)

TERMS (SYNONYMS GIVEN IN PARENTHESES)	DISTINCTIONS AND COMMENTS

3. In each of the following pairs, used in historical cost accounting, the word "cost" appears in one of the terms where "expense" is meant.

Expired Cost vs. Unexpired Cost	The distinction is between *expense* and *asset*.
Product Cost vs. Period Cost	The terms distinguish product cost from period expense. When a given asset is used, is its cost converted into work in process and then finished goods on the balance sheet until the goods are sold or is it an expense shown on this period's income statement? Product costs appear on the income statement as part of cost of goods sold in the period when the goods are sold. Period expenses appear on the income statement with an appropriate caption for the item in the period when the cost is incurred or recognized.

4. The following subdivisions of fixed (historical) costs are used in analyzing operations. The relation between the components of fixed costs is:

Fixed Costs	=	Capacity Costs	+	Programmed Costs

Semifixed Costs	+	Fixed Portions	Standby Costs	+	Enabling Costs
	+	of			
"Pure" Fixed Costs		Semi-variable Costs			

Capacity Cost (Committed Cost)	vs. Programmed Cost (Managed Cost; Discretionary Cost)	Capacity costs give a firm the capability to produce or to sell. Programmed costs, such as for advertising or research and development, may not be essential, but once a decision to incur them is made, they become fixed costs.
Standby Cost	vs. Enabling Cost	Standby costs will be incurred whether capacity, once acquired, is used or not, such as property taxes and depreciation on a factory. Enabling costs, such as for a security force, can be avoided if the capacity is unused.
Semifixed Cost	vs. Semivariable Cost	A cost fixed over a wide range but that can change at various levels is a semifixed cost or "step cost." An example is the cost of rail lines from the factory to the main rail line where fixed cost depends on whether there are one or two parallel lines, but are independent of the number of trains run per day. Semivariable costs combine a strictly fixed component cost plus a variable component. Telephone charges usually have a fixed monthly component plus a charge related to usage.

Exhibit 1-2.   Cost Terminology: Distinctions Among Terms Containing The Word "Cost" (*Continued*)

TERMS (SYNONYMS GIVEN IN PARENTHESES)		DISTINCTIONS AND COMMENTS

5. The following pairs of terms distinguish among economic uses or decision-making uses or regulatory uses of cost terms.

Fully Absorbed Cost	vs.	Variable Cost (Direct Cost)	Fully absorbed costs refer to costs where fixed costs have been allocated to units or departments as required by generally accepted accounting principles. Variable costs, in contrast, may be more relevant for making decisions, such as in setting prices.
Fully Absorbed Cost	vs.	Full Cost	In full costing, all costs, manufacturing costs as well as central corporate expenses (including financing expenses) are allocated to products or divisions. In full absorption costing, only manufacturing costs are allocated to products. Only in full costing will revenues, expenses, and income summed over all products or divisions equal corporate revenues, expenses, and income.
Opportunity Cost	vs.	Outlay Cost (Out-of-Pocket Cost)	Opportunity cost refers to the economic benefit foregone by using a resource for one purpose instead of for another. The outlay cost of the resource will be recorded in financial records. The distinction arises because a resource is already in the possession of the entity with a recorded historical cost. Its economic value to the firm, opportunity cost, generally differs from the historical cost; it can be either larger or smaller.
Future Cost	vs.	Past Cost	Effective decision making analyzes only present and future outlay costs, or out-of-pocket costs. Opportunity costs are relevant for profit maximizing; past costs are used in financial reporting.
Short-Run Cost	vs.	Long-Run Cost	Short-run costs vary as output is varied for a given configuration of plant and equipment. Long-run costs can be incurred to change that configuration. This pair of terms is the economic analog of the accounting pair, see (2) above, variable and fixed costs. The analogy is not perfect because some short-run costs are fixed, such as property taxes on the factory, from the point of view of breakeven analysis.

Exhibit 1-2.   Cost Terminology: Distinctions Among Terms Containing The Word "Cost" (*Continued*)

TERMS (SYNONYMS GIVEN IN PARENTHESES)			DISTINCTIONS AND COMMENTS
Imputed Cost	vs.	Book Cost	In a regulatory setting some costs, for example the cost of owners' equity capital, are calculated and used for various purposes; these are imputed costs. Imputed costs are not recorded in the historical costs accounting records for financial reporting. Book costs are recorded.
Average Cost	vs.	Marginal Cost	The economic distinction equivalent to fully absorbed cost of product and variable cost of product. Average cost is total cost divided by number of units. Marginal cost is the cost to produce the next unit (or the last unit).
Differential Cost (Incremental Cost)	vs.	Variable Cost	Whether a cost changes or remains fixed depends on the activity basis being considered. Typically, but not invariably, costs are said to be variable or fixed with respect to an activity basis such as changes in production levels. Typically, but not invariably, costs are said to be incremental or not with respect to an activity basis such as the undertaking of some new venture. For example, consider the decision to undertake the production of food processors, rather than food blenders, which the manufacturer has been making. To produce processors requires the acquisition of a new machine tool. The cost of the new machine tool is incremental with respect to a decision to produce food processors instead of food blenders, but, once acquired, becomes a fixed cost of producing food processors. If costs of direct labor hours are going to be incurred for the production of food processors or food blenders, whichever is produced (in a scenario when not both are to be produced), such costs are variable with respect to production measured in units, but not incremental with respect to the decision to produce processors rather than blenders. This distinction is often blurred in practice, so a careful understanding of the activity basis being considered is necessary for understanding of the concepts being used in a particular application.

Exhibit 1-2.   Cost Terminology: Distinctions Among Terms Containing The Word "Cost" (*Continued*)

cost-to-cost. The *percentage-of-completion method* in which the firm estimates the fraction of completion as the ratio of costs incurred to date divided by the total costs the firm expects to incur for the entire project.

cost-volume-profit analysis. A study of the sensitivity of *profits* to changes in units sold (or produced) or costs or prices.

cost-volume-prof.it graph (chart). A graph that shows the relation between *fixed costs, contribution per unit, breakeven point,* and *sales. See breakeven chart.*

costing. The process of calculating the cost of activities, products, or services; the British word for *cost accounting.*

counterparty. The term refers to the opposite party in a legal contract. In accounting and finance, a frequent usage arises when an entity purchases (or sells) a *derivative* financial contract, such as an *option, forward contract,* and *futures contract.*

coupon. That portion of a *bond* document redeemable at a specified date for payments. Its physical form resembles a series of tickets; each coupon has a date, and the holder either deposits it at a bank, just like a check, for collection or mails it to the issuer's agent for collection.

coupon rate. Of a *bond,* the total dollar amount of coupons paid in any one year divided by par value. Contrast with *effective rate.*

covenant. A promise with legal validity. A loan covenant specifies the terms under which the lender can force the borrower to repay funds otherwise not yet due. For example, a *bond* covenant could state that the *principal* of a bond issue falls due on December 31, 2010, unless the firm's *debt-equity*

ratio falls below 40 percent, in which case the amount becomes due immediately.

CPA. *See certified public accountant.* The *AICPA* suggests that no periods appear in the abbreviation.

CPI. *Consumer price index.*

CPP. Current purchasing power; usually used, primarily in the UK, as an adjective modifying the word "accounting" to mean the accounting that produces *constant-dollar financial statements.*

Cr. Abbreviation for *credit,* always with initial capital letter. Quiz: what do you suppose *Cr.* stands for? For the answer, *see Dr.*

creative accounting. Selection of *accounting principles* and interpretation of transactions or events designed to manipulate, typically to increase but sometimes merely to smooth, reported *income from continuing operations*; one form of *fraudulent financial reporting.* Many attempts at creative accounting involve premature *revenue recognition.*

credit. As a noun, an entry on the right-hand side of an *account*; as a verb, to make an entry on the right-hand side of an account; records increases in *liabilities, owners' equity, revenues,* and *gains*; records decreases in *assets* and *expenses. See debit and credit conventions.* This term also refers to the ability or right to buy or borrow in return for a promise to pay later.

credit bureau. An organization that gathers and evaluates data on the ability of a person to meet financial obligations and sells this information to its clients.

credit loss. The amount of accounts receivable that the firm finds, or expects to find, *uncollectible.*

credit memorandum. A document used by a seller to inform a buyer that the seller is crediting (reducing) the buyer's account receivable because of *errors*, *returns*, or *allowances*; also, the document provided by a bank to a depositor to indicate that the bank is increasing the depositor's balance because of some event other than a deposit, such as the collection by the bank of the depositor's *note receivable*.

creditor. One who lends. In the UK, *account payable*.

critical accounting judgments. All numbers on a *balance sheet*, except the date, require some judgment or estimate. (The previous sentence passes for a joke in accounting.) The SEC requires that management in its annual report to shareholders identify the accounting issues whose judgments and estimates have potential for significant effect on *earnings* and *financial position*. Examples include *inventory valuation, measurement of goodwill impairment*, accounting for *hedges*, and *revenue recognition*.

critical path method (CPM). A method of *network analysis* in which the analyst estimates normal duration time for each activity within a project. The critical path identifies the shortest completion period based on the most time-consuming sequence of activities from the beginning to the end of the network. Compare *PERT*.

critical success factors. The important things a company must do to be successful; can vary from one company to another.

cross-reference (index). A number placed beside each *account* in a *journal entry* indicating the *ledger* account to which the record keeper posted the entry and placing in the ledger the page number of the journal where the record keeper first recorded the journal entry; used to link the *debit* and *credit* parts of an entry in the ledger accounts back to the original entry in the journal. *See audit trail.*

cross-section analysis. Analysis of *financial statements* of various firms for a single period; contrast with *time-series analysis*, in which analysts examine statements of a given firm for several periods of time.

Crown corporation. Canada and UK: a corporation that is ultimately accountable, through a minister of the Crown, to Parliament or a legislature for the conduct of its affairs.

cum div. (dividend). The condition of shares whose quoted market price includes a declared but unpaid dividend. This condition pertains between the declaration date of the dividend and the record date. Compare *ex div. (dividend)*.

cum rights. The condition of securities whose quoted market price includes the right to purchase new securities. Compare *ex rights*.

cumulative dividend. Preferred stock *dividends* that, if not paid, accrue as a commitment that the firm must pay before it can declare dividends to common shareholders.

cumulative preferred shares. *Preferred* shares with *cumulative dividend* rights.

current assets. *Cash* and other *assets* that a firm expects to turn into cash, sell, or exchange within the normal operating cycle of the firm or one year, whichever is longer. One year is the usual period for classifying asset balances on the balance sheet. Current assets include *cash, marketable securities, receivables, inventory*, and *current prepayments*.

current cost. *Cost* stated in terms of current values (of *productive capacity*) rather than in terms of *acquisition .cost. See net realizable value* and *current selling price.*

current cost accounting. The *FASB's* term for *financial statements* in which the *attribute measured* is *current cost.*

current cost/nominal-dollar accounting. Accounting based on *current cost* valuations measured in *nominal dollars.* Components of *income* include an *operating margin* and *holding gains and losses.*

current exchange rate. The rate at which the holder of one unit of currency can convert it into another at the end of the *accounting period* being reported on or, for *revenues, expenses, gains,* and *losses,* the date of recognition of the transaction.

current exit value. *Exit value.*

current fund. In governmental accounting, a synonym for *general fund.*

current funds. *Cash* and other assets readily convertible into cash; in governmental accounting, funds spent for operating purposes during the current period; includes *general,* special revenue, *debt service,* and *enterprise funds.*

current (gross) margin. *See operating margin based on current costs.*

current liability. A debt or other obligation that a firm must discharge within a short time, usually the *earnings cycle* or one year, normally by expending *current assets.*

current operating performance concept. The notion that reported *income* for a period ought to reflect only ordinary, normal, and recurring operations of that period. A consequence is that *extraordinary* and nonrecurring items are entered directly in the Retained Earnings account. Contrast with *clean surplus concept.* This concept is no longer acceptable. (*See APB Opinion No. 9* and *No. 30.*)

current ratio. Sum of *current assets* divided by sum of *current liabilities. See ratio.*

current realizable value. *Realizable value.*

current replacement cost. Of an *asset,* the amount currently required to acquire an identical asset (in the same condition and with the same service potential) or an asset capable of rendering the same service at a current *fair market price.* If these two amounts differ, use the lower. Contrast with *reproduction cost.*

current selling price. The amount for which an *asset* could be sold as of a given time in an *arm's-length* transaction rather than in a forced sale.

current service costs. *Service costs* of a *pension plan.*

current value accounting. The form of accounting in which all assets appear at *current replacement cost (entry value)* or *current selling price* or *net realizable value (exit value)* and all *liabilities* appear at *present value.* Entry and exit values can differ from each other, so theorists have not agreed on the precise meaning of "current value accounting."

current yield. Of a *bond,* the annual amount of *coupons* divided by the current market price of the bond. Contrast with *yield to maturity.*

currently attainable standard cost. *Normal standard cost.*

curvilinear (variable) cost. A continuous, but not necessarily linear (straight-line), functional relation between activity levels and *costs.*

customer-level activities. Work performed to meet the needs of a specific customer, aggregated over all customers.

customer response time. Period that elapses from the moment a customer places an order for a product or requests service to the moment the firm delivers the product or service to the customer.

customers' ledger. The *ledger* that shows *accounts receivable* of individual customers. It is the *subsidiary ledger* for the *control account* Accounts Receivable.

cutoff rate. *Hurdle rate.*

D

data bank. An organized file of information, such as a customer name and address file, used in and kept current by a processing system.

database. A comprehensive collection of interrelated information stored together in computerized form to serve several applications.

database management system. Generalized software programs used to handle physical storage and manipulation of databases.

days of average inventory on hand. *See ratio.*

days of grace. The days allowed by law or contract for payment of a debt after its due date.

DCF. *Discounted cash flow.*

DDB. *Double declining-balance depreciation.*

debenture bond. A *bond* not secured with *collateral.*

debit. As a noun, an entry on the left-hand side of an *account*; as a verb, to make an entry on the left-hand side of an account; records increases in *assets* and *expenses*; records decreases in *liabilities, owners' equity*, and *revenues*. *See debit and credit conventions.*

debit and credit conventions. The conventional use of the *T-account* form and the rules for debit and credit in

balance sheet accounts (see below). The equality of the two sides of the *accounting equation* results from recording equal amounts of *debits* and *credits* for each *transaction.*

Typical Asset Account	
Opening Balance	
Increase	Decrease
+	−
Dr.	Cr.
Ending Balance	

Typical Liability Account	
	Opening Balance
Decrease	Increase
−	+
Dr.	Cr.
	Ending Balance

Typical Owners' Equity Account	
	Opening Balance
Decrease	Increase
−	+
Dr.	Cr.
	Ending Balance

Revenue and expense accounts belong to the owners' equity group. The relation and the rules for debit and credit in these accounts take the following form:

Owners' Equity	
Decrease	Increase
−	+
Dr.	Cr.

Expenses		Revenues	
Dr.	Cr.	Dr.	Cr.
+	−	−	+
*			*

*Normal balance before closing

debit memorandum. A document used by a seller to inform a buyer that the seller is debiting (increasing) the amount of the buyer's *accounts receivable*. Also, the document provided by a bank to a depositor to indicate that the bank is decreasing the depositor's *balance* because of some event other than payment for a *check*, such as monthly service charges or the printing of checks.

debt. An amount owed. The general name for *notes, bonds, mortgages*, and the like that provide evidence of amounts owed and have definite payment dates.

debt capital. *Noncurrent liabilities. See debt financing* and contrast with *equity financing.*

debt-equity ratio. Total *liabilities* divided by total equities. *See ratio.* Some analysts use only total shareholders' equity in the denominator. Some analysts restrict the numerator to *long-term debt.*

debt financing. *Leverage.* Raising *funds* by issuing *bonds, mortgages*, or *notes.* Contrast with *equity financing.*

debt guarantee. *See guarantee.*

debt ratio. *Debt-equity ratio.*

debt service fund. In governmental accounting, a *fund* established to account for payment of *interest* and *principal* on all general-obligation *debt* other than that payable from special *assessments.*

debt service payment. The payment required by a lending agreement, such as periodic coupon payment on a bond or installment payment on a loan or a lease payment. It is sometimes called "interest payment," but this term will mislead the unwary. Only rarely will the amount of a debt service payment equal the interest expense for the period preceding the payment. A debt service payment will always include some amount for interest, but the payment will usually differ from the interest expense.

debt service requirement. The amount of cash required for payments of *interest*, current maturities of *principal* on outstanding *debt*, and payments to *sinking funds* (corporations) or to the debt service fund (governmental).

debtor. One who borrows; in the UK, *account receivable.*

decentralized decision making. Management practice in which a firm gives a manager of a business unit responsibility for that unit's *revenues* and *costs*, freeing the manager to make decisions about prices, sources of supply, and the like, as though the unit were a separate business that the manager owns. *See responsibility accounting* and *transfer price.*

declaration date. Time when the *board of directors* declares a *dividend.*

declining-balance depreciation. The method of calculating the periodic *depreciation* charge by multiplying the *book value* at the start of the period by a constant percentage. In pure declining-balance depreciation, the constant percentage is $1 - ns/c$, where n is the *depreciable life*, s is *salvage value*, and c is *acquisition cost. See double declining-balance depreciation.*

deep discount bonds. Said of *bonds* selling much below (exactly how much is not clear) *par value.*

defalcation. Embezzlement.

default. Failure to pay *interest* or *principal* on a *debt* when due.

defeasance. Transaction with the economic effect of *debt retirement* that does not retire the debt. When *interest rates* increase, many firms find that the *market value* of their outstanding *debt* has dropped substantially below its *book value.* In *historical cost accounting* for debt retirements, retiring debt with a *cash* payment less than the book value of the debt results in a gain (generally, an *extraordinary item*). Many firms would like to retire the outstanding debt issues and report the gain. Two factors impede doing so: (1) the gain can be a taxable event generating adverse *income tax* consequences; and (2) the transaction costs in retiring all the debt can be large, in part because the firm cannot easily locate all the debt holders or persuade them to sell back their bonds to the issuer. Defeasance serves as the economic equivalent to retiring a debt issue while saving the issuer from adverse tax consequences and from locating and retiring the bonds. The process works as follows: The debt-issuing firm turns over to an independent trustee, such as a bank, amounts of cash or low-risk government bonds sufficient to make all debt service payments on the outstanding debt, including bond retirements, in return for the trustee's commitment to make all debt service payments. The debt issuer effectively retires the outstanding debt. It debits the liability account, credits Cash or Marketable Securities as appropriate, and credits Extraordinary Gain on Debt Retirement. The trustee can retire debt or make debt service payments, whichever it chooses. For income tax purposes, however, the firm's debt remains outstanding. The firm will have taxable interest *deductions* for its still-outstanding debt and taxable interest *revenue* on the investments held by the trustee for debt service. In law, the term "defeasance" means "a

rendering null and void." This process renders the outstanding debt economically null and void, without causing a taxable event.

defensive interval. A financial *ratio* equal to the number of days of normal cash *expenditures* covered by *quick assets.* It is defined as follows:

Quick Assets

(All Expenses Except Amortization and Others Not Using Funds ÷ 365)

The denominator of the ratio is the cash expenditure per day. Analysts have found this ratio useful in predicting *bankruptcy.*

deferral. The accounting process concerned with past *cash receipts* and *payments*; in contrast to *accrual*; recognizing a liability resulting from a current cash receipt (as for magazines to be delivered) or recognizing an asset from a current cash payment (as for prepaid insurance or a long-term depreciable asset).

deferral method. *See flow-through method* (of accounting for the *investment credit*) for definition and contrast.

deferred annuity. An *annuity* whose first payment occurs sometime after the end of the first period.

deferred asset. *Deferred charge.*

deferred charge. *Expenditure* not recognized as an *expense* of the period when made but carried forward as an *asset* to be *written off* in future periods, such as for advance rent payments or insurance premiums. *See deferral.*

deferred cost. *Deferred charge.*

deferred credit. Sometimes used to indicate *advances from customers.*

deferred debit. *Deferred charge.*

deferred expense. *Deferred charge.*

deferred gross margin. *Unrealized gross margin.*

deferred income. *Advances from customers.*

deferred income tax (liability). An *indeterminate-term liability* that arises when the pretax income shown on the tax return is less than what it would have been had the firm used the same *accounting principles* and *cost basis* for *assets* and *liabilities* in tax returns as it used for financial reporting. *SFAS No. 109* requires that the firm debit income tax *expense* and credit deferred income tax with the amount of the taxes delayed by using accounting principles in tax returns different from those used in financial reports. *See temporary difference, timing difference, permanent difference,* and *installment sales.* If, as a result of temporary differences, cumulative taxable income exceeds cumulative reported income before taxes, the deferred income tax account will have a *debit* balance, which the firm will report as a *deferred charge.*

deferred revenue. Sometimes used to indicate *advances from customers.*

deferred tax. *See deferred income tax.*

deficit. A *debit balance* in the Retained Earnings account; presented on the balance sheet in a *contra account* to shareholders' equity; sometimes used to mean negative *net income* for a period.

defined-benefit plan. A *pension plan* in which the employer promises specific dollar amounts to each eligible employee; the amounts usually depend on a formula that takes into account such things as the employee's earnings, years of employment, and age. The employer adjusts its cash contributions and pension expense to *actuarial* experience in the eligible employee group and investment performance of the pension *fund.* This is sometimes called a "fixed-benefit" pension plan. Contrast with *money purchase plan.*

defined-contribution plan. A *money purchase (pension) plan* or other arrangement, based on formula or discretion, in which the employer makes cash contributions to eligible individual employee *accounts* under the terms of a written plan document. The trustee of the funds in the account manages the funds, and the employee-beneficiary receives at retirement (or at some other agreed time) the amount in the fund. The employer makes no promise about that amount. Profit-sharing pension plans are of this type.

deflation. A period of declining *general price-level changes.*

Delphi technique. Forecasting method in which members of the forecasting group prepare individual forecasts, share them anonymously with the rest of the group, and only then compare forecasts and resolve differences.

demand deposit. *Funds* in a *checking account* at a bank.

demand loan. *See term loan* for definition and contrast.

denial of opinion. Canada: the statement that an *auditor,* for reasons arising in the *audit,* is unable to express an opinion on whether the *financial statements* provide *fair presentation.*

denominator volume. Capacity measured in the number of units the firm expects to produce this period; when divided into *budgeted fixed costs,* results in fixed costs applied per unit of product.

department(al) allocation. Obtained by first accumulating *costs* in *cost pools* for each department and then, using separate rates, or sets of rates, for each department, allocating from each cost pool to products produced in that department.

dependent variable. *See regression analysis.*

depletion. Exhaustion or *amortization* of a *wasting asset* or *natural resource.* Also see *percentage depletion.*

depletion allowance. *See percentage depletion.*

deposit intangible. *See core deposit intangible.*

deposit, sinking fund. Payments made to a *sinking fund.*

deposit method (of revenue recognition). A method of *revenue* recognition that is the same as the *completed sale* or *completed contract method.* In some contexts, such as when the customer has the right to return goods for a full refund or in retail land sales, the customer must make substantial payments while still having the right to back out of the deal and receive a refund. When the seller cannot predict with reasonable precision the amount of cash it will ultimately collect and when it will receive cash, the seller must *credit* Deposits, a *liability account*, rather than *revenue.* (In this regard, the accounting differs from that in the completed contract method, in which the account credited offsets the *Work-in-Process* inventory account.) When the *sale* becomes complete, the firm credits a revenue account and *debits* the Deposits account.

deposits (by customers). A *liability* that the firm *credits* when receiving *cash* (as in a bank, or in a grocery store when the customer pays for soda-pop bottles with cash to be repaid when the customer returns the bottles) and when the firm intends to discharge the liability by returning the cash.

Contrast with the liability account *Advances from Customers*, which the firm credits on receipt of cash, expecting later to discharge the liability by delivering goods or services. When the firm delivers the goods or services, it credits a *revenue* account.

deposits in transit. Deposits made by a firm but not yet reflected on the *bank statement.*

depreciable cost. That part of the *cost* of an asset, usually *acquisition cost* less *salvage value*, that the firm will charge off over the life of the asset through the process of *depreciation.*

depreciable life. For an *asset*, the period or units of activity (such as miles driven for a truck) over which the firm allocates the *depreciable cost.* For tax returns, depreciable life can be shorter than estimated *service life.*

depreciation. *Amortization of plant assets*; the process of allocating the cost of an asset to the periods of benefit— the *depreciable life*; classified as a *production cost* or a *period expense*, depending on the asset and whether the firm uses *full absorption* or *variable costing.* Depreciation methods described in this glossary include the *annuity method, appraisal method, composite method, compound interest method, declining-balance method, production method, replacement method, retirement method, straight-line method, sinking fund method*, and *sum-of-the-years'-digits method.*

depreciation reserve. An inferior term for *accumulated depreciation. See reserve.* Do not confuse with a replacement *fund.*

derivative (financial instrument). A financial instrument, such as an option to purchase a security, created from another, such as a security; an instrument, such as a *swap*, whose value depends on the value of another asset called the "underlying"—for example, the right to receive the difference between the interest payments on a fixed-rate five-year loan for $1 million and the interest payments on a floating-rate five-year loan for $1 million. To qualify as a derivative under *FASB* rules, *SFAS No. 133*, the instrument has one or more underlyings, and one or more notional amounts or payment provisions or both, it either does not require an initial net investment or it requires one smaller than would be required for other types of contracts expected to have a similar response to changes in market factors, and its terms permit settlement for cash in lieu of physical delivery or the instrument itself trades on an exchange. *See also forward contract* and *futures contract*.

Descartes' rule of signs. In a *capital budgeting* context, a rule that says a series of cash flows will have a nonnegative number of *internal rates of return*. The number equals the number of variations in the sign of the cash flow series or is less than that number by an even integer. Consider the following series of cash flows, the first occurring now and the others at subsequent yearly intervals: -100, -100, $+50$, $+175$, -50, $+100$. The internal rates of return are the numbers for r that satisfy the following equation:

$$- 100 - \frac{100}{(1 + r)} + \frac{50}{(1 + r)^2} +$$
$$\frac{175}{(1 + r)^3} - \frac{50}{(1 + r)^4} + \frac{100}{(1 + r)^5} = 0.$$

The series of cash flows has three variations in sign: a change from minus to plus, a change from plus to minus, and a change from minus to plus. The rule says that this series

must have either one or three internal rates of return; in fact, it has only one, about 12 percent. But also *see reinvestment rate.*

detection costs. *See appraisal costs.*

detective controls. *Internal controls* designed to detect, or maximize the chance of detection of, errors and other irregularities.

determination. *See determine.*

determine. A term often used (in our opinion, overused) by accountants and those who describe the accounting process. A leading dictionary associates the following meanings with the verb "determine": settle, decide, conclude, ascertain, cause, affect, control, impel, terminate, and decide upon. In addition, accounting writers can mean any one of the following: measure, allocate, report, calculate, compute, observe, choose, and legislate. In accounting, there are two distinct sets of meanings: those encompassed by the synonym "cause or legislate" and those encompassed by the synonym "measure." The first set of uses conveys the active notion of causing something to happen, and the second set of uses conveys the more passive notion of observing something that someone else has caused to happen. An accountant who speaks of cost or income "determination" generally means measurement or observation, not causation; management and economic conditions cause costs and income to be what they are. One who speaks of accounting principles "determination" can mean choosing or applying (as in "determining depreciation charges" from an allowable set) or causing to be acceptable (as in the *FASB*'s "determining" the accounting for *leases*). In the long run, income is cash-in less cash-out, so management and economic conditions "determine" (cause) income to be what it is. In the short run, reported income is a function of accounting principles chosen and applied, so the accountant "determines" (measures) income. A question such as "Who determines income?" has, therefore, no unambiguous answer. The meaning of "an accountant determining acceptable accounting principles" is also vague. Does the clause mean merely choosing one principle from the set of generally acceptable principles, or does it mean using professional judgment to decide that some of the generally accepted principles are not correct under the current circumstances? We try never to use "determine" unless we mean "cause." Otherwise we use "measure," "report," "calculate," "compute," or whatever specific verb seems appropriate. We suggest that careful writers will always "determine" to use the most specific verb to convey meaning. "Determine" seldom best describes a process in which those who make decisions often differ from those who apply technique. The term *predetermined (factory) overhead rate* contains an appropriate use of the word.

development stage enterprise. As defined in *SFAS No. 7*, a firm whose planned principal *operations* have not commenced or, having commenced, have not generated significant *revenue*. The financial statements should identify such enterprises, but no special *accounting principles* apply to them.

diagnostic signal. See *warning signal* for definition and contrast.

differentiable cost. The cost increments associated with infinitesimal changes in volume. If a total cost curve is smooth (in

mathematical terms, differentiable), then we say that the curve graphing the derivative of the total cost curve shows differentiable costs.

differential. An adjective used to describe the change (increase or decrease) in a *cost, expense, investment, cash flow, revenue, profit*, and the like as the firm produces or sells one or more additional (or fewer) units or undertakes (or ceases) an activity. This term has virtually the same meaning as *incremental*, but if the item declines, "decremental" better describes the change. Contrast with *marginal*, which means the change in cost or other item for a small (one unit or even less) change in number of units produced or sold.

differential analysis. Analysis of *differential costs, revenues, profits, investment, cash flow*, and the like.

differential cost. See *differential*.

differential cost analysis. See *relevant cost analysis*.

dilution. A potential reduction in *earnings per share* or *book value* per share by the potential *conversion* of securities or by the potential exercise of *warrants* or *options*.

dilutive. Said of a *security* that will reduce *earnings per share* if it is exchanged for *common shares*.

dip(ping) into LIFO layers. See *LIFO inventory layer*.

direct access. Access to computer storage where information can be located directly, regardless of its position in the storage file. Compare *sequential access*.

direct cost. Cost of *direct material* and *direct labor* incurred in producing a product. *See prime cost*. In some accounting literature, writers use this term to mean the same thing as *variable cost*.

direct costing. Another, less-preferred, term for *variable costing.*

direct-financing (capital) lease. *See sales-type (capital) lease* for definition and contrast.

direct labor (material) cost. Cost of labor (material) applied and assigned directly to a product; contrast with *indirect labor (material).*

direct labor variance. Difference between actual and *standard direct labor* allowed.

direct method. *See statement of cash flows.*

direct posting. A method of bookkeeping in which the firm makes *entries* directly in *ledger accounts*, without using a *journal.*

direct write-off method. *See write-off method.*

disbursement. Payment by *cash* or by *check. See expenditure.*

DISC (domestic international sales corporation). A U.S. *corporation*, usually a *subsidiary*, whose *income* results primarily from exports. The parent firm usually defers paying *income tax* on 50 percent of a DISC's income for a long period. Generally, this results in a lower overall corporate tax for the *parent* than would otherwise be incurred.

disclaimer of opinion. An *auditor's report* stating that the auditor cannot give an opinion on the *financial statements.* Usually results from *material* restrictions on the scope of the audit or from material uncertainties, which the firm could not resolve prior to the audit, regarding the accounts.

disclosure. The showing of facts in *financial statements, notes* thereto, or the *auditor's report.*

discontinued operations. *See income from discontinued operations.*

discount. In the context of *compound interest, bonds* and *notes*, the difference between *face amount* (or *future value*) and *present value* of a payment; in the context of *sales* and *purchases*, a reduction in price granted for prompt payment. *See also chain discount, quantity discount*, and *trade discount.*

discount factor. The reciprocal of one plus the *discount rate.* If the discount rate is 10 percent per period, the discount factor for three periods is $1/(1.10)^3 = (1.10)^{-3} = 0.75131.$

discount rate. *Interest rate* used to convert future payments to *present values.*

discounted bailout period. In a *capital budgeting* context, the total time that must elapse before discounted value of net accumulated cash flows from a project, including potential *salvage value* at various times of assets, equals or exceeds the *present value* of net accumulated cash outflows. Contrast with *discounted payback period.*

discounted cash flow (DCF). Using either the *net present value* or the *internal rate of return* in an analysis to measure the value of future expected cash *expenditures* and *receipts* at a common date. In discounted cash flow analysis, choosing the alternative with the largest *internal rate of return* often yields wrong answers given *mutually exclusive projects* with differing amounts of initial investment for two of the projects. Consider, to take an unrealistic example, a project involving an initial investment of $1, with an *IRR* of 60 percent, and another project involving an initial investment of $1 million, with an IRR of 40 percent. Under most conditions, most firms will prefer the second project to the first, but choosing the project with the larger IRR will lead to undertaking the first, not the second. Usage calls this shortcoming of choosing between alternatives based on the magnitude of the internal rate of return, rather than based on the magnitude of the *net present value* of the cash flows, the "scale effect."

discounted payback period. The shortest amount of time that must elapse before the discounted *present value* of cash inflows from a project, excluding potential *salvage value,* equals the discounted present value of the cash outflows.

discounting a note. *See note receivable discounted* and *factoring.*

discounts lapsed (lost). The sum of *discounts* offered for prompt payment that the purchaser did not take because the discount period expired. *See terms of sale.*

discovery sampling. Acceptance sampling in which the analyst accepts an entire population if and only if the sample contains no disparities.

discovery value accounting. *See reserve recognition accounting.*

discretionary cost center. *See engineered cost center* for definition and contrast.

discretionary costs. *Programmed costs.*

Discussion Memorandum. A neutral discussion of all the issues concerning an accounting problem of current concern to the *FASB.* The publication of such a document usually signals that the FASB will consider issuing an *SFAS* or *SFAC* on this particular problem. The discussion memorandum brings together material about the particular problem to facilitate interaction and comment by those interested in the matter. A public hearing follows before the FASB will issue an *Exposure Draft.*

dishonored note. A *promissory note* whose maker does not repay the loan at *maturity,* for a *term loan,* or on demand, for a *demand loan.*

disintermediation. Moving funds from one interest-earning account to another, typically one promising a higher rate. Federal law regulates the maximum *interest rate* that both banks and savings-and-loan associations can pay for *time deposits.* When free-market interest rates exceed the regulated interest ceiling for such time deposits, some depositors withdraw their funds and invest them elsewhere at a higher interest rate. This process is known as "disintermediation."

distributable income. The portion of conventional accounting net income that the firm can distribute to owners (usually in the form of *dividends*) without impairing the physical capacity of the firm to continue operations at current levels. Pretax distributable income is conventional pretax income less the excess of *current cost* of goods sold and *depreciation* charges based on the replacement cost of *productive capacity* over cost of goods sold and depreciation on an *acquisition cost basis.* Contrast with *sustainable income. See inventory profit.*

distributable surplus. Canada and UK: the statutory designation to describe the portion of the proceeds of the issue of shares without *par value* not alloc3ated to share capital.

distributed processing. Processing in a computer information network in which an individual location processes data relevant to it while the operating system transmits information required elsewhere, either to the central computer or to another local computer for further processing.

distribution expense. *Expense* of selling, advertising, and delivery activities.

dividend. A distribution of assets generated from *earnings* to owners of a corporation. The firm may distribute cash (cash dividend), shares (stock dividend), property, or other securities (dividend in kind). Because UK terminology restricts the word "stock" to *inventory*, we tend to refer to "shares," not "stock," in the context of *capital stock.* In this context, however, almost all refer to "stock dividend," not "share dividend." Dividends, except stock dividends, become a legal liability of the corporation when the corporation's board declares them. Hence, the owner of stock ordinarily recognizes *revenue* when the board of the corporation declares the dividend, except for stock dividends. *See also liquidating dividend* and *stock dividend.*

dividend yield. *Dividends* declared for the year divided by market price of the share as of the time for which the analyst computes the yield.

dividends in arrears. Dividends on *cumulative preferred stock* that the corporation's board has not yet declared in accordance with the preferred stock contract. The corporation must usually clear such arrearages before it can declare dividends on *common shares.*

dividends in kind. *See dividend.*

division. A more or less self-contained business unit that is part of a larger family of business units under common control.

divisional control. *See control system.*

divisional reporting. *See segment reporting.*

division return on investment (ROI). Equals the *division profit* divided by the investment in the division.

dollar sign rules. In accounting statements or schedules, place a dollar sign beside the first figure in each column and beside any figure below a horizontal line drawn under the preceding figure.

dollar-value LIFO method. A form of *LIFO* inventory accounting with inventory quantities (*layers*) measured in dollar, rather than physical, terms. The method adjusts for changing prices by using specific price indexes appropriate for the kinds of items in the inventory.

domestic international sales corporation. *See DISC.*

donated capital. A *shareholders' equity* account credited when the company receives gifts, such as land or buildings, without issuing shares or other owners' equity interest in return. A city might donate a plant site hoping the firm will build a factory and employ local residents. Do not confuse with *contributed capital.*

double declining-balance depreciation (DDB). *Declining-balance depreciation* in which the constant percentage used to multiply by book value in computing the depreciation charge for the year is $2/n$, where n is the *depreciable life* in periods. Omit *salvage value* from the depreciable amount. Thus, if the asset cost $100 and has a depreciable life of five years, the depreciation in the first year would be $40 = 2/5 \times \$100$, in the second year would be $24 = 2/5 \times (\$100 - \$40)$, and in the third year would be $14.40 = 2/5 \times (\$100 - \$40 - \$24)$. By the fourth year, the remaining undepreciated cost could be depreciated under the straight-line method at $10.80 = \frac{1}{2} \times (\$100 - \$40 - \$24 - \$14.40)$ per year for tax purposes. Note that salvage value does not affect these computations except that the method will not depreciate the book value below salvage value.

double entry. In recording transactions, a system that maintains the equality of the accounting equation or the balance sheet. Each entry results in recording equal amounts of *debits* and *credits.*

double taxation. Occurs when the taxing authority (U.S. or state) taxes corporate income as earned (first tax) and then the same taxing authority taxes the aftertax income, distributed to owners as dividends, again as personal income tax (second tax).

doubtful accounts. *Accounts receivable* that the firm estimates to be *uncollectible.*

Dr. The abbreviation for *debit*, always with the initial capital letter. *Dr.* is a shortened from of the word *debitor*, and *Cr.* comes from the word *creditor.* In the early days of double-entry record keeping in the UK, the major asset was accounts receivable, called *creditors*, and the major liability was accounts payable, called *debitors.* Thus the *r* in *Cr.* does not refer to the *r* in *credit* but to the second *r* in *creditor.*

draft. A written order by the first party, called the drawer, instructing a second party, called the drawee (such as a bank) to pay a third party, called the payee. *See also check, cashier's check, certified check, NOW account, sight draft,* and *trade acceptance.*

drawee. *See draft.*

drawer. *See draft.*

drawing account. A *temporary account* used in *sole proprietorships* and *partnerships* to record payments to owners or partners during a period. At the end of the period, the firm closes the drawing account by crediting it and debiting the owner's or partner's share of income or, perhaps, his or her capital account.

drawings. Payments made to a *sole proprietor* or to a *partner* during a period. *See drawing account.*

driver, cost driver. A cause of costs incurred. Examples include processing orders, issuing an engineering change order, changing the production schedule, and stopping production to change machine settings. The notion arises primarily in product costing, particularly *activity-based costing.*

drop ship(ment). Occurs when a distributor asks a manufacturer to send an order directly to the customer (ordinarily a manufacturer sends goods to a distributor, who sends the goods to its customer). Usage calls the shipment a "drop shipment" and refers to the goods as "drop shipped."

dry-hole accounting. *See reserve recognition accounting* for definition and contrast.

dual-transactions assumption (fiction). Occurs when an analyst, in understanding cash flows, views transactions not involving *cash* as though the firm first generated cash and then used it. For example, the analyst could view the issue of *capital stock* in return for the *asset* land as though the firm issued stock for *cash* and then used cash to acquire the land. Other examples of transactions that could involve the dual-transaction assumption are the issue of a *mortgage* in return for a noncurrent asset and the issue of stock to bondholders on *conversion* of their *convertible bonds.*

dual transfer prices. Occurs when the *transfer price charged* to the buying *division* differs from that *credited* to the selling division. Such prices make sense when the selling division has excess capacity and, as usual, the *fair market value* exceeds the *incremental cost* to produce the goods or services being transferred.

duality. The *double entry* record-keeping axiom that every *transaction* must result in equal *debit* and *credit* amounts.

dumping. A foreign firm's selling a good or service in the United States at a price below market price at home or, in some contexts, below some measure of cost (which concept is not clearly defined). The practice is illegal in the United States if it harms (or threatens to harm) a U.S. industry.

E

e. The base of natural logarithms; 2.71828.... If *interest* compounds continuously during a period at stated rate of r per period, then the effective *interest rate* is equivalent to interest compounded once per period at rate i where $i = e^r - 1$. Tables of e^r are widely available. If 12 percent annual interest compounds continuously, the effective annual rate is $e^{.12} - 1 = 12.75$ percent. Interest compounded continuously at rate r for d days is $e^{rd/365} - 1$. For example, interest compounded for 92 days at 12 percent is $e^{.12 \times 92/365} - 1 = 3.07$ percent.

earn-out. For two merging firms, an agreement in which the amount paid by the acquiring firm to the acquired firm's shareholders depends on the future earnings of the acquired firm or, perhaps, of the *consolidated entity*.

earned surplus. A term that writers once used, but no longer use, for *retained earnings*.

earnings. A term with no precise meaning but used to mean *income* or sometimes *profit*. The *FASB*, in requiring that firms report *comprehensive income*, encouraged firms to use the term "earnings" for the total formerly reported as *net income*. Firms will likely only slowly change from using the term "net income" to the term "earnings."

earnings, retained. *See retained earnings.*

earnings cycle. The period of time, or the series of transactions, during which a given firm converts *cash* into *goods* and *services*, then sells goods and services to customers, and finally collects cash from customers. *Cash cycle.*

earnings per share (of common stock). *Net income* to common shareholders (net income minus *preferred dividends)* divided by the average number of *common shares* outstanding; *see also primary earnings per share* and *fully diluted earnings per share. See ratio.*

earnings per share (of preferred stock). *Net income* divided by the average number of *preferred shares* outstanding during the period. This ratio indicates how well income covers (or protects) the preferred dividends; it does not indicate a legal share of *earnings. See ratio.*

earnings statement. *Income statement.*

easement. The acquired right or privilege of one person to use, or have access to, certain property of another. For example, a public utility's right to lay pipes or lines under the property of another and to service those facilities.

EBIT. *Earnings* before *interest* and *(income) taxes*; acronym used by analysts.

EBITDA. *Earnings* before *interest, (income) taxes, depreciation,* and *amortization*; acronym used by analysts to focus on a particular measure of *cash flow* used in valuation. This is not the same as, but is similar in concept to, *cash flow from operations.* Some analysts exclude *nonrecurring* items from this total.

economic consequences. The *FASB* says that in setting *accounting principles*, it should take into account the real effects on various participants in the business world. It calls these effects "economic consequences."

economic depreciation. Decline in *current cost* (or *fair value*) of an *asset* during a period.

economic entity. *See entity.*

economic life. The time span over which the firm expects to receive the benefits of an *asset*. The economic life of a *patent, copyright*, or *franchise* can be less than the legal life. *Service life.*

economic order quantity (EOQ). In mathematical *inventory* analysis, the optimal amount of stock to order when demand reduces inventory to a level called the "reorder point." If *A* represents the *incremental cost* of placing a single order, *D* represents the total demand for a period of time in units, and *H* represents the incremental holding cost during the period per unit of inventory, then the economic order quantity is:

$$EOQ = \sqrt{2AD/H}$$

Usage sometimes calls *EOQ* the "optimal lot size."

economic transfer pricing rule. Transfer at the *differential outlay cost* to the selling division (typically *variable costs*), plus the *opportunity cost* to the company of making the internal transfers ($0 if the seller has idle capacity, or selling price minus variable costs if the seller is operating at capacity).

economic value added (EVA®). The amount of earnings generated above the cost of funds invested to generate those earnings. To calculate economic value added, find the difference between (the net after-tax operating profit) and (the product of the weighted-average cost of capital multiplied by the investment in the economic unit).

ED. *Exposure Draft.*

EDGAR. Electronic Data, Gathering, Analysis, and Retrieval system; rules and systems adopted by the *SEC* in 1993 to ensure that all the paperwork involved in the filings submitted by more than 15,000 public companies are electronically submitted.

EDP. *Electronic data processing.*

effective interest method. In computing *interest expense* (or *revenue*), a systematic method that makes the interest expense (revenue) for each period divided by the amount of the net *liability (asset)* at the beginning of the period equal to the *yield rate* on the liability (asset) at the time of issue (acquisition). Interest for a period is the yield rate (at time of issue) multiplied by the net liability (asset) at the start of the period. The *amortization* of discount or premium is the *plug* to give equal *debits* and *credits*. (Interest expense is a debit, and the amount of debt service payment is a credit.)

effective (interest) rate. Of a liability such as a bond, the *internal rate of return* or *yield to maturity* at the time of issue. Contrast with *coupon rate*. If the borrower issues the bond for a price below *par*, the effective rate exceeds the coupon rate; if it issues the bond for a price greater than par, the effective rate is lower than the coupon rate. In the context of *compound interest*, the effective rate occurs when the *compounding period* on a *loan* differs from one year, such as a nominal interest rate of 12 percent compounded monthly. The effective interest is the single rate that one could use at the end of the year to multiply the *principal* at the beginning of the year and give the same amount as results from compounding interest each period during the year. For example, if 12 percent per year compounds monthly, the effective annual interest rate is 12.683 percent. That is, if you compound $100 each month at 1 percent per month, the $100 will grow to $112.68 at the end of the year. In general, if the nominal rate of r percent per year compounds m times per year, then the effective rate is $(1 + r/m)^m - 1$.

efficiency variance. A term used for the *quantity variance* for materials or labor or *variable overhead* in a *standard costing system*.

efficient capital market. A market in which security prices reflect all available information and react nearly instantaneously and in an unbiased fashion to new information.

efficient market hypothesis. The finance supposition that security prices trade in *efficient capital markets*.

EITF. *Emerging Issues Task Force.*

electronic data processing. Performing computations and other data-organizing steps in a computer, in contrast to doing these steps by hand or with mechanical calculators.

eligible. Under income tax legislation, a term that restricts or otherwise alters the meaning of another tax or accounting term, generally to signify that the related assets or operations can receive a specified tax treatment.

eliminations. In preparing *consolidated statements*, *work sheet* entries made to avoid duplicating the amounts of *assets, liabilities, owners' equity, revenues*, and *expenses* of the consolidated *entity* when the firm sums the accounts of the *parent* and *subsidiaries*.

Emerging Issues Task Force (EITF). A group convened by the *FASB* to deal more rapidly with accounting issues than the FASB's due-process procedures can allow. The task force comprises about 20 members from

public accounting, industry, and several trade associations. It meets every six weeks. Several FASB board members usually attend and participate. The chief accountant of the *SEC* has indicated that the SEC will require that published financial statements follow guidelines set by a consensus of the EITF. The EITF requires that nearly all its members agree on a position before that position receives the label of "consensus." Such positions appear in *Abstracts of the EITF*, published by the FASB. Since 1984, the EITF has become one of the promulgators of *GAAP*.

employee stock option. *See stock option.*

Employee Stock Ownership Trust (or Plan). *See ESOT.*

employer, employee payroll taxes. *See payroll taxes.*

enabling costs. A type of *capacity cost* that a firm will stop incurring if it shuts down operations completely but will incur in full if it carries out operations at any level. Examples include costs of a security force or of a quality-control inspector for an assembly line. Contrast with *standby costs*.

encumbrance. In governmental accounting, an anticipated *expenditure* or *funds* restricted for an anticipated expenditure, such as for outstanding purchase orders. *Appropriations* less expenditures less outstanding encumbrances yields unencumbered balance.

ending inventory. The *cost* of *inventory* on hand at the end of the *accounting period*; often called "closing inventory." Ending inventory from the end of one period becomes the *beginning inventory* for the next period.

endorsee. *See endorser.*

endorsement. *See draft.* The *payee* signs the draft and transfers it to a fourth party, such as the payee's bank.

endorser. A *note* or *draft payee*, who signs the note after writing "Pay to the order of X," transfers the note to person X, and presumably receives some benefit, such as cash, in return. Usage refers to person X as the "endorsee." The endorsee then has the rights of the payee and can in turn become an endorser by endorsing the note to another endorsee.

engineered cost center. Responsibility center with sufficiently well-established relations between inputs and outputs that the analyst, given data on inputs, can predict the outputs or, conversely, given the outputs, can estimate the amounts of inputs that the process should have used. Consider the relation between pounds of flour (input) and loaves of bread (output). Contrast discretionary cost center, where such relations are so imprecise that analysts have no reliable way to relate inputs to outputs. Consider the relation between advertising the corporate logo or trademark (input) and future revenues (output).

engineering method (of cost estimation). To estimate unit cost of product from study of the materials, labor, and *overhead* components of the production process.

enterprise. Any business organization, usually defining the accounting *entity*.

enterprise fund. A *fund* that a governmental unit establishes to account for acquisition, operation, and maintenance of governmental services that the government intends to be self-supporting from user charges, such as for water or airports and some toll roads.

entity. A person, *partnership, corporation,* or other organization. The *accounting entity* that issues accounting statements can differ from the entity defined by law. For example, a *sole proprietorship* is an accounting entity, but the individual's combined business and personal assets are the legal entity in most jurisdictions. Several affiliated corporations can be separate legal entities but issue *consolidated financial statements* for the group of companies operating as a single economic entity.

entity theory. The corporation view that emphasizes the form of the *accounting equation* that says *assets = equities.* Contrast with *proprietorship theory.* The entity theory focuses less on the distinction between *liabilities* and *shareholders' equity* than does the proprietorship theory. The entity theory views all equities as coming to the corporation from outsiders who have claims of differing legal standings. The entity theory implies using a *multiple-step* income statement.

entry value. The *current cost* of acquiring an asset or service at a *fair market price. Replacement cost.*

EOQ. *Economic order quantity.*

EPS. *Earnings per share.*

EPVI. *Excess present value index.*

equalization reserve. An inferior title for the allowance or *estimated liability* account when the firm uses the *allowance method* for such things as maintenance expenses. Periodically, the accountant will debit maintenance *expense* and credit the allowance. As the firm makes *expenditures* for maintenance, it will debit the allowance and credit cash or the other asset used in maintenance.

equities. *Liabilities* plus *owners' equity. See equity.*

equity. A claim to *assets*; a source of assets. *SFAC No. 3* defines equity as "the residual interest in the assets of an entity that remains after deducting its liabilities." Thus, many knowledgeable people use "equity" to exclude liabilities and count only owners' equities. We prefer to use the term to mean all liabilities plus all owners' equity because no other single word serves this useful purpose. We fight a losing battle.

equity financing. Raising *funds* by issuing *capital stock*. Contrast with *debt financing*.

equity method. In accounting for an *investment* in the securities of another company, a method that debits the proportionate share of the earnings of the other company to the investment account and credits that amount to a *revenue* account as earned. When the investor receives *dividends*, it debits *cash* and credits the investment account. An investor who owns sufficient shares of an unconsolidated company to exercise significant control over the actions of that company must use the equity method. It is one of the few instances in which the firm recognizes revenue without an increase in *working capital*.

equity ratio. *Shareholders' equity* divided by total *assets. See ratio.*

equivalent production. *Equivalent units.*

equivalent units (of work). The number of units of completed output that would require the same costs that a firm would actually incur for the production of completed and partially completed units during a period. For example, if at the beginning of a period the firm starts 100 units and by the end of the period has incurred costs for each of these equal to 75 percent of total costs to complete the units, then the equivalent units of work for the period would be 75. This is used primarily in *process costing* calculations to measure in uniform terms the output of a continuous process.

ERISA (Employee Retirement Income Security Act of 1974). The federal law that sets most *pension plan* requirements.

error accounting. *See accounting errors.*

escalator clause. Inserted in a purchase or rental contract, a clause that permits, under specified conditions, upward adjustments of price.

escapable cost. *Avoidable cost.*

ESOP (Employee Stock Ownership Plan). *See ESOT.*

ESOT (Employee Stock Ownership Trust). A trust *fund* created by a corporate employer that can provide certain tax benefits to the corporation while providing for employee stock ownership. The corporate employer can contribute up to 25 percent of its payroll per year to the trust. The corporation can deduct the amount of the contribution from otherwise taxable income for federal *income tax* purposes. The trustee of the assets must use them for the benefit of employees—for example, to fund death or retirement benefits. The assets of the trust are usually the *common shares*, sometimes nonvoting, of the corporate employer. For an example of the potential *tax shelter*, consider the case of a corporation with $1 million of *debt* outstanding, which it wants to retire, and an annual payroll of $2 million. The corporation sells $1 million of common shares to the ESOT. The ESOT borrows $1 million with the loan guaranteed by, and therefore a *contingency* of, the corporation. The corporation uses the $1 million proceeds of the issued shares to retire its outstanding debt. (The debt of the ESOT has replaced the debt of the corporation.) The corporation can contribute $500,000 (= .25 × $2 million payroll) to the ESOT each year and treat the contribution as a deduction for tax purposes. After a little more than two years, the ESOT has received sufficient funds to retire its loan. The corporation has effectively repaid its original $1 million debt with pretax dollars. Assuming an income tax rate of 40 percent, it has saved $400,000 (= .40 × $1 million) of aftertax dollars *if* the $500,000 expense for the contribution to the ESOT for the pension benefits of employees would have been made, in one form or another, anyway. Observe that the corporation could use the proceeds ($1 million in the example) of the shares issued to the ESOT for any of several different purposes: financing expansion, replacing plant assets, or acquiring another company. Basically this same form of pretax-dollar financing through pensions is available with almost any corporate pension plan, with one important exception. The trustees of an ordinary pension trust must invest the assets prudently, and if they do not, they are personally liable to the employees. Current judgment about prudent investment requires diversification—trustees should invest pension trust assets in a wide variety of investment opportunities. (The trustee cannot ordinarily invest more than 10 percent of a pension trust's assets in the parent's common shares.) Thus the ordinary pension trust cannot, in practice, invest all, or even most, of its assets in the parent corporation's shares. This constraint does not apply to the investments of an ESOT. The trustee can invest all ESOT assets in the parent company's shares. The

ESOT also provides a means for closely held corporations to achieve wider ownership of shares without *going public*. The laws enabling ESOTs provide for the independent professional appraisal of shares not traded in public markets and for transactions between the corporation and the ESOT or between the ESOT and the employees to be based on the appraised values of the shares.

estate planning. The arrangement of an individual's affairs to facilitate the passage of assets to beneficiaries and to minimize taxes at death.

estimated expenses. *See after cost.*

estimated liability. The preferred terminology for estimated costs the firm will incur for such uncertain things as repairs under *warranty*. An estimated liability appears on the *balance sheet*. Contrast with *contingency*.

estimated revenue. A term used in governmental accounting to designate revenue expected to accrue during a period independent of whether the government will collect it during the period. The governmental unit usually establishes a *budgetary account* at the beginning of the budget period.

estimated salvage value. Synonymous with *salvage value* of an *asset* before its retirement.

estimates, changes in. *See accounting changes.*

estimation sampling. The use of sampling technique in which the sampler infers a qualitative (e.g., fraction female) or quantitative (e.g., mean weight) characteristic of the population from the occurrence of that characteristic in the sample drawn. *See attribute(s) sampling; variables sampling.*

EURL (entreprise unipersonnelle é responsabilité limitée). France: similar to *SARL* but having only one shareholder.

ex div. (dividend). Said of *shares* whose market price quoted in the market has been reduced by a *dividend* already declared but not yet paid. The *corporation* will send the dividend to the person who owned the share on the *record date.* One who buys the share ex dividend will not receive the dividend although the corporation has not yet paid it.

ex rights. The condition of securities whose quoted market price no longer includes the right to purchase new securities, such rights having expired or been retained by the seller. Compare *cum rights.*

except for. Qualification in *auditor's report,* usually caused by a change, approved by the auditor, from one acceptable accounting principle or procedure to another.

excess present value. In a *capital budgeting* context, *present value* (of anticipated net cash inflows minus cash outflows including initial cash outflow) for a project. The analyst uses the *cost of capital* as the *discount rate.*

excess present value index. *Present value* of future *cash* inflows divided by initial cash outlay.

exchange. The generic term for a transaction (or, more technically, a reciprocal transfer) between one entity and another; in another context, the name for a market, such as the New York Stock Exchange.

exchange gain or loss. The phrase used by the *FASB* for *foreign exchange gain or loss.*

exchange rate. The *price* of one country's currency in terms of another country's currency. For example, the British pound sterling might be worth U.S.$1.60 at a given time. The exchange rate would be stated as "one pound is worth one dollar and sixty cents" or "one dollar is worth £.625" (= £1/$1.60).

excise tax. Tax on the manufacture, sale, or consumption of a commodity.

executory contract. An exchange of promises; an agreement providing for payment by a payor to a payee on the performance of an act or service by the payee, such as a labor contract. Accounting does not recognize benefits arising from executory contracts as *assets,* nor does it recognize obligations arising from such contracts as *liabilities. See partially executory contract.*

exemption. A term used for various amounts subtracted from gross income in computing taxable income. Usage does not call all such subtractions "exemptions." *See tax deduction.*

exercise. Occurs when owners of an *option* or *warrant* purchase the security that the option entitles them to purchase.

exercise price. *See option.*

exit value. The proceeds that would be received if assets were disposed of in an *arm's-length transaction. Current selling price; net realizable value.*

expectancy theory. The notion that people act in ways to obtain rewards and prevent penalties.

expected value. The mean or arithmetic *average* of a statistical distribution or series of numbers.

expected value of (perfect) information. Expected *net benefits* from an undertaking with (perfect) information minus expected net benefits of the undertaking without (perfect) information.

expendable fund. In governmental accounting, a *fund* whose resources, *principal*, and earnings the governmental unit can distribute.

expenditure. Payment of *cash* for goods or services received. Payment can occur at the time the purchaser receives the goods or services or at a later time. Virtually synonymous with *disbursement* except that disbursement is a broader term and includes all payments for goods or services. Contrast with *expense.*

expense. As a noun, a decrease in *owners' equity* accompanying the decrease in *net assets* caused by selling goods or rendering services or by the passage of time; a "gone" (net) asset; an expired cost. Measure expense as the *cost* of the (net) assets used. Do not confuse with *expenditure* or *disbursement*, which can occur before, when, or after the firm recognizes the related expense. Use the word "cost" to refer to an item that still has service potential and is an asset. Use the word "expense" after the firm has used the asset's service potential. As a verb, "expense" means to designate an expenditure—past, current, or future— as a current expense.

expense account. An *account* to accumulate *expenses*; *closed* to *retained earnings* at the end of the accounting period; a *temporary owners' equity* account; also used to describe a listing of expenses that an employee submits to the employer for reimbursement.

experience rating. A term used in insurance, particularly unemployment insurance, to denote changes from ordinary rates to reflect extraordinarily large or small amounts of claims over time by the insured.

expired cost. An *expense* or a *loss.*

Exposure Draft (ED). A preliminary statement of the *FASB* (or the *APB* between 1962 and 1973) showing the contents of a pronouncement being considered for enactment by the board.

external failure costs. *Costs* that a firm *incurs* when it detects nonconforming products and services after delivering them to customers, including warranty repairs, product liability, marketing costs, and *sales allowances.*

external reporting. Reporting to shareholders and the public, as opposed to internal reporting for management's benefit. *See financial accounting,* and contrast with *managerial accounting.*

extraordinary item. A *material expense* or *revenue* item characterized both by its unusual nature and by its infrequency of occurrence; appears along with its income tax effects separately from ordinary income and *income from discontinued operations* on the *income statement.* Accountants would probably classify a *loss* from an earthquake as an extraordinary item. Accountants treat gain (or loss) on the retirement of *bonds* as an extraordinary item under the terms of *SFAS No. 4.*

extrinsic rewards. Rewards that come from outside the individual, such as rewards from a teacher, a parent, an organization, and a spouse; they include grades, money, praise, and prizes. Contrast with *intrinsic rewards.*

F

face amount (value). The nominal amount due at *maturity* from a *bond* or *note* not including the contractual periodic payment that can also come due on the same date. Good usage calls the corresponding amount of a stock certificate the *par* or *stated value,* whichever applies.

facility-level activities. Work that supports the entire organization.

Examples include top management, human resources, and research and development.

factoring. The process of buying *notes* or *accounts receivable* at a *discount* from the holder owed the debt; from the holder's point of view, the selling of such notes or accounts. When the transaction involves a single note, we refer to the process as "discounting a note."

factory. Used synonymously with *manufacturing* as an adjective.

factory burden. *Manufacturing overhead.*

factory cost. *Manufacturing cost.*

factory expense. *Manufacturing overhead. Expense* is a poor term in this context because the item is a *product cost.*

factory overhead. Usually an item of *manufacturing cost* other than *direct labor* or *direct materials.*

fair market price (value). *See fair value.*

fair presentation (fairness). One of the qualitative standards of financial reporting. When the *auditor's report* says that the *financial statements* "present fairly ... ," the auditor means that the accounting alternatives used by the entity all comply with *GAAP.* In recent years, however, courts have ruled that conformity with *generally accepted accounting principles* can be insufficient grounds for an opinion that the statements are fair. *SAS No. 5* requires that the auditor judge the accounting principles used in the statements to be "appropriate in the circumstances" before attesting to fair presentation.

fair value, fair market price (value). Price (value) negotiated at *arm's length* between a willing buyer and a willing seller, each acting rationally in his or her own self-interest. The accountant can estimate this amount in the absence of a monetary transaction. This is sometimes measured as the present value of expected cash flows.

fair-value hedge. A hedge of an exposure to changes in the *fair value* of a recognized *asset* or *liability* or of an unrecognized firm commitment. If the firm uses *hedge accounting*, it will report both the hedged item and the hedging instrument at fair value, with *gains* and *losses* reported in *net income.* If the hedge is effective, the gains and losses on these items will offset each other, although both will appear in net income.

FASAC. *Financial Accounting Standards Advisory Council.*

FASB (Financial Accounting Standards Board). An independent board responsible, since 1973, for establishing *generally accepted accounting principles.* Its official pronouncements are *Statements of Financial Accounting Concepts (SFAC), Statements of Financial Accounting Standards (SFAS),* and *FASB Interpretations. See also Discussion Memorandum* and *Technical Bulletin.* Web site: *www.fasb.org.*

FASB Interpretation FIN. An official *FASB* statement interpreting the meaning of *Accounting Research Bulletins, APB Opinions,* and *Statements of Financial Accounting Standards. FIN 46,* for example, has curtailed the use of *off-balance-sheet financings.*

FASB Technical Bulletin. *See Technical Bulletin.*

favorable variance. An excess of actual *revenues* over expected revenues; an excess of *standard cost* over actual cost.

federal income tax. *Income tax* levied by the U.S. government on individuals and corporations.

Federal Insurance Contributions Act. *See FICA.*

Federal Unemployment Tax Act. *See FUTA.*

feedback. The process of informing employees about how their actual performance compares with the expected or desired level of performance, in the hope that the information will reinforce desired behavior and reduce unproductive behavior.

FEI. *Financial Executives Institute.*

FICA (Federal Insurance Contributions Act). The law that sets *Social Security taxes* and benefits.

fiduciary. Someone responsible for the custody or administration of property belonging to another; for example, an executor (of an estate), agent, receiver (in *bankruptcy*), or trustee (of a trust).

FIFO (first-in, first-out). The *inventory flow assumption* that firms use to compute *ending inventory* cost from most recent purchases and *cost of goods sold* from oldest purchases including beginning inventory. FIFO describes cost flow from the viewpoint of the income statement. From the balance sheet perspective, *LISH* (last-in, still-here) describes this same cost flow. Contrast with *LIFO*.

finance. As a verb, to supply with *funds* through the *issue* of securities, bonds, notes, or mortgages or through the retention of earnings.

financial accounting. The accounting for *assets, equities, revenues*, and *expenses* of a business; primarily concerned with the historical reporting, to external users, of the *financial position* and operations of an *entity* on a regular, periodic basis. Contrast with *managerial accounting.*

Financial Accounting Foundation. The independent foundation (committee), governed by a board of trustees, that raises funds to support the *FASB* and *GASB*.

Financial Accounting Standards Advisory Council (FASAC). A committee of academics, preparers, attestors, and users that give advice to the *FASB* on matters of strategy and emerging issues. The council spends much of each meeting learning about current developments in standard-setting from the FASB staff.

Financial Accounting Standards Board. *FASB.*

Financial Executives Institute (FEI). An organization of financial executives, such as chief accountants, *controllers*, and treasurers, of large businesses. In recent years, the FEI has been a critic of the FASB because it views many of the FASB requirements as burdensome while not *cost-effective.*

financial expense. An *expense* incurred in raising or managing *funds.*

financial flexibility. As defined by *SFAC No. 5*, "the ability of an entity to take effective actions to alter amounts and timing of cash flows so it can respond to unexpected needs and opportunities."

financial forecast. *See financial projection* for definition and contrast.

financial instrument. The *FASB* defines this term as follows.: "Cash, evidence of an ownership interest in an entity, or a contract that both:

> [a] imposes on one entity a contractual obligation (1) to deliver cash or another financial instrument to a second entity or (2) to exchange financial instruments on potentially unfavorable terms with the second entity, and
> [b] conveys to that second entity a contractual right (1) to receive cash or

another financial instrument from the first entity or (2) to exchange other financial instruments on potentially favorable terms with the first entity."

financial leverage. *See leverage.*

financial literacy. The *NYSE* and the *NASDAQ* have required that companies who list their shares with these groups have an audit committee comprising at least three independent board members who are financially literate. The organizations mention the ability to understand the *financial statements*, but leave the definition of financial literacy to the individual boards to define. We think financial literacy in this sense requires the ability to understand the transactions requiring critical accounting judgments or estimates; the accounting issues and choices for those judgments; what management chose, and why; and what opportunities management's choices provide for earnings management. *See critical accounting judgments.*

financial model. Model, typically expressed with arithmetic relations, that allows an organization to test the interaction of economic variables in a variety of settings.

financial position (condition). Statement of the *assets* and *equities* of a firm; displayed as a *balance sheet*.

financial projection. An estimate of *financial position*, results of *operations*, and changes in cash flows for one or more future periods based on a set of assumptions. If the assumptions do not represent the most likely outcomes, then auditors call the estimate a "projection." If the assumptions represent the most probable outcomes, then auditors call the estimate a "forecast." "Most probable" means that management has evaluated the assumptions and that they are management's judg-

ment of the most likely set of conditions and most likely outcomes.

financial ratio. *See ratio.*

financial reporting objectives. Broad objectives that are intended to guide the development of specific *accounting standards*; set out by *FASB SFAC No. 1.*

Financial Reporting Release. Series of releases, issued by the SEC since 1982; replaces the *Accounting Series Release. See SEC.*

financial statements. The *balance sheet, income statement, statement of retained earnings, statement of cash flows,* statement of changes in *owners' equity* accounts, statement of *comprehensive income*, and *notes* thereto.

financial structure. *Capital structure.*

financial vice-president. Person in charge of the entire accounting and finance function; typically one of the three most influential people in the company.

financial year. Australia and UK: term for *fiscal year*.

financing activities. Obtaining resources from (a) owners and providing them with a return on and a return of their *investment* and (b) *creditors* and repaying amounts borrowed (or otherwise settling the obligation). *See statement of cash flows.*

financing lease. *Capital lease.*

finished goods (inventory account). Manufactured product ready for sale; a *current asset* (inventory) account.

firm. Informally, any business entity. (Strictly speaking, a firm is a *partnership*.)

firm commitment. The *FASB*, in *SFAS No. 133*, defines this as "an agreement with an unrelated party, binding on both parties and usually legally enforceable," which requires that the firm promise to pay a specified amount of a currency and that the firm has sufficient disincentives for nonpayment that the firm will probably make the payment. A firm commitment resembles a *liability*, but it is an *executory contract*, so is not a liability. *SFAS No. 133* allows the firm to recognize certain financial *hedges* in the balance sheet if they hedge firm commitments. The *FASB* first used the term in *SFAS No. 52* and *No. 80* but made the term more definite and more important in *SFAS No. 133*. This is an early, perhaps the first, step in changing the recognition criteria for assets and liabilities to exclude the test that the future benefit (asset) or obligation (liability) not arise from an executory contract.

first-in, first-out. *See FIFO.*

fiscal year. A period of 12 consecutive months chosen by a business as the *accounting period* for *annual reports*, not necessarily a *natural business year* or a calendar year.

FISH. An acronym, conceived by George H. Sorter, for *first-in, still-here.* FISH is the same cost flow assumption as *LIFO*. Many readers of accounting statements find it easier to think about inventory questions in terms of items still on hand. Think of LIFO in connection with *cost of goods sold* but of FISH in connection with *ending inventory. See LISH.*

fixed assets. *Plant assets.*

fixed assets turnover. *Sales* divided by average total *fixed assets.*

fixed benefit plan. A *defined-benefit plan.*

fixed budget. A plan that provides for specified amounts of *expenditures* and *receipts* that do not vary with activity levels; sometimes called a "static budget." Contrast with *flexible budget.*

fixed charges earned (coverage) ratio. *Income* before *interest expense* and *income tax expense* divided by interest expense.

fixed cost (expense). An *expenditure* or *expense* that does not vary with volume of activity, at least in the short run. *See capacity costs*, which include *enabling costs* and *standby costs*, and *programmed costs* for various subdivisions of fixed costs. *See cost terminology.*

fixed cost price variance (spending variance). The difference between actual and *budgeted fixed costs.*

fixed interval sampling. A method of choosing a sample: the analyst selects the first item from the population randomly, drawing the remaining sample items at equally spaced intervals.

fixed liability. *Long-term* liability.

fixed manufacturing overhead applied. The portion of *fixed manufacturing overhead cost* allocated to units produced during a period.

fixed overhead variance. Difference between *actual fixed manufacturing costs* and fixed manufacturing costs applied to production in a *standard costing system.*

flexible budget. *Budget* that projects receipts and expenditures as a function of activity levels. Contrast with *fixed budget.*

flexible budget allowance. With respect to manufacturing overhead, the total cost that a firm should have incurred at the level of activity actually experienced during the period.

float. *Checks* whose amounts the bank has *added* to the depositor's bank account but whose amounts the bank has not yet reduced from the *drawer's* bank account.

flow. The change in the amount of an item over time. Contrast with *stock.*

flow assumption. An assumption used when the firm makes a *withdrawal* from *inventory*. The firm must compute the cost of the withdrawal by a flow assumption if the firm does not use the *specific identification* method. The usual flow assumptions are *FIFO*, *LIFO*, and *weighted average*.

flow of costs. *Costs* passing through various classifications within an *entity* engaging, at least in part, in manufacturing activities. See the accompanying diagram for a summary of *product* and *period cost* flows.

Flow of Costs (and Sales Revenue)

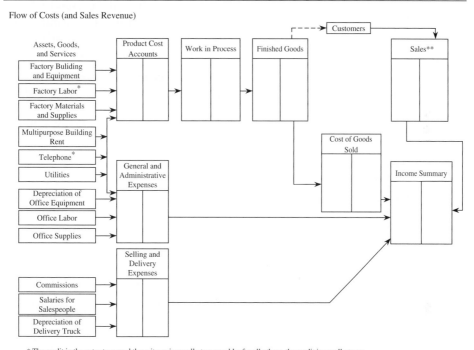

 * The credit in the entry to record these items is usually to a payable; for all others, the credit is usually to an asset, or to an asset contra account.
 ** When the film records sales to customers, it credits the Sales account. The debit is usually to Cash or Accounts Receivable.

flow-through method. Accounting for the *investment credit* to show all income statement benefits of the credit in the year of acquisition rather than spreading them over the life of the asset acquired (called the "deferral method"). The *APB* preferred the deferral method in *Opinion No. 2* (1962) but accepted the flow-through method in *Opinion No. 4* (1964). The term also applies to *depreciation* accounting in which the firm uses the *straight-line method* for financial reporting and an *accelerated depreciation* method for tax reporting. Followers of the flow-through method would not recognize a *deferred tax liability. APB Opinion No. 11* prohibits the use of the flow-through approach in financial reporting, although some regulatory commissions have used it.

FOB. Free on board some location (for example, FOB shipping point, FOB destination). The *invoice* price includes delivery at seller's expense to that location. Title to goods usually passes from seller to buyer at the FOB location.

folio. A page number or other identifying reference used in posting to indicate the source of entry.

footing. Adding a column of figures.

footnotes. More detailed information than that provided in the *income statement, balance sheet, statement of retained earnings*, and *statement of cash flows.* These are an integral part of the statements, and the *auditor's report* covers them. They are sometimes called "notes."

forecast. *See financial projection* for definition and contrast.

foreclosure. Occurs when a lender takes possession of property for his or her own use or sale after the borrower fails to make a required payment on a *mortgage.* Assume that the lender sells the property but that the proceeds of the sale are too small to cover the outstanding balance on the loan at the time of foreclosure. Under the terms of most mortgages, the lender becomes an unsecured creditor of the borrower for the still-unrecovered balance of the loan.

foreign currency. For *financial statements* prepared in a given currency, any other currency.

foreign currency translation. Reporting in the currency used in financial statements the amounts denominated or measured in a different currency.

foreign exchange gain or loss. Gain or loss from holding *net* foreign *monetary items* during a period when the *exchange rate* changes.

foreign sales corporation. *See FSC.*

forfeited share. A share to which a subscriber has lost title because of nonpayment of a *call.*

Form 10-K. *See 10-K.*

Form 20-F. *See 20-F.*

forward contract. An agreement to purchase or sell a specific commodity or financial instrument for a specified price, the *forward price*, at a specified date. Contrast with *futures contract.* Typically, forward contracts are not traded on organized exchanges (unlike *futures contract*), so the parties to the agreement sacrifice liquidity but gain flexibility in setting contract quantities, qualities, and settlement dates.

forward-exchange contract. An agreement to exchange at a specified future date currencies of different countries at a specified rate called the "forward rate."

forward price. The price of a commodity for delivery at a specified future date; in contrast to the "spot price," the price of that commodity on the day of the price quotation.

franchise. A privilege granted or sold, such as to use a name or to sell products or services.

fraudulent conveyance. A transfer of goods or cash that a court finds illegal. *Creditors* of a *bankrupt* firm usually receive less than the firm owed them. For example, a creditor of a bankrupt firm might collect from the trustee of the bankrupt firm only $.60 for every dollar the bankrupt firm owed. Creditors, anticipating bankruptcy, sometimes attempt to persuade the firm to pay the debt in full before the firm declares bankruptcy, reducing the net assets available to other creditors. Bankruptcy laws have rules forbidding such transfers from a near-bankrupt firm to some of its creditors. Such a transfer is called a "fraudulent conveyance." Courts sometimes ask accountants to judge whether a firm had liabilities exceeding assets even before the firm went into bankruptcy.

When the court can find that economic bankruptcy occurred before legal bankruptcy, it will declare transfers of assets to creditors after economic bankruptcy to be fraudulent conveyances and have the assets returned to the trustees (or to a legal entity called the "bankrupt's estate") for redistribution to all creditors.

fraudulent financial reporting. Intentional or reckless conduct that results in materially misleading *financial statements. See creative accounting.*

free cash flow. This term has no standard meaning. Some financial statement analysts use it to mean *cash flow from operations + interest expense + income tax expense.* Others mean the excess of cash flow from operations over cash flow for investing. Usage varies so much that you should ascertain the meaning intended in context by this phrase.

free on board. *FOB.*

freight-in. The *cost* of freight or shipping incurred in acquiring *inventory*, preferably treated as a part of the cost of *inventory*; often shown temporarily in an *adjunct account* that the acquirer closes at the end of the period with other purchase accounts to the inventory account.

freight-out. The *cost* of freight or shipping incurred in selling *inventory*, treated by the seller as a selling *expense* in the period of sale.

FSC (foreign sales corporation). A foreign *corporation* engaging in certain export activities, some of whose *income* the United States exempts from federal *income tax*. A U.S. corporation need pay no income taxes on *dividends* distributed by an FSC out of *earnings* attributable to certain foreign income.

full absorption costing. The *costing* method that assigns all types of manufacturing costs (*direct material, direct labor, fixed* and *variable overhead*) to units produced; required by *GAAP*; also called "absorption costing." Contrast with *variable costing.*

full costing, full costs. The total cost of producing and selling a unit; often used in *long-term* profitability and pricing decisions. Full cost per unit equals *full absorption cost* per unit plus *marketing, administrative, interest,* and other *central corporate expenses,* per unit. The sum of full costs for all units equals total costs of the firm.

full disclosure. The reporting policy requiring that all significant or *material* information appear in the financial statements. *See fair presentation.*

fully diluted earnings per share. For *common stock,* smallest *earnings per share* figure that one can obtain by computing an earnings per share for all possible combinations of assumed *exercise* or *conversion* of *potentially dilutive securities.* This figure must appear on the *income statement* if it is less than 97 percent of earnings available to common shareholders divided by the average number of common shares outstanding during the period.

fully vested. Said of a *pension plan* when an employee (or .his or her estate) has rights to all the benefits purchased with the employer's contributions to the plan even if the employee does not work for this employer at the time of death or retirement.

function. In governmental accounting, said of a group of related activities for accomplishing a service or regulatory program for which the governmental unit has responsibility; in mathematics, a rule for associating a number, called the dependent variable, with another number (or numbers), called independent variable(s).

functional classification. *Income statement* reporting form that classifies *expenses* by function, that is, cost of goods sold, administrative expenses, financing expenses, selling expenses. Contrast with *natural classification*.

functional currency. Currency in which an entity carries out its principal economic activity.

fund. An *asset* or group of assets set aside for a specific purpose. *See also fund accounting*.

fund accounting. The accounting for resources, obligations, and *capital* balances, usually of a not-for-profit or governmental *entity*, which the entity has segregated into *accounts* representing logical groupings based on legal, donor, or administrative restrictions or requirements. The groupings are "funds." The accounts of each fund are *self-balancing*, and from them one can prepare a *balance sheet* and an operating statement for each fund. *See fund* and *fund balance*.

fund balance. In governmental accounting, the excess of assets of a *fund* over its liabilities and reserves; the not-for-profit equivalent of *owners' equity*.

funded. Said of a *pension plan* or other obligation when the firm has set aside *funds* for meeting the obligation when it comes due. The federal law for pension plans requires that the firm fund all *normal costs* when it recognizes them as expenses. In addition, the firm must fund *prior service cost* of pension plans over 30 or over 40 years, depending on the circumstances.

funding. Replacing *short-term* liabilities with *long-term* debt.

funds. Generally *working capital*; current assets less current liabilities; sometimes used to refer to *cash* or to cash and *marketable securities*.

funds provided by operations. *See cash provided by operations*.

funds statement. An informal name often used for the *statement of cash flows*.

funny money. Said of securities, such as *convertible preferred stock, convertible bonds, options*, and *warrants*, that have aspects of *common shares* but that did not reduce reported *earnings per share* before the issuance of *APB Opinion No. 9* in 1966 and *No. 15* in 1969.

FUTA (Federal Unemployment Tax Act). Provides for taxes to be collected at the federal level, to help subsidize the individual states' administration of their unemployment compensation programs.

future value. Value at a specified future date of a sum increased at a specified *interest rate*.

futures contract. An agreement to purchase or sell a specific commodity or financial instrument for a specified price, at a specific future time or during a specified future period. Contrast with *forward contract*. When traded on an organized exchange, the exchange sets the minimum contract size and expiration date(s). The exchange requires that the holder of the contract settle in cash each day the fluctuations in the value of the contract. That is, each day, the exchange marks the contract to market value, called the "(daily) settlement price." A contract holder who has lost during the day must put up more cash, and a holder who has gained receives cash.

G

GAAP. *Generally accepted accounting principles*; a plural noun. In the UK and elsewhere, this means "generally accepted accounting practices."

GAAS. *Generally accepted auditing standards*; a plural noun. Do not confuse with *GAS*.

gain. In *financial accounting* contexts, the increase in *owners' equity* caused by a transaction that is not part of a firm's typical, day-to-day operations and not part of owners' *investment* or *withdrawals*. Accounting distinguishes the meaning of the term "gain" (or *loss*) from that of related terms. First, gains (and losses) generally refer to nonoperating, incidental, peripheral, or nonroutine transactions: gain on sale of land in contrast to *gross margin* on *sale* of *inventory*. Second, gains and losses are *net* concepts, not gross concepts: gain or loss results from subtracting some measure of *cost* from the measure of inflow. *Revenues* and *expenses*, on the other hand, are gross concepts; their difference is a net concept. Gain is nonroutine and net; *profit* or *margin* is routine and net; revenue from *continuing operations* is routine and gross; revenue from *discontinued operations* is nonroutine and gross. Loss is net but can be either routine (loss on sale of inventory) or not (loss on disposal of segment of business).

In *managerial accounting* and lay contexts, gain is the difference between some measure of *revenue* or *receipts* or *proceeds* and some measure of costs, such as direct costs or variable costs or fully absorbed costs or full costs (*see cost terminology*). Because the word can have so many different meanings, careful writers should be explicit to designate one.

gain contingency. *See contingency.*

GAS. *Goods available for sale.* Do not confuse with *GAAS*.

GASB (Governmental Accounting Standards Board). An independent body responsible, since 1984, for establishing accounting standards for state and local government units. It is part of the *Financial Accounting Foundation*, parallel to the *FASB*, and currently consists of five members.

GbR (Gesellschaft des bürgerlichen Rechtes). Germany: a *partnership* whose members agree to share in specific aspects of their own separate business pursuits, such as an office. This partnership has no legal form and is not a separate accounting *entity*.

GDP Implicit Price Deflator (index). A *price index* issued quarterly by the Office of Business Economics of the U.S. Department of Commerce. This index attempts to trace the price level of all *goods and services* composing the *gross domestic product*. Contrast with *Consumer Price Index*.

gearing. U.K.: *financial leverage*.

gearing adjustment. A *revenue* representing part of a *holding gain*. Consider a firm that has part of its assets financed by *noncurrent liabilities* and that has experienced *holding gains* on its *assets* during a period. All the increase in wealth caused by the holding gains belongs to the owners; none typically belongs to the lenders. Some British accounting authorities believe that published *income statements* should show part of the holding gain in *income* for the period. The part they would report in income is the fraction of the gain equal to the fraction that debt composes of total financing; for example, if debt equals 40 percent of total equities and the holding gain equals $100 for the period, the amount to appear in income for the period would be $40. Usage calls that part the "gearing adjustment."

general debt. A governmental unit's debt legally payable from general revenues and backed by the full faith and credit of the governmental unit.

general expenses. *Operating expenses* other than those specifically identified as cost of goods sold, selling, and administration.

general fixed asset (group of accounts). Accounts showing a governmental unit's long-term assets that are not accounted for in *enterprise, trust,* or intragovernmental service funds.

general fund. A nonprofit entity's assets and liabilities not specifically earmarked for other purposes; the primary operating fund of a governmental unit.

general journal. The formal record in which the firm records transactions, or summaries of similar transactions, in *journal entry* form as they occur. Use of the adjective "general" usually implies that the journal has only two columns for cash amounts or that the firm also uses various *special journals*, such as a *check register* or *sales journal.*

general ledger. The name for the formal *ledger* containing all the financial statement accounts. It has equal debits and credits, as evidenced by the *trial balance.* Some of the accounts in the general ledger can be *control accounts*, supported by details contained in *subsidiary ledgers.*

general partner. *Partnership* member who is personally liable for all debts of the partnership; contrast with *limited partner.*

general price index. A measure of the aggregate prices of a wide range of goods and services in the economy at one time relative to the prices during a base period. *See Consumer Price Index* and *GDP Implicit Price Deflator.* Contrast with *specific price index.*

general price level–adjusted statements. *See constant-dollar accounting.*

general price-level changes. Changes in the aggregate prices of a wide range of goods and services in the economy. These price measurements result from using a *general price index.* Contrast with *specific price changes.*

general purchasing power. The command of the dollar over a wide range of goods and services in the economy. The general purchasing power of the dollar is inversely related to changes in a general price index. *See general price index.*

general purchasing-power accounting. *See constant-dollar accounting.*

generally accepted accounting principles (GAAP). As previously defined by the *CAP, APB,* and now the *FASB*, the conventions, rules, and procedures necessary to define accepted accounting practice at a particular time; includes both broad guidelines and relatively detailed practices and procedures. In the United States the FASB defines GAAP to include accounting pronouncements of the *SEC* and other government agencies as well as a variety of authoritative sources, such as this book.

generally accepted auditing standards (GAAS). The *PCAOB* has explicitly stated that it began compiling its auditing promulgations with GAAS, as issued by the AICPA, but "a reference to generally accepted auditing standards in auditors' reports is no longer appropriate or necessary." The phrase has referred to the standards, as opposed to particular procedures, that the *AICPA* promulgated (in *Statements on Auditing Standards*) and that concern "the auditor's professional quantities" and "the judgment exercised by him in the performance of his examination and in his report." Currently, there have been ten such standards: three general ones (concerned with proficiency, independence, and degree of care to be exercised), three standards of field work, and four standards of reporting. The first standard of reporting requires that the *auditor's report* state whether the firm prepared the *financial statements* in accordance with *generally accepted accounting principles.* Thus, before the PCAOB became the auditing rulemaker, the typical auditor's report says that the auditor conducted the examination in accordance with generally accepted auditing standards and that the firm prepared the statements in accordance with generally accepted accounting principles. The report will not refer to the standards of the Public Company Accounting Oversight Board (United States). *See auditor's report.*

geographic segment. A single operation or a group of operations that are located in a particular geographic area and that generate revenue, incur costs, and have assets used in or associated with generating such revenue.

GIE (groupement d'intérêt économique). France: a joint venture, normally used for exports and research-and-development pooling.

GmbH (Gesellschaft mit beschränkter Haftung). Germany: a private company with an unlimited number of shareholders. Transfer of ownership can occur only with the consent of other shareholders. Contrast with *AG.*

goal congruence. The idea that all members of an organization have incentives to perform for a common interest, such as *shareholder* wealth maximization for a *corporation.*

going-concern assumption. For accounting purposes, accountants' assumption that a business will remain in operation long enough to carry out all its current plans. This assumption partially justifies the *acquisition cost* basis, rather than a *liquidation* or *exit value* basis, of accounting.

going public. Said of a business when its *shares* become widely traded rather than being closely held by relatively few shareholders; issuing shares to the general investing public.

goods. Items of merchandise, supplies, raw materials, or finished goods. Sometimes the meaning of "goods" is extended to include all *tangible* items, as in the phrase "goods and services."

goods available for sale. The sum of *beginning inventory* plus all acquisitions of merchandise or finished goods during an *accounting period.*

goods-in-process. *Work-in-process.*

goodwill. The excess of cost of an acquired firm (or operating unit) over the current *fair market value* of the separately identifiable *net assets* of the acquired unit. Before the acquiring firm can recognize goodwill, it must assign a *fair market value* to all identifiable assets, even when not recorded on the books of the acquired unit. For example, if a firm has developed a *patent* that does not appear on its books because of *SFAS No. 2,* if another company acquires the firm, the acquirer will recognize the patent at an amount equal to its estimated fair market value. The acquirer will compute the amount of goodwill only after assigning values to all assets it can identify. Informally, the term indicates the value of good customer relations, high employee morale, a well-respected business name, and so on, all of which the firm or analyst expects to result in greater-than-normal earning power.

goodwill method. A method of accounting for the *admission* of a new partner to a *partnership* when the new partner will receive a portion of capital different from the value of the *tangible* assets contributed as a fraction of tangible assets of the partnership. *See bonus method* for a description and contrast.

Governmental Accounting Standards Advisory Council. A group that consults with the *GASB* on agenda, technical issues, and the assignment of priorities to projects. It comprises more than a dozen members representing various areas of expertise.

Governmental Accounting Standards Board. *GASB.*

GPL (general price level). Usually used as an adjective modifying the word "accounting" to mean *constant-dollar accounting.*

GPLA (general price level–adjusted accounting). *Constant-dollar accounting.*

GPP (general purchasing power). Usually used as an adjective modifying the word "accounting" to mean *constant-dollar accounting.*

graded vesting. Said of a *pension plan* in which not all employees currently have fully *vested* benefits. By law, the benefits must vest according to one of several formulas as time passes.

grandfather clause. An exemption in new accounting *pronouncements* exempting transactions that occurred

before a given date from the new accounting treatment. For example, *APB Opinion No. 17*, adopted in 1970, exempted *goodwill* acquired before 1970 from required *amortization*. The term "grandfather" appears in the title to *SFAS No. 10.*

gross. Not adjusted or reduced by deductions or subtractions. Contrast with *net*, and see *gain* for a description of how the difference between net and gross affects usage of the terms *revenue*, *gain*, *expense*, and *loss.*

gross domestic product (GDP). The market value of all goods and services produced by capital or labor within a country, regardless of who owns the capital or of the nationality of the labor; most widely used measure of production within a country. Contrast with gross national product (GNP), which measures the market value of all goods and services produced with capital owned by, and labor services supplied by, the residents of that country regardless of where they work or where they own capital. In the United States in recent years, the difference between GDP and GNP equals about two-tenths of 1 percent of GDP.

gross margin. *Net sales* minus *cost of goods sold.*

gross margin percent. $100 \times (1 - Cost\ of\ goods\ sold/Net\ sales) = 100 \times (Gross\ margin\ /Net\ sales)$.

gross national product (GNP). *See gross domestic product* for definition and contrast.

gross price method (of recording purchase or sales discounts). The firm records the *purchase* (or *sale*) at the *invoice price*, not deducting the amounts of *discounts* available. Later, it uses a *contra* account to purchases (or sales) to record the amounts of discounts taken. Because information on discounts lapsed will not emerge from this system, most firms should prefer the *net price method* of recording purchase discounts.

gross profit. *Gross margin.*

gross profit method. A method of estimating *ending inventory* amounts. First, the firm measures *cost of goods sold* as some fraction of sales; then, it uses the *inventory equation* to value *ending inventory.*

gross profit ratio. *Gross margin* divided by *net sales.*

gross sales. All *sales* at *invoice* prices, not reduced by *discounts*, *allowances*, *returns*, or other adjustments.

group depreciation. In calculating *depreciation* charges, a method that combines similar assets rather than depreciating them separately. It does not recognize gain or loss on retirement of items from the group until the firm sells or retires the last item in the group. *See composite life method.*

guarantee. A promise to answer for payment of debt or performance of some obligation if the person liable for the debt or obligation fails to perform. A guarantee is a *contingency* of the *entity* making the promise. Often, writers use the words "guarantee" and "warranty" to mean the same thing. In precise usage, however, "guarantee" means some person's promise to perform a contractual obligation such as to pay a sum of cash, whereas "warranty" refers to promises about pieces of machinery or other products. *See warranty.*

H

half-year convention. In *tax accounting* under *ACRS*, and sometimes in *financial accounting*, an assumption that the firm acquired *depreciable assets* at midyear of the year of acquisition. When the firm uses this convention, it computes the *depreciation charge* for the year as one-half the charge that it would have used if it had acquired the assets at the beginning of the year.

hardware. The physical equipment or devices forming a computer and peripheral equipment.

hash total. Used to establish accuracy of data processing; a control that takes the sum of data items not normally added together (e.g., the sum of a list of part numbers) and subsequently compares that sum with a computer-generated total of the same values. If the two sums are identical, then the analyst takes some comfort that the two lists are identical.

Hasselback. An annual directory of accounting faculty at colleges and universities; gives information about the faculty's training and fields of specialization. James R. Hasselback, of Florida State University, has compiled the directory since the 1970s; Prentice-Hall distributes it. Online, you can find it at the Rutgers University accounting Web site: *www.rutgers.edu/Accounting/*.

health-care benefits obligation. At any time, the present value of the non-pension benefits promised by an employer to employees during their retirement years.

hedge. To reduce, perhaps cancel altogether, one risk the entity already bears, by purchasing a security or other financial instrument. For example, a farmer growing corn runs the risk that corn prices will decline before the corn matures and can be brought to market. Such a farmer can arrange to sell the corn now for future delivery, hedging the risk of corn price changes. Suppose a firm has a *receivable* denominated in Euros due in six months. It runs the risk that the exchange rate between the dollar and the Euro will change and the firm will receive a smaller number of dollars in the future than it would receive from the same number of marks received today. Such a firm can hedge its exposure to risk of changes in the exchange rate between dollars and Euros in a variety of ways. *See cash-flow hedge* and *fair-value hedge.* Do not confuse with *hedge accounting.*

hedge accounting. Firms can, but need not, use hedge accounting. If the firm elects hedge accounting and if its hedging instrument is highly effective, it will report *gains* and *losses* on hedging instruments for *cash-flow hedges* in *other comprehensive income*, rather than in *net income*. For *fair-value hedges*, the firm using hedge accounting will report the hedged *asset* or *liability* at *fair value*; it reports the hedging instrument at fair value in any event.

held-to-maturity securities. *Marketable debt securities* that a firm expects to, and has the ability to, hold to *maturity*; a classification important in *SFAS No. 115*, which generally requires the owner to carry marketable securities on the balance sheet at market value, not at cost. Under *SFAS No. 115*, the firm can show held-to-maturity debt securities at *amortized cost.* If the firm lacks either the expectation or the intent to hold the debt security to its maturity, then the firm will show that security at market value as a security *available for sale.*

hidden reserve. An amount by which a firm has understated *owners' equity*, perhaps deliberately. The understatement arises from an undervaluation of *assets* or overvaluation of *liabilities.* By undervaluing assets on this period's *balance sheet*, the firm can overstate *net income* in some future period by disposing of the asset: actual *revenues* less

artificially low cost of assets sold yields artificially high net income. No *account* in the *ledger* has this title.

hire-purchase agreement (contract). U.K.: a *lease* containing a purchase *option.*

historical cost. *Acquisition cost; original cost*; a *sunk cost.*

historical cost/constant-dollar accounting. Accounting based on *historical cost* valuations measured in *constant dollars.* The method restates *nonmonetary items* to reflect changes in the *general purchasing power* of the dollar since the time the firm acquired specific *assets* or incurred specific *liabilities.* The method recognizes a *gain* or *loss* on *monetary items* as the firm holds them over time periods when the general purchasing power of the dollar changes.

historical exchange rate. The rate at which one currency converts into another at the date a transaction took place. Contrast with *current exchange rate.*

historical summary. A part of the *annual report* that shows items, such as *net income, revenues, expenses, asset* and *equity* totals, *earnings per share*, and the like, for five or ten periods including the current one. Usually not as much detail appears in the historical summary as in *comparative statements*, which typically report as much detail for the two preceding years as for the current year. Annual reports can contain both comparative statements and a historical summary.

holdback. Under the terms of a contract, a portion of the progress payments that the customer need not pay until the contractor has fulfilled the contract or satisfied financial obligations to subcontractors.

holding company. A company that confines its activities to owning *shares* in, and supervising management of, other companies. A holding company usually owns a controlling interest in—that is, more than 50 percent of the voting shares of—the companies whose shares it holds. Contrast with *mutual fund. See conglomerate*. In British usage, the term refers to any company with controlling interest in another company.

holding gain or loss. Difference between end-of-period price and beginning-of-period price of an asset held during the period. The financial statements ordinarily do not separately report realized holding gains and losses. Income does not usually report unrealized gains at all, except on *trading securities. See lower of cost or market. See inventory profit* for further refinement, including *gains* on *assets* sold during the period.

holding gain or loss net of inflation. Increase or decrease in the *current cost* of an asset while it is held; measured in units of *constant dollars*.

horizontal analysis. *Time-series analysis.*

horizontal integration. An organization's extension of activity in the same general line of business or its expansion into supplementary, complementary, or compatible products. Compare *vertical integration*.

house account. An account with a customer who does not pay sales commissions.

human resource accounting. A term used to describe a variety of proposals that seek to report the importance of human resources—knowledgeable, trained, and loyal employees—in a company's earning process and total assets.

hurdle rate. Required rate of return in a *discounted cash flow* analysis.

hybrid security. *Security*, such as a *convertible bond*, containing elements of both *debt* and *owners' equity*.

hypothecation. The *pledging* of property, without transfer of title or possession, to secure a loan.

I

IAA. *Interamerican Accounting Association.*

IASB. *International Accounting Standards Board.*

ICMA (Institute of Certified Management Accountants). *See CMA* and *Institute of Management Accountants.*

ideal standard costs. *Standard costs* set equal to those that a firm would incur under the best possible conditions.

IFRS. International Financial Reporting Standard(s). Refers broadly to all the pronouncements of the *IASB* and, with numbers after the letters, to specific reporting standards issued by the IASB.

IIA. *Institute of Internal Auditors.*

IMA. *Institute of Management Accountants.*

impairment. Reduction in *market value* of an *asset*. When the firm has information indicating that its long-lived *assets*, (e.g., *plant*, identifiable *intangibles*, and *goodwill*) have declined in *market value* or will provide a smaller future benefit than originally anticipated, it tests to see if the decline in value is so drastic that the expected future cash flows from the asset have declined below *book value*. If then-current book value exceeds the sum of expected cash flows, an asset impairment has occurred. When the firm judges that an impairment has occurred, the firm writes down the book value of the asset to its then-current *fair value*, which is the market value of the asset or, if the firm cannot assess the market value, the expected *net present value* of the future cash flows.

implicit interest. *Interest* not paid or received. *See interest, imputed.* All transactions involving the deferred payment or receipt of cash involve interest, whether explicitly stated or not. The implicit interest on a single-payment *note* equals the difference between the amount collected at maturity and the amount lent at the start of the loan. One can compute the implicit *interest rate* per year for loans with a single cash inflow and a single cash outflow from the following equation:

$$\left[\frac{\text{Cash Received at Maturity}}{\text{Cash Lent}}\right]^{(1/t)} - 1$$

where t is the term of the loan in years; t need not be an integer.

imprest fund. *Petty cash fund.*

improvement. An *expenditure* to extend the useful life of an *asset* or to improve its performance (rate of output, cost) over that of the original asset; sometimes called "betterment." The firm capitalizes such expenditures as part of the asset's cost. Contrast with *maintenance* and *repair.*

imputed cost. A cost that does not appear in accounting records, such as the *interest* that a firm could earn on cash spent to acquire inventories rather than, say, government bonds. Or, consider a firm that owns the buildings it occupies. This firm has an imputed cost for rent in an amount equal to what it would have to pay to use similar buildings owned by another or equal to the amount it could collect from someone renting the premises from the firm. *Opportunity cost.*

imputed interest. *See interest, imputed.*

in the black (red). Operating at a profit (loss).

in-process R&D. When one firm acquires another, the acquired firm will often have *research and development* activities under way that, following *GAAP*, it has *expensed.* The acquiring firm will pay for these activities to the extent they have value and will then, following GAAP, write off the activities. For each dollar of in-process R&D the acquiring firm identifies and immediately *expenses*, it will have one less dollar of *goodwill* or other assets to *amortize.* Some acquirers have overstated the valuations of acquired in-process R&D in order to increase immediate *write-offs* and subsequent, recurring *income.*

incentive compatible compensation. Said of a compensation plan that induces managers to act for the interests of owners while acting also in their own interests. For example, consider that a time of rising prices and increasing inventories when using a *LIFO* cost flow assumption implies paying lower *income taxes* than using *FIFO.* A bonus scheme for managers based on accounting *net income* is not incentive-compatible because owners likely benefit more under LIFO, whereas managers benefit more if they report using FIFO. *See LIFO conformity rule* and *goal congruence.*

income. *Excess of revenues* and *gains* over *expenses* and *losses* for a period; *net income.* The term is sometimes used with an appropriate modifier to refer to the various intermediate amounts shown in a *multiple-step income statement* or to refer to revenues, as in "rental income." *See comprehensive income.*

income accounts. *Revenue* and *expense accounts.*

income before taxes. On the *income statement*, the difference between all *revenues* and *expenses* except *income tax* expense. Contrast with *net income.*

income determination. *See determine.*

income distribution account. *Temporary account* sometimes debited when the firm declares *dividends*; closed to *retained earnings*.

income from continuing operations. As defined by *APB Opinion No. 30*, all *revenues* less all *expenses* except for the following: results of operations (including *income tax* effects) that a firm has discontinued or will discontinue; *gains* or *losses*, including income tax effects, on disposal of segments of the business; gains or losses, including income tax effects, from *extraordinary items*; and the cumulative effect of *accounting changes*.

income from discontinued operations. *Income*, net of tax effects, from parts of the business that the firm has discontinued during the period or will discontinue in the near future. Accountants report such items on separate lines of the *income statement*, after *income from continuing operations* but before *extraordinary items*.

income (revenue) bond. *See special revenue debt.*

income smoothing. A method of timing business *transactions* or choosing *accounting principles* so that the firm reports smaller variations in *income* from year to year than it otherwise would. Even though some managements set income smoothing as an objective, no standard-setter does.

income statement. The statement of *revenues, expenses, gains,* and *losses* for the period, ending with *net income* for the period. Accountants usually show the *earnings-per-share* amount on the income statement; the *reconciliation* of beginning and ending balances of *retained earnings* can also appear in a combined statement of income and retained earnings. *See income from continuing operations, income from*

discontinued operations, extraordinary items, multiple-step, and single-step.

income summary. In problem solving, an *account* that serves as a surrogate for the *income statement*. In using an income summary, close all *revenue* accounts to the Income Summary as *credits* and all *expense* accounts as *debits*. The *balance* in the account, after all these *closing entries* represents income or loss for the period. Then, close the income summary balance to retained earnings.

income tax. An annual tax levied by the federal and other governments on the income of an entity.

income tax allocation. *See deferred income tax (liability)* and *tax allocation: intrastatement.*

incremental. An adjective used to describe the increase in *cost, expense, investment, cash flow, revenue, profit,* and the like if the firm produces or sells one or more units or if it undertakes an activity. *See differential.*

incremental cost. *See incremental.*

incur. Said of an obligation of a firm, whether or not that obligation is *accrued*. For example, a firm incurs interest expense on a loan as time passes but accrues that interest only on payment dates or when it makes an *adjusting entry*.

indenture. *See bond indenture.*

independence. The mental attitude required of the *CPA* in performing the *attest* function. It implies that the CPA is impartial and that the members of the auditing CPA firm own no shares in the corporation being audited.

independent accountant. The *CPA* who performs the *attest* function for a firm.

independent variable. *See regression analysis.*

indeterminate-term liability. A *liability* lacking the criterion of being due at a definite time. This term is our own coinage to encompass the *minority interest.*

indexation. An attempt by lawmakers or parties to a contract to cope with the effects of *inflation.* Amounts fixed in law or contracts are "indexed" when these amounts change as a given measure of price changes. For example, a so-called escalator clause (COLA— cost of living allowance or adjustment) in a labor contract might provide that hourly wages will be increased as the *Consumer Price Index* increases. Many economists have suggested that the indexation of numbers be fixed in the *income tax* laws. Suppose, for example, the personal *exemption* is $2,500 at the start of the period. If prices rise by 10 percent during the period, and if the personal exemption is indexed, then the personal exemption would automatically rise to $2,750 (= $2,500 + .10 × $2,500) at the end of the period.

indirect cost pool. Any grouping of individual costs that a firm does not identify with a *cost objective.*

indirect costs. Production costs not easily associated with the production of specific goods and services; *overhead costs.* Accountants can *allocate* them on some *arbitrary* basis to specific products or departments.

indirect labor (material) cost. An *indirect cost* for labor (material), such as for supervisors (supplies).

indirect method. *See statement of cash flows.*

individual proprietorship. *Sole proprietorship.*

Industry Audit Guides. A series of *AICPA* publications providing specific accounting and *auditing principles* for specialized situations. Audit guides have been issued covering government contractors, state and local government units, investment companies, finance companies, brokers and dealers in securities, and many other subjects.

inescapable cost. A *cost* that the firm or manager cannot avoid (see *avoidable*) because of an action. For example, if management shuts down two operating rooms in a hospital but still must employ security guards in unreduced numbers, the security costs are "inescapable" with respect to the decision to close the operating rooms.

inflation. A time of generally rising prices.

inflation accounting. Strictly speaking, *constant-dollar accounting.* Some writers incorrectly use the term to mean *current cost accounting.*

information circular. Canada: a document, accompanying the notice of a shareholders' meeting, prepared in connection with the solicitation of proxies by or on behalf of the management of the corporation. It contains information concerning the people making the solicitation, election of directors, appointment of auditors, and other matters to be acted on at the meeting.

information system. A system, sometimes formal and sometimes informal, for collecting, processing, and communicating data that are useful for the managerial functions of decision making, planning, and control and for financial reporting under the *attest* requirement.

inherent interest rate. *Implicit interest* rate.

initial cash flows. *Cash flows* associated with the beginning of an investment project. Often include *asset* cost, freight and installation costs, reduced by cash proceeds form disposing of existing assets made redundant or unnecessary by the new project, and *income tax* effect of *gain (loss)* on disposal of existing assets.

insolvent. Unable to pay debts when due; said of a company even though *assets* exceed *liabilities.*

installment. Partial payment of a debt or partial collection of a receivable, usually according to a contract.

installment contracts receivable. The name used for *accounts receivable* when the firm uses the *installment method* of recognizing revenue. Its *contra account, unrealized gross margin,* appears on the balance sheet as a subtraction from the amount receivable.

installment sales. Sales on account when the buyer promises to pay in several separate payments, called *installments.* The seller can, but need not, account for such sales using the *installment method.* If the seller accounts for installment sales with the sales *basis of revenue recognition* for financial reporting but with the installment method for income tax returns, then it will have *deferred income tax (liability).*

installment (sales) method. Recognizing *revenue* and *expense* (or *gross margin*) from a sales transaction in proportion to the fraction of the selling price collected during a period; allowed by the *IRS* for income tax reporting but acceptable in *GAAP* (*APB Opinion No. 10*) only when the firm cannot estimate cash collections with reasonable precision. *See realized* (and *unrealized*) *gross margin.*

Institute of Certified Management Accountants (ICMA). *See CMA* and *Institute of Management Accountants.*

Institute of Internal Auditors (IIA). The national association of accountants engaged in internal auditing and employed by business firms; administers a comprehensive professional examination. Those who pass the exam qualify to be designated *CIA* (Certified Internal Auditor).

Institute of Management Accountants (IMA). Formerly, the National Association of Accountants, NAA; a society open to those engaged in management accounting; parent organization of the *ICMA,* which oversees the *CMA* program.

insurance. A contract for reimbursement of specific losses; purchased with insurance premiums. "Self-insurance" is not insurance but is merely the noninsured's willingness to assume the risk of incurring losses while saving the premium.

intangible asset. A nonphysical right that gives a firm an exclusive or preferred position in the marketplace. Examples are *copyright, patent, trademark, goodwill, organization costs, capitalized* advertising cost, computer programs, licenses for any of the preceding, government licenses (e.g., broadcasting or the right to sell liquor), *leases,* franchises, mailing lists, exploration permits, import and export permits, construction permits, and marketing quotas. Invariably, accountants define intangible using a "for example" list, as we have just done, because accounting has been unable to devise a definition of intangible that will include items such as those listed above but exclude stock and bond certificates. Accountants classify these items as tangibles, even though they give their holders a preferred position in receiving dividends and interest payments.

Interamerican Accounting Association (IAA). An organization, headquartered in Miami, devoted to facilitating interaction between accounting practitioners in the Americas.

intercompany elimination. *See eliminations.*

intercompany profit. Profit within an organization. If one *affiliated company* sells to another, and the goods remain in the second company's *inventory* at the end of the period, then the first company has not y.et realized a *profit* by a sale to an outsider. The profit is "intercompany profit," and the accountant eliminates it from net *income* when preparing *consolidated income statements* or when the firm uses the *equity method.*

intercompany transaction. *Transaction* between a *parent company* and a *subsidiary* or between subsidiaries in a *consolidated entity*; the accountant must eliminate the effects of such a transaction when preparing *consolidated financial statements. See intercompany profit.*

intercorporate investment. Occurs when a given *corporation* owns *shares* or *debt* issued by another.

interdepartment monitoring. An *internal control* device. The advantage of allocating *service department costs* to *production departments* stems from the incentives that this gives those charged with the costs to control the costs incurred in the service department. That process of having one group monitor the performance of another is interdepartment monitoring.

interest. The charge or cost for using cash, usually borrowed funds. Interest on one's own cash used is an *opportunity cost, imputed interest.* The amount of interest for a loan is the total amount paid by a borrower to a lender less the amount paid by the lender to the borrower. Accounting

seeks to allocate that interest over the time of the loan so that the interest rate (= interest charge/amount borrowed) stays constant each period *See interest rate* for discussion of the quoted amount. *See effective interest rate* and *nominal interest rate.*

interest, imputed. The difference between the face amount and the present value of a promise. If a borrower promises to pay a single amount at a future date, then the face amount the borrower will repay at *maturity* will exceed the present value (computed at a *fair market* interest rate, called the "imputed interest rate") of the promise. *See also imputed cost.*

interest factor. One plus the *interest* rate.

interest method. *See effective interest method.*

interest rate. A basis used for computing the cost of borrowing funds; usually expressed as a ratio between the number of currency units (e.g., dollars) charged for a period of time and the number of currency units borrowed for that same period of time. When the writers and speakers do not state a period, they almost always mean a period of one year. *See interest, simple interest, compound interest, effective (interest) rate,* and *nominal interest rate.*

interest rate swap. *See swap.*

interfund accounts. In governmental accounting, the accounts that show transactions between funds, especially interfund receivables and payables.

interim statements. Statements issued for periods less than the regular, annual *accounting period.* The *SEC* requires most corporations to issue interim statements on a quarterly basis. In preparing interim reports, a problem arises that the accountant can resolve only by understanding whether interim reports should report on the interim period (1) as a self-contained accounting period or (2) as an integral part of the year so that analysts can make forecasts of annual performance. For example, assume that at the end of the first quarter, a retailer has dipped into old LIFO layers, depleting its *inventory*, so that it computes *LIFO cost of goods sold* artificially low and *net income* artificially high, relative to the amounts the firm would have computed if it had made the "normal" purchases, equal to or greater than sales. The retailer expects to purchase inventory sufficiently large so that when it computes cost of goods sold for the year, there will be no *dips into old LIFO layers* and income will not be artificially high. The first approach will compute the quarterly income from low cost of goods sold using data for the dips that have actually occurred by the end of the quarter. The second approach will compute quarterly income from cost of goods sold assuming that purchases were equal to "normal" amounts and that the firm did not dip into old LIFO layers. *APB Opinion No. 28* and the *SEC* require that interim reports be constructed largely to satisfy the second purpose.

internal audit, internal auditor. An *audit* conducted by the firm's own employees, called "internal auditors," to ascertain whether the firm's *internal control* procedures work as planned. Contrast with an external audit conducted by a *CPA*.

internal controls. Policies and procedures designed to provide management with reasonable assurances that employees behave in a way that enables the firm to meet its organizational goals. See *control system*.

internal failure costs. *Costs incurred* when a firm detects nonconforming

products and services before delivering them to customers; these include scrap, rework, and retesting.

internal rate of return (IRR). The discount rate that equates the net *present value* of a stream of cash outflows and inflows to zero.

internal reporting. Reporting for management's use in planning and control. Contrast with *external reporting* for financial statement users.

Internal Revenue Service (IRS). Agency of the U.S. Treasury Department responsible for administering the Internal Revenue Code and collecting income and certain other taxes.

International Accounting Standards Board (IASB). An organization that promotes the international convergence of accounting standards. Web site: *http://whww.iasb.org*. Successor to the International Accounting Standards Committee, IASC, which it superceded in 2001. A good site for tracing developments in international accounting is *http://www.iasplus.com*, maintained by the worldwide Deloitte firm, and recommended by the renowned expert on international accounting, Professor Stephen A. Zeff of Rice University.

International Organization of Securities Commissions. *IOSCO.*

interperiod tax allocation. *See deferred income tax (liability).*

interpolation. The estimation of an unknown number intermediate between two (or more) known numbers.

Interpretations. See FASB Interpretation.

intrastatement tax allocation. *See tax allocation: intrastatement.*

intrinsic rewards. Rewards that come from within the individual, such as the satisfaction from studying hard, providing help to someone in need, or doing a good job. Contrast with *extrinsic rewards.*

inventoriable costs. *Costs* incurred that the firm adds to the cost of manufactured products; *product costs* (*assets*) as opposed to *period expenses.*

inventory. As a noun, the *balance* in an asset *account*, such as raw materials, supplies, work-in-process, and finished goods; as a verb, to calculate the *cost* of goods on hand at a given time or to count items on hand physically.

inventory equation. *Beginning inventory* + Net additions − Withdrawals = *Ending inventory.* Ordinarily, additions are net purchases, and withdrawals are *cost of goods sold.* Notice that ending inventory, appearing on the balance sheet, and cost of goods sold, appearing on the income statement, must add to a fixed sum. As one of those components increases, the other must decrease. In valuing inventories, the firm usually knows beginning inventory and net purchases. Some inventory methods (for example, some applications of the *retail inventory method*) measure costs of goods sold and use the equation to find the cost of ending inventory. Most methods measure cost of ending inventory and use the equation to find the cost of goods sold (withdrawals). In *current cost* (in contrast to *historical cost*) *accounting,* additions (in the equation) include holding gains, whether realized or not. Thus the current cost inventory equation is as follows: Beginning inventory (at current cost) + Purchases (where current cost is historical cost) + Holding gains (whether realized or not) − Ending inventory (at current cost) = Cost of goods sold (current cost).

inventory holding gains. *See inventory profit.*

inventory layer. *See LIFO inventory layer.*

inventory profit. A term with several possible meanings. Consider the data in the following illustration. The firm uses a *FIFO cost flow assumption* and derives its *historical cost* data. The assumed *current cost* data resemble those that the FASB suggested in *SFAS No. 89.* The term *income from continuing operations* refers to revenues less expenses based on current, rather than historical, costs. To that subtotal, add realized holding gains to arrive at realized (conventional) income. To that, add unrealized holding gains to arrive at economic income. The term "inventory profit" often refers (for example, in some *SEC* releases) to the realized holding gain, $110 in the illustration. The amount of inventory profit will usually be material when the firm uses FIFO and when prices rise. Other analysts, including us, prefer to use the term "inventory profit" to refer to the total *holding gain,* $300 (= $110 + $190, both realized and unrealized), but writers use this meaning less often. In periods of rising prices and increasing inventories, the realized holding gains under a FIFO cost flow assumption will exceed those under LIFO. In the illustration, for example, assume under LIFO that the historical cost of goods sold is $4,800, that historical LIFO cost of beginning inventory is $600, and that historical LIFO cost of ending inventory is $800. Then income from continuing operations, based on current costs, remains $350 (= $5,200 − $4,850), realized holding gains are $50 (= $4,850 − $4,800), realized income is $400 (= $350 + $50), the unrealized holding gain for the year is $250 [= ($1,550 − $800) − ($1,100 − $600)], and economic income is $650 (= $350 + $50 + $250). The cost flow assumption has only one real effect on this series of calculations: the split of the total holding gain into realized and unrealized portions. Thus, economic income does not depend on the cost flow assumption. Holding gains total $300 in the illustration. The choice of cost flow assumption determines the portion reported as realized.

Inventory Profit Illustration

	(Historical) Acquisition Cost Assuming FIFO	Current Cost
ASSUMED DATA		
Inventory, 1/1	$ 900	$ 1,100
Inventory, 12/31	1,160	1,550
Cost of Goods Sold for the Year	4,740	4,850
Sales for the Year	$ 5,200	$ 5,200
INCOME STATEMENT FOR THE YEAR		
Sales	$ 5,200	$ 5,200
Cost of Goods Sold	4,740	4,850
(1) Income from Continuing Operations		$ 350
Realized Holding Gains		110[a]
(2) Realized Income = Conventional Net Income (under FIFO)	$ 460	$ 460
Unrealized Holding Gain		190[b]
(3) Economic Income . .		$ 650

[a] Realized holding gain during a period is current cost of goods sold less historical cost of goods sold; for the year the realized holding gain under FIFO is $110 − $4,850 − $4,740. Some refer to this as "inventory profit."
[b] The unrealized holding gain during a period is the unrealized holding gain at the end of the period less the unrealized holding gain prior to this year. The unrealized holding gain at the beginning of the year in this example is $200 = $1,100 − $900.

inventory turnover. Number of times the firm sells the average *inventory* during a period; *cost of goods sold* for a period divided by average inventory for the period. *See ratio.*

invested capital. *Contributed capital.*

investee. A company in which another entity, the "investor," owns stock.

investing activities. Acquiring and selling *securities* or productive *assets* expected to produce *revenue* over several *periods.*

investment. An *expenditure* to acquire property or other *assets* in order to produce *revenue*; the asset so acquired; hence, a *current* expenditure made in anticipation of future income; said of other companies' *securities* held for the long term and appearing in a separate section of the *balance sheet*; in this context, contrast with *marketable securities.*

investment center. A *responsibility center*, with control over *revenues, costs,* and *assets.*

investment credit. A reduction in income tax liability sometimes granted by the federal government to firms that buy new equipment. This item is a credit in that the taxpayer deducts it from the tax bill, not from pretax income. The tax credit has been a given percentage of the purchase price of the assets purchased. The government has changed the rules and rates over the years. As of 1999, there is no investment credit. *See flow-through method* and *carryforward.*

investment decision. The decision whether to undertake an action involving production of goods or services; contrast with financing decision.

investment tax credit. *Investment credit.*

investment turnover ratio. A term that means the same thing as *total assets turnover ratio.*

investments. A balance sheet heading for tangible assets held for periods longer than the operating cycle and not used in revenue production (assets not meeting the definitions of *current assets* or *property, plant, and equipment*).

invoice. A document showing the details of a sale or purchase *transaction*.

IOSCO (International Organization of Securities Commissions). The name, since 1983, of a confederation of regulators of securities and futures markets. Members come from over 80 countries. The IOSCO encourages the *IASB* to eliminate accounting alternatives and to ensure that accounting standards are detailed and complete, with adequate disclosure requirements, and that financial statements are user-friendly.

I.O.U. An informal document acknowledging a debt, setting out the amount of the debt and signed by the debtor.

IRR. *Internal rate of return.*

IRS. *Internal Revenue Service.*

isoprofit line. On a graph showing feasible production possibilities of two products that require the use of the same limited resources, a line showing all feasible production possibility combinations with the same *profit* or, perhaps, *contribution margin.*

issue. A corporation exchange of its shares (or *bonds*) for cash or other *assets*. Terminology says the corporation "issues," not "sells," those shares (or bonds). Also used in the context of withdrawing supplies or materials from inventory for use in operations and of drawing a *check.*

issued shares. Those shares of *authorized capital stock* that a *corporation* has distributed to the shareholders. *See issue.* Shares of *treasury stock* are legally issued but are not *outstanding* for the purpose of voting, *dividend declarations*, and *earnings-per-share* calculations.

J

JIT. *See just-in-time inventory.*

job cost sheet. A schedule showing actual or budgeted inputs for a special order.

job development credit. The name used for the *investment credit* in the 1971 tax law, since repealed, on this subject.

job (-order) costing. Accumulation of *costs* for a particular identifiable batch of product, known as a job, as it moves through production.

jobs. Customized products.

joint cost. Cost of simultaneously producing or otherwise acquiring two or more products, called joint products, that a firm must, by the nature of the process, produce or acquire together, such as the cost of beef and hides of cattle. Generally, accounting allocates the joint costs of production to the individual products in proportion to their respective sales value (or, sometimes and usually not preferred, their respective physical quantities) at the *split-off* point. Other examples include *central corporate expenses* and *overhead* of a department when it manufactures several products. *See common cost* and *sterilized allocation.*

joint cost allocation. *See joint cost.*

joint process. A process that converts a common input into several outputs.

joint product. One of two or more outputs with significant value that a firm must produce or acquire simultaneously. *See by-product* and *joint cost.*

journal. The place where the firm records transactions as they occur; the book of original entry.

journal entry. A dated *journal* recording, showing the accounts affected, of equal *debits* and *credits*, with an explanation of the *transaction*, if necessary.

Journal of Accountancy. A monthly publication of the *AICPA*.

Journal of Accounting and Economics. Scholarly journal published by the William E. Simon Graduate School of Business Administration of the University of Rochester.

Journal of Accounting Research. Scholarly journal containing articles on theoretical and empirical aspects of accounting; published by the Graduate School of Business of the University of Chicago.

journal voucher. A *voucher* documenting (and sometimes authorizing) a *transaction*, leading to an entry in the *journal*.

journalize. To make an entry in a *journal*.

judgment(al) sampling. A method of choosing a sample in which the analyst subjectively selects items for examination, in contrast to selecting them by statistical methods. Compare *random sampling*.

junk bond. A low-rated *bond* that lacks the merit and characteristics of an investment-grade bond. It offers high yields, typically in excess of 15 percent per year, but also possesses high risk of default. Sometimes writers, less pejoratively, call these "high-yield bonds." No clear line separates junk from nonjunk bonds.

just-in-time inventory (production) (JIT). In managing *inventory* for manufacturing, system in which a firm purchases or manufactures each component just before the firm uses it. Contrast with systems in which firms acquire or manufacture many parts in advance of needs. JIT systems have much smaller carrying costs for inventory, ideally none, but run higher risks of incurring *stockout* costs.

K

k. Two to the tenth power (2^{10} or 1,024), when referring to computer storage capacity. The one-letter abbreviation derives from the first letter of the prefix "kilo-" (which means 1,000 in decimal notation).

Kaizen costing. A management concept that seeks continuous improvements, likely occurring in small incremental amounts, by refinements of all components of a production process.

KG (Kommanditgesellschaft). Germany: similar to a general partnership (*OHG*) except that some of its members may limit their liability. One of the partners must be a *general partner* with unlimited liability.

kiting. A term with slightly different meanings in banking and auditing contexts. In both, however, it refers to the wrongful practice of taking advantage of the *float*, the time that elapses between the deposit of a *check* in one bank and its collection at another. In the banking context, an individual deposits in Bank A a check written on Bank B. He (or she) then writes checks against the deposit created in Bank A. Several days later, he deposits in Bank B a check written on Bank A, to cover the original check written on Bank B. Still later, he deposits in Bank A a check written on Bank B. The process of covering the deposit in Bank A with a check written on Bank B and vice versa continues until the person can arrange an actual deposit of cash. In the auditing context, kiting refers to a form of *window dressing* in which the firm makes the amount of the account

Cash in Bank appear larger than it actually is by depositing in Bank A a check written on Bank B without recording the check written on Bank B in the *check register* until after the close of the *accounting period.*

know-how. Technical or business information that is of the type defined under *trade secret* but that a firm does not maintain as a secret. The rules of accounting for this *asset* are the same as for other *intangibles.*

L

labor efficiency variance. Measures labor productivity by multiplying the *standard* labor price times the difference between the standard labor hours and the actual labor hours.

labor price (or wage) variance. Measures the difference between the actual and *standard* labor prices (wage rates).

labor variances. The *price* (or *rate*) and *quantity* (or *usage*) *variances* for *direct labor* inputs in a *standard costing system.*

laid-down cost. Canada and United Kingdom: the sum of all direct costs incurred for procurement of goods up to the time of physical receipt, such as invoice cost plus customs and excise duties, freight and cartage.

land. An *asset* shown at *acquisition cost* plus the *cost* of any nondepreciable *improvements*; in accounting, implies use as a plant or office site rather than as a *natural resource*, such as timberland or farmland.

lapping (accounts receivable). The theft, by an employee, of cash sent in by a customer to discharge the latter's *payable.* The employee conceals the theft from the first customer by using cash received from a second customer. The employee conceals the theft from the second customer by using cash

received from a third customer, and so on. The process continues until the thief returns the funds or can make the theft permanent by creating a fictitious *expense* or receivable write-off or until someone discovers the fraud.

lapse. To expire; said of, for example, an insurance policy or discounts that are made available for prompt payment and that the purchaser does not take.

last-in, first-out. *See LIFO.*

layer. *See LIFO inventory layer.*

lead time. The time that elapses between placing an order and receiving the *goods* or *services* ordered.

learning curve. A mathematical expression of the phenomenon that incremental unit costs to produce decrease as managers and labor gain experience from practice.

lease. A contract calling for the lessee (user) to pay the lessor (owner) for the use of an asset. A cancelable lease allows the lessee to cancel at any time. A noncancelable lease requires payments from the lessee for the life of the lease and usually shares many of the economic characteristics of *debt financing.* Most long-term noncancelable leases meet the usual criteria for classifying them as *liabilities*, and GAAP require the firm to show them as liabilities. *SFAS No. 13* and the *SEC* require disclosure, in notes to the financial statements, of the commitments for long-term noncancelable leases. *See capital lease* and *operating lease.*

leasehold. The *asset* representing the right of the lessee to use leased property. *See lease* and *leasehold improvement.*

leasehold improvement. An *improvement* to leased property. The firm should *amortize* it over the *service life* or the life of the lease, whichever is shorter.

least and latest rule. Paying the least amount of taxes as late as possible within the law to minimize the *present value* of tax payments for a given set of operations. Sensible taxpayers will follow this rule. When a taxpayer knows that tax rates will increase later, the taxpayer can reduce the present value of the tax burden by paying smaller taxes sooner. Each set of circumstances requires its own computations.

ledger. A book of accounts; book of final entry. *See general ledger* and *subsidiary ledger.* Contrast with *journal.*

legal capital. The amount of *contributed capital* that, according to state law, the firm must keep permanently in the firm as protection for creditors.

legal entity. *See entity.*

lender. *See loan.*

lessee. *See lease.*

lessor. *See lease.*

letter stock. Privately placed *common shares*; so called because the *SEC* requires the purchaser to sign a letter of intent not to resell the shares.

leverage. More than proportional result from extra effort or financing. Some measure of output increases faster than the measure of input. "Operating leverage" refers to the tendency of *net income* to rise at a faster rate than sales in the presence of *fixed costs.* A doubling of sales, for example, usually implies a more than doubling of net income. "Financial leverage" (or "capital leverage") refers to an increase in rate of return larger than the increase in explicit financing costs— the increased rate of return on *owners' equity* (*see ratio*) when an *investment* earns a return larger than the after-tax *interest rate* paid for *debt* financing.

Because the interest charges on debt usually do not change, any *incremental* income benefits owners and none benefits debtors. When writers use the term "leverage" without a qualifying adjective, the term usually refers to financial leverage, the use of *long-term* debt in securing *funds* for the *entity.*

leveraged lease. A special form of lease involving three parties: a *lender*, a *lessor*, and a *lessee.* The lender, such as a bank or insurance company, lends a portion, say 80 percent, of the cash required for acquiring the *asset.* The lessor puts up the remainder, 20 percent, of the cash required. The lessor acquires the asset with the cash, using the asset as security for the loan, and leases it to the lessee on a *noncancelable* basis. The lessee makes periodic lease payments to the lessor, who in turn makes payments on the loan to the lender. Typically, the lessor has no obligation for the debt to the lender other than transferring a portion of the receipts from the lessee. If the lessee should default on the required lease payments, then the lender can repossess the leased asset. The lessor usually has the right to benefit from the tax deductions for *depreciation* on the asset, for *interest expense* on the loan from the lender, and for any *investment credit.* The lease is leveraged in the sense that the lessor, who takes most of the risks and enjoys most of the rewards of ownership, usually borrows most of the funds needed to acquire the asset. *See leverage.*

liability. An obligation to pay a definite (or reasonably definite) amount at a definite (or reasonably definite) time in return for a past or current benefit (that is, the obligation arises from a transaction that is not an *executory contract*); a probable future sacrifice of economic benefits arising from present obligations of a particular *entity* to *transfer assets* or to provide services to other entities in the future as a result of past *transactions* or events. *SFAC No. 6* says that "probable" refers to that which we can reasonably expect or believe but that is neither certain nor proved. A liability has three essential characteristics: (1) the obligation to transfer assets or services has a specified or knowable date, (2) the entity has little or no discretion to avoid the transfer, and (3) the event causing the obligation has already happened, that is, it is not executory.

lien. The right of person A to satisfy a claim against person B by holding B's property as security or by seizing B's property.

life annuity. A *contingent annuity* in which payments cease at the death of a specified person(s), usually the *annuitant(s)*.

LIFO (last-in, first-out). An *inventory* flow assumption in which the *cost of goods sold* equals the cost of the most recently acquired units and a firm computes the *ending inventory cost* from the costs of the oldest units. In periods of rising prices and increasing inventories, LIFO leads to higher reported expenses and therefore lower reported income and lower balance sheet inventories than does FIFO. Contrast with *FIFO*. *See FISH* and *inventory profit*.

LIFO conformity rule. The *IRS* rule requiring that companies that use a *LIFO cost flow assumption* for *income taxes* must also use LIFO in computing *income* reported in *financial statements* and forbidding the disclosure of *pro forma* results from using any other cost flow assumption.

LIFO, dollar-value method. *See dollar-value LIFO method*.

LIFO inventory layer. A portion of LIFO inventory cost on the *balance sheet*. The *ending inventory* in physical quantity will usually exceed the *beginning inventory*. The *LIFO cost flow assumption* assigns to this increase in physical quantities a cost computed from the prices of the earliest purchases during the year. The LIFO inventory then consists of layers, sometimes called "slices," which typically consist of relatively small amounts of physical quantities from each of the past years when purchases in physical units exceeded sales in units. Each layer carries the prices from near the beginning of the period when the firm acquired it. The earliest layers will typically (in periods of rising prices) have prices much less than current prices. If inventory quantities should decline in a subsequent period—a "dip into old LIFO layers"—the latest layers enter cost of goods sold first.

LIFO reserve. *Unrealized holding gain* in *ending inventory*: current or *FIFO historical* cost of ending inventory less LIFO *historical cost*. A better term for this concept is "excess of current cost over LIFO historical cost." *See reserve*.

limited liability. The legal concept that shareholders of corporations are not personally liable for debts of the company.

limited partner. A *partnership* member who is not personally liable for debts of the partnership. Every partnership must have at least one *general partner*, who is fully liable.

line-of-business reporting. *See segment reporting*.

line of credit. An agreement with a bank or set of banks for short-term borrowings on demand.

linear programming. A mathematical tool for finding profit-maximizing (or cost-minimizing) combinations of products to produce when a firm has several products that it can produce but faces linear constraints on the resources available in the production processes or on maximum and minimum production requirements.

liquid. Said of a business with a substantial amount (the amount is unspecified) of *working capital*, especially *quick assets*.

liquid assets. *Cash, current marketable securities*, and sometimes, *current receivables*.

liquidating dividend. A *dividend* that a firm declares in the winding up of a business to distribute its assets to the shareholders. Usually the recipient treats this as a return of *investment*, not as *revenue*.

liquidation. Payment of a debt; sale of assets in closing down a business or a segment thereof.

liquidation value per share. The amount each *share* of stock will receive if the *board* dissolves a corporation; for *preferred stock* with a liquidation preference, a stated amount per share.

liquidity. Refers to the availability of *cash*, or near-cash resources, for meeting a firm's obligations.

LISH. An acronym, conceived by George H. Sorter, for *last-in, still-here*. LISH is the same cost flow assumption as *FIFO*. Many readers of accounting statements find it easier to think about inventory questions in terms of items still on hand. Think of FIFO in connection with *cost of goods sold* but of LISH in connection with *ending inventory. See FISH.*

list price. The published or nominally quoted price for goods.

list price method. *See trade-in transaction.*

loan. An arrangement in which the owner of property, called the lender, allows someone else, called the borrower, the use of the property for a period of time, which the agreement setting up the loan usually specifies. The borrower promises to return the property to the lender and, often, to make a payment for the use of the property. This term is generally used when the property is *cash* and the payment for its use is *interest.*

LOCOM. *Lower of cost or market.*

long-lived (term) asset. An asset whose benefits the firm expects to receive over several years; a *noncurrent* asset, usually includes *investments, plant assets*, and *intangibles.*

long run. long term. A term denoting a time or time periods in the future. How far in the future depends on context. For some securities traders, "long-term" can mean anything beyond the next hour or two. For most managers, it means the period of time long enough to allow change in total productive capacity. For government policymakers, it can mean anything beyond the next decade or two. For geologists, it can mean millions of years. In contrast to the *short run.* Use a hyphen when the phrase is an adjective, but no hyphen when it is a noun.

long-term (construction) contract accounting. The *percentage-of-completion method* of *revenue* recognition; sometimes used to mean the *completed contract method.*

long-term debt ratio. *Noncurrent liabilities* divided by total *assets.*

long-term liability (debt). *Noncurrent liability.*

long term. *See long run.*

long-term solvency risk. The risk that a firm will not have sufficient *cash* to pay its *debts* sometime in the *long run.*

loophole. Imprecise term meaning a technicality allowing a taxpayer (or *financial statements*) to circumvent the intent, without violating the letter, of the law (or *GAAP*).

loss. Excess of *cost* over net proceeds for a single transaction; negative *income* for a period; a cost expiration that produced no *revenue. See gain* for a discussion of related and contrasting terms and how to distinguish loss from *expense.*

loss contingency. *See contingency.*

lower of cost or market (LOCOM). A basis for valuation of *inventory* and, formerly in the United States, of *marketable securities.* This basis sets inventory value at the lower of *acquisition cost* or *current replacement cost* (market), subject to the following constraints. First, the market value of an item used in the computation cannot exceed its *net realizable value*— an amount equal to selling price less reasonable costs to complete production and to sell the item. Second, the market value of an item used in the computation cannot be less than the net realizable value minus the normal *profit* ordinarily realized on disposition of completed items of this type. The basis chooses the lower-of-cost-or-market valuation as the lower of acquisition *cost* or replacement cost *(market)* subject to the upper and lower bounds on replacement cost established in the first two steps. Thus,

Market Value = Midvalue of
(Replacement Cost,
Net Realizable Value,
Net Realizable Value
Less Normal Profit
Margin)

Lower of Cost = Minimum
or Market   (Acquisition
Valuation   Cost, Market Value)

The accompanying exhibit illustrates the calculation of the lower-of-cost-or-market valuation for four inventory items. Notice that each of the four possible outcomes occurs once in measuring lower of cost or market. Item 1 uses acquisition cost; item 2 uses net realizable value; item 3 uses replacement cost; and item 4 uses net realizable value less normal profit margin.

	Item			
	1	2	3	4
Calculation of Market Value				
(a) Replacement Cost ...	$92	$96	$92	$96
(b) Net Realizable VAlue	95	95	95	95
(c) Net Realizable Value Less Normal Profit Margin [= (b) − $9]	86	86	86	86
(d) Market = Midvalue [(a), (b), (c)]	92	95	92	95
Calculation of Lower of Cost or Market				
(e) Acquisition Cost	$90	$97	$96	$90
(f) Market [= (d)]	92	95	92	95
(g) Lower of Cost or Market = Minimum [(e), (f)]	90	95	92	90

A taxpayer cannot use the lower-of-cost-or-market basis for inventory on tax returns in combination with a *LIFO cost flow assumption.* In the context of inventory, once the firm writes down the asset, it establishes a new "original cost" basis and ignores subsequent increases in market value in the accounts.

The firm can apply lower of cost or market to individual items of inventory or to groups (usually called *pools*) of items. The smaller the group, the more *conservative* the resulting valuation.

Omit hyphens when you use the term as a noun, but use them when you use the term as an adjectival phrase.

Ltd., Limited. UK: a private limited corporation. The name of a private limited company must include the word "Limited" or its abbreviation "Ltd."

lump-sum acquisition. *Basket purchase.*

M

MACRS. *Modified Accelerated Cost Recovery System. See Accelerated Cost Recovery System.* Since 1986, MACRS has been the accelerated depreciation method required for U.S. income tax purposes.

maintenance. *Expenditures* undertaken to preserve an *asset's* service potential for its originally intended life. These expenditures are *period expenses* or *product costs.* Contrast with *improvement,* and *see repair.*

make money. making money. *See also* discussion under *money.* Avoid these phrases because they can mean any of the following:

1. Earning *income:* "Microsoft made a lot of money last year."

2. Earning *other comprehensive income:* "I still hold the Microsoft share I bought in 1990 and I've made a lot of money on them." This is an *unrealized holding gain,* an increase in wealth, but not an increase in *cash.*

3. Save *opportunity costs or* opportunity losses: "If I'd only sold those shares in 1999, I'd have made more money. I didn't sell the shares, so I lost money." Accounting does not recognize opportuni-

ty costs. This use of the term refers to the lost benefits form not doing something. You rightly feel you'd have been better off selling those shares. If you were to say, "I didn't sell; I lost money as a result," some people who use the phrase would argue you didn't lose money because you failed to make a transaction, but some people would agree with you.

4. Earn revenues: "George Forman has made a lot of money touting his cooking devices on TV." George earned income and received payments, but the user of the term this way subtracts no costs.

5. Earn gross margin: "We at the hardware store make money selling those cooking device than we do selling basic tools, because the cookers have a larger markup." The user understands we need to subtract some costs, but doesn't take into account the indirect cost such as occupancy costs, inventory holding costs, and shrinkage costs.

6. Sell for cash: "You didn't make any money yet from selling those cookers because the customer won't pay for another two months." This user would be better off to know the *allowance method for uncollectibles.* Net revenue, gross sales less expected uncollectibles, better describes what this user has in mind.

7. Generating cash flow from operations. Many companies can have positive income but negative cash flow from operations. Some analysts will say such a company made no money in such a year.

8. And, don't forget *counterfeiting.*

make-or-buy decision. A managerial decision about whether the firm should produce a product internally or purchase it from others. Proper make-or-buy decisions in the short run result only when a firm considers *incremental costs* in the analysis.

maker (of note) (of check). One who signs a *note* to borrow; one who signs a *check*; in the latter context, synonymous with "drawer." *See draft.*

management. Executive authority that operates a business.

management accounting. *See managerial accounting.*

Management Accounting. Monthly publication of the *IMA.*

management audit. An audit conducted to ascertain whether a firm or one of its operating units properly carries out its objectives, policies, and procedures; generally applies only to activities for which accountants can specify qualitative standards. *See audit* and *internal audit.*

management by exception. A principle of management in which managers focus attention on performance only if it differs significantly from that expected.

management by objective (MBO). A management approach designed to focus on the definition and attainment of overall and individual objectives with the participation of all levels of management.

management information system (MIS). A system designed to provide all levels of management with timely and reliable information required for planning, control, and evaluation of performance.

management's discussion and analysis (MD&A). A discussion of management's views of the company's performance; required by the *SEC* to be included in the *10-K* and in the *annual report* to shareholders. The information

typically contains discussion of such items as liquidity, results of *operations, segments,* and the effects of *inflation.*

managerial (management) accounting. Reporting designed to enhance the ability of management to do its job of decision making, planning, and control. Contrast with *financial accounting.*

manufacturing cost. Cost of producing goods, usually in a factory.

manufacturing expense. An imprecise, and generally incorrect, alternative title for *manufacturing overhead.* The term is generally incorrect because these costs are usually *product costs,* not expenses.

manufacturing overhead. General manufacturing *costs* that are not directly associated with identifiable units of product and that the firm incurs in providing a capacity to carry on productive activities. Accounting treats *fixed* manufacturing overhead cost as a *product cost* under *full absorption costing* but as an *expense* of the period under *variable costing.*

margin. *Revenue* less specified expenses. *See contribution margin, gross margin,* and *current margin.*

margin of safety. Excess of actual, or budgeted, sales over *breakeven* sales; usually expressed in dollars but can be expressed in units of product.

marginal cost. The *incremental cost* or *differential cost* of the last unit added to production or the first unit subtracted from production. *See cost terminology* and *differential* for contrast.

marginal costing. *Variable costing.*

marginal revenue. The increment in *revenue* from the sale of one additional unit of product.

marginal tax rate. The amount, expressed as a percentage, by which income taxes increase when taxable income increases by one dollar. Contrast with *average tax rate.*

markdown. *See markup* for definition and contrast.

markdown cancellation. *See markup* for definition and contrast.

market-based transfer price. A *transfer price* based on external market data rather than internal company data.

market price. *See fair value.*

market rate. The rate of *interest* a company must pay to borrow *funds* currently. *See effective rate.*

market value. *Fair market value.*

marketable equity securities. *Marketable securities* representing *owners' equity* interest in other companies, rather than *loans* to them.

marketable securities. Other companies' *stocks* and *bonds* held that can be readily sold on stock exchanges or over-the-counter markets and that the company plans to sell as cash is needed; classified as *current assets* and as part of "cash" in preparing the *statement of cash flows*. If the firm holds these same securities for *long-term* purposes, it will classify them as *noncurrent assets. SFAS No. 115* requires that all marketable equity and all debt securities (except those debt securities the holder has the ability and intent to hold to maturity) appear at market value on the balance sheet. The firm reports changes in market value in income for *trading securities* but debits holding losses (or credits holding gains) directly to owners' equity accounts for *securities available for sale.*

marketing costs. Costs incurred to sell; includes locating customers, persuading them to buy, delivering the goods or services, and collecting the sales proceeds.

mark to market. As a verb, to record an item in the books at *current fair market value.* When used as an adjective, hyphenate the phrase.

markon. *See markup* for definition and contrast.

markup. The difference between the original selling price of items acquired for *inventory* and the cost. Precise usage calls this "markon," although many businesspeople use the term "markup." Because of confusion of this use of "markup" with its precise definition (see below), terminology sometimes uses "original markup." If the originally established retail price increases, the precise term for the amount of price increase is "markup," although terminology sometimes uses "additional markup." If a firm reduces selling price, terminology uses the terms "markdown" and "markup cancellation." "Markup cancellation" refers to reduction in price following "additional markups" and can, by definition, be no more than the amount of the additional markup; "cancellation of additional markup," although not used, is descriptive. "Markdown" refers to price reductions from the original retail price. A price increase after a markdown is a "markdown cancellation." If original cost is $12 and original selling price is $20, then markon (original markup) is $8; if the firm later increases the price to $24, the $4 increase is markup (additional markup); if the firm later lowers the price to $21, the $3 reduction is markup cancellation; if the firm further lowers the price to $17, the $4 reduction comprises $1 markup cancellation and $3 markdown; if the firm later increases the price to $22, the $5 increase comprises $3 of markdown cancellation and $2 of markup (additional markup). Accountants track markup cancellations and markdowns separately because they deduct the former (but not the latter) in computing the selling prices of goods available for sale for the denominator of the *cost percentage* used in the conventional *retail inventory method*.

markup cancellation. *See markup* for definition and contrast.

markup percentage. *Markup* divided by (acquisition cost plus *markup*).

master budget. A *budget* projecting all *financial statements* and their components.

matching convention. The concept of recognizing cost expirations *(expenses)* in the same accounting period during which the firm recognizes related *revenues*; combining or simultaneously recognizing the revenues and expenses that jointly result from the same *transactions* or other events.

material. As an adjective, it means relatively important, capable of influencing a decision (*see materiality*); as a noun, *raw material*.

materiality. The concept that accounting should disclose separately only those events that are relatively important (no operable definition yet exists) for the business or for understanding its statements. *SFAC No. 2* suggests that accounting information is material if "the judgment of a reasonable person relying on the information would have been changed or influenced by the omission or misstatement."

materials efficiency variance. Measures materials waste by multiplying the *standard* materials price times the difference between the standard materials quantity used and the actual materials quantity used.

materials price variance. Measures the difference between the actual and *standard* materials prices.

materials variances. *Price* and *quantity variances* for *direct materials* in *standard costing systems*; difference between actual cost and standard cost.

matrix. A rectangular array of numbers or mathematical symbols.

matrix inverse. For a given square *matrix* A, the matrix, A^{-1} such that $AA^{-1} = A^{-1}A = I$, the identity matrix. Not all square matrices have inverses. Those that do not are "singular"; those that do are nonsingular.

maturity. The date at which an obligation, such as the *principal* of a *bond* or a *note*, becomes due.

maturity value. The amount expected to be collected when a loan reaches *maturity*. Depending on the context, the amount may be *principal* or principal and *interest*.

MBO. *Management by objective.*

MD&A. *Management's discussion and analysis* section of the *annual report*.

measuring unit. *See attribute measured* for definition and contrast.

merchandise. *Finished goods* bought by a retailer or wholesaler for resale; contrast with finished goods of a manufacturing business.

merchandise costs. Costs incurred to sell a product, such as commissions and advertising.

merchandise turnover. *Inventory turnover* for merchandise. *See ratio.*

merchandising business. As opposed to a manufacturing or service business, one that purchases (rather than manufactures) *finished goods* for resale.

merger. The joining of two or more businesses into a single *economic entity*. *See holding company.*

minority interest. A *balance sheet account* on *consolidated statements* showing the *equity* in a less-than-100-percent-owned *subsidiary* company; equity allocable to those who are not part of the controlling (majority) interest; can be classified either as shareholders' equity or as a liability of *indeterminate term* on the consolidated balance sheet. The *income statement* must subtract the minority interest in the current period's income of the less-than-100-percent-owned subsidiary to arrive at consolidated *net income* for the period.

minority investment. A holding of less than 50 percent of the *voting stock* in another corporation; accounted for with the *equity method* when the investor owns sufficient shares that it can exercise "significant influence" and as *marketable securities* otherwise. *See mutual fund.*

minutes book. A record of all actions authorized at corporate *board of directors* or shareholders' meetings.

MIS. *Management information system.*

mix variance. One of the *manufacturing variances*. Many *standard cost* systems specify combinations of inputs—for example, labor of a certain skill and materials of a certain quality grade. Sometimes combinations of inputs used differ from those contemplated by the standard. The mix variance attempts to report the cost difference caused by those changes in the combination of inputs.

mixed cost. A *semifixed* or a *semivariable* cost.

Modified Accelerated Cost Recovery System (MACRS). Name used for the *Accelerated Cost Recovery System*, originally passed by Congress in 1981 and amended by Congress in 1986.

modified cash basis. The *cash basis of accounting* with long-term assets accounted for using the *accrual basis of accounting*. Most users of the term "cash basis of accounting" actually mean "modified cash basis."

monetary assets and liabilities. *See monetary items.*

monetary gain or loss. The firm's *gain* or *loss* in *general purchasing power* as a result of its holding *monetary assets* or liabilities during a period when the *general purchasing power of the dollar* changes; explicitly reported in *constant-dollar accounting*. During periods of *inflation*, holders of net monetary assets lose, and holders of net monetary liabilities gain, general purchasing power. During periods of *deflation*, holders of net monetary assets gain, and holders of net monetary liabilities lose, general purchasing power.

monetary items. Amounts fixed in terms of dollars by statute or contract; *cash, accounts receivable, accounts payable,* and *debt*. The distinction between monetary and nonmonetary items is important for *constant-dollar accounting* and for *foreign exchange gain or loss* computations. In the foreign exchange context, account amounts denominated in dollars are not monetary items, whereas amounts denominated in any other currency are monetary.

monetary-nonmonetary method. *Foreign currency translation* that translates all *monetary items* at the *current exchange rate* and translates all *nonmonetary items* at the *historical rate.*

money. A word seldom used with precision in accounting, at least in part because economists have not yet agreed on its definition. Economists use the term to refer to both a medium of exchange and a store of value. *See cash,* and *monetary items* and *make money.*

"Money" sometimes refers to debits and sometimes to credits; "making money" sometimes means earning accounting income and sometimes avoiding a cost, not reported in accounting, so careful writing about accounting avoids the word.

Focus on the following four sets of questions and see how much difficulty you have in answering the questions associated with **3** and **4**. Assume I start with $10 in cash.

1. I took a cab and it cost $10; I spent money. Did the cabbie earn money? If so, how much?

2. I asked Jerry to give me a ride and he did, so I didn't spend $10. Did I earn money? If so, how much?

3. I decided to walk, so I didn't spend $10. Did I earn money? If so, how much?

4. I canceled the trip, so I didn't spend $10. Did I earn money? If so, how much?

Now, you can better appreciate why careful writers avoid using the word.

Consider a different set of issues concerning the phrase, "*making money.*" Lay terminology uses this to mean "earning *income*" whether, as a result, the firm increased its *cash* balances or other *net assets*. The user does not typically mean that the firm has increased cash equal to the amount of net income, although the unaware listeners often think the phrase means this. Given that usage equates "*making money*" with "earning income," in this sense "money" has a credit balance not a debit balance. Since cash typically has a debit balance, the phrase "*making money*" is even more troublesome. Consider the following language from the U.S. statutes on forfeitures required of some who commit illegal acts: "the

amount of money acquired through illegal transactions." Does the law mean the cash left over after the lawbreaker has completed the illegal transactions the income earned from the transactions or something else? Sometimes "making money" means avoiding a cost, not recognized in financial accounting.

money purchase plan. A *pension plan* in which the employer contributes a specified amount of cash each year to each employee's pension fund; sometimes called a *defined-contribution plan*; contrast with *defined-benefit plan.* The plan does not specify the benefits ultimately received by the employee, since these benefits depend on the rate of return on the cash invested. As of the mid-1990s, most corporate pension plans were defined-benefit plans because both the law and *generally accepted accounting principles* for pensions made defined-benefit plans more attractive than money purchase plans. *ERISA* makes money purchase plans relatively more attractive than they had been. We expect the relative number of money purchase plans to continue to increase.

mortality table. Data of life expectancies or probabilities of death for persons of specified age and sex.

mortgage. A claim given by the borrower (mortgagor) to the lender (mortgagee) against the borrower's property in return for a loan.

moving average. An *average* computed on observations over time. As a new observation becomes available, analysts drop the oldest one so that they always compute the average for the same number of observations and use only the most recent ones.

moving average method. *Weighted-average inventory method.*

multiple-step. Said of an *income statement* that shows various subtotals of *expenses* and *losses* subtracted from *revenues* to show intermediate items such as *operating income*, income of the enterprise (operating income plus *interest* income), income to investors (income of the enterprise less *income taxes*), net income to shareholders (income to investors less interest charges), and income retained (net income to shareholders less dividends). *See entity theory.*

municipal bond. A *bond* issued by a village, town, or city. *Interest* on such bonds is generally exempt from federal *income taxes* and from some state income taxes. Because bonds issued by state and county governments often have these characteristics, terminology often calls such bonds "municipals" as well. These are also sometimes called "tax-exempts."

mutual fund. An investment company that issues its own stock to the public and uses the proceeds to invest in securities of other companies. A mutual fund usually owns less than 5 or 10 percent of the stock of any one company and accounts for its investments using current *market values*. Contrast with *holding company.*

mutually exclusive (investment) projects. Competing investment projects in which accepting one project eliminates the possibility of undertaking the remaining projects.

N

NAARS. *National Automated Accounting Research System.*

NASDAQ (National Association of Securities Dealers Automated Quotation System). A computerized system to provide brokers and dealers with price quotations for securities traded *over the counter* as well as for some *NYSE* securities.

National Association of Accountants (NAA). Former name for the *Institute of Management Accountants (IMA).*

National Automated Accounting Research System (NAARS). A computer-based information-retrieval system containing, among other things, the complete text of most public corporate annual reports and *Forms 10-K.* Users can access the system through the *AICPA.*

natural business year. A 12-month period chosen as the reporting period so that the end of the period coincides with a low point in activity or inventories. *See ratio* for a discussion of analyses of financial statements of companies using a natural business year.

natural classification. *Income statement* reporting form that classifies *expenses* by nature of items acquired, that is, materials, wages, salaries, insurance, and taxes, as well as depreciation. Contrast with *functional classification.*

natural resources. Timberland, oil and gas wells, ore deposits, and other products of nature that have economic value. Terminology uses the term *depletion* to refer to the process of *amortizing* the cost of natural resources. Natural resources are "nonrenewable" (for example, oil, coal, gas, ore deposits) or "renewable" (timberland, sod fields); terminology often calls the former "wasting assets." *See also reserve recognition accounting* and *percentage depletion.*

negative confirmation. *See confirmation.*

negative goodwill. *See goodwill.* When a firm acquires another company, and the *fair market value* of the *net assets* acquired exceeds the purchase price, *APB*

Opinion No. 16 requires that the acquiring company reduce the valuation of noncurrent assets (except *investments* in *marketable securities*) until the purchase price equals the adjusted valuation of the fair market value of net assets acquired. If, after the acquiring company reduces the valuation of noncurrent assets to zero, the valuation of the remaining net assets acquired still exceeds the purchase price, then the difference appears as a credit balance on the balance sheet as negative goodwill. For negative goodwill to exist, someone must be willing to sell a company for less than the fair market value of net current assets and marketable securities. Because such bargain purchases are rare, one seldom sees negative goodwill in the financial statements. When it does appear, it generally signals unrecorded obligations, such as a contingency related to a pending lawsuit.

negotiable. Legally capable of being transferred by *endorsement.* Usually said of *checks* and *notes* and sometimes of *stocks* and *bearer bonds.*

negotiated transfer price. A *transfer price* set jointly by the buying and the selling divisions.

net. Reduced by all relevant deductions.

net assets. Total *assets* minus total *liabilities*; equals the amount of *owners' equity.* Often, we find it useful to split the balance sheet into two parts: owners' equity and all the rest. The "rest" is total assets less total liabilities. For example, consider one definition of *revenue*: the increase in owners' equity accompanying the net assets increase caused by selling goods or rendering services. One could use an alternative, more cumbersome way to say the same thing: the increase in owners' equity accompanying the

assets increase or the liabilities decrease, or both, caused by selling goods or rendering services. Consider the definition of *goodwill*: the excess of purchase price over the fair market value of identifiable net assets acquired in a purchase transaction. Without the phrase "net assets," the definition might be as follows: the excess of purchase price over the fair market value of identifiable assets reduced by the fair market value of identifiable liabilities acquired in a purchase transaction.

net bank position. From a firm's point of view, *cash* in a specific bank less *loans* payable to that bank.

net book value. *Book value.*

net current asset value (per share). *Working capital* divided by the number of common shares outstanding. Some analysts think that when a common share trades in the market for an amount less than net current asset value, the shares are undervalued and investors should purchase them. We find this view naive because it ignores, generally, the efficiency of capital markets and, specifically, unrecorded obligations, such as for executory contracts and contingencies, not currently reported as *liabilities* in the *balance sheet* under *GAAP.*

net current assets.

Working capital = Current assets − Current liabilities

net income. The excess of all *revenues* and *gains* for a period over all *expenses* and *losses* of the period. The FASB is proposing to discontinue use of this term and substitute *earnings. See comprehensive income.*

net loss. The excess of all *expenses* and *losses* for a period over all *revenues* and *gains* of the period; negative *net income.*

net markup. In the context of *retail inventory methods, markups* less markup cancellations; a figure that usually ignores *markdowns* and markdown cancellations.

net of tax method. A nonsanctioned method for dealing with the problem of *income tax allocation*; described in *APB Opinion No. 11.* The method subtracts deferred tax items from specific *asset* amounts rather than showing them as a deferred credit or *liability.*

net of tax reporting. Reporting, such as for *income from discontinued operations, extraordinary items,* and *prior-period adjustments,* in which the firm adjusts the amounts presented in the *financial statements* for all income tax effects. For example, if an extraordinary loss amounted to $10,000, and the marginal tax rate was 40 percent, then the extraordinary item would appear "net of taxes" as a $6,000 loss. Hence, not all of a firm's income taxes necessarily appear on one line of the income statement. The reporting allocates the total taxes among *income from continuing operations, income from discontinued operations, extraordinary items,* cumulative effects of *accounting changes,* and *prior-period adjustments.*

net operating profit. *Income from continuing operations.*

net present value. Discounted or *present value* of all cash inflows and outflows of a project or of an *investment* at a given *discount rate.*

net price method (of recording purchase or sales discounts). Method that records a *purchase* (or *sale*) at its *invoice* price less all *discounts* made available, under the assumption that the firm will take nearly all discounts offered. The purchaser debits, to an *expense* account, discounts lapsed through failure to pay promptly. For purchases, management usually prefers to know about the amount of discounts lost because of inefficient operations, not the amounts taken, so that most managers prefer the net price method to the *gross price method.*

net realizable (sales) value. Current selling price less reasonable costs to complete production and to sell the item. Also, a method for *allocating joint costs* in proportion to *realizable values* of the joint products. For example, joint products A and B together cost $100; A sells for $60, whereas B sells for $90. Then a firm would allocate to A ($60/$150) × $100 = .40 × $100 = $40 of cost and allocate to B ($90/$150) × $100 = $60 of cost.

net sales. Sales (at gross invoice amount) less *returns, allowances,* freight paid for customers, and *discounts* taken.

net working capital. *Working capital;* the term "net" is redundant in accounting. Financial analysts sometimes mean *current assets* when they speak of working capital, so for them the "net" is not redundant.

net worth. A misleading term with the same meaning as *owners' equity.* Avoid using this term; accounting valuations at historical cost do not show economic worth.

network analysis. A project planning and scheduling method, usually displayed in a diagram, that enables management to identify the interrelated sequences that it must accomplish to complete the project.

new product development time. The period between a firm's first consideration of a product and delivery of it to the customer.

New York Stock Exchange (NYSE). A public market in which those who own seats (a seat is the right to participate) trade various corporate *securities*.

next-in, first-out. *See NIFO.*

NIFO (next-in, first-out). A *cost flow assumption*, one not allowed by GAAP. In making decisions, many managers consider *replacement costs* (rather than *historical costs*) and refer to them as NIFO costs.

no par. Said of *shares* without a *par value*.

nominal accounts. *Temporary accounts*, such as *revenue* and *expense* accounts; contrast with *balance sheet accounts*. The firm *closes* all nominal accounts at the end of each *accounting period*.

nominal amount (value). An amount stated in dollars, in contrast to an amount stated in *constant dollars*. Contrast with *real amount (value)*.

nominal dollars. The measuring unit giving no consideration to differences in the *general purchasing power of the dollar* over time. The face amount of currency or coin, a *bond*, an *invoice*, or a *receivable* is a nominal-dollar amount. When the analyst adjusts that amount for changes in *general purchasing power*, it becomes a *constant-dollar* amount.

nominal interest rate. A rate specified on a *debt* instrument; usually differs from the market or *effective rate*; also, a rate of *interest* quoted for a year. If the interest compounds more often than annually, then the *effective interest rate* exceeds the nominal rate.

noncancelable. *See lease.*

nonconsolidated subsidiary. An *intercorporate investment* in which the parent owns more than 50 percent of the shares of the *subsidiary* but accounts for the investment with the *cost method*.

noncontributory. Said of a *pension plan* in which only the employer makes payments to a pension *fund*. Contrast with *contributory*.

noncontrollable cost. A cost that a particular manager cannot *control*.

noncurrent. Of a *liability*, due in more than one year (or more than one *operating cycle*); of an *asset*, the firm will enjoy the future benefit in more than one year (or more than one operating cycle).

nonexpendable fund. A governmental fund whose *principal*, and sometimes earnings, the entity cannot spend.

noninterest-bearing note. A *note* that does not specify explicit interest. The *face value* of such a note will exceed its *present value* at any time before *maturity* value so long as *interest rates* are positive. *APB Opinion No. 21* requires that firms report the present value, not face value, of long-term noninterest-bearing notes as the *asset* or *liability* amount in financial statements. For this purpose, the firm uses the *historical interest rate. See interest, imputed.*

nonmanufacturing costs. All *costs* incurred other than those necessary to produce goods. Typically, only manufacturing firms use this designation.

nonmonetary items. All items that are not monetary. *See monetary items.*

nonoperating. In the *income statement* context, said of *revenues* and *expenses* arising from *transactions* incidental to the company's main line(s) of business; in the *statement of cash flows* context, said of all financing and investing sources or uses of cash in contrast to cash provided by operations. *See operations.*

nonprofit corporation. An incorporated *entity*, such as a hospital, with owners who do not share in the earnings. It usually emphasizes providing services rather than maximizing income.

nonrecurring. Said of an event that is not expected to happen often for a given firm. *APB Opinion No. 30* requires firms to disclose separately the effects of such events as part of *ordinary* items unless the event is also unusual. *See extraordinary* item.

nonvalue-added activity. An activity that causes costs without increasing a product's or service's value to the customer.

normal cost. Former name for *service cost* in accounting for pensions and other postemployment benefits.

normal costing. Method of charging costs to products using actual *direct materials*, actual *direct labor*, and predetermined *factory overhead* rates.

normal costing system. *Costing* based on *actual material* and *labor* costs but using *predetermined overhead* rates per unit of some *activity* basis (such as *direct labor hours* or machine hours) to apply overhead to production. Management decides the rate to charge to production for overhead at the start of the period. At the end of the period the accounting multiplies this rate by the actual number of units of the base activity (such as actual direct labor hours worked or actual machine hours used during the period) to apply overhead to production.

normal spoilage. Costs incurred because of ordinary amounts of spoilage. Accounting prorates such costs to units produced as *product costs.* Contrast with *abnormal spoilage.*

normal standard cost, normal standards. The *cost* a firm expects to incur under reasonably efficient operating conditions with adequate provision for an average amount of rework, spoilage, and the like.

normal volume. The level of production that will, over a time span, usually one year, satisfy purchasers' demands and provide for reasonable *inventory* levels.

note. An unconditional written promise by the maker (borrower) to pay a certain amount on demand or at a certain future time.

note receivable discounted. A *note* assigned by the holder to another. The new holder of the note typically pays the old holder an amount less than the *face value* of the note, hence the word "discounted." If the old holder assigns the note to the new holder with recourse, the old holder has a *contingent liability* until the maker of the note pays the debt. *See factoring.*

notes. Some use this word instead of *footnotes* when referring to the detailed information included by management as an integral part of the *financial statements* and covered by the *auditor's report.*

NOW (negotiable order of withdrawal) account. Negotiable order of withdrawal. A *savings account* whose owner can draw an order to pay, much like a *check* but technically not a check, and give it to others, who can redeem the order at the savings institution.

number of days sales in inventory (or receivables). Days of average inventory on hand (or average collection period for receivables). *See ratio.*

NV (naamloze vennootschap). Netherlands: a public limited liability company.

NYSE. *New York Stock Exchange.*

O

OASDI. *Old Age, Survivors, Disability, and Insurance.*

objective. *See reporting objectives* and *objectivity.*

objective function. In *linear programming*, the name of the profit (or cost) criterion the analyst wants to maximize (or minimize).

objectivity. The reporting policy implying that the firm will not give formal recognition to an event in financial statements until the firm can measure the magnitude of the events with reasonable accuracy and check that amount with independent verification.

obsolescence. An asset's *market value* decline caused by improved alternatives becoming available that will be more *cost-effective.* The decline in market value does not relate to physical changes in the asset itself. For example, computers become obsolete long before they wear out. *See partial obsolescence.*

Occupational Safety and Health Act. *OSHA.*

off-balance-sheet financing. A description often used for an obligation that meets all the tests to be classified a liability except that the obligation arises from an *executory contract* and, hence, is not a *liability.* Consider the following example: Miller Corporation desires to acquire land costing $25 million, on which it will build a shopping center. It could borrow the $25 million from its bank, paying interest at 12 percent, and buy the land outright from the seller. If so, both an asset and a liability will appear on the balance sheet. Instead, it borrows $5 million and purchases for $5 million from the seller an *option* to buy the land from the seller at any time within the next six years for a price of $20 million. The option costs Miller Corporation $5 million immediately and provides for continuing "option" payments of $2.4 million per year, which precisely equal Miller Corporation's borrowing rate multiplied by the remaining purchase price of the land: $2.4 million $= .12 \times$ $20 million. Although Miller Corporation need not continue payments and can let the option lapse at any time, it also has an obligation to begin developing on the site immediately. Because Miller Corporation has invested a substantial sum in the option, will invest more, and will begin immediately developing the land, Miller Corporation will almost certainly exercise its option before expiration. The seller of the land can take the option contract to the bank and borrow $20 million, paying interest at Miller Corporation's borrowing rate, 12 percent per year. The continuing option payments from Miller Corporation will be sufficient to enable the seller to make its payments to the bank. *Generally accepted accounting principles* view Miller Corporation as having acquired an option for $5 million rather than having acquired land costing $25 million in return for $25 million of debt. The firm will likely be able to structure this transaction so that it need not recognize debt on the balance sheet until it borrows more funds to exercise the option.

The *FASB* has curtailed the use of such financings with *FIN 46. See also variable interest entity.*

off-balance-sheet risk. A contract that exposes an entity to the possibility of loss but that does not appear in the financial statements. For example, a *forward-exchange contract* generally does not appear on the balance sheet because it is an *executory contract*. The contract can reduce or increase the entity's exposure to foreign-exchange risk (the chance of loss due to unfavorable changes in the foreign-exchange rate). It can also expose the entity to credit risk (the chance of loss that occurs when the *counterparty* to the contract cannot fulfill the contract terms). *SFAS No. 105* requires entities to describe contracts with off-balance-sheet risk.

OHG (Offene Handelsgesellschaft). Germany: a general *partnership*. The partners have unlimited *liability*.

Old Age, Survivors, Disability, and Insurance, or OASDI. The technical name for Social Security under the Federal Insurance Contributions Act (*FICA*).

on consignment. Said of goods delivered by the owner (the consignor) to another (the consignee) to be sold by the consignee. On delivery of the goods from the consignor to the consignee, the consignor can, but need not, make an entry transferring the goods at cost from Finished Goods Inventory to another inventory account, such as Goods out on Consignment. The consignor recognizes revenue only when the consignee has sold the goods to customers. Under such an arrangement, the owner of the goods bears the inventory holding costs until the ultimate seller (consignee) sells them. The owner also bears the risk that the items will never sell to final customers, but manufacturers or distributors who provide generous return options to their customers can achieve this aspect of consignment sales in an outright sale. The consignment protects the consignor from the consignee's bankruptcy

because the arrangement entitles the owner either to the return of the property or to payment of a specified amount. The goods are assets of the consignor. Such arrangements provide the consignor with better protection than an outright sale on account to the consignee in bankruptcy. In event of bankruptcy, the ordinary seller, holding an account receivable, has no special claim to the return of the goods, whereas a consignor can reclaim the goods without going through bankruptcy proceedings, from which the consignor might recover only a fraction of the amounts owed to it.

on (open) account. Said of a *purchase* (or *sale*) when the seller expects payment sometime after delivery and the purchaser does not give a *note* evidencing the *debt*. The purchaser has generally signed an agreement sometime in the past promising to pay for such purchases according to an agreed time schedule. When the firm sells (purchases) on open account, it *debits* (*credits*) *Accounts Receivable* (*Payable*).

one-line consolidation. Said of an *intercorporate investment* accounted for with the *equity method*. With this method, the *income* and *balance sheet* total *assets* and *equities* amounts are identical to those that would appear if the parent consolidated the investee firm, even though the income from the investment appears on a single line of the income statement and the net investment appears on a single line in the assets section of the balance sheet.

one-write system. A system of bookkeeping that produces several records, including original documents, in one operation by the use of reproductive paper and equipment that provides for the proper alignment of the documents.

on-time performance. The firm delivers the product or service at the time scheduled for delivery.

open account. Any *account* with a nonzero *debit* or *credit balance*. *See on (open) account.*

operating. An adjective used to refer to *revenue* and *expense* items relating to the company's main line(s) of business. *See operations.*

operating accounts. *Revenue, expense,* and *production cost accounts*. Contrast with *balance sheet accounts.*

operating activities. For purposes of the *statement of cash flows*, all *transactions* and *events* that are neither *financing activities* nor *investing activities*. *See operations.*

operating budget. A formal *budget* for the *operating cycle* or for a year.

operating cash flow. *Cash flow from operations.* Financial statement analysts sometimes use this term to mean

> *Cash flow from operations −*
> *Capital expenditures − Dividends.*

This usage leads to such ambiguity that the reader should always confirm the definition that the writer uses before drawing inferences from the reported data.

operating cycle. *Earnings cycle.*

operating expenses. *Expenses* incurred in the course of *ordinary* activities of an *entity*; frequently, a classification including only *selling, general,* and *administrative expenses*, thereby excluding *cost of goods sold, interest,* and *income tax* expenses. *See operations.*

operating lease. A *lease* accounted for by the *lessee* without showing an *asset* for the lease rights (*leasehold*) or a *liability* for the lease payment obligations. The lessee reports only rental payments during the period, as *expenses* of the period. The asset remains on the lessor's *books*, where rental collections appear as *revenues.* Contrast with *capital lease.*

operating leverage. Usually said of a firm with a large proportion of *fixed costs* in its *total costs*. Consider a book publisher or a railroad: such a firm has large costs to produce the first unit of service; then, the *incremental costs* of producing another book or transporting another freight car are much less than the *average cost*, so the *gross margin* on the sale of the subsequent units is relatively large. Contrast this situation with that, for example, of a grocery store, where the *contribution margin* equals less than 5 percent of the selling price. For firms with equal profitability, however defined, we say that the one with the larger percentage increase in income from a given percentage increase in dollar sales has the larger operating leverage. *See leverage* for contrast of this term with "financial leverage." *See cost terminology* for definitions of terms involving the word "cost."

operating margin. *Revenues* from *sales* minus *cost of goods sold* and *operating expenses.*

operating margin based on current costs. *Revenues* from *sales* minus *current cost* of goods sold; a measure of operating efficiency that does not depend on the *cost flow assumption* for *inventory*; sometimes called "current (gross) margin." *See inventory profit* for illustrative computations.

operating ratio. *See ratio.*

operational control. *See control system.*

operational measures of time. Indicators of the speed and reliability with which organizations supply products and services to customers. Companies generally use two operational measures of time: *customer response time* and *on-time performance.*

operations. A word not precisely defined in *accounting.* Generally, analysts distinguish operating activities (producing and selling *goods* or *services*) from financing activities (raising funds) and *investing activities.* Acquiring goods on account and then paying for them one month later, though generally classified as an operating activity, has the characteristics of a financing activity. Or consider the transaction of selling plant assets for a price in excess of book value. On the *income statement,* the gain appears as part of income from operations ("continuing operations" or "discontinued" operations, depending on the circumstances), but the *statement of cash flows* reports all the funds received below the Cash from Operations section as a nonoperating source of cash, "disposition of noncurrent assets." In income tax accounting, an "operating loss" results whenever deductions exceed taxable revenues.

opinion. The *auditor's report* containing an attestation or lack thereof; also, *APB Opinion.*

opinion paragraph. Section of *auditor's report,* generally following the *scope paragraph* and giving the auditor's conclusion that the *financial statements* are (rarely, are not) in accordance with *GAAP* and present fairly the *financial position,* changes in financial position, and the results of *operations.*

opportunity cost. The *present value* of the *income* (or *costs)* that a firm could earn (or save) from using an *asset* in its best alternative use to the one under consideration.

opportunity cost of capital. *Cost of capital.*

option. The legal right to buy or sell something during a specified period at a specified price, called the *exercise* price. If the right exists during a specified time interval, it is known as an "American option." If it exists for only one specific day, it is known as a "European option." Do not confuse employee stock options with *put* and *call* options, traded in various public markets.

ordinary annuity. An *annuity in arrears.*

ordinary income. For income tax purposes, reportable *income* not qualifying as *capital gains.*

organization costs. The *costs* incurred in planning and establishing an *entity;* example of an *intangible* asset. The firm must treat these costs as *expenses* of the period, even though the *expenditures* clearly provide future benefits and meet the test to be *assets.*

organization goals. Broad objectives for an organization established by management.

original cost. *Acquisition cost;* in public utility accounting, the acquisition cost of the *entity* first devoting the *asset* to public use. *See aboriginal cost.*

original entry. Entry in a *journal.*

OSHA (Occupational Safety and Health Act). The federal law that governs working conditions in commerce and industry.

other comprehensive income. According to the FASB, *comprehensive income* items that are not themselves part of earnings. *See comprehensive income.* To define comprehensive income does not convey its essence. To understand comprehensive income, you need to understand how it differs from *earnings* (or *net income),* the concept measured in the *earnings (income) statement*. The term *earnings* (or *net income*) refers to the sum of all components of comprehensive income *minus* the components of other comprehensive income.

outlay. The amount of an *expenditure*.

outlier. Said of an observation (or data point) that appears to differ significantly in some regard from other observations (or data points) of supposedly the same phenomenon; in a *regression analysis*, often used to describe an observation that falls far from the fitted regression equation (in two dimensions, line).

out-of-pocket. Said of an *expenditure* usually paid for with cash; an *incremental* cost.

out-of-stock cost. The estimated decrease in future *profit* as a result of losing customers because a firm has insufficient quantities of *inventory* currently on hand to meet customers' demands.

output. Physical quantity or monetary measurement of *goods* and *services* produced.

outside director. A corporate board of directors member who is not a company officer and does not participate in the corporation's day-to-day management.

outstanding. Unpaid or uncollected; when said of *stock*, refers to the shares issued less *treasury stock*; when said of *checks*, refers to a check issued that did not clear the *drawer's* bank prior to the *bank statement* date.

over-and-short. Title for an *expense account* used to account for small differences between book balances of cash and actual cash and vouchers or receipts in *petty cash* or *change funds*.

overapplied (overabsorbed) overhead. Costs applied, or *charged*, to product

and exceeding actual *overhead costs* during the period; a *credit balance* in an overhead account after overhead is assigned to product.

overdraft. A *check* written on a checking account that contains funds less than the amount of the check.

overhead costs. Any *cost* not directly associated with the production or sale of identifiable goods and services; sometimes called "burden" or "indirect costs" and, in the UK, "oncosts"; frequently limited to manufacturing overhead. *See central corporate expenses* and *manufacturing overhead*.

overhead rate. Standard, or other predetermined rate, at which a firm applies *overhead costs* to products or to services.

over-the-counter. Said of a *security* traded in a negotiated transaction, as on *NASDAQ*, rather than in an auctioned one on an organized stock exchange, such as the *New York Stock Exchange*.

owners' equity. *Proprietorship; assets* minus *liabilities; paid-in capital* plus *retained earnings* of a corporation; partners' capital accounts in a *partnership*; owner's capital account in a *sole proprietorship*.

P

paid-in capital. Sum of balances in *capital stock* and *capital contributed in excess of par (or stated) value* accounts; same as *contributed capital* (minus *donated capital*). Some use the term to mean only *capital contributed in excess of par (or stated value)*.

paid-in surplus. *See surplus*.

P&L. Profit-and-loss statement; *income statement*.

paper profit. A *gain* not yet realized through a *transaction*; an *unrealized holding gain*.

par. *See at par* and *face amount.*

par value. *Face amount* of a *security.*

par value method. In accounting for *treasury stock*, method that *debits* a common stock account with the *par value* of the shares required and allocates the remaining debits between the *Additional Paid-in Capital* and *Retained Earnings* accounts. Contrast with *cost method.*

parent company. Company owning more than 50 percent of the voting shares of another company, called the *subsidiary.*

Pareto chart. A graph of a skewed statistical distribution. In many business settings, a relatively small percentage of the potential population causes a relatively large percentage of the business activity. For example, some businesses find that the top 20 percent of the customers buy 80 percent of the goods sold. Or, the top 10 percent of products account for 60 percent of the revenues or 70 percent of the profits. The statistical distribution known as the Pareto distribution has this property of skewness, so a graph of a phenomenon with such skewness has come to be known as a Pareto chart, even if the underlying data do not actually well fit the Pareto distribution. Practitioners of *total quality management* find that in many businesses, a small number of processes account for a large fraction of the quality problems, so they advocate charting potential problems and actual occurrences of problems to identify the relatively small number of sources of trouble. They call such a chart a "Pareto chart."

partial obsolescence. One cause of decline in *market value* of an *asset.* As technology improves, the economic value of existing *assets* declines. In many cases, however, it will not pay a firm to replace the existing asset with a new one, even though it would acquire the new type rather than the old if it did make a new acquisition currently. In these cases, the accountant should theoretically recognize a loss from partial obsolescence from the firm's owning an old, out-of-date asset, but *GAAP* do not permit recognition of partial obsolescence until the sum of future cash flows from the asset total less than book value; *see impairment.* The firm will carry the old asset at *cost* less *accumulated depreciation* until the firm retires it from service so long as the *undiscounted* future *cash flows* from the asset exceed its book value. Thus management that uses an asset subject to partial obsolescence reports results inferior to those reported by a similar management that uses a new asset. *See obsolescence.*

partially executory contract. *Executory contract* in which one or both parties have done something other than merely promise.

partially funded. Said of a *pension plan* in which the firm has not funded all earned benefits. *See funded* for funding requirements.

partially vested. Said of a *pension plan* in which not all employee benefits have *vested. See graded vesting.*

participating dividend. *Dividend* paid to preferred shareholders in addition to the minimum preferred dividends when the *preferred shares* contract provides for such sharing in earnings. Usually the contract specifies that dividends on *common shares* must reach a specified level before the preferred shares receive the participating dividend.

participating preferred shares. *Preferred shares* with rights to *participating dividends.*

participative budgeting. Using input from lower- and middle-management employees in setting goals.

partner's drawing. A payment made to a partner and debited against his or her share of income or capital. The name of a *temporary account*, closed to the partner's capital account, to record the debits when the partner receives such payments.

partnership. Contractual arrangement between individuals to share resources and operations in a jointly run business. *See general* and *limited partner* and *Uniform Partnership Act.*

patent. A right granted for up to 20 years by the federal government to exclude others from manufacturing, using, or selling a claimed design, product, or plant (e.g., a new breed of rose) or from using a claimed process or method of manufacture; an *asset* if the firm acquires it by purchase. If the firm develops it internally, current *GAAP* require the firm to *expense* the development costs when incurred.

payable. Unpaid but not necessarily due or past due.

pay-as-you-go. Said of an *income tax* scheme in which the taxpayer makes periodic payments of income taxes during the period when it earns the income to be taxed; in contrast to a scheme in which the taxpayer owes no payments until the end of, or after, the period when it earned the income being taxed (called PAYE—pay-as-you-earn—in the UK). The phrase is sometimes used to describe an *unfunded pension plan*, or retirement benefit plan, in which the firm makes payments to pension plan beneficiaries from general corporate funds, not from cash previously contributed to a fund. Under this method, the firm debits expense as it makes payments, not as it

incurs the obligations. This is not acceptable as a method of accounting for pension plans, under *SFAS No. 87*, or as a method of *funding*, under *ERISA.*

payback period. Amount of time that must elapse before the cash inflows from a project equal the cash outflows.

payback reciprocal. One divided by the *payback period.* This number approximates the *internal rate of return* on a project when the project life exceeds twice the payback period and the cash inflows are identical in every period after the initial period.

PAYE (pay-as-you-earn). *See pay-as-you-go* for contrast.

payee. The person or entity who receives a cash payment or who will receive the stated amount of cash on a *check. See draft.*

payout ratio. *Common stock dividends* declared for a year divided by net *income* to common stock for the year; a term used by financial analysts. Contrast with *dividend yield.*

payroll taxes. Taxes levied because the taxpayer pays salaries or wages; for example, *FICA* and unemployment compensation insurance taxes. Typically, the employer pays a portion and withholds part of the employee's wages.

PCAOB. *Public Company Accounting Oversight Board.*

P/E ratio. *Price-earnings ratio.*

Pension Benefit Guarantee Corporation (PBGC). A federal corporation established under *ERISA* to guarantee basic pension benefits in covered pension plans by administering terminated pension plans and placing *liens* on corporate assets for certain unfunded pension liabilities.

pension fund. *Fund*, the assets of which the trustee will pay to retired ex-employees, usually as a *life annuity*; generally held by an independent trustee and thus not an *asset* of the employer.

pension plan. Details or provisions of employer's contract with employees for paying retirement *annuities* or other benefits. *See funded, vested, service cost, prior service cost, money purchase plan,* and *defined-benefit plan.*

per books. An expression used to refer to the *book value* of an item at a specific time.

percent. Any number, expressed as a decimal, multiplied by 100.

percentage depletion (allowance). Deductible *expense* allowed in some cases by the federal *income tax* regulations; computed as a percentage of gross income from a *natural resource* independent of the unamortized cost of the *asset*. Because the amount of the total deductions for tax purposes usually exceeds the cost of the asset being *depleted*, many people think the deduction is an unfair tax advantage or *loophole.*

percentage-of-completion method. Recognizing *revenues* and *expenses* on a job, order, or contract (1) in proportion to the *costs* incurred for the period divided by total costs expected to be incurred for the job or order ("cost to cost") or (2) in proportion to engineers' or architects' estimates of the incremental degree of completion of the job, order, or contract during the period. Contrast with *completed contract method.*

percentage statement. A statement containing, in addition to (or instead of) dollar amounts, ratios of dollar amounts to some base. In a percentage

income statement, the base is usually either *net sales* or total *revenues*, and in a percentage *balance sheet*, the base is usually total *assets.*

period. *Accounting period.*

period cost. An inferior term for *period expense.*

period expense (charge). *Expenditure*, usually based on the passage of time, charged to operations of the accounting period rather than *capitalized* as an asset. Contrast with *product cost.*

periodic cash flows. *Cash flows* that occur during the life of an investment project. Often include *receipts* from *sales*, *expenditures* for *fixed* and *variable production costs*, and savings of *fixed* and *variable* production costs, to name a few. They do not include noncash items, such as *financial accounting depreciation charges* or *allocated* items of *overhead* not requiring *differential* cash expenditures.

periodic inventory. In recording *inventory*, a method that uses data on beginning inventory, additions to inventories, and ending inventory to find the cost of withdrawals from inventory. Contrast with *perpetual inventory.*

periodic procedures. The process of making *adjusting entries* and *closing entries* and preparing the *financial statements*, usually by use of *trial balances* and *work sheets.*

permanent account. An account that appears on the *balance sheet*. Contrast with *temporary account.*

permanent difference. Difference between reported income and taxable income that will never reverse and, hence, requires no entry in the *deferred income tax (liability)* account; for example, nontaxable state and municipal *bond* interest that will appear on the financial statements. Contrast with *temporary difference*. *See deferred income tax liability.*

permanent file. The file of working papers that are prepared by a public accountant and that contain the information required for reference in successive professional engagements for a particular organization, as distinguished from working papers applicable only to a particular engagement.

perpetual annuity. *Perpetuity.*

perpetual inventory. *Inventory* quantity and amount records that the firm changes and makes current with each physical addition to or withdrawal from the stock of goods; an inventory so recorded. The records will show the physical quantities and, frequently, the dollar valuations that should be on hand at any time. Because the firm explicitly computes *cost of goods sold*, it can use the *inventory equation* to compute an amount for what *ending inventory* should be. It can then compare the computed amount of ending inventory with the actual amount of ending inventory as a *control* device to measure the amount of *shrinkages*. Contrast with *periodic inventory.*

perpetuity. An *annuity* whose payments continue forever. The *present value* of a perpetuity in *arrears* is *p/r* where *p* is the periodic payment and *r* is the *interest rate* per period. If a perpetuity promises $100 each year, in arrears, forever and the interest rate is 8 percent per year, then the perpetuity has a value of $1,250 = $100/.08.

perpetuity growth model. *See perpetuity.* A *perpetuity* whose cash flows grow at the rate *g* per period and thus has

present value of $1/(r - g)$. Some call this the "Gordon Growth Model" because Myron Gordon wrote about applications of this formula and its variants in the 1950s. John Burr Williams wrote about them in the 1930s.

personal account. *Drawing account.*

PERT (Program Evaluation and Review Technique). A method of *network analysis* in which the analyst makes three time estimates for each activity— the optimistic time, the most likely time, and the pessimistic time—and gives an expected completion date for the project within a probability range.

petty cash fund. Currency and coins maintained for expenditures that the firm makes with cash on hand.

physical units method. A method of allocating a *joint cost* to the *joint products* based on a physical measure of the joint products; for example, allocating the cost of a cow to sirloin steak and to hamburger, based on the weight of the meat. This method usually provides nonsensical (*see sterilized allocation*) results unless the physical units of the joint products tend to have the same value.

physical verification. *Verification*, by an *auditor*, performed by actually inspecting items in *inventory, plant assets*, and the like, in contrast to merely checking the written records. The auditor can use statistical sampling procedures.

planning and control process. General name for the management techniques comprising the setting of organizational goals and *strategic plans*, *capital budgeting, operations* budgeting, comparison of plans with actual results, performance evaluation and corrective action, and revisions of goals, plans, and budgets.

plant. *Plant assets.*

plant asset turnover. Number of dollars of *sales* generated per dollar of *plant assets*; equal to sales divided by average *plant assets*.

plant assets. *Assets* used in the revenue-production process. Plant assets include buildings, machinery, equipment, land, and natural resources. The phrase "property, plant, and equipment" (though often appearing on balance sheets) is therefore a redundancy. In this context, "plant" used alone means buildings.

plantwide allocation method. A method for *allocating overhead costs* to product. First, use one *cost pool* for the entire plant. Then, allocate all costs from that pool to products using a single overhead *allocation* rate, or one set of rates, for all the products of the plant, independent of the number of departments in the plant.

PLC (public limited company). U.K.: a publicly held *corporation.* Contrast with *Ltd.*

pledging. The borrower assigns *assets* as security or *collateral* for repayment of a loan.

pledging of receivables. The process of using expected collections on *accounts receivable* as *collateral* for a loan. The borrower remains responsible for collecting the receivable but promises to use the proceeds for repaying the debt.

plow back. To retain *assets* generated by earnings for continued investment in the business.

plug. Process for finding an unknown amount. For any *account*, Beginning balance + Additions − Deductions = Ending balance; if you know any three of the four items, you can find the fourth with simple arithmetic, called "plugging." In making a *journal entry*, often you know all *debits* and all but one of the *credits* (or vice versa). Because *double-entry* bookkeeping requires equal debits and credits, you can compute the unknown quantity by subtracting the sum of the known credits from the sum of all the debits (or vice versa), also called "plugging." Accountants often call the unknown the "plug." For example, in amortizing a *discount* on *bonds payable* with the *straight-line depreciation* method, *interest expense* is a plug: Interest expense = Interest payable + *Discount amortization.* *See trade-in transaction* for an example. The term sometimes has a bad connotation for accountants because plugging can occur in a slightly different context. During the process of preparing a *preclosing trial balance* (or *balance sheet*), often the sum of the debits does not equal the sum of the credits. Rather than find the error, some accountants are tempted to force equality by changing one of the amounts, with a plugged debit or credit to an account such as Other Expenses. No harm results from this procedure if the amount of the error is small compared with asset totals, since spending tens or hundreds of dollars in a bookkeeper's or accountant's time to find an error of a few dollars will not be *cost-effective.* Still, most accounting teachers rightly disallow this use of plugging because exercises and problems set for students provide enough information not to require it.

point of sale. The time, not the location, at which a *sale* occurs.

pooling-of-interests method. Accounting for a *business combination* by adding together the *book value* of the *assets* and *equities* of the combined firms; generally leads to a higher reported *net income* for the combined firms than results when the firm accounts for the business combination as a purchase because the *market values* of the merged assets generally exceed their book values. U.S. GAAP do not allow this method, although it previously did, so financial statements still reflect the effects of pooling accounting. Contrast with *purchase method*. Called *uniting-of-interests method* by the *IASB*.

population. The entire set of numbers or items from which the analyst samples or performs some other analysis.

positive confirmation. *See confirmation.*

post. To record entries in an *account* to a *ledger*, usually as transfers from a *journal*.

post-closing trial balance. *Trial balance* taken after the accountant has *closed* all *temporary accounts*.

post-statement events. Events that have *material* impact and that occur between the end of the *accounting period* and the formal publication of the *financial statements*. Even though the events occur after the end of the period being reported on, the firm must disclose such events in notes if the auditor is to give a *clean opinion*.

potentially dilutive. A *security* that its holder can convert into, or exchange for, common shares and thereby reduce reported *earnings per share*; *options, warrants, convertible bonds*, and *convertible preferred stock*.

PPB. *Program budgeting*. The second "P" stands for "plan."

practical capacity. Maximum level at which a plant or department can operate efficiently.

precision. The degree of accuracy for an estimate derived from a sampling process, usually expressed as a range of values around the estimate. The analyst could express a sample estimate in the following terms: "Based on the sample, we are 95 percent sure [confidence level] that the true population value is within the range of X to Y [precision]." *See confidence level.*

preclosing trial balance. *Trial balance* taken at the end of the period before *closing entries*; in this sense, an *adjusted trial balance*; sometimes taken before *adjusting entries* and then synonymous with *unadjusted trial balance*.

predatory prices. Setting prices below some measure of cost in an effort to drive out competitors with the hope of recouping losses later by charging monopoly prices. Illegal in the United States if the prices set are below long-run variable costs. We know of no empirical evidence that firms are successful at recoupment.

predetermined (factory) overhead rate. Rate used in applying *overhead costs* to products or departments developed at the start of a period. Compute the rate as estimated overhead cost divided by the estimated number of units of the overhead allocation base (or *denominator volume*) activity. *See normal costing.*

preemptive right. The privilege of a *shareholder* to maintain a proportionate share of ownership by purchasing a proportionate share of any new securities issues. Most state corporation laws allow corporations to pay shareholders to waive their preemptive rights or state that preemptive rights exist only if the *corporation charter* explicitly grants them. In practice, then, preemptive rights are the exception rather than the rule.

preference as to assets. The rights of *preferred shareholders* to receive certain payments before common shareholders receive payments in case the board dissolves the corporation.

preferred shares. *Capital stock* with a claim to *income* or *assets* after *bondholders* but before *common shares*. *Dividends* on preferred shares are *income distributions*, not *expenses*. *See cumulative preferred stock*.

premium. The excess of issue (or market) price over *par value*. For a different context, *see insurance*.

premium on capital stock. Alternative but inferior title for *capital contributed in excess of par (or stated) value*.

prepaid expense. An *expenditure* that leads to a *deferred charge* or *prepayment*. Strictly speaking, this is a contradiction in terms because an *expense* is a gone asset, and this title refers to past *expenditures*, such as for rent or insurance premiums, that still have future benefits and thus are *assets*. We try to avoid this term and use "prepayment" instead.

prepaid income. An inferior alternative title for *advances from customers*. Do not call an item *revenue* or *income* until the firm earns it by delivering goods or rendering services.

prepayments. *Deferred charges*; assets representing *expenditures* for future benefits. Rent and insurance premiums paid in advance are usually current prepayments.

present value. Value today (or at some specific date) of an amount or amounts to be paid or received later (or at other, different dates), discounted at some *interest* or *discount rate*; an amount that, if invested today at the specified rate, will grow to the amount to be paid or received in the future.

prevention costs. *Costs incurred* to prevent defects in the products or services they produce, including procurement inspection, processing control (inspection), design, quality training and machine inspection.

price. The quantity of one *good* or *service*, usually *cash*, asked in return for a unit of another good or service. *See fair value*.

price-earnings (P/E) ratio. At a given time, the market value of a company's *common share*, per share, divided by the *earnings per* common *share* for the past year. The analyst usually bases the denominator on *income from continuing operations* or, if the analyst thinks the current figure for that amount does not represent a usual situation—such as when the number is negative or, if positive, close to zero—on some estimate of the number. *See ratio*.

price index. A series of numbers, one for each period, that purports to represent some *average* of prices for a series of periods, relative to a base period.

price level. The number from a *price index* series for a given period or date.

price level–adjusted statements. *Financial statements* expressed in terms of dollars of uniform purchasing power. The statements restate *nonmonetary* items to reflect changes in general *price levels* since the time the firm acquired specific *assets* and incurred *liabilities*. The statements recognize a *gain* or *loss* on *monetary items* as the firm holds them over time periods when the general *price level changes*. Conventional financial statements show *historical costs* and ignore differences in purchasing power in different periods.

price variance. In accounting for *standard costs*, an amount equal to (Actual cost per unit − Standard cost per unit) × Actual quantity.

primary earnings per share (PEPS).
Net *income* to common shareholders
plus *interest* (net of tax effects) or
dividends paid on *common-stock
equivalents* divided by (weighted
average of common shares outstanding
plus the net increase in the number of
common shares that would become
outstanding if the holders of all
common stock equivalents were to
exchange them for common shares
with cash proceeds, if any, used to
retire common shares). As of 1997 and
SFAS No. 128, replaced with *basic
earnings per share.*

prime cost. Sum of *direct materials* plus
direct labor costs assigned to product.

prime rate. The loan rate charged by
commercial banks to their
creditworthy customers. Some
customers pay even less than the
prime rate and others, more. The
Federal Reserve Bulletin is the
authoritative source of information
about historical prime rates.

principal. An amount on which *interest*
accrues, either as *expense* (for the
borrower) or as *revenue* (for the lender);
the *face amount* of a *loan*; also, the
absent owner (principal) who hires the
manager (agent) in a "principal-agent"
relationship.

principle. *See generally accepted
accounting principles.*

prior-period adjustment. A *debit* or
credit that is made directly to *retained
earnings* (and that does not affect
income for the period) to adjust
earnings as calculated for prior
periods. Such adjustments are now
rare. Theory suggests that accounting
should correct for errors in accounting
estimates (such as the *depreciable life* or
salvage value of an asset) by adjusting
retained earnings so that statements for
future periods will show correct

amounts. But *GAAP* require that
corrections of such estimates flow
through current, and perhaps future,
*income statements. See accounting
changes* and *accounting errors.*

prior service cost. *Present value* at a
given time of a *pension plan's*
retroactive *benefits.* "Unrecognized
prior service cost" refers to that
portion of prior service cost not yet
debited to *expense. See actuarial accrued
liability* and *funded.* Contrast with
normal cost.

pro forma income. *See pro forma
statements.*

pro forma statements. Hypothetical
statements; financial statements as
they would appear if some event, such
as a *merger* or increased production
and sales, had occurred or were to
occur; sometimes spelled as one word,
"proforma." The phrase "pro forma
income" has come to disrepute, as
some companies have published pro
forma income statements showing
their good news, their recurring
income, and omitting the bad news, as
non-recurring. They have attempted to
focus the investment community on
their own presentation of this good
news, de-emphasizing GAAP net
income. The *SEC* and others have
attempted to make these disclosures
less misleading.

probable. In many of its definitions,
the *FASB* uses the term "probable."
*See, for example, asset, firm commitment,
liability.* A survey of practicing
accountants revealed that the average
of the probabilities that those surveyed
had in mind when they used the term
"probable" was 85 percent. Some
accountants think that any event
whose outcome is greater than
50 percent should be called "probable."
The FASB uses the phrase "more likely

than not" when it means greater than 50 percent.

proceeds. The *funds* received from the disposition of assets or from the issue of securities.

process costing. A method of *cost accounting* based on average costs (total cost divided by the *equivalent units* of work done in a period); typically used for assembly lines or for products that the firm produces in a series of steps that are more continuous than discrete.

product. *Goods* or *services* produced.

product cost. Any *manufacturing cost* that the firm can—or, in some contexts, should—debit to an *inventory* account. *See flow of costs*, for example. Contrast with *period expenses*.

product life cycle. Time span between initial concept (typically starting with research and development) of a good or service and the time when the firm ceases to support customers who have purchased the good or service.

production cost. *Manufacturing cost*.

production cost account. A *temporary account* for accumulating *manufacturing costs* during a period.

production department. A department producing salable *goods* or *services*; contrast with *service department*.

production method (depreciation). One form of *straight-line depreciation*. The firm assigns to the depreciable asset (e.g., a truck) a *depreciable life* measured not in elapsed time but in units of output (e.g., miles) or perhaps in units of time of expected use. Then the *depreciation* charge for a period is a portion of depreciable cost equal to a fraction computed as the actual output produced during the period divided by the expected total output to be produced over the life of the asset.

This method is sometimes called the "units-of-production (or output) method."

production method (revenue recognition). *Percentage-of-completion method* for recognizing *revenue*.

production volume variance. Standard fixed *overhead* rate per unit of normal *capacity* (or base activity) times (units of base activity budgeted or planned for a period minus actual units of base activity worked or assigned to product during the period); often called a "volume variance."

productive capacity. One *attribute measured* for *assets*. The *current cost* of *long-term assets* means the cost of reproducing the productive capacity (for example, the ability to manufacture one million units a year), not the cost of reproducing the actual physical assets currently used (*see reproduction cost*). *Replacement cost* of productive capacity will be the same as reproduction cost of assets only in the unusual case when no technological improvement in production processes has occurred and the relative prices of goods and services used in production have remained approximately the same as when the firm acquired the currently used goods and services.

product-level activities. Work that supports a particular product or service line. Examples include design work, supervision, and advertising that are specific to each type of product or service.

production cycle efficiency. Measures the efficiency of the production cycle by computing the ratio of the time spent processing a unit divided by the *production cycle time*. The higher the percentage, the less the time and costs spent on *non-value-added activities*, such as moving and storage.

production cycle time. The total time to produce a unit. Includes processing, moving, storing, and inspecting.

profit. Excess of *revenues* over *expenses* for a *transaction*; sometimes used synonymously with *net income* for the period.

profit and loss account. UK: *retained earnings*.

profit-and-loss sharing ratio. The fraction of *net income* or loss allocable to a partner in a *partnership;*. need not be the same fraction as the partner's share of capital.

profit-and-loss statement. *Income statement*.

profit center. A *responsibility center* for which a firm accumulates both *revenues* and *expenses*. Contrast with *cost center*.

profit margin. *Sales* minus all *expenses*.

profit margin percentage. *Profit margin* divided by *net sales*.

profit maximization. The doctrine that the firm should account for a given set of operations so as to make reported *net income* as large as possible; contrast with *conservatism*. This concept in accounting differs from the profit-maximizing concept in economics, which states that the firm should manage operations to maximize the present value of the firm's wealth, generally by equating *marginal costs* and *marginal revenues*.

profit plan. The *income statement* portion of a *master budget*.

profit-sharing plan. A *defined-contribution plan* in which the employer contributes amounts based on *net income*.

profit variance analysis. Analysis of the causes of the difference between budgeted profit in the *master budget* and the profits earned.

profit-volume analysis (equation). Analysis of effects, on *profits*, caused by changes in volume or *contribution margin* per unit or *fixed costs*. See *breakeven chart*.

profit-volume graph. *See breakeven chart*.

profit-volume ratio. *Net income* divided by net sales in dollars.

profitability accounting. *Responsibility accounting*.

program budgeting (PPB). Specification and analysis of inputs, outputs, costs, and alternatives that link plans to *budgets*.

programmed cost. A *fixed cost* not essential for carrying out operations. For example, a firm can control costs for research and development and advertising designed to generate new business, but once it commits to incur them, they become fixed costs. These costs are sometimes called managed costs or *discretionary costs*. Contrast with *capacity costs*.

progressive tax. Tax for which the rate increases as the taxed base, such as income, increases. Contrast with *regressive tax*.

project financing arrangement. As defined by *SFAS No. 47*, the financing of an investment project in which the lender looks principally to the *cash flows* and *earnings* of the project as the source of funds for repayment and to the *assets* of the project as *collateral* for the loan. The general *credit* of the project entity usually does not affect the terms of the financing either because the borrowing entity is a *corporation* without other assets or because the financing provides that the lender has no direct *recourse* to the entity's owners.

projected benefit obligation. The *actuarial present value* at a given date of all pension benefits attributed by a *defined-benefit pension* formula to employee service rendered before that date. The analyst measures the obligation using assumptions as to future compensation levels if the formula incorporates future compensation, as happens, for example, when the plan bases the eventual pension benefit on wages of the last several years of employees' work lives. Contrast to "accumulated benefit obligation," where the analyst measures the obligation using employee compensation levels at the time of the measurement date.

projected financial statement. *Pro forma* financial statement.

projection. *See financial projection* for definition and contrast.

promissory note. An unconditional written promise to pay a specified sum of cash on demand or at a specified date.

proof of journal. The process of checking the arithmetic accuracy of *journal entries* by testing for the equality of all *debits* and all *credits* since the last previous proof.

property dividend. A *dividend in kind.*

property, plant, and equipment. *See plant assets.*

proportionate consolidation. Canada: a presentation of the *financial statements* of any investor-investment relation, whereby the investor's pro rata share of each *asset, liability, income* item, and *expense* item appears in the *financial statements* of the investor under the various *balance sheet* and *income statement* headings.

proprietary accounts. *See budgetary accounts* for definition and contrast in the context of governmental accounting.

proprietorship. *Assets* minus *liabilities* of an *entity*; equals *contributed capital* plus *retained earnings.*

proprietorship theory. The corporation view that emphasizes the form of the *accounting equation* that says *assets − liabilities = owners' equity*; contrast with *entity theory.* The major implication of a choice between these theories deals with the treatment of *subsidiaries.* For example, the proprietorship theory views *minority interest* as an *indeterminate-term liability.* The proprietorship theory implies using a *single-step income statement.*

prorate. To *allocate* in proportion to some base; for example, to allocate *service department* costs in proportion to hours of service used by the benefited department or to allocate *manufacturing variances* to product sold and to product added to *ending inventory.*

prorating variances. *See prorate.*

prospectus. Formal written document describing *securities* a firm will issue. *See proxy.*

protest fee. Fee charged by banks or other financial agencies when the bank cannot collect items (such as *checks*) presented for collection.

provision. Part of an *account* title. Often the firm must recognize an *expense* even though it cannot be sure of the exact amount. The entry for the estimated expense, such as for *income taxes* or expected costs under *warranty*, is as follows:

Retained Earnings (Estimated) . . . X

   Liability Increase
   (Estimated) X

American terminology often uses "provision" in the expense account title of the above entry. Thus, Provision for Income Taxes means the estimate of income tax expense. (British terminology uses "provision" in the title for the estimated liability of the above entry, so that Provision for Income Taxes is a balance sheet account.)

proxy. Written authorization given by one person to another so that the second person can act for the first, such as to vote shares of stock; of particular significance to accountants because the *SEC* presumes that management distributes financial information along with its proxy solicitations.

public accountant. Generally, this term is synonymous with *certified public accountant.* Some jurisdictions, however, license individuals who are not CPAs as public accountants.

public accounting. That portion of accounting primarily involving the *attest* function, culminating in the *auditor's report.*

Public Company Accounting Oversight Board. PCAOB. A board established by the Sarbanes-Oxley Act of 2002 which regulates the auditing profession and sets standards for audits of public companies. The *SEC* appoints its members.

PuPU. Acronym for *pur*chasing *p*ower *u*nit; conceived by John C. Burton, former chief accountant of the *SEC.* Those who think that *constant-dollar accounting* is not particularly useful poke fun at it by calling it "PuPU accounting."

purchase allowance. A reduction in sales *invoice price* usually granted because the purchaser received *goods* not exactly as ordered. The purchaser does not return the goods but agrees to keep them for a price lower than originally agreed upon.

purchase discount. A reduction in purchase *invoice price* granted for prompt payment. *See sales discount* and *terms of sale.*

purchase investigation. An investigation of the financial affairs of a company for the purpose of disclosing matters that can influence the terms or conclusion of a potential acquisition.

purchase method. Accounting for a *business combination* by adding the acquired company's assets at the price paid for them to the acquiring company's assets. Contrast with *pooling-of-interests method.* The firm adds the acquired assets to the books at current values rather than original costs; the subsequent *amortization expenses* usually exceed those (and reported income is smaller than that) for the same business combination accounted for as a pooling of interests. U.S. *GAAP* now require that the acquirer use the purchase method, but other countries still allow poolings.

purchase order. Document issued by a buyer authorizing a seller to deliver goods, with the buyer to make payment later.

purchasing power gain or loss. *Monetary gain or loss.*

push-down accounting. An accounting method used in some *purchase transactions.* Assume that Company A purchases substantially all the *common shares* of Company B but that Company B must still issue its own *financial statements.* The question arises, shall Company B change the *basis* for its *assets* and *equities* on its own books to the same updated amounts at which they appear on Company A's *consolidated financial statements*? Company B uses "push-down accounting" when it shows the new asset and equity bases reflecting Company A's purchase, because the method "pushes down" the new bases from Company A (where *GAAP* require them) to Company B (where the new bases would not appear in *historical cost accounting*). Since 1983, the *SEC* has required push-down accounting under some circumstances.

put. An option to sell *shares* of a publicly traded corporation at a fixed price during a fixed time span. Contrast with *call.*

Q

qualified report (opinion). *Auditor's report* containing a statement that the auditor could not complete a satisfactory examination of all things considered relevant or that the auditor has doubts about the financial impact of some *material* item reported in the financial statements. *See except for* and *subject to.*

quality. In modern usage, a product or service has quality to the extent it conforms to specifications or provides customers the characteristics promised them.

quality of earnings. A phrase with no single, agreed-upon meaning. Some who use the phrase use it with different meanings on different occasions. "Quality of earnings" has an accounting aspect and a business cycle aspect.

In its accounting aspect, managers have choices in measuring and reporting *earnings.* This discretion can involve any of the following: selecting *accounting principles* or standards when *GAAP* allow a choice; making estimates in the application of accounting principles; and timing transactions to allow recognizing *nonrecurring* items in earnings. In some instances the range of choices has a large impact on report-

ed earnings and in others, small. (1) Some use the phrase "quality of earnings" to mean the degree to which management can affect reported income by its choices of accounting estimates even though the choices recur every period. These users judge, for example, insurance companies to have low-quality earnings. Insurance company management must reestimate its liabilities for future payments to the insured each period, thereby having an opportunity to report periodic earnings within a wide range. (2) Others use the phrase to mean the degree to which management actually takes advantage of its flexibility. For them, an insurance company that does not vary its methods and estimating techniques, even though it has the opportunity to do so, has high-quality earnings. (3) Some have in mind the proximity in time between *revenue* recognition and cash collection. For them, the smaller the time delay, the higher will be the quality. (4) Still others use the phrase to mean the degree to which managers who have a choice among the items with large influence on earnings choose the ones that result in income measures that are more likely to recur. For them, the more likely an item of earnings is to recur, the higher will be its quality. Often these last two groups trade off with each other. Consider a dealer leasing a car on a long-term *lease*, receiving monthly collections. The dealer who uses *sales-type lease* accounting scores low on proximity of revenue recognition (all at the time of signing the lease) to cash collection but highlights the nonrepetitive nature of the transaction. The leasing dealer who uses *operating lease* accounting has perfectly matching revenue recognition and cash collection, but the *recurring* nature of the revenue gives a misleading picture of a repetitive transaction. The phrase "item of earnings" in (4) is ambiguous. The writer could mean the underlying economic event (which occurs when the lease for the car is signed) or the revenue recognition (which occurs every time the dealer using operating lease accounting receives cash). Hence, you should try to understand what other speakers and writers mean by "quality of earnings" when you interpret what they say and write. Some who refer to "earnings quality" suspect that managers will usually make choices that enhance current earnings and present the firm in the best light, independent of the firm's ability to generate similar earnings in the future.

In the business cycle aspect, management's action often has no impact on the stability and recurrence of earnings. Compare a company that sells consumer products and likely has sales repeating every week with a construction company that builds to order. Companies in noncyclical businesses, such as some public utilities, likely have more stable earnings than ones in cyclical businesses, such as steel. Some use "quality of earnings" to refer to the stability and recurrence of basic revenue-generating activities. Those who use the phrase this way rarely associate earnings quality with accounting issues.

quality of financial position. Because of the *articulation* of the *income statement* with the *balance sheet*, the factors that imply a high (or low) *quality of earnings* also affect the balance sheet. Users of this phrase have in mind the same accounting issues as they have in mind when they use the phrase "quality of earnings."

quantitative performance measure. A measure of output based on an

objectively observable quantity, such as units produced or *direct costs* incurred, rather than on an unobservable quantity or a quantity observable only nonobjectively, like quality of service provided.

quantity discount. A reduction in purchase price as quantity purchased increases. The Robinson-Patman Act constrains the amount of the discount. Do not confuse with *purchase discount.*

quantity variance. *Efficiency variance;* in *standard cost* systems, the standard price per unit times (actual quantity used minus standard quantity that should be used).

quasi-reorganization. A *reorganization* in which no new company emerges or no court has intervened, as would happen in *bankruptcy*. The primary purpose is to rid the balance sheet of a *deficit* (negative *retained earnings*) and give the firm a "fresh start."

quick assets. *Assets* readily convertible into *cash*; includes cash, current marketable securities, and current receivables.

quick ratio. Sum of (cash, current marketable securities, and current receivables) divided by *current liabilities*; often called the "acid test ratio." The analyst can exclude some nonliquid receivables from the numerator. *See ratio.*

R

R^2. The proportion of the statistical variance of a *dependent variable* explained by the equation fit to *independent variable(s)* in a *regression analysis.*

Railroad Accounting Principles Board (RAPB). A board brought into existence by the Staggers Rail Act of 1980 to advise the Interstate Commerce

Commission on accounting matters affecting railroads. The RAPB was the only cost-accounting body authorized by the government during the decade of the 1980s (because Congress ceased funding the CASB during the 1980s). The RAPB incorporated the pronouncements of the CASB and became the government's authority on cost accounting principles.

R&D. *See research and development.*

random number sampling. For choosing a sample, a method in which the analyst selects items from the *population* by using a random number table or generator.

random sampling. For choosing a sample, a method in which all items in the population have an equal chance of being selected. Compare *judgment(al) sampling.*

RAPB. *Railroad Accounting Principles Board.*

rate of return on assets. *Return on assets.*

rate of return on common stock equity. *See ratio.*

rate of return on shareholders' (owners') equity. *See ratio.*

rate of return (on total capital). *See ratio* and *return on assets.*

rate variance. *Price variance,* usually for *direct labor costs.*

ratio. The number resulting when one number divides another. Analysts generally use ratios to assess aspects of profitability, solvency, and liquidity. The commonly used financial ratios fall into three categories: (1) those that summarize some aspect of *operations* for a period, usually a year, (2) those that summarize some aspect of *financial position* at a given moment— the moment for which a balance sheet reports, and (3) those that relate some aspect of operations to some aspect of financial position. Exhibit 1-3 lists common financial ratios and shows separately both the numerator and the denominator for each ratio.

Ratio	Numerator	Denominator
Profitability Ratios		
Rate of return on assets	Net income + Interest expense (net of tax effects)[a]	Average total assets during the period
Profit margin for ROA (before interest effects)	Net income + Interest expense (net of tax effects)[a]	Sales
Various expense ratios	Various expenses	Sales
Total assets turnover ratio	Sales	Average total assets during the period
Accounts receivable turnover ratio	Sales	Average accounts receivable during the period
Inventory turnover ratio	Cost of goods sold	Average inventory during the period
Fixed asset turnover ratio	Sales	Average fixed assets during the period

Exhibit 1-3.   Summary of Financial Statements Ratios

Ratio	Numerator	Denominator
Rate of return on common shareholders' equity	Net income − Preferred stock dividends	Average common share-holders' equity during the period
Profit margin for ROCE (after interest expense and preferred dividends)	Net income − Preferred stock dividends	Sales
Capital structure leverage ratio	Average total assets during the period	Average common share-holders' equity during the period
Earnings per share of common stock[b]	Net income − Preferred stock dividends	Weighted-average number of common shares outstanding
Short-term Liquidity Ratios		
Current ratio	Current assets	Current liabilities
Quick or acid test ratio	Highly liquid assets (cash, marketable securities, and receivables)[c]	Current liabilities
Cash flow from operations to current liabilities ratio	Cash flow from operations	Average current liabilities during the period
Accounts payable turnover ratio	Purchases[d]	Average accounts payable during the period
Days accounts receivable outstanding	365 days	Accounts receivable turnover ratio
Days inventories held	365 days	Inventory turnover ratio
Days accounts payable outstanding	365 days	Accounts payable turnover ratio
Long-term Liquidity Ratios		
Long-term debt ratio	Total long-term debt	Total long-term debt plus shareholders' equity
Debt equity ratio	Total liabilities	Total equities (total liabilities + shareholders' equity = total assets)
Cash flow from operations to total liabilities ratio	Cash flow from operations	Average total liabilities during the period
Interest coverage ratio	Income before Interest and income taxes	Interest expense

Exhibit 1-3.   Summary of Financial Statements Ratios (*Continued*)

[a] If the parent company does not own all of a consolidated subsidiary, the calculation also adds back to net income the minority interest share of earnings.

[b] This calculation is more complicated when there are convertible securities, options, or warrants outstanding.

[c] The calculation could conceivably exclude receivables for some firms and include inventories for others.

[d] Purchases = Cost of goods sold + Ending inventories − Beginning inventories

For all ratios that require an average balance during the period, the analyst often derives the average as one half the sum of the beginning and the ending balances. Sophisticated analysts recognize, however, that particularly when companies use a fiscal year different from the calendar year, this averaging of beginning and ending balances may mislead. Consider, for example, the rate of *return on assets* of Wal-Mart, whose fiscal year ends on January 31. Wal-Mart chooses a January 31 closing date at least in part because inventories are at a low level and are therefore easy to count—it has sold the Christmas merchandise, and the Easter merchandise has not yet all arrived. Furthermore, by January 31, Wal-Mart has collected for most Christmas sales, so receivable amounts are not unusually large. Thus at January 31, the amount of total assets is lower than at many other times during the year. Consequently, the denominator of the rate of return on assets, total assets, for Wal-Mart more likely represents the smallest amount of total assets on hand during the year rather than the average amount. The return on assets rate for Wal-Mart and other companies that choose a fiscal year-end to coincide with low points in the inventory cycle is likely to exceed the ratio measured with a more accurate estimate of the average amounts of total assets.

raw material. Goods purchased for use in manufacturing a product.

reacquired stock. *Treasury shares.*

real accounts. *Balance sheet accounts*, as opposed to *nominal accounts*. *See permanent accounts.*

real amount (value). An amount stated in *constant dollars*. For example, if the firm sells an investment costing $100 for $130 after a period of 10 percent general *inflation*, the *nominal amount* of *gain* is $30 (= $130 − $100) but the real amount of gain is C$20 (= $130 − 1.10 × $100), where "C$" denotes constant dollars of purchasing power on the date of sale.

real estate. *Land* and its *improvements*, such as landscaping and roads, but not buildings.

real interest rate. Interest rate reflecting the productivity of capital, not including a premium for inflation anticipated over the life of the loan.

realizable value. *Fair value* or, sometimes, *net realizable (sales) value.*

realization convention. The accounting practice of delaying the recognition of *gains* and *losses* from changes in the market price of *assets* until the firm sells the assets. However, the firm recognizes unrealized losses on *inventory* (or *marketable securities* classified as *trading securities*) prior to sale when the firm uses the *lower-of-cost-or-market* valuation basis for inventory (or the *fair value* basis for marketable securities).

realize. To convert into *funds*; when applied to a *gain* or *loss*, implies that an *arm's-length transaction* has occurred. Contrast with *recognize*; the firm can recognize a loss (as, for example, on *marketable equity securities*) in the financial statements even though it has not yet realized the loss via a transaction.

realized gain (or loss) on marketable equity securities. An income statement account title for the difference between the proceeds of disposition and the *original cost* of *marketable equity securities.*

realized holding gain. *See inventory profit* for definition and an example.

rearrangement costs. Costs of reinstalling assets, perhaps in a different location. The firm can, but need not, *capitalize* them as part of the assets cost, just as is done with original installation cost. The firm will *expense* these costs if they merely maintain the asset's future benefits at their originally intended level before the relocation.

recapitalization. *Reorganization.*

recapture. Name for one kind of tax payment. Various provisions of the *income tax* rules require a refund by the taxpayer (recapture by the government) of various tax advantages under certain conditions. For example, the taxpayer must repay tax savings provided by *accelerated depreciation* if the taxpayer prematurely retires the item providing the tax savings.

receipt. Acquisition of *cash.*

receivable. Any *collectible*, whether or not it is currently due.

receivable turnover. *See ratio.*

reciprocal holdings. Company A owns stock of Company B, and Company B owns stock of Company A; or Company B owns stock of Company C, which owns stock of Company A.

recognize. To enter a transaction in the accounts; not synonymous with *realize.*

reconciliation. A calculation that shows how one balance or figure derives from another, such as a reconciliation of retained earnings or a *bank reconciliation schedule. See articulate.*

record date. The date at which the firm pays *dividends* on payment date to those who own the stock.

recourse. The rights of the lender if a borrower does not repay as promised. A recourse loan gives the lender the right to take any of the borrower's assets not exempted from such taking

by the contract. *See also note receivable discounted.*

recovery of unrealized loss on trading securities. An *income statement account title* for the *gain* during the current period on *trading securities.*

recurring. Occurring again; occurring repetitively; in accounting, an adjective often used in describing *revenue* or *earnings.* In some contexts, the term "recurring revenue" is ambiguous. Consider a construction contractor who accounts for a single long-term project with the *installment method*, with revenue recognized at the time of each cash collection from the customer. The recognized revenue is recurring, but the transaction leading to the revenue is not. *See quality of earnings.*

redemption. Retirement by the issuer, usually by a purchase or *call*, of *stocks* or *bonds.*

redemption premium. *Call premium.*

redemption value. The price a corporation will pay to retire *bonds* or *preferred stock* if it calls them before *maturity.*

refinancing. An adjustment in the *capital structure* of a *corporation*, involving changes in the nature and amounts of the various classes of *debt* and, in some cases, *capital* as well as other components of *shareholders' equity. Asset* carrying values in the accounts remain unchanged.

refunding bond issue. Said of a *bond* issue whose proceeds the firm uses to retire bonds already *outstanding.*

register. A collection of consecutive entries, or other information, in chronological order, such as a check register or an insurance register that lists all insurance policies owned. If the firm records entries in the register, it can serve as a *journal.*

registered bond. A bond for which the issuer will pay the *principal* and *interest*, if registered as to interest, to the owner listed on the books of the issuer; as opposed to a bearer bond, in which the issuer must pay the possessor of the bond.

registrar. An *agent*, usually a bank or trust company, appointed by a corporation to keep track of the names of shareholders and distributions to them.

registration statement. Required by the Securities Act of 1933, statement of most companies that want to have owners of their securities trade the securities in public markets. The statement discloses financial data and other items of interest to potential investors.

regression analysis. A method of *cost estimation* based on statistical techniques for fitting a line (or its equivalent in higher mathematical dimensions) to an observed series of data points, usually by minimizing the sum of squared deviations of the observed data from the fitted line. Common usage calls the cost that the analysis explains the "dependent variable"; it calls the variable(s) we use to estimate cost behavior "independent variable(s)." If we use more than one independent variable, the term for the analysis is "multiple regression analysis." *See* R^2, *standard error*, and *t-value*.

regressive tax. Tax for which the rate decreases as the taxed base, such as income, increases. Contrast with *progressive tax*.

Regulation S-K. The *SEC*'s standardization of nonfinancial statement disclosure requirements for documents filed with the SEC.

Regulation S-T. The *SEC*'s regulations specifying formats for electronic filing and the *EDGAR* system.

Regulation S-X. The *SEC*'s principal accounting regulation, which specifies the form and content of financial reports to the SEC.

rehabilitation. The improving of a used *asset* via an extensive repair. Ordinary *repairs* and *maintenance* restore or maintain expected *service potential* of an asset, and the firm treats them as *expenses*. A rehabilitation improves the asset beyond its current service potential, enhancing the service potential to a significantly higher level than before the rehabilitation. Once rehabilitated, the asset may be better, but need not be, than it was when new. The firm will *capitalize expenditures* for rehabilitation, like those for *betterments* and *improvements*.

reinvestment rate. In a *capital budgeting* context, the rate at which the firm invests cash inflows from a project occurring before the project's completion. Once the analyst assumes such a rate, no project can ever have multiple *internal rates of return*. *See Descartes' rule of signs.*

relative performance evaluation. Setting performance targets and, sometimes, compensation in relation to the performance of others, perhaps in different firms or divisions, who face a similar environment.

relative sales value method. *See net realizable (sales) value.*

relevant cost. Cost used by an analyst in making a decision. *Incremental cost; opportunity cost.*

relevant cost analysis. Identifies the costs (or *revenues*) relevant to the decision to be made. A cost or revenue is relevant only if an amount differs between alternatives. Also called *differential cost analysis.*

relevant range. Activity levels over which costs are linear or for which *flexible budget* estimates and *breakeven charts* will remain valid.

remit earnings. An expression likely to confuse a reader without a firm understanding of accounting basics. A firm generates *net assets* by earning *income* and retains net assets if it does not declare *dividends* in the amount of net income. When a firm declares dividends and pays the cash (or other net assets), some writers would say the firm "remits earnings." We think the student learns better by conceiving earnings as a *credit balance.* When a firm pays dividends it sends net assets, things with debit balances, not something with a credit balance, to the recipient. When writers say firms "remit earnings," they mean the firms send assets (or net assets) that previous earnings have generated and reduce *retained earnings.*

remittance advice. Information on a *check stub,* or on a document attached to a check by the *drawer,* that tells the *payee* why a payment is being made.

rent. A charge for use of land, buildings, or other assets.

reorganization. In the *capital structure* of a corporation, a major change that leads to changes in the rights, interests, and implied ownership of the various security owners; usually results from a *merger* or an agreement by senior security holders to take action to forestall *bankruptcy.*

repair. An *expenditure* to restore an *asset's* service potential after damage or after prolonged use. In the second sense, after prolonged use, the difference between repairs and maintenance is one of degree and not of kind. A repair is treated as an *expense* of the period when incurred. Because the firm treats repairs and maintenance similarly in this regard,

the distinction is not important. A repair helps to maintain capacity at the levels planned when the firm acquired the *asset.* Contrast with *improvement.*

replacement cost. For an asset, the current fair market price to purchase another, similar asset (with the same future benefit or service potential). *Current cost. See reproduction cost* and *productive capacity. See also distributable income* and *inventory profit.*

replacement cost method of depreciation. Method in which the analyst augments the original-cost *depreciation* charge with an amount based on a portion of the difference between the *current replacement cost* of the asset and its *original cost.*

replacement system of depreciation. *See retirement method of depreciation* for definition and contrast.

report. *Financial statement; auditor's report.*

report form. *Balance sheet* form that typically shows *assets* minus *liabilities* as one total. Then, below that total appears the components of *owners' equity* summing to the same total. Often, the top section shows *current* assets less current liabilities before *noncurrent assets* less noncurrent liabilities. Contrast with *account form.*

reporting objectives (policies). The general purposes for which the firm prepares *financial statements.* The *FASB* has discussed these in *SFAC No. 1.*

representative item sampling. Sampling in which the analyst believes the sample selected is typical of the entire population from which it comes. Compare *specific item sampling.*

reproduction cost. The *cost* necessary to acquire an *asset* similar in all physical respects to another asset for which the analyst requires a *current* *value. See replacement cost and productive capacity* for contrast.

required rate of return (RRR). *Cost of capital.*

requisition. A formal written order or request, such as for withdrawal of supplies from the storeroom.

resale value. *Exit value; net realizable value.*

research and development (R&D). A form of economic activity with special accounting rules. Firms engage in research in hopes of discovering new knowledge that will create a new product, process, or service or of improving a present product, process, or service. Development translates research findings or other knowledge into a new or improved product, process, or service. *SFAS No. 2* requires that firms expense costs of such activities as incurred on the grounds that the future benefits are too uncertain to warrant *capitalization* as an asset. This treatment seems questionable to us because we wonder why firms would continue to undertake R&D if there was no expectation of future benefit; if future benefits exist, then R&D *costs* should be assets that appear, like other assets, at *historical cost.*

reserve. The worst word in accounting because almost everyone not trained in accounting, and some who are, misunderstand it. The common confusion is that "reserves" represent a pool of *cash* or other *assets* available when the firm needs them. Wrong. Cash always has a *debit balance.* Reserves always have a *credit* balance. When properly used in accounting, "reserves" refer to an account that appropriates *retained earnings* and restricts dividend declarations. Appropriating retained earnings is

itself a poor and vanishing practice, so the word should seldom appear in accounting. In addition, "reserve" was used in the past to indicate an asset *contra account* (for example, "reserve for depreciation") or an *estimated liability* (for example, "reserve for warranty costs"). In any case, reserve accounts have *credit* balances and are not pools of *funds*, as the unwary reader might infer. If a company has set aside a pool of *cash* (or *marketable securities*) to serve some specific purpose such as paying for a new factory, then it will call that cash a *fund.* No other word in accounting causes so much misunderstanding by nonexperts as well as by "experts" who should know better. A leading unabridged dictionary defines "reserve" as "cash, or assets readily convertible into cash, held aside, as by a corporation, bank, state or national government, etc. to meet expected or unexpected demands." This definition is absolutely wrong in accounting. Reserves are not funds. For example, the firm creates a contingency fund of $10,000 by depositing cash in a fund and makes the following entry:

Contingency Fund . . . 10,000	
Cash	10,000

The following entry can accompany the previous entry, if the firm wants to appropriate retained earnings:

Retained Earnings . . . 10,000	
Reserve for	
Contingencies . . . 10,000	

The transaction leading to the first entry has economic significance. The second entry has little economic impact for most firms. The problem with the word "reserve" arises because the firm can make the second entry without the first—a company can create a reserve, that is, appropriate retained earnings, without creating a fund. The problem results, at least in part, from the fact that in common usage, "reserve" means a pool of assets, as in the phrase "oil reserves." The *Internal Revenue Service* does not help in dispelling confusion about the term "reserves." The federal *income tax* return for corporations uses the title "Reserve for Bad Debts" to mean "Allowance for Uncollectible Accounts" and speaks of the "Reserve Method" in referring to the *allowance method* for estimating *revenue* or *income* reductions from estimated *uncollectibles*.

reserve recognition accounting (RRA). One form of *accounting* for natural resources. In exploration for natural resources, the problem arises of how to treat the expenditures for exploration, both before the firm knows the outcome of the efforts and after it knows the outcome. Suppose that the firm spends $10 million to drill 10 holes ($1 million each) and that nine of them are dry whereas one is a gusher containing oil with a *net realizable value* of $40 million. Dry hole, or *successful efforts*, accounting would expense $9 million and *capitalize* $1 million, which the firm will *deplete* as it lifts the oil from the ground. *SFAS No. 19*, now suspended, required *successful efforts costing*. Full costing would expense nothing but would capitalize the $10 million of drilling costs that the firm will deplete as it lifts the oil from the single productive well. Reserve recognition accounting would capitalize $40 million, which the firm will deplete as it lifts the oil, with a $30 million *credit* to *income* or *contributed capital*. The *balance sheet* shows the *net realizable value* of proven oil and gas reserves. The *income statement* has three sorts of items: (1) current income

resulting from production or "lifting profit," which is the *revenue* from sales of oil and gas less the expense based on the current valuation amount at which these items have appeared on the balance sheet, (2) profit or loss from exploration efforts in which the current value of new discoveries is revenue and all the exploration cost is expense, and (3) gain or loss on changes in current value during the year, which accountants in other contexts call a *holding gain or loss*.

reset bond. A bond, typically a *junk bond*, that specifies that periodically the issuer will reset the coupon rate so that the bond sells at *par* in the market. Investment bankers created this type of instrument to help ensure the purchasers of such bonds of getting a fair rate of return, given the riskiness of the issuer. If the issuer gets into financial trouble, its bonds will trade for less than par in the market. The issuer of a reset bond promises to raise the interest rate and preserve the value of the bond. Ironically, the reset feature has often had just the opposite effect. The default risk of many issuers of reset bonds has deteriorated so much that the bonds have dropped to less than 50 percent of par. To raise the value to par, the issuer would have to raise the interest rate to more than 25 percent per year. That rate is so large that issuers have declared bankruptcy rather than attempt to make the new large interest payments; this then reduces the market value of the bonds rather than increasing their value.

residual income. In an external reporting context, a term that refers to *net income* to *common shares* (= net income less *preferred stock dividends*). In *managerial accounting*, this term refers to the excess of income for a *division* or *segment* of a company over the product of the *cost of capital* for the company multiplied by the average amount of capital invested in the division during the period over which the division earned the income.

residual security. A *potentially dilutive security. Options, warrants, convertible bonds,* and *convertible preferred securities.*

residual value. At any time, the estimated or actual *net realizable value* (that is, proceeds less removal costs) of an *asset,* usually a depreciable *plant asset.* In the context of depreciation accounting, this term is equivalent to *salvage value* and is preferred to *scrap value* because the firm need not scrap the asset. It is sometimes used to mean net *book value.* In the context of a *noncancelable* lease, it is the estimated value of the leased asset at the end of the lease period. *See lease.*

resources supplied. *Expenditures* made for an activity.

resources used. *Cost driver* rate times cost driver volume.

responsibility accounting. Accounting for a business by considering various units as separate entities, or *profit centers,* giving management of each unit responsibility for the unit's *revenues* and *expenses. See transfer price.*

responsibility center. An organization part or *segment* that top management holds accountable for a specified set of activities. Also called "accountability center." *See cost center, investment center, profit center,* and *revenue center.*

restricted assets. Governmental resources restricted by legal or contractual requirements for specific purpose.

restricted retained earnings. That part of *retained earnings* not legally available for *dividends. See retained earnings, appropriated.* Bond indentures and other loan contracts can curtail the legal ability of the corporation to declare dividends without formally requiring a retained earnings appropriation, but the firm must disclose such restrictions.

retail inventory method. Ascertaining cost amounts of *ending inventory* as follows (assuming *FIFO*): cost of ending inventory = (selling price of *goods available for sale* − sales) × *cost percentage.* The analyst then computes cost of goods sold from the inventory equation; costs of beginning inventory, purchases, and ending inventory are all known. (When the firm uses *LIFO,* the method resembles the *dollar-value LIFO method.) See markup.*

retail terminology. *See markup.*

retained earnings. Net *income* over the life of a corporation less all *dividends* (including capitalization through *stock dividends); owners' equity* less *contributed capital.*

retained earnings, appropriated. An *account* set up by crediting it and debiting *retained earnings;* used to indicate that a portion of retained earnings is not available for dividends. The practice of appropriating retained earnings is misleading unless the firm marks all capital with its use, which is not practicable, nor sensible, since capital is fungible—all the *equities* jointly fund all the *assets.* The use of formal retained earnings appropriations is declining.

retained earnings statement. A *reconciliation* of the beginning and the ending balances in the *retained earnings account;* required by *generally accepted accounting principles* whenever the firm presents *comparative balance sheets* and an *income statement.* This reconciliation can appear in a separate statement, in a combined statement of income and retained earnings, or in the balance sheet.

retirement method of depreciation. A method in which the firm records no entry for *depreciation expense* until it retires an *asset* from service. Then, it makes an entry *debiting* depreciation expense and *crediting* the asset account for the cost of the asset retired. If the retired asset has a *salvage value*, the firm reduces the amount of the debit to depreciation expense by the amount of salvage value with a corresponding debit to cash, receivables, or salvaged materials. The "replacement system of depreciation" is similar, except that the debit to depreciation expense equals the cost of the new asset less the salvage value, if any, of the old asset. Some public utilities used these methods. For example, if the firm acquired ten telephone poles in Year 1 for $60 each and replaces them in Year 10 for $100 each when the salvage value of the old poles is $5 each, the accounting would be as follows:

Retirement Method

Plant Assets	600
Cash	600
To acquire assets in Year 1	
Depreciation Expense . .	550
Salvage Receivable	50
Plant Assets	600
To record retirement and depreciation in Year 10.	
Plant Assets	1,000
Cash	1,000
To record acquisition of new assets in Year 10.	

Replacement Method

Plant Assets	600
Cash	600
To acquire assets in Year 1	
Depreciation Expense . .	950
Salvage Receivable	50
Cash	1,000
To record depreciation on old asset in amount quantified by net cost of replacement asset in Year 10.	

The retirement method is like *FIFO* in that it records the cost of the first assets as depreciation and puts the cost of the second assets on the balance sheet. The replacement method is like *LIFO* in that it records the cost of the second assets as depreciation expense and leaves the cost of the first assets on the balance sheet.

retirement plan. *Pension plan.*

retroactive benefits. In initiating or amending a *defined-benefit pension plan*, benefits that the benefit formula attributes to employee services rendered in periods prior to the initiation or amendment. *See prior service costs.*

return. A schedule of information required by governmental bodies, such as the tax return required by the *Internal Revenue Service*; also the physical return of merchandise. *See also return on investment.*

return on assets (ROA). *Net income* plus after-tax *interest charges* plus *minority interest* in income divided by average total *assets*; perhaps the single most useful ratio for assessing management's overall operating performance. Most financial economists would subtract average noninterest-bearing *liabilities* from the denominator. Economists realize that when liabilities do not provide for explicit interest charges, the creditor adjusts the terms of contract, such as setting a higher selling price or lower discount, to those who do not pay cash immediately. (To take an extreme example, consider how much higher salary a worker who receives a salary once per year, rather than once per month, would demand.) This ratio requires in the numerator the income amount before the firm accrues any charges to suppliers of funds. We cannot measure the interest charges implicit in the noninterest-bearing liabilities because they cause items such as cost of goods sold and salary expense to be somewhat larger, since the interest is implicit. Subtracting their amounts from the denominator adjusts for their implicit cost. Such subtraction assumes that assets financed with noninterest-bearing liabilities have the same rate of return as all the other assets.

return on investment (ROI), return on capital. *Income* (before distributions to suppliers of capital) for a period; as a rate, this amount divided by average total assets. The analyst should add back *interest*, net of tax effects, to *net income* for the numerator. *See ratio.*

revenue. The *owners' equity* increase accompanying the *net assets* increase caused by selling goods or rendering services; in short, a service rendered; *sales* of products, merchandise, and services and earnings from *interest*, *dividends*, *rents*, and the like. Measure revenue as the expected *net present value* of the net assets the firm will receive. Do not confuse with *receipt* of *funds*, which can occur before, when, or after revenue is recognized. Contrast with *gain* and *income*. *See also holding gain.* Some writers use the term *gross income* synonymously with *revenue*; avoid such usage.

revenue center. Within a firm, a *responsibility center* that controls only revenues generated. Contrast with *cost center. See profit center.*

revenue expenditure. A term sometimes used to mean an *expense*, in contrast to a capital *expenditure* to acquire an *asset* or to discharge a *liability*. Avoid using this term; use *period expense* instead.

revenue received in advance. An inferior term for *advances from customers*.

reversal (reversing) entry. An *entry* in which all *debits* and *credits* are the credits and debits, respectively, of another entry, and in the same amounts. The accountant usually records a reversal entry on the first day of an *accounting period* to reverse a previous *adjusting entry*, usually an *accrual*. The purpose of such entries is to make the bookkeeper's tasks easier. Suppose that the firm pays salaries every other Friday, with paychecks compensating employees for the two weeks just ended. Total salaries accrue at the rate of $5,000 per five-day workweek. The bookkeeper is accustomed to making the following entry every other Friday:

(1) Salary Expense	10,000
Cash	10,000
To record salary expense and salary payments.	

If the firm delivers paychecks to employees on Friday, November 25, then the *adjusting entry* made on November 30 (or perhaps later) to record accrued salaries for November 28, 29, and 30 would be as follows:

(2) Salary Expense	3,000
Salaries Payable .	3,000
To charge November operations with all salaries earned in November.	

The firm would close the Salary Expense account as part of the November 30 closing entries. On the next payday, December 9, the salary entry would be as follows:

(3) Salary Expense	7,000
Salaries Payable	3,000
Cash	10,000
To record salary payments split between expense for December (seven days) and liability carried over from November.	

To make entry (3), the bookkeeper must look back into the records to see how much of the debit is to Salaries Payable accrued from the previous month in order to split the total debits between December expense and the liability carried over from November. Notice that this entry forces the bookkeeper both (a) to refer to balances in old accounts and (b) to make an entry different from the one customarily made, entry (1). The reversing entry, made just after the books have been closed for the second quarter, makes the salary entry for December 9 the same as that made on all other Friday paydays. The reversing entry merely *reverses* the adjusting entry (2):

(4) Salaries Payable	3,000	
Salary Expense		3,000

To reverse the adjusting entry.

This entry results in a zero balance in the Salaries Payable account and a credit balance in the Salary Expense account. If the firm makes entry (4) just after it closes the books for November, then the entry on December 9 will be the customary entry (1). Entries (4) and (1) together have the same effect as entry (3).

The procedure for using reversal entries is as follows: the firm makes the required adjustment to record an accrual (*payable* or *receivable*) at the end of an *accounting period*; it makes the closing entry as usual; as of the first day of the following period, it makes an entry reversing the adjusting entry; when the firm makes (or receives) a payment, it records the entry as though it had not recorded an adjusting entry at the end of the preceding period. Whether a firm uses reversal entries affects the record-keeping procedures but not the financial statements.

We also use this term to describe the entry reversing an incorrect entry before recording the correct entry.

reverse stock split. A stock split in which the firm decreases the number of shares *outstanding. See stock split.*

revolving fund. A fund whose amounts the firm continually spends and replenishes; for example, a *petty cash fund.*

revolving loan. A *loan* that both the borrower and the lender expect to renew at *maturity.*

right. The privilege to subscribe to new *securities* issues or to purchase shares. Usually, securities called *warrants* contain the rights, and the owner of the warrants can sell them. *See also preemptive right.*

risk. A measure of the variability of the *return on investment.* For a given expected amount of return, most people prefer less risk to more risk. Therefore, in rational markets, investments with more risk usually promise, or investors expect to receive, a higher rate of return than investments with lower risk. Most people use "risk" and "uncertainty" as synonyms. In technical language, however, these terms have different meanings. We use "risk" when we know the probabilities attached to the various outcomes, such as the probabilities of heads or tails in the flip of a fair coin. "Uncertainty" refers to an event for which we can only estimate the probabilities of the outcomes, such as winning or losing a lawsuit.

risk-adjusted discount rate. Rate used in discounting cash flows for projects more or less risky than the firm's average. In a *capital budgeting* context, a decision analyst compares projects by comparing their net *present values* for a given *interest* rate, usually the cost of capital. If the analyst considers a given project's outcome to be much more or much less risky than the normal undertakings of the company, then the analyst will use a larger interest rate (if the project is riskier) or a smaller interest rate (if less risky) in discounting, and the rate used is "risk-adjusted."

risk-free rate. An interest rate reflecting only the pure interest rate plus an amount to compensate for inflation anticipated over the life of a loan, excluding a premium for the risk of default by the borrower. Financial economists usually measure the risk-free rate in the United States from U.S. government securities, such as Treasury bills and notes.

risk premium. Extra compensation paid to employees or extra *interest* paid to lenders, over amounts usually considered normal, in return for their undertaking to engage in activities riskier than normal.

ROA. *Return on assets.*

ROI. *Return on investment*; usually used to refer to a single project and expressed as a ratio: *income* divided by average *cost* of *assets* devoted to the project.

royalty. Compensation for the use of property, usually a patent, copyrighted material, or natural resources. The amount is often expressed as a percentage of receipts from using the property or as an amount per unit produced.

RRA. *Reserve recognition accounting.*

RRR. Required rate of return. *See cost of capital.*

rule of 69. Rule stating that an amount of cash invested at r percent per period will double in $69/r + .35$ periods. This approximation is accurate to one-tenth of a period for interest rates between $1/4$ and 100 percent per period. For example, at

10 percent per period, the rule says that a given sum will double in $69/10 + .35 = 7.25$ periods. At 10 percent per period, a given sum actually doubles in 7.27+ periods.

rule of 72. Rule stating that an amount of cash invested at r percent per period will double in $72/r$ periods. A reasonable approximation for interest rates between 4 and 10 percent but not nearly as accurate as the *rule of 69* for interest rates outside that range. For example, at 10 percent per period, the rule says that a given sum will double in $72/10 = 7.2$ periods.

rule of 78. The rule followed by many finance companies for allocating earnings on *loans* among the months of a year on the sum-of-the-months'-digits basis when the borrower makes equal monthly payments to the lender. The sum of the digits from 1 through 12 is 78, so the rule allocates 12/78 of the year's earnings to the first month, 11/78 to the second month, and so on. This approximation allocates more of the early payments to interest and less to principal than does the correct, compound-interest method. Hence, lenders still use this method even though present-day computers can make the compound-interest computation as easily as they can carry out the approximation. *See sum-of-the-years'-digits depreciation.*

ruling (and balancing) an account. The process of summarizing a series of entries in an *account* by computing a new *balance* and drawing double lines to indicate that the new balance summarizes the information above the double lines. An illustration appears below. The steps are as follows: (1) Compute the sum of all *debit* entries including opening debit balance, if any—$1,464.16. (2) Compute the sum of all credit entries including opening credit balance, if any—$413.57. (3) If the amount in (1) exceeds the amount in (2), then write the excess as a credit with a checkmark—$1,464.16 − $413.57 = $1,050.59. (4) Add both debit and credit columns, which should both now sum to the same amount, and show that identical total at the foot of both columns. (5) Draw double lines under those numbers and write the excess of debits over credits as the new debit balance with a checkmark. (6) If the amount in (2) exceeds the amount in (1), then write the excess as a debit with a checkmark. (7) Do steps (4) and (5) except that the excess becomes the new credit balance. (8) If the amount in (1) equals the amount in (2), then the balance is zero, and only the totals with the double lines beneath them need appear.

An Open Account, Ruled and Balanced
(Steps Indicated in Parentheses Correspond to Steps Described in "Ruling an Account."

	Date 2004	Explanation	Ref.	Debit (1)	Date 2004	Explanation	Ref.	Credit (2)	
	Jan. 2	Balance	√	100.00					
	Jan. 13		VR	121.37	Sept. 15		J	.42	
	Mar. 20		VR	56.42	Nov. 12		J	413.15	
	June 5		J	1,138.09	Dec. 31	Balance	√	1,050.59	(3)
	Aug. 18		J	1.21					
	Nov. 20		VR	38.43					
	Dec. 7		VR	8.64				———	
(4)	2005			1,464.16	2005			1,464.16	(4)
(5)	Jan. 1	Balance	√	1,050.59					

Rutgers Accounting Web Site. *See http://www.rutgers.edu/Accounting/* for a useful compendium of accounting information.

S

S corporation. A corporation taxed like a *partnership*. Corporation (or partnership) agreements allocate the periodic *income* to the individual shareholders (or partners) who report these amounts on their individual *income tax* returns. Contrast with *C corporation*.

SA (société anonyme). France: A *corporation*.

SAB. *Staff Accounting Bulletin of the SEC.*

safe-harbor lease. A form of *tax-transfer lease*.

safety stock. Extra items of *inventory* kept on hand to protect against running out.

salary. Compensation earned by managers, administrators, and professionals, not based on an hourly rate. Contrast with *wage*.

sale. A *revenue* transaction in which the firm delivers *goods* or *services* to a customer in return for cash or a contractual obligation to pay.

sale and leaseback. A *financing* transaction in which the firm sells improved property but takes it back for use on a long-term *lease*. Such transactions often have advantageous income tax effects but usually have no effect on *financial statement income*.

sales activity variance. *Sales volume variance.*

sales allowance. A sales *invoice* price reduction that a seller grants to a buyer because the seller delivered *goods* different from, perhaps because of damage, those the buyer ordered. The seller often accumulates amounts of such adjustments in a temporary *revenue contra account* having this, or a similar, title. *See sales discount.*

sales basis of revenue recognition. Recognition of *revenue* not when a firm produces goods or when it receives orders but only when it has completed the sale by delivering the goods or services and has received cash or a claim to cash. Most firms recognize revenue on this basis. Compare with the *percentage-of-completion method* and the *installment method*. This is identical with the *completed contract method*, but the latter term ordinarily applies only to *long-term* construction projects.

sales contra, estimated uncollectibles. A title for the contra-revenue account to recognize estimated reductions in income caused by *accounts receivable* that will not be collected. *See bad debt expense, allowance for uncollectibles*, and *allowance method.*

sales discount. A sales *invoice* price reduction usually offered for prompt payment. *See terms of sale* and *2/10, n/30.*

sales return. The physical return of merchandise. The seller often accumulates amounts of such returns in a temporary revenue contra account.

sales-type (capital) lease. A form of *lease. See capital lease.* When a

manufacturer (or other firm) that ordinarily sells goods enters a capital lease as *lessor*, the lease is a "sales-type lease." When a financial firm, such as a bank or insurance company or leasing company, acquires the asset from the manufacturer and then enters a capital lease as lessor, the lease is a "direct-financing-type lease." The manufacturer recognizes its ordinary profit (sales price less *cost of goods sold*, where sales price is the *present value* of the contractual lease payments plus any down payment) on executing the sales-type capital lease, but the financial firm does not recognize profit on executing a capital lease of the direct-financing type.

sales value method. *Relative sales value method. See net realizable value method.*

sales volume variance. Budgeted *contribution margin* per unit times (planned sales volume minus actual sales volume).

salvage value. Actual or estimated selling price, net of removal or disposal costs, of a used *plant asset* that the firm expects to sell or otherwise retire. *See residual value.*

SAR. *Summary annual report.*

Sarbanes-Oxley Act. The law, passed in 2002 in the wake of the Enron and related scandals, to stiffen the requirements for corporate governance, including accounting issues. It speaks, among other things, to the regulation of the accounting profession, the standards for audit committees of public companies, the certifications that managements must sign, and standards of internal control that companies must meet.

SARL (société à responsabilité limitée). France: a *corporation* with limited liability and a life of no more than 99 years; must have at least two and no more than 50 *shareholders.*

SAS. *Statement on Auditing Standards of the AICPA.*

scale effect. *See discounted cash flow.*

scatter diagram. A graphic representation of the relation between two or more variables within a population.

schedule. A supporting set of calculations, with explanations, that show how to derive figures in a *financial statement* or tax return.

scientific method. *Effective interest method* of *amortizing bond discount* or *premium.*

scrap value. *Salvage value* assuming the owner intends to junk the item. A *net realizable value. Residual value.*

SEC (Securities and Exchange Commission). An agency authorized by the U.S. Congress to regulate, among other things, the financial reporting practices of most public corporations. The SEC has indicated that it will usually allow the *FASB* to set accounting principles, but it often requires more disclosure than the FASB requires. The SEC states its accounting requirements in its *Accounting Series Releases (ASR*—replaced in 1982 by the following two), *Financial Reporting Releases, Accounting and Auditing Enforcement Releases, Staff Accounting Bulletins* (these are, strictly speaking, interpretations by the accounting staff, not rules of the commissioners themselves), and *Regulation S-X and Regulation S-K. See also registration statement,* 10-K, *and* 20-F.

secret reserve. *Hidden reserve.*

Securities and Exchange Commission. *SEC.*

securitization. The process of bundling together a group of like *assets,* for example *accounts receivable,* into a single portfolio, then selling that portfolio or partial ownership shares in it. This has roughly the same economic effect as using the assets as *collateral* for a borrowing, but the securitization transaction removes the assets from the *balance sheet.*

security. Document that indicates ownership, such as a *share* of *stock,* or indebtedness, such as a *bond,* or potential ownership, such as an *option* or *warrant.*

security available for sale. According to *SFAS No. 115* (1993), a *debt* or *equity security* that is not a *trading security,* or a debt security that is not a *security held to maturity.*

security held to maturity. According to *SFAS No. 115* (1993), a *debt security* the holder has both the ability and the intent to hold to *maturity;* valued in the *balance sheet* at amortized acquisition cost: the book value of the security at the end of each period is the book value at the beginning of the period multiplied by the historical *yield* on the security (measured as of the time of purchase) less any cash the holder receives at the end of this period from the security.

segment (of a business). As defined by *APB Opinion No. 30,* "a component of an *entity* whose activities represent a separate major line of business or class of customer.... [It can be] a *subsidiary,* a division, or a department, ... provided that its *assets,* results of *operations,* and activities can be clearly distinguished, physically and operationally for financial reporting purposes, from the other assets, results of operations, and activities of the entity." *SFAS No. 14* defines a segment as a "component of an enterprise engaged in promoting a product or service or a group of related products and services primarily to unaffiliated customers … for a profit." *SFAS No. 131* defines operating segments using the "management approach" as components of the enterprise engaging in revenue- and expense-generating business activities "whose operating results are regularly reviewed by the enterprise's chief operating decision maker to make decisions about resources … and asset performance."

segment reporting. Reporting of *sales, income*, and *assets* by *segments of a business*, usually classified by nature of products sold but sometimes by geographical area where the firm produces or sells goods or by type of customers; sometimes called "line of business reporting." The accounting for segment income does not allocate *central corporate expenses* to the segments.

self-balancing. A set of records with equal *debits* and *credits* such as the *ledger* (but not individual accounts), the *balance sheet*, and a *fund* in nonprofit accounting.

self-check(ing) digit. A digit forming part of an account or code number, normally the last digit of the number, which is mathematically derived from the other numbers of the code and is used to detect errors in transcribing the code number. For example, assume the last digit of the account number is the remainder after summing the preceding digits and dividing that sum by nine. Suppose the computer encounters the account numbers 7027261-7 and 9445229-7. The program can tell that something has gone wrong with the encoding of the second account number because the sum of

the first seven digits is 35, whose remainder on division by 9 is 8, not 7. The first account number does not show such an error because the sum of the first seven digits is 25, whose remainder on division by 9 is, indeed, 7. The first account number may be in error, but the second surely is.

self-insurance. *See insurance.*

self-sustaining foreign operation. A foreign operation both financially and operationally independent of the reporting enterprise (owner) so that the owner's exposure to exchange-rate changes results only from the owner's net investment in the foreign entity.

selling and administrative expenses. *Expenses* not specifically identifiable with, or assigned to, production.

semifixed costs. *Costs* that increase with activity as a step function.

semivariable costs. *Costs* that increase strictly linearly with activity but that are positive at zero activity level. Royalty fees of 2 percent of sales are variable; royalty fees of $1,000 per year plus 2 percent of sales are semivariable.

senior securities. *Bonds* as opposed to *preferred shares; preferred shares* as opposed to *common shares.* The firm must meet the senior security claim against *earnings* or *assets* before meeting the claims of less-senior securities.

sensitivity analysis. A study of how the outcome of a decision-making process changes as one or more of the assumptions change.

sequential access. Computer-storage access in which the analyst can locate information only by a sequential search of the storage file. Compare *direct access.*

serial bonds. An *issue* of *bonds* that mature in part at one date, another part on another date, and so on. The various maturity dates usually occur at equally spaced intervals. Contrast with *term bonds.*

service basis of depreciation. *Production method.*

service bureau. A commercial data-processing center providing service to various customers.

service cost, (current) service cost. *Pension plan expenses incurred* during an *accounting period* for employment services performed during that period. Contrast with *prior service cost. See funded.*

service department. A department, such as the personnel or computer department, that provides services to other departments rather than direct work on a salable product. Contrast with *production department.* A firm must allocate costs of service departments whose services benefit manufacturing operations to *product costs* under *full absorption costing.*

service department cost allocation. A procedure in which firms *allocate* the *costs* of operating service departments to other departments.

service life. Period of expected usefulness of an asset; can differ from *depreciable life* for income tax purposes.

service potential. The future benefits that cause an item to be classified as an *asset.* Without service potential, an item has no future benefits, and accounting will not classify the item as an asset. *SFAC No. 6* suggests that the primary characteristic of service potential is the ability to generate future net cash inflows.

services. Useful work done by a person, a machine, or an organization. *See goods.*

setup. The time or costs required to prepare production equipment for doing a job.

SFAC. *Statement of Financial Accounting Concepts* of the *FASB.*

SFAS. *Statement of Financial Accounting Standards. See FASB.*

shadow price. An opportunity cost. A *linear programming* analysis provides as one of its outputs the potential value of having available more of the scarce resources that constrain the production process, for example, the value of having more time available on a machine tool critical to the production of two products. Common terminology refers to this value as the "shadow price" or the "dual value" of the scarce resource.

share. A *security* representing ownership in a corporation.

share premium. U.K.: *additional paid-in capital* or *capital contributed in excess of par value.*

shareholders' equity. *Proprietorship* or *owners' equity* of a corporation. Because *stock* means inventory in Australia, the U.K., and Canada, their writers use the term "shareholders' equity" rather than the term "stockholders' equity."

short run. short term. Contrast with *long run.* Managers mean a period of time long enough to allow change the level of production or other activity within the constraints of current total productive capacity. In a *balance sheet* context, it means *current*, ordinarily due within one year. Use a hyphen when the phrase is an adjective, but no hyphen when it is a noun.

short-term liquidity risk. The risk that an *entity* will not have enough *cash* in the *short run* to pay its *debts.*

short-term operating budget. Management's quantitative action plan for the coming year.

shrinkage. An excess of *inventory* shown on the *books* over actual physical quantities on hand; can result from theft or shoplifting as well as from evaporation or general wear and tear. Some accountants, in an attempt to downplay their own errors, use the term to mean record-keeping mistakes that they later must correct, with some embarrassment, and that result in material changes in reported income. One should not use the term "shrinkage" for the correction of mistakes because adequate terminology exists for describing mistakes.

shutdown cost. Those fixed costs that the firm continues to incur after it has ceased production; the costs of closing down a particular production facility.

side letter. *See channel stuffing.*

sight draft. A demand for payment drawn by Person A to whom Person B owes cash. Person A presents the *draft* to Person B's (the debtor's) bank in expectation that Person B will authorize his or her bank to disburse the funds. Sellers often use such drafts when selling goods to a new customer in a different city. The seller is uncertain whether the buyer will pay the bill. The seller sends the *bill* of lading, or other evidence of ownership of the goods, along with a sight draft to the buyer's bank. Before the warehouse holding the goods can release them to the buyer, the buyer must instruct its bank to honor the sight draft by withdrawing funds from the buyer's account. Once the bank honors the sight draft, it hands to the buyer the bill of lading or other document evidencing ownership, and the goods become the property of the buyer.

simple interest. *Interest* calculated on *principal* where interest earned during periods before maturity of the loan does not increase the principal amount earning interest for the subsequent periods and the lender cannot withdraw the funds before maturity. Interest = principal × interest rate × time, where the rate is a rate per period (typically a year) and time is expressed in units of that period. For example, if the *rate* is annual and the time is two months, then in the formula, use 2/12 for *time*. Economic calculations seldom use simple interest except for periods of less than one year and then only for computational convenience. Contrast with *compound interest*.

single-entry accounting. Accounting that is neither *self-balancing* nor *articulated*. That is, it does not rely on equal *debits* and *credits*. The firm makes no *journal entries* and must *plug* to derive *owners' equity* for the *balance sheet*.

single proprietorship. *Sole proprietorship.*

single-step. Said of an *income statement* in which *ordinary revenue* and *gain* items appear first, with their total. Then come all ordinary *expenses* and *losses*, with their total. The difference between these two totals, plus the effect of *income from discontinued operations* and *extraordinary items*, appears as *net income*. Contrast with *multiple-step* and *see proprietorship theory*.

sinking fund. *Assets* and their earnings earmarked for the retirement of bonds or other long-term obligations. Earnings of sinking fund investments become taxable income of the company.

sinking fund method of depreciation. Method in which the periodic charge is an equal amount each period so that the *future value* of the charges, considered as an *annuity*, will accumulate at the end of the depreciable life to an amount equal to the *acquisition cost* of the asset. The firm does not necessarily, or even usually, accumulate a *fund* of cash. Firms rarely use this method.

skeleton account. *T-account.*

slide. The name of the error made by a bookkeeper in recording the digits of a number correctly with the decimal point misplaced; for example, recording $123.40 as $1,234.00 or as $12.34. If the only errors in a *trial balance* result from one or more slides, then the difference between the sum of the *debits* and the sum of the *credits* will be divisible by nine. Not all such differences divisible by nine result from slides. *See transposition error.*

SMAC (Society of Management Accountants of Canada). The national association of accountants whose provincial associations engage in industrial and governmental accounting. The association undertakes research and administers an educational program and comprehensive examinations; those who pass qualify to be designated CMA (Certified Management Accountants), formerly called RIA (Registered Industrial Accountant).

SNC (société en nom collectif). France: a *partnership.*

soak-up method. The *equity method.*

Social Security taxes. Taxes levied by the federal government on both employers and employees to provide *funds* to pay retired persons (or their survivors) who are entitled to receive such payments, either because they paid Social Security taxes themselves or because Congress has declared them eligible. Unlike a *pension plan*, the Social Security system does not collect funds and invest them for many years. The tax collections in a given year pay primarily for benefits distributed that year. At any given time the system has a multitrillion-dollar unfunded obligation to current workers for their eventual retirement benefits. *See Old Age, Survivors, Disability, and Insurance.*

software. The programming aids—such as compilers, sort and report programs, and generators—that extend the capabilities of and simplify the use of the computer, as well as certain operating systems and other control programs. Compare *hardware.*

sole proprietorship. A firm in which all *owners' equity* belongs to one person.

solvent. Able to meet debts when due.

SOP. *Statement of Position* (of the *AcSEC* of the *AICPA*).

sound value. A phrase used mainly in appraisals of *fixed assets* to mean *fair market price (value)* or *replacement cost* in present condition.

source of funds. Any *transaction* that increases *cash* and *marketable securities* held as *current assets.*

sources and uses statement. *Statement of cash flows.*

SOYD. *Sum-of-the-years'-digits depreciation.*

SP (société en participation). France: a silent *partnership* in which the managing partner acts for the partnership as an individual in transacting with others who need not know that the person represents a partnership.

special assessment. A compulsory levy made by a governmental unit on property to pay the costs of a specific improvement or service presumed not to benefit the general public but only the owners of the property so assessed; accounted for in a special assessment fund.

special journal. A *journal*, such as a sales journal or cash disbursements journal, to record *transactions* of a similar nature that occur frequently.

special purpose entity. The name for a business now known as a *variable interest entity*. *GAAP* never defined this name, but brought it into existence with an *EITF* consensus in 1990. The Enron financial manipulations depended in part on use of these entities to achieve *off-balance-sheet financing*.

special revenue debt. A governmental unit's debt backed only by revenues from specific sources, such as tolls from a bridge.

specific identification method. Method for valuing *ending inventory* and *cost of goods sold* by identifying actual units sold and remaining in inventory and summing the actual costs of those individual units; usually used for items with large unit values, such as precious jewelry, automobiles, and fur coats.

specific item sampling. Sampling in which the analyst selects particular items because of their nature, value, or method of recording. Compare *representative item sampling*.

specific price changes. Changes in the market prices of specific *goods* and *services*. Contrast with *general price-level changes*.

specific price index. A measure of the price of a specific good or service, or a small group of similar goods or services, at one time relative to the price during a base period. Contrast with *general price index*. *See dollar-value LIFO method*.

spending variance. In *standard cost systems*, the *rate* or *price variance* for *overhead costs*.

split. *Stock split*. Sometimes called "split-up."

split-off point. In accumulating and allocating costs for *joint products*, the point at which all costs are no longer *joint costs* but at which an analyst can identify costs associated with individual products or perhaps with a smaller number of *joint products*.

spoilage. *See abnormal spoilage* and *normal spoilage*.

spot price. The price of a commodity for delivery on the day of the price quotation. *See forward price* for contrast.

spreadsheet. For many years, a term that referred specifically to a *work sheet* organized like a *matrix* that provides a two-way classification of accounting data. The rows and columns both have labels, which are *account* titles. An entry in a row represents a *debit*, whereas an entry in a column represents a *credit*. Thus, the number "100" in the "cash" row and the "accounts receivable" column records an entry debiting cash and crediting accounts receivable for $100. A given row total indicates all debit entries to the account represented by that row, and a given column total indicates the sum of all credit entries to the account represented by the column. Since personal-computer software has become widespread, this term has come to refer to any file created by programs such as Lotus 1-2-3® and Microsoft Excel®. Such files have rows and columns, but they need not represent debits and credits. Moreover, they can have more than two dimensions.

squeeze. A term sometimes used for *plug*.

SSARS. *Statement on Standards for Accounting and Review Services.*

stabilized accounting. *Constant-dollar accounting.*

stable monetary unit assumption. In spite of *inflation*, which appears to be a way of life, the assumption that underlies historical cost/nominal-dollar accounting—namely that one can meaningfully add together current dollars and dollars of previous years. The assumption gives no specific recognition to changing values of the dollar in the usual *financial statements*. *See constant-dollar accounting.*

Staff Accounting Bulletin. An interpretation issued by the staff of the chief accountant of the *SEC* "suggesting" how the accountants should apply various *Accounting Series Releases* in practice. The suggestions are part of *GAAP*.

stakeholder. An individual or group, such as employees, suppliers, customers, and shareholders, who have an interest in the corporation's activities and outcomes.

standard cost. Anticipated *cost* of producing a unit of output; a predetermined cost to be assigned to products produced. Standard cost implies a norm—what costs should be. Budgeted cost implies a forecast—something likely, but not necessarily, a "should," as implied by a norm. Firms use standard costs as the benchmark for gauging good and bad performance. Although a firm can similarly use a budget, it need not. A budget can be a planning document, subject to changes whenever plans change, whereas standard costs usually change annually or when technology significantly changes or when costs of labor and materials significantly change.

standard costing. *Costing* based on *standard costs.*

standard costing system. *Product costing* using *standard costs* rather than actual costs. The firm can use either *full absorption* or *variable costing* principles.

standard error (of regression coefficients). A measure of the uncertainty about the magnitude of the estimated parameters of an equation fit with a *regression analysis.*

standard manufacturing overhead. *Overhead costs* expected to be incurred per unit of time and per unit produced.

standard price (rate). Unit price established for materials or labor used in *standard cost systems.*

standard quantity allowed. The direct material or direct labor (inputs) quantity that production should have used if it had produced the units of output in accordance with preset *standards.*

standby costs. A type of *capacity cost*, such as property taxes, incurred even if a firm shuts down operations completely. Contrast with *enabling costs.*

stated capital. Amount of capital contributed by shareholders; sometimes used to mean *legal capital.*

stated value. A term sometimes used for the *face amount* of *capital stock*, when the *board* has not designated a *par value*. Where there is stated value per share, *capital contributed in excess of stated value* can come into being.

statement of affairs. A *balance sheet* showing immediate *liquidation* amounts rather than *historical costs*, usually prepared when *insolvency* or *bankruptcy* is imminent. Such a statement specifically does not use the *going-concern assumption.*

statement of cash flows. A schedule of *cash receipts* and *payments*, classified by *investing, financing*, and *operating activities*; required by the *FASB* for all for-profit companies. Companies can report operating activities with either the direct method (which shows only receipts and payments of cash) or the indirect method (which starts with *net income* and shows adjustments for *revenues* not currently producing cash and for *expenses* not currently using cash). "Cash" includes cash equivalents such as Treasury bills, commercial paper, and *marketable securities* held as *current assets*. This is sometimes called the "funds statement." Before 1987, the FASB required the presentation of a similar statement called the *statement of changes in financial position*, which tended to emphasize *working capital*, not cash.

statement of changes in financial position. As defined by *APB Opinion No. 19*, a statement that explains the changes in *working capital* (or cash) balances during a period and shows the changes in the working capital (or cash) accounts themselves. The *statement of cash flows* has replaced this statement.

statement of charge and discharge. A financial statement, showing *net assets* or *income*, drawn up by an executor or administrator, to account for receipts and dispositions of cash or other assets in an estate or trust.

Statement of Financial Accounting Concepts (SFAC). One of a series of *FASB* publications in its *conceptual framework* for *financial accounting* and reporting. Such statements set forth objectives and fundamentals to be the basis for specific financial accounting and reporting standards.

Statement of Financial Accounting Standards (SFAS). See FASB.

statement of financial position. *Balance sheet.*

Statement of Position (SOP). A recommendation, on an emerging accounting problem, issued by the *AcSEC* of the *AICPA*. The AICPA's Code of Professional Ethics specifically states that *CPAs* need not treat *SOPs* as they do rules from the *FASB*, but a CPA would be wary of departing from the recommendations of an *SOP*.

statement of retained earnings (income). A statement that reconciles the beginning-of-period and the end-of-period balances in the *retained earnings* account. It shows the effects of *earnings, dividend declarations,* and *prior-period adjustments.*

statement of significant accounting policies (principles). A summary of the significant *accounting principles* used in compiling an *annual report*; required by *APB Opinion No. 22.* This summary can be a separate exhibit or the first *note* to the financial statements.

Statement on Auditing Standards (SAS). A series addressing specific auditing standards and procedures. *No. 1* (1973) of this series codifies all statements on auditing standards previously promulgated by the *AICPA*.

Statement on Standards for Accounting and Review Services (SSARS). Pronouncements issued by the *AICPA* on unaudited *financial statements* and unaudited financial information of nonpublic entities.

static budget. *Fixed budget.* Budget developed for a set level of the driving variable, such as production or sales, which the analyst does not change if the actual level deviates from the level set at the outset of the analysis.

status quo. Events or cost incurrences that will happen or that a firm expects to happen in the absence of taking some contemplated action.

statutory tax rate. The tax rate specified in the *income tax* law for each type of income (for example, *ordinary income, capital gain or loss).*

step allocation method. *Step-down method.*

step cost. *Semifixed cost.*

step-down method. In *allocating service department* costs, a method that starts by allocating one service department's costs to *production departments* and to all other service departments. Then the firm allocates a second service department's costs, including costs allocated from the first, to production departments and to all other service departments except the first one. In this fashion, a firm can allocate all service departments costs, including previous allocations, to production departments and to those service departments whose costs it has not yet allocated.

step method. *Step-down method.*

step(ped) cost. *Semifixed cost.*

sterilized allocation. Desirable characteristics of cost allocation methods. Optimal decisions result from considering *incremental costs* only. Optimal decisions never require *allocations* of *joint* or *common costs.* A "sterilized allocation" causes the optimal decision choice not to differ from the one that occurs when the accountant does not allocate joint or common costs "sterilized" with respect to that decision. Arthur L. Thomas first used the term in this context. Because *absorption costing* requires that product costs absorb all manufacturing costs and because some allocations can lead to bad decisions, Thomas (and we) advocate that the analyst choose a sterilized allocation scheme that will not alter the otherwise optimal

decision. No single allocation scheme is always sterilized with respect to all decisions. Thus, Thomas (and we) advocate that decisions be made on the basis of incremental costs before any allocations.

stewardship. Principle by which management is accountable for an *entity's* resources, for their efficient use, and for protecting them from adverse impact. Some theorists believe that accounting has as a primary goal aiding users of *financial statements* in their assessment of management's performance in stewardship.

stock. A measure of the amount of something on hand at a specific time. In this sense, contrast with *flow. See inventory* and *capital stock.*

stock appreciation rights. An employer's promise to pay to the employee an amount of *cash* on a certain future date, with the amount of cash being the difference between the *market value* of a specified number of *shares* of *stock* in the employer's company on the given future date and some base price set on the date the rights are granted. Firms sometimes use this form of compensation because changes in tax laws in recent years have made *stock options* relatively less attractive. *GAAP* compute compensation based on the difference between the market value of the shares and the base price set at the time of the grant.

stock dividend. A so-called *dividend* in which the firm distributes additional *shares* of *capital stock* without cash payments to existing shareholders. It results in a *debit* to *retained earnings* in the amount of the market value of the shares issued and a *credit* to *capital stock* accounts. Firms ordinarily use stock dividends to indicate that they have permanently reinvested earnings in the business. Contrast with a *stock split*, which requires no entry in the capital stock accounts other than a notation that the *par* or *stated value* per share has changed. Because UK terminology restricts the word "stock" to *inventory*, we tend to refer to "shares," not "stock," in the context of capital stock. In this context, however, almost all refer to "stock" dividend, "not" share dividend.

stock option. The right to purchase or sell a specified number of shares of *stock* for a specified price at specified times. Employee stock options are purchase rights granted by a corporation to employees, a form of compensation. Traded stock options are *derivative* securities, rights created and traded by investors, independent of the corporation whose stock is optioned. Contrast with *warrant.*

stock right. *See right.*

stock split(-up). Increase in the number of common shares outstanding resulting from the issuance of additional shares to existing shareholders without additional capital contributions by them. Does not increase the total *value* (or *stated value*) of *common shares* outstanding because the *board* reduces the par (or stated) value per share in inverse proportion. A three-for-one stock split reduces par (or stated) value per share to one-third of its former amount. A stock split usually implies a distribution that increases the number of shares outstanding by 20 percent or more. Compare with *stock dividend.*

stock subscriptions. *See subscription* and *subscribed stock.*

stock warrant. *See warrant.*

stockholders' equity. *See shareholders' equity.*

stockout. Occurs when a firm needs a unit of *inventory* to use in production or to sell to a customer but has none available.

stockout costs. *Contribution margin* or other measure of *profits* not earned because a seller has run out of *inventory* and cannot fill a customer's order. A firm can incur an extra cost because of delay in filling an order.

stores. *Raw materials*, parts, and supplies.

straight-debt value. An estimate of the *market value* of a *convertible bond* if the bond did not contain a conversion privilege.

straight-line depreciation. Method in which, if the *depreciable life* is n periods, the periodic *depreciation* charge is $1/n$ of the *depreciable cost*; results in equal periodic charges. Accountants sometimes call it "straight-time depreciation."

strategic plan. A statement of the method for achieving an organization's goals.

stratified sampling. In choosing a *sample*, a method in which the investigator first divides the entire *population* into relatively homogeneous subgroups (strata) and then selects random samples from these subgroups.

street security. A stock certificate in immediately transferable form, most commonly because the issuing firm has registered it in the name of the broker, who has endorsed it with "payee" left blank.

Subchapter S corporation. A firm legally organized as a *corporation* but taxed as if it were a *partnership*. Tax terminology calls the corporations paying their own income taxes C *corporations.*

subject to. In an *auditor's report*, qualifications usually caused by a *material* uncertainty in the valuation of an item, such as future promised payments from a foreign government or outcome of pending litigation.

subordinated. *Debt* whose claim on income or assets has lower priority than claims of other debt.

subscribed stock. A *shareholders' equity* account showing the capital that the firm will receive as soon as the share-purchaser pays the subscription price. A subscription is a legal contract, so once the share-purchaser signs it, the firm makes an entry *debiting* an *owners' equity contra account* and *crediting* subscribed stock.

subscription. Agreement to buy a *security* or to purchase periodicals, such as magazines.

subsequent events. *Poststatement events.*

subsidiary. A company in which another company owns more than 50 percent of the voting shares.

subsidiary ledger. The *ledger* that contains the detailed accounts whose total appears in a *controlling account* of the *general ledger*.

subsidiary (ledger) accounts. The *accounts* in a *subsidiary ledger*.

successful efforts costing. In petroleum accounting, the *capitalization* of the drilling costs of only those wells that contain gas or oil. *See reserve recognition accounting* for an example.

summary annual report (SAR). Condensed financial statements distributed in lieu of the usual *annual report*. Since 1987, the *SEC* has allowed firms to include such statements in the annual report to shareholders as long as the firm includes full, detailed statements in SEC filings and in *proxy* materials sent to shareholders.

summary of significant accounting principles. *Statement of significant accounting policies (principles).*

sum-of-the-years'-digits depreciation (SYD, SOYD). An *accelerated depreciation* method for an asset with *depreciable life* of n years where the charge in period i ($i = 1, ..., n$) is the fraction $(n + 1 - i)/[n(n + 1)/2]$ of the *depreciable cost*. If an asset has a depreciable cost of $15,000 and a five-year depreciable life, for example, the depreciation charges would be $5,000 ($= 5/15 \times$ $15,000) in the first year, $4,000 in the second, $3,000 in the third, $2,000 in the fourth, and $1,000 in the fifth. The name derives from the fact that the denominator in the fraction is the sum of the digits 1 through n.

sunk cost. Past *costs* that current and future decisions cannot affect and, hence, that are irrelevant for decision making aside from *income tax* effects. Contrast with *incremental costs* and *imputed costs*. For example, the *acquisition cost* of machinery is irrelevant to a decision of whether to scrap the machinery. The current *exit value* of the machinery is the *opportunity cost* of continuing to own it, and the cost of, say, the electricity to run the machinery is an incremental cost of its operation. Sunk costs become relevant for decision making when the analysis requires taking *income taxes (gain* or *loss* on disposal of asset) into account, since the cash payment for income taxes depends on the tax basis of the asset. Avoid this term in careful writing because it is ambiguous. Consider, for example, a machine costing $100,000 with current *salvage* value of $20,000. Some (including us) would say that $100,000 (the *gross* amount) is "sunk"; others would say that only $80,000 (the *net* amount) is "sunk."

supplementary statements (schedules). Statements (schedules) in addition to the four basic *financial statements* (*balance sheet, income statement, statement of cash flows,* and the *statement of retained earnings*).

surplus. A word once used but now considered poor terminology; prefaced by "earned" to mean *retained earnings* and prefaced by "capital" to mean *capital contributed in excess of par (or stated) value.*

surplus reserves. *Appropriated retained earnings.* A phrase with nothing to recommend it: of all the words in accounting, *reserve* is the most objectionable, and *surplus* is the second-most objectionable.

suspense account. A *temporary account* used to record part of a transaction before final analysis of that transaction. For example, if a business regularly classifies all sales into a dozen or more different categories but wants to deposit the proceeds of cash sales every day, it can credit a sales suspense account pending detailed classification of all sales into Durable Goods Sales, Women's Clothing Sales, Men's Clothing Sales, Housewares Sales, and so on.

sustainable income. The part of *distributable income* (computed from *current cost* data) that the firm can expect to earn in the next accounting period if it continues operations at the same levels as were maintained during the current period. *Income from discontinued operations,* for example, can be distributable but not sustainable.

swap. A currency swap is a financial instrument in which the holder promises to pay to (or receive from) the *counterparty* the difference between *debt* denominated in one currency (such as U.S. dollars) and the payments on debt denominated in another currency (such as German marks). An interest-rate swap typically obligates the party and counterparty to exchange the difference between fixed- and floating-rate interest payments on otherwise similar loans.

S-X. *See Regulation S-X.*

SYD. *Sum-of-the-years'-digits depreciation.*

T

T-account. Account form shaped like the letter T with the title above the horizontal line. *Debits* appear on the left of the vertical line, *credits* on the right.

take-home pay. The amount of a paycheck; earned wages or *salary* reduced by deductions for *income taxes, Social Security taxes,* contributions to fringe-benefit plans, union dues, and so on. Take-home pay might be as little as half of earned compensation.

take-or-pay contract. As defined by *SFAS No. 47,* a purchaser-seller agreement that provides for the purchaser to pay specified amounts periodically in return for products or services. The purchaser must make specified minimum payments even if it does not take delivery of the contracted products or services.

taking a bath. To incur a large loss. *See big bath.*

tangible. Having physical form. Accounting has never satisfactorily defined the distinction between tangible and intangible assets. Typically, accountants define intangibles by giving an exhaustive list, and everything not on the list is defined as tangible. *See intangible asset* for such a list.

target cost. *Standard cost.* Sometimes, target price less expected profit margin.

target price. Selling price based on customers' value in use of a good or service, constrained by competitors' prices of similar items.

tax. A nonpenal, but compulsory, charge levied by a government on income, consumption, wealth, or other basis, for the benefit of all those governed. The term does not include fines or specific charges for benefits accruing only to those paying the charges, such as licenses, permits, special assessments, admission fees, and tolls.

tax allocation: interperiod. *See deferred income tax liability.*

tax allocation: intrastatement. The showing of income tax effects on *extraordinary items, income from discontinued operations*, and *prior-period adjustments*, along with these items, separately from income taxes on other income. *See net-of-tax reporting.*

tax avoidance. *See tax shelter* and *loophole.*

tax basis of assets and liabilities. A concept important for applying *SFAS No. 109* on *deferred income taxes.* Two *assets* will have different *book values* if the firm paid different amounts for them, *amortizes* them on a different schedule, or both. Similarly a single asset will have a book value different from what it will have for tax purposes if the firm recorded different *acquisition* amounts for the asset for book and for tax purposes, amortizes it differently for book and for tax purposes, or both. The difference between financial book value and income tax basis becomes important in computing deferred income tax amounts. The adjusted cost in the financial records is the "book basis," and the adjusted amount in the tax records is the "tax basis." Differences between book and tax basis can arise for *liabilities* as well as for assets.

tax credit. A subtraction from taxes otherwise payable. Contrast with *tax deduction.*

tax deduction. A subtraction from *revenues* and *gains* to arrive at taxable income. Tax deductions differ technically from tax *exemptions*, but both reduce gross income in computing taxable income. Both differ from *tax credits*, which reduce the computed tax itself in computing taxes payable. If the tax rate is the fraction t of pretax income, then a *tax credit* of $1 is worth $1/t$ of *tax deductions.*

tax evasion. The fraudulent understatement of taxable revenues or overstatement of deductions and expenses or both. Contrast with *tax shelter* and *loophole.*

tax-exempts. *See municipal bonds.*

tax shelter. The legal avoidance of, or reduction in, *income taxes* resulting from a careful reading of the complex income-tax regulations and the subsequent rearrangement of financial affairs to take advantage of the regulations. Often writers use the term pejoratively, but the courts have long held that a taxpayer has no obligation to pay taxes any larger than the legal minimum. If the public concludes that a given tax shelter is "unfair," then Congress can, and has, changed the laws and regulations. The term is sometimes used to refer to the investment that permits tax avoidance. *See loophole.*

tax shield. The amount of an *expense*, such as *depreciation*, that reduces taxable income but does not require *working capital.* Sometimes this term includes expenses that reduce taxable income and use working capital. A depreciation deduction (or *R&D expense* in the expanded sense) of $10,000 provides a tax shield of $3,700 when the marginal tax rate is 37 percent.

taxable income. *Income* computed according to *IRS* regulations and subject to *income taxes.* Contrast with income, net income, income before taxes (in the *income statement*), and *comprehensive income* (a *financial reporting* concept). Use the term "pretax income" to refer to income before taxes on the income statement in financial reports.

tax-transfer lease. One form of *capital lease.* Congress has in the past provided business with an incentive to invest in qualifying *plant and equipment* by granting an *investment credit*, which, though it occurs as a reduction in *income taxes* otherwise payable, effectively reduces the purchase price of the assets. Similarly, Congress continues to grant an incentive to acquire such assets by allowing the *Modified Accelerated Cost Recovery System* (*MACRS*, form of unusually *accelerated depreciation*). Accelerated depreciation for tax purposes allows a reduction of taxes paid in the early years of an asset's life, providing the firm with an increased *net present value* of *cash flows.* The *IRS* administers both of these incentives through the income tax laws, rather than paying an outright cash payment. A business with no taxable income in many cases had difficulty reaping the benefits of the investment credit or of accelerated depreciation because Congress had not provided for tax refunds to those who acquire qualifying assets but who have no taxable income. In principle, a company without taxable income could lease from another firm with taxable income an asset that it would otherwise purchase. The second firm acquires the asset, gets the tax-reduction benefits from the acquisition, and becomes a lessor, leasing the asset (presumably at a lower price reflecting its own costs lowered by the tax reductions) to the unprofitable

company. Before 1981, tax laws discouraged such leases. That is, although firms could enter into such leases, they could not legally transfer the tax benefits. Under certain restrictive conditions, the tax law now allows a profitable firm to earn tax credits and take deductions while leasing to the firm without tax liability in such leases. These are sometimes called "safe-harbor leases."

Technical Bulletin. The *FASB* has authorized its staff to issue bulletins to provide guidance on financial accounting and reporting problems. Although the FASB does not formally approve the contents of the bulletins, their contents are part of *GAAP.*

technology. The sum of a firm's technical *trade secrets* and *know-how*, as distinct from its *patents.*

temporary account. *Account* that does not appear on the *balance sheet; revenue* and *expense* accounts, their *adjuncts* and *contras, production cost accounts, dividend distribution accounts*, and purchases-related accounts (which close to the various inventories); sometimes called a "nominal account."

temporary difference. According to the *SFAS No. 109* (1992) definition: "A difference between the tax basis of an asset or liability and its reported amount in the financial statements that will result in taxable or deductible amounts in future years." Temporary differences include *timing differences* and differences between *taxable income* and pretax income caused by different cost bases for assets. For example, a plant asset can have a cost of $10,000 for financial reporting but a basis of $7,000 for income tax purposes. This temporary difference could arise because the firm has used an accelerated depreciation method for tax but straight-line for book, or the firm could have purchased the asset in a transaction in which the fair value of the asset exceeded its tax basis. Both situations create a temporary difference.

temporary investments. Investments in *marketable securities* that the owner intends to sell within a short time, usually one year, and hence classifies as *current assets.*

10-K. The name of the annual report that the *SEC* requires of nearly all publicly held corporations.

term bonds. A *bond issue* whose component bonds all mature at the same time. Contrast with *serial bonds.*

terminal cash flows. *Cash flows* that occur at the end of an *investment* project. Often include proceeds of *salvage* of equipment and tax on *gain (loss)* on disposal.

term loan. A loan with a *maturity* date, as opposed to a demand loan, which is due whenever the lender requests payment. In practice, bankers and auditors use this phrase only for loans for a year or more.

term structure. A phrase with different meanings in *accounting* and *financial economics.* In accounting, it refers to the pattern of times that must elapse before *assets* turn into, or produce, *cash* and the pattern of times that must elapse before *liabilities* require cash. In financial economics, the phrase refers to the pattern of interest rates as a function of the time that elapses for loans to come due. For example, if six-month loans cost 6 percent per year and 10-year loans cost 9 percent per year, this is called a "normal" term structure because the longer-term loan carries a higher rate. If the six-month loan costs 9 percent per year and the 10-year loan costs 6 percent per year, the term structure is said to be "inverted." *See yield curve.*

terms of sale. The conditions governing payment for a sale. For example, the terms *2/10, n(et)/30* mean that if the purchaser makes payment within 10 days of the invoice date, it can take a *discount* of 2 percent from *invoice* price; the purchaser must pay the invoice amount, in any event, within 30 days, or it becomes overdue.

theory of constraints (TOC). Concept of improving operations by identifying and reducing bottlenecks in process flows.

thin capitalization. A state of having a high *debt-equity ratio.* Under income tax legislation, the term has a special meaning.

throughput contract. As defined by *SFAS No. 47,* an agreement signed by a shipper (processor) and by the owner of a transportation facility (such as an oil or natural gas pipeline or a ship) or a manufacturing facility that provides for the shipper (processor) to pay specified amounts periodically in return for the transportation (processing) of a product. The shipper (processor) must make cash payments even if it does not ship (process) the contracted quantities.

throughput contribution. Sales dollars minus the sum of all short-run variable costs.

tickler file. A collection of *vouchers* or other memoranda arranged chronologically to remind the person in charge of certain duties to make payments (or to do other tasks) as scheduled.

time-adjusted rate of return. *Internal rate of return.*

time cost. *Period cost.*

time deposit. Cash in bank earning interest. Contrast with *demand deposit.*

time-series analysis. *See cross-section analysis* for definition and contrast.

times-interest (charges) earned. Ratio of pretax *income* plus *interest* charges to interest charges. *See ratio.*

timing difference. The major type of *temporary difference* between taxable income and pretax income reported to shareholders; reverses in a subsequent period and requires an entry in the *deferred income tax* account; for example, the use of *accelerated depreciation* for tax returns and *straight-line depreciation* for financial reporting. Contrast with *permanent difference.*

Toronto Stock Exchange (TSX). A public market where various corporate securities trade.

total assets turnover. *Sales* divided by average total *assets.*

total quality management (TQM). Concept of organizing a company to excel in all its activities in order to increase the quality of products and services.

traceable cost. A *cost* that a firm can identify with or assign to a specific product. Contrast with a *joint cost.*

trade acceptance. A *draft* that a seller presents for signature (acceptance) to the buyer at the time it sells goods. The draft then becomes the equivalent of a *note receivable* of the seller and a *note payable* of the buyer.

trade credit. Occurs when one business allows another to buy from it in return for a promise to pay later. Contrast with "consumer credit," which occurs when a business extends a retail customer the privilege of paying later.

trade discount. A *list price discount* offered to all customers of a given type. Contrast with a *discount* offered for prompt payment and with *quantity discount.*

trade-in. Acquiring a new *asset* in exchange for a used one and perhaps additional cash. *See boot* and *trade-in transaction.*

trade-in transaction. The accounting for a trade-in; depends on whether the firm receives an asset "similar" to (and used in the same line of business as) the asset traded in and whether the accounting is for *financial statements* or for *income tax* returns. Assume that an old asset cost $5,000, has $3,000 of *accumulated depreciation* (after recording depreciation to the date of the trade-in), and hence has a *book value* of $2,000. The old asset appears to have a market value of $1,500, according to price quotations in used asset markets. The firm trades in the old asset on a new asset with a list price of $10,000. The firm gives up the old asset and $5,500 cash *(boot)* for the new asset. The generic entry for the trade-in transaction is as follows:

New Asset	A		
Accumulated Depreciation (Old Asset)	3,000		
Adjustment on Exchange of Asset	B	or	B
Old Asset	5,000		
Cash	5,500		

1. The *list price* method of accounting for trade-ins rests on the assumption that the list price of the new asset closely approximates its market value. The firm records the new asset at its list price (A = $10,000 in the example); B is a *plug* (= $2,500 credit in the example). If B requires a *debit* plug, the Adjustment on Exchange of Asset is a *loss*; if B requires a *credit* plug (as in the example), the adjustment is a *gain.*

2. Another theoretically sound method of accounting for trade-ins rests on the assumption that the price quotation from used-asset markets gives a market value of the old asset that is a more reliable measure than the market value of the new asset determined by list price. This method uses the *fair market price (value)* of the old asset, $1,500 in the example, to determine B (= $2,000 book value − $1,500 assumed proceeds on disposition = $500 debit or loss). The exchange results in a loss if the book value of the old asset exceeds its market value and in a gain if the market value exceeds the book value. The firm records the new asset on the books by plugging for A (= $7,000 in the example).

3. For income tax reporting, the taxpayer must recognize neither gain nor loss on the trade-in. Thus the taxpayer records the new asset for tax purposes by assuming B is zero and plugging for A (= $7,500 in the example). In practice, firms that want to recognize the loss currently will sell the old asset directly, rather than trading it in, and acquire the new asset entirely for cash.

4. *Generally accepted accounting principles (APB Opinion No. 29)* require a variant of these methods. The basic method is (1) or (2), depending on whether the list price of the new asset (1) or the quotation of the old asset's market value (2) provides the more reliable indication of market value. If the basic method requires a debit entry, or loss, for the Adjustment on Exchange of Asset, then the firm records the trade-in as in (1) or (2) and recognizes the full amount of the loss currently. If, however, the basic method requires a credit entry, or gain, for the Adjustment on Exchange of Asset, then the firm recognizes the gain currently if the old asset and the new asset are not "similar." If the assets are similar and the party trading in receives no cash, then it recognizes no gain and the treatment resembles that in (3); that is B = 0, plug for A. If the assets are similar and the firm trading in receives cash—a rare case—then it recognizes a portion of the gain currently. The portion of the gain recognized currently is the fraction cash received/fair market value of total consideration received. (When the firm uses the list price method, (1), it assumes that the market value of the old asset is the list price of the new asset plus the amount of cash received by the party trading in.) A summary of the results of applying *GAAP* to the example follows.

More Reliable Information as to Fair Market Value	Old Asset Compared with New Asset	
	Similar	Not Similar
New Asset List Price	A = $7,500	A = $10,000
	B = 0	B = 2,500 gain
Old Asset Market Price	A = $7,000	A = $ 7,000
	B = 500 loss	B = 500 loss

trade payables (receivables). *Payables (receivables)* arising in the ordinary course of business transactions. Most *accounts payable (receivable)* are of this kind.

trade secret. Technical or business information such as formulas, recipes, computer programs, and marketing data not generally known by competitors and maintained by the firm as a secret; theoretically capable of having an indefinite, finite life. A famous example is the secret process for Coca-Cola® (a registered *trademark* of the company). Compare with *know-how.* The firm will capitalize this intangible asset only if purchased. If this *intangible* has a finite, expected useful life, *GAAP* require amortization over that estimate of its life. If the right has indefinite life, then *GAAP* require no amortization, but annual tests for *impairment.* If the firm develops the intangible internally, the firm will *expense* the costs as incurred and show no asset.

trademark. A distinctive word or symbol that is affixed to a product, its package, or its dispenser and that uniquely identifies the firm's products and services. *See trademark right.*

trademark right. The right to exclude competitors in sales or advertising from using words or symbols that are so similar to the firm's *trademarks* as possibly to confuse consumers. Trademark rights last as long as the firm continues to use the trademarks in question. In the United States, trademark rights arise from use and not from government registration. They therefore have a legal life independent of the life of a registration. Registrations last 20 years, and the holder can renew them as long as the holder uses the trademark. If this *intangible* has a finite, expected useful life, *GAAP* require amortization

over that estimate of its life. If the right has indefinite life, then *GAAP* require no amortization, but annual tests for *impairment.* Under *SFAS No. 2,* the firm must *expense* internally developed trademark rights.

trading on the equity. Said of a firm engaging in *debt financing*; frequently said of a firm doing so to a degree considered abnormal for a firm of its kind. *Leverage.*

trading securities. *Marketable securities* that a firm holds and expects to sell within a relatively short time; a classification important in *SFAS No. 115,* which requires the owner to carry marketable equity securities on the balance sheet at market value, not at cost. Contrast with *available for sale, securities* and *held-to-maturity securities.* Under *SFAS No. 115,* the balance sheet reports trading securities at market value on the balance sheet date, and the income statement reports *holding gains and losses* on trading securities. When the firm sells the securities, it reports realized gain or loss as the difference between the selling price and the market value at the last balance sheet date.

transaction. A *transfer* (of more than promises—*see executory contract*) between the accounting *entity* and another party or parties.

transfer. Under *SFAC No. 6,* consists of two types: reciprocal and nonreciprocal. In a reciprocal transfer, or "exchange," the entity both receives and sacrifices. In a nonreciprocal transfer, the entity sacrifices but does not receive (examples include gifts, distributions to owners) or receives but does not sacrifice (investment by owner in entity). *SFAC No. 6* suggests that the term "internal transfer" is self-contradictory and that writers should use the term "internal event" instead.

transfer agent. Usually a bank or trust company designated by a corporation to make legal transfers of *shares (bonds)* and, perhaps, to pay *dividends (coupons)*.

transfer price. A substitute for a *market*, or *arm's-length, price* used in *profit*, or *responsibility center, accounting* when one segment of the business "sells" to another segment. Incentives of profit center managers will not coincide with the best interests of the entire business unless a firm sets transfer prices properly.

transfer-pricing problem. The problem of setting *transfer prices* so that both buyer and seller have *goal congruence* with respect to the parent organization's goals.

translation adjustment. The effect of *exchange-rate* changes caused by converting the value of a net investment denominated in a *foreign currency* to the entity's reporting currency. *SFAS No. 52* requires firms to translate their net investment in relatively self-contained foreign operations at the *balance sheet* date. Yearly changes in value caused by exchange-rate changes accumulate in an *owners' equity* account, sometimes called the "cumulative translation adjustment."

translation gain (or loss). *Foreign exchange gain (or loss).*

transportation-in. *Freight-in.*

transposition error. An error in record keeping resulting from reversing the order of digits in a number, such as recording "32" for "23." If the only errors in a *trial balance* result from one or more transposition errors, then the difference between the sum of the *debits* and the sum of the *credits* will be divisible by nine. Not all such differences result from transposition errors. *See slide.*

treasurer. The financial officer responsible for managing cash and raising funds.

treasury bond. A bond issued by a corporation and then reacquired. Such bonds are treated as retired when reacquired, and an *extraordinary gain or loss* on reacquisition is recognized. This term also refers to a *bond* issued by the U.S. Treasury Department.

treasury shares. *Capital stock* issued and then reacquired by the corporation. Such reacquisitions result in a reduction of *shareholders' equity* and usually appear on the balance sheet as contra to shareholders' equity. Accounting recognizes neither *gain* nor *loss* on transactions involving treasury stock. The accounting debits (if positive) or credits (if negative) any difference between the amounts paid and received for treasury stock transactions to *additional paid-in capital*. *See cost method* and *par value method.*

treasury stock. *Treasury shares.*

trend analysis. Investigation of sales or other economic trends. Can range from a simple visual extrapolation of points on a graph to a sophisticated computerized time series analysis.

trial balance. A two-column listing of *account balances.* The left-hand column shows all accounts with *debit* balances and their total. The right-hand column shows all accounts with *credit* balances and their total. The two totals should be equal. Accountants compute trial balances as a partial check of the arithmetic accuracy of the entries previously made. *See adjusted, preclosing, post-closing, unadjusted trial balance*, *plug*, *slide*, and *transposition error.*

troubled debt restructuring. As defined in *SFAS No. 15*, a concession (changing of the terms of a *debt*) that is granted by a *creditor* for economic or legal reasons related to the *debtor's* financial difficulty and that the creditor would not otherwise consider.

TSE. *Toronto Stock Exchange.*

***t*-statistic.** For an estimated *regression* coefficient, the estimated coefficient divided by the *standard error* of the estimate.

turnover. The number of times that *assets*, such as *inventory* or *accounts receivable*, are replaced on average during the period. Accounts receivable turnover, for example, is total sales on account for a period divided by the average accounts receivable balance for the period. *See ratio.* In the UK, "turnover" means *sales*.

turnover of plant and equipment. *See ratio.*

***t*-value.** In *regression analysis*, the ratio of an estimated regression coefficient divided by its *standard error*.

20-F. Form required by the *SEC* for foreign companies issuing or trading their securities in the United States. This form reconciles the foreign accounting amounts resulting from using foreign *GAAP* to amounts resulting from using U.S. GAAP.

two T-account method. A method for computing either (1) *foreign-exchange gains and losses* or (2) *monetary gains* or *losses* for *constant-dollar accounting statements*. The left-hand *T-account* shows actual net balances of *monetary items*, and the right-hand T-account shows implied (common) dollar amounts.

2/10, n(et)/30. *See terms of sale.*

U

unadjusted trial balance. *Trial balance* taken before the accountant makes *adjusting* and *closing entries* at the end of the period.

unappropriated retained earnings. *Retained earnings* not appropriated and therefore against which the *board* can declare *dividends* in the absence of retained earnings restrictions. *See restricted retained earnings.*

unavoidable cost. A *cost* that is not an *avoidable cost.*

uncertainty. *See risk* for definition and contrast.

uncollectible account. An *account receivable* that the *debtor* will not pay. If the firm uses the preferable *allowance method*, the entry on judging a specific account to be uncollectible *debits* the allowance for uncollectible accounts and *credits* the specific account receivable. *See bad debt expense* and *sales contra, estimated uncollectibles.*

unconsolidated subsidiary. A *subsidiary* not consolidated and, hence, not accounted for in the *equity method.*

uncontrollable cost. The opposite of *controllable cost.*

underapplied (underabsorbed) overhead. An excess of actual *overhead costs* for a period over costs applied, or charged, to products produced during the period; a *debit balance* remaining in an overhead account after the accounting assigns overhead to product.

underlying document. The record, memorandum, *voucher*, or other signal that is the authority for making an *entry* into a *journal.*

underwriter. One who agrees to purchase an entire *security issue* for a specified price, usually for resale to others.

undistributed earnings. *Retained earnings.* Typically, this term refers to that amount retained for a given year.

unearned income (revenue). *Advances from customers*; strictly speaking, a contradiction in terms because the terms "income" and "revenue" mean earned.

unemployment tax. *See FUTA.*

unencumbered appropriation. In governmental accounting, portion of an *appropriation* not yet spent or encumbered.

unexpired cost. An *asset.*

unfavorable variance. In *standard cost* accounting, an excess of expected revenue over actual revenue or an excess of actual cost over standard cost.

unfunded. Not *funded.* An obligation or *liability*, usually for *pension costs*, exists, but no *funds* have been set aside to discharge the obligation or liability.

Uniform Partnership Act. A model law, enacted by many states, to govern the relations between partners when the *partnership* agreement fails to specify an agreed-upon treatment.

unissued capital shares. *Shares* authorized but not yet issued.

uniting-of-interests method. The *IASB*'s term for the *pooling-of-interests method*. The *IASB* allows uniting of interests only when the merging firms have roughly equal size and the shareholders retain substantially the same, relative to each other, voting rights and interests in the combined entity after the combination as before.

unit-level activities. Work that converts resources into individual products. Examples include *direct materials, direct labor*, and energy to run the machines.

units-of-production method. The *production method of depreciation.*

unlimited liability. The legal obligation of *general partners* or the sole proprietor for all debts of the *partnership* or *sole proprietorship.*

unqualified opinion. *See auditor's report.*

unrealized appreciation. An *unrealized holding gain*; frequently used in the context of *marketable securities.*

unrealized gain (loss) on marketable securities. An *income statement account* title for the amount of *gain (loss)* during the current period on the portfolio of *marketable securities* held as *trading securities. SFAS No. 115* requires the firm to recognize, in the income statement, gains and losses caused by changes in market values, even though the firm has not yet *realized* them.

unrealized gross margin (profit). A *contra account* to *installment accounts receivable* used with the *installment method* of revenue recognition; shows the amount of profit that the firm will eventually realize when it collects the receivable. Some accountants show this account as a *liability.*

unrealized holding gain. *See inventory profit* for the definition and an example.

unrecovered cost. *Book value* of an *asset.*

unused capacity. The difference between resources supplied and resources used.

usage variance. *Efficiency variance.*

use of funds. Any transaction that reduces funds (however "funds" is defined).

useful life. *Service life.*

V

valuation account. A *contra account* or *adjunct account.* When the firm reports *accounts receivable* at expected collectible amounts, it will credit any expected uncollectible amounts to the *allowance for uncollectibles*, a valuation account. In this way, the firm can show both the gross receivables amount and the amount it expects to collect. *SFAC No. 6* says a valuation account is "a separate item that reduces and increases the carrying amount" of an asset (or liability). The accounts are part of the related assets (or liabilities) and are not assets (or liabilities) in their own right.

value. Monetary worth. This term is usually so vague that you should not use it without a modifying adjective unless most people would agree on the amount. Do not confuse with cost. *See fair market price (value), entry value,* and *exit value.*

value added. *Cost* of a product or *work-in-process* minus the cost of the material purchased for the product or work-in-process.

value-added activity. Any activity that increases the usefulness to a customer of a product or service.

value chain. The set of business functions that increase the usefulness to the customer of a product or service; typically including research and development, design of products and services, production, marketing, distribution, and customer service.

value engineering. An evaluation of the activities in the value chain to reduce costs.

value variance. *Price variance.*

variable annuity. An *annuity* whose periodic payments depend on some uncertain outcome, such as stock market prices.

variable budget. *Flexible budget.*

variable costing. In allocating costs, a method that assigns only *variable manufacturing costs* to products and

treats *fixed manufacturing costs* as *period expenses.* Contrast with *full absorption costing.*

variable costs. *Costs* that change as activity levels change. Strictly speaking, variable costs are zero when the activity level is zero. *See semivariable costs.* In accounting, this term most often means the sum of *direct costs* and variable *overhead.*

VIE (variable interest entity). An entity arranged so that one cannot analyze controlling financial interest by analyzing voting interest, because the entity has insufficient *owners' equity* at risk, which means it cannot finance its operations without additional financial support, such as the promises of another entity. The entity's owners' equity lacks attributes associated with equity: the ability to absorb losses, the right to receive residual returns, and the ability, conveyed by voting rights, to make decisions. The entity can have a "primary beneficiary," which absorbs (or receives) a majority of the variability of outcomes of the entity. If there is a primary beneficiary, that business will consolidate the VIE, regardless of ownership.

variable overhead efficiency variance. The difference between the *actual* and *standard cost driver* volume times the standard cost driver rate.

variable overhead price variance. The difference between the *actual* and *standard cost driver* rate times the actual cost driver volume.

variable overhead variance. Difference between actual and *standard variable overhead* costs.

variable rate debt. *Debt* whose interest rate results from the periodic application of a formula, such as "three-month LIBOR [London

Interbank Offered Rate] plus 1 percent [one hundred basis points] set on the 8th day of each February, May, August, and November."

variables sampling. The use of a sampling technique in which the sampler infers a particular quantitative characteristic of an entire population from a sample (e.g., mean amount of accounts receivable). *See also estimation sampling. See attribute(s) sampling* for contrast and further examples.

variance. Difference between actual and *standard costs* or between *budgeted* and actual *expenditures* or, sometimes, *expenses.* The word has completely different meanings in accounting and in statistics, where it means a measure of dispersion of a distribution.

variance analysis. *Variance investigation.* This term's meaning differs in statistics.

variance investigation. A step in managerial control processes. *Standard costing systems* produce *variance* numbers of various sorts. These numbers seldom exactly equal to zero. Management must decide when a variance differs sufficiently from zero to study its cause. This term refers both to the decision about when to study the cause and to the study itself.

variation analysis. Analysis of the causes of changes in financial statement items of interest such as *net income* or *gross margin.*

VAT (Value-added tax). A tax levied on the market value of a firm's outputs less the market value of its purchased inputs.

vendor. A seller; sometimes spelled "vender."

verifiable. A qualitative *objective* of financial reporting specifying that

accountants can trace items in *financial statements* back to *underlying documents*—supporting *invoices,* canceled *checks,* and other physical pieces of evidence.

verification. The auditor's act of reviewing or checking items in *financial statements* by tracing back to *underlying documents*—supporting *invoices,* canceled *checks,* and other business documents—or sending out *confirmations* to be returned. Compare with *physical verification.*

vertical analysis. Analysis of the financial statements of a single firm or across several firms for a particular time, as opposed to *horizontal* or *time-series analysis,* in which the analyst compares items over time for a single firm or across firms.

vertical integration. The extension of activity by an organization into business directly related to the production or distribution of the organization's end products. Although a firm can sell products to others at various stages, a vertically integrated firm devotes the substantial portion of the output at each stage to the production of the next stage or to end products. Compare *horizontal integration.*

vested. An employee's *pension plan* benefits that are not contingent on the employee's continuing to work for the employer.

VIE. *Variable interest entity.*

visual curve fitting method. One crude form of cost *estimation.* Sometimes, when a firm needs only rough approximations of the amounts of *fixed* and *variable costs,* management need not perform a formal *regression analysis* but can plot the data and draw a line that seems to fit the data. Then it can use the parameters of that line for the rough approximations.

volume variance. *Production volume variance*; less often, used to mean *sales volume variance.*

voucher. A document that signals recognition of a *liability* and authorizes the disbursement of cash; sometimes used to refer to the written evidence documenting an *accounting entry*, as in the term *journal voucher.*

voucher system. In controlling *cash*, a method that requires someone in the firm to authorize each *check* with an approved *voucher*. The firm makes no *disbursements* of currency or coins except from *petty cash funds.*

vouching. The function performed by an *auditor* to ascertain that underlying data or documents support a *journal entry.*

W

wage. Compensation of employees based on time worked or output of product for manual labor. But *see take-home pay.*

warning signal. Tool used to identify quality-control problems; only signals a problem. Contrast with *diagnostic signal*, which both signals a problem and suggests its cause.

warrant. A certificate entitling the owner to buy a specified number of shares at a specified time(s) for a specified price; differs from a *stock option* only in that the firm grants options to employees and issues warrants to the public. *See right.*

warranty. A promise by a seller to correct deficiencies in products sold. When the seller gives warranties, proper accounting practice recognizes an estimate of warranty *expense* and an *estimated liability* at the time of sale. *See guarantee* for contrast in proper usage.

wash sale. The sale and purchase of the same or similar *asset* within a short time period. For *income tax* purposes, the taxpayer cannot recognize *losses* on a sale of shares if the taxpayer purchases equivalent shares within 30 days before or after the date of sale.

waste. Material that is a residue from manufacturing operations and that has no sale value. Frequently, this has negative value because a firm must incur additional costs for disposal.

wasting asset. A *natural resource* that has a limited *useful life* and, hence, is subject to *amortization*, called *depletion.* Examples are timberland, oil and gas wells, and ore deposits.

watered stock. Shares issued for *assets* with *fair market price (value)* less than *par* or *stated value.* The firm records the assets on the books at the overstated values. In the law, for shares to be considered watered, the *board of directors* must have acted in bad faith or fraudulently in issuing the shares under these circumstances. The term originated from a former practice of cattle owners who fed cattle ("stock") large quantities of salt to make them thirsty. The cattle then drank much water before their owner took them to market. The owners did this to make the cattle appear heavier and more valuable than otherwise.

weighted average. An average computed by counting each occurrence of each value, not merely a single occurrence of each value. For example, if a firm purchases one unit for $1 and two units for $2 each, then the simple average of the purchase prices is $1.50, but the weighted average price per unit is $5/3 = $1.67. Contrast with *moving average.*

weighted-average cost of capital. Measured as the *weighted-average* of the *after-tax cost* of *long-term debt* and the cost of *equity*.

weighted-average inventory method. Valuing either *withdrawals* or *ending inventory* at the *weighted-average* purchase price of all units on hand at the time of withdrawal or of computation of ending inventory. The firm uses the *inventory equation* to calculate the other quantity. If a firm uses the *perpetual inventory* method, accountants often call it the *moving average method*.

where-got, where-gone statement. A term allegedly used in the 1920s by W. M. Cole for a statement much like the *statement of cash flows*. Noted accounting historian S. Zeff reports that Cole actually used the term "where-got-gone" statement.

wind up. To bring to an end, such as the life of a corporation. The *board* winds up the life of a corporation by following the winding-up provisions of applicable statutes, by surrendering the charter, or by following *bankruptcy* proceedings. *See also liquidation.*

window dressing. The attempt to make financial statements show *operating* results, or a *financial position*, more favorable than they would otherwise show.

with recourse. *See note receivable discounted.*

withdrawals. *Assets* distributed to an owner. *Partner's drawings. See inventory equation* for another context.

withholding. Deductions that are taken from *salaries* or *wages*, usually for *income taxes*, and that the employer remits, in the employee's name, to the taxing authority.

without recourse. *See note receivable discounted.*

work sheet (program). (1) A computer program designed to combine explanations and calculations. This type of program helps in preparing *financial statements* and *schedules.* (2) A tabular schedule for convenient summary of *adjusting* and *closing entries.* The work sheet usually begins with an *unadjusted trial balance.* Adjusting entries appear in the next two columns, one for *debits* and one for *credits.* The work sheet carries the horizontal sum of each line to the right into either the *income statement* or the *balance sheet* column, as appropriate. The *plug* to equate the income statement column totals is, if a debit, the income or, if a credit, a loss for the period. That income will close *retained earnings* on the *balance sheet.* The *income statement credit* columns are the revenues for the period, and the *debit* columns are the *expenses* (and revenue *contras*) that appear on the *income statement.* "Work sheet" also refers to *schedules* for ascertaining other items that appear on the *financial statements* and that require adjustment or compilation.

working capital. *Current assets* minus *current liabilities;* sometimes called "net working capital" or "*net current assets.*"

work(ing) papers. The schedules and analyses prepared by the *auditor* in carrying out investigations before issuing an *opinion* on *financial statements.*

work-in-process (inventory account). Partially completed product; appears on the *balance sheet* as *inventory.*

worth. *Value. See net worth.*

worth-debt ratio. Reciprocal of the *debt-equity ratio. See ratio.*

write down. To *write off*, except that the firm does not charge all the *asset*'s cost to *expense* or *loss*; generally used for nonrecurring items.

write off. To *charge* an *asset* to *expense* or *loss*; that is, to *debit* expense (or loss) and *credit* the asset.

write-off method. For treating *uncollectible accounts*, a method that *debits bad debt expense* and *credits* accounts receivable of specific customers as the firm identifies specific accounts as uncollectible. The firm cannot use this method when it can estimate uncollectible amounts and they are significant. See *bad debt expense, sales contra, estimated uncollectibles*, and the *allowance method* for contrast.

write up. To increase the recorded *cost* of an *asset* with no corresponding *disbursement* of *funds*; that is, to *debit* asset and *credit revenue* or, perhaps, *owners' equity*; seldom done in the United States because currently accepted accounting principles await actual transactions before recording asset increases. An exception occurs in accounting for *marketable equity securities*.

X

XBRL. eXtensible Business Report Language. A language created by over 30 partners, including the *AICPA*, to promote automated processing of business information by software on a computer. The main idea is that the user can access only the data needed for a particular use, without downloading and extracting the needed data from a *balance sheet*. For example, if you download a company's *annual report*, you can go to the balance sheet and copy out the amounts for *current assets* and *current liabilities*, then divide the first by the second to get the *current ratio*. Using XBRL, you would write an arithmetic expression such as tag for current assets[particular company]/tag for current liabilities[same company] Then XBPL would extract from the data just the two numbers, corresponding to the two tags you programmed. The intiative to construc ABRL began around 2000; Microsoft® was the first to prepare, in 2002, financial statement data available for public use in XBRL; and the *SEC*, in 2005, has allowed companies to file financial data at the Sec using XBRL. In 2005, the *PCAOP* issued guildelines for the audit of such XBRL filings at the SEC. We guess that use of XBRL will mushroom over the next decade. It serves users' needs in a way no other widely available system does.

Y

yield. *Internal rate of return* of a stream of cash flows. Cash yield is *cash flow* divided by *book value. See also dividend yield.*

yield curve. The relation between *interest rates* and the term to maturity of loans. Ordinarily, longer-term loans have higher interest rates than shorter-term loans. This is called a "normal" yield curve. Sometimes long-term and short-term rates are approximately the same—a flat yield curve. Sometimes short-term loans have a higher rate than long-term ones—an inverted yield curve. *Term structure* of interest rates.

yield to maturity. At a given time, the *internal rate of return* of a series of *cash flows*; usually said of a *bond*; sometimes called the "effective rate."

yield variance. Measures the input-output relation while holding the standard mix of inputs constant:

(Standard price × Actual amount of input used in the standard mix) − (Standard price × Standard quantity allowed for the actual output). It is the part of the *efficiency variance* not called the *mix variance*.

Z

zero-base(d) budgeting (ZBB). One philosophy for setting budgets. In preparing an ordinary *budget* for the next period, a manager starts with the budget for the current period and makes adjustments as seem necessary because of changed conditions for the next period. Since most managers like to increase the scope of the activities managed and since most prices increase most of the time, amounts in budgets prepared in the ordinary, incremental way seem to increase period after period. The authority approving the budget assumes that managers will carry out operations in the same way as in the past and that next period's expenditures will have to be at least as large as those of the current period. Thus, this authority tends to study only the increments to the current period's budget. In ZBB, the authority questions the process for carrying out a program and the entire budget for the next period. The authority studies every dollar in the budget, not just the dollars incremental to the previous period's amounts. The advocates of ZBB claim that in this way, (1) management will more likely delete programs or divisions of marginal benefit to the business or governmental unit, rather than continuing with costs at least as large as the present ones, and (2) management can discover and implement alternative, more cost-effective ways of carrying out programs. ZBB implies questioning the existence of programs and the fundamental nature of the way that firms carry them out, not only the amounts used to fund them. Experts appear to divide evenly as to whether the middle word should be "base" or "based."

INDEX